D1558614

West's Law School Advisory Board

JESSE H. CHOPER
Professor of Law,
University of California, Berkeley

DAVID P. CURRIE
Professor of Law, University of Chicago

YALE KAMISAR
Professor of Law, University of San Diego
Professor of Law, University of Michigan

MARY KAY KANE
Chancellor, Dean and Distinguished Professor of Law,
University of California,
Hastings College of the Law

LARRY D. KRAMER
Dean and Professor of Law, Stanford Law School

WAYNE R. LaFAVE
Professor of Law, University of Illinois

JONATHAN R. MACEY
Professor of Law, Yale Law School

ARTHUR R. MILLER
Professor of Law, Harvard University

GRANT S. NELSON
Professor of Law,
University of California, Los Angeles

JAMES J. WHITE
Professor of Law, University of Michigan

CASES AND MATERIALS ON

ADVANCED TORTS: ECONOMIC AND DIGNITARY TORTS

BUSINESS, COMMERCIAL AND INTANGIBLE HARMS

By

Dan B. Dobbs
Regents and Rosenstiel Distinguished Professor of Law
University of Arizona

Ellen M. Bublick
Associate Professor of Law
University of Arizona

AMERICAN CASEBOOK SERIES®

Mat #40199282

Thomson/West have created this publication to provide you with accurate and authoritative information concerning the subject matter covered. However, this publication was not necessarily prepared by persons licensed to practice law in a particular jurisdiction. Thomson/West are not engaged in rendering legal or other professional advice, and this publication is not a substitute for the advice of an attorney. If you require legal or other expert advice, you should seek the services of a competent attorney or other professional.

American Casebook Series and West Group are trademarks
registered in the U.S. Patent and Trademark Office.

© 2006 Thomson/West

610 Opperman Drive
P.O. Box 64526
St. Paul, MN 55164–0526
1–800–328–9352

Printed in the United States of America

ISBN–13: 978–0–314–15103–2
ISBN–10: 0–314–15103–6

To Kate, George, Becky, and Jean and to
Hannah, Tim, and Ben.

– Dan Dobbs

To David, Harrison, and Daniel—my joy,

And with abiding thanks to my parents, who gave me
the heart of the watermelon.

– Ellen Bublick

*

Preface

Torts of the kind we call economic and dignitary have always been important. The growth of business tort litigation has made these torts central in civil litigation.

This book attempts to cover the traditional canon of economic and dignitary torts—those not associated with physical harm to person or property. We omit a few torts that are technically economic or dignitary. Wrongful death is technically an economic tort, but it grows directly out of personal injury causing death and seems to have no real place in a book on economic torts.

We have also excluded or given only passing attention to several areas of law that, although involving economic torts, are usually taught in specialized courses. Such torts may involve strong bonds with other topics that would take us far from torts. They may also entail a good deal of criminal and sometimes administrative enforcement. Anti-trust law and employment law are in this category; we touch both but think an attempt to cover those areas would be inappropriate if not impossible.

On the other hand, we have definitely included a brief coverage of the specialized field of intellectual property and unfair competition torts. We've done so partly because those torts are organically related to the core canon, partly because business tort law practice requires knowledge of all the materials we have included, and partly because we hope courses built on this book can provide exposure to these important torts for students who cannot manage to take the more specialized courses.

Coverage we give to particular torts is relative both to the wide coverage we give to other torts and to their shared issues in civil litigation—civil litigation as distinct from criminal and administrative enforcement. On the first point, we can take defamation as one example. A whole casebook could be written on defamation, but that would lose the important connections to other economic torts. With respect to civil litigation, a media-law book would cover many non-tort issues, such as, say, FCC regulation of broadcast media. This casebook, in contrast, reflects the *tort* law grounding of all the economic torts. That means that, still using the defamation example, we do *not* cover FCC regulation of broadcast media; but it also means we *do* cover defamation cases brought against individuals and not merely defamation by media publishers.

Coverage is also dictated by the relation of economic torts to each other. The fact that commercial, non-media enterprises sue and defend defamation suits is one clue to the surprising unity of the subject matter of non-physical torts. Beyond that, lawyers very often assert, in the same suit, some combination of claims for interference with contract, trademark, trade secrets, fraud, libel, and other claims.

The unity of subject matter does not lie only in the fact that practical professionals frequently draw on a wide range of materials of the kind represented in this book. Fundamental policy and theory issues underlie many disparate portions of these materials. For example, concerns of free speech, right of petition, and free association appear in most chapters in the book. Similarly, some of the jurisdictional problems particularly associated with the internet touch libel and intellectual property in similar ways. The role of contract in limiting tort liability is a major issue that spans a number of economic torts in Part II, but it can also make a cameo appearance even in defamation cases. Problems of overlapping torts with different governing rules for the same set of facts arise because some torts are defined by the defendant's conduct, while others are largely defined by the kind of harm done. Almost any tort in this book could be conceived as some other tort. To take an obvious example, malicious prosecution, injurious falsehood, and defamation might all be viewed as an interference with contract or business opportunity when the resulting damage includes loss of a contract or prospective business.

Because there is more unity in the dignitary-economic tort materials than one might expect, there is something to be said for teaching as wide a range of these materials as time permits, taking into account any other related courses students are likely to be taking.

We have followed several editing conventions to simplify reading cases. We drop many citations given in the original cases, without marking those omissions in any way. The same is true for footnotes. We likewise re-paragraph in some cases. Textual omissions are marked by four dots if they run to the end of a sentence or beyond, otherwise three dots. Interior quotation marks are often omitted without any special indication. Finally, when we summarize materials in square brackets, there may be omitted material unrelated to our summary.

Many lawyers who were once our students have contributed enormously to this book (although not to its errors). We cannot name them all, but we must thank especially Alison Bachus, Chadwick Campbell, Jennifer Johnson, and Victoria Levin who contributed their research to earlier drafts, and three current students whose help on this edition has been extraordinary—Suzanne Diaz, Jennifer Thorson, and Travis Wheeler. Ellen Bublick also wishes to thank Professor Jean Braucher and David Jacobs for their helpful readings of her work. Dan Dobbs adds his thanks to Jenna Summerfield for her support of a curmudgeonly scholar at work.

Both Ellen and Dan are grateful to faculty assistants Sandy Davis, Davon May, Melissa Haun, Kristie Gallardo, and Barbara Lopez for their hard work in preparing this book for publication.

DAN B. DOBBS
ELLEN M. BUBLICK
Tucson

January, 2006

Summary of Contents

*

Table of Contents

Page

*

Table of Cases

The principal cases are in bold type. Cases cited or discussed in the text are roman type. References are to pages. Cases cited in principal cases and within other quoted materials are not included.

*

CASES AND MATERIALS ON

ADVANCED TORTS: ECONOMIC AND DIGNITARY TORTS

BUSINESS, COMMERCIAL AND INTANGIBLE HARMS

*

What Are Economic and Dignitary Torts?

This book is about torts that cause economic and intangible losses, not about personal injury torts or even about physical harms to property. Many of the torts covered here can also be identified in narrower ways—as media torts or communicative torts in some cases or business or commercial torts in others.

The common ground, though, is that none of these torts arises out of physical harm or physical contact. The plaintiff instead claims to suffer one of two kinds of non-physical injury—stand-alone economic or commercial harm or stand-alone dignitary affronts akin to or including emotional harms. We say "stand-alone" because these economic or dignitary losses do not arise from physical harms but stand by themselves.

An example of an economic tort is deceit. The defendant fraudulently represents that his house has a new roof and you buy it on that understanding. It turns out that the roof is old and leaky and you must replace it. The defendant has not physically harmed you or even the house, but he has caused you economic harm.

Libel and privacy invasion may cause economic harm because they cause the loss of a job, the loss of business, or damage to the intangible asset of reputation. Libel and privacy invasion often also cause emotional or dignitary harm. The emotional or dignitary harm, like the economic harm, stands alone in the sense that it does not result from physical injury or even the threat of physical injury. Someone publishes defamatory statements about you. Even if you suffer no economic loss such as loss of employment resulting from the libel, your reputation may be sullied and that is ordinarily a sufficient harm to justify a recovery. In that case, the loss is dignitary, a damage to one's rights of personality, not economic. Because torts like libel can and often do cause both kinds of harm, we must say that this book covers some dignitary interests as well as economic losses.

Negligence is seldom an explicit feature in stand-alone economic and dignitary torts. Each of the economic or dignitary torts considered in this book comes with a set of rules of its own. Some may impose strict liability. Others go in the opposite direction and require some kind of intent. But all come with a set of elements that the plaintiff must prove. Traditionally, negligence is not one of those elements.

With physical injury torts, the tort is usually defined by specifying the acts that are forbidden, or at least the kind of fault that must be attributed to the defendant before liability can attach. Some dignitary and economic torts do the same. Other torts in this group, however, emphasize the kind of harm inflicted, such as emotional distress or invasion of privacy or interference with contract. This haphazard conceptual structure leads to strange overlaps from time to time. You might have a claim for libel and if the libel caused interference with contract you might conceivably have two claims, raising the question, which set of rules apply? Is this merely a strategic opportunity for plaintiff's lawyers and lucrative additional work for defense lawyers, or is something wrong if you might get around the limitations on defamation by invoking privacy interests? We want to suggest that the structure of tort law relating to intangible injuries may need serious reconsideration.

Users of this book should be aware up front that when a tort is based upon the defendant's communication to others, special policies may protect the defendant from liability. Free competition is a significant policy in some cases. In others, the First Amendment's right of free speech is the dominant concern. The relation of free speech to communicative torts has been best developed in defamation cases. Consequently, we start with that topic so the First Amendment jurisprudence can be considered when we later come to consider other torts involving economic loss and dignitary damages resulting from communication.

Part I

INTANGIBLE HARMS PRIMARILY TO DIGNITARY OR PERSONAL INTERESTS

Part I examines tort claims that are often primarily based on intangible injuries of a highly personal or dignitary nature. For example, the harms we see in Part I may be associated with reputational damage, emotional distress without either physical injury or the threat of it, or a loss of privacy or sense of self. In contrast, Part II examines torts that are primarily economic in nature, such as interference with contract.

In spite of our division of the torts into those that are more "personal" and those that are more "economic," the fact is that business tort litigation very frequently involves both kinds of tort claims. The lawyer who litigates interference with contract or fraud cases must know defamation law, too.

Free speech issues are at the forefront in many of the cases in Part I. Other issues can be profound. Just how much should we protect intangible and purely dignitary interests? If we should all have a right to privacy, say, just what do we mean by that and how broad should the right be?

We have stated some of the broad themes that will appear in Part I in hopes that such a statement will make it easier for readers to jump into the deep end of tort law, but we don't mean to say that this part of tort law lacks the ordinary legal issues and rules. In fact, along with a concern about structure, we think you might be concerned about the over-complexity with some torts and the under-definition of others.

If all of this seems too broad, then it is time to move into concrete cases, but maybe a glance back at this introduction will be useful later on.

Chapter 1

THE PRIMA FACIE CASE FOR DEFAMATION: COMMON LAW AND STATUTES

---

§ 1. TRADITIONAL DEFAMATION ELEMENTS AND THE ROLE OF FAULT

1. **Defamation and its forms; reputational harm.** Defamation: a derogatory communication about the plaintiff to someone else. One form is libel, roughly speaking, a communication through writing or something analogous to writing. The other form is slander, a communication through oral expression or something analogous to it. Recovery for defamation aims, more or less, to redress harm to the plaintiff's reputation, which in turn may cause financial and emotional harm.

2. **Common law and Constitution in defamation law.** Although free speech concerns are central in many defamation cases, with the result that the outcome may be controlled by Constitutional limits on liability, the common law is still potentially controlling in many cases. Even when Constitutional rules impact a case, the impact occurs only after the plaintiff has made out a common law case of defamation. Lawyers thus invariably use common law rules in asserting and defending defamation claims. This chapter and the next survey those traditional common law rules.

3. **Elements of the plaintiff's case.** "Traditional common law rules in the case of both libel and slander required the plaintiff to prove (1) defendant's publication to a third person (2) of defamatory material (3) of and concerning the plaintiff." 2 DOBBS ON TORTS § 401 (2001 & Supp.). Certain cases of slander, as distinct from libel, traditionally require proof of damages.

CASSIDY V. DAILY MIRROR NEWSPAPERS, LIMITED, [1929], 2 K.B. 331, 69 A.L.R. 720. "Scrutton, L.J. . . . A man named Cassidy, who for some reason also called himself Corrigan and described himself as a General in the Mexican Army, was married to a lady who also called herself Mrs. Cassidy or Mrs. Corrigan. Her husband occasionally came and stayed with her at her flat, and her acquaintances met him. Cassidy achieved some notoriety in racing circles and in indiscriminate relations with women, and at a race meeting he posed, in company with a lady, to a racing photographer, to whom he said he was engaged to marry the lady and the photographer might announce it. The photographer, without any further inquiry, sent the photograph to the Daily Mirror with an inscription: 'Mr. Corrigan, the race horse owner, and Miss X.'—I omit the name—'whose engagement has been announced,' and the Daily Mirror published the photograph and inscription.

"This paper was read by the female acquaintances of Mrs. Cassidy or Mrs. Corrigan, who gave evidence that they understood from it that the lady was not married to Mr. M. Corrigan and had no legal right to take his name, and that they formed a bad opinion of her in consequence. Mrs. Cassidy accordingly brought an action for libel against the newspaper setting out these words with an innuendo, meaning thereby that the plaintiff was an immoral woman who had cohabited with Corrigan without being married to him."

Held: the plaintiff has an action for damages against the publisher. The words were capable of defamatory meaning by suggesting that Mrs. Cassidy was not married to the man who stayed at her flat. And the fact that the newspaper did not know the facts that would permit some persons to draw the defamatory conclusion is no defense. The publisher must take the consequences even if it has no intent to speak about the plaintiff at all.

---

4. **The common law presumptions.** Once the plaintiff proved that the defendant had published defamatory material about the plaintiff—the three elements listed in ¶ 3—the common law of libel inflicted three presumptions on the defendant. First, the publication was presumed false, so the defendant had the burden of proving truth as an affirmative defense. Second, the publication was presumed to cause damages, so the plaintiff never had to prove any actual loss of reputation, much less pecuniary losses. (These presumptions did not apply to the special cases considered in §§ 5 and 6 below.) Third, the publication was presumed to be malicious, so the plaintiff never had to prove fault. Still accepting these rules is *Kiesau v. Bantz,* 686 N.W.2d 164 (Iowa 2004).

5. **Modifications of the presumptions in contemporary law.** Some courts have now modified one or more of these elements directly, with the result that in some states the plaintiff may be required to prove falsity, fault, damage, or some combination of these elements. E.g., *Mathis v. Cannon,* 276 Ga. 16, 573 S.E.2d 376 (2002) (proof of falsity and

fault required); *Costello v. Hardy,* 864 So.2d 129 (La. 2004) (same); *Ravnikar v. Bogojavlensky,* 438 Mass. 627, 782 N.E.2d 508 (2003) (proof of fault and sometimes proof of falsity required). Where not modified, however, any one of these rules can subject defendants to substantial risk. In *Republic Tobacco Co. v. North Atlantic Trading Co., Inc.,* 381 F.3d 717 (7th Cir. 2004), the court, after a reduction, approved an award of $1 million in compensatory damages based solely on the "presumption" of damages in a case involving defamation in private letters.

6. **Role of affirmative defenses.** Is it fair to say that the traditional common law rules imposed liability without fault? Is *Cassidy* an example? When strict liability or near-strict liability is imposed, affirmative defenses that inject issues of fault and fairness become most significant. Besides defenses like the statute of limitations, the law of defamation recognizes a number of privileges to publish material that would be defamatory except for the privilege. Constitutional free speech law may also require fault in many cases. Truth and privilege come up in Chapter 2. The remainder of this chapter looks at the elements of the plaintiff's case for libel and the elements for slander.

§ 2. ELEMENTS: PUBLICATION

GREAT ATLANTIC & PAC. TEA CO. v. PAUL

256 Md. 643, 261 A.2d 731 (1970)

DIGGES, Judge. . . .

[Mr. Paul, a retired police officer suffering from a heart condition, was shopping in the defendant's grocery store. The defendant's employee Parker believed, seemingly without reason, that Mr. Paul was secreting a can of tick spray with intent to avoid payment. The jury could find that the defendant's employee "accosted plaintiff violently in the aisle; falsely accused him loudly and profanely of being a thief; forced him to submit to a frisk with his hands raised in the air, knocking canned goods to the floor; and these actions caused numerous close-by shoppers to turn and stare at him as if they were observing a 'three-ring circus.' " Paul asserted several claims against the defendant, including one for slander. The jury found for Paul and awarded $10,000 in compensatory and $30,000 in punitive damages. The defendant appeals.]

Appellant's sole ground for reversal on the decision of slander is that the element of publication was not satisfied. "Publication" in the law of defamation is the communication of defamatory matter to a third person or persons. This means that for alleged defamatory words to be actionable they must be seen or heard by some person other than the plaintiff and defendant. There is the further qualification that this third person must understand the meaning of the words, the familiar example being that no publication occurs when a third person hears slanderous words spoken in a foreign language he does not understand.

Appellant proposes that publication in the law of slander is a different and stricter requirement than it is in libel. It says that in order for slander to be published the plaintiff must show that the defendant spoke the defamatory words in the hearing of a third person who personally knew or knew of the plaintiff. It concedes, as it must, that publication to any third party is sufficient in libel. It argues that damage to reputation is the gravamen of slander and there can be no actionable tort when defendant does not communicate the defamatory words to someone whose opinion of the plaintiff may reasonably be affected. It further argues the distinction between libel and slander on this point is that written words have a permanent nature and libelous material once distributed may fairly be presumed to reach persons who personally know the plaintiff. We do not think such a distinction exists in law nor do we think there is any requirement in either libel or slander that the publication be to a third person having personal knowledge of the plaintiff.

[Defendant claimed support for its position in Bonkowski v. Arlan's Department Store, 12 Mich.App. 88, 162 N.W.2d 347 (1968).] In Bonkowski, a husband and wife were stopped by a department store security guard as they were about to enter their car on a shopping center parking lot. The guard accused the wife of taking jewelry from the department store without paying and compelled her to empty her pocketbook. She established that there were other persons in the parking lot at that time. The court found that the forced emptying of her pocketbook in the presence of a uniformed guard could constitute a dramatic pantomime implying that Mrs. Bonkowski was a thief. However, the court found no publication to the husband (for reasons not here pertinent) and no publication of the "slander by act" because Mrs. Bonkowski neither "knew or could identify anyone (else) who had been present." Publication not having been established the judgment was reversed. We do not believe this decision is correctly interpreted by appellant. ... [I]t is apparent in their proper context the court was merely stating that there was no proof that any one present in the parking lot either heard the remarks or observed the incident. ...

After a diligent search we have been able to discover no support for appellant's contention either in cases or texts. In S. Bower, A Code of the Law of Actionable Defamation, Art. 6 a (2d ed. 1923), the author states: "It is immaterial, in order to constitute publication in law, whether the communication be made to one or more named or known or specific persons, or to the public at large or a class or number of unknown or undesignated persons. ..."

We note in other jurisdictions that where alleged slanderous remarks are made under circumstances such that it is a reasonable inference that third persons present could have overheard the remarks and understood them to refer to the plaintiff, whether there has been publication is at least a jury question. This is true even when the third persons deny hearing the slanderous statement. ...

[Given the "three-ring circus" created by the defendant's frisking of Mr. Paul and the stares of customers,] it is disingenuous of A & P to claim that no publication took place under these circumstances. . . . Appellant would have us conclude that even where a slanderer directs his remarks to the plaintiff under such circumstances that third persons nearby hear the words and understand them to refer to the plaintiff there can be no recovery unless the defamed person can show that the incident was overheard and seen by someone personally familiar with him. Such is not the law as we can find it stated by a single authority in this country and we hold it is not the law of Maryland. . . .

Judgment affirmed. Costs to be paid by appellant.

---

7. **Publication defined.** To be actionable, defamatory material must be published. This does not connote media publication or widespread dissemination, only communication in some understandable form to one or more persons besides the plaintiff. E.g., *Brown v. Kelly Broadcasting Co.,* 48 Cal.3d 711, 712, 771 P.2d 406, 412, 257 Cal.Rptr. 708, 712 (1989). With publication so broadly defined, defamation actions are not only the constant concern of media publishers; such actions are also open to purely private citizens and to business corporations using defamation actions as part of the arsenal of tools in litigation against competitors. E.g., *Republic Tobacco Co. v. North Atlantic Trading Co., Inc.,* 381 F.3d 717 (7th Cir. 2004). The publication issue is not concerned with the content of the publication, only the fact of publication. It is thus a narrow issue and one that is seldom litigated. The content of the publication is, however, important on other elements.

8. **Intentional or negligent publication required.** The defendant is not responsible for publications made without either intent or negligence. If he talks in his sleep and a burglar in the room hears him slander the plaintiff, the defendant will not be liable. On the other hand, suppose that the outraged employee who frisked Mr. Paul unreasonably believed that the two of them were alone when in fact onlookers were gawking at them. In such a case, negligent publication could readily be found. The requirement of intentional or negligent publication is sometimes characterized as fault, but if it is fault, it is a peculiar kind of fault, because it does not entail an intent to publish a falsehood or even something damaging to the plaintiff's reputation.

9. **Form of publication.** We already know that written and oral publications are sometimes treated differently, but the publication requirement applies to both. From *Paul* we can also see that a publication could be in other forms such as pantomime.

10. **Understanding vs. belief.** As the *Paul* court notes, there is no communication at all unless the material can be understood by at least one recipient of it. But notice that a recipient of a publication in a foreign language might not understand the language, yet might under-

stand the gist of the publication if it is accompanied by gestures. Also notice the requirement of understanding is not a requirement of belief. You might perfectly well understand a publication that accuses your domestic partner of a crime, yet not believe it. Where damages can be presumed (¶ 4, supra), the plaintiff may recover even if no one believes the defamation. *In re Peck,* 295 B.R. 353 (B.A.P. 9th Cir. 2003); see *Plumley v. Landmark Chevrolet, Inc.,* 122 F.3d 308 (5th Cir. 1997); cf. *Bell v. National Republican Congressional Committee,* 187 F.Supp.2d 605, 615 (S.D. W.Va. 2002) (presuming harm to reputation from published defamatory statement even if no recipient shares the plaintiff's interpretation of the defendant's statement).

11. **Privilege vs. publication analysis.** Some courts have said that intra-corporate communications are not publications at all. A similar notion has been applied in some cases of communications to a spouse or a stenographer. Are these approaches consistent with the rule that publication is purely a question whether communication has taken place? Other courts follow the RESTATEMENT (SECOND) OF TORTS § 577 by treating such facts as raising questions of privilege rather than questions of publication. Does it matter which approach a court takes?

12. **Foreseeable or intended republication by others.** The defendant is accountable as a publisher if he authorizes or intends a publication effected by another and also if he so publishes in a way that makes the other's re-publication foreseeable. See RESTATEMENT (SECOND) OF TORTS § 576. In *Tuman v. Genesis Associates,* 894 F.Supp. 183 (E.D. Pa. 1995), the defendant therapists allegedly implanted false memories in their patient, Dianne, which led to Dianne's publication of statements that her parents had committed incest and murder. The parents sued the therapists. The court held that the defendants could be subjected to a defamation claim because they "induced" Dianne to make the publication. Again, distinguish the issue of publication from the issue of privilege: some writers think therapists should be privileged.

13. **Repeater as publisher.** The repeater of a defamatory publication is also a publisher and subject to liability for his publication. RESTATEMENT (SECOND) OF TORTS § 578. This republication is considered to be a separate tort, for which the original publisher and the repeater may both be liable. See *Shively v. Bozanich,* 31 Cal.4th 1230, 80 P.3d 676, 7 Cal.Rptr.3d 576 (2003); *Wright v. Bachmurski,* 29 Kan.App.2d 595, 29 P.3d 979 (2001). This rule is limited only with certain mass publications under the single publication rule, which treats all copies of a single edition of a book as a single publication. See Chapter 6, § 2.

14. **Publication by victim: "compelled self-publication" actionable.** Self-publication is more striking. Suppose the defendant employer discharges the plaintiff employee, saying that the reason was the employee's theft. The employee denies the theft but is discharged anyway. When the employee applies for a new job, the prospective employer asks, "Why did you leave your job?" The employee feels she must answer truthfully by saying that the defendant had asserted theft. The prospec-

tive employer then refuses to hire the plaintiff. Is it possible to think that the original employer is a publisher here? *Lewis v. Equitable Life Assur. Soc. of the U.S.*, 389 N.W.2d 876 (Minn. 1986), and a few other cases have accepted the concept of "self-publication" and it fits the foreseeability test in the employment setting. *Overcast v. Billings Mut. Ins. Co.,* 11 S.W.3d 62 (Mo. 2000), followed the same idea where the defendant fire insurer denied the plaintiff's claim on the assertion that the plaintiff had committed arson. Since a policyholder will foreseeably seek to replace the insurance policy, and to do so must reveal any denied claims, publication to others was foreseeable so the defamatory assertion was actionable.

15. **Rejecting or qualifying compelled self-publication theory.** Most courts have rejected self-publication claims, usually in the employment context. *Cweklinsky v. Mobile Chemical Co.,* 267 Conn. 210, 837 A.2d 759 (2004), rejecting self-publication claims, listed a number of reasons for its position, among them: (1) free communication is a major public policy, (2) a culture of silence in the workplace would be harmful to both employer and employee, (3) the plaintiff's duty to mitigate damages would be undermined by recognition of the claim. The Restatement treats the victim's own publication as publication by the defendant in one limited circumstance—when the plaintiff foreseeably publishes without knowing of the defamatory content, as where his reference is in a sealed envelope. RESTATEMENT (SECOND) OF TORTS § 577, cmt. m. Some courts that otherwise reject the self-publication notion may accept it in the limited circumstances recognized by the Restatement. See *Austin v. Inet Technologies, Inc.,* 118 S.W.3d 491 (Tex. App. 2003).

16. **Failure to remove.** In *Hellar v. Bianco*, 111 Cal.App.2d 424, 244 P.2d 757, 28 A.L.R.2d 1451(1952), an unknown person wrote on the men's room wall of a tavern certain comments about the sexual activity of the plaintiff, a woman. The writer included the plaintiff's home phone number. A man called the plaintiff seeking to take advantage of her advertised inclinations. The plaintiff's husband called the tavern and demanded immediate removal. The bartender was busy and alone and did not immediately remove it. The husband found a constable and went to the premises. The group gathered in the men's room and verified that the writing had not been removed. The plaintiff was allowed to proceed with her suit on the ground that removal was required.

17. **Failure to remove: the Restatement.** The Restatement leveraged *Hellar v. Bianco* into a general rule that one is liable for intentionally and unreasonably failing to remove defamatory matter he knows to be exhibited on his land or chattels. RESTATEMENT (SECOND) OF TORTS § 577(2).

18. **Failure to remove: adoption theory.** If someone writes defamatory matter in your torts casebook what must you do—and how quickly? In *Tacket v. General Motors Corp.,* 836 F.2d 1042 (7th Cir. 1987), Judge Easterbrook commented: "The Restatement suggests that a tavern owner would be liable if defamatory graffiti remained in a

bathroom stall a single hour after their discovery. Section 577 Illustration 15, derived from Hellar v. Bianco. . . . The common law of washrooms is otherwise, given the steep discount that readers apply to such statements and the high cost of hourly repaintings of bathroom stalls. The burden of constant vigilance greatly exceeds the benefits to be had. A person is responsible for statements he makes or adopts, so the question is whether a reader may infer adoption from the presence of a statement. That inference may be unreasonable for a bathroom wall or the interior of a subway car in New York City but appropriate for the interior walls of a manufacturing plant. . . ." Does the adoption theory make it easier to apply the principle?

19. **Failure to remove from a public forum.** Do *Hellar* and the Restatement imply that libraries must remove defamatory materials from their books once they are on notice of the content? What about defamatory material posted on a computer bulletin board? We'll take a look at this problem and the federal legislation on it in Chapter 5 after we've considered privilege and constitutional rules.

REFERENCE: The publication rules are summarized in DOBBS ON TORTS § 402 (2001).

§ 3. ELEMENTS: DEFAMATORY MEANING

(a) The Defamatory Quality of a Publication

20. **Tests of defamatory quality.** The second element of the plaintiff's case for defamation is that the publication means something that counts as "defamatory." With variations in the exact formula, courts traditionally emphasized that a defamatory publication tended to expose the plaintiff to "public scorn, hatred, contempt or ridicule." E.g., *Gohari v. Darvish,* 363 Md. 42, 767 A.2d 321 (2001). That has a faintly old-fashioned ring to it now and the Restatement generalized the definition to cover any publication that tends to lower the plaintiff in the community's esteem *or* to deter others from associating with him. RESTATEMENT (SECOND) OF TORTS § 559. Isn't that just about anything in a large society with diverse beliefs?

TATUR v. SOLSRUD

167 Wis.2d 266, 481 N.W.2d 657 (App. 1992)

LaROCQUE, Judge.

[The plaintiffs were candidates for reelection to the County Board. They were defeated, possibly because of allegedly false statements made by the defendants almost immediately before the election. They sue for defamation. The trial court gave summary judgment for the defendants.]

The issue on appeal is whether the alleged misrepresentations concerning the candidates' voting records are capable of a defamatory meaning. "A communication is defamatory if it tends so to harm the reputation of another as to lower him in the estimation of the community or to deter third persons from associating or dealing with him." In determining whether language is defamatory, "the words must be construed in the plain and popular sense in which they would naturally be understood." It is the function of the court as a matter of law to determine whether a communication is capable of a defamatory meaning.

The candidates allege that the letters sent by Solsrud and Christman to electors contained false statements and misrepresentations regarding how they voted on specific resolutions, the effect of their vote and the procedural and factual backgrounds of the resolutions. ... For the purposes of this appeal, we will assume that all the statements concerning the candidates' voting records are false. Most of the statements concern how the candidates voted on issues regarding expenditures or taxes. Examples of the statements contained in the letters are as follows:

> My opponent, Voted against "Elimination of New Hiring & Replacements" in an effort made to curb more spending and higher taxes. Positions would not have been filled without the full approval of the County Board ... Voted against the repeal of the 6% double penalty on delinquent real estate taxes. There already was a 12% interest rate and the penalty put that much more burden on the taxpayer who could not pay his taxes on time ... Voted to pay $6,184.00 for back retirement tax to State of Wisconsin. This was on top of $16,808.00 payments and interest to the State which have accumulated since 1980 because of a County management oversight.

The candidates contend that Christman and Solsrud, by intentionally misleading the public as to their voting records, attempted to lower the candidates in the estimation of the community and attempted to deter electors from voting for them. While we do not condone such illegal campaign tactics as allegedly used by Christman and Solsrud, misrepresenting how someone votes on an issue is not defamatory as a matter of law because it does not assault a person's character such that it would lower a person's esteem in a community. The situation presented here is analogous to *Frinzi v. Hanson*, 30 Wis.2d 271, 140 N.W.2d 259 (1966).

Frinzi argued that the statement "Dominic Frinzi, by stating that he is considering running as an independent has thrown away all pretense at being a Democrat," was defamatory because it characterized him as "a deceiver, a man unworthy of public confidence, a man having a pretended character and a man who is a premeditated liar." The court held that running as an independent is not disgraceful as to hold a person up to public ridicule or contempt. The court further held that the thrust of the statement implying that Frinzi was not a good Democrat was also not libelous even though it might cause some Democrats not to vote for him. Likewise, how elected officials vote on issues is not disgraceful so that it would lower their esteem in the community even though it might cause some electors not to vote for them. The candidates attempt to distinguish *Frinzi* on the basis that here false factual statements were intentionally made four days before the election in order to persuade voters not to vote for them. However, the fact that the alleged misrepresentations were intended does not render a nondefamatory statement defamatory. . . .

Judgment affirmed.

[Dissenting opinion omitted. The court's decision was affirmed on similar reasoning in *Tatur v. Solsrud,* 174 Wis.2d 735, 498 N.W.2d 232 (1993).]

---

21. **Lowered esteem, social avoidance.** The defamatory quality of many publications is obvious enough. "Plaintiff is a child molester," "the plaintiff is technically a good surgeon but performs many unnecessary surgeries" are statements easily found defamatory. Recall that the Restatement treats words as defamatory if they *either* tend to lower the plaintiff in the community's esteem *OR* tend to cause others to avoid the plaintiff. Does the second clause add anything and if so why? Try applying the standard to these publications:

(A) "Plaintiff is a troublemaker." *McGrath v. TCF Bank Savings, FSB*, 502 N.W.2d 801 (Minn. App. 1993), modified on other points in 509 N.W.2d 365 (Minn. 1993).

(B) "Plaintiff deserted her husband after he lost his hand in an explosion." *Burns v. McGraw–Hill Broadcasting Company, Inc.*, 659 P.2d 1351 (Colo. 1983).

(C) The defendant privately discharges the plaintiff from employment and then escorts her to the door in view of others but without comment. See *Bolton v. Department of Human Services*, 540 N.W.2d 523 (Minn. 1995).

(D) "Plaintiff contracted AIDS when the hospital used infected blood in a transfusion."

(E) "Plaintiff brought a law suit against a rapper claiming that his lyrics iced her sex life." Cf. *Tucker v. Fischbein,* 237 F.3d 275 (3d Cir. 2001); *Tucker v. Philadelphia Daily News,* 577 Pa. 598, 848 A.2d 113 (2004).

22. **Right thinking people?** Lowering esteem with which people in the community? How many people? If it is not defamatory to say of a person that she is a Democrat or a Republican, is that because "right-thinking people" would not think less of a person because she is one of the things named? Many cases, especially older ones, have tested defamatory content by the esteem of "right-thinking" people. E.g., *Columbia Sussex Corp., Inc. v. Hay,* 627 S.W.2d 270 (1981). Could you say instead that it is the esteem of a group that is at least a substantial minority? See, adopting the latter test, *Burns v. McGraw-Hill Broadcasting Com-*

pany, Inc., 659 P.2d 1351 (Colo. 1983) (quoting RESTATEMENT (SECOND) OF TORTS § 559).

23. **Imputations of homosexuality.** Suppose defendant says that the plaintiff is a homosexual or lesbian. This is a difficult subject. If you believe that there is nothing "wrong" with homosexuality, can you logically support liability when a person is falsely named a homosexual?

In *Nazeri v. Missouri Valley College*, 860 S.W.2d 303 (Mo. 1993), the court said: "The harm inflicted by defamation is particularly sensitive to the characteristics and situation of the injured party and of the society that surrounds him or her. Attitudes change slowly and unevenly among different groups. Despite the efforts of many homosexual groups to foster greater tolerance and acceptance, homosexuality is still viewed with disfavor, if not outright contempt, by a sizeable proportion of our population. Moreover, engaging in deviant sexual intercourse with another person of the same sex is still a class A misdemeanor in this state. We hold that a false allegation of homosexuality is defamatory in Missouri."

In *Albright v. Morton,* 321 F.Supp.2d 130 (D. Mass. 2004), the court distinguished *Nazeri* because it was based in part on the idea that homosexual conduct was a crime. "This rationale," the *Albright* court said, "is extinguished by the Supreme Court's recent ruling in *Lawrence v. Texas,* 539 U.S. 558, 123 S.Ct. 2472, 156 L.Ed.2d 508 (2003), finding a Texas statute criminalizing same sex sexual conduct unconstitutional under the Due Process Clause because individuals have a right to privacy to engage in sexual acts in their homes. The Supreme Court overruled *Bowers v. Hardwick,* 478 U.S. 186, 106 S.Ct. 2841, 92 L.Ed.2d 140 (1986), and concluded that continuing that precedent 'demeans the lives of homosexual persons.' Continuing to characterize the identification of someone as a homosexual defamation *per se* has the same effect."

24. **Alternatives.** Given the uncertainties and doubts about what counts as defamatory, why make the defamatory quality of a publication the legal launchpad anyway? Why not simply provide that the plaintiff can recover for any materially untrue personal statement so long as she proves damages of the general kind that would have been foreseeable?

(b) Meaning

As a part of determining whether a publication could reduce the community's esteem for the plaintiff, we will naturally need to know what the communication means. Frequently this is no problem. "He murdered his wife," is rather clear. But other publications are not so clear, so we have questions about what they mean, how meaning is determined, and who makes that determination.

GRANT V. READER'S DIGEST ASS'N, INC., 151 F.2d 733 (2d Cir.1946). The plaintiff was a lawyer. The defendant published a statement saying that the plaintiff represented the Communist Party as a legislative agent or lobbyist. *Held*, "although the words did not say that the plaintiff was a member of the Communist Party, they did say that he had acted on its behalf, and we think that a jury might in addition find that they implied that he was in general sympathy with its objects and methods. The last conclusion does indeed involve the assumption that the Communist Party would not retain as its 'legislative representative' a person who was not in general accord with its purposes; but that inference is reasonable and was pretty plainly what the author wished readers to draw from his words."

FUNDERBURK v. BECHTEL POWER CORP., 103 Wash.2d 796, 698 P.2d 556 (1985). Elledge, a safety supervisor for a large construction project, at a meeting of managers, commented that the first aid station where plaintiffs worked as nurses was a "whore's nest" (or perhaps he said "boar's nest"). He mentioned specifically that the floor was cracked, there was no privacy for patients, and that the station was dirty. The plaintiff-nurses who worked there sued. Elledge said he referred to the station, not to the nurses. The trial court concluded that everyone present understood the comments in this sense and consequently held for the defendant. *Held*, affirmed. "In order for a statement to be defamatory, it must be understood as such by those who heard it. Whether a statement is understood to be defamatory is a question for the trier of fact to determine. The trier of fact in this case, the trial court, concluded that the statement did not refer to the appellants and was understood as not referring to the appellants by those who heard it."

---

25. **The Restatement's blackletter.** The Restatement says that a publication means (a) what the recipient correctly understands that it was intended to express and also (b) what the recipient mistakenly but reasonably understands that it was intended to express. RESTATEMENT (SECOND) OF TORTS § 563.

26. **Jury role.** If reasonable people can differ about the intended or reasonably understood meaning, the issue is for the trier of fact. Illinois law, however, is at least theoretically different. It says that if there is a reasonable innocent construction to the published language the case must be dismissed unless the plaintiff can prove pecuniary loss resulting, even if the other reasonable construction of the language is one that clearly defames the plaintiff. *Bryson v. News America Pubs., Inc.,* 174 Ill.2d 77, 672 N.E.2d 1207, 220 Ill.Dec. 195 (1996); see *Knafel v. Chicago Sun–Times, Inc.,* 413 F.3d 637 (7th Cir. 2005).

27. **Two canons of interpretation.** Routine canons of interpretation tell us that in determining meaning, the whole context must be considered. Perhaps that includes not only the textual context, what went before and came after, but also the social context. See *Gjonlekaj v. Sot,* 308 A.D.2d 471, 764 N.Y.S.2d 278 (App.Div. 2003); *Turner v. KTRK*

Televsion, Inc., 38 S.W.3d 103 (Tex. 2000). Accepted canons also tell us that words are to be taken in the meaning that would be attached to them by ordinary people, seemingly ruling out highly subjective interpretations except where the statements are addressed to specialists or to cultural subgroups. See *November v. Time Inc.,* 13 N.Y.2d 175, 194 N.E.2d 126, 244 N.Y.S.2d 309 (1963).

28. **Meaning and the form of the language.** It seems obvious that language can convey defamatory meaning indirectly, even if, in form, there is no assertion at all. "We must evaluate the effect rather than the form of the language as a whole, for 'Positive assertion of a charge is not necessary to constitute a writing libelous; they may be made in the form of insinuation, allusion, irony, or questions, and the matter will be as defamatory ... as if asserted in positive and direct terms.' " *Spanel v. Pegler,* 160 F.2d 619, 622 (7th Cir. 1947).

29. **Meaning without words.** A "publication" is not necessarily in words or even in pictures. Sometimes conduct expresses a defamatory assertion. Imagine you are handcuffed while shopping and marched out of the store. In addition, figures of speech, expressions of belief, juxtapositions of a headline and photograph—all forms of communication can express meaning that may be defamatory. In speaking of defamatory statements we mean to include any form of expression to which meaning can be attached.

WARD V. ZELIKOVSKY, 136 N.J. 516, 643 A.2d 972 (1994). The defendant's publication was "She's a bitch" and "They don't like Jews." *Held*, not actionable. "Most courts that have considered whether allegations of racism, ethnic hatred or bigotry are defamatory have concluded for a variety of reasons that they are not. The most important reason is the chilling effect such a holding would cast over a person's freedom of expression. In Stevens v. Tillman, 855 F.2d 394 (1988), cert. denied, 489 U.S. 1065, 109 S.Ct. 1339, 103 L.Ed.2d 809 (1989), the Seventh Circuit held that an accusation of bigotry is not actionable unless the statement suggests the existence of defamatory facts. An elementary-school principal sued the president of the local parent teacher association for calling the principal a 'racist.' Judge Easterbrook, writing for a unanimous panel, reasoned that '[a]ccusations of "racism" no longer are "obviously and naturally harmful." The word has been watered down by overuse, becoming common coin in political discourse. ... Formerly a "racist" was a believer in the superiority of one's own race, often a supporter of slavery or segregation, or a fomenter of hatred among the races. ... Politicians sometimes use the term much more loosely, as referring to anyone (not of the speaker's race) who opposes the speaker's political goals—on the "rationale" that the speaker espouses only what is good for the jurisdiction (or the audience), and since one's opponents have no cause to oppose what is beneficial, their opposition must be based on race. The term used this way means only: "He is neither for me nor of our race; and I invite you to vote your race." ... That may be an unfortunate brand of politics, but it also drains the term of its former, decidedly opprobrious, meaning. The term has acquired intermediate meanings too. The speaker may use "she is a racist" to mean "she is condescending to me, which must be because of my race because there is no other reason to condescend" a reaction that attaches racial connotations to what may be an inflated opinion of one's self—or to mean "she thinks all black mothers are on welfare, which is stereotypical." Meanings of this sort fit comfortably within the immunity for name-calling.' . . .

"Not all accusations of bigotry are automatically non-defamatory, however. Instances may arise in which claiming someone is a bigot will become more than non-actionable insult. Whether an accusation of bigotry is actionable depends on whether the statement appeared to be supported by reasonably specific facts that are capable of objective proof of truth or falsity. The statement might explicitly refer to those specific facts or be made in such manner or under such circumstances as would fairly lead a reasonable listener to conclude that he or she had knowledge of specific facts supporting the conclusory accusation. For example, a claim of bigotry could include claims that the selected person had engaged in specific acts such as making racist statements, [or] denying another employment or advancement because of race or religion. . . ."

ROBEL V. ROUNDUP CORP., 148 Wash.2d 35, 59 P.3d 611 (2002). Co-workers, in the hearing of others, called the plaintiff a bitch, snitch, squealer and liar, adding that only idiots did the work she was assigned to do. *Held*: these words are not actionable as defamation. "The vulgarisms, along with the word 'idiot,' were plainly abusive words not intended to be taken literally as statements of fact. To determine whether the words 'snitch,' 'squealer,' and 'liar' should likewise be viewed as nonactionable opinions, we consider the 'totality of the circumstances' surrounding those statements. . . . [A] court should consider at least (1) the medium and context in which the statement was published, (2) the audience to whom it was published, and (3) whether the statement implies undisclosed facts."

---

30. **Headlines: the whole article rule.** Defamation by headline cases usually apply the canon that calls for reading the whole context. Newspaper headlines are thus construed in the light of the remainder of the story, and even if the headline seems defamatory, it is not actionable if the story as a whole negates the defamatory implication. *Central Arizona Light & Power Co. v. Akers*, 45 Ariz. 526, 46 P.2d 126 (1935); see *Ross v. Columbia Newspapers*, 266 S.C. 75, 221 S.E.2d 770 (1976).

31. **Headlines: where text is far removed.** But what is the whole context when the story is a long one? In *Kaelin v. Globe Communications Corp.*, 162 F.3d 1036 (9th Cir. 1998), the jury could find that

the headline implied that the plaintiff was suspected of murdering Nicole Brown Simpson and was libelous. The rest of the story, which might have dispelled the implication, was 17 pages removed. The jury could find that the text so removed would not cure the libel in the headline and could impose liability accordingly.

32. **Headlines: systematic and repeated libel.** In *Sprouse v. Clay Communication, Inc.*, 158 W.Va. 427, 211 S.E.2d 674 (1975), the whole context was a series of headlines printed over a period of time. Liability was imposed for a headline even though the story might have redeemed it, where the publisher systematically, repeatedly, and intentionally printed misleading political headlines.

§ 4. ELEMENTS: "OF AND CONCERNING THE PLAINTIFF"

(a) Publications Defaming the Individual Plaintiff

BINDRIM v. MITCHELL

92 Cal.App.3d 61, 155 Cal.Rptr. 29 (1979)

KINGSLEY, Associate Justice. . . .

Plaintiff is a licensed clinical psychologist and defendant is an author. Plaintiff used the so-called "Nude Marathon" in group therapy as a means of helping people to shed their psychological inhibitions with the removal of their clothes.

Defendant Mitchell had written a successful best seller in 1969 and had set out to write a novel about women of the leisure class. Mitchell attempted to register in plaintiff's nude therapy but he told her he would not permit her to do so if she was going to write about it in a novel. Plaintiff [Defendant?] said she was attending the marathon solely for therapeutic reasons and had no intention of writing about the nude marathon. Plaintiff brought to Mitchell's attention paragraph B of the written contract which reads as follows: "The participant agrees that he will not take photographs, write articles, or in any manner disclose who has attended the workshop or what has transpired. If he fails to do so he releases all parties from this contract, but remains legally liable for damages sustained by the leaders and participants."

Mitchell reassured plaintiff again she would not write about the session, she paid her money and the next day she executed the agreement and attended the nude marathon. Mitchell entered into a contract with Doubleday two months later and was to receive $150,000 advance royalties for her novel. . . . The novel was published under the name "Touching" and it depicted a nude encounter session in Southern California led by "Dr. Simon Herford."

Plaintiff first saw the book after its publication and his attorneys sent letters to Doubleday and Mitchell. Nine months later the New American Library published the book in paperback.

The parallel between the actual nude marathon sessions and the sessions in the book "Touching" was shown to the jury by means of the tape recordings Bindrim had taken of the actual sessions. Plaintiff complains in particular about a portrayed session in which he tried to encourage a minister to get his wife to attend the nude marathon. Plaintiff alleges he was libeled by the passage [in which the fictional psychologist was presented as demanding, in extremely crude terms, that a minister-participant drag his wife to the nude marathon.]

Plaintiff asserts that he was libeled by the suggestion that he used obscene language which he did not in fact use. Plaintiff also alleges various other libels due to Mitchell's inaccurate portrayal of what actually happened at the marathon. Plaintiff alleges that he was injured in his profession and expert testimony was introduced showing that Mitchell's portrayal of plaintiff was injurious and that plaintiff was identified by certain colleagues as the character in the book, Simon Herford.

[The jury gave plaintiff a verdict for $38,000 in compensatory damages, plus a punitive award. The trial judge reduced the compensatory award to $25,000, awarded separately against each defendant.] . . .

Appellants allege that plaintiff failed to show he was identifiable as Simon Herford, relying on the fact that the character in "Touching" was described in the book as a "fat Santa Claus type with long white hair, white sideburns, a cherubic rosy face and rosy forearms" and that Bindrim was clean shaven and had short hair. . . . [T]he only differences between plaintiff and the Herford character in "Touching" were physical appearance and that Herford was a psychiatrist rather than psychologist. Otherwise, the character Simon Herford was very similar to the actual plaintiff. . . . Plaintiff was identified as Herford by several witnesses and plaintiff's own tape recordings of the marathon sessions show that the novel was based substantially on plaintiff's conduct in the nude marathon.

. . . [T]he transcripts of the actual encounter weekend show a close parallel between the narrative of plaintiff's novel and the actual real life events. Here, there were many similarities between the character, Herford, and the plaintiff Bindrim and those few differences do not bring the case under the rule of Middlebrooks. There is overwhelming evidence that plaintiff and "Herford" were one.

. . . The test is whether a reasonable person, reading the book, would understand that the fictional character therein pictured was, in actual fact, the plaintiff acting as described. Each case must stand on its own facts. In some cases, an appellate court can, on examination of the entire work, find that no reasonable person would have regarded the episodes in the book as being other than the fictional imaginings of the author about how the character he had created would have acted. . . . We cannot make any similar determination here. Whether a reader, identifying plaintiff with the "Dr. Herford" of the book, would regard the passages herein complained of as mere fictional embroidering or as reporting actual language and conduct, was for the jury. Its verdict adverse to the defendants cannot be overturned by this court.

Defendants raise the question of whether there is "publication" for libel where the communication is to only one person or a small group of persons rather than to the public at large. Publication for purposes of defamation is sufficient when the publication is to only one person other than the person defamed. Therefore, [it is] irrelevant whether all readers realized plaintiff and Herford were identical. . . .

Bindrim contends that the trial court erred in striking the damage award on the contract count. We are aware of no authority that a professional person can, by contract or otherwise, prevent one of his patients from reporting the treatment that patient received. Since the whole theory of plaintiff's therapy was that of group encounter, what Mitchell saw done to and by other members of the group was part of her own treatment. She was free to report what went on. The limits to her right to report were those involved in the libel counts. Plaintiff has no separate cause of action for the mere reporting. . . .

. . . The judge reduced the verdict against Mitchell from $38,000 to $25,000 on the ground that there was no evidence that the publication of the libel to Mrs. Hoover caused any damage. We agree with the court's determination that Mrs. Hoover was fully aware of what actually happened at the session, and therefore that plaintiff could not have been damaged by any publication to her. . . .

[The court modified the judgment to enter an award for $50,000 jointly and severally against Doubleday and Mitchell; an award of $25,000 in punitive damages was included against Doubleday alone.]

JEFFERSON, Associate Justice (concurring).

. . . The dissent erroneously describes the majority holding as creating a cause of action for libel out of a work of fiction that attacks the techniques of "nude encounter therapy." . . . Had the defendant author of the work of fiction limited her novel to a truthful or fictional description of the techniques employed in nude encounter therapy, I would agree with the dissent that plaintiff had no cause of action for defamation. . . .

FILES, Presiding Justice (dissenting).

This novel, which is presented to its readers as a work of fiction, contains a portrayal of nude encounter therapy, and its tragic effect upon an apparently happy and well-adjusted woman who subjected herself to it. Plaintiff is a practitioner of this kind of therapy. His grievance, as described in his testimony and in his briefs on appeal, is provoked by that institutional criticism. . . .

The decision of the majority upholding a substantial award of damages against the author and publisher poses a grave threat to any future work of fiction which explores the effect of techniques claimed to have curative value. . . .

Defendants' novel describes a fictitious therapist who is conspicuously different from plaintiff in name, physical appearance, age, personality and profession. Indeed the fictitious Dr. Herford has none of the characteristics of plaintiff except that Dr. Herford practices nude encounter therapy. Only three witnesses, other than plaintiff himself, testified that they "recognized" plaintiff as the fictitious Dr. Herford. All three of those witnesses had participated in or observed one of plaintiff's nude marathons. The only characteristic mentioned by any of the three witnesses as identifying plaintiff was the therapy practiced. . . .

Plaintiff has no monopoly upon the encounter therapy which he calls "nude marathon." Witnesses testified without contradiction that other professionals use something of this kind. There does not appear to be any reason why anyone could not conduct a "marathon" using the style if not the full substance of plaintiff's practices.

Plaintiff's brief discusses the therapeutic practices of the fictitious Dr. Herford in two categories: Those practices which are similar to plaintiff's technique are classified as identifying. Those which are unlike plaintiff's are called libelous because they are false. Plaintiff has thus resurrected the spurious logic [of] which Professor Kalven wrote: "There is revealed here a new technique by which defamation might be endlessly manufactured. First, it is argued that, contrary to all appearances, a statement referred to the plaintiff; then, that it falsely ascribed to the plaintiff something that he did not do, which should be rather easy to prove about a statement that did not refer to plaintiff in the first place. . . ."

Even if we accept the plaintiff's thesis that criticism of nude encounter therapy may be interpreted as libel of one practitioner, the evidence does not support a finding in favor of plaintiff.

Whether or not a publication to the general public is defamatory is "whether in the mind of the average reader the publication, considered as a whole, could reasonably be considered as defamatory."

The majority opinion contains this juxtaposition of ideas: "Secondly, defendants' (proposed) instructions that the jury must find that a substantial segment of the public did, in fact, believe that Dr. Simon Herford was, in fact, Paul Bindrim (CT 173, 171), was properly refused. For the tort of defamation, publication to one other person is sufficient, Supra."

The first sentence refers to the question whether the publication was defamatory of plaintiff. The second refers to whether the defamatory matter was published. The former is an issue in this case. The latter is not. Of course, a publication to one person may constitute actionable libel. But this has no bearing on the principle that the allegedly libelous effect of a publication to the public generally is to be tested by the impression made on the average reader. . . .

---

33. **Of and concerning, the test.** The publication must be "of and concerning" the plaintiff. The Restatement says that a statement is concerning the plaintiff when the recipient of the statement "correctly, or mistakenly but reasonably understands that it was intended" as a reference to the plaintiff. RESTATEMENT (SECOND) OF TORTS § 564. Is this helpful?

34. **Testimony.** Should courts admit testimony of individuals who say they thought that the publication referred to the plaintiff? In *Naantaanbuu v. Abernathy,* 746 F.Supp. 378 (S.D.N.Y. 1990), a book recounted Dr. Martin Luther King's last night before he was assassinated, saying he and others went to a dinner at a friend's house and perhaps implying that he had sexual relations with the friend. The plaintiff sued, claiming she was the one referred to, although no names or identifying characteristics were given. The court thought testimony that others thought she was referred to would probably be admissible and refused to dismiss. What if the witnesses can give no objective reasons for thinking that the alleged implications referred to the plaintiff?

35. **Extrinsic facts identifying plaintiff known to few.** Only those people who know facts extrinsic to the book itself could lose esteem for Bindrim. You and I, reading the book and not knowing Bindrim, could not identify him. Does that make the case different from one in which the publisher names a movie star or singer whose name and picture you would recognize but with whom you have no dealings and about whom you care nothing?

36. **Physical descriptions.** In *Carter-Clark v. Random House, Inc.,* 196 Misc.2d 1011, 768 N.Y.S.2d 290 (N.Y. Sup. Ct. 2003), *aff'd* 17 A.D.3d 241, 793 N.Y.S.2d 394 (2005), *Primary Colors,* a book of fiction based on President Clinton's first presidential primary campaign depicted the presidential aspirant visiting a library in Harlem, where, in real life, the plaintiff worked. In the book, the presidential campaigner meets a woman who works there and later the two are depicted coming out of a bedroom arranging their clothes, with the implication of a sexual encounter. The book gives only minimal physical description of the woman. The court held that the plaintiff could not adequately show that the scenes described were of and concerning her, mentioning the sketchy physical description as one of the reasons.

37. **Same name plaintiffs.** Suppose that a real person was named Simon Herford. Could that person sue? Try to determine upon what facts the answer would depend. Would it matter that the book had the usual disclaimer to the effect that it referred to no actual person? In *Bryson v. News America Publications, Inc.,* 174 Ill.2d 77, 672 N.E.2d 1207, 220 Ill.Dec. 195 (1996), a short story about "Bryson" allegedly defamed the plaintiff of the same last name. The identity of name and general location in the state was held sufficient ground for rejecting a motion to dismiss the complaint. But in *Springer v. Viking Press,* 90 A.D.2d 315, 457 N.Y.S.2d 246 (1982), *aff'd,* 60 N.Y.2d 916, 458 N.E.2d

1256, 470 N.Y.S.2d 579 (1983), the defendant's book contained a character named Lisa—the plaintiff's given name—and had her living on 114th Street, where the plaintiff lived. The fictional Lisa had some of the same physical characteristics as the real-life plaintiff. In fact, the defendant author and the plaintiff had been close friends before a rancorous breakup. As to people who knew both plaintiff and defendant and knew of their former relationship, would it be reasonable to think that the book's bad Lisa was the good Lisa of real life? The court held that the plaintiff had not shown that bad Lisa was about her.

38. **Special proof requirements?** Matthew Savare, Comment, *Falsity, Fault, and Fiction: A New Standard for Defamation in Fiction,* 12 U.C.L.A. Ent. L. Rev. 129 (2004), wants to hold as a matter of law that identification is insufficient unless the plaintiff produces clear and convincing evidence showing that "the defendant intentionally used the fiction device as a subterfuge to defame the plaintiff" and was actuated by hatred, ill-will or spite. In addition he would require that the identification be unmistakable.

39. **Counseling libel victims.** Should you counsel a client to sue for libel? That is an important question for lawyers. Although you'll have a better basis for answering as we pursue more material, consider the question now in connection with Bindrim's claim. Was Bindrim well advised to sue? Consider also whether the defendant might have expended more in defense than in paying the judgment.

Reference: On identifying the plaintiff, see 2 Dobbs on Torts § 405 (2001 & Supps.).

(b) Defaming the Individual Plaintiff by "Defaming" a Group

40. **Illustrative problems in group defamation.** *Case 1*: Defendant publishes a book in which authors discuss various persons working at Nieman-Marcus in Dallas. The book says most of the salesmen at Nieman-Marcus in Dallas are fairies. There were 25 salesmen. None was identified or identifiable as being within the target group.

Case 2: Defendant makes derogatory statements about doctors of osteopathy (D.O.s), implicitly comparing them to chiropractors and explicitly asserting that their training is inferior to that of M.D.s. There are almost 20,000 D.O.s in the United States.

41. **Large and small groups.** When the group is small, as in Case 1, courts have sometimes allowed all to sue, even though the libelous language only applies to "most." Recovery on facts of Case 1 was held permissible in *Neiman-Marcus v. Lait,* 13 F.R.D. 311 (S.D.N.Y. 1952). When the group is large and no particular plaintiffs can be identified except by the fact that they are members of the group, recovery is denied. On facts like those in Case 2, recovery was denied in *McCullough v. Cities Service Co.,* 676 P.2d 833, 52 A.L.R.4th 609 (Okla. 1984).

42. **Professor King's proposal.** Professor King proposes categorically to exclude claims when the group exceeds 25 members as well as to

impose other limitations. See Joseph H. King, Jr., *Reference to the Plaintiff Requirements in Defamatory Statements Directed at Groups,* 35 WAKE FOREST L. REV. 343 (2000). What if the group does not have membership cards and cannot be readily or accurately counted? What if the group has 50 members, but everyone thinks it has 25 members, one of which is known to be the plaintiff?

43. **Factors besides size.** Besides the size of the group, courts have listed several factors to be considered in determining whether the group can sue. These include (a) intensity of suspicion, (b) cohesiveness of the group, (c) the nature and intensity of the libel, (d) the prominence of the group and (e) the prominence of individuals within the group. *McCullough,* supra ¶ 41, mentioned some of these factors.

44. **Recovery by all members of the group?** Suppose a defamatory statement is made about a small class of persons: "All the older white male law school teachers at Lexola University have been guilty of sexual harassment of their students at one time or another." Only five men on the Lexola faculty could be considered "older white male" teachers. Can they all recover? Is the answer different if the statement is not that all of them were guilty but only that some or most of them were?

45. **An application: 21 officers.** The defendant newspaper published a column that asked: "Is it true that a Bellingham cop locked himself and a female companion in the back of a cruiser in a town sandpit and had to radio for help?" The Bellingham police department had 21 officers. All 21 sued. The court dismissed the complaint. *Arcand v. The Evening Call Pub. Co.,* 567 F.2d 1163 (1st Cir. 1977). Is this contrary to the *Neiman-Marcus* case where 25 salesmen were allowed to sue?

46. **Identifying the problem.** Is the problem in group libel mainly about (a) the of and concerning problem, (b) whether harm is done, (c) a policy concern? Consider the effect on public discussion if people could be sued for libel for negative statements about lawyers as a whole. On the other hand, consider the effects of systematic libel of minority groups.

(c) Disqualifying Plaintiffs on other Grounds

47. **Public entities and estates of the deceased as plaintiffs.** Besides the problem of identifying the plaintiff as the person who was defamed, a particular plaintiff may be disqualified from suit on at least two other grounds more or less personal to the plaintiff himself.

(1) Public entities may be denied standing to sue for defamation and perhaps for other torts that depend on the defendant's communication. See *Chicago v. Tribune Co.,* 307 Ill. 595, 610, 139 N.E. 86, 91, 28 A.L.R. 1368 (1923); see J. A. Bryant, Jr., *Right of Governmental Entity to Maintain Action for Defamation,* 45 A.L.R.3d 1315 (1972) (reflecting general accord that no such action will be entertained).

(2) An estate of a deceased person usually cannot sue for defamation of the deceased. See Chapter 6, § 1.

§ 5. LIBEL VS. SLANDER

48. **Slander: pecuniary loss generally required.** Slander is, roughly at least, oral defamation. Actions for slander originated in Church Courts of medieval England. Church courts might impose a penance upon the sinning slanderer, but did not assess damages in favor of the victim. The royal courts—that is, the common law courts—eventually began to give relief in slander cases where the plaintiff had suffered temporal damages such as pecuniary loss, since the church courts made no financial award to the victim. Eventually the common law courts took over all slander actions, but they retained the requirement that the plaintiff would have to prove some kind of pecuniary loss. They then held that such a loss could be presumed in several categories of exceptional cases. In these categories the slander is said to be "per se" so that no proof of pecuniary harm is required. (Slander that is not per se is sometimes called slander per quod.)

49. **Classification of publications as libel or as slander.** Defamation can count as libel and thus garner presumed damages even though it is not actually in writing. For instance, Lord Coke once said that a demeaning picture or a person or a gallows-sign scratched on the plaintiff's house might constitute a kind of libel. *De Libelis Famosis*, 50 Co.Rep. 125a, 77 Eng. Rep. 250 (Star Chamber 1605). Making an oral statement by reading aloud from written materials has traditionally qualified as a libel rather than merely a slander. An oral defamatory statement may also result in a libel if the speaker knows, intends, or foresees that it will be reduced to writing or other permanent form, and it is in fact published in such a form. See *Cohen v. Bowdoin,* 288 A.2d 106 (Me. 1972).

What about media publications? Motion pictures and television are visual and comparable to writing and pictures on that ground. What about radio? One solution is to switch from the emphasis upon the visual to an emphasis upon the tangible. Printing and writing, videos and films are all embodied in a tangible medium and might be grouped together on that account. Radio would be classified in the same way if there were a sound recording. But does it seem silly to say that a radio broadcast is libel if it is recorded but slander if not? If so, you might say all media publications, with their potential for mass communication, should be considered as libel. But you are on the slippery slope: what about defamation by an unrecorded loudspeaker at a football stadium where 50,000 people listen intently?

The Restatement adopted flexible "factors" in lieu of a rule or a policy guide. It said that the decision whether to classify as slander or as libel depended upon (a) the breadth or area of dissemination, (b) whether it is premeditated and (c) whether the communication persists over time. RESTATEMENT (SECOND) OF TORTS § 568.

50. **Categories of slander per se.** Courts have generally recognized three or four categories of slander per se. "Slander per se is that which charges (1) a serious criminal offense or one of moral turpitude, (2) a "loathsome" and communicable disease, (3) any matter incompatible with business, trade, profession, or office, and, sometimes, (4) serious sexual misconduct." DAN B. DOBBS, THE LAW OF TORTS § 408 (2000).

51. **Serious criminal offense.** Accusations of crime do not count as slander per se unless they are accusations of a serious crime. The Restatement expresses this by saying that the crime charged must be either punishable by imprisonment or regarded as involving moral turpitude. Ascription to the plaintiff of a criminal character or disposition is not the imputation of a crime—nor is an imputation of conduct that is a crime elsewhere but not at the place published.

52. **Loathsome disease.** A loathsome disease was traditionally a venereal disease or leprosy, two diseases once believed incurable. Today AIDS would easily count. See *McCune v. Neitzel,* 235 Neb. 754, 457 N.W.2d 803 (1990) (AIDS).

53. **Matter incompatible with business, trade, profession.** Two constraints limited this category. First, the bad conduct or character imputed to the plaintiff must be incompatible with the proper conduct of the plaintiff's profession or business. To say a landlord bribes police officers does not say his character is incompatible with his business. See *Liberman v. Gelstein,* 80 N.Y.2d 429, 605 N.E.2d 344, 590 N.Y.S.2d 857 (1992). Second, the slander against the plaintiff must speak to the plaintiff's character, habit, persistent predilection, or ongoing condition, not merely to a one-time or occasional lapse. Do you think a statement that a physician has a terminal illness would qualify? *Ravnikar v. Bogojavlensky,* 438 Mass. 627, 782 N.E.2d 508 (2003). What about a statement that a surgeon got drunk on Saturday night? That she was always intoxicated? Sometimes courts speak of a "single instance rule" as if to say that a single instance could never demonstrate character incompatible with the plaintiff's trade or profession. Is that too extreme? Is there any single act that could be attributed to a lawyer that would make potential client think she is incompetent or untrustworthy?

54. **Serious sexual misconduct.** This category began more narrowly as a kind of gallantry: if you imputed unchastity to a woman, that would be slander per se and damages presumed. This obviously turned on gender distinctions and also on a social insistence upon chastity that is no longer given such a place of esteem. For both reasons, some authorities have reshaped the category to cover only serious sexual misconduct (of either gender). See RESTATEMENT (SECOND) OF TORTS § 574 (1977); *Rejent v. Liberation Publications, Inc.,* 197 A.D.2d 240, 611 N.Y.S.2d 866 (1994).

55. **What counts as pecuniary harm.** Pecuniary harm can be demonstrated by proof of any loss of a thing having pecuniary value,

including loss of income. Loss of reputation may lead to pecuniary loss but it is not pecuniary loss in itself.

BEVERLY ENTERPRISES, INC. v. TRUMP, 182 F.3d 183 (3d Cir. 1999). The plaintiff Dotson was a vice president of an employer, Beverly. He had had a distinguished career as Chairman of the National Labor Relations Board and as an assistant Secretary in the Labor Department. In a large crowd, the defendant, who was a labor leader, allegedly made angry accusations against both Dotson and his employer, to the effect that "you people at Beverly are all criminals," then saying that the vice-president was "part of that World War II generation that danced on the graves of Jews." *Held*: (1) The first statement is not actionable; it is mere name-calling. (2) The second statement imputes racial bigotry but that falls in none of the categories of slander per se. "[T]o survive a motion to dismiss, the plaintiff must go beyond a claim of injury to reputation and allege special damages. Typically considered as a pecuniary loss, special damages are actual and concrete damages capable of being estimated in money, established by specific instances such as actual loss due to withdrawal of trade of particular customers, or actual loss due to refusal of credit by specific persons, all expressed in figures."

---

56. **Pecuniary harm with parasitic damages.** Once the plaintiff establishes pecuniary loss, she can recover all elements of damages, including such nonpecuniary damages as emotional harm. See *Walker v. Grand Central Sanitation, Inc.*, 430 Pa.Super. 236, 634 A.2d 237 (1993). Conversely, proving emotional harm without pecuniary loss does not permit recovery for slander that is not slander per se.

57. **Changing law.** Almost everyone who looks at the law of defamation finds it unsatisfactory or worse. Some changes are seeping in. In *Nazeri v. Missouri Valley College*, 860 S.W.2d 303 (Mo. 1993), the court said: "We hold that in defamation cases the old rules of per se and per quod do not apply. . . . [P]laintiffs need not concern themselves with whether the defamation was per se or per quod, nor with whether special damages exist, but must prove actual damages in all cases." Several other cases have now also abolished the presumption of damages and required proof of reputational harm whether the claim is for libel or slander and whether it was traditionally "per se" or not. See DOBBS ON TORTS § 409 (2000). Commentators have supported such a change. David A. Anderson, *Reputation, Compensation, and Proof*, 25 WM. & MARY L. REV. 747 (1984); see also RODNEY A. SMOLLA, LAW OF DEFAMATION § 7.08. The Constitution and certain statutes may have the effect of requiring proof of actual damages but not necessarily pecuniary loss in certain cases. Statutes governing some special cases may go further by requiring proof of pecuniary loss and perhaps by limiting all recovery to such loss.

58. **Possible alternatives.** If you think change is needed, consider these alternatives to the *Nazeri* rule: (a) the distinction between libel and slander is abolished but damages are presumed in all cases, that is, slander is treated like libel; (b) courts should retain the basic structure of rules but incrementally add to the slander per se categories as required by justice or policy; (c) courts should only modify the slander per se rules to require proof of some actual harm such as actual loss of reputation but should no longer require proof of pecuniary loss.

§ 6. LIBEL PER SE AND PER QUOD

59. **The traditional rule.** The common law rule held that with libel as distinct from slander, damages were presumed once the defamatory quality of a publication was shown. The plaintiff could recover substantial sums without proving (a) any pecuniary loss such as loss of a job or even (b) any actual harm to reputation that caused people to view the plaintiff differently. All libel, then, was libel per se in the sense that no proof of special (or any) damages was required to make the plaintiff's case. RESTATEMENT (SECOND) OF TORTS § 569 (1977).

60. **The rule of libel per quod.** For complex reasons, some courts stumbled into a different rule for libel. Leaving aside wrinkles in the rule, some of these courts came to this position about publications that would be libel if they were defamatory at all:

> (1) Where the publication is seemingly innocent rather than defamatory, the publication is not libelous per se [not libelous in itself]; in such a case, the plaintiff may introduce evidence of extrinsic facts to show that it has a defamatory meaning in spite of its apparent innocence; but
>
> (2) where extrinsic facts were required to show the defamatory quality of the publication, the plaintiff has no action for libel unless she also proves special damages in the form of pecuniary loss.

61. **Example of the extrinsic facts/special damages rule.** A commonly mentioned example goes something like this: The defendant's publication states that Pam had a baby yesterday. The publication is not defamatory on its face. Pam might bring in facts extrinsic to the publication, however, to show that, as everyone in town knows, she is unmarried. Consequently, she might claim that putting the publication together with the readers' knowledge of other facts, the publication becomes libelous. The extrinsic facts/special damages rule, sometimes called the rule of libel per quod, would allow Pam to recover, but only if she had pecuniary loss resulting from the publication.

62. **Caveat: another version of the per quod rule.** Some courts apply the per quod rule to require special damages, not when extrinsic facts are required to show the defamatory quality, but when the publication is ambiguous and one horn of the ambiguity is non-defamatory. See RODNEY A. SMOLLA, LAW OF DEFAMATION § 7:29 (Westlaw database updated May 2005)

63. **Policies, practicalities, and qualifiers.** Although courts seem to have stumbled into adopting a libel per quod rule, it might conceivably be a surrogate for a policy rule. Maybe you can't reasonably presume damages when the facts that make the publication potentially defamatory are not included in the publication. If that's the point to be served by the per quod rule, then maybe New York is right in saying that where everyone already knows the extrinsic facts, you can, after all presume damages in a per quod case. See *Hinsdale v. Orange County Publications, Inc.,* 17 N.Y.2d 284, 217 N.E.2d 650, 270 N.Y.S.2d 592 (1966). Could the per quod rule be an early effort to protect some publishers who were not at fault? (Recall that libel was and sometimes still is a strict liability tort.)

*

Professional and Academic Enhancements
Chapter 1

History and Aims of Defamation Law

Grotesque anomalies. More than one hundred years ago a commentator observed about defamation law:

> [P]erhaps no other branch of the law is as open to criticism for its doubts and difficulties, its meaningless and grotesque anomalies. It is, as a whole, absurd in theory, and very often mischievous in its practical operation.

Van Vechten Veeder, *The History and Theory of the Law of Defamation I*, 3 Colum. L. Rev. 546 (1903) (hereafter Veeder I). This observation may suggest why a little history as well as a lot of analysis may help understand the law of defamation.

Aims and distinctions: insult and honor. The law of defamation permits recovery of damages, ostensibly to redress harm to the plaintiff's reputation, or her loss of esteem in the community. Is it more than that, or less? The idea of reputation is under-defined and easily confused with other ideas. Primitive law may have focused at least part of the time on insult rather than on harm to reputation as such. In primitive societies, insult could lead to blood feud. Legal redress for harsh words or name-calling formalized the victim's vengeance and made the violence of revenge unnecessary. The sting of derogatory words may not have been that someone believed them but that the defendant could get away with making the accusation at all. Reputation would be lost, all right, but only because the plaintiff did not get revenge. A money recovery would provide as good a revenge for words of shame as a blood feud, and more profitably. So "if one calls a man 'wolf' or 'hare' one must pay him three shillings. . . ." 2 Frederick Pollock & Frederick Maitland, The History of English Law 537 (2d ed. 1952). You can see the idea that the defendant must not be allowed to get away with insult, verbal or physical, in the fact that the victim of a physical beating might assert not only injury but dishonor. Veeder I at 549. Today courts and commentators routinely treat defamation law as redress for reputational loss rather than redress for insult or shame. Yet you may doubt that reputation is really the core issue in some cases of libel. At least so far as damages are still presumed, so that the plaintiff is not required to prove lost reputation, the question of what you are protecting by defamation law is open to question.

Sin: slander and the church courts. In the medieval period, church courts in England punished some kinds of slander on the theory that it was sinful to slander your neighbor. In 1222 a Church "constitution" threatened excommunication for anyone who might "for the sake of hatred, profit, or favour . . . maliciously impute a crime to any person who is not of ill fame among good and substantial persons. . . ." R.H. HELMHOLZ, INTRODUCTION, SELECT CASES ON DEFAMATION TO 1600, at xiv-xv (Selden Society 1985). After that, Church courts punished certain slanders as sins. The punishment was penance prescribed by religious law, not a money judgment. The emphasis was not on harm to reputation as such, but on sinfulness of the speaker. The Church imposed a penalty or penance upon the speaker and part of this might include some form of amends to the victim.

Common law courts take over slander. The Church Courts were inquisitorial in method and sometimes corrupt as well. This gave common law courts practical ground for asserting jurisdiction over slander where the plaintiff suffered temporary harm—pecuniary loss—as a result of the slander and in the 1500s they did so. The theory was that the Church could not give damages, so where the plaintiff suffered pecuniary loss, the common law should step in. The common law addition of pecuniary loss in slander cases necessarily injected the idea of objective loss of reputation and moved the concept of defamation away from insult and sin. But vestiges of slander's ontogeny may still cloud our thinking.

Sedition: political libel. As early as 1275, statutes condemned defamation of "great men" like prelates and earls, mainly because such defamation was seen as creating turbulance or sedition. By the early 17th century the printing press was seen as a threat by the English monarchy; printed materials might be both seditious and widely effective. So the Star Chamber, which was in reality more like an arm of royal power than anything we would consider a court, imposed criminal liabilities for printed publications that criticized the government or its officers and also printing that might tend to provoke more private disorders such as duels. The theory of the Star Chamber, Veeder says, was that law could not always obtain the right result, so a court of unrestrained power was required. Veeder I at 562–63. Here the emphasis again was not directly on reputation, but on political stability. Incident to this emphasis on writing, the Star Chamber developed a new distinction between oral slander and written libel. The Star Chamber was abolished in the upheavals leading to the English Civil War, but the law of libel then passed on to the common law courts. After the English Civil War and the Restoration of the monarchy in 1660, courts began to develop the modern law of defamation, with its theoretical emphasis on reputational loss.

In *Telnikoff v. Matusevitch,* 347 Md. 561, 702 A.2d 230 (1997), the Maryland Court summarized England's traditional repressive attitude toward speech in this way:

> Printing was introduced in England in 1476, but the Crown's pervasive control over the press and publications began under the reign of Henry VIII and continued throughout the Tudor period and much of the Stuart period. The control took the form of royal proclamations containing lists of prohibited publications, the grant-

> ing of monopolies or privileges to certain printers, orders by the Privy Council and investigations by the Council into allegedly seditious statements and publications, decrees and prosecutions by the court of the Star Chamber for "seditious libel," and a comprehensive licensing system. Under the Star Chamber Decree of June 23, 1586, "[a]ll books (with the exception of law books and books printed by the queen's printer) were required to be licensed by the Archbishop of Canterbury and the Bishop of London. Law books were to be licensed by the Justices." Fredrick Seaton Siebert, *Freedom of the Press in England 1476–1776,* at 61–62 (1952).

The court added in a footnote that distribution or possession of prohibited publications could be punished by fine, imprisonment, or execution.

Seditious libel in America: Peter Zenger. The Star Chamber, with its prosecutions for truthful speech, was abolished in the 17th century, but some Star Chamber doctrine was saved by the common law courts and transported to America by way of high-handed Colonial governors appointed by the Crown. In the 1730s, New York's British-appointed Governor Cosby controlled the only newspaper in that state. It was a fountain of propaganda for the Governor, his party, and the British. The Governor himself is said to have been avaricious and "shady" but in truth he seems to have been thoroughly corrupt. Citizens decided to set up a politically independent paper, *The New York Weekly Journal*. Peter Zenger was the printer. Cosby was the center of their attack. The *Journal* reported the Governor's misdemeanors and pointed out his attempts to cover up his "shady" dealings.

Cosby responded by attempting to get indictments against the authors who had criticized him, but Grand Juries refused on the ground that they could not identify the authors. Then Cosby burned copies of the paper in front of City Hall, although few citizens or officials would stay to watch. Finally, Cosby decided to prosecute Zenger for libel on the ground that he printed the offending paper. The Governor and Council ordered Zenger held for trial for "seditious libel."

Cosby's forces did not stop there. Bail was set so high that Zenger had to await trial in prison, a total of nine months. (Anna Catherine Zenger, his wife, put the paper out on time during his incarceration.) Then Zenger's lawyers were disbarred for objecting to the court's composition. But a lawyer named Andrew Hamilton (who had migrated to America as an indentured servant) came to his defense.

The trial that eventually followed has been widely published in transcript. In essence, Hamilton attacked the Star Chamber's doctrine that a citizen could be imprisoned for sedition because he published the truth. Although the judge did not agree with Hamilton, Hamilton was able to present the issue to the jury, which found Zenger not guilty on August 4, 1735.

Zenger's acquittal did not establish a free press in the Colonies, but it has ever since been a rallying point against the British scheme of criminal punishment for truthful words.

The events leading up to Zenger's trial, as well as the trial itself, are recounted in VINCENT BURANELLI, THE TRIAL OF PETER ZENGER 3–75 (1957). On the trial, see LEONARD LEVY, FREEDOM OF THE PRESS FROM ZENGER TO JEFFERSON (1966).

When the colonies achieved statehood, their own constitutions sometimes enshrined the feelings that freed Peter Zenger, providing in various ways for protection of free speech. And the Constitution of the United States, in the First Amendment, set out a plan for public discourse about public business opposed to the British system of control over ideas.

For a brief moment under President John Adams, the United States embraced the Star Chamber's use of political libel prosecutions to suppress opposition arguments. In the midst of a threat of war from France, the Congress enacted the Sedition Act in 1798, a statute that made it criminal to defame Congress or the President (John Adams). The statute inaugurated a series of persecutions of Adams' political enemies.

But the American outlook resurfaced. States became alarmed at the "reign of terror" wreaked under the statute. Kentucky and Virginia in effect declared the power of states to resist such unconstitutional actions. Eventually the act was repealed.

Personal defamation. The law of slander and libel reflects both political defamation and highly personal defamation, sometimes combined but often distinct. Personal defamation in America often charges the plaintiff with what the community regards as serious moral failings, crimes, disloyalty to country, lies, hypocrisy, sexual misbehavior or betrayal of the community's core standards. But there is a pragmatic side, too. Defamation is often charges the plaintiff with conduct that it incompatible with the plaintiff's business, trade, or profession and the gist of the complaint is that the plaintiff has suffered or may suffer financial loss. Finally, although personal defamation always theoretically involves reputation, some cases seem to involve little or no reputational harm. Instead, some personal defamation cases may be brought because the plaintiff feels insult or dishonor without any actual loss of reputation. The plaintiff's own privacy, self-image, or identity may be in question but perhaps not her reputation. This is a topic not well identified in most cases, although it raises a fundamental question what we are trying to do with defamation law.

Political and social defamation. The realm of political libel is usually more difficult. On the one hand, with the history of the Elizabethan police state as background, suppression of speech seems a risky business for a democratic society. On the other, defamatory propaganda has been used systematically to ruin individuals and groups as well as to put the defamers in power. See David Riesman, *Democracy and Defamation: Control of Group Libel*, 42 COLUM. L. REV. 727 (1942). The role of courts and damages judgments in these cases demands the most extreme care.

Publication

Publication and Privilege

A privilege is an affirmative defense in the nature of an exception to the general rule of liability. It is a battery if you intend to hit someone in a harmful or offensive way and actually do so. Yet in some cases you are privileged to hit another. For example, when you strike in reasonable self-defense. Privileges in defamation cases are exceptionally important. They are considered in Chapter 2. In the meantime, however, the intersection of privilege and publication is worth a look.

In covering the basic publication rules, we noted that courts sometimes refused to recognize intra-corporate and similar communications publications at all, but that some others treated such communications as publications, perhaps subject to a privilege. What difference does it make whether the judge goes the "no publication" route or the privilege route?

The answer is that if you treat the intra-corporate communication as a publication but say it may be privileged, the judge then becomes focused on the reasons for the privilege and its scope and on whether the privilege was "abused" by, say, the defendant's malice. A ruling that says there is no publication simply puts the plaintiff out of court. A ruling that says there is a publication but that it might be privileged, leads the court to a more considered approach. How would the two approaches work on the following set of facts?

Derringer is manager of a plastics factory. He sends a memo to the company's chief operating officer about plant efficiency. The memo says that a foreman, Adkins, is having an illicit sexual affair with Babson, the spouse of a local minister, and that the company is coming in for bad publicity as a result. "Incidentally," the memo goes on to say, "Babson was already notorious for an affair with another local minister." The accusation is defamatory both to Adkins and Babson. You represent Babson in a suit against Derringer. Derringer moves for summary judgment on the ground that there is no publication.

Publication and Privilege in Evaluation of Self-Publication Issues

Does the possibility of a privilege analysis assist us in evaluating the self-publication problem? Suppose you said that the usual rule of foreseeability governs when the employer gives the employee a defamatory reason for discharge. At least in some cases, re-publication by the employee would be foreseeable, so the employer is a publisher. Maybe that does not sound so radical if you realize that the employer may be privileged to tell the employee his reasons for discharge. If you find publication but also find a privilege, the employer would not be liable unless he was in bad faith or perhaps guilty of a knowing falsehood.

In *Gonsalves v. Nissan Mtr. Corp. in Hawai'i, Ltd.*, 100 Hawai'i 149, 58 P.3d 1196, (2002), the court rejected liability, seemingly on the ground that self-publication is not "publication" at all. The court gave these reasons: (1) Liability would shutdown communications between employer and employee, with potentially harmful results for both; for example, the employer would give no reasons for discharge, so the employee could not rebut false charges; (2) plaintiffs would have no incentive to "mitigate damages," and in fact could keep repeating the defamation for years, generating new law suits constantly; (3) liability would interfere with the employer's right to discharge at will employees. If these are good reasons for non-liability, do they suggest that there was no publication or only that the employer should be privileged and still subject to liability for knowing falsehood?

A Mini–Problem

The defendant, being sued for defamation, wishes to defend on the ground that the plaintiff also published some of the same defamatory material. Do the publication rules assist the defendant?

Meaning

Meaning: Evidence and the Judicial Process

Meaning and inference. Most issues about meaning have to do with inferences that the statement of one thing, innocent in itself, implies another that is defamatory. In *Bell v. National Republican Congressional Committee*, 187 F.Supp.2d 605 (S.D. W.Va. 2002), the defendant issued a political pamphlet with a picture showing the opposition candidate, Humphreys, and an unidentified man. The captain said that "A multi-millionaire trial lawyer, Jim Humphreys has represented rapists and repeat child molesters." The unidentified man was not a rapist or child molester and he sued. The defendant probably did not intend to say he was, but might reasonable people draw the inference that the photograph was depicting a rapist or child molester?

Judge and jury. The judge must decide whether the statements in issue are capable of bearing a defamatory meaning. In the inference case, the judge would decide whether the inference is rationally permissible. If it is not, the case is dismissed. If the judge concludes that reasonable people could draw the inference or find some other defamatory meaning, then the trier of fact must decide what meaning the words conveyed and whether that meaning was defamatory. This rule necessarily means that both judge and jury could recognize multiple meanings in any given statement. What is to be done if the defamatory meaning is permissibly inferred, but only a few people would draw that inference?

The meaning of meaning. As we've seen, the Restatement defines the meaning of a statement as being (a) what the recipient correctly understands that it was intended to express and also (b) what the recipient mistakenly but reasonably understands that it was intended to express. RESTATEMENT (SECOND) OF TORTS § 563. On the subjective test in clause (a), how would you prove what the defendant actually intended except by proving how the statement could reasonably be interpreted?

Testimony about meaning. *(a) Objective meaning.* When the defendant's publication rests on a word not commonly known, or not known to the judge, testimony may be required to explain the meaning of the word. Suppose a witness with appropriate credentials can tell the court the meaning of a foreign word or expression used in the allegedly defamatory statements. Wouldn't it make sense to admit such testimony, assuming the recipients of the publication read and understood the language?

(b) Interpretation or subjective meaning. Once the meaning of the word is known, nothing suggests that the judge must take testimony on the interpretative question. If the judge rules the statement is not capable of a defamatory meaning, the question of testimony on meaning becomes moot. Likewise if the judge rules that the statement is defamatory as a matter of law. However, where the trier of fact can properly find more than one possible meaning in the way known words are used, should witnesses be permitted or even required to testify about the meaning of an allegedly defamatory statement?

Suppose a witness would testify:"I understood the statement to mean that the defendant believed the plaintiff was turning his back on his own family." Judges and juries can decide the meaning of a statement as well as a witness. Unless the witness is basing his understanding on a fact that cannot be fully described, such as the defendant's facial expression at the time he spoke the words, meaning probably should not be determined by purely subjective witness testimony. Equally, the defendant should not be able to avoid liability on the ground that no one has testified to the meaning of the words or pictures used.

(c) Experts. Should an expert be permitted to testimony that "I fired X" means that X was dishonest or at least that it could rationally be interpreted to mean that? In *Seropian v. Forman,* 652 So.2d 490 (Fla. Dist. Ct. App. 1995), the alleged defamation was an accusation of "influence peddling." The plaintiff's expert testified a day and a half on the meaning of that term in the context. The court said: "If influence peddling conveyed the obloquy that plaintiff suggests, that fact should be readily understood by the ordinary jury without a political scientist swearing that it does. We find that the trial judge abused her discretion with regard to this political scientist's testimony."

A Problem in Meaning or Defamatory Quality

The plaintiff was a well-known anti-gangsta rap activist. A rapper named Tupac Shakur allegedly attacked her in an album called *All Eyez On Me*, leading the plaintiff to sue Shakur's estate for intentional infliction of emotional distress, slander, and invasion of privacy. One paragraph added a claim that her "husband, William Tucker has as a result of his wife's injuries, suffered a loss of advice, companionship and *consortium*."

Counsel for the estate, Fischbein, made arguably derisive comments and the media picked up the story. Newsweek wrote that "Even C.

Delores Tucker, the gangsta rap foe, wants a chunk [of Tupac Shakur's estate]. She and her husband claim that a lyrical attack by Tupac iced their sex life." Time, in an article entitled "Shakur Booty" wrote that Tucker was claiming the lyrics "caused her so much distress that she and her husband have not been able to have sex. She wants $10 million." The attorney made more comments for publication on the same assumption.

Tucker sued for defamation. If Fischbein's comments were like Newsweek's, did he get his law right? What do these publications mean? Are they defamatory?

Based on *Tucker v. Fischbein,* 237 F.3d 275 (3d Cir. 2001).

Problem: A Grammarian's Testimony: Smith v. Pickett

Sam Adam Pickett, believing that the Allen Corporation was an evil business, carried pickets on alternate Thursdays attacking those associated with Allen. One picket said:

Smith/Jones
worked for/did the hatchet jobs for
the Allen Corporation

Smith sued Pickett, claiming libel. Pickett offered an expert at grammar as a witness. When the trial judge inquired, Pickett's lawyer said the expert would, if permitted, testify (a) that the picket must be read to mean that Smith worked for the Allen Corporation and that Jones did hatchet jobs for the Allen Corporation and (b) that "worked for" was not defamatory, although "hatchet jobs" was. The trial judge refused to permit the evidence. When both parties rested, Pickett moved for a directed verdict on the ground that no testimony for either party established the meaning of the words. The trial judge denied the motion and submitted the case to the jury, which found the words to be defamatory and gave a verdict for the plaintiff in the amount of $50,000. The judge entered a judgment on the verdict. Estimate Pickett's chances of securing a reversal.

Slander and Libel per Se and per Quod and the Rule of Mitior Sensus

Slander per se and libel per se. How do libel per se and slander per se compare in a jurisdiction that requires proof of special damages when extrinsic facts are required to show that the publication is defamatory? Slander per se is tested by asking whether the publication falls within one of the four categories. Libel per se is tested by asking whether extrinsic facts are required to show the defamatory quality of the publication. The two concepts, though using some of the same words, are not traditionally the same at all.

Confusing slander per se and libel per se. Is defamation law confused enough that a judge might actually use the slander categories as part of the description of libel per se? Or use the libel "on its face" test as a test of slander per se? Yes and yes. See *Aycock v. Padgett,* 134

N.C.App. 164, 516 S.E.2d 907 (1999); *Ward v. Zelikovsky,* 263 N.J.Super. 497, 623 A.2d 285 (1993), overruled on other grounds, *Ward v. Zelikovsky,* 136 N.J. 516, 643 A.2d 972 (1994). Is it confused enough that a judge might decide that all libel is actionable per se without proof of special damages but that some libel was nevertheless libel per quod, meaning nothing at all about special damages? Yes. *Holtzscheiter v. Thomson Newspapers, Inc.,* 332 S.C. 502, 506 S.E.2d 497 (1998). Is it confused enough that a judge might use the slander test based upon categories in one part of the opinion and the libel "on its face" test in another part of the same opinion? Yes. *Moore v. Streit,* 181 Ill.App.3d 587, 130 Ill.Dec. 341, 537 N.E.2d 408 (1989).

Mitior sensus. The adoption of the libel per quod rule may have been prompted in some instances by an entirely different line of cases. Some old English opinions took the view that if a defamatory statement could be construed in an innocent (nondefamatory) way, then such a construction was mandatory. This rule was called the rule of *mitior sensus*. It obviously contradicts the normal rule that leaves disputable meanings to the jury. The Tennessee Court explained the rule thus (citations omitted):

> The courts of this state have consistently followed the prevailing common-law practice of construing the allegedly libelous words in their "plain and natural" import. Other jurisdictions have followed the seventeenth-century English doctrine of Mitior sensu, applicable to slander, which required that words be given an innocent construction whenever humanly possible. The art of construing in Mitior sensu probably reached its zenith (or perhaps its nadir) in the famous case of Holt v. Astrigg, 79 Eng.Rep. 161 (1608). In that case the allegedly slanderous language was: "Sir Thomas Holt struck his cook on the head with a cleaver, and cleaved his head; the one part lay on the one shoulder, and another part on the other." The court held that this was not slanderous per se because "it is not averred that the cook was killed ... [N]otwithstanding such wounding, the party may yet be living; and it is then but trespass." The court was of the opinion that slander "ought to be direct." *Memphis Pub. Co. v. Nichols*, 569 S.W.2d 412 (Tenn. 1978).

This innocent construction doctrine still complicates the law in Illinois (see ¶ 26) and perhaps some other states. It seems clear that the innocent construction rule addresses a set of facts that is quite different from the facts addressed by the per quod rule, but Illinois has seemingly combined the two rules.

Scope of the libel per quod special damages requirement. In a jurisdiction that follows the libel per quod rule, would special damages be required in these situations?

(A) The defendant's publication is ambiguous—capable of a defamatory meaning but also capable of an innocent one. "Joan is a very close friend and strong support for Bob, who is doing time in prison for dealing and is probably still dealing from prison." If a jury could find that this statement implies criminal activity by Joan or is otherwise defamatory, and could also find that the statement implies nothing defamatory, would Joan be required to prove special damages? See *MacLeod v. Tribune Pub. Co., Inc.*, 52 Cal.2d 536, 343 P.2d 36 (1959) (even though the publication may "also be susceptible of an innocent interpretation," special damages are not required; "The test is whether a defamatory meaning appears from the language itself without the necessity of explanation or the pleading of extrinsic facts"). Some statements are to the contrary, suggesting that if defamation can be found only through implication or if there is an innocent construction available for the defendant's language, the plaintiff is required to prove special damages. See *Becker v. Toulmin,* 165 Ohio St. 549, 138 N.E.2d 391 (1956).

(B) The defendant's publication is clearly defamatory on its face but the plaintiff is not named in the publication and she will have to bring in extrinsic facts to show that she was the person referred to. Illinois combines its innocent construction rule with its libel per quod rule and may or may not require the plaintiff who is not named but is arguably identifiable to show pecuniary loss here. See, applying or maybe reworking Illinois law, *Muzikowski v. Paramount Pictures Corp.,* 322 F.3d 918 (7th Cir. 2003).

(C) The defendant's publication uses a word that has defamatory meaning in the plaintiff's industry but that is not known to people generally; expert testimony will be required to explain the meaning of the word.

Rationales for the special damages requirement. The rule of libel per quod did not originate as a considered policy. Still, it might represent a complication in the law of libel that could be justified. Consider these possibilities:

(A) When libel is not apparent in the publication itself, not even by implication, then harm is not very likely or is likely to be small. In these circumstances, the plaintiff should prove pecuniary loss." See *Hinsdale v. Orange County Publications, Inc.,* 17 N.Y.2d 284, 217 N.E.2d 650, 270 N.Y.S.2d 592 (1966) (extrinsic facts known to all readers, special damages proof not required).

(B) When libel is not apparent in the publication itself, the publisher may have no way to recognize that he puts himself at risk for liability by publishing the material and should not be made to pay damages unless the plaintiff suffers pecuniary loss.

Coming at confusing material from a different direction. We cannot ignore the confusions that surround libel per quod because those confusions may shape outcomes. But for a breath of fresh air, consider what a coherent scheme of damages for libel would look like. Here are some options:

(A) Damages are presumed in all cases of published defamation, or at least all cases of libel.

(B) The plaintiff must prove damages in all cases of published defamation, but damages need not be pecuniary; proof of harm to reputation is sufficient.

(C) The plaintiff must prove pecuniary loss in all cases of published defamation.

Notice that any one of these possible rules would simplify the law of defamation. Notice also that we have not previously considered the second possible rule—that damages should be proved, but that "special" or pecuniary damages are not required. This may be the direction in which the courts are headed. Certainly a number of courts have now said that the plaintiff must prove actual harm. E.g., *Schlegel v. Ottumwa-Courier,* 585 N.W.2d 217 (Iowa 1998); *Walker v. Grand Central Sanitation, Inc.,* 430 Pa.Super. 236, 634 A.2d 237 (1993). And some authority is now prepared to take the logic all the way by abolishing the distinction between slander and libel. All plaintiffs would be required to prove actual harm to reputation but not pecuniary loss. See *Nazeri v. Missouri Valley College,* 860 S.W.2d 303 (Mo. 1993).

Other rules for extrinsic fact cases? In spite of the confusions and irritations of per quod talk, there is an underlying problem of no small concern. When a writer's words do not either state or logically imply anything defamatory it is very hard to say that the writer has defamed anyone. Extrinsic facts may allow readers to draw defamatory inferences, but the defamation doesn't come from the writer. Perhaps instead of requiring special pecuniary damages, courts should (a) require fault on the part of the publisher and (b) pay careful attention to truth issues. A little later we will see Constitutional decisions that give these ideas impetus, but for now we continue to examine state law defamation.

Chapter 2

TRUTH AND PRIVILEGE UNDER COMMON LAW AND STATUTES

---

§ 1. TRUTH AS A JUSTIFICATION: A FIRST TAKE

LEMONS V. CHRONICLE PUBLISHING CO., 253 Ill.App.3d 888, 192 Ill.Dec. 634, 625 N.E.2d 789 (1993). The plaintiff was apprehended by a retail store's personnel after he left with concealed merchandise. The plaintiff pulled a knife and the store employees were cut or scratched. As a result, the plaintiff was convicted of several crimes. The defendant newspaper reported the incident and later the conviction, saying the plaintiff had been convicted of stabbing security guards. The plaintiff sued for libel. He argued that (1) he had scratched but not "stabbed" the store employees and that they were not security guards; (2) that the report defamed him because to stab is worse than to scratch and to attack security guards is to attack "the badge." *Held*: the truth defense exonerates the defendant. The defendant's report is substantially true, so defendant's motion to dismiss was properly sustained. The burden of proof is on the defendant to show truth, but substantial truth going to the gist or sting of the libel is all that is required. Literal truth is not required.

---

1. **Burden of proof.** Notice that the common law burden of proof is on the defendant to show truth as an affirmative defense. In certain cases, to be seen in Chapter 4, the Constitution places the burden of proof upon the plaintiff to show falsity in the first instance.

2. **Substantial truth, gist, or sting; tests or standards.** The substantial truth rule, that if the gist or sting is true, the defendant is not liable, is well accepted. Some courts have tried to erect a standard for determining what counts as substantial truth. In *Masson v. New*

Yorker Magazine, Inc., 501 U.S. 496, 111 S.Ct. 2419, 115 L.Ed.2d 447 (1991), Justice Kennedy said:

> [T]he statement is not considered false unless it "would have a different effect on the mind of the reader from that which the pleaded truth would have produced."

Is this test literally correct or only substantially so?

3. **Bad reputation.** If the defendant cannot prove substantial truth, could he still introduce evidence of the plaintiff's bad reputation that falls short of proving substantial truth? To what issue would such evidence be directed? See *Fraser v. Park Newspapers of St. Lawrence Inc.,* 257 A.D.2d 961, 684 N.Y.S.2d 332 (1999).

MEMPHIS PUBLISHING CO. v. NICHOLS

569 S.W.2d 412 (Tenn. 1978)

BROCK, Justice.

On June 5, 1971, the following news article appeared in the Memphis Press–Scimitar:

> WOMAN HURT BY GUNSHOT Mrs. Ruth A. Nichols, 164 Eastview, was treated at St. Joseph Hospital for a bullet wound in her arm after a shooting at her home, police said. A 40-year-old woman was held by police in connection with the shooting with a .22 rifle. Police said a shot was also fired at the suspect's husband. Officers said the incident took place Thursday night after the suspect arrived at the Nichols home and found her husband there with Mrs. Nichols. Witnesses said the suspect first fired a shot at her husband and then at Mrs. Nichols, striking her in the arm, police reported. No charges had been placed.

Ruth Ann Nichols and her husband, Bobby Lee Nichols, filed separate actions, which were consolidated for trial, charging defamation and an invasion of privacy. The crux of plaintiffs' charge is that the article published by the defendant falsely implied that Mrs. Nichols and Mr. Newton, the assailant's husband, were having an adulterous affair, and were "caught" by Mrs. Newton. Plaintiffs charged that "at the time of the publication of the said article the defendant knew, or could have known had it exercised reasonable care, and could have ascertained that the said matters were untrue."

The undisputed proof showed that not only were Mrs. Nichols and Mr. Newton at the Nichols' home but so, also, were Mr. Nichols and two neighbors, all of whom were sitting in the living room, talking, when Mrs. Newton arrived around three o'clock in the afternoon. Hearing a commotion, Mr. Newton went outside to investigate and there his wife fired several shots at him. Mr. Newton then ran behind the Nichols' home whereupon Mrs. Newton entered the house and shot Mrs. Nichols. . . .

[T]he clear implication of the article is that Mrs. Nichols and Mr. Newton had an adulterous relationship and were discovered by Mrs. Newton, thus precipitating the shooting incident. If so read, it can hardly be doubted that Mrs. Nichols' reputation would be injured. . . .

In this case, the defendant newspaper does not assert that Mrs. Nichols and Mr. Newton in truth had an adulterous relationship. Nevertheless, the defendant's principal defense is that all material facts stated in the news article were substantially true, emphasizing in its brief:

> IT IS OF CRUCIAL IMPORTANCE TO NOTE THAT THE RECORD REFLECTS THAT EVERY MATERIAL FACT IN THE ARTICLE QUOTED ABOVE WAS TRUE." Mrs. Nichols was in fact treated at St. Joseph Hospital for a bullet wound in her arm after the shooting. A 40-year-old woman Was in fact held by police in connection with the shooting. A shot Was in fact fired at the suspect's husband. The suspect Did in fact find her husband at the Nichols' home with Mrs. Nichols. The suspect Did in fact fire a shot at her husband and then at Mrs. Nichols and Did in fact strike her in the arm. No charges Had in fact been placed at the time of the writing of the article.

In our opinion, the defendant's reliance on the truth of the facts stated in the article in question is misplaced. The proper question is whether the meaning reasonably conveyed by the published words is defamatory, "whether the libel as published would have a different effect on the mind of the reader from that which the pleaded truth would have produced." The publication of the complete facts could not conceivably have led the reader to conclude that Mrs. Nichols and Mr. Newton had an adulterous relationship. The published statement, therefore, so distorted the truth as to make the entire article false and defamatory. It is no defense whatever that individual statements within the article were literally true. . . .

Mrs. Nichols' libel suit is remanded to the trial court for a new trial. Mr. Nichols' suit for libel is dismissed. . . .

---

4. **Interpreting Nichols.** Would it be correct to say that under the principle in *Nichols* the defendant is held to guarantee not only the truth of what he literally says but also the truth of any reasonably drawn inferences from those statements? That is, the truth of the sting and not merely the truth of the very words used? Cf. *Schiavone Construction Co. v. Time, Inc.*, 847 F.2d 1069 (3d Cir. 1988) (jury to judge truth in light of its own finding as to the scope of the sting). What if the defendant states facts truthfully but omits to state exculpatory facts? See DOBBS ON TORTS § 411 (2001 & Supp.). What if the court thinks the omitted fact would not alter the false impression created by the publication? *Mohr v. Grant,* 153 Wash.2d 812, 108 P.3d 768 (2005).

5. **Testing the interpretation.** If the principle is that broad, will it work justly under the common law regime where no fault is required to establish libel? Suppose the defendant truthfully says any one of the following:

> I fired X.
>
> The X law firm used to represent me, but now I use the Y law firm.
>
> I brought a law suit against X and refused X's settlement offer. Shortly after that I was flying a plane that crashed. I was lucky to survive because someone had tampered with the fuel line.

6. **Truth of quotations.** Abigail Agave tells you that she saw Billy Bath cheating on a law school exam. You write to Cathy Cathcart: "Abigail told me that Billy Bath cheated on an exam." Perhaps you add, "I don't believe it." Billy Bath sues you for libel. What evidence would show that your writing was true? The answer is that repeaters are fully subject to liability. E.g., *Khawar v. Globe International, Inc.,* 19 Cal.4th 254, 965 P.2d 696, 79 Cal.Rptr.2d 178 (1998) (holding a newspaper liable for reporting the assertion in a book that the plaintiff had shot Robert Kennedy). In *Flowers v. Carville,* 310 F.3d 1118 (9th Cir. 2002), some of the defendants allegedly published statements to the effect that an *expert said* that the tapes produced by Gennifer Flowers to prove her connection with former President Clinton "had been edited to enhance Flowers's credibility." The court pointed out that, even if this was a correct statement of the expert's comment, it is a repetition for which the repeaters may be subjected to liability to Flowers. In Billy Bath's case, it is no defense to show that Abigail really did accuse Billy of cheating; you must show instead that Billy in fact cheated.

7. **The truth of opinion statements.** We will see in Chapter 4 that certain kinds of opinion statements are protected. But the protection does not apply to everything labeled opinion. You truthfully state that it is your opinion but only your opinion that Bath cheated. Or, similarly, you truthfully state that you suspect that Bath cheated but you cannot prove it. In *Republic Tobacco Co. v. North Atlantic Trading Co., Inc.,* 381 F.3d 717, 729 (7th Cir. 2004), the court said that "prefacing a defamatory statement with the phrase 'in my opinion' does not shield a defendant from liability, and the same is true for presenting a defamatory statement under a list of 'concerns.' "

8. **Defamatory questions.** You ask a question, "Did Bath cheat on the exam?" Can this be defamatory? The Privy Council once said in a case arising out of New Zealand: "It is defamatory to say of a man that he is suspected of dishonorable conduct. The defendants would, by imputing suspicion, be willing to wound, and yet afraid to strike—an attitude which a New Zealand jury would like no better than an English jury." *"Truth" (N.Z.) Ltd. v. Holloway,* [1960] 1 W.L.R. 997 (Privy Council 1960). Does a question arouse suspicion? *Lutz v. Watson,* 136 A.D.2d 888, 525 N.Y.S.2d 80 (1988).

MALOOF v. POST PUB. CO., 306 Mass. 279, 28 N.E.2d 458 (1940). Suits by four young men. "The alleged libels concerned the four plaintiffs and one James Abdella. The substance of the libels was that the five men were members of a gang of extortionists, and told one Zanditton, a garage proprietor, that they had been hired to kill him but would spare him if he would pay $25, which he paid them. On a later date, the newspapers asserted, they demanded $50 more from him, but before he paid it the police were notified and arrested the five men near Zanditton's garage. At the trial, the jury returned a verdict for the defendant in each of the eight cases. The exceptions of the several plaintiffs bring the cases here." *Held*, the plaintiff's exceptions sustained, new trial.

"The libels complained of charged the several plaintiffs with the crime of extortion. It is not denied that they were defamatory as matter of law. The only defense was the truth of the charge. The burden of proof was on the defendants to maintain that defense by showing the substantial truth of the charge in all material respects. It was not sufficient for the defendants to show that the plaintiffs were arrested on the charge of extortion, for in the present cases the charge was that the plaintiffs actually were guilty of extortion. The fact that the charge was qualified by the words 'it is alleged' or their equivalent, does not absolve the defendants from responsibility for publishing it. An accusation purporting to rest on hearsay is none the less defamatory."

---

9. **"Alleged."** Why isn't it enough to protect the newspaper that its story says "it is alleged" that the men were extortionists? Because the repeater rule in effect means that the defendant must show truth of the underlying facts, not merely truth of the fact that someone made allegations.

10. **Privilege vs. truth.** Distinguish the truth-falsity issue from the defense of privilege. As we'll see, there is a privilege to report official documents and public proceedings like trials. The limits of the truth defense show why such a privilege is needed.

11. **Non-factual ridicule.** The old idea that ridicule would be actionable as defamation has never fit well with the idea that truth could be a defense. Older cases held that truth was irrelevant in ridicule cases, so that the plaintiff could recover even though the ridicule was neither true nor false. In *Burton v. Crowell Pub. Co.*, 82 F.2d 154 (2d Cir. 1936), a picture of the plaintiff was actionable because it made people laugh at the similarity to a man exposing himself, although no one believed plaintiff was doing so. Ridicule that neither asserts nor implies misstatements of a factual nature is probably now constitutionally protected, at least where the target is a public figure or a public issue is involved. *Hustler Magazine v. Falwell,* 485 U.S. 46, 108 S.Ct. 876, 99 L.Ed.2d 41 (1988), below, Chapter 4, § 2.

12. **Strategy: reputation on the line.** Sometimes it may be better not to sue. In *Williams v. District Court*, 866 P.2d 908 (Colo. 1993), the plaintiff was an airline pilot who had been accused by flight attendants of sexual harassment and forced sexual intercourse. The pilot sued the defendant, alleging it was responsible for republication of these charges. The defendant served interrogatories inquiring in great detail about the pilot's past sexual history. The pilot resisted, but the trial judge held that he had put his reputation on the line by suing and that the information was relevant. The Supreme Court of Colorado agreed. "[A] defendant in a defamation action may present any evidence which tends to mitigate damages. Such evidence can include any publications by third persons dealing with the same subject, made before or at about the same time as the date of the publishing by the defendant. In this case, information concerning his past sexual history may lead to evidence of Williams' reputation, and whether it has been harmed by the alleged actions of the defendants." The Supreme Court, however, also held that the trial judge should give privacy interests some weight in determining whether to order the defendant to answer.

13. **Structuring libel claims to avoid reputation issues.** Another reason not to sue for defamation is that the defendant might plead the truth. Even if truth is not established, the evidence presented on truth may harm the plaintiff's reputation further. Suppose you represent the plaintiff and realize that the defendant might prove the truth of his defamatory statements, or might at least prove a preexisting bad reputation. Can you structure your case to avoid the truth and reputation issues?

14. **Defendant's plea of truth, a downside.** Some cases have actually held that a plea of truth is a reaffirmation of the libel and that unless the defendant prevails, the jury would be justified in awarding punitive damages on the theory that the plea of truth in itself shows malice. *Marley v. Providence Journal Co.*, 86 R.I. 229, 134 A.2d 180 (1957). Such a view may not be consonant with contemporary conceptions of free speech, but might it suggest reasons for tactical caution about pleading truth if your evidence is weak? Cf. *Dodson v. Allstate Ins. Co.*, 345 Ark. 430, 47 S.W.3d 866 (2001) (withdrawn counterclaim that had re-asserted the allegedly defamatory statements could be admitted to "impeach" defendant's trial court position that it had never made such statements). If you represent a defendant who wants to argue that his publication was only name-calling and thus not actionable, would you also advise him to attempt a truth defense? See *Bentley v. Bunton*, 94 S.W.3d 561 (Tex. 2002).

References: Strict liability and the galloping presumptions, Dobbs on Torts (2000) § 401; publication, Id., § 402; meaning, Id. § 404; defamatory content, Id. § 403; qualifying as the plaintiff, Id. § 405; group defamation, Id. § 406; the slander rules, Id. § 408; libel per quod, Id.§ 409; truth in general, Id. § 410. At least two helpful books on defamation are kept up to date with regular supplements or revisions:

see Robert D. Sack, Sack on Defamation and Rodney A. Smolla, Law of Defamation.

§ 2. ABSOLUTE PRIVILEGES

(a) Judicial Proceedings

HAWKINS v. HARRIS

141 N.J. 207, 661 A.2d 284 (1995)

O'HERN, J.

[The plaintiff was injured in two separate motor vehicle accidents and brought suit against the motorists. Those suits were tried, then settled. In this action, the plaintiff alleged that insurers for the motorists, their lawyers, and their investigators subjected her to repeated indignities in the course of the preparing for the earlier litigation. The claim at issue here is based on these allegations: "(1) investigator-defendants contacted an attendant at Mrs. Hawkins' health club and asked him how long he had been having an affair with her; (2) investigator-defendants twice contacted Mrs. Hawkins' minister and informed him that she and her husband were committing insurance fraud; and (3) investigator-defendants contacted Mrs. Hawkins' housekeeper and asked her how much money Mrs. Hawkins was paying her to lie." The majority of the Appellate Division held that this claim was absolutely privileged.]

... Although defamatory, a statement will not be actionable if it is subject to an absolute or qualified privilege. A statement made in the course of judicial, administrative, or legislative proceedings is absolutely privileged and wholly immune from liability. That immunity is predicated on the need for unfettered expression critical to advancing the underlying government interest at stake in those settings.

The trouble with privileges is that they are granted to good and bad alike. A legislator has an absolute privilege on the floor of a chamber to revile, to defame, or to distort the truth. Invoking the Speech and Debate Clause, U.S. Const. art. I, § 6, a lawmaker may use this provision "as a cloak of immunity from prosecution while he [is] smearing the reputations and characters of American citizens whom the Bill of Rights [had] been designed to protect." Albert Coates, Preserving the Constitution: *The Autobiography of Senator Sam Ervin*, 63 N.C.L.Rev. 993, 994 (1985) (book review). We accept such a privilege because it is more important to allow a lawmaker to speak and vote freely on matters of public concern than it is to punish the lawmaker as a rogue. The Speech and Debate Clause protects the integrity of the legislative process by preventing the "intimidation of legislators by the Executive and accountability before a possibly hostile judiciary."

A corresponding privilege extends to members of the judiciary in the performance of judicial duties. Few doctrines were more solidly established at common law than the immunity of judges from liability for damages for acts committed within their judicial jurisdiction. ... This immunity applies even when the judge is accused of acting maliciously and corruptly, and it "is not for the protection or benefit of a malicious or corrupt judge, but for the benefit of the public, whose interest it is that the judges should be at liberty to exercise their functions with independence and without fear of consequences." ...

The extension of an absolute privilege to jurors, witnesses, and parties and their representatives is grounded in similar public-policy concerns. ...

The California Supreme Court set forth a useful formulation of the litigation privilege in Silberg v. Anderson, 50 Cal.3d 205, 266 Cal.Rptr. 638, 786 P.2d 365 (1990). ... The absolute privilege applies to "any communication (1) made in judicial or quasi-judicial proceedings; (2) by litigants or other participants authorized by law; (3) to achieve the objects of the litigation; and (4) that have some connection or logical relation to the action." Whether a defendant is entitled to the privilege is a question of law. Because the most difficult question in this case is whether investigator-defendants should be considered "litigants" or "other participants authorized by law," we will address that issue last.

1. Were the Investigator–Defendants' Statements Made in the Course of Judicial Proceedings?

The litigation privilege is not limited to statements made in a courtroom during a trial; "it extends to all statements or communications in connection with the judicial proceeding." For example, the privilege covers statements made during settlement negotiations. The privilege also protects a person while engaged in a private conference with an attorney regarding litigation. Such application of the privilege affords litigants and witnesses "the utmost freedom of access to the courts without fear of being harassed subsequently by derivative tort actions."

Thus, the privilege extends to "preliminary conversations and interviews between a prospective witness and an attorney if they are in some way related to or connected with a pending or contemplated action." One purpose of the privilege is to encourage "open channels of communication and the presentation of evidence" in judicial proceedings. Such open communication is "a fundamental adjunct to the right of access to judicial and quasi-judicial proceedings." The reason has been well explained: A witness' apprehension of subsequent damages liability might induce two forms of self-censorship. First, witnesses might be reluctant to come forward to testify. And once a witness is on the stand, his testimony might be distorted by the fear of subsequent liability. Even within the constraints of the witness' oath there may be various ways to give an account or to state an opinion. These alternatives may be more or less detailed and may differ in emphasis and certainty. A witness who knows that he might be forced to defend a subsequent lawsuit, and perhaps to pay damages, might be inclined to shade his testimony in favor of the potential plaintiff, to magnify uncertainties, and thus to deprive the finder of fact of candid, objective, and undistorted evidence. But the truthfinding process is better served if the witness' testimony is submitted to "the crucible of the judicial process so that the factfinder may consider it, after cross-examination, together with the other evidence in the case to determine where the truth lies." Just as we wish witnesses to have absolute freedom to express the truth as they view it, we wish parties to have an unqualified opportunity to explore the truth of a matter without fear of recrimination.

We are satisfied that the pretrial discussions between the investigator-defendants and the witnesses were made in the course of the underlying personal injury litigation.

2. Were the Investigator–Defendants' Statements Made to Achieve the Objects of the Litigation?

Pretrial investigation is "necessary to a thorough and searching investigation of the truth," and, therefore, essential to the achievement of the objects of litigation. . . .

The investigations took place in the course of the underlying automobile accident litigation. The disputes therefrom were not resolved before trial, but they might have been. We are satisfied that the investigations were undertaken to achieve the objects of the litigation. Whether the statements were made to achieve the objects of the litigation depends on their relationship to the investigation.

3. Did the investigator-defendants' statements have some connection or logical relation to the action?

To be privileged, a defamatory statement must have some relation to the course of the proceedings. "The pertinency thus required is not a technical legal relevancy, such as would, necessarily, justify insertion of the matter in a pleading or its admission into evidence, but rather a general frame of reference and relationship to the subject matter of the action."

That requirement "was never intended as a test of a participant's motives, morals, ethics or intent." . . . The question is whether the three statements at issue were in any way relevant to the proceedings. The allegedly defamatory statements concerning insurance fraud and the subornation of a witness were clearly relevant to the underlying litigation. However, we are less certain about the relevance to the proceedings of plaintiff's claimed infidelity. "[E]xtrajudicial defamatory allegations relating to a party's honesty are not sufficiently 'pertinent' to a judicial proceeding to clothe them with an absolute privilege, when the only basis alleged for finding the allegations pertinent is that the defamed party's credibility was at issue." We shall return to the issue of relevancy in our disposition.

4. Were the investigator-defendants "other participants authorized by law"?

Whether investigators are "other participants authorized by law" is the crucial issue. Had an insurance company for the defendants in the underlying litigation conducted the investigations, the company would have been regarded as a participant authorized by law because of its undoubted interest in the outcome of the proceedings. The immunity that attends judicial proceedings "protects both counsel and other representatives who are employed to assist a party in the course of litigation." ... [I]nsofar as [the investigator] was engaged in a function which would be protected had it been undertaken by an attorney, he is entitled to absolute immunity while acting as an agent of an attorney.

We believe that that is the correct legal analysis. Just as the legislative privilege extends to the aide of the legislator, the litigation privilege should extend to the aide of an attorney in the course of legal proceedings.

Because of their extraordinary scope, absolute privileges "have been limited to situations in which authorities have the power both to discipline persons whose statements exceed the bounds of permissible conduct and to strike such statements from the record." The absolute privilege "does not extend to statements made in situations for which there are no safeguards against abuse." ["[I]n strictly judicial proceedings the potential harm which may result from the absolute privilege is somewhat mitigated by the formal requirements such as notice and hearing, the comprehensive control exercised by the trial judge whose action is reviewable on appeal, and the availability of retarding influences such as false swearing and perjury prosecutions. ..."] A corresponding burden, then, that flows from the benefits of the privilege is an attorney's ethical and professional responsibility for the conduct of aides.

We are satisfied that the privilege should extend to the relevant statements of investigators made in the course of pretrial discovery. Courts have the power and authority to impose sanctions (for example, the suppression of improperly adduced evidence) on parties for an abuse of the discovery process. In addition, some private investigators will be subject to State licensure procedures. Finally, an attorney may be held professionally responsible for a lack of supervision of such investigators.

...

The litigation privilege is not, however, a license to defame. A statement is privileged only if it has some relation to the proceeding. Because of the unusual procedural posture of this case, the trial court may not have fully considered the relevance to the underlying litigation of the investigator's alleged suggestion of plaintiff's adultery. That issue is not before us on this appeal.

The judgment of the Appellate Division is affirmed.

[The dissent of HANDLER, J., is omitted]

---

15. **Burden of proof; the indefeasible absolute privilege.** The defendant bears the burden of proving that the publication was privileged. When the privilege is absolute, publications within its scope are fully protected, even if the defendant uttered the publication with malice.

16. **Absolute privilege for all those engaged in judicial proceeding.** The absolute privilege protects all those appropriately engaged in the judicial task—judges, jurors, lawyers, prosecutors, and witnesses. See RESTATEMENT (SECOND) OF TORTS §§ 585–589.

17. **Perjury.** What if a witness under oath intentionally makes a false and defamatory statement? Courts usually say that no civil action lies for perjury as such. See *Cooper v. Parker–Hughey,* 894 P.2d 1096 (Okla. 1995). Conceivably, the fact of perjury, although not actionable in itself, could be relevant to some other cause of action, and perjury is subject to criminal prosecution.

18. **Judicial documents.** Defamation that occurs in pleadings and other documents is generally privileged or immune in the same way as statements made in court. However, under some circumstances, one who instigates a criminal or civil suit may be liable for malicious prosecution or some similar tort. See Chapter 8. It is also possible to hold that filing a pleading is privileged but that republication of it is not. That topic is considered in § 3 (c) below.

19. **At the edges of the proceeding.** Once absolute immunity is accepted, difficult cases remain on the fringes. Suppose a lawyer solicits clients for a particular litigation, for instance, clients to serve as plaintiffs in a neighborhood suit over zoning. In the course of the solicitation, the lawyer makes defamatory statements about opposing parties. Absolutely privileged? *Finkelstein, Thompson & Loughran v. Hemispherx Biopharma, Inc.,* 774 A.2d 332 (D.C. 2001); *Rubin v. Green,* 4 Cal.4th 1187, 847 P.2d 1044, 17 Cal.Rptr.2d 828 (1993). California has held that its statutory absolute privilege protects even defamatory reports to police or administrative agencies as preparation for "any other proceeding authorized by law." The privilege defeats other tort claims based on communication to law enforcement agencies as well, with the exception of malicious prosecution, which remains actionable, and possibly with the exception of a claim under the state's civil rights statutes. *Hagberg v. California Fed. Bank FSB,* 32 Cal.4th 350, 81 P.3d 244, 7 Cal.Rptr.3d 803 (2004). But *Buchanan v. Maxfield Enters., Inc.,* 130 Cal.App.4th 418, 29 Cal.Rptr.3d 909 (2005), holds that a citizen's arrest that involves no report of crime to the police is not so privileged.

20. **Nonjudicial work by judicial officers; the "functional" test.** It is possible that all responsibility of all federal employees has been terminated by a federal statute. See ¶ 26 below. If that is not the

case, then *Forrester v. White*, 484 U.S. 219, 108 S.Ct. 538, 98 L.Ed.2d 555 (1988), becomes relevant. The Supreme Court in that case held that the absolute privilege protects the judicial function, not the judicial office. It thus recognized that a judge acting in an executive or administrative capacity, as when the judge discharges an employee, is not entitled to the absolute privilege. The judge might still have a qualified privilege, however.

21. **Judicial work by nonjudicial officers.** The functional test works the other way around, too. The absolute immunity applies to protect executive or administrative officers who are not judges at all, so long as they are functioning in a judicial-type capacity in adversary proceedings. See *Butz v. Economou*, 438 U.S. 478, 98 S.Ct. 2894, 57 L.Ed.2d 895 (1978); *Allan and Allan Arts Ltd. v. Rosenblum,* 201 A.D.2d 136, 615 N.Y.S.2d 410 (1994) (zoning appeal board hearing, absolute privilege so long as the hearing is adversarial, applies law to the facts, and is subject to judicial review). Would the absolute immunity apply to a university's formal grievance hearing for employees claiming discrimination or other wrongs? *Overall v. University of Pennsylvania,* 412 F.3d 492 (3d Cir. 2005).

22. **Anti-SLAPP statutes.** In addition to the formal common law privileges, statutes in a number of states now offer a distinct procedural advantage to a defendant who is sued for acts in furtherance of speech rights in connection with public issues. The statutes assume that such suits are meant to harass the defendant, that is, that they are Strategic Law Suits Against Public Participation. The statutes require dismissal of the claim at an early stage unless the plaintiff can affirmatively show a likelihood of prevailing on the merits. A number of statutory terms, which differ somewhat among the states, must be construed, but it seems clear that anti-SLAPP procedure, though potentially providing a complete shield to the defendant, is quite distinct from the complete bar of the absolute litigation privilege. We will encounter the SLAPP statutes and decisions further in later chapters, especially Chapters 7 & 8.

(b) Legislative Business

UNITED STATES CONSTITUTION ARTICLE I, § 6, CLAUSE 1

The Senators and Representatives shall receive a Compensation for their Services, to be ascertained by Law, and paid out of the Treasury of the United States. They shall in all Cases, except Treason, Felony and Breach of the Peace, be privileged from Arrest during their Attendance at the Session of their respective Houses, and in going to and returning from the same; and for any Speech or Debate in either House, they shall not be questioned in any other Place.

---

23. **Scope of the immunity.** Article I, § 6 gives the textual basis for the immunity of federal legislators in defamation and other claims.

Speech and debate in either House includes official business that does not actually transpire on the floor, such as committee business. It does not, however, include press releases or campaign speeches outside the Houses, committees or other official functions. Even republication elsewhere of materials contained in a Senate speech would fall outside the absolute immunity. See *Hutchinson v. Proxmire,* 443 U.S. 111, 99 S.Ct. 2675, 61 L.Ed.2d 411 (1979). However, the privilege does extend to aides engaged in assisting legislators and to legislative committee and other work related to the business of the legislature. See *Gravel v. United States,* 408 U.S. 606, 92 S.Ct. 2614, 33 L.Ed.2d 583 (1972). The Restatement accords witnesses in a legislative proceeding absolute immunity. RESTATEMENT (SECOND) OF TORTS § 590A (1977).

24. **State and local legislative bodies.** State legislators may be provided by state law with essentially the same kind of immunity and sometimes this has been extended to purely local legislative bodies like city councils, too. See DOBBS ON TORTS § 412 (2000). In *Vultaggio v. Yasko,* 215 Wis.2d 326, 572 N.W.2d 450 (1998), the court held that a speaker at a city council's public meeting to get citizen views has only a qualified privilege.

(c) Executive Business

25. **Division of authorities on executive privilege.** The cases are divided as to whether some, none, or all officers of the executive branch may enjoy the absolute privilege when they speak within the course of their official duties, at least under some circumstances. Some authorities protect only high level officers, sometimes cabinet level officers, only. See *Bauer v. State*, 511 N.W.2d 447 (Minn. 1994); RESTATEMENT (SECOND) OF TORTS § 591 (b). Others protect lower level officers. See *Chamberlain v. City of Portland,* 184 Or.App. 487, 56 P.3d 497 (2002) (a police officer was an executive officer who had absolute immunity from defamation suits). Some accord officers only a qualified privilege. *Gibson v. Abbott*, 529 So.2d 939 (Ala. 1988); *Chamberlain v. Mathis*, 151 Ariz. 551, 729 P.2d 905 (Ariz. 1986). Federal officers of any rank are protected so long as they speak within the scope of their federal duties and within the scope of their discretion, *Barr v. Matteo*, 360 U.S. 564, 79 S.Ct. 1335, 3 L.Ed.2d 1434 (1959), and probably also under the rule in the next paragraph.

26. **The Westfall Act affecting federal employees.** In addition to judge-made immunity, the Westfall Act addition to the Federal Tort Claims Act immunizes all federal employees for many acts within the scope of their federal duties. It does so by substituting the government as defendant. In some cases the victim will then be able to proceed against the government, but not in cases of defamation—as to that, the government still retains full immunity. The Act itself seems to provide immunity only to the extent that there is a "remedy against the United States" under the Federal Tort Claims Act. So construed, the statute would leave a claim available for defamation, since there is no remedy against the United States for that. However, the Supreme Court has held

that the Westfall Act immunizes the employee even if the government is also immune under the Federal Tort Claims Act. See *United States v. Smith,* 499 U.S. 160, 111 S.Ct. 1180, 113 L.Ed.2d 134 (1991). In line with this, courts refuse to entertain defamation actions against federal officers. *Simpkins v. District of Columbia Government,* 108 F.3d 366 (D.C. Cir. 1997).

27. **Government contractors.** Should a government contractor be absolutely privileged if he defames someone in the course of a government investigation if a government executive employee in the same position would be so privileged? See *Mangold v. Analytic Services, Incorporated,* 77 F.3d 1442 (4th Cir. 1996).

28. **Civil rights actions against officers.** One of the most fundamental civil rights statutes, 42 U.S.C.A. § 1983, provides for a private federal cause of action against anyone acting under color of law who violates the plaintiff's federal rights. Do citizens have a federal constitutional right not to be defamed by their government officials? *Paul v. Davis,* 424 U.S. 693, 96 S.Ct. 1155, 47 L.Ed.2d 405 (1976), held not because there was simply no specific constitutional right to reputation, although the due process clause might be invoked if official defamation was used to deprive the plaintiff of some specific entitlement. *Paul v. Davis* is a case of no right, not a case of immunity, but it has immunity effects, especially when combined with state law that immunizes officers.

(d) Consent and Other Absolute Privileges

Woodfield v. Providence Hospital, 779 A.2d 933 (D.C.2001). The plaintiff worked as a nurse at Providence Hospital, where the employee manual provided, "Providence Hospital will release only employment dates and last position title." The plaintiff never applied for a promotion and was never disciplined or reprimanded. After she resigned her position, she applied for a position at Suburban Hospital. That hospital offered her a position subject to a background check. She signed a release permitting this check. It authorized Suburban "to investigate my background to determine any and all information of concern to my record, whether same is of record or not. I release employers and persons named in my application from all liability for any damages on account of his/her furnishing said information." Although the supervisor at Providence did not know of this release, she allegedly responded to the investigator by saying that the plaintiff "did not receive any promotions because of her poor performance. Because of her poor performance, I choose not to answer any further questions." Suburban then retracted its job offer and the plaintiff sued Providence for defamation. *Held,* the release is a consent that furnishes at least a qualified privilege. Providence is a third party beneficiary, even though Providence was not aware of the release. And "the breach of any duty created by the employee manual to limit the release of information (assuming the manual creates such a duty) in no way limits the validity or breadth of the release from tortious defamation, which appellant subsequently entered into for the benefit of

Providence Hospital and Easterling. Appellant's consent contained in the release was broader than the provision of the employee manual. Therefore, we conclude that the release is valid and acts as a consent to the assumedly defamatory statements by Providence Hospital and Easterling."

---

29. **As an absolute privilege.** Although the *Woodfield* court was content to say that the privilege was at least a qualified privilege, the Restatement and other cases have characterized the privilege as an absolute one. See *Smith v. Holley,* 827 S.W.2d 433 (Tex. App. 1992); RESTATEMENT (SECOND) OF TORTS § 583.

30. **California rule.** In a situation similar to that in *Woodfield,* the court in *McQuirk v. Donnelley,* 189 F.3d 793 (9th Cir. 1999), held that the release would not bar the employee's defamation claim because of California Civil Code § 1688, which provides that "contracts which have for their object, directly or indirectly, to exempt anyone from responsibility for his own fraud, or willful injury to the person or property of another, or violation of law, whether willful or negligent, are against the policy of the law." The court declared that defamation was an intentional tort, so the consent was invalid.

31. **Organizations' defamation of a member.** What result if the plaintiff is a member of a Fraternal Lodge or labor union. For his criticism of the president of the organization, the president, following rules of the organization disclosed to the member when he joined, publicly "excommunicates" him, stating defamatory "facts" supporting his decision?

32. **Other absolute privileges.** There is no particular limit to the number of absolute privileges or immunities that courts or legislature can create. Two that are more or less formally identified and more or less independent of other privileges are a privilege to publish defamatory matter (1) to one's spouse and (2) when the publication is required by law. RESTATEMENT (SECOND) OF TORTS § 592A. Statutes may add specific immunities. In addition, in Chapter 4 we'll see some "absolute" protections under the Untied States Constitution.

§ 3. QUALIFIED PRIVILEGE

(a) Self, Others, Common Interest, Including Certain Statutory Privileges

GOHARI v. DARVISH

363 Md. 42, 767 A.2d 321 (2001)

HARRELL, J.

[The defendant Darvish operated a group of car dealer franchises. He employed Gohari, who worked his way up in the enterprise, attaining a highly responsible position as vice-president and comptroller of Darcars Toyota, where he was responsible for overseeing the accounting and financial functions of the dealership.]

In August of 1996, Gohari quit his job with Darcars. In November of 1996, he entered into an agreement with James Kline to buy the Kline Arlington Toyota dealership. Needing Toyota's permission to consummate the transaction, Gohari applied to Toyota Motor Sales, Inc.'s (Toyota) local agent, Central Atlantic Toyota Distributors, Inc. (CATD), for approval to own and operate the dealership. According to testimony at trial, CATD was responsible for examining "the credentials of the individual to determine whether or not [he or she] qualified to be a dealer and/or operator."

[Clements, investigating for CATD, got Gohari's permission to interview Darvish. Darvish reportedly told Clements that "Gohari lacked the experience, capacity and character to be considered a qualified candidate" and that Gohari "had suddenly left the DARCARS organization several months ago in an unprofessional manner and with no notice[,] . . . that there was questionable financial manipulation by Mr. Gohari to inflate his compensation[,] and that Mr. Darvish should have terminated Mr. Gohari's employment much earlier but had kept him on out of loyalty."]

CATD ultimately concluded that, because Gohari lacked the necessary operational experience, it would require that he recruit a qualified general manager to oversee the day-to-day retail business of the dealership before it would approve the franchise transfer. Gohari submitted several names as possible general managers, but was unable to procure CATD approval before his contract with Kline expired by its terms.

[Gohari sued Darvish for defamation and interference with contract. The jury awarded the plaintiff $500,000 in compensatory damages for defamation and over $2 million in compensatory damages for interference with contract. The intermediate court reversed on the ground that defendant's statements were qualifiedly privileged.]

A defendant, in a defamation suit, may assert a qualified, or conditional, privilege. *See generally* Dan B. Dobbs, The Law of Torts, §§ 413–414 (2000) [hereinafter The Law of Torts]. . . .

In *Marchesi v. Franchino,* 283 Md. 131, 387 A.2d 1129 (1978), we explained:

> The common law conditional privileges rest upon the notion that a defendant may escape liability for an otherwise actionable defamatory statement, if publication of the utterance advances social policies of greater importance than the vindication of a plaintiff's reputational interest. . . . Specifically, the common law recognized that a person ought to be shielded against civil liability for defamation where, in good faith, he publishes a statement in furtherance of his own legitimate interests, or those shared in common with the

> recipient or third parties, or where his declaration would be of interest to the public in general. . . .

According to one scholar, there are four basic common law qualified privileges:

> (1) The public interest privilege, to publish materials to public officials on matters within their public responsibility; (2) the privilege to publish to someone who shares a common interest, or, relatedly, to publish in defense of oneself or in the interest of others; (3) the fair comment privilege; and (4) the privilege to make a fair and accurate report of public proceedings.

THE LAW OF TORTS, *supra,* § 413, at 1158.

The conditional privilege at issue in the present case involves Professor Dobbs's subsection, *supra,* (2)—"the privilege to publish to someone who shares a common interest, or, relatedly, to publish in defense of oneself or in the interest of others." The standard for common interest is the following:

> An occasion is conditionally privileged when the circumstances are such as to lead any one of several persons having a common interest in a particular subject matter correctly or reasonably to believe that facts exist which another sharing such common interest is entitled to know. . . .

Dobbs has elaborated:

> Common interests are usually found among members of identifiable groups in which members share similar goals or values or cooperate in a single endeavor. . . . The idea is to promote free exchange of relevant information among those engaged in a common enterprise or activity and to permit them to make appropriate internal communications and share consultations without fear of suit. . . . The privilege does not arise in the first place unless the communication relates in some degree to the common interest, and once the privilege arises it is lost if it is abused by malice or excessive publication.

The record in the present case demonstrates a common interest shared by CATD/franchisor and Darvish/franchisee for they share in "business and professional dealings." It was undoubtedly in CATD's business interest to receive an accurate, full, and truthful assessment of the qualifications of a proposed franchisee candidate to operate one of its franchises. A logical person to give such an assessment might be someone like Darvish—Gohari's former employer and an existing franchisee of Toyota, CATD's principal. Furthermore, conceptually it would be in Darvish's professional interest to answer candidly as Darvish must deal with CATD and Toyota on an ongoing basis as a Toyota franchisee. For example, Darvish "reports his sales to CATD and requests inventory from CATD, and it is CATD which, as in this case, holds approval power over the potential sale or transfer of a Toyota franchise." Thus, there is a common interest in maintaining a candid business relationship in furtherance of the franchisee's individual success and the overall success of the franchisor.

We perceive also that a need "to publish ... in the interest of others" arguably is present in this case. The rule regarding the protection of interest of the recipient or a third person has been explained as follows:

> (1) An occasion makes a publication conditionally privileged if the circumstances induce a correct or reasonable belief that
>
> > (a) there is information that affects a sufficiently important interest of the recipient or a third person, and
> >
> > (b) the recipient is one to whom the publisher is under a legal duty to publish the defamatory matter or is a person to whom its publication is otherwise within the generally accepted standards of decent conduct.
>
> (2) In determining whether a publication is within generally accepted standards of decent conduct it is an important factor that unjustify
>
> > (a) the publication is made in response to a request rather than volunteered by the publisher *or*
> >
> > (b) a family or other relationship exists between the parties.

RESTATEMENT (SECOND) OF TORTS § 595, at 268.

It seems patent that information regarding Gohari's qualifications would be important to CATD and Toyota. The information supplied by Darvish also appears to have been supplied within generally accepted standards of decent conduct. [The Restatement] comment states that "[i]t is enough that the circumstances are such as to lead to the reasonable belief that the third person's interest is in danger"....

The fact that the communication is made in response to a request is of particular importance:

> The fact that the recipient has made the request is an indication that he, at least, regards the matter in respect to which information is desired as sufficiently important to justify the publication of any defamatory matter that may be involved in response to the request. In that case, the person requested to give information is not required nicely to evaluate the interest that the person making the request seeks to protect, nor to make that comparison otherwise required of him, between the harm likely to be done to the other's reputation if the defamatory matter is false and the harm likely to be done to the third person's interest if the it should prove true.

RESTATEMENT (SECOND) OF TORTS § 595, at 273–74. ...

In the present case, Darvish was approached by CATD to provide his assessment of his former employee's, Gohari's, qualifications as the prospective owner-operator of a Toyota dealership. ...

The only other jurisdiction to address directly the flagship question presented in this case held that a qualified privilege may be applied to communications in franchisor/franchisee relationships. In *Quinn v. Jewel Food Stores Inc.,* 276 Ill.App.3d 861, 213 Ill.Dec. 204, 658 N.E.2d 1225 (1995), the plaintiff was a former employee of Jewel Food Stores (Jewel) and, while working for Jewel, had received work evaluations in which he was described, in part, as being a con artist. The plaintiff left Jewel and sought a franchise with Southland Corporation (7–Eleven) and White Hen Pantry convenience stores. [Defendant released the evaluation to the prospective franchisors.] The plaintiff was denied a franchise and subsequently sued Jewel for defamation. The Appellate Court of Illinois determined that Jewel had a qualified privilege because the situation involved "some interest of the person to whom the matter is published or of some other third person." In so determining, the Illinois court stated: "[p]laintiff seeks to differentiate the relationships between franchisor-franchisee and employer-employee relationship. However, we believe the difference between the two is in form, rather than substance." . . .

Lastly, Petitioner argues that there can be no qualified privilege because "Darvish, as Gohari's potential competitor, had a powerful interest in destroying Gohari's chances of entering into the same sort of contract with CATD and acquiring his own Toyota dealership," and thus, "[n]o 'social polic[ies]' . . . are advanced by applying a qualified privilege under such circumstances; to the contrary, a qualified privilege would only injure competition and protect individuals whose self-interest lies in defaming innocent parties." We agree that the potential competitive interest of Darvish should not be disregarded. This same competitive interest, however, may exist within the employer/employee relationship. . . .

Whether Respondent made the statements, assuming them to be false for present analysis, because of his competitive interest becomes part of the evaluation concerning whether the qualified privilege has been abused. . . . "[T]he question of whether a defamatory communication enjoys a conditional privilege is one of law for the court, whether it has been forfeited by malice is usually a question for the jury."

[Maryland departs from the common law rules by requiring that a libel plaintiff must prove fault. See *Rosenberg v. Helinski,* 328 Md. 664, 616 A.2d 866 (1992). The plaintiff argued that even if the trial court was in error in failing to permit the qualified privilege defense, the error was harmless because the jury must have found "actual malice" to find liability at all. The court concluded that the jury could have imposed liability under a negligence standard and hence that injection of a privilege, destroyed by malice, might have changed the result.]

Judgment of the court of special appeals affirmed; petitioner to pay the costs.

---

33. **Burden of proof.** As with the absolute privileges, the defendant bears the burden of alleging and proving the bases for qualified privileges. E.g., *Cortez v. Jo–Ann Stores, Inc.,* 827 N.E.2d 1223 (Ind. Ct. App. 2005). Once the defendant succeeds in establishing the privilege, the plaintiff can defeat the privilege and thus recover by showing that the privilege was abused by malice or otherwise. On this, the plaintiff, not the defendant, bears the burden of proof. See *Lundquist v. Reusser,* 7 Cal.4th 1193, 875 P.2d 1279, 31 Cal.Rptr.2d 776 (1994).

34. **Interest of others.** Focus first on the "interest of others" privilege. What do you think of the limitations imposed on the interest of others' privilege?

35. **Incentives to derogate the plaintiff.** Consider the facts of *Gohari.* Wouldn't former employers almost always have an incentive to make derogatory statements about a former employee who is trying to buy a business that will compete with his former employer? If so, should that mean no privilege? Recall that most torts put the burden of proving fault on the plaintiff in the first place and that recognition of a privilege has a similar effect.

36. **Privilege versus no publication.** Recall the publication requirement developed in Chapter 1. As we saw there, courts sometimes say that a communication is not a "publication" and thus negate liability on that ground. This has sometimes been said, for example, with intracorporate communications. Is it now clear why a qualified privilege might be a better tool for dealing with that situation?

SIGAL CONSTRUCTION CORP. V. STANBURY, 586 A.2d 1204 (D.C. App. 1991). Plaintiff applied for work with Stevens as project manager in construction. Acting for Stevens, Lincoln called plaintiff's former employer, Sigal. He talked to Paul Littman, a Sigal project executive, who told him that "Ken seemed detail oriented to the point of losing sight of the big picture." As a result, Stevens did not hire the plaintiff. Plaintiff sued. *Held,* judgment for the plaintiff affirmed. The plaintiff has the burden of showing that the common interest privilege to which defendant was entitled, was abused. Abuse is shown by bad faith, common law malice, or by acting with such gross indifference or recklessness as to amount to wanton and willful disregard of the rights of the plaintiff. Here, because Littman led Lincoln/Stevens to believe he spoke from personal knowledge when in fact he lacked personal knowledge and did not have a traceable source of information, the jury could find the privilege abused.

OLSON V. 3M COMPANY, 188 Wis.2d 25, 523 N.W.2d 578 (App. 1994). C formally complained to her employer that she had been sexually harassed. The employer investigated and as a result discharged two men. The employer issued a press release stating that it had discharged "two production employees" because of an investigation into allegations of harassment and that "incidents of this nature" [not described] are not tolerated. The police department also issued a press release; it referred to sexual assaults and medical treatment for the victims. The men brought the present action for defamation. The evidence in the suit was conflicting. Some evidence warranted the belief that the plaintiffs had engaged in suggestive and harassing activities against C; but other evidence might have warranted the inference that the plaintiff-employees were victims of either C's desire to get revenge for a work-related matter, or her generally provocative manner. Still other evidence suggested that the employer may have wanted to avoid (a) liability to the complainant and (b) loss of federal contracts. *Held*, summary judgment for defendant employer affirmed. (1) Publication to the employees is privileged because the employer has a common interest with employees in a workplace free of sexual harassment and that includes reasonable communications to its employees concerning actions taken. (2) The small-town employer has a privilege in its own self-interest to publish to the community matters sufficiently affecting that interest, where publication will be of service to that interest, as where many community members knew of some of the underlying investigations. (3) The privilege may be lost by knowing or reckless falsehood. (4) Although a privilege might be lost by excessive publication, the publication here is not excessive under the self-interest privilege.

Draghetti v. Chmielewski, 416 Mass. 808, 626 N.E.2d 862 (1994). The plaintiff was a police officer. Defendant was the chief of police. The plaintiff also worked part time teaching at the state's police academy. The police chief-defendant told reporters and they reported that "Chmielewski said there was evidence that Draghetti, who had been hired to teach at the academy last year, intended to collect pay for teaching at the academy while on duty." He also said the matter had been turned over to the district attorney after the police department had completed its own investigation, and this, too, was reported. It would have been criminal for the plaintiff to collect for teaching while he was on duty and he did not in fact collect or attempt to collect.

In the libel suit against the chief of police, the police chief claimed a cluster of privileges: "Chmielewski asserts that as police chief he had a right, even a duty, to speak to the press about Draghetti. We do not agree. In those cases in which we have held that an employer has a conditional privilege to make defamatory statements, the statements were published to a narrow group who shared an interest in the communication. . . . Similarly, a police chief has no official duty to report internal investigations to the press. The conditional privilege to publish defamatory material is designed to allow public officials to speak freely on matters of public importance in the exercise of their official duties. . . . Last, Chmielewski asserts that he and the citizens who read the Union–News share a common interest in the communication which entitles him to a qualified privilege. Such a distortion of the meaning of the "common interest" privilege would create a privilege for virtually all newsworthy statements. We conclude that Chmielewski's remarks to the Union–News were not conditionally privileged.

---

37. **Destruction of common and self-interest privileges.** The common and self-interest privileges are destroyed by "abuse." The traditionally recognized abuse is publication with malice, malice meaning ill-will, spite, or improper purpose. Under the influence of language of the Constitutional cases in a slightly different setting, courts like *Olson* have begun to recognize that knowing or reckless falsehood can also constitute abuse. See *Albert v. Loksen,* 239 F.3d 256 (2d Cir. 2001) (adding that in New York, the privilege is abused only if malice is "the one and only cause for the publication"). Abuse might be found if the publication contains defamatory matter not reasonably necessary to accomplish the purpose of the privilege and also in the case of excessive publication—publication to persons whose interests are outside the privilege. Negligence ordinarily would not suffice to destroy the privilege.

38. **Potential applications?** Which of the following would be good candidates for the common interest privilege?

(A) A church member, at a church meeting, argues that the plaintiff should be stricken from the church's rolls because she is an adulterer.

(B) A union newspaper publishes defamatory comments about an employer with whom the union bargains.

(C) One employee reports defamatory comments about another employee to the employer.

(D) A tenured faculty member makes defamatory statements about a non-tenured faculty member in the course of a review that determines whether to recommend tenure.

39. **Common interest privilege in media publications?** Should the self- or common-interest privilege ever include publications to the public media? In *Konikoff v. Prudential Ins. Co. of America,* 234 F.3d 92 (2d Cir. 2000), Judge Sack, an author of major books on defamation (see Robert D. Sack & Sandra S. Baron, Libel, Slander and Related Problems [2d ed. 1994]) wrote the court's opinion. He recognized that the privilege might be extended to widespread publications, but concluded that New York had not done so.

40. **Statutory privileges, immunities.** Some statutes codify privileges and their scope, sometimes adding detail. See Cal. Civ. Code § 47. Many other statutes erect specific privileges, qualified or absolute. Child abuse reporting is commonly singled out for statutory privileges. California gives an absolute privilege—an immunity—to those who are required to report suspected abuse. However, for those who are not required but merely permitted to make the report of child abuse, the privilege is only a qualified one, destroyed by the reporter's knowledge of

falsity. See Cal. Penal Code § 11172(a). See *Stecks v. Young,* 38 Cal. App.4th 365, 45 Cal.Rptr.2d 475 (1995) (even therapist who "trusted the accusations of a purportedly schizophrenic patient, who had no personal knowledge that the children were being abused, and conveyed those accusations to the authorities" was immune as a mandatory reporter). A federal statute on credit reporting in effect erects a qualified privilege for certain credit information, displacing defamation suits based on that information unless malice or intent to injure is shown. See 15 U.S.C.A. § 1681h.

(b) Communications to Officials and Others—The "Public Interest Privilege"

41. **Privilege to report suspected crime.** Suppose you have observed conduct of X and believe that conduct might be some evidence of criminal activities by X. Should you be privileged to report your suspicions to the police? The issue arises because it might turn out that (a) you are mistaken about facts or (b) even if the facts are right their defamatory implications are untrue.

Although the exact boundaries of the privilege may be indistinct, the privilege definitely exists. It permits reports to any public official charged with taking appropriate action or to receive such reports and process them. It is not necessarily limited to "crimes"; it could include reports that would justify administrative or regulatory action rather than a criminal prosecution. Nor is it necessarily limited to reports to officials. A report to a private person is conceivably privileged if that person could appropriately act to prevent a crime, for example. See Restatement (Second) of Torts § 598. The Restatement calls this the public interest privilege, in reference to the broad idea that it covers reports of information that affects a public interest. The term may be misleading in the light of the many public interests involved in defamation cases, but "report of crime" may be too narrow, so the privilege lacks a good name.

42. **Abuse of privilege.** The common law privilege to report is lost by abuse. Excessive publication, "malice" in the sense of improper purpose or spite, and knowing or reckless falsehood would all suffice to show abuse. See *DeLong v. Yu Enteprises, Inc.,* 334 Or. 166, 47 P.3d 8 (2002) ("actual malice" or bad faith). The California Supreme Court, however, treats statements made to police in the course of a police investigation like testimony of a witness in a judicial or "official" proceeding and thus absolutely privileged, except in a malicious prosecution claim or perhaps a claim for civil rights violation. *Hagberg v. California Fed. Bank FSB,* 32 Cal.4th 350, 81 P.3d 244, 7 Cal.Rptr.3d 803 (2004). *DeLong,* supra, suggested that similar authority in Oregon would be reconsidered in an appropriate case.

43. **Shifting report litigation to the law of malicious prosecution.** If a report to authorities accusing the plaintiff of a crime has some resemblance to judicial testimony, it also looks a great deal like

instigation of a prosecution. The law of malicious prosecution—which might be regarded as a subset of defamation law—has special rules protecting those who instigate prosecutions. One important effect of the qualified privilege to report suspected crime is that the problem is shifted to the rules of malicious prosecution. The protection those rules give to those who report suspected crime is substantial but not absolute. See Chapter 8.

(c) Reporting Public Records and Proceedings—The Fair Report Privilege

DORSEY v. NATIONAL ENQUIRER, INC.

973 F.2d 1431 (9th Cir. 1992)

BEEZER, Circuit Judge:

Arnold Dorsey, better known as Engelbert Humperdinck, sued the National Enquirer, Inc. alleging that an article in its tabloid defamed him. The district court granted summary judgment in favor of the Enquirer and Dorsey appeals. We affirm.

In 1980, Kathy Jetter obtained a determination in New York Family Court that Dorsey was the father of her daughter. The court ordered Dorsey to pay child support and educational expenses. In May, 1988, Jetter petitioned the same court for an increase in child support payments and for an order requiring Dorsey to purchase life insurance naming the girl as his beneficiary.

Dorsey opposed the request and Jetter filed a Reply Affidavit. In the affidavit she stated: "The request for life insurance is of a dire necessity. Upon information and belief, the respondent has AIDS related syndrome and has been treated at Sloan Kettering in New York." Sometime before December 1988, Jetter gave the National Enquirer a copy of this affidavit. In its December 27, 1988 edition, the Enquirer published an article that highlighted the Reply Affidavit's allegation that Dorsey carries the AIDS virus.

The Enquirer's front page displays a photo of Dorsey next to the headline: "Mother of His Child Claims in Court ... Engelbert Has AIDS Virus." The article itself bears the headline: "Mom of Superstar Singer's Love Child Claims in Court ... Engelbert Has AIDS Virus."

The one-page article quotes Jetter's affidavit twice and quotes Jetter as saying: "I never would have filed the court papers if I wasn't 100 percent convinced he has the AIDS virus." Jordan Stevens, a private investigator hired by Jetter, is quoted as saying: "Humperdinck is suffering from the AIDS virus. We have stated that belief in court papers and it is based on an intensive investigation of the singer during the past five years. He was tested positive for the AIDS virus in early 1985. As stated in the court documents, he has had treatment for the AIDS virus at Sloan–Kettering hospital but our information is that the disease remains." The article goes on to explain the ramifications of having the AIDS virus.

The article discusses Jetter and Dorsey's relationship and their previous legal proceedings over child support, leading up to the life insurance request and Reply Affidavit. The third paragraph notes that Dorsey denies the affidavit's AIDS allegation. In the next-to-last paragraph, the Enquirer reports that Dorsey's attorney "said there was no truth whatsoever to the charge that the singer has the AIDS virus and called it an 'utter fabrication.'" The article also includes a picture of Dorsey with the caption: "ENGELBERT DENIES he has the AIDS virus."

Dorsey filed a defamation action against the Enquirer. The Enquirer moved for summary judgment. The district court granted the motion, finding as a matter of law that the article was a fair and true report of allegations made in a judicial proceeding. Thus, it was privileged under California law and protected by the United States Constitution. The district court further held that the incremental harm doctrine shielded the Enquirer from liability. [In a footnote the court said: "The Enquirer does not raise the defense that the published allegations themselves are true. In connection with this lawsuit, a doctor chosen by the Enquirer tested Dorsey for the HIV virus. Dorsey tested 'negative.' Dorsey also filed a declaration asserting that he has never tested positive for the virus and has never received medical treatment of any kind at a Sloan–Kettering hospital facility. The Enquirer does not dispute Dorsey's assertion that he does not have AIDS or 'AIDS related syndrome.' "]

Dorsey timely appealed the summary judgment order. . . .

California law defines an area of reporting which is privileged from defamation actions. Section 47(4) [now § 47(d)] of the state's Civil Code grants the privilege to "a fair and true report in a public journal, of . . . anything said in the course [of a judicial, legislative, or public official proceeding]." The district court applied section 47(4) and found that, as a matter of law, the Enquirer article was a fair and true report of a judicial proceeding.

Dorsey first contends that section 47(4) is inapplicable here because the Enquirer article does not report on a "judicial" proceeding within the meaning of the statute. He asserts that the use of the phrase "other public official proceeding" in section 47(4) demonstrates that the California legislature intended the judicial and legislative privileges to be similarly limited to only those proceedings open to the public. Dorsey further asserts that New York Family Court proceedings are confidential and thus outside the scope of the statutory privilege. . . .

The Second Circuit, sitting in diversity and applying California law, extended the privilege to a report of secret grand jury proceedings. Reeves, 719 F.2d at 605–606. The court commented that the only limitation in section 47(4) concerning judicial proceedings is that the report be fair and accurate. The courts have not read "public" to modify "judicial" in section 47(4). We thus reject Dorsey's argument that the privilege cannot apply to family court proceedings from which the general public is excluded.

Dorsey next contends that the trier of fact should have been allowed to determine whether the Enquirer article is a "fair and true" report of the Reply Affidavit's contents. We disagree. . . .

In crafting their treatment of the "fair and true" issue, the courts have recognized the importance of protecting a free and vigorous press. The California Supreme Court has said that "because unnecessarily protracted litigation would have a chilling effect upon the exercise of First Amendment rights, speedy resolution of cases involving free speech is desirable." Therefore, defamation actions should be disposed of at the earliest possible stage of the proceedings if the facts as alleged are insufficient as a matter of law to support a judgment for the plaintiff.

. . . [T]he district court could determine, as a matter of law, whether the article is a "fair and true" report. . . .

In Kilgore, the California Supreme Court set forth the test for determining whether a publication qualifies as a "fair and true" report. The court held that an article that captures the substance of the proceedings constitutes a "fair and true" report . . . .

The "fair and true" requirement of section 47(4) therefore does not require a media defendant "to justify every word of the alleged defamatory material that is published. The media's responsibility lies in ensuring that the 'gist or sting' of the report—its very substance—is accurately conveyed." Moreover, courts must accord media defendants a "certain amount of literary license" and exercise a "degree of flexibility" in determining what is a "fair report."

Dorsey contends that the article in the Enquirer does not capture the substance of the proceedings in the New York Family Court and thus is not a "fair and true" report. Dorsey first asserts that there is a greater "sting" in the article than in the Reply Affidavit. . . .

Dorsey asserts . . . that the article goes beyond the sting of the Reply Affidavit by including out-of-court statements made by Jetter and her investigator. Dorsey takes issue with Jetter's statement: "I never would have filed the court papers if I wasn't 100 percent convinced he has the AIDS virus." He also takes issue with Stevens' statements: "Humperdinck is suffering from the AIDS virus. We have stated that belief in court papers and it is based on an intensive investigation of the singer during the past five years. He was tested positive for the AIDS virus in early 1985. As stated in the court documents, he has had treatment for the AIDS virus at Sloan–Kettering hospital but our information is that the disease remains."

Dorsey contends that the gist of the Reply Affidavit is that Jetter was not certain about her allegation that Dorsey had contracted the AIDS virus. According to Dorsey, the fact that Jetter prefaced her allegation with the qualifier "Upon information and belief" demonstrates that Jetter was stating that she did not have firsthand knowledge of whether Dorsey has the AIDS virus.

In comparison, Dorsey contends, the article states that Jetter was 100 percent convinced that Dorsey has the AIDS virus. The article also contains statements from her investigator that assert without qualification that Dorsey has the AIDS virus, that Dorsey tested positive in early 1985, and that Jetter's belief is based upon a five-year intensive investigation. Dorsey contends that the gist of these statements overwhelms and contradicts the Reply Affidavit's "information and belief" qualification.

... It is unclear that an average reader would know the full import of qualifying an allegation made in court with the term "information and belief." However, whether the average reader understands the nuances of first versus second hand knowledge, the average reader can be expected to assume that an allegation made in court is made in good faith and based upon some information that gives the declarant reason to believe that the allegation is true.

Accordingly, Jetter's quoted out-of-court statement that she would not have filed the Reply Affidavit were she not 100 percent convinced that her allegation was true, merely confirms the gist of the Reply Affidavit. It confirms that she filed the Reply Affidavit in good faith.

The statements of Jetter's investigator are more problematic because they seem to suggest more certainty than does the affidavit. The investigator specifically states that Dorsey has the AIDS virus and pinpoints when Dorsey allegedly tested positive—early 1985. The investigator also explains that his information stems from an intensive five-year investigation.

The investigator's statements do not, however, go beyond the gist or sting of the affidavit. Dorsey claims the Enquirer article is defamatory because it alleges that he is infected by the AIDS virus. This is the substance of both the affidavit and the investigator's statements. In including Stevens' statements, the Enquirer did not exceed the degree of flexibility and literary license accorded newspapers in making a "fair report" of a judicial proceeding.

Additional support for this conclusion is found in California's expansive view of "judicial proceedings." Under 47(4), out-of-court statements are considered part of the judicial proceeding if they "comprise a history of the proceedings." Newspapers are not required to limit their stories to a verbatim rendition of the judicial proceeding. In adopting section 47(4), California provided a certain amount of breathing room for newspapers to explain the basis of a judicial proceeding without at the same time opening themselves up to exposure for defamation liability. ...

PREGERSON, Circuit Judge, concurring in part and dissenting in part.

I agree with the majority's view that there is no merit to Dorsey's argument that California Civil Code § 47(4) does not apply to family court proceedings from which the general public is excluded.

But I disagree with the majority's view that in the circumstances of this case the "fair and true" issue is one of law which a court can decide on summary judgment. . . .

---

44. **Rationale or policy basis for fair report privilege.** In *Rosenberg v. Helinski,* 328 Md. 664, 616 A.2d 866 (1992), the court summarized what it treated as three separate policy bases for the fair report privilege: "(1) the agency rationale, by which the reporter acts as agent for an otherwise preoccupied public which could, if it possessed the time, energy or inclination, attend the proceeding; (2) the public supervision rationale, by which the reporter provides to the larger community data it needs to monitor government institutions; (3) or the public information rationale, by which the reporter provides information affecting the greater public welfare." Would it ever matter which rationale you adopted? What if a private person reports allegations in a complaint to another private person for business purposes of his own? See *Sahara Gaming Corp. v. Culinary Workers Union Local 226,* 115 Nev. 212, 984 P.2d 164 (1999).

45. **Scope: Public documents and proceedings versus public events.** There is no generally recognized privileged to report public events. However, there is a privilege to report public documents and also to report public proceedings such as city council meetings and trials. Would the privilege cover a police report? See *Dinkel v. Lincoln Pub. (Ohio), Inc.,* 93 Ohio App.3d 344, 638 N.E.2d 611 (1994). What about a reporter's interview with the police chief? Cf. *Yohe v. Nugent,* 321 F.3d 35 (1st Cir. 2003).

46. **Extending the privilege?** The Restatement supports extension of this privilege to include "public meetings" "held for the purpose of discussing . . . matters of public concern." Its illustrations are political meetings at which candidates for public office speak, stockholders' meetings open to the public and the like. RESTATEMENT (SECOND) OF TORTS § 611, cmt. i (1977). Some authority supports a further extension to oral statements made by public officials to reporters. See *Maple Lanes, Inc. v. News Media Corp.,* 322 Ill.App.3d 842, 256 Ill.Dec. 124, 751 N.E.2d 177 (2001).

47. **Abuse of the privilege: inaccuracy or unfairness.** Given the rationales stated above, the fair report privilege would stand even if the reporter published with "malice," so long as the report was both accurate and fair. The idea is that the reporter and publisher are conduits carrying information the public by definition has a right to know, so the reporter's knowledge that statements in public documents he reports are false does not rob him of the privilege. See *Herron v. Tribune Pub. Co.,* 108 Wash.2d 162, 736 P.2d 249 (1987); RESTATEMENT § 611 cmt. a.

However, some cases have said or assumed that malice in some sense would destroy the privilege. *Molnar v. Star–Ledger,* 193 N.J.Super. 12, 471 A.2d 1209 (1984), is such a case, but its precedent value is doubtful at best, because it relied on a case in which malice destroyed the common interest privilege, not the fair report privilege. Precedent in Illinois is in disarray. A recent case holding of an Appellate Court in that state to the effect that "actual malice" will destroy the fair report privilege is *Solaia Technology, LLC v. Specialty Pub. Co.,* 357 Ill.App.3d 1, 292 Ill.Dec. 772, 826 N.E.2d 1208 (2005).

48. **Privilege and truth defense.** The privilege differs from the truth defense, too, in that the traditional truth defense would require the publisher to show that the statement reported—testimony of a witness in a trial, for example—was itself true.

49. **Substantial accuracy.** Perfect accuracy is not required. The report of a public document or proceeding remains privileged if the report is substantially accurate. See DOBBS ON TORTS § 415 (2000).

50. **Fairness.** Sometimes courts distinguish accuracy from fairness, the term accuracy referring to the literal correctness of individual statements and the term fairness referring to distortions in the overall picture presented. In this kind of usage, a news story might be accurate in stating that a suit was brought against an employee for fraud, but unfair if it omitted to add that the suit was later dismissed and the employee allowed to return to work. See *Costello v. Ocean County Observer*, 136 N.J. 594, 643 A.2d 1012 (1994) (discussing such a case: "Defendants do not enjoy the privilege by merely copying unsupported statements contained in court documents. The reporter is bound to explain the context of those statements in a fair and accurate manner"). A literally accurate report of a complaint that is nevertheless vague or ambiguous may lose its privilege if the sting of the report is greater than would result from a fair and accurate report. *Weber v. Lancaster Newspapers, Inc.*, 878 A.2d 63 (Pa. Super. 2005).

51. **Report of pleadings not yet acted upon.** In *Green Acres Trust v. London,* 141 Ariz. 609, 688 P.2d 617 (1984), the court held privilege would not attach to pleadings not yet filed. Consequently, lawyers who released contents of proposed pleadings to a reporter had no immunity. The Restatement restricts the privilege further, providing that it does not apply to protect reports of the content of pleadings filed with the court but not yet judicially acted upon. The Restaters thought that if naked pleadings could be reported with impunity, people would intentionally file defamatory pleadings, then report them. What criticisms could you offer? See DOBBS ON TORTS § 415 (2000). More recent cases reject the Restatement rule. *Newell v. Field Enterprises, Inc.,* 91 Ill.App.3d 735, 415 N.E.2d 434, 47 Ill.Dec. 429, 20 A.L.R.4th 551 (1980).

ROSENBERG v. HELINSKI, 328 Md. 664, 616 A.2d 866 (1992). In a judicial hearing concerning a father's right to visit his female child without supervision, a psychologist testified that in his opinion the father had sexually abused the child. After the hearing, he repeated his views for the benefit of television cameras. Clips of his statements were run on the news, along with the name of the father. The father brought this action against the psychologist. *Held*, the psychologist is privileged to give a fair and accurate report of his own testimony. The Restatement's view that "self-reporting" is not privileged is interpreted to deprive the self-reporter of the privilege only when he orchestrated events to appear in the privileged forum to begin with.

(d) Fair Comment

A.S. ABELL COMPANY v. KIRBY

227 Md. 267, 176 A.2d 340, 90 A.L.R.2d 1264 (1961)

HAMMOND, Judge.

[The plaintiff, Kirby, was a police officer. The Governor was empowered to remove a police commissioner for incompetence or misconduct. The Baltimore City Delegation in the Legislature formally charged that Commissioner Hepbron had been friendly with underworld leaders and had committed various improper acts. There was a hearing of sorts on this matter; 25 witnesses testified, but not under oath and not subject to cross-examination. The governor concluded that Hepbron had committed "indiscretions" but not enough to justify his removal.]

On June 17, 1959, the day after the Governor's decision was announced, his opinion, news stories about it, and the editorial complained of appeared in The Morning Sun.

The editorial was headed "Not Proved." It said . . . that the manager of the "shocking kangaroo court" staged by the City Delegation in the Spring, "at which unsworn witnesses threw everything they had at Mr. Hepbron and the victim was not even allowed to cross-question witnesses or introduce witnesses of his own," was another member of the political leader's "crowd in the Legislature". . . . There followed the paragraph alleged to have been libelous, as follows: "Every important witness against the Police Commissioner, moreover, was a man with a motive. We name especially the infamous Kirby, former Inspector Forrester, and former Chief Inspector Ford whose retirement was requested and granted some time ago with dazzling haste." . . .

[Kirby sued the newspaper for defamation. He recovered $45,000. The defendant appealed.]

Offered in evidence were standard definitions of the word "infamous," including these: "having a reputation of the worst kind, held in abhorrence, base, detestable, nefarious—odious"; and, "One of the strongest adjectives of detestations of persons in the English language. . . . Deprived of all or certain of the rights of a citizen, in consequence of conviction of certain crimes." The writer of the editorial testified he intended by the use of the word to convey the meaning of "the common usage—bad reputation, disgraceful."

It is recognized that a newspaper like any member of the community may, without liability, honestly express a fair and reasonable opinion or comment on matters of legitimate public interest. The reason given is that such discussion is in the furtherance of an interest of social importance, and therefore it is held entitled to protection even at the expense of uncompensated harm to the plaintiff's reputation.

The Courts and the writers have not agreed as to whether fair comment is a qualified privilege (those who say it is rely largely on the fact that actual malice, as in the case of concededly qualified privileges, destroys the otherwise existing immunity) or whether such a publication is merely outside the scope of actionable defamation. In practical effect and result, whichever view is taken would seem to make no difference (except perhaps on the burden of proof), since there is immunity on either basis.

Whether a publication claimed to come within the protection of fair comment is actionable often turns on whether or not it contains misstatements of fact as distinguished from expressions of opinion. The majority of the States (perhaps three-fourths) hold that the immune instances of public discussion are those limited to opinion, comment, and criticism, and do not embrace those in which there is any false assertion of defamatory fact. The minority view, that even false statements of fact are privileged, at least as to public officers and candidates, if they are made for the public benefit with an honest belief in their truth (because the public interest demands that those who are in a position to furnish information about public servants should not be deterred by fear of suit), has long been favored by many commentators but there has been no rush by the Courts to adopt it.

Maryland has consistently followed the majority rule—that defamatory misstatement of fact cannot be defended successfully as fair comment. The distinction between fact and opinion, although theoretically and logically hard to draw, is usually reasonably determinable as a practical matter: Would an ordinary person, reading the matter complained of, be likely be understand it as an expression of the writer's opinion or as a declaration of an existing fact? An opinion may be so stated as to raise directly the inference of a factual basis, and the defense of fair comment usually has been held not to cover an opinion so stated.

The greater number of Courts have held that the imputation of a corrupt or dishonorable motive in connection with established facts is itself to be classified as a statement of fact and as such not to be within the defense of fair comment.

The publisher duly excepted to the failure of the court to instruct the jury that it could consider all the evidence in the case as to Kirby's activities. . . .

[Over a period of years, Kirby made accusations, denied accusations against himself, and testified for persons charged with crime, seemingly under circumstances that would make his name known. Most of the details are omitted in the following excerpt:]

. . . The Judiciary Committee of the Baltimore City Council held a hearing on illegal wire tapping, at which Kirby, on advice of counsel, refused to testify. Later, in five numbers cases in which Kirby had been a witness or involved, those who had been convicted were either released from prison or cleared. Some twenty-one indictments, in nineteen of which Kirby's name appeared among others as a witness, were stetted. In various of the cases Forrester's or Goldstein's name, or both, appeared in the list of witnesses.

On January 28, 1959, Kirby was charged by Hepbron with planting false evidence in one named raided place and of twice refusing to obey orders of a superior, one being the refusal to take the lie detector test. After a three day hearing, at which Meekins was the principal accuser, Hepbron found Kirby guilty and dismissed him from the force. Kirby appealed the dismissal to court and the case was pending when the editorial referring to him as "infamous" was published.

Kirby testified before the City Delegation on March 14, 1959, and before the Governor in May of that year. On both occasions he testified that Hepbron knew of illegal wire tapping practice in the Baltimore Police Department, and that on orders from Lieutenant Goldstein he had gone to the Emerson Hotel where he saw Hepbron and a well known underworld figure walk out of an elevator together, followed by two girls from a night club in the Block in Baltimore.

It is the publisher's contention that the facts just recited were enough to support the characterization of Kirby as infamous and that the preferable and controlling rule of law is that all relevant facts known or readily available to the public are admissible in evidence as a bar to a defamation action under the defense of fair comment, even if they have not been set out or referred to in the publication. . . .

We think that to sustain fair comment, facts which are set out in the publication must be truly stated (if they are unprivileged), and that such a fact which is not set out must both be true and be so referred to in the publication as to be either recognizable or be made identifiable, and be easily accessible. . . .

Aside from the allegations of infamy and corrupt motive, there are no facts in, or referred to in, the editorial before us as to Kirby in respect of anything but the Legislative hearing and the Governor's hearing, and the writer of the editorial admitted there was nothing derogatory to Kirby in connection with those hearings. There is nothing in the editorial to lead the reader to reasons why the writer thought Kirby was infamous or a man with a motive, or why the reader should. The linking of his name to Forrester and Ford was not a sufficient reference to the record relied on by the publisher, and there was nothing in the editorial to lead the reader to that search of the newspaper archives which would have been required to reconstruct that record. . . .

Judgment affirmed, with costs.

PRESCOTT, Judge (dissenting in part). . . .

[Evidence about Kirby's alleged infamy included evidence that] due to the scandals involving Kirby and other members of the Rackets Division, thirty or more gambling indictments were stetted because "of the State's inability to produce the necessary credible evidence required for successful prosecution"; and that he was formally charged by the Commissioner with planting false evidence and of twice refusing to obey orders of a superior officer, found guilty on all three charges and dismissed from the force. Most, if not all, of this was aired in the public press and was readily accessible to the public at large. The record discloses that Kirby's name appeared no less than 183 times in 65 newspaper articles offered in evidence; 23 times his name was in headlines, and three times his photograph accompanied the articles.

To me, the above clearly establishes the fact that Kirby was "infamous," and "a man with a motive" when he appeared against Commissioner Hepbron at the hearing in Annapolis. . . .

People for the Ethical Treatment of Animals v. Bobby Berosini, Ltd., 111 Nev. 615, 895 P.2d 1269 (1995). Defendants published a video tape of Berosini preparing his animals for a show in Las Vegas. The tape showed Berosini punching and hitting the animals. Defendants interpreted this as cruelty and published statements saying he abuses his animals and beats them severely. The statements were made after full disclosure of the tape. *Held,* the statements were "evaluative opinions" involving value judgment based on true information "disclosed to or known by the public" and as such are not actionable.

---

52. **Where facts are misstated.** How does the fair comment privilege work if the publisher states all the "facts" upon which his opinion is based, but one of the "facts" is wrong?

We know that a publisher cannot raise the truth issue merely because he has truthfully attributed defamatory statements to others. See ¶ 6, supra. Distinguish the role of truth where the defense is not truth but fair comment. To get the fair comment privilege, the defendant must truthfully state the facts on which his comment is based, so truth is relevant, but only to establish one of the essential conditions for fair comment. See, *Magnusson v. New York Times Co.,* 98 P.3d 1070 (Okla. 2004) (in determining fair comment privilege, court noted that the defendant truthfully reported what witnesses had said).

53. **Opinions vs. facts?** What counts as opinion and what as a misstatement of fact? Suppose you said, "I watched him testify and in my opinion he was lying?" Suppose instead you showed a video clip of the testimony to your audience and then said "in my opinion the tape shows him lying"?

54. **Unfair comments?** A number of cases have held or stated that a comment is unfair and not protected if it imputes dishonorable motives to the plaintiff, and even that the opinion drawn from the facts must be "reasonable." See *Julian v. American Business Consultants, Inc.*, 2 N.Y.2d 1, 137 N.E.2d 1, 155 N.Y.S.2d 1 (1956); but see *Polanco v. Fager,* 886 F.2d 66 (4th Cir. 1989) (opinion of medical doctor that plaintiff surgeon performed unnecessary operation, plaintiff was doing so out of greed; fair comment privilege applied).

55. **Honest opinions.** Some cases insist that, if the fair comment is to apply, the publication "must be the honest expression of the writer's real opinion." *Leers v. Green,* 24 N.J. 239, 131 A.2d 781 (1957). Given that the publication must deal with an issue of public concern, or one about which the defendant has invited judgment, and given also that the facts must be truly stated, why should a court be inquiring into the defendant's subjective mental state to discover whether he actually held the opinion he stated? And how would the court discover that?

*

Professional and Academic Enhancements
Chapter 2

Federal Civil Rights Claims for Defamation Against State Executives

PAUL v. DAVIS

424 U.S. 693, 96 S.Ct. 1155, 47 L.Ed.2d 405 (1976)

Mr. Justice REHNQUIST delivered the opinion of the Court . . .

Petitioner Paul is the Chief of Police of the Louisville, Ky., Division of Police, while petitioner McDaniel occupies the same position in the Jefferson County, Ky., Division of Police. In late 1972 they agreed to combine their efforts for the purpose of alerting local area merchants to possible shoplifters who might be operating during the Christmas season. In early December petitioners distributed to approximately 800 merchants in the Louisville metropolitan area a "flyer". . . . [The flyer contained "mug shot" photos referring to "active shoplifters." One of the photos was that of the plaintiff-respondent and gave his name.]

Respondent appeared on the flyer because on June 14, 1971, he had been arrested in Louisville on a charge of shoplifting. He had been arraigned on this charge in September 1971, and, upon his plea of not guilty, the charge had been "filed away with leave (to reinstate)," a disposition which left the charge outstanding. Thus, at the time petitioners caused the flyer to be prepared and circulated respondent had been charged with shoplifting but his guilt or innocence of that offense had never been resolved. Shortly after circulation of the flyer the charge against respondent was finally dismissed by a judge of the Louisville Police Court.

[Plaintiff-respondent brought this suit under § 1983 against Chief Paul and others alleged to be responsible. The Court of Appeals held he had stated a viable claim.]

[The plaintiff's] complaint asserted that the "active shoplifter" designation would inhibit him from entering business establishments for fear of being suspected of shoplifting and possibly apprehended, and would seriously impair his future employment opportunities. Accepting that such consequences may flow from the flyer in question, respondent's complaint would appear to state a classical claim for defamation actionable in the courts of virtually every State. . . .

. . . Concededly if the same allegations had been made about respondent by a private individual, he would have nothing more than a claim for defamation under state law. But, he contends, since petitioners are respectively an official of city and of county government, his action is thereby transmuted into one for deprivation by the State of rights secured under the Fourteenth Amendment. . . .

If respondent's view is to prevail, a person arrested by law enforcement officers who announce that they believe such person to be responsible for a particular crime in order to calm the fears of an aroused populace, presumably obtains a claim against such officers under § 1983. And since it is surely far more clear from the language of the Fourteenth Amendment that "life" is protected against state deprivation than it is that reputation is protected against state injury, it would be difficult to see why the survivors of an innocent bystander mistakenly shot by a policeman or negligently killed by a sheriff driving a government vehicle, would not have claims equally cognizable under 1983.

It is hard to perceive any logical stopping place to such a line of reasoning. . . .

The result reached by the Court of Appeals, which respondent seeks to sustain here, must be bottomed on one of two premises. The first is that the Due Process Clause of the Fourteenth Amendment and § 1983 make actionable many wrongs inflicted by government employees which had heretofore been thought to give rise only to state-law tort claims. The second premise is that the infliction by state officials of a "stigma" to one's reputation is somehow different in kind from the infliction by the same official of harm or injury to other interests protected by state law, so that an injury to reputation is actionable under § 1983 and the Fourteenth Amendment even if other such harms are not. We examine each of these premises in turn.

The first premise would be contrary to pronouncements in our cases on more than one occasion with respect to the scope of § 1983 and of the Fourteenth Amendment. . . . "Violation of local law does not necessarily mean that federal rights have been invaded. The fact that a prisoner is assaulted, injured, or even murdered by state officials does not necessarily mean that he is deprived of any right protected or secured by the Constitution or laws of the United States". . . .

[The plaintiff] has pointed to no specific constitutional guarantee safeguarding the interest he asserts has been invaded. Rather, he apparently believes that the Fourteenth Amendment's Due Process Clause should ex propria vigore extend to him a right to be free of injury wherever the State may be characterized as the tortfeasor. But such a reading would make of the Fourteenth Amendment a font of tort law to be superimposed upon whatever systems may already be administered by the States. We have noted the "constitutional shoals" that confront any attempt to derive from congressional civil rights statutes a body of general federal tort law; A fortiori, the procedural guarantees of the Due Process Clause cannot be the source for such law. . . .

The second premise upon which the result reached by the Court of Appeals could be rested that the infliction by state officials of a "stigma" to one's reputation is somehow different in kind from infliction by a state official of harm to other interests protected by state law is equally untenable. The words "liberty" and "property" as used in the Fourteenth Amendment do not in terms single out reputation as a candidate for special protection over and above other interests that may be protected by state law. . . .

Two things appear from the line of cases beginning with Lovett [discussed in omitted portions of the opinion.] The Court has recognized the serious damage that could be inflicted by branding a government employee as "disloyal," and thereby stigmatizing his good name. But the Court has never held that the mere defamation of an individual, whether by branding him disloyal or otherwise, was sufficient to invoke the guarantees of procedural due process absent an accompanying loss of government employment. . . .

[In Wisconsin v. Constantineau, 400 U.S. 433, 91 S.Ct. 507, 27 L.Ed.2d 515 (1971)] the Court held that a Wisconsin statute authorizing the practice of "posting" was unconstitutional because it failed to provide procedural safeguards of notice and an opportunity to be heard, prior to an individual's being "posted." Under the statute "posting" consisted of forbidding in writing the sale or delivery of alcoholic beverages to certain persons who were determined to have become hazards to themselves, to their family, or to the community by reason of their "excessive drinking." The statute also made it a misdemeanor to sell or give liquor to any person so posted.

There is undoubtedly language in Constantineau, which is sufficiently ambiguous to justify the reliance upon it by the Court of Appeals: "Yet certainly where the State attaches 'a badge of infamy' to the citizen due process comes into play. '[T]he right to be heard before being condemned to suffer grievous loss of any kind, even though it may not involve the stigma and hardships of a criminal conviction, is a principle basic to our society.' Where a person's good name, reputation, honor, or integrity is at stake because of what the government is doing to him, notice and an opportunity to be heard are essential."

We think that the ... language in the last sentence quoted, "because of what the government is doing to him," referred to the fact that the governmental action taken in that case deprived the individual of a right previously held under state law the right to purchase or obtain liquor in common with the rest of the citizenry. "Posting," therefore, significantly altered her status as a matter of state law, and it was that alteration of legal status which, combined with the injury resulting from the defamation, justified the invocation of procedural safeguards. The "stigma" resulting from the defamatory character of the posting was doubtless an important factor in evaluating the extent of harm worked by that act, but we do not think that such defamation, standing alone, deprived Constantineau of any "liberty" protected by the procedural guarantees of the Fourteenth Amendment. . . .

This conclusion is reinforced by our discussion of the subject a little over a year later in Board of Regents v. Roth, 408 U.S. 564, 92 S.Ct. 2701, 33 L.Ed.2d 548 (1972). . . .

While Roth recognized that governmental action defaming an individual in the course of declining to rehire him could entitle the person to notice and an opportunity to be heard as to the defamation, its language is quite inconsistent with any notion that a defamation perpetrated by a government official but unconnected with any refusal to rehire would be actionable under the Fourteenth Amendment. . . .

It is apparent from our decisions that there exists a variety of interests which are difficult of definition but are nevertheless comprehended within the meaning of either "liberty" or "property" as meant in the Due Process Clause. These interests attain this constitutional status by virtue of the fact that they have been initially recognized and protected by state law, and we have repeatedly ruled that the procedural guarantees of the Fourteenth Amendment apply whenever the State seeks to remove or significantly alter that protected status. . . .

In each of these cases, as a result of the state action complained of, a right or status previously recognized by state law was distinctly altered or extinguished. It was this alteration, officially removing the interest from the recognition and protection previously afforded by the State, which we found sufficient to invoke the procedural guarantees contained in the Due Process Clause of the Fourteenth Amendment. But the interest in reputation alone which respondent seeks to vindicate in this action in federal court is quite different from the "liberty" or "property" recognized in those decisions. Kentucky law does not extend to respondent any legal guarantee of present enjoyment of reputation which has been altered as a result of petitioners' actions. Rather his interest in reputation is simply one of a number which the State may protect against injury by virtue of its tort law, providing a forum for vindication of those interests by means of damages actions. And any harm or injury to that interest, even where as here inflicted by an officer of the State, does not result in a deprivation of any "liberty" or "property" recognized by state or federal law, nor has it worked any change of respondent's status as theretofore recognized under the State's laws. For these reasons we hold that the interest in reputation asserted in this case is neither "liberty" nor "property" guaranteed against state deprivation without due process of law.

Respondent in this case cannot assert denial of any right vouchsafed to him by the State and thereby protected under the Fourteenth Amendment. That being the case, petitioners' defamatory publications, however seriously they may have harmed respondent's reputation, did not deprive him of any "liberty" or "property" interests protected by the Due Process Clause.

Respondent's complaint also alleged a violation of a "right to privacy guaranteed by the First, Fourth, Fifth, Ninth, and Fourteenth Amendments." . . .

While there is no "right of privacy" found in any specific guarantee of the Constitution, the Court has recognized that "zones of privacy" may be created by more specific constitutional guarantees and thereby impose limits upon government power. ... Respondent's case, however, comes within none of these areas. He does not seek to suppress evidence seized in the course of an unreasonable search. And our other "right of privacy" cases, while defying categorical description, deal generally with substantive aspects of the Fourteenth Amendment. ...

None of respondent's theories of recovery were based upon rights secured to him by the Fourteenth Amendment. Petitioners therefore were not liable to him under § 1983. The judgment of the Court of Appeals holding otherwise is Reversed.

[Justice Brennan's dissent, in which Justice Marshal concurred and in which Justice White concurred in part, is omitted.]

---

1. Would the result in *Paul* be different if the defendants had knowingly published a falsehood about the plaintiff?

2. Under *Paul,* the plaintiff can claim denial of procedural due process only if the defamation causes the loss of a pre-existing right created by the state, such as a right to a job or the right to buy liquor in *Constantineau*. In *Buckey v. County of Los Angeles,* 968 F.2d 791 (9th Cir. 1992), the court held that loss of business reputation was not analogous to loss of a job.

3. In *Benitez v. Rasmussen,* 261 Neb. 806, 626 N.W.2d 209 (2001), a state agency placed plaintiff's name on Registry of those found guilty of child abuse, making it impossible for the plaintiff to engage in her business. The agency refused to expunge her name, and this refusal was regarded as a stigma. "When that stigma is coupled with the claimant's allegation that his or her inclusion in a central registry has placed a 'tangible burden on ... employment prospects,' courts have found that the claimant has stated a cognizable legal claim for a procedural due process violation. Likewise, when familial relations are eroded by an individual's inclusion in the registry, courts have found the 'plus' requirement satisfied." Here, the plaintiff claimed the tangible burden on her prospects is the loss of her child-care business. But she had no state-created interest in the child care business because renewal of licenses is subject to the state agency's rules. Further, the statute forbids renewal of the license upon conviction. Consequently, under the rule of *Paul v. Davis* the plaintiff has no protectible interest here.

PUTNAM v. KELLER

332 F.3d 541(8th Cir. 2003)

Beam, Circuit Judge ...

Putnam was a music instructor and faculty member of the [defendant] College's Columbus campus for twenty-nine years. He was the founder and director of the performance group "Chorale." He retired from these positions in 2000, but he maintained part-time employment as an instructor through the fall of 2000. He also enrolled in an adult continuing education course for the 2000–2001 school year. Putnam was informed in January 2001, that the College was eliminating his part-time position. Around the same time, he received a letter from the College's counsel, informing him that he would be banned from campus until at least June 1, 2003, while he was under investigation for misappropriating school funds, in violation of school policy and perhaps state criminal law. The letter also alleged that Putnam permitted and encouraged Chorale events that had "inappropriate sexual overtones," making the group he directed appear "cult-like." Putnam denied the accusations in his written response to the College, and he asked for the ban to be lifted.

[Putnam sued under § 1983, claiming denial of both procedural and substantive due process and a violation of free speech and free association rights. There was some evidence that the defendants had made the accusations known to other faculty and staff at the college. The trial court dismissed Putnam's substantive due process claim but denied the defendant's summary judgment motion on the other claims.]

Putnam is entitled to procedural due process if he can show that the College officials deprived him of a constitutionally protected liberty or property interest. Winegar v. Des Moines Indep. Cmty. Sch. Dist., 20 F.3d 895, 899 (8th Cir.1994).

An employee's liberty interests are implicated where the employer levels accusations at the employee that are so damaging as to make it difficult or impossible for the employee to escape the stigma of those charges. The requisite stigma has generally been found when an employer has accused an employee of dishonesty, immorality, criminality, racism, and the like.

. . . In order to establish a procedural due process claim for the loss of this protected liberty interest, Putnam must show (1) that he was stigmatized by the allegations which resulted in his discharge; (2) that the College officials made the allegations public; and (3) that he denied the allegations. . . . We agree with the district court that the accusations made against Putnam rise to the level of stigma articulated in *Winegar* and *Coleman*. Additionally, it is undisputed that Putnam denied the accusations against him in a letter from his attorney to the College, in response to the initial "stay-away" letter. [The court also noted evidence that the accusation were published to others in the college.]

[On Putnam's claim that he was denied substantive due process, the court concluded that the defendants were entitled to an immunity.]

Putnam alleges that the College officials' decision to ban him from the campus violated his rights of free speech and association. . . .

We find that the College campus is a designated public forum because the record establishes that the College opened the campus for expressive activities, such as musical performances and other activities available to the public. As such, Putnam has the same First Amendment right of access to the campus as does any other member of the community. In order to ban Putnam from the campus, the College officials must show that the restrictions are narrowly drawn to serve a compelling interest. The officials have made no such showing. Thus, we agree with the district court that Putnam has demonstrated a violation of constitutional rights. We also agree that Putnam's free speech rights were clearly established at the time the College officials banned him from the campus. The officials are not immune from suit on the issue of violations of Putnam's First Amendment rights.

We affirm the denial of qualified immunity to the College officials with respect to Putnam's procedural due process and First Amendment claims, and we affirm the grant of summary judgment in favor of the College officials based on qualified immunity on Putnam's substantive due process claim.

---

1. On the procedural due process claim, the court in *Putnam v. Keller* did not even cite *Paul v. Davis*, much less discuss it. Did the *Putnam* court comply with the *Paul* rules?

2. As *Putnam* shows, reputational interests may be redressed not only through a claim that procedural due process was denied, but also through First Amendment, free speech or free association claims. If the plaintiff is able to prove any constitutional tort against the plaintiff, damages to reputation flowing from that tort would be recoverable as consequential damages. See *Alexander v. DeAngelo,* 329 F.3d 912, 917 (7th Cir. 2003).

3. What if a prison guard publishes an untrue statement that the plaintiff prisoner is a snitch—a statement that endangers the plaintiff because other inmates are likely to attack him. Would that show a constitutional deprivation and thus avoid the impact of *Paul v. Davis*? Or would that just be another case of defamation? See *Benefield v. McDowall,* 241 F.3d 1267 (10th Cir. 2001) (no citation to *Paul*, holding the claim actionable under the Eighth Amendment).

Additional Problems on the Fair Report Privilege and Its Analogs

PHILLIPS V. EVENING STAR NEWSPAPERS CO., 424 A.2d 78 (D.C. App. 1980). A police department, for the convenience of newspapers, not only logged police actions in department but also made aural recordings of such actions that could be reached by reporters on an information hot line that played a recorded message. The plaintiff's wife was shot and he was the only one present. The plaintiff said he had dropped his gun and it went off, killing his wife. Before police accepted the accident theory, they charged the plaintiff with homicide and the hot line so reported, adding that the wife was "shot during an argument." The defendant newspaper accurately reported the hot line information. After the police accepted the accident explanation, the plaintiff sued the newspaper, which pleaded the fair report privilege. "[T]he Star's reliance on the 'hot line' log as an official document to provide occasion for the official report privilege is misplaced and incorrect. This log representing the oral police communication from which the Star composed its article does not carry the dignity and authoritative weight as a record for which the common law sought to provide a reporting privilege. Mere inaccurate business records of some sort, even if the hot line log could gain that status, will not suffice to create an official record to which the reporting privilege will attach.... As to the reach of the reporting privilege to police statements regarding an arrest, the following states the common law rule:

> An arrest by an officer is an official action, and a report of the fact of that arrest, or of the charge of crime made by the officer in making or returning the arrest, is therefore within the conditional privilege covered by this Section (Reports of Official Proceedings and Public Meetings). On the other hand statements made by the police, or by the complainant or other witnesses, or by the prosecuting attorney as to facts of the case or the evidence expected to be given, are not yet part of the judicial proceeding, or of the arrest itself, and are not privileged under this Section.

Restatement (Second) of Torts, § 611, Comment h (Tent. Draft No. 20, 1974)."

MOLNAR v. STAR-LEDGER, 193 N.J.Super. 12, 471 A.2d 1209 (1984). A fire occurred. The defendant newspaper reported a Deputy Fire Chief's statement (in a private interview?) that arson was probable and that the plaintiff had refused to take a lie detector test. The Deputy had said that, but it turned out to be an error. The plaintiff had not in fact refused to take the test. In the plaintiff's suit against the newspaper, *held*, the newspaper is privileged (a) under the common interest privilege; (b) because the statement made by the Deputy Chief "concerned a matter within the scope of his official responsibilities and therefore cannot be any question that the communication was qualifiedly privileged"; and (c) "The qualified privilege to report defamatory words or statements uttered by a public official with respect to matters within the scope of his official responsibility is analogous to the privilege afforded the news media with respect to full, fair and accurate reports of judicial, legislative and other public proceedings."

YOHE v. NUGENT, 321 F.3d 35 (1st Cir. 2003). A reporter asked the police chief why 30 cars had converged on a neighborhood. The chief responded by saying, accurately, that the department had received a report that a man had been drinking all weekend, was heavily armed, and potentially suicidal. The plaintiff was the man referred to but he was not suicidal, a fact established almost immediately thereafter by evaluations at two hospitals. The whole thing came to nothing except that the newspaper defendants published the Chief's statements, properly attributed them to the Chief and its source in a departmental report. *Held*, "[T]he news account of Yohe's arrest was a privileged fair report of governmental conduct."

1. Is there some privilege to report official acts or conduct as distinct from the privilege to report documents and proceedings? If so, should acts or conduct include statements made by officials within the scope of their duties?

2. Are there signs of confusion in these cases? Could they be groping toward a general privilege to report newsworthy items of public concern or public business? Notice that any privilege to report is necessarily an exception to the rule that repeaters are liable for repetition of defamatory statements.

3. What risk to the publisher if the reporter does not attribute the information to the official?

Problem: Seaman v. The Star

Estrella Archer, a reporter for *The Star*, discovered in casual conversation with a member of the grand jury that it was investigating bribery of public officials and had been looking at evidence against Rick Seaman, a local physician. The juror indicated that Seaman may have offered a bribe to a state official in the Health Department, Bob Pinnicle, who is a controversial figure and has been accused in the past of favoring special interests. The grand jury has heard testimony against Seaman, and had examined a writing signed "Rick Seaman." That writing offered Pinnicle $10,000 to get certain regulations passed for the benefit of a local hospital in which Seaman has shares. Archer gave the information to a columnist for The Star, Bruno Cordoba. Cordoba included some of the information item in a column called "We hear . . ." and followed by gossip and newsy tidbits. As published in The Star:

> We hear . . .
>
> The controversial Bob Pinnicle has again been associated with bribery. A local physician, Rick Seaman, has been accused by officials of offering a bribe to Pinnicle and authorities have possession of a note signed with the name "Rick Seaman" offering Pinnicle money. The matter is under investigation.

That was the entire reference to the matter. The state has no Shield Law, so reporters can be required to divulge sources. For this reason, and because grand jury proceedings are secret, the newspaper decided against running the matter as a news story, since had it attributed the information to the juror, the juror would be in trouble and might refuse to make further revelations.

Seaman sued *The Star* for libel. He alleges that the day after the column was published, the grand jury terminated the investigation and did not indict. He also alleged that the note was a forgery, not signed by him at all. On deposition, he admitted that the note referred to existed and was before the grand jury, but insisted that it was a forgery. Conceding that the note was a forgery, *The Star* moved for summary judgment.

Please construct arguments for and against granting the motion. Use principles and policies as well as authorities and rules of law covered in this chapter.

Chapter 3

FREE SPEECH: DISCUSSING PUBLIC PERSONS AND ISSUES

§ 1. THE TIMES-SULLIVAN CASE AND RULES

The history of libel law leaves little doubt that it originated in soil entirely different from that which nurtured ... constitutional values. Early libel was primarily a criminal remedy, the function of which was to make punishable any writing which tended to bring into disrepute the state, established religion, or any individual likely to be provoked to a breach of the peace because of the words. Truth was no defense in such actions and while a proof of truth might prevent recovery in a civil action, this limitation is more readily explained as a manifestation of judicial reluctance to enrich an undeserving plaintiff than by the supposition that the defendant was protected by the truth of the publication. The same truthful statement might be the basis of a criminal libel action.

—Harlan, J., in *Curtis Publishing Co. v. Butts*, 388 U.S. 130, 87 S. Ct. 1975, 18 L.Ed.2d 1094 (1967)

THE FIRST AMENDMENT

Congress shall make no law respecting an establishment of religion, or prohibiting the free exercise thereof; or abridging the freedom of speech, or of the press; or the right of the people peaceably to assemble, and to petition the Government for a redress of grievances.

NEW YORK TIMES COMPANY v. SULLIVAN

376 U.S. 254, 84 S.Ct. 710, 11 L.Ed.2d 686,
95 A.L.R.2d 1412 (1964)

Mr. Justice BRENNAN delivered the opinion of the Court.

[The plaintiff, Sullivan, an elected commissioner in charge of police, sued the New York Times Company and others for libel allegedly contained in a full-page advertisement published in the New York Times. He recovered $500,000 in the Alabama courts after the New York Times Company rejected his demand for retraction. The ad appealed for funds to support the civil rights movement and was signed by a number of well-known persons. It referred to "an unprecedented wave of terror" in the South. It went on as follows:]

"In Montgomery, Alabama, after students sang 'My Country, Tis of Thee' on the State Capitol steps, their leaders were expelled from school, and truckloads of police armed with shotguns and tear-gas ringed the Alabama State College Campus. When the entire student body protested to state authorities by refusing to re-register, their dining hall was padlocked in an attempt to starve them into submission." Sixth paragraph: "Again and again the Southern violators have answered Dr. King's peaceful protests with intimidation and violence. They have bombed his home almost killing his wife and child. They have assaulted his person. They have arrested him seven times—for 'speeding,' 'loitering' and similar 'offenses.' And now they have charged him with 'perjury'—a felony under which they could imprison him for ten years. . . ."

Although neither of these statements mentions respondent by name, he contended that the word "police" in the third paragraph referred to him as the Montgomery Commissioner who supervised the Police Department, so that he was being accused of "ringing" the campus with police. He further claimed that the paragraph would be read as imputing to the police, and hence to him, the padlocking of the dining hall in order to starve the students into submission. As to the sixth paragraph, he contended that since arrests are ordinarily made by the police, the statement "They have arrested (Dr. King) seven times" would be read as referring to him; he further contended that the "They" who did the arresting would be equated with the "They" who committed the other described acts and with the "Southern violators." Thus, he argued, the paragraph would be read as accusing the Montgomery police, and hence him, of answering Dr. King's protests with "intimidation and violence," bombing his home, assaulting his person, and charging him with perjury. Respondent and six other Montgomery residents testified that they read some or all of the statements as referring to him in his capacity as Commissioner.

It is uncontroverted that some of the statements contained in the two paragraphs were not accurate descriptions of events which occurred in Montgomery. . . .

On the premise that the charges in the sixth paragraph could be read as referring to him, respondent was allowed to prove that he had not participated in the events described. Although Dr. King's home had in fact been bombed twice when his wife and child were there, both of these occasions antedated respondent's tenure as Commissioner, and the police were not only not implicated in the bombings, but had made every effort to apprehend those who were. . . .

Respondent made no effort to prove that he suffered actual pecuniary loss as a result of the alleged libel. . . .

[The jury was instructed under the common law rules allowing recovery without proof of actual damages. The trial judge refused to charge that actual malice or intent to harm was required. The Alabama Supreme Court affirmed. On the ground that the Fourteenth Amendment applied only to state action, it rejected the defendant's constitutional arguments. The Supreme Court held, however, that state action could be found because the state courts applied a state rule of law imposing speech restrictions. In addition, given the subject matter, the speech was not merely "commercial speech."]

[Under Alabama law,] [o]nce "libel per se" has been established, the defendant has no defense as to stated facts unless he can persuade the jury that they were true in all their particulars. His privilege of "fair comment" for expressions of opinion depends on the truth of the facts upon which the comment is based. Unless he can discharge the burden of proving truth, general damages are presumed, and may be awarded without proof of pecuniary injury. A showing of actual malice is apparently a prerequisite to recovery of punitive damages, and the defendant may in any event forestall a punitive award by a retraction meeting the statutory requirements. Good motives and belief in truth do not negate an inference of malice, but are relevant only in mitigation of punitive damages if the jury chooses to accord them weight.

The question before us is whether this rule of liability, as applied to an action brought by a public official against critics of his official conduct, abridges the freedom of speech and of the press that is guaranteed by the First and Fourteenth Amendments.

Respondent relies heavily, as did the Alabama courts, on statements of this Court to the effect that the Constitution does not protect libelous publications. Those statements do not foreclose our inquiry here. None of the cases sustained the use of libel laws to impose sanctions upon expression critical of the official conduct of public officials. . . . [L]ibel can claim no talismanic immunity from constitutional limitations. It must be measured by standards that satisfy the First Amendment.

The general proposition that freedom of expression upon public questions is secured by the First Amendment has long been settled by our decisions. The constitutional safeguard, we have said, was fashioned to assure unfettered interchange of ideas for the bringing about of political and social changes desired by the people. The maintenance of the opportunity for free political discussion to the end that government may be responsive to the will of the people and that changes may be obtained by lawful means, an opportunity essential to the security of the Republic, is a fundamental principle of our constitutional system. [I]t is a prized American privilege to speak one's mind, although not always with perfect good taste, on all public institutions," and this opportunity is to be afforded for "vigorous advocacy" no less than "abstract discussion.

The First Amendment, said Judge Learned Hand, "presupposes that right conclusions are more likely to be gathered out of a multitude of tongues, than through any kind of authoritative selection. To many this is, and always will be, folly; but we have staked upon it our all."

Mr. Justice Brandeis, in his concurring opinion in Whitney v. California, gave the principle its classic formulation: "Those who won our independence believed ... that public discussion is a political duty; and that this should be a fundamental principle of the American government. They recognized the risks to which all human institutions are subject. But they knew that order cannot be secured merely through fear of punishment for its infraction; that it is hazardous to discourage thought, hope and imagination; that fear breeds repression; that repression breeds hate; that hate menaces stable government; that the path of safety lies in the opportunity to discuss freely supposed grievances and proposed remedies; and that the fitting remedy for evil counsels is good ones. Believing in the power of reason as applied through public discussion, they eschewed silence coerced by law—the argument of force in its worst form. Recognizing the occasional tyrannies of governing majorities, they amended the Constitution so that free speech and assembly should be guaranteed."

Thus we consider this case against the background of a profound national commitment to the principle that debate on public issues should be uninhibited, robust, and wide-open, and that it may well include vehement, caustic, and sometimes unpleasantly sharp attacks on government and public officials. The present advertisement, as an expression of grievance and protest on one of the major public issues of our time, would seem clearly to qualify for the constitutional protection. The question is whether it forfeits that protection by the falsity of some of its factual statements and by its alleged defamation of respondent.

... The constitutional protection does not turn upon "the truth, popularity, or social utility of the ideas and beliefs which are offered." As Madison said, "Some degree of abuse is inseparable from the proper use of every thing; and in no instance is this more true than in that of the press." ... "[T]he people of this nation have ordained in the light of history, that, in spite of the probability of excesses and abuses, these liberties are, in the long view, essential to enlightened opinion and right conduct on the part of the citizens of a democracy." ... "Whatever is added to the field of libel is taken from the field of free debate."

Injury to official reputation error affords no more warrant for repressing speech that would otherwise be free than does factual error.

Where judicial officers are involved, this Court has held that concern for the dignity and reputation of the courts does not justify the punishment as criminal contempt of criticism of the judge or his decision. This is true even though the utterance contains "half-truths" and "misinformation." Such repression can be justified, if at all, only by a clear and present danger of the obstruction of justice. ... Criticism of their official conduct does not lose its constitutional protection merely because it is effective criticism and hence diminishes their official reputations.

If neither factual error nor defamatory content suffices to remove the constitutional shield from criticism of official conduct, the combination of the two elements is no less inadequate. This is the lesson to be drawn from the great controversy over the Sedition Act of 1798, 1 Stat. 596, which first crystallized a national awareness of the central meaning of the First Amendment. That statute made it a crime, punishable by a $5,000 fine and five years in prison, "if any person shall write, print, utter or publish ... any false, scandalous and malicious writing or writings against the government of the United States, or either house of the Congress ... , or the President ... , with intent to defame ... or to bring them, or either of them, into contempt or disrepute; or to excite against them, or either or any of them, the hatred of the good people of the United States." [The act recognized a truth defense.]

Although the Sedition Act was never tested in this Court, the attack upon its validity has carried the day in the court of history. Fines levied in its prosecution were repaid by Act of Congress on the ground that it was unconstitutional. ... Jefferson, as President, pardoned those who had been convicted and sentenced under the Act and remitted their fines, stating: "I discharged every person under punishment or prosecution under the sedition law, because I considered, and now consider, that law to be a nullity, as absolute and as palpable as if Congress had ordered us to fall down and worship a golden image." ...

There is no force in respondent's argument that the constitutional limitations implicit in the history of the Sedition Act apply only to Congress and not to the States. [The Fourteenth Amendment applies the First Amendment's restrictions to the states by way of the due process clause.]

What a State may not constitutionally bring about by means of a criminal statute is likewise beyond the reach of its civil law of libel. The fear of damage awards under a rule such as that invoked by the Alabama courts here may be markedly more inhibiting than the fear of prosecution under a criminal statute. ...

The state rule of law is not saved by its allowance of the defense of truth. A defense for erroneous statements honestly made is no less essential here than was the requirement of proof of guilty knowledge. ...

A rule compelling the critic of official conduct to guarantee the truth of all his factual assertions—and to do so on pain of libel judgments virtually unlimited in amount—leads to a comparable "self-censorship."

Allowance of the defense of truth, with the burden of proving it on the defendant, does not mean that only false speech will be deterred. Even courts accepting this defense as an adequate safeguard have recognized the difficulties of adducing legal proofs that the alleged libel was true in all its factual particulars. Under such a rule, would-be critics of official conduct may be deterred from voicing their criticism, even though it is believed to be true and even though it is in fact true, because of doubt whether it can be proved in court or fear of the expense of having to do so. They tend to make only statements which "steer far wider of the unlawful zone." The rule thus dampens the vigor and limits the variety of public debate. It is inconsistent with the First and Fourteenth Amendments.

The constitutional guarantees require, we think, a federal rule that prohibits a public official from recovering damages for a defamatory falsehood relating to his official conduct unless he proves that the statement was made with "actual malice"—that is, with knowledge that it was false or with reckless disregard of whether it was false or not. . . .

[Alabama law provides that] where general damages are concerned malice is "presumed." Such a presumption is inconsistent with the federal rule. "The power to create presumptions is not a means of escape from constitutional restrictions." . . .

This Court's duty is not limited to the elaboration of constitutional principles; we must also in proper cases review the evidence to make certain that those principles have been constitutionally applied. . . . We must "make an independent examination of the whole record," so as to assure ourselves that the judgment does not constitute a forbidden intrusion on the field of free expression . . .

Applying these standards, we consider that the proof presented to show actual malice lacks the convincing clarity which the constitutional standard demands, and hence that it would not constitutionally sustain the judgment for respondent under the proper rule of law. [There was no evidence that individual signers of the ad or the New York Times were aware of erroneous statements at the time of publication.]

The Times' failure to retract upon respondent's demand . . . is likewise not adequate evidence of malice for constitutional purposes. Whether or not a failure to retract may ever constitute such evidence, there are two reasons why it does not here. First, the letter written by the Times reflected a reasonable doubt on its part as to whether the advertisement could reasonably be taken to refer to respondent at all. Second, it was not a final refusal, since it asked for an explanation on this point—a request that respondent chose to ignore. . . .

Finally, there is evidence that the Times published the advertisement without checking its accuracy against the news stories in the Times' own files. The mere presence of the stories in the files does not, of course, establish that the Times "knew" the advertisement was false, since the state of mind required for actual malice would have to be brought home to the persons in the Times' organization having responsibility for the publication of the advertisement. With respect to the failure of those persons to make the check, the record shows that they relied upon their knowledge of the good reputation of many of those whose names were listed as sponsors of the advertisement, and upon the letter from A. Philip Randolph, known to them as a responsible individual, certifying that the use of the names was authorized. ... We think the evidence against the Times supports at most a finding of negligence in failing to discover the misstatements, and is constitutionally insufficient to show the recklessness that is required for a finding of actual malice.

We also think the evidence was constitutionally defective in another respect: it was incapable of supporting the jury's finding that the allegedly libelous statements were made "of and concerning" respondent. ...

[The Alabama Supreme Court found sufficient reference to the plaintiff because "the average person knows that municipal agents, such as police and firemen, and others, are under the control and direction of the city governing body, and more particularly under the direction and control of a single commissioner. In measuring the performance or deficiencies of such groups, praise or criticism is usually attached to the official in complete control of the body."]

This proposition has disquieting implications for criticism of governmental conduct. For good reason, "no court of last resort in this country has ever held, or even suggested, that prosecutions for libel on government have any place in the American system of jurisprudence." The present proposition would sidestep this obstacle by transmuting criticism of government, however impersonal it may seem on its face, into personal criticism, and hence potential libel, of the officials of whom the government is composed. ... Raising as it does the possibility that a good-faith critic of government will be penalized for his criticism, the proposition relied on by the Alabama courts strikes at the very center of the constitutionally protected area of free expression. We hold that such a proposition may not constitutionally be utilized to establish that an otherwise impersonal attack on governmental operations was a libel of an official responsible for those operations. Since it was relied on exclusively here, and there was no other evidence to connect the statements with respondent, the evidence was constitutionally insufficient to support a finding that the statements referred to respondent. ...

Reversed and remanded.

Mr. Justice BLACK, with whom Mr. Justice DOUGLAS joins (concurring).

... I base my vote to reverse on the belief that the First and Fourteenth Amendments not merely "delimit" a State's power to award damages to "public officials against critics of their official conduct" but completely prohibit a State from exercising such a power. ...

Mr. Justice GOLDBERG, with whom Mr. Justice DOUGLAS joins (concurring in the result).

... In my view, the First and Fourteenth Amendments to the Constitution afford to the citizen and to the press an absolute, unconditional privilege to criticize official conduct despite the harm which may flow from excesses and abuses. . . .

Notes

1. **Actual malice.** The *Times-Sullivan* Court made it clear that actual malice was not common law malice based on spite, ill-will, or improper purpose. Instead, the Court required the public official to prove that the defamatory publication was made "with knowledge that it was false or with reckless disregard of whether it was false or not." To avoid confusing common law and constitutional "malice," we will try to speak of knowing or reckless falsehood when discussing the *Times-Sullivan* constitutional requirement.

2. **Self-censorship and values of speech.** The *Times-Sullivan* Court aimed to avoid any system of laws that imposes either external or self-censorship. But what, exactly, are the values of free speech that generate this concern?

3. **Free speakers against free speech.** Long ago, David Riesman pointed to the use of speech as propaganda or even brain-washing by powerful groups, Nazi Germany being a central focus. See David Riesman, *Democracy and Defamation: Control of Group Libel*, 42 COLUM. L. REV. 727 (1942). Some current thinkers have enlarged on this theme, perceiving free speech as failing to accomplish their political goals and possibly as antagonistic to them. Since the most effective speech is that wielded by majorities, powerful persons, or media publishers, it can be used, for example, to perpetuate ethnic stereotypes. See among others Richard Delgado and Jean Stefancic, *Images of the Outsider in American Law and Culture: Can Free Expression Remedy Systemic Social Ills?*, 77 CORNELL L. REV. 1258 (1992).

4. **Independent review and convincing clarity.** The Court in *Times-Sullivan* made at least two quasi-procedural rulings of great practical importance. (a) The Court itself would exercise a scope of review greater than federal courts normally exercise, reviewing evidence to determine whether it would be constitutionally sufficient. The idea is complex and outside the scope of this course, but at a minimum it means that the Court would not be limited to review for "clearly erroneous" determinations of fact. (b) The plaintiff's evidence on knowing or reckless falsehood must meet a convincing clarity standard. Perhaps falsity as well as Constitutional "malice" must be proved by the higher standard. See *DiBella v. Hopkins,* 403 F.3d 102 (2d Cir. 2005) (concluding that most courts to consider the issue have so held, and forecasting that New York law would follow this standard even if it is not a Constitutional requirement).

Scope

5. **Public officials and public figures.** *Times-Sullivan* applied only to plaintiffs who were public officials. The Court soon extended the public

official category to cover candidates for public office. *Monitor Patriot Co. v. Roy*, 401 U.S. 265, 91 S.Ct. 621, 28 L.Ed.2d 35 (1971). In 1967, the Court went further, holding that the knowing or reckless falsehood rule of *Times-Sullivan* requiring knowing or reckless falsehood would also apply to *public figures* suing for libel. *Curtis Publishing Co. v. Butts*, 388 U.S. 130, 87 S.Ct. 1975, 18 L.Ed.2d 1094 (1967). The Court was divided on this point, but extension to public figures was justified partly on the ground that public figures influenced public policy: economic and political power are fused, and there is a high degree of interaction among science, industry and government. Later, we'll see the Court embracing a different rationale—that public figures were subject to the rules of *Times-Sullivan* because public figures either become embroiled in public controversy or because they thrust themselves into the public mind. See *Gertz v. Robert Welch, Inc.*, 418 U.S. 323, 94 S.Ct. 2997, 41 L.Ed.2d 789 (1974).

6. **Who is a public official? The *Rosenblatt* case.** In *Rosenblatt v. Baer,* 383 U.S. 75, 86 S.Ct. 669, 15 L.Ed.2d 597 (1966), the Court held that (1) the category is to be determined by federal law, not state definitions; (2) the category includes appointees as well as elected officials; and (3) it includes former public officials when the alleged libel considers them or their performance while in office. The Court went on to say these things:

> (1) [T]he "public official" designation applies at the very least to those among the hierarchy of government employees who have, or appear to the public to have, substantial responsibility for or control over the conduct of governmental affairs. . . .
>
> (2) Where a position in government has such apparent importance that the public has an independent interest in the qualifications and performance of the person who holds it, beyond the general public interest in the qualifications and performance of all government employees . . . the New York Times malice standards apply.

Does the first quotation represent the Court's test for public official status? Could "at the very least" in that quotation possibly mean "only?" In *Mandel v. The Boston Phoenix Inc.,* 322 F.Supp.2d 39 (D. Mass. 2004), the court, purporting to follow *Rosenblatt,* said "only those employees with 'substantial responsibility for or control over the conduct of government affairs' are deemed public officials."

The *Rosenblatt* Court also insisted on a limitation. The employee's position in government would have to be one that would invite public scrutiny apart from the defamatory charge. In other words, you can't publish a libel about a government employee and then invoke the *Times-Sullivan* rules because of the public interest created by your libel. Can a newspaper claim the *Times-Sullivan* protections when it reports an accusation by the Superintendent of Schools that a janitor at the high school is selling drugs to students?

In *Lane v. MPG Newspapers,* 438 Mass. 476, 781 N.E.2d 800 (2003), the plaintiff was a town firefighter and one of 104 elected representatives to the annual town meeting. He did not campaign or raise funds and was elected to the position by receiving 345 votes. The court thought that several factors would be important in determining whether a person was a public official—the public employee's "ability to set policy guidelines that are of importance to public debate; . . . the impact of the government position on everyday life; the potential for social harm from abuse of the government position; as well as the employee's access to the press." But the court also said it could perceive no cases in which an elected person would not be a public official. There is a limit: "[T]o be protected, a defendant's speech must relate to a public official's official conduct or qualifications for office." In this case the plaintiff was accused of stealing town water for his business. Charge of a crime would always bear on fitness for public office, so the plaintiff was required to prove knowing or reckless falsehood with convincing clarity. He couldn't do that, so summary judgment was properly granted.

7. **Suits by public entities.** It is generally thought that public entities cannot sue individuals for defamation for speech addressed to public issues or criticisms of the public entity. See *Nampa Charter School, Inc. v. DeLaPaz,* 140 Idaho 23, 89 P.3d 863 (2004); *Chicago v. Tribune Co.*, 307 Ill. 595, 139 N.E. 86, 28 A.L.R. 1368 (1923) ("This action is out of tune with the American spirit, and has no place in American jurisprudence").

8. **Criminal libel.** A criminal libel prosecution brought against a defendant based upon criticisms of public officials is subject to the *Times-Sullivan* rules requiring proof of knowing or reckless falsehood. See *Garrison v. Louisiana*, 379 U.S. 64, 85 S.Ct. 209, 13 L.Ed.2d 125 (1964) (a prosecution for defaming judges). Criminal libel prosecutions are uncommon, have a bad name, and a doubtful purpose. See, reviewing some of the cases and scholarship, *Ivey v. State,* 821 So.2d 937 (Ala. 2001).

ST. AMANT V. THOMPSON, 390 U.S. 727, 88 S.Ct. 1323, 20 L.Ed.2d 262 (1968). St. Amant, a candidate for the United States Senate, made a speech attacking an opponent by claiming that the opponent had a relationship with Partin, the president of the local Teamsters Union, who in turn was said to be guilty of planned misdeeds. St. Amant said the planned misdeed could not be reported to the police, because Partin had a connection with the Sheriff's office through Herman Thompson, a sheriff's deputy and that money had passed between Partin and Thompson. Thompson brought this action for libel claiming that St. Amant's statement implied serious misconduct. Thompson recovered $5,000 in damages. The Louisiana Supreme Court upheld the award on the ground that he had proved *Times-Sullivan* recklessness, because St. Amant had no personal knowledge and relied on reports of a man whose reputation for veracity was not established in the record, because he did not verify the information, and because "he gave no consideration to whether or not the statements defamed Thompson." On the assumption that Thompson was a public official, that the statements charged him with a crime and were false, *held*, reversed and remanded. "These considerations fall short of proving St. Amant's reckless disregard for the accuracy of his statements about Thompson." Although reckless disregard cannot be fully encompassed in one infallible definition, our cases have emphasized that to show reckless disregard the plaintiff must show the defendant had a high degree of awareness of probable falsity. Recklessness for this purpose is not measured by departure from a prudent person standard. "There must be sufficient evidence to permit the conclusion that the defendant in fact entertained serious doubts as to the truth of his publication. Publishing with such doubts shows reckless disregard for truth or falsity and demonstrates actual malice.

"The defendant in a defamation action brought by a public official cannot, however, automatically insure a favorable verdict by testifying that he published with a belief that the statements were true. The finder of fact must determine whether the publication was indeed made in good faith. Professions of good faith will be unlikely to prove persuasive, for example, where a story is fabricated by the defendant, is the product of his imagination, or is based wholly on an unverified anonymous telephone call. Nor will they be likely to prevail when the publisher's allegations are so inherently improbable that only a reckless man would have put them in circulation. Likewise, recklessness may be found where there are obvious reasons to doubt the veracity of the informant or the accuracy of his reports.

"By no proper test of reckless disregard was St. Amant's broadcast a reckless publication about a public officer."

---

9. **Negligent investigation.** Would negligent investigation ever suffice to show knowing or reckless falsehood under the *St. Amant* test? The Supreme Court insists on more, but in some cases the Court has permitted an inference of knowing or reckless falsehood when the publisher relied upon witnesses known to be untrustworthy and had time to investigate more carefully but failed to do so. See *Curtis Publishing Co. v. Butts,* 388 U.S. 130, 153, 87 S.Ct. 1975, 1991, 18 L.Ed.2d 1094 (1967). Argue pro or con: a rule permitting the trier to draw inferences of knowing falsehood from a bad investigation runs the risk of undercutting the protection announced in *Times-Sullivan* and *St. Amant.*

10. **Purposeful avoidance of the truth.** In *Harte-Hanks Communications, Inc. v. Connaughton,* 491 U.S. 657, 109 S.Ct. 2678, 105 L.Ed.2d 562 (1989), the Court said: "[I]t is likely that the newspaper's inaction was a product of a deliberate decision not to acquire knowledge of facts that might confirm the probable falsity of Thompson's charges. Although failure to investigate will not alone support a finding of actual malice, the purposeful avoidance of the truth is in a different category." In *Bentley v. Bunton,* 94 S.W.3d 561 (Tex. 2002), the defendant, conducting a local public access TV talk-show, repeatedly asserted that the plaintiff, a local judge, was corrupt, discussing eight instances of behavior he claimed showed corruption. But although these accusations stretched out over months, and authoritative sources could have confirmed the charge or exculpated the judge, the defendant never asked them. "All those who could have shown Bunton that his charges were wrong Bunton deliberately ignored." The court also said: "Imagining that something may be true is not the same as belief." But the mere fact that more investigation could be done or that the plaintiff denied the charges before they were published, does not show reckless falsehood. *Hearst Corp. v. Skeen,* 159 S.W.3d 633 (Tex. 2005).

11. **Ill-will or spite.** We know that under *Times-Sullivan*, spite and other forms of enmity are not sufficient and that instead the ultimate fact to be proved is knowing or reckless falsehood. If purposeful avoidance of the

truth is evidence of knowing falsehood, how about personal ill-will? The plaintiff can show that the journalist hates him. Does that evidence, without more, show that what the journalist knew he was writing a falsehood? When some evidence points to possible knowledge of falsity, the defendant's partisanship or ill-will can be viewed as strengthening that interpretation of the evidence by "accumulation" of inferences. In such a case, evidence of such ill-will has been admitted as circumstantial evidence, and may suffice to prove that the defendant had serious doubts about the truth of his statements. *Celle v. Filipino Reporter Enterprises, Inc.,* 209 F.3d 163 (2d Cir. 2000); *Woodcock v. Journal Publishing Company, Inc.*, 230 Conn. 525, 544, 646 A.2d 92, 101 (1994). But if the defendant really is biased against the plaintiff, maybe he really believes all the bad things he wrote. In *Church of Scientology International v. Behar,* 238 F.3d 168 (2d Cir. 2001), the court approved the trial judge's comment that the "speaker's belief in his statements, even his exaggerations, enhances, rather than diminishes, the likelihood that they are protected."

12. **Improbable statements and near misses.** *St. Amant* recognized that some statements are "so inherently improbable that only a reckless man would have put them in circulation." Suppose the opposite: the defendant's statement is a close approximation of the truth even though technically false. Does that tend to negate a finding of knowing or reckless falsehood? See *Annette F. v. Sharon S.,* 119 Cal.App.4th 1146, 15 Cal.Rptr.3d 100 (2004) (fact: a court found Annette had committed domestic abuse and therefore enjoined her; statement: Annette was "convicted" of domestic abuse).

13. **Discovery.** The subjective standard in *St. Amant* has had at least one procedural effect that can affect the outcome of libel suits, especially against media publishers. First, the Court has allowed the plaintiff to use discovery to probe the state of mind of journalists. For example, the plaintiff might use discovery to establish the journalist's state of mind at the time of publication with respect to the veracity of persons interviewed. *Herbert v. Lando,* 441 U.S. 153, 99 S.Ct. 1635, 60 L.Ed.2d 115 (1979).

14. **Summary judgment.** On the other hand, the clear and convincing evidence standard in *New York Times v. Sullivan* gives the journalist and publisher some solid protection, not only at trial but also on motion for summary judgment. "[T]he trial judge's summary judgment inquiry ... will be whether the evidence presented is such that a jury applying that evidentiary standard could reasonably find for either the plaintiff or the defendant. [On the "malice" issue] the appropriate summary judgment question will be whether the evidence in the record could support a reasonable jury finding either that the plaintiff has shown actual malice by clear and convincing evidence or that the plaintiff has not." *Anderson v. Liberty Lobby, Inc.,* 477 U.S. 242, 106 S.Ct. 2505, 91 L.Ed.2d 202 (1986).

15. **Data.** Professor David Logan summarizes data from the Libel Defense Resource Center showing that media defendants win 82% of the cases pretrial, 36% of what remains at jury trial, and still others on appeal. He also reports that most awards are now under $250,000, although huge awards such as $10 million have become more common. Do these figures mean that the Court has successfully protected freedom of speech rights? David A. Logan, *Libel Law in the Trenches: Reflections on Current Data on Libel Litigation,* 87 VA. L. REV. 503 (2001). Don't forget to add in the costs of defending libel actions.

§ 2. PRIVATE PERSONS AND PUBLIC ISSUES

(a) Fault and Damages Required in Suits by Private Persons

Rosenbloom v. Metromedia, Inc., 403 U.S. 29, 91 S.Ct. 1811, 29 L.Ed.2d 296 (1971). The defendant broadcast reports about police seizure of the plaintiff's inventory of nudist magazines, characterizing the magazines as obscene books and referring to "girlie-books" and the "smut literature racket." In the plaintiff's libel action, the jury returned a verdict for the plaintiff. The Court of Appeals reversed, holding that the *Times-Sullivan* rules protected the defendants as a matter of law. *Held,* by an evenly divided Court, the Court of Appeals is affirmed. Per Brennan, J.: "Self-governance in the United States presupposes far more than knowledge and debate about the strictly official activities of various levels of government. The commitment of the country to the institution of private property, protected by the Due Process and Just Compensation Clauses in the Constitution, places in private hands vast areas of economic and social power that vitally affect the nature and quality of life in the Nation. Our efforts to live and work together in a free society not completely dominated by governmental regulation necessarily encompass far more than politics in a narrow sense. 'The guarantees for speech and press are not the preserve of political expression or comment upon public affairs.' ... If a matter is a subject of public or general interest, it cannot suddenly become less so merely because a private individual is involved, or because in some sense the individual did not 'voluntarily' choose to become involved." Clear and convincing evidence of a knowing or reckless falsehood is required when a private individual sues for a defamatory falsehood about his involvement "in an event of public or general concern."

GERTZ v. ROBERT WELCH, INC.

418 U.S. 323, 94 S.Ct. 2997, 41 L.Ed.2d 789 (1974)

Mr. Justice POWELL delivered the opinion of the Court. ...

In 1968 a Chicago policeman named Nuccio shot and killed a youth named Nelson. The state authorities prosecuted Nuccio for the homicide and ultimately obtained a conviction for murder in the second degree. The Nelson family retained petitioner Elmer Gertz, a reputable attorney, to represent them in civil litigation against Nuccio.

Respondent publishes American Opinion, a monthly outlet for the views of the John Birch Society. Early in the 1960's the magazine began to warn of a nationwide conspiracy to discredit local law enforcement agencies and create in their stead a national police force capable of supporting a Communist dictatorship. As part of the continuing effort to alert the public to this assumed danger, the managing editor of American Opinion commissioned an article on the murder trial of Officer Nuccio. For this purpose he engaged a regular contributor to the magazine. In March 1969 respondent published the resulting article under the title "FRAME–UP: Richard Nuccio And The War On Police." The article purports to demonstrate that the testimony against Nuccio at his criminal trial was false and that his prosecution was part of the Communist campaign against the police.

In his capacity as counsel for the Nelson family in the civil litigation, petitioner attended the coroner's inquest into the boy's death and initiated actions for damages, but he neither discussed Officer Nuccio with the press nor played any part in the criminal proceeding. Notwithstanding petitioner's remote connection with the prosecution of Nuccio, respondent's magazine portrayed him as an architect of the "frame-up." According to the article, the police file on petitioner took "a big, Irish cop to lift." The article stated that petitioner had been an official of the "Marxist League for Industrial Democracy, originally known as the Intercollegiate Socialist Society, which has advocated the violent seizure of our government." It labeled Gertz a "Leninist" and a "Communist-fronter." It also stated that Gertz had been an officer of the National Lawyers Guild, described as a Communist organization that "probably did more than any other outfit to plan the Communist attack on the Chicago police during the 1968 Democratic Convention."

These statements contained serious inaccuracies. The implication that petitioner had a criminal record was false. Petitioner had been a member and officer of the National Lawyers Guild some 15 years earlier, but there was no evidence that he or that organization had taken any part in planning the 1968 demonstrations in Chicago. There was also no basis for the charge that petitioner was a "Leninist" or a "Communist-fronter." And he had never been a member of the "Marxist League for Industrial Democracy" or the "Intercollegiate Socialist Society."

The managing editor of American Opinion made no effort to verify or substantiate the charges against petitioner. Instead, he appended an editorial introduction stating that the author had "conducted extensive research into the Richard Nuccio Case." And he included in the article a photograph of petitioner and wrote the caption that appeared under it: "Elmer Gertz of Red Guild harasses Nuccio." Respondent placed the issue of American Opinion containing the article on sale at newsstands throughout the country and distributed reprints of the article on the streets of Chicago.

Petitioner filed a diversity action for libel in the United States District Court for the Northern District of Illinois. He claimed that the falsehoods published by respondent injured his reputation as a lawyer and a citizen. [There was a jury verdict for Gertz, but the District Court then decided that the New York Times standard should govern this case even though Gertz was not a public official or public figure. Accordingly it entered a judgment NOV for the defendant. The Court of Appeals held that *Rosenbloom* imposed the *Times-Sullivan* rules regardless of the plaintiff's status or fame. Since knowing or reckless falsehood had not been shown, the Court of Appeals affirmed the district's court's judgment for the defendant.]

The principal issue in this case is whether a newspaper or broadcaster that publishes defamatory falsehoods about an individual who is neither a public official nor a public figure may claim a constitutional privilege against liability for the injury inflicted by those statements. The Court considered this question on the rather different set of facts presented in Rosenbloom v. Metromedia, Inc., 403 U.S. 29, 91 S.Ct. 1811, 29 L.Ed.2d 296 (1971). . . .

[The opinion here reviewed views of different Justices as stated in *Rosenbloom*, concluding the review by noting the dissents of Justices Marshall and Stewart, which argued that the public interest test for applying the *Times-Sullivan* rules "would involve the courts in the dangerous business of deciding 'what information is relevant to self-government.' "]

We begin with the common ground. Under the First Amendment there is no such thing as a false idea. However pernicious an opinion may seem, we depend for its correction not on the conscience of judges and juries but on the competition of other ideas. But there is no constitutional value in false statements of fact. Neither the intentional lie nor the careless error materially advances society's interest in "uninhibited, robust, and wide-open" debate on public issues. . . .

Although the erroneous statement of fact is not worthy of constitutional protection, it is nevertheless inevitable in free debate. As James Madison pointed out in the Report on the Virginia Resolutions of 1798: "Some degree of abuse is inseparable from the proper use of every thing; and in no instance is this more true than in that of the press." And punishment of error runs the risk of inducing a cautious and restrictive exercise of the constitutionally guaranteed freedoms of speech and press. Our decisions recognize that a rule of strict liability that compels a publisher or broadcaster to guarantee the accuracy of his factual assertions may lead to intolerable self-censorship. . . .

The need to avoid self-censorship by the news media is, however, not the only societal value at issue. . . .

The legitimate state interest underlying the law of libel is the compensation of individuals for the harm inflicted on them by defamatory falsehood. We would not lightly require the State to abandon this purpose, for, as Mr. Justice Stewart has reminded us, the individual's right to the protection of his own good name "reflects no more than our basic concept of the essential dignity and worth of every human being–a concept at the root of any decent system of ordered liberty. The protection of private personality, like the protection of life itself, is left primarily to the individual States under the Ninth and Tenth Amendments. But this does not mean that the right is entitled to any less recognition by this Court as a basic of our constitutional system." . . .

The New York Times standard defines the level of constitutional protection appropriate to the context of defamation of a public person. Those who, by reason of the notoriety of their achievements or the vigor and success with which they seek the public's attention, are properly classed as public figures and those who hold governmental office may recover for injury to reputation only on clear and convincing proof that the defamatory falsehood was made with knowledge of its falsity or with reckless disregard for the truth. This standard administers an extremely powerful antidote to the inducement to media self-censorship of the common-law rule of strict liability for libel and slander. And it exacts a correspondingly high price from the victims of defamatory falsehood. . . . [W]e believe that the New York Times rule states an accommodation between this concern and the limited state interest present in the context of libel actions brought by public persons. For the reasons stated below, we conclude that the state interest in compensating injury to the reputation of private individuals requires that a different rule should obtain with respect to them.

Theoretically, of course, the balance between the needs of the press and the individual's claim to compensation for wrongful injury might be struck on a case-by-case basis. ... But this approach would lead to unpredictable results and uncertain expectations, and it could render our duty to supervise the lower courts unmanageable. Because an ad hoc resolution of the competing interests at stake in each particular case is not feasible, we must lay down broad rules of general application. Such rules necessarily treat alike various cases involving differences as well as similarities. Thus it is often true that not all of the considerations which justify adoption of a given rule will obtain in each particular case decided under its authority.

With that caveat we have no difficulty in distinguishing among defamation plaintiffs. The first remedy of any victim of defamation is self-help—using available opportunities to contradict the lie or correct the error and thereby to minimize its adverse impact on reputation. Public officials and public figures usually enjoy significantly greater access to the channels of effective communication and hence have a more realistic opportunity to counteract false statements then private individuals normally enjoy. Private individuals are therefore more vulnerable to injury, and the state interest in protecting them is correspondingly greater.

More important than the likelihood that private individuals will lack effective opportunities for rebuttal, there is a compelling normative consideration underlying the distinction between public and private defamation plaintiffs. An individual who decides to seek governmental office must accept certain necessary consequences of that involvement in public affairs. He runs the risk of closer public scrutiny than might otherwise be the case. And society's interest in the officers of government is not strictly limited to the formal discharge of official duties. As the Court pointed out in Garrison v. Louisiana, the public's interest extends to "anything which might touch on an official's fitness for office.

... Few personal attributes are more germane to fitness for office than dishonesty, malfeasance, or improper motivation, even though these characteristics may also affect the official's private character."

Those classed as public figures stand in a similar position. ...

Even if the foregoing generalities do not obtain in every instance, the communications media are entitled to act on the assumption that public officials and public figures have voluntarily exposed themselves to increased risk of injury from defamatory falsehood concerning them. No such assumption is justified with respect to a private individual. He has not accepted public office or assumed an "influential role in ordering society." He has relinquished no part of his interest in the protection of his own good name, and consequently he has a more compelling call on the courts for redress of injury inflicted by defamatory falsehood. Thus, private individuals are not only more vulnerable to injury than public officials and public figures; they are also more deserving of recovery.

For these reasons we conclude that the States should retain substantial latitude in their efforts to enforce a legal remedy for defamatory falsehood injurious to the reputation of a private individual. The extension of the New York Times test proposed by the Rosenbloom plurality would abridge this legitimate state interest to a degree that we find unacceptable. And it would occasion the additional difficulty of forcing state and federal judges to decide on an ad hoc basis which publications address issues of "general or public interest" and which do not—to determine, in the words of Mr. Justice Marshall, "what information is relevant to self-government." We doubt the wisdom of committing this task to the conscience of judges. ...

We hold that, so long as they do not impose liability without fault, the States may define for themselves the appropriate standard of liability for a publisher or broadcaster of defamatory falsehood injurious to a private individual. This approach provides a more equitable boundary between the competing concerns involved here. It recognizes the strength of the legitimate state interest in compensating private individuals for wrongful injury to reputation, yet shields the press and broadcast media from the rigors of strict liability for defamation. At least this conclusion obtains where, as here, the substance of the defamatory statement "makes substantial danger to reputation apparent." This phrase places in perspective the conclusion we announce today. Our inquiry would involve considerations somewhat different from those discussed above if a State purported to condition civil liability on a factual misstatement whose content did not warn a reasonably prudent editor or broadcaster of its defamatory potential. ...

[W]e endorse this approach in recognition of the strong and legitimate state interest in compensating private individuals for injury to reputation. But this countervailing state interest extends no further than compensation for actual injury. For the reasons stated below, we hold that the States may not permit recovery of presumed or punitive damages, at least when liability is not based on a showing of knowledge of falsity or reckless disregard for the truth.

The common law of defamation is an oddity of tort law, for it allows recovery of purportedly compensatory damages without evidence of actual loss. ... The largely uncontrolled discretion of juries to award damages where there is no loss unnecessarily compounds the potential of any system of liability for defamatory falsehood to inhibit the vigorous exercise of First Amendment freedoms. Additionally, the doctrine of presumed damages invites juries to punish unpopular opinion rather than to compensate individuals for injury sustained by the publication of a false fact. More to the point, the States have no substantial interest in securing for plaintiffs such as this petitioner gratuitous awards of money damages far in excess of any actual injury.

... It is necessary to restrict defamation plaintiffs who do not prove knowledge of falsity or reckless disregard for the truth to compensation for actual injury. We need not define "actual injury," as trial courts have wide experience in framing appropriate jury instructions in tort actions. Suffice it to say that actual injury is not limited to out-of-pocket loss. Indeed, the more customary types of actual harm inflicted by defamatory falsehood include impairment of reputation and standing in the community, personal humiliation, and mental anguish and suffering. Of course, juries must be limited by appropriate instructions, and all awards must be supported by competent evidence concerning the injury, although there need be no evidence which assigns an actual dollar value to the injury.

We also find no justification for allowing awards of punitive damages against publishers and broadcasters held liable under state-defined standards of liability for defamation. ... [J]uries assess punitive damages in wholly unpredictable amounts bearing no necessary relation to the actual harm caused. And they remain free to use their discretion selectively to punish expressions of unpopular views. Like the doctrine of presumed damages, jury discretion to award punitive damages unnecessarily exacerbates the danger of media self-censorship. ... In short, the private defamation plaintiff who establishes liability under a less demanding standard than that stated by New York Times may recover only such damages as are sufficient to compensate him for actual injury.

Notwithstanding our refusal to extend the New York Times privilege to defamation of private individuals, respondent contends that we should affirm the judgment below on the ground that petitioner is either a public official or a public figure. There is little basis for the former assertion. Several years prior to the present incident, petitioner had served briefly on housing committees appointed by the mayor of Chicago, but at the time of publication he had never held any remunerative governmental position. Respondent admits this but argues that petitioner's appearance at the coroner's inquest rendered him a "de facto public official." Our cases recognized no such concept. Respondent's suggestion would sweep all lawyers under the New York Times rule as officers of the court and distort the plain meaning of the "public official" category beyond all recognition. We decline to follow it.

Respondent's characterization of petitioner as a public figure raises a different question. That designation may rest on either of two alternative bases. In some instances an individual may achieve such pervasive fame or notoriety that he becomes a public figure for all purposes and in all contexts. More commonly, an individual voluntarily injects himself or is drawn into a particular public controversy and thereby becomes a public figure for a limited range of issues. In either case such persons assume special prominence in the resolution of public questions.

Petitioner has long been active in community and professional affairs. He has served as an officer of local civic groups and of various professional organizations, and he has published several books and articles on legal subjects. Although petitioner was consequently well known in some circles, he had achieved no general fame or notoriety in the community. None of the prospective jurors called at the trial had ever heard of petitioner prior to this litigation, and respondent offered no proof that this response was atypical of the local population. We would not lightly assume that a citizen's participation in community and professional affairs rendered him a public figure for all purposes. Absent clear evidence of general fame or notoriety in the community, and pervasive involvement in the affairs of society, an individual should not be deemed a public personality for all aspects of his life. It is preferable to reduce the public-figure question to a more meaningful context by looking to the nature and extent of an individual's participation in the particular controversy giving rise to the defamation.

In this context it is plain that petitioner was not a public figure. He played a minimal role at the coroner's inquest, and his participation related solely to his representation of a private client. He took no part in the criminal prosecution of Officer Nuccio. Moreover, he never discussed either the criminal or civil litigation with the press and was never quoted as having done so. He plainly did not thrust himself into the vortex of this public issue, nor did he engage the public's attention in an attempt to influence its outcome. We are persuaded that the trial court did not err in refusing to characterize petitioner as a public figure for the purpose of this litigation.

We therefore conclude that the New York Times standard is inapplicable to this case and that the trial court erred in entering judgment for respondent. Because the jury was allowed to impose liability without fault and was permitted to presume damages without proof of injury, a new trial is necessary. We reverse and remand for further proceedings in accord with this opinion. . . .

---

16. **Greater fault can be required under state law.** The states are free to provide greater speech protections than the federal Constitution

demands. In *Konikoff v. Prudential Ins. Co. of American,* 234 F.3d 92 (2d Cir. 2000), Judge Sack observed:

> The vast majority of states subsequently decided that the "appropriate standard of liability" left for them to decide by *Gertz* is negligence. The New York State Court of Appeals, however, chose a different path. It held in *Chapadeau* that "where the content of the article is arguably within the sphere of legitimate public concern, which is reasonably related to matters warranting public exposition, the party defamed may recover" if he or she can establish "by a preponderance of the evidence, that the publisher acted in a grossly irresponsible manner without due consideration for the standards of information gathering and dissemination ordinarily followed by responsible parties." *Chapadeau,* 38 N.Y.2d at 199, 341 N.E.2d at 571, 379 N.Y.S.2d at 64.

Some other states have likewise provided greater-than-*Gertz* protections for discussion of public concern issues even when the plaintiff is a private person. E.g., *Beauchamp v. City of Noblesville, Indiana,* 320 F.3d 733 (7th Cir. 2003) (Indiana law); *Rocci v. Ecole Secondaire Macdonald–Cartier,* 165 N.J. 149, 755 A.2d 583 (2000).

17. **Proof of actual damages can be required under state law.** Some states have likewise abolished the common law presumption of damages, not only in libel per quod cases but seemingly in all. In those states, the plaintiff will be required to prove some kind of actual harm and not merely where *Gertz* requires such proof. See *Arthaud v. Mutual of Omaha Ins. Co.,* 170 F.3d 860 (8th Cir. 1999); *Nazeri v. Missouri Valley College,* 860 S.W.2d 303 (Mo. 1993).

18. **What kind of fault—ill-will?** *Gertz* requires only "some fault." Could that conceivably be fault in the sense of ill-will as distinct from fault about discovering or reporting the truth?

19. **Do traditional ideas of negligence work here?** Most courts have turned to negligence as the "some fault" required. What conduct could count as negligence? Consider these types of "negligence" under *Gertz*:

> (A) The journalist fails to investigate or does so poorly. Must the plaintiff show that investigation fell below professional standards, or can the trier make a free-wheeling judgment that the investigation simply should have been better?
>
> (B) The journalist draws and writes up doubtful, impermissible, or irrational inferences from the established facts.
>
> (C) The journalist is credulous; he believes a witness whose testimony might be true but about which most people would be skeptical: he interviews and believes a convict's accusation of another. Cf. *McCoy v. Hearst Corporation,* 42 Cal.3d 835, 727 P.2d 711, 231 Cal.Rptr. 518 (1986) (addressing only the knowing falsehood, not the negligence issue).
>
> (D) The journalist does an excellent investigation but his report is ambiguous and can be read to imply something defamatory. Can the concept of negligence apply to bad writing? A poor word choice? A candidate for sheriff in a county with 84% Hispanic constituency publicly claims that he is especially qualified because he is multicultural. The

newspaper reports the speech as claiming that "No Anglo can be elected sheriff." Does this show (a) knowing or reckless falsehood? or (b) negligence? *Freedom Newspapers of Texas v. Cantu,* 168 S.W.3d 847 (Tex. 2005). Distinguish intentional misstatements in the publication. Cf. *Masson v. New Yorker Magazine, Inc.,* 501 U.S. 496, 111 S.Ct. 2419, 115 L.Ed.2d 447 (1991) (defendant attributed certain statements to the plaintiff, using quotation marks; in fact, the defendant was merely summarizing its interpretation of the meaning; if a false direct quotation made the plaintiff sound worse, the *Times-Sullivan* test is met).

20. **Res ipsa loquitur.** An object under the defendant's control falls from the defendant's window and strikes the plaintiff. Courts say "res ipsa loquitur," the thing speaks for itself and that it says "negligence." Could you say the same for false and defamatory publications or at least some of them? Suppose a report of a public document is inaccurate. Why not res ipsa loquitur? Would the Supreme Court think that Constitutional under *Gertz*?

21. **Comparative fault.** If negligence is to be the basis of liability, does that mean that the plaintiff's damages could be reduced for comparative fault? This would be a wholly new thing in the law of defamation. When could it apply? In *Masson v. New Yorker Magazine, Inc.,* 501 U.S. 496, 111 S.Ct. 2419, 115 L.Ed.2d 447 (1991), a journalist interviewed the plaintiff for a *New Yorker* piece. He may have presented himself in a bad light, but the journalist's article as published arguably presented him in a worse light. Could the plaintiff's interview count as comparative fault that would justify a proportionate reduction in damages?

(b) Determining Who Is a Private Person or Public Figure

Time, Inc. v. Firestone, 424 U.S. 448, 96 S.Ct. 958, 47 L.Ed.2d 154 (1976). Mary Alice married Russell Firestone, of a wealthy, famous family. Eventually, she sued for separate maintenance and Russell counterclaimed for divorce on the grounds of extreme cruelty and adultery. Testimony indicated that each party had engaged in extramarital activities. The trial court decreed a divorce seemingly on the ground that neither party was domesticated. His opinion, however, also said that "bizarre and amatory" "extramarital escapades of the plaintiff [Mary Alice] ... would have made Dr. Freud's hair curl." Time Magazine reported the divorce "on the grounds of extreme cruelty and adultery" (the grounds on which Russell had sought divorce), and mentioned Dr. Freud's curly hair. Time refused a retraction and Mary Alice sued. The court in that case gave judgment for Mary Alice Firestone for $100,000 and the state courts affirmed it. *Held:* Vacated and remanded for a fault determination. (1) Mary Alice was not a public figure; hence the *Times-Sullivan* knowing or reckless falsehood standard does not apply and she is not required to prove malice. (a) The fact that the case was a cause celebre is not enough to make her a public figure; if it were, we would be re-adopting the *Rosenbloom* approach. (b) "Dissolution of a marriage through judicial proceedings is not the sort of 'public controversy' referred to in Gertz." (c) Nor did she "thrust herself to the forefront of any particular public controversy in order to influence the resolution of the issues involved in it." (d) Resort to judicial process was not voluntary in this instance; she had no choice but to resort to the courts for relief. (e) The fact that she held press conferences is not enough, either. She did not use them to thrust herself into the forefront of controversy to influence its resolution. (2) However, *Gertz* requires some fault as a basis for liability. No issue of fault was submitted to the jury. If the Supreme Court of Florida found fault, that is sufficient, as *Gertz* does not require a jury's determination of fault. However, the case is remanded for the Florida court's explicit determination on fault. [Concurrences and dissents are not summarized in this case abstract.]

WOLSTON v. READER'S DIGEST ASSOCIATION, INC.

443 U.S. 157, 99 S.Ct. 2701, 61 L.Ed.2d 450 (1979)

Mr. Justice REHNQUIST delivered the opinion of the Court.

In 1974, respondent Reader's Digest Association, Inc., published a book entitled KGB, the Secret Work of Soviet Agents (KGB), written by respondent John Barron. The book describes the Soviet Union's espionage organization and chronicles its activities since World War II. In a passage referring to disclosures by "royal commissions in Canada and Australia, and official investigations in Great Britain and the United States," the book contains the following statements relating to petitioner Ilya Wolston:

> Among Soviet agents identified in the United States were Elizabeth T. Bentley, Edward Joseph Fitzgerald, William Ludwig Ullmann, William Walter Remington, Franklin Victor Reno, Judith Coplon, Harry Gold, David Greenglass, Julius and Ethel Rosenberg, Morton Sobell, William Perl, Alfred Dean Slack, Jack Soble, Ilya Wolston, Alfred and Martha Stern.*
>
> * No claim is made that this list is complete. It consists of Soviet agents who were convicted of espionage or falsifying information or perjury and/or contempt charges following espionage indictments, or who fled to the Soviet bloc to avoid prosecution. . . .

[The District Court granted summary judgment for defendants on the ground that Wolston was a public figure. The Court of Appeals affirmed.]

We hold that the District Court and the Court of Appeals were wrong in concluding that petitioner was a public figure within the meaning of this Court's defamation cases. Petitioner therefore was not required by the First Amendment to meet the "actual malice" standard of New York Times Co. v. Sullivan, supra, in order to recover from respondents.

During 1957 and 1958, a special federal grand jury sitting in New York City conducted a major investigation into the activities of Soviet intelligence agents in the United States. As a result of this investigation, petitioner's aunt and uncle, Myra and Jack Soble, were arrested in

January 1957 on charges of spying. The Sobles later pleaded guilty to espionage charges, and in the ensuing months, the grand jury's investigation focused on other participants in a suspected Soviet espionage ring, resulting in further arrests, convictions, and guilty pleas. On the same day the Sobles were arrested, petitioner was interviewed by agents of the Federal Bureau of Investigation at his home in the District of Columbia. Petitioner was interviewed several more times during the following months in both Washington and in New York City and traveled to New York on various occasions pursuant to grand jury subpoenas.

On July 1, 1958, however, petitioner failed to respond to a grand jury subpoena directing him to appear on that date. Petitioner previously had attempted to persuade law enforcement authorities not to require him to travel to New York for interrogation because of his state of mental depression. On July 14, a Federal District Judge issued an order to show cause why petitioner should not be held in criminal contempt of court. These events immediately attracted the interest of the news media, and on July 15 and 16, at least seven news stories focusing on petitioner's failure to respond to the grand jury subpoena appeared in New York and Washington newspapers.

Petitioner appeared in court on the return date of the show-cause order and offered to testify before the grand jury, but the offer was refused. A hearing then commenced on the contempt charges. Petitioner's wife, who then was pregnant, was called to testify as to petitioner's mental condition at the time of the return date of the subpoena, but after she became hysterical on the witness stand, petitioner agreed to plead guilty to the contempt charge. He received a 1–year suspended sentence and was placed on probation for three years, conditioned on his cooperation with the grand jury in any further inquiries regarding Soviet espionage. Newspapers also reported the details of the contempt proceedings and petitioner's guilty plea and sentencing. In all, during the 6–week period between petitioner's failure to appear before the grand jury and his sentencing, 15 stories in newspapers in Washington and New York mentioned or discussed these events. This flurry of publicity subsided following petitioner's sentencing, however, and, thereafter, he succeeded for the most part in returning to the private life he had led prior to issuance of the grand jury subpoena. At no time was petitioner indicted for espionage. . . .

[No persuasive power and influence.] Neither respondents nor the lower courts relied on any claim that petitioner occupied a position of such "persuasive power and influence" that he could be deemed one of that small group of individuals who are public figures for all purposes. Petitioner led a thoroughly private existence prior to the grand jury inquiry and returned to a position of relative obscurity after his sentencing. He achieved no general fame or notoriety and assumed no role of special prominence in the affairs of society as a result of his contempt citation or because of his involvement in the investigation of Soviet espionage in 1958.

Instead, respondents argue, and the lower courts held, that petitioner falls within the second category of public figures—those who have "thrust themselves to the forefront of particular public controversies in order to influence the resolution of the issues involved"—and that, therefore, petitioner is a public figure for the limited purpose of comment on his connection with, or involvement in, Soviet espionage in the 1940's and 1950's. Both lower courts found petitioner's failure to appear before the grand jury and citation for contempt determinative of the public-figure issue. [They found that] "by his voluntary action he invited attention and comment in connection with the public questions involved in the investigation of espionage."

[As a limited purpose, thrusting figure.] We do not agree with respondents and the lower courts that petitioner can be classed as such a limited-purpose public figure. First, the undisputed facts do not justify the conclusion of the District Court and Court of Appeals that petitioner "voluntarily thrust" or "injected" himself into the forefront of the public controversy surrounding the investigation of Soviet espionage in the United States. . . . It would be more accurate to say that petitioner was dragged unwillingly into the controversy. The Government pursued him in its investigation. . . . But the mere fact that petitioner voluntarily chose not to appear before the grand jury, knowing that his action might be attended by publicity, is not decisive on the question of public-figure status. . . . It is clear that petitioner played only a minor role in whatever public controversy there may have been concerning the investigation of Soviet espionage. We decline to hold that his mere citation for contempt rendered him a public figure for purposes of comment on the investigation of Soviet espionage. Petitioner's failure to appear before the grand jury and citation for contempt no doubt were "newsworthy," but the simple fact that these events attracted media attention also is not conclusive of the public-figure issue. A private individual is not automatically transformed into a public figure just by becoming involved in or associated with a matter that attracts public attention. To accept such reasoning would in effect re-establish the doctrine advanced by the plurality opinion in Rosenbloom v. Metromedia, Inc. . . .

[One who engages in criminal conduct.] [We] reject the further contention of respondents that any person who engages in criminal conduct automatically becomes a public figure for purposes of comment on a limited range of issues relating to his conviction. We declined to accept a similar argument in Time, Inc. v. Firestone, where we said: "[W]hile participants in some litigation may be legitimate 'public figures,' either generally or for the limited purpose of that litigation, the majority will more likely resemble respondent, drawn into a public forum largely against their will in order to attempt to obtain the only redress available to them or to defend themselves against actions brought by the State or by others. There appears little reason why these individuals should substantially forfeit that degree of protection which the law of defamation would otherwise afford them simply by virtue of their being drawn into a courtroom. . . ." We think that these observations remain sound, and that they control the disposition of this case. To hold otherwise would create an "open season" for all who sought to defame persons convicted of a crime.

Accordingly, the judgment of the Court of Appeals is Reversed.

Mr. Justice BLACKMUN, with whom Mr. Justice MARSHALL joins, concurring in the result. . . .

The passage of time, I believe, often will be relevant in deciding whether a person possesses these two public-figure characteristics. First, a lapse of years between a controversial event and a libelous utterance may diminish the defamed party's access to the means of counter argument. At the height of the publicity surrounding the espionage controversy here, petitioner may well have had sufficient access to the media effectively to rebut a charge that he was a Soviet spy. It would strain credulity to suggest that petitioner could have commanded such media interest when respondents published their book in 1974. Second, the passage of time may diminish the "risk of public scrutiny" that a putative public figure may fairly be said to have assumed. In ignoring the grand jury subpoena in 1958, petitioner may have anticipated that his conduct would invite critical commentary from the press. Following the contempt citation, however, petitioner "succeeded for the most part in returning to . . . private life." Any inference that petitioner "assumed the risk" of public scrutiny in 1958 assuredly is negated by his conscious efforts to regain anonymity during the succeeding 16 years.

This analysis implies, of course, that one may be a public figure for purposes of contemporaneous reporting of a controversial event, yet not be a public figure for purposes of historical commentary on the same occurrence. Historians, consequently, may well run a greater risk of liability for defamation. Yet this result, in my view, does no violence to First Amendment values. While historical analysis is no less vital to the marketplace of ideas than reporting current events, historians work under different conditions than do their media counterparts. A reporter trying to meet a deadline may find it totally impossible to check thoroughly the accuracy of his sources. A historian writing sub specie aeternitatis has both the time for reflection and the opportunity to investigate the veracity of the pronouncements he makes.

For these reasons, I conclude that the lapse of 16 years between petitioner's participation in the espionage controversy and respondents' defamatory reference to it was sufficient to erase whatever public-figure attributes petitioner once may have possessed. Because petitioner clearly was a private individual in 1974, I see no need to decide the more difficult question whether he was a public figure in 1958.

[The dissent of Justice Brennan is omitted.]

---

22. **All purpose public figures.** *Gertz* recognized that some persons might be all purpose public figures simply because of their pervasive power

or influence. As to these people, they would be public figures without thrusting themselves into public affairs. Can you imagine an example?

23. **Thrusting into the vortex.** For the most part, *Gertz* seemed to shift focus away from the plaintiff's importance or impact on public issues. Instead, *Gertz* focused on a kind of assumed risk analysis; a public figure was one who thrust himself into public affairs or controversies. And, because of his involvement in public controversies, such a person would also have access to the media, so her side of the story could be disseminated. Do *Firestone* and *Wolston* exemplify this approach or depart from it?

24. **Timing.** Justice Blackmun thought public figurehood could melt away with the years, a view he recognized would favor current journalists and disfavor historians. But notice that if historians still get the protection of the *Times-Sullivan* rules, the time-frame for their research would mean that an error of a historian might be reckless when the same error of a reporter on a deadline might not be. And academic historians at least are not likely to be writing for profit.

25. **Where the libel defendant generates the controversy.** A different timing issue arose in *Chafoulias v. Peterson,* 668 N.W.2d 642 (Minn. 2003), where lawyer Peterson put up posters asserting her clients' claim that they had been sexually attacked by "Arab" guests at the plaintiff's hotel while the clients had been employed there. The plaintiff issued a press release stating its policy against permitting guests to sexually attack its employees and responded in several other rather mild ways to the suggestion that the plaintiff knew of the attacks and did nothing. After considerable local press and television on the debate about adequate responses to sexual attacks, ABC aired a national television show that allegedly libeled the plaintiff by repeating the suggestion that he knew of the attacks. By the time ABC aired the show, however, there was a controversy and the plaintiff had taken part in it by press release and otherwise, so as to ABC he was a public figure. The plaintiff's libel suit against lawyer Peterson was different, though. She allegedly promoted the controversy in the first place. The court thought that if that were the case, Peterson could not attribute public figure status to the plaintiff on the basis of his participation in the controversy she generated. See also ¶ 6, supra. So the plaintiff was a public figure as to ABC but might not be a public figure as to Peterson.

26. **Criminals as public figures.** (a) Can it be right to say with *Firestone* that one who engages in civil litigation is not a public figure for purposes of discussing that litigation? Or with *Wolston* that one who is charged with crime is not a public figure? Notice that *Wolston* not only removes from public figure status those who are charged with crime but also those who are "convicted" and those who actually engage in criminal conduct. Could states afford greater protection than *Wolston* requires when it comes to publications about those convicted of crime?

(b) Some state decisions have barred the criminal's claim. See *Scottsdale Pub., Inc v. Superior Court (Romano),* 159 Ariz. 72, 764 P.2d 1131 (Ct. App. 1988) (criminal chose a life of crime); *Ruebke v. Globe Communications Corp.,* 241 Kan. 595, 738 P.2d 1246 (1987) (criminal was a public figure, he had somehow participated in the controversy because of intense media coverage of the murder investigation).

27. **Involuntary public figures?** In *Dameron v. Washington Magazine*, 779 F.2d 736 (D.C. Cir. 1985), the plaintiff was an air traffic controller. The defendant published a story about the Air Florida crash in Washington. The story added that most crashes were not the result of controller errors, but that controller errors had been assigned partial blame in a few accidents, including a 1974 crash into Mt. Weather in Virginia. Plaintiff was not named, but he sued claiming libel on the ground that he was the only controller on duty in the Mt. Weather crash and on the further ground that he was not at fault. The author of the story had a National Transportation Safety Board accident report as authority, but did not know that there had been a trial in which Dameron had been absolved. Dameron was found, however, to be a public figure even though he had not thrust or injected himself into controversy.

> This one [thrusting] factor, however, is not the be-all and end-all of public figure status. . . . Persons can become involved in public controversies and affairs without their consent or will. Air-controller Dameron, who had the misfortune to have a tragedy occur on his watch, is such a person. We conclude that Dameron did become an *in*voluntary public figure for the limited purpose of discussions of the Mt. Weather crash.

The court thought this was different from *Firestone* because:

> Dameron was at the center of a controversy involving the loss of many lives in a mishap involving a public carrier. At issue was the management of a program administered by the FAA, an arm of the government. . . . Dameron appeared at . . . hearings and testified for many hours about his role in the crash. . . . We think that, like it or not, Dameron was embroiled in a public controversy.

28. **Government contractors as public officials or public figures.** In *Hutchinson v. Proxmire*, 443 U.S. 111, 99 S.Ct. 2675, 61 L.Ed.2d 411 (1979), the defendant published allegedly defamatory comments about the plaintiff's receipt of public grant money for research on monkeys grinding their teeth. The defendant made fun of the whole research and perhaps implied that the plaintiff's work was useless or worse: "the good doctor has made a fortune from his monkeys and in the process made a monkey out of the American taxpayer." The Court largely ignored the question whether the plaintiff was a public official because he was receiving government grants to do his work. It considered instead whether he was a public figure and concluded he was not. "Hutchinson did not thrust himself or his views into public controversy to influence others. Respondents have not identified such a particular controversy; at most, they point to concern about general public expenditures. But that concern is shared by most and relates to most public expenditures; it is not sufficient to make Hutchinson a public figure. . . . Moreover, Hutchinson at no time assumed any role of public prominence in the broad question of concern about expenditures."

Some state cases seem in accord with the narrow view of public figure status taken in *Hutchison*. E.g., *Saunders v. VanPelt*, 497 A.2d 1121 (Me. 1985) (psychologist contracting with school districts for examinations of students not a public figure). However, in *Dombey v. Phoenix Newspapers, Inc.*, 150 Ariz. 476, 724 P.2d 562 (1986), the plaintiff was an insurance agent for the county who by contract provided specified insurance and insurance advice. He received substantial commissions from public funds. The Arizona Supreme Court found he could be a public figure because he invited public scrutiny by assuming the role he did. See also *Green v. Northern Pub. Co., Inc.*, 655 P.2d 736 (Alaska 1982) (doctor under contract to provide services to jails, on which doctor spent 3/4 time, public figure).

29. **Knowing falsehood on matters related to limited public figure status.** Perhaps in the case of a limited purpose public figure described in *Gertz*, the publisher would have the advantage of *Times-Sullivan* rules only for discussing matters related to that narrow status. Some decisions seem to so assume. See *Annette F. v. Sharon S.,* 119 Cal.App.4th 1146, 15 Cal.Rptr.3d 100, 113–114 (2004). Maybe the publisher would be protected in discussing the profits made by insurers from government as *Dombey* suggests, but would not be protected in discussing the same insurers' private lives or their unrelated profits in non-governmental transactions. Would it be better to recognize the plaintiffs' public figure status in these cases and focus on a narrower question—whether the publication was sufficiently related to the public figure status?

30. **Police and teachers; officials and figures.** Some courts address the public employee-plaintiff's position in terms of public figure rather than in terms of public official status. This is true, for example, both with teachers and police officers. It is fairly clear that police officers are either public officials or public figures, *Fleming v. Rose,* 350 S.C. 488, 567 S.E.2d 857 (2002) (state police lieutenant), though there are a handful of decisions to the contrary. *Kiesau v. Bantz,* 686 N.W.2d 164 (Iowa 2004) (emphasizing that deputy sheriff plaintiff was low level employee). With public school teachers, who may hold the entire future of some students in their hands, some courts have classed them as public officials or figures, as in *Sewell v. Brookbank,* 119 Ariz. 422, 581 P.2d 267 (Ct. App. 1978). But apparently a larger group holds that public school teachers and even principals are not public officials or public figures. E.g., *Beeching v. Levee,* 764 N.E.2d 669 (Ind. Ct. App. 2002). Do you think a distinction should be drawn between cases in which an officer or teacher is suing an employer for defamation or is suing part of her constituency such as students or their parents in the case of a teacher?

31. **Businesses, charities.** A business or charitable entity can sue for defamation. If it does, can it be a public figure? The cases on business and charitable public figures are like the individual cases in that the classification usually turns on facts of the case rather than on the fact that the plaintiff is a business. In *Reader's Digest Ass'n v. Superior Court*, 37 Cal.3d 244, 690 P.2d 610, 208 Cal.Rptr. 137 (1984), a church was found to be a public figure. In *Bank of Oregon v. Independent News*, 298 Or. 434, 693 P.2d 35 (1985), a bank was said not to be a public figure, partly because there was no pre-existing controversy; merely doing business, offering stock for sale, advertising and the like is not sufficient to establish that a corporation is a public figure. Does that sound wrong to you? Could a publicly traded corporation automatically be a public figure regardless whether there is a controversy? See SACK ON DEFAMATION: LIBEL, SLANDER, AND RELATED PROBLEMS § 5.3.7 (2004) (available on Westlaw). Would it matter what issue was under discussion? Distinguish the test for public interest issues under anti-SLAPP statutes (Chapter 2, ¶ 22). See *Ampex Corp. v. Cargle,* 128 Cal.App.4th 1569,

27 Cal.Rptr.3d 863 (2005) (a publicly traded corporation with many investors that promotes itself is itself the subject of public interest so that a SLAPP statute applies.)

32. **Context public figures.** Professor Smolla has argued that courts have not and should not follow the limited notion of public figure coming out of *Firestone, Wolston* and *Hutchinson*. Courts should instead, using the flexibility of common law privileges, recognize what he calls a "context public" figure—a public figure in the context of the particular "marketplaces of ideas." For most citizens, neighborhoods, workplaces and institutions of daily life are the local marketplaces where uninhibited discussion is most relevant. Those who never inject themselves into controversies of national attention, nevertheless may involve themselves in children's schools, in neighborhoods, and in work disputes. Smolla, *Let the Author Beware: The Rejuvenation of the American Law of Libel*, 132 U. of Pa. L. Rev. 1 (1983).

33. **The unimportance of job categories.** An annotation considers 150 job or activity categories such as police officers, factory workers, or funeral directors. As the annotation shows, the category itself is seldom determinative; what the plaintiff has done, or the extent of public controversy of which the plaintiff is a part, is usually far more important than the plaintiff's job or status. See Tracy Bateman, Annotation, *Who Is "Public Figure" for Purposes of Defamation Action*, 19 A.L.R.5th 1. Dobbs on Torts § 418 (2000) summarizes the main points in determining who counts as a public official or public figure.

§ 3. PRIVATE PERSONS AND ISSUES OF PURELY PRIVATE CONCERN

DUN & BRADSTREET, INC. v. GREENMOSS BUILDERS, INC.

472 U.S. 749, 105 S.Ct. 2939, 86 L.Ed.2d 593 (1985)

Justice POWELL announced the judgment of the Court and delivered an opinion, in which Justice REHNQUIST and Justice O'CONNOR joined. . . .

Petitioner Dun & Bradstreet, a credit reporting agency, provides subscribers with financial and related information about businesses. All the information is confidential; under the terms of the subscription agreement the subscribers may not reveal it to anyone else. On July 26, 1976, petitioner sent a report to five subscribers indicating that respondent, a construction contractor, had filed a voluntary petition for bankruptcy. This report was false and grossly misrepresented respondent's assets and liabilities. That same day, while discussing the possibility of future financing with its bank, respondent's president was told that the bank had received the defamatory report. He immediately called petitioner's regional office, explained the error, and asked for a correction. In addition, he requested the names of the firms that had received the false report in order to assure them that the company was solvent.

Petitioner promised to look into the matter but refused to divulge the names of those who had received the report.

After determining that its report was indeed false, petitioner issued a corrective notice on or about August 3, 1976, to the five subscribers who had received the initial report. The notice stated that one of respondent's former employees, not respondent itself, had filed for bankruptcy and that respondent "continued in business as usual." Respondent told petitioner that it was dissatisfied with the notice, and it again asked for a list of subscribers who had seen the initial report. Again petitioner refused to divulge their names.

Respondent then brought this defamation action in Vermont state court. It alleged that the false report had injured its reputation and sought both compensatory and punitive damages. The trial established that the error in petitioner's report had been caused when one of its employees, a 17-year-old high school student paid to review Vermont bankruptcy pleadings, had inadvertently attributed to respondent a bankruptcy petition filed by one of respondent's former employees. Although petitioner's representative testified that it was routine practice to check the accuracy of such reports with the businesses themselves, it did not try to verify the information about respondent before reporting it.

After trial, the jury returned a verdict in favor of respondent and awarded $50,000 in compensatory or presumed damages and $300,000 in punitive damages. Petitioner moved for a new trial. It argued that in Gertz v. Robert Welch, Inc., this Court had ruled broadly that "the States may not permit recovery of presumed or punitive damages, at least when liability is not based on a showing of knowledge of falsity or reckless disregard for the truth," and it argued that the judge's instructions in this case permitted the jury to award such damages on a lesser showing. The trial court indicated some doubt as to whether Gertz applied to "non-media cases," but granted a new trial "[b]ecause of ... dissatisfaction with its charge and ... conviction that the interests of justice require[d]" it. App. 26.

The Vermont Supreme Court reversed. 143 Vt. 66, 461 A.2d 414 (1983). Although recognizing that "in certain instances the distinction between media and nonmedia defendants may be difficult to draw," the court stated that "no such difficulty is presented with credit reporting agencies, which are in the business of selling financial information to a limited number of subscribers who have paid substantial fees for their services." Relying on this distinguishing characteristic of credit reporting firms, the court concluded that such firms are not "the type of media worthy of First Amendment protection as contemplated by New York Times [Co. v. Sullivan, 376 U.S. 254, 84 S.Ct. 710, 11 L.Ed.2d 686 (1964),] and its progeny." It held that the balance between a private plaintiff's right to recover presumed and punitive damages without a showing of special fault and the First Amendment rights of "nonmedia" speakers "must be struck in favor of the private plaintiff defamed by a nonmedia defendant." Accordingly, the court held "that as a matter of federal constitutional law, the media protections outlined in Gertz are inapplicable to nonmedia defamation actions."

... We now affirm, although for reasons different from those relied upon by the Vermont Supreme Court.

... In Gertz v. Robert Welch, Inc., 418 U.S. 323, 94 S.Ct. 2997, 41 L.Ed.2d 789 (1974), we held that the protections of New York Times did not extend as far as Rosenbloom suggested. ... [W]e held that the fact that expression concerned a public issue did not by itself entitle the libel defendant to the constitutional protections of New York Times. These protections, we found, were not "justified solely by reference to the interest of the press and broadcast media in immunity from liability." Rather, they represented "an accommodation between [First Amendment] concern[s] and the limited state interest present in the context of libel actions brought by public persons." In libel actions brought by private persons we found the competing interests different. Largely because private persons have not voluntarily exposed themselves to increased risk of injury from defamatory statements and because they generally lack effective opportunities for rebutting such statements, we found that the State possessed a "strong and legitimate ... interest in compensating private individuals for injury to reputation." Balancing this stronger state interest against the same First Amendment interest at stake in New York Times, we held that a State could not allow recovery of presumed and punitive damages absent a showing of "actual malice." Nothing in our opinion, however, indicated that this same balance would be struck regardless of the type of speech involved.

We have never considered whether the Gertz balance obtains when the defamatory statements involve no issue of public concern. To make this determination, we must employ the approach approved in Gertz and balance the State's interest in compensating private individuals for injury to their reputation against the First Amendment interest in protecting this type of expression. This state interest is identical to the one weighed in Gertz. There we found that it was "strong and legitimate." A State should not lightly be required to abandon it, "for, as Mr. Justice Stewart has reminded us, the individual's right to the protection of his own good name 'reflects no more than our basic concept of the essential dignity and worth of every human being—a concept at the root of any decent system of ordered liberty. The protection of private personality, like the protection of life itself, is left primarily to the individual States under the Ninth and Tenth Amendments. ...' "

The First Amendment interest, on the other hand, is less important than the one weighed in Gertz. We have long recognized that not all speech is of equal First Amendment importance. It is speech on "matters of public concern" that is "at the heart of the First Amendment's protection." As we stated in Connick v. Myers, 461 U.S. 138, 145, 103 S.Ct. 1684, 1689, 75 L.Ed.2d 708 (1983), this "special concern [for speech on public issues] is no mystery":

"The First Amendment was fashioned to assure unfettered interchange of ideas for the bringing about of political and social changes desired by the people. Accordingly, the Court has frequently reaffirmed that speech on public issues occupies the 'highest rung of the hierarchy of First Amendment values,' and is entitled to special protection. In contrast, speech on matters of purely private concern is of less First Amendment concern. As a number of state courts, including the court below, have recognized, the role of the Constitution in regulating state libel law is far more limited when the concerns that activated New York Times and Gertz are absent. In such a case, [t]here is no threat to the free and robust debate of public issues; there is no potential interference with a meaningful dialogue of ideas concerning self-government; and there is no threat of liability causing a reaction of self-censorship by the press. The facts of the present case are wholly without the First Amendment concerns with which the Supreme Court of the United States has been struggling."

While such speech is not totally unprotected by the First Amendment, its protections are less stringent. In Gertz, we found that the state interest in awarding presumed and punitive damages was not "substantial" in view of their effect on speech at the core of First Amendment concern. This interest, however, is "substantial" relative to the incidental effect these remedies may have on speech of significantly less constitutional interest. The rationale of the common-law rules has been the experience and judgment of history that "proof of actual damage will be impossible in a great many cases where, from the character of the defamatory words and the circumstances of publication, it is all but certain that serious harm has resulted in fact." As a result, courts for centuries have allowed juries to presume that some damage occurred from many defamatory utterances and publications. This rule furthers the state interest in providing remedies for defamation by ensuring that those remedies are effective. In light of the reduced constitutional value of speech involving no matters of public concern, we hold that the state interest adequately supports awards of presumed and punitive damages—even absent a showing of "actual malice."

The only remaining issue is whether petitioner's credit report involved a matter of public concern. In a related context, we have held that "[w]hether . . . speech addresses a matter of public concern must be determined by [the expression's] content, form, and context . . . as revealed by the whole record." These factors indicate that petitioner's credit report concerns no public issue. It was speech solely in the individual interest of the speaker and its specific business audience. This particular interest warrants no special protection when—as in this case—the speech is wholly false and clearly damaging to the victim's business reputation. . . .

In addition, the speech here, like advertising, is hardy and unlikely to be deterred by incidental state regulation. It is solely motivated by the desire for profit, which, we have noted, is a force less likely to be deterred than others. Arguably, the reporting here was also more objectively verifiable than speech deserving of greater protection. In any case, the market provides a powerful incentive to a credit reporting agency to be accurate, since false credit reporting is of no use to creditors. Thus, any incremental "chilling" effect of libel suits would be of decreased significance.

We conclude that permitting recovery of presumed and punitive damages in defamation cases absent a showing of "actual malice" does not violate the First Amendment when the defamatory statements do not involve matters of public concern. Accordingly, we affirm the judgment of the Vermont Supreme Court.

It is so ordered.

---

34. **Ad hoc decisions on what is a public concern.** Justice Powell seemed to say in *Gertz* that the Court should not try to determine whether the defamation involved issues of public concern or not, because that would take the Court into ad hoc decision-making based on the *content* of the speech. That might be regarded as dangerous partly because the question of what is important to self-government should not be decided by judges but by the people themselves. Yet in *Dun & Bradstreet*, Justice Powell seems willing to consider whether speech involves issues of public concern. What is the difference? Is it fair to say that Justice Powell did not want to consider public concern as a ground for expanding speech rights but was willing to do so as a ground for narrowing them?

35. **Media vs. non-media defendants.** The Vermont Court in *Dun & Bradstreet* took the view that *Gertz* only applied to *media* defendants. In the Supreme Court, Justice Brennan commented on that point in his dissent: "Such a distinction is irreconcilable with the fundamental First Amendment principle that '[t]he inherent worth of . . . speech in terms of its capacity for informing the public does not depend upon the identity of its source, whether corporation, association, union, or individual.' "

36. **Wisconsin: strict liability for non-media publishers.** Maybe the most extreme case refusing *Gertz* protection to non-media defendants is *Denny v. Mertz*, 106 Wis.2d 636, 318 N.W.2d 141 (1982). Denny had once been employed by the Koehring company but resigned. He was a stockholder who sought to oust management. Mertz, the Chairman of the Board, interviewed by *Business Week* said Denny was a biased source of information because he had been terminated by the company. This was inaccurate and when challenged, Mertz concluded that Denny had resigned. In the meantime, however, *Business Week* published the quotation. The Wisconsin Court held that *Gertz* had no application to non-media defendants. The result was that the individual who was quoted would be strictly liable while the enterprise that quoted him would be liable only for negligence.

37. **Texas: protection for non-media speakers.** In *Casso v. Brand*, 776 S.W.2d 551 (Tex. 1989), a public figure sued a non-media defendant (who was another public figure). The Texas Court said:

> The Supreme Court has yet to decide, however, whether [the *Times-Sullivan*] standard is also constitutionally required when public officials like Brand or public figures sue private individuals like Casso for defamation. . . . The appropriate standard is therefore left to the states for determination. Like the court of appeals, we have no hesitancy in requiring Brand, under Texas common law, to meet the New York Times burden of proof.

38. **What did *Dun* do?** Courts sometimes have formulated the *Dun & Bradstreet* decision in broad terms, holding or implying that the case excuses the plaintiff from the *Gertz* fault rules as well as the *Gertz* damages proof. The Ninth Circuit said rather casually that "a majority of the Justices opined that defamatory statements of untrue fact contained in private figure/private concern speech are unprotected by the first amendment." *Dworkin v. Hustler Magazine Inc.*, 867 F.2d 1188 (9th Cir. 1989). *Dun & Bradstreet* itself only addressed the requirement of actual damages, not the issue of fault. Still, maybe that is the logic of the case's purported balancing of interests. See, arguing that the fault rules and the damages rules go hand in hand, *Snead v. Redland Aggregates Ltd.*, 998 F.2d 1325 (5th Cir. 1993); RODNEY SMOLLA, LAW OF DEFAMATION § 3.02 [5]. On the other hand, *New England Tractor-Trailor Training of Conn., Inc. v. Globe Newspaper Co.*, 395 Mass. 471, 480 N.E.2d 1005 (1985), took the view that "the fault requirement of *Gertz* [remains] intact regardless whether the private parties are suing on matters of public or private concern."

THE MATRIX OF PROTECTIONS AFTER DUN & BRADSTREET

Issues \ Persons	Public	Private
Public Concern	1 *Times-Sullivan*	2 *Gertz*
Private Concern	3 Public official? Public figure?	4 *Dun & Bradstreet*

The Third Box

The Third Box

39. **Is the third box always empty?** Are there any cases that fit in the third box in the matrix, that is, cases in which the plaintiff is a public

figure or official but the defamatory publication is about a private concern issue? In *Dworkin v. Hustler Magazine Inc.*, 867 F.2d 1188 (9th Cir. 1989), the plaintiff was a public figure but asserted that the libel was about a matter of private concern—cartoons depicting lesbian sexual matters, for instance—and that it was therefore not governed by the *Times-Sullivan* regime. The court rejected the argument, saying "we doubt that it is possible to have speech about a public figure but not of public concern."

40. **The Supreme Court.** The Supreme Court has brushed the question obliquely. In *Monitor Patriot Co. v. Roy,* 401 U.S. 265, 91 S.Ct. 621, 28 L.Ed.2d 35 (1971), the newspaper published a statement that a candidate for office was a former small-time bootlegger. The trial judge charged that the *Times-Sullivan* rule would apply to require a showing of knowing or reckless falsehood if the libel concerned official conduct, but left it to the jury to determine whether the bootlegger charge was "a public affair on a par with official conduct." Assuming the statement is false so that truth is not available to defeat the claim, is the trial court's instruction to the jury correct? Is it based on a public-private concern distinction? The Supreme Court thought the instruction error. The Court said:

> In our view, however, the syllogistic manipulation of distinctions between private sectors and public sectors, or matters of fact and matters of law, is of little utility in resolving questions of First Amendment protection.
>
> ... But whether there remains some exiguous area of defamation against which a candidate may have full recourse is a question we need not decide in this case. The trial judge presented the issue to the jury in the form of the question: "Is it more probable than otherwise that the publication that the plaintiff was a former small-time bootlegger was a public affair on a par with official conduct of public officials?" This instruction, and the others like it, left the jury far more leeway to act as censors than is consistent with the protection of the First and Fourteenth Amendments in the setting of a political campaign. ...
>
> We therefore hold as a matter of constitutional law that a charge of criminal conduct, no matter how remote in time or place, can never be irrelevant to an official's or a candidate's fitness for office for purposes of application of the "knowing falsehood or reckless disregard" rule of New York Times Co. v. Sullivan. Since the jury in this case was permitted to make its own unguided determination that the charge of prior criminal activity was not "relevant," and that the New York Times standard was thus inapplicable, the judgment must be reversed and the case remanded for further proceedings not inconsistent with this opinion.

What about a *non*-criminal charge against a public official? If a police officer is a public official and a credit agency reports that he is bankrupt, would *Times-Sullivan* rather than *Dun & Bradstreet* apply?

41. ***Gertz* limited purpose public figure.** The analogous case of a *Gertz* limited purpose public figure, however, seems to fit the third box. Indeed, the idea in *Gertz* seems to be that although few if any issues are of private concern when it comes to a public official, public figures describe their own sphere of privacy by limiting their participation in public affairs.

42. **Public figure/official not identified as such in the publication.** Some courts have said that a public official does not come under the *Times-Sullivan* rule if the official is not identified as an official in the alleged defamation and if he is not well-known as such. *Bufalino v. Associated Press*, 692 F.2d 266 (2d Cir. 1982); *Hinerman v. Daily Gazette Co., Inc.*, 188 W.Va. 157, 423 S.E.2d 560 (1992).

Are these cases correctly decided? Consider *Ocala Star–Banner Co. v. Damron*, 401 U.S. 295, 91 S.Ct. 628, 28 L.Ed.2d 57 (1971). In that case, the newspaper reported that *Leonard* Damron had been charged in federal court with perjury. This was wholly untrue about Leonard, but it was exactly true about his brother *James*. The story did not mention Leonard's official post as mayor of a small town. The trial court refused to apply the *Times-Sullivan* constraints. "The trial judge denied the motion on the ground that New York Times and later cases relating to public officials or public figures in the official conduct of their office or position are not applicable to this cause of action which was founded upon a newspaper publication of the Defendants which was libelous per se and made no reference to the public offices held or sought by the Plaintiff." The Florida appeals court affirmed on the ground that the publication did not criticize Leonard's performance of official duties. The Supreme Court, however, held that *Times-Sullivan* applied because Damron was without question a public official as mayor of the town. Any conduct of officials is relevant to their fitness for office.

At a different level, notice that *Bufalino* is focusing on an extrinsic fact, just as the libel per quod cases did. But the extrinsic fact here is not one that tends to make the statement defamatory; it is instead one that tends to generate a rule of limited liability. If it is right to disregard extrinsic facts (at least some of the time) when they are needed to establish liability, is it equally right to disregard them when they are needed to invoke the *Times-Sullivan* protections?

REFERENCE: The basic constitutional standards evolved from *Times-Sullivan, Gertz*, and *Dun & Bradstreet* are summarized in DOBBS ON TORTS § 417 (2000).

Using the Times–Sullivan Rule in Non–Constitutional Cases: The Labor Preemption Example

A broad question. The rule in *New York Times v. Sullivan*, by its terms, is a Constitutional rule and one that applies only when the plaintiff is a public official or public figure. But might it be used by analogy even in cases where it is not constitutionally required?

Labor dispute law. Under the National Labor Relations Act, a federal labor board has jurisdiction over certain labor disputes. When a union seeks to organize an employer's workers, the National Labor Relations Board (NLRB) supervises an election to determine whether the workers wish to be represented by a union or not. If they do, the union then becomes the agent for the workers in bargaining with the company. Certain practices are declared to be unfair labor practices and the Board can prevent those practices by either side. To prevent state law from interfering with a unified management of these labor disputes, federal law preempts state law, which is not allowed to deal with any matter that would arguably constitute an unfair labor practice and hence would arguably be within the Board's jurisdiction.

The Linn Case. In *Linn v. United Plant Guard Workers of America, Local 114*, 383 U.S. 53, 86 S.Ct. 657, 15 L.Ed.2d 582 (1966), the plaintiff, a manager of the employer (Pinkerton's), brought a state-court suit claiming that the union in the course of an organizing campaign had libeled him in a leaflet. The trial court found that the alleged libel was arguably an unfair labor practice and hence preempted. Accordingly, it dismissed the suit. The Court of Appeals affirmed.

The Supreme Court reversed. It noted that the NLRB generally did not attempt to regulate libelous statements published in organizing campaigns, leaving the resolution to the good sense of the voters. The courts should similarly permit wide open campaigning, but there was no merit in "malicious" campaign statements. So the rules of *New York Times v. Sullivan* were to be adopted by analogy, not because the Constitution required them, but because they furnished appropriate ways to effect the statutory design. The Court added a requirement not imposed by *Times-Sullivan* rules: the plaintiff had to prove something about the harm suffered. Although *Linn* is technically a matter of federal preemption, there is no federal libel law. If the libel was not knowing or reckless, then, federal preemption really means federal limbo and the plaintiff will lose the libel claim.

Extending Linn. Linn was extended in *Old Dominion Branch No. 496, Nat'l Ass'n of Letter Carriers, AFL-CIO v. Austin,* 418 U.S. 264, 94 S.Ct. 2770, 41 L.Ed.2d 745 (1974), to protect a union against libel complaints of employees. The union had already successfully organized employees and was their collective bargaining representative. In the course of an effort to organize the employees who had not joined, it allegedly libeled the non-union employees, who sued. The trial judge's instruction to the jury required "malice," but only in the common law sense, not in the *Times-Sullivan* sense. This was held to be erroneous, because the *Times-Sullivan* knowing or reckless falsehood standard would be applied to determine whether liability under state libel law would be preempted. Dissenters argued that *Linn* covered only "labor disputes" and that there was no real labor dispute here because there was no union-management or union-union conflict; the union defendant was already the collective bargaining agent.

The technicalities of labor-law preemption are interesting enough, but the most interesting thing for libel law is the usefulness of the *Times-Sullivan* formula in non-constitutional cases. Might the formula be used in other cases even when not compelled by the Constitution?

Private Persons and Issues of Purely Private Concern

AYALA v. WASHINGTON

679 A.2d 1057 (D.C. App. 1996)

RUIZ, Associate Judge. . . .

[The plaintiff, Ayala, is an airline pilot. He sued his former lover, Washington, for defamation. The jury found that Washington had published statements to Ayala's employer and to the FAA that Ayala used marijuana and that they were false and published recklessly or knowingly. The trial judge through that the plaintiff had not adequately proved falsity and entered judgment for Washington in spite of the jury's finding. The court on appeal considered whether this was a *Dun & Bradstreet* case involving a private person involved in an issue of purely private concern.]

Whether a statement addresses a matter of public concern is a question of law. . . .

[T]he focus of the phrase "matters of public concern" is not on speech that might be of popular interest because it captures the attention of the public based on its sensational or human interest aspects, but is instead on speech of constitutional interest because it relates to the ordering of government and society at large. This approach is consistent with Gertz, supra, where the Court expressly rejected any test that turns on a judicial determination of whether the content of the defamatory statement attracted public interest. . . .

The determining factor . . . is whether or not the speech addressed the conduct of government. . . .

[The court examined a number of state court cases.]

Although the foregoing cases speak of "striking a balance" between the risk that truthful speech on a particular topic will be inhibited and the risk that injury to reputation will go uncompensated and undeterred, our threshold decision is in essence a decision about who shall strike that balance. If we decide that the First Amendment protects the defamatory statements in this case, then the decision will have been made—the balance struck—at the most fundamental level of national legislation through the Constitution. If we decide, however, that First Amendment protection does not apply to the defamation claim in this case, then we permit the ordinary law-making organs of state and national government to strike the balances they think are best suited to the times and places over which they exercise jurisdiction. Thus, we pause to consider what factors should affect our decision about who should decide.

Where speech concerns the conduct of government or important issues of self-governance, there is a grave danger that those who make and apply the rules at a given time—the governing majority of the moment—will undervalue criticism of the status quo in relation to the reputations of those who represent it. Thus, it is important that the balance in connection with such issues be struck in favor of protection of speech—and against undue government regulation of speech—through the more permanent device of the Constitution. Therefore, such matters are properly treated as of "public concern," and speakers are protected by the First Amendment from the inhibition that they inadvertently may run afoul of defamation laws.

Where the matter is one that affects the interests of all, on the other hand, there is less danger that the value of defamatory speech will be inadequately weighed by the government in the balance against reputation. Applied to the airline safety concern alleged in this case, where the issue is the safety of all and the reputations of a few, it is more likely that the risk of inhibited speech will be overvalued in relation to the risk that damage to the reputations of a few will go unvindicated. Moreover, the danger to public safety posed by various non-governmental actors is one that is subject to significant change over time. Thus, it is more appropriate in that context to use the usual decision-making processes of government to determine which risks should be reduced at the expense of others. Such matters are therefore properly treated as being of "private concern" and speakers are properly subject to the regulation of defamation laws.

In view of the foregoing, we conclude that the content of Washington's letters to Ayala's employer was of private concern, and subject to defamation law, but that the content of her letter to the FAA was incidental to allegations of public concern, and therefore protected by the Constitution. Washington's letters to Ayala's employer merely communicated information regarding the alleged misconduct of a single private individual, albeit misconduct that could have a significant effect on public safety. The allegations did not, however, address any issue concerning the conduct of government or the structure of society or any social issue. There is little danger that government, acting through defamation law, will improperly weigh the social interest in communication of such information against the reputation interest of the subject of such communications. Indeed, for the reasons discussed above, where the subject matter is the safety of all, the weighing is best done through the ordinary processes of government, which are able to respond to shifts in the social value of the competing interests, whether they are caused by changes in circumstances or popular mood. In fact, the interest in airline safety implicated by Washington's communication to Ayala's employer are precisely the sort that are best evaluated and regulated through the usual non-constitutional legislative and judicial processes, because the interests at stake are shared across society.

Washington's letter to the FAA is of a different character, however. In it, she criticizes the FAA's handling of her accusations. She asserts that the agency's failure to give credence to her charges is the result of discrimination against her as a woman and as a non-elite. Such speech is at the very core of the First Amendment; the fact that it was directed to a government agency instead of to the public at large merely brings it within an even more specific clause of the First Amendment–that which prohibits laws "abridging ... the right ... to petition the Government for a redress of grievances." ...

[The court concluded, however, that the plaintiff had made sufficient proof of "malice" and falsity and remanded for proceedings on punitive damages.]

1. Nat Stern, *Private Concerns of Private Plaintiffs: Revisiting a Problematic Defamation Category,* 65 Mo. L. Rev. 597, 629 (2000), criticizes *Ayala's* differentiation between the two communications. He argues that if a pilots use of marijuana is not a matter of public concern when communicated to his employer, it does not become a matter of public concern merely because it is communicated to a public agency and hitched to an unrelated issue about the agency's performance. Suppose, Stern suggests, the publications had accused *Ayala* of fathering an illegitimate child. Would that become a public concern issue because it was reported to a federal agency and "hitched" to other and different matters that would concern the public?

2. We will probably often agree on what issues are and are not issues of public concern. The plaintiff's credit standing probably is not an issue of public concern. Child molestation is. But if we agree on what counts as a public concern issue, a problem remains in characterizing the issue. Suppose a television show is discussing sexual abuse of children and erroneously identifies the plaintiffs as abusers. The plaintiffs are not abusers and not public figures. If the issue is not of public concern, then the plaintiffs can recover without proof of reputational loss. How should we characterize the issue under discussion—is it about child abuse or about the plaintiffs' home life? Cf. *Richie v. Paramount Pictures Corp.,* 544 N.W.2d 21 (Minn. 1996) (on similar facts, actual damages proof required).

Chapter 4

FREE SPEECH: ABSOLUTE PROTECTIONS FOR OPINIONS AND TRUTHFUL SPEECH

The Constitutional rules seen in the last chapter required the plaintiff to produce special evidence and added new elements to be proved before the plaintiff could recover for defamation against certain persons. This chapter considers what you might call "absolute" protections against liability for certain publications. Once it is established that the defendant published only the truth or "opinion," the plaintiff could not establish knowing falsehood or even negligence. The limitations on these protections mainly come instead from definitions of "truth" and "opinion."

§ 1. A CONSTITUTIONAL VIEW OF TRUTH

PHILADELPHIA NEWSPAPERS, INC. v. HEPPS

475 U.S. 767, 106 S.Ct. 1558, 89 L.Ed.2d 783 (1986)

Justice O'CONNOR delivered the opinion of the Court. ...

[The plaintiff Hepps is the principal stockholder of GPI, a franchisor of a chain of stores that sell beer and snacks. The defendant newspaper published a series of articles, the theme of which was that Hepps and related plaintiffs had links to organized crime and used those links to influence legislative and administrative action for the benefit of the beer and snacks stores. The stories associated the plaintiffs with a "a Pittsburgh Democrat and convicted felon," and indicated that federal "investigators have found connections between Thrifty and underworld figures." A grand jury was said to be investigating the "alleged relationship between the Thrifty chain and known Mafia figures," and "[w]hether the chain received special treatment from the [state governor's] administration and the Liquor Control Board." The publication indicated that the grand jury was investigating Mafia links.]

[The plaintiffs sued for defamation. Pennsylvania follows the common law rule in presuming that defamatory statements are false, but in this instance the trial court concluded that the Constitution put the burden of proving falsity on the plaintiff and so instructed the jury. Pennsylvania also had a media shield statute, allowing media employees to refuse to divulge their sources. The trial judge refused to instruct that the jury could draw an inference adverse to the defendant if the shield statute was invoked. The jury found for the defendant. The Supreme Court of Pennsylvania, however, concluded that Gertz required the plaintiff to show fault but that fault could be shown independent of any showing of falsity. Consequently, the defendant had the burden of proving truth and the plaintiff did not have the burden of proving falsity.]

... The [*New York Times v. Sullivan*] Court ... held that the Constitution prohibits a public official from recovering damages for a defamatory falsehood relating to his official conduct unless he proves that the statement was made with "actual malice"—that is, with knowledge that it was false or with reckless disregard of whether it was false or not.

That showing must be made with "convincing clarity," or, in a later formulation, by "clear and convincing proof." Gertz. The standards of New York Times apply not only when a public official sues a newspaper, but when a "public figure" sues a magazine or news service. See Curtis Publishing Co. v. Butts.

[The Court summarized Gertz and Dun & Bradstreet.] One can discern in these decisions two forces that may reshape the common-law landscape to conform to the First Amendment. The first is whether the plaintiff is a public official or figure, or is instead a private figure. The second is whether the speech at issue is of public concern. When the speech is of public concern and the plaintiff is a public official or public figure, the Constitution clearly requires the plaintiff to surmount a much higher barrier before recovering damages from a media defendant than is raised by the common law. When the speech is of public concern but the plaintiff is a private figure, as in Gertz, the Constitution still supplants the standards of the common law, but the constitutional requirements are, in at least some of their range, less forbidding than when the plaintiff is a public figure and the speech is of public concern. When the speech is of exclusively private concern and the plaintiff is a private figure, as in Dun & Bradstreet, the constitutional requirements do not necessarily force any change in at least some of the features of the common-law landscape.

Our opinions to date have chiefly treated the necessary showings of fault rather than of falsity. Nonetheless, as one might expect given the language of the Court in New York Times, a public-figure plaintiff must show the falsity of the statements at issue in order to prevail on a suit for defamation. ...

Here, as in Gertz, the plaintiff is a private figure and the newspaper articles are of public concern. In Gertz, as in New York Times, the common-law rule was superseded by a constitutional rule. We believe that the common law's rule on falsity—that the defendant must bear the burden of proving truth—must similarly fall here to a constitutional requirement that the plaintiff bear the burden of showing falsity, as well as fault, before recovering damages.

There will always be instances when the fact finding process will be unable to resolve conclusively whether the speech is true or false; it is in those cases that the burden of proof is dispositive. Under a rule forcing the plaintiff to bear the burden of showing falsity, there will be some cases in which plaintiffs cannot meet their burden despite the fact that the speech is in fact false. The plaintiff's suit will fail despite the fact that, in some abstract sense, the suit is meritorious. Similarly, under an alternative rule placing the burden of showing truth on defendants, there would be some cases in which defendants could not bear their burden despite the fact that the speech is in fact true. Those suits would succeed despite the fact that, in some abstract sense, those suits are unmeritorious. Under either rule, then, the outcome of the suit will sometimes be at variance with the outcome that we would desire if all speech were either demonstrably true or demonstrably false.

This dilemma stems from the fact that the allocation of the burden of proof will determine liability for some speech that is true and some that is false, but all of such speech is unknowably true or false. Because the burden of proof is the deciding factor only when the evidence is ambiguous, we cannot know how much of the speech affected by the allocation of the burden of proof is true and how much is false. In a case presenting a configuration of speech and plaintiff like the one we face here, and where the scales are in such an uncertain balance, we believe that the Constitution requires us to tip them in favor of protecting true speech. To ensure that true speech on matters of public concern is not deterred, we hold that the common-law presumption that defamatory speech is false cannot stand when a plaintiff seeks damages against a media defendant for speech of public concern.

In the context of governmental restriction of speech, it has long been established that the government cannot limit speech protected by the First Amendment without bearing the burden of showing that its restriction is justified. It is not immediately apparent from the text of the First Amendment, which by its terms applies only to governmental action, that a similar result should obtain here: a suit by a private party is obviously quite different from the government's direct enforcement of its own laws. Nonetheless, the need to encourage debate on public issues that concerned the Court in the governmental-restriction cases is of concern in a similar manner in this case involving a private suit for damages: placement by state law of the burden of proving truth upon media defendants who publish speech of public concern deters such speech because of the fear that liability will unjustifiably result. Because such a "chilling" effect would be antithetical to the First Amendment's protection of true speech on matters of public concern, we believe that a private-figure plaintiff must bear the burden of showing that the speech at issue is false before recovering damages for defamation from a media defendant. To do otherwise could "only result in a deterrence of speech which the Constitution makes free."

We recognize that requiring the plaintiff to show falsity will insulate from liability some speech that is false, but unprovably so. Nonetheless, the Court's previous decisions on the restrictions that the First Amendment places upon the common law of defamation firmly support our conclusion here with respect to the allocation of the burden of proof. In attempting to resolve related issues in the defamation context, the Court has affirmed that "[t]he First Amendment requires that we protect some falsehood in order to protect speech that matters." Here the speech concerns the legitimacy of the political process, and therefore clearly "matters." ... We therefore do not break new ground here in insulating speech that is not even demonstrably false.

We note that our decision adds only marginally to the burdens that the plaintiff must already bear as a result of our earlier decisions in the law of defamation. The plaintiff must show fault. A jury is obviously more likely to accept a plaintiff's contention that the defendant was at fault in publishing the statements at issue if convinced that the relevant statements were false. As a practical matter, then, evidence offered by plaintiffs on the publisher's fault in adequately investigating the truth of the published statements will generally encompass evidence of the falsity of the matters asserted.

We recognize that the plaintiff's burden in this case is weightier because of Pennsylvania's "shield" law, which allows employees of the media to refuse to divulge their sources. But we do not have before us here the question of the permissible reach of such laws. Indeed, we do not even know the precise reach of Pennsylvania's statute. The trial judge refused to give any instructions to the jury as to whether it could, or should, draw an inference adverse to the defendant from the defendant's decision to use the shield law rather than to present affirmative evidence of the truthfulness of some of the sources. That decision of the trial judge was not addressed by Pennsylvania's highest court, nor was it appealed to this Court. In the situation before us, we are unconvinced that the State's shield law requires a different constitutional standard than would prevail in the absence of such a law.

For the reasons stated above, the judgment of the Pennsylvania Supreme Court is reversed, and the case is remanded for further proceedings not inconsistent with this opinion.

Justice BRENNAN, with whom Justice BLACKMUN joins, concurring.

... I write separately only to note that, while the Court reserves the question whether the rule it announces applies to non-media defendants, I adhere to my view that such a distinction is "irreconcilable with the fundamental First Amendment principle that '[t]he inherent worth of ... speech in terms of its capacity for informing the public does not depend upon the identity of the source, whether corporation, association, union, or individual.' "

Justice STEVENS, with whom THE CHIEF JUSTICE, Justice WHITE, and Justice REHNQUIST join, dissenting.

The issue the Court resolves today will make a difference in only one category of cases—those in which a private individual can prove that he was libeled by a defendant who was at least negligent. For unless such a plaintiff can overcome the burden imposed by Gertz v. Robert Welch, Inc., 418 U.S. 323, 347, 94 S.Ct. 2997, 3010, 41 L.Ed.2d 789 (1974), he cannot recover regardless of how the burden of proof on the issue of truth or falsity is allocated. By definition, therefore, the only litigants—and the only publishers—who will benefit from today's decision are those who act negligently or maliciously.

... [Most of this dissent is omitted.]

In my view, as long as publishers are protected by the requirement that the plaintiff has the burden of proving fault, there can be little, if any, basis for a concern that a significant amount of true speech will be deterred unless the private person victimized by a malicious libel can also carry the burden of proving falsity. The Court's decision trades on the good names of private individuals with little First Amendment coin to show for it.

I respectfully dissent.

---

1. **State law on the burden of proof.** (a) Some states now appear to put the burden on the plaintiff to prove falsity in all cases. Be warned, however, that opinions sometimes speak loosely. In *Yohe v. Nugent,* 321 F.3d 35 (1st Cir. 2003), the court defined defamation as a "publication ... of a statement concerning the plaintiff which is false and causes damage to the plaintiff." Does this put the burden on the plaintiff to prove falsity in all cases?

2. **To what cases does the *Hepps* rule apply?** Lawyers need to know to which cases *Hepps* applies in its shifting of the common law proof burden on the truth-or-falsity issue. What can you say for sure about that?

3. **Implications about constitutional fault requirements?** Did any of the Justices in *Hepps* imply that a plaintiff could sometimes meet the burden of proving fault by proving ill-will rather than by proving negligent, reckless, or intentional falsehood? Both the O'Connor and the Stevens opinion appear to assume that the constitutionally required fault could be found even if no falsehood was demonstrated.

§ 2. THE CONSTITUTIONAL VIEW OF "OPINION" AND SOME RELATED IDEAS

> Under the First Amendment there is no such thing as a false idea. However pernicious an opinion may seem, we depend for its correction not on the conscience of judges and juries but on the competition of other ideas.
>
> —*Gertz v. Robert Welch, Inc.*

GREENBELT COOPERATIVE PUBLISHING ASS'N v. BRESLER, 398 U.S. 6, 90 S.Ct. 1537, 26 L.Ed.2d 6 (1970). The plaintiff, Bresler, was negotiating with the city to obtain zoning variances that would permit high-rise construction. At the same time, the city was negotiating to acquire another tract of land owned by Bresler for the construction of a new high school. These negotiations evoked substantial controversy. At a tumultuous city council meeting, some citizens "characterized Bresler's negotiating position as blackmail." The defendant, reporting the meeting in its newspaper, included the blackmail statement. Bresler was concededly a public figure. The trial judge defined malice to include spite or ill-will, and the jury found for Bresler. The Maryland Court affirmed a libel judgment in Bresler's favor. *Held,* reversed. "[A]s a matter of constitutional law, the word 'blackmail' in these circumstances was not slander when spoken, and not libel when reported. ... [E]ven the most careless reader must have perceived that the word was no more than rhetorical hyperbole, a vigorous epithet used by those who considered Bresler's negotiating position extremely unreasonable. Indeed, the record is completely devoid of evidence that anyone in the city of Greenbelt or anywhere else thought Bresler had been charged with a crime."

HUSTLER MAGAZINE v. FALWELL

485 U.S. 46, 108 S.Ct. 876, 99 L.Ed.2d 41 (1988)

Chief Justice REHNQUIST delivered the opinion of the Court. ...

The inside front cover of the November 1983 issue of Hustler Magazine featured a "parody" of an advertisement for Campari Liqueur that contained the name and picture of respondent and was entitled "Jerry Falwell talks about his first time." This parody was modeled after actual Campari ads that included interviews with various celebrities about their "first times." Although it was apparent by the end of each interview that this meant the first time they sampled Campari, the ads clearly played on the sexual double entendre of the general subject of "first times." Copying the form and layout of these Campari ads, Hustler's editors chose respondent as the featured celebrity and drafted an alleged "interview" with him in which he states that his "first time" was during a drunken incestuous rendezvous with his mother in an outhouse. The Hustler parody portrays respondent and his mother as drunk and immoral, and suggests that respondent is a hypocrite who preaches only when he is drunk. In small print at the bottom of the page, the ad contains the disclaimer, "ad parody—not to be taken seriously." The magazine's table of contents also lists the ad as "Fiction; Ad and Personality Parody."

[Falwell sued. The trial court directed a verdict for defendants on the privacy claim. The jury found against Falwell on the libel claim because it concluded "that the ad parody could not reasonably be understood as describing actual facts about Falwell or actual events in which he participated." However, the jury found for Falwell on the intentional infliction of emotional distress claim, and awarded $100,000 in compensatory damages, as well as $50,000 in punitive damages against each defendant. The Court of Appeals affirmed.]

Respondent would have us find that a State's interest in protecting public figures from emotional distress is sufficient to deny First Amendment protection to speech that is patently offensive and is intended to inflict emotional injury, even when that speech could not reasonably have been interpreted as stating actual facts about the public figure involved. This we decline to do.

[The Court here discussed many of the libel cases and the First Amendment standards and policies.]

In respondent's view, and in the view of the Court of Appeals, so long as the utterance was intended to inflict emotional distress, was outrageous, and did in fact inflict serious emotional distress, it is of no constitutional import whether the statement was a fact or an opinion, or whether it was true or false. It is the intent to cause injury that is the gravamen of the tort, and the State's interest in preventing emotional harm simply outweighs whatever interest a speaker may have in speech of this type.

Generally speaking the law does not regard the intent to inflict emotional distress as one which should receive much solicitude, and it is quite understandable that most if not all jurisdictions have chosen to make it civilly culpable where the conduct in question is sufficiently "outrageous." But in the world of debate about public affairs, many things done with motives that are less than admirable are protected by the First Amendment. In Garrison v. Louisiana, 379 U.S. 64, 85 S.Ct. 209, 13 L.Ed.2d 125 (1964), we held that even when a speaker or writer is motivated by hatred or ill will his expression was protected by the First Amendment. . . .

Were we to hold otherwise, there can be little doubt that political cartoonists and satirists would be subjected to damages awards without any showing that their work falsely defamed its subject. [The Court reviewed the history of satiric political cartoons and their role in public debate.]

Despite their sometimes caustic nature, from the early cartoon portraying George Washington as an ass down to the present day, graphic depictions and satirical cartoons have played a prominent role in public and political debate. . . .

Respondent contends, however, that the caricature in question here was so "outrageous" as to distinguish it from more traditional political cartoons. There is no doubt that the caricature of respondent and his mother published in Hustler is at best a distant cousin of the political cartoons described above, and a rather poor relation at that. If it were possible by laying down a principled standard to separate the one from the other, public discourse would probably suffer little or no harm. But we doubt that there is any such standard, and we are quite sure that the pejorative description "outrageous" does not supply one. "Outrageousness" in the area of political and social discourse has an inherent subjectiveness about it which would allow a jury to impose liability on the basis of the jurors' tastes or views, or perhaps on the basis of their dislike of a particular expression. An "outrageousness" standard thus runs afoul of our longstanding refusal to allow damages to be awarded because the speech in question may have an adverse emotional impact on the audience. . . . [T]he sort of expression involved in this case does not seem to us to be governed by any exception to the general First Amendment principles stated above.

We conclude that public figures and public officials may not recover for the tort of intentional infliction of emotional distress by reason of publications such as the one here at issue without showing in addition that the publication contains a false statement of fact which was made with "actual malice," i.e., with knowledge that the statement was false or with reckless disregard as to whether or not it was true. This is not merely a "blind application" of the New York Times standard, it reflects our considered judgment that such a standard is necessary to give adequate "breathing space" to the freedoms protected by the First Amendment.

Here it is clear that respondent Falwell is a "public figure" for purposes of First Amendment law. . . . The Court of Appeals interpreted the jury's finding to be that the ad parody "was not reasonably believable," and in accordance with our custom we accept this finding. Respondent is thus relegated to his claim for damages awarded by the jury for the intentional infliction of emotional distress by "outrageous" conduct. But for reasons heretofore stated this claim cannot, consistently with the First Amendment, form a basis for the award of damages when the conduct in question is the publication of a caricature such as the ad parody involved here. The judgment of the Court of Appeals is accordingly

Reversed.

Justice KENNEDY took no part in the consideration or decision of this case.

Justice WHITE, concurring in the judgment.

As I see it, the decision in New York Times Co. v. Sullivan has little to do with this case, for here the jury found that the ad contained no assertion of fact. But I agree with the Court that the judgment below, which penalized the publication of the parody, cannot be squared with the First Amendment.

4. **First Amendment and other communicative torts.** At a very broad level, *Hustler-Falwell* shows that the First Amendment speech protections seem to apply not only in defamation but also with other communicative torts. In this case, the other communicative tort is the intentional infliction of emotional distress, but we'll see still others, such as invasion of privacy and interference with contract or business by communicative behavior.

5. **Contrasting disbelief of factual assertions.** Distinguish: (1) the defendant asserts facts but the jury does not believe them; (2) the defendant asserts no factual material at all, even if it is presented in factual form. Suppose a mainstream newspaper publishes a column in which the columnist asserts that he has investigated and found that Rev. Nemo has committed incest. Suppose also that the jury found it was not true and further found that no one believes it to be true. Would such a case come under the *Hustler-Falwell* rule?

New Times, Inc. v. Isaacks, 91 S.W.3d 844 (Tex. App. 2002), on appeal, 146 S.W.3d 144 (Tex. 2004). The defendant, an alternative newspaper, satirized a judge and district attorney for holding a teenager in juvenile detention because he had written a story in school depicting the murder of a teacher. The satire presented a fictional detention of a six-year old: " '[A] diminutive 6–year old,' was arrested during 'story-time' in her class at Ponder Elementary School for a book report she had written about an award-winning children's classic, *Where the Wild Things Are,* by Maurice Sendak. According to the article, Judge Whitten [a plaintiff] ordered Cindy detained for ten days at the Denton County Juvenile Detention Center while prosecutors decided whether to file charges." The article went on to say that Cindy appeared subdued when she stood before Judge Whitten dressed in 'blue jeans, a Pokemon T-shirt, handcuffs and ankle shackles.' Judge Whitten was quoted as chastising Cindy from the bench: 'Any implication of violence in a school situation, even if it was just contained in a first-grader's book report, is reason enough for panic and overreaction,' Whitten said from the bench. 'It's time for you to grow up, young lady, and it's time for us to stop treating kids like children.' " And further: "Sources say courthouse security officers ordered the shackles after they reviewed [Cindy's] school disciplinary record, which included reprimands for spraying a boy with pineapple juice and sitting on her feet. Welch also confirmed reports that school representatives will soon join several local faith-based organizations, including God-Fearing Opponents of Freedom (GOOF), and ask publishers to review the content guidelines for children's books. 'Parents must understand that zero tolerance means just that,' [Gov. George W. Bush] said. 'We won't tolerate anything.' "

In the Court of Appeals, Held, (1) If reasonable people would understand the publication as satire or parody, it would be constitutionally protected, but it is a jury question whether a reasonable person would take it as a literal news report. (2) Apart from the satire-opinion rules, the actual malice standard applies, but it does not warrant summary judgment for the defendant here because "a jury could find that the defendant "knew or strongly suspected that the article could be misleading."

In the Texas Supreme court, held, reversed. (1) No reasonable reader could think that the story was to be interpreted as stating actual facts because of the many humorous absurdities and because, in line with the general rule, the publication had to be read as a whole. The objective reasonable reader is not a dullard; the reader is certainly not the lowest common denominator. The fact that some particular reader might not read the entire publication or might not get the joke was irrelevant, given that the objective standard of a reasonable reader was the test. (2) "[E]vidence of intent to ridicule is not evidence of actual malice. Rather, actual malice concerns the defendant's attitude toward the truth, not toward the plaintiff."

MILKOVICH v. LORAIN JOURNAL

497 U.S. 1, 110 S.Ct. 2695, 111 L.Ed.2d 1 (1990)

Chief Justice REHNQUIST delivered the opinion of the Court. . . .

[The wrestling team of Maple Heights High School was involved in an altercation at a home wrestling match with a team from Mentor High School. People were injured. The Ohio High School Athletic Association, after a hearing, criticized the action of Maple Heights' Coach Milkovich and made the Maple Heights team ineligible for the state tournament. Parents and wrestlers sued the Athletic Association for a restraining order. Coach Milkovich testified. The court ultimately overturned the Association's probation and ineligibility orders on due process grounds.]

The day after the court rendered its decision, respondent Diadiun's column appeared in the News-Herald, a newspaper which circulates in Lake County, Ohio, and is owned by respondent Lorain Journal Co. The column bore the heading "Maple beat the law with the 'big lie.' " [The Court quoted passages from the column, some of which, reformatted, follow.]

If you get in a jam, lie your way out. . . . Anyone who attended the meet, whether he be from Maple Heights, Mentor, or impartial observer, knows in his heart that Milkovich and Scott lied at the hearing after each having given his solemn oath to tell the truth. But they got away with it. Is that the kind of lesson we want our young people learning from their high school administrators and coaches? I think not.

[Superintendent Scott sued but lost in the Ohio Supreme Court. Milkovich also sued. He lost because the Ohio Court of Appeals, following the Ohio Supreme Court's decision in the Scott case, held that Milkovich could not recover. The Supreme Court granted certiorari.]

[The *Ollman* Factors]

The Scott court decided that the proper analysis for determining whether utterances are fact or opinion was set forth in the decision of the United States Court of Appeals for the District of Columbia Circuit in Ollman v. Evans, 242 U.S.App.D.C. 301, 750 F.2d 970 (1984). Under that analysis, four factors are considered to ascertain whether, under the "totality of circumstances," a statement is fact or opinion. These factors are: (1) "the specific language used"; (2) "whether the statement is verifiable"; (3) "the general context of the statement"; and (4) "the broader context in which the statement appeared." The court found that application of the first two factors to the column militated in favor of deeming the challenged passages actionable assertions of fact. That potential outcome was trumped, however, by the court's consideration of the third and fourth factors. With respect to the third factor, the general context, the court explained that "the large caption 'TD Says' . . . would indicate to even the most gullible reader that the article was, in fact, opinion." As for the fourth factor, the "broader context," the court reasoned that because the article appeared on a sports page—"a traditional haven for cajoling, invective, and hyperbole"—the article would probably be construed as opinion. . . .

[Common Law Rules]

The common law generally did not place any additional restrictions on the type of statement that could be actionable. Indeed, defamatory communications were deemed actionable regardless of whether they were deemed to be statements of fact or opinion. See, e.g., Restatement of Torts, supra, §§ 565–567. . . . However, due to concerns that unduly burdensome defamation laws could stifle valuable public debate, the privilege of "fair comment" was incorporated into the common law as an affirmative defense to an action for defamation. "The principle of 'fair comment' afford[ed] legal immunity for the honest expression of opinion on matters of legitimate public interest when based upon a true or privileged statement of fact." 1 F. Harper & F. James, Law of Torts § 5.28, p. 456 (1956). . . . "According to the majority rule, the privilege of fair comment applied only to an expression of opinion and not to a false statement of fact, whether it was expressly stated or implied from an expression of opinion."

[The Court discussed *New York Times* and its progeny, including *Greenbelt-Bresler*, *Hustler-Falwell* and another case].

The Court has also determined "that in cases raising First Amendment issues . . . an appellate court has an obligation to 'make an independent examination of the whole record' in order to make sure that 'the judgment does not constitute a forbidden intrusion on the field of free expression.' . . .

[Special Protections for "Opinion" Speech?]

Respondents would have us recognize, in addition to the established safeguards discussed above, still another First Amendment-based protection for defamatory statements which are categorized as "opinion" as opposed to "fact." For this proposition they rely principally on the following dictum from our opinion in Gertz:

"Under the First Amendment there is no such thing as a false idea. However pernicious an opinion may seem, we depend for its correction not on the conscience of judges and juries but on the competition of other ideas. But there is no constitutional value in false statements of fact."

Judge Friendly appropriately observed that this passage "has become the opening salvo in all arguments for protection from defamation actions on the ground of opinion, even though the case did not remotely concern the question." Cianci v. New Times Publishing Co., 639 F. 2d 54, 61 (2d Cir. 1980). Read in context, though, the fair meaning of the passage is to equate the word "opinion" in the second sentence with the word "idea" in the first sentence. Under this view, the language was merely a reiteration of Justice Holmes' classic "marketplace of ideas" concept. . . .

Thus we do not think this passage from Gertz was intended to create a wholesale defamation exemption for anything that might be labeled "opinion." Not only would such an interpretation be contrary to the tenor and context of the passage, but it would also ignore the fact that expressions of "opinion" may often imply an assertion of objective fact.

If a speaker says, "In my opinion John Jones is a liar," he implies a knowledge of facts which lead to the conclusion that Jones told an untruth. Even if the speaker states the facts upon which he bases his opinion, if those facts are either incorrect or incomplete, or if his assessment of them is erroneous, the statement may still imply a false assertion of fact. Simply couching such statements in terms of opinion does not dispel these implications; and the statement, "In my opinion Jones is a liar," can cause as much damage to reputation as the statement, "Jones is a liar." As Judge Friendly aptly stated: "[It] would be destructive of the law of libel if a writer could escape liability for accusations of [defamatory conduct] simply by using, explicitly or implicitly, the words I think." It is worthy of note that at common law, even the privilege of fair comment did not extend to "a false statement of fact, whether it was expressly stated or implied from an expression of opinion."

Apart from their reliance on the Gertz dictum, respondents do not really contend that a statement such as, "In my opinion John Jones is a liar," should be protected by a separate privilege for "opinion" under the

First Amendment. But they do contend that in every defamation case the First Amendment mandates an inquiry into whether a statement is "opinion" or "fact," and that only the latter statements may be actionable. ... But we think the "breathing space which freedoms of expression require in order to survive," is adequately secured by existing constitutional doctrine without the creation of an artificial dichotomy between "opinion" and fact.

[*Hepps* and the Provably False Standard]

Foremost, we think Hepps stands for the proposition that a statement on matters of public concern must be provable as false before there can be liability under state defamation law, at least in situations, like the present, where a media defendant is involved. Thus, unlike the statement, "In my opinion Mayor Jones is a liar," the statement, "In my opinion Mayor Jones shows his abysmal ignorance by accepting the teachings of Marx and Lenin," would not be actionable. Hepps ensures that a statement of opinion relating to matters of public concern which does not contain a provably false factual connotation will receive full constitutional protection.

["Actual facts" vs. "loose, figurative language"]

Next, the Bresler–Letter Carriers–Falwell line of cases provide protection for statements that cannot "reasonably [be] interpreted as stating actual facts" about an individual. Falwell, 485 U. S. at 50. This provides assurance that public debate will not suffer for lack of "imaginative expression" or the "rhetorical hyperbole" which has traditionally added much to the discourse of our Nation.

The New York Times—Butts and Gertz culpability requirements further ensure that debate on public issues remains "uninhibited, robust, and wide-open." Thus, where a statement of "opinion" on a matter of public concern reasonably implies false and defamatory facts regarding public figures or officials, those individuals must show that such statements were made with knowledge of their false implications or with reckless disregard of their truth. Similarly, where such a statement involves a private figure on a matter of public concern, a plaintiff must show that the false connotations were made with some level of fault as required by Gertz. Finally, the enhanced appellate review required by Bose Corp., provides assurance that the foregoing determinations will be made in a manner so as not to "constitute a forbidden intrusion of the field of free expression."

[Application to this case]

...The dispositive question in the present case then becomes whether or not a reasonable fact finder could conclude that the statements in the Diadiun column imply an assertion that petitioner Milkovich perjured himself in a judicial proceeding. We think this question must be answered in the affirmative. As the Ohio Supreme Court itself observed, "the clear impact in some nine sentences and a caption is that [Milkovich] 'lied at the hearing after ... having given his solemn oath to tell the truth.'" This is not the sort of loose, figurative or hyperbolic language which would negate the impression that the writer was seriously maintaining petitioner committed the crime of perjury. Nor does the general tenor of the article negate this impression.

We also think the connotation that petitioner committed perjury is sufficiently factual to be susceptible of being proved true or false. A determination of whether petitioner lied in this instance can be made on a core of objective evidence by comparing, inter alia, petitioner's testimony before the OHSAA board with his subsequent testimony before the trial court. As the Scott court noted regarding the plaintiff in that case, "[w]hether or not H. Don Scott did indeed perjure himself is certainly verifiable by a perjury action with evidence adduced from the transcripts and witnesses present at the hearing. Unlike a subjective assertion the averred defamatory language is an articulation of an objectively verifiable event." So too with petitioner Milkovich.

[Addressing the appropriate balance between protection of speech and protection of reputation, the Court quoted Justice Stewart as follows:]

> The right of a man to the protection of his own reputation from unjustified invasion and wrongful hurt reflects no more than our basic concept of the essential dignity and worth of every human being—a concept at the root of any decent system of ordered liberty.
>
> ...

We believe our decision in the present case holds the balance true. The judgment of the Ohio Court of Appeals is reversed and the case remanded for further proceedings not inconsistent with this opinion.

HORSLEY V. RIVERA, 292 F.3d 695 (11th Cir. 2002). Plaintiff is an anti-abortion activist who maintained a website listing names of abortion doctors, graying out those who had been wounded and x-ing out those who had been killed. Soon after one doctor was murdered, Rivera interviewed Horsley on a television show. Rivera said "what you are doing, in my opinion is aiding and abetting a homicide" and "You are an accomplice to homicide." In Horsley's suit for libel, *held*, Rivera's statements are rhetorical hyperbole as a matter of law, partly because Horsley in the same interview recognized as much by using similar figurative language and partly because, given the context of a heated debate on an emotional topic, the accusation looks more like an expression of outrage than a literal accusation of murder.

---

6. **Traditional common law; fair comment.** The traditional common law protected opinion statements only under the fair comment

and the name-calling rules. Traditional fair comment rules protected speech on matters of public interest and when the defendant had somehow submitted himself to public opinion. The constitutional rule in *Milkovich* seems to offer similar protections. Maybe that is what some courts meant by saying that the fair comment rule has been "superseded" by the constitutional rules. E.g., *Ryan v. Herald Ass'n, Inc.,* 152 Vt. 275, 284, 566 A.2d 1316, 1321 (1989). But nothing in the constitutional cases prevents state courts from continuing to decide cases under the common law rules, or from expanding those rules to protect opinion statements independent of what the constitution requires. See, protecting the defendant under the common law fair comment rules, *Magnusson v. New York Times Co.,* 98 P.3d 1070 (Okla. 2004). If the common law rules are broadened to use different tests for determining "probably false" or to protect more than the constitutional rules protect, then they may add to the defendant's collection of shields against liability. If the common law rules are not broader than the constitutional rules, could it ever matter whether the judge holds for the defendant under common law rules or under constitutional rules?

7. **"Actual facts" and "provably false."** Did the *Milkovich* Court erect two alternative tests, so that statements are protected when they cannot be reasonably interpreted as stating actual facts and also when they are not provably false? Or do these two "tests" merely reflect different ways of saying the same thing?

8. **Facts on which opinion based are true or privileged and fully stated.** The fair comment privilege might protect statements of "opinion" where the facts on which the opinion were true or privileged and also fully stated. Does the *Milkovich* Court appear to think that a conclusion based on truthfully stated facts would be protected under the Constitution?

9. **Meaning of *Milkovich*.** What would count as a protected statement that is not provably false under *Milkovich*? Perhaps that case "means that the statement must be the kind that could be verified or falsified through the senses if witnesses had been present at all times. In contrast, statements that could be judged and evaluated but not neutrally determined by touch, vision, or hearing, would not be provably false. Although circumstantial evidence might be required to prove falsity of some statements, the circumstantial evidence itself would presumably have to be factual rather than evaluative." DOBBS ON TORTS § 420 (2000). Professor Gray, referring to the Restatement Second of Torts, suggests that its opinion rule refers to comment on facts but not to degrees of conviction about the existence of facts. 2 F. HARPER, F. JAMES, & O. GRAY, THE LAW OF TORTS § 5.8 (1986 & Supps.). Judge Sack lists a number of ideas about fact and opinion. One of them is that opinion statements are subjective, while factual statements are objective. Courts sometimes rely on this idea in concluding that no provably false fact was published. See *Aviation Charter, Inc. v. Aviation Research Group/US,* 416 F.3d 864 (8th Cir. 2005). Judge Sack also notes that an inference of fact based on another fact is not opinion. See Robert D. Sack, *Protection of Opinion*

under the First Amendment: Reflections on Alfred Hill, "Defamation and Privacy under the First Amendment," 100 COLUM. L. REV. 294 (2000).

10. **Scope of constitutional protection dictated by the scope of Hepps?** Is there any argument for the proposition that *Milkovich* goes only where *Hepps* goes? If *Hepps* turns out *not* to apply in a *Dun & Bradstreet* type case, would that mean that a private, *Dun & Bradstreet* plaintiff could recover for pure statements of opinion that imply no unstated facts? To illustrate the issue, imagine that one neighbor, referring to the plaintiff, says to another: "Joan is a bitch!" Is that constitutionally protected or must the defendant rely upon state law? See Robert D. Sack, *Protection of Opinion under the First Amendment: Reflections on Alfred Hill, "Defamation and Privacy under the First Amendment,"* 100 COLUM. L. REV. 294, 326–327 (2000).

11. **Common law—expanding protection for privilege?** The states can protect "opinion" statements whether or not the Constitution does so. See *Wilkow v. Forbes,* Inc., 241 F.3d 552 (7th Cir. 2001) (Illinois law); *Lubin v. Kunin,* 117 Nev. 107, 17 P.3d 422 (2001); *Immuno AG v. Moor–Jankowski,* 77 N.Y.2d 235, 566 N.Y.S.2d 906, 567 N.E.2d 1270, 1273 (1991); *Finck v. City of Tea,* 443 N.W.2d 632 (S.D. 1989). In determining whether a statement was opinion or not, the *Immuno* court said it would consider, not merely the words alone, but "the content of the whole communication, its tone and apparent purpose." Ohio has taken a similar view under its Constitution, considering the context in which statements appear (such as an editorial column), the linguistic context (sarcasm, hyperbole), and specific language, and verifiability. *Vail v. Plain Dealer,* 72 Ohio St.3d 279, 649 N.E.2d 182 (1995). New Jersey has also provided strong protection for opinion-like statements, taking off from fair comment rules but also permitting protection for misstatements of fact, at least where issues are of public interest. See *Dairy Stores, Inc. v. Sentinel Publishing Co., Inc.*, 104 N.J. 125, 516 A.2d 220 (1986).

12. **Heated debate.** In *Horsley,* the court pointed to the "heated debate" as a ground for considering the defendant's statement as an opinion and not provably false. *Horsley* is not alone. See, e.g., *Lieberman v. Fieger,* 338 F.3d 1076 (9th Cir. 2003). What is there about heated debate or excitement that could convert a pure statement of fact into an opinion that is not provably false? Distinguish the argument that an arguably factual assertion appearing in a stream of rhetorical hyperbole can take on the coloration of the hyperbole that surrounds it. This argument was also made in *Lieberman v. Fieger*, supra, where the defendant said the plaintiff was crazy, nuts, and Looney Toons; the Looney Toons statement suggested that his assertion of mental unbalance was to be taken as the same kind of rhetoric.

REFERENCE: The constitutional truth-opinion rules are summarized briefly in DOBBS ON TORTS § 420 (2000).

§ 3. PROTECTIONS UNDER THE FREEDOM OF RELIGION CLAUSES

THE FIRST AMENDMENT

Congress shall make no law respecting an establishment of religion, or prohibiting the free exercise thereof. . . .

GOODMAN V. TEMPLE SHIR AMI, INC., 712 So.2d 775 (Fla. Dist. Ct. App. 1998). The defendants were considering whether to renew the plaintiff's contract for services as a rabbi at the Temple. An individual defendant said at the Temple's board meeting that the plaintiff, Rabbi Goodman, "had committed a crime by striking the senior Rabbi at a temple in Chicago where Rabbi Goodman was then employed, following which Rabbi Goodman's employment was terminated by the Chicago temple. [Rabbi Goodman sued on several grounds, including defamation.] We conclude that the trial court correctly dismissed the claims (with the exception of that for breach of the first contract, which we will shortly discuss). In order for the trial court to have resolved these disputes, it would have had to immerse itself in religious doctrines and concepts and 'determine' whether the religious disagreements were a 'valid' basis for the termination of Rabbi Goodman's services. The allegedly defamatory report and tortious interference occurred as part of this religious dispute and would require the trial court to weigh their effect on the board members as compared to the effects of the other considerations which clearly are religious disagreements. Inquiring into the adequacy of the religious reasoning behind the dismissal of a spiritual leader is not a proper task for a civil court."

13. **Finding religious doctrine issues in Goodman.** On the surface it is hard to see what issue in Rabbi Goodman's defamation suit would require the court to immerse itself in or even consider religious doctrine. The truth or falsity of the statement that Goodman struck a senior Rabbi is not itself a matter of religion. Maybe the court became so focused on the wrongful termination claim that it failed to recognize that the defamation claim might be different. Or maybe the court really had some concern other than the potential immersion in religious doctrine. Before reaching either of those conclusions, though, it is worth an effort to see how religious doctrine could be involved in a decision on the merits of the defamation claim by working out the issues that would arise as this slander case made its way through trial.

CHA v. KOREAN PRESBYTERIAN CHURCH OF WASHINGTON

262 Va. 604, 553 S.E.2d 511 (2001)

HASSELL, Justice. . . .

[The plaintiff was one of the pastors of the church. After some concerns in the church about financial improprieties, one of the deacons of the church, speaking to other deacons, said of the plaintiff that he had "borrowed over $100,000 from believers and has not returned the money." The plaintiff's employment at the church was terminated. He sued the church and individuals claiming wrongful termination of contract and interference with contract. He sued those individuals who said he had "borrowed" money for defamation.]

The United States Supreme Court, applying the First Amendment, has held that generally civil courts are not a constitutionally permissible forum for a review of ecclesiastical disputes. Even though there are limited exceptions to this constitutional principle, it is well established that a civil court may neither interfere in matters of church government nor in matters of faith and doctrine. . . .

The United States Court of Appeals for the Fourth Circuit has held, and we agree, that the "right to choose ministers without government restriction underlies the well-being of religious community ... for perpetuation of a church's existence may depend upon those whom it selects to preach its values, teach its message, and interpret its doctrines both to its own membership and to the world at large. Any attempt by government to restrict a church's free choice of its leaders thus constitutes a burden on the church's free exercise rights."...

Upon our review of the pleadings in this case, we hold that the plaintiff's allegations of defamation against the individual defendants cannot be considered in isolation, separate and apart from the church's decision to terminate his employment. The individual defendants who purportedly uttered defamatory remarks about the plaintiff were church officials who attended meetings of the church's governing bodies that had been convened for the purpose of discussing certain accusations against the plaintiff. We can only conclude that if a civil court were to exercise jurisdiction of the plaintiff's motion for judgment under these circumstances, the court would be compelled to consider the church's doctrine and beliefs because such matters would undoubtedly affect the plaintiff's fitness to perform pastoral duties and whether the plaintiff had been prejudiced in his profession. Neither the Free Exercise Clause nor Article I, § 16 of the Constitution of Virginia permits a civil court to undertake such a role.

Indeed, most courts that have considered the question whether the Free Exercise Clause divests a civil court of subject matter jurisdiction to consider a pastor's defamation claims against a church and its officials have answered that question in the affirmative. See Higgins v. Maher, 210 Cal.App.3d 1168, 258 Cal.Rptr. 757, 761 (1989) ("[i]f our civil courts enter upon disputes between bishops and priests because of allegations of defamation ... it is difficult to conceive the termination case which could not result in a sustainable lawsuit"); McManus v. Taylor, 521 So.2d 449, 451 (La.Ct. App.1988) ("[t]o allow defamation suits to be litigated to the fullest extent against members of a religious board who are merely discharging the duty which has been entrusted to them by their church could have a potentially chilling effect on the performance of those duties'').

---

14. **A middle way?** If you are convinced by the chill argument as distinct from the interference argument, why not apply the rule in *Times-Sullivan* where we first encountered chill arguments? In *McNair v. Worldwide Church of God,* 197 Cal.App.3d 363, 242 Cal.Rptr. 823 (1987), an individual officer of the church was expounding church doctrine to a group of church leaders. In doing so, he allegedly defamed the former wife of an important church officer. For that situation, at least, the court accommodated the competing interests—reputation on the one hand and free exercise of religion on the other—by requiring the plaintiff to produce special evidence. First, it had to be clear and convincing evidence. Second it had to show that the defendants published with knowledge that the defamatory statements were false, or at least in reckless disregard of falsity.

Kliebenstein v. Iowa Conference of the United Methodist Church, 663 N.W.2d 404 (Iowa 2003). Defendant, an ordained minister and district superintendent of the United Methodist Church, sent a letter both to members of the Shell Rock, Iowa church and to others in the community. The letter expressed unhappiness about a named member of the congregation, Jane Kliebenstein, and appeared to associate her ''with the 'spirit of Satan.' '' She sued for defamation. The trial court granted summary judgment for the defendant. *Held,* reversed. The Free Exercise and Establishment Clauses of both federal and state constitutions preclude civil court interference in the disciplinary and governance matters of a religious entity. The ''defense rests on the general rule that '[d]efamation actions are precluded by the First Amendment when an examination of the truth of the allegedly defamatory statements would require an impermissible inquiry into church doctrine and discipline.' Defendants contend that in order to determine whether the term 'spirit of Satan' is defamatory—or truthful—as applied to Kliebenstein, a factfinder would necessarily be required to study and interpret church theology and beliefs concerning Satan. ... Because we are convinced that the phrase 'spirit of Satan' has a secular, as well as sectarian, meaning, and because the accusatory phrase was used by defendants to describe Jane Kliebenstein in a communication published to more than just church members, we hold plaintiffs' claim of defamation should not have been summarily dismissed by the district court on constitutional grounds.''

*

Professional and Academic Enhancements
Chapter 4

Opinion and the Disclosure of Facts Behind It

RILEY v. HARR

292 F.3d 282 (1st Cir. 2002)

LIPEZ, Circuit Judge. . . .

[Defamation action by Riley, a person depicted in the best-selling book, *A Civil Action*, which recounts litigation brought for the death of a number of persons around Woburn, Massachusetts. The trial court gave summary judgment for defendants on all claims that now remain in issue.] The Book tells the story of the *Anderson* litigation primarily from the perspective of the plaintiffs' attorney, Jan Schlichtmann, recounting his struggle to prove that Riley's tannery and defendant Grace were responsible for the contamination of Wells G and H. The Book describes evidence which, in Schlichtmann's view, tended to show that the tannery had dumped waste laced with TCE on the fifteen acres, and repeatedly suggests that Riley's denials that such dumping had occurred were false.

Statement C describes Schlichtmann's reaction to the discovery of a document indicating that tannery waste had been deposited on the fifteen acres in 1956:

> This document was thirty years old and it dealt only with tannery waste, which might or might not have contained TCE. But even so, Schlichtmann thought it had great value. Riley had sworn at his deposition that he had never dumped anything on the fifteen acres. Riley had lied then, and Schlichtmann—who didn't need much convincing—believed that Riley was also lying about using TCE.

The assertion in Statement C that Riley had lied in the course of the *Anderson* litigation is, in principle, "provable as false." *Milkovich,* 497 U.S. at 19, 110 S.Ct. 2695. A statement is not actionable, however, if "it is plain that the speaker is expressing a subjective view, an interpretation, a theory, conjecture, or surmise."

[The passage represents] Schlichtmann's conclusion, not Harr's. As Harr points out, "[t]he law does not force writers to clumsily begin each and every sentence with 'Schlichtmann felt' " in order to indicate that a statement is being attributed to Schlichtmann. As Statement C is cast as Schlichtmann's assessment of Riley's testimony, and follows a summary of the evidence upon which it is based (the document reporting the discovery of tannery waste on the fifteen acres), it amounts to 'a subjective view, an interpretation, a theory, conjecture, or surmise,' not an assertion of objective fact based on undisclosed evidence.

Moreover, even if we accepted Riley's premise that the statement "Riley had lied then" constitutes Harr's own declaration that Riley had uttered a falsehood, the statement would still be protected under the First Amendment. Like the allegedly defamatory newspaper articles in *Phantom Touring, Inc. v. Affiliated Publications,* 953 F.2d 724 (1st Cir.1992)], the Book "not only discussed ... the facts underlying [Harr's] views but also gave information from which readers might draw contrary conclusions."

[The court considered numerous individual statements and also several theories besides defamation, then affirmed the summary judgment for defendants.]

Analysis of "Opinion"

In Milkovich, the Supreme Court reviewed and seemingly rejected, the multi-factor analysis in *Ollman v. Evans,* 750 F.2d 970 (1984). That analysis may have permitted judges a wide latitude in characterizing the defendant's statement as either unprotected fact or as protected opinion.

In *Ollman* itself, the defendants published a newspaper column that described the plaintiff as a Marxist professor, which was true, and suggested that from quotations from his works, he would use the classroom to attempt to convert students to socialism. The column quoted an anonymous political scientist in a major university to the effect that the plaintiff, "has no status within the profession, but is a pure and simple activist. ..." These statements were held to be opinion and absolutely protected.

In another case of the same era, *Janklow v. Newsweek,* 788 F.2d 1300 (8th Cir. 1986), the libel allegedly arose because the defendant implied that the plaintiff, a public prosecutor, had initiated prosecution of a man named Banks because Banks had charged him with raping a Native American girl. But in fact, the prosecution had begun before the rape charge was made. Could the misstatement about when prosecution began possibly be a statement of opinion? Using the *Ollman* factors, the *Janklow* court argued that the time statement itself was not the important thing, it was the implication of revenge—and that was opinion.

Among the questions lawyers and judges must consider are: (1) Has *Milkovich* changed (a) outcomes in the cases? (b) the methodology or approach to analysis? (2) Has *Milkovich* induced courts to over-elaborate opinion issues? (3) Have courts begun to use "opinion" analysis with its several factors simply to get a desired result, perhaps often to protect speech for reasons not much associated with "opinion"? (4) Are the real issues those that must resolved, not by rules of law but by analysis of the facts and words case by case, for instance, whether some assertion of fact is implied by the words used?

GUILFORD TRANSP. INDUS. INC. v. WILNER, 760 A.2d 580 (D.C. 2000). The defendant authored an Op–Ed piece about the plaintiff railroad. It was published in an influential trade publication. Defendant said that after the plaintiff took over the railroad system, "a bitter labor-management conflict was [quickly] ignited when Guilford bolted from traditional national wage and benefits negotiations. Local negotiations with the Brotherhood of Maintenance of Way Employees culminated in an almost three-month strike that required Congressional intervention." There was a good deal more in the same vein with arguably loaded words like "quickly" and "bolted." Testimony indicated that there was nothing quick about the appearance of the labor dispute and that the plaintiff had not bolted from, but simply never opted into the national negotiations. The plaintiff claims that the piece implied that the plaintiff was hostile to labor and that shippers reading the piece feared that hostility to labor meant unreliable transport for their goods, hence would seek alternative carriers.

Held, summary judgment for defendant affirmed. As *Ollman* recognized, "[t]he reasonable reader who peruses [a] column on the editorial or Op–Ed page is fully aware that the statements found there are not 'hard' news like those printed on the front page or elsewhere in the news sections of the newspaper. . . . Although the Supreme Court has made it clear, since *Ollman* was decided, that statements of 'opinion' are not constitutionally protected if they assert provably false and defamatory facts, [citing *Milkovich*], the constitutional principles that animate the passage we have quoted from *Ollman* remain equally compelling and equally good law today. . . . Under *Milkovich,* 'statements of opinion can be actionable if they imply a provably false fact, or rely upon stated facts that are provably false.' '[B]ut if it is plain that a speaker is expressing a subjective view, an interpretation, a theory, conjecture, or surmise, rather than claiming to be in possession of objectively verifiable facts, the statement is not actionable.' '[A] statement of opinion is actionable only if it has an explicit or implicit factual foundation and is therefore objectively verifiable.' . . . '*Milkovich* did not disavow the importance of context,' and it therefore remains critical to our inquiry that the allegedly defamatory utterances in this case appeared in an Op–Ed column in which Wilner was commenting on matters of substantial public concern. . . . [W]hether or not any of the remaining statements . . . are in fact inaccurate, Wilner's basic theme is not provably false. Whether the plaintiffs are hostile to labor is not an issue of fact susceptible of objective proof. '[I]t is the defamatory *implication*—not the underlying assertions giving rise to the implication—which must be examined to discern whether the statements are entitled to full constitutional protection.' "

JEFFERSON COUNTY SCHOOL DIST. NO. R–1 v. MOODY'S INVESTOR'S SERVS., INC.

175 F.3d 848 (10th Cir. 1999)

HENRY, Circuit Judge. . . .

In 1993, the School District decided to refinance part of its bonded indebtedness by issuing refunding bonds, thereby obtaining the benefit of lower interest rates. Even though it had retained Moody's in the past, the School District selected two other agencies to rate its bonds. As a result, it paid no fee to Moody's and provided Moody's with no information about its current financial condition.

The School District brought the bonds to market on October 20, 1993. Initially, they sold well, and the District received subscriptions for the purchase of substantially all of the issue. However, less than two hours into the sales period, Moody's published an article regarding the bonds in its "Rating News," an electronically distributed information service sent to subscribers and news services. Moody's stated that although it had not been asked to rate the bonds, it intended to assign a rating to the issue subsequent to the sale. Moody's then discussed the bonds and the School District's financial condition, concluding that "[t]he outlook on the district's general obligation debt is negative, reflecting the district's ongoing financial pressures due in part to the state's past underfunding of the school finance act as well as legal uncertainties and fiscal constraints. . . ." Within minutes, "The Dow Jones Capital Market Reports," an electronic publication owned and operated by Dow Jones & Company, issued an electronic communication repeating the Moody's statement about the refunding bonds" "negative outlook."

The School District alleges that Moody's statement was materially false in that it indicated that the School District's financial condition was not creditworthy and conveyed the impression that Moody's assessment was based on current information. The School District further maintains that the most recent financial information that it had sent to Moody's was more than a year old. According to the School District, Moody's published the article in order to retaliate against it for deciding to use other credit rating agencies, and the article had a significant effect on the marketing of the bonds: purchase orders ceased, several buyers canceled prior orders, and the School District was forced to reprice the bonds at a higher interest rate in order to complete the sale, thereby causing it to suffer a net loss of $769,000. [The trial court granted defendants' motion to dismiss the claim.]

Milkovich distinguishes between what one scholar has labeled evaluative and deductive opinion. *See* Kathryn Dix Sowle, *A Matter of Opinion: Milkovich Four Years Later,* 3 Wm. & Mary Bill of Rights Journal 467, 474 (1994). According to Professor Sowle, evaluative opinions are those that are not provably false, and a writer or speaker may not be held liable on a defamation claim for expressing them. In contrast, deductive opinions are those that state or imply assertions that may be proven false; the First Amendment does not immunize them from defamation claims.

Although the distinction between these two kinds of opinions is sometime difficult to draw, consideration of the following factors has proven useful: (1) the phrasing of the allegedly defamatory statement; (2) the context in which the statement appears; (3) the medium through which it is disseminated; and (4) the circumstances surrounding its publication. A review of decisions applying *Milkovich* illustrates how courts have applied these factors in determining whether allegedly defamatory statements constitute protected expressions of opinion.

In some instances, allegedly defamatory statements have been deemed too indefinite to be proven true or false. For example, in *Biospherics, Inc. v. Forbes, Inc.,* 151 F.3d 180, 184–85 (4th Cir.1998), the Fourth Circuit concluding that a magazine article's statement that optimistic projections about a company's stock were based on "hype and hope" represented the kind of irreverent and indefinite language that indicated that the writer was not stating actual facts. Similarly, *Keohane v. Stewart,* 882 P.2d 1293, 1300–01 (Colo.1994) (en banc), the Colorado Supreme Court concluded that letters to the editor accusing a trial judge of conspiring to "let off" the defendant could not be reasonably interpreted as stating actual facts because the letters were replete with speculative and hyperbolic language and because the context in which they appeared indicated that the writer was stating his opinion.

Other statements have been found to be protected by the First Amendment because their underlying factual premises have been fully disclosed. *See, e.g., Biospherics,* 151 F.3d at 185–86 (concluding that a magazine article's statements that investors "would sour" on a particular company and that "the few independent analysts who follow the company think its stock is worth $2 on current business" were protected by the First Amendment because the article disclosed the basis for its conclusions); *Moldea v. New York Times,* 22 F.3d 310, 317 (D.C.Cir.1994) (en banc) (holding that a statement in a book review that the author had engaged in "sloppy journalism" was protected by the First Amendment because the statement was "supported by revealed premises that we cannot hold to be false in the context of a book review"); *Living Will Center,* 879 P.2d at 11–12 (Colo.1994) (en banc) (concluding that a news broadcast that referred to the marketing of a living will package as a "scam" was protected expression of opinion because the facts on which the broadcaster based his assessment were disclosed in the broadcast and there was no hint that the assessment was based on undisclosed information).

Finally, in other instances, courts have concluded that, due to the subject matter involved, there is simply no objective evidence that could prove that an allegedly defamatory statement was false. *See, e.g, Living Will Center,* 879 P.2d at 13–14 (concluding that the statement that a product was not worth the price was not verifiable because "[t]he worth of a given service or product is an inherently subjective measure which turns on myriad considerations and necessarily subjective economic, aesthetic, and personal judgments"); *James v. San Jose Mercury News, Inc.,* 17 Cal.App.4th 1, 20 Cal.Rptr.2d 890, 898 (1993) (concluding that the statement "when the legal community turns on kids, it doubles their trauma" was protected under *Milkovich* because it was not verifiable and asking, rhetorically, "When does 'the legal community' 'turn on' 'kids'? What is 'trauma' in this context, and how can its increments be measured?").

In contrast to these decisions, courts have also applied *Milkovich* to conclude that certain statements, even though couched as expressions of opinion, are provably false and therefore are not protected from defamation claims by the First Amendment. For example, the Ninth Circuit has concluded that a statement in a broadcast that a product "didn't work" could be reasonably interpreted to refer to the performance of specific functions, a matter that could be assessed by evaluating objective evidence. *Unelko Corp. v. Rooney,* 912 F.2d 1049, 1053–55 (9th Cir.1990). . . .

We begin by examining the allegedly false statements that the School District maintains were implied by the Moody's article. The first of these statements—that the School District was not credit-worthy—is no more specific than Moody's statement about the refunding bonds' "negative outlook." Like the statement of a product's value, a statement regarding the creditworthiness of a bond issuer could well depend on a myriad of factors, many of them not provably true or false. . . . We therefore conclude that, in light of its failure to identify a more specific statement, the School District has failed to demonstrate that Moody's implied statement about its creditworthiness is provably false.

Because the alleged statement about a lack of creditworthiness is so vague, the School District's interpretation of Moody's article would be plausible only if it could establish that the article implied some other specific (but as yet unidentified) false assertions about the School District's financial condition. Although the School District maintains that the case should be allowed to proceed because it may be able to identify such statements, the article's use of the phrase "ongoing financial pressures" undermines that argument. The range of factors that could cause "ongoing financial pressures" is vast, ranging from constitutional and statutory changes, court decisions, property values, inflation, and labor costs to many other factors too numerous to catalogue. In order for the School District to prove that Moody's article implied an assertion about the factors causing the District's "ongoing financial pressures," it would first need to identify one or several of these many possible factors. It would then need to demonstrate that a reasonable reader of Moody's Rating News could discern these assertions from the general references to the refunding bonds' "negative outlook" and the School District's "ongoing financial pressures." Finally, the School District would be required to prove that those specific assertions were false. The allegations of the School District's complaint do not permit such strained inferences.

The School District's additional allegation—that the Rating News article implied that it was based on current information—does not remedy the deficiencies of the First Amended Complaint. As Moody's has observed, the School District has not alleged that Moody's evaluation of the factors expressly identified as causing the bonds'' ''negative outlook'' (Amendment I and the underfunding of the School Finance Act) was based on outdated information. Accordingly, the School District's allegation amounts to a contention that Moody's evaluation was based on unspecified, outdated information about unnamed factors causing the bonds' negative outlook. Again, such speculative conclusions cannot be drawn by a reasonable reader from the text of Moody's article.

We emphasize that the phrases ''negative outlook'' ''ongoing financial pressures'' are not necessarily too indefinite to imply a false statement of fact. If coupled with specific factual assertions, such statements might not be immunized from defamation claims by the First Amendment. Moreover, the fact that Moody's article describes its evaluation as an opinion is not sufficient, standing alone, to establish that Moody's statements are protected. Moody's sells its opinions much as a title attorney would sell a title opinion. . . . If such an opinion were shown to have materially false components, the issuer should not be shielded from liability by raising the word ''opinion'' as a shibboleth. However, in this case, the School District's failure to identify a specific false statement reasonably implied from Moody's article, combined with the vagueness of the phrases ''negative outlook'' and ''ongoing financial pressures'' indicates that Moody's article constitutes a protected expression of opinion. . . .

Accordingly, the judgment of the district court in favor of Moody's and against the School District is AFFIRMED.

GROSS v. NEW YORK TIMES CO.

82 N.Y.2d 146, 623 N.E.2d 1163, 603 N.Y.S.2d 813 (1993)

TITONE, Judge.

This dispute has its origin in a series of investigative reports published by defendant New York Times between January of 1985 and February of 1986. The articles in question charged plaintiff, the former Chief Medical Examiner of the City of New York, with having mishandled several high profile cases and having used his authority to protect police officers and other city officials from suspicion after individuals in their custody had died under questionable circumstances. Defendants' articles spawned four separate criminal investigations into plaintiff's conduct, each of which terminated with findings that there was no evidence of professional misconduct or criminal wrongdoing by plaintiff. Plaintiff thereafter commenced the present action for libel. The issue at this early, preanswer stage of the litigation is whether plaintiff's pleadings sufficiently allege false, defamatory statements of *fact* rather than mere nonactionable statements of *opinion*. . . .

Plaintiff's 59-page complaint cites essentially eight "false and defamatory" articles as the basis for his libel action. The opening two paragraphs [of the first article] asserted that, as the City's Chief Medical Examiner, plaintiff had "produced a series of misleading or inaccurate autopsy reports on people who died in custody of the police, according to colleagues in the Medical Examiner's office and pathologists elsewhere." Further, according to the article, plaintiff had "instituted a policy of special handling for police-custody cases," had "performed the autopsies himself" in many such cases and "[i]n others, documents show[,] he intervened to alter the findings of other pathologists."

The article, which also discussed the purported disarray in the Medical Examiner's office, reported on interviews conducted with several pathologists, who both described and characterized plaintiff's specific actions in relation to cases handled by the Medical Examiner's office. One pathologist who had worked with plaintiff asserted for example, that, in the case of the man who had allegedly been beaten by the police, plaintiff had changed the autopsy findings to state that death had resulted from a procedure performed by doctors after the incident rather than from a fractured skull. The pathologist was then quoted as asserting: "What Gross has done is bend over backwards to help the police" and "[i]t's weaseling." Another pathologist, who had not worked with plaintiff but who had been asked to review some of the disputed autopsy findings, was quoted as saying: "If he did these cases honestly, Dr. Gross is unbelievably incompetent"; "[i]f he has done this deliberately—and I believe he has—he may well be looking for a way out for the police". . . . The over-all thrust of the series was that plaintiff had issued false or misleading reports about deaths occurring within his jurisdiction in order to protect the police and that his conduct ranged from "highly suspicious" . . . to "possibly illegal". . . .

The Appellate Division affirmed the trial court's determination, stressing that the "articles complained of report accusatory opinions together with a recitation of the facts upon which they are based" and that "[e]specially when attributed to a source, the average reader will recognize that criticisms, allegations and accusations are not statements of fact but rather expressions of opinion". . . . We now reverse and hold that the complaint should have been sustained, since, in addition to the expressed opinions and conclusions, the articles contain defamatory assertions that a reasonable reader would understand to be advanced as statements of fact. . . .

While the Supreme Court has rejected the notion that there is a special categorical privilege for expressions of opinion as opposed to assertions of fact, it has recognized that "a statement of opinion relating to matters of public concern which does not contain a provably false factual connotation will receive full constitutional protection" [Citing *Milkovich*.] Further, this Court has adopted a similar view under our own State Constitution and has embraced a test for determining what constitutes a nonactionable statement of opinion that is more flexible and is decidedly more protective of "the cherished constitutional guarantee of free speech.

The dispositive inquiry, under either Federal or New York law, is "whether a reasonable [reader] could have concluded that [the articles were] conveying facts about the plaintiff." In our State the inquiry, which must be made by the court, entails an examination of the challenged statements with a view toward (1) whether the specific language in issue has a precise meaning which is readily understood; (2) whether the statements are capable of being proven true or false; and (3) whether either the full context of the communication in which the statement appears or the broader social context and surrounding circumstances are such as to "signal . . . readers or listeners that what is being read or heard is likely to be opinion, not fact."

This is not to suggest that the wisdom to be derived from the formerly utilized common-law analysis has been completely discarded. To the contrary, although the terminology may have fallen out of favor, the seasoned common-law categories for actionable and nonactionable reportage have been invoked to inform our modern constitutional analysis.

Thus, in determining whether a particular communication is actionable, we continue to recognize and utilize the important distinction between a statement of opinion that implies a basis in facts which are not disclosed to the reader or listener and a statement of opinion that is accompanied by a recitation of the facts on which it is based or one that does not imply the existence of undisclosed underlying facts [citing *Ollman v. Evans* and other authorities]. The former are actionable not because they convey "false opinions" but rather because a reasonable listener or reader would infer that "the speaker [or writer] knows certain facts, unknown to [the] audience, which support [the] opinion and are detrimental to the person [toward] whom [the communication is directed]." In contrast, the latter are not actionable because, as was noted by the dissenting opinion [in *Milkovich*], a proffered hypothesis that is offered after a full recitation of the facts on which it is based is readily understood by the audience as conjecture.

Applying these principles to plaintiff's cause is not a simple task because plaintiff's pleadings cite the whole series of articles, each in its entirety, as the basis for plaintiff's defamation claim. . . .

We conclude, however, that the courts below erred in dismissing the complaint, since the articles it cited contain many assertions of objective fact that, if proven false, could form the predicate for a maintainable libel action. Additionally, although the articles contain many assertions that would be understood by the reasonable reader as mere hypotheses premised on stated facts, there are also actionable charges made in the articles—such as the charges that plaintiff engaged in cover-ups, directed the creation of "misleading" autopsy reports and was guilty of "possibly illegal'' conduct—that, although couched in the language of hypothesis or conclusion, actually would be understood by the reasonable reader as assertions of fact.

Contrary to the Appellate Division's conclusion, these assertions are not too vague to constitute concrete accusations of criminality. ...

In *Silsdorf v. Levine,* 59 N.Y.2d 8, 16, 462 N.Y.S.2d 822, 449 N.E.2d 716, we merely held that an accusation of criminality that, read in context, is set forth as a fact is not transformed into a nonactionable expression of opinion merely because it is couched ''in the form of [an] opinion.'' To illustrate, if the statement ''John is a thief'' is actionable when considered in its applicable context, the statement ''*I believe* John is a thief'' would be equally actionable when placed in precisely the same context. By the same token, however, the assertion that ''John is a thief'' could well be treated as an expression of opinion or rhetorical hyperbole where it is accompanied by other statements, such as ''John stole my heart,'' that, taken in context, convey to the reasonable reader that something other than an objective fact is being asserted.

Similarly, even when uttered or published in a more serious tone, accusations of criminality could be regarded as mere hypothesis and therefore not actionable if the facts on which they are based are fully and accurately set forth and it is clear to the reasonable reader or listener that the accusation is merely a personal surmise built upon those facts. ...

In this case, the assertion that plaintiff engaged in ''corrupt'' conduct in his capacity as Chief Medical Examiner cannot be treated as a mere rhetorical flourish or the speculative accusation of an angry but ill-informed citizen made during the course of a heated debate. Rather, the accusation was made in the course of a lengthy, copiously documented newspaper series that was written only after what purported to be a thorough investigation. Having been offered as a special feature series rather than as coverage of a current news story, the disputed articles were calculated to give the impression they were ''the product of some deliberation, not of the heat of [the] moment.'' Moreover, since the articles appeared in the news section rather than the editorial or ''op-ed'' sections, the common expectations that apply to those more opinionated journalistic endeavors were inapplicable here. Thus, the circumstances under which these accusations were published ''encourag[ed] the reasonable reader to be less skeptical and more willing to conclude that [they] stat[ed] or impl[ied] facts''. ...

Accordingly, the order of the Appellate Division, insofar as appealed from, should be reversed, with costs, and the motion of the Times defendants to dismiss causes of action 1 through 5 and 8 through 13 of the complaint denied.

RODRIGUEZ V. PANAYIOTOU, 314 F.3d 979 (9th Cir. 2002). The plaintiff is a police officer. He alleged that in checking on complaints of ''lewd acts'' in the men's restroom in Will Rogers Park, Beverly Hills, California, he entered a stall in the restroom and when he exited he saw the defendant "fully exposed and engaging in a lewd act." The plaintiff arrested and charged the defendant. The defendant is a famous singer under a different name, George Michael. "Michael released a new song and music video entitled *Outside,* which made vague references to and parodied the incident. A few months later, in a series of magazine and television interviews to promote his new album, Michael responded to questions regarding the arrest with allegations that Rodriguez had entrapped him. Michael claimed that Rodriguez had induced him to engage in the lewd act for which he was arrested by first exposing himself to and masturbating in front of him." Some of his language was "colorful." "There's a man standing there, six feet two, great-looking, and waiving [sic] his dick about and staring at me." The plaintiff sued, labeling his claim as "slander." The trial court dismissed the claim, "holding that Michael's statements were non-actionable, non-defamatory expressions of opinion." *Held,* over a dissent, reversed and remanded. "To determine whether an alleged defamatory statement implies a factual assertion, we examine the 'totality of the circumstances' in which the statement was made. We look at the statement both 'in its broad context,' considering 'the general tenor of the entire work, the subject of the statements, the setting, and the format of the work,' and in its 'specific context,' noting the 'content of the statements,' the 'extent of figurative or hyperbolic language used,' and 'the reasonable expectations of the audience in that particular situation.' In applying this test, the 'court must place itself in the position of the ... reader, and determine the sense of meaning of the statement according to its natural and popular construction and the 'natural and probable effect [it would have] upon the mind of the average reader.' Michael's comments to the media, which imply the belief that he had been entrapped by Rodriguez, constitute his interpretation of the law. 'Absent a clear and unambiguous ruling from a court or agency of competent jurisdiction, statements by laypersons that purport to interpret the meaning of a statute ... are opinion statements, and not statements of fact.' " As to the other statements, however, "Michael's statements went well beyond generalized accusations, subjective comments, or other 'classic rhetorical hyperbole. Instead, Michael's statements asserted the precise factual nature of his accusation, and charged Rodriguez with the specific and objectively verifiable acts of genital exposure and masturbation. These are provably false factual assertions of what Rodriguez was accused of having committed. Similarly, the colorful and humorous language Michael used to speak about the incident did not 'negate the impression that [Michael] was seriously maintaining [that Rodriguez] committed [the lewd act].' "

MATHIS v. CANNON, 276 Ga. 16, 573 S.E.2d 376 (2002). Defendant posted messages about Cannon on a web site. Two of the messages read: (1) "**cannon a crook___?** by: *duelly41* explain to us why us got fired from the calton company please ___? want hear your side of the story cannon!!!!!!!!" (2) "**cannon a crook** by: *duelly 41* hey cannon why u got fired from calton company___? why does cannon and lt governor mark taylor think that crisp county needs to be dumping ground of the south___ u be busted man crawl under a rock and hide cannon and poole!!! if u deal with cannon u a crook too!!!!!!! so stay out of crisp county and we thank u for it." *Held*, plaintiff was not entitled to summary judgment. "[A]ny person reading the postings on the message board—written entirely in lower case replete with question marks, exclamation points, misspellings, abbreviations, and dashes—could not reasonably interpret the incoherent messages as stating actual facts about Cannon, but would interpret them as the late night rhetorical outbursts of an angry and frustrated person opposed to the company's hauling of other people's garbage into the county. [Citing Milkovich.]"

Chapter 5

EXTENDING SPEECH PROTECTIONS AND REFORMING DEFAMATION

§ 1. COMMON LAW PRIVILEGE AND THE CONSTITUTIONAL RULES

1. **Re-defining the malice that destroys a common law privilege.** Some common law privileges are lost (or never established) merely because the defendant has reported facts inaccurately or has failed to report facts at all. The privilege to report public documents is in the first category; fair comment is in the second. Other common law privileges are lost because the defendant harbors evil motives, bad thoughts, hatred, ill-will, spite, or improper purposes. The common interest privilege is an example. Should the common law privileges be adjusted to integrate them better with either *Times-Sullivan* or *Gertz*? A number of courts now either define the common law malice needed to defeat a privilege as knowing or reckless falsehood rather than spite, ill-will, or improper purpose, e.g., *Eckman v. Cooper Tire & Rubber Co.,* 893 So.2d 1049, 1053 (Miss. 2005); or at least say that knowing or reckless falsehood is sufficient proof of common law malice. E.g., *Rockwood Bank v. Gaia,* 170 F.3d 833 (8th Cir. 1999). Are there cases in which courts could drop the whole privilege analysis and simply require the plaintiff to prove the appropriate fault in the first place?

2. **The plaintiff proves *Times-Sullivan* fault—effect on common law privileges.** The plaintiff proves *Times-Sullivan* knowing falsehood. Knowing falsehood assuredly qualified to destroy the privilege at common law, so proof of knowing falsehood would be counted as within the concept of common law malice and the privilege would be destroyed before it arises if the plaintiff has made *Times-Sullivan* proof. In this case courts could dispense with talk of common law privilege.

3. **The plaintiff proves Gertz' "some fault"—effect on common law privileges.** Suppose the plaintiff is a private person who is defamed on a matter of public concern, like Mr. Gertz. The Fraternal Order of Beagles publishes a newsletter for its membership. In one

edition it publishes an editorial by DuBois proposing to oust member Perez, saying he was guilty of several specifically named unpatriotic crimes in time of war. In fact, Perez did not commit any of the acts charged and he sued the defendant for libel. The defendant pleaded the common interest privilege. Perez can prove "some fault"—sufficient to meet the *Gertz* Constitutional requirement, but he cannot prove either *Times-Sullivan* knowing or reckless falsehood or common law malice in the sense of ill-will. Negligence or "some fault" was not usually enough to destroy privileges. In light of the Constitutional decisions consider whether courts should

(A) Retain the common law privilege as is and hold it is lost when the defendant is guilty of either knowing or reckless falsehood or common law malice such as spite or ill will.

(B) Simplify the law by consolidating the common law privilege with *Gertz* rules to hold the privilege is lost by proof of whatever fault the state requires in *Gertz*-type cases.

(C) Simplify the law by consolidating the common law privilege with *Times-Sullivan* rules to hold that the privilege is lost *only* by proof of knowing or reckless falsehood.

4. **The fair report privilege and the constitutional requirements.** The *Daily World* publishes a purported summary of a complaint filed by Telemann against Phelen, a private citizen, saying Telemann charged Phelen with offering bribes to a public officer. Phelen sues the *Daily World* for defamation on the ground that it is false and defamatory to say he offered bribes and on the further ground that the Telemann complaint should not be understood as saying bribes were offered. This might fall into the *Gertz* category in the sense that the plaintiff seems to be a private person but the issue is one of public concern. If we focus on that, we come up with the idea that the plaintiff could establish liability (as far as the Constitution is concerned) by proving "some fault." However, the common law privilege in fair report cases is broader—it protects the publication regardless of fault if it is fair and accurate. This case is thus quite different from cases like in the ¶ 3, where both Constitutional and common law are destroyed by some species of fault regarding the truth or falsity of the statement's sting. The newer Constitutional rules, then, do not seem to suggest possible changes in the fair report privilege.

§ 2. ARE NEW PROTECTIONS STILL DEVELOPING?

(a) Neutral Reporting

EDWARDS v. NATIONAL AUDUBON SOCIETY, INC.

556 F.2d 113 (2d Cir. 1977)

IRVING R. KAUFMAN, Chief Judge. . . .

The DDT debate. The publication fifteen years ago of Rachel Carson's Silent Spring set off a furious controversy that, even today, continues to rage around the insecticide DDT. Naturalists and environmentalist groups like the National Audubon Society have vigorously opposed DDT because, in their view, use of the chemical endangers bird life. Proponents of the pesticide deny this charge and forcefully urge that, without DDT, millions of human beings will die of insect-carried diseases and starvation caused by the destruction of crops by insect pests.

As might be expected when such fundamental questions of value enter the debate, at times the DDT controversy has exceeded the limits of temperance and good manners. Naturalists have insinuated that many proponents of DDT are unduly influenced by the selfish interests of the pesticide industry. On the other hand, such an outstanding advocate of DDT as appellee Dr. J. Gordon Edwards, has characterized a ban on export of the insecticide, supported by the Audubon Society, as "deliberately genocidal." Accusations of scientific bad faith have unfortunately become almost commonplace on both sides.

Arbib's "Foreword" to American Birds. The scientists who advocate continued use of DDT respond to charges that the chemical destroys bird life by citing the annual Audubon Society Christmas Bird Count, which shows a steady increase in bird sightings despite the growing employment of pesticides in the last thirty years. The Audubon Society believes this is an invalid use of its statistics because there are many more bird counters now and because bird watchers have grown more skillful in recent years with better access to observation areas. This dispute over the interpretation of the Society's statistics lies at the heart of the controversy over DDT's threat to bird life.

By 1972 the DDT controversy was raging at peak intensity, and the Audubon Society was acutely alarmed at what it considered the persistent misuse of its Bird Count data. Accordingly, Robert S. Arbib, Jr., a highly respected amateur ornithologist and editor of the Society's publication American Birds, determined to preface his report of the 1971 Christmas Count with a warning against distortion of the results. His foreword to the April, 1972, issue of American Birds, contained the following comment on the Count's significance:

> We are well aware that segments of the pesticide industry and certain paid "scientist-spokesmen" are citing Christmas Bird Count totals ... as proving that the bird life of North America is thriving, and that many species are actually increasing despite the widespread and condemned use of DDT and other non-degradable hydrocarbon pesticides. This, quite obviously, is false and misleading, a distortion of the facts for the most self-serving of reasons. The truth is that many species high on the food chain, such as most bird-eating raptors and fisheaters, are suffering serious declines in numbers as a direct result of pesticide contamination; there is now abundant evidence to prove this. ... With increased local coverage by the press of Christmas Bird Count activities, it is important that Count spokesmen reiterate the simple and truthful fact that what we are seeing is result of not more birds, but more birders. Any time you hear a "scientist" say the opposite, you are in the presence of someone who is being paid to lie, or is parroting something he knows little about. ...

The New York Times Article. Arbib's general accusations came to the attention of New York Times nature reporter John Devlin in late July, 1972. Devlin immediately realized that the Audubon Society's charges were a newsworthy development in the already acrimonious DDT debate, and he accordingly telephoned Arbib to obtain the names of those the Society considered "paid liars". Arbib was initially reluctant to identify any individuals as the people referred to in his article. But, as a result of Devlin's persistent urging that many eminent persons associated with the pesticide industry might be hurt unnecessarily by the Society's indiscriminate attack, Arbib eventually promised to furnish the names of specific individuals whom he felt were justly subject to the Society's charges.

Arbib, of course, did not know of anyone in particular whom he could with assurance call a "paid liar." [He obtained names of "those who had most persistently misused the Bird Count data" from a colleague, Clement. Arbib said he believed it would be all right to give the names to Mr. Devlin as long as we qualified this by saying, "We don't have any knowledge of anyone being paid liars, and all we want to say is that they have been consistent misinterpreters of the information in American Birds."]

When Devlin telephoned again for the names, Arbib was prepared. ... But, Devlin and Arbib sharply disagreed at trial regarding the ensuing conversation. Arbib insisted that he [said in essence that the named scientists were] not necessarily "paid liars". Devlin flatly denied that Arbib so cautioned him. He testified that Arbib made it clear that the scientists whose names were furnished to the Times were the persons referred to in Arbib's "Foreword" to American Birds. The list included the names of the [plaintiffs.] All of the accused were eminent scientists, though none were ornithologists.

Upon receiving these names from Arbib, Devlin attempted to secure comments from each of the five accused. He succeeded in reaching three. ... All of these scientists categorically denied the charges, and Dr. Spencer even referred to them as "almost libelous". [Two scientists] sent Devlin voluminous supporting materials setting forth their side of the DDT debate. None of this material, however, responded directly to the Audubon Society's criticism of the use of Bird Count data by these scholars; it dealt almost entirely with the general merits of the pesticide controversy.

Having thus in good faith elicited both sides of the story to the best of his ability, Devlin wrote the article which is the sole ground for the libel judgment against the Times and the principal basis for the judgment against Clement. Devlin's story was published in the Times on August 14, 1972.

Pesticide Spokesmen Accused Of 'Lying' on Higher Bird Count

By JOHN DEVLIN

> Segments of the pesticide industry and certain "scientist-spokesmen," are accused in the current issue of American Birds of "lying" by saying that bird life in America is thriving despite the use of DDT. [The article continued, giving accurate detail of the Arbib's statements, the controversy, and the foreword, naming the plaintiffs who were named by Arbib and accurately quoting their responses. Several filed this action for defamation.]

[T]he jury was instructed that the Times could be found guilty of actual malice if Devlin had serious doubts about the truth of the statement that the appellees were paid liars, even if he did not have any doubt that he was reporting Arbib's allegations faithfully. The jury returned a verdict against both the Times and Clement, but exonerated Arbib. It awarded $20,000 damages to Dr. Jukes and Dr. White–Stevens, respectively, and $21,000 to Dr. Edwards.

... Implicit in the jury's verdict against Clement is the finding, which we must accept, that the Times accurately reported the five scientists whose names were furnished by Arbib were the "paid liars" referred to in the American Birds Foreword. We believe that a libel judgment against the Times, in the face of this finding of fact, is constitutionally impermissible.

At stake in this case is a fundamental principle. Succinctly stated, when a responsible, prominent organization like the National Audubon Society makes serious charges against a public figure, the First Amendment protects the accurate and disinterested reporting of those charges, regardless of the reporter's private views regarding their validity. See Time, Inc. v. Pape, 401 U.S. 279, 91 S.Ct. 633, 28 L.Ed.2d 45 (1971). What is newsworthy about such accusations is that they were made. We do not believe that the press may be required under the First Amendment to suppress newsworthy statements merely because it has serious doubts regarding their truth. Nor must the press take up cudgels against dubious charges in order to publish them without fear of liability for defamation. The public interest in being fully informed about controversies that often rage around sensitive issues demands that the press be afforded the freedom to report such charges without assuming responsibility for them.

The contours of the press's right of neutral reportage are, of course, defined by the principle that gives life to it. Literal accuracy is not a prerequisite: if we are to enjoy the blessings of a robust and unintimidated press, we must provide immunity from defamation suits where the journalist believes, reasonably and in good faith, that his report accurately conveys the charges made. Time, Inc. v. Pape. It is equally clear, however, that a publisher who in fact espouses or concurs in the charges made by others, or who deliberately distorts these statements to launch a personal attack of his own on a public figure, cannot rely on a privilege of neutral reportage. In such instances he assumes responsibility for the underlying accusations.

It is clear here, that Devlin reported Audubon's charges fairly and accurately. He did not in any way espouse the Society's accusations: indeed, Devlin published the maligned scientists' outraged reactions in the same article that contained the Society's attack. The Times article, in short, was the exemplar of fair and dispassionate reporting of an unfortunate but newsworthy contretemps. Accordingly, we hold that it was privileged under the First Amendment.

Even absent the special protection afforded to neutral reportage, see Time, Inc. v. Pape, the evidence adduced at trial was manifestly insufficient to demonstrate "actual malice" on the part of the Times. It is uncontested that Devlin was unaware of the baselessness of the Audubon Society's dramatic allegations. Nor was there a shred of evidence from which the jury might have found that Devlin entertained serious doubts concerning the truth of Arbib's charge that the appellees were "paid liars."

It is conceded that the Times might have published the Audubon Society's accusations without fear of liability had Devlin but refrained from eliciting the views of the Society's victims. ...

We do not believe ... that the scientists' responses to Devlin's inquiries could be found sufficient to warn Devlin of the probable falsity of the Society's charges. Surely liability under the "clear and convincing proof" standard of New York Times v. Sullivan cannot be predicated on mere denials, however vehement; such denials are so commonplace in the world of polemical charge and countercharge that, in themselves, they hardly alert the conscientious reporter to the likelihood of error. ...

KHAWAR V. GLOBE INTERNATIONAL, INC., 19 Cal.4th 254, 965 P.2d 696, 79 Cal.Rptr.2d 178 (1998). A book published by Morrow argued that the plaintiff, not Sirhan Sirhan, assassinated Robert Kennedy. A tabloid,

Globe, published a summary of the book's claims. The plaintiff sued Globe. Globe sought to defend on the neutral reportage privilege. *Held*, the privilege does not apply. The plaintiff took no part in any controversy and did not thrust himself into public affairs; he was merely a private individual nearby when Kennedy was shot. The neutral reportage principle does not apply to reports of accusations against private figures. If it did apply, it would "emasculate the Gertz distinction between private and public figure plaintiffs." Furthermore, the fact that the accuser is a public figure is not enough. Although the public is entitled to know what accusations public figures make, because their accusations reflect the kinds of persons they are, the focus must be upon the status of the plaintiff if the Gertz distinctions are to be maintained.

---

5. **Repeaters rule.** The defendant needed to invoke the neutral reportage privilege in *Edwards* because truth of the fact that an accusation was made is no defense under the repeaters rule, Chapter 1, ¶ 13.

NORTON V. GLENN, 860 A.2d 48 (Pa. 2004). Media defendants reported defamatory statements made by Glenn, a member of the Parkersburg Borough Council, about another Council member, Norton, and the Mayor, Wolfe that included a statement that some were "queers and child molesters." Although some statements were made in the council chamber, the comments at issue were made outside the chamber. The trial judge concluded that the media defendants were protected by the neutral reportage rule, which made actual malice irrelevant, and therefore precluded evidence that the media defendants had published with actual malice. The Superior Court reversed. In the Supreme Court of Pennsylvania, *held,* the Superior Court is affirmed. The United States Constitution does not require the neutral reportage privilege. "The *Edwards* court's reliance on [*Time, Inc. v. Pape*] was ill-placed. In *Time,* the media defendant repeated statements regarding a public official that had been made in a civil rights report. The Court did not absolve the media defendant of liability on the basis that the defendant acted merely as a neutral conduit for statements of a third party; rather, the Court found that the defendant escaped liability because the public official-plaintiff could not establish that the defendant had acted with actual malice. Thus, *Time* did not explicitly or even impliedly adopt a privilege whereby the press could with impunity republish statements made by public figures or officials, escaping liability even where it could be shown that the press published these statements with actual malice. Indeed, *Time* applied the actual malice standard to the matter before it."

6. ***Time, Inc. v. Pape.*** *Time v. Pape,* 401 U.S. 279, 91 S.Ct. 633, 28 L.Ed.2d 45 (1971), as the *Norton* court said, turned on the absence of evidence that the defendant published the defamation with "actual malice." The case arose when Time Magazine reported on an official

document of the United States Civil Rights Commission. The Commission's document was perhaps ambiguous, but one reading was that the plaintiff had been guilty of serious police misconduct. That was what Time reported the document as saying. If a fair reading of the official document charged the plaintiff with police misconduct, would the common law fair report privilege protect the publisher? Would the same fair report privilege protect the publisher in *Edwards* and *Norton*?

7. **The status of *Edwards*.** Although *Edwards* has been cited many times, only a few courts, few of them courts of last resort, have actually adopted the privilege. A few others have rejected it. Most courts have not decided the issue and a few have purposefully avoided it by deciding on other grounds. See DOBBS ON TORTS § 415 (2000).

8. **Creeping towards an *Edwards* rule?** Some decisions that do not adopt *Edwards* nevertheless provide protection "by expanding the fair report privilege to include report of things like a witness' repetition for television cameras of testimony he gave in court, a governor's press conference, a private meeting, and even to unofficial remarks of a congressman. Such decisions come increasingly close to a newsworthiness privilege...." DOBBS, supra, ¶ 7.

Some other decisions, without mentioning *Edwards* or neutral reportage, make broad statements that might be read as supporting an *Edwards* rule of neutral reportage even for private figures. In *Green v. CBS Inc.,* 286 F.3d 281 (5th Cir. 2002), the defendant broadcast a television show reporting on the effects of winning a lottery. The show focused on the plaintiff's former husband, but quoted allegations of others that the plaintiff fabricated charges against the former husband to get some of the lottery money. The court dismissed this claim on the ground that the statements "are non-actionable because they merely report allegations." Since the plaintiff was a private person, that language goes beyond even the *Edwards* principle and appears to be at odds with the common law liability of repeaters.

9. **Reliance on wire service reports.** In addition to expanded fair comment privilege, there is the fact that a publisher might be reasonable in relying upon a source. A newspaper's publication of a wire service report, or a fair paraphrase of it, is not likely to be negligent, much less a knowing or reckless falsehood. Thus both public figure plaintiffs and *Gertz* plaintiffs would fail in such a case because the minimum level of fault is not proved. See *Appleby v. Daily Hampshire Gazette,* 395 Mass. 32, 478 N.E.2d 721 (1985). Sometimes this is referred to as "the wire service defense," but as you can see, it is not an affirmative defense or privilege but merely an application of the fault requirement in *Times-Sullivan* and *Gertz* cases. Viewed in this light, the repeater-publisher's reliance on any apparently reliable source, wire-service or not, would negate the fault element. In *Karaduman v. Newsday, Inc.,* 51 N.Y.2d 531, 435 N.Y.S.2d 556, 416 N.E.2d 557 (1980), the defendant published a book based on previously published newspaper pieces. Although the court referred to a "privilege," its actual holding

was that the plaintiff had the burden of proving New York's fault requirement ("gross irresponsibility"). Since the plaintiff had not shown why the book publisher should have questioned the accuracy of the newspaper articles, summary judgment for the book publisher was appropriate. Is this essentially the same as the neutral reportage privilege or something different?

10. **Status of the parties under an *Edwards* rule.** *Edwards* limits the protection (a) to public figure plaintiffs and (b) to cases in which the publisher reports accusations of "a responsible, prominent organization like the National Audubon Society." Is either limitation sustainable if you adopt the thrust of *Edwards*? What if a newspaper reports accusations of a group of homeless people that the CIA encouraged them to distribute drugs?

11. **Controversy and investigative reporting.** A few courts have focused not only on the responsible status of the accuser as a condition for protection under the *Edwards* rule, but have also insisted that there must be an existing controversy to report and that the protection cannot apply if the accusation is elicited by the reporter. The idea is that *Edwards* was not meant to cover investigative reporting. See *Levin v. McPhee*, 119 F.3d 189 (2d Cir. 1997).

(b) Secondary Publication and Carriers

12. **General rule.** Recall the ground rules—(a) that an original publisher is liable for intended or foreseeable republication by others; and, (b) that in the absence of a privilege, a repeater is liable for his repetition (Chapter 1, ¶ ¶ 12 & 13). Contemporary discussions now often use a three-fold classification of those who make information available: (1) publishers or primary publishers (like newspapers); (2) secondary publishers or distributors or disseminators (like newsstands and libraries); and (3) common carriers, conduits, or transmitters (like the telephone company). Publishers, as we know, are subject to liability in the absence of a privilege, even if they are repeating what someone else said. Secondary publishers, however, are not liable unless they know of the defamatory content. See RESTATEMENT §§ 578, 581 (repeater's liability, with exemption for innocent secondary publisher). Common carriers of information may not be liable even if they know of the defamatory content. See *Anderson v. New York Telephone Co.,* 35 N.Y.2d 746, 320 N.E.2d 647, 361 N.Y.S.2d 913 (1974) (opinion of Gabrielli, J.) (telephone company equipment used to play recorded defamatory messages to anyone who dialed the numbers, company was not a publisher merely because it failed to terminate lease of equipment after hearing the defamatory message).

13. **Constitutionalizing the common law rules?** Although the library that provides defamatory books to its readers is protected so long as it knows nothing of the defamatory content, the implication is that it might be liable as a repeater if it circulates books after knowing of that content. In the light of the constitutional developments we have seen,

should all distributors be treated like common carriers, merely as conduits with no responsibility for content?

14. **Internet publishers.** With the advent of computer bulletin boards and Internet services, new versions of the conduit/secondary publisher problem arise. A federal statute now provides: "No provider or user of an interactive computer service shall be treated as the publisher or speaker of any information provided by another information content provider." 47 U.S.C.A. § 230(c)(1) (dubbed the Communications Decency Act or CDA). Content providers—those who actually create or develop the defamatory material, are not immunized. That will be no solace to plaintiffs who are defamed by anonymous postings on the defendant's website. On the other hand, will the statute help defendants operating interactive web sites if, given the nature of the internet, foreign countries without similar protections can acquire personal jurisdiction over internet defendants?

(c) Implications and Inferences—A Final Take on "Truth", Opinion, and Extrinsic Facts

WHITE v. FRATERNAL ORDER OF POLICE

909 F.2d 512 (D.C. Cir. 1990)

MIKVA, Circuit Judge.

Robert C. White appeals a grant of summary judgment in favor of the defendants. White, a Captain in the Washington, D.C. Metropolitan Police Department ("MPD") sued the appellees, the Fraternal Order of Police ("FOP"), The Washington Post Company ("the Post"), and National Broadcasting Company, Inc. ("NBC") for invasion of privacy and defamation. . . .

In April 1985, then-Lieutenant White was nominated for promotion to Captain in the MPD and required to pass a physical exam, including a urine test for drugs. White submitted a urine sample to the Police and Fire Department Clinic. There, the sample was subjected to an Enzyme Multiple Immunoassay Test ("EMIT test"), which showed a positive result for marijuana. The standard operating procedure when an EMIT test showed a positive result was to forward the urine sample to the CompuChem laboratory in North Carolina for confirmation of the initial result. Instead, White was notified of the positive result and brought back to the Clinic to submit a second sample.

The next day, White's original and second urine samples were hand-carried by a member of the MPD to the CompuChem lab in North Carolina. Such hand-delivery by a member of the MPD was also a departure from normal procedures as was the testing of the second sample by CompuChem without first subjecting it to an EMIT test at the Clinic. The CompuChem lab found both samples to be drug-free. White was promoted to Captain, and later became head of the Department's narcotics squad.

[Receiving information about these events from two employees of the Department's Clinic, the FOP reported the information to the U.S. Attorney and to Mayor Barry.]

After describing the irregular procedures employed for White's drug tests, the letters stated that Lieutenant Noyes, the Administrative Lieutenant at the Clinic, said to Richardson: "I am giving you a direct order not to tell anyone about what went on." The letters also reported that Lieutenant Noyes accompanied White to the men's room when he gave his second urine sample, that the urine samples were removed from the clinic and returned later the same day by an officer who normally would not handle urine samples, and that the top lock on the laboratory door was then left unsecured overnight before the samples were sent to CompuChem.

The letters stated that the EMIT test on the first urine sample indicated a high level of cannabinoids that "should easily have been confirmed" by the CompuChem lab, and that it was "highly unusual" for such a result not to be confirmed. The letters concluded [that high ranking officials were involved in the incident with Captain White and suggested "that drug testing procedures have been subverted to protect one and possibly more MPD officials from the results of positive urinalysis tests. ..." The letter referred specifically to possible violation of bribery and tampering with evidence statutes. An internal investigation was conducted by Cox and a committee. As a result, the Chief reprimanded several high level officers, not including White.]

On August 25, 1987 and on eight occasions thereafter, the Post published articles concerning the FOP's allegations and the Cox Committee's investigation of those allegations. ...

On September 28, 1987, NBC's WRC-TV (Channel 4) broadcasted a report which mentioned White by name and displayed his photograph. Pat Collins delivered the report on location in front of the Police and Fire Clinic. Using dramatic intonation, Collins presented an account of the questionable handling of White's drug tests. Collins' facts were essentially the same as those presented in the FOP letters, but he did not attribute the facts to the letters or the Cox Committee investigation. Upon completion of the report, the broadcast cut to anchorman Jim Vance in the studio who offered a terse conclusion: "A three-man task force assigned to investigate the matter is expected to issue a report soon." ...

[The District Court gave summary judgment for the defendants. On appeal, the court first considered and rejected certain invasion of privacy claims by White.]

In an action for defamation, the courts are charged with the responsibility of determining whether a challenged statement is "capable of conveying a defamatory meaning." If, at the summary judgment stage, the court determines that the publication is capable of bearing a defamatory meaning, a jury must determine whether such meaning was attributed in fact. Under District of Columbia defamation law, which governs this diversity case, a court's power to find that a statement is not defamatory as a matter of law is limited: It is only when the court can say that the publication is not reasonably capable of any defamatory meaning and cannot be reasonably understood in any defamatory sense that it can rule as a matter of law, that it was not libelous. . . .

This case draws us into an area fraught with subtle complexities: the law of defamation by implication. A defamation by implication stems not from what is literally stated, but from what is implied. Adding to the complexity of this case is the fact that the reports at issue contain materially true accounts of what transpired. This court has recognized, however, that "District of Columbia law . . . clearly contemplates the possibility that a defamatory inference may be derived from a factually accurate news report."

White concedes that much of the information published in the FOP letters and provided in the news reports was true. The core theory underlying his defamation claims is that even concededly accurate information is capable of bearing a defamatory meaning. He asserts that the FOP letters were defamatory by implication and that the respective news reports effected defamation by the omission of certain crucial facts. Before evaluating these claims, we set out our understanding of the law of defamation by implication as applied to materially accurate news reports.

In entertaining claims of defamation by implication, courts must be vigilant not to allow an implied defamatory meaning to be manufactured from words not reasonably capable of sustaining such meaning. The difficulty lies in applying a standard that has both subjective and objective components:

> The usual test applied to determine the meaning of a defamatory utterance is whether it was reasonably understood by the recipient of the communication to have been intended in the defamatory sense. . . . When one uses language, one is held to the construction placed on it by those who hear or read, if that construction is a reasonable one.

[Harper, James, & Gray, The Law of Torts § 5.4, pp. 48–49 (1986)]. Under this standard, in order to prevail on a defamation claim, the language used must, as a matter of law, be reasonably capable of a defamatory interpretation and a jury must find that the language was actually understood by the recipient in that sense. It is no defense that the defendant did not actually intend to convey the defamatory meaning, so long as the defamatory interpretation is a reasonable one. At bottom, "[t]he meaning of a communication is that which the recipient correctly, or mistakenly but reasonably, understands that it was intended to express." Restatement (Second) of Torts § 563 (1977).

Application of this general standard becomes even more difficult where the reported facts are materially true and the alleged defamation is not stated explicitly. If the speaker or author has not uttered the alleged defamation explicitly, how is the court to discern whether it would be reasonable to understand the alleged defamatory meaning to have been intended? We believe it is possible to extract a standard from the cases addressing the defamatory character, *vel non*, of materially true reports.

In McBride [v. Merrell, Dow and Pharmaceuticals, Inc., 717 F.2d 1460, 1465 (D.C.Cir.1983)], we held that the true statement that Dr. McBride received $5,000 a day for his expert testimony might support the implied defamatory meaning that "the plaintiff's case was so weak they had to pay that much to get any expert to testify, and hence that Dr. McBride's testimony was for sale." That implied defamatory meaning arose not out of mere reporting of the $5,000 payment, but from the juxtaposition of that figure with the fees which the defendant normally paid such experts. The McBride court noted this direct comparison. The publication read: "These expert witnesses included William McBride ... who was paid $5,000 a day to testify in Orlando. In contrast, Richardson-Merrell pays witnesses $250 to $500 a day, and the most it has ever paid is $1,000 a day."

[The cases] suggest that if a communication, viewed in its entire context, merely conveys materially true facts from which a defamatory inference can reasonably be drawn, the libel is not established. But if the communication, by the particular manner or language in which the true facts are conveyed, supplies additional, affirmative evidence suggesting that the defendant intends or endorses the defamatory inference, the communication will be deemed capable of bearing that meaning.

In McBride, the author's juxtaposition of two classes of expert fees supplied the affirmative evidence rendering it reasonable to impute a defamatory meaning to the publication. ... In sum, the court must first examine what defamatory inferences might reasonably be drawn from a materially true communication, and then evaluate whether the author or broadcaster has done something beyond the mere reporting of true facts to suggest that the author or broadcaster intends or endorses the inference. We emphasize that the tortious element is provided by the affirmative conduct of the author or broadcaster, although it is immaterial for purposes of finding defamatory meaning whether the author or broadcaster actually intends or endorses the defamatory inference.

The FOP letters also do more than merely present the facts supporting an inference that White played an improper role in the irregularities surrounding his drug tests. By raising the specter of criminal violations, including bribery, the FOP provided a clear signal from which a reader could conclude, rightly or wrongly, that the defamatory inference was intended or endorsed. ...

Because the letters, viewed in their entirety, are thus capable of bearing implied defamatory meanings and of placing White in a false light, we proceed to discuss whether any of the statements in the FOP letters are privileged or protected as expressions of opinion. ...

What the district court and the FOP apparently fail to understand is that it is the defamatory implication—not the underlying assertions giving rise to the implication—which must be examined to discern whether the statements are entitled to full constitutional protection. Prosser makes this clear in discussing defamation by implication: "[I]f the defendant juxtaposes [a] series of facts so as to imply a defamatory connection between them, or [otherwise] creates a defamatory implication ... he may be held responsible for the defamatory implication, unless it qualifies as an opinion, even though the particular facts are correct. Prosser, The Law of Torts § 116, 5th Ed. (Supp.1988)." ... A defamation by implication, therefore, is not treated any differently than a direct defamation once the publication has been found capable of a defamatory meaning. A defendant may escape liability if the defamatory meaning is established as true or as constitutionally protected expression.

[The court concluded that the letters were not protected "expressions" in the light of *Milkovich*; so far as publications reported the internal investigation, that investigation was "not sufficiently judicial in nature to warrant application of the absolute privilege." The qualified privilege issues required trial. The Court then considered liability of the media defendants.]

First, as we noted above, [White's] reliance on Memphis Publishing Co. v. Nichols, 569 S.W.2d 412 (Tenn.1978), to establish a defamation by omission is misplaced. There, omissions were relevant only to establish falsity, not defamatory meaning. More importantly, we find that any omissions by the Post were immaterial because the same impressions would have been created if the omitted material had been included. If all of the articles had mentioned that CompuChem did not confirm the EMIT results on the first sample, a reader who concluded that the second sample had been tampered with would no doubt draw the same conclusion as to the first sample because the report of mishandling would apply to both samples. ...

[W]e also find the articles incapable of bearing a defamatory meaning based on the text of the articles themselves. The Post merely reported true facts from which a reader might infer that White used drugs. But we find no evidence in the text of the articles to suggest that it would be reasonable for a reader to conclude that the Post intended the defamatory inference. Beyond unpleasant but true facts, the articles are devoid of any suggestive juxtapositions, turns of phrase, or incendiary headlines. ...

[As to NBC's broadcast the same kind of analysis applies, and] we conclude that Pat Collins' dramatic intonation, standing alone or in combination with other factors, was not sufficiently distinctive to convey a clear implication to the viewers. We therefore conclude that the broadcast is not capable of conveying a defamatory meaning. As with the Post, we reject the false light claim against NBC because the picture created, though unpleasant, was substantially accurate.

[The court's discussion of qualified privilege for the media is omitted.]

---

15. **Gist.** Recall that a statement is treated as "true" if the gist or sting is true. Can we say that the other side of the coin is that a publication taken as a whole is false if the gist or sting is false, even if each individual statement in it is literally true? *Turner v. KTRK Television, Inc.*, 38 S.W.3d 103 (Tex. 2000), took that position. The court there said:

> Two other states' high courts have held that the First Amendment interest of robust, uninhibited discussion prevents a public figure from claiming defamation based on the whole of a communication when all its individual statements are literally or substantially true. Other courts have held that a public figure may not sue for defamation based on the publication as a whole unless it omits material facts. . . .
>
> We respectfully reject the approach of these states. Nothing in the United States Supreme Court's jurisprudence precludes a public figure from claiming defamation based on a publication as a whole. . . . Like a statement of opinion, a publication may by omission or misleading juxtaposition connote false facts even though it does not state them directly.

16. **Intent to express a given meaning vs. a new conception of truth.** The *White* court relies heavily on the Restatement's idea that a reader's correct or reasonable understanding of the publisher's intent, as shown by some objective manifestation beyond the publication of true facts that are loaded with defamatory implications. Is this disingenuous? Maybe what the court is really saying is that truth of the facts reported counts as truth, even if the defamatory implication is false, so long as the publisher does not endorse the defamatory implication. This would represent not merely a technical interpretation of the "meaning" but a new idea about what counts as truth. Could *Edwards* also be interpreted as a new version of what counts as truth?

17. **Fair comment privilege.** Stating facts about public figures truthfully (or under a privilege) and then commenting on the stated facts is privileged as to public figures at common law. Why wouldn't it be privileged to state the facts as in *White without* adding the comment? Is it that the defamatory implication or inference is not a "comment" or "opinion," whether it is expressed by the publisher or merely understood by the reader? The omitted portions of *White* did not discuss fair comment, only fair and accurate report of governmental proceedings.

18. **Fair report privilege.** Suppose the defendant reports that police are investigating whether the plaintiff, a public figure, was guilty of official misdeeds. There is in fact such an investigation, but the defendant's report might imply that serious allegations have been made

against the plaintiff and that they might even be true. The defendant might prevail if the court only requires truth of the literal report rather than truth of the underlying implications. If the court rejects that approach, the defendant might prevail if a police investigation is a species of public proceeding so that the fair report privilege might apply. *Dolcefino v. Randolph,* 19 S.W.3d 906 (Tex. App. 2000), seemed to take the view that a report was literally true and protected for that reason. Judge Sack, however, seems to justify the decision as a fair report privilege. See ROBERT D. SACK, SACK ON DEFAMATION: LIBEL, SLANDER, AND RELATED PROBLEMS § 7.3.2 (2001) (available on Westlaw). But some cases simply can't be explained that way. In *Green v. CBS Inc.,* 286 F.3d 281 (5th Cir. 2002), the court protected the defendant's report of defamatory third person allegations even though (a) the plaintiff was a private person and (b) the report was not a report of any official action, proceeding, document or quotation.

19. **Proof of fault.** The plaintiff in *White* was a police officer—usually classed as a public official or public figure—so he would presumably be required to prove knowing or reckless falsehood. Unless the publishers in *White* had some additional facts to show that the defamatory inference of a rigged test was a false one, why doesn't White's claim fail under the *Times-Sullivan* test? How could the plaintiff prove knowing falsehood or other fault? In *Turner v. KTRK Television, Inc.,* 38 S.W.3d 103 (Tex. 2000), a broadcaster omitted important facts that would have put the victim of the newscast in a materially better light. The broadcaster knew of the facts, but the court thought that the plaintiff, a public figure, had not shown malice. The court said:

> For an omission to be evidence of actual malice, however, the plaintiff must prove that the publisher knew or strongly suspected that it could create a substantially false impression. On this record, we cannot say that Dolcefino's failure to include these facts is clear and convincing evidence that he knew the broadcast would present a false impression or that he entertained serious doubts to that effect. ... Dolcefino's failure to include all the relevant details regarding Turner's participation in the estate suggests negligence, but under these circumstances we cannot conclude that it establishes actual malice with convincing clarity.

20. **Reference.** On the problem of defamatory implications drawn from truthful statements, see Dienes and Levine, *Implied Libel, Defamatory Meaning, and State of Mind: The Promise of New York Times Co. v. Sullivan,* 78 IOWA L. REV. 237 (1993); DOBBS ON TORTS § 411 (2000).

§ 3. REFORMING DEFAMATION

Almost everyone agrees that defamation law, to put it simply, is a mess. What is to be done?

When substantive law concepts become too difficult to manage, reformers almost always resort to process changes or to remedial changes. The most far-reaching proposals for reform of defamation law limits or eliminates the money judgment. Could you simply substitute a declaratory judgment for the ordinary money damages remedy? What would you have the declaratory judgment say? How could plaintiffs afford to sue for a declaratory judgment? If lawyers would have no contingent fee prospects, they could sue for defamation only if those victimized by defamation paid cash fees or lawyers devoted their pro bono time to defamation cases—unless the defendant who lost the declaratory judgment suit had to pay the plaintiff's reasonable attorney fees.

The Annenberg proposals, discussed in Smolla, *The Annenberg Libel Reform Proposal: The Case for Enactment*, 31 Wm. & Mary L. Rev. 25 (1989) and Ron Smolla, The Law of Defamation § 9.13 (4) (1989), would have attempted to resolve the libel controversy through retraction or reply. If that was unsuccessful, then declaratory judgment would become a possibility. In the summer of 1993, the Commissioners on Uniform Laws promulgated the Uniform Correction or Clarification of Defamation Act, which plays with some of the same ideas. North Dakota adopted a version of the Uniform Act in 1995. N.D. Cent. Code §§ 32–43–01 et seq. The English Defamation Act of 1996 seems to share some of the goals and some of the techniques of the Uniform Act. Instead of permitting the aggrieved party to demand correction, the English statute permits the publisher to offer "amends." After that, the act becomes complicated. Do you think some combination of (a) declaratory judgment and (b) retraction would suffice if defendants could be made liable for the plaintiff's attorney fees?

*

PROFESSIONAL AND ACADEMIC ENHANCEMENTS
Chapter 5

Secondary Publication and Carriers

ZERAN v. AMERICA ONLINE, INC.

129 F.3d 327 (4th Cir. 1997)

WILKINSON, Chief Judge. . . .

[Someone posted a message on defendant's internet bulletin board advertising T shirts that glorified Tim McVeigh's bombing of the Murrah Federal Building in Oklahoma City. For example, the trial judge's opinion reported, shirts saying "Visit Oklahoma . . . It's a BLAST!!!", "Putting the kids to bed . . . Oklahoma 1995," and "McVeigh for President 1996." The notice said to call Ken at the plaintiff's home number. He was deluged with calls. AOL promised to remove the posting, but in fact someone continued to post other similar messages for a period of days. Another defendant, a radio station in Oklahoma learned of the posted matter and broadcast the information, including the plaintiff's number. By this time, he was getting threatening calls every two minutes. The radio station retracted after two weeks and the calls subsided somewhat. The plaintiff sued the radio station and AOL separately, the latter case being transferred to a federal court in Virginia. The trial judge granted AOL's motion for judgment on the pleadings.]

"No provider or user of an interactive computer service shall be treated as the publisher or speaker of any information provided by another information content provider." 47 U.S.C. § 230(c)(1).[2] By its plain language, § 230 creates a federal immunity to any cause of action that would make service providers liable for information originating with a third-party user of the service. Specifically, § 230 precludes courts from entertaining claims that would place a computer service provider in a publisher's role. Thus, lawsuits seeking to hold a service provider liable for its exercise of a publisher's traditional editorial functions—such as

2. Section 230 defines "interactive computer service" as "any information service, system, or access software provider that provides or enables computer access by multiple users to a computer server, including specifically a service or system that provides access to the Internet and such systems operated or services offered by libraries or educational institutions." 47 U.S.C. § 230(e)(2). The term "information content provider" is defined as "any person or entity that is responsible, in whole or in part, for the creation or development of information provided through the Internet or any other interactive computer service." Id. § 230(e)(3). The parties do not dispute that AOL falls within the CDA's "interactive computer service" definition and that the unidentified third party who posted the offensive messages here fits the definition of an "information content provider."

deciding whether to publish, withdraw, postpone or alter content—are barred.

The purpose of this statutory immunity is not difficult to discern. Congress recognized the threat that tort-based lawsuits pose to freedom of speech in the new and burgeoning Internet medium. The imposition of tort liability on service providers for the communications of others represented, for Congress, simply another form of intrusive government regulation of speech. Section 230 was enacted, in part, to maintain the robust nature of Internet communication and, accordingly, to keep government interference in the medium to a minimum. In specific statutory findings, Congress recognized the Internet and interactive computer services as offering "a forum for a true diversity of political discourse, unique opportunities for cultural development, and myriad avenues for intellectual activity." Id. § 230(a)(3). . . .

None of this means, of course, that the original culpable party who posts defamatory messages would escape accountability. While Congress acted to keep government regulation of the Internet to a minimum, it also found it to be the policy of the United States "to ensure vigorous enforcement of Federal criminal laws to deter and punish trafficking in obscenity, stalking, and harassment by means of computer." Id. § 230(b)(5). Congress made a policy choice, however, not to deter harmful online speech through the separate route of imposing tort liability on companies that serve as intermediaries for other parties' potentially injurious messages.

. . . It would be impossible for service providers to screen each of their millions of postings for possible problems. Faced with potential liability for each message republished by their services, interactive computer service providers might choose to severely restrict the number and type of messages posted. Congress considered the weight of the speech interests implicated and chose to immunize service providers to avoid any such restrictive effect.

Another important purpose of § 230 was to encourage service providers to self-regulate the dissemination of offensive material over their services. . . .

Congress enacted § 230 to remove the disincentives to selfregulation created by the Stratton Oakmont decision. Under that court's holding, computer service providers who regulated the dissemination of offensive material on their services risked subjecting themselves to liability, because such regulation cast the service provider in the role of a publisher. Fearing that the specter of liability would therefore deter service providers from blocking and screening offensive material, Congress enacted § 230's broad immunity. . . .

Zeran argues, however, that the § 230 immunity eliminates only publisher liability, leaving distributor liability intact. Publishers can be held liable for defamatory statements contained in their works even absent proof that they had specific knowledge of the statement's inclusion. According to Zeran, interactive computer service providers like

AOL are normally considered instead to be distributors, like traditional news vendors or book sellers. Distributors cannot be held liable for defamatory statements contained in the materials they distribute unless it is proven at a minimum that they have actual knowledge of the defamatory statements upon which liability is predicated. Zeran contends that he provided AOL with sufficient notice of the defamatory statements appearing on the company's bulletin board. This notice is significant, says Zeran, because AOL could be held liable as a distributor only if it acquired knowledge of the defamatory statements' existence.

Because of the difference between these two forms of liability, Zeran contends that the term "distributor" carries a legally distinct meaning from the term "publisher." Accordingly, he asserts that Congress' use of only the term "publisher" in § 230 indicates a purpose to immunize service providers only from publisher liability. He argues that distributors are left unprotected by § 230 and, therefore, his suit should be permitted to proceed against AOL. We disagree. Assuming arguendo that Zeran has satisfied the requirements for imposition of distributor liability, this theory of liability is merely a subset, or a species, of publisher liability, and is therefore also foreclosed by § 230.

... Although Zeran attempts to artfully plead his claims as ones of negligence, they are indistinguishable from a garden variety defamation action. ...

In this case, AOL is legally considered to be a publisher. "[E]very one who takes part in the publication ... is charged with publication." Even distributors are considered to be publishers for purposes of defamation law. ...

AOL falls squarely within this traditional definition of a publisher and, therefore, is clearly protected by § 230's immunity.

Zeran contends that decisions like Stratton Oakmont and Cubby, Inc. v. CompuServe Inc., 776 F.Supp. 135 (S.D.N.Y.1991), recognize a legal distinction between publishers and distributors. He misapprehends, however, the significance of that distinction for the legal issue we consider here. It is undoubtedly true that mere conduits, or distributors, are subject to a different standard of liability. As explained above, distributors must at a minimum have knowledge of the existence of a defamatory statement as a prerequisite to liability. But this distinction signifies only that different standards of liability may be applied within the larger publisher category, depending on the specific type of publisher concerned. To the extent that decisions like Stratton and Cubby utilize the terms "publisher" and "distributor" separately, the decisions correctly describe two different standards of liability. Stratton and Cubby do not, however, suggest that distributors are not also a type of publisher for purposes of defamation law. ...

If computer service providers were subject to distributor liability, they would face potential liability each time they receive notice of a potentially defamatory statement—from any party, concerning any message. ... Because service providers would be subject to liability only for the publication of information, and not for its removal, they would have a natural incentive simply to remove messages upon notification, whether the contents were defamatory or not. Thus, like strict liability, liability upon notice has a chilling effect on the freedom of Internet speech.

Similarly, notice-based liability would deter service providers from regulating the dissemination of offensive material over their own services. Any efforts by a service provider to investigate and screen material posted on its service would only lead to notice of potentially defamatory material more frequently and thereby create a stronger basis for liability. Instead of subjecting themselves to further possible lawsuits, service providers would likely eschew any attempts at self-regulation.

More generally, notice-based liability for interactive computer service providers would provide third parties with a no-cost means to create the basis for future lawsuits. . . .

For the foregoing reasons, we affirm the judgment of the district court.

BLUMENTHAL v. DRUDGE, 992 F.Supp. 44 (D.D.C. 1998). Drudge wrote political gossip for regular posting on the internet. AOL paid him $3,000 a month to write and post the gossip and advertised that the Druge Report was available to members as an enticement to join AOL. Drudge had no other source of income. He posted gossip asserting that the plaintiff, a new high-level White House employee, had a spousal abuse past. It was pure rumor and gossip, unsubstantiated by Drudge and eventually retracted by him with an apology. *Held*, AOL is immune. "Congress decided not to treat providers of interactive computer services like other information providers such as newspapers, magazines or television and radio stations, all of which may be held liable for publishing or distributing obscene or defamatory material written or prepared by others . . . AOL acknowledges both that § 230(c)(1) would not immunize AOL with respect to any information AOL developed or created entirely by itself and that there are situations in which there may be two or more information content providers responsible for material disseminated on the Internet–joint authors, a lyricist and a composer, for example. . . . AOL maintains that there simply is no evidence here that AOL had any role in creating or developing any of the information in the Drudge Report. The Court agrees. . . . Any attempt to distinguish between 'publisher' liability and notice-based 'distributor' liability and to argue that § 230 was only intended to immunize the former would be unavailing. Congress made no distinction between publishers and distributors in providing immunity from liability."

1. **Provided by "another."** The statute immunizes the service provider as to any information "provided by another information content provider." Is material that AOL hires another to write "provided by another" or is it provided by AOL itself? AOL is not a human being. How can AOL provide content without hiring someone to provide it?

What if AOL's full time employee wrote the material as requested by AOL? What if the same employee wrote it along with Drudge?

2. **"Provided" by another.** Instead of asking who is "another," ask what it means to say one has "provided" the content? In *Batzel v. Smith,* 333 F.3d 1018 (9th Cir. 2003), a man named Smith sent an email to a museum group, indicating that the plaintiff was a descendant of a high-ranking Nazi and possessed looted paintings. Smith later said he did not send the email to the address reserved for publication and had not expected it to be published. In fact, however, the museum group did published the email in its electronic newsletter and on its website. The plaintiff sued the museum group as well as Smith. The court held that the museum group could be immune under the statute, even though it selected which emails to publish, but that it would not be immune unless Smith fell within the concept of a provider."If information is provided to those individuals in a capacity unrelated to their function as a provider or user of interactive computer services, then there is no reason to protect them with the special statutory immunity." Free speech would not be promoted by immunizing providers and users of interactive computer services who actually know or have reason to know "that the information provided was not intended for publication on the Internet. Quite the contrary: Users of the Internet are likely to be discouraged from sending e-mails for fear that their e-mails may be published on the web without their permission."

3. **ISP interacting with or editing content.** In *Carafano v. Metrosplash.com, Inc.,* 207 F.Supp.2d 1055 (C.D. Cal. 2002), the court thought a website operator was a content provider and thus subject to liability because it created multiple choice questions and answer choices that formed the basis for member profiles which were then posted on the site for access by other members. An unknown person, purporting to be the plaintiff, posted her profile, answering questions to present her as a "licentious" person looking for a one-night stand. The plaintiff was a well-known actress. "The users of the Matchmaker website do not simply post whatever information they desire. Rather, a profile for each user is created from the questions asked by Matchmaker and the answers provided." That reasoning left the defendant unprotected by the statutory immunity, but on appeal, the Ninth Circuit held that the defendant was not a content provider merely because its questions prompted responses by third persons. The court said: "[S]o long as a third party willingly provides the essential published content, the interactive service provider receives full immunity regardless of the specific editing or selection process. The fact that some of the content was formulated in response to Matchmaker's questionnaire does not alter this conclusion. Doubtless, the questionnaire facilitated the expression of information by individual users. However, the selection of the content was left exclusively to the user. . . . Matchmaker cannot be considered an 'information content provider' under the statute because no profile has any content until a user actively creates it." *Carafano v. Metrosplash.Com. Inc.,* 339 F.3d 1119, 1124 (9th Cir. 2003). What if the interactive computer service selectively deletes messages and thus affects

the overall content? *Donato v. Moldow,* 374 N.J.Super. 475, 865 A.2d 711 (2005) (immunity remains).

4. **Suing anonymous libelers.** Anonymity encourages frank exploration of the truth, but also manifestations of the John Doe's own psychic problems, as anyone can see by exploring the internet. If the publisher of internet libel created by others is immune, what about the possibility of suing the anonymous libeler? Could that at least discourage further attacks? In *Public Relations Soc'y of America, Inc. v. Road Runner High Speed Online,* 8 Misc.3d 820, 799 N.Y.S.2d 847 (Sup. Ct. 2005), the court ordered the internet provider to produce records that would identify an anonymous emailer of libel. *Dendrite Int'l, Inc. v. Doe,* 342 N.J.Super. 134, 775 A.2d 756 (2001), set out a series of requirements that must be met before disclosure would be ordered, including a requirement that the plaintiff make out a prima facie case of liability and notice to the anonymous poster that would permit him to oppose the motion for disclosure. The trial court must then balance First Amendment rights to speak anonymously against the harm to the plaintiff. In *Dendrite,* the plaintiff lost because it did not prove actual harm.

Some commentators emphasize that the freedom to defame behind a cloak of anonymity has great social value because it encourages good as well as libelous speech. Lyrissa Barnett Lidsky, *Silencing John Doe: Defamation & Discourse in Cyberspace,* 49 DUKE L.J. 855 (2000), expresses the view we forecast when we took up *Times-Sullivan*—that the internet empowers individuals with limited resources to publish their views on matters of public concern. Focusing on corporate libel victims and anonymous individual "critics," Lidsky suggests that Joe Doe libelers should have expansive protection. The relevant culture uses the internet to blow off steam, she says. That fact, the shrill tone of the messages, and the fact that most of those posting messages don't pretend first-hand knowledge, leads readers to expect no "buttoned-down analyses." Consequently, we ought to treat many such messages as pure opinion for which there is no liability as long as they deal with public issues.

We raise three points to consider. (1) Is it hard to agree on the trashy character of internet messages and at the same time find they have great social value? (2) In emphasizing the low character of internet postings and the anonymity of the libelers, Professor Lidsky argues that these things relate to context which in turn suggests we ought to take the statements as non-factual and thus as protected "opinion." Our question is whether this is really a matter of context bearing on factual vs. non-factual meaning or whether it is a matter of belief. When she suggests that anonymity of the poster is itself "a cue to discount their statements," isn't she talking about whether we should *believe* the statements rather than what they mean? And wouldn't belief or degree of conviction go to questions of damages rather than to privilege or immunity? (3) Finally, if you can be attacked repeatedly on the internet without the ability to identify and confront your attacker, the attacker's speech is not chilled; but what about yours? Is your only hope to keep your head down and to stay out of public affairs altogether?

Chapter 6

THE PROCEDURAL AND REMEDIAL SIDE OF DEFAMATION

§ 1. DEATH AND SURVIVAL

GILLIKIN V. SPRINGLE, 254 N.C. 240, 118 S.E.2d 611 (1961); GILLIKIN V. BELL, 254 N.C. 244, 118 S.E.2d 609 (1961). Louie Elmer Gillikin was killed in an auto-truck collision. The truck was owned by Springle and driven by his agent. Springle was coroner of the county. Springle allegedly prevented an appropriate police investigation and refused to hold an inquest. Springle brought suit against the administrator of Gillikin's estate for property damage. The administrator counterclaimed for wrongful death. The judge non-suited the administrator, who later brought the present claim. The present claim asserts that the administrator was nonsuited as a result of Springle's "'wicked and wrongful scheming' and the wrongful use of 'the functions and prerogatives of his office as coroner,' coercion of witnesses, and concealment of truth, a conspiracy with others to show the collision was caused by the negligence of intestate. . . ." In particular, the conspirators allegedly "coerced one Knudson, an occupant of the automobile, to give perjured testimony in the trial of the case and assisted in securing other false testimony" and falsified evidence by planting a beer can and a 7–Up bottle in a "prominent position in the car and directed a commercial photographer, who had been called to the scene of the accident, to make faked-up and trumped-up pictures to not only defame and degrade the good name and reputation of Louie Elmer Gillikin. . . ." The photographer allegedly exposed the private parts of the deceased and made a picture of his body so exposed, which was then widely circulated in the county. The trial court dismissed the claim. *Held,* affirmed.

(1) "Perjured testimony and the subornation of perjured testimony are criminal offenses, but neither are torts supporting a civil action for damages."

(2) "It is a misdemeanor at common law, punishable on indictment with fine and imprisonment, to write and publish defamatory matter of

any person deceased, provided it be published with the malevolent purpose to injure his family and posterity, and to expose them to contempt and disgrace. . . ." However, "[t]he cases are practically unanimous in holding that no" tort claim exists for defamation of the dead. "The Legislature has the power to modify the common law and permit an action for damages for defamation of a dead person, designating the person who may sue and how the sums recovered shall be distributed. Until the Legislature authorizes such actions, we feel impelled to adhere to the common law denying a right of action."

---

1. **Defaming the living by defaming the dead.** Defendant says of the deceased, a government official: "Danny Dedmon took a bribe from Patty Plangent." Plangent is obviously defamed. On the other hand, Dedmon's family, though perhaps embarrassed or distressed, are not defamed. See *Decker v. Princeton Packet, Inc.*, 116 N.J. 418, 561 A.2d 1122 (1989). Might the family have a claim for infliction of emotional distress, intentional or negligent? *Gugliuzza v. K.C.M.C., Inc.*, 606 So.2d 790 (La. 1992), refused to recognize a mental anguish claim based on defamation of the dead.

2. **Survival or not.** Not only is there no tort for defamation of the dead, the defamation claims of living persons do not ordinarily survive the death of either the plaintiff or the defendant, although some statutes permit survival of reputational claims. See *Plumley v. Landmark Chevrolet, Inc.*, 122 F.3d 308 (5th Cir. 1997). In addition, Pennsylvania has held that a survival statute is constitutionally required to permit survival of defamation claims if it permits survival of other claims. See *Moyer v. Phillips*, 462 Pa. 395, 341 A.2d 441 (1975); Annot., 75 A.L.R.3d 741; 77 A.L.R.3d 1339.

§ 2. THE STATUTE OF LIMITATIONS

3. **Periods.** Statutes of Limitation for libel and slander are often very short. Although a number of states use a two-year period, many others impose a one-year limitation.

4. **Traditional rule starting the statutory clock.** The traditional rule in defamation cases started the statute of limitations running at publication. E.g., *Morgan v. Hustler Magazine, Inc.*, 653 F.Supp. 711 (N.D. Ohio 1987); *Wagner, Nugent, Johnson, Roth, Romano, Erikson & Kupfer v. Flanagan*, 629 So.2d 113 (Fla. 1993). One problem under this rule is that the plaintiff may not actually know of the libel until the statute of limitations has run. The other is that injury may not occur until long after the libel.

5. **Accepting the discovery rule for "hidden" publication.** A few cases have applied a discovery rule to defamation claims, starting the statute running only when the publication was actually discovered or

should have been discovered by the plaintiff. E.g., *Dulude v. Fletcher Allen Health Care, Inc.*, 174 Vt. 74, 807 A.2d 390 (2002). In *Clark v. Airesearch Mfg. Co. of Arizona, Inc.*, 138 Ariz. 240, 673 P.2d 984 (Ct. App. 1983), the court concluded in principle that "the rule of discovery should be applied in those situations in which the defamation is published in a manner in which it is peculiarly likely to be concealed from the plaintiff, such as in a confidential memorandum or a credit report." This looks like a trend. See *Digital Design Group, Inc. v. Information Builders, Inc.*, 24 P.3d 834 (Okla. 2001).

6. **Open publication barring claims for all prior publications.** Like the decisions in ¶ 5, California holds that the discovery rule usually applies only when the libel is "hidden from view." This leads California to say that the discovery rule is not available to the plaintiff where the libel is published in books, magazines, or newspapers. Suppose defamatory publication No. 1 was made by A four years ago and was hidden from view so that P neither knew nor could know about it. A year later, B published a book quoting the first libel. P did not discover either publication until she read the book two years ago. P now sues, three years after the book's publication. Under a one-year statute of limitation, P is clearly barred from claiming against B. Will the discovery rule permit a suit against A even though suit against B is barred? *Shively v. Bozanich,* 31 Cal.4th 1230, 80 P.3d 676, 7 Cal.Rptr.3d 576 (2003), on somewhat similar facts, said not. The court in effect held that general publication of a book is always the latest moment for accrual of a cause of action for libel it contains, including earlier and previously hidden iterations of the libel by others.

KEETON V. HUSTLER MAGAZINE, INC., 131 N.H. 6, 549 A.2d 1187 (1988). "At common law, the multiple publication rule accorded the plaintiff a separate cause of action for each sale or delivery of a copy of the offending publication. Under this rule, a defendant was potentially subject to many suits based on distribution of a single edition of a book or magazine; the rule likewise required the plaintiff to bring many suits in order to recover damages in full. With the advent of modern-day mass publication, this rule became increasingly burdensome, both to the parties and to the judicial system itself. The potential number and geographic dispersion of libel suits, coupled with the possibility that they might be based upon distribution over a long period of time, was particularly burdensome for defendants. In response, the majority of courts have adopted the so-called single publication rule.

"The Restatement (Second) of Torts states the single publication rule as follows: '(3) Any one edition of a book or newspaper . . . or similar aggregate communication is a single publication. (4) As to any single publication, (a) only one action for damages can be maintained; (b) all damages suffered in all jurisdictions can be recovered in the one action; and (c) a judgment for or against the plaintiff upon the merits of any action for damages bars any action for damages between the same parties in all jurisdictions.' Restatement (Second) of Torts § 577A. The Uniform Single Publication Act of 1952, 14 U.L.A. 353 (1980), also embodies this rule, and has been adopted by seven States.

"Operation of the single publication rule is perhaps best explained in comment e to § 577A of the Restatement: '[T]he plaintiff has only one cause of action for the publication. In his single action he may recover damages for the publication to all persons whom the communication has reached or may be expected to reach, whether before or after trial, until its circulation has terminated or the statute of limitations has run against the cause of action. This is true even though the publication has crossed state lines and has been read, heard or seen in every state and in foreign countries; and all damages sustained in all jurisdictions may be recovered in the one action. The purpose of the rule is to include in the single suit all damages resulting anywhere from the single aggregate publication.' States adopting the rule generally hold, in addition, that the plaintiff's cause of action accrues for limitations purposes on the first date that the publisher releases the finished product for sale.

"We recognize the wisdom, in light of modern publishing practices, of adopting the single publication rule as described above. Without the rule, the burden that libel suits would place on parties and the courts might well be intolerable. We therefore join [t]he great majority of States [that] now follow [the] rule in libel actions."

7. **Single publication rule: the number and timeliness of suits.** The logic of the single publication rule has two important effects. First, once a claim for defamation in any single edition of a book or periodical has gone to judgment, no other claim can be brought even though the book circulates and causes harm for years. Second, the statute of limitations begins to run from the first day the edition is published. See *Pitts v. City of Kankakee, Illinois,* 267 F.3d 592 (7th Cir. 2001) (applying the rule by analogy in a civil rights claim where the city had posted "a single sign, put up on one day and left undisturbed for a period of time"). Most states follow the single publication rule. There is a Uniform Act on the subject as well.

8. **Limited publication.** We've seen that a hidden publication might justify using the discovery rule to delay accrual of the action. Could the fact that publication is limited or hidden also affect the single publication rule? In *Shively,* supra ¶ 6, the court regarded the discovery rule as antithetical to the single publication rule and thought that where the single publication rule applies, the discovery rule cannot. At the same time, however, the court said that publication for purposes of the single publication rule occurs at the "first general distribution of the publication to the public." Would that mean that the single publication rule would not start the clock running when the defendant publishes a defamatory book only to scholarly research libraries? Something like that allegedly happened in *Hebrew Academy of San Francisco v. Goldman,* 129 Cal.App.4th 391, 28 Cal.Rptr.3d 515 (2005). The court conclud-

ed that the single publication rule did not apply but that the discovery rule did.

9. **Publication elsewhere.** An interstate publication like a national magazine might hit the newsstands in New York on Wednesday but not be offered for sale in Tennessee until the following Monday. If the plaintiff lives in Tennessee should we say the relevant first publication occurs only when distribution begins in Tennessee? *Applewhite v. Memphis State University*, 495 S.W.2d 190 (Tenn. 1973), took this approach.

10. **Single publication rule on the Web; what is a single edition?** Should the single publication rule apply to libel posted on a website? The cases say so. See *Traditional Cat Ass'n, Inc. v. Gilbreath,* 118 Cal.App.4th 392, 13 Cal.Rptr.3d 353 (2004); *Churchill v. State,* 378 N.J.Super. 471, 876 A.2d 311 (2005); *Firth v. State,* 98 N.Y.2d 365, 775 N.E.2d 463, 747 N.Y.S.2d 69 (2002). In a way that question relates to another—what IS a single edition? Would a second printing of a book count, or would it be a second edition only if changes in content or format were made? What about the constant additions to a web site?

Three Other Procedural Points

11. **Pleadings.** The common law rule is that libel must be pleaded verbatim. Maybe nowadays that would be understood as a requirement of specificity rather than literal word-for-word requirement.

12. **Discovery.** The Constitutional rules in public official and public figure cases are understood to mean that the plaintiff can use discovery to question media publishers about their state of mind to determine knowing or reckless falsehood. See *Herbert v. Lando,* 441 U.S. 153, 99 S.Ct. 1635, 60 L.Ed.2d 115 (1979). Equally, the plaintiff might seek to discover the reporter's sources, because if the reporter had none, that would tend to show a knowing or reckless falsehood as well as a negligent one. But what if the reporter invokes a privilege, recognized by statute or common law, to keep sources confidential? In *Downing v. Monitor Pub. Co. Inc.,* 120 N.H. 383, 415 A.2d 683 (1980), the court held that "when a defendant in a libel action, brought by a plaintiff who is required to prove actual malice under New York Times, refuses to declare his sources of information upon a valid order of the court, there shall arise a presumption that the defendant had no source." A little other authority supports this presumption or some variant of it. See Robert G. Berger, *The 'No–Source' Presumption: The Harshest Remedy,* 36 Am. U. L. Rev. 603 (1987). Before permitting discovery or the no-source presumption, should the court first require the plaintiff to prove falsehood in a bifurcated trial?

13. **Summary judgment standards.** The clear and convincing evidence standard in public figure cases requires the plaintiff to show that a jury could not only find knowing or reckless falsehood but could do so by clear and convincing evidence; this in turn is to be considered

by the judge in passing on a motion for summary judgment. *Anderson v. Liberty Lobby, Inc.*, 477 U.S. 242, 106 S.Ct. 2505, 91 L.Ed.2d 202 (1986).

§ 3. REMEDIES

(a) Surveying the Remedies

14. **Reviewing the status of presumed damages.** (a) Recall that in *Gertz*-type cases, damages can no longer be presumed. *Gertz v. Robert Welch, Inc.*, 418 U.S. 323, 94 S.Ct. 2997, 41 L.Ed.2d 789 (1974). However, *Gertz* did not require pecuniary loss. It is enough under *Gertz* if the plaintiff shows she suffered reputational loss or mental anguish. *Gertz* specifically said that the plaintiff need not produce evidence that assigns a dollar value to the reputational injury.

(b) In the *Dun & Bradstreet*-type case, states are permitted but not required to award the common law presumed damages. A number of states continue to follow this practice. E.g., *Maison de France v. Mais Oui!, Inc.*, 126 Wash.App. 34, 108 P.3d 787 (2005).

(c) Seemingly, a private-person plaintiff who proves knowing or reckless falsehood can also recover presumed damages. *Martin v. Griffin Television, Inc.*, 549 P.2d 85 (Okla. 1976) (to recover presumed damages, a private person plaintiff must prove actual malice under the *New York Times* test).

(d) A number of states have discarded the common law presumed damages and now require proof of actual harm even when the Constitution makes no such requirement. *Arthaud v. Mutual of Omaha Ins. Co.*, 170 F.3d 860 (8th Cir. 1999); *United Ins. Co. of America v. Murphy,* 331 Ark. 364, 961 S.W.2d 752 (1998); *Walker v. Grand Central Sanitation, Inc.*, 430 Pa.Super. 236, 634 A.2d 237 (1993). In addition, state statutes may require proof of actual damages in particular cases, and state slander rules often still require proof not merely of actual damages but actual pecuniary loss.

15. **Compensatory damages.** Courts permit juries to decide "fair compensation for actual damages, including emotional distress and harm to reputation." Equally, juries may award proven consequential damages that are not too remote. See *Ayash v. Dana–Farber Cancer Inst.*, 443 Mass. 367, 822 N.E.2d 667, 697 (2005) (articles impugning the plaintiff affected her career, causing emotional harm and loss of income); *Bolduc v. Bailey,* 586 F.Supp. 896 (D. Colo. 1984) (cost of clearing name). Several courts have recognized that the victim's spouse may recover for any proven loss of consortium as in other cases, e.g., *Roche v. Egan,* 433 A.2d 757 (Me. 1981), although a Texas court has held otherwise. *Carr v. Mobile Video Tapes, Inc.*, 893 S.W.2d 613 (Tex. App. 1995) (based on Texas law requiring physical injury of the victim to support a lost consortium claim).

16. **Punitive damages.** If the plaintiff proves that the defendant was guilty of publishing knowing or reckless and defamatory falsehood,

is that a sufficient basis for recovery of punitive in addition to compensatory damages? In *Prozeralik v. Capital Cities Communications, Inc.*, 82 N.Y.2d 466, 626 N.E.2d 34, 605 N.Y.S.2d 218 (1993), the court said not. It thought that punitive damages would be justified only if the defendant had a malicious motive for the publication. Would it not be a fair inference that the defendant had a malicious motive or "evil mind" if the defendant knew he was publishing false and defamatory material? In *Taskett v. King Broadcasting Co.,* 86 Wash.2d 439, 546 P.2d 81, 86 (1976), the court declared that "under No circumstances will we allow a jury to award Punitive damages." (the court's capitalization). On the other hand, some courts treat proof of knowing or reckless falsehood as sufficient evidence to warrant an award of punitive damages. *Mitchell v. Griffin Television, L.L.C.,* 60 P.3d 1058 (Okla. Ct. Civ. App. 2002). In evaluating these different approaches, consider whether *Prozeralik* or *Taskett* would be justified (a) by First Amendment principles or (b) by punitive damages rules. If punitive damages are allowed, they are subject to the constitutional due process constraints imposed by *State Farm Mut. Auto. Ins. Co. v. Campbell,* 538 U.S. 408, 123 S.Ct. 1513, 155 L.Ed.2d 585 (2003) (limiting total punitive awards by considering several factors and establishing a rule of thumb that "few awards exceeding a single-digit ratio between punitive and compensatory damages, to a significant degree, will satisfy due process").

17. **Radio broadcast statutes.** Many states have enacted "radio" statutes, offering certain protections to broadcasters. E.g., N.Y. Civ. Rights Law § 75. The statute may codify the position of broadcasters as secondary publishers or distributors, thus protecting the broadcaster from liability for utterances of others unless the broadcaster is negligent in failing to exclude such utterances. See Fla. Stat. Ann. § 770.04. Statutes may also provide that the plaintiff must prove actual damages. Ga. Code Ann. § 51–5–10 ("only such actual, consequential, or punitive damages as have been alleged and proved").

18. **Retraction statutes.** Many states have also enacted retraction statutes. Under the California statute, applicable to newspapers and broadcasters, the "plaintiff shall recover no more than special damages unless a correction be demanded and be not published or broadcast." Cal. Civil Code § 48a. There are some variations and there is room for debate about what counts as a correction or retraction. One court held a retraction statute unconstitutional so far as it barred "general" damages for reputation loss and emotional distress merely because a retraction was published. *Boswell v. Phoenix Newspapers, Inc.*, 152 Ariz. 9, 730 P.2d 186 (1986) (saying the statute effectively deprives of a remedy great classes of persons who will have no special damages, such as the elderly, the retired, homemakers, children and the unemployed).

19. **Right of reply and compelled publication.** A limited experiment with a right of reply remedy—which allowed the allegedly defamed person to use the defaming media to publish his own response—was struck down by the Supreme Court in *Miami Herald Pub. Co. v.*

Tornillo, 418 U.S. 241, 94 S.Ct. 2831, 41 L.Ed.2d 730 (1974), as an unconstitutional intrusion on editorial rights of the press.

20. **Emotional harm as parasitic damages.** *Gertz* permits proof of non-pecuniary damages, so long as they are "actual" rather than presumed. Cases have allowed recovery for mental distress as parasitic to defamation claims, or as one element of damage resulting from harm to reputation. That means the special limitations attached to stand-alone mental distress claims do not apply once the plaintiff makes out a case for defamation. See *Southern Baptist Hospital of Florida, Inc. v. Welker,* 908 So.2d 317 (Fla. 2005). In *Prozeralik v. Capital Cities Communications*, 188 A.D.2d 178, 593 N.Y.S.2d 662 (1993), the court affirmed a recovery of $4 million for "humiliation, mental anguish and injury to plaintiff's reputation," although the case was later remanded for new trial on issues of falsity. *Prozeralik v. Capital Cities Communications, Inc.,* 82 N.Y.2d 466, 626 N.E.2d 34, 605 N.Y.S.2d 218 (1993).

21. **Firestone's emotional harm as substitute for reputational loss.** The Supreme Court in *Firestone* went further; it allowed the plaintiff to drop the reputation claim altogether and recover for mental distress, while still calling the claim one for libel. Commentators have criticized the *Firestone* rule as a means of allowing the plaintiff to recover presumed damages under another name. Anderson, *Reputation, Compensation, and Proof*, 25 WM. & MARY L. REV. 747, 758 (1984); see also DAN B. DOBBS, LAW OF REMEDIES § 7.2 (6) (1993). Some state courts have rejected the *Firestone* approach, and instead require reputational harm as a predicate for other damages in a libel action. See *Little Rock Newspapers, Inc. v. Dodrill*, 281 Ark. 25, 660 S.W.2d 933 (1983); *Schlegel v. Ottumwa Courier,* 585 N.W.2d 217 (Iowa 1998); *Richie v. Paramount Pictures Corporation*, 544 N.W.2d 21 (Minn. 1996); *Kenney v. Wal–Mart Stores, Inc.*, 100 S.W.3d 809 (Mo. 2003).

22. **Restitution—the defendant's profits.** Conceivably the defendant's libel is profitable to him, as with a book that libels a public figure throughout and sells because it is scandalous. Could the plaintiff base her recovery on the defendant's profits rather than on damages for the plaintiff's loss of reputation?

23. **Injunctions.** Courts are clearly reluctant to prohibit speech by injunction, and generally refuse injunctions as a matter of local law, albeit with free speech in mind. E.g., *Kramer v. Thompson*, 947 F.2d 666 (3d Cir. 1991) (holding that injunction must be denied under Pennsylvania law even though a jury had previously found the statements libelous and had awarded damages; a compulsory retraction was equally unacceptable); *High Country Fashions, Inc. v. Marlenna Fashions, Inc.,* 257 Ga. 267, 357 S.E.2d 576 (1987) ("we follow the general rule that 'equity will not enjoin libel and slander'"). This long tradition is not necessarily limited to "prior restraint" or other Constitutional ideas.

(b) The Libel-Proof Plaintiff

BROOKS v. AMERICAN BROADCASTING COMPANIES, INC.

932 F.2d 495 (6th Cir. 1991)

RYAN, Circuit Judge. . . .

ABC television personality Geraldo Rivera traveled to Akron, Ohio, to investigate rumors that a local judge persuaded women to have sex with him by offering the women favorable rulings in certain cases. Rivera suspected that Brooks, an Akron resident with a substantial and slightly publicized criminal background, was assisting the judge by attempting to frighten the women out of testifying against him. Rivera persuaded Brooks to meet Rivera at a hotel. As soon as Brooks got out of his taxi, Rivera emerged from the hotel and rapidly asked Brooks a series of questions concerning Brooks's suspected role as "hitman" for the judge.

After this questioning, during which Brooks may not have known that ABC was recording his answers, Rivera summoned a camera crew from a nearby van. Muttering some obscenities, Brooks fled, with Rivera and camera crew in close pursuit. On a 1980 episode of ABC's television program "20/20," the network broadcast Rivera's and other persons' negative comments concerning Brooks and his alleged involvement with the judge. The remarks were to the effect that the judge employed Brooks as a "hitman," that five witnesses attested to his role, and that Brooks was a "pimp," "betrayed" by the judge, a "muscleman," and a "street knowledgeable jive turkey." Before the broadcast of the "20/20" segment, a grand jury indicted Brooks on charges related to obstruction of justice.

Over the years, police had taken Brooks into custody 20 times on suspicion of various misdeeds. Brooks's criminal history included convictions for 1) breaking and entering, 2) grand larceny, 3) first-degree manslaughter, and 4) carrying a concealed weapon under disability. Adverse publicity had compromised Brooks's reputation severely prior to the "20/20" broadcast. The Akron Beacon Journal publicized Brooks's convictions in four articles. In addition to reporting the convictions, the Beacon Journal also had noted Brooks's "involvement" in a 1979 Akron slaying. Ten days before the "20/20" broadcast, the newspaper reported Brooks's indictment for intimidation of witnesses and obstruction of justice in relation to the judge, and referred to Brooks as "the man police suspect of being the so-called 'hit-man' in the sex case involving [the judge]. . . ." According to Brooks, potential employers had become wary of hiring him as a result of his prior convictions.

In 1981, Brooks filed a complaint in the United States District Court invoking diversity jurisdiction and alleging that ABC and others libeled him by broadcasting Rivera's derogatory and allegedly false remarks.

Brooks sought $20 million in compensatory and $20 million in punitive damages. ...

[The trial court granted summary judgment for the defendant on the libel claim and refused to permit Brooks to amend his complaint to add some other theories.]

In dismissing Brooks's libel claim, the district court agreed with the defendants that, as a matter of law, Brooks was "libel-proof," a rather loose-woven legal conception of the federal courts. At the federal appellate level, the "libel-proof" concept makes its home only in the Second Circuit, although the Eighth, Third, and Fifth Circuits have referred to the concept as if those circuits might apply it under the right circumstances.[3] Ray v. United States Dept. of Justice, 658 F.2d 608, 611 (8th Cir. 1981); Marcone v. Penthouse Int'l Magazine, 754 F.2d 1072, 1078–79 (3d Cir. 1985); Zerangue v. TSP Newspapers, Inc., 814 F.2d 1066, 1074 (5th Cir. 1987). Restated in its most viable form, defendant's argument is as follows: due to his prior publicized criminal acts and due to other publicity concerning the "hitman" allegations, any additional damage to Brooks's reputation that might have occurred due to the "20/20" broadcast was de minimis as a matter of law.

In a critical case in the libel-proof doctrine's evolution, the Second Circuit held: "We consider as a matter of law that appellant is, for purposes of this case, libel-proof, i.e., so unlikely by virtue of his *life as a habitual criminal* to be able to recover anything other than nominal damages as to warrant dismissal of the case." Cardillo v. Doubleday & Co., 518 F.2d 638, 639 (2d Cir. 1975) (emphasis added). At the time of the appeal, Cardillo was serving a 21-year sentence for assorted federal felonies. Id. at 640. A subsequent Second Circuit opinion further defined the contours of the libel-proof concept: The libel-proof plaintiff doctrine is to be applied with caution, since few plaintiffs will have so bad a reputation that they are not entitled to obtain redress for defamatory statements, even if their damages cannot be quantified and they receive only nominal damages. But *in those instances where an allegedly libelous statement cannot realistically cause impairment of reputation because the person's reputation is already so low ..., even nominal damages are not to be awarded*. Instead, the claim should be dismissed so that the costs of defending against the claim of libel, which can themselves impair vigorous freedom of expression, will be avoided. Guccione v. Hustler Magazine, Inc., 800 F.2d 298, 303 (2d Cir.1986) (emphasis added). Criminal convictions are the well-worn path to achieving libel-proof status, but a specific reputation obtained through means such as newspaper and magazine articles also will suffice. See id. Courts even have admitted

3. Thus far the Ninth Circuit has adopted only the "incremental harm branch" of the libel-proof doctrine. Masson v. New Yorker Magazine, Inc., 881 F.2d 1452, 1457 (9th Cir.1989). "This doctrine measures the incremental reputational harm inflicted by the challenged statements beyond the harm imposed by the nonactionable remainder of the publication; if that 'incremental harm' is ... nominal or nonexistent, the statements are dismissed as not actionable." Id. at 1458 (quotation omitted).

articles published as much as five to eight years before the fact, to show that a plaintiff is libel-proof. Id. at 304.

In contrast to the Second Circuit, the District of Columbia Circuit has rejected libel-proof notions: "Because we think it [libel-proof theory] a fundamentally bad idea, we are not prepared to assume that it is the law of the District of Columbia; nor is it part of federal constitutional law." Liberty Lobby, Inc. v. Anderson, 746 F.2d 1563, 1569 (D.C.Cir. 1984) (Scalia, J.), vacated on other grounds, 477 U.S. 242, 106 S.Ct. 2505, 91 L.Ed.2d 202 (1986). The Liberty Lobby court implied that in applying libel-proof doctrine, the federal courts were spinning loose-woven legal theory not firmly attached to the loom of state law. Id. at 1568–69.

In the only relevant appellate case in this circuit, we affirmed without opinion the district court's dismissal for failure to state a claim. Ray v. Time, Inc., 452 F.Supp. 618 (W.D.Tenn.1976) (Wellford, J.), aff'd without opinion, 582 F.2d 1280 (6th Cir.1978). Plaintiff James Earl Ray, the notorious assassin of Martin Luther King, Jr., brought action for libel against Time and others for publishing false information concerning Ray and his crimes. With respect to the allegedly false information that Ray was a narcotics addict and narcotics peddler as well as a robber, the district court concluded: The Court is persuaded, in the light of all the circumstances in this cause and in the public record involved in the other cases mentioned, that ... James Earl Ray is libel-proof, as that term was used in Cardillo v. Doubleday & Co., Inc., 518 F.2d 638, 639 (2d Cir.1975). ... Ray, as Cardillo, is a convicted habitual criminal and is unlikely to be able to recover damages to his reputation as to warrant dismissal of his libel claim in the light of First Amendment considerations attendant to publication of material dealing with his background and criminal activities. As in [another Second Circuit case], this Court agrees ... that all the circumstances indicate this action is frivolous. Id. at 622.

Although we may question whether all aspects of the libel proof doctrine are sound policy, in this diversity action, our task is to anticipate how the Supreme Court of Ohio would rule if confronted with Brooks's claim. Unfortunately, to date the Ohio courts have not addressed the libel-proof concept.

In any event, regardless of whether the Supreme Court of Ohio would endorse some version of the libel-proof theory, we cannot affirm the district court's summary judgment on the basis of such a concept. In our view, genuine issues of material fact remain as to whether defendants' statements could have done further damage to Brooks's already tarnished reputation. While prior to the broadcast, some Akron residents knew Brooks as an occasionally violent criminal, no popular nationwide television program or other publicity had portrayed Brooks as a "hit-man" for a corrupt judge, a "pimp," a "muscleman," or a "street knowledgeable jive turkey." We leave it to a trier of fact to determine whether, and to what extent, the "20/20" episode damaged Brooks's reputation.

Accordingly, we remand this case to the district court for further proceedings. On remand, the district court may conclude that a trial is necessary to resolve the question of Brooks's libel-proofness. On the other hand, the district court may grant summary judgment for defendants on the basis of one or more of the several alternative grounds, not based upon the libel-proof concept, that defendants have advanced.

[Summary judgment for the defendant is vacated.]

24. **"Incremental" vs. "issue-specific" versions.** The court's reference to the incremental version of the libel-proof plaintiff doctrine is based on a law review note that created the terminology and distinguished the "issue-specific" from "incremental" versions of the libel-proof plaintiff doctrine. Note, *The Libel–Proof Plaintiff Doctrine*, 98 HARV. L. REV. 1909 (1985). The issue-specific version involves a reputation already tarnished on the issue in question. For instance, the defendant publishes that plaintiff tested positively for drugs and this is false; but plaintiff has admitted he is a drug user. The "incremental" version inspects the communication itself. *Id.* at 1912. If the challenged statement harms the reputation less than true or privileged statements in the same document, the judge can find there are no cognizable damages.

25. **Is the issue one of truth?** In *Desnick v. American Broadcasting Companies, Inc.*, 44 F.3d 1345 (7th Cir. 1995), ABC ran a television show criticizing Desnick and his Eye Center. The show stated or implied that Desnick did unnecessary surgery, changed patient records, and otherwise carried on Medicare fraud. It also charged that Desnick or his business tampered with an opthalmic glare machine so that patients would see glares (a symptom of cataracts) and would then accept cataract surgery. Desnick sued for libel, but only for the charges of tampering with the glare machine. Since the charges together might be understood as charges of medicare fraud and/or medical malpractice, the glare machine charge might seem like more of the same, adding little or nothing to the harm done by the uncontested charges. But Judge Posner, characterizing the problem as one of substantial truth, held that dismissal was improper. First, he observed that the charges against Desnick "neither are admitted nor are established.... Given the obstacles to proving defamation, the failure to mount a legal challenge to a defamatory statement cannot be considered an admission that the statement is true." He thought that dismissal of the libel claim was therefore error. Second, the glare machine statements might be understood by the trier to add something because they could not so easily be explained away.

26. **Is the issue one of damages?** In *Davis v. The Tennessean,* 83 S.W.3d 125 (Tenn. Ct. App. 2001), the plaintiff, convicted of aiding a murder, was serving a 99-year sentence for it; the newspaper erroneously reported that plaintiff himself had fired the gun. "Before leaving, Davis shot the owner as he lay on the floor." The court denied recovery.

It said: "His character reputation with the public was established and could not be harmed by inaccurate attribution to him of conduct which was part of the crime in which he participated."

27. **Jury role.** Maybe *Desnick* is simply recognizing the appropriate role of the trier of fact. In *Armistead v. Minor,* 815 So.2d 1189 (Miss. 2002), the court thought that summary judgment on the libel-proof doctrine would require "the Court to make factual findings regarding plaintiff's reputation for a particular trait. . . . While it may be said that some reputations are easily assessed, it still requires consideration of credibility issues, and this is not something the trial judge should undertake."

28. **The *Masson-New Yorker* case.** In *Masson v. New Yorker Magazine, Inc.*, 501 U.S. 496, 111 S. Ct. 2419, 115 L. Ed. 2d 447 (1991), *The New Yorker* attributed statements to the plaintiff in quotations. Although the quotations might be rational interpretations of the statements he actually made, some of the words used were not in fact his. What if the words in quotation marks only made Masson sound "incrementally" worse than the words he actually used? This issue was not reached because it was considered to be a matter of state law, not constitutional law. Presumably this means the Court thought the libel-proof plaintiff was a kind of damages issue, not a truth issue, since *truth* does have constitutional ramifications.

*

PROFESSIONAL AND ACADEMIC ENHANCEMENTS
Chapter 6

The Procedural and Remedial Side of Defamation

Problems of Widespread Publication

Choice of Law

WELLS v. LIDDY, 186 F.3d 505 (4th Cir. 1999). Wells, the plaintiff, a resident of Louisiana, was a secretary at the Democratic National Committee in Washington's Watergate complex for a short time in 1972. During that period, there was a political burglary of the DNC office. Gordon Liddy allegedly coordinated the burglaries and Liddy was "tried on multiple counts of burglary, conspiracy, and interception of wire and oral communications, was found guilty, and received a sentence of six to twenty years imprisonment." After serving 52 months in prison, Liddy retained his fame by writing books and regularly making speeches. In 1997, Wells sued Liddy in a Maryland federal district court, claiming defamation based on several distinct publications: a speech in Virginia; a speech on a cruise ship at sea; comments on a radio program; and comments on a web site. The trial court gave partial summary judgment on the ground that Wells could not prove knowing or reckless falsehood as required by the law of Louisiana even for private persons. Federal courts apply the choice of law rules of the state in which they sit, and the court thought Maryland would apply Louisiana law as the place of the harm and that the plaintiff could not succeed under Louisiana law.

Held, reversed. *(1) Liddy's Virginia speech.* This speech was not broadcast; only the audience present heard it. "In defamation actions, the place of the harm has traditionally been considered to be the place where the defamatory statement was published, i.e., seen or heard by non-parties." So Virginia law would control and the statements were capable of defamatory meaning under Virginia law.

(2) Liddy's cruise ship speech. "The district court's application of Louisiana law to a case of defamation at sea was incorrect. All cases involving a tort committed on navigable water, whether brought under federal admiralty jurisdiction, in state court under the saving-to-suitors clause, or in federal court under diversity jurisdiction, are governed by admiralty law." General maritime law is "[d]rawn from state and federal sources, the general maritime law is an amalgam of traditional common-law rules, modifications of those rules, and newly created rules." Because uniformity is important here, choice of law rules referring to state law are inappropriate.

But "there is no well-developed body of general maritime law of defamation. In such a situation, it is clear that the general maritime law may be supplemented by either state law or more general common law principles. Because great diversity exists among the states' defamation laws, we conclude that it would be more appropriate to apply general common law tort principles rather than the specific law of a single state. [W]e determine that the common law as compiled in the Restatement (Second) of Torts should control our evaluation of Wells's claim of shipboard defamation ... [and specifically] whether Liddy's cruise ship speech is capable of defamatory meaning." On this basis, the court concluded that the speech was capable of defamatory meaning.

(3) *The Don and Mike radio show comments.* "Because of the widespread simultaneous publication of the allegedly defamatory statement in many different jurisdictions, application of the traditional *lex loci delicti* rule becomes cumbersome, if not completely impractical." The court forecasts that Maryland, though it still retains lex loci rules, would consider alternatives here. "The Second Restatement contains a specific section addressing multistate defamation that provides:

> (1) The rights and liabilities that arise from defamatory matter in any ... broadcast over radio or television ... or similar aggregate communication are determined by the local law of the state which, with respect to the particular issue, has the most significant relationship to the occurrence and the parties under the principles stated in § 6.
>
> (2) When a natural person claims that he has been defamed by an aggregate communication, the state of most significant relationship will usually be the state where the person was domiciled at the time, if the matter complained of was published in that state.

Restatement (Second) of Conflict of Laws § 150 (1971). Wells notes that the Don and Mike show was broadcast in Louisiana, the state of her domicile. Therefore, following the Second Restatement, Louisiana law applies to the Don and Mike show claim." Under Louisiana law applied to the broadcast, the statements were not capable of defamatory meaning.

(4) *Web site defamation.* This is another instance of multistate defamation and hence Louisiana law applies as the plaintiff's domicile and the most significant connection. The statements on the web site were capable of defamatory meaning, but the statements were not published by Liddy.

1. **A local publication.** Suppose that the defendant, located in New York, publishes a libel about the plaintiff, who lives in Nevada. The only publication takes place in Minnesota. When sued, the defendant pleads a common law privilege, such as a privilege of fair comment or a privilege to give a report of ongoing litigation proceedings. The three states involved give significantly different scope to those privileges. Which one should apply? Where the publication is in a single state, the Restatement applies the local law of the state where the publication

occurs unless, with respect to some particular issue, some other state has a "more significant relationship" to the parties and the events. RESTATEMENT OF CONFLICT OF LAWS § 149 (1971). What if the publication took place in Minnesota about a court proceeding then pending in New York?

2. **Procedural and semi-procedural rules of law.** The law of the forum state—that is, the place where the case is tried—usually governs one set of issues associated with procedure and door-closers like the statute of limitations, even though some other state's law might govern "substantive" issues.

CONDIT V. DUNNE, 317 F.Supp.2d 344 (S.D. N.Y. 2004). Gary Condit was a Congressman from California, who spent most of his working time in Washington D.C. After a female friend of his, Chandra Levy, disappeared in Washington, he became the object of intense interest. The defendant make several defamatory remarks about Condit, implying his involvement in Levy's disappearance. His remarks were published at various times on a radio talk show, Larry King Live, and in print media, some of which allegedly emanated from Washington, Connecticut, Los Angeles and elsewhere. The defendant lived in New York and Condit brought suit there. In addition, the defendant claims that most of the statements emanated from New York. The main issue on choice of law focused on whether New York or California law should apply. (New York law might give broader protection to speech under its opinion rules than the federal Constitution would required, while California's "opinion" protection went no further than Constitutionally required.) The court recognized a number of factors potentially relevant in determining significant relationship to a state, asking (1) "where plaintiff suffered the greatest injury;" (2) "where the statements emanated and were broadcast; (3) where the activities to which the allegedly defamatory statements refer took place;" and (4) what "policy interests" the states might have in applying their own law. *Held*, California law will apply. "Weighing the factors, the Court finds that California has the most significant interest in the litigation. Certainly New York's interest in the litigation is not insignificant, but none of the conduct about which defendant spoke took place in New York, and plaintiff has no specific connection to New York. Moreover, defendant's comments also have no specific connection to New York, except that defendant happened to be physically present in New York when he uttered the statements that were broadcast nationwide."

1. **Factors.** How can you know that New York's interest in protecting opinion-like speech weighs less than California's interest in protecting citizens from defamation? Does the use of factors always make the outcome indeterminate until trial of the issue, and if so, is that in itself chill on speech?

2. **State of publication, defendant's domicile.** In *Levin v. McPhee,* 917 F.Supp. 230, 236 (S.D. N.Y. 1996), aff'd on other grounds,

119 F.3d 189 (2nd Cir. 1997), the plaintiff was seemingly a Russian who claimed to have been libeled by American publications about events in Russia. The court concluded that "the conduct at issue—publication of the allegedly libelous statements—took place in New York, where the author resides and where both publishers are headquartered. New York law therefore governs the question of liability." Is this essentially contrary to the *Condit* decision or does it merely show that factors can justify any choice the court makes?

3. **Law applied to foreign publications.** Defendant publishes defamation in America and also in a foreign country, Ruritania. The plaintiff, a citizen of Ruritania, sues in the United States. What law applies? According to one case, the law of the foreign country will apply except that this will be limited by the First Amendment rules. See *DeRoburt v. Gannett Co. Inc.*, 83 F.R.D. 574 (D. Haw. 1979). If the foreign publication by an American publisher defames a foreign public official, should the *Times-Sullivan* rules offer any protection when the foreign official brings suit in this country against the American publisher? Or is that some kind of Constitutional imperialism? In *Desai v. Hersh*, 719 F.Supp. 670 (N.D. Ill. 1989), the court thought that if you publish in a foreign country you abandon American constitutional protections. Suppose the foreign official sued in her own country. Should that country voluntarily choose to apply American law?

Jurisdiction in Interstate Libel Cases

KEETON v. HUSTLER MAGAZINE, INC.

465 U.S. 770, 104 S.Ct. 1473, 79 L.Ed.2d 790 (1984)

Justice REHNQUIST delivered the opinion of the Court. . . .

Petitioner Keeton is a resident of New York. Her only connection with New Hampshire is the circulation there of copies of a magazine that she assists in producing. The magazine bears petitioner's name in several places crediting her with editorial and other work. Respondent Hustler Magazine, Inc., is an Ohio corporation, with its principal place of business in California. Respondent's contacts with New Hampshire consist of the sale of some 10 to 15,000 copies of Hustler magazine in that State each month. Petitioner claims to have been libeled in five separate issues of respondent's magazine published between September, 1975, and May, 1976. [An earlier suit by Keeton in Ohio had been held barred by the Ohio statute of limitations. The New Hampshire statute was unique—using a six-year period—and apparently the statute had run against the plaintiff's claim in all other states.] . . .

We conclude that the Court of Appeals erred when it affirmed the dismissal of petitioner's suit for lack of personal jurisdiction. Respondent's regular circulation of magazines in the forum State is sufficient to support an assertion of jurisdiction in a libel action based on the contents of the magazine. This is so even if [the plaintiff could recover damages from publications taking place throughout the United States.]

The Court of Appeals acknowledged that petitioner was suing, at least in part, for damages suffered in New Hampshire. And it is beyond dispute that New Hampshire has a significant interest in redressing injuries that actually occur within the State. A state has an especial interest in exercising judicial jurisdiction over those who commit torts within its territory. This is because torts involve wrongful conduct which a state seeks to deter, and against which it attempts to afford protection, by providing that a tortfeasor shall be liable for damages which are the proximate result of his tort. This interest extends to libel actions brought by nonresidents. False statements of fact harm both the subject of the falsehood and the readers of the statement. New Hampshire may rightly employ its libel laws to discourage the deception of its citizens. There is no constitutional value in false statements of fact.

New Hampshire may also extend its concern to the injury that in-state libel causes within New Hampshire to a nonresident. The tort of libel is generally held to occur wherever the offending material is circulated. Restatement (Second) of Torts § 577A, Comment a (1977). The reputation of the libel victim may suffer harm even in a state in which he has hitherto been anonymous. The communication of the libel may create a negative reputation among the residents of a jurisdiction where the plaintiff's previous reputation was, however small, at least unblemished. . . .

The Court of Appeals also thought that there was an element of due process "unfairness" arising from the fact that the statutes of limitations in every jurisdiction except New Hampshire had run on the plaintiff's claim in this case. Strictly speaking, however, any potential unfairness in applying New Hampshire's statute of limitations to all aspects of this nationwide suit has nothing to do with the jurisdiction of the Court to adjudicate the claims. The issue is personal jurisdiction, not choice of law. The question of the applicability of New Hampshire's statute of limitations to claims for out-of-state damages presents itself in the course of litigation only after jurisdiction over respondent is established, and we do not think that such choice of law concerns should complicate or distort the jurisdictional inquiry. . . .

Finally, implicit in the Court of Appeals' analysis of New Hampshire's interest is an emphasis on the extremely limited contacts of the plaintiff with New Hampshire. But we have not to date required a plaintiff to have "minimum contacts" with the forum State before permitting that State to assert personal jurisdiction over a nonresident defendant. On the contrary, we have upheld the assertion of jurisdiction where such contacts were entirely lacking. . . .

The judgment of the Court of Appeals is reversed and the cause is remanded for proceedings consistent with this opinion.

1. **Choice of law in *Keeton*.** The fact that New Hampshire has jurisdiction does not necessarily mean that (a) it would apply its local law or (b) that it would be constitutionally permissible for it to do so. In fact, however, New Hampshire did decide to apply its *procedural* laws, including its statute of limitations, in the *Keeton* litigation. See *Keeton v. Hustler Magazine, Inc.,* 131 N.H. 6, 549 A.2d 1187 (1988). Yet even that decision would not mean that New Hampshire would or constitutionally could apply its substantive law rules.

2. **Jurisdiction over internet libels; totality of contacts approach.** The internet has a potent potential for defamation and it has also raised new problems of jurisdiction. If Keeton were defamed by a statement on a website originating in California, would every court in the United States have jurisdiction over her claim? Some courts have mostly focused on the totality of the defendant's contacts with the state where jurisdiction is asserted, rejecting jurisdiction where the defendant merely publishes on a passive web site, without seeking to do business in the state or engaging in an active web site with substantial interchange of information. In other words, the facts that people in the plaintiff's home state might find the defamation on the web is not by itself enough. In *Bailey v. Turbine Design, Inc.,* 86 F.Supp.2d 790 (W.D. Tenn. 2000), plaintiff, located in Tennessee, was a competitor with defendant, located in Florida. The defendant's web site referred to the plaintiff as a con artist, then said "*Click here to do some due diligence.*" Clicking on the displayed link took the user to a mug shot of the plaintiff along with the plaintiff's arrest records from 1991. But this was not "interactive," and not enough to warrant jurisdiction in Tennessee. A number of cases are reviewed in the legal literature. E.g., John Di Bari, *A Survey of the Internet Jurisdiction Universe,* 18 N.Y. INT'L L. REV. 123 (2005).

3. **Jurisdiction over internet libels; the effects test.** In *Calder v. Jones,* 465 U.S. 783, 104 S.Ct. 1482, 79 L.Ed.2d 804 (1984), a California plaintiff sued the author and editor of an allegedly defamatory article published in the National Enquirer in Florida, which circulated a substantial number of copies in California. The author and editor objected to California's jurisdiction, but the Untied States Supreme Court held that jurisdiction was proper. The article "concerned the California activities of a California resident. It impugned the professionalism of an entertainer whose television career was centered in California. The article was drawn from California sources, and the brunt of the harm, in terms both of respondent's emotional distress and the injury to her professional reputation, was suffered in California. In sum, California is the focal point both of the story and of the harm suffered. Jurisdiction over petitioners is therefore proper in California based on the 'effects' of their Florida conduct in California." Although the author and editor were not in charge of publishing or marketing, they "are not charged with mere untargeted negligence. Rather, their intentional, and allegedly tortious, actions were expressly aimed at California."

The effects test may negate jurisdiction in some cases. In *Pavlovich v. Superior Court,* 29 Cal.4th 262, 58 P.3d 2, 127 Cal.Rptr.2d 329 (2002), the court emphasized that "merely asserting that a defendant knew or should have known that his intentional acts would cause harm in the forum state is not enough to establish jurisdiction under the effects test. . . . Instead, the plaintiff must also point to contacts which demonstrate that the defendant *expressly aimed* its tortious conduct at the forum. . . ."

Some courts have used the effects test in support of jurisdiction in internet defamation cases, but sometimes alongside the totality of contacts test. In *Blumenthal v. Drudge*, 992 F.Supp. 44 (D.D.C. 1998), the defendant, with a base of operations in Los Angeles, published an electronic gossip column, focusing on Hollywood and Washington, D.C. He allegedly defamed people in Washington, D.C. in the publication. The court upheld jurisdiction in Washington, partly because he was targeting people there but also partly because the web site was interactive, so that he could be perceived as engaging in acts there.

Robert J. Condin, *"Defendant Veto" or "Totality of the Circumstances"? It's Time for the Supreme Court to Straighten out the Personal Jurisdiction Standard Once Again,* 54 CATH. U. L. REV. 53 (2004), is very helpful in discussing the effects and uncertainties of *Calder* in libel and related cases.

The Jurisdiction of Foreign Countries

The Gutnick Case

In *Dow Jones & Co. v. Gutnick*, (2002) HCA 56, 194 A.L.R. 433 (2002), the plaintiff, who lived in Victoria, Australia, sued Dow Jones in the state of Victoria for defamation allegedly contained on a subscription website owned by Dow Jones and managed in New Jersey, but read in Australia as well as other places. The Australia High Court upheld the jurisdiction of the Victoria court and the application of Australian law.

The law of Australia does not emphasize free speech as American law does. As one of the High Court judges said: "Australian defamation law, and, for that matter, English defamation law also, and the policy underlying them are different from those of the United States. There is no doubt that the latter leans heavily, some might say far too heavily, in favour of defendants." The same judge added that what Dow Jones sought was "to impose upon Australian residents . . . an American legal hegemony in relation to Internet publications. The consequence, if the appellant's submission were to be accepted would be to confer upon one country, and one notably more benevolent to the commercial and other media than this one, an effective domain over the law of defamation, to the financial advantage of publishers in the United States, and the serious disadvantage of those unfortunate enough to be reputationally damaged outside the United States." (Callinan, J.)

Australia, of course, is not required to use the same approaches taken by American case law. To get a handle on *Gutnick's* assertion of jurisdiction, however, consider what result American courts would reach under the totality of contacts or the effects tests if the tables were turned and an American citizen sued an Australian internet publisher.

The Yahoo! Case

One more foreign decision is worth noting. *Yahoo!, Inc. v. La Ligue Contre le Racisme et L'Antisemitisme,* 169 F.Supp.2d 1181(N.D. Cal. 2001), reflects an order of a French court. Yahoo! is an internet service provider. It provides a site in which people can offer items for sale in an internet auction and reports the highest offered price to the seller, who then can make his own arrangements with the would-be buyer. Yahoo! does not operate the auction. French law prohibits the exhibition of any Nazi artifacts or propaganda, and a French court held that the auction site violated French law because, although the site did not appear in the French "edition" (Yahoo.fr), French citizens could reach the site and see the sale offers. The French court ordered the American Yahoo! to cease auctioning such items and announced in advance a fine of over $13,000 each day of violation. Although *Yahoo!* is not a libel case, it suggests the potential that was realized in *Gutnick*. (On the technical side of the case, Yahoo! sought a declaratory judgment that the order was not enforceable. The trial judge granted the order, but the Ninth Circuit, in a panel decision, reversed on the ground that the French associations sued were not subject to personal jurisdiction. *Yahoo! Inc. v. La Ligue Contre Le Racisme Et L'Antisemitisme,* 379 F.3d 1120 (9th Cir. 2004). Then the Ninth Circuit granted rehearing en banc, 399 F.3d 1010, and that's where the matter stands as of August, 2005.

Enforcement of Defamation Awards Made in Foreign Countries

General Principles

The Full Faith and Credit Clause of the Constitution requires that each state give full faith and credit to the judgments of sister states, enforcing them much as they would enforce their own judgments, so long as the court rendering the judgment had jurisdiction.

Could American courts simply refuse to enforce an Australian libel judgment in the United States? That would be a critical question if Mr. Gutnick could not find Dow Jones assets in Australia and wanted to register the judgment in the United States to reach Dow Jones' assets at its home.

Absent a treaty obligation, American courts are not required to enforce judgments of courts of foreign countries. However, American courts generally do in fact enforce foreign money judgments as a matter of comity and as an important element in world-wide commerce, provided that the foreign court had jurisdiction of the parties. Even if the foreign court does not recognize important rights like the right to jury trial or the right to cross examination, American law generally enforces the foreign judgment.

The *Telnikoff* Case

In spite of the strong policy of enforcing foreign judgments, American courts hold that, as a matter of discretion, they may refuse enforcement of foreign judgments that are fundamentally inconsistent with the state's public policy. In *Telnikoff v. Matusevitch,* 347 Md. 561, 702 A.2d 230 (1997), the Maryland Court considered an English judgment against Matusevitch, who had been born in America but who had lived in the Soviet Union for a long period before fleeing that country. At the time of the Maryland decision, he was resident in Maryland and had worked in the District of Columbia for an American corporation during the entire period involved in the case. Matusevitch was sued in England by Telnikoff, who had been born in Leningrad in 1937, and who emigrated to Israel but who became an English citizen at some point. Both men dealt with radio broadcasts to Russia. Telnikoff recovered a judgment against Matusevitch in the English courts for £240,000 based upon Matusevitch's letters in an English publication criticizing Telnikoff's proposals as racist. The Maryland court held that enforcement of the English judgment would be repugnant to Maryland's free speech policy. The court observed that the plaintiff was in a species of public official, that the publication was not a knowing or reckless falsehood, and indeed, that it was in the nature of comment or rhetorical hyperbole.

Is *Telnikoff* right and will it be followed? In answering that question, consider this. American free speech policy is fundamental, but does it apply (a) to publications made in foreign countries or (b) to judgments of foreign countries? On the second point, it has been suggested that enforcement of a foreign, speech-restrictive judgment is no more a matter of American constitutional law than enforcement of a speech restrictive contract. See Molly S. Van Houweling, *Enforcement of Foreign Judgments, the First Amendment, and Internet Speech: Notes for the Next Yahoo! v. LICRA*, 24 Mich. J. Int'l L. 697 (2003); Mark D. Rosen, *Exporting the Constitution,* 53 Emory L. J. 171 (2004). On the first point, consider the argument that the Constitution of the United States simply does not protect publishers from foreign law. Or has the internet changed everything?

How would you compare or contrast *Telnikoff* and the trial court's decision in *Yahoo!*?

1. **New directions?** Some of the cases presented above and some of the issues have provoked a good deal of comment, often associated with the burgeoning global economy as it is abetted by the internet. The issues generated by internet libel are paralleled by similar issues in other fields, notably trademarks on the web. Should American courts be more cosmopolitan, recognizing the value of being a part of the global community and respecting the judgments of others? Paul Schiff Berman, *Towards a Cosmopolitan Vision of Conflict of Laws: Redefining Governmental Interests in a Global Era,* 153 U. Pa. L. Rev. 1819 (2005) (suggesting a cosmopolitan as opposed to parochial view would recognize "the possibility that people can hold multiple, sometimes nonterritorial,

community affiliations'' and a pluralist view that acknowledges ''that forms of legal (or quasi-legal) jurisdiction can be asserted by communities beyond those represented by official state-sanctioned courts'').

Another Path: The European Court of Human Rights

Among Europeans, or any group of foreign states bound by treaties, disregard of speech-restrictive judgments stands on a different footing. Consider *Miloslavsky v. United Kingdom,* 20 E.H.R.R. 442 (Euro. Ct. Human Rts 1995). Miloslavsky, a history professor in England, wrote a pamphlet about the decision in 1945 (at the end of World War II) to turn over 70,000 Cossack refugees to the Soviets and Titoists. It was generally understood, he said, that this would mean the refugees, men, women and children, would be massacred, as indeed they were. Miloslavsky placed heavy responsibility for the decision upon Lord Aldington. Lord Aldington recovered a large judgment in the English Courts, which also enjoined any further publication of the statements. Miloslavsky, then brought suit against England in the European Court of Human Rights. Relying on a Convention to which England was a party, the court concluded that England had denied Miloslavsky a basic right of free speech and held England liable for Miloslavsky's losses in the suit.

If the *Miloslavsky* decision in the European Court is a sound one, would it not also be sound to refuse enforcement of the English judgment against Miloslavsky?

As of now, enforcement of foreign judgment is a matter for the states to decide. This may change in the near future. One idea is that a federal statute should control. Another is that an international treaty could govern the issue .. If you represent publishers—in print, on the internet, or otherwise—these are most significant matters.

Libel-Proof Plaintiffs

CHURCH OF SCIENTOLOGY INTERNATIONAL v. BEHAR

238 F.3d 168 (2d Cir. 2001)

JOHN M. WALKER, Jr., Chief Judge. . . .

On May 6, 1991, Time magazine published a 10-page, 7500-word cover article entitled ''Scientology: The Cult of Greed'' (the ''Article''). The Article, written by defendant-appellee Richard Behar (''Behar''), was highly critical of Scientology, which it described as ''pos[ing] as a religion'' but being ''really a ruthless global scam,'' and narrated various instances of wrongdoing by a number of individual Scientologists. CSI filed a complaint alleging libel against Behar and defendants-appellees Time Inc. Magazine Co. and its parent company Time Warner, Inc.

(collectively, "Time"). [The alleged libels are numerous; what follows is an incomplete sample.]

Paragraph 40 of the Complaint

1. "[T]he church ... survives by intimidating members and critics in a Mafia-like manner."

2. "Scientology is quite likely the most ruthless, the most classically terroristic ... cult the country has ever seen."

3. "Those who criticize the church—journalists, doctors, lawyers and even judges—often find themselves ... framed for fictional crimes, beaten up or threatened with death." ...

Paragraph 52 of the Complaint

5. "One source of funds for the Los Angeles-based church is the notorious, self-regulated stock exchange in Vancouver, British Columbia, often called the scam capital of the world."

6. "Baybak, 49, who runs a public relations company staffed with Scientologists, apparently has no ethics problem with engineering a hostile takeover of a firm he is hired to promote."

7. "What these guys do is take over companies, hype the stock, sell their shares, and then there's nothing left. ... They stole this man's property." ...

Paragraph 58 of the Complaint

8. "THE LOTTICKS LOST THEIR SON, Noah, who jumped from a Manhattan hotel clutching $171, virtually the only money he had not yet turned over to Scientology. His parents blame the church and would like to sue but are frightened by the organization's reputation for ruthlessness."

9. "His death inspired his father Edward, a physician, to start his own investigation of the church. 'We thought Scientology was something like Dale Carnegie,' Lottick says. 'I now believe it's a school for psychopaths. Their so-called therapies are manipulations. They take the best and brightest people and destroy them.' " ...

[The plaintiff conceded that it was a public figure. Evidence indicated that, as to most of the alleged libels, the author of the publication relied upon extensive investigation, including interviews with many people. The court concluded that no reasonable person could find that the author entertained serious doubts about the truth of the statements and hence that no malice had been shown as to most statements.]

The VSE [Vancouver Stock Exchange] *Statements: Subsidiary Meaning*. The district court ultimately dismissed the VSE Statement based on the subsidiary meaning doctrine established by this court in Herbert v. Lando, 781 F.2d 298 (2d Cir.1986). In Herbert, we held that when a "published view" of a plaintiff is not actionable as libel, other statements made in the same publication are not "actionable if they merely imply the same view, and are simply an outgrowth of and subsidiary to those claims upon which it has been held that there can be no recovery." Relying on the Supreme Court's holding in Masson v. New Yorker Magazine, Inc., 501 U.S. 496, 111 S.Ct. 2419, 115 L.Ed.2d 447 (1991), that the related "incremental harm" doctrine is not a creature of federal constitutional law, CSI argues that (1) the subsidiary meaning doctrine can be applied here only if it is part of the relevant body of state law, and (2) neither California nor New York law, one of which presumably applies to this case, recognizes this doctrine. Because the subsidiary meaning doctrine is merely a gloss on constitutional actual malice, we disagree.

The incremental harm doctrine at issue in Masson reasons that when unchallenged or non-actionable parts of a publication are damaging, an additional statement, even if maliciously false, might be non-actionable because it causes no appreciable additional harm. In Masson, the Supreme Court reject[ed] any suggestion that the incremental harm doctrine is compelled as a matter of First Amendment protection for speech ... [because t]he question of incremental harm does not bear upon whether a defendant has published a statement with knowledge of falsity or reckless disregard of whether it was false or not.

By contrast with the incremental harm doctrine, the subsidiary meaning doctrine does "bear upon" whether a defendant has acted with actual malice. In Herbert, for example, this court held that nine of eleven allegedly libelous statements were not actionable because they were not maliciously published; the published statements were backed by evidence that was not known to be false, and as to the reliability of which the defendants had not shown reckless disregard. Because the defendants' overall "view" of the plaintiff rested on such evidence, we held that they "could not be said to have had actual malice in publishing [it]." In light of this conclusion, it would have been illogical to hold, based on other statements, that the plaintiffs in fact had such actual malice. To avoid that contradiction, we enunciated the subsidiary meaning doctrine. It follows that the doctrine, as articulated in Herbert and as relevant here, "bear[s] ... upon" whether a "view" was published with actual malice. It is thus a question of federal constitutional law, not state law, and it remains good law after Masson.

Our holding in Herbert is still the law of this Circuit, and we therefore conclude that the district court properly held that the VSE Statement was subsidiary in meaning to the larger thrust of the Article, which asserted that "Scientology, rather than being a bona fide religion, is in fact organized for the purpose of making money by means legitimate and illegitimate." We believe that the import of statements 6 and 7, which were included in the Article's VSE sidebar, is also subsidiary to the general message of the Article, and therefore CSI's claims with respect to those statements were properly dismissed. ...

1. **Libel-proof plaintiff as a truth issue?** Can we say that there is no special libel proof plaintiff doctrine? Perhaps you can make a case

that the libel-proof plaintiff doctrine turns out to be nothing more than (a) application of the substantial truth rules, (b) a requirement of actual damages in the form of reputational harm, or (c) an application of the *Times-Sullivan* "malice" rules, depending upon the facts. A less sophisticated summary of the libel proof plaintiff problem is presented in Dobbs on Torts § 422 (2000).

2. **Comparing non-libel cases.** In *Etheredge v. District of Columbia*, 635 A.2d 908 (D.C. App. 1993), the plaintiff sued for false arrest and other torts. The officers charged the plaintiff with assault upon an officer with a deadly weapon, but for that charge they lacked probable cause. The court noted that "Historically, '[a]n arrest for one offense cannot be justified by proof of another, even though intimately connected in time and place.'" But it thought that there were circumstances in which the rule should be not mechanically applied. "Borrowing a phrase from the world of sports, we advert to the rule of 'no harm, no foul.' Where a technical charging error by the police in characterizing the plaintiff's conduct did not affect what subsequently happened to the plaintiff, there is no reasonable basis for imposing liability. If, for example, police arrest a man who has entered a home and raped the occupant, and charge the man with burglary (but not with rape), the rapist ought not to be permitted to recover damages if it subsequently appears that probable cause as to burglary was lacking, when probable cause existed to charge the plaintiff with rape, and he could and would have been arrested for that offense anyway." So the issue would be on retrial whether the plaintiff suffered any detention under the wrong charge that he would not have suffered under a correct one. Which form of the libel proof plaintiff doctrine does this resemble—the one emphasizing the truth rules, the damages rules, or the malice rules?

Chapter 7

INVASION OF PRIVACY

INTRODUCTORY NOTE

Invasion of privacy is not only big business, it is a big subject. Where an entire course is taught on privacy, many means of privacy invasion—via internet "cookies," compilations of credit records (sometimes erroneous), medical and government information, for example—can be considered. Likewise, the effect, or lack of effect, of many statutes can be considered in such courses. This book more modestly attempts to cover basic common law rights of privacy, with a nod to an occasional statute.

Origins. Privacy law as a separate body of rules got its start with the publication of Samuel D. Warren and Louis D. Brandeis, *The Right to Privacy*, 4 HARV. L. REV. 193 (1890). Up until then, privacy interests were protected by various legal doctrines like trespass and common law copyright. After that article was published, courts began to recognize the commercial appropriation form of privacy invasion.

Commercial appropriation and other forms. Commercial appropriation is illustrated by the kind of case in which an advertiser uses your picture without your permission. Although a commercial appropriation may be demeaning to personhood, this book will consider such an appropriation as at least partly an economic tort analogous to an appropriation of intellectual property, and it will be considered in that context. New York enacted a privacy statute that was limited to such appropriation. N.Y. CIV. RTS. L. § 50. With a few exceptions, other courts, however, have tended to recognize three other forms of privacy invasion, accomplished by (1) intruding upon privacy, e.g., eavesdropping, (2) placing the plaintiff in a false light, e.g., by publishing a non-defamatory falsehood, and (3) publishing "private facts" about the plaintiff.

§ 1. FORMS OF PRIVACY INVASION

(a) Intrusion

MILLER v. BROOKS

123 N.C.App. 20, 472 S.E.2d 350 (1996)

LEWIS, Judge.

[Plaintiff was defendant's husband, but the parties had had marital difficulties and were living apart. The defendant wife had surrendered her key to the house.]

In February 1993, defendant Annette Miller made arrangements with defendant Gregory Brooks, a private investigator with defendant Brooks Investigations, Inc., for a surveillance camera to be placed in the Buck Lane residence. Brooks hired defendants Massaroni and Hite to assist. On 5 February 1993, Brooks contacted a locksmith who met defendants Miller, Brooks, and Massaroni at the house and made a key to the house. On or about 16 or 17 February 1993, when plaintiff was not home, defendants Massaroni and Brooks entered the Buck Lane house, altered the wiring, and installed a hidden videotape camera in the bedroom ceiling.

On 17 February 1993, plaintiff returned home and discovered a pile of dust or dirt on the floor indicating that someone had been in his house. He engaged a private detective who helped him locate and remove the camera and videotape. They watched the videotape which showed pictures of plaintiff in his bedroom, getting undressed, taking a shower, and going to bed. The tape also showed defendants Brooks and Hite in plaintiff's bedroom. After discovering the camera, plaintiff became fearful for his life, moved out of his house temporarily, and carried a loaded shotgun in his car. He suspected he was being investigated by federal officials and went into hiding. Later, defendants Miller, Massaroni, and Hite went to the house to change the videotape and discovered that the camera and tape had been removed.

In mid-February 1993, defendant Miller, representing herself as a resident, asked the local post office to hold the mail for 2400 Buck Lane. Afterwards, she regularly picked up plaintiff's mail at the post office, sorted through and discarded portions of it, and placed the remainder in plaintiff's mailbox. Defendant Massaroni picked up the mail for her once. Postal employees discovered that defendant Miller was not living at the Buck Lane house and contacted plaintiff.

[Plaintiff's suit for invasion of privacy, infliction of distress, and trespass was terminated on summary judgment for all defendants.]

Our Supreme Court has held that a right of privacy exists in North Carolina and has recognized the first type of privacy tort, i.e., invasion of privacy by the unauthorized appropriation of a plaintiff's photographic likeness for a defendant's advantage as part of an advertisement or commercial enterprise. However, the Court has refused to recognize the third type, invasion of privacy by disclosure of private facts, or the fourth type, invasion of privacy by placing a plaintiff in a false light before the public. See Renwick, 310 N.C. at 322, 326, 312 S.E.2d at 411, 413.

In Smith v. Jack Eckerd Corp., 101 N.C.App. 566, 400 S.E.2d 99 (1991), we defined the intrusion tort as follows: "[o]ne who intentionally intrudes, physically or otherwise, upon the solitude or seclusion of another or his private affairs or concerns, is subject to liability to the other for invasion of his privacy, if the intrusion would be highly offensive to a reasonable person." . . .

Plaintiff had every reasonable expectation of privacy in his mail and in his home and bedroom. A jury could conclude that these invasions would be highly offensive to a reasonable person.

Unlike the privacy torts based on public disclosure of private facts and false light publicity, the intrusion tort does not implicate the First Amendment concerns addressed in Renwick and Hall. Recognition of this tort also does not duplicate other tort claims. An offensive physical contact is not required for the intrusion tort as it is for battery. Severe emotional distress is not an element of this tort as it is for intentional and negligent infliction of emotional distress. The intrusion tort also does not duplicate trespass since trespass requires proof of an unauthorized entry on land possessed by another and this tort does not. Thus, we conclude that the intrusion tort is actionable in this State.

We reject defendants' assertion that the marital relationship between plaintiff and defendant Annette Miller precludes plaintiff from asserting an intrusion claim. [T]here is evidence that, at the time of the intrusions, plaintiff and defendant Miller were living separately and had agreed that only plaintiff would live in the marital residence. The evidence raises a genuine issue of material fact as to whether plaintiff had authorized her to enter his house without his permission. Furthermore, there is no evidence that plaintiff authorized his wife or anyone else to install a video camera in his bedroom or to intercept and open his mail.

Although a person's reasonable expectation of privacy might, in some cases, be less for married persons than for single persons, such is not the case here where the spouses were estranged and living separately. Further, the marital relationship has no bearing on the acts of defendants Brooks, Hite, Brooks Investigations, and Massaroni. Plaintiff's marriage to defendant Miller did nothing to reduce his expectations that his personal privacy would not be invaded by perfect strangers. The acts of installing the hidden video camera and the interception of plaintiff's mail as alleged and forecasted are sufficient to sustain plaintiff's claims for invasion of privacy by intrusion on his seclusion, solitude, or private affairs. Plaintiff has offered sufficient proof of these acts, many of which are admitted in defendants' depositions, to survive summary judgment.

Plaintiff also asserts that the trial court erred by granting summary judgment to defendants on his trespass claim. We agree. . . .

There is abundant record evidence showing that defendants, on more than one occasion, intentionally entered the Buck Lane house and premises and that plaintiff had possession at that time. The key issue in dispute is whether these entries were authorized.

. . . Even if [defendant wife] had permission to enter the house and to authorize others to do so, there is also evidence to create a genuine issue of material fact as to whether defendants' entries exceeded the scope of any permission given.

We further conclude that plaintiff's marriage to defendant Annette Miller does not automatically preclude his action for trespass. N.C. Gen.Stat. section 52–5 (1991) provides that a husband and wife may sue each other for damages sustained to their person or property as if they were unmarried. . . .

"The essence of a trespass to realty is the disturbance of possession." Matthews, 235 N.C. at 283, 69 S.E.2d at 555. If plaintiff had the right of possession at the time of the entries and if defendant Miller had no such right, any entries made by her without plaintiff's consent, or by the other defendants, constitute trespass. This is true even if defendants entered the premises with a bona fide belief that they were entitled to enter the property since such a belief is no defense to trespass. . . .

Plaintiff further asserts that the court erred by granting summary judgment to defendants on his claim for intentional infliction of emotional distress. . . . Here, plaintiff has forecast sufficient evidence of these elements to survive summary judgment. A jury could reasonably find that the conduct of defendants in breaking into plaintiff's house and installing a hidden video camera was "extreme and outrageous conduct." . . .

Plaintiff has also forecast sufficient evidence of severe and disabling emotional distress to survive summary judgment. . . .

[Summary judgment for the defendants on the claim of punitive damages.] Plaintiff's evidence of aggravated conduct includes the following: (1) that defendants knew plaintiff had paranoid tendencies making him particularly susceptible to their intrusions; (2) that defendants Brooks and Massaroni altered the wiring of his house although neither of them were licensed electricians; (3) that defendants placed the camera in the bedroom rather than in a less private area of the house; (4) that they went back into the house even after they discovered that the camera had been removed. Given this evidence, summary judgment was not proper on plaintiff's prayer for punitive damages.

Reversed and remanded.

SCHILLER V. MITCHELL, 357 Ill.App.3d 435, 828 N.E.2d 323, 293 Ill.Dec. 353 (2005). The defendant affixed a video camera to his home, pointing toward the garage door and side door of his next door neighbor, the plaintiff. He taped more or less constantly, using the tapes to lodge many, many complaints to police and the neighborhood association, for example, that plaintiff's sprinkler got water on the defendant's land and plaintiff swept his garage in the morning. Plaintiff sued on several theories, including intrusive invasion of privacy. The trial judge dismissed all claims. *Held*, affirmed. As to invasion of privacy: "The complaint does not explain why a passerby on the street or a roofer or a tree trimmer could not see what the camera saw, only from a different angle. We conclude that plaintiffs have not pleaded facts that satisfy the privacy element of the tort of intrusion upon the seclusion of another."

PEOPLE FOR THE ETHICAL TREATMENT OF ANIMALS V. BOBBY BEROSINI, LTD., 111 Nev. 615, 895 P.2d 1269 (1995). Berosini prepared his animals for a show at the Stardust Hotel in Las Vegas. He had insisted as part of his arrangement with Stardust that he and his animals would be left alone for a period of time immediately preceding each show. His stated purpose was to keep the animals from distraction and to focus their attention. Defendant secretly made a video tape of Berosini's treatment of the animals during these periods. This treatment led some but not all observers to think the animals were abused. Berosini lost his libel claim based on publication of the video and comments about it. He also claimed intrusive invasion of privacy. *Held*, the intrusion must be one that would be offensive to a reasonable person and in addition it must invade a reasonable expectation of privacy. Berosini's expectation of privacy was limited to an expectation that the animals would not be distracted. Hence the taping, which was secret, "did not intrude upon Berosini's expected seclusion."

REID V. PIERCE COUNTY, 136 Wash.2d 195, 961 P.2d 333 (1998). Several plaintiffs in different suits alleged that several different county employees took or copied official autopsy photos of the plaintiffs' deceased relatives, then used or retained those photos for personal purposes. One allegedly kept a scrapbook; another allegedly used the photos in teaching road safety. *Held*, the plaintiffs have no claim for intentional or negligent infliction of emotional distress because the plaintiffs were not present when the conduct took place, but "the immediate relatives of a decedent have a protectable privacy interest in the autopsy records of the decedent. That protectable privacy interest is grounded in maintaining the dignity of the deceased."

Personal Harassment

1. **Debt collection.** Some forms of personal harassment are sometimes considered to be intrusive invasions of privacy. Although offensive

and harassing debt collection tactics might readily be considered under the rules for intentional infliction of emotional distress, some such cases have talked of privacy invasion. There is a federal statute regulating debt collection methods and tactics. Fair Debt Collection Practices Act, 15 U.S.C.A. § 1692.

2. **Telemarketers.** In *Irvine v. Akron Beacon Journal,* 147 Ohio App.3d 428, 770 N.E.2d 1105 (2002), appeal denied, 96 Ohio St.3d 1491, 774 N.E.2d 765 (2002), the court upheld a privacy invasion and a statutory violation claim against a newspaper that programmed autodial calling in such a way as to result in predictably repeated calls to the same numbers. There is a federal statute, the Telephone Consumer Protection Act or TCPA, 47 U.S.C.A. § 227. It gains what strength it has from FCC rules based on it. See 47 C.F.R. § 64.1200. State statutes may also create some limited privacy rights against telemarketers.

3. **Other forms of harassment.** In *Phillips v. Smalley Maintenance Services*, 435 So.2d 705 (Ala. 1983) an employer repeatedly made sexual demands and asked sexual questions of an employee. The court said this was an invasion of privacy by invasion of psychological solitude. Why not simply say it was an intentional infliction of mental distress?

Employee Testing

4. **Lie detector tests.** Employees come in for a large amount of scrutiny by employers. Should an employer faced with theft losses be permitted to demand that all his employees take a lie detector or polygraph test? Absent statute, threats, or other improprieties, use of a polygraph alone does not seem to be a tort. See *Gibson v. Hummel*, 688 S.W.2d 4 (Mo. App. 1985). State statutes sometimes forbade the employer's use, however, and now a federal statute does too. Under the federal statute, the employer may not use a polygraph to test either employees or prospective employees. The federal statute creates a private right of action for violations and authorizes job reinstatement as well as damages. 29 U.S.C. § 2005(c). The statute makes it unlawful to "require, request, [or] suggest" any such test, or to use any such test provided by others or even to ask about it. 29 U.S.C. § 2002.

5. **Governmental drug testing.** Governmental employers who test employees for drugs are conducting "searches" within the meaning of the Fourth Amendment. Thus testing must be reasonable. That normally requires an individualized suspicion of those tested, or in the alternative, special needs and a compelling governmental interest in suspicionless testing. The work of some governmental employees is dangerous or "special" enough to permit testing under these standards. *Skinner v. Railway Labor Executives' Ass'n,* 489 U.S. 602, 109 S.Ct. 1402, 103 L.Ed.2d 639 (1989) (railroad employees after accidents). But general drug testing of candidates for high office, however, is impermissible. *Chandler v. Miller,* 520 U.S. 305, 117 S.Ct. 1295, 137 L.Ed.2d 513 (1997).

6. **Private employer drug testing.** Since the United States Constitution limits government but not private actors, private employers are constitutionally free to test employees even without a suspicion of wrongdoing. States could, however, impose limits in the interest of privacy. Should they? In *Twigg v. Hercules Corp.,* 185 W.Va. 155, 406 S.E.2d 52 (1990), an employee refused a suspicionless drug test and was discharged. He sued for wrongful discharge on the theory that it was against public policy to discharge a person for resisting an invasion of privacy. The court agreed, holding that employers in West Virginia could test whenever they had either (a) reasonable and good faith suspicion (not necessarily probable cause) or (b) the job responsibility involved public safety or the safety of others. Some other cases have taken a similar view but have found on the facts that safety considerations justified the invasion of privacy. See *Hennessey v. Coastal Eagle Point Oil Co.,* 129 N.J. 81, 609 A.2d 11 (1992) (so holding and reviewing cases). Other states, by statute or decision, however, in effect eliminate privacy invasion claims based on employer drug testing. E.g., ARIZ. REV. STAT. § 23–493.04.

Other Information Gathering

7. **Systematic information gathering.** Traditionally, privacy concerns focused on governmental intrusion. Hence the Fourth Amendment's guarantee against governmental intrusion on "the right of the people to be secure in their persons, houses, papers, and effects. . . ." Today, however, government, large corporations, and individual pirates are engaged in massive gathering and storage of information about citizens, through the legal and illegal use of computers, information sharing among businesses, and direct governmental investigations. Some private businesses are of course in the business of gathering and selling information about private individuals, both wholesale (as with mailing lists) and retail (details such as finances, social security numbers, and various preferences) about particular individuals. Sometimes these intrusions lead only to more telemarketing or spam, sometimes to loss of funds and credit, and sometimes to serious misinformation that can cause harm to reputation, or even physical harm. See ¶ 13, below.

8. **Eavesdropping.** Eavesdropping is a basic example of intrusive privacy invasion. Some telephonic eavesdropping is prohibited by federal statute, which prescribes a tort suit with guaranteed minimum damages. 18 U.S.C. § 2520 creates a civil cause of action for wiretapping and electronic and cordless phone interceptions prohibited in the statute's other sections. The victim can recover damages specified in a schedule or actual damages, whichever is higher, and also punitive damages and a reasonable attorney fee. States have also enacted similar statutes. Other kinds of eavesdropping can easily count as a common law tort. See *Hamberger v. Eastman*, 106 N.H. 107, 206 A.2d 239 (1964) (landlord had a recording device in tenants' bedroom).

9. **Some statutory actions.** Some intrusion attempts are crimes under federal or state law, and some statutes create a cause of action. At

best, statutory protection is piecemeal and often ineffective. A federal statute forbids your video store from revealing the names of films you rent and gives you a cause of action with a minimum of $2500 if the store tells anyone beside the government agent with a warrant or court order. 18 U.S.C.A. § 2710. Companies you do business with are allowed to share information they have about you with others, provided only that they give you a "privacy notice." Some statutes impose burdens on businesses to give their customers privacy notices explaining how they will use information about their customers without really providing privacy protection for the customers. Some other statutes are mentioned in ¶ ¶ 1, 2, and 4 above and in ¶ 10, below.

10. **Accessing another's electronically stored materials.** A more substantial federal statute, 18 U.S.C.A. § 2707(a), authorizes a civil action against anyone who accesses a facility and obtains electronically stored information without authorization. This allows actions, for example, against someone who manages to access copies of your email stored by your Internet Service Provider. In *Theofel v. Farey-Jones,* 359 F.3d 1066 (9th Cir. 2004), the defendants, who were involved in commercial litigation with ICA, subpoenaed all of the email of that company in the hands of the ISP, NetGate. The subpoena was grossly overbroad and was invalid for that reason. But NetGate, which had no interest of its own, did not contest it. The defendant thus accessed many private emails of individuals associated with ICA. These individuals sued under the statute. Judge Kozinski recognized that privacy interests were involved, but repeatedly analogized the case to one of trespass. The court held that NetGate's consent was procured by a mistake obvious to the defendants, so that its consent was not an authorization that protected the defendants. The court said: "The subpoena power is a substantial delegation of authority to private parties, and those who invoke it have a grave responsibility to ensure it is not abused. ... Fighting a subpoena in court is not cheap, and many may be cowed into compliance with even overbroad subpoenas, especially if they are not represented by counsel or have no personal interest at stake. Because defendants procured consent by exploiting a mistake of which they had constructive knowledge, the district court erred by dismissing based on that consent."

SANDERS v. AMERICAN BROADCASTING COS. INC.

20 Cal.4th 907, 85 Cal.Rptr.2d 909, 978 P.2d 67 (1999)

WERDEGAR, J.

Defendant Stacy Lescht, a reporter employed by defendant American Broadcasting Companies, Inc. (ABC), obtained employment as a "telepsychic" with the Psychic Marketing Group (PMG), which also employed plaintiff Mark Sanders in that same capacity. While she worked in PMG's Los Angeles office, Lescht, who wore a small video camera hidden in her hat, covertly videotaped her conversations with several coworkers, including Sanders.

Sanders sued Lescht and ABC for, among other causes of action, the tort of invasion of privacy by intrusion. [Claims against ABC based upon publication of the videotaped material were disposed of without trial and are not involved here.]

In 1992, plaintiff Mark Sanders was working as a telepsychic in PMG's Los Angeles office, giving "readings" to customers who telephoned PMG's 900 number (for which they were charged a per-minute fee). The psychics' work area consisted of a large room with rows of cubicles, about 100 total, in which the psychics took their calls. Each cubicle was enclosed on three sides by five-foot-high partitions. The facility also included a separate lunch room and enclosed offices for managers and supervisors. During the period of the claimed intrusion, the door to the PMG facility was unlocked during business hours, but PMG, by internal policy, prohibited access to the office by nonemployees without specific permission. An employee testified the front door was visible from the administration desk and a supervisor greeted any nonemployees who entered.

Defendant Stacy Lescht, employed by defendant ABC in an investigation of the telepsychic industry, obtained employment as a psychic in PMG's Los Angeles office. When she first entered the PMG office to apply for a position, she was not stopped at the front door or greeted by anyone until she found and approached the administration desk. Once hired, she sat at a cubicle desk, where she gave telephonic readings to customers. Lescht testified that while sitting at her desk she could easily overhear conversations conducted in surrounding cubicles or in the aisles near her cubicle. When not on the phone, she talked with some of the other psychics in the phone room. Lescht secretly videotaped these conversations with a "hat cam," i.e., a small camera hidden in her hat; a microphone attached to her brassiere captured sound as well. Among the conversations Lescht videotaped were two with Sanders, the first at Lescht's cubicle, the second at Sanders's.

During the first conversation, Sanders and, after a period, a third employee, were standing in the aisle just outside Lescht's cubicle. They talked in moderate tones of voice, and a fourth employee, passing by, joined in the conversation at one point. Sanders conceded there was a "possibility" the psychic in the next cubicle beyond Lescht could have overheard the first conversation if he tried, although in Sanders's view that was very unlikely because he had no reason to eavesdrop. The second conversation, which took place with both Lescht and Sanders seated in Sanders's cubicle, was conducted in relatively soft voices and was interrupted once by Sanders's receiving a customer call and once by a passing coworker's offer of a snack. During this second, longer conversation, Sanders discussed his personal aspirations and beliefs and gave Lescht a psychic reading.

Sanders pled two causes of action against Lescht and ABC based on the videotaping itself: violation of Penal Code section 632 (hereafter section 632) and the common law tort of invasion of privacy by intrusion. The court ordered trial on these counts bifurcated, with the section 632 count tried first. [Section 632 generally prohibits the nonconsensual recording of communications, but does not apply where the parties may reasonably expect that the conversation may be overheard or recorded]. In a special verdict form, the jury was asked whether the conversation upon which defendants allegedly intruded was conducted "in circumstances in which the parties to the communication may reasonably have expected that the communications may have been overheard." Based on the jury's affirmative answer to this question, the trial court ordered judgment entered for defendants on the section 632 cause of action. [The jury found for the plaintiff on the common law privacy claim and awarded $335,000 in compensatory and $300,000 in punitive damages. The Court of Appeals reversed on the ground that the plaintiff had no reasonable expectation of privacy.]

In Shulman, we adopted the definition of the intrusion tort. ... The cause of action, we held, has two elements: (1) intrusion into a private place, conversation or matter, (2) in a manner highly offensive to a reasonable person. The first element, we stated, is not met when the plaintiff has merely been observed, or even photographed or recorded, in a public place. Rather, the plaintiff must show the defendant penetrated some zone of physical or sensory privacy surrounding, or obtained unwanted access to data about, the plaintiff. The tort is proven only if the plaintiff had an objectively reasonable expectation of seclusion or solitude in the place, conversation or data source.

While Shulman reiterated the requirement that an intrusion plaintiff have a reasonable expectation of privacy, neither in Shulman nor in any other case have we stated that an expectation of privacy, in order to be reasonable for purposes of the intrusion tort, must be of absolute or complete privacy. Indeed, our analysis of the issues in Shulman suggested, to the contrary, that mass media videotaping may constitute an intrusion even when the events and communications recorded were visible and audible to some limited set of observers at the time they occurred. In Shulman, a television producer had fitted a rescue nurse with a small microphone, by which the nurse's conversation with a severely injured accident victim was recorded. Although a number of other persons were participating in the rescue, the record on summary judgment, we noted, left unclear whether any nonparticipant members of the general public were present or could overhear any of the patient's communications to the nurse and other rescuers. Partly on that basis, we found triable issues of fact as to the patient's reasonable expectation of privacy in her conversation with the nurse and other rescuers. We thereby implied the plaintiff patient could have a reasonable expectation of privacy in her communications even if some of them may have been overheard by those involved in the rescue, but not by the general public.

Shulman's discussion of possible bases for a reasonable expectation of privacy on the patient's part also suggests that a person may reasonably expect privacy against the electronic recording of a communication, even though he or she had no reasonable expectation as to confidentiality of the communication's contents. While one who imparts private information risks the betrayal of his confidence by the other party, a substantial distinction has been recognized between the secondhand repetition of the contents of a conversation and its simultaneous dissemination to an unannounced second auditor, whether that auditor be a person or a mechanical device. ... [S]uch secret monitoring denies the speaker an important aspect of privacy of communication—the right to control the nature and extent of the firsthand dissemination of his statements.

This case squarely raises the question of an expectation of limited privacy. On further consideration, we adhere to the view suggested in Shulman: privacy, for purposes of the intrusion tort, is not a binary, all-or-nothing characteristic. There are degrees and nuances to societal recognition of our expectations of privacy: the fact the privacy one expects in a given setting is not complete or absolute does not render the expectation unreasonable as a matter of law. Although the intrusion tort is often defined in terms of "seclusion," the seclusion referred to need not be absolute. Like "privacy," the concept of "seclusion" is relative. The mere fact that a person can be seen by someone does not automatically mean that he or she can legally be forced to be subject to being seen by everyone.

Dietemann v. Time, Inc., supra, 449 F.2d 245 (9th Cir. 1971), upon which the trial court relied, does, indeed, exemplify the idea of a legitimate expectation of limited privacy. Reporters for a news magazine deceitfully gained access to a quack doctor's home office, where they secretly photographed and recorded his examination of one of them. The court held the plaintiff could, under California law, reasonably expect privacy from press photography and recording, even though he had invited the reporters—unaware of their true identity—into his home office: "Plaintiff's den was a sphere from which he could reasonably expect to exclude eavesdropping newsmen. He invited two of defendant's employees to the den. One who invites another to his home or office takes a risk that the visitor may not be what he seems, and that the visitor may repeat all he hears and observes when he leaves. But he does not and should not be required to take the risk that what is heard and seen will be transmitted by photograph or recording, or in our modern world, in full living color and hi-fi to the public at large. ..."

Equally illustrative of the general principle is Huskey v. National Broadcasting Co., Inc., 632 F.Supp. 1282 (N.D.Ill.1986). The defendant's camera crew, visiting a federal prison, filmed plaintiff Huskey, an inmate, in the prison's "exercise cage," wearing only gym shorts and exposing his distinctive tattoos. The federal court rejected the defendant's contention no intrusion could have occurred because Huskey was "not secluded." "Of course Huskey could be seen by guards, prison personnel and inmates, and obviously he was in fact seen by NBC's camera operator. But the mere fact a person can be seen by others does not mean that person cannot legally be 'secluded.' ... Further, Huskey's visibility to some people does not strip him of the right to remain secluded from others. Persons are exposed to family members and invited guests in their own homes, but that does not mean they have opened the door to television cameras." Whether the exercise cage could be considered an area of limited seclusion within the prison was a factual question for trial.

Similarly, in a famous early case, the presence of an unnecessary male observer at the home delivery of the plaintiff's child was held to be an intrusion, even though the delivery was also observed by the plaintiff's husband, the attending doctor and a woman assistant. The existence of such limited privacy is not dependent on the plaintiff being in his or her home. ...

Defendants' claim, that a "complete expectation of privacy" is necessary to recover for intrusion, thus fails as inconsistent with case law as well as with the common understanding of privacy. Privacy for purposes of the intrusion tort must be evaluated with respect to the identity of the alleged intruder and the nature of the intrusion. As seen below, moreover, decisions on the common law and statutory protection of workplace privacy show that the same analysis applies in the workplace as in other settings; consequently, an employee may, under some circumstances, have a reasonable expectation of visual or aural privacy against electronic intrusion by a stranger to the workplace, despite the possibility the conversations and interactions at issue could be witnessed by coworkers or the employer. ...

[The court noted that "the United States Supreme Court has recognized, in the Fourth Amendment context, that even employees without personal offices may have a reasonable, but limited, expectation of privacy against intrusions by strangers to the workplace." See Mancusi v. DeForte (1968) 392 U.S. 364, 369, 88 S.Ct. 2120, 20 L.Ed.2d 1154 (Union employee who shared a single large office with several other union officials had a privacy interest in the office sufficient to challenge its warrantless search by state officers. ...).]

To summarize, we conclude that in the workplace, as elsewhere, the reasonableness of a person's expectation of visual and aural privacy depends not only on who might have been able to observe the subject interaction, but on the identity of the claimed intruder and the means of intrusion. For this reason, we answer the briefed question affirmatively: a person who lacks a reasonable expectation of complete privacy in a conversation, because it could be seen and overheard by coworkers (but not the general public), may nevertheless have a claim for invasion of privacy by intrusion based on a television reporter's covert videotaping of that conversation.

Defendants warn that "the adoption of a doctrine of *per se* workplace privacy would place a dangerous chill on the press' investigation of abusive activities in open work areas, implicating substantial First Amendment concerns." (Italics in original.) We adopt no such per se doctrine of privacy. We hold only that the possibility of being overheard by coworkers does not, as a matter of law, render unreasonable an employee's expectation that his or her interactions within a nonpublic workplace will not be videotaped in secret by a journalist. In other circumstances, where, for example, the workplace is regularly open to entry or observation by the public or press, or the interaction that was the subject of the alleged intrusion was between proprietor (or employee) and customer, any expectation of privacy against press recording is less likely to be deemed reasonable. Nothing we say here prevents a media defendant from attempting to show, in order to negate the offensiveness element of the intrusion tort, that the claimed intrusion, even if it infringed on a reasonable expectation of privacy, was justified by the legitimate motive of gathering the news. As for possible First Amendment defenses, any discussion must await a later case, as no constitutional issue was decided by the lower courts or presented for our review here. . . .

The judgment of the Court of Appeal is reversed, and the cause is remanded to that court for further proceedings consistent with our opinion.

MED. LAB. MGMT. CONSULTANTS v. AMERICAN BROADCASTING COS., INC.

306 F.3d 806 (9th Cir. 2002)

HUG, Circuit Judge.

[Journalists for American Broadcasting Company made secret video recordings (by way of a camera in a wig) of the plaintiff and his place of business, airing 52 seconds of videotape inside the lab in a sensational-type television presentation on labs that fail to identify cervical cancer in pap smear slides. The plaintiff dropped a claim for false light invasion of privacy and concentrated largely on intrusive invasion instead, partly because an ABC representative misrepresented herself as a person interested in opening a similar lab in another part of the country. The trial court gave summary judgment for the broadcaster.]

[On the intrusive invasion of privacy claim, a plaintiff must prove] (1) an intentional intrusion into a private place, conversation, or matter (2) in a manner highly offensive to a reasonable person. To prevail on the first prong, the plaintiff must show (a) an actual, subjective expectation of seclusion or solitude in the place, conversation, or matter, and (b) that the expectation was objectively reasonable. . . . The subjective expectation of privacy may be tested by any outward manifestations that Devaraj expected his dealings with the ABC representatives to be private. A comparison of what precautions he took to safeguard his privacy interest with the precautions he might reasonably have taken, is appropriate. [Here,] Devaraj's ready exposure of other parts of Medical Lab's administrative offices to the ABC representatives signals that he did not regard these parts as private places. . . .

Devaraj also claims that he had an expectation of privacy in the contents of his conversation with the ABC representatives, particularly in the contents of the conversation that transpired in the conference room. . . . Devaraj did not reveal any information about his personal life or affairs, but only generally discussed Medical Lab's business operations, the pap smear testing industry, and Gordon's supposed plans to open her own laboratory. This information was, at most, company confidential, not private to Devaraj himself. Privacy is personal to individuals and does not encompass any corporate interest. . . .

Lastly, Devaraj argues that he expected that the three undercover ABC representatives were not surreptitiously videotaping his dealings with them for broadcast to the general public. Devaraj's argument implicates the privacy interest that the California Supreme Court has termed the "expectation of limited privacy," which is an expectation of privacy against the electronic recording of a communication even though the speaker lacks an expectation of complete privacy in the communication. [Citing *Sanders*.] The notion of limited privacy recognizes that although an individual may be visible or audible to some limited group of persons, the individual may nonetheless expect to remain secluded from other persons and particularly from the public at large. . . .

Devaraj undeniably held the subjective expectation that the ABC representatives were not secretly videotaping his conversation with them for television broadcast. Devaraj's ignorance of the covert videotaping was essential to ABC's operation of undercover, investigative journalism. Thus, although Devaraj lacked an expectation of complete privacy in his conversation with three strangers during a business meeting, he could have reasonably expected that the conversation would be confined to them for the most part, and not widely exposed to the public at large. In imparting information to strangers, one inevitably risks its secondhand repetition. . . .

We conclude that the Arizona Supreme Court would not recognize as broad an interest in limited privacy as the California Supreme Court has done. In reaching this conclusion, we find significant the differences between the California and Arizona law in the area of electronic eavesdropping. [California's Privacy Act] prohibits the electronic recording of any "confidential communication" without the consent of all parties to the communication. Under California law, a "confidential communication" includes "any communication carried on in circumstances as may reasonably indicate that any party to the communication desires it to be confined to the parties thereto."

In Arizona, any person present at a conversation may record the conversation without obtaining the consent of the other parties to the conversation. . . . Arizona law thus reflects a policy decision by the state that the secret recording of a private conversation by a party to that conversation does not violate another party's right to privacy. Under

Arizona law, then, Devaraj could have no reasonable expectation that the ABC representatives were not surreptitiously videotaping his communications with them.

However, even if we assume that the Arizona Supreme Court would embrace an interest in limited privacy as broad as that articulated by the California Supreme Court, we still conclude that as a matter of law Devaraj's privacy expectation was not reasonable. ... Unlike the "internal" conversation between coworkers in *Sanders,* an "external" conversation between a workplace insider, such as a proprietor, and a workplace outsider, like a customer, is more probably business-related and thus not sufficiently private and personal in character to make any privacy expectation reasonable.

Given that Devaraj cannot assert a privacy right on behalf of Medical Lab, Devaraj could have no reasonable expectation of limited privacy in a workplace interaction with three strangers that was purely professional and touched upon nothing private and personal to Devaraj himself.

We conclude that while Devaraj may have maintained a subjective expectation of privacy over the location of his conversations with the undercover ABC representatives, an expectation of privacy in the contents of the conversation, and an expectation that against the ABC's secret videotaping of his communication for future broadcast to the general public, these expectations were not objectively reasonable....

[In addition,] [a]ny intrusion by the ABC representatives was *de minimis* and thus not highly offensive to a reasonable person. The covert videotaping of a business conversation among strangers in business offices does not rise to the level of an exceptional prying into another's private affairs, which the Restatement's illustrations indicate is required for "offensiveness."

[Affirmed]

---

11. **Corporate "privacy."** (a) *Medical Lab Management* is in accord with many other cases in saying that business corporations have no protectible privacy interests, on the ground that privacy rights are dignitary in nature, designed to protect sensibilities and feelings. See David A. Elder, Privacy Torts § 1:4 (2002 & Supps.).

(b) However, corporations may be protected from intangible, electronic intrusions under some theory besides privacy invasion. For instance, in one case, the defendant allegedly posted false job listings on the internet, resulting in large volumes of emails to the plaintiff, adversely affecting the company's computer resources. Although the court rejected a privacy claim, it held that the plaintiff stated a claim for trespass to chattels—traditionally a claim for physical interference with a tangible chattel. *School of Visual Arts v. Kuprewicz,* 3 Misc.3d 278, 771

N.Y.S.2d 804 (Sup. Ct. 2003). Other courts have likewise expanded the old trespass to chattels tort to protect against various electronic intrusions. For example, see *Thrifty-Tel, Inc. v. Myron Bezenek,* 46 Cal. App.4th 1559, 54 Cal.Rptr.2d 468 (1996) (computer hackers breaking into telephone company's long-distance system, using confidential access code, and making calls was trespass to chattels). Distinguish electronic intrusions that are disruptive because their volume affects computer performance from those that are disruptive because of their content. In a split decision, the California Supreme Court rejected the trespass theory where only content was at issue. *Intel Corp. v. Hamidi,* 30 Cal.4th 1342, 71 P.3d 296, 1 Cal.Rptr.3d 32 (2003). Even here, though, some other tort theory may work—perhaps a claim for interference with economic prospects, discussed in Chapters 11 & 12 below. Should courts restate the rule that corporations have no protectible privacy interests?

12. **Newsgathering: publication vs. intrusion.** Newsgathering activities may be protected by First Amendment considerations when the privacy claim is based upon publication, but the mere fact that the defendant is acting for the newsmedia has not generally provided a privilege for a trespass or, presumably, an intrusive invasion of privacy. See *Desnick v. American Broadcasting Companies, Inc.,* 44 F.3d 1345 (7th Cir. 1995); cf. *Wilson v. Layne,* 526 U.S. 603, 119 S.Ct. 1692, 143 L.Ed.2d 818 (1999) (civil rights action against officer who invited journalists into plaintiff's home). After *Sanders,* though, is there some kind of legal protection in intrusion cases if the privacy-invader can say "I was gathering news"?

13. **Reasonable expectation of privacy, or of non-recordation?** In *Hornberger v. American Broadcasting Cos., Inc.,* 351 N.J.Super. 577, 799 A.2d 566 (2002), the defendant arranged for young African-American men to cruise in expensive cars to see if police would discriminate against them. The defendant secretly made video and audio tapes. After the police had stopped some of the test drivers and had them get out of the car, police began a search inside the car. The defendant caught some of their conversation between the parties on tape. The police officers sued for privacy invasion of the false light variety, but the court concluded that they had no claim because they had no reasonable expectation of privacy, even if they had a reasonable expectation that their conversation would not be recorded.

In *Remsburg v. Docusearch, Inc.,* 149 N.H. 148, 816 A.2d 1001 (2003), a private internet investigator was in the business of selling personal information to unknown clients for unknown purposes. Youens paid Docusearch to tell him Amy Lynn Boyer's social security number and also where she worked. Docusearch obtained the social security number from a credit report and provided it to Youens. Docusearch then had a woman make a pretextual phone call to Boyer. The caller's pretense worked; she was able to elicit the workplace address. Docusearch provided the information to Youens, who went to her place of work, shot her dead, then killed himself. Boyer's mother sued, claiming wrongful death and invasion of privacy. Could Boyer have had a reasonable expectation of privacy in either her social security number or her workplace address? The court answered yes as to social security but no as to her workplace address. It held, however, that the pretextual phone call violated the state's consumer protection statute.

14. **Discerning expectations of partial privacy or good motive.** Can courts really discern the expectation of partial privacy based upon motive or purpose of the defendant? Notice that in *Sanders* the plaintiff knows the defendant is present and hearing his words; he is ignorant only of her motive or purpose. Are all persons who are talking to you invading your privacy if they have unrevealed motives? Suppose an employer casually chats with an employee but has secret hopes that the employee will reveal information about other employees or private information about herself. Or a psychiatrist takes secret pleasure in hearing the nutty details of an obsessive patient or hopes to publish a best seller about his patients?

15. **Restroom privacy.** *Johnson v. Allen,* 272 Ga.App. 861, 613 S.E.2d 657 (2005) says that a defendant who installs a surveillance camera in a public restroom is invading privacy of users, but that if a public restroom is used for sex, the user has no expectation of privacy. Has "expectation of privacy" become a kind of code phrase for some kind of policy judgment? There are probably more restroom cases than anyone wants to read about. *Hougum v. Valley Mem. Homes,* 574 N.W.2d 812 (N.D. 1998) summarizes a number, reflecting the view that liability is appropriate when the surveillance is planned or intentional. But in *Hougum* itself, the court said there was no intent to intrude upon seclusion when a security guard "inadvertently" saw a minister in the next stall masturbating, then made a citizen's arrest.

(b) False Light

SOLANO v. PLAYGIRL, INC.,

292 F.3d 1078 (9th Cir. 2002)

FISHER, Circuit Judge.

The January 1999 issue of Playgirl magazine featured a cover photograph of actor Jose Solano, Jr., best known for his role as "Manny Gutierrez" on the syndicated television program "Baywatch" from 1996 to 1999. Solano was shown shirtless and wearing his red lifeguard trunks, the uniform of his "Baywatch" character, under a heading reading: "TV Guys. PRIMETIME'S SEXY YOUNG STARS EXPOSED." Playgirl, ostensibly focused on a female readership, typically contains nude photographs of men in various poses emphasizing their genitalia, including some showing them engaged in simulated sex acts. The magazine also contains written editorial features. Although Solano—who did not pose for or give an interview to Playgirl—did not in fact appear nude in the magazine, he sued Playgirl alleging it deliberately created the false impression that he did so, making it appear he was willing to degrade himself and endorse such a magazine. . . .

As indicated above, Solano appeared bare-chested wearing his red trunks, dominating the cover. In the upper left corner was a red circle containing the words, "TV Guys," followed by the headline, "Prime-time's Sexy Young Stars Exposed," which ran across the top of Solano's head. Immediately to the left of Solano's picture, the magazine proclaimed, "12 Sizzling Centerfolds Ready to Score With You." The "s" in "Centerfolds" was superimposed on Solano's right shoulder. Also placed to the left of Solano, running down the left margin, the cover touted "Countdown to Climax: Naughty Ways to Ring in the New Year," "Toyz in the Hood: The Best in Erotic Home Shopping" and "Bottoms Up!: Hot Celebrity Buns." In the cover's lower right hand corner was the headline, "Baywatch's Best Body, Jose Solano."

Solano's sole appearance inside the magazine was on page 21, in a quarter-page, head-and-shoulders photograph—showing him fully dressed in a tee shirt and sweater—alongside a brief, quarter-page profile of the actor. Solano's profile included information about his "Baywatch" character, facts about his life before he began acting and a quote in which he says that with two younger brothers he strives to be a positive role model and hopes to encourage others to pursue their dreams. Solano's photograph and profile were part of a five-page feature entitled "TV Guys," consisting of photographs and short profiles of 10 popular television actors. Neither Solano nor any of the other actors was shown nude. Significantly, Playgirl issues are displayed on newsstands packaged in plastic wrap to prevent potential customers from flipping through the pages to view the magazine's contents.

[The district court granted Playgirl summary judgment and Solano appeals.]

Solano argues that Playgirl's use of his photograph along with suggestive headlines on the cover conveyed the false message that Solano voluntarily posed nude for the magazine and, in doing so, implicitly endorsed the magazine and its sexually explicit content. To prevail on this false light claim, Solano must show that: (1) Playgirl disclosed to one or more persons information about or concerning Solano that was presented as factual but that was actually false or created a false impression about him; (2) the information was understood by one or more persons to whom it was disclosed as stating or implying something highly offensive that would have a tendency to injure Solano's reputation; (3) by clear and convincing evidence, Playgirl acted with constitutional malice; and (4) Solano was damaged by the disclosure.

Solano contends that when the photograph and headlines on the cover are viewed in context—that of a magazine that features sexually suggestive nude pictures of men—there is a triable issue of fact regarding the falsity of the message conveyed by Playgirl. We agree. We addressed a publication's creating an implied false message in *Eastwood v. Nat'l Enquirer, Inc.*, 123 F.3d 1249 (9th Cir.1997), and *Kaelin v. Globe Communications Corp.*, 162 F.3d 1036 (9th Cir.1998). In *Eastwood* the tabloid magazine National Enquirer's cover page headline advertised an

"Exclusive Interview" with actor/director Clint Eastwood. The magazine contained an article with quotes allegedly attributable to Eastwood, cast as if Eastwood had been speaking directly to the bylined Enquirer editor. Eastwood in fact had never given any interview to the Enquirer—exclusive or otherwise. Although the magazine never expressly stated that Eastwood actually had given it the interview, this court nevertheless reasoned that the Enquirer had "signal[ed], through text and graphics, that he had willingly talked to the Enquirer." *Kaelin* involved a defamation action brought by Kato Kaelin, the hapless houseguest of O.J. Simpson, against the Globe tabloid for publishing a front-page headline announcing, "COPS THINK KATO DID IT ... he fears they want him for perjury, say pals." Kaelin argued the "IT" implied the two brutal murders for which Simpson was tried and acquitted; the magazine claimed the word referred only to perjury, because the article inside the magazine explained that the police suspected Kaelin of having committed perjury. We were unpersuaded by the Globe's argument: "Even assuming that such a [perjury] reading is reasonably possible, it is not the only reading that is reasonably possible as a matter of law. So long as the publication is reasonably susceptible of a defamatory meaning, a factual question for the jury exists." ...

Solano contends that his bare-chested, three-quarter-length photograph alongside the suggestive headlines on the Playgirl cover created the false impression that readers could expect to find more photographs of him inside the magazine, nude—"exposed"—in Playgirl's typical sexually explicit and revealing mode of depicting its "sexy" male subjects. Moreover, the placement of the "12 Sizzling Centerfolds—Ready to Score With You" line, which appeared in large bold letters immediately to the left of and just touching Solano's shoulder, could reasonably be interpreted to encompass Playgirl's cover subject, Solano. It is well-established that "[a] defendant is liable for what is insinuated as well as for what is stated explicitly." ...

That Solano's profile inside the magazine was of a relatively innocent and nonsexual nature is of little significance. In *Kaelin,* we concluded that the accuracy and truth of the Globe article discussing the suspicion that Kaelin had perjured himself did not cure the false impression conveyed by the cover headline, which implied he was suspected of murder. We held that the issue was one for the jury to decide. ...

[A] jury reasonably could conclude that the Playgirl cover conveyed the message that Solano was not the wholesome person he claimed to be, that he was willing to—or was "washed up" and had to—sell himself naked to a women's sex magazine.

Although Solano has established a genuine issue as to whether the cover created a false impression, to survive summary judgment he must, as a public figure, also establish by clear and convincing evidence that Playgirl's editors knowingly or recklessly created this false impression. The third element necessary to establish a claim for false light, therefore, is the constitutional requirement of actual malice. Specifically,

Solano must show that Playgirl either deliberately cast [its] statements in an equivocal fashion in the hope of insinuating a [false] import to the reader, or that [it] knew or acted in reckless disregard of whether [its] words would be interpreted by the average reader as [false] statements of fact. As we noted in *Eastwood,* proving actual malice by clear and convincing evidence is a heavy burden, "far in excess of the preponderance sufficient for most civil litigation."

[The court alluded to the rule that the defendant must have made the false publication with a high degree of awareness of probable falsity, or must have entertained serious doubts as to the truth of his publication.]

Against this backdrop, we now turn to the conflicting evidence regarding the existence of actual malice on the part of Playgirl editors in assembling the January 1999 issue. Playgirl associate editor Theresa O'Rourke testified in her deposition that at an October 1998 meeting to discuss the January 1999 cover, Playgirl senior vice president Carmine Bellucci generally instructed the editorial staff to "sex up" the magazine to imply that there was more nudity in the magazine than actually was there. She stated that Bellucci wanted to "bang [readers] over the head with something like, hey, this is sexy young stars exposed" so that "people are going to want to pick up the magazine more." According to O'Rourke, "we definitely weren't trying to be subtle, and we knew it." She stated that there had been discussion in the cover meetings that the cover layout implied Solano appeared nude in a centerfold inside the magazine. She said the "Primetime's Sexy Young Stars Exposed" headline specifically sparked debate at the meetings "[b]ecause some of us did not feel like it was fair to do that." Editor-in-chief Claire Viguerie Harth testified that the magazine's intent with the headline was "to make a line that was sexy enough [that] people would be intrigued and want to look inside, but not to say something that the magazine was showing something that it didn't have." . . .

O'Rourke also recalled that someone raised a concern about the "12 Sizzling Centerfolds: Ready to Score with You" headline because it occupied the space where the headline relating to the cover subject often is placed. She believed "someone's going to think that he's naked in there." O'Rourke said that Bellucci tended to just "blow off" such comments and concerns. Bellucci agreed in his deposition that Solano was a "primetime sexy young star" as those words were used in the cover headline, but denied that the editors used Solano's photograph and the cover headlines falsely to imply that Solano appeared nude in the magazine.

[T]he testimony of O'Rourke and Spiezio serve to prove that during the editorial process *someone* raised concerns about the use of Solano's photograph alongside the suggestive headlines; [editors] were aware of some staffers' concerns that the cover might falsely imply that Solano appeared nude inside the magazine. Given that awareness and the evidence that Bellucci wanted to "sex up" the magazine to imply nudity, plainly to promote magazine sales, a jury could conclude Playgirl's editors knowingly or recklessly published the misleading cover. Such evidence is sufficient to satisfy the actual malice standard.

... Viewing the evidence in the light most favorable to Solano and taking into account the typical Playgirl content, we believe Solano at this stage of the proceedings raises a genuine issue as to whether Playgirl's editorial staff produced the January 1999 cover knowing, or with reckless disregard for whether, Solano's bare-chested photograph and various suggestive headlines would falsely imply that he voluntarily posed for and appeared nude inside the magazine.

The final element necessary to prove a case for false light is damages. A plaintiff may collect actual damages and general damages for humiliation and mental anguish and suffering. [Citing *Gertz*.] Playgirl argues that Solano cannot prove any damages. Solano admitted in his deposition that he did not seek therapy or any other type of treatment from any medical professional, although he did seek spiritual counseling from his father, a minister. He testified to both personal and familial humiliation and embarrassment because of the publication of his picture in the magazine. He claimed that several possibilities for appearing on various television programs failed to materialize after the publication of the Playgirl issue, yet he was unable to provide evidence that any lost job was related to his appearance in the magazine. Solano's current and previous agent and previous manager all stated that no one ever has mentioned the Playgirl issue to them—especially in relation to a job for Solano. Solano also argues that his invitations to charity events declined after the publication of the Playgirl issue, but again he admitted that he could only speculate—and had no proof—that there is a connection between the two events.

In *Eastwood,* we rejected the contention that the jury's award of $150,000 was unsupported by a record that detailed Eastwood's extensive efforts to maintain his privacy. There we held that a jury finding that "fans would think him (1) a hypocrite for giving the Enquirer an 'exclusive interview' about his private life (plus access to an 'exclusive' baby picture), and/or (2) essentially washed up as a movie star if he was courting publicity in a sensationalist tabloid ... would have been sufficiently damaging to Eastwood's reputation to support an award of [$150,000]."

[Reversed and remanded.]

CAIN v. HEARST CORPORATION

878 S.W.2d 577 (Tex. 1994)

Justice GONZALEZ delivered the opinion of the Court, in which Chief Justice PHILLIPS, Justice HECHT, Justice CORNYN and Justice ENOCH join.

This case comes to us on certified questions from the United States Court of Appeals for the Fifth Circuit. . . .

Clyde Cain is a prison inmate in the Texas Department of Corrections serving a life sentence for murder. He sued the Hearst Corporation, d/b/a the Houston Chronicle Publishing Company, claiming that a newspaper article invaded his privacy by placing him in a false light. The article, which appeared in the Chronicle on June 30, 1991, referred to Cain as a burglar, thief, pimp, and killer. In recounting Cain's criminal record the article, in summary, states that: Cain is believed to have killed as many as eight people; Cain killed one of his lawyers in 1973 and married the lawyer's widow a few months later; Cain killed a 67 year old man in 1977; in 1983 he "bought" a prostitute from a friend to help finance his activities; Cain persuaded the prostitute to marry a trailer park owner named Anderson, so that Cain could kill Anderson and share the prostitute's inheritance from Anderson; when the prostitute balked, Cain threatened to kill her 5 year old daughter and "deliver her daughter's head in a wastepaper basket"; the prostitute married Anderson 3 days later, and on January 5, 1985 Cain killed Anderson. Cain's sole complaint is that the article printed false information that he was a member of the "Dixie Mafia" and that he had killed as many as eight people. Cain asserted that these statements put him in a false light with the public. Suit was filed in state court one and one-half years after the article was published.

[The federal court certified questions of Texas law to the Supreme Court of Texas.] . . .

The Restatement (Second) of Torts, Section 652E defines false light invasion of privacy as follows: "One who gives publicity to a matter concerning another that places the other before the public in a false light is subject to liability to the other for invasion of his privacy, if (a) the false light in which the other was placed would be highly offensive to a reasonable person, and (b) the actor had knowledge of or acted in reckless disregard as to the falsity of the publicized matter and the false light in which the other would be placed." Restatement (Second) of Torts § 652E (1977). . . .

We reject the false light invasion of privacy tort for two reasons: 1) it largely duplicates other rights of recovery, particularly defamation; and 2) it lacks many of the procedural limitations that accompany actions for defamation, thus unacceptably increasing the tension that already exists between free speech constitutional guarantees and tort law.

. . . Although not explicitly required by the Restatement definition, most jurisdictions, including the lower Texas courts that have recognized the action, require that a statement be false if it is to be cognizable under the false light doctrine. The falsity requirement is sensible, considering that the "revelation of private facts" invasion of privacy tort purports to grant relief for the disclosure of true statements that adversely affect the plaintiff.

If we were to recognize a false light tort in Texas, it would largely duplicate several existing causes of action, particularly defamation.

... [T]he elements of damages that have been recognized in false light actions are similar to those awarded for defamation. The principal element of actual damages for false light claims is typically mental anguish, but physical illness and harm to the plaintiff's commercial interests have also been recognized. These are essentially the types of damages sought in defamation actions. Thus many, if not all, of the injuries redressed by the false light tort are also redressed by defamation. ...

[T]he false light tort bears remarkable similarities to defamation. However, the torts are not wholly identical for two reasons: (1) defamation actions are subject to a number of procedural requirements to which invasion of privacy actions are not subject, and (2) certain publications not actionable under a defamation theory might be actionable under false light. Far from persuading us that these distinctions justify a separate tort, we believe they demonstrate that adopting a false light tort in this State would unacceptably derogate constitutional free speech rights under both the Texas and the United States Constitution. ...

[T]echnical restrictions [in defamation actions] serve to safeguard the freedom of speech. Every defamation action that the law permits necessarily inhibits free speech. As the Supreme Court stated with respect to political speech in New York Times v. Sullivan, "[w]hatever is added to the field of libel is taken from the field of free debate." While less compelling, these same considerations are also at play in private, non-political expression. Thus, the defamation action has been narrowly tailored to limit free speech as little as possible.

Courts in many jurisdictions have preserved their protection of speech by holding false light actions to the same strictures as defamation actions. Permitting plaintiffs to bring actions for false light without the limits established for defamation actions may inhibit free speech beyond the permissible range. On the other hand, no useful purpose would be served by the separate tort if these restrictions are imposed. ...

In theory, the false light action may provide a remedy for certain non-defamatory speech against which there may be no other remedy in tort law. This rationale, however, does not persuade us to recognize the false light tort.

It is questionable whether a remedy for non-defamatory speech should exist at all. ...

The class of speech restricted by defamation is only that which defames. False light may be brought against any untruth to which the subject of the speech takes umbrage. Editors for the media may guard against defamation by being alert to facts which tend to diminish reputation; under false light, any fact in the story, no matter how seemingly innocuous, may prove to be the basis for liability.

The Restatement adds an element not associated with defamation, the requirement that the statement places the subject in a false light "highly offensive" to the reasonable person. The distinction fails to draw reasonably clear lines between lawful and unlawful conduct, however. A law forbidding or requiring conduct in terms so vague that men of common intelligence must necessarily guess at its meaning and differ as to its application violates due process.... On balance, the marginal benefit to be achieved by permitting recovery against non-defamatory speech not addressed by any existing tort is outweighed by the probable chilling effect on speech and, in some cases, on freedom of the press, that would result from recognition of the false light tort. For the reasons expressed in this opinion, we expressly decline to recognize the tort of false light.

[Dissenting opinions omitted]

---

16. **Requirements where the tort is recognized.** The *Cain* court quotes the elements required by the Restatement § 652E—the plaintiff is placed in a false light in a way that would be highly offensive to a reasonable person and the defendant knows the falsity or acts in reckless disregard of it. One requirement may not be obvious. Mere publication as the term is used in defamation law is not enough; the defendant must give *publicity* to the false light, meaning that the communication must go to the public at large or to enough people that it will almost certainly reach the public at large. E.g., *Cole v. Chandler,* 752 A.2d 1189 (Me. 2000).

17. **A pre-*Gertz* Supreme Court decision.** Before *Gertz* was decided, the Supreme Court applied a *Times-Sullivan* knowing or reckless falsehood standard in a false light privacy case, even though the plaintiff there was not a public official or public figure. *Time v. Hill*, 385 U.S. 374, 87 S.Ct. 534, 17 L.Ed.2d 456 (1967). Persons knowledgeable in the field usually think that this would be corrected in the case of a private person plaintiff so that the privacy rule would match the *Gertz* rule. The Court itself has noted the asymmetry. Since it is not particularly controversial, the Court would presumably bring false light into line with defamation rules. See *Cantrell v. Forest City Pub. Co.*, 419 U.S. 245, 95 S.Ct. 465, 42 L.Ed.2d 419 (1974).

18. **Constitutional restrictions on the tort.** Since false light privacy, unlike intrusive privacy, depends upon publishing something about the plaintiff, constitutional restrictions analogous to those imposed in defamation cases will apply. *Fellows v. National Enquirer, Inc.*, 42 Cal.3d 234, 228 Cal.Rptr. 215, 57 A.L.R.4th 223, 721 P.2d 97 (1986); *West v. Media General Convergence, Inc.*, 53 S.W.3d 640 (Tenn. 2001) (a negligence standard for private plaintiffs, a *Times-Sullivan* standard for public officials or figures); RESTATEMENT, § 652E, cmt. d. On matters of public interest, at least, both the requisite fault and falsity of fact are

required, so that opinion statements would not be actionable as false light. *Veilleux v. National Broadcasting Co.,* 206 F.3d 92 (1st Cir. 2000).

19. **Newsworthiness.** New York does not recognize a false light privacy claim, only a claim for using the plaintiff's name or likeness. On that claim, New York law may treat newsworthiness as a defense, even if the publication is misleading and puts the plaintiff in a false light. See *Messenger v. Gruner + Jahr Printing and Pub.,* 208 F.3d 122 (2d Cir. 2000).

20. **Gender discrimination by publication.** Title VII claims by a protected group such as women often assert that discrimination takes place because the work environment is hostile in a discriminatory way. To a large extent, these claims are based upon communicative behavior. Liability in such cases protects national policy against discrimination and economic rights of women and minorities, but the injuries are also closely related to claims for defamation, privacy invasion, and intentional infliction of distress and are sometimes coupled with these common law claims. What is the role of the First Amendment in dealing with "severe or pervasive" communication that belittles women or minorities in the workplace? In *DeAngelis v. El Paso Municipal Police Officers Ass'n,* 51 F.3d 591 (5th Cir. 1995) the plaintiff, who was the first female police sergeant on the El Paso force, was subjected to ridicule which she and other females on the force interpreted as demeaning. This came in a column of the police association's newsletter. The court was concerned whether, in the light of the First Amendment, expressions of opinion could count as violations of Title VII. It sidestepped the issue by finding that the evidence was insufficient to support a finding that the workplace was sexually harassing.

21. **Abolishing or rejecting the tort.** In some states statutory codification of a limited privacy right is deemed to exclude rights not included. As a result, in some states only the commercial appropriation right is recognized. See *Costanza v. Seinfeld,* 279 A.D.2d 255, 719 N.Y.S.2d 29 (2001); *WJLA-TV v. Levin,* 264 Va. 140, 564 S.E.2d 383 (2002). The result is that false light and other types of privacy claims have no standing. Apart from such states, the false light tort has been rejected in the highest courts of Colorado, North Carolina and Minnesota as well as Texas. See *Denver Pub. Co. v. Bueno,* 54 P.3d 893 (Colo. 2002); *Renwick v. News & Observer Pub. Co.,* 310 N.C. 312, 312 S.E.2d 405 (1984); *Lake v. Wal-Mart Stores, Inc.,* 582 N.W.2d 231 (Minn. 1998). A number of other courts have expressed doubts about the tort and may have been suggesting that they would reject it should the occasion arise.

22. **The Godbehere Case.** *Godbehere v. Phoenix Newspapers, Inc.,* 162 Ariz. 335, 783 P.2d 781 (1989), is a case that expressly retains the false light tort, saying that it does not duplicate defamation claims or imperil free speech. Explaining its reasons for believing that a false light claim was needed in addition to a libel claim, the Arizona Court said (all citations omitted):

"Although both defamation and false light invasion of privacy involve publication, the nature of the interests protected by each action differs substantially. A defamation action compensates damage to reputation or good name caused by the publication of false information. To be defamatory, a publication must be false and must bring the defamed person into disrepute, contempt, or ridicule, or must impeach plaintiff's honesty, integrity, virtue, or reputation.

"Privacy, on the other hand, does not protect reputation but protects mental and emotional interests. Indeed, [t]he gravamen of [a privacy] action ... is the injury to the feelings of the plaintiff, the mental anguish and distress caused by the publication. ... The remedy is available to protect a person's interest in being let alone and is available when there has been publicity of a kind that is highly offensive. ... Under this theory, a plaintiff may recover even in the absence of reputational damage, as long as the publicity is unreasonably offensive and attributes false characteristics. However, to qualify as a false light invasion of privacy, the publication must involve a major misrepresentation of [the plaintiff's] character, history, activities or beliefs, not merely minor or unimportant inaccuracies.

"Another distinction between defamation and false light invasion of privacy is the role played by truth. ... A false light cause of action may arise when something untrue has been published about an individual, or when the publication of true information creates a false implication about the individual. In the latter type of case, the false innuendo created by the highly offensive presentation of a true fact constitutes the injury. Thus, although defamation and false light often overlap, they serve very different objectives. The two tort actions deter different conduct and redress different wrongs. A plaintiff may bring a false light invasion of privacy action even though the publication is not defamatory, and even though the actual facts stated are true. Several examples in comment b to Restatement § 652E also illustrate the practical differences between a false light action and defamation and demonstrate how, in a certain class of cases, the false light action is the only redress available. It is these considerations, we believe, that lead the vast majority of other jurisdictions, including the United States Supreme Court, to recognize the distinction between defamation and false light. ..."

23. **Non-defamatory statements under *Godbehere*.** The *Godbehere* Court, to illustrate why non-defamatory statements should be actionable under a false light theory, gave the following illustrations from the Restatement (§ 652E):

> 3. A is a renowned poet. B publishes in his magazine a spurious inferior poem, signed with A's name. Regardless of whether the poem is so bad as to subject B to liability for libel, B is subject to liability to A for invasion of privacy.
>
> 4. A is a Democrat. B induces him to sign a petition nominating C for office. A discovers that C is a Republican and demands that B

remove his name from the petition. B refuses to do so and continues public circulation of the petition, bearing A's name. B is subject to liability to A for invasion of privacy.

5. A is a war hero, distinguished for bravery in a famous battle. B makes and exhibits a motion picture concerning A's life, in which he inserts a detailed narrative of a fictitious private life attributed to A, including a non-existent romance with a girl. B knows this matter to be false. Although A is not defamed by the motion picture, B is subject to liability to him for invasion of privacy.

FELLOWS V. NATIONAL ENQUIRER, INC., 42 Cal.3d 234, 228 Cal.Rptr. 215, 57 A.L.R.4th 223, 721 P.2d 97 (1986). The defendant National Enquirer carried a photograph of plaintiff Arthur Fellows and actress Angie Dickinson over the caption, "ANGIE DICKINSON. Dating a producer." The accompanying "article" was two sentences long: "Gorgeous Angie Dickinson's all smiles about the new man in her life—TV producer Arthur Fellows. Angie's steady-dating Fellows all over TinselTown, and happily posed for photographers with him as they exited the swanky Spago restaurant in Beverly Hills." Fellows advised the defendant that the article was "false because Mr. Fellows has never dated Miss Dickinson, is not 'the new man in her life,' and has been married to Phyllis Fellows for the last 18 years." The defendant refused to retract. Fellows sued, ultimately relying on a false light privacy claim. The trial court dismissed the claim because Fellows had not pleaded special damages. The intermediate appellate court reversed, holding that the plaintiff could proceed on the privacy claim without special damages. *Held,* the trial court correctly dismissed the claim. "In order to be actionable, the false light in which the plaintiff is placed must be highly offensive to a reasonable person. Although it is not necessary that the plaintiff be defamed, publicity placing one in a highly offensive false light will in most cases be defamatory as well. The substantial overlap between the two torts raised from the outset the question of the extent to which the restrictions and limitations on defamation actions would be applicable to actions for false light invasion of privacy." The appellate court's initial premise was that interests protected by privacy law and those protected by defamation law are different. But "where a complaint is based on a defamatory publication, this conceptual difference in the two torts does not justify making actionable an otherwise protected statement." Consequently, California's statutory rule of libel per quod applies in a false light privacy action. "Section 45a manifests a legislative determination that liability imposed for a publication which affords no warning of its defamatory nature, and has not caused actual pecuniary injury, would place too great a burden on the editorial process and would hamper the free dissemination of the news. The fact that plaintiff had deleted injury to reputation from his prayer and is seeking to recover only for injury to his sensibilities, does not alter the legislative judgment that such injuries alone are inadequate to outweigh the burden on a free press."

24. **Are any limitations on defamation recoveries applicable to false light claims?** If a court accepts the false light tort as distinct from libel and slander, are there any limitations drawn from defamation law besides those based upon free speech considerations? *West v. Media General Convergence, Inc.,* 53 S.W.3d 640 (Tenn. 2001), made a point of insisting that the false light claim was "personal" to the plaintiff, was not actionable by business entities, did not survive the victim's death, could not be assigned, and was subject to the statute of limitations for libel or slander. Most decisions agree that the false light claim does not survive, although there are a few decisions going the other way. Equally, survivors ordinarily have no claim of their own. See *Tyne v. Time Warner Entertainment Co., L.P.,* 336 F.3d 1286 (11th Cir. 2003). In *Tyne,* the plaintiffs were survivors of men lost at sea. They claimed that the defendant's movie, *The Perfect Storm*, depicted the men in a false light and that, as a result, their own privacy was invaded. Although Florida intermediate appellate courts had recognize a limited "relational right of privacy" where the defendant's conduct was egregious, the facts in *Tyne* could not be made to fit that rule. The non-survival rule matches the rule often applied in defamation cases. See Chapter 6, ¶ 2, supra.

(c) Private Facts

25. **Highly offensive publicity of truth.** The invasion of privacy by revealing private facts requires publication and hence also implicates the First Amendment. As a common law matter, the Restatement requires, as with false light, not merely communication but "publicity" in the sense communicating to the public at large or "many persons." See *Bodah v. Lakeville Motor Express, Inc.,* 663 N.W.2d 550 (Minn. 2003) (distribution of private information about employees to 16 freight terminals across six states was not "publicity," because it was not published to so many persons that it would become public knowledge); RESTATEMENT § 652D.

26. **Some qualifications of the publicity requirement.** There are probably some qualifications. Where the defendant obtains the information improperly in the first place, perhaps by misrepresenting his own identity or purpose, maybe widespread publicity should not be required. And if the disclosure to one person creates a risk of physical harm, the requirement of widespread publicity seems totally irrelevant. Both these qualifications are suggested by the facts in *Remsburg v. Docusearch, Inc.,* 149 N.H. 148, 816 A.2d 1001 (2003), summarized supra ¶ 13. On an entirely different track, liability for disclosure in breach of contract or a relationship of confidence is presumably shaped by the contract or the confidence, not by the Restatement's publicity rule. A physician who discloses his patient's private medical information might well be held for breach of confidence even if he disclosed the information only to one person. See ¶ ¶ 38 & 39 below. Finally, some authority takes the view that disclosure to a small group of people is sufficient "if those people have a special relationship with the plaintiff that makes the

disclosure as devastating as disclosure to the public at large." *Karraker v. Rent-A-Center, Inc.*, 411 F.3d 831(7th Cir. 2005).

27. **Falsity.** Liability for giving publicity to private facts does not require proof of either derogatory information or falsity. On the contrary, the damage is done because the information is true but "highly offensive" and "not of legitimate concern to the public." Is it really possible, absent contract or special confidential relationship, to impose liability for truthful communications?

Doe v. Mills, 212 Mich.App. 73, 536 N.W.2d 824 (1995). The allegations: Plaintiffs intended to have abortions at the Women's Advisory Center and they regarded this fact as private and confidential. Defendants were protesting at the abortion clinic, carrying large signs held up for public view. These signs identified the plaintiffs by name and implored them by name printed on the signs not to kill their babies (by having abortions). The defendants had gained this information from a third person who had rummaged in a dumpster and found a paper that indicated to him that plaintiffs might be obtaining an abortion. The plaintiffs claimed intrusive and private facts privacy invasion and intentional infliction of emotional distress. The trial judge gave summary judgment for the defendants, apparently reasoning that the information was not highly offensive and that since the issue of abortion was of public interest, the facts were not protected from disclosure. *Held,* although there is no intrusive privacy invasion because the defendants did not themselves or by an agent search through the rubbish, the allegations state a claim for revelation of private facts. Matters touching medical and sexual information are usually considered private. The jury may find that this revelation would be offensive to a reasonable person and that the facts are private in nature. The facts do not establish that the plaintiffs knowingly waived any right of privacy. In addition, the facts state a claim for intentional infliction of emotional distress.

BONOME v. KAYSEN

17 Mass.L.Rptr. 695, 2004 WL 1194731 (Mass. Super. Ct. 2004).

[The plaintiff, Bonome, operated a landscaping business operating in the Cambridge, Massachusetts area. Kaysen, the author of a book that became the basis of the movie, *Girl, Interrupted*, began having an affair with Bonome and eventually he divorced his wife and moved in with Kaysen. While they were living together, she began writing a memoir. The other defendant, Random House, published the book. It described her sexual and emotional relationship with her "boyfriend," sometimes graphically. The defendant had vaginal pain that doctors could not diagnose, and much of her memoir was about that pain and the effect of the pain on her relationship with the "boyfriend." At one point, the book presents a scene in which "the boyfriend is physically forceful in an attempt to engage her in sex. This scene is followed by ruminations about whether the relationship had exceeded the bounds of consensual sexual relations into the realm of coerced non-consensual sex. 'For a short time I indulged myself in this idea. He was trying to rape me. But he wasn't really, was he?' " There was more in this vein. Bonome sued, claiming he was readily recognized and suffered humiliation. Defendants moved to dismiss.]

[The book] explores the issue of when undesired physical intimacy crosses the line into non-consensual sexual relations in the context of her condition. These broader topics are all matters of legitimate public concern, and it is within this specific context that the explicit and highly personal details of the relationship are discussed. Thus, the defendants had a legitimate and protected interest to publish these facts.

As noted above, there is an additional interest in this case: Kaysen's right to disclose her own intimate affairs. In this case, it is critical that Kaysen was not a disinterested third party telling Bonome's personal story in order to develop the themes in her book. Rather, she is telling *her own* personal story—which inextricably involves Bonome in an intimate way. In this regard, several courts have held that where an autobiographical account related to a matter of legitimate public interest reveals private information concerning a third party, the disclosure is protected so long as there is a sufficient nexus between those private details and the issue of public concern.

Where one's own personal story involves issues of legitimate public concern, it is often difficult, if not impossible, to separate one's intimate and personal experiences from the people with whom those experiences are shared. Thus, it is within the context of Bonome and Kaysen's lives being inextricably bound together by their intimate relationship that the disclosures in this case must be viewed. Because the First Amendment protects Kaysen's ability to contribute *her own* personal experiences to the public discourse on important and legitimate issues of public concern, disclosing Bonome's involvement in those experiences is a necessary incident thereto. . . .

[Motion granted.]

Notes

28. **Public concern and the right to tell one's own story.** Would there be a public concern issue involved if there were no scene in which "the boyfriend is physically forceful in an attempt to engage her in sex"? If not, would Kaysen's right to discuss herself in print justify publication of truly reported facts about the relationship and her feelings about it? Maybe that's the wrong question. In the absence of confidential relationship or a contractual obligation to keep facts confidential (¶ ¶ 41–42, below), should we simply say that anyone can always tell the truth whether or not it is a part of one's own story?

THE FLORIDA STAR v. B.J.F.

491 U.S. 524, 109 S.Ct. 2603, 105 L.Ed.2d 443 (1989)

Justice MARSHALL delivered the opinion of the Court.

Florida Stat. § 794.03 (1987) makes it unlawful to "print, publish, or broadcast ... in any instrument of mass communication" the name of the victim of a sexual offense. Pursuant to this statute, appellant The Florida Star was found civilly liable for publishing the name of a rape victim which it had obtained from a publicly released police report. The issue presented here is whether this result comports with the First Amendment. We hold that it does not.

The Florida Star is a weekly newspaper which serves the community of Jacksonville, Florida, and which has an average circulation of approximately 18,000 copies. A regular feature of the newspaper is its "Police Reports" section. That section, typically two to three pages in length, contains brief articles describing local criminal incidents under police investigation.

On October 20, 1983, appellee B.J.F. reported to the Duval County, Florida, Sheriff's Department (the Department) that she had been robbed and sexually assaulted by an unknown assailant. The Department prepared a report on the incident which identified B.J.F., by her full name. The Department then placed the report in its press room. The Department does not restrict access either to the press room or to the reports made available therein.

A Florida Star reporter-trainee sent to the press room copied the police report verbatim, including B.J.F.'s full name, on a blank duplicate of the Department's forms. A Florida Star reporter then prepared a one-paragraph article about the crime, derived entirely from the trainee's copy of the police report. The article included B.J.F.'s full name. It appeared in the "Robberies" subsection of the "Police Reports" section on October 29, 1983, one of fifty-four police blotter stories in that day's edition. The article read:

> [B.J.F.] reported on Thursday, October 20, she was crossing Brentwood Park, which is in the 500 block of Golfair Boulevard, en route to her bus stop, when an unknown black man ran up behind the lady and placed a knife to her neck and told her not to yell. The suspect then undressed the lady and had sexual intercourse with her before fleeing the scene with her 60 cents, Timex watch and gold necklace. Patrol efforts have been suspended concerning this incident because of a lack of evidence.

In printing B.J.F.'s full name, The Florida Star violated its internal policy of not publishing the names of sexual offense victims.

On September 26, 1984, B.J.F. filed suit in the Circuit Court of Duval County against the Department and The Florida Star, alleging that these parties negligently violated § 794.03. See supra, n. 1. Before trial, the Department settled with B.J.F. for $2,500. The Florida Star moved to dismiss, claiming, inter alia, that imposing civil sanctions on the newspaper pursuant to § 794.03 violated the First Amendment. The trial judge rejected the motion.

At the ensuing day-long trial, B.J.F. testified that she had suffered emotional distress from the publication of her name. She stated that she had heard about the article from fellow workers and acquaintances; that her mother had received several threatening phone calls from a man who stated that he would rape B.J.F. again; and that these events had forced B.J.F. to change her phone number and residence, to seek police protection, and to obtain mental health counseling. In defense, The Florida Star put forth evidence indicating that the newspaper had learned B.J.F.'s name from the incident report released by the Department, and that the newspaper's violation of its internal rule against publishing the names of sexual offense victims was inadvertent.

At the close of B.J.F.'s case, and again at the close of its defense, The Florida Star moved for a directed verdict. On both occasions, the trial judge denied these motions. [The District Court of Appeal affirmed. The Supreme Court of Florida denied review.]. . . .

The parties to this case frame their contentions in light of a trilogy of cases which have presented, in different contexts, the conflict between truthful reporting and state-protected privacy interests. In Cox Broadcasting Corp. v. Cohn, 420 U.S. 469, 95 S.Ct. 1029, 43 L.Ed.2d 328 (1975), we found unconstitutional a civil damages award entered against a television station for broadcasting the name of a rape-murder victim which the station had obtained from courthouse records. In Oklahoma Publishing Co. v. District Court, 430 U.S. 308, 97 S.Ct. 1045, 51 L.Ed.2d 355 (1977), we found unconstitutional a state court's pretrial order enjoining the media from publishing the name or photograph of an 11–year-old boy in connection with a juvenile proceeding involving that child which reporters had attended. Finally, in Smith v. Daily Mail Publishing Co., 443 U.S. 97, 99 S.Ct. 2667, 61 L.Ed.2d 399 (1979), we found unconstitutional the indictment of two newspapers for violating a state statute forbidding newspapers to publish, without written approval of the juvenile court, the name of any youth charged as a juvenile offender. The papers had learned about a shooting by monitoring a police band radio frequency, and had obtained the name of the alleged juvenile assailant from witnesses, the police, and a local prosecutor.

. . . Appellee counters that the privacy trilogy is inapposite, because in each case the private information already appeared on a "public record," and because the privacy interests at stake were far less profound than in the present case. In the alternative, appellee urges that Cox Broadcasting be overruled and replaced with a categorical rule that publication of the name of a rape victim never enjoys constitutional protection.

We conclude that imposing damages on appellant for publishing B.J.F.'s name violates the First Amendment, although not for either of the reasons appellant urges. Despite the strong resemblance this case bears to Cox Broadcasting, that case cannot fairly be read as controlling here. The name of the rape victim in that case was obtained from courthouse records that were open to public inspection, a fact which Justice White's opinion for the Court repeatedly noted. Significantly, one of the reasons we gave in Cox Broadcasting for invalidating the challenged damages award was the important role the press plays in subjecting trials to public scrutiny and thereby helping guarantee their fairness. That role is not directly compromised where, as here, the information in question comes from a police report prepared and disseminated at a time at which not only had no adversarial criminal proceedings begun, but no suspect had been identified.

Nor need we accept appellant's invitation to hold broadly that truthful publication may never be punished consistent with the First Amendment. Our cases have carefully eschewed reaching this ultimate question, mindful that the future may bring scenarios which prudence counsels are not resolving anticipatorily. Indeed, in Cox Broadcasting, we pointedly refused to answer even the less sweeping question "whether truthful publications may ever be subjected to civil or criminal liability" for invading "an area of privacy" defined by the State. Respecting the fact that press freedom and privacy rights are both "plainly rooted in the traditions and significant concerns of our society," we instead focused on the less sweeping issue of "whether the State may impose sanctions on the accurate publication of the name of a rape victim obtained from public records—more specifically, from judicial records which are maintained in connection with a public prosecution and which themselves are open to public inspection." We continue to believe that the sensitivity and significance of the interests presented in clashes between First Amendment and privacy rights counsel relying on limited principles that sweep no more broadly than the appropriate context of the instant case.

In our view, this case is appropriately analyzed with reference to such a limited First Amendment principle. It is the one, in fact, which we articulated in Daily Mail in our synthesis of prior cases involving attempts to punish truthful publication: "[I]f a newspaper lawfully obtains truthful information about a matter of public significance then state officials may not constitutionally punish publication of the information, absent a need to further a state interest of the highest order." According the press the ample protection provided by that principle is supported by at least three separate considerations, in addition to, of course, the overarching public interest, secured by the Constitution, in the dissemination of truth. The cases on which the Daily Mail synthesis relied demonstrate these considerations.

First, because the Daily Mail formulation only protects the publication of information which a newspaper has "lawfully obtain[ed]," the government retains ample means of safeguarding significant interests upon which publication may impinge, including protecting a rape victim's anonymity. To the extent sensitive information rests in private hands, the government may under some circumstances forbid its nonconsensual acquisition, thereby bringing outside of the Daily Mail principle the publication of any information so acquired. To the extent sensitive information is in the government's custody, it has even greater power to forestall or mitigate the injury caused by its release. The government may classify certain information, establish and enforce procedures ensuring its redacted release, and extend a damages remedy against the government or its officials where the government's mishandling of sensitive information leads to its dissemination. Where information is entrusted to the government, a less drastic means than punishing truthful publication almost always exists for guarding against the dissemination of private facts. . . .

A second consideration undergirding the Daily Mail principle is the fact that punishing the press for its dissemination of information which is already publicly available is relatively unlikely to advance the interests in the service of which the State seeks to act. It is not, of course, always the case that information lawfully acquired by the press is known, or accessible, to others. But where the government has made certain information publicly available, it is highly anomalous to sanction persons other than the source of its release. We noted this anomaly in Cox Broadcasting: "By placing the information in the public domain on official court records, the State must be presumed to have concluded that the public interest was thereby being served." The Daily Mail formulation reflects the fact that it is a limited set of cases indeed where, despite the accessibility of the public to certain information, a meaningful public interest is served by restricting its further release by other entities, like the press. As Daily Mail observed in its summary of Oklahoma Publishing, "once the truthful information was 'publicly revealed' or 'in the public domain' the court could not constitutionally restrain its dissemination."

A third and final consideration is the "timidity and self-censorship" which may result from allowing the media to be punished for publishing certain truthful information. Cox Broadcasting noted this concern with over deterrence in the context of information made public through official court records, but the fear of excessive media self-suppression is applicable as well to other information released, without qualification, by the government. A contrary rule, depriving protection to those who rely on the government's implied representations of the lawfulness of dissemination, would force upon the media the onerous obligation of sifting through government press releases, reports, and pronouncements to prune out material arguably unlawful for publication. This situation could inhere even where the newspaper's sole object was to reproduce, with no substantial change, the government's rendition of the event in question.

Applied to the instant case, the Daily Mail principle clearly commands reversal. The first inquiry is whether the newspaper "lawfully obtain[ed] truthful information about a matter of public significance." It is undisputed that the news article describing the assault on B.J.F. was accurate. In addition, appellant lawfully obtained B.J.F.'s name. Appellee's argument to the contrary is based on the fact that under Florida law, police reports which reveal the identity of the victim of a sexual offense are not among the matters of "public record" which the public, by law, is entitled to inspect. But the fact that state officials are not required to disclose such reports does not make it unlawful for a newspaper to receive them when furnished by the government. Nor does the fact that the Department apparently failed to fulfill its obligation under § 794.03 not to "cause or allow to be ... published" the name of a sexual offense victim make the newspaper's ensuing receipt of this information unlawful. Even assuming the Constitution permitted a State to proscribe receipt of information, Florida has not taken this step. It is, clear, furthermore, that the news article concerned "a matter of public significance," in the sense in which the Daily Mail synthesis of prior cases used that term. That is, the article generally, as opposed to the specific identity contained within it, involved a matter of paramount public import: the commission, and investigation, of a violent crime which had been reported to authorities.

The second inquiry is whether imposing liability on appellant pursuant to § 794.03 serves "a need to further a state interest of the highest order." Appellee argues that a rule punishing publication furthers three closely related interests: the privacy of victims of sexual offenses; the physical safety of such victims, who may be targeted for retaliation if their names become known to their assailants; and the goal of encouraging victims of such crimes to report these offenses without fear of exposure.

At a time in which we are daily reminded of the tragic reality of rape, it is undeniable that these are highly significant interests, a fact underscored by the Florida Legislature's explicit attempt to protect these interests by enacting a criminal statute prohibiting much dissemination of victim identities. We accordingly do not rule out the possibility that, in a proper case, imposing civil sanctions for publication of the name of a rape victim might be so overwhelmingly necessary to advance these interests as to satisfy the Daily Mail standard. For three independent reasons, however, imposing liability for publication under the circumstances of this case is too precipitous a means of advancing these interests to convince us that there is a "need" within the meaning of the Daily Mail formulation for Florida to take this extreme step.

First is the manner in which appellant obtained the identifying information in question. As we have noted, where the government itself provides information to the media, it is most appropriate to assume that the government had, but failed to utilize, far more limited means of guarding against dissemination than the extreme step of punishing truthful speech. ... Where, as here, the government has failed to police itself in disseminating information, it is clear under Cox Broadcasting, Oklahoma Publishing, and Landmark Communications that the imposition of damages against the press for its subsequent publication can hardly be said to be a narrowly tailored means of safeguarding anonymity. ...

That appellant gained access to the information in question through a government news release makes it especially likely that, if liability were to be imposed, self-censorship would result. Reliance on a news release is a paradigmatically routine newspaper reporting techniqu[e]. . . .

A second problem with Florida's imposition of liability for publication is the broad sweep of the negligence per se standard applied under the civil cause of action implied from § 794.03. Unlike claims based on the common law tort of invasion of privacy, civil actions based on § 794.03 require no case-by-case findings that the disclosure of a fact about a person's private life was one that a reasonable person would find highly offensive. On the contrary, under the per se theory of negligence adopted by the courts below, liability follows automatically from publication. This is so regardless of whether the identity of the victim is already known throughout the community; whether the victim has voluntarily called public attention to the offense; or whether the identity of the victim has otherwise become a reasonable subject of public concern—because, perhaps, questions have arisen whether the victim fabricated an assault by a particular person. Nor is there a scienter requirement of any kind under § 794.03, engendering the perverse result that truthful publications challenged pursuant to this cause of action are less protected by the First Amendment than even the least protected defamatory falsehoods: those involving purely private figures, where liability is evaluated under a standard, usually applied by a jury, of ordinary negligence. . . .

Third, and finally, the facial underinclusiveness of § 794.03 raises serious doubts about whether Florida is, in fact, serving, with this statute, the significant interests which appellee invokes in support of affirmance. Section 794.03 prohibits the publication of identifying information only if this information appears in an "instrument of mass communication," a term the statute does not define. Section 794.03 does not prohibit the spread by other means of the identities of victims of sexual offenses. An individual who maliciously spreads word of the identity of a rape victim is thus not covered, despite the fact that the communication of such information to persons who live near, or work with, the victim may have consequences equally devastating as the exposure of her name to large numbers of strangers.

When a State attempts the extraordinary measure of punishing truthful publication in the name of privacy, it must demonstrate its commitment to advancing this interest by applying its prohibition evenhandedly, to the small time disseminator as well as the media giant. Where important First Amendment interests are at stake, the mass scope of disclosure is not an acceptable surrogate for injury. . . .

Reversed.

[Justice Scalia's opinion, concurring in part and concurring the judgment is omitted; Justice White's dissenting opinion, in which the Chief Justice and Justice O'Connor joined, is omitted.]

29. **Disclosure of the truth.** Liability for disclosure of private facts is liability for disclosure of the truth. Which is more persuasive to you:

(A) You have a constitutional right to publish the truth, period; or

(B) You have a constitutional right to publish the truth about public affairs or any matter of public concern; or

(C) Your constitutional right to publish is limited by the state's power to protect interests of the highest order, but the privacy of rape victims is not one of those interests; or

(D) No one has a constitutional right to publish the truth if it will foreseeably hurt another person and does actually do so.

30. **Emotional distress claim as an end run around "lawfully obtained"?** Allegations in *Burgess v. Busby,* 142 N.C.App. 393, 544 S.E.2d 4 (2001), asserted that the plaintiffs had all been jurors in a medical malpractice case in which Dr. Busby had been a defendant. The jurors found one doctor negligent, but not Dr. Busby. Busby then sent out a letter listing the jurors with their addresses as jurors who had found a doctor guilty of negligence. The letter went to medical practitioners in the county. The plaintiffs alleged that Busby had done so in retaliation and for the purpose of encouraging doctors to refuse or limit medical care to the plaintiffs. They claimed intentional infliction of emotional distress, a common law obstruction of justice tort, and invasion of privacy. As North Carolina refuses to recognize the private fact and false light versions of privacy invasion, the plaintiffs asserted that this was an intrusive invasion of privacy. The court held it was not an intrusive invasion and hence denied the privacy claim. But it permitted the plaintiff to proceed on the emotional distress theory and the obstruction of justice theory. *Florida Star* was not cited, nor was the *Cox Broadcasting* case. Would those cases not forbid the emotional distress claim?

31. **Restricting publication at the source.** In the light of comments in *Florida Star*, can the states simply declare public records off bound to citizens of the Republic? Are there no constitutional limits on *that*?

In *Los Angeles Police Dept. v. United Reporting Pub. Corp.,* 528 U.S. 32, 120 S.Ct. 483, 145 L.Ed.2d 451 (1999), a statute permitted police to release addresses of arrested persons only to private investigators and to persons who claimed, under penalty of perjury, a "scholarly, journalistic, political, or governmental purpose." One requesting information was also required to declare that it would not be used directly or indirectly to sell a product or service. Even then, some addresses remained confidential. The plaintiff was a commercial entity in the business of supplying names of recently arrested person to attorneys, counselors, and others. The majority upheld the statute. One group of Justices did so on the ground that the plaintiff was not entitled to rely upon unconstitutional effects it might have on others such as substance abuse counselors. Another group thought the statute was simply valid as a "a restriction on access to government information, not as a restriction on protected speech. . . . [T]he statute at issue does not restrict speakers from conveying information they already possess. Anyone who comes upon arrestee address information in the public domain is free to use that information as she sees fit." (Ginsburg, J., concurring.) The only discussion of privacy interests came from dissenters, Justice Stevens and Kennedy, who thought that the government's interest in protecting privacy could not serve to protect the statute in light of the fact that the information was available to journalists and could be widely published.

If you aren't sure about the propriety of restricting public information, try the shoe on the other foot. Suppose a prosecutor has received a complaint about an assault by the plaintiff. He has not charged the plaintiff with any crime (and never does), but he reveals the complaint and his negotiation with the plaintiff's attorney to a news reporter. Is every citizen who becomes a suspect subject to official exposure? *Svaldi v. Anaconda-Deer Lodge County,* 325 Mont. 365, 106 P.3d 548 (2005), discussing similar facts partly in terms of negligence, held the plaintiff had no claim.

32. **Statutory privacy and right to public information.** A number of statutes, state and federal, provide for privacy rights and corresponding restrictions upon access or publication. There are certain privacy protections in the federal Freedom of Information Act. 5 U.S.C. § 552a. The federal Privacy Act, 5 U.S.C. § 552a, lists some nondisclosable materials about individuals, and a separate statute, the Family Educational and Privacy Rights Act, 20 U.S.C. § 1232g, addresses privacy and access to records of institutions which received federal funds, in particular, educational institutions. With certain exceptions, education records are not to be released. Federal tax statutes create a civil cause of action for damages for improper disclosure of tax records. 26 U.S.C.A. § 7431.

States often have two minds on the topic, providing for access to public records on the one hand, but sealing them in some cases on the other. Ariz. Rev. Stats. § 39–121 provides that "public records and other matters" are open to inspection. A cause of action for damages is granted if access is denied. Ariz. Rev. Stats. § 39–121.02. But the statute does not define a public record.

33. **Expungement.** Could a citizen seeking privacy rights obtain an injunction to require a governmental agency to seal or expunge records? Suppose you were arrested for some horrible crime, say child molesting, but were released when prosecutors decided they had no evidence. Could you require the police department to expunge your arrest records, your photographs, and your fingerprints?

34. **Abuse or misuse of privacy?** Is it possible that privacy rights are sometimes too extensive? In *Bryson v. Banner Health Sys.,* 89 P.3d 800 (Alaska 2004), a man named Kompkoff had a very long history

of serious violence, beginning with slashing and stabbing people with knives, and graduating to rape. He was repeatedly paroled and repeatedly committed serious violent crimes on parole. The Family Recovery Center put Kompkoff in a group treatment program, but did not warn the group of his dangerous character because it was forbidden to reveal the history of any person in the group. The utterly predictable thing happened: a woman in the group, not warned of the danger, gave Kompkoff a ride. He attempted to rape her at gunpoint and eventually shot her. Is this a case of overprotecting privacy, in effect requiring people to imply false assurances of safety?

GATES v. DISCOVERY COMMUNICATIONS, INC.

34 Cal.4th 679, 101 P.3d 552, 21 Cal.Rptr.3d 663 (2004)

WERDEGAR, J. ...

Plaintiff served a prison sentence of three years (with time off for good behavior) that was imposed after he was convicted upon pleading guilty in 1992 to being an accessory after the fact to a murder for hire that occurred in 1988. The victim was an automobile salesman who was shot and killed by hired "hitmen" at the door of his Southern California home. A prominent automobile dealer was convicted of masterminding the murder in order to deter a class action lawsuit the victim had filed against an automobile dealership owned by the dealer's parents. Plaintiff, who was employed as the automobile dealers assistant manager at the time of the murder, originally was charged as a coconspirator, but the charges were later reduced. Defendants are television production and transmission companies that aired an account of the crime in 2001—more than a dozen years after the crime occurred.

After defendants' documentary was broadcast, plaintiff filed this action, pleading causes of action for defamation and invasion of privacy. ...

Defendants demurred to both causes of action, contending plaintiff was a limited-purpose public figure and could not demonstrate that defendants had made any defamatory statements with malice. Defendants also filed a special motion to strike the invasion of privacy claim under Code of Civil Procedure section 425.16 (section 425.16), the anti-SLAPP statute.[4]

[The trial court sustained the demurrer to the defamation action, but overruled the demurrer and the anti-SLAPP motion to the privacy action. The Court of Appeals reversed, holding that the privacy action could not proceed.]

[The plaintiffs rely on *Briscoe v. Reader's Digest Ass'n, Inc.*, 4 Cal.3d 529, 93 Cal.Rptr. 866, 57 A.L.R.3d 1, 483 P.2d 34 (1971).] *Briscoe* involved an action for invasion of privacy brought against a magazine

4. The anti-SLAPP statute requires an expedited dismissal of claims based on the defendant's exercise of rights of speech or petition unless the plaintiff can show a probability of success. See Chapter 8, § 4 below.–ed.

publisher. The dispute arose when the defendant published an article disclosing that the plaintiff had committed a truck hijacking 11 years previously. The plaintiff alleged that his friends and his 11-year-old daughter, after learning for the first time from the defendant's article these true but embarrassing facts about his past life, had scorned and abandoned him. Conceding the truth of the disclosures, the plaintiff nevertheless contended that because the offense had occurred many years earlier and he had subsequently led a lawful, obscure life and achieved a place in respectable society, the use of his name in the defendant's article was not "newsworthy" and constituted therefore a tortious invasion of his privacy.

In a unanimous opinion authored by Justice Peters, we held the plaintiff had stated a cause of action ..... Recognizing the potential conflict between freedom of the press and the right of privacy, we distinguished between reports of "hot news," items of possible immediate public concern or interest that are [p]articularly deserving of First Amendment protection and reports of the facts of *past* crimes and the identification of *past* offenders with respect to which reports of the facts ... are newsworthy but identification of the *actor* ... usually serves little independent public purpose. ... Accordingly, we reasoned, a truthful publication is protected only if it is newsworthy and does not reveal facts so offensive as to shock the community's notion of decency. We also discussed factors for determining whether an incident is newsworthy: [1] the social value of the facts published, [2] the depth of the article's intrusion into ostensibly private affairs, and [3] the extent to which the party voluntarily acceded to a position of public notoriety.

Applying the foregoing, we concluded in *Briscoe* that "a jury could reasonably find that plaintiff's identity as a former hijacker was not newsworthy". ...

[The court here reviewed a series of decisions of the United States Supreme Court beginning with *Cox Broadcasting Corp. v. Cohn*, 420 U.S. 469, 95 S.Ct. 1029, 43 L.Ed.2d 328 (1975), and including *Florida Star*.]

We conclude that the high court's decision in *Cox* and its subsequent pronouncements in [other cases] have fatally undermined *Briscoe's* holding that a media defendant may be held liable in tort for recklessly publishing true but not newsworthy facts concerning a rehabilitated former criminal insofar as that holding applies to facts obtained from public official court records. As explained, the high court in *Cox* flatly stated that "the States may not impose sanctions on the publication of truthful information contained in official court records open to public inspection."

It is true that in subsequently articulating the more general principle of which *Cox's* rule is an instance—viz., that "state officials may not constitutionally punish publication of [truthful] information" that "a newspaper lawfully obtains ... about a matter of public significance" (*Daily Mail, supra,* 443 U.S. at p. 103, 99 S.Ct. 2667)—the high court excepted circumstances involving "a need to further a state interest of the highest order" (*ibid.;* see also *The Florida Star, supra,* 491 U.S. at p. 533, 109 S.Ct. 2603. . . .) But in light of the needs and interests the high court, as previously noted, has determined *not* to be "of the highest order" for these purposes, we conclude, contrary to plaintiff's suggestion, that any state interest in protecting for rehabilitative purposes the long-term anonymity of former convicts falls similarly short.

Plaintiff requests that we distinguish *Cox* and its progeny on their facts, principally the fact that "all of these cases involve situations in which the events reported on occurred within a few days, weeks or months of the offending publication, not years after the fact as in *Briscoe*. . . ." But as the Court of Appeal below recognized, the high court has never suggested, in *Cox* or in any subsequent case, that the fact the public record of a criminal proceeding may have come into existence years previously affects the absolute right of the press to report its contents. . . .

Neither that defendants' documentary was of an historical nature nor that it involved "reenactments," rather than firsthand coverage, of the events reported, diminishes any constitutional protection it enjoys. [T]he constitutional guarantees of freedom of expression apply with equal force to the publication whether it be a news report or an entertainment feature. And, as the high court of a sister state recently observed in deciding a similar privacy case, "[t]here is no indication that the First Amendment provides less protection to historians than to those reporting current events." (*Uranga v. Federated Publs., Inc.*, (2003) 138 Idaho 550, 556, 67 P.3d 29, 35). . . .

Accordingly, following *Cox* and its progeny, we conclude that an invasion of privacy claim based on allegations of harm caused by a media defendant's publication of facts obtained from public official records of a criminal proceeding is barred by the First Amendment to the United States Constitution. . . .

It follows that defendants' anti-SLAPP motion should have been granted, because, as a matter of law, plaintiff cannot prevail on his invasion of privacy claim. The trial court erred insofar as it concluded to the contrary.

The judgment of the Court of Appeal is affirmed.

---

35. **Retreat from the spotlight.** Recall that in *Wolston*, Chapter 3, § 2 (b), Justice Blackmun argued that one could retreat from the spotlight and cease to be a public figure. If the Supreme Court were to grant certiorari in *Gates,* on what grounds might it decide that *Florida Star* does not foreclose Mr. Gates' suit?

36. **Newsworthy events or figures.** Constitutional issues aside, courts usually recognize some kind of right or privilege to publish "newsworthy" materials when the claim is private fact privacy and

sometimes when the claim is for commercial appropriation as well. For this purpose, the plaintiff is a kind of common law public figure if she is involved in a newsworthy event, even if it is not one of her own making. The common law conception of newsworthiness seems considerably broader than the constitutional concept of public concern. See David A. Elder, Privacy Torts § 3:17. It is certainly broader than the concept of public controversy as expressed in *Time v. Firestone* in Chapter 3. The Restatement, for example, tells us customary views and the mores of the community will determine what counts as news. Restatement Second of Torts § 652D, cmt. g.

37. **Involuntary involvement in news; Sipple's case.** A private citizen named Oliver Sipple became famous when he obstructed an effort to shoot former President Gerald Ford. Two days later, a columnist publicly revealed that Sipple was a homosexual. Sipple was thereafter subjected to many and various humiliations, some at the hands of his own family. His invasion of privacy claim was rejected, in part because his sexual preference was regarded as newsworthy. "Newsworthy" turned out to be a matter of the publisher's subjective motive. The court thought that the publisher's purpose to dispel false ideas about gays by using Sipple's life as an example showed that the publisher had no motive based upon sensational prying, and that, for the court, seemed to make the story newsworthy as a matter of law. *Sipple v. Chronicle Publ'g Co.*, 154 Cal.App.3d 1040, 1049, 201 Cal.Rptr. 665, 670 (1984). Contrast the outcome in *Diaz v. Oakland Tribune, Inc.*, 139 Cal.App.3d 118, 188 Cal.Rptr. 762 (1983), where another California court held that it was not newsworthy to reveal that a student body president involved in a dispute with a college was a transsexual. Is newsworthiness a concept sufficiently precise to protect both privacy and First Amendment values? To escape judicial manipulation? What about taking (and publishing) a picture of a person walking down the street for no particular reason? Cf. *Arrington v. New York Times Co.*, 55 N.Y.2d 433, 449 N.Y.S.2d 941, 434 N.E.2d 1319 (1982) (picture made on the street used to illustrate article, no claim).

38. **AIDS/HIV privacy.** AIDS and HIV status has given rise to a number of privacy claims of the private facts variety. Some states have imposed stringent statutory rules against revealing names of HIV or AIDS victims. New York's statute has been construed to create an implied tort action against a doctor who reveals a patient's HIV status, with the possibility of a punitive damages award. *Doe v. Roe*, 190 A.D.2d 463, 599 N.Y.S.2d 350 (1993). Notice that on these facts, however, the common law confidential relationship cases would have dictated liability regardless of the statute. What result if a newspaper publishes, truthfully, that the plaintiff has AIDS? *Cruz v. Latin News Impacto*, 216 A.D.2d 50, 627 N.Y.S.2d 388 (1995).

In *Estate of Behringer v. Medical Center at Princeton*, 249 N.J.Super. 597, 592 A.2d 1251 (1991), the court viewed AIDS as a handicap within the meaning of a statute that forbade discrimination against handicapped. Nevertheless, it held that a hospital where an AIDS-victim doctor worked was authorized to insist that the doctor reveal his AIDS status to any patient with whom he worked in the hospital.

AIDS privacy has been raised defensively by suppliers of blood when they are sued for defective or contaminated blood causing AIDS after a transfusion. The blood suppliers defend their refusal to exclude donors who are in high-risk groups for AIDS on the basis of the donors' privacy rights. Similarly, some courts have refused to permit the plaintiff-victim of AIDS blood transfusions to use discovery to find the name or AIDS status of donors.

39. **Abolishing the private facts tort.** In *Hall v. Post*, 323 N.C. 259, 372 S.E.2d 711 (N.C. 1988), Burley Mitchel, J., said:

> First ... the private facts branch of the invasion of privacy tort is, at the very best, constitutionally suspect. ... Second, the constitutionally suspect private facts branch of the invasion of privacy tort will almost never provide a plaintiff with any advantage not duplicated or overlapped by the tort of intentional infliction of emotional distress and possibly by other torts such as trespass or intrusive invasion of privacy.

In *Doe v. Methodist Hospital*, 690 N.E.2d 681 (Ind. 1997), the defendant, by word of mouth, reported accurately that the plaintiff had tested positive for HIV. The court concluded that this did not count as publicizing to a substantial group of people and would not be actionable as a private facts invasion of privacy for that reason. A plurality also appeared to say that the private facts claim should not be recognized at all unless the elements necessary for intentional infliction of emotional distress were proven. "[W]e cannot see any relevant difference between emotional injuries resulting from public disclosures of private facts and those arising from other sources."

FOOD LION, INC. V. CAPITAL CITIES/ABC, INC., 194 F.3d 505 (4th Cir. 1999). ABC reporters, applied for job at Food Lion, a grocery chain, to investigate suspected practices involving selling of unwholesome food. They used hidden video cameras to tape various scenes and some of the footage, purportedly showing use of expired beef, was shown on ABC. Food Lion sued the reporters and ABC claiming fraud, trespass, and breach of fiduciary duty by the employees. The jury awarded $1 against each reporter for the trespass. The trial judge refused to permit the jury to award substantial damages based on harm done by publication. Food Lion urged on appeal that it was error to deny it the right to recover reputational harm from publication. *Held*, affirmed on this point. Food Lion could not have sued for defamation without proving knowing or reckless falsehood. It cannot be permitted to make an end run around the First Amendment protection by suing for trespass, then claiming publication or reputational damages. That is the message of *Hustler Magazine v. Falwell.*

---

40. **Trespass and its discontents.** The reporters in *Food Lion* might be considered trespassers if they gained "consent" of Food Lion by fraud which deluded Food Lion about the nature of the transaction involved. *Desnick v. American Broadcasting Companies, Inc.,* 44 F.3d 1345, 1352 (7th Cir. 1994), says, though, that even so, the plaintiff can recover only for invasion of interests the tort right is designed to protect. In *Desnick*, more ABC reporters fraudulently represented themselves as patients for an eye clinic in order to establish ABC's claims that the clinic systematically promoted unnecessary surgery of medicare patients. The court thought that fraud did not vitiate the clinic's consent to their presence. It said:

> There was no invasion . . . of any of the specific interests that the tort of trespass seeks to protect. The test patients entered offices that were open to anyone expressing a desire for ophthalmic services and videotaped physicians engaged in professional, not personal, communications with strangers (the testers themselves). The activities of the offices were not disrupted. Nor was there any inva[sion of] a person's private space. . . .

A case that reached a contrary result was distinguished: "Dietemann was not in business, and did not advertise his services or charge for them. His quackery was private." This reasoning largely disposed of the privacy claim as well. But the interests that the tort of trespass seeks to protect surely include privacy, so shouldn't ABC have been liable for the trespass?

41. **Abuse of confidence.** In *Humphers v. First Interstate Bank of Oregon*, 298 Or. 706, 696 P.2d 527 (1985), the court imposed liability upon a doctor who revealed an adopted child's identity, saying this was a violation of confidence, not an invasion of privacy. In *McCormick v. England,* 328 S.C. 627, 494 S.E.2d 431(1998), the court said: "The jurisdictions that recognize the duty of confidentiality have relied on various theories for the cause of action, including invasion of privacy, breach of implied contract, medical malpractice, and breach of a fiduciary duty or a duty of confidentiality." The court went on to say that even if the plaintiff had an invasion of privacy claim against her physician for revealing her personal medical information in letter to a court, her claim for breach of a duty of confidence remained viable "in the absence of a compelling public interest or other justification for the disclosure." In *Horne v. Patton*, 291 Ala. 701, 287 So.2d 824 (1973), a doctor's breach of his duty of confidence by giving the patient's medical information to the plaintiff's employer was held for invasion of privacy. In *Doe v. Roe*, 93 Misc.2d 201, 400 N.Y.S.2d 668 (1977), it was a psychiatrist who published a book about therapy in which some of plaintiff's verbatim statements were used. Although the patient's name was not used, she claimed she was recognized. The court said the doctor had violated the implied covenant of confidence and that the First Amendment was no bar to the claim. Inducing the release of confidential information is treated in the same way. *Anker v. Brodnitz*, 98 Misc.2d 148, 413 N.Y.S.2d 582 (Sup. Ct. 1979), aff'd, 73 A.D.2d 589, 422 N.Y.S.2d 887 (1979).

42. **Unlawfully obtained, breach of contract?** In *Cohen v. Cowles Media Co.,* 501 U.S. 663, 111 S.Ct. 2513, 115 L.Ed.2d 586 (1991), the plaintiff gave a newspaper certain political information after receiving a promise of confidentiality, which the newspaper promptly breached by publishing the information and the plaintiff's name as the source. The Supreme Court held that no constitutional considerations prevented liability of the newspaper under the general doctrine of promissory estoppel, since that doctrine is one of general applicability. In cases like *Florida Star* "the State itself defined the content of publications that would trigger liability. Here, by contrast, Minnesota law simply requires those making promises to keep them." What about the "lawfully obtained" formulation? "[I]t is not at all clear that respondents obtained Cohen's name 'lawfully' in this case, at least for purposes of publishing it. Unlike the situation in *Florida Star,* where the rape victim's name was obtained through lawful access to a police report, respondents obtained Cohen's name only by making a promise that they did not honor."

43. **Lawfully obtained? Receiving stolen goods.** Suppose Roberts robs the plaintiff's office, unlawfully obtaining information about him, then gives the information to defendant newspaper, which publishes it. Does *Florida Star* permit the courts to impose liability upon either Roberts or the newspaper? In *Bartnicki v. Vopper,* 532 U.S. 514, 121 S.Ct. 1753, 149 L.Ed.2d 787 (2001), the defendant published some illegally taped conversations on matters of public concern. The court assumed that the defendant knew that the information had been obtained in violation of federal statutes. Since the matter was one of public concern, however, and since the defendant did not himself have any role in the law violation, he could not constitutionally be held liable for the publication. Is it accurate to say that (1) some lawfully obtained materials do not after all receive protection (*Cohen v. Cowles Media,* supra) and that (2) some unlawfully obtained materials DO receive protection *(Bartnicki,* supra)?

What other wrongful means might justify liability?

MADDEN v. CREATIVE SERVICES, INC.

84 N.Y.2d 738, 622 N.Y.S.2d 478, 646 N.E.2d 780 (1995)

KAYE, Chief Judge. . . .

[P]laintiff George Madden founded a neighborhood coalition to oppose construction of a 12-screen movie theater complex by defendant National Amusements, Inc., a movie theater chain, in a residential area of the Town of Pittsford. Madden enlisted Francis E. Kenny, a partner in the Rochester firm of Nixon, Hargrave, Devans & Doyle, to provide pro bono legal services to the coalition, which included petitioning the Town Board to deny the rezoning application filed by National. National in turn retained defendant Creative Services, Inc., a private investigative firm. According to plaintiffs, the purpose was to intimidate and discredit them; according to defendants, the purpose was to uncover any possible connection between Madden and National's competitor Loews Theaters, Inc., also a Nixon, Hargrave client.

On November 14, 1991, Creative dispatched Ralph Douglas Howe, Jr. and Michael Sean Cole—Massachusetts-based investigators not licensed in New York—to place Madden and his wife, plaintiff Roseanne Cohen, under surveillance. The investigators allegedly followed and photographed plaintiffs without their knowledge. Posing as prospective home buyers, Howe and Cole also made an appointment with a real estate agent to visit plaintiffs' residence.

After business hours the next day—Friday, November 15—Howe and Cole entered the Nixon, Hargrave offices claiming to have lost a ring. They gained access to Kenny's office, where building personnel found them photographing purportedly privileged documents about the zoning dispute. When briefly left alone in the offices, Howe and Cole fled but were spotted at a local motel and arrested the following morning. The arrest preempted the scheduled visit to plaintiffs' residence. Defendants never developed the photographs, and no disclosure of documents or information is alleged by plaintiffs. Defendant employers deny authorizing or knowing of the investigators' conduct.

Charged with third degree burglary and petit larceny, Howe and Cole each pleaded guilty to trespass. Additionally, an action was instituted by Attorney Kenny against the investigators and their employers.

Plaintiffs commenced the present action in the United States District Court [against Creative, National, and others, alleging these claims among others: intentional interference with the attorney-client privilege; intentional infliction of emotional distress; conversion of documents; unlawful search and seizure; intentional interference with the right to petition governmental agencies. They sought $1 million in compensatory damages "for their feelings of personal insecurity, fear of being followed, emotional distress, increased anxiety and nightmares," $2 million in punitive damages, and an amount for lost consortium. The district court dismissed the complaint for failure to state a claim; the federal Court of Appeals certified a question (1) whether a cause of action existed for invasion of the attorney-client privilege and (2) if so whether economic loss was required to establish such an action.]

That a proposed cause of action has not previously been recognized by us, or indeed by any other court in the Nation, is itself inconclusive, for it is the strength of the common law to respond, albeit cautiously and intelligently, to the demands of common sense justice in an evolving society.

. . . [P]laintiffs urge that a new tort claim be created for third-party intrusions because, as a matter of public policy, the confidentiality of attorney-client communications is of supervening societal importance. In plaintiffs' words, damages are necessary in order "to vindicate fully the attorney-client privilege and to send a message to those who would invade the privilege that they do so at their peril." On the facts before us, we cannot agree that either the protection of plaintiffs' right or the prosecution of defendants' wrong requires that we recognize the proposed new claim for damages.

Tort liability of course depends on balancing competing interests: "the question remains who is legally bound to protect [plaintiffs' right] at the risk of liability. ... [To] identify an interest deserving protection does not suffice to collect damages from anyone who causes injury to that interest" (Humphers v. First Interstate Bank, 298 Or. 706, 713–716, 696 P.2d 527, 530–533). Not every deplorable act—as the intentional trespass here surely was—is redressable in damages.

Imposing a new tort duty, and tort liability for compensatory and punitive damages, is unquestionably a part of this Court's important common-law tradition and responsibility. We exercise that responsibility with care, mindful that a new cause of action will have foreseeable and unforeseeable consequences, most especially the potential for vast, uncircumscribed liability.

The potential expanse of the proposed cause of action is evident. A claim for third-party intrusions on attorney-client confidences necessarily envelops damage claims against attorneys themselves, which we have yet to recognize. Additionally, such claims could hardly be confined to attorney-client confidences; certainly no rational distinction could be made among the privileged relationships recognized by the Legislature. Of concern as well is that, under existing tort law, proven emotional injury is ordinarily as fully compensable as economic injury.

... The professed basis for plaintiffs' claim is protection of the attorney-client privilege, yet in this case they allege no harm that is tied to violation of the attorney-client privilege, no injury [suffered] as a result of the unauthorized examination of the documents in Kenny's office. ... The alleged damage resulting from the third-party intrusion is solely a generalized fear for personal safety and security that might accompany a theft or trespass on one's property. A new cause of action for intrusion on the attorney-client privilege should at least require some element of harm to plaintiffs that arises directly from a breach of this privilege.

It is perhaps because of the adequacy of existing remedies to deter third-party invasions of the attorney-client privilege that no court before us has been asked to impose the liability plaintiffs now seek.

... Those who attempt an unlawful intrusion by fraud, trespass or force, and those in complicity with them, may face criminal penalties; private investigators are additionally subject to license revocation or, if unlicensed, criminal sanctions (see, General Business Law art. 7). Attorneys are encouraged by available disciplinary sanctions and negligence law to secure clients' privileged documents adequately, and might even themselves be subject to damages for breach of confidence. There are existing causes of action, such as intentional infliction of emotional distress and conversion, simply not made out on the facts before us. Finally, had defendants' examination of confidential documents prejudiced plaintiffs in a zoning or other proceeding, sanctions could have been sought.

In the end, it is clear that plaintiffs would by this new cause of action, the functional equivalent of a common-law privacy tort, merely circumvent established privacy law. In this case, that is neither necessary to protect the private interest at issue nor prudent as a matter of public policy.

Accordingly, certified question No. 1 should be answered in the negative and certified question No. 2 not answered as unnecessary.

§ 2. DAMAGES

44. **Constitutional limits.** As indicated in § 1, the Constitution will almost certainly apply to privacy claims involving speech elements in ways that are parallel to its application in libel cases.

45. **Elements of damages.** The Restatement tells us vaguely that the plaintiff can recover damages for "the harm to his interest in privacy" and in addition any mental distress suffered if it is the kind normally resulting from such an invasion, plus any consequential damages legally caused by the invasion. RESTATEMENT (SECOND) OF TORTS § 652H.

46. **Emotional distress.** The chief component of harm in privacy cases is usually some form of emotional distress, for which the plaintiff is permitted to recover "general," unspecified, and nonpecuniary damages. The intangible, emotional harm may be expressed in varied terms—embarrassment, anxiety, humiliation, shame, a feeling of powerlessness or degradation and so on—but the bottom line is that the jury is permitted to award a sum of money which, like the money awarded for pain and suffering and that awarded in libel cases, has no connection to any pecuniary loss.

47. **Relation to the action for intentional infliction of distress.** Although emotional distress is the usual element of damages, it is in effect presumed from the finding that privacy was invaded. In *Godbehere v. Phoenix Newspapers, Inc.*, 162 Ariz. 335, 783 P.2d 781 (1989), the Court held that one could recover for false light invasion of privacy (and perhaps any invasion of privacy) without showing the "outrageous" conduct and severe emotional distress required to recover for intentional infliction of mental distress. Similarly, in *Sabrina W. v. Willman,* 4 Neb.App. 149, 540 N.W.2d 364 (1995), the court held that the plaintiff could recover for emotional distress resulting from an intrusive invasion of privacy without proving that it was "severe" as required in the tort of intentional infliction of distress, even though the court also thought that the very "gravamen" of the privacy tort was injury to the plaintiff's feelings.

*

Chapter 7

Expunging Public Records

V.C. v. CASADY

262 Neb. 714, 634 N.W.2d 798 (2001)

GERRARD, J.

V.C., the appellant, sued Thomas K. Casady, chief of the Lincoln Police Department (LPD), and Don Leuenberger, director of the Nebraska Department of Health and Human Services (DHHS), seeking an order directing Casady and Leuenberger to expunge any record of an LPD investigation into an allegation that the appellant had sexually molested a child, C.C., who was then 9 years old. The district court determined that it had jurisdiction to issue such an order, but that the appellant was not entitled to relief. The appellant filed this appeal.

[C.C.'s mother was involved in a custody dispute over the child. Through her custody-suit attorney and then personally, she raised the possibility with a police officer that V.C., a friend of the child's father, might have sexually abused the child.]

As part of his investigation, the police officer interviewed C.C. at C.C.'s school. The police officer also spoke to the counselor at C.C.'s school and reviewed a deposition of the father that had been in the possession of the mother's attorney. The police officer then dictated a supplemental investigation report. The police officer concluded that there was no evidence of a sexual assault. Since there was no evidence of a crime, no charges were filed.

Briefly summarized, the police officer's supplementary investigation report states that while there was no evidence that the appellant had abused C.C., the police officer did find the appellant's relationship with the child to be peculiar and inappropriate and expressed these concerns to C.C. and the father. The report recounts the mother's explanation of the situation to the police officer as follows: The mother had been employed in the appellant's office, and the appellant became acquainted with C.C. when the mother brought C.C. to work. The appellant became C.C.'s godfather and became extremely involved in C.C.'s life. The mother became concerned and began restricting the appellant's contact with C.C. The mother then left the appellant's employment. According to the police officer's recitation of the mother's statements, the appellant then befriended the father and provided the father with substantial financial support in exchange for being permitted to spend time with C.C.

Casady testified regarding the LPD's retention and use of police reports. Generally, Casady drew a distinction between incident reports and investigation reports.

Incident reports are maintained as both a hard copy of a written report and as an electronic record containing some of the information on the officer's written report. Incident reports contain the name of the victim, but not the name of any suspects. The incident report in this case, contained in exhibit 3, identifies only C.C. as the victim and the LPD officer who prepared the report.

. . . Police incident reports are public records, available to the general public upon request. In addition, the FBI is provided with and maintains records of code numbers, the nature of the event, and the date of each incident report for the purpose of compiling national crime statistics, but the FBI does not have access to the report and is not given any identifying information.

A supplementary investigation report is a narrative report about any case or information that an officer cares to prepare. Such a report names all the persons involved in the case, including suspects. These reports are electronic records and are not regularly kept as hard copies. They may be accessed by the LPD's police officers and civilian employees who need to access them. Case investigation reports and additional case investigation reports are maintained as hard copies, and not as electronic records. They include names and details of the investigation.

Investigation reports are not available to the general public, including victims, without a subpoena or a court order. Governmental officials or agencies charged with criminal investigatory responsibilities may be provided with copies of such reports upon request. . . .

The LPD has extensive rules and regulations about the distribution of information that are rigorously enforced. Reports are kept in a secure area and, when discarded, are securely recycled and destroyed.

Casady also testified at length regarding the utility of such records to the LPD. Casady stated that the reports document the LPD's investigation in the event that questions arise about whether an investigation has been handled properly; for instance, Casady noted that police investigations sometimes result in litigation. Casady also stated that the reports preserve a record of the investigation in case allegations are made in the future, either by C.C. or against the appellant. Casady also testified that the reports would provide documentation if C.C. was ever convicted of a crime and his childhood history was a relevant issue in sentencing.

Casady stated that if anyone ever wanted testimony from the investigating police officer or anyone else at the LPD regarding the investigation, the police reports would provide the only record. Casady also testified that the reports help him to provide oversight to ensure competent investigations, noting that there is occasionally a need to investigate the death of a child regarding whom there have been previous reports or referrals. Casady testified that in his opinion, there is a valid place in police reports for clearly noted opinions.

Casady admitted that if there was some way of guaranteeing that nothing would ever come up in the future that would involve this case, then the police reports would have no continuing utility.

The appellant filed an "Amended Petition in Equity" against Casady, alleging that the LPD reports on file were untrue and injurious to his reputation. The appellant sought to require Casady to deliver to him all of the LPD documents and records in the case. The appellant also asked the district court to order Casady to purge the LPD records and to identify all the persons who had been informed of the records. The appellant's petition also named Leuenberger and the Lancaster County Attorney as parties and sought to compel those parties to purge their records as well. . . .

At trial, the appellant made several offers of proof regarding evidence that was intended to undermine the credibility of the facts and conclusions stated in the police reports. A lawyer, who defended the appellant with respect to charges made by the mother in a separate civil proceeding, would have testified that the mother's attorney told this lawyer that if the appellant stopped helping the father in his custody proceeding, another civil action brought by the mother against the appellant would "go away." This testimony was excluded as irrelevant.

A licensed clinical psychologist would have testified that he had met with and assessed the appellant to determine if there was evidence of pedophilic tendencies. The psychologist would have testified that he reviewed the police report and concluded that there was no evidence that the appellant had pedophilic tendencies. Casady's relevance objection was sustained.

C.C.'s father would have testified about his contact with the LPD investigating officer and the events of the investigation. The appellant would have testified about his relationship with C.C. and why the appellant took the interest in C.C. that he did. Relevance objections were sustained to this proffered testimony. Attempts to attack the accuracy of statements in the reports were also made during the investigating officer's testimony, but Casady's objection was sustained, and the testimony was stricken. . . .

The appellant was permitted to testify at trial regarding the potential harm to him of the continued existence of the reports. The appellant recalled that he was required, on application to another state's bar, to have police records sent to the other state's bar association. The appellant also testified that he has on several occasions obtained security clearances. [He testified to several similar risks.]

The appellant assigns that it was error for the trial court to (1) find that the LPD and DHHS have a legitimate need to retain the reports sought to be expunged; (2) fail to find harm or potential harm to the appellant's basic legal interests; and (3) exclude evidence relevant and material to a determination of the competence, reliability, and accuracy of the investigation that provides the basis for the generation of the records. . . .

[T]o the extent that the appellant's petition addresses information maintained in the Abused or Neglected Child Registry, there is a statutory remedy available that allows for the expunction of such information, but there is no indication in the record that the appellant followed the statutory procedure. Where a statute provides an adequate remedy at law, equity will not entertain jurisdiction, and the statutory remedy must be exhausted before one may resort to equity. . . .

Assuming, arguendo, that expunction is available as an equitable remedy, the first question is under what circumstances the power of a court to expunge may be invoked.

Most of the reported cases that address the propriety of expunction as an equitable remedy have done so in the context of arrest records, rather than police reports. In cases upholding the theory of "inherent equitable power to expunge," the expunction of such records is a process of weighing the interests of society and of the individuals involved.

Courts which recognize an inherent power to expunge arrest records have tempered this power by requiring that it be exercised sparingly and only in extraordinary circumstances. Notably, no court has questioned the legitimacy or importance of the government's interest in obtaining and retaining records dealing with individuals who pass through our criminal justice system, none has viewed inherent judicial authority to expunge as a power to be used routinely, and none has suggested that the government's interest in maintaining accurate criminal histories can be outweighed in any but exceptional circumstances. . . .

Where constitutional questions are involved, the litigant has the right to raise them in a court of equity and such court has the right to consider them. In cases to which a statutory scheme does not extend, however, the court's inherent power is limited to instances where the petitioner's constitutional rights may be seriously infringed by retention of his or her records.

For instance, a number of courts have ordered expunction of local police records as an appropriate remedy in the wake of police action in violation of constitutional rights.

Assuming, then, that expunction is an available remedy for a court of equity, the issue facing this court is whether the appellant's evidence, taken as true as required by our standard of appellate review, establishes the extraordinary circumstances necessary for expunction to be ordered. Because the appellant's evidence, taken as true, fails to establish the invasion of a legally protected right, we conclude that the appellant did not prove the extraordinary circumstances that would be necessary to support an order expunging the police investigative reports at issue. . . .

The appellant argues that the LPD's retention of the police reports deprives him of liberty without due process of law, in violation of the

Due Process Clause of the U.S. Constitution. However, the only injury identified in the appellant's petition is harm to his reputation. It is well established that an injury to reputation alone is not enough to create a liberty interest, protected by the Due Process Clause, apart from some more tangible interests such as employment. . . .

[The plaintiff also failed to establish an invasion of the right to privacy.] The appellant's argument is premised on the possibility that the police investigative reports will be disseminated and cause him harm. In the first place, we note that the uncontradicted evidence presented at trial indicates that the police reports are not public records and are disseminated only to other law enforcement agencies or when subject to legal process. . . .

In the instant case, the evidence does not indicate, and the appellant does not argue, that the police investigative reports at issue were generated in violation of the appellant's constitutional rights. While the appellant sought to impeach the information in the reports, he does not claim, and the evidence would not support concluding, that the investigation was undertaken in bad faith or that the reports were the result of actionable police misconduct.

While the appellant claims that the information contained in the police investigative reports is embarrassing to him, those reports do not contain confidential information and explicitly exonerate the appellant of any illegal conduct. . . . Accepting the appellant's argument would require the judiciary to become the arbiter of what is and is not good police work, and to edit police reports to remove conclusions over which there is disagreement. This is simply not an appropriate judicial function.

Police reports summarize the facts surrounding an event and constitute a necessary log of police activity. The hallmark of our system of government calls for the preservation of accurate official records rather than suppression of information. If a record of involvement with criminal process is expunged, the traces literally vanish and no indication is left behind that information has been removed. Therefore, it is possible that the judicial editing of history could produce a greater harm than that sought to be corrected by the expunction of certain information from a police report. . . .

We conclude that the trial court erred in excluding the appellant's proffered evidence to the extent that it was relevant to the truth of the conclusions set forth in the police reports. As noted above, expunction of police records is a process of weighing the interests of society and of the individual involved. Whether the facts set forth in a police report are true or false will directly bear on the interests of the individual involved, as the harm done to the individual's legally protected interest may vary depending upon the veracity of the information that is disseminated. Furthermore, the utility of a police record to law enforcement may depend on the reliability of the information contained in the report. Thus, while we cannot countenance the use of the courts as a forum for questioning the competence of an investigation, evidence bearing on the reliability of a police report is certainly relevant to the analysis necessary to determine if expunction is appropriate.

However, we conclude that this error does not require reversal, as it does not affect the issue that the district court and this court have determined to be dispositive. ... Even if the appellant's evidence had been accepted ... his evidence would still fail to establish the invasion of a legally protected right. Absent such proof, the appellant is not entitled to the remedy of expunction.

Assuming, without deciding, that expunction of police records is an available remedy under extraordinary circumstances when an individual's legally protected rights have been invaded, the appellant's evidence, taken as true, failed to establish such circumstances. The district court did not err in dismissing the appellant's petition at the close of his evidence, and we therefore affirm the judgment of the district court.

1. **No power to expunge.** Some courts say that, at least for some kinds of records, they have no power or jurisdiction to order expungement. See *United States v. Flowers,* 389 F.3d 737 (7th Cir. 2004), holding that federal courts have no "jurisdiction to order an Executive Branch agency to expunge what are admittedly accurate records of a person's indictment and conviction."

2. **Reaching the merits on a balancing test.** The *Flowers* case, supra, also held that it had jurisdiction to order expungement of records kept by the *judicial* branch of government. Here, the court would weigh dangers to the individual against the public interest in keeping the records. But the "unwarranted adverse consequences to the individual must be uniquely significant in order to outweigh the strong public interest in maintaining accurate and undoctored records. ... the weight of the public interest can be seen in the long tradition of open proceedings and public records, which is the essence of a democratic society." The plaintiff seeking expungement there had been guilty of the crime as an 18-year-old, but had since achieved a college degree, and some professional status. But the court said that the mere fact that judicial records might interfere with her employment prospects was not extraordinary and would not justify expungement.

3. **Comparing and contrasting *Cassady*.** Notice that *Cassady* involved records of the executive branch and assumed jurisdiction. Are there any facts in *Cassady* that would make it a better or worse case for expungement than *Flowers*?

4. **Statutory provisions.** There are a number of statutes regulating expungement of particular records concerning the plaintiff, including records that put the plaintiff on a list of child molesters. Colorado once held that a suit for expungement of arrest records brought by a woman who had been charged and found not guilty stated a cause of action. *Davidson v. Dill,* 180 Colo. 123, 503 P.2d 157 (1972). However, in that case the plaintiff had been charged with only a minor infraction—loitering—and no evidence was developed by the record custodian at trial to show any need to keep the records of arrest or the ability of the police

department to keep them confidential. Later, the Colorado legislature set up a statutory scheme that would permit some persons caught up in the criminal justice system to seek a judicial order sealing records rather than destroying them. That statute added that once a record was sealed by judicial order, state officials "may properly reply, upon any inquiry in the matter, that no such records exist with respect to such person." COLO. REV. STAT. ANN. § 24–72–308. How do you look at this—a case of simple protection of privacy or a state's re-writing history and deliberately lying to its citizens?

5. "If government can be carried out secretly by invoking privacy rights of individuals, government will not be open or democratic. This point has led to concerns when courts or legislatures seal or expunge records, although their purpose is always said to be laudable." 2 DOBBS ON TORTS § 427 (2001), citing Franklin & Johnsen, *Expunging Criminal Records: Concealment and Dishonesty in an Open Society,* 9 HOFSTRA L. REV. 733 (1981). If the quotation is right, it is nevertheless too one-sided?

6. One argument for expungement or sealing records of conviction is that the continued existence of accurate records will "continue the degradation beyond the endpoint of a criminal justice sanction. They makes the full rehabilitation of ex-offenders impossible. . . ." Nora V. Demleitner, *Is There a Future for Leniency in the U.S. Criminal Justice System?,* 103 MICH. L. REV. 1231, 1246 (2005) (Book review).

7. Consider the fact that you might need access to a person's arrest record if you are considering hiring him to work in a child care center. Or if you are litigating against that person? See *State ex rel. Herget v. Circuit Court for Waukesha Co.,* 84 Wis. 2d 435, 267 N.W.2d 309 (1978) (juvenile proceeding records involving same damage allegedly done to the plaintiff who is now suing civilly). A denial of access to records of a witness who may be testifying as part of a plea bargain might be denial of due process. See *Davis v. Alaska,* 415 U.S. 308, 94 S.Ct. 1105, 39 L.Ed.2d 347 (1974).

8. **Distinguishing records.** Consider (a) records of investigation and/or arrest where no prosecution ever took place; (b) records of investigation and conviction; and (c) records of arrest and investigation where the trier has found the plaintiff not guilty. Would you distinguish among these or other similar categories? Notice that in one of the cases listed here, expungement is in accord with the truth, while in others it is in effect an official lie.

Civil Rights Actions for Privacy Invasion

YORK v. STORY

324 F.2d 450 (9th Cir. 1963)

HAMLEY, Circuit Judge. . . .

[The complaint alleged that the plaintiff] went to the police department of Chino for the purpose of filing charges in connection with an assault upon her. Appellee Ron Story, an officer of that police department, then acting under color of his authority as such, advised appellant that it was necessary to take photographs of her. Story then took appellant to a room in the police station, locked the door, and directed her to undress, which she did. Story then directed appellant to assume various indecent positions, and photographed her in those positions. These photographs were not made for any lawful or legitimate purpose.

Appellant objected to undressing. She stated to Story that there was no need to take photographs of her in the nude, or in the positions she was directed to take, because the bruises would not show in any photograph. A policewoman was present at the police station but was not requested to be present in the room where the pictures were taken, and was not present. No person except appellant and Story was present in the room when the pictures were taken.

Later that month, Story advised appellant that the pictures did not come out and that he had destroyed them. Instead, Story circulated these photographs among the personnel of the Chino police department. In April, 1960, two other officers of that police department, appellee Louis Moreno and defendant Henry Grote, acting under color of their authority as such, and using police photographic equipment located at the police station made additional prints of the photographs taken by Story. Moreno and Grote then circulated these prints among the personnel of the Chino police department. Appellant did not learn of the described actions of Story, Moreno and Grote in distributing these photographs until December, 1960. [The plaintiff's complaint specifically said that the acts described had "violated and deprived plaintiff of her right to privacy and liberty and constituted an unreasonable search and seizure contrary to and prohibited by the Fourth and Fourteenth Amendments to the United States Constitution and the Federal Civil Rights Act." The trial court dismissed the complaint.]

A complaint states a claim under section 1979 [42 U.S.C. § 1983], if the facts alleged show that the defendant: (1) while acting under color of state or local authority, (2) subjected the plaintiff, or caused the plaintiff to be subjected, to the deprivation of any rights, privileges or immunities secured to the plaintiff by the Constitution and laws of the United States. . . .

The district court's determination that this pleading does not state a claim under section 1979 rests solely upon the ground that, under the allegations of the amended complaint, appellant had not been deprived of any federally-protected right.

Contending that the district court erred in this regard, appellant advances alternative arguments, as follows: (1) under the facts alleged there was an unreasonable search within the meaning of the Fourth Amendment and since the guarantee against unreasonable searches and seizures contained in the Fourth Amendment has been made applicable to the states by reason of the Due Process Clause of the Fourteenth Amendment, she was protected from such a search at the hands of city police officers; (2) the Fourth Amendment is premised upon a basic right of privacy, made available to appellant as against city police officers by reason of the Due Process Clause of the Fourteenth Amendment, which right was violated without regard to whether such violation constituted an unreasonable search in the Fourth Amendment sense; and (3) the alleged acts of appellees constituted such an invasion of appellant's privacy as to amount to a deprivation of liberty, without due process of law, as guaranteed to her by the Due Process Clause of the Fourteenth Amendment.

The alleged act of Story in taking photographs of appellant in the nude, if proved, may or may not constitute an unreasonable search in the Fourth Amendment sense. But if we should hold that it does, this would not dispose of the whole case for the alleged subsequent acts of Story and Moreno in distributing prints of these photographs, of which appellant also complains, could hardly be characterized as unreasonable searches.

It is therefore necessary, in any event, to reach appellant's second or third argument, or both, relating to invasions of privacy. Accordingly, we turn at once to appellant's third contention—that all of these acts constituted such invasions of her privacy as to amount to deprivations of liberty without due process of law, guaranteed to her by the Due Process Clause of the Fourteenth Amendment.

We are not called upon to decide as an original proposition whether "privacy," as such, is comprehended within the "liberty" of which one may not be deprived without due process of law, as used in the Due Process Clause of the Fourteenth Amendment. For it has already been declared by the Supreme Court that the security of one's privacy against arbitrary intrusion by the police is basic to a free society and is therefore "implicit in the concept of ordered liberty," embraced within the Due Process Clause of the Fourteenth Amendment.

What we must decide, however, is whether the acts of the police, as here alleged, constitute an arbitrary invasion upon the security of one's privacy in the Due Process sense.

We cannot conceive of a more basic subject of privacy than the naked body. The desire to shield one's unclothed figured from view of strangers, and particularly strangers of the opposite sex, is impelled by elementary self-respect and personal dignity. A search of one's home has been established to be an invasion of one's privacy against intrusion by the police, which, if "unreasonable," is arbitrary and therefore banned under the Fourth Amendment. We do not see how it can be argued that the searching of one's home deprives him of privacy, but the photographing of one's nude body, and the distribution of such photographs to strangers does not.

Nor can we imagine a more arbitrary police intrusion upon the security of that privacy than for a male police officer to unnecessarily photograph the nude body of a female citizen who has made complaint of an assault upon her, over her protest that the photographs would show no injuries, and at a time when a female police officer could have been, but was not, called in for this purpose, and to distribute those photographs to other personnel of the police department despite the fact that such distribution of the photographs could not have aided in apprehending the person who perpetrated the assault.

But granting all of that, must it still be held that the particular intrusions here alleged are not secured against by the Due Process Clause of the Fourteenth Amendment because they are not expressly proscribed in the Bill of Rights?

We think not. In the field of civil rights litigation the cases are not infrequent in which law enforcement action not banned in terms by any provision of the Bill of Rights had been made the subject of a successful claim.

All of the cases just cited involved persons who were in police custody at the time of the incident complained of. This circumstance, however, is indicative only of the infrequency of a case such as this, in which one not in custody is the alleged victim of arbitrary police action. No statute, decision or principle that we know of makes the Civil Rights Act available to those in the toils of the law, but closes the federal courthouse to law-abiding citizens who have suffered just as grievous a deprivation of constitutional rights. . . .

Appellees assert that appellant has a civil remedy in the courts of California. But it is immaterial, insofar as the right to pursue remedies under the Civil Rights Act is concerned, that state remedies may also be available.

We therefore conclude that, under the allegations of the amended complaint, appellant has laid a foundation for proving, if she can, not only that appellees were acting under color of local authority at the times in question, but that such acts constituted an arbitrary intrusion upon the security of her privacy, as guaranteed to her by the Due Process Clause of the Fourteenth Amendment. It was therefore error to dismiss the action on the ground that the amended complaint did not state a claim upon which relief can be granted.

The judgment is reversed and the cause is remanded for further proceedings.

[The dissenting opinion is omitted.]

Notes

1. *Paul v. Davis,* 424 U.S. 693, 96 S.Ct. 1155, 47 L.Ed.2d 405 (1976), Chapter 2, ¶ 28, held that no federal civil rights action would lie for a state official's publication of a libel about the plaintiff. The same case held that no civil rights action would lie for the official's publication on a privacy theory either. The Court said in part:

> While there is no "right of privacy" found in any specific guarantee of the Constitution, the Court has recognized that "zones of privacy" may

> be created by more specific constitutional guarantees and thereby impose limits upon government power. See *Roe v. Wade*. ... Respondent's case, however, comes within none of these areas. He does not seek to suppress evidence seized in the course of an unreasonable search. And our other "right of privacy" cases, while defying categorical description, deal generally with substantive aspects of the Fourteenth Amendment. In Roe the Court pointed out that the personal rights found in this guarantee of personal privacy must be limited to those which are "fundamental" or "implicit in the concept of ordered liberty". ... The activities detailed as being within this definition were ones very different from that for which respondent claims constitutional protection matters relating to marriage, procreation, contraception, family relationships, and child rearing and education. In these areas it has been held that there are limitations on the States' power to substantively regulate conduct.

York v. Story was decided before *Paul v. Davis*. Can it survive *Paul's* holding?

2. *York* is not alone in holding that disclosures of private facts by state officials can violate a federal civil rights act, § 1983. In *James v. City of Douglas, Ga.*, 941 F.2d 1539 (11th Cir. 1991), officers took a video tape from a suspect; it showed the suspect and the plaintiff engaged in sexual acts. Someone in the police made a copy and a number of officials watched the tape. The court, citing the constitutional right of privacy vaguely recognized in *Paul* and other cases, held that the right was well enough established that the defendant did not have the immunity that protects officers when the constitutional right claimed by the plaintiff is not well established. In *Arakawa v. Sakata*, 133 F.Supp.2d 1223 (D. Haw. 2001), an officer released the plaintiff's social security number, which was widely disseminated. The court held that this violated the plaintiff's constitutional right of privacy and would be actionable under § 1983 unless privileged.

Wilson v. Layne, 526 U.S. 603, 119 S.Ct. 1692, 143 L.Ed.2d 818 (1999). In the pre-dawn hours, U.S. Marshals, attempting to execute a warrant for Dominic Wilson, entered a home where they believed he was living. They also took with them media representatives, including a reporter and photographer from the Washington Post. The home was actually the home of Dominic's parents, who were roused from bed by the presence of armed men in their home. Dominic was not there. The Wilson's sued the marshals under *Bivens*, claiming a federal violation of civil rights arising from the fact that Marshals brought along persons not needed to effectuate the warrant. *Held,* (1) Where the warrant does not authorize third persons and such persons are not required to assist in effecting the warrant, official invitation to third persons to enter violates the Fourth Amendment. "In his Commentaries on the Laws of England, William Blackstone noted that 'the law of England has so particular and tender a regard to the immunity of a man's house, that it stiles it his castle, and will never suffer it to be violated with impunity: agreeing herein with the sentiments of ancient Rome. ... For this reason no doors can in general be broken open to execute any civil process; though, in criminal causes, the public safety supersedes the private.'" William Blackstone, 4 Commentaries on the Laws of England 223 (1765–1769).

"The Fourth Amendment embodies this centuries-old principle of respect for the privacy of the home: 'The right of the people to be secure in their persons, houses, papers, and effects, against unreasonable searches and seizures, shall not be violated, and no Warrants shall issue, but upon probable cause, supported by Oath or affirmation, and particularly describing the place to be searched, and the persons or things to be seized.' "

---

1. Some privacy is protected under ordinary rules of trespass. Some is protected under the Fourth Amendment. Fourth Amendment claims against state officers and municipalities are redressed under 42 U.S.C.A. § 1983. No corresponding statute applies to federal officers, but the Supreme Court remedied that deficiency by recognizing that victims of federal civil rights violations could sue directly under the constitution. This is the *Bivens* action, so-called from *Bivens v. Six Unknown Named Agents of Federal Bureau of Narcotics,* 403 U.S. 388, 91 S.Ct. 1999, 29 L.Ed.2d 619 (1971).

2. The Supreme Court has long recognized what it calls a qualified privilege that protects officers against liability for constitutional violations unless the specific application of the constitutional right in question was clearly established at the time officers violated it. In *Wilson v. Layne* the Court concluded that while the abstract constitutional rights of the Fourth Amendment were well-established, the specific holding that the rights were violated by the invitation of outsiders was not. Hence the officer there were "privileged" and not liable.

3. Some other authority has condemned the intrusion by ride-along press as a matter of common law. *Prahl v. Brosamle,* 98 Wis.2d 130, 295 N.W.2d 768 (1980) (officer trespassed by inviting press into plaintiff's property). A Florida case went the other way on the peculiar ground that there was a custom to permit press to enter scenes of public interest and that consent by the homeowner could be implied from that custom. *Florida Publishing Co. v. Fletcher,* 340 So.2d 914 (Fla. 1976). That case is criticized in DOBBS ON TORTS § 96 (2000). *Fletcher* has no general acceptance and may be itself a dead letter after the Supreme Court's decision in *Wilson v. Layne.* In addition, courts, including *Wilson,* have rejected the argument that the First Amendment gives the press a right to enter private property not otherwise open to the public merely because newsworthy events occur there. E.g., *Stahl v. State,* 665 P.2d 839 (Okla. 1983).

Chapter 8

TORTIOUS LITIGATION AND TACTICS

---

§ 1. MALICIOUS PROSECUTION OF A CRIMINAL CHARGE

(a) Malicious Prosecution and Other Torts

1. **Elements.** Malicious prosecution of a criminal charge against the person who is now the plaintiff is actionable as a tort only if the plaintiff proves:

(1) That the defendant instituted or instigated a prosecution;

(2) without probable cause; and

(3) with malice; and

(4) that the criminal proceeding terminated favorably to the plaintiff; and

(5) the plaintiff suffered damages as a result.

2. **Damages.** The main component of recoverable damages is usually the plaintiff's cost of defending the criminal charge, including reasonable attorney fees. See *Tri-State Hospital Supply Corp. v. United States,* 341 F.3d 571 (D.C. Cir. 2003). Recovery of attorney fees as damages incurred because of the earlier wrongful litigation is not barred by the general American rule barring recovery of fees incurred in the present action. See Leubsdorf, *Recovering Attorney Fees As Damages,* 38 Rutgers L. Rev. 439 (1986); Dan B. Dobbs, The Law of Remedies § 3.10(3) (2d ed. 1993).

3. **False arrest or imprisonment.** Malicious prosecution differs greatly from false arrest.

(1) False arrest is a seizure of the person and a trespassory tort (like trespass to land, battery, and assault), so proof of the fact of arrest makes a prima facie case. Malicious prosecution, though it may follow an arrest, is a separate step and entails no seizure of the person at all. Proof of prosecution, then, is not prima facie proof of a tort.

(2) As the first point implies, in a false arrest case, the burden is upon the defendant who seizes or confines the plaintiff to justify his deed, for example, by showing that he was an officer acting under a warrant or with probable cause to believe the plaintiff committed a crime. But if the claim is for malicious prosecution, the burden is the other way around—the plaintiff whose case is based upon indictment or arraignment must prove a want of probable cause.

(3) Damages for false arrest are damages for the confinement, not for the prosecution. Once the prosecution is begun, or the plaintiff is held under legitimate process, damages for false arrest cease to accrue and the plaintiff will ordinarily be required to show malicious prosecution to recover damages from that time. See *Asgari v. City of Los Angeles,* 15 Cal.4th 744, 937 P.2d 273, 63 Cal.Rptr.2d 842 (1997).

4. **Libel.** Malicious prosecution, in spite of its factual connection with false arrest, is in some respects is closer to libel. The prosecution, whether instituted by the official prosecutor or instigated by a citizen who prevails upon the officials to make a prosecution, always accuses the plaintiff of a crime. That would presumably always be defamatory. It would probably count as libel rather than slander, too, since the accuser can foresee that the accusation will be published in written form by way of information or indictment or criminal complaint. See Casebook Chapter 1, ¶ 49; THOMAS M. COOLEY, TORTS 225 (2d ed. 1888). Why doesn't the plaintiff who has been wrongfully prosecuted simply sue for libel, then? Part of the answer is that the privilege to report to authorities gets in the way of the defamation suit. Another part is that as a matter of policy, courts do not wish to inhibit or chill appropriate resort to courts for prosecutions or the resolution of civil disputes. Consequently, malicious prosecution is a "disfavored tort," see *Sheldon Appel Company v. Albert & Oliker,* 47 Cal.3d 863, 765 P.2d 498, 254 Cal.Rptr. 336 (1989), and courts have demanded that the plaintiff prove all five of the elements listed above, none of which would have been required to make a prima facie case in libel.

(b) Institution or Instigation

McCRANEY v. BARBERI

677 So.2d 355 (Fla. App. 1996)

VAN NORTWICK, Judge.

Christina McCraney appeals a final summary judgment entered in her malicious prosecution action against James A. Barberi, appellee....

On March 17, 1993, Christina McCraney issued a worthless check to Barberi Radio & TV in the amount of $293.56. Upon learning that the check had been returned for insufficient funds, she issued a money order to Barberi in the face amount of $296.56, the amount of the worthless check plus a $3 bank charge. In the meantime, Safe-Check Services, with whom Barberi Radio & TV contracted for recovery of returned checks, had begun collection efforts regarding the check written by McCraney.

Florida law permits Barberi to seek recovery of a $20 service charge for collection efforts regarding worthless checks. Barberi and Safe–Check Services decided to pursue recovery of the $20. The parties differ as to whether McCraney was notified that she still owed $20: Barberi and Safe–Check Services maintain that she was, McCraney maintains that she was not. Nevertheless, Barberi and Safe–Check Services jointly prepared and Barberi submitted a worthless check affidavit to the state attorney's office. This affidavit states that McCraney issued a worthless check in the amount of $293.56. The affidavit nowhere reveals that McCraney subsequently delivered the $296.56 money order to Barberi. Barberi contends that he attached a copy of the money order to the worthless check affidavit and that, when he submitted the affidavit, he told the state attorney's office he was only seeking payment of the $20 service charge allowed him by statute. The worthless check affidavit in the record, however, does not include a copy of the money order as an attachment.

The record includes the affidavit of the assistant state attorney who prosecuted McCraney's case. In this affidavit, the assistant state attorney states that, upon receipt of the worthless check affidavit, he decided to prosecute McCraney. This affidavit does not state, however, that the state attorney's office made the decision to prosecute McCraney with the knowledge that the full amount of the check had been paid by McCraney. The record indicates that, once the state attorney's office became aware that McCraney had paid the amount of the worthless check, a decision was made to nol prosse the felony worthless check charge against McCraney.

McCraney filed suit against Barberi and Safe–Check Services for malicious prosecution, contending that they had falsely and knowingly instituted a criminal proceeding against her for the entire face value of the worthless check when she had paid the face value plus bank charges. Thereafter, the trial court granted summary judgment in favor of Barberi. . . .

To prevail in an action for malicious prosecution, a plaintiff must show: (i) that an original criminal or civil judicial proceeding was commenced or continued, (ii) that the defendant was the legal cause of the judicial proceeding, (iii) that the judicial proceeding was terminated in the plaintiff's favor, (iv) that probable cause for the proceeding was absent, (v) that malice was present, and (vi) that the plaintiff suffered resulting damage.

The issues here relate to whether Barberi was the legal cause of McCraney's prosecution. . . . The general rule is that if the defendant merely gives a statement to the proper authorities, leaving the decision to prosecute entirely to the uncontrolled discretion of the officer or if the officer makes an independent investigation, the defendant is not regarded as having instigated the proceeding. However, if the defendant's persuasion is the determining factor in inducing the officer's decision or if he gives information which he knew to be false and so unduly influences the authorities, then the defendant may be held liable. In the instant case, a primary question is whether Barberi's affidavit was knowingly false and unduly influenced the authorities to prosecute the appellant McCraney. . . .

When Barberi's worthless check affidavit is considered in the light most favorable to the plaintiff McCraney, it creates an issue of material fact whether Barberi truthfully advised the state attorney's office that the full amount of the check, plus an additional bank charge, had been paid by McCraney. Further, an issue of material fact remains concerning whether the assistant state attorney would have elected to prosecute McCraney if the state attorney's office had known that the full amount of the worthless check, plus a \$3 bank charge, had been paid by McCraney, and that a maximum of only \$20 was due and owing to Barberi. Because factual conflicts remain to be resolved, the summary judgment was erroneously entered.

REVERSED and REMANDED for further proceedings consistent with this opinion.

---

5. **Prosecutorial immunity.** One who institutes a prosecution is potentially subject to a malicious prosecution suit, but official prosecutors will usually enjoy an absolute immunity for any acts within the scope of prosecutorial duties. See *DeLaurentis v. City of New Haven,* 220 Conn. 225, 597 A.2d 807 (1991). The immunity becomes a qualified one only when the prosecutor performs other functions, as when the prosecutor acts as an investigating officer. *McCollum v. Garrett,* 880 S.W.2d 530 (1994). But see *Orso v. City and County of Honolulu,* 56 Haw. 241, 534 P.2d 489 (1975) (holding a city liable for tortious prosecutorial activity on the ground that the prosecutor is an executive and not immune).

6. **Continuing a prosecution.** Because the official prosecutor is usually immune, the malicious prosecution plaintiff often focuses on an individual who "instigates" the prosecution indirectly, as Barberi did in the *McCraney* case, or as a police officer might do in filing an affidavit. Alternatively, the plaintiff may focus on someone who did not instigate the prosecution but who continued it after the error in doing so became manifest.

7. **The real criminal as a cause.** The most extreme case is *Seidel v. Greenberg*, 108 N.J.Super. 248, 260 A.2d 863 (1969). Arsonists set a fire to collect insurance on a lumberyard. Police suspected the plaintiff, as perhaps was inevitable under the circumstances, though plaintiff in fact had nothing to do with the fire. He was prosecuted, but the real arsonists were eventually discovered. The plaintiff then sued the arsonists. Their only connection with the plaintiff's prosecution is that they committed the crime of which he was accused. The court imposed liability upon the arsonists. Does this fit the requirement of instigation?

8. **A charge that does not constitute a crime.** In a few cases, the plaintiff is charged with an act that is not a crime or before a tribunal that has no authority. Should this count as instigation of a proceeding?

(c) Termination

CANTALINO v. DANNER

96 N.Y.2d 391, 754 N.E.2d 164, 729 N.Y.S.2d 405 (2001)

Chief Judge KAYE. . . .

This case arises out of the bitterly contested divorce of plaintiff from her husband. The husband, a lieutenant in the New York City Police Department, was living with defendant—his girlfriend, who was also a police officer. While the divorce action was pending in Kings County Supreme Court, the husband purported to obtain a divorce in the Dominican Republic and marry defendant. He then repeatedly failed to comply with orders entered in the Kings County divorce proceeding.

Plaintiff moved to have her husband held in contempt, and Supreme Court ordered that he be personally served. One service attempt was unsuccessful when defendant allegedly grabbed the papers from the process server. On another occasion, the officers at the husband's precinct apparently thwarted a service attempt by informing the process server that he was not at work and sending the process server to a false location. On yet a third occasion, the Police Department allegedly refused to provide a police escort so that plaintiff could serve her husband at his home in Staten Island.

Following these failed attempts, Supreme Court ordered that service be made on the husband by "nailing [the papers] to the door" of his home and sending them by regular and certified mail to that address. Pursuant to that order, plaintiff, accompanied by her process server, Rosalie Perez, went to his home, armed with a hammer and nails. In the course of nailing the papers, they damaged the screen door. Defendant came out of the house, and an altercation ensued. Defendant called the police, claiming that plaintiff had pushed her and threatened her with the hammer. As a result, the police arrested both plaintiff and Perez. Plaintiff spent the night in jail; Perez was given a desk appearance ticket and released.

[The plaintiff was charged with assault, menacing, and possession of a weapon. The court dismissed the charge in the interest of justice, stating that the plaintiff in following the court's order to nail process on the door could not have had criminal intent.] In addition, the court noted that dismissing the complaint "would have a positive effect on the community," and that "[i]ndeed to continue this prosecution would demonstrate an abuse of the criminal justice system by those police officers charged with enforcing the law". . . .

Plaintiff then brought the present malicious prosecution action against defendant. [The Appellate Division ordered dismissal of this action,] holding that a dismissal in the interest of justice is not a "judicial determination of the accused's innocence on the merits." We now reverse and reinstate the complaint....

In *Smith-Hunter,* this Court held that any termination of a criminal prosecution, such that the criminal charges may not be brought again, qualifies as a favorable termination, so long as the circumstances surrounding the termination are not inconsistent with the innocence of the accused. The Court rejected the notion that the termination must affirmatively demonstrate the accused's innocence, stating that the law "should not require one who is falsely and maliciously accused to proceed to trial—incurring additional financial and emotional costs—as a prerequisite to recovery for malicious prosecution."

As we noted in *Smith-Hunter,* however, several types of terminations do not qualify as "favorable" at common law, since they are fundamentally inconsistent with innocence. For instance, where a prosecution fails to go forward because of misconduct by the accused preventing a proper trial, the termination cannot be considered favorable. Similarly, if a prosecution ends because of a compromise with the accused, the termination is not favorable. The same rule applies if charges are dismissed out of mercy, since mercy presupposes the guilt of the accused.

Applying these principles to the case at hand, the dismissal of criminal charges against plaintiff was a favorable termination because it was not inconsistent with her innocence. Far from implying guilt, the Criminal Court Judge made clear that he dismissed the charges because plaintiff was innocent and the prosecution groundless....

To be sure, there are circumstances where a dismissal in the interest of justice is inconsistent with innocence because it represents mercy requested or accepted by the accused....

[T]he question is whether, under the circumstances of each case, the disposition was inconsistent with the innocence of the accused. A case-specific rule is particularly appropriate for dismissals in the interest of justice, since the trial court is required to state on the record its reasons for dismissing the criminal charges. And here, as noted, the Criminal Court's statement of reasons makes clear that it dismissed the charges against plaintiff because they were groundless—not out of mercy or compassion....

---

9. **Favorable termination requirement.** Courts agree that a favorable termination is required, but not on how that is defined. In *Ash v. Ash,* 72 Ohio St.3d 520, 651 N.E.2d 945 (1995), the court thought there was termination "in favor of the accused only when its final disposition indicates that the accused is innocent."

10. **Plaintiff settles the criminal charge.** Plaintiff, long a customer of defendant, writes a check for $6.38. The check bounces. The defendant, without consulting plaintiff, executes an affidavit for a warrant in which he charges plaintiff with intentionally issuing a check without sufficient funds to cover it. Plaintiff goes to the justice of the peace, pays court costs and pays off the check, saying it was all a mistake in writing on the wrong bank account. He then sues defendant for malicious prosecution. Some courts say there is no "termination" here because there was a dismissal by the plaintiff-accused without a trial on the merits, or because this was a compromise. See *Cimino v. Rosen*, 193 Neb. 162, 225 N.W.2d 567 (1975).

11. **Unexplained nolle prosqui.** "[A] criminal prosecution is terminated in favor of the plaintiff when the district attorney formally abandons the criminal proceedings by a nolle prosequi or a motion to dismiss, as in this case. However, the reasons stated for the nolle prosequi or dismissal must be consistent with the innocence of the accused." *Wynne v. Rosen*, 391 Mass. 797, 464 N.E.2d 1348 (1984). If the plaintiff does not prove the reasons, the court may assume that the nolle prosqui is a compromise and reject the plaintiff's malicious prosecution claim accordingly. See *Tucker v. Duncan*, 499 F.2d 963, (4th Cir. 1974).

(d) Probable Cause

12. **The objective test.** The common definitions of probable cause, taken from *Bacon v. Towne*, 58 Mass. (4 Cush.) 217 (1849), emphasize an objective test:

"Probable cause is such a state of facts in the mind of the prosecutor as would lead a man of ordinary caution and prudence to believe, or entertain an honest and strong suspicion, that the person arrested is guilty."

Notice the objective nature of this test. No mention is made of what the accuser himself personally believes.

13. **A subjective test.** A number of cases so phrased the test as to require both an objective (reasonable) belief in guilt and a subjective ("honest") belief in guilt. E.g. *Torian v. Ashford*, 216 Ala. 85, 112 So. 418 (1927). Would this mean that you should not mention strong evidence of guilt to appropriate officers if you yourself disbelieved it?

14. **Attacking the subjective test.** The subjective test was attacked in Dobbs, *Belief and Doubt in Malicious Prosecution and Libel*, 21 Ariz. L. Rev. 607 (1980). California, citing the attack and giving its own complete analysis, rejected any element of subjectivity in *Sheldon Appel Co. v. Albert & Oliker*, 47 Cal.3d 863, 765 P.2d 498, 254 Cal.Rptr. 336 (1989). Citing the same article, the Michigan Court also supported the objective test in *Matthews v. Blue Cross and Blue Shield of Michigan*, 456 Mich. 365, 572 N.W.2d 603 (1998).

15. **Probable cause: judge and jury.** The most peculiar rule about probable cause is that the probable cause issue is for the judge to

determine, not the jury. At the same time, the facts upon which that determination must be based are to be decided by the jury. How is this possible?

16. **Factual analysis.** The question of probable cause is often a matter of detailed factual analysis. The point is to determine whether the facts as they appeared to the accuser at the time would warrant a reasonable inference that the accused was guilty of a crime. It is possible to argue both for and against probable cause in the following problem?

Problem: Callman v. Discount, Inc.

The plaintiff, Louise Callman, and her husband Jack, who lived in another state, were visiting with Jack's mother, Mildred Ferson. Louise and Mildred went to the defendant's large discount store to shop. A store security guard, Evelyn Maple, saw them come in together, talking to each other, then part company. Maple tried to keep both in sight, but couldn't do so. She kept Louise in sight most of the time. She could not explain later why she did so or what made her notice the two women, but she did observe that Louise had an exceptionally large purse, one that could hold, say, 8 x 10 picture frames, or a package of pillow cases. She saw Louise pick up a carton of cigarettes and carry it through the store. Soon thereafter she saw Louise get together with Mildred, and saw the two enter a checkout lane. Mildred paid for her goods but the clerk told Louise she would have to pay for the cigarettes at a different counter. As Maple observed, Louise and Mildred went back into the store, Louise was still carrying the cigarettes. Instead of leaving through another checkout aisle where they could pay for the cigarettes, the two women went to a different part of the store and shopped some more. Ten minutes later (in Maple's estimation), Louise looked at her watch and the two women walked hurriedly toward the exits. They were not required to pass through a checkout counter and Louise walked out with the carton of cigarettes, unpaid for, still in her hand. Outside, the two women stood in front of the store and waited about three minutes until Jack drove up in his pickup. They loaded their purchases in the bed of the pickup, except that Louise kept the carton in her hand and put it in the front seat. At that point, Maple approached Louise and said: "You haven't paid for those cigarettes." Louise was flustered, apologized, and said she'd go right in and pay for them. Maple insisted on calling the police and pressed shoplifting charges. At trial the jury acquitted Louise. Louise sued Maple and Discount for malicious prosecution. The defendants argued that Louise could not prove a want of probable cause. What facts can be emphasized to support a conclusion one way or the other?

(e) Malice

17. **Common law malice.** The "malice" required in malicious prosecution is common law malice—any improper purpose, spite, ill-will or the like. Any purpose other than to bring the offender to justice will qualify as malice. Malice can be inferred from the instigator's conduct. For example, the instigator's conduct in failing to reveal to authorities

evidence that exculpates the now-plaintiff may suffice to show malice. *South Arkansas Petroleum Co. v. Schiesser,* 343 Ark. 492, 36 S.W.3d 317 (2001). But while misstatements to the police may show malice, they do not show any want of probable cause and malice alone will not sustain a cause of action. *First Valley Bank of Los Fresnos v. Martin,* 144 S.W.3d 466 (Tex. 2004).

18. **Less than malice?** As a matter of fact, the cases seldom seem to involve hatred or ill-will. Most often they appear to represent milder human frailties. For instance, the store security officer might come to believe that a customer is stealing and then refuse to hear the customer's explanation of events. That conduct, considering all the circumstances, was sufficient for a finding of malice in *Lambert v. Sears, Roebuck & Co.,* 280 Or. 123, 570 P.2d 357 (1977). In *Martin v. City of Albany,* 42 N.Y.2d 13, 396 N.Y.S.2d 612, 364 N.E.2d 1304 (1977), a police officer lost his temper when the plaintiff sought to intervene in an arrest he was making. He wrongfully charged the plaintiff with interfering with arrest. He was quite obnoxious, but seems to have acted out of excess of self-importance, or perhaps from a lack of self-assurance. These facts were sufficient to show malice. Cases like these two suggest that malice might include abuse of power or oppressive conduct.

19. **Inferring malice from want of probable cause.** The general rule is that the trier of fact may infer the existence of malice from the absence of probable cause, but not the other way around—the trier definitely cannot infer a want of probable cause from the existence of malice. Since the jury decides malice and the judge decides probable cause, how can the jury draw the inference?

(f) Defenses

20. **Guilt-in-fact.** Even if the defendant lacked probable cause, he can raise an affirmative defense that the plaintiff was guilty in fact, somewhat analogous to the truth defense in common law defamation cases.

21. **Prosecutorial immunities.** Judicial officers are generally absolutely immune so long as they are exercising discretionary decisions, such as the decision whether to prosecute. This insulates judges and prosecutors in most instances from the malicious prosecution suit.

22. **Police officers: immunity, instigation.** Police officers are seldom immune (or absolutely privileged) in malicious prosecution cases. The officer, like any other witness, enjoys absolute immunity for testimony given in court. That immunity does not extend to protect him for charges made to institute the prosecution. See *Hinchman v. Moore,* 312 F.3d 198 (6th Cir. 2002). To the extent an officer is protected by a qualified immunity, that immunity falls when bad faith is exhibited, and this is more or less the same as "malice," which must be proved in any event. Is there room to argue that a police officer in recommending prosecution (as distinct from making an arrest) is functioning as a prosecutor and should share the prosecutor's absolute immunity? In

Malley v. Briggs, 475 U.S. 335, 106 S.Ct. 1092, 89 L.Ed.2d 271 (1986), the Supreme Court held that an officer could be liable for a civil rights violation when he instituted a prosecution on the basis of an irrational interpretation of evidence, even though he presented the evidence to a magistrate who issued a warrant.

23. **Release in exchange for dropped prosecution.** A student is arrested at the instigation of the defendant and prosecution is begun. It is terminated when the student pleads for mercy, but in exchange for the termination the prosecutor demands a release in which the student agrees not to assert any claims against the arresting officers or the instigator of the prosecution. Conceivably this is not a termination, but if it is a termination of the criminal prosecution, is the release a bar? Or would it be against public policy to bar a claim like this? The Supreme Court has held that the release is a good one in civil rights litigation, at least in the absence of facts showing that it was exacted without adequate public purpose or without voluntary assent of the accused. *Town of Newton v. Rumery,* 480 U.S. 386, 107 S.Ct. 1187, 94 L.Ed.2d 405 (1987). Accord: *Hoines v. Barney's Club, Inc.,* 28 Cal.3d 603, 620 P.2d 628, 170 Cal.Rptr. 42 (1980). States would be free to take a different view on state tort law causes of action. Can you construct an argument?

§ 2. TORTIOUS CIVIL LITIGATION AND TACTICS

24. **Terminology.** When plaintiff sues for prosecution of a prior civil suit, many courts will continue to call the claim malicious prosecution. Others may use different terminology. "Wrongful use of civil proceedings" is the Restatement's choice, but there are variations in the cases.

25. **Elements.** The plaintiff who claims that a prior civil action was maliciously prosecuted against her must prove all the same elements required when the claim is based on a prior criminal action—participation in the instigation or continuation of the prior action, a favorable termination of that action, a want of probable cause, malice, and damages. In some jurisdictions, there is one further element, discussed in *Joeckel v. Disabled American Veterans,* below. Continuing a suit after it becomes clear that there is no probable cause meets the instigation requirement, though damages would accrue only from the time a want of probable cause became apparent. See *Zamos v. Stroud,* 32 Cal.4th 958, 12 Cal.Rptr.3d 54, 87 P.3d 802 (2004).

26. **Instigation—non-litigants' potential liability.** One who actively participates in the initiation of the prior suit may be held liable as an instigator of the suit, even if he was never actually a party. See Restatement (Second) of Torts § 674 (1977). What counts as participation? Advice and encouragement? Providing substantial funds for the prior suit? In *Valles v. Silverman,* 135 N.M. 91, 84 P.3d 1056 (Ct.App. 2003), the court said that liability of a non-litigant would depend on

showing that his conduct was "the determining factor in the decision to file the lawsuit." Yet the court also said that the defendant's conduct need not be a but-for cause of the prior suit. The court thought substantial funding by a non-litigant might well be found to be the determining factor.

27. **Probable cause.** Common law is developed and honed through civil actions. Consequently, courts find probable cause quite readily when the plaintiff in the first suit has a plausible ground for believing he might succeed. See *Roop v. Parker Northwest Paving Co.,* 194 Or.App. 219, 94 P.3d 885, 897 (2004) ("standard for probable cause to bring a civil action is less stringent than that required to prosecute a criminal action"); DOBBS ON TORTS § 436 (2000).

28. **Probable cause—advice of counsel.** Would a client who retains an attorney to pursue a claim be liable for malicious prosecution when the claim is defeated or does reliance on her attorney's advice in suing show that she has probable cause? "Non-lawyers may judge appearances by relying in good faith upon advice of fully informed counsel who is admitted to the bar in the state or otherwise appears to be reasonably competent." See DOBBS ON TORTS § 436 (2000). However, "if the defendant acted in bad faith or withheld facts from counsel he or she knew or should have known would have defeated the cause of action, probable cause is not established. Counsel's advice must be sought in good faith and not as a mere cloak to protect one against suit for malicious prosecution." *Palmer v. Zaklama*, 109 Cal.App.4th 1367, 1383, 1 Cal.Rptr.3d 116, 128 (2003).

29. **Favorable termination.** In *Lackner v. LaCroix*, 25 Cal.3d 747, 602 P.2d, 393, 159 Cal.Rptr. 693 (1979), the physician plaintiffs alleged that lawyers had brought a malpractice action barred by the statute of limitations and that the physicians had won a favorable termination of the malpractice action for that reason. The court held that this was not a favorable termination. "It is not essential to maintenance of an action for malicious prosecution that the prior proceeding was favorably terminated following trial on the merits. However, termination must reflect on the merits of the underlying action." *Palmer Dev. Corp. v. Gordon,* 723 A.2d 881 (Me. 1999), took the same line, rejecting the argument that a vexatious suit brought by a plaintiff who knows the statute has run should be actionable.

30. **Counterclaims for malicious prosecution.** Suppose that a patient sues his physician for malpractice and the physician counterclaims for malicious civil litigation. In light of the termination rule, can the doctor prevail on the counterclaim? Cases say not. E.g., *Hatch v. Davis,* 102 P.3d 774 (Utah Ct. App. 2004). What problems, if any, do you see in permitting the counterclaim for malicious prosecution? *Distinguish:* Plaintiff sues for malicious prosecution of the defendant's counterclaim in an earlier suit. *Crosson v. Berry,* 829 N.E.2d 184 (Ind. Ct. App. 2005).

31. **Malice.** Malice no doubt includes pursuit of a claim known to be false, but more commonly has referred to ill-will, spite, improper

purpose. As in the criminal-case predicate for malicious prosecution, malice might be inferred from the defendant's conduct. A landlord files an eviction suit, mistakenly naming an individual rather than the corporation that was actually the tenant. He has every right to evict the tenant, but his purpose is to drive the tenant out of business. Does this qualify as malice to support the individual's malicious prosecution claim? See *Willis v. Parker,* 814 So.2d 857 (Ala. 2001).

32. **Constitutional constraints?** Since malicious prosecution turns on publication that adversely affects reputation, would *New York Times v. Sullivan* apply if the plaintiff were a public figure?

JOECKEL v. DISABLED AMERICAN VETERANS

793 A.2d 1279 (D.C. 2002)

RUIZ, Associate Judge....

Appellant served as National Adjutant of DAV from 1988 to 1993, having risen from a position as a clerk to one of DAV's highest ranking positions over the span of his 18 years as an employee for the veterans service organization. During Joeckel's tenure as National Adjutant, DAV paid $80,000 to a DAV employee and his wife as part of the settlement of a lawsuit which alleged that Joeckel had sexually harassed the employee's wife after a business meeting sponsored by DAV. In the wake of controversy over the use of DAV funds to settle the suit, DAV ultimately terminated Joeckel's employment....

Subsequently, DAV sought recovery of the $80,000, which it alleged Joeckel had misappropriated, under the employee theft provisions of its insurance policy with Fireman's Fund Insurance Company (FFIC). When FFIC refused to indemnify DAV, the organization brought suit against the insurer in Jefferson County Circuit Court in Louisville, Kentucky. In the same Kentucky court, DAV also filed suit against Joeckel, seeking recovery of the $80,000 on theories of conversion, breach of fiduciary duty, fraud, and various equitable theories. Joeckel counterclaimed for damages and equitable relief associated with his discharge and the revocation of his DAV membership.

DAV eventually settled its claim against FFIC, but not for the full amount for which it had sought indemnification. The organization thus continued to pursue its action against appellant which culminated, after a full trial, in a jury verdict in favor of Joeckel on all of DAV's claims. With legal victory in hand, Joeckel then filed a one-count complaint for malicious prosecution in the Superior Court of the District of Columbia, alleging that DAV's "initiation and prosecution of the Kentucky lawsuit against [him] was unfounded and known to be so by DAV, and was done unlawfully, willfully, maliciously and without probable cause, and with an intent to injure [him]." Joeckel asserted that, as a proximate result of DAV's actions, he had suffered "economic damages and losses, humiliation and embarrassment, emotional damages, and injury to his reputation," as well as "other damages."

[The trial court granted DAV's motion for summary judgment.]

We have long held that in order to support an action for malicious prosecution in the District of Columbia, a plaintiff must plead and be able to prove: 1) that the underlying suit terminated in plaintiff's favor; 2) malice on the part of the defendant; 3) lack of probable cause for the underlying suit; and 4) special injury occasioned by plaintiff as the result of the original action. The special injury required has been defined as arrest, seizure of property, or injury which would not necessarily result from suits to recover for like causes of action. In the District of Columbia, injuries to reputation, emotional distress, loss of income, and substantial expense in defending have all been held to fall outside the scope of the definition of special injury.

Appellant does not argue that our law is otherwise. Rather, he contends that the same rationale underlying the determination of special injury in *Soffos v. Eaton,* 80 U.S.App.D.C. 306, 152 F.2d 682 (1945), should allow him to proceed to trial on the merits of his malicious prosecution claim. In *Soffos,* the court reviewed the dismissal of a malicious prosecution action on the basis that special injury had not been pled by the plaintiff. There, the plaintiff had been subjected to four consecutive suits by her landlord which the plaintiff alleged had been brought "maliciously without just cause and in bad faith." Recognizing that the common law of the District did not allow an action to lie for the recovery of damages sustained by the prosecution of a civil action with malice unless the complainant had incurred special injury such as arrest or seizure of property, the court nevertheless allowed the plaintiff in that case to continue with her suit, stating that "[s]ome sort of balance ha[d] to be struck between the social interest in preventing unconscionable suits and in permitting honest assertion of supposed rights." The court further explained that because "the right to litigate is not the right to become a nuisance[,] ... [t]he burden of being compelled to defend successive unconscionable suits is not one which would necessarily result in all suits prosecuted to recover for like causes of action," and therefore, held the court, the appellant's complaint stated a claim upon which relief could be granted.

... Joeckel contends that *Soffos* recognizes that a "balance" has to be struck and that there is evident imbalance when the expenses incurred in defending an action are excessively disproportionate to the original plaintiff's litigation objectives.... Joeckel claims that in pursuing its frivolous action against him, after obtaining $50,000 from its insurance company and having only $30,000 left to recover, the DAV deliberately caused him to spend almost $200,000 to defend himself, and that this disproportion between the DAV's purported damages and the amount he had to expend constitutes special injury.

[The court discussed its decision in *Davis v. Boyle Bros.,* 73 A.2d 517 (D.C.1950), which allowed the plaintiff to pursue her claim against a department store which had admitted its error in suing the plaintiff, had promised her it would stop its collection efforts, yet continued to pursue a default judgment against her. But it said both *Davis* and *Soffos* involved blatant harm "beyond that which would normally be incurred in such litigations" and were thus distinguishable from Joeckel's claim.]

. . . [W]e believe any theory that "special injury is present when the expenses of litigation [prosecution or] defense are excessively disproportionate," would be impracticable as articulated by appellant. Whether it be the original plaintiff's expenses which are the focus of a disproportionality assessment or the expenses of the original defendant, there are many reasons, some beyond the control of litigating parties, why expenses incurred in sustaining or defending a legal action may surpass the amount originally sought in the suit itself. For example, an employer may legitimately bring a costly action against a former employee who has misappropriated funds, not merely to recover the actual losses sustained as a result of the employee's misconduct, but also with the hope of deterring similar future misconduct by other employees. Conversely, the fact that an employee may defend such an action to its fullest and most costly extent, even if that cost surpasses the amount originally sought by the employer, does not necessarily mean that the employee has suffered the special injury necessary to sustain a malicious prosecution claim as such costs could result from the choice of defense counsel or defense strategy employed, as well as the sometimes unpredictable ways in which litigation develops.

We note that this court has declined prior invitations to abandon or modify the special injury rule based on the long-held belief that it best promotes this jurisdiction's policy of encouraging free access to the courts. Appellant's brief presents serious arguments why the special injury rule, which has been rejected by a majority of the states, is unnecessary, and may even be contrary, to that goal. [But the court could abandon the special injury requirement only in an *en banc* proceeding.]

Accordingly, for all of the foregoing reasons, the judgment is *Affirmed.*

---

33. **Special injury.** Is the special injury requirement equivalent to (a) the special damages requirement in slander cases, or (b) the actual damages requirement in *Gertz* cases?

34. **Injury to reputation.** When attorneys or doctors are sued for malpractice, they may suffer harm to their reputations regardless of the outcome. Is this special injury? No. See *Ammerman v. Newman*, 384 A.2d 637 (D.C. App. 1978) (doctor); *Madda v. Reliance Ins. Co.*, 53 Ill.App. 3d 67, 11 Ill.Dec. 29, 368 N.E.2d 580 (1977) (lawyer).

35. **Legislatively sanctifying doctors' reputation.** The Illinois legislature intervened to eliminate the special injury rule, but only for the benefit of health care providers who have been sued for medical malpractice. In *Miller v. Rosenberg,* 196 Ill.2d 50, 749 N.E.2d 946, 255

Ill.Dec. 464 (2001), a periodontist sued his former patient, Rosenberg, for malicious prosecution, claiming she had sued him for failure to diagnose a problem when in fact he had referred her to a surgeon for that very problem. The periodontist claimed injury to reputation, mental anguish, and economic costs of defense, but not special injury. He was allowed to proceed because under the statute the special injury rule was waived for health care providers. The statute was held constitutional as against challenges under the Illinois Constitution based on special legislation and equal protection. The court said the statute had a rational basis—to discourage medical malpractice actions.

36. **Malicious defenses.** There was no traditional common law action against a defendant for interposing malicious defenses. Van Patten & Willard, *The Limits of Advocacy: A Proposal for the Tort of Malicious Defense in Civil Litigation,* 35 HASTINGS L.J. 891 (1984), argued that such an action should be recognized and *Aranson v. Schroeder,* 140 N.H. 359, 671 A.2d 1023 (1995), accepted the invitation to create one. Try stating the first premise for an argument on either side.

§ 3. "ABUSE OF PROCESS"

UNION NATIONAL BANK OF LITTLE ROCK v. KUTAIT

312 Ark. 14, 846 S.W.2d 652 (1993)

NEWBERN, Justice.

[Ed Kutait borrowed money from the Union National Bank to start a furniture manufacturing business. Conflicts arose between these parties and the business went into bankruptcy. Ed Kutait and others brought a federal suit against the bank for $15 million. In the meantime, the bank still claimed the debt due on the original loan. While this federal action against the bank was pending, the bank brought suit against Ed Kutait's brother, Dr. Kemel Kutait, seeking $5 million in damages on several theories, including a claim that Dr. Kemel Kutait had guaranteed his brother's loan, a claim of fraud, and claims of interference with contract.]

The Bank's claims against Dr. Kutait were all arguably time barred or lacking in a factual basis. Dr. Kutait contended the claims accusing him of dishonesty and deceit caused distress which was exacerbated by the $5 million in damages sought in the suit. His counsel sought to have the case dismissed for lack of a sound legal basis. During the process of negotiations counsel for the Bank allegedly suggested it would dismiss the suit if Dr. Kutait would influence his brother to drop his federal court claim against the Bank.

Dr. Kutait refused to attempt to influence his brother. On August 25, 1988, shortly before trial the Bank dropped its claim against Dr. Kutait by taking a voluntary nonsuit. The Bank could have refiled its claim against Dr. Kutait within one year, but it did not do so. Dr. Kutait filed this malicious prosecution and abuse of process action two months after the federal court jury returned a verdict for Ed Kutait against the Bank in excess of $5 million. He sought compensatory and punitive damages arguing that the institution of the 1987 lawsuit was without probable cause.

At the trial, testimony was presented supporting the allegation that the Bank's counsel said the suit against Dr. Kutait would be dropped if he used his influence to get his brother to drop his federal court claim....

The nature of abuse of process was considered in Smith & McAdams, Inc. v. Nelson, 255 Ark. 641, 501 S.W.2d 769 (1973). We quoted with approval from W. Prosser, Law of Torts § 121 (4th Ed.1971), three requirements to sustain an abuse of process action. There must be: (1) a legal procedure set in motion in proper form, even with probable cause, and even with ultimate success, but, (2) perverted to accomplish an ulterior purpose for which it was not designed, and (3) a wilful act in the use of process not proper in the regular conduct of the proceeding.

In that case and others we have determined that abuse of process is somewhat in the nature of extortion or coercion. The key is improper use of process after issuance, even when issuance has been properly obtained. In the Smith & McAdams, Inc., case we stated, "The test of process abuse is not whether the process was originally issued with malice and without probable cause. The remedy in that situation would be an action for malicious prosecution which was asserted in the case at bar." ...

The Bank argues that the evidence presented failed to support all the elements of the claim. We agree there was no "process" abused subsequent to the initiation of the action and, therefore, the third of the elements of the claim failed. The only process issued in the 1987 suit was the summons which accompanied the complaint served on Dr. Kutait. It was the fact of the filing of the lawsuit against him which formed the basis for Dr. Kutait's complaint and not a specific abusive use of any "process" like the issuance of summons, serving of an arrest warrant, or improper actions in the process used to obtain discovery....

Dr. Kutait urges an expansion of our definition of abuse of process to include the filing of parallel litigation to accomplish an ulterior coercive purpose. He cites a variety of cases from other jurisdictions generally supportive of his position that the filing of litigation for a perverse purpose is sufficient process. The Bank counters with citations from other jurisdictions which hold to the contrary and reject the mere filing of litigation as satisfying the requirements for abuse of process.

We need not resort to the law in other jurisdictions as the opinion and holding in the Farm Service Cooperative case provide ample guidance. To sustain an abuse of process claim, there must have been issuance of process subsequent to initiation of suit, and the additional process must have been utilized for a coercive or improper purpose. While that may seem a mechanical sort of rule, this case demonstrates the wisdom of it. Were we to hold that the filing of the action satisfied the "process" requirement we would put ourselves in the position of holding that one may be liable for the filing of an action with probable cause. Even if the Bank had an ulterior motive for suing Dr. Kutait, and even if that motive had been improper, we would not wish to say that any citizen is precluded from bringing an action when there is probable cause to do so. Abuse of process issued thereafter is a different matter, and that did not occur here.

Reversed and dismissed.

---

37. **Damages required.** In addition to the elements listed by the *Kutait* court, the plaintiff probably must also prove actual damages, as some courts have said. E.g., *Thomas v. Marion County,* 652 N.W.2d 183, 186 (Iowa 2002).

38. **Probable cause and favorable termination.** Why require want of probable cause and favorable termination in the malicious prosecution suit, but then allow the plaintiff to sue for "abuse of process" even when the defendant had probable cause to bring the prior suit?

39. **Abuse of process "act after" requirement.** Courts often say that the defendant is liable for abuse of process only if he commits some "act after" process is issued and the act is one intended to obtain some improper collateral advantage. This may be coupled with the statement that *issuance* of process, as distinct from some act *after* issuance, is never an abuse of process. See *Bell ex rel. Snyder v. Icard, Merrill, Cullis, Timm, Furen and Ginsburg, P.A.,* 986 S.W.2d 550 (Tenn. 1999).

40. **Illustrating "act after" rule.** In *Melton v. Rickman,* 225 N.C. 700, 36 S.E.2d 276 (1945), the defendant loaned the plaintiff $25 for two weeks at an interest rate of 65%. The plaintiff had no bank account, but the defendant took a check from the plaintiff as "evidence" of the debt. The defendant then instigated a warrant for the plaintiff's arrest on a bad check charge. The justice of the peace found the plaintiff guilty but withheld judgment for a week to permit payment, which the plaintiff then made. The plaintiff sued the money lender for abuse of process but lost because the moneylender had committed no act after the arrest warrant was issued. Didn't the moneylender in *Melton v. Rickman* implicitly offer a release from the arrest if payment was made?

41. **Process.** The "process" in abuse of process may be viewed broadly or narrowly. In its narrowest sense, process refers to enforceable orders such as a summons, subpoena, attachments, warrant for arrest or the like. Some courts have even suggested that a summons and complaint cannot count as process that can be abused. Besides *Kutait,* see *Bell ex rel. Snyder v. Icard, Merrill, Cullis, Timm, Furen and Ginsburg, P.A.,* 986 S.W.2d 550 (Tenn. 1999). Given the "enforceable order"

conception of process, a court may hold that filing a wrongful lis pendens is not a tort because lis pendens is not a process. Other courts, however, take process to include all the procedures in litigation and thus include lis pendens as process, so that abuse is actionable. Such a view holds that repeated filings in the wrong venue and even abusive discovery techniques or oppressive litigation tactics can be an abuse of process. See *General Refractories Co. v. Fireman's Fund Ins. Co.,* 337 F.3d 297 (3d Cir. 2003) (defendant obstructing discovery efforts); DAN B. DOBBS, THE LAW OF TORTS § 438 (2000). In *Givens v. Mullikin,* 75 S.W.3d 383 (Tenn. 2002), the Tennessee Court said the act-after rule "only demands that a plaintiff show some additional abuse of process after the *original* processes of the court, *i.e.,* the complaint, summons, and responsive pleadings, have been issued." Consequently, *Givens* upheld a complaint that defendant issued many, many unjustified subpoenas to various records custodians requiring them to produce records the plaintiff said were duplicative and irrelevant. The wrong evidently was issuance of the process (subpoenas), not any act after, but that was sufficient.

42. **Abuse of process patterns.** Should the "act after" requirement apply in every kind of abuse of process case? There are three more or less distinct patterns of process abuse.

(a) *Extortion.* Defendant, having instigated a prosecution or suit against the plaintiff, offers to drop the proceeding if the plaintiff will marry the defendant. See *Melton v. Rickman,* supra, n. 37. In this pattern of abuse of process, the plaintiff who uses judicial process to obtain relief to which he is entitled has committed no tort, even if his motive for obtaining his entitlement is unworthy. See *Schmit v. Klumpyan,* 264 Wis.2d 414, 663 N.W.2d 331 (App. 2003) (partition action would pressure defendants in that action to sell, as the plaintiffs there wished, but that is not actionable as that is what the plaintiff is entitled to in a partition action).

(b) *Excessive attachment.* The defendant sues for a small debt but attaches property of the plaintiff worth many times the amount of the debt, but he makes no explicit extortionate demand. This may be regarded as wrongful (1) because the demand is implicit but obvious or (2) because excessive attachment or the like is wrongful in itself and without any demand. The same might be true if the process server falsifies an affidavit of service.

(c) *Harassment in litigation.* The defendant uses process to harm the plaintiff for the sake of harm alone, without any extortion by either express or implied demand. For instance, a lawyer suing a school system issues subpoenas for every single teacher in the system to appear on the same day merely to impose expense upon his adversary.

43. **Attorneys: debt collection practices.** Unfair debt collection practices, some of which involve process, are regulated by a federal

statute. See 15 U.S.C. § 1692i. The statute may apply to attorneys who seek to collect consumer debts.

CRACKEL V. ALLSTATE INS. CO., 208 Ariz. 252, 92 P.3d 882 (Ct.App. 2004). The plaintiffs suffered minor injuries when their car was struck while stopped at a stop light. The car was rear-ended by an Allstate insured. Liability was virtually certain and the damages claim was small, but Allstate stonewalled. In several ways, Allstate made it expensive for the plaintiffs to pursue their small claims. Written evidence and behavior of Allstate made it a jury question whether Allstate pursued these tactics for the purpose of making claims so expensive to pursue that they would be dropped. After an arbitration award for the plaintiffs, Allstate insisted on a trial and a settlement conference, all of which added to the plaintiffs delay and expense, but Allstate eventually settled for the amount awarded by the arbitrator. The plaintiffs then brought this action for abuse of process and a jury returned a verdict in plaintiffs' favor. *Held,* affirmed. (a) Any specific process in litigation can be the subject of actionable abuse. (b) Defendants as well as plaintiffs may abuse process. (c) A process is abused when it is used to achieve goals inconsistent with the purpose for which the litigation recognized. (d) If Allstate attempted to force sustained and expensive litigation as a club to coerce small claims plaintiffs to surrender their causes of action, that would be an improper purpose. (e) Considering all the evidence, a jury could find that to be Allstate's purpose in inflicting high litigation costs in a small claim where liability was virtually certain. (f) Although evidence of various tactics and policies was considered to establish improper purpose, there must be evidence that Allstate abused some specific process. There was evidence that, at a mandatory settlement conference, Allstate "(1) intentionally refused to abide by the local rule requiring distribution of pretrial memoranda to opposing counsel in preparation for the conference, (2) told the trial court that nothing the court could say would affect Allstate's negotiating position, and (3) misrepresented the conclusions of Allstate's expert on whether it had been reasonable for Drannan to seek medical attention after the accident. Based on [attorney] Gaub's comments during the settlement conference and his previous efforts to cancel that proceeding altogether, the jury could have reasonably concluded Gaub had engaged in the sanctioned behavior precisely to convey his resolve to litigate the case in conformity with Allstate's official policy for dealing with minor soft tissue injuries." (f) "Because abuse-of-process claims involve no standard-of-care requirement, because expert witnesses are expensive for plaintiffs to secure, and because a jury is capable of deciding whether a legal process has been primarily used to pursue an improper purpose, we decline Allstate's invitation to require expert testimony to support an abuse-of-process claim."

DeVANEY v. THRIFTWAY MARKETING CORP.

124 N.M. 512, 953 P.2d 277 (1997)

MINZNER, Justice.

Thriftway owns and operates several convenience stores within the boundaries of the Navajo Nation, in Farmington, and in surrounding communities. DeVaney was formerly a manager at a Thriftway store located within the Navajo Nation. An article appeared in the September 19, 1991, edition of the Navajo Times, a newspaper circulated and read throughout the Navajo Nation and surrounding communities including Farmington and Gallup. The article stated that DeVaney made the following negative comments about Thriftway: "I don't think the company [Thriftway] really cares about the Navajo people even though they have a lot of stores here on the reservation," and, "They [Thriftway] had cut their prices so much in Farmington that they weren't making any money so they had to increase the price of the gasoline on the reservation to bring in the profits."

The article also contained comments to the effect that Thriftway practiced a course of conduct in which store managers were fired after only a year or two of service without regard for the wishes of the communities in which they worked and that Thriftway was insensitive to the Navajo culture both by hiring employees without regard for their ability to understand Navajo culture and by failing to provide any training on Navajo culture after they were hired.

Thereafter, Thriftway sued DeVaney for defamation and interference with business relations, alleging that it was damaged by DeVaney's comments because they caused public contempt for the company. Specifically, Thriftway believed that its then-pending negotiations with the Navajo Nation to complete a business transaction failed because of the negative comments DeVaney made publicly.

In the action initiated by Thriftway, DeVaney moved to dismiss both counts. Devaney asserts that, at a hearing, the judge indicated that he would dismiss the count for intentional interference with business relations but would not dismiss the count for defamation. Thriftway then filed a motion for default judgment before the expiration of the time limitation on the filing of DeVaney's answer. The court did not grant Thriftway's motion. Additionally, DeVaney alleges that one of Thriftway's employees failed to appear for a scheduled out-of-town deposition. Thriftway also resisted requests for discovery of relevant information within the exclusive control of Thriftway. Specifically, Thriftway refused to produce documents containing information about Thriftway's gas prices within the Navajo Nation compared with those in Farmington and other communities and documents pertaining to Thriftway's personnel practices in relation to its managers. When the court compelled disclosure of the necessary information, Thriftway dismissed its suit.

In the present complaint against Thriftway for malicious prosecution and abuse of process, DeVaney alleged that Thriftway "filed the lawsuit without probable cause or reasonable grounds to believe that it had been slandered, libelled or defamed, without probable cause or reasonable grounds to believe that any of its contractual or business relations had been interfered with, and without probable cause or reasonable grounds to believe that it had been damaged by any act of [DeVaney]." DeVaney alleged that Thriftway's suit was filed in order to silence his criticism of Thriftway's business practices and to obtain a retraction of the criticisms. He contends on appeal that these motives provide a basis for a claim of malicious prosecution as well as abuse of process. DeVaney highlighted Thriftway's actions of prematurely filing a default motion, abusing discovery and dismissing the suit in response to an order compelling discovery, as instances of improper conduct during its suit against him.

Thriftway moved for summary judgment, seeking to show that DeVaney could not establish one or more of the essential elements of the torts on which he based his complaint.... The district court granted Thriftway's motion for summary judgment and dismissed Devaney's complaint.... On the abuse of process claim, the Court of Appeals assumed existence of an improper motive, but held that a subsequent improper act "amount[ing] to extortion," was required in addition to filing the complaint. On the malicious prosecution claim, the Court of Appeals did not decide whether Thriftway had reasonable grounds to sue DeVaney, but held that DeVaney failed to prove "special damages," a required element for the tort....

[The elements of malicious (civil) prosecution and abuse of process are similar.] Abuse of process requires an improper act, a primary improper motive, and damages. Malicious prosecution requires initiation of proceedings, a lack of probable cause, favorable termination, malice, and damages. While these elements may appear and even sometimes, on particular facts, actually may be distinguishable, they serve similar interests. The requirements of improper purpose for abuse of process and of malice for malicious prosecution are substantially similar. The institution of proceedings without probable cause, an element of malicious prosecution, can be characterized as an act not proper in the regular course of proceedings, an element of abuse of process. Also, the requirement of a favorable termination represents a procedural and evidentiary safeguard with respect to a showing of lack of probable cause. Cult Awareness Network v. Church of Scientology Int'l, 177 Ill.2d 267, 226 Ill.Dec. 604, 610, 685 N.E.2d 1347, 1353 (1997) ("[A] favorable termination is limited to only those legal dispositions that can give rise to an inference of lack of probable cause."). As this similarity of elements shows, malicious prosecution probably is better understood as a specific application of the more general tort of abuse of process.

Finally, two recent developments have further obscured the differences between these two torts. First, the "American Rule" rejection of the requirement of special damages, which we adopt today, removes any potential distinction between the two torts under the element of damages. Second, this Court has allowed a claim for abuse of process without requiring an act subsequent to the filing of a complaint, making abuse of process even less distinguishable from malicious prosecution.

Based on these similarities, we believe that there is no longer a principled reason for characterizing these two forms of misuse of process as separate causes of action.... As a result, we conclude that these torts should be restated as a single cause of action, which shall be known as "malicious abuse of process," and which shall be defined by the following elements: (1) the initiation of judicial proceedings against the plaintiff by the defendant; (2) an act by the defendant in the use of process other than such as would be proper in the regular prosecution of the claim; (3) a primary motive by the defendant in misusing the process to accomplish an illegitimate end; and (4) damages. In short, there must be both a misuse of the power of the judiciary by a litigant and a malicious motive.

... While we believe malicious prosecution and abuse of process should no longer be separate causes of action, we recognize that many of the traditional elements of both torts continue to serve important purposes. Specifically, the traditional elements of a lack of probable cause under the former tort of malicious prosecution and of an act not proper in the regular prosecution of a claim under the former tort of abuse of process serve to protect the important interest of access to the courts, thereby preventing any chilling effect on the legitimate use of process.

... An improper act, or misuse of process, need not occur subsequent to the filing of a complaint and might, in fact, be found in the complaint itself, or even precede the filing of a complaint, see Prosser & Keeton, supra, § 121, at 898 ("[A] demand for collateral advantage that occurs before the issuance of process may be actionable, so long as process does in fact issue at the defendant's behest, and as a part of the attempted extortion.") Nevertheless, the filing of a proper complaint with probable cause, and without any overt misuse of process, will not subject a litigant to liability for malicious abuse of process, even if it is the result of a malicious motive.

This is the position of the majority of states addressing the issue. E.g., ... Oren Royal Oaks, 232 Cal.Rptr. at 575, 728 P.2d at 1209 ("[T]he mere filing or maintenance of a lawsuit—even for an improper purpose—is not a proper basis for an abuse of process action...."). In order to satisfy the misuse of process requirement, then, we conclude that there must be an overt act that is irregular or improper in the normal course of proceedings. There are two independent means of demonstrating a misuse of process.

... [T]o demonstrate the overt act required in an action for malicious abuse of process, a plaintiff may show the defendant filed an action against that plaintiff without probable cause.... The second general method of demonstrating a misuse of process is through some irregularity or impropriety suggesting extortion, delay, or harassment, conduct formerly actionable under the tort of abuse of process. Under this method, the act might be a procedural irregularity, or might be an act that otherwise indicates the wrongful use of proceedings, such as an extortion attempt....

DeVaney ... alleged two overt acts, a lack of probable cause and procedural improprieties, that could, separately, support the misuse of process element for malicious abuse of process. We conclude that there are genuine issues of material fact as to both types of misuse of process....

At the time the [DeVaney] article was published, Thriftway was negotiating with the Navajo Nation Economic Development Council (Council) for the sale of Thriftway's stores within the Navajo Nation. There were several articles appearing in the newspaper discussing Thriftway's business practices in relation to the negotiations both before and after the publication of the article with DeVaney's statements. In addition, the buyout would affect more than merely the direct participants in the negotiations.... Based on these facts, we conclude that the subject of the buyout was a matter of public concern and created a public controversy in which Thriftway voluntarily injected itself.... Thus, Thriftway should have known that it would have the burden of proving both that the statements were false and that DeVaney made the statements with knowledge of falsity or with a reckless disregard of the truth.

... Thriftway could not reasonably anticipate carrying its burden of proof in the defamation action without having to disclose the information requested. In this context, Thriftway's refusal to comply with the discovery request may have been a misuse of process. The fact that Thriftway dismissed its suit after being compelled by the court to produce the documents could support an inference that there was not a legitimate basis for the failure to produce.

[Remanded for trial]

---

44. **Reforming malicious prosecution and abuse of process law.** The *DeVaney* case went on to root out other traditional rules. It abolished the special injury requirement and eliminated the favorable termination requirement. By eliminating the termination requirement, it intentionally opened the door to counterclaims for its combined malicious prosecution/abuse of process tort. And added a complication: if the person complaining of malicious abuse of process raises that issue before favorable termination, for instance by a counterclaim, and she also claims that the wrongful act in that suit was brought without probable cause, then she must prove a want of probable cause by clear and convincing evidence. If she waits until termination of the original suit, a preponderance of the evidence will do.

§ 4. FREE SPEECH IMPACTS ON MALICIOUS PROSECUTION OR ABUSE OF PROCESS

PROFESSIONAL REAL ESTATE INVESTORS, INC. v. COLUMBIA PICTURES INDUSTRIES, INC.

508 U.S. 49, 113 S.Ct. 1920, 123 L.Ed.2d 611 (1993)

Justice THOMAS delivered the opinion of the Court....

Petitioners Professional Real Estate Investors, Inc., and Kenneth F. Irwin (collectively, PRE) operated La Mancha Private Club and Villas, a resort hotel in Palm Springs, California. Having installed videodisc players in the resort's hotel rooms and assembled a library of more than 200 motion picture titles, PRE rented videodiscs to guests for in-room viewing. PRE also sought to develop a market for the sale of videodisc players to other hotels wishing to offer in-room viewing of prerecorded material. Respondents, Columbia Pictures Industries, Inc., and seven other major motion picture studios (collectively, Columbia), held copyrights to the motion pictures recorded on the videodiscs that PRE purchased. Columbia also licensed the transmission of copyrighted motion pictures to hotel rooms through a wired cable system called Spectradyne. PRE therefore competed with Columbia not only for the viewing market at La Mancha but also for the broader market for in-room entertainment services in hotels.

[Columbia sued PRE claiming copyright infringement through the rental of videodiscs for viewing in hotel rooms. PRE counterclaimed. It asserted a federal antitrust claim. It said that the copyright infringement suit itself was brought with intent to monopolize and restrain trade and that the suit was a violation of the Sherman Act, 15 U.S.C. §§ 1–2. This was especially so in the light of Columbia's threat to file similar copyright suits to intimidate other hotels and resorts from adopting similar video rental programs and other anticompetitive practices. Litigation established that in-room playing was not a public performance and that PRE was not infringing. In the second round of litigation, the trial court held that Columbia's suit was not a sham and dismissed PRE's claims under antitrust laws. The Court of Appeals affirmed.]

Those who petition government for redress are generally immune from antitrust liability. We first recognized in Eastern R. Presidents Conference v. Noerr Motor Freight, Inc., 365 U.S. 127, 81 S.Ct. 523, 5 L.Ed.2d 464 (1961), that "the Sherman Act does not prohibit ... persons from associating together in an attempt to persuade the legislature or the executive to take particular action with respect to a law that would produce a restraint or a monopoly." In light of the government's "power to act in [its] representative capacity" and "to take actions ... that operate to restrain trade," we reasoned that the Sherman Act does not punish "political activity" through which "the people ... freely inform the government of their wishes." Nor did we "impute to Congress an intent to invade" the First Amendment right to petition.

Noerr, however, withheld immunity from "sham" activities because application of the Sherman Act would be justified when petitioning activity, ostensibly directed toward influencing governmental action, is a mere sham to cover ... an attempt to interfere directly with the business relationships of a competitor. In Noerr itself, we found that a publicity campaign by railroads seeking legislation harmful to truckers was no sham in that the "effort to influence legislation" was "not only genuine but also highly successful."

In California Motor Transport Co. v. Trucking Unlimited, 404 U.S. 508, 92 S.Ct. 609, 30 L.Ed.2d 642 (1972), we elaborated on Noerr in two relevant respects. First, we extended Noerr to "the approach of citizens ... to administrative agencies ... and to courts." Second, we held that the complaint showed a sham not entitled to immunity when it contained allegations that one group of highway carriers "sought to bar ... competitors from meaningful access to adjudicatory tribunals and so to usurp that decision making process" by "institut[ing] ... proceedings and actions ... with or without probable cause, and regardless of the merits of the cases." We left unresolved the question presented by this case—whether litigation may be sham merely because a subjective expectation of success does not motivate the litigant. We now answer this question in the negative and hold that an objectively reasonable effort to litigate cannot be sham regardless of subjective intent.

Our original formulation of antitrust petitioning immunity required that unprotected activity lack objective reasonableness. Noerr rejected the contention that an attempt to influence the passage and enforcement of laws might lose immunity merely because the lobbyists' sole purpose ... was to destroy [their] competitors.... In short, Noerr shields from the Sherman Act a concerted effort to influence public officials regardless of intent or purpose....

Since California Motor Transport, we have consistently assumed that the sham exception contains an indispensable objective component....

In sum, fidelity to precedent compels us to reject a purely subjective definition of "sham." The sham exception so construed would undermine, if not vitiate, Noerr. And despite whatever "superficial certainty" it might provide, a subjective standard would utterly fail to supply "real intelligible guidance."

We now outline a two-part definition of "sham" litigation. First, the lawsuit must be objectively baseless in the sense that no reasonable litigant could realistically expect success on the merits. If an objective litigant could conclude that the suit is reasonably calculated to elicit a favorable outcome, the suit is immunized under Noerr, and an antitrust claim premised on the sham exception must fail.... Under this second part of our definition of sham, the court should focus on whether the baseless lawsuit conceals an attempt to interfere directly with the business relationships of a competitor, through the use [of] the governmental process—as opposed to the outcome of that process—as an anticompetitive weapon. This two-tiered process requires the plaintiff to disprove the challenged lawsuit's legal viability before the court will entertain evidence of the suit's economic viability. Of course, even a plaintiff who defeats the defendant's claim to Noerr immunity by demonstrating both the objective and the subjective components of a sham must still prove a substantive antitrust violation. Proof of a sham merely deprives the defendant of immunity; it does not relieve the plaintiff of the obligation to establish all other elements of his claim....

We conclude that the Court of Appeals properly affirmed summary judgment for Columbia on PRE's antitrust counterclaim. Under the objective prong of the sham exception, the Court of Appeals correctly held that sham litigation must constitute the pursuit of claims so baseless that no reasonable litigant could realistically expect to secure favorable relief.

The existence of probable cause to institute legal proceedings precludes a finding that an antitrust defendant has engaged in sham litigation. The notion of probable cause, as understood and applied in the common law tort of wrongful civil proceedings requires the plaintiff to prove that the defendant lacked probable cause to institute an unsuccessful civil lawsuit and that the defendant pressed the action for an improper, malicious purpose. Probable cause to institute civil proceedings requires no more than a reasonabl[e] belie[f] that there is a chance that [a] claim may be held valid upon adjudication.... Just as evidence of anticompetitive intent cannot affect the objective prong of Noerr's sham exception, a showing of malice alone will neither entitle the wrongful civil proceedings plaintiff to prevail nor permit the factfinder to infer the absence of probable cause. When a court has found that an antitrust defendant claiming Noerr immunity had probable cause to sue, that finding compels the conclusion that a reasonable litigant in the defendant's position could realistically expect success on the merits of the challenged lawsuit. Under our decision today, therefore, a proper probable cause determination irrefutably demonstrates that an antitrust plaintiff has not proved the objective prong of the sham exception and that the defendant is accordingly entitled to Noerr immunity.

[Affirmed]

Justice STEVENS, with whom Justice O'CONNOR joins, concurring in the judgment.

While I agree with the Court's disposition of this case and with its holding "that an objectively reasonable effort to litigate cannot be sham regardless of subjective intent," I write separately to disassociate myself from some of the unnecessarily broad dicta in the Court's opinion. Specifically, I disagree with the Court's equation of "objectively baseless" with the answer to the question whether any "reasonable litigant could realistically expect success on the merits." ...

The distinction between abusing the judicial process to restrain competition, and prosecuting a lawsuit that, if successful, will restrain competition, must guide any court's decision whether a particular filing, or series of filings, is a sham. The label "sham" is appropriately applied to a case, or series of cases, in which the plaintiff is indifferent to the outcome of the litigation itself, but has nevertheless sought to impose a collateral harm on the defendant by, for example, impairing his credit, abusing the discovery process, or interfering with his access to governmental agencies. It might also apply to a plaintiff who had some reason to expect success on the merits but because of its tremendous cost would not bother to achieve that result without the benefit of collateral injuries imposed on its competitor by the legal process alone. Litigation filed or pursued for such collateral purposes is fundamentally different from a case in which the relief sought in the litigation itself would give the plaintiff a competitive advantage or, perhaps, exclude a potential competitor from entering a market with a product that either infringes the plaintiff's patent or copyright or violates an exclusive franchise granted by a governmental body.

[Justice Souter's concurring opinion is omitted.]

---

45. **First Amendment.** The First Amendment provides: "Congress shall make no law respecting an establishment of religion, or prohibiting the free exercise thereof; or abridging the freedom of speech, or of the press; or the right of the people peaceably to assemble, and to petition the Government for a redress of grievances." In *Noerr* and *California Motor Freight*, discussed by Justice Thomas, the Court construed the antitrust statutes to exempt petitions to the government, first in the form of lobbying and second in the form of lawsuits.

46. **Noerr line: statutory construction or constitutional rule?** The *Noerr* line of cases involves construction of the antitrust statutes, but those statutes are construed in the light of the right to petition government. In *Titan America, LLC v. Riverton Investment Corp.,* 264 Va. 292, 569 S.E.2d 57 (2002), the court held that the *Noerr* line established Constitutional, First Amendment protections, not merely protections derived from construing the antitrust statute. In *Structure Bldg. Corp. v. Abella,* 377 N.J.Super. 467, 873 A.2d 601 (2005), the court applied the *Noerr* line as a matter of state common law, dismissing a real estate developer's suit against neighbors who had pursued legal actions to oppose the development. The trial judge's analysis, approved by the appellate court, included the observation that "if we didn't have Noerr–Pennington Doctrine, the Court would have to create one."

47. **Sham lawsuits.** Sham lawsuits are not protected under *PRE*. Is it fair to say that for some justices the lawsuit is a sham when it looks like abuse of process, while others would require it to look like malicious prosecution?

48. **Abuse of process affected by the *Noerr* line?** In *DirectTV v. Zink,* 286 F.Supp.2d 873 (E.D. Mich. 2003), the court concluded that *PRE* could not be invoked to bar an abuse of process claim, as distinct from a claim for wrongful civil proceedings, because filing a objectively justified lawsuit should not protect the plaintiff from charges of abuse of process after suit is filed. "Since petitioning courts to enforce the law is a protected right for all, applying the Noerr-Pennington doctrine in the situation described above would infringe on the defendant's right to petition the courts in the name of protecting an activity not truly part of the plaintiff's petition."

DIXON v. SUPERIOR COURT

30 Cal.App.4th 733, 36 Cal.Rptr.2d 687 (1994)

WALLIN, Associate Justice....

At the heart of this controversy is a 22-acre portion of the California State University at Long Beach (CSULB) campus long believed by many Native American Indians to be part of an ancient Indian village known as Puvunga. In 1974, following nomination by petitioner Keith Dixon, an archaeologist and Professor Emeritus of Anthropology at CSULB, the Puvunga site was accepted for inclusion on the National Register of Historic Places.

[About 1980, the University commissioned Scientific Resource Surveys (SRS) to make "archaeological tests" on a part of the Puvunga site because the University wished to build a Japanese Garden there. SRS made a report favorable to the University's wishes. SRS' report incurred the criticism of Professor Emeritus Dixon who wrote that it was poorly done, biased, and should be withdrawn. However, the university seems to have proceeded with the Japanese Garden anyway.

[Years later, in 1992, the University planned "to construct a strip mall" and a parking lot on the Puvunga site. It was required by California's Environmental Quality Act (CEQA) to obtain a study first. This time it commissioned Envicom Corporation to do the site study. Envicom reported that the proposed project "would not significantly impact the local environment, result in alteration or destruction of an archaeological site, or affect cultural values or sacred or religious uses in that area." Based on those findings, the report recommended CSULB adopt a negative declaration. Dixon again objected. The negative declaration that the environment would not be affected, he argued, was based on an earlier error-filled and sub-professional report. Thereafter, he continued to complain about SRS's work and its effect on the current strip mall question.]

SRS responded by filing the underlying lawsuit against Dixon. The complaint sought $570,000 in damages for intentional and negligent interference with contractual relations and prospective economic advantage, libel, slander and trade libel. SRS alleged its contractual relationship with CSULB had been destroyed by Dixon's oral and written statements....

After filing his answer, Dixon moved to strike the complaint, which he characterized as a SLAPP suit, under Code of Civil Procedure section 425.16, subdivision (b). That section provides that any

> cause of action against a person arising from any act of that person in furtherance of the person's right of petition or free speech under the United States or California Constitution in connection with a public issue shall be subject to a special motion to strike, unless the court determines that the plaintiff has established that there is a probability that the plaintiff will prevail on the claim.

In support of the motion, Dixon attached his declaration in which he averred that the statements he made to CSULB officials were for the sole purpose of participating in the CEQA public comment and review process by informing them about the cultural, historical and archaeological significance of the Puvunga site and the potential environmental effects that further excavation and commercial development would cause. His statements regarding the quality of SRS's work and their competence as an archeological firm were not based on personal animosity; rather, they were based on a professional review of the documents SRS generated. He denied any participation in the NAHC proceedings regarding CSULB's proposed development or discussing his opinion of SRS's work with any member of the Native American community....

The typical SLAPP suit involves citizens opposed to a particular real estate development. The group opposed to the project, usually a local neighborhood, protests by distributing flyers, writing letters to local newspapers, and speaking at planning commission or city council meetings. The developer responds by filing a SLAPP suit against the citizen group alleging defamation or various business torts. (Barker, Common–Law and Statutory Solutions to the Problem of SLAPPS (1993) 26 Loyola L.A.L.Rev. 395, 396.) SLAPP plaintiffs do not intend to win their suits; rather, they are filed solely for delay and distraction (id. at p. 397), and to punish activists by imposing litigation costs on them for exercising their constitutional right to speak and petition the government for redress of grievances. (See Comment, SLAPP Suits: Weaknesses in First Amendment Law and in the Court's Responses to Frivolous Litigation (1992) 39 UCLA L.Rev. 979.)

And [w]hile SLAPP suits masquerade as ordinary lawsuits the conceptual features which reveal them as SLAPP's are that they are generally meritless suits brought by large private interests to deter common citizens from exercising their political or legal rights or to punish them for doing so. [Citations.] Because winning is not a SLAPP plaintiff's primary motivation, defendants' traditional safeguards against meritless actions, (suits for malicious prosecution and abuse of process, requests for sanctions) are inadequate to counter SLAPP's. Instead, the SLAPPer considers any damage or sanction award which the SLAPPee might eventually recover as merely a cost of doing business. By the time a SLAPP victim can win a "SLAPP-back" suit years later the SLAPP plaintiff will probably already have accomplished its underlying objective....

In 1992, the Legislature responded to the problem of SLAPP suits by enacting Code of Civil Procedure section 425.16....

Acts "in furtherance" of a person's First Amendment rights are defined in section 425.16 to include, "any written or oral statement or writing made before a legislative, executive, or judicial proceeding, or any other official proceeding authorized by law; any written or oral statement or writing made in connection with an issue under consideration or review by a legislative, executive, or judicial body, or any other official proceeding authorized by law; or any written or oral statement or writing made in a place open to the public or a public forum in connection with an issue of public interest." (Code of Civ.Proc., § 425.16, subd. (e).)

The party moving to strike a complaint under Code of Civil Procedure section 425.16 has the burden of making a prima facie showing that the lawsuit arises from any act of [defendant] in furtherance of [defendant's] right of petition or free speech under the United States or California Constitution in connection with a public issue.

There is no dispute the proposed development of the Puvunga site and its related CEQA proceedings were matters of public concern. What is in dispute is whether Dixon's allegedly tortious statements were made in connection with those proceedings. SRS argues they were not because ... they were directed against SRS, which was not part of the CEQA proceedings....

SRS has been involved with the Puvunga site since 1980, when it performed archaeological tests on another portion of the site CSULB sought to develop.... Given SRS's involvement with the Puvunga site and its position as to its archaeological significance (or lack thereof), it strains credulity for SRS to argue it was not involved in the CEQA proceedings.

... We conclude the comments made by Dixon were in connection with a public issue and fall within the statutory definition of Code of Civil Procedure section 425.16. That being so, the burden shifted to SRS to establish a probability of prevailing on its claim....

SRS argues [it met its burden] by offering evidence that the statements made by Dixon were made with actual malice [and] with knowledge of their falsity or with reckless disregard for their truth....

In McDonald, an unsuccessful candidate for appointment as United States Attorney sued an individual who had sent letters to the President of the United States and other members of the administration falsely accusing the candidate of violating the civil rights of various individuals, fraud, extortion and blackmail. The complaint alleged the defendant knew the statements were false and they were made with malice. In rejecting the defendant's claim of absolute immunity, the Supreme Court held the right to petition is "cut from the same cloth" as other guarantees of the First Amendment. And to grant absolute immunity would improperly elevate the right to petition above other First Amendment guarantees. Under the law of the state in which the complaint was brought, plaintiff was entitled to damages on a showing of malice. Dixon contends, and we agree, that McDonald does not apply where, as here, a statute exists which expressly invites public comment....

Here, as in Matossian, the statutory invitation for public participation bars any inquiry into the motives behind the statements or comments made. To bring himself within the protection of section 425.16, all Dixon had to do was show his statements were made in response to a matter of public concern. He did. Therefore, SRS could not, as a matter of law, have established a probability of prevailing at trial because even if it proved Dixon acted with malice, his statements are still entitled to absolute immunity.

Finally, SRS raises several constitutional challenges to Code of Civil Procedure section 425.16. It first contends the section violates its right to due process by requiring a plaintiff to establish probability of success without the opportunity to conduct discovery. Specifically, it argues if it were permitted to conduct discovery, it would be able to show a triable issue of fact as to malice. But, as we hold, Dixon's motivation in making the complained of statements is irrelevant; thus, proof of malice is not material in this case.

SRS also contends the statute unconstitutionally deprives it of the right to trial by jury by requiring the court to weigh the evidence in ruling on the motion to strike. But the court does not weigh the evidence in ruling on the motion; instead, it accepts as true all evidence favorable to the plaintiff. Moreover, the right to trial by jury pertains solely to questions of fact. Here, there was no question of fact to be decided by the trial court. Even if all of SRS's evidence is accepted as true, that is, that Dixon was waging a personal vendetta against SRS and was doing so maliciously, SRS still could not make a prima facie showing because Dixon's statements were entitled to absolute immunity.

The alternative writ is dissolved. Let a peremptory writ of mandate issue directing the trial court to vacate its order denying petitioner's motion to strike the complaint and enter a new order granting the motion and dismissing the complaint.

---

49. **Origin and expansion of Anti–SLAPP statutes.** The statutes are largely the result of persistent efforts of two writers, who saw suits by developers against those opposed to development as an effort to squash opposition and a chill on the right of citizens to petition government or otherwise exercise free speech. See George W. Pring and Penelope Canan, SLAPPs: Getting Sued for Speaking Out (1996); Penelope Canan and George W. Pring, *Studying Strategic Lawsuits Against*

Public Participating: Mixing Quantitative and Qualitative Approaches, 22 L. & SOC'Y REV. 385 (1988). The statutes are not by terms limited to developers and courts have applied them in other kinds of cases. For example, in *Fabre v. Walton,* 436 Mass. 517, 781 N.E.2d 780 (2002), the plaintiff, a female, obtained a protective order against the defendant, who then sued for abuse of process. His abuse suit was dismissed under an anti-SLAPP statute. "The filing of a complaint for an abuse protection order and the submission of supporting affidavits are petitioning activities. . . ."

50. **Anti-SLAPP predicate requirements.** Massachusetts has observed more than once that in dismissing the plaintiff's complaint before factual development, the statute protects "one party's exercise of its right of petition [but] impinges on the adverse party's exercise of its right to petition. . . ." *Baker v. Parsons,* 434 Mass. 543, 750 N.E.2d 953 (2001). The *Baker* court held that the defendant raising the anti-SLAPP defense would have to make a threshold showing that the claim against him was based upon his rights of petition. Once that was done, though, the court said that the plaintiff would be required to show by a preponderance of the evidence—not merely some evidence—that the defendant's petitioning activity was "devoid of any reasonable factual support or any arguable basis in law." To similar effect is *Jarrow Formulas, Inc. v. LaMarche,* 31 Cal.4th 728, 74 P.3d 737, 3 Cal.Rptr.3d 636 (2003).

51. **Constitutionality of anti-SLAPP statutes.** In *Opinion of the Justices (SLAPP Suit Procedure),* 138 N.H. 445, 641 A.2d 1012 (1994), the court concluded that a statute like California's would violate New Hampshire's right to jury trial because it would require the trial judge hearing the motion to strike to weigh evidence and to dismiss if the plaintiff merely had a possibility of winning rather than a probability. It concluded by saying: "The question before us is whether the legislative response itself imperils constitutional rights. A solution cannot strengthen the constitutional rights of one group of citizens by infringing upon the rights of another group."

52. **A different type of anti-SLAPP.** New York's statute is different. It authorizes a defendant like Dixon to maintain an action or counterclaim to recover damages, including attorney fees, provided the SLAPP suit "was commenced or continued without a substantial basis in fact and law and could not be supported by a substantial argument for the extension, modification or reversal of existing law" and "other compensatory damages" may be recovered only if the action was "for the purpose of harassing, punishing or otherwise maliciously inhibiting" speech, petition, and association right. Punitive damages can be recovered only upon additional proof: that the action was initiated solely to harass, punish or the like. N.Y. CIV. RTS. § 70–a.

Professional and Academic Enhancements
Chapter 8

Tortious Litigation and Tactics

A Mini-Problem

Denton, a creditor of Albert's, holds a judgment against Albert. To collect, Denton followed a valid statutory procedures by having the sheriff levy on Albert's personal property located in Albert's house. One item was a valuable painting by Niccolo Bellini. In fact the painting belonged to Albert's's friend, Perlman. Albert was merely keeping it while Perlman was in Pago Pago. Does Perlman, the owner, have an action against Denton, the creditor, or against the sheriff? Must malice be shown?

Civil Rights: Prosecution without Probable Cause

NEWSOME v. McCABE

256 F.3d 747 (7th Cir. 2001)

EASTERBROOK, Circuit Judge.

James Newsome spent 15 years in prison for murder. The killing and associated crimes (armed robbery and armed violence) occurred in October 1979. Newsome was arrested in November 1979 when police, who were holding him on other charges, noted his resemblance to a composite sketch of the person who in the course of a robbery shot and killed Mickey Cohen. Newsome was convicted of that crime in September 1980, and his efforts to obtain collateral relief were unavailing until December 1994, when a state court vacated his conviction. In 1995, after the State's Attorney declined to put Newsome on trial a second time, the Governor of Illinois concluded that Newsome is innocent and pardoned him. Newsome then filed this suit under 42 U.S.C. § 1983 against five officers of the Chicago Police Department. He could not seek damages for wrongful arrest and detention; that claim accrued in 1979, so the statute of limitations expired in 1981. But a claim based on wrongful conviction and imprisonment did not accrue until the pardon, and Newsome tried to take advantage of the newly opened window for suit. Absolute immunity forecloses any action against the prosecutors and judges, but Newsome has tried to avoid that doctrine by suing the investigating officers, arguing that the police were complicit in a wrongful prosecution. He calls this a claim of "malicious prosecution" and contends that the police must pay for failing to halt the criminal prosecution. The defendants responded by arguing that Newsome's theory is legally deficient and that, at all events, qualified immunity prevents an award of damages.

[The trial court allow the claim to go forward as to only two defendants, John McCabe and Raymond McNally, on evidence that they "failed to alert the prosecutors that Newsome's fingerprints did not match those they had obtained at the scene of the crime" and other evidence that they coached witnesses at a lineup and withheld that fact from the prosecutor. The trial court thought there was a constitutional tort when a state actor was guilty of state-law malicious prosecution and the accused was deprived of liberty.]

Whether there is a constitutional right not to be prosecuted without probable cause—the question that the district court saw through the lens of malicious prosecution—was addressed and answered in the negative by seven Justices in [Albright v. Oliver, 510 U.S. 266, 114 S.Ct. 807, 127 L.Ed.2d 114 (1994)]. The problem is that they did not agree on the reason. Four Justices concluded that probable cause is the exclusive domain of the fourth amendment, and that unless the plaintiff can establish that his arrest was unlawful there is no further constitutional claim. Newsome had a potential fourth amendment claim, but as we mentioned at the outset the time to pursue it expired almost 20 years ago. One Justice preferred to analyze the subject in terms of substantive due process, an approach that could leave room for Newsome's claim but doomed *Albright's* because he did not argue that the police engaged in egregious misconduct. Two more Justices believed that the right approach lies in due *process* without substantive coloration—whether the person seized by the state had an adequate opportunity to defend himself in the criminal prosecution and, if not, an adequate opportunity to obtain compensation in state court. [Justices Kennedy and Thomas.] A jury might conclude that McCabe and McNally deprived Newsome of an adequate chance to defend himself in the criminal prosecution. But Justices Kennedy and Thomas concluded that in such circumstances the federal Constitution still does not supply a damages remedy, unless the state courts refuse to do so.... Justices Kennedy and Thomas conclude that due process of law is afforded by the opportunity to pursue a claim in state court, and four other Justices do not think that the due process clause applies in the first place....

Claims of malicious prosecution should be analyzed not under the substantive due process approach ... but under the language of the Constitution itself and, if state law withholds a remedy, under the approach ... adopted by Justices Kennedy and Thomas in *Albright*. ... [T]here is nothing but confusion to be gained by calling the legal theory "malicious prosecution."

Where does this leave Newsome? Certainly not with a constitutional claim founded on malicious prosecution. Nor does he have a viable fourth amendment claim, for the statute of limitations expired long ago. But he does have a due process claim in the original sense of that phrase—he did not receive a fair trial if the prosecutors withheld material exculpatory details. Although the State's Attorney did not have in his file details about the fingerprints and the means McCabe and McNally used to influence the identification, a prosecutor is responsible for learning of and disclosing all exculpatory evidence known to the police. Defendants recognize that a claim along these lines states a genuine constitutional tort. [Such a violation occurs at trial, not at arrest, and consequently, under prior decisions, the claim does not accrue until pardon.] Nonetheless, defendants contend, if the claim is recast in this fashion then they prevail because *they* did not withhold evidence; the prosecutor did so (even if they were to blame). Because injury depended on the action of the prosecutor they either are not substantively liable or possess a derivative form of immunity, the line of argument concludes.

Buckley v. Fitzsimmons, 20 F.3d 789 (7th Cir.1994), provides the principal support for this contention. It holds that responsibility rests on the prosecutor, rather than the police, when there would have been no injury but for a prosecutorial decision that is protected by absolute immunity. ... But Newsome's suit does not present the *Buckley* issue, and defendants' reliance on that decision is unavailing, for a fundamental reason: *Buckley* supposed that the police had been forthcoming with the prosecutors, so that injury really could be traced to prosecutorial decisions.... If officers are not candid with prosecutors, then the prosecutors' decisions—although vital to the causal chain in a but-for sense—are not the important locus of action. Pressure must be brought to bear elsewhere. Prosecutors kept in the dark by the police (and not negligent in failing to hire other persons to investigate the police) won't improve their performance with or without legal liability for their conduct. Requiring culpable officers to pay damages to the victims of their actions, however, holds out promise of both deterring and remediating violations of the Constitution.

... If Newsome can prove what he alleges, then ... he will establish a violation of the due process clause, a kind of violation for which officers McCabe and McNally do not have immunity. This is not the basis of the district court's order, nor is it Newsome's preferred theory—malicious prosecution is not tenable as an independent constitutional—but we may affirm a decision on any ground that the record supports. The decision of the district court rejecting defendants' affirmative defense of qualified immunity is accordingly

Affirmed.

1. ***Newsome's* Subsequent history.** In a later appeal, the court affirmed a judgment for Newsome for $15 million in damages and $850,000 in attorney fees and costs. *Newsome v. McCabe,* 319 F.3d 301 (7th Cir. 2003).

2. ***Albright's* limitation on civil rights suits.** *Albright v. Oliver,* 510 U.S. 266, 114 S.Ct. 807, 127 L.Ed.2d 114 (1994), referred to in *Newsome,* offered no less than six opinions. No opinion was signed by a majority. The Justices differed a great deal, but most did agree that

Albright could not successfully assert a substantive due process violation based on prosecution without probable cause.

3. **Fourth Amendment as a basis.** *Albright* left open the possibility that a plaintiff prosecuted without probable cause might, at least in some circumstances, have a § 1983 claim based on the Fourth Amendment's prohibition of unreasonable seizure. Perhaps some of the Justices had in mind the fact that Albright had actually been subjected to arrest without probable cause before the prosecution stage was reached. But it is also possible to conceive of prosecution itself as a form of seizure, at least if bond is required to secure freedom pending trial, or travel restrictions are imposed as a condition of bail. The court took that approach in *Gallo v. City of Philadelphia,* 161 F.3d 217 (3d Cir. 1998), thus permitting the § 1983 claim brought by a plaintiff who was prosecuted without probable cause and restricted in travel by his bail conditions, even though he was never arrested. Justice Ginsburg, writing a lonely concurring opinion in *Albright* also developed an elaborate theory that once seizure occurs, the prosecuted individual remains seized until the trial is over. These concepts of seizure may be constitutionally sound or not, but they do not match the common law's careful distinctions between arrest (seizure) and malicious prosecution.

4. **Procedural due process.** Among the many things *Albright* did not determine was whether a prosecution without probable cause could be, or at least lead to, a deprivation of procedural due process. Is that what *Newsome* recognizes as a basis for the § 1983 claim?

5. **Adequate state remedy.** Justice Kennedy's concurring opinion in *Albright* argued that "a state actor's random and unauthorized deprivation of that interest cannot be challenged under 42 U.S.C. § 1983 so long as the State provides an adequate postdeprivation remedy." Some authority has applied this idea to exclude procedural due process claims where the state permits a malicious prosecution action that would be an adequate remedy. *Nieves v. McSweeney,* 241 F.3d 46 (1st Cir. 2001). But Justice Kennedy seemed to distinguish a prosecution without probable cause from a constitutional violation that deprived the prosecuted plaintiff of fundamental fair trial on the issue of guilt. See *Albright v. Oliver,* 510 U.S. 266, 283, 114 S.Ct. 807, 818, 127 L.Ed.2d 114 (1994) (Kennedy, J. Concurring). The adequate state remedy rule probably does not bar the civil rights claim based on denial of a fair trial. *Castellano v. Fragozo,* 352 F.3d 939 (5th Cir. 2003) (fact of adequate state remedy would not be enough to bar due process claim based on alleged fabrication of evidence plus perjury at trial).

6. **Immunity.** Recall that witnesses are immune from liability for trial testimony. So if the officers had lied on the witness stand instead of withholding exculpatory evidence, they would be immune, and no constitutional civil rights claim could be asserted based on their fabricated evidence. *McCullah v. Gadert,* 344 F.3d 655 (7th Cir. 2003). Consider these variations: (a) The officer fabricates evidence to obtain a warrant?

(b) The prosecutor knowingly uses fabricated testimony at trial? (c) The prosecutor has a policy of using fabricated evidence at trial?

7. **Other confusions.** Courts have sometimes confused all this even more by referring to some of these civil rights suits for constitutional violation as "§ 1983 malicious prosecution" claims, by saying they are Fourth Amendment claims even though the Fourth Amendment seems to address unreasonable seizure rather than prosecution pursuant to legal process, and by saying that even in a Fourth Amendment action for unreasonable seizure, the plaintiff must prove the common law elements of malicious prosecution to make out a constitutional violation. See DOBBS ON TORTS § 440A–440D (Supp.).

42 U.S.C.A. § 1981

(a) Statement of equal rights

All persons within the jurisdiction of the United States shall have the same right in every State and Territory to make and enforce contracts, to sue, be parties, give evidence, and to the full and equal benefit of all laws and proceedings for the security of persons and property as is enjoyed by white citizens, and shall be subject to like punishment, pains, penalties, taxes, licenses, and exactions of every kind, and to no other.

(b) "Make and enforce contracts" defined

For purposes of this section, the term "make and enforce contracts" includes the making, performance, modification, and termination of contracts, and the enjoyment of all benefits, privileges, terms, and conditions of the contractual relationship.

(c) Protection against impairment

The rights protected by this section are protected against impairment by nongovernmental discrimination and impairment under color of State law.

PHILLIP v. UNIVERSITY OF ROCHESTER

316 F.3d 291 (2d Cir. 2003)

POOLER, Circuit Judge. . . .

Nigel S. Phillip, Bernard Schmidt, St. Patrick Reid, and Grant Gittens are African-Americans and were, at the time of the pertinent events, students at the University of Rochester, a private university. In the early morning of April 30, 1999, the plaintiffs and other students, most of whom were minorities, gathered to socialize in the lobby of the university library. Within minutes, James Clukey, a university security officer, came up to the students and told them to "break it up" and "take it outside." Although the students attempted to comply with Clukey's order, he demanded that Gittens show his university identification and asked the other individuals whether they were students at the university. One of the students, Elizabeth Pena, reached into Gittens' pocket, pulled out his university identification and said, "there, you see he's a student here. We are all students here." Clukey snatched Gittens' identification card and radioed the Rochester Police Department ("RPD") for assistance. The officer also followed the students outside. Soon afterwards Raymond Pipitone, a university security supervisor, came to the scene along with other security officers.

Phillip tried to end the confrontation by bringing Gittens to a friend's car. Just as the car was about to leave the parking lot, Clukey placed himself in front of the car, would not allow it to leave, and began to copy its license plate.

Several police units then arrived. Police officers arrested the four plaintiffs, apparently based on conduct that the officers had observed. The plaintiffs stayed in jail overnight but received adjournments in contemplation of dismissal the following morning. Charges against all plaintiffs have been dismissed....

Plaintiffs sued the university, Pipitone, and Clukey, claiming false arrest and imprisonment, battery and excessive use of force, assault, malicious prosecution, intentional and negligent infliction of emotional distress, and violation of the equal benefit clause of Section 1981. Defendants moved pursuant to Fed.R.Civ.P. 12(b)(6) to dismiss several of these claims including the Section 1981 claim. The district court dismissed plaintiffs' Section 1981 claim along with several of their other claims. With respect to the Section 1981 equal benefit clause claim, the court found plaintiffs could not prevail because they failed to allege state action....

To assess the need for state action in a Section 1981 equal benefit claim, we begin with the language of the statute both in its original form and as amended in 1991.

Before November 1991, Section 1981 provided only that

> All persons within the jurisdiction of the United States shall have the same right in every State and Territory to make and enforce contracts, to sue, be parties, give evidence, and to the full and equal benefit of all laws and proceedings for the security of persons and property as is enjoyed by white citizens, and shall be subject to like punishment, pains, penalties, taxes, licenses, and exactions of every kind, and to no other.

42 U.S.C. § 1981.

In 1991, Congress enacted amendments to Section 1981. The text just quoted now is denominated as subsection (a). A new subsection (b) repudiates *Patterson v. McLean Credit Union,* 491 U.S. 164, 109 S.Ct. 2363, 105 L.Ed.2d 132 (1989), in which the Supreme Court held that breaches of contract are outside the scope of the "make and enforce contracts" clause of Section 1981. And, pertinent to this appeal, a new subsection (c) provides: "The rights protected by this section are protected against impairment by nongovernmental discrimination and impairment under color of State law." 42 U.S.C. § 1981(c).

On the face of the amended statute, it would seem that the answer to the question this appeal presents is clear: No state action is required for a Section 1981 claim.

Despite the apparent clarity of the statutory language, the courts of appeals to have considered whether the amended statute requires state action for an equal benefit clause claim have answered yes. *Youngblood v. Hy—Vee Food Stores, Inc.,* 266 F.3d 851, 855 (8th Cir.2001), *cert. denied,* 535 U.S. 1017, 122 S.Ct. 1606, 152 L.Ed.2d 621 (2002); *Brown v. Philip Morris Inc.,* 250 F.3d 789, 799 (3d Cir.2001). As we explain, we do not find *Youngblood, Brown,* or their sources sufficiently persuasive to displace the clear words of the statute.

Mahone, the primary and largely unexamined source for the holdings in *Youngblood* and *Brown,* merits close examination. In *Mahone,* the Third Circuit held that police officers who physically and verbally abused African–Americans, falsely arrested them, and gave false testimony against them could be sued under Section 1981's equal benefit clause. *Mahone,* 564 F.2d at 1028–29. In response to defendants' argument that construing Section 1981 to encompass their actions would federalize tort law, the court said in dicta that there was no such danger because the equal benefit clause requires state action. Although the court acknowledged that the "make and enforce contracts" clause of Section 1981 does not require state action, it said that the rights to "make and enforce contracts" and to enjoy the "full and equal benefit of all laws and proceedings for the security of persons and property as is enjoyed by white citizens" [was] different.... Because it is individuals who ordinarily make contracts, the court reasoned that individuals should be held liable for the racially motivated infringement of the contracts they make. In contrast, the court said that the equal benefit clause "suggest[s] a concern with relations between the individual and the state, not between two individuals" because states, not individuals, make laws and only the state can take away the protection of the laws it created.

Because we do not agree with the premise of *Mahone,* we do not find its logic persuasive. Although the phrasing of the equal benefit clause does suggest that there must be some nexus between a claim and the state or its activities, the state is not the only actor that can deprive an individual of the benefit of laws or proceedings for the security of persons or property.

Having determined that individuals can deprive others of the equal benefit of laws and proceedings designed to protect the personal freedoms and property rights of the citizenry, we see no principled basis for holding that state action is required for equal benefit clause claims but not for contract clause claims. We therefore reject the analysis in *Mahone.* ...

Even assuming that the Third Circuit correctly decided *Mahone,* we believe that the 1991 amendment removes any doubt that the conduct of private actors is actionable under the equal benefit clause of Section

1981. Thus, we respectfully differ with the contrary conclusion reached by the Eighth and Third Circuits....

We do not here attempt to define the universe of laws and proceedings for the security of persons and property, believing this task best resolved case by case. However, we do hold that plaintiffs here adequately alleged a deprivation of a law or proceeding for the security of persons and property. Accepting the truth of plaintiffs' allegations and according those allegations the most generous interpretation they support, defendants refused to allow Gittens and his friends to leave an area where they were peacefully assembled, confiscated Gittens' identification, and then called the police. We also accept the plausible inference that the police were called either to criminally investigate plaintiffs' behavior or to restore peace. We have no difficulty categorizing either a criminal investigation or the restoration of peace as a "proceeding for the security of persons and property" at the Rule 12(b)(6) stage.... We hold that, assuming that Section 1981 requires a nexus to state proceedings or laws but not state action, plaintiffs' allegations are sufficient because plaintiffs claim that defendants attempted to trigger a legal proceeding against plaintiffs but would not have taken the same action had white students engaged in the same conduct.

We hold that the equal benefit clause of Section 1981(a) does not require state action. We also find that plaintiffs' allegations state a claim that defendants, who were motivated by racial discrimination, attempted to deprive them of the "full and equal benefit" of a state proceeding "for the security of persons and property." Therefore, we vacate and remand. We emphasize that our holding is limited to the facts before us, and we intimate no view of the appropriate outcome for factual allegations less directly linked to "laws [or] proceedings for the security of persons and property."

Malicious Prosecution Suits against and by Attorneys

1. **Suit against the losing attorney for wrongful or negligent suits.** Suppose you, as an attorney, bring suit against X on behalf of your client. After you lose, X sues you personally, claiming you acted unreasonably when you should have known that X was not liable or was the wrong person. Liability in cases like this is doubly deniable—first because negligence is generally insufficient for economic harm claims and second because to hold the attorney liable for representation of his client would likely interfere in the long run with full and vigorous representation of clients. See *Beecy v. Pucciarelli,* 387 Mass. 589, 441 N.E.2d 1035 (1982).

The lawyer's violation of a disciplinary rule or ethical-duty statute adds nothing to validate the opposing party's claim against him. See *Bob Godfrey Pontiac v. Roloff,* 291 Or. 318, 630 P.2d 840 (1981). But other cases hold that the attorney is subject to liability to his client's adversary if the attorney lacks probable cause and the other elements of the malicious prosecution claim are met. E.g., *Manuel v. Wilka,* 610 N.W.2d 458 (S.D. 2000).

2. **Suit by the winning attorney who has been sued while litigation is pending.** Suppose X, your client's adversary, sues you personally while your client's claim against X is still pending. X might claim, for example, that your representation of your client interfered with X's contract rights with your client. Now you must pursue your client's claims against X and also defend yourself from X's attack. On the latter, your client will not be paying the bills and you may find yourself with conflicts of interest because you might want to settle your client's suit cheaply to persuade X to drop his claim against you. This looks like a serious interference with the adversary system. Now suppose you win your client's claim and also successfully defend X's suit against you. Can you recover for wrongful civil litigation brought by X if you are in a state requiring special injury? *Engel v. CBS, Inc.,* 93 N.Y.2d 195, 689 N.Y.S.2d 411, 711 N.E.2d 626 (1999), on somewhat similar facts, reiterates New York's special injury requirement and holds that the harm suffered by the lawyer is not a special injury. What about the harm to the adversary system?

Right to Petition and Law Suits that Discriminate

United States v. Scott, 788 F.Supp. 1555 (D. Kan. 1992). The federal Fair Housing Act, 42 U.S.C.A. § 3604(f) makes it unlawful "[t]o discriminate in the sale or rental, or to otherwise make unavailable or deny, a dwelling to any buyer or renter because of a handicap" of the renter or buyer or those associated with him. The statute creates a claim on behalf of persons aggrieved by violation. The Haberers lived in a single family residence protected by restrictive covenants providing that only single-families (related persons) could live there. The Haberers agreed to sell to a "Developmental Services" organization, who intended to use the house as a group home for six unrelated and mentally disabled individuals. Neighbors, including Scott, became concerned. Before the sale took place, they brought suit in state court to enforce the covenant by enjoining the sale. The state court concluded that the proposed use would not violate the covenants and denied the request for injunction. The court also concluded that the action was not frivolous or meritless. After this suit was dismissed, the sale proceeded, some 19 days later than the original closing date. The United States, acting on behalf of the Haberers, then brought suit against Scott and other neighbors under the Fair Housing Act. *Held,* the United States is entitled to partial summary judgment. The defendants, though not acting in bad faith or frivolously, nevertheless by their suit made housing "unavailable" to persons because of their handicap.

1. Would the neighbors have been liable if they had picketed in exercise of their free speech rights and if the picketing had caused the same delay?

2. Does *Professional Real Estate Investors, Inc.* bear on the federal statute as interpreted in *United States v. Scott*?

WHITE v. LEE

227 F.3d 1214 (9th Cir. 2000)

REINHARDT, Circuit Judge....

On May 12, 1992, a local nonprofit housing developer, Resources for Community Development (RCD), applied for a use permit from Berkeley's Zoning Adjustment Board. RCD sought to convert the Bel Air Motel, a property on University Avenue, to a multi-family housing unit for homeless persons. The use permit required approval by both the Zoning Adjustment Board and the Berkeley City Council.

The plaintiffs lived close to the Bel Air Motel and were opposed to its proposed conversion. They expressed their opposition in a variety of ways. They wrote to the Berkeley City Council, spoke out before the Zoning Adjustment Board and at other public meetings, and published a newsletter with articles critical of the project. The front page of the February 1993 issue of the plaintiffs' newsletter, Flatland News, for example, contained an article titled "City Forcing Bel Air Project Down Our Throats." The plaintiffs discussed their opposition to the project with the local press and attempted to persuade merchants on University Avenue to oppose the Bel Air project also.

The Zoning Adjustment Board granted RCD its use permit on October 1, 1992. An appeal to the Berkeley City Council failed, by a 4–4 vote, in April 1993. That same month, a coalition in which plaintiffs were involved ("the Coalition of Neighborhood Groups Opposing the Bel Air Conversion") filed a lawsuit against Berkeley and RCD in state court.... It alleged that one of the Zoning Adjustment Board's members, Linda Maio, was also a member of RCD's board and, because of this conflict of interest, improperly participated in the Zoning Adjustment Board's hearings. [The plaintiffs ultimately lost the conflict of interest lawsuit but the developer encountered difficulties in financing.]

[Marianne Lawless, executive director of Housing Rights, Inc. ("HRI"), a Berkeley housing rights advocacy group, wrote the San Francisco office of HUD, complaining of discrimination by the neighbors who opposed the project, referring to flyers handed out by the neighbors. The neighbors are White and other plaintiffs in this action.]

The [plaintiffs'] flyers made a variety of points about the project. One, titled "Who are the Homeless?", showed a pie chart dividing the homeless into three, presumably discrete categories—economic, mentally ill, and substance abusers—and complained about the "inequitable distribution" of Berkeley housing and services for the homeless in poor areas or commercial corridors "with high ethnic concentrations." Another listed projects planned for the area near the intersection of University and Shattuck Avenues, stated that these projects would provide beds for "90 mentally ill and 90 'stabilized' substance abusers," and concluded,

"This is commercial suicide! Impacts MUST be assessed!" A third flyer contended that inadequate information had been provided about the Bel Air project for the Berkeley City Council to make a "fair, complete and proper evaluation"; regarding the project's tenant population, it stated, "At least 71% will be homeless, but no details as to mentally ill, substance abusers, dual diagnosis, etc." ...

[T]he local HUD office drafted an administrative complaint asserting that HRI had been "[i]ntimidated, interfered [with], or coerced ... to keep [HRI] from the full benefit of the Federal Housing Law" and that the plaintiffs had engaged in discrimination on the basis of mental handicap....

In early November 1993, the San Francisco Office sent letters to White, Deringer, and Graham. The office enclosed HRI's complaint and stated that the plaintiffs could file an answer within ten days. HUD, the letters stated, would "commence an investigation of this complaint, and simultaneously encourage all parties involved to conciliate the matter." If conciliation failed and HUD's investigation produced "evidence to substantiate a finding that there is reasonable cause to believe that you have engaged in an unlawful discriminatory housing practice," HUD would issue a charge against them, at which point they would be exposed to certain penalties—including damages as great as $100,000—and could elect to have their case heard by an administrative law judge or referred for trial in U.S. District Court. The plaintiffs filed answers to the complaint on November 12.

[The court recited details of HUD's effort to stop the plaintiffs from speaking. The immediately following paragraph is a summary taken from a later portion of the opinion.]

The HUD officials carried out an investigation that lasted more than eight months, substantially longer than the presumptive 100–day time limit set by [statute]. During the investigation, defendant Zurowski conveyed a conciliation proposal requiring the plaintiffs to cease all litigation and publications regarding the Bel Air project and advised the plaintiffs to accept it because they had violated the Fair Housing Act by distributing "discriminatory" flyers. Defendants Lee and Smith directed the plaintiffs under threat of subpoena to produce all their publications regarding the Bel Air project, minutes of relevant meetings, correspondence with other organizations, and the names, addresses, and telephone numbers of persons who were involved in or had witnessed the alleged discriminatory conduct. Smith interrogated the plaintiffs, again under threat of subpoena, about their views and public statements in opposition to the Bel Air project. In a letter drafted by Smith, defendant Gillespie asserted HUD's purported authority to investigate "allegations that individuals have engaged in speech advocating illegal acts, including discrimination against persons based on their physical or mental disabilities" and stated that the plaintiffs had violated the Fair Housing Act by writing "news articles which referenced the mental disability of the intended residents of the proposed project as a reason for denial of the project." Defendant Phillips told a major metropolitan newspaper that the plaintiffs had "broken the law." We conclude that these actions would have chilled or silenced a person of ordinary firmness from engaging in future First Amendment activities....

[The Washington office of HUD ultimately concluded that there were no grounds to proceed and the matter was dropped.]

The plaintiffs filed their complaint in May 1995. They alleged that defendants Gillespie, Smith, Lee, Zurowski, and Phillips investigated and harassed them solely because of the exercise of their First Amendment rights to free speech and to petition the government for a redress of grievances. The plaintiffs sued these defendants in their official and individual capacities, pursuant to Bivens v. Six Unknown Named Agents of Federal Bureau of Narcotics, 403 U.S. 388, 91 S.Ct. 1999, 29 L.Ed.2d 619 (1971), and requested declaratory and injunctive relief, damages, and attorneys' fees. They sued defendant Julian only in her official capacity, for declaratory and injunctive relief....

[The trial court granted summary judgment for the plaintiff on the issue of liability.]

Here, the plaintiffs wrote and distributed flyers and published a newsletter in the advocacy of a politically controversial viewpoint—"the essence of First Amendment expression." They organized and participated in a coalition of neighbors who shared their views, admirable or not. The right to expressive association includes the right to pursue, as a group, discriminatory policies that are antithetical to the concept of equality for all persons. See Boy Scouts of America v. Dale, 530 U.S. 640, 659–61, 120 S.Ct. 2446, 2457–58, 147 L.Ed.2d 554 (2000).

The First Amendment also guarantees the right "to petition the Government for a redress of grievances." The plaintiffs exercised this right by attending and speaking out at Zoning Adjustment Board hearings and by challenging in the courts the board's decision to grant a use permit for the Bel Air project. Regardless of what we might think of their objectives, the plaintiffs "were doing what citizens should be encouraged to do, taking an active role in the decisions of government."

It is important to emphasize that a person's speech or petitioning activity is not removed from the ambit of First Amendment protection simply because it advocates an unlawful act. The First Amendment does not permit government "to forbid or proscribe advocacy of the use of force or of law violation except where such advocacy is directed to inciting or producing imminent lawless action and is likely to incite or produce such action"....

The investigation by the HUD officials unquestionably chilled the plaintiffs' exercise of their First Amendment rights....

[Officials also argued that their investigation was justified by the neighbors' state-court-conflict-of-interest lawsuit.]

With respect to petitions brought in the courts, the Supreme Court has held that a lawsuit is unprotected only if it is a "sham"—i.e., "objectively baseless in the sense that no reasonable litigant could realistically expect success on the merits. . . ."

Applying these principles to the present case, it follows that the plaintiffs' state-court lawsuit could have amounted to a discriminatory housing practice only in the event that (1) no reasonable litigant could have realistically expected success on the merits, and (2) the plaintiffs filed the suit for the purpose of coercing, intimidating, threatening, or interfering with a person's exercise of rights protected by the FHA. Because, in the present case, the first requirement cannot be sustained, we need not even consider the second. . . . The lawsuit filed by the plaintiffs was unquestionably not objectively baseless. Far from it: it challenged a rather egregious conflict of interest by a person who was simultaneously a member of both the Zoning Adjustment Board and the board for the developer seeking the Bel Air use permit. . . .

We agree that the San Francisco Office was justified in accepting HRI's complaint. Furthermore, the mere fact that the officials provided the plaintiffs with a copy of HRI's complaint and informed them of their rights and duties under the FHA, pursuant to § 3610(a)(1)(B)(ii), did not in itself violate the plaintiffs' rights under the First Amendment. As we have explained earlier, however, the critical issue is not whether the HUD officials were justified in accepting HRI's complaint and initiating some form of limited investigation, but whether the manner in which they actually conducted their eight-month investigation violated the plaintiffs' First Amendment rights. . . .

Because the plaintiffs' lawsuit could have been actionable under the FHA if and only if it were a sham, the officials were obligated to first determine that the suit was objectively baseless before proceeding with any potentially chilling investigation into the plaintiffs' protected speech and other petitioning activity—even for the stated purpose of determining whether the plaintiffs had filed the suit with an unlawful discriminatory intent. . . .

The HUD officials completely failed to satisfy this threshold requirement. From the time they initiated their investigation until the time they submitted their final report to the Washington office, the officials made little or no effort to investigate the basis for the plaintiffs' suit. Instead, their investigation focused almost exclusively on what the officials considered to be the plaintiffs' discriminatory speech. . . .

For the reasons stated, we affirm all the rulings of the district court challenged on the appeals and cross-appeal.

Buster v. George W. Moore, Inc., 438 Mass. 635, 783 N.E.2d 399 (2003). Defendants, collectively called Duffy, acquired various properties over many years and eventually had a package of property together for building a retail shopping center. The plaintiff, Buster, owed property abutting the proposed shopping center. The plaintiff intended development of his property for commercial tenants. The town conservation commission heard Buster's objection that his property would be adversely affected, but eventually gave appropriate approval to Duffy's shopping center. Buster appealed and obtained a stay of the approval that could delay work on the shopping center for up to three years while appeals went forward. Duffy, considering the appeals to be economic blackmail, learned that the plaintiff's property was mortgaged and that Buster was in default on the mortgage. Duffy purchased the note and mortgage from the mortgagee and then proposed a foreclosure, but offered to forbear if Buster would drop the appeal and permit the shopping center development to proceed. Buster rejected this proposal and the defendants then began foreclosure proceedings. Before the foreclosure sale, however, Buster filed for bankruptcy which triggered an automatic stay of the foreclosure. Duffy then moved to lift the stay, and while that motion was pending, they instigated a safety inspection of the plaintiff's property by the town. The town found various and serious violations; it ordered all construction to stop on the plaintiff's property and also elimination of all occupancy. Thereupon Buster stipulated to lift the foreclosure stay, to drop the appeals delaying the defendant's shopping center development, and to accept in exchange a reduction of Buster's obligations on the note now owed by the defendants. Buster then filed this action against defendants claiming, among other things, (a) violation of a state civil rights statute by means of threats and coercion and (b) violation of state deceptive practices legislation.

Held, summary judgment for defendants affirmed.

(1) *Civil rights.* Economic coercion may be actionable under the state civil rights act, but not in this case. "The defendants were lawfully entitled to foreclose and it made economic sense to do so. Although they were willing to 'trade' foreclosure for a deal involving Buster's voluntary dismissal of all appeals, the offer to negotiate on those terms could not be deemed 'threats, intimidation or coercion' where the proffered deal potentially put the plaintiffs in a better position than they would have been in relation to a more 'disinterested' holder of the mortgage.... 'Generally, by itself, a threat to use lawful means to reach an intended result is not actionable [under the civil rights statute].' ... Although we must await subsequent cases to determine more exactly the actionable bounds of economic coercion under the act, economic loss occasioned by a plaintiff's own conduct, such as when the plaintiff defaults on a note and mortgage, is beyond these bounds."

(2) *Deceptive practices statute.* Buster argued that unfair competition, deceptive practices statute was violated (a) by Duffy's purchase of the note and mortgage and (b) by instigating inspection of Buster's property without revealing the true motives for doing so. As to the first argument, Duffy "initially sought, acquired, and utilized a legitimate competitive advantage to weaken Buster's economic position" but that does not lead to the conclusion that the Duffys acted unfairly or deceptively, particularly where, as we have seen, the plaintiffs' business vulnerabilities were so clearly the result of their own conduct. It has long been noted that the market is a rough and tumble place where a competitor's lack of courtesy, generosity, or respect is neither uncommon nor in itself unlawful." Instigation of inspection is not actionable either.

"As mortgagees of the property, the Duffys had an obvious, independent, and legitimate business interest in limiting their own liability. They chose a traditional means to do so—having city inspectors determine whether the mortgagor was complying with applicable safety codes."

The *Buster* court made no mention of either abuse of process or the Massachusetts SLAPP statute.

Alternatives to the Traditional Actions

What alternatives are there to tort suits for various forms of unjustified litigation? Consider the following:

1. There are a number of situations in which you can seek a "provisional remedy"—that is, a remedy before you actually have a trial and establish your right. Examples are temporary restraining orders, preliminary injunctions, receivers appointed before trial, attachments and garnishments before trial and the like. In most of these cases statutes require that, in order to obtain such a remedy, you must post a bond to guarantee payment of damages suffered by the defendant in case it turns out on trial that you really were not entitled to the remedy. Damages in such cases include attorney fees, but not damages for emotional harm or other presumed damages. Liability, in effect, is strict; but in most states it is limited to the amount set in the bond approved by the judge before the remedy is granted. See Dobbs, *Should Security be Required as a pre-Condition to Provisional Injunctive Relief*, 52 N.C.L. Rev. 1091 (1974).

2. Some cases seem to have extended strict liability to such cases even where no bond has been imposed. See *Braun v. Pepper*, 224 Kan. 56, 578 P.2d 695 (1978) (receiver appointed before trial, honest and reasonable mistake but liability imposed); Cf. *Smith v. Coronado Foothills Estates Homeowners Assn., Inc.*, 117 Ariz. 171, 571 P.2d 668 (1977) (temporary restraining order, liability not limited to the amount of the bond).

3. Although the general rule in America holds that the losing party in litigation is not required to pay the winner's attorney fees, there are several exceptions. Indeed, the tort suit for unjustified litigation is one of those exceptions. Suppose the plaintiff sues under a statute which allows the prevailing party to recover attorney fees. Suppose the plaintiff then loses. Does the existence of a statutory right to attorney fees in favor of the prevailing defendant suggest that the defendant could not recover for unjustified litigation? What if the defendant recovers attorney fees by motion in the case and then brings a separate suit for malicious prosecution?

4. Would it be better to dispense with the tort suit altogether and simply deal with the problem of unjustified litigation by assessing

attorney fees against the losing party at the end of the unjustified litigation?

5. To what extent can a claim for infliction of emotional distress be substituted for a malicious prosecution claim, or, for that matter, for a defamation claim? In *Sacco v. High Country Independent Press Inc.*, 271 Mont. 209, 896 P.2d 411 (1995), the plaintiff's former employer and its shareholders told a police officer that Sacco had stolen photographs and proof sheets from the erstwhile employer. Then they or some of them informed others as well. Criminal charges were filed as a result and later terminated in Sacco's favor. The court permitted the plaintiff to proceed on (a) a claim for malicious prosecution, (b) a claim for defamation, and (c) a claim for negligence and/or intentional infliction of emotional distress. See also *Sands v. Living Word Fellowship,* 34 P.3d 955 (Alaska 2001). Can you comment?

Chapter 9

INTERFERENCE WITH FAMILY RELATIONSHIPS

§ 1. ALIENATION OF AFFECTIONS AND CRIMINAL CONVERSATION

DAN B. DOBBS, THE LAW OF TORTS § 441 (2000)[1]

Criminal conversation. Criminal conversation merely meant adultery or sexual relations. The defendant who engaged in adultery with the plaintiff's spouse would be liable to the plaintiff. The authorities state the elements of the tort with almost alarming simplicity: the tort is said to consist of having sexual relations with one spouse. "The fact that the wife consented, that she was the aggressor, that she represented herself as single, that she was mistreated or neglected by her husband, that she and her husband were separated through no fault of her own, or that her husband was impotent, were not valid defenses." The only defense was the nonparticipating spouse's own consent. In other words, the defendant was liable to the husband although he had committed no tort to the wife and was guilty of no fraud, force, or deception.

Alienation of affections. If the defendant deprived one spouse of the other's affections but did not engage in sexual relations, that, too, became a tort by the latter half of 19th century. The defendant here must ordinarily have known of the marital relationship and acted for the purpose of affecting it adversely, but neither sexual nor romantic involvement was required. Indeed, the defendant could be held liable though he was only a minister or a family member who, without a privilege, urged one spouse to leave the other....

Abolishing the torts. Criminal conversation and alienation of affections have now been abolished in the great majority of states, either by explicit legislation or by judicial decision. Only four or five states have continued to give full scope to the alienation action and some of those have abolished the criminal conversation claim.

1. Footnotes omitted.

1. **Saving families?** William R. Corbett, *A Somewhat Modest Proposal to Prevent Adultery and Save Families: Two Old Torts Looking for a New Career,* 33 ARIZ. ST. L.J. 985 (2001), argues against total abolition of the torts. He thinks that a revised and more modest version of the torts should be recognized. His proposed revision would require adultery and knowledge by the defendant that the adulterous partner was married. Professor Corbett argues that recognizing such a tort would "prevent adultery and save families."

HELSEL V. NOELLSCH, D.C., 107 S.W.3d 231 (Mo. 2003). Suit by former wife against husband's paramour for alienation of actions. *Held*, the action is abolished in Missouri. "The original justification for the tort of alienation of affection lies in the antiquated concept that husbands had a proprietary interest in the person and services of their wives. Although modern courts no longer justify the tort of alienation of affection in these terms, the tort has remained fundamentally unchanged . . . Even though the original property concepts remain inextricably bound to the tort, some still argue that suits for alienation of affection must be retained as a useful means of preserving marriages and protecting families. While these are laudable goals, it is unlikely that suits for alienation of affection actually serve this purpose. First, suits for alienation of affection are almost exclusively brought after the marriage is either legally dissolved or irretrievably broken. Revenge, not reconciliation, is the often the primary motive."

2. **Where the actions are still viable.** In a few states, the alienation of affection action or the criminal conversation action or both have been retained. They can be enforced with vigor. In *Jones v. Swanson,* 341 F.3d 723 (8th Cir. 2003), applying South Dakota law, the jury awarded a husband compensatory and punitive damages of $450,000 and $500,000 respectively against a defendant who had an affair with his wife, even though the wife had pursued another man and had for months expressed dissatisfaction with her husband and a desire for divorce. The court did reduce damages on both counts to a total of $400,000. In *Nunn v. Allen,* 154 N.C.App. 523, 574 S.E.2d 35 (2002), the plaintiff's wife had long since ceased sleeping in the same room as her husband and had actually separated from him with a formal agreement in September. There was some evidence that she had a sexual relationship with the defendant just before the formal separation agreement and afterward. The court upheld a judgment for the husband against the paramour, saying that post-separation conduct could support an inference of pre-separation alienation, and a claim for criminal conversation could be based on post-separation sexual relations.

FIGUEIREDO-TORRES V. NICKEL, 321 Md. 642, 584 A.2d 69 (1991). H and W sought marriage counseling from the defendant, a psychologist. The defendant allegedly used his counseling with W to embark on a sexual relationship with her, which led to dissolution of the marriage defendant had been retained to improve. The state has abolished both criminal conversation and alienation of affections actions. *Held,* the plaintiff stated valid claims for (1) professional malpractice and (2) intentional infliction of emotional distress. "[T]he allegations of improper sexual conduct set forth in Torres' complaint may constitute criminal conversation; however, if in addition, the sexual activity violated the professional standard of care which Nickel owed to Torres, it is sufficient to support a cause of action for professional negligence.... The defendant was not 'the milkman, the mailman, or the guy next door'; he was [the plaintiff's] psychologist and marriage counselor."

3. **A distinction.** Suppose that in *Figueiredo-Torres,* only the wife had been the defendant's patient—same result?

4. **Claims independent of family relationship.** Abolition of the tort actions for alienation does not logically bar claims based upon some duty independent of the family relationship. For instance, defamation may be actionable even though defamation of a spouse may alienate the other spouse's affections. *Ellis v. Price,* 337 Ark. 542, 990 S.W.2d 543 (1999). But what about a claim for emotional distress based on the defendant's intentional alienation of affections or criminal conversation? See *Quinn v. Walsh,* 49 Mass. App. Ct. 696, 732 N.E.2d 330 (2000). Or a claim for emotional distress based on the allegation that the wife misrepresented for 12 years that the husband was the father of the wife's child? In *Day v. Heller,* 264 Neb. 934, 653 N.W.2d 475 (2002) the court rejected that claim on policy grounds—that a trial would put the child at the center of litigation to the detriment of his best interests.

§ 2. ABDUCTION, HARBORING, OR ALIENATION OF CHILDREN

5. **Enticement or abduction of a spouse.** A defendant who abducts the plaintiff's spouse is liable to the direct victim for any tort (such as false imprisonment) committed against her. He is also liable to the spouse of the direct victim. Where alienation remains actionable, the same is true when he merely entices one spouse to leave the other, since that is essentially a form of alienation of affections. Dan B. Dobbs, The Law of Torts § 441 (2000).

6. **Enticing, abducting or harboring a minor; interference with custody rights.** When the minor child is enticed, or abducted, or "harbored," the parents having custody of the child are entitled by common law or statute to recover. See Dan B. Dobbs, supra, § 443. Damages nowadays may include awards for the parents' distress, their loss of the child's society, and the expenses incurred in recovering custody as well as punitive damages in an appropriate case.

Wolf v. Wolf, 690 N.W.2d 887 (Iowa 2005). Timothy and Joan were parents of Ashley, who was born in 1985. In 1990 the parents divorced. Iowa courts initially awarded joint custody with primary care to Joan, but later awarded primary care to Timothy, who has been entitled to the physical custody continuously since 1998. Joan moved to Arizona with Ashley and asked Arizona courts to award her primary care. They refused. Joan and Ashley remained in Arizona. In 2000, Timothy, armed with a writ of habeas corpus, went to Arizona and retrieved Ashley, taking her back to Iowa. After less than two months, Joan had provided Ashley with a plane ticket, cell phone, and credit card, thus securing her return to Arizona. Arizona courts again refused to alter the primary care. Joan then filed a petition in the Iowa courts to give her primary care and appeared in Iowa to testify. The judge ordered her to remain in Iowa until the rights of the parties were determined, and she promised to do so, but in fact she fled with Ashley back to Arizona. The judge confirmed primary care in Timothy. Timothy then sued Joan in tort. The trial judge awarded compensatory and punitive damages against Joan. *Held,* liability for compensatory and punitive damages affirmed. One who abducts, compels, or induces a minor child to leave a parent legally entitled either to custody or to primary care, is subject to liability, both under common law and statute. The tort claim "can, more effectively than any of the alternative sanctions [such as the Uniform Child Custody Jurisdiction Act, kidnaping prosecution, and contempt], serve both to prevent child-snatching and to pick up the pieces if it does occur."

7. **Suits parents and their allies.** Most courts have allowed the victimized parent with custodial rights to recover against the parental kidnaper and or those who aid and abet the kidnaper. E.g., *Weirich v. Weirich,* 833 S.W.2d 942 (Tex. 1992). However, a Minnesota case rejected the action on the ground that litigation might not be in the child's best interests. *Larson v. Dunn,* 460 N.W.2d 39 (Minn. 1990). In turn, *Stone v. Wall,* 734 So.2d 1038 (Fla. 1999) rejected *Larson* with the observation "those who would bypass the legal system by taking children from those who have a superior right to legal custody cause a far greater affront to our system of justice. Such conduct has the potential for causing far greater harm to the children than litigation." The court went on to quote another judge, saying that "[i]f one principle stands paramount in our system of jurisprudence, it is that no one person, mother, father, president or pauper stands above the law." One comment on *Larson* suggested that the conflict in the cases "may represent a conflict of two legal cultures, one associated with tort practice and emphasizing rights and responsibilities, the other associated with family law practice and emphasizing a kind of social work role for judges and court staff." DAN B. DOBBS, supra § 443.

8. **Parents without custody.** Courts have given little recognition to rights of the parent who lacks custody, or, as in *Wolf,* the right of primary care. In many states, then, the custodial parent is free to interfere with court-ordered visitation rights. Should courts distinguish between the minor guerrilla warfare between divorced parents and a sustained deprival of a child over a period of months or years?

9. **Seduction of a minor child.** "When a minor female child was seduced, old common law recognized a claim by the father both for medical expenses and/or loss of his daughter's services resulting from the seduction. The seduction claim belonged to the father, not the child. The loss of services here became the fictional basis of the action which in reality was a reflection of judicial outrage coupled with the belief that the father had legal rights in his female children. Social change brought more independence to women and procedural reforms required suit to be brought by the real party in interest. After these changes, and sometimes as a result of explicit statutes, courts began to permit the seduced woman to bring her own suit. The effect was to convert the relational injury claim into a kind of battery claim, or perhaps one for fraud, but either way to be pursued by the immediate victim. In a battery claim, the plaintiff's valid consent would bar the claim, but not if the consent had been procured by fraud." DOBBS, supra, § 443.

10. **Kidnaping statutes.** Statutes dealing with the parental kidnaping problem are mostly procedural and jurisdictional. When parents take a kidnaped child across state lines or international boundaries, courts in their new home may modify the original custody decree so that it is now favorable to the kidnaper. Contemporary statutes attempt to stop this kind of modification and to give courts more powers in dealing with the kidnaper. A federal statute, The Parental Kidnaping Prevention Act, 28 U.S.C.A. § 1738A, attempts to limit second state second guessing of custody decrees. It also authorizes FBI assistance in locating felonious parent-kidnapers, and the use of some limited federal information that may assist in locating the felon. Two Uniform Acts deal with the subject as well. The first and older is the Uniform Child Custody Jurisdiction Act, some form of which is adopted in all states. The second is the Uniform Child Custody Jurisdiction & Enforcement Act. Both attempt to give and limit jurisdiction of courts to second guess the original decree. Details are left for the courses in Family Law.

11. **International kidnaping.** International kidnaping is also a serious problem. An international convention attempts to deal with it. The United States is a signatory. 42 U.S.C.A. § 11601 et seq. (providing procedures for implementing the Convention on Civil Aspects of International Child Abduction). Children wrongfully removed from one country ordinarily are to be repatriated unless that would put the child at grave risk.

12. **Alienation of a child's affections.** What about an action for alienation of a child's affections without actually enticing the child away from her family? In *Bouchard v. Sundberg,* 80 Conn.App. 180, 834 A.2d 744 (2003), the court held that a statute abolishing the alienation action generally had the effect of abolishing any action for alienation of a child's affection, too. One line of cases involves therapists who, allegedly, help a grown child create false memories of abuse. See DOBBS, supra, § 444.

*

Part II

INTANGIBLE HARMS PRIMARILY TO ECONOMIC INTERESTS

An Introduction to Economic Torts

Part II continues to look at torts that do not cause physical harms to the plaintiff or the plaintiff's property, although we'll see some cases in which the plaintiff suffers stand-alone economic harm because some *other* person's property is physically damaged.

Lawyers who deal with economic torts need to know defamation law, if for no other reason than because hundreds, perhaps thousands of cases, assert both defamation and some economic tort. Yet, Part II differs from Part I in significant ways. Although the torts in Part I often caused economic harm, they were also often suffused with highly personal elements related to emotional distress or a sense of personal dignity. In Part II, we turn to the other side of the coin—to torts that primarily involve stand-alone economic harm, and only secondarily involve highly personal harm—except, of course, in the sense that loss of money is always distressing.

Some recurring themes

One or two issues recur through various chapters in Part II. The free speech or First Amendment issues we saw in Part I will crop up again in Part II, but perhaps with less force and pervasiveness, because commercial speech is usually given somewhat less protection. Another issue we've touched on will also appear in Part II—what to do about tort theories that overlap with other tort theories. For instance, if defamation law says "no" to a claim, can the plaintiff perhaps still prevail by claiming tortious interference with contract arising out of the same defamatory communication?

Another important issue in Part II is to determine the basis of liability. This is an issue in all tort law, of course, since the law must always determine what kind of fault is required to establish liability or whether any fault is required. But with economic torts in a free society, where people are expected to seek their own economic betterment, what counts as fault is not necessarily a straightforward matter. In fact, what counts as a "right" that should be protected against interference can itself be deeply disputed.

A new issue related to the determination of economic rights is more focused and it will appear repeatedly in Part II. Does tort law trump contract law, or vice versa? For instance, where plaintiff and defendant are in a contractual relationship, does the contract limit the plaintiff's rights, or does she have a tort claim that trumps the contract limitations? And, sometimes relatedly, we will ask whether negligence without more will ever suffice to support a tort claim for stand-alone economic loss.

The tort-contract question is now often expressed by accepting, rejecting, or qualifying "the economic loss rule." We have resisted the temptation to introduce Part II with a chapter on the economic loss rule because we believe the application or rejection of rule becomes meaningful, mainly in particular situations that will appear from time to time as we move through Part II. However, although different thinkers may hold different conceptions of the rule, there is no need to be mysterious about its main outlines. The economic loss rule tells us that, at least where the plaintiff and defendant are in a contractual relationship, tort claims arising out of the contract matters are not to be permitted. As you might expect, any rule that broad may turn out to have exceptions, or at least qualifications.

Along with the themes we've summarized here, there are plenty of important legal rules, and some of them require comparisons or contrasts with materials in Part I. We begin with a claim that looks a little like an unusual form of a defamation claim.

Chapter 10

SOME NOMINATE TORTS—DISPARAGEMENT, BAD FAITH, FIDUCIARY BREACH AND CONVERSION OF INTANGIBLES

With this chapter, we begin to examine harms that are primarily economic or commercial in nature. We do not consider all such torts here; some specific wrongs are considered later in special settings, such as those associated with intellectual property, unfair competition, misrepresentation, or lawyer malpractice. As elsewhere in this book, we are concerned with non-physical harms only, not, for example, with economic harm resulting to the plaintiff from her own personal injury or property damage.

It is important here to notice that in this chapter, the conduct forbidden is defined (although sometimes somewhat broadly). That will contrast with some of the rules we'll see in the next chapter, where some perfectly lawful conduct is actionable, provided only that the defendant intended economic harm to result.

§ 1. INJURIOUS FALSEHOOD

GREGORY'S, INC. v. HAAN

545 N.W.2d 488 (S.D. 1996)

KONENKAMP, Justice.

Charles Haan built and sold homes in Watertown. Northland Building Center supplied materials for Haan's housing projects and even acted as general contractor in some instances. Haan and Northland had agreed that payment for materials supplied to Haan would not be due upon receipt, but when the matter came to court the parties contradicted each other on precisely when Haan's payments were due. According to Northland, when the homes were "done and enclosed" Haan was to settle his account. Haan contends the accounts were not due until after the homes were completed and sold and after Northland gave a thirty day "notice of request for payment." Haan also asserts Northland agreed not to file a materialman's lien until after giving Haan a thirty-day notice. These agreements, Haan concedes, were "all oral."

On January 6, 1993 when Haan sold one of the homes for which Northland had supplied materials, he spent the sale proceeds without satisfying his account. He sold another house on January 29, again without settling his account. Haan claims Northland agreed to defer payment and forbear filing liens until March 15, 1993. Nonetheless, in February, Northland filed materialman's liens against the two properties for which it had supplied materials. On March 12, Northland also filed a lien against lots five and six and the east two feet of lot four in block six of Haan's First Addition. Indisputably, lot six was vacant and unimproved; however, Northland asserts lot six was connected to lot five and the east two feet of lot four, for which it supplied materials. Northland filed a lien on Haan's personal home too, but it had supplied no labor or materials on that property for over two years. The right to file a lien statement ceases at the end of 120 days after the last labor or materials were supplied.

As a result of these lien filings, Haan alleges his lenders cancelled his credit line, two home buyers sued him for breach of warranty of title, and he lost money on other projects in progress. Northland brought suit to enforce the liens and collect Haan's arrearages. Haan counterclaimed: Count I alleged breach of contract based upon the thirty-day notice agreements; Count II alleged "slander of title" for the liens on lot six and Haan's home ... The trial court granted Northland's summary judgment motion on Count I and dismissed the remaining counts....

[The South Dakota statute provided that agreements for an extension of credit are not enforceable unless in writing.] [W]e conclude Haan's alleged thirty-day notice agreements with Northland were contracts for further extensions of credit. Delaying payment for thirty days beyond a "notice of request for payment" or suspending the right to file a lien for thirty days after notice, effectively defers collecting or enforcing a debt. Thus Haan sought damages for the breach of an unenforceable oral contract for an extension of credit. SDCL 53–8–2. We uphold the trial court's grant of summary judgment on Count I .....

Will the common law support a disparagement of title claim in South Dakota?.... This Court has specifically recognized a slander of title cause of action for filing a false mechanic's lien.... Other states have likewise recognized this action at common law. The rule is expressed in Restatement (Second) Torts (1977):

> § 623A. Liability for Publication of Injurious Falsehood—General Principle.
>
> One who publishes a false statement harmful to the interests of another is subject to liability for pecuniary loss resulting to the other if

(a) he intends for publication of the statement to result in harm to interests of the other having a pecuniary value, or either recognizes or should recognize that it is likely to do so, and

(b) he knows that the statement is false or acts in reckless disregard of its truth or falsity.

§ 624. Disparagement of Property—Slander of Title.

The rules on liability for the publication of an injurious falsehood stated in § 623A apply to the publication of a false statement disparaging another's property rights in land, chattels or intangible things, that the publisher should recognize as likely to result in pecuniary harm to the other through the conduct of third persons in respect to the other's interests in the property.

To establish disparagement of title, it must be shown that publication of the falsehood: (1) was derogatory to the title to plaintiff's property, its quality, or plaintiff's business in general, calculated to prevent others from dealing with plaintiff or to interfere with plaintiff's relations with others to plaintiff's disadvantage (often stated as malice); (2) was communicated to a third party; (3) materially or substantially induced others not to deal with plaintiff; and (4) resulted in special damage. W. PAGE KEETON ET AL., PROSSER AND KEETON ON THE LAW OF TORTS § 128 at 967 (5th Ed.1984). Haan's complaint stated a cause of action under the common law. Now the question is whether the filing of a false materialman's lien is privileged.

. . . Some jurisdictions deduce the filing of mechanic's lien is part of a judicial proceeding [hence possibly subject to the absolute privilege]. In South Dakota, a materialman's lien may be ancillary to judicial action—the filing is a prerequisite to a lien foreclosure. Still, a lawsuit will not necessarily follow from filing a lien and often does not. Yet the lien may remain a valid encumbrance on the property for many years and the property owner must take action to force its removal. We conclude the filing of materialman's lien is not a judicial proceeding, so the privilege accorded under SDCL 20–11–5(2) will not apply. The law, however, indulges another privilege in these circumstances.

Many jurisdictions recognize a conditional privilege (sometimes expressed in different terms) to file good faith claims in the public records. The privilege is subsumed in the requirement that the person suing for disparagement of title must show malice or that the lien filer had an illegitimate purpose. Under this privilege, even if a lien filing was erroneous, it will not support a disparagement of title action if the person who filed acted in the reasonable belief that the filing was valid. Mere negligence in filing a false lien statement is insufficient to surmount the privilege; knowledge or reckless disregard of falsity is required. Northland's lien filings carry a conditional privilege and to overcome it Haan must show they were false and not filed in good faith.

The circuit court incorrectly dismissed Haan's disparagement of title counterclaim ruling the filing of the lien statements were absolutely privileged, when in fact a conditional privilege applied. We therefore reverse and remand for further proceedings consistent with this opinion.

1. **Injurious falsehood elements.** Historically, Hahn's claim was an "action on the case" for any special damages they could prove, provided they established that the defendant (1) had communicated (2) a false statement likely to cause pecuniary damages (3) with "malice"; (4) and that pecuniary harm resulted. Put differently, there must be either a knowing or reckless falsehood *or* spite, ill-will, or the like. This tort is now often called "injurious falsehood." In the form seen in *Gregory's Inc. v. Hahn,* it is more commonly called slander of title—"slander," even though the publication is in written form.

2. **Privilege talk.** Is there any reason at all to have a privilege destructible by bad faith if reckless falsehood or ill-will is required in the first place?

3. **A tort to intangible economic interests.** Injurious falsehood is sometimes conceived of as a tort to property interests, but no harm is done to the property. Rather, the harm comes in the form of interference with contract or economic opportunity. The slander of title version of injurious falsehood seen in *Gregory's* protects economic interests associated with clear title. An attack on the plaintiff's fee title is not required; a falsehood about the plaintiff's security interests might suffice. Likewise, any kind of "property," including intangible property, can be protected from the "slander of title." For instance, the plaintiff's interest in a trademark. See *Macia v. Microsoft Corp.,* 152 F.Supp.2d 535 (D. Vt. 2001).

4. **Recording claims against property: potential theories of liability.** In the specific case of slander of title by way of recording instruments that show an interest in the plaintiff's land, at least three theories might be invoked against one who records a *lis pendens** or asserts some similar claim affecting vendibility of the property. These are: (a) injurious falsehood, (b) wrongful civil proceedings/abuse of process, and (c) interference with contract. If a court uses the abuse of process or wrongful civil proceeding theory, it may circumvent the special damages requirement attached to slander of title cases. In *Ruiz v. Varan,* 110 N.M. 478, 797 P.2d 267 (1990), the court found a *lis pendens* notice actionable because there was no claim against the property, only a contract claim; "the only purpose the filing of the lis pendens served was to place a cloud upon the title . . . to force settlement of the claims of Mr. Ruiz," and that the filing was done with an ulterior motive. The court found "nominal" damages of $5,000, but no actual damages.

5. **Rejecting the absolute privilege to resort of judicial process.** Because recording a *lis pendens*, or a deed or an option, is a

* A statutory *lis pendens* is a formal notice, made part of property records, that a suit has been filed claiming some interest in specified property. It makes any purchaser of the property subject to the outcome of the pending suit. The result is very much like a lien on the property, since would-be purchasers will not normally go through with a purchase knowing that the lawsuit between other persons may affect title.

unilateral act, not resort to judicial process at all, such a filing would cloud title without judicial action. Should the privilege of resort to judicial process, so important in the wrongful civil proceedings case, be limited when the defendant can cause harm without adjudication? Some courts and legislatures think so. Thus one who knows his option to purchase land is void but who records it anyway, is liable for injurious falsehood of the slander of title variety. *Peckham v. Hirshfeld*, 570 A.2d 663 (R.I. 1990); cf. *Jeffrey v. Cathers,* 104 S.W.3d 424 (Mo. App. 2003) (filing wrongfully altered document to establish mechanic's lien). Statutes may impose a minimum damages award or treble damages. See Ariz. Rev. Stats. § 33–420; *Wyatt v. Wehmueller*, 167 Ariz. 281, 806 P.2d 870 (1991). Cf. *Lugar v. Edmondson Oil Co.*, 457 U.S. 922, 102 S.Ct. 2744, 73 L.Ed.2d 482 (1982) (attachment of property before judgment could be unconstitutional deprivation of property actionable under civil rights statute).

6. **Applying the absolute privilege to use judicial process.** But some courts have invoked the absolute judicial privilege. *General Elec. Co. v. Sargent & Lundy*, 916 F.2d 1119 (6th Cir. 1990) (presuit statements protected). When so invoked, it defeats a claim of wrongful *lis pendens*, whether it is asserted on an abuse of process theory, *Kopp v. Franks*, 792 S.W.2d 413, 425 (Mo. App. 1990), or on a slander of title theory. *Stewart v. Fahey,* 14 Ariz. App. 149, 481 P.2d 519 (1971). Similarly, the absolute privilege, or a qualified one, has been invoked to defeat interference with contract claims based on *lis pendens* filings. See *Westfield Development Co. v. Rifle Investment Associates*, 786 P.2d 1112 (1990) (qualified privilege to file notice of *lis pendens* offered protection in interference with contract claim.); *Levin, Middlebrooks, Mabie, Thomas, Mayes & Mitchell v. United States Fire Ins. Co.*, 639 So.2d 606 (Fla. 1994) (absolute privilege in interference claim, although case did not involve injurious falsehood).

AUVIL v. CBS "60 MINUTES"

67 F.3d 816 (9th Cir. 1995)

PER CURIAM....

On February 26, 1989, CBS's weekly news show "60 Minutes" aired a segment on daminozide, a chemical growth regulator sprayed on apples.... Scientific research had indicated that daminozide, more commonly known by its trade name, Alar, breaks down into unsymmetrical dimethylhydrazine (UDMH), a carcinogen.

The segment opened with the following capsule summary from Ed Bradley, a "60 Minutes" commentator: The most potent cancer-causing agent in our food supply is a substance sprayed on apples to keep them on the trees longer and make them look better. That's the conclusion of a number of scientific experts. And who is most at risk? Children, who may someday develop cancer from this one chemical called daminozide. Daminozide, which has been sprayed on apples for more than 20 years, breaks down into another chemical called UDMH....

Following the "60 Minutes" broadcast, consumer demand for apples and apple products decreased dramatically. The apple growers and others dependent upon apple production lost millions of dollars. Many of the growers lost their homes and livelihoods.

In November 1990, eleven Washington State apple growers, representing some 4,700 growers in the Washington area, filed a complaint in Washington State Superior Court against CBS, local CBS affiliates, the NRDC, and Fenton Communications, Inc., a public relations firm used by the NRDC in 1989. The growers asserted, among others, a claim for product disparagement.

... The district court denied the growers' motions but granted summary judgment to CBS because the growers did not produce evidence sufficient to create a triable issue of fact as to the falsity of the broadcast....

To establish a claim of product disparagement, also known as trade libel, a plaintiff must allege that the defendant published a knowingly false statement harmful to the interests of another and intended such publication to harm the plaintiff's pecuniary interests. Restatement (Second) of Torts § 623A. Accordingly, for a product disparagement claim to be actionable, the plaintiff must prove, inter alia, the falsity of the disparaging statements. See Restatement (Second) of Torts §§ 623A, 651(1)(c).

Existing case law on product disparagement provides little guidance on the falsity prong. Nonetheless, as a tort whose actionability depends on the existence of disparaging speech, the tort is substantively similar to defamation. Therefore, we reference defamation cases to arrive at a decision in the instant matter.

[The plaintiffs claimed that the CBS report was false in asserting that Alar was a "cancer-causing agent" and that it would cause cancer in thousands of children. They proved that "no studies have been conducted to test the relationship between ingestion of daminozide and incidence of cancer in humans." However, the court considered animal laboratory tests, which supported CBS, to be a legitimate means for assessing cancer risks in humans. Similarly, the absence of specific studies about cancer in children did not prove the falsity of the statement about them, especially since children consume more apples relative to body weight than adults.]

Despite their inability to prove that statements made during the broadcast were false, the growers assert that summary judgment for CBS was improper because a jury could find that the broadcast contained a provably false message, viewing the broadcast segment in its entirety. They further argue that, if they can prove the falsity of this implied message, they have satisfied their burden of proving falsity.

The growers' contentions are unavailing. Their attempt to derive a specific, implied message from the broadcast as a whole and to prove the falsity of that overall message is unprecedented and inconsistent with

Washington law. No Washington court has held that the analysis of falsity proceeds from an implied, disparaging message. It is the statements themselves that are of primary concern in the analysis. For example, in Lee v. Columbian, Inc., 64 Wash.App. 534, 826 P.2d 217 (1991), the plaintiff brought a defamation suit against a newspaper, claiming that the headline and lead sentence of a newspaper article defamed him. He conceded that both statements were true on their face; nevertheless, he argued that the statements were false and capable of defamatory meaning. He contended that "using irony and innuendo, the headline and lead sentence both strongly implied that Plaintiff was using a tax loophole to improperly reduce his taxes." The Washington Court of Appeals found the plaintiff's argument to be merit less because

> [d]efamatory meaning may not be imputed to true statements. The defamatory character of the language must be apparent from the words themselves. Washington courts are "bound to invest words with their natural and obvious meaning and may not extend language by innuendo or by the conclusions of the pleader."

The Washington courts' view finds support in the Restatement, which instructs that a product disparagement plaintiff has the burden of proving the "falsity of the statement." Restatement (Second) of Torts § 651(1)(c). This standard refers to individual statements and not to any overall message. Therefore, we must reject the growers' invitation to infer an overall message from the broadcast and determine whether that message is false.

We also note that, if we were to accept the growers' argument, plaintiffs bringing suit based on disparaging speech would escape summary judgment merely by arguing, as the growers have, that a jury should be allowed to determine both the overall message of a broadcast and whether that overall message is false. Because a broadcast could be interpreted in numerous, nuanced ways, a great deal of uncertainty would arise as to the message conveyed by the broadcast. Such uncertainty would make it difficult for broadcasters to predict whether their work would subject them to tort liability. Furthermore, such uncertainty raises the specter of a chilling effect on speech.

[Affirmed]

---

7. **Commercial disparagement; trade libel; Sirloin Slander.** *Auvil* represents the commercial disparagement, product disparagement, or trade libel form of injurious falsehood. "[F]ood suppliers have aggressively lobbied for and obtained legislation sometimes called veggie libel laws or sirloin slander bills. These statutes, using varied language, permit claims based upon false statements about food products. If the defendant publishes a statement that apples are sprayed with a product that can cause cancer and it turns out that the evidence does not support the cancer fear, the statute may permit *all* apple producers to sue for

damages. The statutes jeopardize all public discussion of health risks and consequently raise quite serious constitutional issues. Particular statutes differ, but to the extent that they permit a claim by individuals who are not referred to, fail to require knowing or reckless falsehood, put the burden of proving truth upon the defendant, or make opinion actionable, they run the risk of constitutional infringement. If the statutes do not run these constitutional risks, they may add little or nothing to the common law of injurious falsehood." 2 DOBBS ON TORTS § 407 (2001 & Supps.) (footnotes omitted). In *Texas Beef Group v. Winfrey,* 11 F.Supp.2d 858 (N.D. Tex. 1998), the plaintiffs were a number of Texas cattle growers suing Oprah Winfrey over a televised discussion of mad cow disease, although neither the growers nor even the State of Texas was mentioned in the discussion. The case ultimately went off on a finding that no knowingly false statements were made. *Texas Beef Group v. Winfrey,* 201 F.3d 680 (5th Cir. 2000).

8. **Distinguishing defamation—or not.** Would the claim against CBS be one for defamation rather than commercial disparagement if CBS had said the apple growers knew they were using a cancer-causing substance? In *Harwood Pharmacal Co. v. National Broadcasting Co.,* 9 N.Y.2d 460, 174 N.E.2d 602, 214 N.Y.S.2d 725 (1961), a television performer held up a package labeled Snooze, the name of the plaintiff's product. The performer allegedly said: "Snooze, the new aid for sleep. Snooze is full of all kinds of habit-forming drugs. Nothing short of a hospital cure will make you stop taking Snooze. You'll feel like a run-down hound dog and lose weight." The court said this was libel, not disparagement because it did not merely criticize the product; instead, it attributed misconduct to the manufacturer. Yet the distinction can be a fine one. This is reflected in the Digest's classification of injurious falsehood cases in the topic Libel and Slander. Courts themselves sometimes address disparagement or slander of title claims purely in terms of libel or slander. Cf. *Pro Golf Mfg., Inc. v. Tribune Review Newspaper Co.,* 570 Pa. 242, 809 A.2d 243 (2002) (Pennsylvania has generally called the tort libel or slander; the slander statute of limitations applies). Suppose the defendant impugns the plaintiff's credit. Libel or disparagement? See, e.g., *Student Loan Fund of Idaho, Inc. v. Duerner,* 131 Idaho 45, 951 P.2d 1272 (1998).

9. **Disparagement as unfair competition or violation of the Lanham Act.** Although disparagement is or has been a common law tort, state statutes regulating trade sometimes also create a statutory disparagement action, albeit under the name of unfair competition or deceptive trade practices. If that was not enough, Congress amended the basic federal trademark statute, effective in 1989, to create a federal cause of action for product disparagement. See 15 U.S.C. § 1125(a) [§ 43(a)], printed in Chapter 13, § 4 below. That statute only applies to "commercial" advertising about commercial activities, however, not, for example, to statements in an art magazine attacking the authenticity of art owned by the plaintiff. *Boule v. Hutton,* 328 F.3d 84 (2d Cir. 2003).

10. **Injurious falsehood and the Constitutional constraints on defamation.** The same First Amendment rules that limit recovery for defamation would presumably apply if the plaintiff turned out to be a public figure. See Chapter 3, ¶ 31. In *Suzuki Motor Corp. v. Consumers Union of United States, Inc.*, 330 F.3d 1110, 1133–34 (9th Cir. 2003), the court noted that "[t]he parties do not dispute that for Suzuki to recover in this case, it must, as a public-figure plaintiff, prove by clear and convincing evidence that CU published disparaging statements about the Samurai with actual malice." It cited with approval an earlier circuit court case for the proposition that claims for product disparagement "are subject to the same first amendment requirements that govern actions for defamation." Does it matter, or do the common law requirements for injurious falsehood already duplicate the *Times-Sullivan* rules requiring a knowing or reckless falsehood?

11. **The pecuniary damages requirement.** Independent of constitutional rules, tort law requires the plaintiff suing for injurious falsehood to prove not only that the defendant "maliciously" made a false statement but also that the plaintiff suffered special or pecuniary damages. This rule is not about the *amount* of recovery; without proof of pecuniary loss, the plaintiff has no cause of action at all. See *Rite Aid Corp. v. Lake Shore Inv.*, 298 Md. 611, 471 A. 2d 735 (1984). Some cases have required the plaintiff to prove pecuniary loss by adducing evidence of specific lost customers; the plaintiff's loss of business or diminution of the value of the plaintiff's business is insufficient. On the other hand, the rule might be avoided if the court is willing to say the claim is really one for libel or for slander per se with its presumed damages. See *Fashion Boutique of Short Hills, Inc. v. Fendi USA, Inc.*, 314 F.3d 48 (2d Cir. 2002). Perhaps in many states today, the specific customer rule would be obsolete where lawyers put on high quality evidence of real loss. Actually, specific losses are not always in the form of lost customers. In *Jeffrey v. Cathers*, 104 S.W.3d 424 (Mo. App. 2003), the court held that if slander of title prevented the plaintiff from obtaining funds to which he was otherwise entitled, and necessitated expenses to obtain those funds, the plaintiff would have a cause of action. See DAN B. DOBBS, THE LAW OF REMEDIES § 6.8(2) (2d ed. 1993) (hereafter DOBBS ON REMEDIES).

12. **Attorney fees.** The American Rule on attorney fees gives the prevailing party no claim against the losing party for attorney fees reasonably expended. Instead, the prevailing party recovers statutory "costs," relatively small sums listed in the governing statute. However, with a few torts, courts recognize that the core harm to the plaintiff is the cost of litigation necessitated by the defendant's tortious acts. Malicious prosecution is an example. So is slander of title. In the latter, the plaintiff can recover the reasonable costs of clearing title or otherwise reducing the harm done by the disparagement, including attorney fees. Attorney fees so incurred count as special, pecuniary damages, too. *Paidar v. Hughes*, 615 N.W.2d 276 (Minn. 2000).

§ 2. BAD FAITH BREACH OF CONTRACT AS A TORT

13. **The implied promise of good faith; tort and contract.** The Restatement of Contracts states as a rule of law that "[e]very contract imposes upon each party a duty of good faith and fair dealing in its performance and its enforcement." RESTATEMENT (SECOND) OF CONTRACTS § 205 (1981). However, the rule seems aimed principally at interpreting the parties' agreement, not at imposing an unwanted term. Suppose I buy your business and promise to pay you for it, but only from the profits of the business. The contract seems to imply that I will use reasonable efforts to operate the business profitably. Cf. *Emerson Radio Corp. v. Orion Sales, Inc.,* 253 F.3d 159 (3d Cir. 2000). If I do not make efforts to operate the business and it makes no profits, you would get nothing under the express terms of the contract, but it is fair to regard my inaction as a breach of the implied promise to use effort. The implication is that I must not in bad faith deprive you of the performance you are due. Such a claim is a contract claim and invokes contract remedies. However, in some situations some courts have now held that the implied covenant can create a tort obligation that invokes tort remedies and perhaps expands the jury's role in determining duties where economic loss is inflicted.

14. **Insurance bad faith—tort liability for "third party," failure to settle within policy limit.** The idea of *tort* liability for contract breach arose first in insurance cases, where the insurer in bad faith failed to pay a valid claim. Two types of cases arose. In the first, the insurer covered the insured for liability up to a stated limit, but the insured was sued by an injured person for amounts are in excess of the policy limit. The insurer had an opportunity to settle reasonably within its policy limit but unreasonably or in bad faith failed to do so. In effect, the insurer was gambling with the insured's money, knowing it could not be held under the policy for any sum more that the policy limit and knowing also that if the judgment exceeded that, the insured would be personally liable. Courts came to insist on good faith by the insurer in such cases to settle within its policy limits if it reasonably could. Bad faith edges close to negligence in these cases: "To prove a bad faith claim based on the failure to settle, a plaintiff must demonstrate that in the investigation, evaluation, and processing of the claim, the insurer acted unreasonably and either knew or was conscious of the fact that its conduct was unreasonable." *Twin City Fire Ins. Co. v. Burke,* 204 Ariz. 251, 63 P.3d 282 (2003). Because the liability is conceptualized as tort rather than contract liability, punitive damages may be available. In *State Farm Mut. Auto. Ins. Co. v. Campbell,* 538 U.S. 408, 123 S.Ct. 1513, 155 L.Ed.2d 585 (2003), the Supreme Court held that, for various reasons, an award of $145 million for bad faith failure to settle within policy limits was constitutionally excessive. On remand, the Utah Supreme Court still approved an award approaching $10 million. *Campbell*

v. State Farm Mutual Automobile Insurance Co., 98 P.3d 409 (Utah 2004).

15. **Insurance bad faith—"first party" insurance claim denied.** In the second type of insurance case, the insured had "first party" rather than liability coverage, for example, fire or medical insurance. The insurer would reject the claim in bad faith, thus depriving the insured of the very benefit insurance was designed to achieve—certainty and promptitude of payment. Although this looks like a breach of contract, most courts now hold that the insurer's bad faith denial of the claim is actionable as a tort. *Gruenberg v. Aetna Ins. Co.,* 9 Cal.3d 566, 108 Cal.Rptr. 480, 510 P.2d 1032 (1973); *Universe Life Ins. Co. v. Giles,* 950 S.W.2d 48 (Tex. 1997). That might be so even if, later, it paid the claim. See *Rawlings v. Apodaca,* 151 Ariz. 149, 726 P.2d 565 (1986).

16. **Expanding bad faith tort claims outside the insurance field, or maybe not.** Proponents of a bad faith tort got a big boost with the decision in *Seaman's Direct Buying Service, Inc. v. Standard Oil Co.,* 36 Cal.3d 752, 206 Cal.Rptr. 354, 686 P.2d 1158 (1984). The plaintiff there claimed that defendant had contracted to supply petroleum products for the plaintiff's dealership. A major shortage occurred, and the defendant, who had not yet begun supplying the plaintiff, refused to do so, denying that its negotiations amounted to a contract. The court said the plaintiff could recover in tort on the covenant of good faith and fair dealing when "in addition to breaching the contract, [a party] seeks to shield itself from liability by denying, in bad faith and without probable cause, that the contract exists."

17. **Criticizing the expansion.** Judge Kozinski commented on *Seaman's:* "Nowhere but in the Cloud Cuckooland of modern tort theory could a case like this have been concocted. One large corporation is complaining that another obstinately refused to acknowledge they had a contract. For this shocking misconduct it is demanding millions of dollars in punitive damages. I suppose we will next be seeing lawsuits seeking punitive damages for maliciously refusing to return telephone calls or adopting a condescending tone in interoffice memos." *Oki America, Inc. v. Microtech International, Inc.,* 872 F.2d 312 (9th Cir. 1988). Under *Seaman's,* would you dare deny a contract if the plaintiff asserted you had one? On that, you might want to know that the jury awards in Seaman's, rounded, were: breach of contract, $400,000; tortious bad faith breach, $400,000; punitive damages for bad faith, $11 million; interference with contract damages, $1.5 million; punitive damages for interference with contract, $11 million.

18. **Withdrawing from the expansion.** The California court quickly withdrew from *Seaman's* tort liability for bad faith breach of contract. See *Freeman & Mills, Inc. v. Belcher Oil Co.,* 11 Cal.4th 85, 900 P.2d 669, 44 Cal.Rptr.2d 420 (1995) (the bad faith breach claim in tort will be limited to the insurance cases and those in which some independently tortious conduct is demonstrated). Very little support now exists for a tort action based on bad faith breach of contract outside the

insurance field. For instance, Montana, which once embraced the *Seaman's* tort, has now said that the tort action will lie only under special conditions—the parties' bargaining power is unequal, the contract is one for a non-profit motivation such as security and peace of mind, the plaintiff is vulnerable and the defendant is aware of it. *Story v. City of Bozeman,* 242 Mont. 436, 791 P.2d 767 (1990).

Can we say that the rejection or limitation of *Seaman's* means that the courts will honor the contract, with whatever limitations it imposes?

UPTOWN HEIGHTS ASSOCIATES LIMITED PARTNERSHIP V. SEAFIRST CORP., 320 Or. 638, 891 P.2d 639 (1995). The plaintiffs are developers who built an apartment complex financed by a construction loan of $7.5 million from the defendant bank. The rental market dropped badly at the time of completion and the plaintiffs had difficulty meeting interest payments when due. The bank extended the loan six months but refused a second extension. The plaintiffs attempted to sell the complex in order to pay off the loan and asked the bank not to foreclose as it had offers that would cover its indebtedness. Foreclosure would (a) hurt the plaintiff's business reputation and (b) drive away purchasers. The bank foreclosed anyway, although it knew that a purchaser had agreed to purchase based on a formula that would produce a price of $8.1 to $8.6 million. Upon foreclosure the buildings were sold to the same purchaser for $7.8 million, the indebtedness to the bank. The plaintiff claimed partly on the theory that the bank breached the implied covenant of good faith.

"This court recently addressed the scope of the duty of good faith in Pacific First Bank v. New Morgan Park Corp., 319 Or. 342, 876 P.2d 761 (1994). Pacific First Bank involved a lease agreement that prevented a tenant from transferring the lease without the landlord's approval. In that case, the tenant merged into its wholly owned subsidiary, thus effecting a transfer of the lease requiring the landlord's consent. The landlord refused to grant consent. This court held that, although a duty of good faith applied to the lease agreement, the landlord did not breach that duty, because the landlord's refusal did not contravene the 'reasonable expectations' of the parties as manifested in the express terms of the lease agreement at issue.

"This court reiterated in Pacific First Bank that every contract contains an implied duty of good faith. That duty 'is to be applied in a manner that will effectuate the reasonable contractual expectations of the parties.' ... [T]he court also restated the precept that the duty of good faith cannot serve to contradict an express contractual term.... Since the contract here authorized foreclosure for default, even when the lender's security was not threatened, the bank did not breach any good faith duty."

19. **Bad faith termination of at-will employment.** The tort claim of at-will employees that termination of employment would violate the covenant of good faith and fair dealing got some support in the broad language of earlier cases, but it that language was quickly whittled down

to eliminate or severely restrict the bad faith tort claim. See *Howard v. Dorr Woolen Co.*, 120 N.H. 295, 414 A.2d 1273 (1980) (down-reading earlier "bad faith" language). In *Foley v. Interactive Data Corp.*, 47 Cal.3d 654, 254 Cal.Rptr. 211, 765 P.2d 373 (1988), the plaintiff was discharged from his employment, possibly because he made reference to his understanding that a new supervisor was under investigation for embezzlement. He sued the employer, claiming in tort for breach of the covenant of good faith. The court recognized that an employment contract might expressly or impliedly require the employer to discharge the employee only for good cause. However, the implied covenant of good faith and fair dealing would not support an action in tort. The court held firmly that the employment relation was not like insurance, partly because the employer, after all, had economic interests in retaining good employees. Other courts are mostly in accord. See *Murphy v. American Home Products Corp.*, 58 N.Y.2d 293, 448 N.E.2d 86, 461 N.Y.S.2d 232 (1983) (right of action for breach of covenant of good faith would be inconsistent with employer's right to terminate at-will employee for any reason); *Finch v. Farmers Co-Op Oil Co. of Sheridan*, 109 P.3d 537 (Wyo. 2005) (tort liability "only in rare and exceptional cases," when "a special relationship of trust and reliance exists between the employer and the employee seeking recovery").

20. **Contract liability and its limits.** Although tort liability for bad faith breach is rejected, contract liability like that illustrated in ¶ 13 remains possible. In *Fortune v. National Cash Register Co.*, 373 Mass. 96, 364 N.E.2d 1251 (1977), the plaintiff was an at-will employee who was terminated so that the employer would avoid payment of bonuses earned. This was held actionable as a breach of the implied covenant of good faith and fair dealing. What the plaintiff recovered, however, was the bonus he had already earned, not the salary he would have earned had he not been fired. The duty of good faith is not violated merely because the defendant insists upon a right he has under the contract, including the right to terminate employment at will. See *Cromeens, Holloman, Sibert, Inc. v. AB Volvo*, 349 F.3d 376 (7th Cir. 2003) (franchisees); *Wagenseller v. Scottsdale Mem. Hosp.*, 147 Ariz. 370, 710 P.2d 1025 (1985). So an at-will employee does not keep his at-will employment, nor does he get a damages substitute. Continued employment was not promised to him and consequently there is no violation of the covenant of good faith. The same is true with franchisees whose franchises are terminable on notice, as in *Cromeens*, supra.

21. **Discharge of an employee in violation of public policy.** Bad faith tort claims by at-will employees are now mostly rejected, but we should round out the employee picture by recognizing that even the at-will employee cannot be discharged in violation of a statute or strong and clear public policy. For example, if a company discharges an employee because the employee refuses to carry out an illegal scheme of the employer, the discharge would violated public policy and would be actionable. "A few courts have limited this claim to a contract theory and exclude tort damages, but most treat it as a tort. In most cases the

employer fires the at will employee for refusing to engage in illegal conduct, for blowing the whistle on the employer's illegal conduct, or for asserting her rights, as where she claims workers' compensation benefits for an employment injury." DOBBS ON TORTS § 454 (2001 & Supps.) (citations omitted).

The public policy cases raise issues about what counts as public policy that is strong enough to warrant such legal relief that contravenes the employment at-will rule. Suppose a medical group discharges a physician because he refuses to refer his patients to specialists in the group—on the ground that those specialists provide inadequate care. Should the physician have a public policy cause of action against his former employer? *LoPresti v. Rutland Regional Health Servs., Inc.,* 865 A.2d 1102 (Vt. 2004).

22. **A civil rights claim?** 42 U.S.C.A. § 1985 creates a federal civil rights cause of action distinct from the better-known § 1983. Section 1985 addresses intimidation against witnesses and jurors to coerce or retaliate for testimony or verdicts "with intent to deny to any citizen the equal protection of the laws, or to injure him or his property for lawfully enforcing, or attempting to enforce, the right of any person, or class of persons, to the equal protection of the laws." In *Haddle v. Garrison,* 525 U.S. 121, 119 S.Ct. 489, 142 L.Ed.2d 502 (1998), an employer and others indicted for federal Medicare fraud allegedly conspired to discharge the plaintiff, an at-will employee, in retaliation for the plaintiff's cooperation with the investigation and perhaps to deter his testimony at the criminal trial. Although the employee had no constitutionally protected property interest—he was an at-will employee, like most who claim wrongful discharge—the Supreme Court held that he had a civil rights action under § 1985 (not § 1983). "The gist of the wrong at which § 1985(2) is directed is not deprivation of property, but intimidation or retaliation against witnesses in federal-court proceedings."

§ 3. BREACH OF FIDUCIARY DUTY

NOTE: SOME BEDROCK BASICS

23. **The relevance of fiduciary status.** A fiduciary's breach of fiduciary duty may be a tort in itself. Or it may be a way of committing some more specific tort, such as fraudulent misrepresentation or appropriation of trade secrets. In this section we consider the breach of fiduciary duty as itself a wrong, observing how fiduciary status imposes new duties, how those duties may related to contractual arrangements between the parties, and how breach may be remedied. The platform for considering these issues is the information we review in this Note.

24. **Fiduciary duties.** (a) Fiduciary duties may vary somewhat depending on individual facts and the general factual setting. See Deborah A. DeMott, *Beyond Metaphor: An Analysis of Fiduciary Obligation,* 1988 DUKE L. J. 879 (1988). Some of the particular duties owed are not so

different from ordinary duties of care. For example, the fiduciary must keep appropriate records of transactions for and with the beneficiary and exercise care in pursuing claims for the beneficiary's benefit. *Murphy v. Wakelee,* 247 Conn. 396, 721 A.2d 1181 (1998) is an example of the latter.

(b) The fiduciary duties most discussed are aimed at securing the fiduciary's financial devotion to the beneficiary. In contrast to ordinary economic transactions in which each party seek to further his own interest, fiduciaries within the scope of the fiduciary relationship, owe duties of loyalty and good faith; they must put the beneficiary's interest first. See RESTATEMENT (SECOND) OF AGENCY § 393, cmt. b (1958) ("In the usual case, it is the agent's duty to further his principal's interests even at the expense of his own in matters connected with the agency. Thus, an agent to buy or to sell for the principal must not buy or sell in competition with the principal, unless it is so agreed"); RESTATEMENT (THIRD) OF RESTITUTION § 43, cmt. b (Tentative Draft 2000). To some extent, fiduciaries must avoid a conflict of interest. See for example, RESTATEMENT (THIRD) OF THE LAW GOVERNING LAWYERS § 121 (2000). Specific duties of a fiduciary may include the duty not to take any secret profits from his position, see *Williams Electronics Games, Inc. v. Garrity,* 366 F.3d 569 (7th Cir. 2004), printed below, and to disclose a great deal of relevant information to the beneficiary that arms' length bargainers need not disclose. See Chapter 14 below. The other side of that coin, as we saw in the chapter on privacy, is that the fiduciary, or one in a relation of confidence, must not breach the duty of confidentiality. Sometimes, too, the burden falls on the fiduciary to justify his actions, at least once he is perceived to have a conflict of interest or otherwise put his loyalty in doubt. See *Ledbetter v. First State Bank & Trust Co.,* 85 F.3d 1537 (11th Cir. 1996) (addressing a formal trust: "If trustee places itself in a position where its interests *might* conflict with the interests of the beneficiary, the law presumes that the trustee acted disloyally; inquiry into such matters as whether the transaction was fair is foreclosed and the burden shifts to the trustee to show it received no benefit"); *Trieweiler v. Sears,* 268 Neb. 952, 689 N.W.2d 807 (2004).

25. **Limiting fiduciary duties.** (a) Can fiduciary duties override a contract provision between the parties? In *Labovitz v. Dolan,* 189 Ill.App.3d 403, 416, 545 N.E.2d 304, 313, 136 Ill.Dec. 780, 789 (1989), a general partner, by contract with the others, had the sole right to distribute or withhold distribution of the profits. He refused to distribute any of the partnership's enormous income, but the other partners were taxed on the partnership income as though they had received it. The suggestion was that the managing partner was trying to squeeze out the others. They sued. The managing partner pointed to the contract provision giving him sole power over case distributions and the trial court dismissed the complaint on that ground. On appeal, the court reversed, saying:

> [A]lthough the Articles clearly gave the general partner the sole discretion to distribute cash as he deemed appropriate, that discre-

tion was encumbered by a supreme fiduciary duty of fairness, honesty, good faith and loyalty to his partners.

(b) Yet to an uncertain degree, the contractual arrangement between the parties and their reasonable expectations can create or limit fiduciary duties. For instance, fiduciaries must not compete with their beneficiaries; it is *not* a "violation of the agent's duty if the principal understands that the agent is to compete; a course of dealing between the parties may indicate that this is understood." RESTATEMENT (SECOND) OF AGENCY § 393, cmt. a (1958).

Lawyers cannot ethically represent clients who are adverse to each other; that is a conflict of interest. Yet they may proceed with some conflicting representations if they secure waivers from the client. E.g., *VISA U.S.A., Inc. v. First Data Corp.*, 241 F.Supp.2d 1100 (2003) (given a waiver, the firm could represent VISA against First Data, although the firm had previously represented both parties and held confidential materials concerning First Data). Both the lawyer and the agent example show that contract or expectations can to some extent limit fiduciary duty.

(c) Apart from contract, corporation law has increasingly permitted directors to have a conflict of interest with the corporations they "serve," sometimes requiring disclosure of the conflict to disinterested directors or shareholders, but sometimes not even requiring disclosure. See Douglas M. Branson, *Assault on Another Citadel: Attempts to Curtail the Fiduciary Standard Of Loyalty Applicable to Corporate Directors,* 57 FORDHAM L. REV. 375 (1988). In fact, corporate directors, are seldom held legally accountable. See Lisa M. Fairfax, *Spare the Rod, Spoil the Director? Revitalizing Directors' Fiduciary Duty Through Legal Liability,* 42 HOUS. L. REV. 393 (2005).

26. **Who is a fiduciary?** The classic model of a fiduciary is a trustee, who is held to the most exacting standards. Anyone who undertakes to act for the benefit of another and not for himself, however, can be a fiduciary. Courts have come to treat a number of particular actors as fiduciaries as a matter of law—corporate director to shareholder, lawyer to client, partner to partner, and in fact, any agent to principal. There are others, such as the executor of an estate and the guardian of an incompetent. In addition, one can become a fiduciary by undertaking fiducial duties and—more or less—by inducing special confidence. Statutes sometimes impose fiduciary status on designated persons. For instance, by the federal statute known as ERISA, the administrator of employee benefit plans are fiduciaries. 29 U.S.C.A. § 1102.

27. **Confidential relationships.** When one person, usually a dominant one, gains the special confidence of another, usually a vulnerable or reliant person, the two are in a confidential relationship, usually conceived of as falling short of a fiduciary relationship. But courts sometime actually treat the relationship as a fiduciary one and impose something like fiduciary duties on the dominant party. See *Roman Catholic Diocese of Jackson v. Morrison,* 905 So.2d 1213 (Miss. 2005).

Bank cases are illustrative. Banks and their customers are in debtor-creditor relationships, not fiduciary relationship, and a bank and its customers equally stand at arm's length in negotiating a loan. Yet confidential or fiduciary elements may arise in particular situations. In *Groob v. KeyBank,* 155 Ohio App.3d 510, 801 N.E.2d 919 (2003), the plaintiff applied for a loan from the bank in order to purchase a company. He presented bank with financial research on the company, but the bank rejected the loan and the plaintiff gave up. The bank officer then used the information to purchase the company for himself. The court held that in spite of the general rule, "a fiduciary relationship may arise from a particular relationship where both parties understand that a special trust or confidence exists between them." That was the case here. Cf. *ADT Operations, Inc. v. Chase Manhattan Bank,* 173 Misc.2d 959, 662 N.Y.S.2d 190 (Sup. Ct. 1997) (while bank could finance a hostile takeover of its customer, it could not supply customer's confidential information to corporation attempting acquisition of the plaintiff).

Suppose the bank were you've banked for years and which has advised you repeatedly on investments suggests you should invest in a grocery store. The bank that touts the investment does not reveal that the grocery store has been losing money. Nor does it reveal that that the bank wants your investment, which would be guaranteed, so it can get out of a losing loan to the grocery? Something like that happened in *Buxcel v. First Fidelity Bank,* 601 N.W.2d 593 (S.D. 1999), where the plaintiff was allowed to get out of his deal with the bank because of the bank's nondisclosure. See also *Susan Fixel, Inc. v. Rosenthal & Rosenthal, Inc.,* 842 So.2d 204 (Fla. Dist. Ct. App. 2003) (recognizing that under special circumstances lender may be fiduciary even to commercial borrower).

WEADICK v. HERLIHY

16 A.D.3d 223, 792 N.Y.S.2d 25 (2005)

SAXE, J.P., ELLERIN, NARDELLI, SWEENY, JJ. . . .

This is a dispute among the individual parties as loft tenants, one of whom (defendant Herlihy) is an attorney, who were seeking to purchase the building they occupy. Herlihy, who was originally a member of the tenants' venture to purchase, opted out at the last moment and made the deal to purchase a half interest in the building for herself alone. Thereafter, plaintiffs, with a new business ally, purchased the other half interest in the building. Claiming that Herlihy was their fiduciary (having represented them in negotiations with the seller) as well as a co-venturer, plaintiffs seek to impose a constructive trust on her interest and compel its conveyance to them. [The trial judge overruled the defendant Herlihy's motion for summary judgment.]

Contrary to defendants' contention, it is immaterial whether plaintiffs imparted any confidences to the attorney co-venturer or whether they relied on her as a result of their lesser business sophistication, since these jural fiduciary relationships, unlike informal confidential ones, do not depend on dominance and related factors. While the client's subjective belief as to the existence of an attorney-client relationship is not dispositive, the history of the parties and their negotiations for purchase of this building, as well as the procedural posture, distinguish the situation here from that in Fleissler v. Bayroff, 266 A.D.2d 34, 698 N.Y.S.2d 19 [1999], upon which defendants rely. Termination of the parties' relationship does not insulate a fiduciary from the consequences of conduct engaged in while a fiduciary. Here, questions exist, including whether the attorney diverted the opportunity to herself and was unjustly enriched as a result.

Facts supporting the imposition of a constructive trust were sufficiently set forth. The motion court aptly recognized the flexibility of the equitable doctrine. . . .

[Affirmed.]

28. **Breach of fiduciary duty a tort.** The Restatement provides expressly that violation of a fiduciary duty is a tort. It adds that one who knowingly assists a fiduciary in committing a breach of trust is also subject to liability. Restatement (Second) of Torts § 874 (1979).

29. **Tort damages—or constructive trust?** To say that breach of fiduciary duty is a tort is not to say that the remedy will always be the remedy "at law" for damages. The plaintiffs in *Weadick v. Herlihy* did not seek tort damages and the court nowhere characterized the action as one in tort. Instead, the plaintiff's sought a constructive trust. Constructive trust language represents a historical way of conceptualizing the role of a person who has wrongfully taken or received something of value that in good conscience belongs to the plaintiff. The language assimilates the wrongdoer to a trustee. A trustee has legal title (like Herlihy), but is compelled to hold it as a fiduciary for the victim. Usually that means the constructive trustee must convey the thing wrongfully obtained to the victim.

30. **Basis for constructive trust.** Breach of fiduciary duty resulting in things of value in the fiduciary's hands is one ground, and a major one, for imposing a constructive trust. It is not the only ground, however. The point is to prevent unjust enrichment, whether it occurs by fiducial breach, fraud, or even mistake. See *Foster v. Hurley,* 444 Mass. 157, 826 N.E.2d 719 (2005) ("a court will declare a party a constructive trustee of property for the benefit of another if he acquired the property through fraud, mistake, breach of duty, or in other circumstances indicating that he would be unjustly enriched"); *Flanigan v. Munson,* 175 N.J. 597, 818 A.2d 1275 (2003); Dobbs on Remedies § 4.3 (2).

31. **Accounting for profits.** If the defendant no longer has the wrongfully acquired property or an identifiable fund resulting from the wrong, the plaintiff may seek an equitable accounting for profits instead of a constructive trust. This would give the plaintiff a money decree

rather than a direct transfer of the property (since the defendant no longer had property identified with the wrong), but if the degree would still be based on the defendant's wrongful gains rather than the plaintiff's loss.

32. **Damages differences.** Constructive trusts and equitable accountings for profits are forms of "restitution" or disgorgement. Those remedies prevent the defendant's unjust enrichment and they are entirely distinguishable from "damages," which are measured by the plaintiff's loss, not the defendant's gain. Which kind of remedy would the plaintiff want if (a) the value of the loft had skyrocketed after Herlihy bought a half interest? (b) the value of the loft had plummeted after Herlihy had purchased? What could the plaintiff get if Herlihy had sold her interest in the loft before suit could be brought?

33. **"Equity" and law.** (a) The old separate equity courts invented the law of trusts. Trusts and constructive trusts became the province of the separate equity courts, not law courts. Most states have now combined law and equity courts, but by tradition, equity procedures and equity culture continue to apply in cases that once were exclusively equitable. That includes claims for constructive trust. In contrast, an ordinary damages suits is regarded as an act "at law," meaning that ordinary procedures of "law" cases would apply.

(b) Differences between equity and law might have major consequences. One notable difference is that while jury trial is usually a matter of right in cases "at law," historic equity courts never let a jury determine the facts. See DOBBS ON REMEDIES § 2.6 (2). Other differences are possible, too, for example, defenses, including the statute of limitations and the scope of appellate review (usually de novo in equity matters). Would the remedy you sought for fiduciary breach determine whether you got a jury trial or not?

WILLIAMS ELECTRONICS GAMES, INC. v. GARRITY

366 F.3d 569 (7th Cir. 2004)

POSNER, Circuit Judge.

[Williams, the manufacturer of *Mortal Kombat* and other video games, sued two of its component suppliers, Arrow and Milgray, and James Garrity, a salesman for Arrow. Williams alleged that Arrow and Milgray, partly through Garrity, bribed one of Williams' buyers, Greg Barry, to buy components from them Arrow and Milgray rather than from others. Barry received more than $100,000 in cash bribes from these defendants. The Counterclaims by some of the defendants were ultimately dismissed. The case was tried to a jury, which awarded $78,000 to Williams against Garrity personally, but found in favor of the other defendants. On this appeal, the court found that the trial judge had erred in instructing the jury on defenses for the two company defendants.]

The defendants argue that if we reverse the judgment in their favor, damages should be capped at $78,000, the amount of the verdict against Garrity.... It happens that that was the amount of the bribes that Garrity paid. But it corresponds neither to the damages that Williams may have sustained as a result of Garrity's bribing Barry (and remember that Milgray as well as Arrow bribed him) nor to the profits that the defendants may have made from the bribery by overcharging Williams, though the bribes might as we'll see be a lower-bound estimate of the damages that Arrow, Garrity's employer—and Arrow alone—inflicted on Williams. The $78,000 figure is a token of the jury's confusion and an unreliable guide to either Williams's total loss or the defendants' gain.

We have mentioned the defendants' gain as well as Williams's loss because in addition to seeking damages for the fraud perpetrated upon it, Williams asked the judge to impose a constructive trust in its favor on the profits that the defendants had made from their bribery. The victim of commercial bribery, who usually as here is the principal of an agent who was bribed, can obtain by way of remedy either the damages that he has sustained (the damages remedy) or the profits that the bribe yielded (the restitution or unjust enrichment remedy). 2 Dan B. Dobbs, *Dobbs Law of Remedies, Damages–Equity–Restitution* § 10.6, p. 698 (2d ed.1993). The total profits would consist of the bribe itself (received by Barry, of course, not by Garrity or Arrow), plus the revenue that the bribe generated for the briber, minus the cost of goods sold and any other variable costs incurred in making the sales that generated that revenue.

Commercial bribery is a deliberate tort, and one way to deter it is to make it worthless to the tortfeasor by stripping away all his gain, since if his gain exceeded the victim's loss a damages remedy would leave the tortfeasor with a profit from his act. *Id.* at 1120. The amount of the bribe paid is of course not a profit to the briber, but an expense, and it should not enter into the net profit calculation sketched above. It can be used as a minimum estimate of damages, however, on the theory that no one would pay a bribe who didn't anticipate garnering net additional revenue at least equal to the amount of the bribe; and that additional revenue is, at least as a first approximation, an additional expense to the person whose agent was bribed. Arrow presumably jacked up its prices to Williams by at least $78,000 to cover the cost of the bribes that it was paying Barry to swing business its way, as otherwise it would have lost rather than made money from bribing him. The implication is that had it not been for the bribes, Arrow's prices to Williams would have been at least $78,000 lower. So that amount is a minimum estimate of the loss to Williams caused by Arrow's bribing Barry.

Restitution is available in any intentional-tort case in which the tortfeasor has made a profit that exceeds the victim's damages (if the damages exceed the profit, the plaintiff will prefer to seek damages instead), whether or not the tort involved a breach of fiduciary duty, though commercial bribery normally will involve such a breach. The only thing that turns on the precise character of the defendant's wrongdoing is, in some cases, the availability of equitable as distinct from legal restitution. Just as damages can be obtained either in a suit at law, or, in an equity suit, under the "clean up" doctrine, or by the imposition of a constructive trust on moneys wrongfully withheld from the plaintiff, or by surcharging a trustee for the losses that he has caused to the trust, so restitution, too, can be awarded in either a suit at law or a suit in equity. If as in this case the wrong consists of a breach of fiduciary obligation—the kind of breach traditionally actionable in suits in equity (fiduciary obligations were an invention of the English chancery court,—the usual form that restitution takes is to impress a constructive trust on the profits of wrongdoing, with the defendant the trustee and the plaintiff, of course, the beneficiary.

But if all that the plaintiff is seeking is a sum of money equal to the defendant's profit, an order of restitution will do fine, and the device of a constructive trust is surplus; the device comes into its own only when the plaintiff is seeking title to specific property in the defendant's hands. Which means, by the way, that the imposition of a constructive trust can be sought as an equitable remedy for a legal as well as an equitable wrong just as, in a suit for damages for breach of contract, the court can order an equitable accounting if the computation of damages involves complexities that would baffle a jury. For completeness, we note that when restitution is sought in a law case and the plaintiff is not seeking to impress a lien on particular property, but just wants an award of profits, he cannot obtain a constructive trust, because there is no *res* (that is, no fund or other specific piece of property) for the trust to attach to. He can still get restitution in such a case, but as a legal remedy for a legal wrong, not as an equitable remedy for a legal or an equitable wrong.

Williams's situation was in between. It was not seeking to impose a lien on particular property, so it had no basis for seeking a constructive trust. But the wrong for which it was seeking a remedy (properly described as restitution, or, what is synonymous as a practical matter, an accounting for profits, rather than as the imposition of a constructive trust) was an equitable wrong, a breach of fiduciary obligation, and so Williams was entitled to seek equitable restitution. And therefore it could seek (legal) damages from a jury and then, if it thought it could obtain a larger recovery by way of restitution, an order of restitution from the judge, since equitable remedies are determined by judges rather than by juries. Of course it could not keep both damages and profits, only the larger of the two. And of course when an equitable remedy is sought in conjunction with a legal remedy the legal claim is tried first and the jury's findings bind the judge, in order to vindicate the right to a jury trial on legal claims.

[Judgment for the defendants is reversed and the case remanded for further proceedings.]

34. **Commercial bribery.** "The taking of a bribe or 'secret commission' is condemned, without regard to economic injury, because it

poses a risk of divided loyalty." RESTATEMENT (THIRD) OF RESTITUTION § 43, cmt. d (Tentative Draft No. 4, 2005). Thus the fiduciary who accepts a bribe, whether it is called a gift, rebate, or commission, has breached his fiduciary duty. Accordingly, both the fiduciary and the briber who aids him in the breach are liable. *Kewaunee Scientific Corp. v. Pegram,* 130 N.C. App. 576, 503 S.E.2d 417 (1998).

Persons not entitled to the agent's loyalty may conceivably have an action when the agent is bribed, although it will not be an action for breach of fiduciary duty. Suppose the agent accepts a bribe to purchase from Supplier A instead of from A's competitor, Supplier B. Supplier B loses sales as a result. Perhaps Supplier B, though not entitled to the agent's loyalty, has an action based on antitrust laws or some unfair competition statutes. See 15 U.S.C.A. § 13 (c); *Diamond Triumph Auto Glass, Inc. v. Safelite Glass Corp.,* 344 F.Supp.2d 936 (M.D.Pa. 2004). Bribery is also a crime and may figure in liability under the Racketeer Influenced and Corrupt Organizations (RICO) Act, covered in Chapter 15.

35. **Recovery without damages.** Can the plaintiff recover in a commercial bribery or any fiduciary breach case even if she has no damages? In addition to authorities considered above, see *Sears, Roebuck & Co. v. American Plumb. & Supply Co.,* 19 F.R.D. 334 (E.D. Wis. 1956). If the plaintiff sues for damages, not the profits gained by the wrongdoing fiduciary, perhaps actual damages would have to be proven. See *Amerco v. Shoen,* 184 Ariz. 150, 907 P.2d 536 (Ariz. Ct. App. 1995) (no nominal damages for corporate director's breach of fiduciary duty; plaintiff must prove compensatory damages or restitution claim); *Gibbs v. Breed, Abbott & Morgan,* 271 A.D.2d 180, 710 N.Y.S.2d 578 (2000) (partner's breach of confidence not shown to cause damages, no liability without that showing); *Meyer v. Maus,* 626 N.W.2d 281 (N.D. 2001) (no liability for lawyer's conflict of interest because that conflict did not cause damages, which would have occurred even had plaintiff secured independent counsel). However, in *Lane County v. Wood,* 298 Or. 191, 691 P.2d 473 (1984), the court held that a public official guilty of fiduciary breach could be liable for nominal damages, and once liable for that, could be subjected to punitive damages.

36. **Allowing the plaintiff to sue "at law."** In *Williams Electronics*, Judge Posner seems to make it clear that, at least in a court where law and equity powers are combined in a single judge, the plaintiff could sue for "damages" resulting from a fiduciary breach and have a jury trial, or alternatively, could ask the judge to exercise his equitable powers to impose a constructive trust. In fact, he says, the plaintiff can take whichever remedy, damages or constructive trust, proves most desirable. Other cases have entertained actions at law for breach of fiduciary duties where the plaintiff sought damages rather than an equitable form of restitution like a constructive trust. *Moore v. Moore,* 360 S.C. 241, 599 S.E.2d 467 (2004) (first partner as fiduciary was liable under a jury verdict for profits lost by second partner when first partner refused to go through with partnership purchase of business). In *Union*

Nat'l Life Ins. Co. v. Crosby, 870 So.2d 1175 (Miss. 2004), the court went so far as to say that breach of fiduciary duty is a tort and that equity courts could not entertain suits for breach of that duty, even when the plaintiff seeks a constructive trust.

37. **Disallowing a suit at law.** A cloudy dictum in *Kinzer v. City of Chicago,* 128 Ill.2d 437, 539 N.E.2d 1216, 132 Ill.Dec. 410 (1989), might conceivably furnish a basis for arguing that a tort action for damages could not be brought, only a suit in equity. And in *Kann v. Kann,* 344 Md. 689, 690 A.2d 509 (1997), a beneficiary's claim against the trustee of an express trust, the court held that the claimant could not have a jury trial but instead had to proceed in equity, suggesting, however, that some kinds of fiduciary breach might call for a different answer.

38. **Remedial flexibility in addressing fiduciary breach.** Notwithstanding the caution of the *Kinzer* and *Kann* courts, flexibility is the keynote of remedial thinking. Instead of ordering a constructive trust to remedy the fiduciary breach by a majority shareholder in a closely held corporation, the court might conclude that the best remedy would be to order the majority shareholder/fiduciary to buy the minority shareholder's shares. *G & N Aircraft, Inc. v. Boehm,* 743 N.E.2d 227 (2001). Or, the court may decide that although the case is a traditional equitable case, the damages remedy is more suited to the facts, and consequently might limit the plaintiff to the damages remedy. See *In re Guardianship and Conservatorship of Jordan,* 616 N.W.2d 553, 561 (Iowa 2000) (guardian as fiduciary liable for damages). Likewise, although equity courts traditionally rejected awards of punitive damages, see DOBBS ON REMEDIES § 3.11 (1), nowadays you can find plenty of cases permitting punitive awards based on breach of fiduciary duty, both in suits brought "in equity," *G & N Aircraft, Inc. v. Boehm,* 743 N.E.2d 227 (2001) (equity suit by minority shareholder, court could fashion remedy in compensatory and punitive damages); *Cooper v. Cooper,* 173 Vt. 1, 783 A.2d 430 (2001) (mortgage foreclosure, traditionally equitable, punitive damages against one cotenant/fiduciary who tried to freeze out the other), and "at law." *Jordan v. Holt,* 362 S.C. 201, 608 S.E.2d 129 (2005).

39. **Why fiduciary breach is relevant in *Williams*.** We observed earlier that fiduciary breach is not the only basis for a constructive trust. Judge Posner adds that the plaintiff could sue either in law or equity for the breach and recover either the "legal" or "equitable" remedy, whichever is best. Given these views, does fiduciary breach have any relevance at all? At a minimum, it forms a basis for finding liability; and if no misrepresentation or breach of contract can be proved, it may be the *only* basis. Look at at *Weadick* and see if you think the tenants could have proved misrepresentation or contract breach.

Problem: Javelinda Corp. v. Ulrich

Javelinda Corporation hired Jason Ulrich ten years ago to work in its Green Springs office. Jason was very good and was promoted quickly.

Eight years ago, he became general manager. The one-year contracts were always renewed with appropriate pay increase and bonus. For the past five years, at renewal time, Jason spoke to the home office about moving on to some other work, but each year he was encouraged to stay and given good raises. Six months ago, when the renewal contract came in for Jason's signature, he did not sign it. When the term was up, he left Javelinda's employment. Jason did not take or misuse any information, but his knowledge of office procedures, computer codes, and the like was essential to operation of the business and Javelinda was put to a great deal of expense and suffered some heavy local business losses as a result of the disruption.

It is clear that Jason breached no contract, but Javelinda's corporate counsel asks you to determine whether, under applicable law, Javelinda can recover against Jason for breach of fiduciary duty.

40. **Injunctions.** Even if Jason had breached the contract, the usual rule is that courts will not issue an injunction to force an employee to work. For one thing, it is probably impractical to compel someone to work reasonably well against her will. For another, "people must be permitted to work out their own destinies and form their own personal associations without official direction from judges." DOBBS ON REMEDIES § 12.22 (2) (2d ed. 1993).

41. **A question about agent's liability for breach of fiduciary duty.** Agents are fiduciaries, no question about that. Do you think it would be a breach of fiduciary duty to quit without notice, leaving the employer, to whom the duty is owed, in a terrible position?

42. **The role of the contract.** If you are of the opinion that Jason did not breach a fiduciary duty, is that because the contract made no provision for notice when the term was up? If that is your view, consider whether Javelinda would have a claim for fiduciary breach if the contract had in fact required 30-days notice before terminating employment, regardless whether the contract had been renewed or not.

§ 4. CONVERSION OF INTANGIBLE PROPERTY OR ECONOMIC RIGHTS

MILLER v. HEHLEN

209 Ariz. 462, 104 P.3d 193 (Ct. App. 2005)

PELANDER, Chief J. . . .

For approximately fifteen years, up to 2001, Miller operated her business as an H & R Block ("Block") franchise under a franchise agreement she and Block had executed. Miller employed Hehlen in that business as an income tax return preparer for five tax seasons, 1997 through 2001. At the beginning of each tax season, including 2001, Hehlen and Miller executed a form employment agreement that Block not only supplied but also required under its franchise agreement with Miller. Block terminated Miller's franchise in April 2001, which Miller is currently challenging in a separate, federal court action, and thereafter Miller operated her business under the name, "MJM & Associates."

In the course of her business, Miller maintained a database of customer information, including customer data sheets. Until 2001, when Miller asked him to stop, Hehlen kept a customer list he had created from those data sheets on a spreadsheet on his home computer. After Miller instructed Hehlen not to take the customer data sheets home, he surreptitiously began writing customer names on copies of receipts that he had been permitted to keep to track revenue generation. He then added the names to his computer spreadsheet at home. After Hehlen's employment with Miller had ended, in June 2001 Miller provided him with substantially the same customer list in connection with a pay dispute between them.

In December 2001, Miller sent her existing clients a postcard that referred to "Bill" as one of her associates, even though Hehlen no longer worked for her at that time. In 2002, Hehlen went to work at another Block office operated directly by Block in Oro Valley. At or near the beginning of the tax season that year, purportedly in response to the postcard Miller had sent out, Hehlen began contacting the customers whose names he had obtained from Miller's office, using a calling script and recording the results of the calls on his spreadsheet. When Miller became aware of those calls in February 2002, she sent Hehlen a cease and desist letter and subsequently filed this action. [The trial judge entered summary judgment for the defendant. In this appeal, the court rejected Miller's claims for breach of contract, violation of trade secret rights, interference with business relations, and defamation.]

Miller further argues that the material facts support a claim that "Hehlen converted her customer list by taking her customer information and interfering with the relationships Miller established with those customers." Arizona has adopted the following definition of conversion, which is in the Restatement (Second) of Torts § 222A(1) (1965): "Conversion is an intentional exercise of dominion or control over a chattel which so seriously interferes with the right of another to control it that the actor may justly be required to pay the other the full value of the chattel." If those elements are shown, a court must then consider the seriousness of the interference and whether the offending party must pay full value. *See* Restatement (Second) of Torts § 222A(2).

Even if the customer list constituted a "chattel," the record does not support a finding that Hehlen's actions rose to the level of a conversion. An action for conversion ordinarily lies only for personal property that is tangible, or to intangible property that is merged in, or identified with, some document. Miller did not allege that Hehlen took a customer list in the form of a single, unified document that had value as tangible property. Nor does a customer list constitute intangible property merged with a document in the same sense as a stock certificate or an insurance policy. Thus, neither rationale supports a claim of conversion based on taking a customer list.

Further, the record does not establish that Hehlen exercised intentional dominion or control over the customer list in such a way that he interfered with Miller's rights to the extent that he should be required to pay the full value of the list, whatever that might be. That is particularly so in light of the terms of Miller's franchise agreement with Block.

[Summary judgment for defendant affirmed.]

43. **Conversion and trespass to chattels.** Conversion was traditionally a tort involving tangible chattels only. It was accomplished when the defendant exercised dominion over the property in a way seriously inconsistent with the plaintiff's right to possession of it. If the defendant was liable, he was in effect an involuntary purchaser—he paid the full value of the converted item. Trespass to chattels was a more limited tort redressing less serious interference with tangible chattels. Trespass to chattels would lie unless the chattel was actually damaged or taken from the plaintiff's possession.

44. **Tangible goods or documents representing them.** The historical rule recognized the action for conversion only as to tangible property. The right of recovery was extended as recognized in *Miller* to cover cases in which rights in tangible chattels were "merged" in or represented by a document. If you could not sell your car without the paper "title," or could not collect on your bonds without paper bond, we could say the right of possession and owner is merged in the car title or the bond. So conversion of a document like a negotiable instrument came to be treated as a conversion of the economic right it represented. In contrast, conversion of a writing that is merely evidence of your right looks like conversion of a piece of paper, not a conversion of the contract rights. Likewise, an interference with your contract rights without dominion over a tangible chattel or an instrument that controlled the right to that chattel, would not be a conversion. See *Shebester v. Triple Crown Insurers,* 826 P.2d 603 (Okla. 1992) ("chose in action" not subject to conversion).

45. **Contemporary cases requiring tangibility.** Here are examples of recent cases applying the tangibility rule:

- *Express One International, Inc. v. Steinbeck,* 53 S.W.3d 895 (Tex. App. 2001), the defendant allegedly used a name similar to plaintiff's trade name, but the court held that this could not be a conversion of the name, which is intangible and not merged into a document.
- The principal case, *Miller v. Hehlen,* of course reflects a similar view about a list of customers.
- In *DIRECTV, Inc. v. Kitzmiller,* 2004 WL 692230 (E.D. Pa. 2004), the court held that no action for conversion would lie against a defendant who used a device to circumvent the encryption in a

satellite TV transmission, thus obtaining the defendant's programs with paying.

- Finally, in *Famology.com Inc. v. Perot Systems Corp.,* 158 F.Supp.2d 589 (E.D. Pa. 2001), the plaintiff claiming to own an internet domain name, sued the defendant for falsely claiming ownership of the name, which caused the plaintiff expenses. The court held that a web domain name cannot be converted because it is not customarily merged into a document.

46. **Alternative remedies: restitution.** When a tangible chattel was converted, the plaintiff was allowed to "waive the tort and sue in assumpsit," meaning the plaintiff could conceptualize her claim as a "quasi-contract" claim for restitution. In this context, restitution means a recovery of the gains made by the defendant, not damages for the plaintiff's loss. See DOBBS ON REMEDIES §§ 5.18 (1) & 5.18 (2) (2d ed. 1993).

47. **Alternative causes of action: freestanding restitution.** Even if no tort is committed by the defendant, it is possible that the defendant is unjustly enriched and should be liable to disgorge his unjust gains on that ground. In that case, liability might be imposed without positing a conversion or any other tort. In *Greenberg v. Miami Children's Hospital Research Inst., Inc.,* 264 F.Supp.2d 1064 (S.D. Fla. 2003), the plaintiffs had provided information to the defendants for the purpose of finding causes and treatment of a disease. The defendants used the information to discover the gene sequence causing the disease and patented the sequence, earning royalties whenever others wanted to use the patented information to test patients. The plaintiffs sued for conversion and unjust enrichment. The court rejected the conversion claim but refused to dismiss the unjust enrichment claim.

48. **Rejecting conversion where other bodies of law address the plaintiff's interests.** The outcomes in *Miller* and the cases summarized in ¶ 45 might have been justified less by the rule that the document converted must be merged with or represent the owner's property interest than by the fact that other bodies of law deal more appropriately with the interest asserted by the plaintiff in those cases. We do not reach trademarks and trade secrets until Chapter 13, but it is easy to imagine that *Express One* is appropriately addressed by trademark and unfair competition law, while *Miller* itself might be best addressed by trade secret law. The *DirectTV* claim might be and actually was supported by federal anti-pirating statutes. In addition, the facts there might be appropriately analyzed under the unjust enrichment rules. The allegations in *Famology* might make you think of civil versions of malicious prosecution or maybe abuse of process, or maybe of an interference with business opportunity claim seen in the next chapter. Quite possibility conversion with its emphasis on dominion of the plaintiff's property is not so appropriate as one of the more specialized tort claims. Is the case different and should the merger-representation requirement be dropped

when no other body of law addresses the interest asserted by the plaintiff?

KREMEN v. COHEN

337 F.3d 1024 (9th Cir. 2003)

KOZINSKI, Circuit Judge....

"Sex on the Internet?," they all said. "*That'll* never make any money." But computer-geek-turned-entrepreneur Gary Kremen knew an opportunity when he saw it. The year was 1994; domain names were free for the asking.... With a quick e-mail to the domain name registrar Network Solutions, Kremen became the proud owner of sex.com. He registered the name to his business, Online Classifieds, and listed himself as the contact.

Con man Stephen Cohen, meanwhile, was doing time for impersonating a bankruptcy lawyer. He, too, saw the potential of the domain name. Kremen had gotten it first, but that was only a minor impediment for a man of Cohen's boundless resource and bounded integrity. Once out of prison, he sent Network Solutions what purported to be a letter he had received from Online Classifieds. It claimed the company had been "forced to dismiss Mr. Kremen," but "never got around to changing our administrative contact with the internet registration [sic] and now our Board of directors has decided to *abandon* the domain name sex.com." Why was this unusual letter being sent via Cohen rather than to Network Solutions directly? It explained:

> Because we do not have a direct connection to the internet, we request that you notify the internet registration on our behalf, to delete our domain name sex.com. Further, we have no objections to your use of the domain name sex.com and this letter shall serve as our authorization to the internet registration to transfer sex.com to your corporation.

Despite the letter's transparent claim that a company called "*Online* Classifieds" had no Internet connection, Network Solutions made no effort to contact Kremen. Instead, it accepted the letter at face value and transferred the domain name to Cohen. When Kremen contacted Network Solutions some time later, he was told it was too late to undo the transfer. Cohen went on to turn sex.com into a lucrative online porn empire.

[Kremen sued Cohen and recovered a judgment ordering a constructive trust and disgorgement of profits. The court awarded $40 million in compensation damages, $25 million in punitive damages. Cohen departed and moved his money offshore. Neither Cohen nor his money have been reached.]

[Kremen sued Network Solutions on both contract and conversion theories. The trial judge granted summary judgment in favor of the defendant on all claims. In this appeal, the court rejected the contract-based claims.]

Kremen's conversion claim is another matter. To establish that tort, a plaintiff must show "ownership or right to possession of property, wrongful disposition of the property right and damages." The preliminary question, then, is whether registrants have property rights in their domain names. Network Solutions all but concedes that they do.... The district court agreed with the parties on this issue, as do we.

Property is a broad concept that includes every intangible benefit and prerogative susceptible of possession or disposition. We apply a three-part test to determine whether a property right exists: First, there must be an interest capable of precise definition; second, it must be capable of exclusive possession or control; and third, the putative owner must have established a legitimate claim to exclusivity. Domain names satisfy each criterion. Like a share of corporate stock or a plot of land, a domain name is a well-defined interest. Someone who registers a domain name decides where on the Internet those who invoke that particular name—whether by typing it into their web browsers, by following a hyperlink, or by other means—are sent. Ownership is exclusive in that the registrant alone makes that decision. Moreover, like other forms of property, domain names are valued, bought and sold, often for millions of dollars....

Finally, registrants have a legitimate claim to exclusivity. Registering a domain name is like staking a claim to a plot of land at the title office. It informs others that the domain name is the registrant's and no one else's. Many registrants also invest substantial time and money to develop and promote websites that depend on their domain names. Ensuring that they reap the benefits of their investments reduces uncertainty and thus encourages investment in the first place, promoting the growth of the Internet overall.

... The district court nevertheless rejected Kremen's conversion claim. It held that domain names, although a form of property, are intangibles not subject to conversion. This rationale derives from a distinction tort law once drew between tangible and intangible property: Conversion was originally a remedy for the wrongful taking of another's lost goods, so it applied only to tangible property. Virtually every jurisdiction, however, has discarded this rigid limitation to some degree. Others reject it for some intangibles but not others. The *Restatement,* for example, recommends the following test:

> (1) Where there is conversion of a document in which intangible rights are merged, the damages include the value of such rights.
>
> (2) One who effectively prevents the exercise of intangible rights of the kind customarily *merged in a document* is subject to a liability similar to that for conversion, even though the document is not itself converted.

Restatement (Second) of Torts § 242 (1965) (emphasis added). An intangible is "merged" in a document when, by the appropriate rule of law, the right to the immediate possession of a chattel and the power to acquire such possession is *represented by* [the] document, or when an intangible obligation [is] *represented by* [the] document, which is regarded as equivalent to the obligation ....

We conclude that California does not follow the *Restatement*'s strict merger requirement. Indeed, the leading California Supreme Court case rejects the tangibility requirement altogether. In *Payne v. Elliot,* 54 Cal. 339, 1880 WL 1907 (1880), the Court considered whether shares in a corporation (as opposed to the share certificates themselves) could be converted. It held that they could, reasoning: "[T]he action no longer exists as it did at common law, but has been developed into a remedy for the conversion of *every species of personal property.*"(emphasis added). While *Payne*'s outcome might be reconcilable with the *Restatement,* its rationale certainly is not: It recognized conversion of shares, not because they are customarily represented by share certificates, but because they are a species of personal property and, perforce, protected....

Were it necessary to settle the issue once and for all, we would toe the line of *Payne* and hold that conversion is "a remedy for the conversion of every species of personal property." But we need not do so to resolve this case. Assuming *arguendo* that California retains some vestigial merger requirement, it is clearly minimal, and at most requires only *some* connection to a document or tangible object—not representation of the owner's intangible interest in the strict *Restatement* sense.

Kremen's domain name falls easily within this class of property. He argues that the relevant document is the Domain Name System, or "DNS"—the distributed electronic database that associates domain names like sex.com with particular computers connected to the Internet. We agree that the DNS is a document (or perhaps more accurately a collection of documents). That it is stored in electronic form rather than on ink and paper is immaterial. It would be a curious jurisprudence that turned on the existence of a *paper* document rather than an electronic one. Torching a company's file room would then be conversion while hacking into its mainframe and deleting its data would not. That is not the law, at least not in California.

The DNS also bears some relation to Kremen's domain name.... Change the information in the DNS, and you change the website people see when they type "www.sex.com." ...

Kremen's domain name is protected by California conversion law, even on the grudging reading we have given it. Exposing Network Solutions to liability when it gives away a registrant's domain name on the basis of a forged letter is no different from holding a corporation liable when it gives away someone's shares under the same circumstances....

[T]here is nothing unfair about holding a company responsible for giving away someone else's property even if it was not at fault. Cohen is obviously the guilty party here, and the one who should in all fairness pay for his theft. But he's skipped the country, and his money is stashed in some offshore bank account. Unless Kremen's luck with his bounty hunters improves, Cohen is out of the picture. The question becomes whether Network Solutions should be open to liability for its decision to hand over Kremen's domain name. Negligent or not, it was Network Solutions that gave away Kremen's property. Kremen never did anything. It would not be unfair to hold Network Solutions responsible and force *it* to try to recoup its losses by chasing down Cohen. This, at any rate, is the logic of the common law, and we do not lightly discard it.

The district court was worried that "the threat of litigation threatens to stifle the registration system by requiring further regulations by [Network Solutions] and potential increases in fees." Given that Network Solutions's "regulations" evidently allowed it to hand over a registrant's domain name on the basis of a facially suspect letter without even contacting him, "further regulations" don't seem like such a bad idea. And the prospect of higher fees presents no issue here that it doesn't in any other context. A bank could lower its ATM fees if it didn't have to pay security guards, but we doubt most depositors would think that was a good idea.

The district court thought there were "methods better suited to regulate the vagaries of domain names" and left it "to the legislature to fashion an appropriate statutory scheme." The legislature, of course, is always free (within constitutional bounds) to refashion the system that courts come up with. But that doesn't mean we should throw up our hands and let private relations degenerate into a free-for-all in the meantime. We apply the common law until the legislature tells us otherwise. And the common law does not stand idle while people give away the property of others.

The evidence supported a claim for conversion, and the district court should not have rejected it. [Reversed on the conversion claim.]

---

49. **Expanding conversion to cover stand-alone economic harm.** *Kremen* is not alone in expanding the conversion action to cover intangibles, even when the intangible is not fully represented by a document. Here are three examples:

- *Schafer v. RMS Realty,* 138 Ohio App.3d 244, 741 N.E.2d 155 (2000) upheld the plaintiff's claim for breach of fiduciary duty by partners who used their power to make it financially impossible for the plaintiff to retain all of his share of the partnership; the court then also approved a claim on the same facts as a conversion claim, saying the defendant had converted the plaintiff's partnership interest.
- *DeLong v. Osage Valley Elec. Cooperative Ass'n,* 716 S.W.2d 320 (Mo. App. 1986) supported the idea a conversion claim by an

electricity producer against a customer who circumvented the meter to take electricity, although that case might be explained on unjust enrichment grounds.

- *Mundy v. Decker,* 1999 WL 14479 (Neb. App. 1999) said it was allowing a "conversion" claim against a departing employee who deleted all the computer files, but the plaintiff actually had copies of the files, so the information itself was not converted; rather the court seems to have had in mind the inconvenience and costs of restoring the files. Damages were in fact based on time spent in that effort, not on the value of the information itself, so the case looks more like a trespass to chattels case than one for conversion.

50. **Expanding trespass to chattels to cover stand-alone economic harm.** Trespass to chattels has also been expanded to reach intangible invasions such as the burden of spam electronically thrust into a company's computer, *School of Visual Arts v. Kuprewicz,* 3 Misc.3d 278, 771 N.Y.S.2d 804 (Sup. Ct. 2003) (causing large volume of email interfering with use of plaintiff's computers), or hacking into a telephone company's computer to make free calls). *Thrifty-Tel, Inc. v. Myron Bezenek,* 46 Cal.App.4th 1559, 54 Cal.Rptr.2d 468 (1996) (computer hackers breaking into telephone company's long-distance system, using confidential access code, and making calls was trespass to chattels).

51. **Scope of Kreman: is merger or representation in a document relevant?** It has been argued that a document representing the plaintiff's intangible interests may help provide reliable indication that those interests should be characterized as property and thus protected, but that courts can decide the property question without imposing a strict requirement of merger or representation. See Courtney W. Franks, Comment, *Analyzing the Urge to Merge: Conversion of Intangible Property and the Merger Doctrine in the Wake of Kremen v. Cohen,* 42 HOUSTON L. REV. 489 (2005). If the intangible interest is not protected under other laws, what should lead a court to recognize it as a property interest?

52. **Scope of Kreman: where other law addresses the plaintiff's interests.** In ¶ 48, supra, we noted a number of cases rejecting the conversion claim in which other legal rules addressed the plaintiff's intangible interest. Would the plaintiff's interest in the domain name in *Kreman* be covered by any other sets of legal rules besides conversion? The law of copyright, trade secrets, or trademark probably do not address the right claimed by the plaintiff, much less afford relief. What about the law of unjust enrichment? Can we say that the plaintiff's claim on a conversion theory is more likely to be justified where no other rule-sets address the claim?

To turn the question around, consider what should be done about the conversion claim if some other set of legal rules *do* address the plaintiff's interest, either to support it or to reject it. Suppose the plaintiff sues for conversion of her good name based on publication of serious accusations about her. Should courts following the relatively open approach suggested in the first part of *Kreman* allow such an action, in effect treating "good name" as intangible property? If the plaintiff can recover under defamation law, why should the court add a new theory to brief? If the plaintiff cannot recover under defamation law, maybe that is because defamation law has addressed her claim and found it wanting. On this point, look back at *Miller* and see if you think *Miller* and *Kremen* could both be right.

*

Professional and Academic Enhancements
Chapter 10

A Remedies Problem in Injurious Falsehood Cases

Padilla owned Blackacre, land with a residential structure. He agreed to sell to Tallman for $500,000, subject to title check. Tallman's title check turned up a judgment in favor of DuMond against Padilla for $640,000. A judgment is an encumbrance on land of the person against whom the judgment runs. Tallman immediately cancelled the contract (as he had the right to do when the encumbrance was discovered). Tallman purchased Whiteacre from Goodman instead. The judgment was genuine, but it had been paid by Padilla's insurer. DuMond should have endorsed the judgment as satisfied when payment was made, but did not do so and for some reason the insurer failed to make satisfaction of the judgment a precondition to payment. Padilla, having lost the sale, considers suing DuMond. He still owns Blackacre. One appraiser tells you that Blackacre is worth $500,000. Another says it is worth $450,000. Still a third says it is worth $550,000. Can Padilla prove special damages?

Dan B. Dobbs, The Law of Remedies § 6.8 (2) (2d ed. 1993)*

. . . The requirement in disparagement cases that the plaintiff prove special damages is not only a requirement of pecuniary loss. It is also a requirement that the plaintiff has realized the loss or that he is likely to realize it at some point in the future; paper losses are not enough. The point of the special damages requirement can be seen in an important English decision, [*Malachy v. Soper*, 3 Bing.N.C. 371, 132 Eng.Repr. 453 (1936).] The defendant there erroneously reported that a court decision had been rendered, the effect of which was that the plaintiff was not the owner of shares of stock. While this erroneous report was outstanding, the plaintiff's share of stock were worthless, since he could not sell them. But the report was promptly corrected, and when it was the plaintiff's shares could be sold at their market value. The court held that the plaintiff's unrealized paper losses could not be a basis for liability; instead, special damages would have to be shown.

If the plaintiff in *Malachy* had actually *sold* his shares while they were worth little or nothing, he would have had a realized loss easily computed by measuring the sale price against their true market value. This would count as special damages. [Restatement Second of Torts

* Footnotes omitted.

§ 633, Comment f (1977).] On the other hand, the loss of a prospective sale during the period of depressed prices would not show special damages. And it would be sound to deny recovery for the loss of the sale since the plaintiff would still have his stock, and it would now be sellable at its true value. Cases like *Malachy* differ in this respect from the case of the retailer who loses customers because his goods are maligned. A customer who quits buying groceries from the plaintiff because he is told they are unfit will buy his groceries elsewhere. And since the grocer can ordinarily supply a more or less unlimited quantity, he does indeed have a loss when the customer fills his needs at another store. The difference is that in *Malachy* the owner of the shares could only have suffered a postponement of the sale while in the grocer's case the grocer has actually lost a sale as soon as the customer buys groceries elsewhere.

Special damages need not take the form of lost sales, however. If the stockholder in *Malachy* had to postpone an intended sale because of the published falsehood, he might have special damages in the delay, presumably measured as interest. Expenses of clearing the title, or surveying expense when title to land has been put in doubt, or damages incurred because sale could not be made at the time planned would all represent realized loss and special damages. Even the cost of correcting the disparagement by advertising or otherwise might be an appropriate element of recovery in some cases.

The point of *Malachy v. Soper* was that realized pecuniary loss had to be shown, not that any particular level of proof was required to show it. But in some cases the plaintiff was required to prove the realized loss by a demanding rule, namely that he must show the loss of identifiable customers. In the case of the shares of stock this would be easy enough if a potential buyer had actually been lost. But in the case of a manufacturer or retailer whose goods have been impugned, the loss of specific buyers would be difficult to show indeed. Yet some cases demanded such proof and rejected proof of a general decline in sales following upon the heels of the disparagement.

Proof of business loss today is usually not so demanding, partly because lawyers now tend to produce a high quality proof. Probably it is safe to say the rule permits proof of special damages by any ordinary, credible evidence that would suffice in any other claim of lost profits, though the value of the evidence in any given case would be subject to careful assessment. For example, proof of declining profits following the publication of the falsehood might be insufficient in itself, but such proof coupled with proof that industry profits as a whole remained the same in the relevant time period along with proof that the defendant's profits rose, might be sufficiently convincing that the falsehood caused the loss. Expert testimony by market analysts and others has also tipped the scale in favor of the plaintiff.

Breach of Fiduciary Duty and Franchises

ARNOTT v. AMERICAN OIL CO.

609 F.2d 873 (8th Cir. 1979)

STEPHENSON, Circuit Judge.

Defendant-appellant, American Oil Company (Amoco), appeals from a judgment entered against it by the district court upon a jury verdict of $100,000 (trebled by the court under the antitrust laws to $300,000 plus attorney fees and costs) and punitive damages of $25,000. Numerous issues are raised, including insufficiency of the evidence to create submissible jury issues on plaintiff's claims. We affirm on condition that plaintiff-appellee, George Arnott, file a remittitur of all damages exceeding $125,000 plus interest and costs.

This action involves the relationship between a major oil company, Amoco (often referred to in the record as Standard Oil), and George Arnott, one of its service station dealers. On August 6, 1973, Amoco terminated Arnott as a Standard Oil dealer by terminating his lease and evicting him from the service station. Arnott's complaint alleged, and the jury found in answer to special interrogatories accompanying the general verdict, that . . . (2) Amoco breached the fiduciary duty owed to Arnott by terminating his lease without good cause and by not dealing with Arnott in good faith during the term of the lease agreement. . . .

The record when viewed most favorably to the jury verdict for Arnott discloses the following. In October 1971 Arnott was operating a Standard Oil station in Minneapolis, when he was approached by Amoco's sales manager for the Sioux Falls district, Dick Lucas, about operating a Standard station at an interstate location in Sioux Falls, South Dakota. Arnott declined [but eventually agreed.] He entered into a lease agreement dated February 18, 1972, for a one-year period. It was then a standard policy of Amoco to issue only one-year leases, but there was also evidence at the trial that these leases were routinely renewed on an annual basis if the dealer operated the station in a reasonable manner. Arnott testified that it was his understanding that as long as he operated the station in a reasonable manner and it was a profitable venture for himself and Standard Oil, he could have it for as long as he wanted, which was in accord with his experience as a Standard Oil dealer. . . .

[Amoco gave dealers a Statement of Policy.] The Statement of Policy contained several provisions which were repeatedly violated by Amoco employees The Policy provisions which the record discloses were violated by Amoco may be summarized as follows: (1) Arnott would be an independent businessman who would have the right to run his station free from coercion or pressure on the part of any company representative; (2) no company representative would bring any pressure to bear on Arnott if he chose to handle competitive brands of motor oils; (3) with respect to tires, batteries, and accessories, Arnott would have complete freedom to buy these products from whomever he chose; the company would not tolerate coercion, harassment, or improper pressure of any kind by its salesmen in the sale of these products; (4) Arnott would have the absolute right to set his own resale price with respect to all Standard Oil products, including gasoline, and would be free to display and promote all products as he saw fit; and (5) Arnott would not be pressured into participating in advertising, sales promotions, or merchandising programs sponsored by the company.

On several occasions when Arnott placed competitive brands on display along with Standard Oil products, he was instructed by Amoco to remove the same. [The court gives many details about this an similar pressures exerted by Amoco, to Arnott's detriment.]

Arnott signed a new lease agreement on December 8, 1972, effective February 19, 1973, for an additional one-year term.... He was advised by Amoco representatives that he was on probation and would not be given a lease unless he agreed to abide by the prices set by Amoco and to participate in their promotional programs. Arnott agreed to be cooperative in order to secure the lease renewal.

However, the problems continued....

During the last two weeks of his operation [during a nationawide gas shortage in 1973], Arnott ran out of gasoline most evenings and eventually closed the station because it was not profitable to remain open. In addition, customers became very irate after pulling into the station only to find gasoline unavailable.

Arnott advised Amoco of his situation and that he was closing down from 10:00 p. m. to 6:00 a. m. However, Amoco advised Arnott that he was in violation of the lease in failing to maintain a 24-hour operation.

Arnott became frustrated, and on July 17, 1973, he signed a cancellation agreement to voluntarily leave the station. Later in the day he reconsidered his position and called an Amoco representative to rescind his consent to the cancellation. A few days later Amoco marketing representative, Clint Bucklin, told Arnott that if he cooperated with Amoco's policies, he could keep the station. The next day Bucklin advised Arnott that Bucklin apparently had acted without authority and that Arnott would be removed August 6, 1973. A formal letter to that effect dated July 26, 1973, was mailed to Arnott, who then retained counsel. Amoco was advised by letter that its August 6 takeover was being treated by Arnott as an involuntary cancellation of the lease. Arnott left the station August 6, 1973. On that date Amoco hand-delivered a letter to Arnott advising him that his lease was being cancelled effective September 5, 1973, because of violation of the 24-hour clause in the lease....

Arnott alleged that Amoco breached the fiduciary duty owed to Arnott by terminating his lease without good cause and by not dealing with Arnott in good faith during the lease term. The court instructed the jury that a fiduciary relationship existed between the defendant and the plaintiff. [The instruction, printed in the court's footnote 6, is as follows.]

> (Y)ou are instructed that a fiduciary relationship existed between the defendant and the plaintiff. A fiduciary relationship is one founded on trust or confidence placed by one person in the integrity and fidelity of another person. Out of such a relation, the law requires that neither party exert undue influence or pressure upon the other, take selfish advantage of his trust or deal with the subject matter of the trust in such a way as to benefit himself or prejudice the other except in the exercise of the utmost good faith and with the full knowledge and consent of the other person involved.

Amoco contends that the evidence does not support the existence of a fiduciary relationship and that the court erred in instructing that the relationship existed as a matter of law. Further, Amoco argues that it properly terminated Arnott's lease for failure to maintain a 24-hour operation as set out in the lease.

Although the existence of a fiduciary relationship is a close question, the dealer-oil company relationship has been the subject of much recent litigation, and the current trend of authority recognizes that a franchise relationship exists between a service station dealer and the oil company whose trademark the dealer is promoting. Inherent in a franchise relationship is a fiduciary duty....

It is likewise clear that Arnott was not pursuing solely his own business interests in his relationship with Amoco. Arnott sold Amoco products under the Amoco trademark, was expected to remain open twenty-four hours a day, was responsible for hiring adequate help, and was subject to inspections from Amoco representatives.... Obviously, a franchise relationship in which Arnott and Amoco had a common interest and profit in the activities of each other, and not the typical landlord-tenant relationship, existed.

A franchisee, unlike a tenant pursuing his own interests, builds the goodwill of his own business and the goodwill of the franchisor. This facet of the relationship has led to the recognition that the franchise relationship imposes a duty upon franchisors not to act arbitrarily in terminating the franchise. [Citing several cases.]

In light of the undisputed facts in this case, it is our view that the district court did not err in instructing that a fiduciary relationship existed between the parties and in instructing that the law requires that neither party exert undue influence or pressure upon the other....

We are satisfied that the evidence amply supports the jury's finding that Amoco breached its "fiduciary" duty of good faith and fair dealing with Arnott in terminating its lease agreement with Arnott without good cause and that as a direct and proximate result of the termination Arnott suffered damages....

1. **Authority opposed to *Arnott*.** Most fiduciary duties run from persons who are in a broad sense agents to persons who are principals. It

is no surprise, then, that most courts have refused to recognize a fiduciary duty running from franchisors to franchisees, although as we'll see statutes may add a measure of protection. See, rejecting a fiduciary duty in termination cases, *Crim Truck & Tractor Co. v. Navistar Int'l Transp. Corp.,* 823 S.W.2d 591 (Tex. 1992).

2. **Authority supporting *Arnott.*** *Arnott* has some slight support in the cases, although here again, statutes may affect the issue. The most extreme case was *Shell Oil Co. v. Marinello,* 63 N.J. 402, 307 A.2d 598 (1973). Shell Oil Company, leased its service station to the plaintiff for three years, with a provision that the lease and franchising agreement could be terminated on 30 days' notice. The court, without using the term fiduciary, directly held that the termination provisions were against public policy and that Shell could not terminate the original lease-franchise without good cause. It could not even fail to renew without good cause. The effect was that a three-year renewable business arrangement became a permanent obligation. Do you think *Arnott* went this far?

3. **Statutory protections for dealers and franchisees.** Although the courts have mainly rejected *Arnott,* a number of legislatures, state and federal, have passed franchising statutes that in various degrees provide protection against termination. Some statutes are general, some are aimed at particular industries or dealerships, such as beer dealers or farm equipment sellers. Some prohibit termination without good causes; some even prohibit nonrenewal of the contract without good cause. E.g., CAL. BUS. & PROF. CODE § 22902 & 22903; TEX. ALCOHOLIC BEV. Code § 102.74. Some federal statutes protect particular franchisees. The Petroleum Marketing Practices Act, 15 U.S.C.A. § 2802 prohibits both termination and nonrenewal of a franchise such as a service station unless one of the grounds spelled out in the statute is demonstrated. Within its scope, this statute preempts state law dealing with termination or nonrenewal, perhaps even state common law based on the implied covenant of good faith and fair dealing. See *Clark v. BP Oil Co.,* 137 F.3d 386 (6th Cir. 1998). Another federal statute protects automobile dealers from bad faith nonrenewal of a dealership. 15 U.S.C.A. § 1222, although here this provision may be construed narrowly to limit its scope. See *Autohaus Brugger, Inc. v. Saab Motors, Inc.,* 567 F.2d 901 (9th Cir. 1978).

SIMS WHOLESALE CO., INC. V. BROWN-FORMAN CORP., 251 Va. 398, 468 S.E.2d 905 (1996). The Virginia Wine Franchise Act provided that a winery could not "cancel, terminate or refuse to continue to renew any agreement" with their wholesalers unless the winery gave notice and also had good cause. A winery decided that it would market more effectively with fewer wholesalers, and that was a sound business decision made in good faith. In accord with that decision, it terminated the contracts with a number of wholesalers. The wholesalers petitioned the Virginia Alcoholic Beverage Control Board, which is the state agency regulating such matters. The Board concluded that the winery lacked good cause for termination under the statute. That decision was appealed to a court of general jurisdiction, and on up to the Court of Appeals. Now, before the Supreme Court of Virginia, *held,* consolidation or down-sizing, though in good faith and based on sound business judgment, is not good cause under the statute. Good cause is not limited to causes based on some deficiency of the wholesaler, but neither can good cause be found merely because good business judgment was exercised. Implications of the statute's specific good cause provisions are that consolidation or down-sizing is not itself good cause. Consequently, the wholesalers must be compensated.

1. **Good cause.** What counts as good cause depends upon the specific statutory wording, but many of the statutes are at pains to recognize a number of specific grounds for termination or nonrenewal that are justified. In *River Valley Truck Ctr., Inc. v. Interstate Companies,* 680 N.W.2d 99 (Minn. Ct. App. 2004), the court recited a number of such grounds under Minnesota's Heavy and Utility Equipment Manufacturers and Dealers Act—bankruptcy of the dealer, the dealer's change in location, his conviction of a felony, or his conduct detrimental to customers. In addition, good cause for termination can be found if the dealer requirements for "reasonable market penetration based on the manufacturer's experience in other comparable marketing areas, consistently fails to meet the manufacturer's market penetration requirements."

2. **De-tortification.** Notice that the *Sims* statute comes up in an administrative action and its review, not a tort suit. Notice also that the damages do not sound like tort damages. Do you think that franchisors would have supported some of these statutes on the ground that they don't impose that much liability and that it is better from them than tort law would be?

3. **Other franchisee-franchisor conflicts.** Besides termination and nonrenewal issues, the franchisee-franchisor relationship is full of difficulties. Franchisees are sometimes dismayed to find that they are required to use certain materials to be purchased from the franchisor, but that the materials are not readily available, or that the franchisor sets up a competing franchise a few blocks away. Is there any reason these issues should not be resolved under the contract provisions or the law of misrepresentation? Although the law of franchising takes us too far away from the fiduciary topic, you should know that state statutes regulate many aspects of franchising and that the Federal Trade Commission also has rules concerning disclosures the proposed franchisor must make.

4. **Some policy questions.** Now let's renew our focus on fiduciary duties. If the courts were right in mostly rejecting fiduciary duties to franchisees, are the legislatures wrong? Does the legislation reflect a pervasive lack of confidence in voluntary contracts? Why would legislatures treat franchisees better than at-will employees, who, as we saw in

the last section, can be discharged without cause. Or should we re-think the right of employers to discharge at-will employees for no reason?

5. **Does contract trump tort?** Put more broadly, the questions about legislation raised in the last paragraph come down to asking whether fiduciary standards should trump the contract limitations. In *Shell Oil*, supra Note 2 following *Arnott,* Shell thought it was making a three year contract; the contract itself said so. But the court ended up treating the franchise and lease as a conveyance of a permanent property right, subject to defeasance only if Shell had good cause to terminate. The court gave the franchisee-lessee something he had never bargained for and in fact something the contract said he was not entitled to. If you think *Shell Oil* was wrong and that the contract between the parties should control, would you go one other step and hold that whenever the parties are in a contractual relationship, the only claim the aggrieved party can assert is breach of contract? In other words, would the mere existence of contractual duties, express or implied, negate fiduciary duties enforceable in tort? Or do you think that the parties should be able to contract against the background of fiduciary duties without having to spell out all those duties in the contract?

Chapter 11

INTENDED INTERFERENCE WITH CONTRACTS AND ECONOMIC OPPORTUNITIES

Introduction to the Chapter

In the realm of stand-alone economic harm, the plaintiff usually suffers because the defendant has in some way interfered with the plaintiff's relations, or prospective relations with others.

One form of interference goes under various names such as interference with prospective advantage, or interference with economic opportunities. An example: the defendant induces retail customers of the plaintiff's grocery store to buy their goods from the defendant's grocery instead. Sometimes interference with economic opportunities (to sell groceries, in the example) is actionable, but it is not in this example because the defendant usually has a right to pursue his economic self-interest (by competition in this example), so long as he interferes with economic prospects only, not with an existing contract. We will put this kind of tort aside until we reach § 3 and concentrate in the first two sections on interference with an enforceable contract rather than mere prospects.

Interference with contract is actually the older form of interference. An example of such interference: the defendant induces the plaintiff's chief executive officer to breach his contract with the plaintiff and go to work for the defendant instead. Very likely that is tortious and the plaintiff, who could sue the CEO for breach of contract, can choose to sue the defendant for tort instead.

In the early cases, intentional interference with a known contract seems to have been actionable in itself. The intended interference was considered malicious and actionable. It was not justified by the fact that the defendant was competing with the plaintiff for, say, the services of the CEO. You can contrast the courts' approval of competition in the interference with economic opportunity cases, where the plaintiff had no enforceable contract with prospective customers.

Still considering interference with contract (not mere economic opportunities), we can say that two things changed over time. One was that courts began to think that *some* interferences were justified or "privileged." They held that proof of intended interference with a known contract was prima facie actionable, but that the defendant could escape liability if he carried the burden of proving he had a privilege. Unfortunately, there was little guidance about what interferences were "wrong" and what interferences were "right" or privileged.

The second change, and it is one that is still in progress, was that some courts began to think that the plaintiff should have the burden of proof to show wrongful or improper interference in the first place. Courts accepting that view shifted the burden of proof back to the plaintiff. But they left the same uncertainty that existed when the burden was on the defendant—what counts as an "improper" interference.

On the question of improper interference, what we can say with some assurance, no matter who had the burden of proof, is that the defendant's interference could be deemed improper if the defendant used improper means, such as threats of bodily harm or fraud, and also if his motive or purpose was considered unacceptable. Courts view a motive to compete with the plaintiff as quite insufficient to justify interference with contract, even though the same motive justifies an interference with economic prospects.

This state of the law leaves us with some difficult questions to be pursued in the materials that follow. Are we honoring contract properly by allowing the promisor to breach but then permitting suit against third parties who encouraged that breach? If the interference is accomplished by communication, what about free speech rights? Can courts really justify putting the burden on the defendant to justify interference, as if to say they presumed guilt, not innocence? What counts as improper (or unprivileged) interference and why should motive or purpose condemn an act that is otherwise legitimate?

§ 1. INTERFERING WITH THE PERFORMANCE OWED THE PLAINTIFF

RESTATEMENT (SECOND) OF TORTS § 766

Copyright 1979 by the American Law Institute
Reprinted by permission

Intentional Interference With Performance Of Contract By Third Person

One who intentionally and improperly interferes with the performance of a contract (except a contract to marry) between another and a third person by inducing or otherwise causing the third person not to perform the contract, is subject to liability to the other for the pecuniary loss resulting to the other from the failure of the third person to perform the contract.

1. **Physical harm to the promisor.** In the earliest cases, a miscreant beat the master's servant. At some periods, this was likely to cause the master harm. The master might be required to continue providing food and shelter for an apprentice, for example, even if the apprentice could not provide services. So the master recovered from the tortfeasor for loss of the servant's services. The miscreant's behavior, though originating in a physical and trespassory tort, was one form of interference with contract, or at least something closely analogous, because it deprived the master of economic value to which he was entitled under the indenture without physically harming the master or his property.

2. **British serfdom.** A big development occurred when the plague created a labor shortage. The feudal powers of the day enacted a statute that no person, unless independently wealthy or engaged in a craft, could leave his work. To back this up, the statute provided also that no other employer could hire him. So in a time of labor shortage, when workers might otherwise have expected competitive wages, they were instead virtually imprisoned and their wages limited. See The Ordinance of Labourers, 23 Edw. III (1349). Significantly, the statute created a regime that recognized rights in the master even when no physical harm had been done or threatened and when the only threat was economic activity of a competitor.

LUMLEY v. GYE, 2 El. & Bl. 216, 118 Eng. Rep. 749 (1853). The plaintiff operated an opera theater. He had retained a singer, Wagner, to perform exclusively at his theater. Before the term of her contract was up, the defendant, knowing of the contract, "enticed" or induced Wagner to cease further performance for the plaintiff and to perform at the defendant's theater instead, to the plaintiff's damage. The plaintiff sued the defendant claiming that inducing a breach of contract was a tort. *Held*, for the plaintiff. Erle, J.: "[P]rocurement of the violation of the right is a cause of action, and... when this principle is applied to a violation of a right arising upon a contract of hiring, the nature of the service contracted for is immaterial."

3. **Reasons for suing the breach-inducer.** Aside from personal anger or ill-will, would the plaintiff in *Lumley* have economic motives for suing the breach inducer instead of simply suing the contract breacher?

4. **Malice or motive.** The judges and lawyers in *Lumley v. Gye* used some form of the word malice more than 50 times, but malice in the sense of spite or ill-will was not required in the traditional claim for interference with contract. You can see this from the succinct statement of Erle, J. Thus it was enough in *Lumley* if the defendant, knowing of the contract, intentionally induced its breach. In particular, the defen-

dant's economic self-interest did not justify his interference with another's contract. Today's courts may reach results like *Lumley's* on the ground that malice is not required or on the ground that malice is defined to include any intentional, unjustified and hurtful act. See *Dowlen v. Weathers,* 2005 WL 1160627 (Tenn. Ct. App. 2005); *Chaves v. Johnson,* 230 Va. 112, 335 S.E.2d 97 (1985).

5. **Intent.** The Restatement Second of Torts ascribed intent to the defendant if he had a purpose to cause the consequences of his act and also if the defendant believed that the consequences were substantially certain to follow. See RESTATEMENT SECOND OF TORTS § 8 A (1965). As applied to interference with contracts, this would mean that the defendant need not act for the *purpose* of causing a third person to breach his contract with the plaintiff. Instead, it would be enough if the defendant believed his acts would have that effect. In *Korea Supply Co. v. Lockheed Martin Corp.,* 29 Cal.4th 1134, 63 P.3d 937, 131 Cal.Rptr.2d 29 (2003), the court rejected the defendant's argument that only a purpose or desire to cause the interference would suffice.

6. **Inducing or otherwise causing breach.** *Lumley* involved a defendant who induced breach of contract. However, liability may attach just as well if the defendant's interference causes damages by supporting or facilitating breach. In *Fowler v. Printers II, Inc.,* 89 Md.App. 448, 598 A.2d 794 (1991), an employee breached her covenant not to compete with her employer by leaving employment and accepting a job with a competitor who knew nothing of the covenant. After the new employer learned of the covenant not to compete, it continued employing the breaching employee. This was enough to make the new employer liable for interfering with the original employer's contract with the employee.

7. **Considering Lumley v. Gye.** *Lumley v. Gye* is the basic case establishing a general tort for inducing another to breach a contract. Notice that Lumley did not claim that Gye used any wrongful means or method to secure Wagner's breach. He did not use fraud or defamation, for example, only persuasion. Why would the court impose liability upon Gye? The plaintiff paid Wagner to secure his contract rights against her and has a breach of contract action against her. But the plaintiff paid nothing to the defendant. Why should the plaintiff be permitted to recover in tort for Wagner's breach from someone who had promised him nothing?

8. **Elements: the prima facie tort and the shifted burden of proof.** In *Korea Supply Co. v. Lockheed Martin Corp.,* 29 Cal.4th 1134, 63 P.3d 937, 131 Cal.Rptr.2d 29 (2003), the court observed that "intentionally interfering with an existing contract is a wrong in and of itself." This means that if the defendant knew of the contractual relationship between the plaintiff and another person, intentionally and successfully interfered with that relationship, and thereby caused economic harm to the plaintiff, the plaintiff has established a prima facie case for liability. Under this traditional form of thinking, the rule in *Lumley v. Gye* exemplifies a prima facie tort. See Mark P. Gergen, *Tortious Interference:*

How it Is Engulfing Commercial Law, Why this Is Not Entirely Bad, and a Prudential Response, 38 ARIZ. L. REV. 1175 (1996). The prima facie tort idea is that if you intentionally (maybe just knowingly) cause economic harm to another, you are prima facie guilty of a tort. Almost all economic activity fits that definition. The effect is that the burden of proof is shifted to the defendant to justify his action, although what justifications will be recognized is sometimes uncertain. We'll see more of the prima facie tort idea in § 7, below.

9. **Elements: the Restatement and "improper" interference.** *Lumley* and the very strong tradition it generated allowed the plaintiff to recover merely upon showing an intentional interference. Some contemporary cases continue to state the rule in that manner. The rule of Restatement § 766, printed above, is different, isn't it? It imposed liability upon a defendant who "intentionally and improperly interferes" with the contract. For instance, it has been held that a lawyer negotiating a settlement agreement for his client is not acting improperly and is not liable even though he knows that the settlement will interfere with the plaintiff-insurer's contractual right to cooperation from its insured. *Safeway Ins. Co., Inc. v. Guerrero,* 210 Ariz. 5, 106 P.3d 1020 (2005). The Restatement's "improper" test raises questions about what counts as "improper" interference and what does not. The Restatement and many cases contemplate that the court could find "improper" interference either (a) because the defendant used improper means to interfere or (b) because, even if the means were legitimate, the defendant had an improper motive. We'll look further into this element in ¶ 12, below.

10. **Privilege—the burden of proof issue.** The traditional rule made the defendant prima facie liable if he intentionally interfered with an existing contract. However, the defendant could still assert a privilege to interfere or "justification" for interference. See *Foster v. Churchill,* 87 N.Y.2d 744, 665 N.E.2d 153, 642 N.Y.S.2d 583 (1996). The privilege was an affirmative defense, with the burden of proof on the defendant to justify his interference. *Commerce Funding Corp. v. Worldwide Security Servs. Corp.,* 249 F.3d 204 (4th Cir. 2001). For example, an appropriate agent would be privileged to advise the principal to breach an undesirable contract as long as he is acting in the interest of the principal and not out of personal motives. See ¶ 49, below. The defendant's assertion of a justification for interference in effect says that neither the means he used nor the motive with which he acted were improper under the circumstance.

Under the more contemporary approach, the defendant's improper motive or conduct must be proved by the plaintiff, not as a privilege raised by the defendant. See *Sisters of Providence in Washington v. A.A. Pain Clinic, Inc.,* 81 P.3d 989 (Alaska 2003); *Buster v. George W. Moore,* Inc., 438 Mass. 635, 783 N.E.2d 399 (2003); *National Employment Serv. Corp. v. Olsten Staffing Serv., Inc.,* 145 N.H. 158, 761 A.2d 401 (2000). Either way, "improper" usually becomes a central issue and "privilege" is merely the way of discussing that issue in courts that put the burden upon the defendant rather than the plaintiff.

11. **Wrongful motive or means; violation of preexisting independent duty.** The easy case for finding that interference with contract is wrongful or improper occurs when the defendant interferes by violating some preexisting or independent duty. Suppose a corporation holds an option to buy Blackacre from T. The defendant is a director of the corporation and hence owes it a fiduciary duty. Nevertheless, the defendant secretly induces T to sell Blackacre to him personally, thus inducing T to breach his option contract with the corporation. This sounds like a breach of fiduciary duty by the defendant director, and liability should follow for that tort, as we saw in Chapter 10, supra. Cf. *Northeast Harbor Golf Club, Inc. v. Harris,* 661 A.2d 1146 (Me. 1995) (director used corporate opportunity to secretly acquire property for herself). In *Northeast Women's Center, Inc. v. McMonagle*, 868 F.2d 1342 (3d Cir. 1989), defendants, who were protesting an abortion clinic and repeatedly invading its equipment, were found guilty both of interference and of a civil RICO violation.

12. **Wrongful motive or means without violation of preexisting duty; factors.** When the defendant interferes with a contract without committing any independent tort, what conduct or motive would count as wrongful or improper? In *Bogle v. Summit Investment Co., LLC,* 137 N.M. 80, 107 P.3d 520, 528, 529 (2005), the court observed that liability would be appropriate if the defendant "acted with either an improper motive or by use of improper means," and went on to say that "[i]mproper means includes not only tortious behavior, but any 'predatory' behavior, including behavior that is wrongful based on an established standard of a trade or profession."

A contemporary generalization is: "The interference with a contractual relationship must be both intentional and improper. Interference with a contract is intentional if the defendant either interferes with the contract on purpose or knows the conduct is substantially certain to interfere with the contract. In determining whether an interference is improper, consideration is given to the following factors: (a) the nature of the actor's conduct, (b) the actor's motive, (c) the interests of the other with which the actor's conduct interferes, (d) the interests sought to be advanced by the actor, (e) the social interests in protecting the freedom of action of the actor and the contractual interests of the other, (f) the proximity or remoteness of the actor's conduct to the interference and (g) the relations between the parties." *Hill v. Winnebago Industries, Inc.*, 522 N.W.2d 326 (Iowa App. 1994) (derived from RESTATEMENT (SECOND) OF TORTS § 767).

Can an enterprise know what economic conduct is acceptable under these factors? Should motive really be considered if the conduct is otherwise permissible?

13. **Applying the "wrongful or improper" factors.** (1) In *Duff v. Engelberg*, 237 Cal.App.2d 505, 47 Cal.Rptr. 114 (1965), the plaintiffs were African-Americans who had contracted to purchase a lot from McCoy. Neighbors Engelberg and Campbell did not want the plaintiffs to

live in the neighborhood and induced the McCoys to convey the lot to the Campbells instead of honoring their contract. Should the plaintiffs be permitted to recover damages from the breach-inducers Engelberg and Campbell as well as specific performance against the seller who reneged? How would the case stack up if defendants had talked the McCoys out of selling for reasons unrelated to the buyers' race, for example, because the neighbors didn't like the buyers' personalities or because they did like the McCoys and wanted them to stay?

(2) In *Fikes v. Furst,* 134 N.M. 602, 81 P.3d 545 (2003), both plaintiff and defendant were anthropologists. They had a contentious relationship for many years. Fikes prepared a book manuscript containing statements about Furst's work, including this: "I discovered what may be the most complicated and fascinating anthropological hoax of the 20th century." Dr. Fikes had a contract with Madison Books to publish the manuscript. "Dr. Furst found out about it, and wrote to the publisher threatening to sue for libel if the book was published. Madison Books then canceled the contract with Dr. Fikes to publish the book." Fikes sued on several grounds. On the interference with contract ground Furst argued that he was not motivated by ill-will or a desire to harm but by a desire to protect his own interest—his professional reputation and livelihood. Do you think that the interference with contract was improper under the factors listed above? Would you say that protecting one's own economic interests is always enough to negate bad motive? What about *Lumley*?

14. **Marriage and illegal contracts.** The principle that one could be liable for intended interference with a contract was limited in two respects. No liability attached for interference with illegal contracts and no liability was attached for interference with marriage contracts.

15. **Importing rights or privileges from other torts.** Would it be fair and desirable to say that the defendant's conduct is proper (or privileged) whenever it would be protected by the rules of some other tort? Suppose the alleged interference is that the defendant files a law suit that prevented or delayed performance of a contract beneficial to the plaintiff but the defendant would not be liable under the rules for tortious civil litigation. Or suppose that the defendant interfered with the plaintiff's contract by defaming the plaintiff. In *Blatty v. New York Times Co.,* 42 Cal.3d 1033, 232 Cal.Rptr. 542, 728 P.2d 1177 (1986), the court said that at least if the gravamen of the interference claim is falsehood, then the rules limiting defamation actions apply to limit the claim.

16. **Free speech.** When a defendant induces someone to breach a contract with the plaintiff but does nothing that is independently wrongful, should his honest speech—the persuasion to breach—be protected under the First Amendment? The defendant's speech is normally commercial speech that currently receives less protection than other speech. Even under the lessened protection for commercial speech, however, the Court protects the speech unless there is a substantial state interest in

curtailing it and the regulation imposed directly advances that interest. In addition, the restriction on speech must represent a "reasonable fit" or appropriate scope to deal with the problem. A distinguished torts professor believes that these rules would protect against the kind of common law liability imposed in *Lumley*. David A. Anderson, *Torts, Speech, and Contracts,* 75 TEX. L. REV. 1499 (1997).

17. **The Restatement on speech rights.** The Second Restatement, in a curt nod to the First Amendment, recognizes that truthful "information" cannot by itself form the basis for an interference claim. Restatement § 772. So what is "improper" about inducing breach of contract if the defendant does not do so by false statements? Would the truthful statement "I'll pay you more money to sing for me" provide the basis for an intentional interference claim under the Second Restatement?

ADLER, BARISH, DANIELS, LEVIN AND CRESKOFF v. EPSTEIN

482 Pa. 416, 393 A.2d 1175, 1 A.L.R.4th 1144 (1978)

ROBERTS, Justice....

From the formation of Adler Barish in February, 1976, through March of the next year, appellees were salaried associates of Adler Barish. Appellees were under the supervision of Adler Barish partners, who directed appellees' work on cases which clients brought to the firm.

While still working for Adler Barish, appellees decided to form their own law firm and took several steps toward achieving their goal. They retained counsel to advise them concerning their business venture, sought and found office space, and early in March, 1977, signed a lease.

Shortly before leaving Adler Barish, appellees procured a line of $150,000 from First Pennsylvania Bank. As security, appellees furnished bank officials with a list of eighty-eight cases and their anticipated legal fees, several of which were higher than $25,000, and together exceeded $500,000. No case on the list, however, was appellees'. Rather, each case was an Adler Barish case on which appellees were working.

Appellee Alan Epstein's employment relationship with Adler Barish terminated on March 10, 1977. At his request, Epstein continued to use offices of Adler Barish until March 19. During this time, and through April 4, when Adler Barish filed its complaint, Epstein was engaged in an active campaign to procure business for his new law firm. He initiated contacts, by phone and in person, with clients of Adler Barish with open cases on which he had worked while a salaried employee. Epstein advised the Adler Barish clients that he was leaving the firm and that they could choose to be represented by him, Adler Barish, or any other firm or attorney.

Epstein's attempt to procure business on behalf of the firm did not stop with these contacts. He mailed to the clients form letters which could be used to discharge Adler Barish as counsel, name Epstein the client's new counsel and create a contingent fee agreement. Epstein also provided clients with a stamped envelope addressed to Epstein. [Other appellees were either aware of Epstein's efforts and made no attempt to stop them, or made similar efforts themselves.]

Thus, clients of Adler Barish served a dual purpose in appellees' effort to start their own law firm. First, while appellees still worked for Adler Barish, Adler Barish cases formed the basis for appellees' obtaining bank credit. Then, appellees, as they left Adler Barish, made a concentrated attempt to procure the cases which had been used to obtain credit.

[The trial court granted an injunction; the Superior Court reversed. The case is here before the Supreme Court.]

An examination of this case in light of Restatement (Second) of Torts, § 766, reveals that the sole dispute is whether appellees' conduct is "improper." ... In assessing whether appellees' conduct is "improper," we bear in mind what this Court stated in Glenn v. Point Park College, where we analyzed "privileges" in conjunction with the closely related right of action for intentional interference with prospective contract relations:

> The absence of privilege or justification in the tort under discussion is closely related to the element of intent. As stated by Harper & James, The Law of Torts, § 6.11, at 513–14: "... where, as in most cases, the defendant acts at least in part for the purpose of protecting some legitimate interest which conflicts with that of the plaintiff, a line must be drawn and the interests evaluated. This process results in according or denying a privilege which, in turn, determines liability." What is or is not privileged conduct in a given situation is not susceptible of precise definition. Harper & James refer in general to interferences which "are sanctioned by the 'rules of the game' which society has adopted, and to the area of socially acceptable conduct which the law regards as privileged"....

We are guided, too, by Section 767 of Restatement (Second) of Torts, which focuses on what factors should be considered in determining whether conduct is "improper"....

We find nothing in the " 'rules of the game' which society has adopted" which sanctions appellees' conduct. Indeed, the rules which apply to those who enjoy the privilege of practicing law in this Commonwealth expressly disapprove appellees' method of obtaining clients ....

It is true that, upon termination of their employment relationship with Adler Barish, appellees were free to engage in their own business venture. See Restatement (Second) of Agency, § 396(a) (1958) ("[u]nless otherwise agreed, after termination of the agency, the agent ... has no duty not to compete with the principal"). But appellees' right to pursue their own business interests is not absolute. "[U]nless otherwise agreed, after the termination of the agency, the agent ... has a duty to the principal not to take advantage of a still subsisting *confidential* relation created during the prior agency relation"). Restatement (Second) of Agency, supra at § 396(d).

Appellees' contacts were possible because Adler Barish partners trusted appellees with the high responsibility of developing its clients' cases. From this position of trust and responsibility, appellees were able to gain knowledge of the details, and status, of each case to which appellees had been assigned. In the atmosphere surrounding appellees' departure, appellees' contacts unduly suggested a course of action for Adler Barish clients and unfairly prejudiced Adler Barish. No public interest is served in condoning use of *confidential* information which has these effects. Clients too easily may suffer in the end....

[Injunction reinstated. The dissent is omitted.]

---

18. **Free speech and solicitation.** At one time, disciplinary rules prohibited lawyers from soliciting clients. It is now held that the First Amendment protects solicitation, at least when the client is not solicited in person. See *Shapero v. Kentucky Bar Ass'n*, 486 U.S. 466, 108 S.Ct. 1916, 100 L.Ed.2d 475 (1988). So under current law, Epstein's solicitation does not seem to violate the professional disciplinary rules in that respect.

19. **Where solicitation is proper.** If solicitation is not itself improper, on what basis could you find improper motive or means? Consider *Lamorte Burns & Co., Inc. v. Walters,* 167 N.J. 285, 770 A.2d 1158 (2001). Two employees assembled the employer's confidential data while they were planning to resign and compete. They even secretly formed their new business while they were employed. The court thought that, as a matter of law, the employees had committed these torts: breach of their duty of loyalty to their employer, misappropriation of trade secrets or confidential information, interference with the employer's contracts with customers, and unfair competition.

20. **Inducing breach of an invalid non-competition covenant.** Suppose employees, in violation of their non-competition covenant, go to work for the original employer's competitor. The competitor knows of the non-competition contract and hence is intentionally inducing the employees' breach. The non-competition covenant is invalid because it is unreasonable on the facts. Could the original employer nevertheless recover against the new employer for inducing breach? What would be wrongful motive or means? See *National Employment Serv. Corp. v. Olsten Staffing Serv., Inc.*, 145 N.H. 158, 761 A.2d 401 (2000).

HANNIGAN v. SEARS, ROEBUCK AND CO.

410 F.2d 285 (7th Cir. 1969)

HASTINGS, Senior Circuit Judge....

Hannigan conceived of a new idea for outdoor storage, i.e., an outdoor metal storage cabinet or locker. After negotiations, Hannigan and John Columbini, president of Fabricated, entered into an agreement on July 17, 1958 whereby Fabricated contracted to manufacture these cabinets exclusively for Hannigan; in consideration thereof, Hannigan agreed to purchase all such outdoor storage cabinets from Fabricated. The contract placed no limitations on Fabricated's right to manufacture and sell its metal outdoor storage buildings, and Fabricated continued to manufacture and to sell such storage buildings to various customers, including defendant Sears and plaintiff Tru-Han....

[In 1959, Sears attempted to persuade Fabricated to sell the lawn lockers directly to Sears.] Sears' avowed purpose for inviting Fabricated into a direct purchasing relationship was to avoid and to eliminate the profit of the middle-man, Tru-Han. Respecting its contractual obligation, Fabricated declined this invitation. [In 1960, Sears attempted to get Hannigan to reduce the price of lawn lockers he sold Sears. When he would not, Sears contracted for a supply from another company, Pemco, but Pemco went out of business.]

During July or August of 1962, Mitchell, in an apparent effort to meet Sears' lawn locker needs, attempted to persuade Fabricated to sell lockers directly to Sears. To perfect such an arrangement, Mitchell told Columbini, with full knowledge of Fabricated's exclusive lawn locker contract with Hannigan, that Sears "... wanted one supplier of the entire line (both utility buildings and lawn lockers), ..., and if he (as president of Fabricated) couldn't supply it that way I would have to look to the other people that I was dealing with." There was also testimony Mitchell told Columbini that Fabricated could "make more money" on the sale of the lockers by selling directly to Sears and bypassing plaintiffs.

Mitchell suggested that Columbini work out something with plaintiffs so Fabricated could serve as Sears' source for both lawn lockers and utility buildings.

At the time Mitchell advised Columbini of Sears' plan to purchase lockers and buildings from a common source, Fabricated was in large measure economically dependent upon Sears. Fabricated was selling utility buildings directly to Sears, and 60% Of Fabricated's "business was devoted to Sears as a customer." Columbini told Mitchell that "... if we lost the Sears business (as a result of the single source plan) that we couldn't exist. We couldn't continue to make cabinets for Tru-Han or any other customer for that matter."

After talking with Mitchell and learning of Sears' common source purchasing plan, Columbini contacted Hannigan and told him that "...

we had to make some agreement or understanding with each other with respect to selling these cabinets directly with Sears, . . . (otherwise), we would stand a chance of losing the entire line of cabinets and buildings, ..."

Thereafter, Hannigan did submit to a new arrangement under which Fabricated would sell lockers directly to Sears and Hannigan would receive a 10% commission on the sale of each such locker. Under this modified arrangement, Sears purchased lockers at a lower price, and Hannigan received significantly less on the sale of each locker.

In substance, plaintiffs alleged that Sears wrongfully and intentionally interfered with their contractual rights by inducing Fabricated to amend its contract with Hannigan and coercing Hannigan into involuntarily agreeing to such amendment. . . .

Without attempting to assess the jury's reasoning in reaching its verdict, it would not be unreasonable for it to have concluded: that Sears, in an effort to obtain an adequate number of lockers at a lower price than it was paying Tru-Han, induced Fabricated to seek a modification of its contractual obligations with Hannigan; and that Sears knew Hannigan had no practical alternative but to acquiesce in the contractual modification.

It is evident that if Hannigan had refused to assent to the modification, Fabricated would have lost all of Sears' business. Because of its economic dependency upon Sears, Fabricated would have been forced out of business leaving plaintiffs in the precarious economic position of being without their sole source of lawn lockers. . . .

To us, there is no legally significant distinction between unabashed third party conduct which induces one party to outrightly repudiate and breach its contract with another and subtle third party conduct which achieves essentially the same result through the equally questionable means of coercing a contractual modification. Both approaches are equally tortious in nature and similarly interfere with the contractual relationships of others.

To distinguish between conduct which directly causes a breach of contract and unjustifiable coercive conduct which effects the same result without a breach would overly limit the significance of the tort of inducing breach of contract and invite today's superior economic forces to freely interfere with contractual relationships without fear of legal reprisal. . . .

In the instant case, it is undeniable that there was an existing contract between Hannigan and Fabricated and that defendant Sears had knowledge of this contract. It is also true that at different times and in varying ways, Sears, for purely private business reasons, encouraged Fabricated to either breach or alter its contract with Hannigan. In its effort to induce Fabricated to sell lawn lockers directly to it, Sears threatened Fabricated with severe economic hardships and offered Fabricated greater economic opportunities. Though Sears' overtures did not cause Fabricated to outrightly repudiate and breach its contractual obligations to plaintiffs, Sears accomplished an equivalent result by economically coercing the parties into modifying their original agreement. As a result of this coercion, Hannigan suffered monetarily. Under these circumstances, Sears could reasonably have been found to have induced a breach of contract within the true meaning of that tort by coercively interfering with Hannigan's contractual relationship with Fabricated....

[The court affirmed Hannigan's judgment of $30,000 compensatory and $90,000 exemplary damages.]

---

21. **Perlman criticizes Hannigan.** *Hannigan* was criticized in Harvey S. Perlman, *Interference with Contract and Other Economic Expectancies: a Clash of Tort and Contract Doctrine*, 49 U. CHI. L. REV. 61, 110 (1982). Perlman thought it was "unwise" to impose liability for inducing a modification of a contract unless the defendant used illegal means. Hannigan could have let Fabricated breach the exclusive distributorship clause and then sued Fabricated. If Fabricated went bankrupt, Hannigan would not recover, but then that would be because the prices fixed were "artificial" and could not be maintained under competitive pressure. Besides, he argued, liability would also make it less likely that the parties and others can take advantage of new opportunities that might put them all in better position than the original transaction.

22. **Types of contract deserving protection against interference?** Another economist has argued that two kinds of contracts deserve the protection afforded by imposing liability for interference. Lillian R. BeVier, *Reconsidering Inducement,* 76 VA. L. REV. 877 (1990). The two types are:

(a) Promisee acquires contract-specific information. If you consider buying controlling shares in a corporation, you will need to acquire a great deal of information that will have no use to you when you consider buying shares in a different corporation. Acquiring information is costly. You don't want to expend the money unless, if the information is favorable, you can be assured that a contract is protected against outside interference.

(b) Relational contracts. The second kind of contract worth protecting against breach-inducers is the relational contract. In relational contracts, the parties do not set up a specific deal and do not allocate all the risks. Instead, they set up a long-term relationship expected to evolve over time. Manufacturer and distributors, franchisors and franchisees, and even employers and high level employees are examples of relational contracts. Such contracts often involve contract-specific information and in that respect are a subset of the first category. In addition, though, there are some specialized problems in relational contracts. For instance, you might invest a great deal in training a high level employee, while the

employee invests little in accepting employment with you. That might make you vulnerable to raiding by other employers, so maybe you need to be assured that breach inducers would be held liable.

What would Professor BeVier think about Dean Perlman's analysis of *Hannigan?*

23. **Factual patterns: cutting out the middleman.** Cases fall into more than one pattern. Factually, *Hannigan* involves liability for cutting out the middleman. This happens regularly with people in the position of brokers. For example, a purchaser of real property may attempt to make a side deal with the owner to avoid the broker's commission. In such a case, the purchaser who knows of the broker's contract is interfering with the contract and liable for the commission in the absence of a defense. *Century 21 Academy Realty, Inc. v. Breland,* 571 So.2d 296 (Ala. 1990). Similarly, a distributor who passes on the manufacturer's goods to a retailer, may be vulnerable if he is not providing services valuable enough to prevent the manufacturer from selling directly to the retailer. Should the retailer be liable for inducing the manufacturer to sell directly to the retailer? The middle could also be a lessee. Suppose a tenant has an opportunity to sell his business at a profit. The landlord refuses to permit a sublease, so the tenant is unable to sell. The landlord's refusal is unreasonable; his purpose is not to assure a financially responsible tenant but to use the occasion to force higher rent or an extra payment from the sublease. Cases have held the landlord liable on similar facts. See *Campbell v. Westdahl,* 148 Ariz. 432, 715 P.2d 288 (App. 1986).

24. **Is there a public interest?** Suppose you work for a public interest law firm that focuses mainly on consumer protection and welfare. Your firm has a chance to submit an amicus brief in a case like *Hannigan.* Should the firm take a position and if so which position?

§ 2. INTERFERING WITH THE PLAINTIFF'S PERFORMANCE

RESTATEMENT (SECOND) OF TORTS § 766A

Copyright 1979 by the American Law Institute
Reprinted by permission

Intentional Interference With Another's Performance Of His Own Contract

One who intentionally and improperly interferes with the performance of a contract (except a contract to marry) between another and a third person, by preventing the other from performing the contract or causing his performance to be more expensive or burdensome, is subject to liability to the other for the pecuniary loss resulting to him.

WINDSOR SECURITIES, INC. v. HARTFORD LIFE INS. CO.

986 F.2d 655 (3d Cir. 1993)

SCIRICA, Circuit Judge.

In the early 1980s, Hartford offered for sale under the trade name "Director" an Individual Flexible Premium Variable Annuity Contract. Under its terms the contract owner paid a premium to Hartford which was placed into an account ("Separate Account Two") until the annuity or death benefit was paid or the contract canceled by its owner.

The contract gave each contract owner the right to have premium payments and accumulated earnings placed in seven different sub-accounts of Separate Account Two and to determine the percentage of accumulated earnings and premium payments allocated to each sub-account. Contract owners had the right to "reallocate amounts held in the Sub–Accounts at any time." These sub-accounts were invested in certain mutual funds sponsored by Hartford. Management of the funds was overseen by a board of directors, a majority of which were outside directors.

In 1986, Paul Prusky, an investment advisor and broker, as well as president and sole shareholder of Windsor Securities, Inc., purchased a contract in his own name. Prusky claimed to have been seeking a variable annuity contract which would allow him to make unlimited transfers among sub-accounts on behalf of his clients. Such flexibility was important to his market timing investment strategy. After managing his own contract for six months, Prusky solicited his clients to purchase Hartford contracts which he then managed under investment management agreements.

Between June 1987 and March 1989, Prusky managed forty-one contracts on behalf of thirty-five clients pursuant to investment management agreements. Each client's contract application included a form letter to Hartford signed by the purchaser stating that "Prusky or other authorized Windsor Securities personnel had the contract owner's power of attorney to transfer funds on the contract owner's behalf." The letters also stated that "monies may be moved into any such sub-account available ... as often as Windsor Securities, Inc. deems necessary." Hartford did not object to these letters.

In September 1988, Walter Arader, a Prusky client, purchased three contracts on Prusky's recommendation and executed an investment management agreement with Windsor.

Between June 1987 and May 1990, Prusky managed his clients' contract accounts by telephoning transfer instructions to Hartford and trading on average twice a week. Hartford honored Prusky's trading instructions on behalf of his clients during this period. By the end of May 1990, Hartford had 18,887 contracts in force and Windsor managed contracts on behalf of 45 contract owners.

Beginning in 1988, Hartford and its independent fund advisor, Wellington Management Company, began to observe a negative impact caused by market timing activity: increased trading and transaction costs, disruption of planned investment strategies, forced and unplanned portfolio turnover, lost opportunity costs, and large asset swings in a fund's asset base that adversely affected Hartford's ability to provide maximal investment return to all contract owners.

Hartford monitored market timing activity in 1988 and 1989. In meetings from late 1989 into early 1990, the funds' board of directors was apprised of the adverse effects of market timing upon the funds' performance. On April 24, 1990, the funds' board determined that market timing harmed contract owners as a whole and adopted a resolution directing Hartford to ameliorate the negative impact of market timing on the funds' performance.

... Hartford instituted restrictions calculated to protect the investments of all contract owners. These restrictions required that any third party desiring to effect transfers among sub-accounts on behalf of multiple contract owners, whose aggregate values exceeded $2 million, sign a "Third Party Transfer Services Agreement" ("TPTSA") and obtain a power of attorney from each contract owner in a form acceptable to Hartford. The TPTSA restricted the ability of third parties to transfer funds among the sub-accounts on behalf of contract owners by placing a $5 million cap on the total amount which a third party agent could transfer on behalf of his clients in any given day. The TPTSA also gave Hartford the right to impose additional restrictions upon thirty days prior written notice.

On May 11, 1990, Hartford sent Prusky a letter explaining the restrictions would become effective June 1, 1990. The letter made clear that after June 1, Hartford would no longer accept instructions from any person or firm that had not executed a TPTSA and power of attorney. Prusky (and hence Windsor) refused to accede. On May 14, 1990, Hartford advised Arader of the need for a TPTSA. Arader refused to execute the limited power of attorney or to instruct Prusky to execute the TPTSA.

[Windsor, Arader, and Prusky sued Hartford in the United States District Court of the Eastern District of Pennsylvania. Windsor and Prusky claimed interference with the management contract and Arader claimed breach of his contract. The trial court granted summary judgment in favor Windsor and Arader but granted summary judgment for Hartford on Prusky's claims. Later, the trial court found that Windsor and Arader failed to mitigate damages, reduced Windsor's award and eliminated Arader's. Its final judgment was an award of $265,490 for Windsor and in favor of Hartford otherwise. Hartford appealed and Windsor and Arader cross-appealed.]

The district court granted summary judgment to Windsor on its claim that Hartford's restrictions tortiously interfered with its existing contracts. Relying on Adler, Barish, Daniels, Levin & Creskoff v. Epstein, the district court held the Pennsylvania Supreme Court would apply § 766A of the Restatement (Second) of Torts and found that Hartford's imposition of the restrictions intentionally and improperly made "Windsor's performance of services for its clients more expensive and/or more burdensome. . . ."

Both § 766 and § 766A involve interference with an existing contract. Section 766 "states the rule for the actor's intentional interference with a third person's performance of his existing contract with the plaintiff." Restatement (Second) of Torts § 766A Comment a. Section 766A, by contrast, states the rule where an actor intentionally interferes with "plaintiff's performance of his own contract, either by preventing that performance or making it more expensive or burdensome." Thus, the sections focus on different targets of interfering conduct. Section 766 addresses disruptions caused by an act directed not at the plaintiff, but at a third person: the defendant causes the promisor to breach its contract with the plaintiff. Section 766A addresses disruptions caused by an act directed at the plaintiff: the defendant prevents or impedes the plaintiff's own performance. . . .

Adler, Barish involved the paradigm interference tort in which a defendant induces or causes a third party to breach its contract with the promisee-plaintiff. . . . The parties have not cited nor have we discovered any Pennsylvania cases recognizing a separate cause of action for preventing or hindering plaintiff's performance of its own contract. . . .

We also note the two tort theories embodied in §§ 766 and 766A may have different effects and justifications. In the § 766 inducement case, the effect of tort liability is to encourage voluntary transactions. [Citing Lillian R. BeVier, *Reconsidering Inducement,* 76 VA.L.REV. 877, 881 n. 10, 889 n. 46, 893, 896, 915–29 (1990); Richard A. Epstein, *Inducement of Breach of Contract as a Problem of Ostensible Ownership,* 16 J. LEGAL STUD. 1, 30–33 (1987).] If an "inducer" wishes to receive a promisee's promised advantage, then the inducer must bargain directly with the promisee. This "bargain-forcing" aspect of inducement liability protects the security of transactions, reduces monitoring costs, encourages consensual rearrangements of contractual obligations, and avoids the negotiation and litigation costs that arise where an inducer causes a promisor to breach its contract with its promisee.

However, in the § 766A "hindrance" case, this "bargain-forcing" justification appears absent. Imposition of liability under this theory does not encourage the third party to bargain with the promisee. In cases where a third-party's conduct "burdens" but does not prevent the plaintiff-promisor's performance, plaintiff's performance is rendered more expensive. The question becomes not whether plaintiff will perform but rather at what cost. This dispute does not involve the promisee.

In cases where plaintiff's performance is prevented, the third party's actions are directed at the plaintiff-promisor. Yet where the defendant prevents plaintiff's performance, plaintiff will presumably not be a willing participant. Generally, such cases will involve force, fraud, or other independently actionable conduct; adverse effects on contract rights will become an element of damages subject only to the usual limitations of causation, mitigation, and reasonable certainty. As Professor Prosser points out,

> [t]he bulk of the cases involving interference as distinct from inducement involve ... physical interference with person or property and also involve the commission of some independent tort, as where the defendant interferes with the plaintiff's rights by converting goods to which the plaintiff was entitled under the contract, or commits an injurious falsehood of the kind sometimes called slander of title. Methods tortious in themselves are of course unjustified and liability is appropriately imposed where the plaintiff's contract rights are invaded by violence, threats and intimidation, defamation, misrepresentation, unfair competition, bribery and the like. Constitutional violations have been put in the same category. Thus in many cases interference with contract is not so much a theory of liability in itself as it is an element of damage resulting from the commission of some other tort, or the breach of some other contract.

W. Page Keeton et al., Prosser and Keeton on the Law of Torts § 129, at 992 (5th ed. 1984)....

Thus, in non-inducement cases, expanding the tortious interference principle to recognize a § 766A "hindrance" cause of action may duplicate protection already afforded through tort and contract. But duplication comes at a cost. It risks chilling socially valuable conduct and creates new liability of uncertain dimensions. Some commentators have criticized the amorphous nature of the tortious interference principle, warning that its expansion is ill-conceived, threatening both fairness and efficiency. These concerns counsel some caution in expanding tortious interference liability.

We need not decide, however, whether the Pennsylvania Supreme Court would embrace or reject § 766A. For even if Pennsylvania would adopt § 766A, we believe Hartford cannot be held liable under that section for the reasons expressed below.

Assuming the Supreme Court of Pennsylvania would adopt § 766A, we must determine whether Hartford's conduct in imposing the restrictions on third party transfers constituted tortious interference with Windsor's investment management contracts. Windsor had the burden of establishing (1) a contractual relationship; (2) Hartford's intent to harm Windsor by interfering with contractual relations; (3) the impropriety of the interference; (4) harm resulting from the conduct....

In determining whether an actor's conduct is "proper," Pennsylvania courts are guided by the following factors derived from the Restatement (Second) of Torts § 767 (1979): (a) the nature of the actor's conduct, (b) the actor's motive, (c) the interests of the other with which the actor's conduct interferes, (d) the interests sought to be advanced by the actor, (e) the social interests in protecting the freedom of action of the actor and the contractual interests of the other, (f) the proximity or remoteness of the actor's conduct to the interference, and (g) the relations between the parties.

The nature of a defendant's conduct is a chief factor in determining whether the conduct is improper or not. Restatement (Second) of Torts § 767 Comment c. According to Windsor: There are two types of tortious interference claims—(1) those in which the conduct of the defendant is independently wrongful ... ; and (2) those in which the defendant's conduct was not independently wrongful.... Our case falls into the former category, since the misconduct at issue in Windsor's claim for tortious interference with contract also constitutes, independently, a breach of the Director II contracts as against Windsor's clients.

We find Windsor's argument untenable. "Wrongful" conduct requires something more than mere breach of contract.... Breach of contract, without more, is not a tort.... see also 3 E. Allan Farnsworth, Contracts § 12.8, at 194–95 (2d ed. 1990) ("Most courts have not infringed on the freedom to keep or to break a contract traditionally afforded a party by the common law and endorsed by the notion of efficient breach")....

Nor do any of the cases advanced by Windsor demonstrate that breach of contract constitutes "independently wrongful" conduct. They suggest the opposite conclusion. All involve innately wrongful conduct such as torts, deprivation of civil rights, and violation of ethical codes....

The concept of independently wrongful conduct becomes useless if breach of contract alone constitutes independently wrongful conduct under § 767. Most interferences with contract and every instance of successful inducement entail a breach of contract.

In sum, we are persuaded that Hartford's conduct in imposing the restrictions was neither tortious nor illegal. Because there is no evidence that Hartford's conduct was wrongful by any measure external to the interference itself, we conclude that Hartford's conduct was not wrongful.

Our cases accord substantial deference to defendants whose conduct, despite its conflict with plaintiff's interest, protects an existing legitimate business concern.

Thus, in Nathanson v. Medical College of Pennsylvania, we attached significance to the fact that defendant's interfering conduct was directed at protecting its legitimate business interests. There, a medical student admitted to defendant MCP, after matriculating, obtained a one-year leave of absence. During the course of her leave, the student applied and was accepted to Georgetown Medical School. When MCP learned of her acceptance to Georgetown, MCP informed Georgetown that plaintiff held a position in MCP's entering class. Georgetown subsequently withdrew its offer of admission and plaintiff sued MCP for tortious interference based on MCP's communication with Georgetown.

The district court, emphasizing the interests sought to be advanced by MCP, found that MCP had acted to "protect" its own contractual interest. We affirmed the district court, observing that "MCP was simply complying with the standard 'traffic rules' followed by medical schools. . . ."

We also emphasized the importance of allowing actors freedom to protect their legitimate business interests in Green v. Interstate United Management Services Corp., 748 F.2d 827 (3d Cir. 1984). There, the defendants determined that their wholly-owned subsidiary had entered "a bad bargain" when it negotiated a lease with plaintiff. The defendants instructed their subsidiary not to sign the lease even though the subsidiary had orally agreed to sign. Overturning a jury verdict of tortious interference, we reasoned that defendants' "motive, plainly, was to prevent dissipation of the resources of their wholly-owned subsidiary. In this case, 'the social interests in protecting the freedom of the actor' outweigh 'the contractual interests of the other.' " . . .

[These and other cases] support Hartford's contention that where an actor is motivated by a genuine desire to protect legitimate business interests, this factor weighs heavily against finding an improper interference. These cases also make clear the social interest in allowing an actor freedom to protect its legitimate business interests. See Restatement of Torts (Second) § 767(e).

Here the district court analyzed Hartford's motive in implementing the restrictions and concluded that Hartford was actuated by a genuine desire to protect its own financial interests and those of non-market timer contract owners, toward whom Hartford bore a fiduciary obligation. Hartford clearly had a proper motive.

Hartford also sought to advance important and legitimate business interests. Hartford and its independent fund advisor, Wellington Management Company, determined that market timing caused increased trading and transaction costs, disruption of planned investment strategies, forced and unplanned portfolio turnover, lost opportunity costs, and subjected a fund's asset base to large asset swings that diminished a fund's ability to provide a maximized return to all contract owners.

Hartford's concern with market timing was understandable. Market timer contracts represented only a small fraction of Hartford's 18,887 contracts, but the risks and costs associated with market timing were borne by all contract owners—few shared in market timing's benefits yet all bore its costs. As a fiduciary charged with protecting the interests of all contract owners, Hartford sought to eliminate or diminish the adverse consequences timing activity imposed on contract owners. . . .

In sum, nothing indicates that the interests Hartford sought to advance were illegitimate, or that Hartford, in advancing these interests, acted with an improper motive or through impermissible means. Others in the mutual fund industry shared Hartford's concern with market timing's untoward effects. For these reasons, we hold that Hartford's conduct in imposing the restrictions did not constitute improper interference. We therefore will reverse summary judgment on the tortious interference with contract claim and direct entry of summary judgment in favor of Hartford.

The district court determined that Hartford's imposition of restrictions breached its contract with Arader.... We believe the district court correctly construed the contested contractual language....

For the foregoing reasons, we will reverse the district court's grant of summary judgment in favor of Windsor on the tortious interference claim and we will direct entry of judgment in favor of Hartford. We will affirm the district court's final judgment in favor of Hartford on Arader's contract claim [because Arader failed to mitigate damages].

---

25. **The Restatement's claim of supporting authorities.** Some of the cases cited by the Reporter as supporting the Restatement Second's new § 766A seem to fall woefully short. For instance, in some, the defendant had prevented the plaintiff's performance of a contract with another by deliberately damaging the property plaintiff used in performance—easily a tort even to people who have never heard of liability for interference with contract. These and other authorities claimed to support the Restatement are considered in DOBBS ON TORTS § 448 (2000 & Supps.).

26. **Approving § 766A liability.** Although the Restatement relied inappropriately on some authorities to justify its § 766A, a number of contemporary courts do say they accept § 766A. See *Plattner v. State Farm Mut. Auto. Ins. Co.,* 168 Ariz. 311, 812 P.2d 1129 (Ct. App. 1991); *Shafir v. Steele,* 431 Mass. 365, 727 N.E.2d 1140 (2000).

27. **The Restatement as Overstatement.** One reason for caution or scepticism about Restatement § 766A is the breadth of its formulation. You could make the plaintiff's performance more burdensome by literally millions of everyday acts. Imagine that a bus driver decides to sleep late one day and consequently his bus runs late. To a certainty, he knows that passengers will either lose work time or take an expensive taxi to work. Is he not intentionally making his passengers' performance of their contracts more burdensome? And is it not absurd to say so? Yet this comment suggests that the blackletter rule has been overstated, not that its underlying principle is necessarily wrong. Should legal professionals who do such things tinker with the rule? Or at least clarify what counts as "improper" interference?

28. **Rejecting or refusing to apply § 766A.** A number of cases implicitly or explicitly reject § 766A by requiring the plaintiff to show (a) a breach of contract or its equivalent, not merely hindrance or burden, or (b) conduct "directed at" a third person rather than "directed at" the plaintiff. See *George A. Fuller Co. v. Chicago College of Osteopathic Med.,* 719 F.2d 1326 (7th Cir. 1983) (Illinois law); *Callis, Papa, Jackstadt & Halloran v. Norfolk & Western Ry.,* 195 Ill.2d 356, 748 N.E.2d 153, 254

Ill.Dec. 707 (2001) (seemingly but perhaps ambiguously); *Pettit v. Paxton*, 255 Neb. 279, 583 N.W.2d 604 (1998) (also suggesting that causation of damages either was not or could not be shown in a § 766A case). Preventing performance of a contract may be equivalent to a breach under these cases. *Havoco of America, Ltd. v. Sumitomo Corp. of America,* 971 F.2d 1332 (7th Cir. 1992). Some other courts have cautiously avoided applying or passing on whether § 766A would be acceptable. *Koehler v. County of Grand Forks,* 658 N.W.2d 741 (N.D. 2003).

§ 3. INTERFERING WITH ECONOMIC OPPORTUNITY AND BAD MOTIVE

RESTATEMENT (SECOND) OF TORTS § 766B

Copyright 1979 by the American Law Institute
Reprinted by permission

Intentional Interference With Prospective Contractual Relation

One who intentionally and improperly interferes with another's prospective contractual relation (except a contract to marry) is subject to liability to the other for the pecuniary harm resulting from loss of the benefits of the relation, whether the interference consists of

(a) inducing or otherwise causing a third person not to enter into or continue the prospective relation or

(b) preventing the other from acquiring or continuing the prospective relation.

29. **Causation and damages.** Notice that § 766B of the Restatement does not require interference with an existing contract. A prospective contractual relationship is sufficient. However, it implicitly requires proof of pecuniary harm resulting from the interference. What if the plaintiff showed that the defendant's interference prevented the plaintiff from bidding on a public construction project in which three other contractors were allowed to bid? See *Santana Products Inc. v. Bobrick Washroom Equip. Inc.,* 401 F.3d 123 (3d Cir. 2005).

ALYESKA PIPELINE SERVICE CO. v. AURORA AIR SERVICE, INC.

604 P.2d 1090 (Alaska 1979)

CONNOR, Justice ....

On May 14, 1974, Alyeska and RCA executed a contract which provided that RCA would construct, operate, and maintain a communications system along the Trans-Alaska Pipeline. The contract set forth that RCA would furnish all supervision, engineering, labor, and transportation necessary to perform the contract. In fulfilling the transportation requirements of the Alyeska-RCA contract, RCA executed a contract on October 3, 1974, with Aurora.

The Aurora-RCA contract, in part, provided: Contractor hereby agrees to furnish one (1) Cessna 207 aircraft with pilot, parts, and accessories to provide aircraft service to transport RCA-Alascom equipment, supplies, and personnel along the pipeline route as designated by RCA-Alascom.

Article 13 of the contract, "Optional Termination," provided that the contract could be terminated at RCA's option.

Prior to the execution of the Aurora-RCA and Alyeska-RCA contracts, Aurora and Alyeska had a contractual relationship under which it was agreed that Aurora would provide non-exclusive air service to Alyeska. In the spring of 1975 a payment dispute arose under this contract between Aurora and Alyeska. Shortly after Aurora commenced a suit seeking recovery, Alyeska paid Aurora the sum it claimed was due.

In October, 1975 Alyeska took over the transportation requirements of its contract with RCA pursuant to a provision in the contract.... Shortly thereafter RCA, prompted by Alyeska's election to take over the air transportation service, exercised its option to terminate its contract with Aurora....

[Aurora sued Alyeska for interference with its "contractual relationship" with RCA by taking over the transportation work itself. The trial judge rejected Alyeska's motion for summary judgment and the jury awarded Aurora $362,901.]

The unilateral right to modify the Alyeska-RCA contract, accepting the superior court's ruling that there was no ambiguity in regard to the interpretation of "work," was vested in Alyeska, but it had to be exercised in good faith. We reject Alyeska's contention that a privilege arising from a contractual right is absolute and may be exercised regardless of motive. It is a recognized principle that a party to a contract has a cause of action against a third party who has intentionally procured the breach of that contract by the other party without justification or privilege. The weight of recent authority holds that even though a contract is terminable at will, a claim of unjustifiable interference can still be made, for "[t]he wrong for which the courts may give redress includes also the procurement of the termination of a contract which otherwise would have (been) continued in effect." Smith v. Ford Motor Co., 289 N.C. 71, 221 S.E.2d 282 (1976).

We choose to follow this trend and thus adopt the view espoused by Prosser: "Since Lumley v. Gye there has been general agreement that a purely 'malicious' motive, in the sense of spite and a desire to do harm to the plaintiff for its own sake, will make the defendant liable for interference with a contract. The same is true of mere officious intermeddling for no other reason than a desire to interfere. On the other hand, in the few cases in which the question has arisen, it has been held that where the defendant has a proper purpose in view, the addition of ill will toward the plaintiff will not defeat his privilege. It may be suggested that here, as in the case of mixed motives in the exercise of a privilege in defamation and malicious prosecution, the court may well look to the predominant purpose underlying the defendant's conduct." Prosser, Law of Torts, § 129, at 943 (4th ed. 1971).

Alternatively, Alyeska asserts that its overriding economic and safety interests constituted a sufficient privilege to require dismissal of Aurora's action as a matter of law. One is privileged to invade the contractual interest of himself, others, or the public, if the interest advanced by him is superior in social importance to the interest invaded. 1 Harper & James, The Law of Torts, § 6.12, at 514 (1956); Restatement of the Law of Torts, § 733 (1939). However, if one does not act in a good faith attempt to protect his own interest or that of another but, rather, is motivated by a desire to injure the contract party, he forfeits the immunity afforded by the privilege. Smith v. Ford Motor Co., 221 S.E.2d at 296.

The question of justification for invading the contractual interest of another is normally one for the trier of fact, particularly when the evidence is in conflict. In the case at bar, the central factual issue, as to which there was evidentiary conflict, was whether Alyeska was genuinely furthering its own economic and safety interests or was using them as a facade for inflicting injury upon Aurora. There was sufficient evidence upon which the jury could properly find that Alyeska was acting out of ill will towards Aurora, rather than to protect a legitimate business interest. The trial judge correctly denied Alyeska's motion for summary judgment and submitted this issue to the jury....

Alyeska argues that Aurora's evidence of the termination of its contract, intentionally procured, made out a prima facie case, that the burden of proof shifted to Alyeska to show justification, and that Alyeska satisfied that requirement by producing evidence of its contract with RCA and its primary interest in the performance of the RCA contract. It is urged that if, in spite of such evidence, the good faith of Alyeska was still a valid issue, the burden of proving Alyeska's lack of good faith should have shifted back to Aurora.

... The issue presented here was whether Alyeska really did exercise its rights in good faith or whether it acted from an ulterior motive. We think that such proof goes to the question of justification, and that it was not part of Aurora's prima facie case, which only requires a showing that a breach was intentionally procured. Nor do we think that Alyeska has submitted sufficient proof of justification to trigger another shifting of the burden of proof and to require Aurora to rebut such evidence. There may be exceptional situations in which such a treble shifting of burdens should occur, but we do not view this case as one of them. On this point there was no error....

Alyeska asserts that it was error to submit the question of punitive damages to the jury. Given the nature of the theory on which Aurora proceeded in this case, that Alyeska purposely destroyed Aurora's contractual relationship with RCA, the trial court was entirely correct in submitting this question to the jury.

---

30. **At-will contracts, economic prospects, or business relations.** The tort involved in *Alyeska* is usually called interference with prospective economic advantage, interference with opportunity, or something similar to distinguish it from the tort of interference with contract. What is the difference? A contract, courts say, deserves protection through tort law, but an economic relationship not cemented by contract is entitled to much less protection. An at-will contract is in reality only a prospective economic expectancy, not an enforceable contract. *Reeves v. Hanlon,* 33 Cal.4th 1140, 95 P.3d 513, 17 Cal.Rptr.3d 289 (2004). Did *Alyeska* treat Aurora's contract as if it were not subject to termination by others?

31. **Alyeska: business opportunities trump contract rights?** Alyeska had a contract right to terminate RCA's transport services. Aurora had no contract right, either with RCA or Alyeska, to continue to provide services. Did Aurora's mere prospect of continued work trump Alyeska's contract right? Does this fit at all with the principle that prospects deserve less protection than contracts? In *Carvel Corp. v. Noonan,* 3 N.Y.3d 182, 818 N.E.2d 1100, 785 N.Y.S.2d 359 (2004), franchisees claimed their franchisor interfered with franchisees' sales when the franchisor sold directly to supermarkets and gave customers coupons that made supermarket purchases cheaper. The court observed that the contract addressed the general subject matter of competition, but failed to deal one way or the other with any of the franchisor's acts involved here. "This, like any other form of price competition, should be regulated, if at all, by the franchisor-franchisee contract."

32. **Alyeska: the role of spite or bad motives in limiting a legal right.** Doesn't everyone feel anger or a sense of ill-will at others on occasion? Should we lose our rights under contract if we have those negative feelings? Another case in which a court examined the defendant's motive for exercising its contractual right was *Smith v. Ford Motor Co.,* 289 N.C. 71, 221 S.E.2d 282 (1976). In that case, Ford, using its economic power, induced its franchisee to discharge an at-will manager. The court said that while Ford had a privilege to protect its own business interests, the privilege was lost if Ford had a "wrong purpose," in that instance, a purpose to get rid of managers who supported an alliance of Ford dealers. See also *Cromeens, Holloman, Sibert, Inc. v. AB Volvo,* 349 F.3d 376 (7th Cir. 2003) (under Illinois law, a defendant's conduct in aid of his own economic interest would not be privileged if he was "motivated solely by malice or ill will").

33. **The mixed motive problem: a but-for test of motive.** If motive (or a bad mental attitude) must count against the defendant, what is to be done when the defendant has several different motives, some of them not bad at all? Could you say there is no liability unless, without the bad motive, the interference would not have taken place? That is, that the defendant would not be liable if he would have taken the same action on the basis of the acceptable motive? In civil rights cases under § 1981, when the same kind of mixed motive issues arose, the Supreme Court took that view. In *Mt. Healthy City Sch. Dist. Bd. of*

Ed. v. Doyle, 429 U.S. 274, 97 S.Ct. 568, 50 L.Ed.2d 471 (1977), a school board discharged a teacher because (a) of his obscene gestures to female students and other untoward incidents and (b) because he revealed certain information to a radio station. Considering the latter to involve First Amendment protected speech, the trial court held that the teacher was entitled to reinstatement and back pay. The Supreme Court, however, took a different view. "The constitutional principle at stake is sufficiently vindicated if such an employee is placed in no worse a position than if he had not engaged in the conduct. A borderline or marginal candidate should not have the employment question resolved against him because of constitutionally protected conduct. But that same candidate ought not to be able, by engaging in such conduct, to prevent his employer from assessing his performance record and reaching a decision not to rehire on the basis of that record, simply because the protected conduct makes the employer more certain of the correctness of its decision." In other words, the teacher could not have his job back if the board would have fired him for the obscene gestures alone (assuming those gestures to be outside the scope of free speech protection). The court might allocate the burden of proof to the employer to show that he would have made the same decision in the absence of discrimination. See *Price Waterhouse v. Hopkins*, 490 U.S. 228, 109 S.Ct. 1775, 104 L.Ed.2d 268 (1989). However, in Title VII cases, Congress took a different view. In the Civil Rights Act of 1991, Congress established that "an unlawful employment practice is established when the complaining party demonstrates that race, color, religion, sex, or national origin was a motivating factor for any employment practice, even though other factors also motivated the practice." 42 U.S.C.A. § 2000e. This legal change applies to actions brought under Title VII, but not to § 1981 claims. See *Mabra v. United Food and Commercial Workers Local Union No. 1996,* 176 F.3d 1357 (11th Cir. 1999). In the context of civil rights claims, all this might be affected by statutes, but these cases show options that could be used in the interference cases. Which view of mixed motives would be preferable in the context of interference with prospects?

34. **Interpreting the Civil Rights Act on causal motives.** Could the standard in the Civil Rights Act of 1991 possibly be an enactment of the but-for test, eliminating liability if, without the motive, the practice complained of would have occurred anyway? See *Foster v. Arthur Andersen, LLP,* 168 F.3d 1029 (7th Cir. 1999).

35. **The mixed motive problem: an analogous case of post-discharge discovery of grounds for discharge.** A technically distinct but substantially similar problem arises when an employer discriminatorily discharges an employee in violation of statute, but after the discharge discovers employee misconduct that would have led the employer to fire her anyway. Although distinguishing mixed motive cases on the ground that in after-acquired evidence cases only one motive exists, the Supreme Court nevertheless held that at least generally speaking, "neither reinstatement nor front pay is an appropriate remedy. It would be both inequitable and pointless to order the reinstatement of someone the

employer would have terminated, and will terminate, in any event and upon lawful grounds." *McKennon v. Nashville Banner Pub. Co.*, 513 U.S. 352, 115 S.Ct. 879, 130 L.Ed.2d 852 (1995). In *Alyeska*, what if that company's safety concerns arose after the contract termination and resulting litigation? Would *Alyeska* still have to maintain the RCA contract or pay damages?

36. **Good motive exculpating the defendant.** If bad motive is ground for making the defendant liable for a sound business decision, does good motive relieve a defendant whose improper act causes the plaintiff the loss of an expectancy? In *Macke v. Pierce,* 266 Neb. 9, 661 N.W.2d 313 (2003), a physician concluded that the patient was not able to do her railroad job in light of her pain. He told the patient so, but then, in breach of patient-physician duty confidentiality, the physician called the railroad and told it she should be restricted to sedentary activity. The railroad discharged the plaintiff. Her suit against the physician for breach of confidence failed for procedural reasons. She then sued for interference with business prospects or relations. The trial court submitted the Restatement's long list of abstract factors to the jury, which found for the defendant doctor. The Nebraska court upheld the jury verdict on the ground that evidence was sufficient to show that the physician's revelation of the medical confidence "was motivated by protecting his patient from harm, and therefore, his communication with the railroad was not unjustified." Should motive play such an important role in this litigation?

DELLA PENNA v. TOYOTA MOTOR SALES, U.S.A., INC.

11 Cal.4th 376, 45 Cal.Rptr.2d 436, 902 P.2d 740 (1995)

ARABIAN, Justice....

John Della Penna, an automobile wholesaler doing business as Pacific Motors, brought this action for damages against Toyota Motor Sales, U.S.A., Inc., and its Lexus division, alleging that certain business conduct of defendants both violated provisions of the Cartwright Act, California's state antitrust statute (Bus. & Prof. Code, § 16700 et seq.), and constituted an intentional interference with his economic relations. The impetus for Della Penna's suit arose out of the 1989 introduction into the American luxury car market of Toyota's Lexus automobile. Prior to introducing the Lexus, the evidence at trial showed, both the manufacturer, Toyota Motor Corporation, and defendant, the American distributor, had been concerned at the possibility that a resale market might develop for the Lexus in Japan. Even though the car was manufactured in Japan, Toyota's marketing strategy was to bar the vehicle's sale on the Japanese domestic market until after the American roll-out; even then, sales in Japan would only be under a different brand name, the "Celsior." Fearing that auto wholesalers in the United States might re-export Lexus models back to Japan for resale, and concerned that, with production and the availability of Lexus models in the American market limited, re-exports would jeopardize its fledgling network of American Lexus dealers, Toyota inserted in its dealership agreements a "no export" clause, providing that the dealer was "authorized to sell [Lexus automobiles] only to customers located in the United States. [Dealer] agrees that it will not sell [Lexus automobiles] for resale or use outside the United States. [Dealer] agrees to abide by any export policy established by [distributor]."

Following the introduction into the American market, it soon became apparent that some domestic Lexus units were being diverted for foreign sales, principally to Japan. To counter this effect, Toyota managers wrote to their retail dealers, reminding them of the "no-export" policy and explaining that exports for foreign resale could jeopardize the supply of Lexus automobiles available for the United States market. In addition, Toyota compiled a list of "offenders"—dealers and others believed by Toyota to be involved heavily in the developing Lexus foreign resale market—which it distributed to Lexus dealers in the United States. American Lexus dealers were also warned that doing business with those whose names appeared on the "offenders" list might lead to a series of graduated sanctions, from reducing a dealer's allocation to possible reevaluation of the dealer's franchise agreement.

During the years 1989 and 1990, plaintiff Della Penna did a profitable business as an auto wholesaler purchasing Lexus automobiles, chiefly from the Lexus of Stevens Creek retail outlet, at near retail price and exporting them to Japan for resale. By late 1990, however, plaintiff's sources began to dry up, primarily as a result of the "offenders list." Stevens Creek ceased selling models to plaintiff; gradually other sources declined to sell to him as well.

In February 1991, plaintiff filed this lawsuit against Toyota Motors, U.S.A., Inc., alleging both state antitrust claims under the Cartwright Act and interference with his economic relationship with Lexus retail dealers. At the close of plaintiff's case-in-chief, the trial court granted Toyota's motion for nonsuit with respect to the remaining Cartwright Act claim (plaintiff had previously abandoned a related claim—unfair competition—prior to trial). The tort cause of action went to the jury, however, under the standard BAJI instructions applicable to such claims with one significant exception. At the request of defendant and over plaintiff's objection, the trial judge modified BAJI No. 7.82—the basic instruction identifying the elements of the tort and indicating the burden of proof—to require plaintiff to prove that defendant's alleged interfering conduct was "wrongful."

The jury returned a divided verdict, nine to three, in favor of Toyota. After Della Penna's motion for a new trial was denied, he appealed. In an unpublished disposition, the Court of Appeal unanimously reversed the trial court's judgment, ruling that a plaintiff alleging intentional interference with economic relations is not required to establish "wrongfulness" as an element of its prima facie case, and that it was prejudicial error for the trial court to have read the jury an amended instruction to that effect....

As a number of courts and commentators have observed, the keystone of the liability imposed in Lumley and Temperton, ... appears to have been the "malicious" intent of a defendant in enticing an employee to breach her contract with the plaintiff, and damaging the business of one who refused to cooperate with the union in achieving its bargaining aims. While some have doubted whether the use of the word "malicious" amounted to anything more than an intent to commit an act, knowing it would harm the plaintiff, Dean Keeton, assessing the state of the tort as late as 1984, remarked that "[w]ith intent to interfere as the usual basis of the action, the cases have turned almost entirely upon the defendant's motive or purpose and the means by which he has sought to accomplish it. As in the cases of interference with contract, any manner of intentional invasion of the plaintiff's interests may be sufficient if the purpose is not a proper one." ...

One consequence of this superficial kinship [to intentional torts] was the assimilation to the interference torts of the pleading and burden of proof requirements of the "true" intentional torts: the requirement that the plaintiff need only allege a so-called "prima facie tort" by showing the defendant's awareness of the economic relation, a deliberate interference with it, and the plaintiff's resulting injury. By this account of the matter—the traditional view of the torts and the one adopted by the first Restatement of Torts—the burden then passed to the defendant to demonstrate that its conduct was privileged, that is, "justified" by a recognized defense such as the protection of others or, more likely in this context, the defendant's own competitive business interests....

Because the plaintiff's initial burden of proof was such a slender one, amounting to no more than showing the defendant's conscious act and plaintiff's economic injury, critics argued that legitimate business competition could lead to time consuming and expensive lawsuits (not to speak of potential liability) by a rival, based on conduct that was regarded by the commercial world as both commonplace and appropriate. The "black letter" rules of the Restatement of Torts surrounding the elements and proof of the tort, some complained, might even suggest to "foreign lawyers reading the Restatement as an original matter [that] the whole competitive order of American industry is prima facie illegal." (Statement of Professor Carl Auerbach at ALI Proceedings, quoted in Perlman, Interference with Contract and Other Economic Expectancies: A Clash of Tort and Contract Doctrine (1982) 49 U.Chi.L.Rev. 61, 79, fn. 89) ...

Calls for a reformulation of both the elements and the means of establishing the economic relations tort reached a height around the time the Restatement Second of Torts was being prepared for publication and are reflected in its departures from its predecessor's version. Acknowledging criticism, the American Law Institute discarded the prima facie tort requirement of the first Restatement. A new provision, section 766B, required that the defendant's conduct be "improper," and adopted a multifactor "balancing" approach, identifying seven factors for the trier of fact to weigh in determining a defendant's liability. The Restatement Second of Torts, however, declined to take a position on the issue of which of the parties bore the burden of proof, relying on the "considerable disagreement on who has the burden of pleading and proving certain matters" and the observation that "the law in this area has not fully congealed but is still in a formative stage." In addition, the Restatement Second provided that a defendant might escape liability by showing that his conduct was justifiable and did not include the use of "wrongful means."....

Over the past decade or so, close to a majority of the high courts of American jurisdictions have [explicitly approved a rule requiring] the plaintiff in such a suit to plead and prove the alleged interference was either "wrongful," "improper," "illegal," "independently tortious" or some variant on these formulations....

The courts provide a damage remedy against third party conduct intended to disrupt an existing contract precisely because the exchange of promises resulting in such a formally cemented economic relationship is deemed worthy of protection from interference by a stranger to the agreement. Economic relationships short of contractual, however, should stand on a different legal footing as far as the potential for tort liability is reckoned. Because ours is a culture firmly wedded to the social rewards of commercial contests, the law usually takes care to draw lines of legal liability in a way that maximizes areas of competition free of legal penalties.

A doctrine that blurs the analytical line between interference with an existing business contract and interference with commercial relations less than contractual is one that invites both uncertainty in conduct and unpredictability of its legal effect. The notion that inducing the breach of an existing contract is simply a subevent of the "more inclusive" class of acts that interfere with economic relations, while perhaps theoretically unobjectionable, has been mischievous as a practical matter. Our courts should, in short, firmly distinguish the two kinds of business contexts, bringing a greater solicitude to those relationships that have ripened into agreements, while recognizing that relationships short of that subsist in a zone where the rewards and risks of competition are dominant.

Beyond that, we need not tread today. It is sufficient to dispose of the issue before us in this case by holding that a plaintiff seeking to recover for alleged interference with prospective economic relations has the burden of pleading and proving that the defendant's interference was wrongful "by some measure beyond the fact of the interference itself." It follows that the trial court did not commit error when it modified BAJI No. 7.82 to require the jury to find that defendant's interference was "wrongful." And because the instruction defining "wrongful conduct" given the jury by the trial court was offered by plaintiff himself, we have no occasion to review its sufficiency in this case. The question of whether additional refinements to the plaintiff's pleading and proof burdens merit adoption by California courts—questions embracing the precise scope of "wrongfulness," or whether a "disinterested malevolence" ... is an actionable interference in itself, or whether the underlying policy justification for the tort, the efficient allocation of social resources, justifies including as actionable conduct that is recognized as anticompetitive under established state and federal positive law (see, e.g., Perlman, Interference with Contract and Other Economic Expectancies; A Clash of Tort and Contract Doctrine, supra, 49 U.Chi.L.Rev. 61)—are matters that can await another day and a more appropriate case....

MOSK, Justice, concurring....

It is the prima facie tort doctrine that is the basis of the tort of intentional interference with prospective economic advantage....

The prima facie tort doctrine exhibits a general deficiency.... "The idea is that 'intentional infliction of harm' is, prima facie, a tort. The problem is that almost any legitimate act can cause 'intentional' harm...." Therefore, "[i]t must be understood that intentional infliction of harm ... covers a multitude of desirable acts as well as a multitude of sins." "The prima facie tort rule, then, is not a rule about wrongdoing at all. It seems to be a philosophical effort to state all"—or at least much of—"tort law in a single sentence rather than an effort to state a meaningful principle." [I]t is a principle that is peculiarly empty.

The prima facie tort doctrine exhibits a specific deficiency with regard to the tort of intentional interference with prospective economic advantage. "Since not all interference [is] actionable, or even morally wrong, it cannot be said that there [is] some principle against interference. Since there is no hint in such abstract statements of liability as to what might constitute a defense it is difficult to believe that there is actually any principle involved at all. It has rather the faded ambience of a 'universal truth' once thought to be discoverable in law. In any event, this [leaves] the defendant in an interference case knowing he [is] entitled to some defense, but not knowing what defenses would be accounted sufficient." (Dobbs, Tortious Interference With Contractual Relationships, supra, 34 Ark.L.Rev. at p. 345) ...

The tort's "protectionist" premise, however, is at war with itself. ... Why should the interfered-with party's acquisitive efforts be elevated to a kind of property interest, good against the world, while those of the interfering party are deemed illegitimate? It is "often assumed ... that interference ... should produce liability because it is wrong to interfere. This is, however, very much the same as saying it is wrong because it is wrong." Reason supports the conclusion that, even when there is a breach of contract, the interfered-with party should not be preferred over the interfering party: the breach may be "efficient."

Further, liability under the tort may threaten values of greater breadth and higher dignity than those of the tort itself.

One is the common law's policy of freedom of competition. Another of these values expresses itself in the guaranty of freedom of speech in the First Amendment to the United States Constitution. ... The interfering party, however, often interferes by means of words. It has been said that, "so far as tort liability is imposed for the communication of facts, opinions or arguments, that liability is simply inconsistent with the law's long commitment to free speech.... [Justice Mosk also discussed free association and right to petition.]

A third reason for the common law's near-incoherence on the tort of intentional interference with prospective economic advantage may be discovered in its focus on the interfering party's motive, that is, why he seeks whatever it is that he seeks through his interference, and on his moral character as revealed thereby....

In spite of the many words devoted to the topic, the focus on the interfering party's motive is simply inappropriate. That is because, for present purposes, motive is altogether immaterial....

Even if it were not inappropriate, the focus on the interfering party's motive surely has a tendency to yield untoward results.... Certainly, motive may be spoken of as a fact. But it implicates a rich variety of values. As a result, it allows and perhaps even invites the trier of fact to pass a kind of moral judgment on the interfering party as such—a judgment that, whether scrupulously fair and strictly impartial, on the one side, or passionately sympathetic or blindly prejudiced, on the other, is simply of no consequence here. For the "law has no roving commission to root out bad people or people whose minds may harbor bad thoughts." (Id. at pp. 347–348.) Neither does it undertake to select for reward people of the opposite sort. Indeed, it has "generally shared" "the belief ... that it is impermissible for" it "to judge one's person rather than one's conduct." (Id. at p. 347.) Thus, it treats all as equal before its bar, whether some may seem to be "small dealers and worthy men" ... and others "rapacious monopolists"....

I would not adopt the "standard" of "wrongfulness." As I have noted, the term and its cognates are inherently ambiguous. They should probably be avoided. They should surely not be embraced....

Second, if I were to adopt such a "standard," I would not allow it to remain undefined .... Any definition of the "standard," of course, should avoid suggesting that the interfering party's motive might be material for present purposes. As I have explained, the focus on this issue is inappropriate.... To reiterate: "The law has no roving commission to root out bad people or people whose minds may harbor bad thoughts." (Dobbs, Tortious Interference With Contractual Relationships, supra, 34 Ark.L.Rev. at pp. 347–348.)....

CARVEL CORP. V. NOONAN, 3 N.Y.3d 182, 818 N.E.2d 1100, 785 N.Y.S.2d 359 (2004). "[A]s a general rule, the defendant's conduct must amount to a crime or an independent tort. Conduct that is not criminal or tortious will generally be 'lawful' and thus insufficiently 'culpable' to create liability for interference with prospective contracts or other nonbinding economic relations.... [A]n exception has been recognized where a defendant engages in conduct 'for the sole purpose of inflicting intentional harm on plaintiffs' but that exception clearly does not apply here. It is undisputed that Carvel's motive in interfering with the franchisees' relationships with their customers was normal economic self-interest.... [We do not decide] whether there can ever be other instances of conduct which, though not a crime or tort in itself, was so 'culpable' ... that it could be the basis for a claim of tortious interference with economic relations. That is a question we leave for another day, because no such egregious conduct was shown here."

Corcoran v. Land O'Lakes, Inc., 39 F.Supp.2d 1139 (N.D. Iowa 1999). "[P]roof of improper purpose for the tort of interference with *prospective* contractual relationships requires proof that the actor's sole or primary purpose [was] to injure or destroy the plaintiff."

Reeves v. Hanlon, 33 Cal.4th 1140, 95 P.3d 513, 17 Cal.Rptr.3d 289 (2004). The two defendants had been lawyer-employees of the plaintiff law firm. Without notice, defendants left the firm and induced a number of the at-will staff employees to leave as well. Both defendants were under a fiduciary duty to the firm. They left no status reports on pending matters they had dealt with and they deleted and destroyed plaintiff's computer files containing client documents and forms, and misappropriated confidential information. In this suit for interference with the employment of at-will employees, the trial judge gave judgment for the plaintiffs. The Court of Appeal affirmed. *Held,* affirmed. "[T]o recover for a defendant's interference with an at-will employment relation, a plaintiff must plead and prove that the defendant engaged in an independently wrongful act—i.e., an act proscribed by some constitutional, statutory, regulatory, common law, or other determinable legal standard.... Adopting this standard of recovery in the context of at-will employment relations is particularly appropriate. Not only will it guard against unlawful methods of competition in the job market, but it will promote the public policies supporting the right of at-will employees to pursue opportunities for economic betterment and the right of employers to compete for talented workers. In this regard, it is clear from the standard that one commits no actionable wrong by merely soliciting or hiring the at-will employee of another." The plaintiff's proof, however, showed that the "defendants did not simply extend job offers to plaintiffs' at-will employees. Rather, defendants purposely engaged in unlawful acts that crippled plaintiffs' business operations and caused plaintiffs' personnel to terminate their at-will employment contracts."

Wal-Mart Stores, Inc. v. Sturges, 52 S.W.3d 711 (Tex. 2001). Wal-Mart owned a store on parcel 1 and had the right to reject any modification of a site plan on the adjoining land, parcel 2. That plan limited the size of any building to 36,000 square feet. Hearing that Fleming Foods wanted a store in the area, the plaintiff obtained an option to purchase parcel 2, then a tentative commitment from Fleming to lease it. But Fleming wanted 51,000 square feet. Wal-Mart, wishing to expand its store, refused to consent to the change in the site plan and told Fleming that if

Wal-Mart could not expand into parcel 2, Wal-Mart would move. That was indeed Wal-Mart's policy—expand by preference but move to a larger store if necessary. Fleming, needing Wal-Mart, had no interest in moving to that location if Wal-Mart moved. Fleming therefore cancelled its tentative agreement with the plaintiff and the plaintiff sued Wal-Mart for interference with prospects. *Held,* (1) interference with prospects is a radically different tort from interference with contract; (2) "[L]awful conduct is not made tortious by the actor's ill will towards another, nor does an actor's lack of ill will make his tortious conduct any less so." (3) "The concepts of malice, justification, and privilege have not only proved to be overlapping and confusing, they provide no meaningful description of culpable conduct" required. (4) Hence, the interference with prospects claim cannot be maintained unless the plaintiff proves that the defendant was guilty of independently tortious conduct such as fraud or defamation addressed to a third person that leads the third person to cease doing business with the plaintiff. Such conduct need not necessarily be actionable by the third person; for example, the third person might not rely upon the fraud. However, the independently tortious conduct is not ground for an interference with prospects claim if that conduct was privileged.

37. **Competition or economic self-interest as privileged or proper.** Even in states that only use the vague "improper act" and bad motive standards, the defendant is free to interfere with economic prospects of others in order to compete or to protect his own economic interests, so long as he does so without improper means or motive. Under a prima facie tort approach, this protection for competition is expressed as a privilege. Under a rule requiring proof of improper conduct in the first place, neither competition nor a truthful statement is improper when the plaintiff has prospects but not a contract right. A number of other contemporary cases besides *Della Penna* and *Wal-Mart v. Sturges* have taken this latter approach on the burden of proof. Yet under the traditional view, when the plaintiff's interests are protected by a valid existing contract, the defendant is acting improperly or without privilege when he intentionally interferes with the contract, even though he is doing nothing that is otherwise wrong. This view, which is predominate in interference with contract cases, is that interference is "a wrong in and of itself" and no independent act of wrongdoing is required. *Korea Supply Co. v. Lockheed Martin Corp.,* 29 Cal.4th 1134, 63 P.3d 937, 131 Cal.Rptr.2d 29 (2003).

38. **Competition and motive.** Some courts still sometimes adhere to a kind of protectionist philosophy. Consider *Deauville Corp. v. Federated Dept. Stores, Inc.,* 756 F.2d 1183 (5th Cir. 1985). Federated was actively developing a large shopping mall and had some anchor tenants. Ward was looking for a place to set up a retail store at a shopping mall in the area and talked some, inconclusively, with Federated. At that point Deauville began trying to get together a mall in the same general area and Ward signed a deal with Deauville to become a joint venturer in that project. However, as it was far from clear that

Deauville would actually proceed, Ward had the option of backing out. Federated then offered Ward a spot as one of its several anchor tenants. Ward accepted the offer. It utilized its option to back out of the Deauville contract. Deauville's project collapsed and Deauville sued Federated for interference. The court agreed that the contract was one at will and competition would be a permissible interference, and agreed as well that Federated's action was competitive. However, it thought that because a jury could find that Federated's motive was "only to harm Deauville" liability was a jury question. What is its premise? Competitive acts are not competitive if done with a bad motive? The Restatement Third of Unfair Competition § 1, cmt. c (1995), notes that the public benefits of competition do not correlate with motive of the actors. Does that make a point one way or the other about *Deauville*?

39. **Requirement that specific opportunity or customer be lost.** Some courts say that the opportunity interfered with must be represented by a specific person or persons: "Illinois courts have stated that the first element of a prima facie case for tortious interference, that plaintiff had a valid business expectancy, requires allegations of business relationships with specific third parties." *Du Page Aviation Corp. v. Du Page Airport Authority*, 229 Ill.App.3d 793 (803), 171 Ill.Dec. 814, 594 N.E.2d 1334, 1340 (1992); see also *Associated Underwriters of Am. Agency, Inc. v. McCarthy,* 356 Ill.App.3d 1010, 826 N.E.2d 1160, 292 Ill.Dec. 724 (2005). Or that the plaintiff must identify specific lost customers or economic relationships. *McGill v. Parker,* 179 A.D.2d 98, 582 N.Y.S.2d 91 (1992); *Table Steaks v. First Premier Bank, N.A.,* 650 N.W.2d 829 (S.D. 2002). Why such a rule?

40. **Independent tort or wrongdoing; two actions or one?** As already noted, a defendant might interfere with contract or opportunity by breaching his fiduciary duty to the plaintiff, for example, secretly taking an opportunity for himself when he was obliged to provide that opportunity to the plaintiff. (See ¶ 11, supra.) Likewise, a defendant might interfere with a contract or opportunity by defaming the plaintiff, thereby causing others to cease doing business with the plaintiff. See *Centro Nautico Representacoes Nauticas, LDA. v. International Marine Co–Op, Ltd.,* 719 So.2d 967 (Fla. Dist. Ct. App. 1998). In such cases, should the court submit both claims to the jury, where the interference claim is based on the defamatory publication?

41. **Independent tort or wrongdoing; which rules apply.** If constitutional rules or state-law privileges would bar the libel action, do the same rules bar the interference action when the independent tort or wrongdoing behind the interference action is the same libel? A number of cases say the libel rule will control and that if the plaintiff cannot recover under those rules, she cannot recover by asserting the same conduct under an interference theory. See *Fontani v. Wells Fargo Investments, LLC.,* 129 Cal.App.4th 719, 28 Cal.Rptr.3d 833 (2005) (statutory privilege for defamation applies equally to protect against interference claim); *Lakeshore Community Hosp., Inc. v. Perry,* 538 N.W.2d 24 (Mich. Ct. App. 1995) (*New York Times v. Sullivan* rule bars

interference claim based on publication); *Binkewitz v. Allstate Ins. Co.*, 222 N.J.Super. 501, 537 A.2d 723 (1988) (qualified privilege under state law); *Caruso v. Local U. No. 690, Int. Bro. of Teamsters*, 100 Wash.2d 343, 670 P.2d 240 (1983).

42. **Crime or tort to fourth person.** Suppose the defendant interferes with a business prospect (not a contract) by committing a crime or an independent tort to a third person. Would that be adequate to satisfy the requirement of independent unlawful act? In *Korea Supply Co. v. Lockheed Martin Corp.*, 29 Cal.4th 1134, 63 P.3d 937, 131 Cal.Rptr.2d 29 (2003), the plaintiff was a "broker" representing a Canadian Corporation bidding to supply Korea with a SAR radar system. The plaintiff would gain a $30 million commission if the sale went through. The odds looked good—the Canadian client bid millions less than the defendant, a company in the United States. And, according to reports, the Canadian system was better. But Korea chose to spend more for less, according to the plaintiff's complaint, and bought the defendant's system instead, because the defendant had bribed important Korean officials with large sums of money and the provision of sexual favors. Accordingly, the plaintiff lost its hoped-for commission. The defendant's conduct violated a federal statute against bribing foreign officials. The California Supreme Court held that the defendant could only be liable for intentional interference, but that intent could be found based on substantial certainty of the consequences; the plaintiff could recover even if the defendant's misconduct was not "directed at" the plaintiff. Under this rule, the defendant will not be liable for unforeseeable harm "since the plaintiff must prove that the defendant knew that the consequences were substantially certain to occur. For example, if the president of [the Canadian company] stood to receive a bonus if the company secured the SAR contract, it would be unlikely that Lockheed Martin would have known this with substantial certainty." Is the court saying, then, that if the defendant had known of bonuses that would be distributed to 30 employees of the Canadian Company, then the defendant would be liable to those 30 employees? How far should this go?

43. **Interference with lawyer-client privilege.** A private detective gains access to a lawyer's office and reads documents related to the client's claim. The detective is employed by the client's adversary. No economic loss is alleged. Does the client, as distinct from the lawyer, have a claim against the intruder? Look back at *Madden v. Creative Services, Inc.*, 84 N.Y.2d 738, 622 N.Y.S.2d 478, 646 N.E.2d 780 (1995), in the privacy chapter.

44. **A case to consider.** The plaintiff owns a fishing boat. He and his crew have partly circled a catch with a seine or net. The defendant intrudes within the partial circle with his own boat and net and takes the catch, in the process ramming the plaintiff's boat and causing physical harm to it. The plaintiff is entitled to recover for damages to his boat. He is also entitled to recover something for conversion of the catch. However, at least as between the captain and the crew, the crew is entitled to share in the proceeds of the catch. Has the crew any claim

against the defendant? If only the captain is a party plaintiff, can he recover the crew's interest?

45. **The Restatement's list of permitted interferences.** Lacking any objective standards, the Restatement falls back on a list factors that seem to furnish no guidance, and a list of cases in which the defendant's interference is either not improper in the first place or is privileged. The cases, roughly, are these:

- You are free to compete for prospective business or clients, so long as you use no wrongful means and violate no laws, provided that at least some part of your purpose is justifiable as competitive. § 768.
- Under similar circumstances, you are free to induce T not to enter into a contract with the plaintiff, if you have an interest in T's financial affairs. § 769.
- You are free to protect a person for whose welfare you are responsible by interfering either with a prospective or existing contract on behalf of that person, but here again this does not protect you if you use wrongful means. § 770.
- Some other forms of competitive or business or economic interests are said to justify interference with the plaintiff's business so long as that interference does not actually cause a breach of contract. § 771 (influencing business policy of the plaintiff by inducing T not to enter into business relations with the plaintiff).
- You can give "truthful information" even if it results in causing T to breach a contract with the plaintiff. Honest advice is a little different. This is also not improper, provided it is asked for and provided the advice is within the scope of the request. Both points are covered in § 772. Gye persuades Wagner to leave Lumley and work for Gye by telling Wagner, "I will pay you twice as much." Is this truthful information? What if Wagner says, "What do you think I should do?" and Gye replies, "You should work for me; you'll make twice as much."
- You can assert a claim in good faith, even though you know the presence of your claim will interfere with a prospective or existing contract. Suppose you say, in good faith, "you can't buy that land from the plaintiff; it's my land."

46. **Interference by a religious organization.** Suppose a church discharges an employee who is not a member of the clergy, then interferes with her employment in a church college by truthfully advising the college that she has been discharged and that she has sued the church. Would the church have a First Amendment argument against liability? Could it couch its argument in terms of the Restatement's factors? See *Brazauskas v. Fort Wayne—South Bend Diocese, Inc.*, 796 N.E.2d 286 (Ind. 2003).

§ 4. DEFENDANT'S BREACH OF HIS OWN CONTRACT—TORT OR CONTRACT?

MACHINE MAINTENANCE & EQUIPMENT CO. v. COOPER INDUSTRIES, INC.

661 F.Supp. 1112 (E.D. Mo. 1987)

GUNN, District Judge....

Beginning in 1976, plaintiff Machine Maintenance & Equipment Co. (plaintiff or MM & E) was a distributor for the sale, repair and replacement of defendant Cooper Industries, Inc.'s (defendant or Cooper) Gardner-Denver product line of industrial compressors. In October 1980 the parties entered into a new written distributorship agreement extending this relationship. The agreement contained a termination clause whereby either party could terminate the agreement without cause upon ninety (90) days notice in writing to the other party and that Cooper could terminate it with cause under certain enumerated circumstances upon one day's notice in writing. These circumstances included breach of the agreement by MM & E or any action on its part deemed by Cooper to be detrimental to Cooper's best interests.

By letter dated July 28, 1983 Cooper notified MM & E that the Dealership Agreement was to be terminated for cause on August 3, 1983 because MM & E had not fulfilled its obligations under the Agreement. Specifically, the letter stated that MM & E's sales had steadily declined, that MM & E had not maintained an adequate supply of parts, had not provided service, had not paid its accounts when due, had not sufficiently promoted the sale and use of Cooper's products, and had been the subject of customer complaints. On July 24, 1983 two key MM & E salesmen, Curt Hertel and Jack Bertlesmeyer, had resigned MM & E and formed their own corporation, Power Supply, Inc. (PSI). On August 2, 1983 PSI formally proposed to Cooper that it be granted MM & E's distributorship. On August 19, 1983 Cooper accepted this proposal.

[The jury found for the plaintiff on claims that defendant violated a federal antitrust act—the Sherman Act—by attempting to eliminate the plaintiff as a competitor and on a "tortious interference" claim. On the latter, it awarded $1.8 million dollars in damages and $10 million in punitive damages. The court ultimately rejected the antitrust claim.]

Defendant argues that it is entitled to judgment notwithstanding the verdict on plaintiff's claim of tortious interference with business relations, because plaintiff failed to introduce sufficient evidence on each of the essential elements of such a claim....

Under Missouri law, a party alleging tortious interference must show: existence of a contract or valid business relationship or expectation; the interferer's knowledge of that relationship; intentional interference which induces the breach; absence of justification for the interference; and damages....

A justification for interference with business relations recognized by Missouri courts is competition between business rivals, as long as that competition meets the standards for appropriate conduct established in § 768 of the Restatement [2d] of Torts....

In the present case the business relationships with which plaintiff alleges wrongful interference are not those between plaintiff and its former salesmen but rather those between plaintiff and its customers. Considering the evidence in accordance with the above-cited standard for j.n.o.v., the Court concludes that the jury could have reasonably believed the following:

Defendant terminated its distributorship agreement with plaintiff without cause with only 34 [sic] days notice rather than 90 days notice as provided for in the agreement. Defendant did not give the full 90 days notice so that plaintiff would have a difficult time in securing an alternate supplier. Without a steady supply of compressors and parts plaintiff would not have been able to serve its customers. Defendant's action was motivated by the hope that customers thereby dissatisfied with plaintiff's service would leave plaintiff and switch to PSI, defendant's new distributor. At the same time, defendant acting in concert with Hertel and Bertlesmeyer, actively contacted plaintiff's regular customers using plaintiff's sales records, told the customers that plaintiff was terminated as a distributor for defendant because it was not doing its job and urged the customers to deal with PSI instead of plaintiff. There was sufficient evidence for the jury to believe that on several occasions such contacts were made even before notice of termination was given to plaintiff and during the 34 day notice period.

The Court concludes that defendant's conduct, as a reasonable juror could have found it to be, slips over to the improper side of the "wrongful means" line. The absence of justification element for tortious interference has therefore been supported by sufficient evidence.

The Court further concludes that plaintiff presented sufficient evidence on the other elements of tortious interference to support the jury verdict in favor of plaintiff. The Court concludes that a reasonable juror could have found from the evidence that but for defendant's "interference" (manner plus contacts and representations to plaintiff's customers), plaintiff's customers would have continued doing business with it as a distributor for a competing quality product. There was also credible evidence that because of defendant's actions plaintiff was unable to secure an alternate product line until January 1984 and that by then plaintiff's customer structure was undermined. The finding that plaintiff sustained actual damages in the form of lost profits as a result of defendant's interference was thus supported by sufficient evidence.

Accordingly, defendant's motion for j.n.o.v. on plaintiff's claim for tortious interference is denied.... [The court ordered a remittitur of punitive damages to $100,000.]

47. **General rule against tort liability of contracting parties.** Most courts routinely say that when a party to the contract interferes

with performance, he is liable for contract breach, but not for tort. E.g., *Applied Equipment Corp. v. Litton Saudi Arabia Limited,* 7 Cal.4th 503, 28 Cal.Rptr.2d 475, 869 P.2d 454 (1994), *Colorado Nat'l Bank of Denver v. Friedman,* 846 P.2d 159 (Colo. 1993).

48. **Conspiring with others to interfere with one's own contract.** Illogically, some courts that accept this rule nevertheless impose liability upon a promisor who "conspires" with others to cause a breach of his own contract. See, summarizing the positions on this, *Joseph P. Caulfield & Associates, Inc. v. Litho Prods., Inc.,* 155 F.3d 883 (7th Cir. 1998).

49. **Protection for agent of a contracting party.** Agents are privileged to advise their principals to breach a contract or interfere with economic relations, at least as long as the agent is acting for his principal and not solely for himself. *HPI Health Care Servs., Inc. v. Mt. Vernon Hosp., Inc.,* 131 Ill.2d 145, 545 N.E.2d 672, 137 Ill.Dec. 19 (1989). Some courts express their protection for the agent by saying that the agent, who is identified with his principal, is not a "third person" and is thus not liable for the interference, especially when the employer is a corporation, which can only act through its agents. See *Latch v. Gratty, Inc.,* 107 S.W.3d 543 (Tex. 2003). Perhaps both approaches leave open the possibility that the agent will be liable not only if he uses improper means to interfere, but also if he acts with an improper motive.

50. **Cases approving liability for interference by a contracting party.** A few cases have said that a contracting party may be liable for interfering with his promisee's contract or opportunities with others. *Leigh Furniture and Carpet Co. v. Isom,* 657 P.2d 293 (Utah 1982), is such a case. Leigh sold his furniture store to Isom, who made a down payment and took possession under an agreement to pay the balance due over a ten-year period. On numerous occasions, Leigh entered the store to cross-examine Isom and his workers about payments and similar matters, demanding accountings at inappropriate seasons. Eventually Leigh refused to accept Isom's tender of payment of the balance due and brought this action. Isom counterclaimed for interference with prospects. Isom recovered $65,000 in compensatory damages and the court affirmed. It said that Leigh would not be liable for interfering with his own contract with Isom; but he may be held liable for interfering with Isom's prospective customers, even though that interference occurs by Leigh's breach of or interference with his own contract. Because of inherent problems in proof of motive, it is "prudent for commercial conduct to be regulated for the most part by the improper means alternative. . . ." Evidence here supports the view that Leigh sought to destroy the business for his own long-range purposes—to profitably resell the building free of Isom's interest. Improper means can be found because Leigh forced Isom to defend two groundless lawsuits. In addition, "a breach of contract committed for the immediate purpose of injuring the other contracting party is an improper means that will satisfy this element. . . ." See also *Campbell v. Westdahl,* 148 Ariz. 432, 715 P.2d 288 (App. 1986); *Jolicoeur Furniture Co., Inc. v. Baldelli,* 653 A.2d 740 (R.I.

1995); *Cherberg v. Peoples Nat. Bank of Washington*, 88 Wash.2d 595, 564 P.2d 1137 (1977).

51. **Evaluating tort recoveries for interfering with own contract.** Consider *Leigh* and *Machine Maintenance*. Every breach of one's own contract can cause damages by interfering with the promisee's opportunities. That is the essence of a breach of contract claim for lost profit. But if a promisor is liable for interference with his own contract, all or most contract claims will be tort claims for interference as well. Worse, the promisor might be liable for "interference" even when his interference is not breach at all but is in fact permitted by the contract terms. Was there anything more in *Leigh* and *Machine Maintenance*? For instance, could you find a tort independent of the contract breach?

52. **Bad faith tort claim?** The tort (not the contract) claim for bad faith breach of the covenant of good faith and fair dealing is similar to the interference claim in certain ways. Both sidestep the limits on contract remedies. Both create new rights that did not obviously exist otherwise. So they are in some ways connected or analogous. See Mark P. Gergen, *Tortious Interference: How It Is Engulfing Commercial Law, Why This is Not Entirely Bad, and a Prudential Response,* 389 Ariz. L. Rev. 1175, 1187–88 (1996). Would some claims that have been presented on a theory that the defendant interfered with his own contract make more sense if they were presented on a bad faith theory? Would that make the claims any more justifiable?

§ 5. INTERFERING BY BREACHING PUBLIC DUTIES OR INVADING PUBLIC INTERESTS

Jackson v. Stanfield, 137 Ind. 592, 36 N.E. 345 (1894). The plaintiff, Jackson, was a lumber broker. He maintained no lumber warehouse, but simply arranged direct shipments of lumber from mills to retail buyers. He operated the kind of business that today would be a home office business run by telephone and computer orders. Lumber retailers such as ordinary lumber yards, maintained warehouses and supplies and therefore had expenses that Jackson did not have. They felt threatened by Jackson's mode of operation. To exclude him from the retail market, they organized an association. The association threatened the wholesaler with whom both they and Jackson dealt, as follows: Any wholesaler who sold to or through Jackson would be "fined" by the association; if it did not pay, then the dealers would refuse to buy from the wholesaler. Jackson's supplies from the wholesalers were being cut off as a result of these threats. *Held*, Jackson had a cause of action against the dealers both for damages and injunction. They were in a conspiracy to suppress competition in restraint of trade, which is unlawful.

53. **Anticompetitive interference.** The defendants' tortious conduct in *Jackson* was anticompetitive because it was likely to eliminate their competition. Competition would be weakened, not strengthened, if

the defendants could act as they did to cut off supplies of a successful competitor. Notice also that if the defendants had been successful, they would not have eliminated competition by providing more efficient service, better goods, or cheaper prices, but rather by excluding a competitor from the market. Hence such acts are not only an interference with contract or prospects at common law, but are a violation of antitrust laws. *Eastern States Retail Lumber Dealers' Ass'n v. United States*, 234 U.S. 600, 34 S.Ct. 951, 58 L.Ed. 1490 (1914) (similar facts). In this sense, the defendants were breaching a public duty when they harmed Jackson. Lawyers frequently assert both interference with contract claims and antitrust claims arising from the same set of facts, as in *Santana Products, Inc. v. Bobrick Washroom Equip., Inc.*, 401 F.3d 123 (3d Cir. 2005).

54. **Concerted action.** One of the things that makes the defendants' conduct in *Jackson* especially threatening and therefore more likely to be anticompetitive, is that the refusal to deal was *concerted*. An individual can normally deal with anyone she likes, and equally can refuse to deal with anyone, apart from a statute to the contrary.

In *Quelimane Co., Inc. v. Stewart Title Guaranty Co.*, 19 Cal.4th 26, 77 Cal.Rptr.2d 709, 960 P.2d 513 (1998), the plaintiff alleged that all of the title insurance companies in the county conspired to refuse to insure titles obtained by tax deeds—land forfeited to the state for nonpayment of taxes and eventually sold by the state at auction. Although no individual company was obliged to insure titles it did not want to insure, the complaint stated a claim against the companies for a conspiracy in restraint of trade and also for interference with existing contracts to resell the land covered by tax deeds, which could not be completed if title insurance was unavailable.

55. **"Secondary" boycotts.** Another characteristic of *Jackson* that is arguably important is that the dealer-defendants there did not simply themselves refuse to deal with Jackson. They used the economic power generated by their concerted agreement to induce someone *else* not to deal with Jackson. This of course describes many interference with contract cases. The process can be chained indefinitely: A might threaten to refuse to deal with B unless B threatens to refuse to deal with C unless C stops dealing with P. Is there anything wrong with secondary boycotts?

56. **Bad motive, bad acts, and anticompetitive results.** The common law of interference has tended to make liability turn on the defendant's vaguely conceived "improper" acts or even the defendant's "improper" motives or attitudes. Cases like *Jackson* suggest an alternative. Maybe courts should really be concerned only if the defendant's conduct seriously undermines competition. This is the focus of antitrust law and policy. That focus leads to analysis of potential economic effects, not to moral judgements about the defendant's state of mind. In addition, the antitrust focus aims to encourage competition, even though competition may be economically destructive to some competitors. The

common law interference torts, on the other hand, by focusing on motive, may themselves discourage appropriate competition by imposing liabilities for sound competitive behavior. "Once judges condemn the motive, they are likely to regard competitive behavior as tortious." DAN B. DOBBS, THE LAW OF TORTS § 447 (2000). See Myers, *The Differing Treatment of Efficiency and Competition in Antitrust and Tortious Interference Law*, 77 MINN. L. REV. 1097 (1993).

57. **Doctors boycotting doctors.** Suppose a group of doctors at a hospital, having enough power in the hospital to do so, deny staff privileges to the plaintiff, another doctor. Or that they announce that they will not work with him or deliver babies of patients who have used that doctor for prenatal care. Does that implicate the concerns seen in *Jackson*?

In *Krebsbach v. Henley*, 725 P.2d 852 (Okl. 1986), the plaintiff doctor did prenatal work but was on the local hospital staff only for prenatal care, not for obstetrics. After prenatal care, he sent patients to the hospital for delivery by others. The defendants were doctors who had been delivering babies at the hospital for the plaintiff's patients. Eventually they refused to continue this practice. They indicated they would refuse future referrals from the plaintiff, refuse to deliver women who planned to use the plaintiff as their obstetrician and refuse to make referrals to him. He sued for interference with contract. The court held for the defendants. It quoted *Pontius v. Children's Hospital*, 552 F.Supp. 1352 (W.D. Pa. 1982):

> In the area of physician referrals and staffing decisions, it is obvious that behavior which might, in a normal commercial sphere, be considered a group boycott subject to the per se rules of illegality may well be dictated by "public service and ethical norms." We are simply not prepared to hold that a group of physicians who decide that they do not want to refer patients to a particular surgeon, because they doubt his qualifications, have committed a per se violation of the Sherman Act. . . .

Do courts have a bias in favor of "professionals"? Are doctors any more worthy of protection than lumber dealers?

TUTTLE V. BUCK, 107 Minn. 145, 119 N.W. 946 (1909). The plaintiff owned a barber shop in a small town. Defendant, a man of wealth, allegedly started a barber shop for the sole purpose of driving the plaintiff out of business. The plaintiff's business was ruined by this. *Held,* the complaint states a cause of action. "[W]hen a man starts an opposition place of business, not for the sake of profit to himself, but regardless of loss to himself, and for the sole purpose of driving his competitor out of business, and with the intention of himself retiring upon the accomplishment of his malevolent purpose, he is guilty of a wanton wrong and an actionable tort."

Note: Labor Strikes

In earlier days, labor strikes were held to be actionable as interferences with the employer's economic interests. Indeed, the labor-management disputes of the 19th and early 20th Centuries may have been one of the reasons why *Lumley v. Gye* was so readily accepted.

In *O'Brien v. People ex rel. Kellogg Switchboard & Supply Co.*, 216 Ill. 354, 75 N.E. 108 (1905), business agents for a union presented a contract to the employer. The employer resisted and the union threatened to strike if the employer would not agree to its terms. Listen to the Supreme Court of Illinois tell us why the union's bargaining was illegal:

> [T]hese business agents sought to obtain the signing of the contract by threats, or to induce the company to sign it in order to avoid a strike. A contract executed under duress is voidable, and duress is present where a party is constrained, under circumstances which deprive him of the exercise of free will, to agree to or to perform the act sought to be avoided. ... [A]ny attempt to compel an individual, firm, or corporation to execute an agreement to conduct his or its business through certain agencies or by a particular class of employees is not only unlawful and actionable, but is an interference with the exercise of the highest civil right.... It is clear that it is unlawful and actionable for one man from unlawful motives to interfere with another's trade by fraud, misrepresentation, or by molesting his customers or [by causing workers to leave his employment by various means, including] persuasion, with an intent to inflict an injury which causes loss.... The principles herein announced are sustained by the weight of authority in England and in this country. Lumley v. Gye....

By about 1930, federal statutes were beginning to protect the right to strike by various devices. To a large extent, federal labor laws now preempt many issues associated with labor disputes, and it is unlikely that the common law rules of interference will have much effect on labor strikes today.

Note: Social and Political Boycotts

Even after statutes legitimized labor strikes, the underlying idea persisted that, except for the purpose of pursuing a business, it was illegal for people to combine in ways that caused an interference with business prospects of others.

In *A.S. Beck Shoe Corp. v. Johnson*, 153 Misc. 363, 274 N.Y.S. 946 (1934), the plaintiff operated a large retail store in Harlem, a section of New York city with a "a large community of negroes." The defendants complained because the store hired no African-Americans. When the store refused to do so, the defendants picketed the store with banners asking people not to buy at the store because it refused to hire negroes. The court noted that "The old English cases and the early American cases condemned as criminal all acts of employees carried on in concert against their employer, as a criminal conspiracy," but that a broad liberal policy had reversed the wholesale condemnation of labor unions. Nevertheless, that policy extended *only* to union activities or labor disputes and it did not protect the defendants who sought racial justice. Accordingly, an injunction was issued.

Cases like *A.S. Beck* suggest some apparent contradictions. You are liable for persuading another person to break a contract; and you are liable for taking part in concerted action that interferes with contracts or even with economic opportunities. Yet the gist of the wrong in both cases turns on your speech. You persuade by speech without committing misrepresentation or libel or making impermissible threats. Or you join an association of others for a common purpose to persuade others. In light of the First Amendment, how can any of this count as a tort? Even if no public persons are involved, *Gertz* appeared to demand falsity in fact and some fault by the defendant in failing to publish truthfully. Does this idea disappear if instead of causing economic and dignitary harm by harming reputation you directly harm the plaintiff's economic opportunities *without* defaming him?

NAACP v. Claiborne Hardware Co., Inc., 458 U.S. 886, 102 S.Ct. 3409, 73 L.Ed.2d 1215 (1982). African-Americans in a Mississippi county boycotted the white businesses by concerted action as a means of seeking social and economic gains. The boycott group also sought to induce all blacks to join the boycott. Individuals supporting the boycott used verbal threats, coercive actions and some direct violence (one case of spanking), to induce other African-Americans to make the boycott unanimous.

The Mississippi courts imposed substantial tort liabilities on individuals associated with the boycott and on associations or groups associated with it. *Held:* reversed. So far as the boycott is nonviolent, it is protected by the First Amendment. Banding together to express political views and achieve political ends is a right of association protected by the Constitution and it is not lost because some members engage in violent or unprotected activities. Speech itself, although intended to persuade and coerce, is also protected. The fact that speech is offensive or intimidating does not remove the protection. Picketing is protected as speech. Government regulation may incidentally affect economic speech, as in labor picketing, but it may not limit political speech. *Noerr*, involving petition of government, is demonstrative that bad purpose or intent to cause economic harm will not allow regulation of First Amendment rights. Where First Amendment speech is mixed with violence, precision of regulation is required and only those damages proximately caused by the wrongful conduct are chargeable to defendants, not those chargeable to speech itself. The Mississippi Courts violated this principle and the judgment against defendants cannot stand.

---

58. **Individuals interfering with contract for political or social reasons.** *Claiborne Hardware* seems to vindicate free speech rights and accordingly to limit the use of tort law under the interference

doctrines. Would it be pretty strange if *Claiborne Hardware* protected concerted action but not individuals? Suppose, after *Claiborne Hardware* was decided, a movie director named Allman persuades an actor named Ballman not to work in a movie made by a director named Callman on the ground that Callman refuses to hire African-American actors. How does such a case differ if at all (a) from *Claiborne Hardware* and (b) *Lumley v. Gye*?

59. **Secondary labor boycotts and free speech.** Do you think *Claiborne Hardware* forecasts any rights to combine with others in purely economic boycotts? Federal labor law prohibits some kinds of secondary boycotts as unfair labor practices. If those secondary boycotts are carried out by speech, are they protected in spite of the federal statute? In *International Longshoremen's Assoc. v. Allied International*, 456 U.S. 212, 102 S.Ct. 1656, 72 L.Ed.2d 21 (1982), a union, to protest Russian actions in Afghanistan, refused to provide longshoremen for unloading ships which carried goods from Russia. Plaintiff was a shipping concern, which regularly carried wood from Russia to American ports. Plaintiff, facing difficulties in getting ships unloaded, sued the union for damages. The Court held that this stated a cause of action under the statute that make secondary boycotts illegal. The purpose is to let the union pressure the employer with whom it has a primary dispute but to shield neutral employers from being drawn into controversies not their own. The union had no dispute with the shipper or the shipping company. There was no exception for political boycotts under the statute.

60. **Residential picketing.** Residential picketing has become a common tactic used by some groups to express political-social-religious ideas. It is especially common in abortion protests. If a physician whose home is picketed by protestors claims the picketing interfered with his prospects or contracts, would you expect the courts to reject the claim because picketing is a matter of free speech under *NAACP v. Claiborne Hardware*? Or would privacy interests in the home warrant liability? Courts have used injunction to create buffer zones to restrict some residential picketing. Does that suggest that damages liability could be imposed for interference with prospects?

§ 6. INTERFERING WITH NON-COMMERCIAL PROSPECTS

61. **Interference with inheritance.** We've seen that courts give defendants more leeway to compete and follow their own self-interests when the plaintiff's interest is merely a prospect rather than an existing contract. Courts have shown a tendency to limit or exclude protection for a number of non-commercial prospects, but not all. Some courts have allowed the interference action when the defendant interferes with the expectancy of inheritance, for example, by influencing the plaintiff's ancestor to convey all her property to the defendant before her death.

See *Carlton v. Carlton*, 575 So.2d 239 (Fla. Dist. App. 1991); *Harmon v. Harmon*, 404 A.2d 1020 (Me. 1979) (both permitting the claim during the lifetime of the ancestor). It may be that some kind of independently tortious conduct will be required to establish such a claim, for example, fraud, duress, or undue influence. See *Doughty v. Morris*, 117 N.M. 284, 871 P.2d 380 (1994). These cases can be troublesome where the effect of the tort suit is to subvert the careful formalities required of wills, or the dead man's statute, or the statute of frauds. See *Holt v. First Nat. Bank of Mobile*, 418 So.2d 77 (Ala. 1982) (requiring writing).

62. **Elections and other sporting events.** In *Gold v. Los Angeles Democratic League*, 49 Cal.App.3d 365, 122 Cal.Rptr. 732 (1975), the plaintiff was running for office as city comptroller. The defendants allegedly put out a handbill representing that the democratic party endorsed the plaintiff's opponent, which was false, since it was the plaintiff who was a democrat and defendant who was a republican. The plaintiff lost the election. Has he a claim, or is this whole thing too uncertain?

Later, in *Youst v. Longo*, 43 Cal.3d 64, 233 Cal.Rptr. 294, 729 P.2d 728 (1987), the plaintiff owned a horse entered in a harness race. Defendant, a competitor in the race, allegedly drove his horse into the path of the plaintiff's horse and struck the plaintiff's horse with his whip, causing the horse to break stride and lose the race. Can the plaintiff recover for interference with his prospects of winning? The California Supreme Court held not. It thought causation not sufficiently provable and that regulation by administrative agency was a better solution. It appeared to think that sporting events generally, should be excluded from this kind of legal action. Does this make you think that the California Supreme Court might not accept liability in *Gold*?

63. **Interference with litigation prospects by a party to litigation: spoliation of evidence.** (a) When a party to litigation intentionally deprives his adversary of access to important evidence by destroying, altering or disposing of it, his adversary may be unable to prove her case or defense. Could this count as a tort for which the adversary could recover, especially if it prevents her from prevailing? A number of courts say not. They believe that trial judges can usually deal fairly with the loss of evidence by allowing the jury to presume or infer that the evidence would have been unfavorable to the one who destroyed it. In that situation, the strong preference of many courts is to use the presumption or some other trial sanction and not to recognize a tort. *Cedars–Sinai Med. Center v. Superior Court,* 18 Cal.4th 1, 74 Cal.Rptr.2d 248, 954 P.2d 511 (1998); *Trevino v. Ortega,* 969 S.W.2d 950 (Tex. 1998). The trial judge's sanctions against the spoliator might be quite strong. In *Gath v. M/A–Com, Inc.,* 440 Mass. 482, 802 N.E.2d 521 (2003), the trial judge permitted the adverse inference and also prohibited the spoliator from offering evidence or argument on certain related issues. In *Verchot v. General Motors Corp.,* 812 So.2d 296 (Ala. 2001), the plaintiff was treated as a spoliator and the court thought that justified dismissing the plaintiff's claim altogether. On the other hand, if the spoliation is not an

intentional interference with existing or reasonably anticipated litigation, the inference would not be available. See *Wal-Mart Stores, Inc. v. Johnson,* 106 S.W.3d 718 (Tex. 2003).

(b) On the other hand, a few courts have taken the view that intentional destruction of evidence important to the adversary's case is a very serious business and warrants a tort claim, not merely the adverse inference at trial of the underlying action. This view might give the aggrieved party a little more leverage because of the possibility of punitive damages. See *Hannah v. Heeter,* 213 W.Va. 704, 584 S.E.2d 560 (2003).

64. **Spoliation of evidence by a nonparty.** When a third person—one who is not a party to the underlying litigation and not acting for any party—destroys the evidence, the case is different. T's destruction of evidence that might have assisted P would hardly warrant a presumption against D who has done nothing wrong. In this situation, some courts have allowed an independent tort action. See *Hannah v. Heeter,* 213 W.Va. 704, 584 S.E.2d 560 (2003). Many others, however, have rejected the claim against non-parties, even though the injury cannot be redressed in such cases by an adverse inference or other sanction. *Temple Community Hospital v. Superior Court,* 20 Cal.4th 464, 84 Cal.Rptr.2d 852, 976 P.2d 223 (1999) (a 4–3 decision); *Fletcher v. Dorchester Mutual Insurance Company,* 437 Mass. 544, 773 N.E.2d 420 (2002); *Richardson v. Sara Lee Corp.,* 847 So.2d 821 (Miss. 2003). What could be the basis for this result? Courts have mentioned relitigation by disappointed losers and the danger of speculation on the causation issue. In addition, it is sometimes said that when the property destroyed belongs to the spoliator, he has every right to do with his own property as he likes. As to negligent spoliation, see Chapter 12, ¶ 23.

65. **Interference with litigation prospects: witnesses.** We know that perjury, though a crime, is not recognized as a tort. See Chapter 2, ¶ 17. Consequently, a witness's false testimony in itself provides no basis for action. A witness's defamatory testimony would also be protected by the absolute judicial privilege seen in Chapter 2. Suppose the witness's testimony operates to interfere with the plaintiff's claim or defense. Could the plaintiff claim that testimony, pleadings, or motions interfered with the plaintiff's prospect of winning the lawsuit, or would such a claim also be met with the absolute privilege? *Trau–Med of America, Inc. v. Allstate Ins. Co.,* 71 S.W.3d 691 (Tenn. 2002), took the view that the absolute judicial privilege applied only to defamation claims, and that the defendant could be held liable for interference with business prospects. Can this be right? Look back at ¶ 41. As to negligent interference with prospects in litigation or otherwise, see Chapter 12.

§ 7. A GENERIC PRIMA FACIE TORT?

66. **Holmes' prima facie tort.** Holmes once advanced an idea that might seem inconsistent with a free society. He said: "It has been

considered that, prima facie, the intentional infliction of temporal damages is a cause of action, which ... requires a justification if the defendant is to escape." *Aikens v. Wisconsin*, 195 U.S. 194, 25 S.Ct. 3, 5, 49 L.Ed. 154 (1904). Perhaps Holmes' idea of "intentional infliction" was a purpose or motive to inflict harm rather than a mere substantial certainty that harm would result. But either way, his statement taken literally would seem to require you to justify all kinds of everyday actions, even voting in a referendum against a bill that would be profitable for the plaintiff or practicing law vigorously in competition with other lawyers in hope that their clients would turn to you. And is there a bit of the Big Brother implicit in Holmes' view? Someone in authority would always be on call to be judging your motives.

ADVANCE MUSIC CORP. V. AMERICAN TOBACCO CO., 296 N.Y. 79, 70 N.E.2d 401 (1946). The plaintiff alleged: Plaintiff was a publisher of sheet music. The defendants were a company that sponsored a popular radio program and the advertising agency responsible for that program. The program broadcast the ten most popular songs of the week in order of sales as established by a survey. Jobbers and resellers of music place their orders largely on the basis of popularity claimed by the radio program. The defendant passes over songs published by the plaintiff or ranks them as less popular for a given week than they really are. This causes dealers in the plaintiff's music to make premature returns of stocks and otherwise to cause the plaintiff pecuniary losses. The defendants are wantonly causing harm to the plaintiff in a way that warrants an inference that they intend such damages.

Held, these allegations suffice to state a cause of action. "In Skinner & Co. v. Shew & Co. (1893), 1 Ch. 413, 422, Lord Justice Bowen said: 'At Common Law there was a cause of action whenever one person did damage to another wilfully and intentionally, and without just cause or excuse' .... On the other hand, the view that all intentional wrongdoing is prima facie tortious has been rejected by other high authorities who contrariwise maintain that every plaintiff must bring his case under some accepted head of tort liability.... In New York, earlier authority adopted the view of Justice Holmes "that 'prima facie, the intentional infliction of temporal damages is a cause of action, which ... requires a justification if the defendant is to escape.' " The allegations here state a claim for a prima facie tort.

SCHMITZ v. SMENTOWSKI

109 N.M. 386, 785 P.2d 726 (1990)

BACA, Justice....

In 1979, the Mocks purchased two adjacent ranches from the Pogues and the Edmondsons ... as part of a three-party land exchange. [As part of this deal, the Mocks sold a feed lot and farm to Schmitz. They received some cash from Schmitz and a promissory note for $230,000. The

Pogues, one of those who sold to Mock, received full cash payment. The Edmondsons were paid partly in cash with the remainder payable in annual installments. To secure the Edmondsons, the Mocks gave them a mortgage. The Mocks expected to use payments on the note from Schmitz to pay the Edmondsons. The Schmitz note was not actually payable to the Mocks, however, but to one Smentowski. Smentowski was acting as a legitimate straw to facilitate the three-way tax-free exchange of the lands. So Smentowski held legal title in trust for the Mocks and paid the income from the note directly to the Edmondsons.]

In 1981, Smentowski received a loan from the Bank. The Bank took possession of the note, so that the Smentowski loan would appear to bank examiners to be backed by more collateral than it in fact was. The evidence indicates that all parties to the transaction, including the Bank, had actual knowledge that Smentowski did not have any beneficial interest in the note—thus, the Bank knew that it had no interest in the note as collateral and that others had claims and defenses to the note. However, despite this knowledge, in 1986, when Smentowski defaulted on his loan, the Bank attempted to collect the balance due on the note from Schmitz. The Bank notified Schmitz of Smentowski's default and requested that he direct future payments on the note into the court. Edmondsons thus did not receive their mortgage payments; they accelerated the mortgage and threatened foreclosure against the Mocks. The Mocks were forced to borrow on their cattle line of credit to prevent foreclosure, and this prevented them from using the line of credit to pursue their business of cattle raising.

[Schmitz brought an interpleader suit and brought in all parties. The Mocks asserted claims, among them a claim against the Bank for prima facie tort. The jury found for the Mocks and they were awarded the note itself and damages for the bank's prima facie tort.]

The Bank contends that we should refuse this opportunity to recognize prima facie tort. It claims that the two jurisdictions that have recognized prima facie tort as a specific tort cause of action, New York and Missouri, have found prima facie tort to be arcane and unworkable, spawning much litigation without appreciable benefit to plaintiffs. . . .

The theory underlying prima facie tort is that a party that intends to cause injury to another should be liable for that injury, if the conduct is generally culpable and not justifiable under the circumstances. With variations in the several jurisdictions that have adopted the tort, its elements are generally recognized to be: 1. An intentional, lawful act by defendant; 2. An intent to injure the plaintiff; 3. Injury to plaintiff, and 4. The absence of justification or insufficient justification for the defendant's acts.

Although the concept that unjustified intentionally caused harm should be the basis for liability has been utilized without denominating the theory as prima facie tort throughout recent jurisprudence, New York was the first state to adopt prima facie tort as a specific cause of action. The cause of action as it developed in New York, became stylized, as courts added requirements; for example, that special damages be proven, that the complaint not plead any other tortious conduct, that the activity complained of be otherwise lawful and not fit into any other established tort category, and that the activity complained of be motivated by a solely malicious intent. In recent years, New York has retreated somewhat from these requirements, allowing alternative pleadings and expanding the definition of prima facie tort.

Restatement (Second) of Torts § 870 (1977) has adopted a much more general theory of prima facie tort, providing that: "One who intentionally causes injury to another is subject to liability to the other for that injury, if his conduct is generally culpable and not justifiable under the circumstances. This liability may be imposed although the actor's conduct does not come within a traditional category of tort liability."

The Restatement approach embodies a balancing process, because "not every intentionally caused harm ... deserves a remedy in tort." Thus, the activity complained of is balanced against its justification and the severity of the injury, weighing: (1) the injury; (2) the culpable character of the conduct; and (3) whether the conduct is unjustifiable under the circumstances. The dual nature of the determination is manifested by the requirement that the conduct be both culpable—wrongful or improper in general—and unjustifiable—under the circumstances no privilege should apply.

The Restatement further breaks down the analytical process into four considerations that should be considered in balancing the above factors: "(1) the nature and seriousness of the harm to the injured party, (2) the nature and significance of the interests promoted by the actor's conduct, (3) the character of the means used by the actor and (4) the actor's motive."

It is apparent from a discussion of the Restatement view that, although it considers the same factors as do the New York courts, it does so in a more flexible way, by balancing the factors rather than by creating stylized requirements.

Instructive to this court in our consideration of prima facie tort is the Missouri experience. In Porter v. Crawford & Co., 611 S.W.2d 265 (Mo.Ct.App.1980), the court addressed the issue we consider today: whether to allow recovery in tort for a lawful act performed maliciously and with the intent to injure the plaintiff. Porter involved an automobile accident, where the defendant-insurance agent settled the plaintiff's claim and delivered a check to plaintiff in release of claims. Plaintiff deposited the draft and wrote checks against it, while, without plaintiff's knowledge, the defendant canceled the draft. Plaintiff incurred injuries as a consequence, and brought suit alleging that, by acting with careless and reckless disregard for plaintiff's rights and without just cause, the defendant had maliciously acted with intent to injure plaintiff.

The Missouri court examined the New York experience and the Restatement view, and fashioned a prima facie tort doctrine that combined the fundamental policy view of the Restatement with the analytically consistent aspects of the New York experience. We feel that their approach was analytically sound, and we adopt it, with refinements as discussed below.

To constitute a prima facie tort, the tort-feasor must act maliciously, with the intent to cause injury, and without justification or with insufficient justification. One early development in New York was that the defendant was required to have acted with "disinterested malevolence"—the intent to harm being the sole motivation for the action. This was a means to determine if otherwise lawful conduct was done without any beneficial end but solely to injure the plaintiff.

We reject this approach in favor of the balancing approach sanctioned by the Restatement. A sole intent to injure is, by definition, unjustifiable—a purpose other than to injure the plaintiff is a justification for the act. Thus, if a defendant offers a purpose other than the motivation to harm the plaintiff as justification for his actions, that justification must be balanced to determine if it outweighs the bad motive of the defendant in attempting to cause injury.... but see Rodgers v. Grow-Kiewit Corp.-Mk., 535 F.Supp. 814, 816 (S.D.N.Y.), aff'd 714 F.2d 116 (2d Cir.1982) ("[M]otives of profit, economic self-interest or business advantage are by their terms not malicious, and their presence, even if mixed with malice or personal animus, bars recovery under prima facie tort.")

We believe that to allow a defendant to escape liability solely because he can demonstrate some economic benefit to himself from the complained of act would defeat the policy behind our recognition of prima facie tort—to allow a plaintiff to recover for intentionally committed acts that, although otherwise lawful, are committed with the intent to injure. Thus, we hold that the act must be committed with the intent to injure plaintiff, or, in other words, without justification, but it need not be shown that the act was solely intended to injure plaintiff.

We also accept the view held by New York and Missouri that prima facie tort may be pleaded in the alternative; however, if at the close of the evidence, plaintiff's proof is susceptible to submission under one of the accepted categories of tort, the action should be submitted to the jury on that cause and not under prima facie tort. Thus, double recovery may not be maintained, and the theory underlying prima facie tort—to provide remedy for intentionally committed acts that do not fit within the contours of accepted torts—may be furthered, while remaining consistent with modern pleading practice.

Contemporary scholarship recognizes that there exists a residue of tort liability, which has escaped categorization in the forms of tort action, that is available for development into recognized torts as the need arises. In recognizing the tort of prima facie tort, this court is acting well within the tradition of the development of tort law in this jurisdiction. New Mexico has recognized that tort law is not static—it must expand to recognize changing circumstances that our evolving society brings to our attention. Thus, in other areas, we have recognized that intentional, malicious conduct that injures another, even though it may not have been recognized by the heretofore accepted areas of intentional tort, can serve as a basis for tort liability. We have also been very willing to adopt the view of the Restatement of Torts to assist our development of new tort areas.

Accordingly, New Mexico has recognized as tortious inducing a breach of contract, adopting the view promulgated in Restatement. We have adopted the cause of action of intentional interference with prospective contractual relations. These torts reflect the underlying theory of prima facie tort as applied to contractual relations—the underlying malicious motive of a defendant's actions, done without justification, makes an otherwise lawful act, competition, tortious . . .

All that remains is for us to determine whether the Bank committed a prima facie tort against the Mocks. It is uncontradicted that the Bank was acting in an otherwise lawful manner. It took possession of a note as collateral on a loan, and when Smentowski defaulted on the loan, it moved to protect its interest and notified the payor to send its payment directly to the Bank.

It is also uncontradicted that the Mocks were injured by the Bank's actions. The mortgage on their ranch was not paid in a timely manner because the proceeds of the note were not turned over to Edmondson, precipitating a foreclosure action. To prevent the loss of the ranch, the Mocks were forced to borrow on their line of credit that they otherwise would have used to purchase cattle, and they thereby lost profit and were forced to under-utilize their land.

The second element of prima facie tort raises more substantial problems. The tort requires that the defendant not only intend the act, but that he also intend the harm. The Bank contends that the Mocks have not demonstrated that the Bank was motivated solely by a malicious intention to harm the Mocks; that the Bank, because it was motivated at least in part by economic self-interest, cannot be liable. As discussed above, we have rejected the requirement that the action be solely motivated by the intent to harm, as accepted by New York, in favor of the Restatement's balancing approach, whereby motives such as economic self-interest are weighed as an issue of justification.

The Bank contends that, nevertheless, our precedent dictates that we should adopt a standard of sole motivation to harm, citing M & M Rental Tools, 94 N.M. 449, 612 P.2d 241 (Ct.App.1980). However, M & M dealt with interference with prospective contract; the rights involved with prospective contract are speculative, and more concrete rights are entitled to a greater degree of protection. The rights implicated by a prima facie tort are not prospective—real, concrete damages must be proven, and we see no reason to adopt a higher standard of intent. . . .

The Mocks contend that a prima facie tort requires nothing more than a showing that the act complained of was wrongful, intentional, and without justification, and that the injury was a natural and foreseeable consequence of the act. In other words, they argue that it is not necessary that the Bank possessed ill will or a malicious motive, i.e. that it intended to harm them, as long as it intended the act that caused the harm. Thus, they claim that because the Bank intended to move against the note, because this act was wrongful and unjustified under the circumstances, and because it caused the Mocks financial injury, the Bank is liable for prima facie tort.

We disagree with this analysis. To allow such a lax standard would be to invite every victim of an intentional act to bring an action in prima facie tort and would subvert the purpose of prima facie tort by eliminating the element requiring that a defendant intended injury to the plaintiff.

Nevertheless, we do agree that the Bank's actions did rise to the level of intending to commit the harm. Thus, we hold that, when a defendant, such as the Bank, has intentionally acted with the certainty that injury will necessarily result, the intent to injure has sufficiently been proved to allow a court to resort to the Restatement's balancing approach to determine whether the tort has been committed. This approach differs from that adopted to New York, yet we believe that the balancing approach allows this lessened degree of proof of intent to be considered. . . .

[Affirmed]

---

67. **Questioning existence of a nominate tort in Schmitz.** Was there really no nominate tort in *Schmitz*? Put differently, if New Mexico had not recognized the prima facie tort, what claim would the plaintiff be making in *Schmitz*?

68. **Where rules of a nominate tort exclude liability on the facts.** What if the plaintiff presents a case in which all nominate torts fail because some limiting rule excludes liability? Suppose, for example, that in a jurisdiction requiring special grievance or injury in wrongful civil litigation cases, the plaintiff can prove all the elements of that tort except special injury. Can the plaintiff then turn to the prima facie tort theory? See *Engel v. CBS, Inc.,* 93 N.Y.2d 195, 689 N.Y.S.2d 411, 711 N.E.2d 626 (1999). A New Mexico court has held that where the claim of tortious interference with contract is the claim that best fits the facts, the plaintiff cannot use New Mexico's prima facie tort theory, even though the plaintiff could not prevail on the interference claim. *Bogle v. Summit Investment Co., LLC,* 137 N.M. 80, 107 P.3d 520 (2005).

69. **Applying prima facie tort theory.** A franchisor grants a franchise to A, who operates profitably, selling many goods to T, who lives in the adjoining county. The franchisor induces T to accept a franchise of his own, covering County B. T accepts and consequently ceases purchasing from A. Has the franchisor committed a nominate tort? A prima facie tort? *Bandag of Springfield, Inc. v. Bandag, Inc.,* 662 S.W.2d 546 (Mo. App. 1983).

70. **States supporting prima facie tort theory.** Courts in New York, Missouri, and New Mexico have more or less subscribed to the prima facie tort theory.

Professional and Academic Enhancements
Chapter 11

Breach of Duty to the Principal with Harm to Another

Harper v. Adametz, 142 Conn. 218, 113 A.2d 136, 55 A.L.R.2d 334 (1955). Tesar owned 80 acres of land in Haddam, Connecticut. Adametz, real estate agent for Tesar, advertised a portion of the property for sale. The plaintiff responded and Adametz showed the plaintiff the eighty-acre farm and told him that the seller was asking $8500 for it but that the buildings and a smaller acreage could be bought for less. Adametz wrote Tesar saying that he had a client who had offered $6500 cash for the farm (meaning eighty acres) and asked for an immediate reply. Tesar (through an attorney) told Adametz that he accepted. Knowing nothing of this, the plaintiff offered Adametz $7000 for the entire farm. Later Adametz told the plaintiff that his offer was rejected but that the plaintiff could buy the buildings and part of the land. The plaintiff then made an offer of $6000 for seventeen acres, including the buildings, and Adametz accepted the offer. The plaintiff was satisfied with his purchase. Adametz then arranged for Tesar to convey the entire property to third persons, for which Tesar received the $6500 he had agreed to accept. The third persons conveyed the 17 acres agreed upon to the plaintiff and the balance to Adametz' son. Tesar had not learned of the plaintiff's offer and the plaintiff had not learned that his offer was never presented. Adametz' son got the 63 acres for nothing and Adametz got $325 in commission. The plaintiff, eventually learning the facts, sued for fraud. *Held*, for the plaintiff. Adametz was Tesar's agent, not the plaintiff's; his fraud was fraud upon Tesar. But even so, "the plaintiff has been denied the right to have his bona fide offer of $7000 submitted to Tesar.... Equity will not permit these defendants to keep a benefit which came to them by reason of Jere's fraudulent conduct. It is true that Tesar has not acted to right the wrong done to him. Had he done so, it is probable that the plaintiff could have had the farm. This should not prevent the plaintiff, in his own right, from having a remedy for the wrong done to him.... Upon the payment of this sum into court, to await further order, an order should enter directing the defendant Walter to convey the sixty-three acres to the plaintiff."

Notes

1. **Interpreting and questioning Harper v. Adametz.** The dissenter thought that, since Adametz was Tesar's agent and not the plaintiff's, "neither the defendant's conduct nor his silence about it presents an

instance of actionable fraud." Since the real estate agent's fraud was not aimed at the plaintiff, and since the plaintiff is not shown to have received less than represented, a fraud claim is difficult to accept here. Adametz was unjustly enriched, and that is ground for recovery, but his enrichment was at the expense of Tesar, his principal, not at the plaintiff's expense. Is *Harper v. Adametz* then really only a case of interference with prospective contract? See 2 Dan B. Dobbs, Law of Remedies § 6.6 (3) (2d ed. 1993). What about Tesar's rights? He, after all, was admittedly the direct victim of Adametz' fraud. Perhaps he, not Harper, should recover the 63 acres. What is the best solution?

2. **Authorities supporting Harper v. Adametz.** There are some similar cases holding for the plaintiff. See *Ward v. Taggart*, 51 Cal.2d 736, 336 P.2d 534 (1959); *Nguyen v. Scott*, 206 Cal.App.3d 725, 253 Cal.Rptr. 800 (1988).

Remedies

ZIPPERTUBING CO. v. TELEFLEX INC.

757 F.2d 1401 (3d Cir. 1985)

[Zippertubing was negotiating a contract to provide certain work and materials to a general contractor, Nab, who was doing work for the New York Transit Authority. Nab was agreeable to Zippertubing's terms, but postponed signing a contract until it could be assured of Zippertubing's sub-suppliers. Zippertubing therefore arranged for supplies from Teleflex and in the course of making that arrangement revealed Nab's name. Teleflex then went to Nab directly and obtained the work for itself.

[Had the job gone through under Teleflex's original bid to Zippertubing, Teleflex would have made about $715,000 net profit. When it got the job for itself, it modified the contract with Nab and ended up with a net profit of more than $2 million. The jury awarded Zippertubing and a related subcontractor $2,000,000 in "compensatory damages" and $750,000 in punitive damages. The trial court added $345,862.96 to the award in the form of prejudgment interest. On appeal, the court first concluded that the defendant was properly held liable for interference with business prospects because it had been given Nab's name in confidence. It then addressed the remedies available.]

The plaintiffs presented evidence from which the jury could reasonably have inferred that Zippertubing and Surf lost anticipated profits. They did not attempt, however, to establish the amount of their lost profits. Instead they proved the amount of profits made by Teleflex as a result of its wrongdoing....

It is undoubtedly so that in most instances in which a New Jersey plaintiff has established liability for interference with a prospective advantage the judgment has been for the plaintiff's lost profits. Probably that is because in most instances the amount of plaintiff's loss and defendant's gain is the same. In the one case dealing with the question in New Jersey, however, the Court of Errors and Appeals held that an accounting for profits is an appropriate remedy for interference with a prospective advantage.

... The remedy applied in Schechter v. Friedman, supra, is consistent with constructive trust principles, and "it is possible to think of the accounting for profits in this kind of case as simply a special form of constructive trust." D. Dobbs, Remedies 253 (1973).... All of these closely related damage rules are consistent with the policy of discouraging tortious conduct by depriving the tortfeasor of the opportunity to profit from wrongdoing. Consistent with that policy, the trial court properly permitted the plaintiffs to prove as damages the amount of Teleflex's profits. The court charged: "The law says that when one has unlawfully deprived another of a contract or a business opportunity and has made that opportunity his own, he is not to be permitted to retain any of the profits, any of the benefits of his unlawful conduct." ...

Teleflex points out that its negotiations with Zippertubing involved extrusion of five specific diameters of closeable insulation. It later contracted with Nab not only to supply closeable insulation, but also to furnish some seamless insulation, and tie-wraps for the closeable insulation. Teleflex urges that the profits derived from the sale of these products should not have been included in the damage award. The measure of damages in tort cases includes those reasonably foreseeable at the time of the commission of the tortious act or omission. It was certainly reasonably foreseeable that in procuring insulation Nab would elect to deal with a single source of supply, and that, but for the tort, that source would have been Zippertubing. The jury could have so concluded based on inferences drawn from Simpson's testimony regarding Nab's customary practices in dealing with contractors, App. 1432, and from evidence that Nab did, in fact, purchase the seamless insulation and tie-wraps from its closeable insulation supplier. Thus, it was not error to permit the jury to base its award on the entire Teleflex–Nab transaction....

Teleflex next contends on appeal that the court erred in submitting the plaintiffs' claim for punitive damages to the jury. Teleflex points out that it has been punished as a wrongdoer by being forced to disgorge its profits, and that the award of punitive damages is duplicative and an excessive punishment. The problem with this argument, of course, is that it is equally applicable to any case in which both compensatory and punitive damages may be awarded. It is conceivable, for example, that a business-tort plaintiff seeking its own lost profits rather than those gained by the wrongdoer, might prove and recover more than the wrongdoer gained from the transaction. Such a defendant would undoubtedly also feel "doubly punished" if assessed with punitive damages. The fact that a disgorgement of profits or unjust enrichment measure was applied with respect to compensatory damages cannot be dispositive. See D. Dobbs, Remedies, 224 (1973).

Teleflex also urges that the plaintiffs' evidence was insufficient under New Jersey law to permit the punitive damage claim to go to the jury. Under that law a tortfeasor may be assessed punitive damages if there is evidence from which the fact finder may infer "actual malice, which is nothing more or less than intentional wrongdoing—an evil-minded act . . . or an act accompanied by a wanton and willful disregard of the rights of another." . . .

The trial court instructed the jury: "You may award [punitive] damages if you determine that the defendant's act or acts were actuated by actual malice, which is nothing less than the intentional wrongdoing, an evil minded act, or an act accompanied by a wanton and wilful disregard of the rights of another." Teleflex did not object to this instruction, and does not urge here that it misstates the elements necessary under New Jersey law for the award of punitive damages.

We have held . . . that the circumstances surrounding the transactions between the parties provided sufficient evidence to permit a jury to find that a relationship of confidentiality arose, and that Teleflex breached its resulting duty by using the identity of Zippertubing's customer, Nab, in contravention of Zippertubing/Surf's prospective advantage. We need not decide whether, from the very nature of the tort, its elements would in any event support punitive damages, since there was ample additional evidence in this case from which malice could be inferred. The jury could find that Coneys and Perrera, with full knowledge that the customer name had been disclosed in confidence, undertook what they knew to be an improper breach of the resulting duty. [The court summarized some of the evidence that permitted such a finding.]

[Judgment affirmed.]

1. **Restitution of the interferor's profits.** Accord, that the interferor's profits are recoverable, *Colorado Interstate Gas Co. v. Natural Gas Pipeline Co. of America,* 885 F.2d 683 (10th Cir. 1989) ($8,000,839 in "restitutionary damages;" "the weight of authority holds that restitutionary damages are available for tortious interference with contract"); *National Merchandising Corp. v. Leyden,* 370 Mass. 425, 348 N.E.2d 771, 5 A.L.R.4th 1266 (1976). The restitutionary claim for the interferor's gains was rejected in *Developers Three v. Nationwide Ins. Co.,* 64 Ohio App.3d 794, 582 N.E.2d 1130 (1990). The court reasoned: "We recognize the incongruity of a court labeling a defendant's conduct as wrongful and yet permitting the defendant 'to retain some part of his ill gotten gains.' On the other hand, there is also something incongruous about putting a plaintiff in a better position than if no tort had been committed. . . ."

2. **Damages required.** Courts have repeatedly said that the plaintiff must show he has sustained harm in some degree to sustain the action for interference. If the plaintiff shows no harm at all, the historical logic is that he has no cause of action, and in accord with that some courts have said that he cannot recover even nominal damages. *Morochnick v. Quigley,* 17 Mass. App. 1035, 461 N.E.2d 1220 (1984);

Centre Equities, Inc. v. Tingley, 106 S.W.3d 143 (Tex. App. 2003); cf. *Eichman v. Fotomat Corp.,* 880 F.2d 149 (9th Cir. 1989) (actual damages not proven, summary judgment therefore proper). But if the plaintiff shows he suffered actual harm of an undeterminable amount, he can recover at least nominal damages. See *Sisters of Providence in Washington v. A.A. Pain Clinic, Inc.,* 81 P.3d 989 (Alaska 2003). And the absence of actual *damages* probably does not preclude *restitution* of the defendant's profits.

3. **Measuring damages.** In *International Minerals and Resources, S.A. v. Pappas,* 96 F.3d 586, 597 (2d Cir. 1996), the court summarized damages for a valid tort claim for interference with contract by saying that a plaintiff "may recover in an appropriate case: (1) general damages based on the difference between contract price and market value of the thing promised, where the interference prevents the performance of the thing promised; (2) special or consequential damages subject to the rules of proximate cause ... and subject also to the requirements of the reasonable certainty and avoidable consequences rules; (3) punitive damages where the defendant's conduct and state of mind warrant punishment; and (4) emotional distress damages in a limited class of cases," citing Dobbs on Remedies § 6.6 (2) (2d ed. 1993). Similarly, the plaintiff can recover for losses she would have avoided had the contract been performed. And proximate cause—or sometimes the contemplation of the parties rule of contract law—sets a limit on recoveries. The plaintiff may be required to minimize damages if she can reasonably do so, but evidently is not required to do so by seeking specific performance from the breaching party. On these items, see 2 Dan B. Dobbs, Law of Torts § 455 (2000).

4. **Proof of damages.** If the plaintiff claims damages, as distinct from restitution of the defendant's profits or gains, the plaintiff will be required to prove that he suffered a loss and also a reasonable basis for determining the amount of that loss. It is easy to imagine that the plaintiff could fail to make such proof, especially in the case of lost prospects. In *American Family Life Assurance Co. of Columbus v. Teasdale,* 733 F.2d 559 (8th Cir. 1984), a state governor issued a press release attacking cancer insurance business. A cancer insurer brought suit claiming interference with contracts and prospects. The plaintiff sued in federal court under § 1983, claiming the press release violated a property right to have a hearing to which it was constitutionally entitled. The insurer proved that after the press release was issued, it did in fact lose some customers, but it did not prove any connection between the release and the loss. The court refused to permit a recovery, partly because the defendant was not shown to have been in bad faith, but also because the plaintiff failed to show that damages resulted in fact from the alleged tort.

5. **Emotional distress damages.** You might expect interference with economic prospects to be an economic tort only, or to afford no relief beyond that available for breach of contract. However, some cases have permitted recovery for emotional distress as well as for proven lost

reputation resulting from the tort. See *Nesler v. Fisher and Company, Inc.*, 452 N.W.2d 191 (Iowa 1990) ("we hold that it was a proper element of damage, despite the defendants' protestation that such an element of damage should not be allowed in a commercial interference case"; end of discussion); RESTATEMENT (SECOND) OF TORTS § 774A (1977) (if emotional distress is reasonably to be expected). *Mooney v. Johnson Cattle Co., Inc.*, 291 Or. 709, 634 P.2d 1333 (1981), hedged recovery this way: "The mental distress, injured reputation, or other consequential harm not only must have occurred, and have resulted from defendant's interference, it also must have been an injury of a kind that should have been expected as a common and predictable accompaniment of disrupting the type of relationship with which the defendant interfered." A Texas court rejected emotional distress claims in contract interference cases altogether. See *Delgado v. Methodist Hosp.*, 936 S.W.2d 479 (Tex.Ct.App. 1996).

6. **Punitive damages.** Courts have also permitted recovery of punitive damages for interference with contract or economic prospects, subject to all the constitutional and common law rules restricting the occasion and amount of such damages. See, e.g., *Texaco, Inc. v. Pennzoil Co.*, 729 S.W.2d 768 (Tex. App. 1987) ($1 billion for interfering with a contract by offering a seller more money than the plaintiff had offered).

7. **Where the contract limits damages.** Should damages be limited to those that would be recoverable for breach of the contract with which the defendant interfered? In *Sulzer Carbomedics, Inc. v. Oregon Cardio-Devices, Inc.*, 257 F.3d 449 (2001), the defendant interfered with a contract between the plaintiff and Clark. A limitation of damages clause in the contract applied to Clark, who as a result was liable for nothing for his breach. But the defendant who induced the breach was held liable for all damages. Should efficient breach policy protect the interfering defendant? Other courts have held that if the plaintiff's recovery against the contract breacher is limited by a liquidated damages clause, the tortfeasor's liability would also be limited. *Western Oil & Fuel Co. v. Kemp*, 245 F.2d 633 (8th Cir. 1957); *Memorial Gardens v. Olympian Sales & Manag.*, 690 P.2d 207 (Colo. 1984) The positive side might be that the plaintiff could recover the liquidated damages sum from the tortfeasor if no actual damages could be proven. See *Koehring Co. v. E.D. Etnyre & Co.*, 254 F.Supp. 334 (N.D. Ill. 1966).

8. **Injunction.** The rule that the plaintiff must suffer some pecuniary harm in order to recover (¶ 2, supra) is probably not meant to exclude injunctive relief. Courts have in fact permitted injunctions against future interference. See 2 DAN B. DOBBS, LAW OF REMEDIES § 6.6 (4) (2d ed. 1993).

9. **Contribution or indemnity?** Could the plaintiff recover in contract against the breacher and also in tort against the interferer? What contribution or indemnity claims should be allowed between the breach-inducer and the promisor? Relatedly, suppose that P sued the breacher and recovered all compensatory damages; could P then recover anything from the tortious interferer? See RESTATEMENT (SECOND) OF

TORTS § 774A(2) (1977) (damages of the interferor are reduced by payments actually made by the breacher).

Interfering with One's Own Contract—the Case of Parent and Subsidiary Corporations

WASTE CONVERSION SYSTEMS, INC. v. GREENSTONE INDUSTRIES, INC.

33 S.W.3d 779 (Tenn. 2000)

HOLDER, J.

[Based upon facts stated, a federal court certified questions of Tennessee law to this court.]

Waste Conversion Systems, Inc. ("WCS") alleges that it entered into a long-term contract to sell waste paper and similar fiber materials to Greenstone Industries-Atlanta, Inc. ("GSI-A"), the wholly-owned subsidiary of Greenstone Industries, Inc. ("GSI"). It also alleged that the contract specified that GSI-A would purchase a minimum quantity of fiber per month at a fixed price. Had the market price of fiber moved higher during the course of the contract, GSI-A would have benefitted by having a guaranteed source of supply at a low fixed price. However, the market price of fiber fell. It is WCS's contention that, without any legal justification whatsoever, GSI-A refused to accept fiber from WCS so that GSI-A could purchase fiber on the open market at a lower price. The claim against GSI is that it willfully and maliciously induced GSI-A to breach this same contract....

The first question certified to this Court is whether a parent corporation can be held liable for inducing a wholly-owned subsidiary to breach a contract. Courts from other jurisdictions hold that a parent corporation has a privilege pursuant to which it can cause a wholly-owned subsidiary corporation to breach a contract without becoming liable for inducement of breach of contract. However, the courts do not portray the privilege as an unqualified one, indicating that it can be lost in one of two ways. In *T.P. Leasing Corp. v. Baker Leasing Corp.*, 293 Ark. 166, 732 S.W.2d 480 (1987), the Supreme Court of Arkansas provided an insightful description of the privilege:

> We think the correct rule is that a parent corporation's privilege permits it to interfere with another's contractual relations when the contract threatens a present economic interest of its wholly owned subsidiary, absent clear evidence that the parent employed wrongful means or acted with an improper purpose.

Other jurisdictions have adopted similar rules.

The reason for acknowledging the privilege of a parent corporation to interfere in its wholly-owned subsidiary's contractual relations is the usual identity of interests between the subsidiary and its parent. This relationship between the parent and the subsidiary corporation is illustrated in *American Medical International, Inc. v. Giurintano,* 821 S.W.2d 331 (Tex.Ct.App.1991), as follows:

> [A] parent and a subsidiary are so closely aligned in business interests as to render them, for tortious interference purposes, the same entity. The court thus ignored the fact that the two were separate entities and held that neither could tortiously interfere with the other because their financial interests were identical, since the parent controlled the subsidiary and its profits.

This illustration corresponds to the analysis by the United States Supreme Court. In *Copperweld Corp. v. Independence Tube Corp.,* 467 U.S. 752, 104 S.Ct. 2731, 81 L.Ed.2d 628 (1984), the Court analyzed the relationship between a parent and subsidiary corporation:

> A parent and its wholly owned subsidiary have a complete unity of interest. Their objectives are common, not disparate; their general corporate actions are guided or determined not by two separate corporate consciousnesses, but one. They are not unlike a multiple team of horses drawing a vehicle under the control of a single driver. With or without a formal "agreement," the subsidiary acts for the benefit of the parent, its sole shareholder.... [I]n reality a parent and a wholly owned subsidiary always have a "unity of purpose or a common design." They share a common purpose whether or not the parent keeps a tight rein over the subsidiary; the parent may assert full control at any moment if the subsidiary fails to act in the parent's best interests.

Even though the Court provided this reasoning in the context of an antitrust case, we believe the underlying relationship between the two corporations would be no different in a tortious interference of contract case.

Courts in Tennessee have not addressed this issue directly, but, in an earlier case, we suggested the direction we are now taking. In *Forrester v. Stockstill,* 869 S.W.2d 328 (Tenn. 1994), this Court dealt with the issue of whether an officer, director, or employee of a corporation could be held liable for wrongfully interfering with an at-will employee's employment relationship with such corporation.... [W]e stated that the wrongful interference with the at-will employment by a third person is actionable only if that person stood as a third party to the employment relationship at the time. Since a corporation can act only upon the advice of its officers and agents and since important societal interests are served by corporations receiving candid advice from these persons, we held that officers, directors, and employees were immune from claims of intentional interference with employment if they act within the general range of their authority and their actions were substantially motivated by an intent to further the interest of the corporation. The case, in the end, was decided in favor of the officers because there was insufficient proof that the officers were not acting in furtherance of the corporation's interest....

The second certified question calls upon us to decide whether a parent corporation can lose immunity for acting contrary to its wholly-owned subsidiary's interest and where the burden of proof should lie. Courts in other jurisdictions generally acknowledge that acting contrary to the subsidiary's interest is one of the ways in which a corporate parent loses its privilege to interfere in its subsidiary's contractual relationship.... A parent corporation acting contrary to its wholly-owned subsidiary's economic interests can be considered a third party to its subsidiary's contractual relationship and can be held liable for tortiously interfering with that relationship.

With respect to the question of who bears the burden of proof, it is a general principle in Tennessee that the burden rests on the party who affirms, not on the party who denies....

In the case before us, the plaintiff, WCS, is the party attempting to recover from a parent corporation that was not a participant in the contract. The plaintiff is the party affirming the facts regarding the parent's interference with the contract as well as its unlawfulness in doing so. Therefore, once it is established that the subsidiary is wholly-owned by the defendant parent corporation (either as conceded in the plaintiff's complaint or as demonstrated by the defendant), the plaintiff should bear the burden of proof to show that the parent acted detrimentally to the subsidiary's economic interests. This fact should be demonstrated by the plaintiff in addition to the elements of the cause of action. The majority of our sister jurisdictions also place the burden on plaintiffs in this situation.

The third certified question asks us to decide whether the loss of the parent corporation's privilege can be caused by its use of wrongful means and what constitutes wrongful means. Cases from other jurisdictions indicate that a corporate parent loses its privilege to interfere in its wholly-owned subsidiary's contractual relations if it employs "wrongful means." The privilege can be lost even if the parent does not act contrary to the subsidiary's best interests....

In defining the meaning of "wrongful means," the court in *Paglin* stated as follows:

> In the context of interference with contractual relations, "wrongful means" is defined to include acts which are wrongful in and of themselves, such as "misrepresentations of facts, threats, violence, defamation, trespass, restraint of trade, or any other wrongful act recognized by statute or common law.

The Second Circuit in *Boulevard Associates* also characterized the term in a narrow manner to include "fraud, misrepresentation, intimidation or molestation." We find the holdings of both of these cases persuasive and believe that a broad definition encompassing both rules should apply in Tennessee. We also believe that the burden of pleading and proving that the defendant parent corporation acted with wrongful means in causing its wholly-owned subsidiary to breach a contract should be on the plaintiff, once it is established that the defendant corporation owns 100 percent of the stock of the subsidiary in question.

Based on the certified questions posed to this Court, we hold that a parent corporation is privileged to interfere in the contractual relations of a wholly-owned subsidiary and that it is immune from liability for inducing to breach a contract with another party. This privilege, however, can be lost either by acting contrary to such subsidiary's economic interests or by using wrongful means. For this purpose, the definition of wrongful means includes fraud, misrepresentation, threats, violence, defamation, trespass, restraint of trade, intimidation, molestation, or any other wrongful act recognized by statute or common law. Once it is established that the defendant corporation owns 100 percent of the stock of the subsidiary in question, the plaintiff bears the burden of proof to demonstrate that the defendant has lost its privilege by acting contrary to its wholly-owned subsidiary's economic interests or by employing wrongful means in inducing its wholly-owned subsidiary to breach a contract. The clerk will transmit a copy of this opinion in accordance with Tenn.Sup.Ct.R. 23(8). The costs in this Court will be taxed to the respondents, Waste Conversion Systems, Inc.

1. **Interfering with one's own contract.** Would it be correct to say that the premise behind *Waste Conversion Systems* is that you cannot ordinarily be held liable in tort for interfering with your own contract?

2. **Wholly owned subsidiary or not.** In *Phil Crowley Steel Corp. v. Sharon Steel Corp.*, 782 F.2d 781 (8th Cir. 1986), the parent corporation owned subsidiaries A and B. The parent sold steel to both subsidiaries, who resold the steel to others. Subsidiary A had contracts for resale of steel to the plaintiff. The profit on A's resale contracts was low, but the profit on B's resale contracts was high. The parent therefore told A to breach its contracts so that the parent could sell all its steel through B, the more profitable subsidiary. Subsidiary A accordingly refused to perform its contract for sale to the plaintiff, who first recovered full contract damages from Subsidiary A, then sued the parent corporation in tort. Although Subsidiary A might suffer as a result, the total corporate structure would gain. Since Subsidiary A was wholly owned, none of its shareholders would suffer. First, what case is to be made for or against tort recovery from the parent? Second—and maybe this is related—if recovery is allowed, what damages should the plaintiff recover?

3. **Whose interests justify the parent's conduct?** When the parent corporation's conduct in inducing breach is protected, is it because (a) the parent's interest justifies interference or (b) the subsidiary's interest justifies it? Some judicial opinions seem to have in mind the parent corporation's interest as a justification for its action. See *Williams v. B & K Med. Sys., Inc.*, 49 Mass.App.Ct. 563, 732 N.E.2d 300 (2000). *Phil Crowley Steel Corp.*, supra, has caused trouble on this point. Its language seems clearly to focus on the interests of the interfering parent corporation, but the case is confusing because it identified those

interests exclusively with the breaching subsidiary, not with the overall performance of the connected corporations as a whole. Other cases, like *Waste Conversion Systems*, seem mostly to think that interference must be justified, if at all, by protection of the subsidiary's interests. Besides *Waste Conversion*, see *T.P. Leasing Corp. v. Baker Leasing Corp.*, 293 Ark. 166, 732 S.W.2d 480 (1987). Maybe either the interests of the subsidiary *or* the interests of the parent should suffice. Judge Calabresi left that possibility open in *Boulevard Associates v. Sovereign Hotels, Inc.*, 72 F.3d 1029 (2d Cir. 1995).

4. **Unity theory.** You can see why the parent might be privileged to pursue its own interests by inducing a subsidiary to breach its contracts and pay damages. What is the logic that says it is privileged to do so only if the breach would be in the subsidiary's best interest? Perhaps the logic is that the privilege arises only because the two corporations, though formally distinct, are in substance one and the same—but only where their interests are the same, and hence if interests diverge so that the parent can help itself by hurting the subsidiary, the parent must be regarded as a third person. If that is it, doesn't this logic forsake policy and justice in favor of empty conceptions about how many legal persons are parties to the contract?

Civil Rights

HAMPTON v. DILLARD DEPT. STORES, INC.

247 F.3d 1091 (10th Cir. 2001)

HENRY, Circuit Judge....

On April 5, 1996, Ms. Hampton and her niece, Demetria Cooper, both African Americans, were shopping for an Easter outfit for Ms. Cooper's one-year-old son in the Dillard's children's department in Overland Park, Kansas. The plaintiffs had four children with them: Ms. Cooper's son, Ms. Hampton's eight-month-old and seven-year-old daughters, and her elder daughter's friend.

Shortly after they entered the store, Tom Wilson, a Dillard's security officer, noticed them. He observed them for more than fifteen minutes. Mr. Wilson testified that he paid close attention to the party, in part, because they had a stroller with them, because Ms. Cooper had a rolled-up dark cloth item in her hand, and because Ms. Cooper kept looking up at the ceiling and glancing around, as if to check to see if she was being watched. Because his suspicions were aroused, he asked fellow employee Pam Fitzgerel to continue the surveillance in a fitting room in the children's department, where the plaintiffs were trying clothing on Ms. Cooper's one-year-old son. At trial, Ms. Fitzgerel testified that Ms. Cooper was holding a rolled-up cloth item in the fitting room; that she later saw an item under Ms. Cooper's jacket; and that, believing the item to be store merchandise, she contacted Mr. Wilson and told him that she was positive that Ms. Cooper had put something under her coat.

The group left the fitting room and Ms. Hampton proceeded to purchase an outfit for Ms. Cooper's son from the salesclerk in the children's department. When she did so, the sales associate gave Ms. Hampton and Ms. Cooper each a coupon that was redeemable at the fragrance counter for cologne samples. The shopping group then proceeded on to the fragrance counter, which is located where the Dillard's store ends and opens into the Oak Park Mall, to redeem their fragrance coupons.

While the women were in the process of redeeming their coupons and while the women were in a conversation with fragrance consultant Betty Chouteau, Mr. Wilson interrupted them. Referring to Ms. Cooper, he advised Ms. Hampton that "the ... black female had been observed placing something in her coat." He asked to look inside the Dillard's bag carried by Ms. Hampton, took the bag, and emptied the contents on the fragrance counter. Mr. Wilson checked the items against the receipt and determined that they corresponded. Ms. Chouteau testified that she perceived it to be "a rather embarrassing situation" for the women and, upon Mr. Wilson's intervention, she "turned and started talking to other people."

While Mr. Wilson was matching up items to the receipt, Ms. Hampton became visibly upset and told Mr. Wilson that, as a regular customer of Dillard's, she did not appreciate being accused of shoplifting and she did not deserve to be treated this way. Mr. Wilson told her to calm down or he would call the Overland Park police and have her removed from the store. Ms. Hampton asked Mr. Wilson his name and the location of the customer service counter. She then proceeded to the customer service counter and had no more contact with Mr. Wilson. The encounter with Mr. Wilson lasted approximately five minutes. Ms. Hampton and Ms. Cooper subsequently filed suit against Dillard's, alleging false imprisonment under Kansas law and a violation of 42 U.S.C. § 1981.

Ms. Hampton and Ms. Cooper based their state tort claims on their detention by Mr. Wilson. They based their § 1981 claims on the observation and detention by Mr. Wilson and on the store's disparate security practices of "arresting or detaining African-American shoppers at a significantly greater rate than it arrests or detains white shoppers." They alleged that their "detention was a part of this pattern or practice." ... Noting that our § 1981 jurisprudence requires that the action interfered with must be based on a contract, the district court decided to bifurcate the trial. In the first phase, the jury was to determine whether the fragrance sample was a benefit of Ms. Hampton's purchase from Dillard's and whether Dillard's intentionally interfered with the redemption of the coupon. If the jury found the coupon was a benefit of purchase and that Dillard's intentionally interfered, it would proceed to phase two, in which it would determine whether the store's intentional interference was racially motivated. The jury found for Ms. Hampton on all of the issues presented in both phases, and awarded her $56,000 in compensatory damages and $1.1 million in punitive damages. The district court entered judgment in accordance with the verdict and rejected

Dillard's Motion for Judgment as a Matter of Law, or Alternatively for a New Trial or Remittitur....

In addition, Ms. Cooper appeals the district court's dismissal of her § 1981 claim and her state law claim. The Lawyer's Committee for Civil Rights has filed an amicus curiae brief in support of (1) affirmance of the verdict and judgment in favor of Ms. Hampton and (2) reversal of the dismissal of Ms. Cooper's claims. Beginning with the defendant's appeal, we shall review each contention in turn.

With respect to 42 U.S.C. § 1981, to establish a prima facie case of discrimination under § 1981, [FN2] the plaintiff must show:

(1) that the plaintiff is a member of a protected class;

(2) that the defendant had the intent to discriminate on the basis of race; and

(3) that the discrimination interfered with a protected activity as defined in § 1981.

Typically, most litigation involving § 1981 claims has emanated from the right to make and enforce employment contracts. However, the statute has been applied to discrimination claims arising in the retail sector and restaurant industry, when a contract has been established....

Dillard's challenges whether the fragrance coupon was a benefit of Ms. Hampton's contractual relationship for the purchase of children's wear. According to Dillard's, the coupons were promotional invitations, handed out indiscriminately and not exclusively in connection with a purchase. Dillard's maintains that the coupon was a gift and that it was never intended to confer a right upon its recipient. In addition, Dillard's points to Ms. Cooper's receipt of a coupon as evidence that a purchase was not required to receive the gift.

In rebuttal, Ms. Hampton argues that we must be mindful of the jury's appraisal of the credibility of the witnesses as well as the jury's resolution of factual issues. She and Ms. Cooper testified that, during the time they shopped at the Dillard's store (over an hour), they never saw anyone receive a coupon and saw no one distributing the coupons. The first they saw of the coupons was *after* Ms. Hampton had purchased merchandise. Furthermore, the sales representative from the fragrance company, Ms. Chouteau, testified that the purpose of the promotional coupon, handed out after a customer of Dillard's had made a purchase, was "to entice the shoppers to come to the fragrance [counter] so that we could talk to them about our product." ...

Ms. Hampton contends that she performed the steps necessary to act in compliance with the terms and conditions of the offer from Dillard's: she completed a purchase and presented the coupon to the fragrance counter. The performance of these acts, she argues, either constitutes an acceptance or entitles her to "the enjoyment of all benefits, privileges, terms, and conditions of the contractual relationship," as the statute says.

Clearly, the purpose of the statute is to make it clear that the right to make and enforce contracts free from race discrimination [is] protected by section 1981. Furthermore, the list set forth in subsection (b) of the statute, which gives examples of what might constitute the "making" or "enforcing" of a [contract] under the Act, is intended to be illustrative rather than exhaustive. We have clarified that a § 1981 claim for interference with the right to make and enforce a contract must involve the actual loss of a contract interest, not merely the possible loss of future contract opportunities....

Here, Dillard's offered a variance of an option or unilateral contract to Ms. Hampton, and she completed the invited performance in accordance with the terms of the offer.

Dillard's also contends that Ms. Cooper's receipt of a coupon undermines the jury's finding that the coupon was a benefit of Ms. Hampton's purchase contract. We disagree. Ms. Cooper, whose child received the clothing, was a part of the shopping party, and perhaps the store clerk thought Ms. Cooper too should receive the coupon. The jury weighed testimony regarding the receipt of such coupons by nonpurchasing customers and determined that the evidence weighed in favor of Ms. Hampton, *i.e.,* the coupon was a benefit of Ms. Hampton's contractual relationship with Dillard's.

... [W]e cannot say that the jury's conclusion that the coupon was a benefit of Ms. Hampton's contract with Dillard's was unreasonable.

Dillard's also sought judgment as a matter of law because Ms. Hampton suffered no actual loss of a contract right or interest.... At trial, Mr. Wilson testified on behalf of Dillard's that he stopped the women while they were approaching the store's exit and that he did not believe them to be exchanging their coupons for fragrance samples.

A recollection of Mr. Wilson's testimony may explain why the jury and district court reached the decisions that they did.... [A] trained security guard [was] claiming that he did not notice that the women were redeeming a coupon. Indeed, he did not notice that they were shopping or even talking with a salesperson.

This testimony was directly contested by Ms. Hampton and Ms. Cooper. The jury could have resolved this conflict based on their evidence, but the silver bullet may have been the testimony of Ms. Chouteau, the perfume consultant:

Q: [D]o you recall Paula Hampton and Demetria Cooper and their children coming up to the cosmetics counter?

A: I do.

Q: Do you recall that their discussion with you was interrupted by a Dillard's security officer?

A: Yes, I do.

....

Q: When [O]fficer Wilson came up and spoke, what did you do then?

A: Well, because it was a rather embarrassing situation and because I was very busy with a lot of other things going on, I turned and started talking to other people at the time with my back to them.

Q: With your back to whom?

A: To the officer and Paula. I mean, I just felt like it was an embarrassing situation for them and I felt uncomfortable, you know, watching, so I turned and went ahead and did what I was supposed to be doing.

Once again, the evidence in the record is sufficient for the jury to determine that Mr. Wilson deliberately interfered with Ms. Hampton's redemption of the coupon and that she suffered an actual loss of a privilege of her contract because of this interruption....

The jury concluded that, had there been no interference, Ms. Hampton would have received the service of [her] redemption of the coupon....

The dissent notes that Mr. Wilson's testimony does not suggest he had the subjective intent to prevent the redemption of the coupon. We agree, but note that § 1981 protects enjoyment of the benefits of a contract from *any* impairment, so long as the impairment arises from intentional discrimination. Thus the proper focus is on whether the defendant had the intent to discriminate on the basis of race, and whether that discrimination interfered with the making or enforcing of a contract.

Even under the dissent's suggestion that subjective intent to interfere with a contract is required, a reasonable juror could find a legally sufficient evidentiary basis to support such a finding, if it disbelieved Mr. Wilson's testimony. As to the issue of Dillard's intent, the court correctly instructed the jury during the first phase of the trial that Ms. Hampton had the burden of proving by a preponderance of the evidence that "defendant [i.e. Dillard's] intentionally prevented her from redeeming [the] coupon...." We note that, because "[t]he issue of intent ... is one that is often not susceptible to direct proof," the jury correctly "consider[ed] all conflicting inferences" that the circumstantial evidence presented....

[The court also upheld the finding that the acts were racially discriminatory.]

Dillard's contends that the compensatory damages award of $56,000 is not supported by the evidence and must be set aside. When a party complains there was insufficient evidence to support a damage award, we must determine whether the damage award is supported by substantial evidence.

Dillard's states that any emotional damages Ms. Hampton suffered resulted from Mr. Wilson's belief that her niece was shoplifting and not from any alleged § 1981 interference with her contract. In addition, Dillard's contends that Ms. Hampton's emotional distress, if any, is unsupported by the record.

Ms. Hampton counters that the damages from the accusation and interference with the contract were substantial: she felt humiliated and disgraced by the accusations. Clearly the accusation, though directed at her niece, implicated her as part of the entourage in the dressing room. In addition, Ms. Hampton claims that she, too, was accused of stealing. She contends that her emotional damages were immediately evident, as she was visibly upset after the incident, as well as lasting, as she is now unable to shop with her children for fear of future ridicule and humiliation. Ms. Hampton also claimed her daughter had repeated nightmares regarding the incident.

We note first that any economic damage that resulted from the store's intentional interference with the redemption of the fragrance sample was negligible. Our review of compensatory damages is limited to Ms. Hampton's testimony regarding her emotional suffering....

We conclude that the award of compensatory damages was well within the district court's discretion.

Dillard's also seeks to reduce or eliminate the $1.1 million punitive damage award. Dillard's argues that there was insufficient evidence for the jury to conclude that the defendant discriminated against plaintiff willfully or maliciously, which is required for an award of punitive damages under § 1981....

Based on the testimony presented, the jury could reasonably find that Dillard's took part in the intentional discriminatory conduct. ... The jury's findings as a whole are sufficient to establish that the discrimination by Dillard's, acting through Mr. Wilson, was malicious, willful, and in gross disregard of Ms. Hampton's rights. We will not disturb the decision to award punitives.

Dillard's also argues that the severity of the punitive damage award violates its constitutional right to due process ..... "First, and most important, is the reprehensibility of [the] defendant's conduct." Next is the ratio of the punitive damage award to the compensatory damage award. Third is the measure of the punitive damage award in relation to awards for comparable misconduct. We also must keep in mind the deterrent goal of punitive damages in conjunction with the impact the size of the award will have on a defendant and with the wealth and size of the defendant as relevant factors.

The availability of punitive damages under § 1981 is well established. Applying the three factors—reprehensibility, ratio, and comparability—to this case, we are unpersuaded by the store's arguments. Dillard's had ample notice it was subject to punitive damages for conduct that was malicious, willful, and in gross disregard of plaintiff's rights.

. . . [T]he jury was presented with evidence about the coding and close surveillance of African-American shoppers. The jury must have agreed with Ms. Hampton that the store's surveillance tactics are particularly reprehensible.

Dillard's next contends that the punitive damages ratio of approximately 20 to 1 is impermissibly excessive and unconstitutionally disproportionate. Dillard's relies primarily on the *BMW* Court's admonitions regarding economic damage cases, where a ratio of 10:1 was cited with approval. Ms. Hampton counters that in cases where " 'the injury is hard to detect [and] the monetary value of noneconomic harm . . . [is] difficult to determine,' " a higher ratio of punitive damages to compensatory damages is justified.

As stated above, the economic injury suffered here was nominal, but the actual injury is more difficult to quantify. "[B]oth the Supreme Court and this court acknowledge that low awards of compensatory damages may support a higher ratio if a particularly egregious act has resulted in a small amount of economic damages. Additionally, . . . where the injury is primarily personal, a greater ratio [than 10:1] may be appropriate." Looking at the harm that might result from the store's conduct in relation to the harm that actually occurred, and eschewing mathematical formulae, we hold that the punitive damage award in this case is justified. . . .

We agree with the district court that Ms. Cooper's receipt of the coupon did not establish a contractual relationship between Ms. Cooper and Dillard's. . . . We are aligned with all the courts that have addressed the issue that there must have been interference with a contract beyond the mere expectation of being treated without discrimination while shopping.

Because there is no dispute as to a material fact regarding Ms. Cooper's failure to make or attempt to make a purchase at Dillard's, we hold that the district court correctly dismissed Ms. Cooper's claims as a matter of law.

In the alternative, Ms. Cooper argues that, as the recipient of the purchased clothing and as a part of the shopping party, her receipt of the coupon conferred upon her the status of a third-party beneficiary. We disagree.

A contract is a stipulation *pour autrui* [for others] if it clearly reveals that the intent of the contracting parties was to provide a benefit to a third party. Ms. Cooper's presence at the register was fortuitous and, as noted above, her receipt of the coupon from the sales clerk did not dilute Ms. Hampton's § 1981 claim. However, an incidental benefit is not enough to confer contractual rights under the contract; there must also be consideration for the contract. . . .

For the reasons stated above we AFFIRM the district court's denial of Dillard's motion for judgment as a matter of law and motion for a new trial; we AFFIRM the district court's award of compensatory and punitive damages; we AFFIRM the district court's grant of summary judgment dismissing Ms. Cooper's claims; and we AFFIRM the district court's award of attorney's fees to Ms. Hampton.

[Dissent omitted.]

Immunity. Civil rights suits against officers and individuals for interference with contract type interests are rare. Distinguish suits against governmental entities, which are likely to be protected by immunities. The Federal Tort Claims Act, which creates the right to sue the federal government in tort, specifically excludes liability for interference with contract as well as liability for most other economic torts. A state statute's exclusion of governmental entity liability for intentional torts may also exclude interference with contract as an intentional tort. *Swanset Development Corp. v. City of Taunton,* 423 Mass. 390, 668 N.E.2d 333 (1996). If the exclusion is based on intentional tort, would that mean that a negligent interference claim would be entertained against an entity?

Chapter 12

UNINTENDED INTERFERENCE WITH ECONOMIC INTERESTS

---

§ 1. PRODUCTS AND THE ECONOMIC LOSS RULE(S)

A Preliminary Note on Products Liability

Products liability law grew up mostly in personal injury cases, not economic tort cases. In the 19th Century, a person who was injured by a negligently made product she purchased from a dealer would usually be denied any relief against the manufacturer on the ground that she and the manufacturer were not in privity. That rule began to disappear after Cardozo's famous decision in *MacPherson v. Buick Motor Co.*, 217 N.Y. 382, 111 N.E. 1050 (1916), leaving the plaintiff free to prove negligence if she could.

Proof of negligence against a remote manufacturer, though, was difficult. Sometimes plaintiffs would sue for breach of express or implied warranty instead of for negligence. This kind of suit was thought of as a contract suit, because the liability was created by the seller's promise (or analogously, by the seller's representation of fact) about the character of the goods. As with contract liability generally, liability turned, not on fault of the seller, but on deviation from the promised quality—a kind of strict liability that was potentially more favorable to the plaintiff than a negligence suit.

The trouble with the warranty claim was that, viewed as a contract claim, it required privity. So the plaintiff who purchased a defective Buick from a dealer could pursue the warranty claim against the dealer, with whom she was in privity, but not against the manufacturer, with whom she was not in privity. The bystander who was injured when the Buick's steering defect caused it to head for the sidewalk would be in privity with no one and thus would have no warranty action.

From this point on the law addressed the privity problem in two distinct ways. First, a limited number of cases and then the Uniform

Commercial Code, adopted by the states in the 1950s and 1960s, liberalized the privity rules without wholly abolishing the privity requirement. (A new revision of the Code was approved in 2002, but state adoption of the revision may take a while. See DAVID G. OWEN, PRODUCTS LIABILITY LAW § 4.1 (2005).) Section 2–318 of the UCC offered the states three versions of a more user-friendly privity rule, in increasing levels of liberality. These were that, for persons injured by breach of the warranty, the privity rules would no longer bar claims—

> [Alternative A] ... by a "natural person" (as distinct from corporations), if the person was in the family or household of the buyer, or was a guest in the household and could be expected to be affected by the goods sold by the defendant.
>
> [Alternative B] ... by a "natural person" who might be expected to use or be affected by the goods sold.
>
> [Alternative C] ... by any person who might be expected to use or be affected by the goods.

The second major approach to the privity problem began with Judge Traynor's opinion in *Greenman v. Yuba Power Products, Inc.*, 59 Cal.2d 57, 27 Cal.Rptr. 697, 377 P.2d 897 (1963). It was hard to abolish the privity rules altogether for contract-warranty claims, but Judge Traynor saw another route to strict liability. His decision in *Greenman* created a strict liability in tort. Under this rule, litigation turned away from considering whether the product departed from the warranted character and toward a consideration whether the product was "defective," something to be determined by rules of law.

The result of this development was that most states adopted a strict tort liability rule for personal injury cases. The Restatement (Second) of Torts § 402A quickly supported that development and said liability for personal injury would be determined by asking whether the product was defective. But the Restatement muddied the water by saying that defectiveness would be judged by the consumers' reasonable expectations of safety—which sounds like a test that might have come from the old contractual warranties.

From there the personal injury cases began to recognize several kinds of "defect" in products that caused injury. These were mainly (1) a manufacturing flaw, cases in which the product is well-designed but some particular products are not made well, leading to injury; (2) a design defect, cases in which the product is dangerously designed; and (3) warning or information defects, cases in which the product can be reasonably safe and non-defective, but only if proper instruction or warning is given.

As it panned out, courts had special difficulty in applying strict liability to design defects. How would you know what design was "defective" under the consumer expectation test? What if the consumer knew nothing about the safety features of the design or what the alternatives were? These questions and others like them led courts to test design defects, not by the consumer expectation test, but by a risk-utility test patterned after Judge Hand's famous decision in *United States v. Carroll Towing Co.,* 159 F.2d 169 (2d Cir. 1947). So design defect decisions began to turn on questions of reasonableness—how dangerous was the product? Could it be made safer at reasonable cost? These questions seemed to turn the strict liability of design defect cases back into negligence cases. Thus the newest Restatement on products drops all references to strict liability. See RESTATEMENT (THIRD) PRODUCTS LIABILITY, §§ 1 & 2 (1998).

In personal injury products claims, courts have generally held that the seller or manufacturer cannot effectively disclaim liability. This is the rule for warranty claims under the UCC § 2–318 and the judicial rule for "strict" tort liability for personal injury cases. This rule means that in personal injury cases, tort rules trump the contract.

With this background, we turn to stand-alone economic or commercial loss caused by products.

SEELY v. WHITE MOTOR CO.

63 Cal.2d 9, 403 P.2d 145, 45 Cal.Rptr. 17 (1965).

[The plaintiff purchased a heavy-duty truck from a dealer, Southern. The truck was manufactured by White Motor Co., and White issued an express warranty guaranteeing the vehicle to be free from defects in material and workmanship and limiting its obligation under the warranty replacement of parts. The truck was a serious problem and for 11 months, the dealer, with guidance from White, tried to fix it, to no avail. The plaintiff sued White, seeking to recover the amounts paid on the price, the lost profits, and an unrelated item. The trial judge ruled for the plaintiff on both claims and both parties appealed.]

[The court first held that, although the plaintiff did not know it was White rather than the dealer who had issued the warranty, he relied on the warranty and that was sufficient.]

Defendant contends that its limitation of its obligation to repair and replacement, and its statement that its warranty "is expressly in lieu of all other warranties, expressed or implied," are sufficient to operate as a disclaimer of responsibility in damages for breach of warranty. This contention is untenable. When, as here, the warrantor repeatedly fails to correct the defect as promised, it is liable for the breach of that promise as a breach of warranty. Since there was an express warranty to plaintiff in the purchase order, no privity of contract was required. . . .

It is contended that the foregoing legislative scheme of recovery has been superseded by the doctrine of strict liability in tort. . . . We cannot agree with this contention. The law of sales has been carefully articulated to govern the economic relations between suppliers and consumers of goods. The history of the doctrine of strict liability in tort indicates that it was designed, not to undermine the warranty provisions of the sales act or of the Uniform Commercial Code but, rather, to govern the distinct problem of physical injuries....

Although the rules of warranty frustrate rational compensation for physical injury, they function well in a commercial setting. These rules determine the quality of the product the manufacturer promises and thereby determine the quality he must deliver. In this case, the truck plaintiff purchased did not function properly in his business. Plaintiff therefore seeks to recover his commercial losses: lost profits and the refund of the money he paid on the trunk. White is responsible for these losses only because it warranted the truck to be "free from defects in material and workmanship under normal use and service." ... Had defendant not warranted the truck, but sold it "as is," it should not be liable for the failure of the truck to serve plaintiff's business needs.

Under the doctrine of strict liability in tort, however, the manufacturer would be liable even though it did not agree that the truck would perform as plaintiff wished or expected it to do.... If under these circumstances defendant is strictly liable in tort for the commercial loss suffered by plaintiff, then it would be liable for business losses of other truckers caused by the failure of its trucks to meet the specific needs of their businesses, even though those needs were communicated only to the dealer. Moreover, this liability could not be disclaimed, for one purpose of strict liability in tort is to prevent a manufacturer from defining the scope of his responsibility for harm caused by his products. The manufacturer would be liable for damages of unknown and unlimited scope. Application of the rules of warranty prevents this result. Defendant is liable only because of its agreement as defined by its continuing practice over eleven months. Without an agreement, defined by practice or otherwise, defendant should not be liable for these commercial losses.

... A consumer should not be charged at the will of the manufacturer with bearing the risk of physical injury when he buys a product on the market. He can, however, be fairly charged with the risk that the product will not match his economic expectations unless the manufacturer agrees that it will. Even in actions for negligence, a manufacturer's liability is limited to damages for physical injuries and there is no recovery for economic loss alone....

Here, plaintiff, whose business is trucking, could have shopped around until he found the truck that would fulfill his business needs. He could be fairly charged with the risk that the product would not match his economic expectations, unless the manufacturer agreed that it would. Indeed, the Uniform Commercial Code expressly recognizes this distinction by providing that limitation of damages is prima facie unconscionable in personal injury cases, but not in cases of commercial loss....

The judgment is affirmed, each side to bear its own costs on these appeals.

1. **The economic loss rule.** Courts widely support the view taken by Justice Traynor in *Seely*. See, e.g., *Moorman Mfg. Co. v. National*

Tank Co., 91 Ill.2d 69, 61 Ill.Dec. 746, 435 N.E.2d 443 (1982) (grain storage tank); accord, RESTATEMENT (THIRD) OF TORTS: PRODUCTS LIABILITY § 21 (1998). However, the economic loss rule, as it is called, may be formulated in various ways and given greater or lesser scope. If the tort claim is excluded under the economic loss rule (ELR), then the plaintiff's only possible claim is on the contract and subject to the law of contract, for example, the rules permitting the seller to disclaim warranties or limit remedies in claims for pure economic loss.

2. **Economic loss in consumer transactions.** As the *Seely* facts suggest, the ELR in this context is not limited to transactions between entrepreneurs; it can also bar consumers' tort recovery. See, specifically so holding, *Werwinski v. Ford Motor Co.,* 286 F.3d 661 (3d Cir. 2002). A few cases have said or suggested otherwise.

3. **Economic loss where personal injury was risked by the product's defect or occurred in a sudden event.** Some courts that follow the economic loss rule created an exception that allowed the plaintiff to sue in tort where the stand-alone economic loss results from conduct that also risks personal injury and/or is caused by a sudden, violent event. The Supreme Court rejected these cases for Admiralty cases and stuck with a plain vanilla rule against recovery of economic loss in tort. It thought that approaches of this kind were "too indeterminate to enable manufacturers easily to structure their business behavior." *East River Steamship Corp. v. Transamerica Delaval, Inc.,* 476 U.S. 858, 106 S.Ct. 2295, 90 L.Ed.2d 865 (1986). The leading case for the exception has been undermined and it seems to have little current support. See *Aloe Coal Co. v. Clark Equipment Co.,* 816 F.2d 110 (3d Cir. 1987).

4. **Damage to other property, including asbestos cases.** Many courts agree with Justice Traynor's view expressed in *Seely,* that physical damage to property should be treated like physical harm to persons. That means the economic loss rule would not protect the defendant if its product damages property other than the product itself. That happened in *A.J. Decoster Co. v. Westinghouse Electric Corp.,* 333 Md. 245, 634 A.2d 1330 (1994), where the plaintiff, a commercial chicken-and-egg producer, lost 140,000 chickens when a power failure eliminated ventilation in the chicken houses. The backup system did not work, allegedly because of a defective switch manufactured by Westinghouse. If the allegation is true, the switch caused physical harm not merely to the switch itself but to other property, so the economic loss rule does not apply and the plaintiff can proceed in a tort claim for negligence or otherwise.

When asbestos is incorporated into a building, causing economic loss in the value of the building or the cost of asbestos removal, courts have been willing to impose liability in tort. E.g., *United States Gypsum Co. v. Mayor and City Council of Baltimore,* 336 Md. 145, 647 A.2d 405 (1994). Is this to be regarded as something of an exception to the economic loss rule? Or should we see it as damage to property distinct from the product?

5. **Damage to the product itself.** Where the product's defect causes the product to damage itself, the usual view is that the economic loss rule bars recovery in tort. See *East River Steamship Corp. v. Transamerica Delaval, Inc.*, supra, ¶ 3 (turbines powering four ships and costing $1.4 million each destroyed themselves, *held*, economic loss rule bars tort recovery).

WAUSAU TILE, INC. v. COUNTY CONCRETE CORP.

226 Wis.2d 235, 593 N.W.2d 445 (1999)

N. PATRICK CROOKS, J....

Wausau Tile, Inc. (Wausau Tile) manufactures, sells and distributes "Terra" pavers to entities around the country. Pavers are concrete paving blocks made of cement, aggregate, water, and other materials for use mainly in exterior walkways. Wausau Tile's pavers have been installed in various locations throughout the nation.

Wausau Tile contracted with Medusa Corporation (Medusa) to supply the cement for the pavers and arranged for County Concrete Corporation (County Concrete) to supply the aggregate. Wausau Tile's contract with Medusa contained warranties providing that Medusa would remedy or replace cement which did not meet particular specifications. [The warranty from Medusa to Wausau Tile stated in part: "These express warranties are in lieu of and exclude all other warranties, express or implied, oral or statutory, of merchantability and fitness for a particular purpose. Seller [Medusa] shall remedy or replace, free of charge, any cement which does not comply with the aforesaid specifications and shall have no further obligation or liability for general, special or consequential damages arising out of a breach of the aforesaid express warranties."]

On April 16, 1996, Wausau Tile filed suit in Marathon County Circuit Court against Medusa, County Concrete, and their insurers, alleging breach of warranty, breach of contract, negligence, indemnification, contribution and strict liability claims. Wausau Tile claimed that several of the installed pavers had suffered "excessive expansion, deflecting, curling, cracking and/or buckling." Wausau Tile asserted that these problems were caused by alkali-silica gel reactions which resulted from high levels of alkalinity in Medusa's cement and high concentrations of silica in County Concrete's aggregate.

Wausau Tile claimed that the expansion and cracking of the pavers had led to problems and property damages which have given rise to "various claims, demands and suits against Wausau Tile." Wausau Tile alleged that it had "sustained monetary damages in remedying the property damage claims, is facing claims for personal injuries, and has suffered and will continue to suffer lost business and profits."....

[Travelers Indemnity Company, Medusa's insurer, moved to dismiss the negligence, indemnification and contribution claims and for a declaration that it was not obliged to defendant Medusa on the contract claims. The strict liability claims added later were also brought under consideration. The trial court ruled for Travelers on both and the Court of Appeals affirmed.]

The economic loss doctrine precludes a purchaser of a product from employing negligence or strict liability theories to recover from the product's manufacturer loss which is solely economic. Economic loss is the loss in a product's value which occurs because the product is inferior in quality and does not work for the general purposes for which it was manufactured and sold.

Economic loss may be either direct or consequential. Direct economic loss is loss in value of the product itself. All other economic loss caused by the product defect, such as lost profits, is consequential economic loss.

The economic loss doctrine does not preclude a product purchaser's claims of personal injury or damage to property other than the product itself. Similarly, claims which allege economic loss in combination with non-economic loss are not barred by the doctrine. In short, economic loss is damage to a product itself or monetary loss caused by the defective product, which does not cause personal injury or damage to other property.

In *Daanen,* this court identified three policies supporting the application of the economic loss doctrine to commercial transactions. First, the economic loss doctrine preserves the fundamental distinction between tort law and contract law. Second, application of the doctrine protects the parties' freedom to allocate economic risk by contract. Third, the doctrine encourages the purchaser, which is the party best situated to assess the risk of economic loss, to assume, allocate, or insure against that risk.

The first of these policies recognizes that contract law rests on bargained-for obligations, while tort law is based on legal obligations. In contract law, the parties' duties arise from the terms of their particular agreement; the goal is to hold parties to that agreement so that each receives the benefit of his or her bargain. The aim of tort law, in contrast, is to protect people from misfortunes which are unexpected and overwhelming. The law imposes tort duties upon manufacturers to protect society's interest in safety from the physical harm or personal injury which may result from defective products. Thus, where a product fails in its intended use and injures only itself, thereby causing only economic damages to the purchaser, the reasons for imposing a tort duty are weak and those for leaving the party to its contractual remedies are strong.

In this case, the damages sought by Wausau Tile can be grouped into three categories: (1) the costs of repairing and replacing cracked, buckled or expanded pavers; (2) the costs of satisfying third parties' claims that the defective pavers either caused personal injury or damaged property adjoining the pavers, such as curbs, mortar beds and walls; and (3) lost profits and business. We consider each of these types of damages in turn.

Repair and replacement costs are typical measures of economic loss. However, it is not the measure of damages which determines whether a claim alleges solely economic loss. Physical harm to property other than the product itself may also be measured by the cost of repair or replacement of the product. Consequently, we must determine whether Wausau Tile has alleged repair or replacement costs as a measure of harm to property other than the defective product.

Wausau Tile argues that the costs of repairing and replacing the pavers do not constitute economic loss because the pavers themselves are property other than the defective product (Medusa's cement). We are not persuaded by that argument.

Damage by a defective component of an integrated system to either the system as a whole or other system components is not damage to "other property" which precludes the application of the economic loss doctrine. Comment e of the Restatement (Third) of Torts § 21 acknowledges this "integrated system" rule....

In the instant case, it is undisputed that the pavers were integrated systems comprised of several component materials, including Medusa's cement. The circuit court determined that Medusa's "concrete is an indistinguishable, integral part of the pavers" which "cannot be separately identified from the finished product." Other courts have held that various substances incorporated into finished products constitute integral components of those products. *See, e.g., Casa Clara,* 620 So.2d at 1247 (Fla. 1993) (holding that defective concrete became an integral part of homes purchased by the plaintiff such that the homes were not "other property"). Because the inference that Medusa's cement was an integral component of the pavers reasonably follows from the facts alleged in the complaint, we must regard it as true. Accordingly, we reject Wausau Tile's contention that the pavers constitute property other than the defective cement.

We conclude that the crux of Wausau Tile's claim for repair and replacement costs is that the pavers were damaged because one or more of their ingredients was of insufficient quality and did not work for Wausau Tile's intended purpose. This is the essence of a claim for economic loss.

Second, Wausau Tile claims damages in the amounts it expended, or anticipates that it will expend, in remediation of third parties' claims of damage to property adjoining the pavers and pedestrians' claims of personal injury. These claims do not allege any personal injury or property damages on Wausau Tile's part. Rather, as Wausau Tile acknowledges in its brief, these claims are an attempt to recoup the commercial costs of settling the claims of third parties which resulted from the product defect. As such, the claims allege consequential economic loss....

Finally, Wausau Tile claims lost business and profits. Wausau Tile's lost business and profits are indirect losses attributable to the inferior quality of the pavers. Accordingly, they constitute economic loss which is not recoverable in tort.

We conclude that Wausau Tile's complaint alleges only economic loss. Therefore, the first policy set forth by this court in *Daanen* supports the application of the economic loss doctrine in this case. Wausau Tile's claims involve failed economic expectations, which are the province of contract law.

The second policy reason for applying the economic loss doctrine is to protect parties' freedom to allocate economic risk via contract. Allowing purchasers to elect recovery under tort theories instead of requiring them to rely on their contractual remedies "rewrites the agreement by allowing a party to recoup a benefit that was not part of the bargain." It strips sellers of the ability to protect themselves from foreseeable risk by negotiating sales agreements.

Wausau Tile and Medusa entered into a contract with a warranty which specifically addressed the suitability of the cement for use in the pavers. We do not find it appropriate to address whether the warranty covers Wausau Tile's alleged damages; the breach of warranty and breach of contract claims are still pending. It is clear, however, that Wausau Tile had the opportunity to negotiate a warranty and did so. Presumably, Wausau Tile paid a price commensurate with the warranty it received. If Wausau Tile were permitted to reap the benefits of a broader warranty by recovering its damages in tort, it would receive more than it bargained for (and paid for) and Medusa would receive less than it bargained for (and was paid for). Consequently, the second policy set forth in *Daanen* also supports the application of the economic loss doctrine in this case.

The third policy reason for applying the economic loss doctrine is that the doctrine encourages the party with the best understanding of the attendant risks of economic loss, the commercial purchaser, to assume, allocate, or insure against the risk of loss caused by a defective product. Purchasers are generally better equipped than sellers to anticipate the economic loss which a defective product could cause their particular businesses. Accordingly, courts have required purchasers to guard against foreseeable economic loss by allocating the risk by contract or by purchasing insurance. The result is a more efficient, more predictable marketplace. If tort recovery were permitted, sellers of products would be potentially liable for unbargained-for and unexpected risks, leading eventually to higher prices for consumers.

Wausau Tile should reasonably have expected that it might receive defective or unsuitable cement. Because cement is one of the main components of pavers, Wausau Tile should also have foreseen that defective cement might produce defects in the pavers. Evidently, Wausau Tile did foresee this risk because it attempted to allocate the risk contractually with Medusa. Wausau Tile may not now turn to tort law in hopes of obtaining benefits for which it may not have bargained....

6. **Rationales in *Wausau Tile*.** In *Wausau Tile*, the contract expressly limited the defendant's liability. A fair reading of that clause might be that tort liability is excluded along with any contract liability not expressly agreed upon. In that case, tort liability would be at war with the parties' expressed intent. Did *Wausau Tile* merely hold that contract clauses like this trump tort rules or did it create a broader rule that would exclude tort liability even where the parties had not done so by contract? In *Indemnity Ins. Co. of North America v. American Aviation, Inc.*, 891 So.2d 532 (Fla. 2004), the court offered this rationale: "The prohibition against tort actions to recover solely economic damages for those in contractual privity is designed to prevent parties to a contract from circumventing the allocation of losses set forth in the contract by bringing an action for economic loss in tort." Is this rationale narrower than, say, the third policy in *Wausau Tile*?

7. **Components separately bargained for?** In *Trans States Airlines v. Pratt & Whitney Canada, Inc.*, 177 Ill.2d 21, 682 N.E.2d 45, 224 Ill.Dec. 484 (1997), the defendant manufactured an aircraft engine and sold it to an aircraft manufacturer who installed it on a commercial airplane, which was then sold to a buyer. The plaintiff, operating an airline, was in the legal position of a buyer of the airplane, and the engine warranty ran directly to the plaintiff. While the plane was in flight, the engine bolts fractured and flew off, damaging the turbine blades and causing a fire. This in turn damaged the airplane itself, caused some personal injury to passengers, and lost profits for the airline operating the plane. Could the plaintiff airline recover against the engine manufacturer for damage to the airframe, given that the two products were made and warranted separately and that other engines could be substituted for the engine in question? The test, the court said, was whether the plaintiff bargained separately for the engine and for the airframe. Here, the "plaintiff bargained for and received a fully integrated aircraft. Plaintiff did not bargain separately for an engine and separately for an airframe. Had plaintiff done so, then damage to the airframe by the engine could be perceived as damage to 'other property.'" Would this test call for a different outcome in *Wausau Tile*?

Palmetto Linen Serv., Inc. v. U.N.X., Inc., 205 F.3d 126 (4th Cir. 2000). Palmetto operated a commercial laundry. It supplied clean linens to hotels and restaurants. One of the defendants sold the Palmetto a computerized system for injecting chemicals into the wash. The system malfunctioned and destroyed $200,000 worth of linens. The trial court dismissed Palmetto's negligence claims against both the dealer and the manufacturer of the computerized pump. *Held*, affirmed. Palmetto argued "that defendants are liable because they breached a legal duty of care separate and apart from their contractual obligations. We disagree. The economic loss rule bars a negligence action 'where duties are created *solely* by contract.' ... Palmetto finally argues that the 'other property' exception to the economic loss rule permits it to proceed in tort. We reject this argument as well. Although the economic loss rule generally 'does not apply where other property damage is proven,'... in the context of a commercial transaction between sophisticated parties, injury to other property is not actionable in tort if the injury was or should have been reasonably contemplated by the parties to the contract. In such cases the 'failure of the product to perform as expected will necessarily cause damage to other property,' rendering the other property damage inseparable from the defect in the product itself...." [Citing a case in which a tort claim for theft of coin collection caused by defect in safe was barred because "essence" of plaintiff's complaint was that safe did not meet economic expectations.]

SOMMER V. FEDERAL SIGNAL CORP., 79 N.Y.2d 540, 593 N.E.2d 1365, 583 N.Y.S.2d 957 (1992). A number of claims were consolidated as the result of a fire in a 42-story Manhattan skyscraper, including a claim by the owner of the building against the defendant fire alarm company. Allegedly, Holmes, the alarm company was negligent in deactivating its warning system, as a result of which there was a delay in notifying the fire department. In consequence of that, a small, containable fire went out of control and caused serious damage to the building. The fire alarm company's duty arose out of its contract with the owner, and the contract provided that the alarm company would not be liable for damages "caused by performance or non-performance of obligations imposed by this contract or by negligent acts or omissions" of the alarm company. But *held,* the plaintiff can sue in tort. "[A] contracting party may be charged with a separate tort liability arising from a breach of a duty distinct from, or in addition to, the breach of contract.... A legal duty independent of contractual obligations may be imposed by law as an incident to the parties' relationship. Professionals, common carriers and bailees, for example, may be subject to tort liability for failure to exercise reasonable care, irrespective of their contractual duties...." In this case, the defendant's "duty to act with reasonable care is not only a function of its private contract ... but also stems from the nature of its services. New York City's comprehensive scheme of fire-safety regulations requires certain buildings [including the plaintiff's] to have central station fire service. Central station operators, in turn, are franchised and regulated by the City, and may be penalized for failing to transmit alarm signals, provide qualified operators, and other acts and omissions.... Fire alarm companies thus perform a service affected with a significant public interest; failure to perform the service carefully and competently can have catastrophic consequences. The nature of Holmes' services and its relationship with its customer therefore gives rise to a duty of reasonable care that is independent of Holmes' contractual obligations." Consequently, the plaintiff may sue in tort. The defendant's second argument, that the contract clause bars the tort suit, is unavailing. "It is the public policy of this State, however, that a party may not insulate itself from damages caused by grossly negligent conduct."

8. **Scope of the economic loss rule—services and construction contracts?** If you thought that the economic loss rule only required judges to give effect to contract limitations so they would not be circumvented by tort law, you would not need to ask whether the economic loss rule applied only in products cases. You would instead look at the contract to determine what the parties intended about limitations. But many courts seem to think the economic loss rule is independent of the parties' reasonable expectations under their contract. Recall that *Wausau Tile* stated the rule as one governing claims by a purchaser of a product, not as one based on interpretation of the parties' contract. In *Insurance Co. of North America v. Cease Elec. Inc.,* 276 Wis.2d 361, 688 N.W.2d 462 (2004), also a Wisconsin case, the plaintiff contracted with the defendant to construct and wire a ventilation system for its barns. The defendant was allegedly negligent and the system failed, resulting in loss of chickens worth $40,000 and the loss of profits. The plaintiff was allowed to proceed on a negligence claim on the ground that the bar of the economic loss rule did not apply to services contracts as opposed to contracts for products. Some other courts have said that the economic loss rule bars tort claims against negligent service providers as well as against product suppliers. See *BRW, Inc. v. Dufficy & Sons, Inc.,* 99 P.3d 66 (Colo. 2004); *Trans-Gulf Corp. v. Performance Aircraft Servs, Inc.,* 82 S.W.3d 691 (Tex. App. 2002). However, some cases in this category, although relying on some form of economic loss rule, may be in fact appealing to a tort no-duty rule seen in the next section.

9. **Torts "independent" of the contract.** Courts recognize that some torts committed by one of the contracting parties may be "independent" of or unrelated to the contract and its risk allocations. *Robinson Helicopter Co., Inc. v. Dana Corp.,* 34 Cal.4th 979, 102 P.3d 268, 22 Cal.Rptr.3d 352 (2004); *Indemnity Ins. Co. of North American v. American Aviation, Inc.,* 891 So.2d 532 (Fla. 2004). Phrased differently, the tort duty, to be actionable, must not be interwoven with the contract. *Huron Tool and Eng'g Co. v. Precision Consulting Servs., Inc.,* 209 Mich.App. 365, 532 N.W.2d 541 (1995). If the duty is independent and not "interwoven" with the contract obligation, the ELR does not bar the tort suit. What would an independent duty be and how would you know that it is independent of the contract? Does *Sommer* help decide that?

10. **Professional services.** A number of courts in effect treat professional duties to a client as independent of the contract. Consequently, clients can sue their lawyers in tort for malpractice causing stand-alone economic harm, even though the representation arose out of a lawyer-client contract. *Collins v. Reynard,* 154 Ill.2d 48, 607 N.E.2d 1185 (1992); *Clark v. Rowe,* 428 Mass. 339, 701 N.E.2d 624 (1998) (noting the lawyer's fiduciary relation to client and observing that the economic loss rule is usually applied only when the parties are in a position to bargain freely concerning risk allocation, not the case with attorney and client). The idea has been extended to other professionals,

such as engineers, *Hydro Investors, Inc. v. Trafalgar Power Inc.,* 227 F.3d 8 (2d Cir. 2000); *Moransais v. Heathman,* 744 So.2d 973 (Fla. 1999), and accountants, *Congregation of the Passion, Holy Cross Province v. Touche Ross & Co.,* 159 Ill.2d 137, 636 N.E.2d 503, 201 Ill.Dec. 71 (1994). *BRW, Inc. v. Dufficy & Sons, Inc.,* 99 P.3d 66, 74 (Colo. 2004), took a slightly different view: "Our economic loss rule requires the court to focus on the contractual relationship between the parties, rather than their professional status, in determining the existence of an independent duty of care." In that case, the court thought the professional duties of an engineer to contractors on the job were those of the contract, not an independent tort.

11. **Economic loss rule barring claims of noncontracting plaintiff; privity.** So far, we've seen the economic loss rule come into issue only when the plaintiff and defendant are in a contractual relationship with each other. Could it ever apply to bar a tort claim when the parties are *not* in a contractual relationship and there is no privity between them? Some courts seem to say so. *Carstens v. City of Phoenix,* 206 Ariz. 123, 75 P.3d 1081 (Ariz. Ct. App. 2003), held that the economic loss rule barred a claim against city building inspectors who had a duty but who failed to find and disclose gross defects in a $2 million construction that the plaintiff later bought in reliance on their inspection. Florida sometimes requires privity to invoke the economic loss rule and sometimes not. The Florida court says that the ELR will bar the tort claim even if the parties are not in privity, provided the claim is for a product defect causing economic harm. However, if the claim is not based on a product defect, the ELR will not bar the tort claim when the parties have no contractual relationship. *Indemnity Ins. Co. of North America v. American Aviation, Inc.,* 891 So.2d 532 (Fla. 2004). The next section takes up a different rule about economic loss. See if you think that some cases invoking the ELR without privity could have been confusing the different rule in that section.

§ 2. NEGLIGENT INTERFERENCE WITH ECONOMIC INTERESTS

ROBINS DRY DOCK & REPAIR CO. v. FLINT

275 U.S. 303, 48 S.Ct. 134, 72 L.Ed. 290 (1927)

Mr. Justice HOLMES delivered the opinion of the Court.

This is a libel by time charterers of the steamship Bjornefjord against the Dry Dock Company to recover for the loss of use of the steamer between August 1 and August 15, 1917. The libelants recovered in both Courts below. . . .

By the terms of the charter party the steamer was to be docked at least once in every six months, and payment of the hire was to be suspended until she was again in proper state for service. In accordance with these terms the vessel was delivered to the petitioner and docked, and while there the propeller was so injured by the petitioner's negligence that a new one had to be put in, thus causing the delay for which this suit is brought. The petitioner seems to have had no notice of the charter party until the delay had begun, but on August 10, 1917, was formally advised by the respondents that they should hold it liable. It settled with the owners on December 7, 1917, and received a release of all their claims.

The present libel in a cause of contract and damage seems to have been brought in reliance upon allegation that the contract for dry docking between the petitioner and the owners was made for the benefit of the libelants and was incidental to the aforesaid charter party, etc. But it is plain, as stated by the Circuit Court of Appeals, that the libelants, respondents here, were not parties to that contract or in any respect beneficiaries and were not entitled to sue for a breach of it even under the most liberal rules that permit third parties to sue on a contract made for their benefit. Before a stranger can avail himself of the exceptional privilege of suing for a breach of an agreement, to which he is not a party, he must, at least, show that it was intended for his direct benefit. Although the respondents still somewhat faintly argue the contrary this question seems to us to need no more words. But as the case has been discussed here and below without much regard to the pleadings we proceed to consider the other grounds upon which it has been thought that a recovery could be maintained.

The District Court allowed recovery on the ground that the respondents had a "property right" in the vessel, although it is not argued that there was a demise, and the owners remained in possession. This notion also is repudiated by the Circuit Court of Appeals and rightly. The question is whether the respondents have an interest protected by the law against unintended injuries inflicted upon the vessel by third persons who know nothing of the charter. If they have, it must be worked out through their contract relations with the owners, not on the postulate that they have a right in rem against the ship.

Of course the contract of the petitioner with the owners imposed no immediate obligation upon the petitioner to third persons as we already have said, and whether the petitioner performed it promptly or with negligent delay was the business of the owners and of nobody else. But as there was a tortious damage to a chattel it is sought to connect the claim of the respondents with that in some way. The damage was material to them only as it caused the delay in making the repairs, and that delay would be a wrong to no one except for the petitioner's contract with the owners. The injury to the propeller was no wrong to the respondents but only to those to whom it belonged. But suppose that the respondent's loss flowed directly from that source. Their loss arose only through their contract with the owners—and while intentionally to bring about a breach of contract may give rise to a cause of action, no authority need be cited to show that, as a general rule, at least, a tort to the person or property of one man does not make the tortfeasor liable to another merely because the injured person was under a contract with that other unknown to the doer of the wrong. The law does not spread its protection so far. A good statement, applicable here, will be found in Elliott Steam Tug Co., Ltd. v. The Shipping Controller, (1922) 1 K. B. 127, 139, 140; Byrd v. English, 117 Ga. 191, 43 S.E. 419, 64 L.R A. 94; The Federal No. 2 (C. C. A.) 21 F. (2d) 313.

The decision of the Circuit Court of Appeals seems to have been influenced by the consideration that if the whole loss occasioned by keeping a vessel out of use were recovered and divided a part would go to the respondents. It seems to have been thought that perhaps the whole might have been recovered by the owners, that in that event the owners would have been trustees for the respondents to the extent of the respondents' share, and that no injustice would be done to allow the respondents to recover their share by direct suit. But justice does not permit that the petitioner be charged with the full value of the loss of use unless there is some one who has a claim to it as against the petitioner. The respondents have no claim either in contract or in tort, and they cannot get a standing by the suggestion that if some one else had recovered it he would have been bound to pay over a part by reason of his personal relations with the respondents. The whole notion of such a recovery is based on the supposed analogy of bailees who if allowed to recover the whole are chargeable over, on what has been thought to be a misunderstanding of the old law that the bailees alone could sue for a conversion and were answerable over for the chattel to their bailor. Whether this view be historically correct or not there is no analogy to the present case when the owner recovers upon a contract for damage and delay. The Winkfield, (1902) P. 42; Brewster v. Warner, 136 Mass. 57, 59, 49 Am. Rep. 5.

Decree reversed.

12. **Conceptualizing the rule in *Robins*.** You can think of the *Robins* rule as a rule that the law imposes no duty in tort to exercise reasonable care to prevent stand-alone economic loss. See *Duquesne Light Co. v. Pennsylvania American Water Co.,* 850 A.2d 701 (Pa. Super. 2004) (as derived from *Robins,* the rule is that "no cause of action exists for *negligence* that causes only economic loss"). Or maybe you can say that the *Robins* no-duty rule only holds that there is no duty to the plaintiff to exercise reasonable care to protect the property of some other person for the benefit of the plaintiff. Which do you think more accurate? Either way, is it clear that *Robins* is a no-duty-in-tort rule and not a rule that subordinates tort to contract?

13. **A landlubber hypothetical.** Suppose that the following occurred in a jurisdiction that always follows the *Robins* rule: Landlord leases a house to Tenant for one year, reserving the right to have repairs made to a septic tank. Landlord hires the defendant to repair the septic tank, but he does so in a negligent way, destroying the tank, with the result that Tenant cannot use the house for two weeks while a new tank is installed. Does *Robins* foreclose the tenant's recovery?

14. **Type of damages claimed.** It is not very clear in *Robins* exactly what the plaintiff claimed. Would it matter whether it was (a) lost rental value or (b) lost profits?

LOUISIANA EX REL. GUSTE V. M/V TESTBANK, 752 F.2d 1019, 88 A.L.R. Fed. 239 (5th Cir. 1985). The M/V Testbank collided with another ship in the Mississippi River Gulf outlet. A white haze of hydrobromic acid developed on impact. Containers on the Testbank went overboard, dumping 12 tons of pentachlorophenol, PCP into the waters. The Coast Guard closed the outlet to navigation and all fishing, shrimping, and related activity was temporarily suspended in the outlet and four hundred square miles of surrounding marsh and waterways. Forty-one consolidated suits asserted claims by shipping interests, marina and boat rental operators, wholesale and retail seafood enterprises not actually engaged in fishing, seafood restaurants, tackle and bait shops, and recreational fishermen.

The trial court granted summary judgment as to claims of economic loss without physical damage to property except those asserted by commercial oystermen, shrimpers, crabbers, and fishermen who had been making a commercial use of the embargoed waters. The district court found these commercial fishing interests deserving of a special protection akin to that enjoyed by seamen. *Held*, affirmed.

If *Robins* sought to avoid open-ended liability, its limits apply even more so here where the defendants interfere with mere economic opportunities, not an existing contract. Although liability could be limited by applying proximate cause or foreseeability rules case by case, the value of having a rule for all cases is significant. "Courts can decide cases without preexisting normative guidance but the result becomes less judicial and more the product of a managerial, legislative or negotiated function. . . . The vessel delayed in St. Louis may be unable to fulfill its obligation to haul from Memphis, to the injury of the shipper, to the injury of the buyers, to the injury of their customers." In drawing the line where liability must stop, the court would be acting as a manager or administrator but not as an adjudicator. Deterrence is desirable, but it becomes less effective when limits of liability are unknowable; from an actuarial viewpoint, it is not practical to fix a reasonable premium on a risk that cannot be assessed. In contrast, each business, knowing the limits of its economic risk, can insure for its own economic losses.

Characterizing the claim as one for public nuisance with private harm does not help. "The problem in public nuisance theory of determining when private damages are sufficiently distinct from those suffered by the general public so as to justify recovery is as difficult, if not more so, as determining which foreseeable damages are too remote to justify recovery in negligence. . . . Given the difficulty of this task, we see no jurisprudential advantage in permitting the use of nuisance theory to skirt the *Robins* rule."

[A number of concurring and dissenting opinions were filed. Judge Wisdom, joined by four others, argued that the majority's rule "conflicts with conventional tort principles of foreseeability and proximate cause." He would use proximate cause together with the particular damage requirement of public nuisance law to limit liability.]

15. **Testbank: the federal oil statutes.** The Trans-Alaska Pipeline Authorization Act created strict liability, including liability for pure economic loss, for spills of Alaskan oil. See 43 U.S.C.A. § 1653. It has been construed to permit the states to impose such liability in spite of *Robins*. See *Slaven v. BP America, Inc.,* 786 F.Supp. 853 (C.D. Cal. 1992); *Kodiak Island Borough v. Exxon Corp.,* 991 P.2d 757 (Alaska 1999).

The federal Oil Pollution Act (OPA), 33 U.S.C. § 2701 et seq., was enacted in August 1990. It is addressed to oil discharges into navigable waters or adjoining shorelines from a vessel or facility. The responsible parties are liable for removal costs but also liable for damages to "any claimant." § 2702(b)(2)(E) provides:

> Damages equal to the loss of profits or impairment of earning capacity due to the injury, destruction, or loss of real property, personal property, or natural resources, which shall be recoverable by any claimant.

In *South Port Marine, LLC v. Gulf Oil Limited Partnership,* 234 F.3d 58 (1st Cir. 2000), the court approved a recovery of economic losses of a marina resulting from an oil spill—lost slip revenues and costs of diverted labor force, but held that punitive damages were not available under the statute.

The federal statutory liability is different from any common law liability you might project: it limits liability. The limitation for some vessels is based on the higher of a fixed amount for each gross ton or a fixed limit ($10 million for vessels over 3000 gross tons). 33 U.S.C. § 2704(a).

J'AIRE CORPORATION v. GREGORY

24 Cal.3d 799, 157 Cal.Rptr. 407, 598 P.2d 60 (1979)

BIRD, Chief Justice. . . .

The facts as pleaded are as follows. Appellant, J'Aire Corporation, operates a restaurant at the Sonoma County Airport in premises leased from the County of Sonoma. Under the terms of the lease the county was to provide heat and air conditioning. In 1975 the county entered into a contract with respondent for improvements to the restaurant premises, including renovation of the heating and air conditioning systems and installation of insulation.

As the contract did not specify any date for completion of the work, appellant alleged the work was to have been completed within a reasonable time as defined by custom and usage. Despite requests that respondent complete the construction promptly, the work was not completed within a reasonable time. Because the restaurant could not operate during part of the construction and was without heat and air conditioning for a longer period, appellant suffered loss of business and resulting loss of profits.

Appellant alleged two causes of action in its third amended complaint. The first cause of action was based upon the theory that it was a third party beneficiary of the contract between the county and respondent. The second cause of action sounded in tort and was based upon negligence in completing the work within a reasonable time. Damages of $50,000 were claimed. [The trial court sustained the defendant's demurrer.]

This court has held that a plaintiff's interest in prospective economic advantage may be protected against injury occasioned by negligent as well as intentional conduct. For example, economic losses such as lost earnings or profits are recoverable as part of general damages in a suit for personal injury based on negligence. Where negligent conduct causes injury to real or personal property, the plaintiff may recover damages for profits lost during the time necessary to repair or replace the property.

Even when only injury to prospective economic advantage is claimed, recovery is not foreclosed. Where a special relationship exists between the parties, a plaintiff may recover for loss of expected economic advantage through the negligent performance of a contract although the parties were not in contractual privity. Biakanja v. Irving (1958) 49 Cal.2d 647, 320 P.2d 16 [and other cases] held that intended beneficiaries of wills could sue to recover legacies lost through the negligent preparation of the will.

In each of the above cases, the court determined that defendants owed plaintiffs a duty of care by applying criteria set forth in Biakanja v. Irving. Those criteria are (1) the extent to which the transaction was intended to affect the plaintiff, (2) the foreseeability of harm to the plaintiff, (3) the degree of certainty that the plaintiff suffered injury, (4) the closeness of the connection between the defendant's conduct and the injury suffered, (5) the moral blame attached to the defendant's conduct and (6) the policy of preventing future harm.

Applying these criteria to the facts as pleaded, it is evident that a duty was owed by respondent to appellant in the present case. (1) The contract entered into between respondent and the county was for the renovation of the premises in which appellant maintained its business. The contract could not have been performed without impinging on that business. Thus respondent's performance was intended to, and did, directly affect appellant. (2) Accordingly, it was clearly foreseeable that any significant delay in completing the construction would adversely affect appellant's business beyond the normal disruption associated with such construction. Appellant alleges this fact was repeatedly drawn to respondent's attention. (3) Further, appellant's complaint leaves no doubt that appellant suffered harm since it was unable to operate its business for one month and suffered additional loss of business while the premises were without heat and air conditioning. (4) Appellant has also alleged that delays occasioned by the respondent's conduct were closely connected to, indeed directly caused its injury. (5) In addition, respondent's lack of diligence in the present case was particularly blameworthy since it continued after the probability of damage was drawn directly to respondent's attention. (6) Finally, public policy supports finding a duty of care in the present case. The wilful failure or refusal of a contractor to prosecute a construction project with diligence, where another is injured as a result, has been made grounds for disciplining a licensed contractor. Although this section does not provide a basis for imposing liability where the delay in completing construction is due merely to negligence, it does indicate the seriousness with which the Legislature views unnecessary delays in the completion of construction.

In light of these factors, this court finds that respondent had a duty to complete construction in a manner that would have avoided unnecessary injury to appellant's business, even though the construction contract was with the owner of a building rather than with appellant, the tenant. It is settled that a contractor owes a duty to avoid injury to the person or property of third parties. As appellant points out, injury to a tenant's business can often result in greater hardship than damage to a tenant's person or property. Where the risk of harm is foreseeable, as it was in the present case, an injury to the plaintiff's economic interests should not go uncompensated merely because it was unaccompanied by any injury to his person or property.

To hold under these facts that a cause of action has been stated for negligent interference with prospective economic advantage is consistent with the recent trend in tort cases. This court has repeatedly eschewed overly rigid common law formulations of duty in favor of allowing compensation for foreseeable injuries caused by a defendant's want of ordinary care. [Citing cases of liability for a mother's emotional distress when her child was killed by defendant's negligence; for a host's injury to a social guest on premises; for a driver's injury to nonpaying passenger; and for loss of consortium.] Rather than traditional notions of duty, this court has focused on foreseeability as the key component necessary to establish liability. . . .

In addition, this holding is consistent with the Legislature's declaration of the basic principle of tort liability, embodied in Civil Code section 1714, that every person is responsible for injuries caused by his or her lack of ordinary care. That section does not distinguish among injuries to one's person, one's property or one's financial interests. . . .

Respondent cites Fifield Manor v. Finston, (1960) 54 Cal.2d 632, 7 Cal.Rptr. 377, 354 P.2d 1073, for the proposition that recovery may not be had for negligent loss of prospective economic advantage. Fifield concerned the parallel tort of interference with contractual relations. There a nonprofit retirement home that had contracted with Ross to provide him with lifetime medical care sued a driver who negligently struck and killed Ross. The plaintiff argued it had become liable under the contract for Ross' medical bills and sought recovery from the driver, on both a theory of direct liability and one of subrogation. Recovery was denied.

The critical factor of foreseeability distinguishes Fifield from the present case. Although it was reasonably foreseeable that defendant's negligence might cause injury to Ross, it was less foreseeable that it would injure the retirement home's economic interest. Defendant had not entered into any relationship or undertaken any activity where negligence on his part was reasonably likely to affect plaintiff adversely. Thus, the nexus between the defendant's conduct and the risk of the injury that occurred to the plaintiff was too tenuous to support the imposition of a duty owing to the retirement home. In contrast, the nexus in the present case between the injury that occurred and respondent's conduct is extremely close. Fifield does not entirely foreclose recovery for negligent interference with prospective economic advantage.

Respondent also relies on Adams v. Southern Pac. Transportation Co. (1975) 50 Cal.App.3d 37, 123 Cal.Rptr. 216. In Adams plaintiff employees were held unable to sue the railroad whose cargo of bombs exploded, destroying the factory where they worked. It should be noted that the Court of Appeal in Adams clearly believed that plaintiffs should be permitted to maintain an action for negligent interference with prospective economic interests. It reluctantly held they could not only under the belief that Fifield precluded such recovery. Adhering to the Fifield rule, the Court of Appeal in Adams did not determine whether the railroad owed plaintiffs a duty of care. In the present case, plaintiff's injury stemmed directly from conduct intended to affect plaintiff and was more readily foreseeable than the damage to the employer's property in Adams. To the extent that Adams holds that there can be no recovery for negligent interference with prospective economic advantage, it is disapproved.

The chief dangers which have been cited in allowing recovery for negligent interference with prospective economic advantage are the possibility of excessive liability, the creation of an undue burden on freedom of action, the possibility of fraudulent or collusive claims and the often speculative nature of damages. Central to these fears is the possibility that liability will be imposed for remote consequences, out of proportion to the magnitude of the defendant's wrongful conduct.

However, the factors enumerated in Biakanja and applied in subsequent cases place a limit on recovery by focusing judicial attention on the foreseeability of the injury and the nexus between the defendant's conduct and the plaintiff's injury. These factors and ordinary principles of tort law such as proximate cause are fully adequate to limit recovery without the drastic consequence of an absolute rule which bars recovery in all such cases. Following these principles, recovery for negligent interference with prospective economic advantage will be limited to instances where the risk of harm is foreseeable and is closely connected with the defendant's conduct, where damages are not wholly speculative and the injury is not part of the plaintiff's ordinary business risk.

Accordingly, this court holds that a contractor owes a duty of care to the tenant of a building undergoing construction work to prosecute that work in a manner which does not cause undue injury to the tenant's business, where such injury is reasonably foreseeable. The demurrer to appellant's second cause of action should not have been sustained. The judgment of dismissal is reversed.

16. **Confusion about *J'Aire*.** *J'Aire* caused confusion. Some lawyers, noting that *J'Aire* did not mention *Seely,* wondered whether *Seely* had been silently overruled or whether it was distinguishable. After *J'Aire,* the California Supreme Court returned to *Seely's* emphasis on the contract. The court overruled its *Seaman's* case, which had created a tort for bad faith breach of a contract (Chapter 10, ¶¶ 16–18). In so doing it adopted "a general rule precluding tort recovery for noninsurance contract breach, at least in the absence of violation of 'an independent duty arising from principles of tort law.'" *Freeman & Mills, Inc. v. Belcher Oil Co.,* 11 Cal.4th 85, 900 P.2d 669, 44 Cal.Rptr.2d 420 (1995). *J'Aire* was not mentioned.

17. ***J'Aire* as contract liability?** *J'Aire* drew commentary from big guns in the torts arsenal. Gary Schwartz, *Economic Loss in American Tort Law: The Examples of J'Aire and of Products Liability*, 23 San Diego L. Rev. 37 (1986), argued that *J'Aire* was wrong in allowing recovery on a negligence theory, but could properly have been decided on a third-party beneficiary theory. Robert Rabin similarly noted that *J'Aire* was no surprise because the defendant had been "engaged specifically to confer a benefit on plaintiff . . . namely, to enhance the suitability of the premises." See Rabin, *Tort Recovery for Negligently Inflicted Economic Loss: A Reassessment*, 37 Stan. L. Rev. 1513, 1521 (1985).

18. **Negligent interference—the American majority.** Although *Robins Dry Dock,* supra, was a federal Admiralty case, the states as well as federal courts have generally accepted its principle. Either under *Robins* or under the purported auspices of the economic loss rule, most courts appear to reject liability for negligent interference with stand-alone economic interests in the absence of special circumstances. E.g., *Casa Clara Condominium Ass'n, Inc. v. Charley Toppino & Sons, Inc.*, 620 So.2d 1244 (Fla. 1993) (defective supplies for construction work, no negligence liability to ultimate purchaser of real property); *In re Chicago Flood Litigation*, 176 Ill.2d 179, 223 Ill.Dec. 532, 680 N.E.2d 265 (1997) (flooded tunnel caused economic harm); *Garweth Corp. v. Boston Edison Co.*, 415 Mass. 303, 613 N.E.2d 92 (1993) (added work for plaintiff as result of oil spill). Similarly, employees who are out of work because the defendant has negligently damaged their workplace or made it too risky, have no claim against that negligent defendant. See *United Textile Workers of America, AFL-CIO v. Lear Siegler Seating Corp.*, 825 S.W.2d 83 (Tenn. App. 1992).

19. **Negligent interference—the American minority.** Several American cases appear to have adopted a general rule like *J'Aire's,* that liability may be imposed for negligent interference with economic interests, such as the prospects of restaurant income in *J'Aire. Mattingly v. Sheldon Jackson College*, 743 P.2d 356 (Alaska 1987); *People Express Airlines, Inc. v. Consolidated Rail Corp.*, 100 N.J. 246, 495 A.2d 107 (1985).

Exceptions to the Majority Rule—or Not

20. **Medical Care Recovery Act; actions per quod.** At one time the master could recover pecuniary losses he suffered as a result of negligent injury to his servant. This action fell into disuse and seems now to be actively rejected by courts that have considered it. California held that a corporation could not recover either for medical expenses it was obligated to pay on behalf of an injured employee or for the corporation's lost profits due to his inability to work when he was negligently injured. *I.J. Weinrot and Son, Inc. v. Jackson*, 40 Cal.3d 327, 220 Cal.Rptr. 103, 708 P.2d 682 (1985). Only *Mattingly v. Sheldon Jackson College*, 743 P.2d 356 (Alaska 1987), seems to permit recovery. Although the common law seems to have discarded liability to the master for injury to the servant, the Federal Medical Care Recovery Act, 42 U.S.C.A. § 2651, allows the federal government to recover from the tortfeasor for medical expenses it has incurred on behalf of a person (such as a service person or family member).

21. **Limited liability cases.** Plangent contracts with Thermidor to keep Thermidor's private road in repair for a stated price per year. Dumas, a building contractor, trespasses on the road to take a short cut; routing heavy machinery over the road, he virtually destroys it. The plaintiff is required by his contract to repair the road and thus has an added expense due to defendant's trespass. Has the plaintiff a claim? Suppose *Robins* really is only a practical limit to avoid indeterminate and unlimited downstream liabilities. Would indeterminancy of liability be a problem if Thermidor's claim is allowed?

22. **Contractor-architect-engineer cases.** Liability for negligently inflicted economic injury might be justified on contract grounds under a third-party beneficiary theory. A tort version of the idea is somewhat similar—a duty of care might be found if the defendant "undertakes" to exercise care for the benefit of the plaintiff or if the defendant and the plaintiff are in a special relationship that generates such a duty. The contractors, architects, and engineers who are hired by landowners to work cooperatively with each other and not as adversaries may be expected to exercise reasonable care for the interests of others in the project. So some courts have said that an engineer or architect hired to design or supervise a construction project is liable for negligence causing economic harm to contractors. *Tommy L. Griffin Plumbing & Heating Co. v. Jordan, Jones & Goulding, Inc.*, 320 S.C. 49, 463 S.E.2d 85 (1995); *Eastern Steel Constructors, Inc. v. City of Salem*, 209 W.Va. 392, 549 S.E.2d 266 (2001) (permitting negligence claim, subject to duty

limitations imposed in the architect-owner contract; also claim based upon implied warranty of skill and care, but not third-party beneficiary claim); 2 DOBBS ON TORTS § 452 (2000 & Supps.). But *BRW, Inc. v. Dufficy & Sons, Inc.*, 99 P.3d 66, 74 (Colo. 2004), regarded the owner's contract with the engineer as an implicit part of the subcontractor's contract, and applied the contract version of the ELR to bar a tort claim by the subcontractor.

23. **Negligent spoliation of evidence.** We've seen cases of liability for intentional spoliation of evidence (which of course interferes with the legal rights or lawsuit opportunities of the victim). What about negligent spoliation by a non-party? A few courts have accepted liability in this situation, provided the defendant was under a duty to preserve the evidence. A duty might arise under a contract or undertaking or by virtue of a special relationships between the parties. See *Boyd v. Travelers Ins. Co.*, 166 Ill.2d 188, 209 Ill.Dec. 727, 652 N.E.2d 267 (1995); *Hannah v. Heeter,* 213 W.Va. 704, 584 S.E.2d 560 (2003). These courts thought that the plaintiff need not pursue and lose the underlying claim. *Boyd* said it was enough if the plaintiff would probably lose the underlying claim without the evidence; *Hannah* thought it was enough if "the spoliated evidence was vital to a party's ability to prevail in a pending or potential civil action." Once this and other elements of the claim were proved, the *Hannah* court thought a presumption arose that the loss of the evidence caused loss of the case. Apparently the plaintiff would still be required to prove the amount of damages he would have or should have recovered. In *Boyd,* the property/evidence lost was the plaintiff's own. In *Callahan v. Stanley Works,* 306 N.J.Super. 488, 703 A.2d 1014 (1997), the property lost belonged to the defendant, but it had nevertheless undertaken to preserve the property as evidence. If the defendant owns the property/evidence and has not undertaken to preserve it, does he have an absolute right to destroy it? See *Austin v. Consolidation Coal Co.*, 256 Va. 78, 501 S.E.2d 161 (1998) (employer's instrument injured employee; employer destroyed the instrument, preventing the employee from suing its manufacturer).

24. **Public nuisance with private economic harm.** A public nuisance occurs when the defendant interferes with some public right, as where he blocks a street or pollutes a waterway. Private individuals who suffer peculiar harm, beyond that suffered by the general public, can sue for damages in such cases. In a few of these cases, the landowner-plaintiff has been permitted to recover from one whose nuisance blocked access to the landowner's business and thus reduced the landowner's profits. See *Stop & Shop Companies, Inc. v. Fisher,* 387 Mass. 889, 444 N.E.2d 368 (1983). On the other hand, in *532 Madison Avenue Gourmet Foods, Inc. v. Finlandia Center, Inc.*, 96 N.Y.2d 280, 750 N.E.2d 1097, 727 N.Y.S.2d 49 (2001), the wall of a 39-story building on Madison Avenue in New York collapsed into the street, blocked traffic for weeks along a 15-block area. This reduced customers of a number of businesses in the vicinity. The court first held that the economic loss rule would bar any negligence claim. It then held that the claim based on public-

nuisance-with-special-harm would not lie, either. The ground: plaintiff's injury was not different in kind from that suffered by others in the neighborhood or "community." The public-nuisance-special-harm-rule is at odds with the economic loss rule, isn't it?

---

25. **Public nuisance and public economic harm.** In *City of Flagstaff v. Atchison, Topeka & Santa Fe Ry.,* 719 F.2d 322 (9th Cir. 1983), a railroad derailed its tank cars carrying gas. The city incurred costs of evacuating people from the danger area and sued the railroad to recover those costs. Although the court recognized that the city could recover the cost of abating a public nuisance, it held that costs of fire or police protection and other governmental services were not recoverable. Those costs would be borne by the public as a whole, not by the tortfeasor. This "cost recovery rule" or "free public services doctrine," holding that a public entity cannot recover for economic costs of supplying services made necessary by a tortfeasor's tort, has gained recognition in a number of courts. E.g., *County of San Luis Obispo v. Abalone Alliance,* 178 Cal.App.3d 848, 223 Cal.Rptr. 846 (1986) (trespassing demonstrators, county could not recover law enforcement costs); *Koch v. Consolidated Edison Co. Of New York, Inc.,* 62 N.Y.2d 548, 468 N.E.2d 1, 479 N.Y.S.2d 163 (1984) (increased costs for police and other services resulting from complete blackout caused by the defendant's negligence; no recovery). What criticisms? Are courts that adopt this rule merely subsidizing industrial wrongdoers at the expenses of taxpayers? See Timothy D. Lytton, *Should Government Be Allowed to Recover the Costs of Public Services From Tortfeasors?: Tort Subsidies, the Limits of Loss Spreading, and the Free Public Services Doctrine,* 76 TUL. L. REV. 727 (2002). Or should we think of this rule as no more than a particular manifestation of the general rule that negligently inflicted pure economic loss is not actionable?

26. **Gun violence causing public economic harm.** (a) In a number of cases, public entities have asserted that their costs of police and health services have been increased because some gun manufacturers have deliberately marketed guns to criminals likely to engage in violence. Notice that, as to the public entities, this is stand-alone economic harm. A respectable group of cases have allowed such claims to go forward on the theory of nuisance or otherwise. *City of Gary ex rel. King v. Smith & Wesson Corp.,* 801 N.E.2d 1222 (Ind. 2003); *City of Boston v. Smith & Wesson Corp.,* 12 Mass.L.Rptr. 225 (Mass. Super. 2000); *James v. Arms Technology, Inc.,* 359 N.J.Super. 291, 820 A.2d 27 (2003); *City of Cincinnati v. Beretta U.S.A. Corp.,* 95 Ohio St.3d 416, 768 N.E.2d 1136 (2002).

(b) Perhaps more often, liability has been rejected. Sometimes the rejection is based on the facts of the particular case, such as the absence of causal evidence. See *In re Firearm Cases,* 126 Cal.App.4th 959, 24 Cal.Rptr.3d 659 (2005), but a number of cases have excluded such recoveries under rules of law, saying, for example, that negligent marketing of guns is not a nuisance, that the gun maker has no duty to control criminals, and that considerations of proximate cause and foreseeability forbid liability. See *District of Columbia v. Beretta, U.S.A. Corp.*, 872 A.2d 633 (D.C. 2005); *City of Philadelphia v. Beretta U.S.A. Corp.*, 277 F.3d 415 (3d Cir. 2002); *Camden County Bd. of Chosen Freeholders v. Beretta U.S.A. Corp.*, 123 F.Supp.2d 245 (D. N.J. 2000), aff'd, 273 F.3d 536 (2001).

(c) In *City of Chicago v. Beretta U.S.A. Corp.*, 213 Ill.2d 351, 821 N.E.2d 1099, 290 Ill.Dec. 525 (2004), the court rejected liability partly on the basis of the economic loss rule. The court recognized that the ELR "is rooted in the theory of freedom of contract," but also thought "it has grown beyond its original contract-based policy justifications. . . ." In particular, the court thought "the policy underlying the economic loss rule" now extends to concern over the "virtually endless" and uninsurable economic consequences that might result from the defendant's conduct. The same court fully embraced the cost recovery rule (¶ 25, supra) as a separate ground for excluding liability.

27. **Suits against the federal government.** The federal tort claims act waives some but not all government immunity. It specifically retains immunity as to several torts, including some economic and dignitary torts. One of those for which immunity is retained is interference with contract. 28 U.S.C.A. § 2680(h). In addition, the jurisdictional section, 28 U.S.C.A. § 1346, provides only for jurisdiction over civil actions "on claims against the United States, for money damages . . . for injury or loss of property, or personal injury or death. . . ." Suppose the government negligently sets fire to its own forest lands but, foreseeably, the fire spreads to lands owned by private individuals. The state spends hundreds of thousands of dollars containing and extinguishing the fire outside forest lands. Would the federal court have jurisdiction to hear a claim against the government? Several Ninth Circuit cases, such as *Oregon v. United States*, 308 F.2d 568 (9th Cir. 1962), have said not. Is it clear what argument can be made for this position?

28. **Physical harms with resulting economic loss.** The economic loss rule, when applied, only forbids recovery for stand-alone economic loss. If the defendant causes physical harms which in turn result in economic loss, the economic loss rule does not forbid recovery. This might occur, for example, if the defendant's negligence causes a power outage and interruption of electricity to the plaintiff's factory, which in turn causes damages to the plaintiff's machines or goods, with resulting loss of profits. *British Celanese, Ltd. v. A. H. Hunt, Ltd.*, [1969] 1 W. L. R. 959 [1969] 2 All E.R. 1252 (Q.B. Div.) (allowing recovery because the solidified mass in the machines was physical injury). This does not mean that the plaintiff will prevail in such such claims. The courts may still exclude recovery on the ground that lost profits are not adequately proven, see *Dunlop Tire & Rubber Corp. v. FMC Corp.*, 53 A.D.2d 150, 385 N.Y.S.2d 971 (1976), or on the broader ground that the entire loss, including physical harms, were unforeseeable.

GREG ALLEN CONSTRUCTION CO. v. ESTELLE

798 N.E.2d 171 (Ind. 2003)

SHEPARD, Chief Justice. . . .

Daniel and Sondra Estelle contracted with Greg Allen Construction, Inc. for renovations to the Estelles' home in Ladoga, Indiana. Greg Allen, president, shareholder, and employee of Allen Construction, signed the contract in his representative capacity. Allen did all the electrical, plumbing and carpentry work, and supervised the other facets of the project.

Over the course of renovations, the Estelles questioned the quality of work being performed. Eventually, the two parties deadlocked on the issue of payment for the substandard work, and suit was filed. The Estelles alleged that both Allen Construction and Greg Allen breached the contract and were negligent.

Because he was acting as president and employee of Allen Construction, the trial court found that Allen was not individually liable to the Estelles. The Court of Appeals disagreed, holding that because Allen participated in and supervised the negligent acts, he was personally liable in tort. . . .

The Estelles and Allen Construction entered into a contract under which Allen Construction would provide home renovations. The claimed wrong is Allen Construction's failure to satisfy its part of the agreement—a quintessential contract claim. The Estelles' complaint says:

> Defendant Company has breached its contract with Plaintiffs in the following respects:
>
> a) Defendant failed or refused to complete the work on schedule as agreed.
>
> b) Defendant's materials and workmanship are of poor quality and Plaintiffs will be forced to hire another contractor to redo Defendant's negligent and poor quality work.
>
> c) Defendant's work does not meet construction code requirements nor does it meet normal construction industry standards in many respects and necessary code permits have not been secured.
>
> . . . Plaintiffs have suffered damages and will suffer damages in an amount which cannot be determined at this time but include unnecessary interest charges on their construction loan, the cost of repair and completion of the work, the cost of redoing Defendants' faulty work, and attorney fees and costs.

The whole of the alleged wrong, deficient home improvements, centered on the performance required by the contract created by Allen Construction and the Estelles. Any duty Allen had to perform his individual duties flowed solely from this contract.

Whatever negligence is attributed to Allen was performed in the course of his duties as an employee of the corporation. Under the traditional respondeat superior doctrine, if Allen is liable in negligence to the Estelles, then so is his principal, the corporation. . . .

The basic theory underlying the distinction between contract and tort is that tort liability is imposed by law and that contract liability is the product of an agreement of the parties. But only the principal, who is a party to the contract, has agreed to perform the obligations of the agreement. To impose "the same" liability on the agent is to make the agent the promisor when the parties had arranged their affairs to put the principal, and only the principal, on the line.

A defendant's exposure to tort liability is best framed in terms of what the defendant did. The proper formulation of the reason Allen is not liable here is that his negligence consisted solely of his actions within the scope of his authority in negligently carrying out a contractual obligation of the corporation as his employer. Nothing he did, and therefore nothing the corporation did, constituted an independent tort if there were no contract. Under those circumstances the Estelles should be remitted to their contract claim against the principal, and they should not be permitted to expand that breach of contract into a tort claim against either the principal or its agents by claiming negligence as the basis of the breach. . . .

To be sure, a number of authorities have expressed the point in terms of "economic loss." Section 357 of the Second Restatement of Agency provides that "[a]n agent who intentionally or negligently fails to perform duties to his principal is not thereby liable to a person whose economic interests are thereby harmed." This follows the more general rule of Section 352 that "[a]n agent is not liable for harm to a person other than his principal because of his failure adequately to perform his duties to his principal, unless physical harm results from reliance upon performance of the duties by the agent, or unless the agent has taken control of land or other tangible things." Illustration two under Section 352 is this case:

> P, who has agreed to build a house for T, employs A to build it. A is careless in the construction of the house, so that the house does not conform to the contract. A is not thereby liable to T for the failure to construct the house in accordance with the contract.

Together, these Restatement sections lead to the conclusion that an agent is not liable for economic loss to anyone except his principal.

Nevertheless, phrasing this issue in terms of nonliability for "economic loss" overstates the point somewhat. In certain statutory settings, an agent may be liable for torts committed by the agent within the scope of his employment. *See State Civil Rights Comm'n v. County Line Park*, 738 N.E.2d 1044, 1050 (Ind. 2000). And there are some common law fields, for example product disparagement by negligent communication of a known false statement, in which a wrong may inflict only "economic loss" but may nevertheless be tortious. *See Restatement (Second) of Torts*

§ 630, cmt. a. Similarly, negligent misrepresentation may be actionable and inflict only economic loss. If so, the agent/servant may be individually liable. *See Restatement (Second) of Agency* § 343, cmt. b ("[a]n agent who . . . defames . . . another . . . is not excused by the mere fact that he is acting as an agent.")

. . . Allen could be individually liable to the Estelles if he negligently burned their house down while working with a blowtorch whether this work was on the Estelles' house under a contract with them, or the project was a neighbor's house and had no contractual relationship to the Estelles. The reason is that this negligence goes beyond failure to perform up to contractual standards, and constitutes a tort even if there were no contractual relationship between the Estelles and either Allen or his corporation. Moreover, describing the reason for the non-liability in this case (and liability for the fire in that hypothetical) as turning on the presence or absence of duty states the conclusion without giving a reason.

The same result can be restated as the law's imposing a duty to avoid injury to person or property. The rule of law is that a party to a contract or its agent may be liable in tort to the other party for damages from negligence that would be actionable if there were no contract, but not otherwise. Typically, damages recoverable in tort from negligence in carrying out the contract will be for injury to person or physical damage to property, and thus "economic loss" will usually not be recoverable. But that is only the usual case, not the uniform rule.

We affirm the judgment of the trial court as to Greg Allen's personal liability. In all other respects, we summarily affirm the decision of the Court of Appeals.

29. **Agent's liability for committing a tort.** An agent who commits what is otherwise a tort does not escape liability merely because he acted in the scope of employment or at the command of his principal. There are potential exceptions: the agent is privileged to do for his principal what the principal could rightfully do for himself. RESTATEMENT (SECOND) OF AGENCY § 343. Otherwise, the agent is liable for his own torts, whether he is acting within the scope of employment or not. Is the general rule stated in this paragraph contrary to *Greg Allen*?

30. **Agent having no duties to the plaintiff; undertakings.** A defendant who owes no duty to the plaintiff is, of course, not liable to the plaintiff. Can we say that one usually owes no duty to use care to prevent stand-alone economic harm to others? Does Greg Allen the individual owe a duty to the plaintiffs because his employer, Greg Allen the corporation, owes such a duty? The Agency Restatement recognizes that agents may voluntarily undertake a duty of care and that breach of such duties is actionable if the plaintiff relies upon the undertaking; but the Restatement confines this rule to undertakings for the physical safety of persons or things. See RESTATEMENT (SECOND) OF AGENCY § 354.

Thus the Restatement provides that an agent is not liable for inadequate performance of his duties to his employer—unless physical harm results through the plaintiff's reliance. RESTATEMENT SECOND OF AGENCY § 352. But why can't the agent undertake to exercise due care as to the plaintiff's stand-alone economic interests? Do you think the plaintiffs thought Greg Allen the individual was undertaking to exercise a professional or craftsman-like level of care?

31. **Scope of *Greg Allen* rule.** (A) Able, employed by the Able Construction Co., which has contracted to do renovations on the plaintiffs' house, negligently sets a fire that burns the house down.

(B) The plaintiff is libeled by a news release written and provided to the newspapers by Bill Zimmer, Jr., an employee of the Zimmer Corporation. He was acting at the direction of the CEO, Bill Zimmer, Sr. Cf. *Cosmas v. Bloomingdales Bros., Inc.,* 442 Pa. Super. 476, 660 A.2d 83 (1995) (employee of department store, acting within scope of her employment, allegedly published defamatory material concerning the plaintiff). What about the editor of a newspaper who writes a defamatory editorial that is then published by his employer? *Phoenix Newspapers, Inc. v. Church,* 24 Ariz.App. 287, 537 P.2d 1345 (1975). See Chapter 1, ¶ 12.

(C) Plaintiff is employed by a public agency. When the plaintiff reports suspected wrongdoing by officers in the agency, the agency discharges him in violation of public policy after a personnel committee composed of individual employees in the agency recommends his termination. In *Ballinger v. Delaware River Port Auth.,* 172 N.J. 586, 800 A.2d 97 (2002), on somewhat similar facts, the court held that the individual employees are liable for their own torts, and, citing the Restatement (Second) of Agency, that "[a]n agent who does an act otherwise a tort is not relieved from liability by the fact that he acted at the command of the principal or on account of the principal." Can you really make a distinction between this case and *Greg Allen*?

32. **Considering versions of the economic loss rule.** We saw a contract version of the economic loss rule in § 1, but Greg Allen the individual had no contract with the plaintiff here and that's what got him off. Then in *Robins* we saw a different version of the economic loss rule, one that may have been based on the very real possibility that economic harm has a domino effect, causing a lengthy chain of traceable economic harms to others. But that doesn't seem to be the case in *Greg Allen*. We could likewise recognize that Greg Allen the individual should not be liable for mere nonfeasance—if he had taken no steps toward building the house. That's not the case here, either. Why not liability for work done badly? Does the result necessarily rest on a normative perception that even if one engages in actively negligent conduct, he owes no duty to protect the economic interests of others?

§ 3. UNINTENDED INTERFERENCE CAUSING REPUTATIONAL LOSS

JORGENSEN v. MASSACHUSETTS PORT AUTHORITY

905 F.2d 515 (1st Cir. 1990)

BOWNES, Senior Circuit Judge. . . .

[Hertzfeldt was first officer and Langley was the captain of a World Airways DC–10 jet that skidded off the end of an icy Logan Airport runway on January 23, 1982. The plane plunged partially into Boston Harbor, killing two persons and injuring many others. Hertzfeldt and Langley asserted that Massport had negligently maintained the runway, causing the skid. They sued for injuries, including lost of future earning capacity and "emotional distress because of harm to reputation and earning capacity." The jury found for both plaintiffs, but the trial judge set aside part of the awards for lost earning capacity and emotional distress stemming from harm to reputation on the grounds that reputational loss was not recoverable in an ordinary negligence case, such as this, involving claims arising from an accident that produced physical injuries and that even if such damages were recoverable, plaintiffs had introduced insufficient evidence to support their claims.]

. . . The absence of Massachusetts precedent leaves Jimenez-Nieves, 682 F.2d 1, as the only authority discussing the issue in this jurisdiction. In Jimenez-Nieves, the plaintiff premised his tort claim on the Social Security Administration's conduct in erroneously stopping payment on certain benefit checks. As a result of this action by Social Security, the plaintiff was suspected by others of fraud and also suffered severe financial hardship. He sued Social Security under the FTCA, claiming, among other things, public humiliation, injury to his credit rating, and other reputation-related harm. We held that insofar as the plaintiff's claim alleged injury to reputation, it was barred under the FTCA because it sounded in defamation, despite plaintiff's characterization of it as a general tort action. We found the claim to resound in the "heartland" of defamation because: (1) the injury was to reputation, and (2) the challenged conduct involved the communication of an idea. We defined "communication" as bringing an idea to the perception of another, either explicitly or implicitly, and observed that the Social Security Administration's conduct in stopping payment on plaintiff's checks constituted communication because it had brought defamatory ideas about the plaintiff (presumably, that he had committed welfare fraud or was a poor credit risk) to the perception of others. See Jimenez-Nieves, 682 F.2d at 6. We specifically declined to follow the reasoning of the Third Circuit in Quinones, which had found a claim for the negligent maintenance of employment records to sound outside the realm of defamation, and thus to be cognizable under the FTCA.

Although it is possible to construe Jimenez-Nieves as holding that all claims alleging injury to reputation sound in defamation, it is not clear that Massachusetts courts necessarily would construe it this broadly or even choose to apply it if it were so construed. As we read Jimenez-Nieves, it holds that where the injury is to reputation and the conduct is the communication of an idea, the claim sounds in defamation. See Jimenez-Nieves, 682 F.2d at 6. Thus, it is not simply the element of injury to reputation that makes conduct sound in defamation. There also must be a communication, defined as conduct that brings an idea to the perception of others.

Some courts have emphasized the injury to reputation element more heavily than the communication element in ruling that claims alleging harm to reputation sound in defamation rather than in ordinary negligence or any other tort. Arguably, no such communication existed here. Unlike in Jimenez-Nieves, the defendant's conduct here is not what conveyed to others the idea that caused harm to the plaintiffs' reputations. Massport's failure to clear the runway of ice did not bring to the minds of others the concept that Hertzfeldt and Langley were not capable pilots. Rather, Massport's conduct caused a result—the accident—which then could have caused others to question plaintiffs' skills as pilots. Because the defendant's conduct was one step removed from the alleged injury to reputation, there arguably was no communication. And without a communication, plaintiffs' claims do not sound in defamation under the reasoning of Jimenez–Nieves.

One could attempt to turn this distinction of Jimenez-Nieves against the plaintiffs by arguing that in the absence of a communication, plaintiffs are impermissibly trying to recover for defamation without proving all the elements of defamation. This argument has some validity. We are not fully persuaded, however, that Massachusetts would stretch Jimenez-Nieves this far. Jimenez-Nieves states only that where there is an alleged injury to reputation and a communication, the plaintiff's claim sounds in defamation despite any attempt to characterize it otherwise. Jimenez-Nieves does not state that without a communication, and hence without defamation, there can be no cognizable action for reputation damages of any sort. To so hold would eliminate an important distinction between the tortious wrong alleged by a plaintiff and the items of damages flowing from the tortious wrong. See Black v. Sheraton Corp. of America, 564 F.2d 531, 540–41 (D.C.Cir.1977) (describing this distinction). Defamation is a type of tortious wrong. Injury to reputation is a particular item of damages. We are not convinced that Massachusetts would hold that damages for injury to reputation may only be recovered in a defamation action. Cf. Kleeblatt v. Business News Publishing Co., 678 F.Supp. 698, 701–03 (N.D.Ill.1987) (dismissing a defamation claim on the ground that no communication had occurred, but upholding a negligence-based reputation claim). Accordingly, we find that neither Jimenez-Nieves nor any other authority provides a basis for concluding that Massachusetts necessarily would find defamation to encompass or preempt all claims alleging injury to reputation. We thus must address the question whether, assuming no preemption, Massachusetts would recognize the validity of a reputation-damage claim in a general negligence setting.

Plaintiffs' emphasis on the compensatory objectives of tort law is not sufficient to persuade us that Massachusetts would recognize their reputation-damage claims. There are widely acknowledged limits on the scope of tort liability—limits that are motivated by policy considerations such as the need to prevent costly, meritless litigation, the desire to avoid disproportionality between liability and fault, and the goal of only allowing liability or damages when the prospect of injury was reasonably foreseeable to the defendant.

Our research has disclosed two cases where courts invoked such policy considerations to reject ordinary negligence reputation-damage claims similar to those made by plaintiffs here. In Greives v. Greenwood, 550 N.E.2d 334 (Ind.Ct.App.1990), the court rejected a negligence claim alleging injury to reputation as a cattle raiser made by a plaintiff whose cattle were negligently inoculated with a fatal virus by the defendant veterinarian. The court stated: "Damages for loss of reputation are only available in actions for libel, slander, abuse of process, malicious prosecution and third party contract interference. These intentional torts afford this remedy because the result is foreseeable. Foreseeability means that which it is objectively reasonable to expect, not merely what might conceivably occur."

Similarly, in Hamilton v. Powell, Goldstein, Frazer & Murphy, 167 Ga.App. 411, 306 S.E.2d 340 (1983), aff'd, 252 Ga. 149, 311 S.E.2d 818 (1984), the court rejected a negligence claim alleging malpractice and injury to reputation made by a plaintiff against a law firm for erroneous securities law advice that had resulted in the arrest of the plaintiff for securities fraud. Like Greives, the court in Hamilton stated that reputation damages were only available in "actions alleging intentional or wanton misconduct." Although the court did not say so explicitly, foreseeability concerns would appear to underlie this result.

There are, however, other cases that have allowed reputation damages in negligence settings. . . .

Massachusetts very well could invoke these foreseeability concerns as justification for not recognizing reputation-damage claims in the ordinary negligence setting. It is also conceivable that Massachusetts courts could choose to satisfy foreseeability concerns by applying an approach analogous to that taken by us in Redgrave v. Boston Symphony Orchestra, Inc., 855 F.2d 888 (1st Cir.1988). In Redgrave, we observed that Massachusetts usually did not recognize damages for injury to reputation in contract actions because such damages are remote, speculative, and not within the contemplation of the parties. We held, however, that if a plaintiff could show specific lost job opportunities proximately resulting from the defendant's breach of contract, such a showing would distinguish the claim from more general reputation claims and would constitute a cognizable cause of action because such specific lost job opportunities could have been within the reasonable contemplation of the parties.

Although Redgrave was a contract case rather than a tort case, the concern about awarding damages not within the contemplation of the parties is analogous to the concern about foreseeability in the tort context. It seems conceivable to us, therefore, that Massachusetts might follow the approach of Redgrave and decide to respond to these foreseeability concerns not by rejecting reputation-damage claims entirely, but by allowing them if plaintiffs can show specific identifiable lost job opportunities or an equivalently particular form of injury.

We do not mean to express any opinion as to whether Massachusetts should follow a Redgrave-type approach. As the concurrence notes, this is an issue on which it is the responsibility of the Massachusetts courts, not the federal courts, to make the law. We simply indicate our view that uncertainty exists as to which approach Massachusetts might follow. . . .

Although we decline to state definitively our view as to whether Massachusetts would recognize a claim for injury to reputation in an ordinary negligence setting, we affirm the district court on the narrower ground that plaintiffs failed to adduce sufficient evidence that Massport's negligence proximately caused the losses claimed by plaintiffs.

---

33. **Defamation by acts.** A merchant, suspecting the plaintiff of shoplifting, attempts to detain him. When the plaintiff resists, the merchant's security guards handcuff him and march him through the store to the security office. Is the defendant's act the publication of a defamatory statement for which the defendant is liable even if it had a privilege to detain or arrest in some less flamboyant manner? If we think the act is a communicative act and that defamation results, should we consider it as slander or as libel? *K-Mart Corporation v. Washington*, 109 Nev. 1180, 866 P.2d 274 (1993). In *Bolton v. Department of Human Services,* 540 N.W.2d 523 (Minn. 1995), an employer discharged an employee, had him pick up his personal belongings, then escorted him to the door without a word. Other employees may have seen these acts. If the discharge itself was not improper, would the escort to the door be actionable?

34. **A lawyer's failure to adduce exculpatory evidence.** In *Bolte v. Joy*, 150 Wis.2d 744, 443 N.W.2d 23 (1989), a lawyer failed to produce a witness in client's suit against a fire insurer; the jury believed that the client had set the fire himself and this led to a loss in the client's reputation. The client's sued the lawyer for reputational loss. The court held that recovery was impermissible because there would be no stopping place.

35. **Libel and slander as exclusive torts for reputational harm.** Courts have usually said that defamation and some related theories form the exclusive bases for a damaged reputation claim. E.g.,

Ross v. Gallant, Farrow & Co., 27 Ariz.App. 89, 551 P.2d 79 (1976); *Lawrence v. Grinde,* 534 N.W.2d 414 (Iowa 1995); *Morrison v. National Broadcasting Co., Inc.*, 19 N.Y.2d 453, 280 N.Y.S.2d 641, 227 N.E.2d 572 (1967). On the other hand, there is *Redgrave v. Boston Symphony Orchestra, Inc.*, 855 F.2d 888 (1st Cir. 1988), mentioned by the *Jorgensen* court. In that case, the Boston Symphony Orchestra had contracted for a performance by Vanessa Redgrave. It breached its contract after symphony patrons objected to her because of her political views. The court ultimately held that Redgrave could recover for reputational loss that resulted, but only for specific lost professional opportunities that could be shown to result from BSO's breach.

36. **Malicious prosecution and reputational harm.** And in the malicious prosecution chapter we saw *Seidel v. Greenberg*, 108 N.J.Super. 248, 260 A.2d 863, 40 A.L.R.3d 987 (1969), where a criminal committed arson under circumstances that made it likely that the plaintiff would come under suspicion for the crime. After the plaintiff cleared himself of criminal responsibility, he successfully sued the arsonist. See also *Singer v. Jefferies & Co., Inc.*, 160 A.D.2d 216, 553 N.Y.S.2d 346 (1990).

DUNCAN v. AFTON, INC.

991 P.2d 739 (Wyo. 1999)

Golden, Justice. . . .

Duncan was an employee of Solvay Minerals in Sweetwater County. Solvay contracted with Afton to collect urine specimens of Solvay's employees from time to time for drug and alcohol testing. Solvay separately contracted with a laboratory, Northwest Toxicology, Inc. of Salt Lake City, Utah, to analyze the specimens and report the results to Solvay.

On December 15, 1997, Solvay ordered Duncan to submit a urine specimen for drug and alcohol testing. Duncan was randomly selected for the test in accordance with Solvay's substance abuse policy. Defendant Leigh Ann Shears, an employee of Afton, supervised the collection of a urine specimen from Duncan at Solvay's place of business.

. . . Duncan alleges that upon providing a urine specimen to Shears in an unsealed container, Shears directed him to return to the restroom to wash his hands. While Duncan was in the restroom, the specimen remained unsealed and out of Duncan's direct sight for that period of time. He alleges that upon his return from the restroom, Shears proceeded to seal the urine specimen and to obtain Duncan's initials on the specimen label. Shears failed to note the temperature of the specimen at the time it was taken as required by standard testing protocol. Duncan further alleges that Afton and Shears subsequently altered the chain of custody documents to make it appear that the temperature had been properly tested.

Solvay received a report that Duncan's specimen had a urine alcohol content of .32, which Duncan alleges is an amount that would have rendered him so intoxicated that he would have been unable to function and would have appeared blatantly intoxicated. The specimen was collected approximately ten hours into Duncan's twelve-hour shift. Duncan denies consuming alcohol that day. Duncan claims that grievous errors in the collection process and the inherent unreliability of the process of testing urine for alcohol content caused the test result.

Based on the .32 report, Solvay terminated Duncan's employment on December 23, 1997. He filed suit in June of 1998, naming Afton and Shears as defendants, claiming that Afton negligently instructed and trained Shears; failed to employ proper collection and handling procedures for urinalysis of alcohol content; failed to inform Solvay that urinalysis is unreliable if specific procedures are not followed; and misrepresented to Solvay the accuracy and reliability of urine alcohol testing. [The trial judge dismissed the action.]

The privity requirement has long been imposed to eliminate the threat of indeterminate, unchecked liability for economic damages. Without a contractual relationship between Afton and Duncan, the privity requirement would prohibit imposing liability. We have previously ruled, however, that the privity requirement should be discarded when the legal theory is negligence or negligent misrepresentation:

> Traditionally, attempts by injured third parties to recover for damages arising out of the negligent performance of a contractual duty fail because of lack of privity. Courts first discarded the requirement of privity in product liability cases based on negligence. The basis of liability may be negligent misrepresentation. Damages in product liability suits have not been limited to physical injury; recovery has also been permitted for economic loss. See Santor v. A & M Karagheusian, Inc., 44 N.J. 52, 207 A.2d 305 (1965). ... Courts, upon abandonment of the privity requirement, expanded tort liability by holding that a third party, not in privity of contract with a professional person or entity, may recover for negligence which proximately causes a foreseeable economic injury to him. The general principle is delineated in Restatement (Second) Torts, supra, § 552 (Topic 3. Negligent Misrepresentation).

Century Ready-Mix Co., 816 P.2d at 804–05 (footnote omitted).

Duncan has advanced both negligence and negligent misrepresentation theories; therefore, privity concerns are not presented in this case. Under ordinary negligence principles, we must explore whether a third party stands in such a relationship with collection agencies that policy considerations require that tort liability should be imposed.

On the several occasions that courts have addressed the liability of parties performing drug and alcohol testing, variations in the particular facts, the legal theories advanced, and the rationale employed resulted in few decisions containing a comprehensive duty of care analysis. Courts have divided in deciding whether a party involved in performing drug and alcohol testing of employees and potential employees owes a duty of care to those persons.

As support for the proposition that it owes no duty of reasonable care to the employee, Afton relies on the reasoning of Smithkline Beecham Corp. v. Doe, 903 S.W.2d 347 (Tex.1995). Smithkline ruled that a drug tester retained by an employer to screen a potential employee owes no duty to that potential employee to warn her about the possible effects of consuming poppy seeds prior to the test. Rationalizing that it was impossible either to inform a test subject of all possible causes of positive results other than using drugs or to warn that test results might be misinterpreted, the Texas Supreme Court determined that any duty of care was a burden more properly placed with employers, the clients of Smithkline. . . .

When this Court has considered whether a duty should be imposed based on a particular relationship, we have balanced numerous factors to aid in that determination:

> (1) the foreseeability of harm to the plaintiff, (2) the closeness of the connection between the defendant's conduct and the injury suffered, (3) the degree of certainty that the plaintiff suffered injury, (4) the moral blame attached to the defendant's conduct, (5) the policy of preventing future harm, (6) the extent of the burden upon the defendant, (7) the consequences to the community and the court system, and (8) the availability, cost and prevalence of insurance for the risk involved.

[The court examined applied each factor to the case. Only some of the factor discussions are printed here.]

. . . We find that Afton could foresee that improper collecting and handling of the specimen could contribute to a false positive result and could injure an employee. It is foreseeable that in recommending testing to an employer, Afton's failing to inform the employer about the proper interpretation and procedures when positive results occur could injure an employee.

In assessing the moral blame factor, several considerations make it appropriate to impose a duty of reasonable care upon a collection company: its direct financial benefit in providing alcohol testing services to Duncan's employer; its direct control over establishing and ensuring proper collection and handling procedures; its ability to hire and train competent personnel to perform services; and its ability to contract with the employer to ensure test results are properly interpreted and utilized.

Perhaps the most important factor in this analysis is whether the policy of preventing future harm is at issue. Afton does not present an argument on this particular factor. Companies like Afton provide services that present a risk of harm great enough to hold them accountable. The particular services provided demand adequate protection of employees' interests to prevent future harm, and the imposition of a duty to act reasonably will reduce the likelihood of injury. There is little question that our ruling that Afton owes a duty places a burden upon Afton to act in a "scientifically reasonable manner" and guard against human error; however, Afton is in the best position to guard against employee injury arising from its collection and handling procedures. . . .

We reverse the district court's order dismissing the action and remand for further proceedings.

---

37. **Misrepresentation reasoning in *Duncan*.** The misrepresentation claim in *Duncan* is a little odd. A misrepresentation claim can be successfully asserted only by one who relies upon the misrepresentation. Duncan seems not to have relied on Afton's alleged misrepresentation to Solvay. Are there nevertheless firm reasons for liability that you could articulate if you were the judge (or the judge's law clerk)?

38. **Authority on point.** (a) Some kinds of employee testing is forbidden by statute, although not necessarily for the purpose of protecting reputation or privacy. For example, the Americans with Disabilities Act, 42 U.S.C.A. § 12112(d) forbids pre-employment medical tests to discover mental or physical disabilities. In *Karraker v. Rent-A-Center, Inc.,* 411 F.3d 831 (7th Cir. 2005), an employer's use of the MMPI was held to be a medical test, so that the employees had a claim under the ADA.

(b) Illegal testing aside, the cases in situations similar to *Duncan* are somewhat divided. In *Hall v. United Parcel Service of America, Inc.*, 76 N.Y.2d 27, 556 N.Y.S.2d 21, 555 N.E.2d 273, 89 A.L.R.4th 515 (1990), the defendant was allegedly negligent in administering a lie detector test to the plaintiff, an employee of UPS. The negligently obtained result then allegedly led to employee's loss of job. Since the claim was not actionable as defamation, the court held it was not actionable on other theories. And the court that decided *Duncan* later held that a psychologist hired to examine a combative employee and make recommendations owed no duty to the employee, with the result that when, following the recommendations, the employee was discharged, he had no claim against the psychologist. *Erpelding v. Lisek,* 71 P.3d 754 (Wyo. 2003).

In *Mission Petroleum Carriers, Inc. v. Solomon,* 106 S.W.3d 705 (Tex. 2003), a trucking company-employer was the drug tester. It discharged Solomon, who sued claiming damage to his reputation prevented him from obtaining other trucking jobs. The court held that the federal trucking regulations on drug testing appropriately balanced all the concerns, and that because Solomon could challenge the drug testing under administrative procedures, the court would give no relief.

On the other hand, *Duncan* has support in several other cases. In *Sharpe v. St. Luke's Hospital,* 573 Pa. 90, 821 A.2d 1215 (2003), FedEx contracted with a hospital for drug testing of FedEx employees. The hospital was allegedly negligent in handling the urine samples and produced a false positive for cocaine in the plaintiff. As a result, FedEx discharged her. The employee sued the hospital, which argued it had no duty of care to her. The court thought otherwise, emphasizing that there was a relationship between plaintiff and the hospital, harm was foreseeable, and that the hospital could limit its liability by simply exercising ordinary care.

Washington State Physicians Ins. Exchange & Association v. Fisons Corporation, 122 Wash.2d 299, 858 P.2d 1054 (1993). A small child suffered seizures and severe permanent brain damage as a result of taking a drug manufactured by the defendant. The drug had been prescribed by her pediatrician, Dr. Klicpera. Her suit against Dr. Klicpera and the drug company has been settled. In this action, Dr. Klicpera is in effect the plaintiff and the drug company is in effect the defendant.

Evidence indicated that years before the child's injury, the drug company knew that the drug could be life-threatening to children and for not quite so long had known that the dosage recommendations were simply wrong. There was also evidence that dosage recommendations originated with a consultant who was "heavily into" stocks for such drugs.

Klicpera claimed several items of damages. One of the jury's awards was $1,085,000 for injury to his reputation. "Under the Consumer Protection Act, a physician whose reputation is injured has standing to sue a drug company which engaged in an unfair or deceptive trade practice by failing to warn the physician of the dangers of its drug about which it had knowledge." The statute creates a private right of action for "unfair or deceptive" acts or practices.

"With regard to the injury element, we have held that damage to business reputation and loss of goodwill are compensable damages under the CPA. The trial court's instructions properly allowed the jury to consider damage to professional reputation in regard to the CPA cause of action. . . . We therefore conclude that the damages the jury awarded for loss of reputation are compensable under the Consumer Protection Act claim, so long as the damages are supported by the evidence. However, the damages awarded for the physician's mental pain and suffering (and its objective physical manifestations) are not compensable under the CPA."

39. **Similar cases.** Several cases are similar to *Fisons*. In *Adirondack Combustion Technologies, Inc. v. Unicontrol, Inc.,* 17 A.D.3d 825, 793 N.Y.S.2d 576 (2005), a broker who sold the defendant's boiler controller to a buyer, was allowed to pursue a claim for harm to reputation when the controller failed to perform properly and ultimately caused damage to the boiler. In *Cargill, Inc. v. Boag Cold Storage Warehouse, Inc.,* 71 F.3d 545 (6th Cir. 1995), the plaintiff sold frozen turkeys to buyers, who stored them in the defendant's cold storage warehouse. The turkeys carried the plaintiff's brand name. The defen-

dant allowed them to thaw, resulting in spoiled turkeys in the hands of buyers. The plaintiff had a costly recall and reputational damages. The court approved the plaintiff's cause of action, saying the economic loss rule only applied to sales of goods. See also *Oksenholt v. Lederle Labs.*, 294 Or. 213, 656 P.2d 293 (1982); *Kennedy v. McKesson Co.*, 58 N.Y.2d 500, 504, 507, 462 N.Y.S.2d 421, 423, 425, 448 N.E.2d 1332, 1334, 1336 (1983).

But in *Cloverhill Pastry-Vend Corp. v. Continental Carbonics Products, Inc.*, 214 Ill.App.3d 526, 158 Ill.Dec. 286, 574 N.E.2d 80 (1991), a baker purchased a machine that left small chips of metal in the dough. When the baker sold baked goods with metal chips in them, it lost reputation or good will with its own customers. But the baker was denied recovery against the machine manufacturer under the economic loss rule. Accord: *Advanced Drainage Systems, Inc. v. Lowman,* 210 Ga.App. 731, 437 S.E.2d 604 (1993); *Waggoner v. Town & Country Mobile Homes, Inc.*, 808 P.2d 649 (Okl. 1990) (manufacturer's failure to provide proper warranty repairs on product hurt dealer's reputation, no recovery; this is merely negligent interference with business prospects); see also *Fetick v. American Cyanamid Co.,* 38 S.W.3d 415 (Mo. 2001) (doctor's claim of fraud against manufacturer whose vaccine allegedly caused harm to doctor's patient, but emotional distress damages are not recoverable for ordinary fraud and emotional harm was not medically diagnosable as required by the state's tort rule).

HUGGINS V. CITIBANK, N.A., 355 S.C. 329, 585 S.E.2d 275 (2003). Huggins sued defendant banks in federal court, alleging that the banks negligently issued a credit card in Huggins' name to an imposter, then attempted to collect the charges from Huggins himself, damaging Huggins' credit and hounding him, causing distress and requiring expenditures in an attempt to clear his credit. The federal court certified this question to the South Carolina Supreme Court: "Does South Carolina recognize the tort of negligent enablement of imposter fraud and, if so, what are the elements of the tort and does plaintiff's complaint state an actionable claim for the tort?" *Held*, question answered "no." The defendants were under no duty of care to non-customers. "Duty arises from the relationship between the alleged tortfeasor and the injured party. ... We are greatly concerned about the rampant growth of identity theft and financial fraud in this country. Moreover, we are certain that some identity theft could be prevented if credit card issuers carefully scrutinized credit card applications. Nevertheless, we ... decline to recognize a legal duty of care between credit card issuers and those individuals whose identities may be stolen. The relationship, if any, between credit card issuers and potential victims of identity theft is far too attenuated to rise to the level of a duty between them. Even though it is foreseeable that injury may arise by the negligent issuance of a credit card, foreseeability alone does not give rise to a duty. ... [W]e conclude the legislative arena is better equipped to assess and address the impact of credit card fraud on victims and financial institutions alike."

40. Duty and relationships. Is it true that duty arises only from a relationship? How about the duty of care owed by an automobile driver to people he has never heard of or even seen, such as a homeowner injured when the driver negligently runs into the plaintiff's house? And isn't it anomalous that the existence of a contractual relationship between the parties excludes a duty of care under the economic loss rule (see § 1, supra), and the absence of a relationship excludes the duty in *Huggins*?

Problem: Prestige Frozen Foods v. Fridgiclean Mfg. Corp.

Defendant Fridgiclean manufactures a substitute for freon called Preon, a liquid used in refrigeration. The liquid is poisonous, but, possibly because the liquid is used internally in the refrigeration mechanisms, the manufacturer gave no warning of the poisonous nature of Preon. Tomasina's Refro Trucking is a carrier who has purchased refrigeration units for its trucks. These units use Preon, which is replaced periodically by Industrial Truck Service, the company that services Tomasina's trucks. The refrigeration machinery leaked Preon during a long haul. Some of it contaminated containers of Prestige Frozen Dinners, food being transported in Tomasina's trucks. The food poisoned by the Preon caused death to persons who later ate it. The food company, Prestige Frozen Dinners, suffered a loss of reputation and loss of sales. Is Fridgiclean liable for the economic losses to Prestige?

41. **Carriers.** Carriers are normally liable only for breach of their contract of carriage or for their negligence. Unless Tomasina's was negligent, it is not likely to be held liable. In addition, 49 U.S.C. § 11707 provides that liability of carriers is limited to "the actual loss or injury to the property" carried. This provision appears on its face to exclude liability for reputational loss. But see *Eastman Kodak Co. v. Westway Motor Freight, Inc.*, 949 F.2d 317 (10th Cir. 1991). With these limitations in mind, focus on the potential liability of the manufacturer.

42. **Characterizing the facts.** In focusing on Fridgiclean's liability, consider first how you might characterize the facts. For example, is it a case of products liability? A case of reputational harm? Are there other characterizations possible?

43. **Reference.** This problem is suggested by one of The Tilburg Hypotheticals, Case 5, presented in J. Spier (ed), The Limits of Expanding Liability 20 (1998).

PROFESSIONAL AND ACADEMIC ENHANCEMENTS
Chapter 12

Unintended Interference with Economic Interests

BRUCE v. BYRNE–STEVENS & ASSOCS. ENG'RS., INC.

113 Wash.2d 123, 776 P.2d 666 (1989)

DORE, Justice. . . .

Respondents Bruce and Smallwood own separate parcels of property on Clear Lake in Pierce County. In 1979 a neighbor, John Nagle, conducted excavation work on his property, resulting in subsidence in the soil of the Bruce and Smallwood properties. They sued Nagle and retained petitioner Byrne-Stevens & Associates Engineers, Inc. (Byrne-Stevens) to calculate and testify as to the cost of stabilizing the soil on their land. The principal of the firm, Patrick J. Byrne, testified at the trial that the cost of restoring lateral support would be $10,020 on the Bruce property and $11,020 on the Smallwood property. The respondents obtained a judgment against Nagle for damages of $10,020 to Bruce and $11,020 to Smallwood.

Bruce and Smallwood sued Byrne-Stevens and Byrne alleging that the cost of restoring lateral support later proved to be double the amount of Byrne's estimate at trial. They contend that Byrne was negligent in preparing his analysis and testimony and that, but for Byrne's low estimate of the cost of restoring lateral support, they would have obtained judgment against Nagle for the true cost of the restoration.

The trial court granted the defendants' motion to dismiss based on witness immunity. The Court of Appeals reversed. . . .

As a general rule, witnesses in judicial proceedings are absolutely immune from suit based on their testimony. . . . The purpose of the rule is to preserve the integrity of the judicial process by encouraging full and frank testimony. . . .

In addition to the benefits obtained by extending immunity, the rule also rests on the safeguards against false or inaccurate testimony which inhere in the judicial process itself. A witness' reliability is ensured by his oath, the hazard of cross-examination and the threat of prosecution for perjury. . . .

[As to privately retained expert witnesses:] The Washington case most on point here is Bader v. State, 43 Wash. App. 223, 716 P.2d 925 (1986). In Bader, Eastern State Hospital evaluated a criminal defendant,

Morris Roseberry, for the purpose of determining whether he was competent to stand trial. Roseberry was diagnosed as paranoid schizophrenic and manic depressive, but was found competent to stand trial. Roseberry was acquitted and released, conditioned on his submitting to treatment. He later murdered a neighbor and the victim's estate sued Eastern State for negligence in its evaluation of Roseberry.

[The Court of Appeals thought Bader was distinguishable from the case of a privately retained witness. However, in] the Bader case, Eastern State was immune, not because it partook of the judge's immunity, but because it took part in judicial proceedings.

In this light, it is immaterial that an expert witness is retained by a party rather than appointed by the court. The basic policy of ensuring frank and objective testimony obtains regardless of how the witness comes to court.

... In addition, the Court of Appeals is simply wrong to say that an expert witness "does not act on the court's behalf." ...

[U]nless expert witnesses are entitled to immunity, there will be a loss of objectivity in expert testimony generally. The threat of civil liability based on an inadequate final result in litigation would encourage experts to assert the most extreme position favorable to the party for whom they testify. It runs contrary to the fundamental reason for expert testimony, which is to assist the finder of fact in a matter which is beyond its capabilities. To the extent experts function as advocates rather than impartial guides, that fundamental policy is undermined.

[I]mposing civil liability on expert witnesses would discourage anyone who is not a full-time professional expert witness from testifying. Only professional witnesses will be in a position to carry insurance to guard against such liability. The threat of liability would discourage the 1-time expert—the university professor, for example—from testifying. Such 1-time experts, however, can ordinarily be expected to approach their duty to the court with great objectivity and professionalism. ...

In sum, the fact that an expert witness is retained by a party has no bearing on the underlying rationale of witness immunity. That basic rationale—ensuring objective, reliable testimony—dictates in favor of immunity for experts. As a policy matter, the economics of expert testimony generally also favor immunity as a means of ensuring that a wide cross section of impartial experts are not deterred from testifying by the threat of liability. ...

[Trial court's order of dismissal reinstated. One judge concurred in the result only. Three judges dissented.]

MARROGI v. HOWARD

805 So.2d 1118 (La. 2002)

CALOGERO, Chief Justice. ...

[Dr. Marrogi had performed professional services for Tulane, but claimed Tulane had underbilled or failed to bill for his services and consequently owed Dr. Marrogi for the shortfall. Dr. Marrogi retained the services of Ray Howard and his firm to provide pretrial analysis and litigation support services. Howard held himself out as an expert in medical billing and coding. Howard was to review the records, submit affidavits, and testify in depositions and hearings. He was paid a total of $7,000 to $10,000.

On the basis of calculations presented by Howard, Marrogi moved to compel discovery of certain Tulane billing records. Tulane objected, pointing out numerous mathematical errors in Howard's affidavit. Howard then presented a revised opinion that reduced the amount he claimed Tulane owed Marrogi to $392,740. Tulane deposed Howard and forced him to admit to additional errors in his revised opinion. At that point Howard refused to participate in the remainder of the deposition in progress or to provide other supported services he had contracted to furnish. The trial court dismissed Marrogi's suit against Tulane. Thereafter, Marrogi brought this action against Howard.]

One court that has applied the doctrine of witness immunity to preclude suits against a "friendly" expert witness is the Washington Supreme Court in Bruce v. Byrne-Stevens & Associates Engineers, Inc., 113 Wash.2d 123, 776 P.2d 666 (1989). ... A plurality of the Washington Supreme Court found that absolute immunity precluded suit against the expert witness for his testimony in judicial proceedings and that such immunity attached to acts and communications that occur in connection with the preparation of that testimony. The court opined that, in the absence of immunity, two forms of indirect censorship would develop: (1) the imposition of liability would discourage anyone who is not a full-time professional expert witness from testifying, because one-time or infrequent experts might not carry the necessary insurance to cover the liability risk in testifying, and (2) the expert witness might shade or distort his testimony out of fear of subsequent liability, perhaps losing objectivity or adopting the most extreme position favorable to his client. These latter tendencies, the court believed, would deprive the finder of fact of candid, objective, and undistorted evidence. The court concluded that the imposition of witness liability was not necessary to secure accurate information for the finder of fact, because expert witness reliability is adequately ensured by the witness's oath, the hazard of cross-examination, and the threat of a perjury prosecution.

While the Washington Supreme Court applied the privilege to a retained expert, the majority of the other courts that have addressed this issue have not applied the privilege of witness immunity to retained experts. In a case factually similar to the instant case, the Pennsylvania Supreme Court concluded that the doctrine of witness immunity does not extend to bar professional malpractice actions against professionals hired to perform services related to litigation. *LLMD of Michigan, Inc. v. Jackson-Cross Co.*, 559 Pa. 297, 740 A.2d 186 (1999). ... While cautioning that the substance of the expert's opinion testimony may not form the basis for a subsequent suit, the court concluded that the judicial process is enhanced by holding an expert witness to the degree of care, skill, and proficiency commonly exercised by members of his or her profession.

After reviewing the cases from the courts of our sister states, as well as the applicable policy considerations, we hold that claims in connection with a retained expert's alleged failure to provide competent litigation support services are not barred by the doctrine of witness immunity. The privilege of witness immunity in Louisiana has been applied in defamation and defamation-like cases, as well as retaliation cases against adverse witnesses, expert and otherwise. The policy underlying that rule is that witnesses must be permitted to speak freely and without fear of exposure to vexatious litigation where a search for the truth is before the fact-finder. However, that laudable objective is not advanced by immunizing the incompetence of a party's retained expert witness simply because he or she provides professional services, including testimony, in relation to a judicial proceeding. Witness immunity itself is an exception to tort liability. . . . [I]mmunity from tort liability is, generally, recognized only to promote an overarching public purpose.

We agree that the finder of fact must be able to rely on candid, objective, and undistorted evidence. However, we do not believe that shielding a client's own professional witness from malpractice liability is necessary to ensure that frank and objective testimony is presented to the fact-finder. A party's retained expert witness, rather than a court-appointed expert, for example, contracts for monetary remuneration with a party to assist in preparing and presenting his case not only in the best light possible but also, surely, in a competent fashion. Thus, the retained expert's function is not only to assist the court or fact-finder in understanding complicated matters, but also to render competent assistance in supporting his client's action against the client's opponent. The *Bruce* court assumed that in the absence of immunity, the expert would be motivated not simply by frankness and objectivity, but by the fear of exposure to civil liability among other considerations. Properly viewed, however, the roles of "hired gun" and servant of the court are not necessarily incompatible. In reality, the expert retained for litigation is hired to present truthful and competent testimony that puts his client's position in the best possible light. The expert witness's oath, the heat of cross-examination, the threat of a perjury prosecution, and, not least, the expert's professional ethics code all serve to limit the feared excesses of an expert subject to malpractice liability. Moreover, the absence of immunity will not only encourage the expert witness to exercise more care in formulating his or her opinion but also protect the litigant from the negligence of an incompetent professional. Given these considerations, witness immunity does not serve an overarching public purpose in barring a client's suit against his own hired professional who deficiently performs agreed upon litigation support services.

. . . Dr. Marrogi has made the allegation that the defendant was negligent, not in having a particular opinion, but in formulating his opinion, i.e., the defendant was negligent in performing professional services such as calculations upon which his expert opinion testimony would ultimately be based. That defendant Howard's erroneous calculations were, in this case, presented in an affidavit and in deposition testimony, rather than, say, a written report, does not change our view that an expert witness hired to perform litigation support services, but who performs those services in a negligent manner, cannot hide from civil liability to his client behind the shield of witness immunity.

... The Washington Supreme Court in *Bruce* speculated that the lack of immunity will result in less truthful expert testimony.[21] With no sanction for incompetent preparation, however, an expert witness is free to prepare and testify without regard to the accuracy of his data or opinion. We do not see how the freedom to testify negligently will result in more truthful expert testimony. Without some overarching purpose, it would be illogical, if not unconscionable, to shield a professional, who is otherwise held to the standards and duties of his or her profession, from liability for his or her malpractice simply because a party to a judicial proceeding has engaged that professional to provide services in relation to the judicial proceeding and that professional testifies by affidavit or deposition. In this case, cross-examination during the deposition succeeded in revealing excesses or inaccuracies in defendant Howard's opinion testimony. The truth-finding function of the judicial system was thus protected. Though defendant Howard contends he is effectively being punished for telling the truth, i.e., confessing to his errors, we see no valid reason why the judicial system should immunize him from liability to his client for his alleged negligence in making calculations and formulating his opinion. ...

We therefore answer the question certified to us in the negative: Witness immunity or privilege in Louisiana does not bar a claim against a retained expert witness asserted by a party who in prior litigation retained the expert, which claim arises from the expert's allegedly negligent performance of his agreed upon duties to provide litigation support services.

1. Most cases that have addressed the point have rejected *Bruce*. *Bruce* rejected, what obstacles remain for the plaintiff?

2. Try to imagine what kind of proof on causation you'd have to adduce if you represent a plaintiff suing the witness she retained.

21. The concern that all but full-time experts will be driven from the courtroom is unrealistic. We have no doubt either that appropriate hold-harmless agreements can protect one-time experts seeking such protection or that the insurance industry can meet the needs of experts, whether full-time or not, for errors and omissions coverage.

Chapter 13

INTELLECTUAL PROPERTY AND UNFAIR COMPETITION

PRELIMINARY SCOPE NOTE

Although intellectual property issues arise in general practice, many lawyers in the field are specialists. In fact, many lawyers specialize in some particular form of intellectual property such as copyright or patent law. Whole treatises, sometimes in multi-volumes, are written on copyright, unfair competition and trademark, patents and so on. The development of the internet has created many additional technical problems. Coverage in this book must be limited to an elementary introduction; far more is left out than is covered. For example, in the copyright area, we will concentrate mainly on print and visual media, omitting the esoterica of music and architectural copyrights almost altogether.

§ 1. COPYRIGHT

(a) Copyright Basics

BUCKLEW v. HAWKINS, ASH, BAPTIE & CO., LLP

329 F.3d 923 (7th Cir. 2003)

POSNER, Circuit Judge. . . .

Local housing authorities that want grants from the federal department of Housing and Urban Development have to complete forms prescribed by HUD. The forms require not only specific basic data such as salaries and other categories of proposed expenditure by the grant applicant but also simple arithmetical transformations of the data, such as adding the numbers in particular cells in the table of basic data. Bucklew developed and copyrighted software, intended to be used in conjunction with standard spreadsheet applications such as Lotus 1–2–3 and Excel, for doing these transformations and displaying them in tables. The essential transformation involves entering the basic data in an electronic copy of the HUD-prescribed form and applying to those data an algorithm that picks out the relevant cells and performs the relevant operation (namely addition) on them and displays the results in tabular form. Standard spreadsheet applications make this transformation relatively easy to program because they include functions such as DSUM, a simple command for adding up the numbers in the cells identified by a criterion specified by the programmer and displaying the results of the addition. Bucklew does not claim copyright in either the spreadsheet applications or DSUM. But there is more, though not a great deal more, to his product than these programs. Decisions have to be made regarding choice and size of font, the size of cells and columns, whether and where to use color, the wording of labels and headings (other than those prescribed by the HUD forms), and whether to use boldface or italics for column headings. These decisions were made by Bucklew. The ones we have named all involve the appearance of the forms, but software that is read only by the computer and not by its human user is also copyrightable, and Bucklew does claim copyright in the "construction" as well as display of his forms; but it is unexplained what he means by this or whether it has been infringed.

The trial focused on one of the four forms (as the parties refer to the conversion of a prescribed HUD form into an electronic form that computes and displays the arithmetic manipulations that HUD requires) copyrighted by Bucklew that he claimed were copied by HAB. This form is a transformation of HUD form 52566, which requires salary data; the other three forms require data for other categories of expenditure. HAB grudgingly concedes that the evidence compels an inference that it copied Bucklew's form 52566 to create its own form 52566. Some similarities between a copyrighted work and a work alleged to infringe it are consistent with an inference of independent creation, and in that case evidence that the alleged infringer had access to (that is, saw or at least could have seen) the copyrighted work is indispensable. But when the similarities concern details of such an arbitrary character that the probability that the infringer had duplicated them independently is remote, an inference of copying may be drawn without any additional evidence. These cases say that access can be inferred from a sufficiently striking similarity between the two works, and that is true; but . . . it is more straightforward to say that in some cases proof of access isn't required.

It is in order to avoid having to prove access that mapmakers will sometimes include a fictitious geographical feature in their maps; if that feature (what is called in the trade a "copyright trap") is duplicated in someone else's map, the inference of copying is compelling. And that is the case with regard to form 52566. Bucklew's version contains an arbitrary pattern of boldfacing of cells; HAB's duplicates it exactly. Bucklew's form also contains an "output range," an intermediate table that he carried over from a previous spreadsheet program but that has no function in his current program—or in HAB's. Had HAB written its program from scratch, it would have had no reason to include an output range—yet it did. [The court recites other similar evidence, then discusses the copying evidence about the other three forms.]

With respect to all four forms HAB argues that even if there was copying there was no infringement. It appeals primarily to the copyright doctrines of merger and scènes à faire. The first of these confusing labels refers to the situation in which there is only one feasible way of expressing an idea, so that if the expression were copyrightable it would mean that the idea was copyrightable, and ideas are not copyrightable. The standard citation remains *Baker v. Selden,* 101 U.S. 99, 25 L.Ed. 841 (1879). *Selden* had published (and copyrighted) a book describing a bookkeeping system that he had invented, and he illustrated the book with blank bookkeeping forms. Baker copied the forms, rearranging columns and using different headings, and sold them to people who wanted to use Selden's system. This was held not to be copyright infringement, even though Baker had copied part of a copyrighted work, since otherwise Selden would have had a monopoly over his bookkeeping system (which was an idea, and hence not copyrightable) that he could have exploited by insisting that anyone wanting to use the system buy the forms necessary for using it from him. If Bucklew were claiming copyright in the tabular presentation of the summary data required by HUD, this case would be governed by *Baker v. Selden.* But he is not. He is claiming copyright in tables configured in an optional way, tables that are the product of format choices that are not unavoidable, for which indeed there were an immense number of alternative combinations any one of which HAB was free to use in lieu of Bucklew's.

The fact that Bucklew's formatting choices do not reflect a high degree of originality is irrelevant. When as in this case a work in which copyright is claimed is based on work in the public domain, the only "originality" required for the new work to be copyrightable (the very term is a misnomer) is enough expressive variation from public-domain or other existing works to enable the new work to be readily distinguished from its predecessors. "Originality in this context means little more than a prohibition of actual copying." That undemanding requirement is satisfied in this case; any more demanding requirement would be burdensome to enforce and would involve judges in making aesthetic judgments, which few judges are competent to make.

The doctrine of scènes à faire (another confusing label, literally "scenes for action," which the *Oxford English Dictionary* tells us is a theatrical term meaning "the most important scene in a play or opera, made inevitable by the action which leads up to it"—which is not the legal doctrine at all) teaches, sensibly enough, that a copyright owner can't prove infringement by pointing to features of his work that are found in the defendant's work as well but that are so rudimentary, commonplace, standard, or unavoidable that they do not serve to distinguish one work within a class of works from another. Every expressive work can be decomposed into elements not themselves copyrightable—the cars in a car chase, the kiss in a love scene, the dive bombers in a movie about Pearl Harbor, or for that matter the letters of the alphabet in any written work. The presence of such elements obviously does not forfeit copyright protection of the work as a whole, but infringement cannot be found on the basis of such elements alone; it is the combination of elements, or particular novel twists given to them, that supply the minimal originality required for copyright protection.

A more fundamental limitation on the scope of copyright infringement is, as we have already noted, that copyright protects only expression and not what is expressed, the "idea," which in the case of fiction is more likely to be a plot or situation than, as in *Baker v. Selden,* an algorithm or other abstraction. Suppose one wanted to prove that the Tom Hanks–Meg Ryan movie *You've Got Mail* infringed the Jimmy Stewart–Margaret Sullavan movie *The Shop Around the Corner.* You could point to the fact that in both movies the hero falls in love with the heroine on the basis of correspondence (letters in the earlier movie, email in the later) without having met her and without realizing that it is someone he knows—and dislikes (and the feeling is reciprocated)—though everything comes right in the end. But it would not be evidence of infringement that both movies were love stories, or that they were comedies, or that the lead actors were a man and a woman. These are generic characteristics, obtained by abstracting the commonest features of the specific work; they do not indicate uniqueness. They are at the opposite extreme from the arbitrary details, such as the pattern of boldfacing in Bucklew's form 52566, that contribute such originality as a new expressive work may have. The format choices that Bucklew made were not generic. It is not as if everyone who writes programs of this sort uses Swiss font or displays an output range or uses a particular pattern of boldfacing.

Nor is it important that after copying Bucklew's form 52566 and using it as the template for the other three forms, HAB introduced a number of variations in its version of form 52566. Variants that result from tinkering with a copied form are derivative works from that form, and it is a copyright infringement to make or sell a derivative work without a license from the owner of the copyright on the work from which the derivative work is derived. In some cases, however, though derivative in a literal sense, is so utterly transformed as to bear no traces of the original; and then there is no infringement. Such cases are in fact common, though they are rarely litigated. Suppose one copied a long passage from a copyrighted work and then edited it to produce a paraphrase so loose that it would not be similar enough to the original to constitute an infringement. The fact that the paraphrase had been "derived" in a genetic sense from a copyrighted original would not make it infringing. Similarly, if the original expression added by the unauthorized preparer of a derivative work is clearly detachable from the original work itself, so that no confusion, or disruption of the copyright owner's plans for the exploitation of his work, would be created by allowing the unauthorized preparer to copyright his original expression, the unauthorized preparer might be allowed to do so. ... But HAB does not argue that its alterations of the copied form went so far as to bring it within the scope of either of these qualifications of the general rule concerning derivative works.

[The court concluded that the other three forms did not infringe the plaintiff's copyright.]

After the judge reduced the jury's award by granting a remittitur that Bucklew accepted, the award consisted of four items: $100,000 for Bucklew's lost profits; $125,000 for HAB's profits from the infringing forms; $70,000 for a savings in time that HAB obtained as a result of the infringement; and $100,000 for profits obtained by HAB on separate products by virtue of its being able to offer its customers "one-stop shopping," i.e., a complete line of HUD financial software, including the copied forms.

A copyright owner can sue for his losses or for the infringer's profits, but not for the sum of the two amounts. That would be double counting. The profits that HAB obtained from selling forms copied from Bucklew came at his expense; his loss was HAB's gain. If the infringer is a more efficient producer, his gain may exceed the copyright owner's loss. If he is not more efficient, his gain is likely to be less than the copyright owner's loss because competition will tend to force price down to cost, minimizing the infringer's profits but depriving the copyright owner of the supracompetitive return that he enjoyed before he faced competition from the seller of an exact substitute for his product. The copyright owner is allowed to waive damages (lost profits) and sue for the infringer's gain. Copyright infringement unlike patent infringement is an intentional tort, and by forcing the infringer to disgorge his profit should it exceed the copyright owner's loss the law discourages infringement and encourages the would-be infringer to transact with the copyright owner rather than "steal" the copyrighted work. But there is no basis in the law for requiring the infringer to give up more than his gain when it exceeds the copyright owner's loss. Such a requirement would add a punitive as distinct from a restitutionary element to copyright damages, and while the copyright statute does authorize statutory damages unrelated to losses or gains, see 17 U.S.C. § 504(c), these were not sought here and—a point to which we shall return—the statute contains no provision for punitive damages. But, astonishingly, HAB has failed to complain about double counting, and so it has booted away a winning issue. . . .

Once the plaintiff proves his losses, or the defendant's profits, from the defendant's sale of an infringing work, the burden shifts to the defendant to apportion the profits or losses between the infringing and noninfringing features of the defendant's work. HAB failed to do that.

[The court discussed further problems in the measurement of damages.]

Besides all these problems with the computation of damages, it will be necessary on remand to apportion damages between the infringing form and what we have determined to be the three noninfringing forms.

The cross-appeal need not detain us for long. Bucklew seeks punitive damages for fraud and conversion under Wisconsin law. He argues that HAB obtained a computer disk containing his copyrighted program by falsely representing that it wanted merely to evaluate the program with a view toward possibly licensing it from Bucklew, and having thus obtained the program by false pretenses then copied it, with the consequences earlier. We may assume that this is a good claim under Wisconsin law. But Bucklew is not asking to have the disk returned, or for damages equal to the value of the disk plus punitive damages proportioned to that value. The compensatory damages that he seeks for the fraud and conversion are identical to the damages that it seeks for copyright infringement, so that its request for punitive damages is in fact a request for punitive damages for copyright infringement. The copyright statute does not authorize such damages, as we have noted, and the statute's preemption clause forbids states to add sanctions for a wrongful act that is identical to a violation of the statute.

[The RICO claim was also rejected.]

Affirmed in Part, Reversed in Part, and Remanded.

---

1. **Sources of copyright law.** The Constitution itself authorizes Congress to prepare a copyright law. U.S. Const. Art. 1, § 8, cl. 8. The current statute is 17 U.S.C. §§ 101 and following. Copyright law is exclusively federal law, not state law. It is subject to some treaties, notably the recent Berne Convention. Common law copyright no longer exists.

2. **Limited time monopoly.** Copyright gives "authors" a protected interest in their work. This is a form of monopoly, but it is one for a limited time period. The general rule, varied in particular cases, is that the copyright "endures for a term consisting of the life of the author and 70 years after the author's death." 17 U.S.C. § 302(a).

3. **Protections provided.** The copyright owners—the author unless the copyright has been assigned—is protected against unconsented-to copying, or as the statute put it, he has the exclusive right to reproduce copies of the work. That is not all. He also has the exclusive right to prepare derivative works, to distribute copies, and to display and perform the work. Thus if A copies the author's work and B merely distributes copies made by A, both are infringers.

4. **What is copyrightable.** Copyright can cover a wide range of works—writing, musical composition, dramas, pictures, sculptures, movies and recordings, for example. But, unless especially provided for otherwise, the copyright can only cover "original works of authorship fixed in any tangible medium of expression" as long as the work can be perceived, reproduced or otherwise communicated.

5. **Form, not substance, idea or fact.** As Judge Posner insists in *Bucklew,* copyright protects the particular form of expression, not the underlying idea. You might copyright the phrase "the dawn came up like thunder" but not the idea that the dawn was impressive. Ideas and facts as such cannot be copyrighted, only the particular expression. Similarly, you cannot copyright a procedure, process, or method of operation. See 17 U.S.C.A. § 102 (b); *Lotus Development Corp. v. Borland International, Inc.,* 49 F.3d 807 (1st Cir. 1995), aff'd per curiam, 516 U.S. 233, 116 S.Ct. 804, 133 L.Ed.2d 610 (1996). Another way to say this is to say that facts and ideas are in the public domain, as are many words and shapes. See *Tufenkian Import/Export Ventures, Inc. v. Einstein Moomjy, Inc.,* 338 F.3d 127 (2d Cir. 2003).

6. **Originality.** Very little originality is required to give copyright protection, as *Bucklew* shows. The work to be copyrighted must be original in the sense of originating with the author. Although facts and ideas cannot be copyrighted, facts might be compiled by selecting, organizing and coordinating them in a useful way. If so, the organization may be a work of authorship subject to copyright. So a simple alphabetical listing of names and telephone numbers—the telephone book—is not subject to copyright, *Feist Publications, Inc. v. Rural Tel. Service Co., Inc.,* 499 U.S. 340, 111 S.Ct. 1282, 113 L.Ed.2d 358 (1991), but a more complex arrangement might be. This means that the originality required need not be creative in any artistic sense. Many quite mundane expressions are copyrighted, including most of those in this book.

7. **Procedure.** If your work is copyrightable—not merely an idea, for example—your copyright attaches from the moment you fix the work in tangible form. "Copyright protection subsists . . . in original works of authorship fixed in any tangible medium of expression. . . ." 17 U.S.C.A. § 102 (a). However, you can't sue for infringement of your copyright until you register the copyright with the Register of Copyrights. 17 U.S.C.A. § 411 (a) ("no action for infringement of the copyright in any United States work shall be instituted until registration of the copyright claim has been made in accordance with this title"). This is a simple filing, and in fact you can get the forms from the Copyright Office on the Web. See http://www.copyright.gov/. Distinguish registration from the *notice* of copyright. You are not required to include a notice of copyright on the published work of authorship, but it is virtually costless, and it demolishes any argument by the defendant that he is an innocent infringer. 17 U.S.C. § 401(d).

8. **Infringement—substantial similarity of the copy.** To prove infringement, the plaintiff must show that the copy is "substantially similar" to the copyrighted expressions. But it need not be identical. What counts as substantially similar is a major issue troubling copyright lawyers and federal judges, especially where the plaintiff's work is composed of both copyrighted and uncopyrighted material. See, e.g., *Tufenkian Import/Export Ventures, Inc. v. Einstein Moomjy, Inc.,* 338 F.3d 127 (2d Cir. 2003); PAUL GOLDSTEIN, COPYRIGHT § 7.3 (2d ed. Supps.);

MELVILLE B. NIMMER & DAVID B. NIMMER, NIMMER ON COPYRIGHT § 13.03 (looseleaf, Supps.).

9. **Infringement and "contributory infringement" as torts.** Infringement of copyright is a statutory tort for which both damages and injunctive relief are given. The defendant is liable for direct infringement when, without a defense, he copies or distributes copyrighted material. The defendant is also liable as a "contributory infringer" when he encourages or abets infringement by others. Likewise, the defendant is "vicariously" liable for another's infringement when the defendant has the right and ability to control others' use of the copyrighted materials and also a financial interest in exploiting the copyrighted material. See *A&M Records, Inc. v. Napster, Inc.,* 239 F.3d 1004 (9th Cir. 2001), aff'd by 284 F.3d 1091 (9th Cir. 2002).

METRO-GOLDWYN-MAYER STUDIOS INC. v. GROKSTER, LTD., ___ U.S. ___, 125 S.Ct. 2764, 162 L.Ed.2d 781 (2005). Napster was a centralized file-sharing service that allowed its subscribers to download copyrighted music without the permission of the copyright owners. After this was held to be an infringement, Grokster and other defendants here set up a de-centralized, peer-to-peer service that could be used to achieve the same end. The defendants would supply free software to users, who would then be able to search computers of all other individuals who had the same software. Each subscriber could ultimately load the desired music from another individual's computer to his own computer without the permission of the copyright owners. This peer-to-peer (P2P) service was not limited to music; the subscriber might load non-music as well as music files from the peer computers. The defendants did not own or control the files; those belonged to individual subscribers. The defendants' role was to supply the software for P2P searching and loading and to stream ads to its subscribers. Its ad revenue would increase with the number of uses. Copyright owners sued several providers like Grokster. The Ninth Circuit approved summary judgment for the defendants, holding that they were not contributory infringers because there were other substantial uses for its software besides infringing copyright. The Ninth Circuit relied on *Sony Corp. of America v. Universal City Studios, Inc.,* 464 U.S. 417, 104 S.Ct. 774, 78 L.Ed.2d 574 (1984), where manufacturers of video tape recorders were held not to be contributory infringers because, although copyrighted television programs might be taped and even distributed by users of the recorders, there were other substantial non-infringing uses for them. In the Supreme Court, *held,* summary judgment for the defendants was error. "*Sony*'s rule limits imputing culpable intent as a matter of law from the characteristics or uses of a distributed product. But nothing in *Sony* requires courts to ignore evidence of intent if there is such evidence. . . . The classic case of direct evidence of unlawful purpose occurs when one induces commission of infringement by another. . . . [A]dvertisement or solicitation that broadcasts a message designed to stimulate others to commit violations [is inducement.]" Here the defendants were "aiming to satisfy a known source of demand for copyright infringement'' by advertising to former Napster users. Their failure to develop filtering tools to discourage copyright infringement by users is also some evidence that they intentionally facilitated their subscribers' copyright infringement. Finally, the fact that the defendants' ad revenue increases with greater use by subscribers, together with evidence that much of the subscribers' use is infringing, is also relevant as bearing on the defendant's probable intent.

10. **The Digital Millennium Copyright Act: the prequel to infringement.** A federal statute creates liability that can arise *before* any infringement—for circumventing digital protection systems such as software encryption or password protection. The statute also prohibits trafficking in systems for circumventing digital protection. 17 U.S.C.A. § 1201. The statute authorizes federal-court actions with injunctive and damages remedies. The judge has discretion to award attorney fees to the prevailing party. 17 U.S.C.A. § 1203. In *Universal City Studios, Inc. v. Corley,* 273 F.3d 429 (2d Cir. 2001), the court upheld an injunction against publishing or linking to a computer code that defeated DVD encryption and made widespread copying easy. The court held that computer code was speech subject to the First Amendment, but that in this case, at least, the code was mainly functional, and the statute was serving a substantial governmental interest unrelated to speech content.

11. **Federal jurisdiction.** Federal jurisdiction over copyright infringement suits is exclusive. However, state courts may entertain some suits over contract rights in copyrights.

12. **Preemption.** The copyright statute preempts state law as to any equivalent rights in protected subject matter. That may leave states the power to protect live performances that are not reduced to a tangible medium. But maybe a lot of protection is not such a good idea. See David W. Melville, Harvey S. Perlman, *Protection for Works of Authorship Through the Law of Unfair Competition: Right of Publicity and Common Law Copyright Reconsidered*, 42 St. Louis U. L.J. 363 (1998) (arguing for protection based only upon contract or confidentiality).

(b) Free Speech and Fair Use

13. **Using copyrighted material.** A lawyer writes a brief and an article, quoting Professor Wooley's article on the *Times-Sullivan* rule. His article, including footnotes, runs to 40 pages in the *Libel Review.* The lawyer's quotation is approximately equal to one page in the law review. The article is copyrighted and the lawyer has no permission to use it or any part. Later, the lawyer quotes the same material at a political rally. Is the lawyer infringing the copyright? If so, how does this fit with free speech?

14. **Fair use.** The copyright statute recognizes ''fair use'' defense for limited copying of limited amounts. Section 107 provides:

> . . . the fair use of a copyrighted work . . . for purposes such as criticism, comment, news reporting, teaching (including multiple copies for classroom use), scholarship, or research, is not an in-

fringement of copyright. In determining whether the use made of a work in any particular case is a fair use the factors to be considered shall include—

(1) the purpose and character of the use, including whether such use is of a commercial nature or is for nonprofit educational purposes;

(2) the nature of the copyrighted work;

(3) the amount and substantiality of the portion used in relation to the copyrighted work as a whole; and

(4) the effect of the use upon the potential market for or value of the copyrighted work.

The fact that a work is unpublished shall not itself bar a finding of fair use if such finding is made upon consideration of all the above factors.

15. **A case of public political information.** Former President Ford wrote memoirs to be published by the plaintiff. The plaintiff contracted with *Time* to permit that magazine to publish a pre-publication selection, for which *Time* was to pay $25,000. The *Nation* somehow got a copy of the manuscript and summarized it in its own publication, also quoting directly between 300–400 words. This led *Time* to back out of its pre-publication contract and the book publisher sued *Nation* for copyright infringement. Consider the four factors above. Was this an infringement or a "fair use"? Do you make anything of the fact the information involved public affairs? Do you make anything of the fact that the copyright holder had not published at all, so that the infringer preempted the right of first publication? The Supreme Court attached great significance to this latter point on the ground that there can be only one "first time." It held that the Nation's appropriation was an infringement, not a fair use in spite of the public interest in the materials. *Harper & Row, Publishers, Inc. v. Nation Enterprises*, 471 U.S. 539, 105 S.Ct. 2218, 85 L.Ed.2d 588 (1985).

16. **The Salinger letters.** J.D. Salinger, a famous author, wrote letters to various persons, including Learned Hand. Those persons at various times donated their papers to various research libraries. A biographer of Salinger, who was writing a serious biography but against Salinger's will, inspected the letters and quoted from them extensively. Salinger objects. What can he do? Salinger copyrighted the letters, then sued to enjoin publication. The physical paper belongs to others, but the right of first use belongs to the author, at least after he copyrights. The injunction forced removal of the quotations from the book because they were infringing his copyright and too substantial in content for fair use, since the biographer could convey their idea content without quoting. Although the nature of the use was scholarly, the first publication rights, so weighty in *Harper & Row,* are again involved here. *Salinger v. Random House, Inc.*, 811 F.2d 90 (2d Cir. 1987).

17. **Judge Leval's "transformative" quotations.** Almost all art, written or visual, owes something to the past. Judge Leval suggests that a use of copyrighted material might be fair if it is "transformative," by employing the appropriated material in a different manner or for a different purpose. Even directly quoted material might be fairly used if it adds new values, insights, or understandings. Leval, *Toward a Fair Use Standard*, 103 HARV. L. REV. 1105 (1990). In particular, he thought that the *Salinger* court had restricted the biographer's use of quotations too much. He pointed to a post-*Salinger* decision which even prevented the use of quotations to argue that the speaker was a paranoid liar. This raises the question whether appropriation of copyrighted material for the purpose of social commentary on public issues should enjoy any special fair use protection.

ROGERS v. KOONS

960 F.2d 301 (2d Cir. 1992)

CARDAMONE, Circuit Judge. . . .

Plaintiff, Art Rogers, a 43-year-old professional artist-photographer, has a studio and home at Point Reyes, California, where he makes his living by creating, exhibiting, publishing and otherwise making use of his rights in his photographic works. . . .

In 1980 an acquaintance, Jim Scanlon, commissioned Rogers to photograph his eight new German Shepherd puppies. When Rogers went to his home on September 21, 1980, he decided that taking a picture of the puppies alone would not work successfully, and chose instead to include Scanlon and his wife holding them. Substantial creative effort went into both the composition and production of "Puppies," a black and white photograph. At the photo session, and later in his lab, Rogers drew on his years of artistic development. He selected the light, the location, the bench on which the Scanlons are seated and the arrangement of the small dogs. He also made creative judgments concerning technical matters with his camera and the use of natural light. He prepared a set of "contact sheets," containing 50 different images, from which one was selected.

After the Scanlons purchased their prints for $200, "Puppies" became part of Rogers' catalogue of images available for further use, from which he, like many professional photographers, makes his living. "Puppies" has been used and exhibited a number of times. A signed print of it has been sold to a private collector, and in 1989 it was licensed for use in an anthology called "Dog Days." Rogers also planned to use the picture in a series of hand-tinted prints of his works. In 1984 Rogers had licensed "Puppies", along with other works, to Museum Graphics, a company that produces and sells note cards and postcards with high quality reproductions of photographs by well-respected American photographers including, for example, Ansel Adams. Museum Graphics has produced and distributed the "Puppies" note card since 1984. The first printing was of 5,000 copies and there has been a second similar size printing.

Defendant Jeff Koons is a 37-year-old artist and sculptor residing in New York City. After receiving a Bachelor of Fine Arts degree from Maryland Institute College of Art in 1976, he worked at a number of jobs, principally membership development at the Museum of Modern Art in New York. While pursuing his career as an artist, he also worked until 1984 as a mutual funds salesman, a registered commodities salesman and broker, and a commodities futures broker. In the ten years from 1980 to 1990 Koons has exhibited his works in approximately 100 Group Exhibitions and in eleven one-man shows. His bibliography is extensive. Koons is represented by Sonnabend Gallery, New York, Donald Young Gallery, Chicago, and Galerie Max Hetzler, Cologne, Germany. His works sell at very substantial prices, over $100,000. He is a controversial artist hailed by some as a "modern Michelangelo," while others find his art "truly offensive." A *New York Times* critic complained that "Koons is pushing the relationship between art and money so far that everyone involved comes out looking slightly absurd."

After a successful Sonnabend show in 1986, Koons began creating a group of 20 sculptures for a 1988 exhibition at the same gallery that he called the "Banality Show." He works in an art tradition dating back to the beginning of the twentieth century. This tradition defines its efforts as follows: when the artist finishes his work, the meaning of the original object has been extracted and an entirely new meaning set in its place. An example is Andy Warhol's reproduction of multiple images of Campbell's soup cans. Koons' most famous work in this genre is a stainless steel casting of an inflatable rabbit holding a carrot. During 1986 and 1987 the sculptor traveled widely in Europe looking at materials and workshops where he might fabricate materials for the Banality Show. He decided to use porcelain, mirrors and wood as mediums. Certain European studios were chosen to execute his porcelain works, other studios chosen for the mirror pieces, and the small Demetz Studio, located in the northern hill country town of Ortessi, Italy, was selected to carve the wood sculptures.

Koons acknowledges that the source for "String of Puppies" was a Museum Graphics note card of "Puppies" which he purchased in a "very commercial, tourist-like card shop" in 1987. After buying the card, he tore off that portion showing Rogers' copyright of "Puppies." Koons saw certain criteria in the note card that he thought made it a workable source. He believed it to be typical, commonplace and familiar. The note card was also similar to other images of people holding animals that Koons had collected. Thus, he viewed the picture as part of the mass culture—"resting in the collective sub-consciousness of people regardless of whether the card had actually ever been seen by such people."

Appellant gave his artisans one of Rogers' note cards and told them to copy it. But in order to guide the creation of a three-dimensional sculptural piece from the two-dimensional photograph, Koons communicated extensively with the Demetz Studio. He visited it once a week during the period the piece was being carved by the workers and gave them written instructions. In his "production notes" Koons stressed that he wanted "Puppies" copied faithfully in the sculpture. For example, he told his artisans the "*work must be just like photo*—features of photo must be captured;" later, "*puppies need detail in fur*. Details—Just Like *Photo*!;" other notes instruct the artisans to "*keep man in angle of photo*—mild lean to side & mildly forward—same for woman," to "keep woman's big smile," and to "keep [the sculpture] very, very realistic;" others state, "*Girl's nose is too small. Please make larger as per photo*;" another reminds the artisans that "The puppies must have variation in fur as per photo—not just large area of paint—variation *as per photo*." (emphasis supplied).

To paint the polychromed wood "String of Puppies" sculptures, Koons provided a chart with an enlarged photocopy of "Puppies" in the center; painting directions were noted in the margin with arrows drawn to various areas of the photograph. The chart noted, "Puppies, painted in shades of blue. Variation of light-to-dark *as per photo*. Paint realistic as per photo, but in blues." and "Man's hair, white with shades of grey *as per black and white photo*!" (emphasis supplied).

When it was finished, "String of Puppies" was displayed at the Sonnabend Gallery, which opened the Banality Show on November 19, 1988. Three of the four copies made were sold to collectors for a total of $367,000; the fourth or artist's copy was kept by Koons. Defendant Koons' use of "Puppies" to create "String of Puppies" was not authorized by plaintiff. . . .

[Rogers learned of the Koons production and sued for copyright infringement. Except as to damages, there were no factual disputes and the trial judge heard cross-motions for summary judgment. The judge found that the copying was not fair use and therefore found infringement. The judge held that Sonnabend as well as Koons would be liable for infringing profits and issued an injunction prohibiting both Koons and Sonnabend from selling or other dealings in the work or any derivative works. The defendants were ordered to deliver all infringing copies to the plaintiff within 20 days.]

When defendants failed to comply with the turn-over order, Rogers moved to hold defendant Koons in contempt. The proceedings on that motion revealed that nine days after the injunction was issued, Koons had loaned the fourth copy of "String of Puppies" to a museum in Germany and arranged for its shipment out of the United States. After a hearing on May 8, 1991, the district court held Koons in contempt, directed him to do whatever was necessary to effect the sculpture's return from Germany, and imposed a daily fine for continued noncompliance to commence eight days later.

On May 28, 1991, we denied Koons' motion to stay the injunction and the contempt penalty pending appeal, but delayed the commencement of the daily fine until June 7, 1991. From the finding of copyright infringement, the granting of a permanent injunction, and the turn-over order appellants Koons and Sonnabend appeal. Rogers cross-appeals from the denial of an award prior to trial for infringing profits. We affirm. . . .

. . . [C]opyright protection extends only to those components of the work that are original to the creator. But the quantity of originality that need be shown is modest—only a dash of it will do. M. Nimmer & D. Nimmer, Nimmer on Copyright § 1.08[C][1] (1991) (Nimmer). Elements of originality in a photograph may include posing the subjects, lighting, angle, selection of film and camera, evoking the desired expression, and almost any other variant involved. To the extent that these factors are involved, "Puppies" is the product of plaintiff's artistic creation. . . .

Plaintiff next must demonstrate that defendant Koons copied his protected work without authorization. . . . Here, the trial court found original elements of creative expression in the copyrighted work were copied and that the copying was so blatantly apparent as not to require a trial. We agree that no reasonable juror could find that copying did not occur in this case. First, this case presents the rare scenario where there is direct evidence of copying. Koons admittedly gave a copy of the photograph to the Italian artisans with the explicit instruction that the work be copied. . . . Further, even were such direct evidence of copying unavailable, the district court's decision could be upheld in this case on the basis that defendant Koons' access to the copyrighted work is conceded, and the accused work is so substantially similar to the copyrighted work that reasonable jurors could not differ on this issue.

Substantial similarity does not require literally identical copying of every detail. Such similarity is determined by the ordinary observer test: the inquiry is "whether an average lay observer would recognize the alleged copy as having been appropriated from the copyrighted work." . . .

We recognize that ideas, concepts, and the like found in the common domain are the inheritance of everyone. What is protected is the original or unique way that an author expresses those ideas, concepts, principles or processes. Hence, in looking at these two works of art to determine whether they are substantially similar, focus must be on the similarity of the expression of an idea or fact, not on the similarity of the facts, ideas or concepts themselves. It is not therefore the idea of a couple with eight small puppies seated on a bench that is protected, but rather Roger's expression of this idea—as caught in the placement, in the particular light, and in the expressions of the subjects—that gives the photograph its charming and unique character, that is to say, makes it original and copyrightable.

Thus, had appellant simply used the idea presented by the photo, there would not have been infringing copying. But here Koons used the identical expression of the idea that Rogers created; the composition, the poses, and the expressions were all incorporated into the sculpture to the extent that, under the ordinary observer test, we conclude that no reasonable jury could have differed on the issue of substantial similarity. For this reason, the district court properly held that Koons "copied" the original.

Moreover, no copier may defend the act of plagiarism by pointing out how much of the copy he has not pirated. Thus, where substantial similarity is found, small changes here and there made by the copier are unavailing. ... Koons' additions, such as the flowers in the hair of the couple and the bulbous noses of the puppies, are insufficient to raise a genuine issue of material fact with regard to copying in light of the overwhelming similarity to the protected expression of the original work. ...

... Section 107 states that an original work copied for purposes such as criticism or comment may not constitute infringement, but instead may be a fair use. The section provides an illustrative—but not exhaustive—list of factors for determining when a use is "fair." These factors include (1) the purpose and character of the use, (2) the nature of the copyrighted work, (3) the amount and substantiality of the work used, and (4) the effect of the use on the market value of the original. 17 U.S.C. § 107. ...

The first factor, purpose and character of the use, asks whether the original was copied in good faith to benefit the public or primarily for the commercial interests of the infringer. Knowing exploitation of a copyrighted work for personal gain militates against a finding of fair use. And—because it is an equitable doctrine—wrongful denial of exploitative conduct towards the work of another may bar an otherwise legitimate fair use claim. Relevant to this issue is Koons' conduct, especially his action in tearing the copyright mark off of a Rogers note card prior to sending it to the Italian artisans. This action suggests bad faith in defendant's use of plaintiff's work, and militates against a finding of fair use.

The Supreme Court has held that copies made for commercial or profit-making purposes are presumptively unfair. ...

The Act expressly provides that comment on or criticism of a copyrighted work may be a valid use under the fair use doctrine. We must analyze therefore whether "String of Puppies" is properly considered a comment on or criticism of the photograph "Puppies." Koons argues that his sculpture is a satire or parody of society at large. He insists that "String of Puppies" is a fair social criticism and asserts to support that proposition that he belongs to the school of American artists who believe the mass production of commodities and media images has caused a deterioration in the quality of society, and this artistic tradition of which he is a member proposes through incorporating these images into works of art to comment critically both on the incorporated object and the political and economic system that created it. These themes, Koons states, draw upon the artistic movements of Cubism and Dadaism, with particular influence attributed to Marcel Duchamp, who in 1913 became the first to incorporate manufactured objects (ready-made) into a work of art, directly influencing Koons' work and the work of other contemporary American artists. We accept this definition of the objective of this group of American artists.

... Parody or satire, as we understand it, is when one artist, for comic effect or social commentary, closely imitates the style of another artist and in so doing creates a new art work that makes ridiculous the style and expression of the original. Under our cases parody and satire are valued forms of criticism, encouraged because this sort of criticism itself fosters the creativity protected by the copyright law. We have consistently held that a parody entitles its creator under the fair use doctrine to more extensive use of the copied work than is ordinarily allowed under the substantial similarity test.

Hence, it must first be determined whether "String of Puppies" is a parody of Rogers' work for purposes of the fair use doctrine. We agree with the district court that it is not. It is the rule in this Circuit that though the satire need not be only of the copied work and may, as appellants urge of "String of Puppies," also be a parody of modern society, the copied work must be, at least in part, an object of the parody, otherwise there would be no need to conjure up the original work. See MCA, Inc. v. Wilson, 677 F.2d at 185; 3 Nimmer, § 13.05[C] n. 60.9.

... By requiring that the copied work be an object of the parody, we merely insist that the audience be aware that underlying the parody there is an original and separate expression, attributable to a different artist. This awareness may come from the fact that the copied work is publicly known or because its existence is in some manner acknowledged by the parodist in connection with the parody. ...

The problem in the instant case is that even given that "String of Puppies" is a satirical critique of our materialistic society, it is difficult to discern any parody of the photograph "Puppies" itself. We conclude therefore that this first factor of the fair use doctrine cuts against a finding of fair use. The circumstances of this case indicate that Koons' copying of the photograph "Puppies" was done in bad faith, primarily for profit-making motives, and did not constitute a parody of the original work.

The next fair use factor asks what is the nature of the work that has been copied. Where the original work is factual rather than fictional the scope of fair use is broader. ... Since "Puppies" was creative and imaginative and Rogers, who makes his living as a photographer, hopes to gain a financial return for his efforts with this photograph, this factor militates against a finding of fair use.

Where the amount of copying exceeds permissible levels, summary judgment has been upheld. ... Here, the essence of Rogers' photograph was copied nearly in toto, much more than would have been necessary even if the sculpture had been a parody of plaintiff's work. In short, it is not really the parody flag that appellants are sailing under, but rather the flag of piracy. ...

Koons went well beyond the factual subject matter of the photograph to incorporate the very expression of the work created by Rogers. We find that no reasonable jury could conclude that Koons did not exceed a permissible level of copying under the fair use doctrine.

The fourth factor looks at the effect of the use on the market value of the original. The Supreme Court in Stewart, 495 U.S. 207, 110 S.Ct. 1750, 109 L.Ed.2d 184, stated that the fourth factor "is the 'most important, and indeed, central fair use factor.'" Under this factor a balance must be struck between the benefit gained by the copyright owner when the copying is found an unfair use and the benefit gained by the public when the use is held to be fair. The less adverse impact on the owner, the less public benefit need be shown to sustain non-commercial fair use. It is plain that where a use has no demonstrable impact on a copyright owners' potential market, the use need not be prohibited to protect the artist's incentive to pursue his inventive skills. Yet where the use is intended for commercial gain some meaningful likelihood of future harm is presumed.

... In this case, of course, the copy was in a different medium than the original: one was a three-dimensional piece of sculpture, and the other a two-dimensional black and white photo. But the owner of a copyright with respect to this market-factor need only demonstrate that if the unauthorized use becomes "widespread" it would prejudice his potential market for his work. The reason for this rule relates to a central concern of copyright law that unfair copying undercuts demand for the original work and, as an inevitable consequence, chills creation of such works. Hence the inquiry considers not only harm to the market for the original photograph, but also harm to the market for derivative works. It is obviously not implausible that another artist, who would be willing to purchase the rights from Rogers, would want to produce a sculpture like Rogers' photo and, with Koons' work extant, such market is reduced. Similarly, defendants could take and sell photos of "String of Puppies," which would prejudice Rogers' potential market for the sale of the "Puppies" note cards, in addition to any other derivative use he might plan.

Further, in discussing this fourth factor, the leading scholar in this area of the law uses an example that closely parallels the facts of the present case and demonstrates the irrelevance of copying in a different medium when analyzing this factor: a movie adaptation is made of a book. Even though the movie may boost book sales, it is an unfair use because of the effect on the potential sale of adaptation rights. 3 Nimmer, § 13.05[B]. ...

[The court held that victims of copyright infringement are entitled to recover damages, statutory damages, or some or all of the infringer's profits. The court remanded for a determination as to the portion of profits Rogers should recover and any deductible expenses Koons might have had. As to Rogers' actual damages, the court suggested that a reasonable license fee best approximates the injury suffered. But Rogers could still elect statutory damages, which might be "enhanced" due to Koons' "wilful" behavior. The contempt order was entirely proper.]

---

18. **Images of images.** A substantial and recognized theory in some contemporary art is based on what artists call "appropriation." The artistic and legal connotations of that word are quite different. Lawyers think of appropriation negatively, as *mis*appropriation. Artists think of it as the subject matter of "postmodern" art, a starting place that is transformed by their art. Appropriation in this sense is sometimes a matter of social commentary or at least a depiction of the environment in which they live. The "environment" or referent of such art is not the physical person or physical environment but the image environment which saturates contemporary life. See Carlin, *Culture Vultures: Artistic Appropriation and Intellectual Property Law*, 13 Colum.-VLA Art & The Law 103 (1988). When people's lives were dominated by thoughts of saints, artists depicted saints; when their lives are dominated by icons and symbols, artists like Andy Warhol depict the familiar image of Campbell's Soup labels. Does any of this matter on the copyright issue?

19. **Indirect social commentary: parody.** Putting aside whatever you might think of Koons' attitude, concepts, and mass production methods, consider whether he should be entitled to a fair use protection. First, consider why parody is given some kind of protection in fair use decisions. Second, consider why the protection is limited to parody of the copyrighted work itself and does not extend to satire of society, or social values. The court's reason seems to be mainly pragmatic, but is it also right in principle? If I wish to criticize society why should I be permitted to appropriate some your property to do it? Or is this the wrong question because the fair use issue is not about my right to use your property but about the extent of your property right in the first place?

In *Campbell v. Acuff-Rose Music, Inc.*, 510 U.S. 569, 114 S.Ct. 1164, 127 L.Ed.2d 500 (1994), a rap music group called 2 Live Crew performed a parody of a copyrighted "rock ballad" called "Pretty Woman." The Supreme Court held that the parody, although commercial, may nonetheless be a fair use and thus not actionable as an infringement of copyright. Parody is or can be a species of comment and criticism. If the new work is "transformative," that is, alters the original with new expression, meaning, or message, commercialism of the new work may be a less important and certainly not dispositive factor. Even if 2 Live Crew copied the "heart" of the music and words, "heart" is what lends itself to parody and the target at which parody aims. In the light of these observations, the lyric copying was not excessive. Whether the music copying was excessive is a fact question to be determined upon remand. The fact of commercial use does not justify a presumption that the 2 Live Crew work caused market harm to the copyright owners.

20. **Direct social commentary: the copyrighted outhouse.** Remember the lawyers' friend, *Hustler Magazine*? Remember Reverend Falwell's suit against the publisher for mental distress? Not only did Reverend Falwell bring that suit against the publisher, he used the "outhouse" ad on which he sued as part of mailings to potential donors. He sent it to 500,000 rank and file members of the Moral Majority, 27,000 major donors, and 750,000 supporters of the Old Time Gospel Hour. The material from *Hustler* was of course copyrighted. (There is no test of truth or moral quality for copyright). *Hustler's* publisher sued for copyright infringement. Is Falwell liable or is this fair use under the four factors? Falwell was undoubtedly using the magazine's own words (and pictures) to criticize and attack the magazine. The court held that the use was fair, considering the four statutory factors. The chief factor was that Falwell's use would not be likely to undermine sales of the magazine. *Hustler Magazine, Inc. v. Moral Majority, Inc.*, 796 F.2d 1148 (9th Cir. 1986). But the facts fit another pattern, too. They involve use of copyrighted material to make direct, explicit criticisms of (a) pornography in general and (b) the copyrighted work as an exemplar of pornography. Is this different from the artistic appropriation in *Koons* beyond the fact that the criticism is more obvious or explicit?

(c) "Moral Rights of Artists"

21. **Moral rights.** The "droit moral" of French law (with counterparts in other civil law countries) refers to intangible rights. Specifically, it refers to the idea that the author of a work—usually a work of visual art such as a painting or sculpture—retains some intangible or moral rights in the work even after the work is unconditionally sold. The rights were mainly (1) to display or publish, (2) to retract or withhold when the work was considered no longer representative, (3) to have the work properly attributed, and (4) to maintain the integrity of the work. The last right is perhaps the one most discussed in the United States today.

22. **The Berne Convention and moral rights.** The Berne Copyright Convention recognizes moral rights in this language:

> (1) Independently of the author's economic rights, and even after the transfer of the said rights, the author shall have the right to claim authorship of the work and to object to any distortion, mutilation or other modification of, or other derogatory action in relation to, the said work, which would be prejudicial to his honor or reputation.

23. **Traditional American law.** Traditional American law did not recognize any general "moral rights" of artists, as such, but of course artists, like others, enjoyed free speech rights (the right to display).

Would an artist (or author) have a right of attribution, that is, the right to have his work ascribed to him and not to someone else? In *Dastar Corp. v. Twentieth Century Fox Film Corp.*, 539 U.S. 23, 123 S.Ct. 2041, 156 L.Ed.2d 18 (2003), the copyright lapsed on a television series, *Crusade in Europe*. The defendant copied the series, edited it, and produced a video from it. The defendant sold the video as its own. The plaintiff, holding rights associated with the original production, sued under trademark laws, claiming that the defendant was falsely designating the origin of the work by not crediting the originators. The Court held that this did not violate trademark laws by failing to credit creative authorship. Instead, the trademark laws were concerned with the origin of the physical goods and the defendant was in fact the origin of the tangible product. So if American law recognizes a right of attribution, it will not be in the federal trademark law.

The most-discussed "moral right" recognized in European law is the visual artist's right to maintain the integrity of the art work. Traditional American law was probably quite clear to the contrary. If a purchaser of an art work choose to repaint it or remove it from public display or destroy it, the purchaser had every right to do so, since the work was mere property.

24. **Visual Artists Rights Act.** With the American adherence in 1988, the Berne Convention became (more or less) a part of American copyright law, effective in 1989. Effective in May, 1991, a new federal act, the Visual Artists Rights Act (VARA), codified as part of the copyright statute, specifically recognized a limited moral right in artists, principally in 17 U.S.C. § 106A. There are also state statutes, perhaps to some extent preempted by the federal statute. The potential for VARA claims is significant. "The VARA subsection that affords rights against destruction of a work of visual art, is expressly limited in coverage to works of 'recognized stature.' However, the VARA subsection that affords rights against mutilation or modification, contains no such express limitation. Since Pollara invoked both subsections, the insufficient stature of her banner could not (as the district court suggested) serve as an independent ground for dismissal of all of her VARA claims." *Pollara v. Seymour,* 344 F.3d 265 (2d Cir. 2003).

25. **Limitations.** Visual art is defined in § 101 to exclude most mass produced items, but it may include limited edition prints or photographs or the like. Some additional limitations on the right provided in 17 U.S.C. § 113 deal with removal of art from buildings. Some protections apply only to artists of recognized stature. The artist's "moral rights" cannot be transferred, but they can be waived.

26. **Policy.** The statute accords artists rights to control property after it is sold, rights no other sellers have. What is the policy? Preservation of cultural values? Somehow vindicating damage to the human spirit as Professor Kwall suggests? See Roberta Rosenthal Kwall, *Preserving Personality and Reputational Interests of Constructed Personas Through Moral Rights: a Blueprint for the Twenty-first Century,* 2001 U. Ill. L. Rev. 151, 152 (2001). Or would the policy be to encourage production of art that otherwise would not be produced? Or maybe to give artists a better economic return than the market will give them?

27. **First amendment problems?** Moral rights claims worry museums, not to mention other public institutions which own art, partly for

practical reasons (can we alter a painting to repair damage? Could we retouch the ceiling in the Sistine Chapel?) Are there free speech problems, too? What if a church decides a fresco painted on its walls by an artist commissioned for the task, conveys the wrong religious message and wants to destroy it? Or Rockefeller destroys a mural of Diego Rivera because it included a depiction of Lenin? What if Koons had tried to show his contempt by defacing a copy of the Rogers photograph, then exhibiting it as transformed art of his own?

§ 2. TRADE SECRETS

> "The word 'property' as applied to trademarks and trade secrets is an unanalyzed expression of certain secondary consequences of the primary fact that the law makes some rudimentary requirements of good faith."–Holmes, J. in *E.I. Du Pont de Nemours Powder Co. v. Masland,* 244 U.S. 100, 37 S.Ct. 575, 61 L.Ed. 1016 (1917).

28. **An illustrative trade secret problem.** An illustration of a trade secret problem is the case in which an employee, often a white-collar one, takes his company's secret chemical formula and starts a business on his own using that formula to compete with his former employer.

29. **Trade secrets defined.** Any information that can be used to economic advantage in the operation of an enterprise can qualify as a trade secret. See RESTATEMENT (THIRD) OF UNFAIR COMPETITION § 39 (1993). Examples: a chemical formula, a computer program, knowledge about a production technique. Trade secrets have economic value in part because the information is not generally known or ascertainable by competitors and it is in fact kept secret or at least its users make reasonable efforts to keep it secret. See UNIFORM TRADE SECRETS ACT, § 1 (4). Even secret combinations of well-known non-secret processes may have enough utility to count as trade secrets. But there are limits. Some courts refuse to hold that customer lists are trade secrets.

30. **Trade secrets vs. patents.** A trade secret is subject to legal protection even though (a) it is not patented and (b) it is not subject to patent. For example, a trade secret may have no element of novelty or inventiveness. In that case, it could not be patented. Or it might be information that could not count as an invention in any event, such as a list. You might actually prefer to protect your business information as a trade secret rather than through the patent process simply because the patent monopoly is for a limited number of years while a secret is good until someone discovers it.

31. **Trade secrets as property—confidential information requirement.** Trade secrets are often regarded as property. If the government takes trade secrets from the owner, for example, it must provide compensation, just as it must with any other property it takes. Nevertheless, Holmes is right: the "property" interest is one we perceive only as a

way of talking about protecting rights in information that arise out of confidential relationships, contract, or some independent tort.

32. **Basis of liability.** The defendant is potentially subject to liability for acquiring, using, or disclosing information he knows or has reason to know is a trade secret or has been acquired by improper means. This means that one who is not himself in a confidential relationship with the trade secret owner may be held liable if he knowingly acquires or uses a trade secret by improper means—burglarizing the plaintiff's plant, hacking into the plaintiff's computers, or bribing the plaintiff's employees, are examples. See RESTATEMENT (THIRD) OF UNFAIR COMPETITION § 40 (1993) (requiring breach of confidence or the like).

33. **No confidential relationship.** If the plaintiff's information is not protected by some means such as patent or copyright, then any duty to protect the information must arise from contract or confidential relationship. In the absence of contract or confidence, the defendant is free to use or reveal the information. If you give a bank your financial information not protected by a confidentiality agreement or a fiduciary relationship, the bank might be free to use that information for itself, say, in making a loan to your competitor. See *Read & Lundy, Inc. v. Washington Trust Co. of Westerly,* 840 A.2d 1099 (R.I. 2004). On confidential relationships with bankers, see Chapter 10, ¶ 27.

Information revealed to prospective purchasers is particularly vulnerable if care is not taken. In *Snead v. Redland Aggregates Ltd.*, 998 F.2d 1325 (5th Cir. 1993), the plaintiff had developed a new type of device and, to induce a purchaser to buy it, revealed its secrets. The purchasers, having learned the necessary details from these negotiations, built their own version of the device and marketed it. This was not a violation of trade secret rights because the seller and buyer had no confidential relationship. Should the seller have insisted on a contract calling for confidence before revealing the secrets? How about an implied contract of good faith and fair dealing or an implied contract of confidence? See *Phillips v. Frey*, 20 F.3d 623 (5th Cir. 1994).

34. **Information must be secret.** The information is not protected unless it is secret. If it is known publicly it is not protected.

35. **Reverse engineering.** When a product is manufactured by a secret process or design, a competitor could often buy the product, take it apart, measure it, and work backwards to a set of plans. This is legitimate. If a defendant does this, he is not liable for taking a trade secret. He has taken public information—the product—and his own skill and effort to construct the product. If the product is not patentable, this is not a tort. However, the fact that the competitor *could* reverse engineer the product is not a defense if in fact he took the information in breach of confidence. *Reingold v. Swiftships, Inc.,* 126 F.3d 645 (5th Cir. 1997).

36. ***Use* of trade secret.** An employee who simply quits his job after properly learning of the employer's trade secrets has committed no

wrong. However, under some circumstances, courts have thought that disclosure or use, though not proven directly, would be inevitable or that an inference of use or disclosure is justified where the plaintiff's former employee, holding trade secrets for production of a product, goes into a competing business manufacturing that very product. See *AutoMed Technologies, Inc. v. Eller,* 160 F.Supp.2d 915 (N.D. Ill. 2001).

37. **Displacement of other claims.** The Uniform Trade Secret Act is adopted in some form in most states. Section 7 of that statute permits the plaintiff to assert contractual claims, but displaces other legal theories of relief for appropriation of trade secrets. So the plaintiff could not sue for "conversion" of the trade secret but would instead be required to sue under the statute. On the other hand, if the defendant beat the plaintiff to extract the trade secret, the plaintiff could sue for the beating independent of the trade secret's appropriation.

38. **Free speech interests.** Are there any free speech, First Amendment interests in revealing trade secrets? In *CBS Inc. v. Davis,* 510 U.S. 1315, 114 S.Ct. 912, 127 L.Ed.2d 358 (1994), CBS induced an employee of a meat processing plant to secretly videotape the plant in operation. The plant owner sought and obtained a preliminary injunction to prevent airing the tape. Justice Blackmun granted a stay of the injunction, however, on the ground that it imposed a prior restraint. Although the tape might reveal trade secrets and might have been obtained in violation of trade secret laws, Justice Blackmun seemed to think that was not enough to warrant a prior restraint on publication, at least on the facts of the case. But in *DVD Copy Control Ass'n, Inc. v. Bunner,* 31 Cal.4th 864, 75 P.3d 1, 4 Cal.Rptr.3d 69 (2003), the court thought that an injunction could be issued against revealing a computer code that defeated DVD encryption, holding that an injunction to protect trade secrets would be constitutionally permissible, on the ground among others that "[t]he First Amendment does not prohibit courts from incidentally enjoining speech in order to protect a legitimate property right."

39. **Remedies and attorney fees.** The Uniform Trade Secrets Act defines trade secrets and authorizes injunctions to prevent their use or misappropriation, as well as damages against one who has already misappropriated them. It provides for preservation of the trade secret during litigation. Recall that some torts, like malicious prosecution, allow the *prevailing plaintiff* to recover reasonable attorney fees incurred as *damages.* The Uniform Trade Secrets Act, § 4, permits the prevailing defendant to recover reasonable attorney fees if the plaintiff's claim is brought in bad faith and the prevailing plaintiff to recover such fees if the defendant's misappropriation of trade secrets was "willful and malicious."

§ 3. MISAPPROPRIATION AND PREEMPTION

INTERNATIONAL NEWS SERVICE V. ASSOCIATED PRESS, 248 U.S. 215, 39 S.Ct. 68, 63 L.Ed.2d 211 (1918). AP and INS were competitors, each collecting news at its source and supplying news accounts to subscriber newspapers, which then published the news in their columns. During World War I, AP was able to get news from Europe, but INS was prohibited by foreign governments from doing so. According to the AP claim, INS provided the news to its subscribers by copying the AP news bulletins on public view in newspaper offices located in the eastern United States, or by copying the AP news as printed in eastern newspapers. This was then sent to INS's western subscribers, where it was still fresh news because of the time difference between the East and West Coasts. AP brought this suit to enjoin the copying and republication. The items were not copyrighted. Any other person could have read the AP bulletins from the same source and, since the bulletins were not copyrighted, could have published them. But the Supreme Court of the United States *held,* for AP. It conceded that AP had no general property interest in the stories against the public in general, but it thought that as against competitors the question was different. INS, operating in this manner against a competitor, was guilty of unfair competition in using news material generated by AP. INS "in appropriating it and selling it as its own is endeavoring to reap where it has not sown. . . ." Holmes and Brandeis dissented separately.

Sears, Roebuck & Co. v. Stiffel Co., 376 U.S. 225, 84 S.Ct. 784, 11 L.Ed.2d 661 (1964). Stiffel secured a design and mechanical patent on a pole lamp, which proved to be a hot seller. Sears made an identical lamp and sold it cheaper. Stiffel sued for patent infringement and, under Illinois state law, unfair competition by confusion. It turned out that the patents were invalid for want of "invention," but the trial court issued an injunction against Sears on the strength of Illinois' conception of unfair competition. The Court of Appeals agreed, noting that a likelihood of public confusion would be sufficient to make out a case. The Supreme Court reversed, holding Sears had a right to make copies of unprotected designs. The patent and copyright laws are supreme and they and they alone fix conditions upon which patents and copyrights can be granted. A patent is a statutory monopoly, but for a limited term of years. The states could not extend the life of the patent or patent an article denied a patent under federal law. They cannot do so indirectly under "unfair competition" laws. An unpatentable article is like one on which the patent has expired: it is in the public domain. Sears thus has every right to copy the unpatentable article, and state unfair competition laws cannot give protection unlimited in time without encroaching on the federal patent system. "[M]ere inability of the public to tell two identical articles apart is not enough to support an injunction against copying or an award of damages for copying that which the federal patent laws permits to be copied." Labeling may be required, but no penalty can attach to the copying itself.

ZACCHINI V. SCRIPPS-HOWARD BROADCASTING CO., 433 U.S. 562, 97 S.Ct. 2849, 53 L.Ed.2d 965 (1977). Zacchini performed an act as a human cannonball. He was one of the acts shown in the Geauga County Fair in Ohio. The act consisted of Zacchini's being shot from a cannon into a net 200 feet away. Like too many other performances, the climax was splendid, but the entire performance took only 15 seconds. The show took place in an area open to all those who had properly entered the fair grounds. There was no separate charge. Defendant filmed the entire act, against Zacchini's express wishes. The film was shown on the defendant's television news. The "entire act" was shown. Television commentary was favorable and recommended seeing the act in person. Zacchini sued. The Ohio Court concluded that, under Ohio law, the defendant was guilty of the kind of privacy invasion Prosser had identified as commercial appropriation and which is sometimes called a right of publicity. It thought, however, that recovery was barred by the First Amendment and that the publisher was "privileged" to provide an accurate report. But the Supreme Court reversed and held that the Constitution did not provide any privilege to the publisher of the film. If Ohio has a preference for enforcing property interests in this act, that does not offend the decisions in *Times-Sullivan* and *Gertz*. Those decisions did not deal with the appropriation of an entire act.

> The Constitution no more prevents a State from requiring [a defendant] to compensate [a plaintiff] for broadcasting his act on television that it would privilege [a defendant] to film and broadcast a copyrighted dramatic work. . . .

The policy of recognizing a property interest here is partly to compensate for efforts already made, but more significantly to provide economic incentive to do further work of interest to the public. These are indeed the policies behind the copyright and patent statutes. Thus Ohio is free to impose liability if it so chooses.

Time v. Hill, which applied *Times-Sullivan* constraints to a privacy claim, does not control because that case did not involve publicity rights. The state's interest in providing a cause of action in each case differs. One involves interests in reputation, the other interests similar to patent and copyright interests. Also the two torts differ in the degree in which they intrude on dissemination of information to the public. Right of publicity cases only affect who gets to publicize.

BONITO BOATS, INC. V. THUNDER CRAFT BOATS, INC., 489 U.S. 141, 109 S.Ct. 971, 103 L.Ed.2d 118 (1989). Bonito developed a new boat hull. A Florida statute enacted thereafter prohibited copying boat hulls by direct molding of fiberglass and prohibited selling such copied hulls. Thunder Craft allegedly copied by this method. Bonito sued for injunction, damages, and accounting for profits. Arguing *Sears* and related cases, Thunder Craft moved to dismiss. The trial court granted the motion, and the Florida Supreme Court, over dissents, ultimately affirmed. In the United States Supreme Court, *held*, affirmed. The patent clause effects a balance between encouragement of innovation and avoidance of anti-competitive monopolies; it grants and it limits. Limits on the monopoly and the ultimate development of public goods are seen by statutory requirements for patents including: (A) requirement of novelty and usefulness; (B) requirement of ultimate disclosure in specific plans and models; (C) exclusion of patents on articles in prior use and even on those that have been *described* before; (D) exclusion of patents even on novel articles when they are obvious extensions of prior art. The system created by these rules must be attractive and effective to induce both creative effort and disclosure of the results. This can be so only if there is free competition in the exploitation of *un*patented designs and innovations. When an inventor discloses designs in response to market inducements additional protection is not appropriate because it will not induce disclosure and it will deprive the public of the building blocks for further development. "To a limited extent, the federal patent laws must determine not only what is protected, but also what is free for all to use." The limit on state power to strike a different balance is illustrated by the case of the expired patent. After expiration of the federal patent, states may not add protection because the public has "paid the congressionally mandated price for disclosure" and the states may not "render the exchange fruitless by offering patent-like protections" after the price has been paid by giving the 17-year monopoly. This does not exclude state protection for trade secrets, however. States could also prohibit unfair competition by protecting consumers from confusion as to the source of the product. The state may protect non-functional elements of a design, but not functional ones. Focus on consumer protection is central to unfair competition. The Florida statute is not an unfair competition statute; instead, it offers patent-like protection for unlimited years and regardless of merits or novelty of design, and regardless of disclosure. So it goes beyond protection against unfair competition.

40. **Is the misappropriation doctrine viable?** In *McKevitt v. Pallasch,* 339 F.3d 530 (7th Cir. 2003), Judge Posner commented that the *INS* case was no longer "legally authoritative because it was based on the federal courts' subsequently abandoned authority to formulate common law principles in suits arising under state law though litigated in federal court. But the doctrine it announced has been adopted as the common law of a number of states. . . ." But doesn't the reasoning in *Bonito Boats* apply equally to copyright, and if so how can the misappropriation doctrine still protect uncopyrighted materials?

41. **Misappropriation in the Restatement.** Misappropriation doctrine is no longer an independent ground for recovery under the contemporary Restatement rules. The misappropriation doctrine is expressly discarded because the scope of legitimate protection is limited to protection of rights recognized in trade secret rules, the right of publicity rules, and the copyright statute. Restatement of Unfair Competition § 38 (1995). Apart from the weakness of the doctrinal support in the courts, the Restatement observed:

> Protection against the misappropriation of intangible trade values insures an incentive to invest in the creation of intangible assets and prevents the potential unjust enrichment that may result from the appropriation of an investment made by another. However, the recognition of exclusive rights in intangible trade values can impede access to valuable information and restrain competition. Unlike appropriations of physical assets, the appropriation of information or other intangible asset does not ordinarily deprive the originator of simultaneous use. The recognition of exclusive rights may thus deny to the public the full benefits of valuable ideas and innovations by limiting their distribution and exploitation. In addition, the principle of unjust enrichment does not demand restitution of every gain derived from the efforts of others. A small shop, for example, may freely benefit from the customers attracted by a nearby department store. . . .

Id., cmt. b.

42. **Intangible "trespasses" and misappropriation.** Recall that some courts have found electronic intrusions, such as those causing excessive demand on a company's computers, to be a trespass. (Chapter 7, ¶ 11(b)). Would such a "trespass" be better conceived as a special, and actionable, type of misappropriation?

§ 4. TRADEMARKS AND UNFAIR COMPETITION

Note: Passing Off, Unfair Competition and Trademark Law

Trademark law, based on statutes, grew out of common law unfair competition and in particular the common law liability for "passing off." The defendant passed off his goods as those of the plaintiff, for example, if customers ask a pharmacist for, say, a drug manufactured by Lilly but the pharmacist systematically substitutes a drug he compounds himself, Lilly could sue him for passing off. With the identification of goods and their source by marks and names, state law and federal pre-*Erie* law developed a common law of trademarks or "unfair competition." The Lanham Trademark Act then provided for federal registration of trademarks and permitted statutory actions for infringement of registered marks. The federal statutory protections have gradually expanded. Although state law is still viable, most claims are pursued and defended under federal law.

15 U.S.C. § 1114 [§ 32 of the Lanham Trademark Act].
[Liability for infringement of registered mark]

(1) Any person who shall, without the consent of the registrant

(a) use in commerce any reproduction, counterfeit, copy, or colorable imitation of a registered mark in connection with the sale, offering for sale, distribution, or advertising of any goods or services on or in connection with which such use is likely to cause confusion, or to cause mistake, or to deceive; . . .

(b) . . . shall be liable in a civil action by the registrant for the remedies hereinafter provided. . . .

43. **Acquiring trademark rights.** Under copyright law, you own the copyright in works you author, whether they are published or not. Trademark law is different. You acquire rights in a mark only by using the mark in commerce to identify yourself as the commercial source of the goods you produce.

44. **Federal registration of trademarks.** Notice that § 1114 speaks of a "registrant." That is because it is providing protection for federally registered marks. Registration on the principal register is not necessary to receive protection, but it does give the mark owner some advantages, for example, a presumption that the plaintiff is the owner of the mark and that the mark is distinctive and capable of identifying the plaintiff's goods. See 15 U.S.C.A. § 1115(a). Registration, unlike the simple filing for copyright mentioned in ¶ 7, requires judgments by the Patent and Trademark Office and may be denied if, for example, the mark is merely descriptive, if it is already in use or is too similar to one that is. Trademark registration differs from copyright registration in another way, by excluding registration for marks containing "immoral" matter. 15 U.S.C.A. § 1052. This chapter is concerned with substantive rights, not the process of registration itself or the various kinds of registration available. You can follow the process and apply online from a site created by the U.S. Patent and Trademark Office, www.uspto.gov/teas.

QUALITEX CO. v. JACOBSON PRODUCTS CO., INC.*

514 U.S. 159, 115 S.Ct. 1300, 131 L.Ed.2d 248 (1995)

JUSTICE BREYER delivered the opinion of the Court. . . .

The case before us grows out of petitioner Qualitex Company's use (since the 1950's) of a special shade of green-gold color on the pads that it makes and sells to dry cleaning firms for use on dry cleaning presses. In 1989 respondent Jacobson Products (a Qualitex rival) began to sell its own press pads to dry cleaning firms; and it colored those pads a similar green-gold. In 1991 Qualitex registered the special green-gold color on press pads with the Patent and Trademark Office as a trademark. Registration No. 1,633,711 (Feb. 5, 1991). Qualitex subsequently added a trademark infringement count, 15 U.S.C. § 1114(1), to an unfair competition claim, § 1125(a), in a lawsuit it had already filed challenging Jacobson's use of the green-gold color.

Qualitex won the lawsuit in the District Court. But, the Court of Appeals for the Ninth Circuit set aside the judgment in Qualitex's favor

*. Blackletter catch lines were inserted by the editors.

on the trademark infringement claim because, in that Circuit's view, the Lanham Act does not permit Qualitex, or anyone else, to register "color alone" as a trademark. . . .

Lanham Act basics. The Lanham Act gives a seller or producer the exclusive right to "register" a trademark, 15 U.S.C. § 1052, and to prevent his or her competitors from using that trademark, § 1114(1). Both the language of the Act and the basic underlying principles of trademark law would seem to include color within the universe of things that can qualify as a trademark. The language of the Lanham Act describes that universe in the broadest of terms. It says that trademarks "includ[e] any word, name, symbol, or device, or any combination thereof." § 1127. Since human beings might use as a "symbol" or "device" almost anything at all that is capable of carrying meaning, this language, read literally, is not restrictive. The courts and the Patent and Trademark Office have authorized for use as a mark a particular shape (of a Coca-Cola bottle), a particular sound (of NBC's three chimes), and even a particular scent (of plumeria blossoms on sewing thread). If a shape, a sound, and a fragrance can act as symbols why, one might ask, can a color not do the same?

Descriptive vs. fanciful. A color is also capable of satisfying the more important part of the statutory definition of a trademark, which requires that a person "us[e]" or "inten[d] to use" the mark "to identify and distinguish his or her goods, including a unique product, from those manufactured or sold by others and to indicate the source of the goods, even if that source is unknown." 15 U.S.C. § 1127. True, a product's color is unlike "fanciful," "arbitrary," or "suggestive" words or designs, which almost automatically tell a customer that they refer to a brand. The imaginary word "Suntost," or the words "Suntost Marmalade," on a jar of orange jam immediately would signal a brand or a product "source"; the jam's orange color does not do so. But, over time, customers may come to treat a particular color on a product or its packaging (say, a color that in context seems unusual, such as pink on a firm's insulating material or red on the head of a large industrial bolt) as signifying a brand. And, if so, that color would have come to identify and distinguish the goods—i.e. "to indicate" their "source"—much in the way that descriptive words on a product (say, "Trim" on nail clippers or "Car-Freshner" on deodorizer) can come to indicate a product's origin. In this circumstance, trademark law says that the word (e.g., "Trim"), although not inherently distinctive, has developed "secondary meaning." Again, one might ask, if trademark law permits a descriptive word with secondary meaning to act as a mark, why would it not permit a color, under similar circumstances, to do the same?

Consistency with trademark law goals. We cannot find in the basic objectives of trademark law any obvious theoretical objection to the use of color alone as a trademark, where that color has attained "secondary meaning" and therefore identifies and distinguishes a particular brand (and thus indicates its "source"). In principle, trademark law, by preventing others from copying a source-identifying mark, "reduce[s] the customer's costs of shopping and making purchasing decisions," 1 J. McCarthy, McCarthy on Trademarks and Unfair Competition § 2.01[2], p. 2–3 (3d ed. 1994) (hereinafter McCarthy), for it quickly and easily assures a potential customer that this item—the item with this mark—is made by the same producer as other similarly marked items that he or she liked (or disliked) in the past. At the same time, the law helps assure a producer that it (and not an imitating competitor) will reap the financial, reputation-related rewards associated with a desirable product. The law thereby "encourage[s] the production of quality products," and simultaneously discourages those who hope to sell inferior products by capitalizing on a consumer's inability quickly to evaluate the quality of an item offered for sale. It is the source-distinguishing ability of a mark—not its ontological status as color, shape, fragrance, word, or sign—that permits it to serve these basic purposes. And, for that reason, it is difficult to find, in basic trademark objectives, a reason to disqualify absolutely the use of a color as a mark.

Functionality doctrine. Neither can we find a principled objection to the use of color as a mark in the important "functionality" doctrine of trademark law. The functionality doctrine prevents trademark law, which seeks to promote competition by protecting a firm's reputation, from instead inhibiting legitimate competition by allowing a producer to control a useful product feature. It is the province of patent law, not trademark law, to encourage invention by granting inventors a monopoly over new product designs or functions for a limited time, 35 U.S.C. §§ 173, after which competitors are free to use the innovation. If a product's functional features could be used as trademarks, however, a monopoly over such features could be obtained without regard to whether they qualify as patents and could be extended forever (because trademarks may be renewed in perpetuity). Functionality doctrine therefore would require, to take an imaginary example, that even if customers have come to identify the special illumination-enhancing shape of a new patented light bulb with a particular manufacturer, the manufacturer may not use that shape as a trademark, for doing so, after the patent had expired, would impede competition—not by protecting the reputation of the original bulb maker, but by frustrating competitors' legitimate efforts to produce an equivalent illumination-enhancing bulb. This Court consequently has explained that, "[i]n general terms, a product feature is functional," and cannot serve as a trademark, "if it is essential to the use or purpose of the article or if it affects the cost or quality of the article," that is, if exclusive use of the feature would put competitors at a significant non-reputation-related disadvantage. Although sometimes color plays an important role (unrelated to source identification) in making a product more desirable, sometimes it does not. And, this latter fact—the fact that sometimes color is not essential to a product's use or purpose and does not affect cost or quality—indicates that the doctrine of "functionality" does not create an absolute bar to the use of color alone as a mark.

Shade confusion argument. ... Jacobson says that, if the law permits the use of color as a trademark, it will produce uncertainty and unresolvable court disputes about what shades of a color a competitor may lawfully use. Because lighting (morning sun, twilight mist) will affect perceptions of protected color, competitors and courts will suffer from "shade confusion." ...

We do not believe, however, that color, in this respect, is special. Courts traditionally decide quite difficult questions about whether two words or phrases or symbols are sufficiently similar, in context, to confuse buyers. They have had to compare, for example, such words as "Bonamine" and "Dramamine" (motion-sickness remedies). ...

Limited supply of colors argument. Second, Jacobson argues, as have others, that colors are in limited supply. Jacobson claims that, if one of many competitors can appropriate a particular color for use as a trademark, and each competitor then tries to do the same, the supply of colors will soon be depleted. ...

This argument is unpersuasive, however, largely because it relies on an occasional problem to justify a blanket prohibition. When a color serves as a mark, normally alternative colors will likely be available for similar use by others. Moreover, if that is not so—if a "color depletion" or "color scarcity" problem does arise—the trademark doctrine of "functionality" normally would seem available to prevent the anticompetitive consequences that Jacobson's argument posits, thereby minimizing that argument's practical force.

The functionality and aesthetic functionality answer. The functionality doctrine, as we have said, forbids the use of a product's feature as a trademark where doing so will put a competitor at a significant disadvantage because the feature is "essential to the use or purpose of the article" or "affects [its] cost or quality." The functionality doctrine thus protects competitors against a disadvantage (unrelated to recognition or reputation) that trademark protection might otherwise impose, namely their inability reasonably to replicate important non-reputation-related product features. For example, this Court has written that competitors might be free to copy the color of a medical pill where that color serves to identify the kind of medication (e.g., a type of blood medicine) in addition to its source. ... The Restatement (Third) of Unfair Competition adds that, if a design's "aesthetic value" lies in its ability to "confe[r] a significant benefit that cannot practically be duplicated by the use of alternative designs," then the design is "functional." Restatement (Third) of Unfair Competition § 17, Comment c, pp. 175–176 (1995). The "ultimate test of aesthetic functionality," it explains, "is whether the recognition of trademark rights would significantly hinder competition."

The upshot is that, where a color serves a significant nontrademark function—whether to distinguish a heart pill from a digestive medicine or to satisfy the "noble instinct for giving the right touch of beauty to common and necessary things," courts will examine whether its use as a mark would permit one competitor (or a group) to interfere with legitimate (nontrademark-related) competition through actual or potential exclusive use of an important product ingredient. That examination should not discourage firms from creating aesthetically pleasing mark designs, for it is open to their competitors to do the same. But, ordinarily, it should prevent the anticompetitive consequences of Jacobson's hypothetical "color depletion" argument, when, and if, the circumstances of a particular case threaten "color depletion."

Why older cases do not control. Third, Jacobson points to many older cases—including Supreme Court cases—in support of its position. . . .

These Supreme Court cases, however, interpreted trademark law as it existed before 1946, when Congress enacted the Lanham Act. The Lanham Act significantly changed and liberalized the common law to "dispense with mere technical prohibitions," most notably, by permitting trademark registration of descriptive words (say, "U-Build-It" model airplanes) where they had acquired "secondary meaning." The Lanham Act extended protection to descriptive marks by making clear that (with certain explicit exceptions not relevant here), "nothing ... shall prevent the registration of a mark used by the applicant which has become distinctive of the applicant's goods in commerce." 15 U. S. C. § 1052(f). This language permits an ordinary word, normally used for a nontrademark purpose (e.g., description), to act as a trademark where it has gained "secondary meaning." Its logic would appear to apply to color as well. Indeed, in 1985, the Federal Circuit considered the significance of the Lanham Act's changes as they related to color and held that trademark protection for color was consistent with the "jurisprudence under the Lanham Act developed in accordance with the statutory principle that if a mark is capable of being or becoming distinctive of [the] applicant's goods in commerce, then it is capable of serving as a trademark."

In 1988 Congress amended the Lanham Act, revising portions of the definitional language, but left unchanged the language here relevant. . . .

This history undercuts the authority of the precedent on which Jacobson relies. . . .

Fourth, Jacobson argues that there is no need to permit color alone to function as a trademark because a firm already may use color as part of a trademark, say, as a colored circle or colored letter or colored word, and may rely upon "trade dress" protection, under § 43(a) of the Lanham Act, if a competitor copies its color and thereby causes consumer confusion regarding the overall appearance of the competing products or their packaging. [The Court also rejected this argument.]

... [W]e conclude that the Ninth Circuit erred in barring Qualitex's use of color as a trademark. For these reasons, the judgment of the Ninth Circuit is

Reversed.

---

45. **Source confusion.** If a competitor uses a symbol closely similar to the plaintiff's mark, buyers may be confused as to the *source* of the goods. If a producer imitated Campbell's distinctive soup labels, you might buy soup thinking its "source" was Campbell's when in fact it was not. Trademark protection aims to prevent the likelihood of consumer confusion. Look back as 15 U.S.C.A. § 1114(a)(1) above to see the statutory language.

46. **Distinctiveness requirement; generic terms.** Consumers will not be confused about the source of a product merely because two or more producers use the same generic term for the product. The word "lumber" is a generic term for certain wood products; the word does not distinguish the plaintiff's lumber from a competitor's lumber. The rule is that if consumers generally regard a term as generic, that term cannot be a trademark because it is not distinctive. Many terms that began life as trademarks became generic because consumers adopted those terms to cover the product as a whole. Aspirin, once a trademark, is now merely a generic term that anyone can use to describe the product.

47. **Distinctiveness and acquired or "secondary" meaning.** "In evaluating the distinctiveness of a mark ... courts have held that a mark can be distinctive in one of two ways. First, a mark is inherently distinctive if '[its] intrinsic nature serves to identify a particular source.' In the context of word marks, courts have applied the now-classic test originally formulated by Judge Friendly, in which word marks that are 'arbitrary' ('Camel' cigarettes), 'fanciful' ('Kodak' film), or 'suggestive' ('Tide' laundry detergent) are held to be inherently distinctive. Second, a mark has acquired distinctiveness, even if it is not inherently distinctive, if it has developed secondary meaning, which occurs when, 'in the minds of the public, the primary significance of a [mark] is to identify the source of the product rather than the product itself.' " *Wal-Mart Stores, Inc. v. Samara Bros.,* 529 U.S. 205, 120 S.Ct. 1339, 146 L.Ed.2d 182 (2000).

48. **Strong and weak trademarks.** Fanciful marks—wholly contrived words like "Kodak," for example—are said to be strong marks. So are arbitrary marks like "Camel" for a cigarette. The word camel is not coined or fanciful, but it is used in a wholly arbitrary way and thus distinctive. Suggestive marks, like "Tide" for a laundry soap might call up images of water associated with washing so they are not wholly arbitrary, but neither are they merely descriptive of the product or its characteristics. These marks, too, are "inherently" distinctive. Marks that are descriptive might acquire distinctiveness through use and identification by the public, but these are likely to be much weaker. The classification scheme is a good rough index to strength, but the fame of

the mark—its recognition among consumers—is ultimately the test. See J. Thomas McCarthy, Trademarks and Unfair Competition (4th ed. 2004).

49. **Significance of the strong-weak distinction.** What is the significance of saying that a mark is strong or weak? First, if your client's mark is a strong one, it will be inherently distinctive and you won't have to prove it has a secondary or acquired meaning to the public if you are in litigation over use of the mark. Second, if someone who is not a competitor uses your client's strong mark on entirely different products, there still might be customer confusion, so the strong mark might be protected. If your client's mark is weak, however, there may be no confusion at all when a similar mark is used on a different product. A weak mark like "Blue Ribbon" might be applied to, say, a dog kennel, without causing confusion with a beer using the same mark. Thus weak marks might be used by a number of different producers of goods. Could the owner of the mark "Plus," used on vitamins, health and beauty aids, enjoin use of the "Plus" as a mark for foods sold at a discount grocery? See *Plus Products v. Plus Discount Foods, Inc.,* 722 F.2d 999 (2d Cir. 1983).

50. **Sponsorship confusion.** The law of trademark and unfair competition originally protected against source confusion. Trade dress cases do not differ in that respect. If the defendant uses the plaintiff's mark but no source confusion is likely to result, should courts nevertheless prohibit the defendant's use? A leading case involved the use of the term "Seventeen." One marketer applied it to a magazine. Another applied it to a girdle (an undergarment that people once wore to constrain or mold their bodies). The two marketers were not in competition and no one would ever buy a girdle thinking it was a magazine or vice versa. Still, it was possible that a girdle buyer would think the girdle was endorsed or sponsored by the magazine of the same name. That was sponsorship confusion and that was enough to be actionable. *Triangle Publications, Inc. v. Rohrlich,* 167 F.2d 969 (2d Cir. 1948). Are we on a slippery slope?

TY INC. v. PERRYMAN

306 F.3d 509 (7th Cir. 2002)

POSNER, Circuit Judge.

Ty Inc., the manufacturer of Beanie Babies, the well-known beanbag stuffed animals, brought this suit for trademark infringement against Ruth Perryman. Perryman sells second-hand beanbag stuffed animals, primarily but not exclusively Ty's Beanie Babies, over the Internet. Her Internet address ("domain name"), a particular focus of Ty's concern, is bargainbeanies.com. She has a like-named Web site (http://www.bargainbeanies.com) where she advertises her wares. Ty's suit is based on the federal antidilution statute, 15 U.S.C. § 1125(c), which protects "famous" marks from commercial uses that cause "dilution of the distinctive quality of the mark." The district court granted summary judgment in favor of Ty and entered an injunction that forbids the defendant to use "BEANIE or BEANIES or any colorable imitation thereof (whether alone or in connection with other terms) within any business name, Internet domain name, or trademark, or in connection with any non-Ty products." Perryman's appeal argues primarily that "beanies" has become a generic term for beanbag stuffed animals and therefore cannot be appropriated as a trademark at all, and that in any event the injunction (which has remained in effect during the appeal) is overbroad.

The fundamental purpose of a trademark is to reduce consumer search costs by providing a concise and unequivocal identifier of the particular source of particular goods. The consumer who knows at a glance whose brand he is being asked to buy knows whom to hold responsible if the brand disappoints and whose product to buy in the future if the brand pleases. This in turn gives producers an incentive to maintain high and uniform quality, since otherwise the investment in their trademark may be lost as customers turn away in disappointment from the brand. A successful brand, however, creates an incentive in unsuccessful competitors to pass off their inferior brand as the successful brand by adopting a confusingly similar trademark, in effect appropriating the goodwill created by the producer of the successful brand. The traditional and still central concern of trademark law is to provide remedies against this practice.

Confusion is not a factor here, however, with a minor exception discussed at the end of the opinion. Perryman is not a competing producer of beanbag stuffed animals, and her Web site clearly disclaims any affiliation with Ty. But that does not get her off the hook. The reason is that state and now federal law also provides a remedy against the "dilution" of a trademark, though as noted at the outset of this opinion the federal statute is limited to the subset of "famous" trademarks and to dilutions of them caused by commercial uses that take place in interstate or foreign commerce. . . .

But what is "dilution"? There are (at least) three possibilities relevant to this case, each defined by a different underlying concern. First, there is concern that consumer search costs will rise if a trademark becomes associated with a variety of unrelated products. Suppose an upscale restaurant calls itself "Tiffany." There is little danger that the consuming public will think it's dealing with a branch of the Tiffany jewelry store if it patronizes this restaurant. But when consumers next see the name "Tiffany" they may think about both the restaurant and the jewelry store, and if so the efficacy of the name as an identifier of the store will be diminished. Consumers will have to think harder—incur as it were a higher imagination cost—to recognize the name as the name of the store. So "blurring" is one form of dilution.

Now suppose that the "restaurant" that adopts the name "Tiffany" is actually a striptease joint. Again, and indeed even more certainly than in the previous case, consumers will not think the striptease joint under common ownership with the jewelry store. But because of the inveterate tendency of the human mind to proceed by association, every time they think of the word "Tiffany" their image of the fancy jewelry store will be tarnished by the association of the word with the strip joint. So "tarnishment" is a second form of dilution. Analytically it is a subset of blurring, since it reduces the distinctness of the trademark as a signifier of the trademarked product or service.

Third, and most far-reaching in its implications for the scope of the concept of dilution, there is a possible concern with situations in which, though there is neither blurring nor tarnishment, someone is still taking a free ride on the investment of the trademark owner in the trademark. Suppose the "Tiffany" restaurant in our first hypothetical example is located in Kuala Lumpur and though the people who patronize it (it is upscale) have heard of the Tiffany jewelry store, none of them is ever going to buy anything there, so that the efficacy of the trademark as an identifier will not be impaired. If appropriation of Tiffany's aura is nevertheless forbidden by an expansive concept of dilution, the benefits of the jewelry store's investment in creating a famous name will be, as economists say, "internalized"—that is, Tiffany will realize the full benefits of the investment rather than sharing those benefits with others—and as a result the amount of investing in creating a prestigious name will rise.

This rationale for antidilution law has not yet been articulated in or even implied by the case law, although a few cases suggest that the concept of dilution is not exhausted by blurring and tarnishment, and the common law doctrine of "misappropriation" might conceivably be invoked in support of the rationale that we have sketched. The validity of the rationale may be doubted, however. The number of prestigious names is so vast (and, as important, would be even if there were no antidilution laws) that it is unlikely that the owner of a prestigious trademark could obtain substantial license fees if commercial use of the mark without his consent were forbidden despite the absence of consumer confusion, blurring, or tarnishment. Competition would drive the fee to zero since, if the name is being used in an unrelated market, virtually every prestigious name will be a substitute for every other in that market.

None of the rationales we have canvassed supports Ty's position in this case. Perryman is not producing a product, or a service, such as dining at a restaurant, that is distinct from any specific product; rather, she is selling the very product to which the trademark sought to be defended against her "infringement" is attached. You can't sell a branded product without using its brand name, that is, its trademark. Supposing that Perryman sold *only* Beanie Babies (a potentially relevant qualification, as we'll see), we would find it impossible to understand how she could be thought to be blurring, tarnishing, or otherwise free riding to any significant extent on Ty's investment in its mark. To say she was would amount to saying that if a used car dealer truthfully advertised that it sold Toyotas, or if a muffler manufacturer truthfully advertised that it specialized in making mufflers for installation in Toyotas, Toyota would have a claim of trademark infringement. Of course there can be no aftermarket without an original market, and in that sense sellers in a trademarked good's aftermarket are free riding on the trademark. But in that attenuated sense of free riding, almost everyone in business is free riding. . . .

It is true that Web search engines do not stop with the Web address; if Perryman's Web address were www.perryman.com but her Web page mentioned Beanies, a search for the word "Beanies" would lead to her Web page. Yet we know from the events that led up to the passage in 1999 of the Anticybersquatting Consumer Protection Act, 15 U.S.C. § 1125(d), that many firms value having a domain name or Web address that signals their product. (The "cybersquatters" were individuals or firms that would register domain names for the purpose of selling them to companies that wanted a domain name that would be the name of their company or of their principal product.) After all, many consumers search by typing the name of a company in the Web address space (browser) on their home page rather than by use of a search engine. We do not think that by virtue of trademark law producers own their aftermarkets and can impede sellers in the aftermarket from marketing the trademarked product. . . .

We surmise that what Ty is seeking in this case is an extension of antidilution law to forbid commercial uses that accelerate the transition from trademarks (brand names) to generic names (product names). Words such as "thermos," "yo-yo," "escalator," "cellophane," and "brassiere" started life as trademarks, but eventually lost their significance as source identifiers and became the popular names of the product rather than the name of the trademark owner's brand, and when that happened continued enforcement of the trademark would simply have undermined competition with the brand by making it difficult for competitors to indicate that they were selling the same product—by rendering them in effect speechless. Ty is doubtless cognizant of a similar and quite real danger to "Beanie Babies" and "Beanies." Notice that the illustrations we gave of trademarks that became generic names are all descriptive or at least suggestive of the product, which makes them better candidates for genericness than a fanciful trademark such as "Kodak" or "Exxon." Ty's trademarks likewise are descriptive of the product they denote; its argument that "Beanies" is "inherently distinctive" (like Kodak and Exxon), and therefore protected by trademark law without proof of secondary meaning, is nonsense. A trademark that describes a basic element of the product, as "Beanies" does, is not protected unless the owner can establish that the consuming public accepts the word as the designation of a brand of the product (that it has acquired, as the cases say, secondary meaning). As the public does with regard to "Beanies"—for now. But because the word is catchier than "beanbag stuffed animals," "beanbag toys," or "plush toys," it may someday "catch on" to the point where the mark becomes generic, and then Ty will have to cast about for a different trademark.

Although there is a social cost when a mark becomes generic—the trademark owner has to invest in a new trademark to identify his brand—there is also a social benefit, namely an addition to ordinary language. . . . An interpretation of antidilution law as arming trademark owners to enjoin uses of their mark that, while not confusing, threaten to render the mark generic may therefore not be in the public interest. Moreover, the vistas of litigation that such a theory of dilution opens up are staggering. Ty's counsel at argument refused to disclaim a right to sue the publishers of dictionaries should they include an entry for "beanie," lower-cased and defined as a beanbag stuffed animal, thus accelerating the transition from trademark to generic term. He should have disclaimed such a right.

We reject the extension of antidilution law that Ty beckons us to adopt, but having done so we must come back to the skipped issue of confusion. For although 80 percent of Perryman's sales are of Ty's products, this means that 20 percent are not, and on her Web page after listing the various Ty products under such names as "Beanie Babies" and "Teenie Beanies" she has the caption "Other Beanies" and under that is a list of products such as "Planet Plush" and "Rothschild Bears" that are not manufactured by Ty. This is plain misdescription, in fact false advertising, and supports the last prohibition in the injunction, the prohibition against using "Beanie" or "Beanies" in connection with any non-Ty products. That much of the injunction should stand. But Ty has not demonstrated any basis for enjoining Perryman from using the terms in "any business name, Internet domain name, or trademark."...

So the judgment must be vacated and the case remanded for the formulation of a proper injunction. ... [W]e cannot imagine a state of facts consistent with the extensive record compiled in the summary judgment proceeding that could possibly justify an injunction against Perryman's representing in her business name and Internet and Web addresses that she is doing what she has a perfect right to do, namely sell Beanie Babies. We therefore direct that the proceedings on remand be limited to the reformulation of the injunction in conformity with this opinion.

---

51. **Imagination costs?** Judge Posner seemed to think that not much was required to establish blurring of a famous mark, but the Supreme Court's decision in *Moseley v. V Secret Catalogue,* Inc., 537 U.S. 418, 123 S.Ct. 1115, 155 L.Ed.2d 1 (2003), requires something more than two similar marks. The court held that there must be evidence of actual dilution because the statute "unambiguously requires a showing of actual dilution, rather than a likelihood of dilution." The plaintiff need not prove actual lost sales, but "at least where the marks at issue are not identical, the mere fact that consumers mentally associate the junior user's mark with a famous mark is not sufficient to establish actionable dilution," because "mental association will not necessarily reduce the capacity of the famous mark to identify the goods of its owner, the statutory requirement for dilution." Evidence here showed that a reader was offended by the defendant's ad, but that he did not change his conception of Victoria's Secret, consequently a decision below for the plaintiff was reversed.

52. **Diluting weak marks.** Notice that the federal antidilution statute only protects "famous" marks. Let's distinguish tarnishment from blurring a mark without tarnishment. Can we take it as given that you cannot dilute by blurring a mark that is already diluted because it is weak? How could you blur a mark like Allied or Blue Ribbon?

53. **"Fair use."** (a) The Lanham Act recognizes "fair use" defenses both in confusion cases and in dilution cases.

(b) The statute recognizes what courts are calling the "classic fair use" doctrine. This occurs when the defendant uses the plaintiff's mark to describe the *defendant's* own goods or services. Plaintiff holds the trademark in "Micro Colors." The term "microcolor" is also a description of a kind of pigment and defendant describes its own product in part with the term microcolor. This can be a classic fair use. *KP Permanent Make-Up, Inc. v. Lasting Impression I, Inc.*, 328 F.3d 1061 (9th Cir. 2003), rev'd on other grounds, 543 U.S. 111, 125 S.Ct. 542, 160 L.Ed.2d 440 (2004). A mechanic advertises: "I service Volkswagens." The same? The exact scope of this defense may be arguable. See J. THOMAS MCCARTHY, TRADEMARKS AND UNFAIR COMPETITION § 11:45 (4th ed. 2005) (available on Westlaw).

(c) Courts can also recognize a different version, this one called a "nominative fair use," where the defendant uses the plaintiff's trademark to identify the *plaintiff's* product as the subject matter of discussion. For instance, the defendant might run a contest using the trademark "New Kids" and asking, "Which of the New Kids is your favorite?" In *New Kids on the Block v. News America Publishing, Inc.*, 971 F.2d 302 (9th Cir. 1992), Judge Kozinski, said that such uses of trademarks were permissible because they only involved "a non-trademark use" to which "the infringement laws simply do not apply." Why not? "Because it does not implicate the source-identification function that is the purpose of trademark...." The *New Kids* court said that protection in such a case would be granted only if the plaintiff's product or services could not readily be identified without using the plaintiff's trademark, if no more of the mark was used than necessary, and if nothing suggested sponsorship or endorsement by the plaintiff.

(d) Is all this really an affirmative defense or is it merely about whether the plaintiff has proved confusion or dilution? The plaintiff still has the burden of proving confusion, at least in some cases. *KP Permanent Make-Up, Inc. v. Lasting Impression I, Inc.*, 543 U.S. 111, 125 S.Ct. 542, 160 L.Ed.2d 440 (2004); *Century 21 Real Estate Corp. v. Lendingtree, Inc.*, 425 F.3d 211 (3d Cir. 2005).

54. **Criticizing antidilution.** One practicing lawyer has objected to the antidilution statute partly on the ground that in some cases it will

"transfer wealth from consumers to already rich mark holders" and transfer power to the already powerful. Malla Pollack, *Time to Dilute the Dilution Statute and What Not to Do When Opposing Legislation*, 78 J. PAT. & TRADEMARK OFF. SOC'Y 518 (1996). As to the power, it is the power to control cultural perceptions. On this point Pollack cites the Gay Olympics case, ¶ 68 below.

As to the wealth, Pollack instances the sale of promotional goods such as T-shirts bearing a sports team's trademarked emblems. Under the antidilution act, commercial sports teams or their licensees will be able to stop unlicensed sales of T-shirts even though such shirts do not confuse the buying public about source or sponsorship. That will mean that the price will inevitably be higher. Some courts might already get the same result without relying on antidilution statutes; they can simply insist that confusion is inevitable in such cases. See *Boston Professional Hockey Ass'n, Inc. v. Dallas Cap & Emblem Mfg., Inc.*, 510 F.2d 1004 (5th Cir. 1975). In a jurisdiction that takes a more moderate view, however, the antidilution statute creates a monopoly that will exact higher costs. What is your opinion of Pollack's two "practical" arguments?

---

15 U.S.C. § 1125 (a) [§ 43(a) of the Lanham Trademark Act]. [False advertising or unfair competition]

(a) Civil action

(1) Any person who, on or in connection with any goods or services, or any container for goods, uses in commerce any word, term, name, symbol, or device, or any combination thereof, or any false designation of origin, false or misleading description of fact, or false or misleading representation of fact, which—

(A) is likely to cause confusion, or to cause mistake, or to deceive as to the affiliation, connection, or association of such person with another person, or as to the origin, sponsorship, or approval of his or her goods, services, or commercial activities by another person, or

(B) in commercial advertising or promotion, misrepresents the nature, characteristics, qualities, or geographic origin of his or her or another person's goods, services, or commercial activities,

shall be liable in a civil action by any person who believes that he or she is or is likely to be damaged by such act.

15 U.S.C. § 1117 [§ 35]. [Equating § 32 and § 43(a) claims]

When a violation of any right of the registrant of a mark registered in the Patent and Trademark Office, or a violation under section 1125(a) [§ 43(a)] of this title, shall have been established in any civil action arising under this chapter, the plaintiff shall be entitled, subject to the provisions of sections 1111 and 1114 of this title, and subject to the principles of equity, to recover (1) defendant's profits, (2) any damages sustained by the plaintiff, and (3) the costs of the action. ... The court in exceptional cases may award reasonable attorney fees to the prevailing party.

Courtenay Communications Corp. v. Hall, 334 F.3d 210 (2d Cir. 2003). Plaintiff, suing under § 43(a), claimed rights in the unregistered mark "iMarketing News." "iMarketing" is generally understood to mean "internet marketing." The defendant argued that the mark was unprotectible because it was generic. The initial "i" in the mark was lower case, red, and in a yellow circle. The trial judge concluded that the mark was generic and dismissed the complaint. *Held,* reversed. (1) "Although CCC has not registered its mark, an unregistered mark is entitled to Lanham Act protection if it would qualify for registration. To qualify for registration, 'a mark must be capable of distinguishing the applicant's goods from those of others.' To qualify for protection, a mark must either be (1) 'inherently distinctive' or (2) distinctive by virtue of acquired secondary meaning. In contrast, generic marks ... are not registrable as trademarks. ... Essentially, a mark is generic if, in the mind of the purchasing public it does not distinguish products on the basis of source but rather refers to the type of product....

In support of its conclusion that CCC's mark is generic, the district court relied on *CES Publ'g Corp. v. St. Regis Publ'ns, Inc.* In that case, this Court determined that 'Consumer Electronics Monthly' was not a protectable trademark as a matter of law because 'consumer electronics' was a generic term describing electronic equipment. ... [But, the court noted, the mark in the present case was not a word-only mark.] [W]e conclude that whether a composite mark, which must be treated as a whole for classification purposes, is generic presents an issue of fact that cannot be resolved on the pleadings ... even if the words "iMarketing News" are generic, CCC may nonetheless be entitled to trademark protection for its composite mark as a whole. There are many examples of legally protected marks that combine generic words with distinctive lettering, coloring, or other design elements. See, e.g., *In re Miller Brewing Co.*, (holding that the genericness of the word 'LITE' did not render unprotectable Miller's use of the word with distinctive lettering). ..."

Unregistered Marks Under § 43(a)

55. **Unfair competition under § 43(a).** Section 43(a) has become the workhorse of many trademark-related claims. Initially, it extended protections of § 32 to non-registered marks. Infringement of the unregistered mark protection under § 43(a) is often called unfair competition. State laws also protect against unfair competition, that is, infringement of marks not federally registered.

False Advertising/Disparagement Claims Under § 43(a)

56. **False advertising under § 43(a).** Since the 1988 amendments, § 43(a) covers false advertising about the products of others as well as about the products of the advertiser. Does it displace common law disparagement?

57. **Limits on false advertising claims—commercial promotions.** There is a limit on what publication can count as false advertising under § 43(a). A false and disparaging ad about your product may be actionable, but only because it is a part of "commercial advertising or promotion." The same disparaging statement made in, say, a book review, does not generate liability under § 43(a). (Look at the statute for the textual basis for this rule.) The result looks like about the same protection for speech we will see in the right of publicity cases in the next section.

58. **Limits on false advertising claims—puffing.** Advertising that merely "puffs" the product is not actionable under § 43(a) unless the puffing implies some specific assertion of verifiable fact. "Puffery exists in two general forms: (1) exaggerated statements of bluster or boast upon which no reasonable consumer would rely; and (2) vague or highly subjective claims of product superiority, including bald assertions of superiority." *American Italian Pasta Co. v. New World Pasta Co.,* 371 F.3d 387 (8th Cir. 2004). What about advertising that the defendant's product is the world's best? What if the defendant falsely added that a scientific test showed that customers agreed?

59. **Limits on false advertising claims—consumer suits.** So far, consumers with no special status have been denied standing to sue under § 43(a). See J. THOMAS MCCARTHY, TRADEMARKS AND UNFAIR COMPETITION § 27:398 (4th Ed. 2004). However, states may permit suits by individual consumers to redress public and consumer interests in honest advertising. *Keimer v. Buena Vista Books, Inc.,* 75 Cal.App.4th 1220, 89 Cal.Rptr.2d 781(1999), printed in Ch. 15, is such a case.

Trade Dress and Product Designs as Marks Under § 43(a)

60. **Trade dress functioning as a protected mark under § 43(a).** Under § 43(a) and as a general principle of unfair competition, "a distinctive overall appearance of a container, label, or means of packaging a product can work as a trademark independent of any specific trademark accompanying such packaging." DOBBS ON TORTS § 458 (2001 & Supps.). Trade dress, like a formal mark, can even be inherently distinctive, so that it can be protected even if it has no acquired or secondary meaning. See *Two Pesos, Inc. v. Taco Cabana, Inc.,* 505 U.S. 763, 112 S.Ct. 2753, 120 L.Ed.2d 615 (1992) (restaurant decor).

61. **Product design functioning as a protected mark.** Recall the *Qualitex* discussion of functionality. If a product's design is functional, the design itself cannot be protected as a mark. Suppose, however, that the product's design is not functional. Can the design be an inherently distinctive mark? Suppose a fashion designer produces this

year's line of upscale garments sold at high prices. A discount store copies them and sells closely similar garments at low prices. Would the fashion designer have a claim that the discounter infringed its trade dress or would some additional evidence be required? See *Wal-Mart Stores, Inc. v. Samara Bros., Inc.,* 529 U.S. 205, 120 S.Ct. 1339, 146 L.Ed.2d 182 (2000) (designs are not inherently distinctive and must acquire a secondary meaning before protection can be afforded).

62. **Protection for nonfunctional designs.** *Bonito* makes it clear that trademark interests in product design or trade dress can be protected under one specific and important condition—that is, when the product design is not functional. Because if the design is functional, the free competition rules for unpatented items must control. *Qualitex* recognizes this point. It is an important limitation on what can be protected under the Lanham Act or the state laws of unfair competition.

63. **What is functional?** A design is functional if it is beneficial to the marketer in some way besides identifying the source of the product or services, and it assists in effective competition and if no other design can perform the same function efficiently. See RESTATEMENT (THIRD) OF UNFAIR COMPETITION § 17. What about frozen beads of ice cream of a specific size? See *Dippin' Dots, Inc. v. Frosty Bites Distribution, LLC.,* 369 F.3d 1197 (11th Cir. 2004) (dot size contributed to product's creamy taste, hence functional). If the plaintiff's product had once been patented but the patent had expired, would that show the product was functional? See *Traffix Devices, Inc. v. Marketing Displays, Inc.,* 532 U.S. 23, 121 S.Ct. 1255, 149 L.Ed.2d 164 (2001).

ROGERS v. GRIMALDI

875 F.2d 994 (2d Cir. 1989)*

JON O. NEWMAN, Circuit Judge.

Appellant Ginger Rogers and the late Fred Astaire are among the most famous duos in show business history. Through their incomparable performances in Hollywood musicals, Ginger Rogers and Fred Astaire established themselves as paragons of style, elegance, and grace. A testament to their international recognition, and a key circumstance in this case, is the fact that Rogers and Astaire are among that small elite of the entertainment world whose identities are readily called to mind by just their first names, particularly the pairing "Ginger and Fred." This appeal presents a conflict between Rogers' right to protect her celebrated name and the right of others to express themselves freely in their own artistic work. Specifically, we must decide whether Rogers can prevent the use of the title "Ginger and Fred" for a fictional movie that only obliquely relates to Rogers and Astaire. . . .

[A]ppellees produced and distributed in the United States and Europe a film entitled "Ginger and Fred," created and directed by famed

* Excerpts are in proper sequence but not all omissions are indicated.

Italian film-maker Federico Fellini. The film tells the story of two fictional Italian cabaret performers, Pippo and Amelia, who, in their heyday, imitated Rogers and Astaire and became known in Italy as "Ginger and Fred." The film focuses on a televised reunion of Pippo and Amelia, many years after their retirement. Appellees describe the film as the bittersweet story of these two fictional dancers and as a satire of contemporary television variety shows.

[Rogers claims under § 43(a) of the Lanham Act and also under state-law right of publicity.] The District Court ruled that because of First Amendment concerns, the Lanham Act cannot apply to the title of a motion picture where the title is "within the realm of artistic expression," and is not "primarily intended to serve a commercial purpose." Use of the title "Ginger and Fred" did not violate the Act, the Court concluded, because of the undisputed artistic relevance of the title to the content of the film. In effect, the District Court's ruling would create a nearly absolute privilege for movie titles, insulating them from Lanham Act claims as long as the film itself is an artistic work, and the title is relevant to the film's content. We think that approach unduly narrows the scope of the Act.

Movies, plays, books, and songs are all indisputably works of artistic expression and deserve protection. Nonetheless, they are also sold in the commercial marketplace like other more utilitarian products, making the danger of consumer deception a legitimate concern that warrants some government regulation. The purchaser of a book, like the purchaser of a can of peas, has a right not to be misled as to the source of the product. Thus, it is well established that where the title of a movie or a book has acquired secondary meaning—that is, where the title is sufficiently well known that consumers associate it with a particular author's work—the holder of the rights to that title may prevent the use of the same or confusingly similar titles by other authors. Indeed, it would be ironic if, in the name of the First Amendment, courts did not recognize the right of authors to protect titles of their creative work against infringement by other authors.

Though First Amendment concerns do not insulate titles of artistic works from all Lanham Act claims, such concerns must nonetheless inform our consideration of the scope of the Act as applied to claims involving such titles. Titles, like the artistic works they identify, are of a hybrid nature, combining artistic expression and commercial promotion. The title of a movie may be both an integral element of the film-maker's expression as well as a significant means of marketing the film to the public. The artistic and commercial elements of titles are inextricably intertwined. Film-makers and authors frequently rely on word-play, ambiguity, irony, and allusion in titling their works. Furthermore, their interest in freedom of artistic expression is shared by their audience. The subtleties of a title can enrich a reader's or a viewer's understanding of a work. Consumers of artistic works thus have a dual interest: They have an interest in not being misled and they also have an interest in enjoying the results of the author's freedom of expression. For all these reasons, the expressive element of titles requires more protection than the labeling of ordinary commercial products.

Because overextension of Lanham Act restrictions in the area of titles might intrude on First Amendment values, we must construe the Act narrowly to avoid such a conflict.

Rogers contends that First Amendment concerns are implicated only where a title is so intimately related to the subject matter of a work that the author has no alternative means of expressing what the work is about. This "no alternative avenues of communication" standard derives from Lloyd Corp. v. Tanner, 407 U.S. 551, 566–67, 92 S.Ct. 2219, 2227–28, 33 L.Ed.2d 131 (1972). . . . In Lloyd, the issue was whether the First Amendment provided war protesters with the right to distribute leaflets on a shopping center owner's property. The Supreme Court held that it did not. But a restriction on the location of a speech is different from a restriction on the words the speaker may use. . . .

Thus, the "no alternative avenues" test does not sufficiently accommodate the public's interest in free expression, while the District Court's rule—that the Lanham Act is inapplicable to all titles that can be considered artistic expression—does not sufficiently protect the public against flagrant deception. We believe that in general the Act should be construed to apply to artistic works only where the public interest in avoiding consumer confusion outweighs the public interest in free expression. In the context of allegedly misleading titles using a celebrity's name, that balance will normally not support application of the Act unless the title has no artistic relevance to the underlying work whatsoever, or, if it has some artistic relevance, unless the title explicitly misleads as to the source or the content of the work.

[Sponsorship confusion.] Many titles, however, include a well-known name without any overt indication of authorship or endorsement—for example, the hit song "Bette Davis Eyes," and the recent film "Come Back to the Five and Dime, Jimmy Dean, Jimmy Dean." To some people, these titles might implicitly suggest that the named celebrity had endorsed the work or had a role in producing it. Even if that suggestion is false, the title is artistically relevant to the work. In these circumstances, the slight risk that such use of a celebrity's name might implicitly suggest endorsement or sponsorship to some people is outweighed by the danger of restricting artistic expression, and the Lanham Act is not applicable.

[Source confusion.] [M]any titles with a celebrity's name make no explicit statement that the work is about that person in any direct sense; the relevance of the title may be oblique and may become clear only after viewing or reading the work. As to such titles, the consumer interest in avoiding deception is too slight to warrant application of the Lanham Act. Though consumers frequently look to the title of a work to determine what it is about, they do not regard titles of artistic works in the same way as the names of ordinary commercial products. Since consumers expect an ordinary product to be what the name says it is, we apply

the Lanham Act with some rigor to prohibit names that misdescribe such goods. But most consumers are well aware that they cannot judge a book solely by its title any more than by its cover. We therefore need not interpret the Act to require that authors select titles that unambiguously describe what the work is about nor to preclude them from using titles that are only suggestive of some topics that the work is not about. Where a title with at least some artistic relevance to the work is not explicitly misleading as to the content of the work, it is not false advertising under the Lanham Act.

[Common law "right of publicity" claims.] The common law right of publicity, where it has been recognized, grants celebrities an exclusive right to control the commercial value of their names and to prevent others from exploiting them without permission. Because the right of publicity, unlike the Lanham Act, has no likelihood of confusion requirement, it is potentially more expansive than the Lanham Act. Perhaps for that reason, courts delineating the right of publicity, more frequently than in applying the Lanham Act, have recognized the need to limit the right to accommodate First Amendment concerns. . . .

We think New York would recognize similar limits in Oregon law on the right of publicity. We note, for example, that the Oregon Supreme Court has on occasion interpreted the free speech clause of the Oregon Constitution as providing broader protection for free expression than that mandated by the federal Constitution. . . .

64. **Titles in copyright law.** Although the copyright statute does not so provide, courts have refused to give copyright protection to literary titles standing alone. See J. THOMAS MCCARTHY, TRADEMARKS AND UNFAIR COMPETITION § 10:34 (4th Ed. 2004)(on Westlaw). Yet according to the *Rogers* court, the title may be "an integral element of the film-maker's expression," and "authors frequently rely on word-play, ambiguity, irony, and allusion in titling their works." Doesn't that sound like plenty of reason to apply copyright protection?

65. **Titles as marks under § 43(a).** But, as *Rogers v. Grimaldi* says, even a title that is not fanciful or arbitrary may come to have secondary meaning and thus distinctively identify the plaintiff's works. In that case, the title can be a protected as a trademark or under § 43(a). Such an outcome is easiest to understand when the title refers to a series of books, magazines, or television shows, see *Herbko Int'l, Inc. v. Kappa Books, Inc.,* 308 F.3d 1156 (Fed. Cir. 2002) ("title of a single book cannot serve as a source identifier"); but maybe even a single title could be protected under § 43(a). See *EMI Catalogue Partnership v. Hill, Holliday, Connors, Cosmopulos Inc.,* 228 F.3d 56 (2d Cir. 2000) (song title, "Sing, Sing, Sing (With a Swing)," associated with Big Band and swing era, may be protected against commercial use in a golf club commercial using swing music and the legend "Swing, Swing, Swing").

66. **Corporate and personal names or persona.** Firm names and even personal names, may be protected against unfair competition under § 43(a), provided that the name has acquired a secondary mean-

ing identifying the source or origin of the "product." See *White v. Samsung Electronics America, Inc.*, 971 F.2d 1395 (9th Cir. 1992) (in some cases at least, the "mark" means the celebrity's persona); *Flynn v. AK Peters, Ltd.*, 377 F.3d 13 (1st Cir. 2004) (but secondary meaning of plaintiff's personal name not established on the evidence).

67. **Speech rights: Stop Olympic Prison.** The U. S. Olympic Committee is chartered by Congress. Its symbols and the term "Olympic" and its variations are given all the protections of the Lanham Act. (36 U. S. C. § 380.) A group known as Stop the Olympic Prison (STOP) was opposed to plans to convert Olympic Village in Lake Placid, N.Y., into a federal prison. It was a non-profit group whose sole purpose was this campaign. It published posters advertising its position. These reflected some of the protected Olympic symbols, including the distinctive five interlocked rings. After the Committee demanded that STOP cease using these symbols, STOP sued for declaratory judgment, claiming free speech rights. The court found that the poster did not violate the statute or infringe trademark rights because there was no confusion as to either source or sponsorship. *Stop the Olympic Prison v. U.S. Olympic Com.*, 489 F.Supp. 1112 (S.D.N.Y. 1980).

68. **Speech rights: Gay Olympics.** In *San Francisco Arts & Athletics, Inc. v. United States Olympic Committee*, 483 U.S. 522, 107 S.Ct. 2971, 97 L.Ed.2d 427 (1987), the defendant sponsored the Gay Olympic Games, which were to parallel the Olympic Games in activities, location and style. The plaintiffs, US Olympic and International Olympic Committees, sued to enjoin use of the protected term "Olympic." The trial court granted a TRO and preliminary injunction and ultimately a permanent injunction. The Ninth Circuit affirmed. The Supreme Court affirmed the Ninth Circuit. The special Olympic Games statute was read to mean that the term and symbol are protected even if their use does not cause confusion. The Lanham Act defenses are not incorporated. Is the protection so extended unconstitutional? Petitioner argues that it would be unconstitutional to protect a generic word, and that Olympic is such a word; and that the first amendment prohibits protection of any term in the absence of a likelihood of confusion.

> This Court has recognized that words are not always fungible, and that the suppression of particular words runs[s] a substantial risk of suppressing ideas in the process. The SFAA argues that this principle prohibits Congress from granting the USOC exclusive control of uses of the word "Olympic," a word that the SFAA views as generic. Yet this recognition always has been balanced against the principle that when a word acquires value "as the result of organization and expenditure of labor, skill, and money" by an entity, that entity constitutionally may obtain a limited property right in the word. *International News Service v. Associated Press*, 248 U.S 215, 239, 39 S.Ct. 68, 63 L.Ed. 211 (1918).

The petitioner also argued that the way in which USOC enforced its proprietary rights was discriminatory and thus violated the Fifth

Amendment. But the Court held that the USOC, though chartered by the government, is not a governmental entity and there is no governmental action here. Hence discriminatory enforcement need not be considered.

69. **Speech rights: dilution/tarnishment.** Suppose the defendant sells posters for such uses as dorm room decoration. One poster shows a girl scout, in uniform, very, very pregnant. Another, using the one-time slogan of United Airlines, shows two ducks coupling in flight with the slogan "Fly United." Another, using a script familiar to soft-drink purchasers, says "Enjoy Cocaine." Perhaps all these posters tarnish a trademark by associating it with something undesirable or at least with something that detracts from the mark. Claims in such cases have been held actionable. You might evaluate the desirability of tarnishment claims by considering what courts would say if you brought the claim under the law of defamation. Imagine, for instance, that it was Campari, not Falwell, who sued Hustler Magazine for its disgusting "First Time" ad parody. (*Hustler Magazine v. Falwell,* 485 U.S. 46, 108 S.Ct. 876, 99 L.Ed.2d 41 (1988), Chapter 4, § 5).

70. **Speech rights: non-commercial speech.** The Lanham Act § 32, supra, refers to commercial use, and more specifically, to the use of a mark "in connection with the sale, offering for sale, distribution, or advertising of any goods or services." We saw in *Ty,* supra and in ¶ 53, supra, that nominative, non-confusing uses of a mark are not actionable. The same point can be made by saying that the use must be commercial, in connection with sale or advertizing of goods or services. That rule is a speech protector. In *Bosley Med. Institute, Inc. v. Kremer,* 403 F.3d 672 (9th Cir. 2005), the defendant used the plaintiff's mark in leveling criticisms of the plaintiff's services. The court held this use was non-commercial and not actionable.

---

§ 5. THE RIGHT OF PUBLICITY—PRIVACY

71. **Commercial appropriation—the dignitary interest.** The right of privacy conceived as four torts included one usually called commercial appropriation. The model for this tort came from early privacy cases in which the plaintiff's name, face, or figure was used in commercial advertising. The earliest plaintiffs suing for commercial appropriation were private individuals whose likeness was used in advertising apparently because it happened to be available as an illustration. These cases had nothing to do with any particular fame of the plaintiff, who indeed seems to have had none. The emphasis in the courts was upon the plaintiff's liberty interest—her right to choose privacy over publicity—her dignitary interests, and her feelings. See *Pavesich v. New England Life Ins. Co.,* 122 Ga. 190, 50 S.E. 68 (1905). The 1977 RESTATEMENT (SECOND) characterized the plaintiff's interests as one of

property, and also foreclosed liability for any "incidental" use of the plaintiff's name. RESTATEMENT § 552C, cmts. a & d. In some states there is a statutory claim for commercial appropriation of name or likeness for commercial or advertising purposes. In *Tyne v. Time Warner Ent'mt Co., L.P.*, 901 So.2d 802 (Fla. 2005), a movie, *The Perfect Storm*, was a fictionalized version of a real event in which several men died. Their survivors, aggrieved at the fictional depiction of the men and of themselves, sued under such a statute. But the court held that a movie that does not promote the sale of a product is not a commercial or advertising purpose.

CARSON V. HERE'S JOHNNY PORTABLE TOILETS, INC., 698 F.2d 831 (6th Cir. 1983). Plaintiff John W. Carson is a famous entertainer, whose "Tonight Show" on television was introduced with the phrase "Here's Johnny." The phrase is generally associated with Carson and the show by a substantial segment of the television viewing public. Carson has authorized use of the phrase by others, who have used it to identify restaurants, men's clothing and men's toiletries. The defendant is a corporation which rents and sells portable toilets under the name "Here's Johnny." The founder was aware of the television significance of the phrase when he adopted it for the toilets. Carson sued. The trial court dismissed the claim. *Held*, vacated and remanded for further proceedings. (1) The "Here's Johnny" mark is a relatively "weak" mark, so that its use on other goods should not be entirely foreclosed, and there is insufficient evidence to establish a likelihood of confusion. Consequently the trademark claim fails. (2) Prosser delineated four types of the right of privacy, including intrusion upon solitude, public disclosure of embarrassing private facts, publicity that places one in a false light, and commercial appropriation of one's name for the defendant's advantage. The first three involve the right to be let alone, but the fourth is best referred to, not as a privacy claim, but as a right of publicity. In this case there is no violation of any real right to privacy, even though Carson may be embarrassed to be associated with the defendant's product. However, there is an invasion of the right of publicity, since the plaintiff's identity is valuable in the promotion of products and he has an interest in preventing unauthorized commercial exploitation of that identity.

MIDLER V. FORD MOTOR CO., 849 F.2d 460 (9th Cir. 1988). Midler is a famous actress-singer. She does not do commercials. The defendant wished to do a commercial with Midler singing a "signature song" closely identified with her, but her agent refused. The defendant then produced the commercial with another person imitating Midler's distinctive voice. The defendant had licensed the copyright of the song and Midler only claims that her identity was appropriated. *Held,* the defendant's appropriation of Midler's voice is actionable under California law. When a distinctive voice of a professional singer is widely known and deliberately imitated to sell a product, the sellers have appropriated property and thus have committed a California tort.

---

72. **Market value of one's name or likeness.** If the plaintiff's only interest is a property interest, can it be argued that a private plaintiff who enjoys no fame or public standing has no market for her name or likeness and hence has no action for commercial appropriation? In *Cox v. Hatch,* 761 P.2d 556 (Utah 1988), Senator Orin Hatch, as part of a reelection campaign, posed for photos with federal postal workers. They consented to pose but did not consent to use of their photos in the campaign. Senator Hatch nevertheless used pictures in his political campaign. But the Utah Court concluded that the workers' likenesses had no "intrinsic value" and that one worker was, for this purpose, pretty much interchangeable with another, so that Senator Hatch was not liable for the appropriation. That view converts the dignitary tort rights to a species of intangible property with damages limited by the value of that property—nothing for a nobody. See also *Dwyer v. American Express Co.*, 273 Ill.App.3d 742, 210 Ill.Dec. 375, 652 N.E.2d 1351 (1995). Could courts recognize both kinds of appropriation and award damages appropriate to the facts? The Supreme Court of Colorado thought that the plaintiff would have the dignitary claim for distress even if she had no identity of commercial value. *Joe Dickerson & Assocs., LLC v. Dittmar,* 34 P.3d 995 (Colo. 2001). Another possibility is that the plaintiff might recover an award based on restitution—the defendant's gain rather than on the plaintiff's loss. See Restatement (Third) of Unfair Competition § 49(1) (1995).

73. **"Noncommercial" use.** Would Midler be entitled to recover if a comic used her voice or mannerisms in a comic skit? If a biographer wrote a biography over her objection? If a newspaper publishes a photograph of her attending an award dinner? The right of publicity is a right to control one's identity in commercial matters or matters of "trade." This is understood to exclude any right to control use of identity in news reporting or commentary, biography, or fiction. The Restatement also excludes "entertainment" and advertising incidental to it. Restatement (Third) of Unfair Competition § 47. Compare the non-commercial and nominative uses of trademark.

74. **Forms of invasion.** At least two more or less distinct forms of invasion can be seen in the cases. (a) The first and most common is the use of elements of the plaintiff's identity in selling something. The defendant might use a personality element of the plaintiff in advertising, as in *Midler*. As to this there is room for litigation over what, besides name or likeness, counts as identity. The defendant might also use elements of the plaintiff's personality as the very thing to be sold. A direct sale of the plaintiff's image would hardly be less intrusive on the plaintiff's commercial rights, so that if the defendant makes posters or

prints for sale to the plaintiff's admirers, this too may be a violation of the right of publicity.

(b) The second is associated with style, mannerisms and other qualities involved in presenting a persona. McCarthy refers to these as "performance values." J. Thomas McCarthy, *The Human Persona as Commercial property: The Right of Publicity*, 19 COLUM.-VLA J.L. & ARTS 129 (1995). Should people be forbidden to put on shows dressed like the Beatles or attempting to look like Elvis Presley?

75. **Intent.** Intent to infringe the right of publicity or even to identify the plaintiff is not required to establish the tort. RESTATEMENT (THIRD) OF UNFAIR COMPETITION § 46, cmt. e.

76. **Duration.** In trademark cases, the mark can lapse if the plaintiff ceases using it to identify the product. In copyright and patent cases the statutes and the courts have made it clear that the time limitation on the monopoly is an important element in the right. Should courts impose a time-limit on the right of publicity? Or should they forever enjoin Elvis imitators from their nefarious public entertainments throughout eternity?

Authority is divided. In *Martin Luther King, Jr., Center for Social Change, Inc. v. American Heritage Products, Inc.*, 250 Ga. 135, 296 S.E.2d 697 (1982), the defendant was making and selling busts of Dr. King after his death. The administrator of his estate and Motown Record Corporation as assignee of rights during King's lifetime claimed an infringement of their property rights in King's identity. The court held that the right of publicity survived death of the person holding that right and that it did so even if the celebrity did not exploit the right during his lifetime and that this property right could be transferred by will or inheritance. "Recognition of the right of publicity rewards and thereby encourages effort and creativity. If the right of publicity dies with the celebrity, the economic value of the right of publicity during life would be diminished because the celebrity's untimely death would seriously impair, if not destroy, the value of the right of continued commercial use." Statutes in some states provide for descendibility of the right of publicity. In *Comedy III Productions, Inc. v. Gary Saderup, Inc.,* 25 Cal.4th 387, 21 P.3d 797, 106 Cal.Rptr.2d 126 (2001), the rights of publicity of the men known as the Three Stooges had passed to a corporation on their death. The corporation successfully sued an artist who sketched pictures of the Three on tee shirts and was entitled to recover the artist's profits.

77. **Do we need the right of publicity?** Could you fairly protect all legitimate interests of celebrities by dropping the right of publicity and relying instead on trademark or copyright law? Personal names can function as trademarks under the ordinary trademark rules, provided the name has acquired secondary meaning. See J. THOMAS MCCARTHY, TRADEMARKS AND UNFAIR COMPETITION § 12:2 (4th ed. 2004). Midler presumably cannot copyright her unique voice because it is not fixed in a tangible medium. She could make a recording of her voice and copyright

that, which would give her rights of performance. But recall that in her claim against Ford Motor Company, she did not own the copyright to the song and apparently did not own the copyright to any recording of a performance. Since copyright law preempts state law equivalents and conflicting laws, you might even argue that her claim was preempted. But the *Midler* court held not, because, it said, "A voice is not copyrightable. The sounds are not 'fixed.' What is put forward as protectible here is more personal than any work of authorship."

WHITE v. SAMSUNG ELECTRONICS AMERICA, INC.

971 F.2d 1395 (9th Cir. 1992)

GOODWIN, Senior Circuit Judge. . . .

Plaintiff Vanna White is the hostess of "Wheel of Fortune," one of the most popular game shows in television history. An estimated forty million people watch the program daily. Capitalizing on the fame which her participation in the show has bestowed on her, White markets her identity to various advertisers.

The dispute in this case arose out of a series of advertisements prepared for Samsung by Deutsch. The series ran in at least half a dozen publications with widespread, and in some cases national, circulation. Each of the advertisements in the series followed the same theme. Each depicted a current item from popular culture and a Samsung electronic product. Each was set in the twenty-first century and conveyed the message that the Samsung product would still be in use by that time. By hypothesizing outrageous future outcomes for the cultural items, the ads created humorous effects. For example, one lampooned current popular notions of an unhealthy diet by depicting a raw steak with the caption: "Revealed to be health food. 2010 A.D." Another depicted irreverent "news"-show host Morton Downey Jr. in front of an American flag with the caption: "Presidential candidate. 2008 A.D."

The advertisement which prompted the current dispute was for Samsung video-cassette recorders (VCRs). The ad depicted a robot, dressed in a wig, gown, and jewelry which Deutsch consciously selected to resemble White's hair and dress. The robot was posed next to a game board which is instantly recognizable as the Wheel of Fortune game show set, in a stance for which White is famous. The caption of the ad read: "Longest-running game show. 2012 A.D." Defendants referred to the ad as the "Vanna White" ad. Unlike the other celebrities used in the campaign, White neither consented to the ads nor was she paid.

Following the circulation of the robot ad, White sued Samsung and Deutsch in federal district court under: (1) California Civil Code § 3344; (2) the California common law right of publicity; and (3) § 43(a) of the Lanham Act, 15 U.S.C. § 1125(a). The district court granted summary judgment against White on each of her claims. White now appeals.

I. Section 3344

White first argues that the district court erred in rejecting her claim under section 3344. Section 3344(a) provides, in pertinent part, that "[a]ny person who knowingly uses another's name, voice, signature, photograph, or likeness, in any manner, ... for purposes of advertising or selling, ... without such person's prior consent ... shall be liable for any damages sustained by the person or persons injured as a result thereof."

White argues that the Samsung advertisement used her "likeness" in contravention of section 3344. ...

In this case, Samsung and Deutsch used a robot with mechanical features, and not, for example, a manikin molded to White's precise features. Without deciding for all purposes when a caricature or impressionistic resemblance might become a "likeness," we agree with the district court that the robot at issue here was not White's "likeness" within the meaning of section 3344. Accordingly, we affirm the court's dismissal of White's section 3344 claim.

II. Right of Publicity

White next argues that the district court erred in granting summary judgment to defendants on White's common law right of publicity claim. ...

Even though Prosser focused on appropriations of name or likeness in discussing the right of publicity, he noted that "[i]t is not impossible that there might be appropriation of the plaintiff's identity, as by impersonation, without the use of either his name or his likeness, and that this would be an invasion of his right of privacy." At the time Prosser wrote, he noted however, that "[n]o such case appears to have arisen."

Since Prosser's early formulation, the case law has borne out his insight that the right of publicity is not limited to the appropriation of name or likeness. [Citing and discussing *Carson*, *Midler* and another case.]

Indeed, if we treated the means of appropriation as dispositive in our analysis of the right of publicity, we would not only weaken the right but effectively eviscerate it. The right would fail to protect those plaintiffs most in need of its protection. Advertisers use celebrities to promote their products. The more popular the celebrity, the greater the number of people who recognize her, and the greater the visibility for the product. The identities of the most popular celebrities are not only the most attractive for advertisers, but also the easiest to evoke without resorting to obvious means such as name, likeness, or voice. ...

Television and other media create marketable celebrity identity value. Considerable energy and ingenuity are expended by those who have achieved celebrity value to exploit it for profit. The law protects the celebrity's sole right to exploit this value whether the celebrity has achieved her fame out of rare ability, dumb luck, or a combination thereof. We decline Samsung and Deutch's invitation to permit the evisceration of the common law right of publicity through means as facile as those in this case. Because White has alleged facts showing that Samsung and Deutsch had appropriated her identity, the district court erred by rejecting, on summary judgment, White's common law right of publicity claim.

[The court also held that White had made a jury issue on her Lanham Act claim as to whether there was "confusion," specifically whether it implied her endorsement of the product.]

IV. The Parody Defense

In defense, defendants cite a number of cases for the proposition that their robot ad constituted protected speech. The only cases they cite which are even remotely relevant to this case are Hustler Magazine v. Falwell, 485 U.S. 46, 108 S.Ct. 876, 99 L.Ed.2d 41 (1988) and L.L. Bean, Inc. v. Drake Publishers, Inc., 811 F.2d 26 (1st Cir.1987). Those cases involved parodies of advertisements run for the purpose of poking fun at Jerry Falwell and L.L. Bean, respectively. This case involves a true advertisement run for the purpose of selling Samsung VCRs. The ad's spoof of Vanna White and Wheel of Fortune is subservient and only tangentially related to the ad's primary message: "buy Samsung VCRs." Defendants' parody arguments are better addressed to non-commercial parodies. The difference between a "parody" and a "knock-off" is the difference between fun and profit.

ALARCON, Circuit Judge, Concurring and dissenting. . . .

The effect of the majority's holding on expressive conduct is difficult to estimate. The majority's position seems to allow any famous person or entity to bring suit based on any commercial advertisement that depicts a character or role performed by the plaintiff. Under the majority's view of the law, Gene Autry could have brought an action for damages against all other singing cowboys. Clint Eastwood would be able to sue anyone who plays a tall, soft-spoken cowboy, unless, of course, Jimmy Stewart had not previously enjoined Clint Eastwood. . . . May Black and Decker, maker of the "Dustbuster" portable vacuum, now sue "Bust-dusters," the Los Angeles topless cleaning service. Can the Los Angeles Kings hockey team state a cause of action against the City of Las Vegas for its billboards reading "L.A. has the Kings, but we have the Aces." . . .

WHITE v. SAMSUNG ELECTRONICS AMERICA, INC.

989 F.2d 1512 (9th Cir. 1993)

KOZINSKI, Circuit Judge, with whom Circuit Judges O'SCANNLAIN and KLEINFELD join, dissenting from the order rejecting the suggestion for rehearing en banc. . . .

Private property, including intellectual property, is essential to our way of life. It provides an incentive for investment and innovation; it stimulates the flourishing of our culture; it protects the moral entitlements of people to the fruits of their labors. But reducing too much to private property can be bad medicine. Private land, for instance, is far more useful if separated from other private land by public streets, roads and highways. Public parks, utility rights-of-way and sewers reduce the amount of land in private hands, but vastly enhance the value of the property that remains.

So too it is with intellectual property. Overprotecting intellectual property is as harmful as under protecting it. Creativity is impossible without a rich public domain. Nothing today, likely nothing since we tamed fire, is genuinely new: Culture, like science and technology, grows by accretion, each new creator building on the works of those who came before. Overprotection stifles the very creative forces it's supposed to nurture.

The panel's opinion is a classic case of overprotection. Concerned about what it sees as a wrong done to Vanna White, the panel majority erects a property right of remarkable and dangerous breadth: Under the majority's opinion, it's now a tort for advertisers to remind the public of a celebrity. Not to use a celebrity's name, voice, signature or likeness; not to imply the celebrity endorses a product; but simply to evoke the celebrity's image in the public's mind. This Orwellian notion withdraws far more from the public domain than prudence and common sense allow. It conflicts with the Copyright Act and the Copyright Clause. It raises serious First Amendment problems. It's bad law, and it deserves a long, hard second look. . . .

Consider how sweeping this new right is. What is it about the ad that makes people think of White? It's not the robot's wig, clothes or jewelry; there must be ten million blond women (many of them quasi-famous) who wear dresses and jewelry like White's. It's that the robot is posed near the "Wheel of Fortune" game board. Remove the game board from the ad, and no one would think of Vanna White. But once you include the game board, anybody standing beside it—a brunette woman, a man wearing women's clothes, a monkey in a wig and gown—would evoke White's image, precisely the way the robot did. It's the "Wheel of Fortune" set, not the robot's face or dress or jewelry that evokes White's image. The panel is giving White an exclusive right not in what she looks like or who she is, but in what she does for a living.

This is entirely the wrong place to strike the balance. Intellectual property rights aren't free: They're imposed at the expense of future creators and of the public at large. Where would we be if Charles Lindbergh had an exclusive right in the concept of a heroic solo aviator? If Arthur Conan Doyle had gotten a copyright in the idea of the detective story, or Albert Einstein had patented the theory of relativity? If every author and celebrity had been given the right to keep people from mocking them or their work? Surely this would have made the world poorer, not richer, culturally as well as economically. . . .

Moreover, consider the moral dimension, about which the panel majority seems to have gotten so exercised. Saying Samsung "appropriated" something of White's begs the question: Should White have the exclusive right to something as broad and amorphous as her "identity"? Samsung's ad didn't simply copy White's schtick—like all parody, it created something new. True, Samsung did it to make money, but White does whatever she does to make money, too; the majority talks of "the difference between fun and profit," but in the entertainment industry fun is profit. Why is Vanna White's right to exclusive for-profit use of her persona—a persona that might not even be her own creation, but that of a writer, director or producer—superior to Samsung's right to profit by creating its own inventions? Why should she have such absolute rights to control the conduct of others, unlimited by the idea-expression dichotomy or by the fair use doctrine? ...

The panel, however, does more than misinterpret California law: By refusing to recognize a parody exception to the right of publicity, the panel directly contradicts the federal Copyright Act. Samsung didn't merely parody Vanna White. It parodied Vanna White appearing in "Wheel of Fortune," a copyrighted television show, and parodies of copyrighted works are governed by federal copyright law. ...

The majority's decision decimates this federal scheme. It's impossible to parody a movie or a TV show without at the same time "evok[ing]" the "identit[ies]" of the actors. You can't have a mock Star Wars without a mock Luke Skywalker, Han Solo and Princess Leia, which in turn means a mock Mark Hamill, Harrison Ford and Carrie Fisher. ... The public's right to make a fair use parody and the copyright owner's right to license a derivative work are useless if the parodist is held hostage by every actor whose "identity" he might need to "appropriate." ...

The majority's decision also conflicts with the federal copyright system in another, more insidious way. ... [T]he right of publicity isn't geographically limited. A right of publicity created by one state applies to conduct everywhere, so long as it involves a celebrity domiciled in that state. If a Wyoming resident creates an ad that features a California domiciliary's name or likeness, he'll be subject to California right of publicity law even if he's careful to keep the ad from being shown in California.

The broader and more ill-defined one state's right of publicity, the more it interferes with the legitimate interests of other states. A limited right that applies to unauthorized use of name and likeness probably does not run afoul of the Copyright Clause, but the majority's protection of "identity" is quite another story. Under the majority's approach, any time anybody in the United States—even somebody who lives in a state with a very narrow right of publicity—creates an ad, he takes the risk that it might remind some segment of the public of somebody, perhaps somebody with only a local reputation, somebody the advertiser has never heard of. ...

Finally, I can't see how giving White the power to keep others from evoking her image in the public's mind can be squared with the First Amendment. Where does White get this right to control our thoughts? The majority's creation goes way beyond the protection given a trademark or a copyrighted work, or a person's name or likeness. All those things control one particular way of expressing an idea, one way of referring to an object or a person. But not allowing any means of reminding people of someone? That's a speech restriction unparalleled in First Amendment law. . . .

What's more, I doubt even a name-and-likeness-only right of publicity can stand without a parody exception. The First Amendment isn't just about religion or politics—it's also about protecting the free development of our national culture. Parody, humor, irreverence are all vital components of the marketplace of ideas. The last thing we need, the last thing the First Amendment will tolerate, is a law that lets public figures keep people from mocking them, or from "evok[ing]" their images in the mind of the public.

The majority dismisses the First Amendment issue out of hand because Samsung's ad was commercial speech. Id. at 1401 & n. 3. So what? Commercial speech may be less protected by the First Amendment than noncommercial speech, but less protected means protected nonetheless. And there are very good reasons for this. Commercial speech has a profound effect on our culture and our attitudes. Neutral-seeming ads influence people's social and political attitudes, and themselves arouse political controversy. "Where's the Beef?" turned from an advertising catchphrase into the only really memorable thing about the 1984 presidential campaign. Four years later, Michael Dukakis called George Bush "the Joe Isuzu of American politics."

In our pop culture, where salesmanship must be entertaining and entertainment must sell, the line between the commercial and noncommercial has not merely blurred; it has disappeared. Is the Samsung parody any different from a parody on Saturday Night Live or in Spy Magazine? Both are equally profit-motivated. Both use a celebrity's identity to sell things—one to sell VCRs, the other to sell advertising. Both mock their subjects. Both try to make people laugh. Both add something, perhaps something worthwhile and memorable, perhaps not, to our culture. Both are things that the people being portrayed might dearly want to suppress.

For better or worse, we are the Court of Appeals for the Hollywood Circuit. Millions of people toil in the shadow of the law we make, and much of their livelihood is made possible by the existence of intellectual property rights. But much of their livelihood—and much of the vibrancy of our culture—also depends on the existence of other intangible rights: The right to draw ideas from a rich and varied public domain, and the right to mock, for profit as well as fun, the cultural icons of our time. . . .

---

78. **McCarthy on Kozinski.** McCarthy, the leading author on the right of publicity, did not agree with Judge Kozinski. He thought commercial speech was never likely to receive the protection Judge Kozinski wanted and in any event that his notion of protecting the ad as parody was wrong. The analogy to parody on Saturday Night Live was wrong because Saturday Night Live was not "touting a product." J. Thomas McCarthy, *The Human Persona as Commercial property: The Right of Publicity*, 19 COLUM.-VLA J.L. & ARTS 129, 137–38 (1995).

79. **Tootsie revisited.** In *Hoffman v. Capital Cities/ABC, Inc.*, 255 F.3d 1180 (9th Cir. 2001), the Ninth Circuit, which decided both *Midler* and *Samsung,* considered a claim by the actor Dustin Hoffman. In the motion picture *Tootsie*, he played an actor who could get a job only by posing as a woman, with striking results and a new appreciation of the difficulties women faced in the workaday world. A memorable still photo showed him as that woman in a red sequined dress. Los Angeles Magazine ran a fashion feature, using a computer to graft new fashion designs onto famous Hollywood figures. The result was Hoffman's face from the red dress photo, but a new gown. The feature was not an advertisement, but the magazine carried a Ralph Lauren ad and the new composite photo of Hoffman had him wearing Ralph Lauren shoes. A Shopper's Guide elsewhere in the magazine listed stores and prices for the shoes and gown. The court approached the right of publicity claim (coupled with a Lanham Act claim) by first declaring that the publication was not commercial, then deciding that *Times-Sullivan* knowing or reckless falsehood would be required for liability. That meant on these facts that "[t]he evidence must clearly and convincingly demonstrate that LAM knew (or purposefully avoided knowing) that the photograph would mislead its readers into thinking that the body in the altered photograph was Hoffman's." The evidence fell short, and the award of $3 million in compensatory and punitive damages was reversed and the trial court was directed to enter judgment for the defendant.

RESTATEMENT (THIRD) OF UNFAIR COMPETITION § 47 (1995)

Copyright © 1995–2004 by the American Law Institute

The name, likeness, and other indicia of a person's identity are used "for purposes of trade" under the rule stated in § 46 if they are used in advertising the user's goods or services, or are placed on merchandise marketed by the user, or are used in connection with services rendered by the user. However, use "for purposes of trade" does not ordinarily include the use of a person's identity in news reporting, commentary, entertainment, works of fiction or nonfiction, or in advertising that is incidental to such uses.

Comment c . . . Use of another's identity in a novel, play, or motion picture is also not ordinarily an infringement. The fact that the publisher or other user seeks or is successful in obtaining a commercial advantage from an otherwise permitted use of another's identity does not render the appropriation actionable. However, if the name or likeness is used solely to attract attention to a work that is not related to the identified person, the user may be subject to liability for a use of the other's identity in advertising. . . .

WINTER v. DC COMICS

30 Cal.4th 881, 69 P.3d 473, 134 Cal.Rptr.2d 634 (2003)

CHIN, J. . . .

In the 1990's, DC Comics published a five-volume comic miniseries featuring "Jonah Hex," a fictional comic book "anti-hero." The series contains an outlandish plot, involving giant worm-like creatures, singing cowboys, and the "Wilde West Ranch and Music and Culture Emporium," named for and patterned after the life of Oscar Wilde. The third volume ends with a reference to two new characters, the "Autumn brothers," and the teaser, "Next: The Autumns of Our Discontent." The cover of volume 4 depicts the Autumn brother characters, with pale faces and long white hair. (See append., *post;* the Autumn brothers are the two lower figures.) One brother wears a stovepipe hat and red sunglasses, and holds a rifle. The second has red eyes and holds a pistol. This volume is entitled, Autumns of Our Discontent, and features brothers Johnny and Edgar Autumn, depicted as villainous half-worm, half-human offspring born from the rape of their mother by a supernatural worm creature that had escaped from a hole in the ground. At the end of volume 5, Jonah Hex and his companions shoot and kill the Autumn brothers in an underground gun battle.

Plaintiffs, Johnny and Edgar Winter, well-known performing and recording musicians originally from Texas, sued DC Comics and others alleging several causes of action including, as relevant here, appropriation of their names and likenesses under Civil Code section 3344. They alleged that the defendants selected the names Johnny and Edgar Autumn to signal readers the Winter brothers were being portrayed; that the Autumn brothers were drawn with long white hair and albino features similar to plaintiffs'; that the Johnny Autumn character was depicted as wearing a tall black top hat similar to the one Johnny Winter often wore; and that the title of volume 4, Autumns of Our Discontent, refers to the famous Shakespearian phrase, "the winter of our discontent." They also alleged that the comics falsely portrayed them as "vile, depraved, stupid, cowardly, subhuman individuals who engage in wanton acts of violence, murder and bestiality for pleasure and who should be killed."

[After extended litigation, the Court of Appeal held for the defendant on all claims except the "misappropriation" or right of publicity claim. The court has that claim for review here.]

[In Comedy III Productions, Inc. v. Gary Saderup, Inc. 25 Cal.4th 387, 396, 106 Cal.Rptr.2d 126, 21 P.3d 797 (2001) (Comedy III)], we held that some, although not all, uses of celebrity likenesses are entitled to First Amendment protection. "When artistic expression takes the form of a literal depiction or imitation of a celebrity for commercial gain, directly trespassing on the right of publicity without adding significant expression beyond that trespass, the state law interest in protecting the fruits of artistic labor outweighs the expressive interests of the imitative artist." Thus, "depictions of celebrities amounting to little more than the appropriation of the celebrity's economic value are not protected expression under the First Amendment." ...

We developed a test to determine whether a work merely appropriates a celebrity's economic value, and thus is not entitled to First Amendment protection, or has been transformed into a creative product that the First Amendment protects. The "inquiry is whether the celebrity likeness is one of the 'raw materials' from which an original work is synthesized, or whether the depiction or imitation of the celebrity is the very sum and substance of the work in question. We ask, in other words, whether a product containing a celebrity's likeness is so transformed that it has become primarily the defendant's own expression rather than the celebrity's likeness. And when we use the word 'expression,' we mean expression of something other than the likeness of the celebrity." These "transformative elements or creative contributions that require First Amendment protection are not confined to parody and can take many forms, from factual reporting to fictionalized portrayal from heavy-handed lampooning to subtle social criticism; "an artist depicting a celebrity must contribute something more than a merely trivial variation, [but must create] something recognizably his own, in order to qualify for legal protection." [W]hen an artist's skill and talent is manifestly subordinated to the overall goal of creating a conventional portrait of a celebrity so as to commercially exploit his or her fame, then the artist's right of free expression is outweighed by the right of publicity."

We made two important cautionary observations. First, "the right of publicity cannot, consistent with the First Amendment, be a right to control the celebrity's image by censoring disagreeable portrayals. Once the celebrity thrusts himself or herself forward into the limelight, the First Amendment dictates that the right to comment on, parody, lampoon, and make other expressive uses of the celebrity image must be given broad scope. The necessary implication of this observation is that the right of publicity is essentially an economic right. What the right of publicity holder possesses is not a right of censorship, but a right to prevent others from misappropriating the economic value generated by the celebrity's fame through the merchandising of the name, voice, signature, photograph, or likeness of the celebrity." Second, "in determining whether the work is transformative, courts are not to be concerned with the quality of the artistic contribution—vulgar forms of expression fully qualify for First Amendment protection." ...

We also cautioned against "wholesale importation of the fair use doctrine [of copyright law] into right of publicity law," although it provides some guidance. We explained that one factor of the fair use test, "the effect of the use upon the potential market for or value of the copyrighted work ... bears directly on this question. We do not believe, however, that consideration of this factor would usefully supplement the test articulated here. If it is determined that a work is worthy of First Amendment protection because added creative elements significantly transform the celebrity depiction, then independent inquiry into whether or not that work is cutting into the market for the celebrity's images ... appears to be irrelevant." Moreover, we explained that even if the work's marketability and economic value derive primarily from the fame of the celebrity depicted, the work may still be transformative and entitled to First Amendment protection. However, if the marketability and economic value of the challenged work do *not* derive primarily from the celebrity's fame, "there would generally be no actionable right of publicity. When the value of the work comes principally from some source other than the fame of the celebrity—from the creativity, skill, and reputation of the artist—it may be presumed that sufficient transformative elements are present to warrant First Amendment protection." ...

Application of the test to this case is not difficult. We have reviewed the comic books and attach a copy of a representative page. We can readily ascertain that they are not just conventional depictions of plaintiffs but contain significant expressive content other than plaintiffs' mere likenesses. Although the fictional characters Johnny and Edgar Autumn are less-than-subtle evocations of Johnny and Edgar Winter, the books do not depict plaintiffs literally. Instead, plaintiffs are merely part of the raw materials from which the comic books were synthesized. ... [T]he Autumn brothers are but cartoon characters—half-human and half-worm—in a larger story, which is itself quite expressive. The characters and their portrayals do not greatly threaten plaintiffs' right of publicity. ... The comic books are similar to the trading cards caricaturing and parodying prominent baseball players that have received First Amendment protection. Cardtoons v. Major League Baseball Players, 95 F.3d 959 (10th Cir. 1996). ...

The distinction between parody and other forms of literary expression is irrelevant to the Comedy III transformative test. It does not matter what precise literary category the work falls into. What matters is whether the work is transformative, not whether it is parody or satire or caricature or serious social commentary or any other specific form of expression.

Plaintiffs also argue, and the Court of Appeal found, that the record contains evidence that defendants were trading on plaintiffs' likenesses and reputations to generate interest in the comic book series and increase sales. This, too, is irrelevant to whether the comic books are constitutionally protected. The question is whether the work is transformative, not how it is marketed. If the work is sufficiently transformative to receive legal protection, it is of no moment that the advertisements may have increased the profitability of the [work]. If the challenged work is transformative, the way it is advertised cannot somehow make it nontransformative. ...

The artist in Comedy III, supra, essentially sold, and devoted fans bought, pictures of The Three Stooges, not transformed expressive works by the artist. Here, by contrast, defendants essentially sold, and the buyers purchased, DC Comics depicting fanciful, creative characters, not pictures of the Winter brothers. This makes all the difference. The comic books here are entitled to First Amendment protection.

Accordingly, we reverse the judgment of the Court of Appeal and remand the matter for further proceedings consistent with our opinion.

DOE v. TCI CABLEVISION

110 S.W.3d 363 (Mo. 2003)

Stephen N. LIMBAUGH, JR., Judge. . . .

[The plaintiff, Tony Twist, has been a professional hockey player and became "notorious for his violent tactics on the ice." Describing Twist, a *Sports Illustrated* writer said: "It takes a special talent to stand on skates and beat someone senseless, and no one does it better than the St. Louis Blues left winger." Twist had been quoted as saying, "I want to hurt them. I want to end the fight as soon as possible and I want the guy to remember it." Twist was immensely popular with fans and tried to position himself to become a sports commentator and product endorser when his playing career was over. Defendant McFarlane created a comic book called *Spawn*.]

Spawn is "a dark and surreal fantasy" centered on a character named Al Simmons, a CIA assassin who was killed by the Mafia and descended to hell upon death. Simmons, having made a deal with the devil, was transformed into the creature Spawn and returned to earth to commit various violent and sexual acts on the devil's behalf. In 1993, a fictional character named "Anthony 'Tony Twist' Twistelli" was added to the *Spawn* storyline. The fictional "Tony Twist" is a Mafia don whose list of evil deeds includes multiple murders, abduction of children and sex with prostitutes. The fictional and real Tony Twist bear no physical resemblance to each other and, aside from the common nickname, are similar only in that each can be characterized as having an "enforcer" or tough-guy persona. . . .

In October 1997, Twist filed suit against McFarlane and various companies associated with the *Spawn* comic book (collectively "respondents"), seeking an injunction and damages for, *inter alia*, misappropriation of name and defamation, the latter claim being later dismissed. McFarlane and the other defendants filed motions for summary judgment asserting First Amendment protection from a prosecution of the misappropriation of name claim, but the motions were overruled. [The jury brought in a verdict for Twist for more than $24 million, but the trial judge entered judgment NOV, partly because there was no evidence that the defendants intended to injure Twist's marketability.]

Several approaches have been offered to distinguish between expressive speech and commercial speech. [The opinion discusses the Restatement (Third) of Unfair Competition, § 47, cmt. c, which describes a "relatedness" test.]

California courts use a different approach, called the "transformative test," that was most recently invoked in Winter v. DC Comics, 30 Cal.4th 881, 134 Cal.Rptr.2d 634, 69 P.3d 473 (2003), a case with a remarkably similar fact situation. ... Concluding that the comic book characters "Johnny and Edgar Autumn" "are not just conventional depictions of plaintiffs but contain significant expressive content other than plaintiffs' mere likenesses," the Court held that the characters were sufficiently transformed so as to entitle the comic book to full First Amendment protection.

The weakness of the Restatement's "relatedness" test and California's "transformative" test is that they give too little consideration to the fact that many uses of a person's name and identity have both expressive and commercial components. These tests operate to preclude a cause of action whenever the use of the name and identity is in any way expressive, regardless of its commercial exploitation. Under the relatedness test, use of a person's name and identity is actionable only when the use is solely commercial and is otherwise unrelated to that person. Under the transformative test, the transformation or fictionalized characterization of a person's celebrity status is not actionable even if its sole purpose is the commercial use of that person's name and identity. Though these tests purport to balance the prospective interests involved, there is no balancing at all—once the use is determined to be expressive, it is protected. At least one commentator, however, has advocated the use of a more balanced balancing test—a sort of predominant use test—that better addresses the cases where speech is both expressive and commercial:

> If a product is being sold that predominantly exploits the commercial value of an individual's identity, that product should be held to violate the right of publicity and not be protected by the First Amendment, even if there is some "expressive" content in it that might qualify as "speech" in other circumstances. If, on the other hand, the predominant purpose of the product is to make an expressive comment on or about a celebrity, the expressive values could be given greater weight.

[Citing Mark S. Lee, *Agents of Chaos: Judicial Confusion in Defining the Right of Publicity—Free Speech Interface,* 23 Loy. L.A. Ent. L. Rev. 471 (2003).]

The relative merit of these several tests can be seen when applied to the unusual circumstances of the case at hand. As discussed, Twist made a submissible case that respondents' use of his name and identity was for a commercial advantage. Nonetheless, there is still an expressive component in the use of his name and identity as a metaphorical reference to tough-guy "enforcers." And yet, respondents agree (perhaps to avoid a defamation claim) that the use was not a parody or other expressive comment or a fictionalized account of the real Twist. As such, the metaphorical reference to Twist, though a literary device, has very little literary value compared to its commercial value. On the record here, the use and identity of Twist's name has become predominantly a ploy to sell comic books and related products rather than an artistic or literary expression, and under these circumstances, free speech must give way to the right of publicity. . . .

[Although the JNOV was error, a new trial was required for error in an instruction that permitted the jury to find liability without first finding an intent to obtain commercial advantage by using Twist's name.]

Town & Country Properties, Inc. v. Riggins, 249 Va. 387, 457 S.E.2d 356 (1995). The plaintiff, John Riggins, was a prominent professional football player, inducted into the Pro Football Hall of Fame in 1992. He now earns his livelihood by charging fees for endorsements and appearances. Upon divorce, Riggins' wife took title to their former home. Wishing to sell the house, she and a realtor arranged an open house, which was advertised by a flyer distributed to other brokers. The flyer said in part: "Come see . . . John Riggins' Former Home." The Riggins name was set out in large type on a line of its own. There was a photo of the house and the advertised price of $849,500. A note said "Register to win an autographed football." The flyer included a menu of food to be served and directions on getting to the house. Riggins said when he saw the flyer he was angry and humiliated and felt a loss of integrity and dignity. He also said that he would not be able to earn money if such a use of his name was possible. In Riggins' suit for damages, the defendants argued that what they said was true, since the home was Riggins' former home, and that as a true statement of fact, the publication was constitutionally protected. *Held*, (1) the publication is actionable under Virginia's right of publicity statute and is not constitutionally protected. Commercial speech is protected only when it performs an informational function. Use of plaintiff's name was not information, only promotional because the name was not relevant to physical condition of the house, architectural features, or the quality of the home. (2) The plaintiff also has a claim based on the theory of conversion, since rights in a name count as property.

Montana v. San Jose Mercury News, Inc., 34 Cal.App.4th 790, 40 Cal. Rptr.2d 639 (1995). The plaintiff, Joe Montana, was a successful quarterback for the San Francisco 49'ers football team, leading the team to a stunning victory in Super Bowl XXIII and again in Super Bowl XXIV. The defendant published a newspaper in the Bay Area and devoted attention to Montana and the team's success. After the team's four championships, the defendant ran a special souvenir section devoted to the "team of destiny" and carrying an artist's rendition of Montana on its front page. This page was later reproduced as a poster and sold and given away, partly or wholly to advertise the newspaper. Montana sued. *Held*, summary judgment for defendant affirmed. The First Amendment protects the posters because the posters report a newsworthy item of public interest and because the newspaper has a constitutional right to promote itself by reproducing its originally protected articles or photographs so long as no endorsement is implied.

STERN V. DELPHI INTERNET SERVICES CORP., 165 Misc.2d 21, 626 N.Y.S.2d 694 (Sup. Ct. 1995). Howard Stern is a famous and controversial talk show celebrity. He announced his candidacy for governor of New York. He also posed for a photograph in leather pants which "largely exposed his buttocks," presumably as a play on his name rather than to demonstrate his essential character. Delphi is an on-line computer service providing news and bulletin boards to subscribers. It set up a bulletin board to discuss Stern's candidacy. Being in a happy rather than a stern frame of mind, Delphi ran an ad using the Stern photograph and inviting participation in its bulletin board discussion. Stern sued but does not claim that Delphi obtained the photo by improper means. *Held,* summary judgment for defendant granted. Media disseminating news may incidentally use the identity of newsworthy subjects in advertising. Delphi's bulletin board service is a news disseminator and the topic, although also related to entertainment, is a matter of public interest. What drives the incidental use exception is the First Amendment and the Stern candidacy is well within the range of subjects protected.

Chapter 13

Moral Rights

POLLARA v. SEYMOUR

344 F.3d 265 (2d Cir. 2003)

JACOBS, Circuit Judge. . . .

Pollara is a professional artist in Albany, New York, who is frequently commissioned to create large painted banners and installations for use at events such as bar mitzvahs, corporate gatherings, and private parties. The work at issue in this case was created for the Gideon Coalition ("Gideon"), a non-profit group that provides legal services to the poor. . . . In 1999, Gideon arranged to set up an information table in Empire State Plaza, a public space in downtown Albany that is surrounded by a complex of New York State government office buildings. The information table was planned as part of Gideon's annual one-day legislative effort known as Lobbying Day. Gideon paid Pollara $1800 to paint a banner, approximately ten feet high and thirty feet long, which was to be erected as a backdrop to the table. Pollara worked more than 100 hours, applying latex paint to heavy-gauge photographer's paper that was reinforced along its edges by duct tape.

The completed banner, in three or four colors, depicts a tableau of two dozen stylized people, with few salient features, standing on line against a background of shut doors labeled "PUBLIC DEFENDER," "LEGAL AID," and "PRISONERS LEGAL SERVICES." They patiently await entry, at left, of an open door marked "LAWYER," inside which sits a person, wearing a jacket and tie. The person sits behind a brown desk, beside which is a trash can. Many of the people on line are depicted to suggest different ethnicities, possible immigrant status, youth and age, and both sexes—one person carries an infant and two have children in tow; the rest are in silhouette. Many are holding rectangles of paper, evidently summonses, correspondence, and the like. Large lettering across the top and left read: "EXECUTIVE BUDGET THREATENS RIGHT TO COUNSEL" and "PRESERVE THE RIGHT TO COUNSEL—NOW MORE THAN EVER!"

Pollara and several helpers erected the banner in Empire State Plaza on March 15, 1999, the evening before Lobbying Day was scheduled to begin. The banner was taped to two ten-foot-high steel supporting poles. Through no fault of Pollara's and without her knowledge, Gideon had failed to obtain a valid permit for Pollara to erect the banner or leave it there overnight.

Defendant Thomas E. Casey is employed by the State's Office of General Services ("OGS") as manager of Empire State Plaza. A supervisor advised Casey by phone at around nine that evening that some kind of banner or poster had been erected at the plaza, and directed Casey to investigate. Casey went there, made inquiry, and ordered several OGS employees to remove the banner. During removal, it was torn vertically into three pieces. . . .

On June 14, 1999, Pollara sued Casey and Joseph J. Seymour (who was the Commissioner of OGS and Casey's ultimate supervisor, although not the same supervisor who had contacted Casey by phone). Pollara's complaint asserted claims under VARA, as well as under 42 U.S.C. § 1983 (for the violation of her First Amendment rights). The VARA claims alleged that Casey and Seymour acted deliberately, willfully, wantonly, intentionally, and/or with gross negligence in mutilating and destroying the banner. After discovery, Pollara dropped her First Amendment claim, and both defendants moved for summary judgment on the VARA claims. . . .

After a bench trial, the district court entered judgment for Casey, ruling (*inter alia*) that the banner was not a "work of visual art" subject to protection under VARA because it constituted advertising or promotional material, categories expressly excluded from VARA's sweep. . . .

The district court also ruled that the banner was not a "work of recognized stature," and suggested that this ruling was sufficient to support entry of judgment as a matter of law in favor of Casey. The VARA subsection that affords rights against destruction of a work of visual art, 17 U.S.C. § 106A(a)(3)(B), is expressly limited in coverage to works of "recognized stature." However, the VARA subsection that affords rights against mutilation or modification, 17 U.S.C. § 106A(a)(3)(A), contains no such express limitation. Since Pollara invoked both subsections, the insufficient stature of her banner could not (as the district court suggested) serve as an independent ground for dismissal of all of her VARA claims. We need not consider this issue further, however, because we resolve the case on other grounds.

As a threshold matter, Pollara argues that we should remand for a new trial before a jury. Pollara relies on *Feltner v. Columbia Pictures Television, Inc.*, 523 U.S. 340, 118 S.Ct. 1279, 140 L.Ed.2d 438 (1998), which held that jury trials are required in certain suits for statutory damages under the Copyright Act, held that the Constitution affords a jury trial for claims involving traditional copyright violations, because the Seventh Amendment guarantees a jury in all "actions brought to enforce statutory rights that are analogous to common-law causes of action ordinarily decided in English law courts in the late 18th century, as opposed to those customarily heard by courts of equity or admiralty. It is an open question whether the Seventh Amendment affords a jury trial right in suits brought under VARA, which appear to lack any analog in common law.

We need not decide whether the Constitution protects the right to a jury trial for claims brought under VARA. ... [The issue is moot, however, because other issues are determinative.]

VARA was enacted in 1990 as an amendment to the Copyright Act, to provide for the protection of the so-called "moral rights" of certain artists. [M]oral rights afford protection for the author's personal, non-economic interests in receiving attribution for her work, and in preserving the work in the form in which it was created, even after its sale or licensing. VARA provides that the author of a "work of visual art," "shall have the right," for life,

> (A) to prevent any intentional distortion, mutilation, or other modification of that work which would be prejudicial to his or her honor or reputation, and any intentional distortion, mutilation, or modification of that work is a violation of that right, and
>
> (B) to prevent any destruction of a work of recognized stature, and any intentional or grossly negligent destruction of that work is a violation of that right.

17 U.S.C. §§ 106A(a)(3), (A), (B), (d)(3).

Not every artist has rights under VARA, and not everything called "art" is protected by such rights. As the quoted text reflects, VARA confers rights only on artists who have produced works of "recognized statute," or whose "honor or reputation" is such that it would be prejudiced by the modification of a work. And VARA protects only things defined as "work[s] of visual art,"—a definition that is "a critical underpinning of the limited scope of the [Act]."

Congress instructed courts to "use common sense and generally accepted standards of the artistic community in determining whether a particular work falls within the scope of the definition [of a 'work of visual art']," and explicitly stated that "whether a particular work falls within the definition should not depend on the medium or materials used. Protection of a work under VARA will often depend, as it does here, upon the work's objective and evident purpose. VARA does not protect advertising, promotional, or utilitarian works, and does not protect works for hire, regardless of their artistic merit, their medium, or their value to the artist or the market. VARA may protect a sculpture that looks like a piece of furniture, but it does not protect a piece of utilitarian furniture, whether or not it could arguably be called a sculpture. Drawings and paintings are protected, but only if they do not advertise or promote. Tellingly, only certain still photographs are protected, depending upon their intended use: Congress explicitly limited VARA's protection to works "intended for exhibition use only," as opposed to works intended for use in a publication or the photographer's photo album. In each case, VARA's protections are limited depending on the purpose of the work. [In a footnote here, the court commented: "Congress could not have intended that every representation by lines (even if doodled on a napkin) or every image in paint would be protected from modification or destruction without the express consent of the person who made it."]

The undisputed facts demonstrate that Pollara's banner falls outside the protections of the Act. The banner was created for the purpose of drawing attention to an information desk, as part of a lobbying effort, and the banner overtly promotes in word and picture a lobbying message. The banner was commissioned and paid for by Gideon, and Gideon determined in advance the banner's content, including its explicit textual message. Gideon's specification of content is insufficient on its own to make the banner a "work for hire;" but the directions given by Gideon evidence the promotional and advertising purpose that bring the banner outside the scope of VARA. While Gideon's name did not appear on the banner, the banner's planned installation adjacent to Gideon's information table, and its explicit lobbying message leave no doubt as to the banner's purpose as promotional and advertising material for Gideon's lobbying effort.

Pollara argues that it is significant that the Banner was commissioned by a political advocacy organization, and that the banner had a political message. According to Pollara, the non-commercial nature of the banner distinguishes it from the sorts of commercial advertising materials that Congress intended to exclude from VARA's protections. Contrary to Pollara's position, however, the term "advertising" contains no such limitation. There is a lot of public interest advertising, including advertising for museums and art. There is political advertising. And "promotion" has an even broader exclusionary sweep. . . .

We steer clear of an interpretation of VARA that would require courts to assess either the worth of a purported work of visual art, or the worth of the purpose for which the work was created. Congress chose to protect in VARA only a narrow subset of the many different forms and types of what can be called art, and expressly left unprotected works created for the primary purpose of promoting or advertising. Having concluded that the banner is such a work, our task is done.

For the foregoing reasons, the judgment of the district court is affirmed. [Concurring opinion is omitted.]

Noncommercial Use of Trademark? Just a Click Away

BOSLEY MED. INSTITUTE, INC. v. KREMER

403 F.3d 672 (9th Cir. 2005)

SILVERMAN, Circuit Judge.

Defendant Michael Kremer was dissatisfied with the hair restoration services provided to him by the Bosley Medical Institute, Inc. In a bald-faced effort to get even, Kremer started a website at www.BosleyMedical.com, which, to put it mildly, was uncomplimentary of the Bosley Medical Institute. The problem is that "Bosley Medical" is the registered trademark of the Bosley Medical Institute, Inc., which brought suit against Kremer for trademark infringement and like claims. Kremer argues that noncommercial use of the mark is not actionable as infringement under the Lanham Act. Bosley responds that Kremer is splitting hairs. . . .

Bosley Medical provides surgical hair transplantation, restoration, and replacement services to the public. Bosley Medical owns the registered trademark "BOSLEY MEDICAL," [and some related marks].

In January 2000, Kremer purchased the domain name www.BosleyMedical.com, the subject of this appeal, as well as the domain name www.BosleyMedicalViolations.com, which is not challenged by Bosley. Five days after registering the domain name, Kremer went to Bosley Medical's office in Beverly Hills, California and delivered a two-page letter to Dr. Bosley, Founder and President of Bosley Medical. The first page read:

> Let me know if you want to discuss this. Once it is spread over the internet it will have a snowball effect and be too late to stop. M. Kremer [phone number]. P.S. I always follow through on my promises. . . .

Kremer began to use www.BosleyMedical.com in 2001. His site summarizes the Los Angeles County District Attorney's 1996 investigative findings about Bosley, and allows visitors to view the entire document. It also contains other information that is highly critical of Bosley. Kremer earns no revenue from the website and no goods or services are sold on the website. There are no links to any of Bosley's competitors' websites. BosleyMedical.com does link to Kremer's sister site, BosleyMedicalViolations.com, which links to a newsgroup entitled alt.baldspot, which in turn contains advertisements for companies that compete with Bosley. BosleyMedical.com also contained a link to the Public Citizen website. Public Citizen is the organization that represents Kremer in this case. [Bosley brought this suit alleging trademark infringement, dilution and state law claims. The trial court gave summary judgment for the defendant on the trademark claims and dismissed the state-law claims under the state's Anti-SLAPP statute.]

The Trademark Act of 1946 ("Lanham Act") prohibits uses of trademarks, trade names, and trade dress that are likely to cause confusion about the source of a product or service. *See* 15 U.S.C. §§ 1114, 1125(a). In 1996, Congress amended § 43 of the Lanham Act to provide a remedy for the dilution of a famous mark. *See* 15 U.S.C. § 1125(c).

Infringement claims are subject to a commercial use requirement. The infringement section of the Lanham Act, 15 U.S.C. § 1114, states that any person who "use[s] in commerce any reproduction, counterfeit, copy, or colorable imitation of a registered mark in connection with the sale, offering for sale, distribution, or advertising of any goods or services on or in connection with which such use is likely to cause confusion, or to cause mistake, or to deceive . . ." can be held liable for such use. [The antidilution sections make somewhat similar requirements for commercial use.]

The inclusion of these requirements in the Lanham Act serves the Act's purpose: "to secure to the owner of the mark the goodwill of his business and to protect the ability of consumers to distinguish among competing producers. ...

The district court ruled that Kremer's use of Bosley's mark was noncommercial. To reach that conclusion, the court focused on the "use in commerce" language rather than the "use in connection with the sale of goods" clause. This approach is erroneous. "Use in commerce" is simply a jurisdictional predicate to any law passed by Congress under the Commerce Clause. ... Therefore, the district court should have determined instead whether Kremer's use was "in connection with a sale of goods or services" rather than a "use in commerce." ... The question before us, then, boils down to whether Kremer's use of Bosley Medical as his domain name was "in connection with a sale of goods or services." If it was not, then Kremer's use was "noncommercial" and did not violate the Lanham Act.

Bosley argues that it has met the commercial use requirement in three ways. First, it argues that a mark used in an otherwise noncommercial website or as a domain name for an otherwise noncommercial website is nonetheless used in connection with goods and services where a user can click on a link available on that website to reach a commercial site. *Nissan Motor Co. v. Nissan Computer Corp.*, 378 F.3d 1002 (9th Cir.2004). However, Bosley's reliance on *Nissan* is unfounded.

In *Nissan,* Nissan Motor Company sued Nissan Computer Corporation for using the Internet websites www.Nissan.com and www.Nissan.net. In *Nissan,* however, commercial use was undisputed, as the core function of the defendant's website was to advertise his computer business. Additionally, the defendant in *Nissan* ... placed links to other commercial businesses directly on their website. Kremer's website contains no commercial links, but rather contains links to a discussion group, which in turn contains advertising. This roundabout path to the advertising of others is too attenuated to render Kremer's site commercial. At no time did Kremer's BosleyMedical.com site offer for sale any product or service or contain paid advertisements from any other commercial entity.

Bosley also points out that Kremer's site contained a link to Public Citizen, the public interest group representing Kremer throughout this litigation. We hold that Kremer's identification of his lawyers and his provision of a link to same did not transform his noncommercial site into a commercial one.

Bosley's second argument that Kremer's website satisfies the "in connection with the sale of goods or services" requirement of the Lanham Act is that Kremer created his website to enable an extortion scheme in an attempt to profit from registering BosleyMedical.com. In *Panavision International, L.P. v. Toeppen,* 141 F.3d 1316 (9th Cir.1998), this court held that a defendant's "commercial use was his attempt to sell the trademarks themselves." Similarly, in *Intermatic Inc. v. Toeppen*, 947 F.Supp. 1227 (N.D.Ill.1996), the court found that "Toeppen's intention to arbitrage the 'intermatic.com' domain name constitute[d] a commercial use." *Id.* at 1239; *see also Boston Prof'l Hockey Ass'n, Inc. v. Dallas Cap & Emblem Mfg., Inc.*, 510 F.2d 1004, 1010 (5th Cir.1975) (holding that trademark law protects the trademark itself, despite the fact that only "a reproduction of the trademark itself is being sold, unattached to any other goods or services").

However, in this case, there is no evidence that Kremer was trying to sell the domain name itself. The letter delivered by Kremer to Bosley's headquarters is a threat to expose negative information about Bosley on the Internet, but it makes no reference whatsoever to ransoming Bosley's trademark or to Kremer's use of the mark as a domain name. . . .

Bosley's third and final argument that it satisfied the commercial use requirement of the Lanham Act is that Kremer's use of Bosley's trademark was in connection with *Bosley's* goods and services. In other words, Kremer used the mark "in connection with goods and services" because he prevented users from obtaining the plaintiff's goods and services. *See People for the Ethical Treatment of Animals v. Doughney*, 263 F.3d 359 (4th Cir.2001) ("*PETA*"). In *PETA*, defendants created a site that promoted ideas antithetical to those of the PETA group. The Fourth Circuit held that the defendant's parody site, though not having a commercial purpose and not selling any goods or services, violated the Lanham Act because it "prevented users from obtaining or using PETA's goods or services."

However, in *PETA*, the defendant's website "provide[d] links to more than 30 commercial operations offering goods and services." To the extent that the *PETA* court held that the Lanham Act's commercial use requirement is satisfied because the defendant's use of the plaintiff's mark as the domain name may deter customers from reaching the plaintiff's site itself, we respectfully disagree with that rationale. While it is true that www.BosleyMedical.com is not sponsored by Bosley Medical, it is just as true that it is *about* Bosley Medical. The *PETA* approach would place most critical, otherwise protected consumer commentary under the restrictions of the Lanham Act. Other courts have also rejected this theory as over-expansive.

The *PETA* court's reading of the Lanham Act would encompass almost all uses of a registered trademark, even when the mark is merely being used to identify the object of consumer criticism. This broad view of the Lanham Act is supported by neither the text of the statute nor the history of trademark laws in this country.

. . . Kremer is not Bosley's competitor; he is their critic. His use of the Bosley mark is not in connection with a sale of goods or services—it is in connection with the expression of his opinion *about* Bosley's goods and services.

The dangers that the Lanham Act was designed to address are simply not at issue in this case. The Lanham Act, expressly enacted to be applied in commercial contexts, does not prohibit all unauthorized uses of a trademark. Kremer's use of the Bosley Medical mark simply cannot mislead consumers into buying a competing product—no customer will mistakenly purchase a hair replacement service from Kremer under the belief that the service is being offered by Bosley. Neither is Kremer capitalizing on the good will Bosley has created in its mark. Any harm to Bosley arises not from a competitor's sale of a similar product under Bosley's mark, but from Kremer's criticism of their services. Bosley cannot use the Lanham Act either as a shield from Kremer's criticism, or as a sword to shut Kremer up.

In 1999, Congress passed the Anticybersquatting Consumer Protection Act ("ACPA"), 15 U.S.C. § 1125(d), as an amendment to the Lanham Act to prohibit cybersquatting. [C]ybersquatting occurs when a person other than the trademark holder registers the domain name of a well known trademark and then attempts to profit from this by either ransoming the domain name back to the trademark holder or by using the domain name to divert business from the trademark holder to the domain name holder. The ACPA states:

> A person shall be liable in a civil action by the owner of a mark ... if, without regard to the goods or services of the parties, that person (i) has a bad faith intent to profit from that mark ...; and (ii) registers, traffics in, or uses a domain name [that is confusingly similar to another's mark or dilutes another's famous mark].

15 U.S.C. § 1125(d)(1)(A) (2004).

The district court dismissed Bosley's ACPA claim for the same reasons that it dismissed the infringement and dilution claims—namely, because Kremer did not make commercial use of Bosley's mark. However, the ACPA does not contain a commercial use requirement, and we therefore reverse.

Kremer argues that the "noncommercial use" proviso that appears in the dilution portion of § 1125 applies to cybersquatting claims with equal force. Admittedly, the language in § 1125 is confusing. 15 U.S.C. § 1125(c)(4) reads: "The following shall not be actionable under this section: ... (B) Noncommercial use of a mark." 15 U.S.C. § 1125(c)(4)(B). Kremer asserts that by using the word "section," rather than the more precise term "subsection," Congress meant for the proviso to apply to all of § 1125, as opposed to subsection (c).

This argument fails for two reasons. The noncommercial use exception, which appears in a different part of the Lanham Act, is in direct conflict with the language of the ACPA. The ACPA makes it clear that "use" is only one possible way to violate the Act ("registers, traffics in, *or* uses"). Allowing a cybersquatter to register the domain name with a bad faith intent to profit but get around the law by making noncommercial use of the mark would run counter to the purpose of the Act. ... It is a well-established canon of statutory construction that a court should go beyond the literal language of a statute if reliance on that language would defeat the plain purpose of the statute.

Additionally, one of the nine factors listed in the statute that courts must consider is the registrant's "bona fide noncommercial or fair use of the mark in a site accessible under the domain name." 15 U.S.C. § 1125(d)(1)(B)(i)(IV). This factor would be meaningless if the statute exempted all noncommercial uses of a trademark within a domain name. . . .

The district court erred in applying the commercial use requirement to Bosley's ACPA claim. Rather, the court should confine its inquiry to the elements of the ACPA claim listed in the statute, particularly to whether Kremer had a bad faith intent to profit from his use of Bosley's mark in his site's domain name. Bosley has met the first prong of the ACPA (that the domain name is identical to the mark) because Kremer used an unmodified version of Bosley's mark as his domain name. . . .

In 1993, responding to the "disturbing increase in lawsuits brought primarily to chill the valid exercise of the constitutional rights of freedom of speech and petition for the redress of grievances," the California Legislature enacted the Anti–Strategic Lawsuit Against Public Participation ("anti-SLAPP") statute. Cal.Civ.Proc.Code § 425.16(a). "The hallmark of a SLAPP suit is that it lacks merit, and is brought with the goals of obtaining an economic advantage over a citizen party by increasing the cost of litigation to the point that the citizen party's case will be weakened or abandoned, and of deterring future litigation." The anti-SLAPP statute was designed to curtail these lawsuits by establishing a procedure to promptly expose and dismiss meritless and harassing claims seeking to chill protected expression. The statute provides that a defendant may move to strike a plaintiff's complaint if it "aris[es] from any act of that person in furtherance of the person's right of petition or free speech under the United States or California Constitution in connection with a public issue."

A defendant filing an anti-SLAPP motion to strike must make an initial prima facie showing that the plaintiff's suit arises from an act in furtherance of defendant's right of petition or free speech. The defendant need not show that plaintiff's suit was brought with the intention to chill defendant's speech; the plaintiff's intentions are ultimately beside the point.

The district court ruled that Bosley was seeking to limit Kremer's free speech and granted Kremer's anti-SLAPP motion to strike Bosley's state law trademark claims. We now reverse. An infringement lawsuit by a trademark owner over a defendant's unauthorized use of the mark as his domain name does not *necessarily* impair the defendant's free speech rights. As noted by the Second Circuit, "[d]omain names ... *per se* are neither automatically entitled to nor excluded from the protections of the First Amendment, and the appropriate inquiry is one that fully addresses particular circumstances presented with respect to each domain name." In *Panavision,* we stated that "[a] significant purpose of a domain name is to identify the entity that owns the web site,'' and we explained in *Mattel* that a source identifier is not entitled to full First Amendment protection. While a summary judgment motion might have been well-taken, an anti-SLAPP motion to strike was not. We reverse the grant of the anti-SLAPP motion to strike and remand to the district court for further proceedings on the state law claims. . . .

Chapter 14

MISREPRESENTATION AND RELATED TORTS: ADVERSARIAL AND QUASIADVERSARIAL BARGAINERS

§ 1. THE TORT OF MISREPRESENTATION DISTINGUISHED FROM ACTS OF MISREPRESENTATION

NEUROSURGERY AND SPINE SURGERY, S.C. v. GOLDMAN

339 Ill.App.3d 177, 790 N.E.2d 925, 274 Ill.Dec. 152 (2003)

[The plaintiff Rabin was a neurosurgeon. The defendant and third-party plaintiff Goldman was a patient of Rabin's partner. Rabin treated Goldman in the hospital. She later allegedly called the hospital and complained that Rabin had forced his way into her room while she was undressed and examined her with the door open. She also told the hospital that Rabin had been dismissed from the staff of other named hospitals for similar conduct. Rabin and his corporation sued Goldman for defamation in making that complaint. Goldman responded in part by bringing a third party complaint against Nancy Skaletsky. Goldman alleged that Skaletsky had told Goldman that Rabin had been dismissed from other hospitals for similar alleged conduct and that Goldman had relied on the statement in making her call to the hospital. Goldman also alleged that Skaletsky's purpose was to induce Goldman to publish the false statement to the hospital. The trial court dismissed Goldman's complaint against Skaletsky. Only those portions of the opinion relating to this claim are included here.]

We begin our discussion by noting that the tort of fraudulent misrepresentation is often surrounded by unnecessary confusion, because misrepresentations themselves often play large roles in a variety of other torts. For instance, an untrue assertion may be at the heart of an action for false imprisonment. A misrepresentation is the essence of torts such as defamation, interference with contractual relations, and malicious prosecution. A malicious, outrageous lie may give rise to a cause of action for intentional infliction of emotional distress. In summary, a great number of causes of action stem from misrepresentations.

However, not every misrepresentation gives rise to a cause of action for fraudulent misrepresentation. The origin of fraudulent misrepresentation lies in the common law action of deceit, which was a very narrow tort. See *Pasley v. Freeman,* 100 Eng. Rep. 450 (K.B.1789); *Derry v. Peek,* 14 A.C. 337 (H.L.1888). Prior to the eighteenth century, recovery on the action of deceit was not available unless the misrepresentation was part of some contractual dealing between the parties. Then, in 1789, in *Pasley,* it was held that one who fraudulently induced a third party to extend credit to a person known to be untrustworthy was liable to the defrauded party. Deceit, as a distinct tort, thus came into being, independent of any contractual relationship.

In 1889, in *Peek,* deceit became the tort we today refer to as fraudulent misrepresentation. . . .

Historically, the torts of deceit and fraudulent misrepresentation have been limited to cases involving business or financial transactions between parties, right down to the first recorded cases, *Pasley* and *Peek.* See W. Prosser, Torts § 105 (4th ed.1971). The United States Supreme Court has similarly observed:

> [M]any familiar forms of . . . conduct may be said to involve an element of "misrepresentation," in the generic sense of that word, but "[s]o far as misrepresentation has been treated as giving rise in and of itself to a distinct cause of action in tort, it has been identified with the common law action of deceit," and has been confined "very largely to the invasion of interests of a financial or commercial character, in the course of business dealings." *United States v. Neustadt,* 366 U.S. 696, 711 n. 26, 81 S.Ct. 1294, 1302 n. 26, 6 L.Ed.2d 614, 624 n. 26 (1961), quoting W. Prosser, Torts § 85, at 702–03 (1941).

The tort of fraudulent misrepresentation has also historically been limited to cases where a plaintiff has suffered a pecuniary harm. . . . Indeed, fraudulent misrepresentation is purely an economic tort under which one may recover only monetary damages. "Although the invasion of an economic interest by tort or by contract breach will often cause the plaintiff personal distress, the interest ordinarily protected in such cases is purely an economic interest and does not include interests in personality. Accordingly the usual rule is that the plaintiff must show pecuniary loss in misrepresentation cases and the damages are limited to such pecuniary loss, with no recovery for emotional distress." D. Dobbs, Remedies § 9.2(4), at 559–60 (2d ed.1993).

. . . Simply put, fraudulent misrepresentation has emerged as a tort distinct from the general milieu of negligent and intentional wrongs and applies only to interferences with financial or commercial interests where a party suffers some pecuniary loss. . . .

Goldman's allegations fail to properly state a cause of action for fraudulent misrepresentation for several reasons. First, Goldman's allegations do not involve a business or financial transaction. The issue of a fraudulent misrepresentation claim in a noncommercial, nonfinancial setting is one of first impression in Illinois. However, as noted above, the tort of fraudulent misrepresentation has always, since being codified in the House of Lords by Lord Hershell in *Peek,* centered around a business or financial transaction. Finding the foreign authorities and treatises cited above very persuasive, this court declines to extend the tort of fraudulent misrepresentation to encompass noncommercial and nonfinancial dealings between parties.

Second, even had the plaintiff alleged a scenario within a setting involving some commercial or financial transaction, the plaintiff fails to sufficiently allege the damages element of a fraudulent misrepresentation action. As discussed earlier, Goldman may not recover on her allegations of physical and emotional distress under an economic tort such as fraudulent misrepresentation. The maker of a fraudulent misrepresentation is subject to liability for pecuniary losses only.

Goldman's remaining allegation concerning pecuniary damages was insufficient. With regard to pecuniary damages, Goldman alleged that she "incurred legal fees and other costs as a result of her reliance upon Nancy Skaletsky's false representations." This allegation that Nancy Skaletsky caused her to incur fees and costs constituted nothing more than an unsupported conclusion. Moreover, this allegation fails to conform to the requirement that each element of a fraudulent misrepresentation action be pleaded with specificity and particularity.... In summary, we hold that the trial court did not err in dismissing count I of Goldman's third-party complaint.

In so ruling, we note that the Goldman's third-party complaint appears to be a subterfuge for an action for contribution from Nancy Skaletsky. Under the Joint Tortfeasor Contribution Act, one tortfeasor can be held liable to a joint tortfeasor, for contribution, for his or her *pro rata* share of damages in causing or contributing to causing a plaintiff's injuries. However, in *Gerill Corp. v. Jack L. Hargrove Builders, Inc.,* 128 Ill.2d 179, 206, 131 Ill.Dec. 155, 538 N.E.2d 530 (1989), our supreme court held that contribution is unavailable to intentional tortfeasors. Although defamation can be predicated on recklessness or negligence, in this case, the plaintiffs' defamation *per se* and *per quod* actions against Goldman were solely predicated on specific intent, alleging that Goldman had intended to defame and acted with malice. ... For the foregoing reasons, the judgment of the circuit court of Du Page County is affirmed.

---

1. **Misrepresentations causing physical or emotional harm.** Although the *tort* of "misrepresentation" or "fraud" is usually concerned with economic losses only, the *act* of misrepresentation may count as some other kind of tort. Some misrepresentations may count as ordinary negligence because they create risks of physical harm. Other misrepresentations might count as intentional or negligent infliction of emotional distress. But to recover for physical harm or emotional distress, the plaintiff will usually be required prove the elements appropriate to those torts, even if the court calls the action one for misrepresentation. For example, the plaintiff asserting fraud or misrepresentation may be required to prove severe distress just as she is required to do so in a claim for infliction of emotional distress. *McConkey v. Aon Corp.*, 354 N.J.Super. 25, 804 A.2d 572 (2002). Or in some jurisdictions the plaintiff may be required to prove physical harm along with the distress. See *M.H. v. Caritas Family Servs.*, 488 N.W.2d 282 (Minn. 1992). But see, advocating expanded liability for emotional distress in misrepresentation cases, Andrew L. Merritt, *Damages for Emotional Distress in Fraud Litigation: Dignitary Torts in a Commercial Society,* 42 VAND. L. REV. 1 (1989).

2. **Misstatements in bargaining transactions.** In this chapter, misrepresentation usually involves arms' length bargainers, two people who do not especially trust one another and who recognize that each will strive to put his own interests first. However, some misrepresentation claims are brought against fiduciaries and those who share a confidential relationship of some kind. In those cases, the defendant may be held to higher standards. And in a few cases, a third person who is not part of the bargaining may make a representation that induces one of the bargainers to act. *Exclusions*: Sometimes misrepresentation is associated with "fraud," and that term does indeed describe intentional misrepresentations. However, there are many acts that courts are likely to call fraud that do not involve any clear misrepresentation—secretly misappropriating property of the plaintiff, for example. This chapter does not cover such "frauds," only misrepresentations. Further, it covers only misrepresentations in bargaining transactions.

§ 2. COMMON LAW DECEIT: THE INTENT REQUIREMENT

ST. FRANCIS DE SALES FEDERAL CREDIT UNION v. SUN INS. CO. OF NEW YORK

818 A.2d 995 (Me. 2002)

CLIFFORD, J. . . .

[The plaintiffs are credit unions that receive deposits of checks.] The Credit Unions contracted with Maine Armored Car to transport those checks to Lewiston for processing. Pursuant to that agreement, Maine Armored Car installed and maintained a locked metal box that was bolted to an exterior wall of the St. Francis De Sales Federal Credit Union building. At the end of each business day, the Credit Unions deposited the checks into the metal box, and Maine Armored Car picked up the checks and delivered them in Lewiston.

The agreement required Maine Armored Car to carry insurance against the loss of Credit Union property. To meet this requirement, Maine Armored Car purchased an armored car transportation insurance policy through Sun. [The policy excluded losses arising from theft from the lock box except where the thief used a master key or other special keys.]

Annually, at Maine Armored Car's request, Sun issued to each Credit Union a certificate of insurance to verify that Sun had issued a policy of insurance to Maine Armored Car for loss of property of its customers from any cause. . . .

The certificates then described the coverage in the underlying policy as "[c]overing the liability assumed by [Maine Armored Car] for loss or damage, *from any cause whatsoever,* to property of customers, consisting of . . . Checks, Drafts, Notes . . . and all other Commercial Papers, and other Documents and Papers of value." (Emphasis added.) The certificates then listed a number of exclusions not relevant to this case, but did not mention any exclusions for theft. Sun issued Certificates from August 1, 1991 to August 1, 1992.

On May 22, 1992, an unknown thief forcefully broke into the lock box attached to the St. Francis Credit Union building and stole the checks. Maine Armored Car submitted a claim to Sun in connection with the theft. Because of the circumstances surrounding the theft from the lock box, i.e., access to the lock box was not gained through the "use of a master key, dial rim lock key, guard key or combination," Sun denied coverage for the loss.

[The credit unions recovered judgments against Maine Armored Car for the lost checks, but they have been unable to collect the judgments. They then sued Sun, alleging that the false representations in Sun's certificates were fraudulent and that the credit unions had relied on those statements to their loss.]

. . . Sun contends that it is entitled to judgments as a matter of law on the Credit Unions' fraud claims because there is insufficient evidence of fraud.

A defendant is liable for fraud if the plaintiff establishes the following elements by clear and convincing evidence:

> [The defendant] (1) makes a false representation (2) of a material fact (3) with knowledge of its falsity or in reckless disregard of whether it is true or false (4) for the purpose of inducing another to act or to refrain from acting in reliance upon it, and (5) the plaintiff justifiably relies upon the representation as true and acts upon it to his damage.

When clear and convincing evidence is required, plaintiffs bear the burden of persuasion to "place in the ultimate factfinder an abiding conviction that the truth of [their] factual contentions are highly probable." ...

The certificates of insurance stated that Sun had issued a policy to Maine Armored Car, "[c]overing the liability assumed by [Maine Armored Car] for loss or damage, *from any cause whatsoever,* to property of customers, consisting of ... Checks, Drafts, Notes ... and all other Commercial Papers, and other Documents and Papers of value." (Emphasis added.) The certificates also listed exclusions from coverage but did not mention exclusions pertaining to theft. The actual *policies* issued by Sun to Maine Armored Car, however, did *not* cover losses "from any cause whatsoever." Rather, the policies did provide coverage for theft, but only thefts committed in a particular manner, and did not cover the kind of theft that occurred in this case. Thus, viewing the evidence in the light most favorable to the Credit Unions, a jury could conclude to a high probability that the representations in the certificates stating that Maine Armored Car was fully covered for losses from any cause whatsoever were false. ...

In order to succeed in an action for fraud, a plaintiff must also prove that the defendant's false misrepresentation was made with knowledge of its falsity, or in reckless disregard of its accuracy. Sun wrote the insurance policies and subsequently issued the certificates of insurance through an insurance broker. The representations in the certificates that Maine Armored Car had insurance to cover its customer losses "from any cause whatsoever" were not mere casual comments or off-hand remarks; rather the representations contained formalized statements of fact concerning insurance coverage, complete with seals and signatures that conveyed credibility.

The certificates vary in several important respects from the language of the policies. Given the significance of these differences, and viewed in a light most favorable to the Credit Unions, a fact finder could reasonably infer that the representations contained in the certificates were made in reckless disregard of their truth or falsity.

... Accordingly, Sun is not entitled to judgments as a matter of law.

---

3. **Warranty and third persons.** Notice that in *St. Francis De Sales* the defendant never had a bargaining relationship with the plaintiff and certainly never had a contract, yet may be held liable for misrepresentation. This observation reflects the fact that warranty and misrepresentation parted company long ago. Warranty claims came to be conceived of as claims more or less contractual in nature and available only to a plaintiff who is in privity with the defendant. Misrepresentation was and is conceived of as a tort; no privity is required. See DOBBS

on Torts § 480 (2001 & Supp.). Actually, however, could the plaintiff here claim on warranty as a third party beneficiary?

4. **Elements: purpose or intent to induce reliance.** Notice that the Maine court said the defendant must have a *purpose* to induce reliance on his false statement. Many authorities say instead that the defendant must have an *intent* to induce reliance. E.g., *Lindberg v. Roseth,* 137 Idaho 222, 46 P.3d 518 (2002); *First American Title Ins. Co. v. Lawson,* 177 N.J. 125, 827 A.2d 230 (2003). The Restatement Second of Torts uses the term "intent" in § 531 but "purpose" in § 525. Could the difference in language conceivably matter?

5. **Scienter or knowing, reckless falsehood.** The requirement of scienter—knowing or reckless falsehood—has been generally accepted since it was imposed in *Derry v. Peek,* 14 Appeals Cases 337 (House of Lords 1889). The scienter requirement is imposed not only in common law fraud cases but in some of the most important kinds of securities fraud claims under federal statutes. See *Ernst & Ernst v. Hochfelder,* 425 U.S. 185, 96 S.Ct. 1375, 47 L.Ed.2d 668 (1976) (something like scienter required, negligence is not enough). See also Chapter 15.

6. **Comparing *Times-Sullivan.*** The knowing or reckless falsehood in *Times-Sullivan* was obviously based on this earlier use of that test in misrepresentation cases. Even the heightened burden of proof—by clear and convincing evidence—is the same. What factors in *St. Francis De Sales*, if any, justify the conclusion that the falsehood was knowing or reckless? If Sun's certificate had somehow libeled someone by asserting its insurance coverage, would courts so readily find knowing or reckless falsehood?

SIDELIGHT: THE HEIGHTENED PLEADING REQUIREMENT UNDER FEDERAL SECURITIES LAWS

Federal securities laws create causes of action for misrepresentation and sometimes other deceptive and unfair conduct. Scienter is usually required for misrepresentation claims. Effective in 1995, Congress provided that when a state of mind (such as knowing misrepresentation) is required,

> the complaint shall, with respect to each act or omission alleged to violate this chapter, state with particularity facts giving rise to a strong inference that the defendant acted with the required state of mind.

The Private Securities Litigation Reform Act of 1995 (PSLRA), 15 U.S.C.A. § 78u–4(b)(2). The requirement appears to go beyond the clear and convincing evidence rule often applied in common law cases, requiring that the plaintiff plead evidentiary facts showing a "strong" inference of scienter. In *Gompper v. VISX, Inc.,* 298 F.3d 893 (9th Cir. 2002), the court held that in judging whether a strong inference had been shown by pleaded facts, it would not ignore competing inferences, but would instead decide against the plaintiff on the pleadings if, on balance, possible contrary inferences could be drawn from the pleadings, even though no trier had actually drawn the contrary inference.

A warning: In another statute, the Securities Litigation Uniform Standards Act of 1998 (SLUSA), 15 USCA § 78bb(f), Congress preempted many class actions brought as *state-law* securities fraud claims, forcing them into federal court and then requiring their dismissal. For such actions, that leaves the unique pleading requirement almost, though not quite, completely controlling. See *Dabit v. Merrill Lynch, Pierce, Fenner & Smith, Inc.*, 395 F.3d 25 (2d Cir. 2005).

7. **Comparing *St. Amant*.** Recall that *St. Amant* defined reckless publication of a false statement as entailing a high degree of subjective awareness on the defendant's part that the statement was probably false. Publishing with serious doubts about the truth would qualify as reckless. Did *St. Francis De Sales* take a more relaxed approach and if so is that warranted because fraud differs from libel?

8. **Scienter and conscious ignorance.** Suppose a real estate agent, told by the seller that the roof of a house is brand new, tells the same to a prospective buyer, who, in reliance, buys the house, only to discover that the roof is about to fall in and will require extensive repairs. Is the real estate broker chargeable with scienter fraud? If the broker is aware that he does not actually know the roof's condition, but makes as statement as if he does, isn't he knowingly lying about at least one thing? Courts impose liability when the defendant knows he doesn't know the facts but implies that he does. See DOBBS ON TORTS § 471 (2001 & Supps.).

9. **Scienter and "intent to deceive."** Some courts have expressed the scienter rule by saying the defendant must have an intent to deceive. In *Nielsen v. Adams,* 223 Neb. 262, 388 N.W.2d 840 (1986), the defendant sold her house to the plaintiff after representing that the basement had never had water damage. After the plaintiff moved into the house he discovered that the water leakage had been so bad that studs behind the walls were rotten. The defendant sought to avoid liability for this fraud by arguing that she had no intent to deceive on any relevant point—the relevant point to her being that there was no current water problem because she had fixed it. The trial judge charged the jury in part on intent to deceive and the jury found for the defendant. This was reversed and intent to deceive dropped out of the court's list of elements. A similar argument that the defendant told the ultimate truth by lying about details was rejected in *Bangert Bros. Construction Co. v. Kiewit Western Co.,* 310 F.3d 1278 (10th Cir. 2002).

§ 3. NEGLIGENT MISREPRESENTATION

ONITA PACIFIC CORP. v. BRONSON TRUSTEES

315 Or. 149, 843 P.2d 890 (1992)

PETERSON, Justice.

[The following summary is a simplified statement of the facts. The defendant owned the right to develop a parcel of land owned by Camomile. Upon development, lots would be sold to purchasers and part of the purchase price had to be devoted to paying down the the remaining debt to Camomile. Lots could not be released for sale until development was completed. Defendant told the plaintiffs that they could purchase a share of this development enterprise for a little over $1 million and that the $1 million would be used to pay off Camomile so that lots could be sold and the price received for them used to finance development. This was error; the defendant was obliged to make full development before lots could be sold. The plaintiffs invested, but when it turned out that lots could not be sold there was no income with which to proceed with development or to repay the money borrowed by the plaintiffs to enter into this plan. The plaintiffs' lender foreclosed on their interest in the deal as a whole. So the plaintiffs lost their investment.]

. . . [T]he trial court granted defendants' motion for directed verdict on the fraud claim. The jury thereafter returned a verdict in favor of plaintiffs on their negligent misrepresentation claim. [The trial court granted defendants' motion for new trial.] . . . The Court of Appeals reversed. Concerning the tort of negligent misrepresentation, the Court of Appeals held that defendants' conduct was actionable and that the jury's verdict was supported by evidence in the record. . . .

Plaintiffs' claim for negligent misrepresentation is based on Restatement (Second) of Torts § 552 (1977). [The court's footnote here reads:] Restatement (Second) of Torts § 552 provides:

> (1) One who, in the course of his business, profession or employment, or in any other transaction in which he has a pecuniary interest, supplies false information for the guidance of others in their business transactions, is subject to liability for pecuniary loss caused to them by their justifiable reliance upon the information, if he fails to exercise reasonable care or competence in obtaining or communicating the information. . . .

[The plaintiffs] assert that "a party who supplies false information should be liable for misrepresentations that are made negligently." Defendants contend that, as between parties to an arm's-length transaction, one party should not be held liable to another party for economic losses caused by the latter's reliance on the former's negligent misrepresentations.

. . . We now state that, under some circumstances, one may be liable for economic loss sustained by others who rely on one's representations negligently made. ... [M]any American courts recognize the tort of negligent misrepresentation, but the scope of recovery for economic loss varies widely. The rule stated in Restatement (Second) of Torts § 552 is close to the mark. But, for the reasons that follow, rather than adopting a black letter "rule," we opt to develop the scope of the duty and the scope of recovery on a case-by-case basis, in the light of related decisions of this court.

Our precedents establish that a negligence claim for the recovery of economic losses caused by another must be predicated on some duty of the negligent actor to the injured party beyond the common law duty to exercise reasonable care to prevent foreseeable harm. ...

[O]ne ordinarily is not liable for negligently causing a stranger's purely economic loss without injuring his person or property. It does not suffice that the harm is a foreseeable consequence of negligent conduct that may make one liable to someone else, for instance to a client. Some source of a duty outside the common law of negligence is required. Hence, where the recovery of economic losses is sought on a theory of negligence, the concept of duty as a limiting principle takes on a greater importance than it does with regard to the recovery of damages for personal injury or property damage.

Having recognized the existence of the tort, the central question in the present case becomes whether, during the parties' arm's-length negotiations, in addition to a duty of honesty, defendants owed plaintiffs a duty to exercise reasonable care in communicating factual information to prevent economic losses to plaintiffs. To resolve this, we examine the nature of the parties' relationship and compare that relationship to other relationships in which the law imposes a duty on parties to conduct themselves reasonably, so as to protect the other parties to the relationship.

The law imposes a duty of care in the attorney-client relationship. ... Unlike parties who are negotiating at arm's length, the attorney is engaged by the client to use his or her expertise for the benefit and protection of the client's interests. The attorney generally does not and should not have any pecuniary interest that is adverse to the client. ...

Other professional or contractual relationships may also give rise to a tort duty to exercise reasonable care on behalf of another's interests. Engineers and architects are among those who may be subject to liability to those who employ (or are the intended beneficiaries of) their services and who suffer losses caused by professional negligence.

Other examples may be cited. An agent owes duties of care and loyalty to his or her principal. ...

In the above relationships, the professional who owes a duty of care is, at least in part, acting to further the economic interests of the "client," the person owed the duty of care. In contrast, the present case involves two adversarial parties negotiating at arm's length to further their own economic interests.

... [W]e conclude that, in arm's-length negotiations, economic losses arising from a negligent misrepresentation are not actionable. This conclusion is in accord with the opinions of some commentators. Professors Harper, James, and Gray have noted the desirability of limiting the class of persons to whom the duty of care is owed in the context of negligent misrepresentations causing economic losses. "On the whole, as indicated above, courts have provided a remedy for negligent misrepresentation principally against those who advise in an essentially nonadversarial capacity. As against sellers and other presumed antagonists, on the other hand, the tendency of most courts has instead been either to rely on deceit with the requirement of scienter, however expanded, or to shift (by analogy to restitution or warranty) to strict liability. ..." 2 Harper, James & Gray, The Law of Torts 412–13, § 7.6 (2d ed 1986). ...

Our conclusion also is consistent with Restatement (Second) of Torts § 552. The text of section 552 and the comments and illustrations thereto suggest that the editors, in using the words "[o]ne who, in the course of his business, profession or employment, or in any other transaction in which he has a pecuniary interest, supplies false information for the guidance of others in their business transactions," had in mind relationships other than the relationship between persons negotiating at arm's length. The comments provide no illustrations dealing with business adversaries in the commercial sense. ...

In the case at bar, defendants and their representative did not owe any duty to plaintiffs during the negotiations by virtue of a contractual, professional, or employment relationship or as a result of any fiduciary or similar relationship implied in the law. Here, the relationship was adversarial. In an arm's-length negotiation, a negligent misrepresentation is not actionable. Hence, plaintiffs cannot maintain their claim for negligent misrepresentation against defendants. ...

The decision of the Court of Appeals reinstating the verdict is reversed, and the case is remanded to the Court of Appeals for further consideration consistent with this opinion.

[Dissents omitted.]

Sain v. Cedar Rapids Community Sch. Dist., 626 N.W.2d 115 (Iowa 2001). Allegations: The plaintiff was a high school senior and a basketball star. He needed three approved English courses to be eligible for a college basketball scholarship. The school's guidance counselor advised him that a course in Technical Communications would qualify, although objective facts show that it had not been approved for this purpose and was never submitted for approval. The plaintiff took the course and was offered a scholarship at a university, but the offer was withdrawn when the NCAA determined that the plaintiff had not taken the required approved courses. The plaintiff sued for negligence and negligent misrepresentation. *Held,* over dissents, the plaintiff has stated a claim good against summary judgment motion. "Our examination of both [Restatement]

§ 552 and our own cases reveals the business or commercial requirement for the tort does not actually concern the subject matter of the transaction between the plaintiff and the defendant, but requires the defendant to be in the business or profession of supplying information for the guidance of others. This is the fundamental requirement to support the imposition of a duty, which is essential for all negligence claims." "Although the Restatement supports a broader view, we have determined that this duty arises only when the information is provided by persons in the business or profession of supplying information to others. Thus, when deciding whether the tort of negligent misrepresentation imposes a duty of care in a particular case, we distinguish between those transactions where a defendant is in the business or profession of supplying information to others from those transactions that are arm's length and adversarial."

JORDAN V. EARTHGRAINS COMPANIES, INC., 576 S.E.2d 336 (N.C. App. 2003). Anheuser, through a wholly-owned subsidiary, Campbell, owned Earthgrains. Anheuser decided to spin off the stock to individual Anheuser shareholders. Earthgrains employees were concerned about their job futures. Beracha, an officer of Campbell, allegedly told employees that the company was profitable and their jobs were secure. In fact the company was losing money and a few months after the alleged representation, the plant was closed. The employees sued Anheuser and Campbell for negligent misrepresentation. *Held,* summary judgment for defendants was proper. "In his position as the director of a corporation, Beracha only owed a duty of care to the corporation and not to individual employees. . . . [The plaintiffs' allegations] fail to show that defendants had a pecuniary interest by allegedly informing plaintiffs that the Charlotte plant was profitable. [The plaintiffs got a special termination bonus when the plant was closed.] [D]efendants would obviously lose money by advising plaintiffs to continue employment, close the plant, and then negotiate a bonus package for plaintiffs. The . . . agreement is inconsistent with plaintiff's argument that defendants obtained a pecuniary interest by inducing plaintiffs to continue employment with defendants."

---

10. **The *International Products* decision.** The leading case establishing liability for negligent misrepresentation was *International Products Co. v. Erie R.R. Co.,* 244 N.Y. 331, 155 N.E.2d 662 (1927). The plaintiff there was an importer expecting a consignment of goods to arrive by steamer. The defendants were to store the goods until the plaintiff could reship them. The plaintiff wanted to insure the goods while they were in storage with the defendant, and for the purpose of correctly designating their location in the insurance policy, the plaintiff asked where they were stored. The defendant told the plaintiff "Dock F", but in fact the goods were stored at Dock D. They were destroyed by

fire, but the plaintiff was unable to collect the insurance because their location was not correctly described. The plaintiff sued the defendant for negligent misrepresentation and was allowed to recover. Notice that the relationship of the parties is definitely not "arm's length" or adversarial: the defendant had no self-interest to serve by lying and maybe more important perhaps had some affirmative self-interest to serve by taking the trouble to be accurate.

11. **Specialized expertise or position of confidence.** In *Kimmell v. Schaefer,* 89 N.Y.2d 257, 675 N.E.2d 450, 652 N.Y.S.2d 715 (1996), New York appeared to formulate its rule a little more carefully. First, it excluded casual responses. Second, it said that liability for negligent misrepresentation would be imposed "only on those persons who possess unique or specialized expertise, or who are in a special position of confidence and trust with the injured party such that reliance on the negligent misrepresentation is justified." Not surprisingly, it recognized liability for the negligent misrepresentations of lawyers and others who are retained for the very purpose of getting accurate information. Unfortunately, *Kimmell* sends mixed messages, because while its language is narrow, the courts actually imposed liability for negligent financial statements by a defendant who had an interest in selling the plaintiffs a share in a venture and who was not hired to provide the plaintiff with accurate information. Nor does it seem likely that he was in a position of special trust or confidence. At best, the reasons why the defendant came under a duty were vague.

Some cases that purport to support general liability for negligent misrepresentation actually seem to involve defendants who are in a special, confidential, or fiducial relationship to the plaintiff. *Arizona Title Ins. & T. Co. v. O'Malley Lumber Co.*, 14 Ariz.App. 486, 484 P.2d 639 (1971) (escrow agent, possibly a version of the conscious ignorance principle). Short of fiduciary or confidential relationship, one party may have special expertise on which the other reasonably relies. Would this generate a duty of reasonable care? See DOBBS ON TORTS § 472. Even if the parties would otherwise look like adversary bargainers? See *Westby v. Gorsuch,* 112 Wash.App. 558, 50 P.3d 284 (2002).

12. **Dissonance? Employers and prospective employers.** In some cases courts have recognized or assumed that prospective employers were under a duty of care in making representations to prospective employees and thus could be liable for negligent misrepresentations inducing an employee to accept employment. See, e.g., *Van Buren v. Pima Community College Dist.,* 113 Ariz. 85, 546 P.2d 821 (1976); *Pollmann v. Belle Plaine Livestock Auction, Inc.,* 567 N.W.2d 405 (Iowa 1997); *Griesi v. Atlantic General Hosp. Corp.,* 360 Md. 1, 756 A.2d 548 (2000) (emphasizing intimate nexus between prospective employer and prospective employee and prospective employee's need for accurate facts, no discussion of pecuniary interests as such). Is *Jordan v. Earthgrains Companies* contra? The pecuniary interest is plain enough here, but what about the fact that in bargaining for employment, the prospective employer and the prospective employee are adversarial?

In *Conway v. Pacific University,* 324 Or. 231, 924 P.2d 818 (1996), a university administrator, offering a tenure track position to a temporary professor with low student evaluations, told him the student evaluations would be no problem to tenure. The professor quit his permanent post at another school and began his tenure track work for the university. His student evaluations never improved over the years and the university denied him tenure. He claimed negligent misrepresentation but the Oregon court that decided *Onita* concluded that the university owed the professor no duty of care to make an accurate statement. Couldn't you accept *Onita* and still rule for the plaintiff in *Conway?*

In *Barmettler v. Reno Air, Inc.,* 114 Nev. 441, 956 P.2d 1382 (1998), the employer stated an intention to keep confidential any employee's participation in chemical dependency programs. Relying upon its interpretation of Restatement § 552, the court concluded that a claim for negligent misrepresentation would not lie because this representation was not "commercial" even though it was a part of employment. But wait. The employer and employee were not adversarial on this issue were they?

13. **Open-ended liability for negligence?** Should courts simply say there is always a duty of reasonable care to represent facts truthfully? Then the questions would be (a) whether the defendant's false statement was unreasonable under the circumstances, considering the relationship of the parties and the type of transaction involved; and (b) whether the plaintiff was justified in relying on the statement, likewise considering the relationship of the parties and type of transaction. See *Williams Ford, Inc. v. Hartford Courant Co.,* 232 Conn. 559, 657 A.2d 212 (1995).

14. **Rejecting negligence as a basis of liability.** At the other extreme, Arkansas rejected liability for negligent misrepresentation altogether in *South County, Inc. v. First Western Loan Co.,* 315 Ark. 722, 871 S.W.2d 325 (1994). Could this be the right solution under the economic loss doctrine, at least if the parties actually enter into a contract which deals with the matters allegedly misrepresented? *Home Valu, Inc. v. Pep Boys,* 213 F.3d 960 (7th Cir. 2000) (economic loss doctrine bars both negligent and intentional fraud claims). Would the economic loss doctrine bar the high school student's claim for lost scholarship in *Sain*?

15. **The Glanzer ambiguity.** In *Glanzer v. Shepard,* 233 N.Y. 236, 135 N.E. 275 (1922), the defendant was in the business of weighing commercial goods that were bought and sold by weight. A seller of beans hired the defendant to weigh beans to be sold by weight. The defendant certified that the beans weighed over 228,000 pounds. The buyer paid accordingly, but in fact the beans weighed almost 12,000 pounds less. The buyer was allowed to recover for his loss. The ambiguity: was the weigher negligent "in act" or "in word;" in weighing or in communicating the result? Was the weigher's interest adverse to those of the buyer? Would it even be plausible to impose warranty liability upon the weigher?

16. **Negligence and conscious ignorance.** Are some cases of "conscious ignorance" (or unconscious ignorance) merely cases of negligent representation? Is it possible that some cases of ignorance are truly cases of scienter fraud while others are cases of negligence, while still others are cases of no fault at all? What difference would it make?

17. **Comparative fault reductions.** If the claim rests upon negligent rather than fraudulent representation, would the plaintiff's comparative fault reduce damages? Most courts addressing the issue appear to think so. See *Florenzano v. Olson*, 387 N.W.2d 168 (Minn. 1986). Some comparative fault statutes affect only cases of personal injury and property damage. That would seem to exclude pure economic harm, but *ESCA Corp. v. KPMG Peat Marwick,* 135 Wash.2d 820, 959 P.2d 651 (1998), held that such a statute permitted comparative responsibility assessments in negligent misrepresentation cases. *Braswell v. People's Credit Union,* 602 A.2d 510, 22 A.L.R.5th 868 (R.I. 1992), adopted a "minority view," refusing to reduce or bar for contributory fault of the consumer-plaintiff. One judicial opinion, without noting the comparative fault statute's limitation to personal injury and death, applied comparative fault in an intentional fraud claim. *Bangert Bros. Construction Co. v. Kiewit Western Co.,* 310 F.3d 1278 (10th Cir. 2002) (forecasting Colorado law).

18. **Emotional harm.** We've seen that courts are disinclined to impose liability for emotional harm for intentional misrepresentations in transactions that are predominantly economic and we could expect the same result even more certainly in negligent misrepresentation cases. But what if the defendant undertakes to make a truthful representation on a matter affecting mental tranquility? In *Friedman v. Merck & Co., Inc.,* 107 Cal.App.4th 454, 131 Cal.Rptr.2d 885 (2003), the manufacturer of a TB test assured a potential user, known to be an "ethical Vegan," that the test contained nothing derived from animals. The user then agreed to be tested, but later found that the representation was not correct. He claimed serious emotional harm. The court found no cases supporting liability for serious emotional harm based on negligent representation.

Reference: For a summary of law on negligent misrepresentation see Dobbs on Torts § 472 (2000).

§ 4. INNOCENT REPRESENTATION

19. **Innocent representation generally not grounds for tort damages.** Possibly a few cases support some kind of liability for innocent misrepresentation, but if so, they are rare; liability for innocent representation, is almost never tort liability. Liability, sometimes said to be liability for innocent representation, is imposed in the four limited cases identified in ¶ ¶ 20–23.

20. **Innocent representation as warranty.** If the defendant's representation amounts to a warranty, liability is imposed under warran-

ty rules without regard to whether the representation (warranty) is innocent or not. However, representations in arms' length bargaining are usually considered warranties only when the representation is so described or is made by a seller of tangible goods. Occasional cases find a warranty in other settings.

21. **Conscious ignorance rule as an innocent representation rule.** Some courts say they are imposing strict responsibility when the defendant makes a representation on his "personal knowledge or under circumstances in which he necessarily ought to have known the truth or untruth of the statement." *Schurmann v. Neau,* 240 Wis.2d 719, 624 N.W.2d 157 (Ct. App. 2000). Does that sound like liability for an innocent and non-negligent misrepresentation?

22. **Rescission for innocent representation.** A plaintiff who is induced to enter into a contract by a mutual and basic mistake might rescind, return what he received, and get back what he gave in the deal. When the defendant makes an innocent representation of basic fact that induces a deal, that is an instance of mutual and basic mistake and the courts may permit the plaintiff to have restitution. See DOBBS ON TORTS § 473 (2001 & Supp.). The claim might be defeated under rules for restitution, for example, if the plaintiff is not in a position to restore what he received or delayed too long in seeking restitution. Subject to the expansive possibilities reflected in ¶¶ 81–84, below, restitution is a recovery of what the plaintiff gave in the transaction, perhaps considerably less than the plaintiff's tort damages, which are based on what the plaintiff lost.

23. **Tort damages measured or limited by the restitution measurement.** Since rescission is available for an innocent representation, maybe the tort action for damages could be substituted for rescission if damages are limited so that they would be no more onerous than a rescission would be. Vendor sells Blackacre for $100,000, Purchaser relying upon the innocent representation that water under Blackacre is potable and suitable for raising cattle. In fact the representation is false so that Blackacre is worth only $80,000. If Purchaser rescinds, she will return Blackacre (worth $80,000) and get back her purchase price ($100,000). Since she can do this, is there any reason not to permit her to sue simply for the equivalent in damages, $20,000? The Restatement specifically approves this limited kind of strict liability. RESTATEMENT § 552C. Some courts call this "rescissionary damages." See, spelling it out, DOBBS ON TORTS § 483 (2001 & Supp.)

24. **Statutory liability.** Some statutes impose strict liability in particular settings or transactions. See Chapter 15 below.

§ 5. NONDISCLOSURE AND CONCEALMENT

BLAINE v. J.E. JONES CONSTRUCTION CO.

841 S.W.2d 703 (Mo. App. 1992)

SATZ, Judge.

This is a tort action in fraud. Plaintiffs are owners of homes in Westglen Farms Subdivision in St. Louis County. They purchased their homes from defendant, J.E. Jones Construction Company (Jones Company), the company that developed the subdivision and constructed their homes. Plaintiffs sued the Jones Company for fraud, alleging they were induced into purchasing their homes by the Jones Company's fraudulent concealment of its intent to build an apartment complex in the subdivision near their homes. . . .

Early on, it was said that fraud will not lie for "tacit nondisclosure." Prosser and Keeton, The Law of Torts, § 106 at 737 (5th ed. 1984). This statement reflects the business ethic of caveat emptor together with a touch of the old tort notion that there can be no liability for nonfeasance, or merely doing nothing.

This statement has been mitigated by limitations and exceptions which almost swallow it up. Thus, we do impose a duty to disclose information where a classical fiduciary relationship exists, or, in an extension of that relationship, where one party expressly or by clear implication places a special confidence in the other. The latter exception is quite often loosely characterized as a relationship where one of the parties has superior knowledge which is not within the fair and reasonable reach of the other. In these situations, the passive nondisclosure of information, one party has an affirmative duty to disclose information, and that party's failure to disclose the information serves as a substitute for the false representation element required in fraud. But, in these situations, the real question is, as it is here, when is there a duty to speak and disclose. . . .

. . . Stripped to its essentials, plaintiffs' claim is based upon the silence of the Jones Company; the silence, plaintiffs contend, of a party to the transactions more knowledgeable than plaintiffs.

To state the obvious, silence alone is neutral. But, silence can be made meaningful by surrounding facts. . . .

[Jones and a partner recorded a Planned Environmental Unit document with St. Louis county. It reflected the possibility that 150 multi-family dwellings would be built somewhere on the tract, along with single-family homes. The recorded document did not state whether the multi-family dwellings would be condominiums or apartments. The plat of the larger tract was not so specific; it marked a portion of the land "Future Development" without mention of multi-family dwellings.]

For the purpose of our discussion, we have assumed, without deciding, that the Jones Company did intend to build apartments when plaintiffs purchased their homes; therefore, it did have superior knowledge of this fact. Nonetheless, we still find it had no duty to disclose that fact.

First, there is no indication that any party's intelligence was superior to another. Plaintiffs were college educated. Second, the parties did not bear any special relation to each other beyond their status as buyer and seller. There was no evidence that a confidential relationship of any sort developed between the parties or that the parties were in a fiduciary relationship, such as executor and beneficiary of an estate, or attorney and client. The existence of such a relationship makes it more likely that a duty to disclose would be found. However, here the transactions at issue were the normal arm's length sales of homes.

Third, the nature of the fact not disclosed is an extrinsic fact, not an intrinsic defect. In sales contracts, if the vendor conceals an intrinsic defect not discoverable by reasonable care, there is a greater likelihood that a duty to disclose will be found than if the fact is something extrinsic to the property likely to affect market value. The intent to build apartments in the future is not a defect in plaintiffs' houses which is not discoverable by reasonable care; rather, the intent is a fact that normally can be ascertained by reasonable inquiry. And, as will be explained in detail under the sixth factor, "materiality", the alleged false representations allegedly made by the Jones Company or its agent Gundaker is not relevant to the Jones Company's passive nondisclosure.

Fourth, the contract is an arm's length sales contract for property, it is not a release or contract of insurance where arguably, all material facts must be disclosed. Fifth, the concealer in this case is a seller. A seller is more likely to have a duty to disclose than a buyer.

The sixth factor is the importance or materiality of the fact not disclosed. Admittedly, a developer's intent to build apartments on nearby property could have an effect on a reasonable buyer's decision to buy a house, and, thus, intent is an important fact. However, the significance of this fact is lessened by its extrinsic nature. The fact may affect the market value of the house, but is not a defect in the house itself. Moreover, the Jones Company's intent to build apartments was a decision about the use of land zoned multi-family which could have changed at any time. The actual layout of the multi-family buildings in fact did change from the time of the original PEU to the actual constructed buildings. Furthermore, a developer could reasonably expect that a potential buyer would inquire about the zoning of his and nearby undeveloped property, as well as potential uses for the undeveloped property. . . .

Finally, the seventh factor is the respective knowledge of the parties of the fact and their means of acquiring this knowledge. There is no question in this case that the existence of multi-family zoning and a proposed layout of the multi-family buildings were a part of the public record. Plaintiffs and potential buyers had access to the information, and indeed plaintiff Ronck did get zoning information from St. Louis County.

Admittedly, the multi-family buildings were not designated as any particular type of multi-family building. Such a designation was not required by St. Louis County.

Here, again, however, the public disclosure of zoning for multi-family units puts a reasonable purchaser of a house in close proximity on notice to inquire about the type of multi-family units to be built. Indeed, plaintiffs here testified they made this inquiry. . . .

A developer in the marketplace should not be saddled with the duty to disclose that, as one of the available options under multi-family zoning, he intends to build apartments. The Jones Company, as any other developer, could assume, quite sensibly and rationally, that a buyer would check the public record or ask the developer or its agent to acquire information about the zoning of his and nearby property. It is not unreasonable for an innocent developer with no intent to deceive to believe that the disclosure of multi-family zoning is sufficient notice to a rational buyer of a house near a then undeveloped multi-family zone. . . .

[Judgment to be entered for Jones Company.]

---

25. **No duty to disclose rule.** The traditional common law rule is that one is under no duty to disclose facts and is not liable for fraud or misrepresentation merely because disclosure would have provided another person a more accurate picture. See Dobbs on Torts § 481 (2000).

26. **Disclosure duties—example.** A seller of a commercial building does not reveal that its only tenant is about to become insolvent and give up its lease. The buyer, who expects to finance the purchase through the tenant's rent payments is left high and dry when the tenant quits its business. Cf. *Greenery Rehabilitation Group, Inc. v. Antaramian*, 36 Mass.App.Ct. 73, 628 N.E.2d 1291 (1994).

27. **Active concealment.** For a brief moment in 1963, a car-buyer got the better of a used car dealer. He traded in a car with a cracked block, concealing the crack with a sealant. However, the dealer eventually lost money on the car when the crack was discovered and sued for fraud. This was not mere passive nondisclosure but an active concealment and the dealer was allowed to recover. *Lindberg Cadillac Co. v. Aron*, 371 S.W.2d 651 (Mo. App. 1963). The Restatement recognizes this liability of one who "intentionally prevents" the plaintiff from acquiring material information. Restatement (Second) of Torts § 550.

28. **Half-truth.** A half-truth can be more misleading than a lie in some cases. Suppose a land seller tells the buyer that there is a small easement over one edge of the land, but says nothing of a large easement down the middle. Can't the buyer reasonably think that reference to the small easement indicates that no other easements exist? The Restatement imposes affirmative duties to speak when the defendant knows

facts that are needed to prevent a partial or ambiguous statement from being misleading. Restatement § 551(2)(b).

29. **Subsequently acquired information.** Sometimes a person's statements are true when they are made but become untrue later. Courts usually recognize that one who has asserted a fact must correct it if the fact becomes untrue later. The same principle requires the speaker to correct a statement that was untrue all along but that he honestly thought was true when he made it. See Restatement § 551(2)(c) & (d).

30. **Fiduciaries and those in positions of trust and confidence.** Fiduciaries are under a duty to make full disclosure to their beneficiaries. In contrast to "arm's length" bargainers, fiduciaries are expected to act in the best interests of others, not for themselves. See *Burkons v. Ticor Title Ins. Co. of California*, 168 Ariz. 345, 813 P.2d 710 (1991) (escrow agent's duty to reveal evidence of fraud by one of the parties upon the other). In some instances, the fiducial obligation may even arise in pre-contract negotiations to set up a fiduciary relationship. *Martin v. Heinold Commodities, Inc.*, 163 Ill.2d 33, 205 Ill.Dec. 443, 643 N.E.2d 734 (1994) (agency discussions with potential broker about fees; broker owed duty to disclose commissions on foreign options). It has even been held that the fiduciary obligation to disclose may continue after the fiduciary relationship itself has terminated. "He could not doff his obligations so readily. He was bound to reveal his defalcations before he could be absolved." *Pacelli Brothers Transportation, Inc. v. Pacelli*, 189 Conn. 401, 456 A.2d 325 (1983). Those who stand in a relationship of trust and confidence are under similar duties to disclose. See *Stewart v. Phoenix Nat'l Bank*, 49 Ariz. 34, 64 P.2d 101, 106 (1937) (bank-depositor relationship normally one of debtor-creditor, but if depositor places special confidence in the bank, based on bank's past treatment as friend and financial advisor, the relationship of confidence may arise in which the bank is under a duty to affirmatively disclose facts in its transactions with the customer).

31. **Nondisclosure and mistake of fact.** Recall that certain mutual mistakes of fact justify rescission and that an innocent representation on one side and a mistake on the other is equivalent to a mutual mistake. What about the case in which the seller makes no mistake but knows or has reason to know that the plaintiff is making one, yet remains silent?

MAYBEE v. JACOBS MOTOR CO., INC.

519 N.W.2d 341 (S.D. 1994)

HENDERSON, Justice. . . .

In October 1988, James Phipps traded his 1984 Chevrolet van to Jacobs Motor Company for another vehicle. The van's engine, however, had been previously replaced with a rebuilt engine using an engine block which had been manufactured in approximately 1966. This replacement engine used a canister-style oil filter, a type that has not been used on passenger vehicles since the late 1960s. Phipps maintains that he informed Jacobs Motor of the engine because he believed a rebuilt engine on a used vehicle to be a strong selling point.

During the van's ten months on the used car lot, Jacobs Motor added approximately 7,000 miles to the odometer, which included a round trip to Houston, Texas. Despite a standard policy of changing the oil and filter on trade-ins, Jacobs Motor asserts that such a service was never performed on the van. Because of this oversight, Jacobs Motor contends that the out-dated canister-style filter was never noticed by its employees.

Maybee and her husband visited Jacobs Motor Company in August of 1989. Salesman Paul Mitchell showed Maybee the van and invited her to take the van home overnight. Although Maybee had the opportunity to ask questions and have the van inspected by her own mechanic, she declined. Conversely, no employee of Jacobs Motor volunteered any information about the van's dieseling problem, oil leak problems, or the engine. However, when asked about the representations of Mitchell, Maybee testified, "He just said that it was an '84 van that was in good condition and that they had used it around the business." When Maybee purchased the van for $8,700.00, not knowing that the 1984 van had a 1966 engine, she signed a contract disclaiming all express and implied warranties.

Over a month after the purchase, Maybee's husband took the van to a mechanic because of oil leakage. The mechanic noticed the canister-style filter and, upon investigation, discovered that the engine had been manufactured in 1966 and was completely worn. Additionally, Maybee's expert testified: It's a high compression engine. It requires a higher octane and better grade of fuel than you can buy today, unless you go to an airport and buy aviation fuel. Maybee contended before the jury that the proper engine had been switched with a 1966 engine, the engine was worn out, it did not run efficiently because of a high compression ratio, and the 1966 engine would stall out or cut out. Ultimately, Maybee testified the vehicle was parked in the yard because it "didn't work."

At trial, all nine witnesses from the auto dealership denied any knowledge, prior to the sale to Maybee, that the van's engine had been rebuilt with the 1966 engine block. Although not all service records for the van could be located, service personnel at Jacobs Motor denied ever changing the oil in the van.

Following a week-long trial, the jury found Jacobs Motor guilty of fraud and deceit and awarded compensatory damages of $14,700.00 and punitive damages of $75,000.00. Because the compensatory damages award was almost ten times the $1,450.00 cost of replacing the engine, the trial court, refusing to rule out mathematical errors or passion or prejudice by the jury, granted a new trial on damages. Jacobs Motor appeals the issue of liability. Maybee appeals the grant of a new trial on damages. . . .

Jacobs Motor maintains that the trial court's actions [in submitting the claim to the jury] are tantamount to overturning Taggart v. Ford Motor Credit Co., 462 N.W.2d 493, 499 (S.D.1990), which held, "This court has never imposed a duty to disclose information on parties to an arm's-length business transaction, absent an employment or fiduciary relationship." In Taggart, the defendants were not parties to the transaction; but in Ducheneaux v. Miller, 488 N.W.2d 902 (S.D.1992), both parties were parties to the transaction. We distinguished Taggart and applied Restatement (Second) of Torts § 551(2)(e):

> (2) One party to a business transaction is under a duty to exercise reasonable care to disclose to the other before the transaction is consummated. . . .
>
> > (e) facts basic to the transaction, if he knows that the other is about to enter into it under a mistake as to them, and that the other, because of the relationship between them, the customs of the trade or other objective circumstances, would reasonably expect a disclosure of those facts.

Thus, the jury was properly left to decide if the engine's age and condition were facts basic to the Maybee–Jacobs Motor transaction.

Finally, Jacobs Motor employs, as a defense, Maybee's signed disclaimer of all express and implied warranties as a safety net for any wrongdoing, an affirmative defense, so to speak. Although "as is" clauses place the risk upon the buyer to accept the product with all its faults, this does not grant the seller a license to mislead the buyer or conceal facts. 37 Am.Jur.2d Fraud and Deceit § 158 (1968).

When a person purchases a 1984 vehicle, is the presence, within that vehicle, of an engine built for a 1966 model vehicle which requires a fuel not typically used by vehicles on the road today, a fact basic to the transaction? The jury so found and this Court finds that the evidence can support such a finding.

[The court ordered a new trial, however, because the damages award was excessive.]

---

32. **Example.** A real estate broker offers T's house for sale. The broker finds the plaintiff as a potential buyer and concludes a sale with the plaintiff. No one ever mentions a hazardous waste dump located nearby. Is the broker liable for this nondisclosure? See *Strawn v. Canuso,* 140 N.J. 43, 657 A.2d 420, 41 A.L.R.5th 859 (1995).

33. **Fault basis.** Is nondisclosure, where actionable at all, (a) an intentional tort, (b) a negligent tort, or (c) a strict liability tort? The Restatement § 550 seems to treat active concealment as an intentional misrepresentation. But § 552 (2) speaks of "a duty to exercise reason-

able care to disclose" matters known to him as a fiduciary, matters necessary to avoid misleading by half-truth, subsequently acquired information, and basic facts. Does this mean that the nondisclosure claim is always one for "negligence"? And therefore that the comparative negligence rule could always reduce recovery in nondisclosure cases? Suppose the house seller knows of a serious defect in the roof that will soon require major expense, says nothing, and prays the buyer won't ask. He very definitely hopes to mislead the buyer by his silence. Is this any less an intentional tort than an active misrepresentation that the roof is in good condition?

34. **Duty to tell or duty to ask?** Does it matter whether the seller is obliged to disclose or the buyer obliged to ask? After all, a buyer can ask whether the house has termites or could even demand a warranty that it does not. But what all should the buyer ask about? Could you expect the buyer to ask whether anyone has recently died in the house with bubonic plague?

35. **Buyers' duties of disclosure.** How do you feel about a buyer's nondisclosure? It is generally said that buyers are under no duty to disclose facts. The land speculator may purchase Blackacre without informing its owner that oil has been found nearby. See, e.g., *Harrell v. Powell*, 249 N.C. 244, 106 S.E.2d 160 (1958) ("A vendee, who knows that there is a gold mine on the land, is not compelled to disclose that fact to the vendor," quoting). *Laidlaw v. Organ*, 15 U.S. (2 Wheat.) 178, 4 L.Ed. 214 (1817) is a leading case. The buyer of cotton learned that peace had been declared, with the likelihood that prices of some goods would go up. The seller knew nothing of the fact and the buyer did not tell him. In this situation, courts may suggest that the buyer is entitled to use his entrepreneurial skills, investigation, and knowledge for his own benefit. Why isn't the same true about the seller's skills and information?

36. **The buying fiduciary.** The fiduciary in the same situation must disclose the facts to the vendor. *Dolan v. Cummings*, 116 App.Div. 787, 102 N.Y.S. 91 (1907), aff'd, 193 N.Y. 638, 86 N.E. 1123 (1909); Annotation, 56 A.L.R. 419 (1928). In the *Dolan* case, a brother had an offer for land owned by his siblings. He bought the land from them without revealing the offer. This was held to be a violation of the confidential relationship between them.

37. **Testing the buyer's-duty rule.** Suppose (a) the prospective buyer knows that the violin the seller is offering for sale for $100 is really a Stradivarius worth hundreds of times as much; (b) the prospective buyer of the seller's land knows that a new tax bill just passed that will make it very profitable to hold the land.

38. **Statutes.** Statutes frequently impose duties of disclosure and otherwise affect rules of common law fraud. See Chapter 15 below.

§ 6. RELIANCE, MATERIALITY, AND THE REQUIREMENT OF A FACTUAL REPRESENTATION

39. **Reliance rules.** (1) No misrepresentation is actionable as such unless the victim in fact relied upon the misrepresentation to his or her detriment. (2) Even if the victim in fact relies upon a representation, the reliance must in some sense be justified. (3) As a matter of law, reliance upon immaterial representations is not justified. (4) Neither is reliance upon nonfactual statements and implications, for instance, upon pure opinion or statements about the future. Although these rules can be expressed in terms of reliance or its justification, most of them can also be expressed independently of the reliance rule. See generally, DOBBS ON TORTS §§ 474–479 (2000).

(a) Reliance in fact

ST. PAUL FIRE & MARINE INS. CO. v. RUSSO BROTHERS, INC.

641 A.2d 1297 (R.I. 1994)

SHEA, Justice.

[The Russos operated a wholesale tobacco business. They needed a commercial bond that would guarantee to the state that tobacco taxes would be paid. St. Paul, for a premium, furnished such a bond on an annual basis. When the Russos' financial position seemed to deteriorate, St. Paul refused to continue providing annual bonds unless the Russos agreed to sign an indemnity agreement under which they would repay St. Paul should it become liable. The Russos executed the agreement. Under the bond, St. Paul was eventually required to pay the state the Russos' taxes. It then sued the Russos on the indemnity agreement. The trial judge gave summary judgment for St. Paul.]

The defendants claim that they are not liable under the indemnity agreement because of alleged misrepresentations by insurance agent Chase at the time they executed the agreement. They contend that prior to executing the agreement, Chase repeatedly assured them the indemnity agreement was effective for only one year. The parties do not dispute that the express language of the agreement requires defendants to indemnify St. Paul if it is found liable under the bond at any time. ... The trial justice found that the indemnity agreement was clear and unambiguous and that the parol evidence rule precluded admitting evidence of a contemporaneous agreement that limited the indemnification to only one year.

... We acknowledge that defendants generally would not be barred from challenging a contract because of fraud, even though they were negligent in signing the contract without reading it. Continental Illustrating Co. v. Longley Motor Sales Co., 43 R.I. 552, 553, 113 A. 869, 869–70 (1921). However, even when the record in this case is viewed in the light most favorable to defendants, neither of these arguments supports defendants' position.

The parol evidence rule is a well-settled rule of substantive law. It provides that, "in the absence of fraud or mistake, parol or extrinsic evidence is not admissible to vary, alter or contradict a written agreement." Chase's alleged oral representations that the indemnity agreement would be effective for only one year constitute extrinsic evidence contradicting the unambiguous terms of the written contract. Although the parol evidence rule would ordinarily bar such extrinsic evidence, defendants argue that the rule is inapplicable to Chase's alleged statements because the statements are evidence of fraud or misrepresentation affecting the contract's validity.

. . . Nowhere in the pleadings and materials properly before the trial justice did defendants allege they were induced to execute the indemnity agreement by the alleged misrepresentations. In his deposition Mr. Russo did not testify that he would not have signed the indemnity agreement if he knew it would be effective for more than one year. Instead, Mr. Russo stated, "I had no choice, because if I didn't receive that bond I'd be out of business then and there, at that moment." Thus the uncontradicted testimony before the trial justice was that Mr. Russo signed the indemnity agreement to stay in business, not because Chase's misrepresentations induced him to sign.

The trial justice properly entered summary judgment because defendants failed to properly assert that the alleged misrepresentation induced them to execute the indemnity agreement. Absent a sufficient pleading of reliance on the alleged misrepresentation, the parol evidence rule precludes evidence of a contemporaneous oral agreement to vary the terms of the written agreement. . . .

---

40. **A problem for evaluation.** Construction Company builds a building for Beyer. After completion, Beyer hires T to make changes. T's work is defective and requires repair. Beyer claims that Construction Company did the defective work and sues for the defects, falsely attributing them to Construction Company. Construction Company, forced to defend a lengthy suit, counterclaims for fraudulent misrepresentations. *DeBry v. Cascade Enterprises*, 879 P.2d 1353 (Utah 1994). Does the company have a good counterclaim?

41. **Relief without damages?** Suppose a misrepresentation leads the victim to purchase something entirely different from the thing she thought she was getting, but she gets something worth as much. Defendant falsely assures the plaintiff that a painting is by Giorgione when in fact is by Bellini and the plaintiff buys in reliance on the assurance. The

painting's value is equal to the value it would have had if it had been painted by Giorgione.

42. **Reliance on nondisclosure; two cases.** How does the reliance requirement work in nondisclosure cases? Suppose a homeowner, selling a house to you, says nothing about termite infestation of which he knows. You buy the house. *Ford New Holland, Inc. v. Proctor–Russell Tractor Co., Inc.*, 630 So.2d 395 (Ala. 1993), denied recovery in a nondisclosure case because, even though the defendant had a duty to disclose, the plaintiff failed to prove that he "had been deceived by the false representation and . . . that [he] had been induced to act in reliance on the defendant's misrepresentation." Can you say you relied upon a representation when you bought the termite-infested house?

In *Lovejoy v. AT&T Corp.*, 92 Cal.App.4th 85, 111 Cal.Rptr.2d 711 (2001), the plaintiff, operating a business with an 800 number provided by Pac Bell, alleged that AT&T falsely represented to Pac Bell that plaintiff wished to switch to AT&T. He went on to allege that his 800 number was then switched, but charges for it were hidden in his AT&T long distance charges. When his long distance service was terminated, so was his 800 number, but he didn't know it. AT&T assigned the number to another user and the plaintiff's business suffered as no calls came through. Did the plaintiff rely? Could you argue that Pac Bell was the plaintiff's agent for the purpose of switching and that the agent's reliance is reliable by the principal?

43. **Reliance on others besides the defendant.** In *Bulbman, Inc. v. Nevada Bell*, 108 Nev. 105, 825 P.2d 588 (1992), the plaintiff consulted an independent expert in choosing a telephone system. On the basis of the expert's recommendations, the plaintiff decided on a Centrex system. He then contacted Nevada Bell, which made representations that Centrex could be installed in thirty minutes and other representations about cost and reliability. The plaintiff then purchased the Centrex system from Nevada Bell, but lost orders because in fact it was not working properly within thirty minutes. The court appeared to think that the plaintiff could not have relied upon the Nevada Bell representations. Can that be correct?

44. **Fraud on the market; plaintiff's reliance on integrity of the market.** Corporate insiders or others disseminate false economic information about a corporation whose shares are sold on major stock markets. If the information shows, say, increase in corporate sales, the market price may rise, but, when the information proves false months later, the market price may drop precipitously. Suppose the plaintiff never hears of the information about increased sales, but does happen to buy shares after that information has been made public and the market price has risen. A few months later, though, the truth is told and the shares fall in value, leaving the plaintiff the loser. Can she recover from the fraudulent insiders on the theory that she relied indirectly by relying on the integrity of the market, which was undermined by the defendants' lies? The Supreme Court has given limited approval of this "fraud

on the market" theory in certain federal securities cases, provided that the fraud did actually affect market price. *Basic Inc. v. Levinson,* 485 U.S. 224, 108 S.Ct. 978, 99 L.Ed.2d 194 (1988). State courts, starting with *Mirkin v. Wasserman,* 5 Cal.4th 1082, 858 P.2d 568, 23 Cal.Rptr.2d 101 (1993), have so far rejected this theory for fraud claims under state common law or state securities statutes. One reason is that they doubt that markets are affected by any one piece of information. Another is that federal statutes enacted in the 1990s have placed substantial impediments in the way of plaintiffs who wish to sue under federal securities laws, and state courts are reluctant to create a hiatus in the protection Congress has seen fit to provide to defendants charged with making misrepresentations. See *Kaufman v. i-Stat Corp.,* 165 N.J. 94, 754 A.2d 1188 (2000).

NATAROS V. FINE ARTS GALLERY OF SCOTTSDALE, INC., 126 Ariz. 44, 612 P.2d 500 (1980). Plaintiff read an auction ad stating items from the McCune estate would be auctioned off. There was a fine print note disclosing that other items would also be included. P attended. He revealed the absence of artistic information but the presence of a desire to acquire art as a hedge against inflation. An employee of the gallery represented that he was knowledgeable and gave P a list of items with price ranges for each, saying it would be a bargain if P could purchase at the lower end. P engaged in competitive bidding, which was not rigged, and purchased some $577,000 in "art" items. Shortly thereafter he stopped payment, and after some bargaining, issued a new check for $286,777 and returned some items.

The items did not originate with the McCune estate but with a New York art dealer. After about a year, the plaintiff had the items appraised by Sotheby's. The appraisals were substantially lower than prices he paid at auction. For instance, a painting by Sargent was appraised at $25–30,000, but P had paid $85,000.

Held: Directed verdict for D affirmed. Under the Arizona Consumer Fraud Act, reliance may not be required. However, falsity is still required and so is resulting actual harm. There was no evidence that if the goods had come from the McCune estate they would have been worth more, so there was no damage. So far as common law claims are concerned, the plaintiffs have not shown that the market value estimates were false. "In this case, the estimated market value given by Mr. Goald for each of the items purchased by Mr. Nataros was in the range of that actually established by free and open bidding at auction. There is no contention that the auction was contrived or that the other bidders were other than bona fide prospective purchasers seeking the same end as Mr. Nataros to obtain the object at the least possible price. Nor was there evidence that Mr. Goald's estimates of values had the ring of self-fulfilling prophesies, that is, that all other bidders were operating under Mr. Goald's pre-established values. In short, the open market place established the truth or falsity of Mr. Goald's representations. At least, in Scottsdale, Arizona in January, 1973, the open market place established that those representations were accurate."

---

45. **Circumventing the reliance rules by contract?** In some fields and under some theories, the role of the reliance in fact requirement may be diminished or eliminated even apart from statutory rules. Consider:

(A) A parent applies for a life policy on a child, "warranting" in the application that the child had never required medical attention. The policy is issued and the child dies shortly thereafter. Investigation shows that the child has in fact had medical attention but the parent says he forgot it. Has the company a defense based on fraud? What if the parent was honest? What if the company did not rely on the applications? Statutes may now provide that the policy is not voided unless the insurer actually relies upon the statement. See ARIZ. REV. STATS. § 20–1109.

(B) Suppose fire insurance policies contain a provision like this:

> If, either before or after a loss, the insured wilfully conceals or misrepresents any materials facts or circumstances concerning this insurance or the subject thereof, or in case of any false swearing by the insured, the entire policy shall be void.

After a fire the insured swears out a proof of loss for $50,000 when in fact the value of the building and goods was not more than $25,000. The company does not pay at all, but argues that this is false swearing and the policy is void. This is usually upheld and liability is avoided. Obviously this does not require reliance by the insurer. See ANNOTATION, 16 A.L.R.3d 774 (1967).

(b) Justified reliance

46. **Requirement of "justified reliance."** According to the usual statement, the plaintiff must prove not only misrepresentation and reliance in fact, but also that reliance was "justified" or reasonable. This does not seem to be a rule of contributory negligence, but what is it, then? The rule does not necessarily call for investigation of facts, but it does seem to require reasonable skepticism about inherently improbable statements. Perhaps the rule is best understood as a generalization about more specific rules of materiality, opinion, and prediction.

47. **Requirement of materiality.** The Restatement rule is that the plaintiff can recover for pecuniary losses for misrepresentation only if her reliance upon the representation is justified, and that it is not justified unless the representation is material. A fact is material if a reasonable person would "attach importance" to it in deciding on a choice of action. It is also material if the defendant knows or has reason to know that the plaintiff personally attaches significance to the matter, even though an objectively reasonable person would not. This is formally spelled out in Restatement § 538. Cases often offer similar formulations.

E.g., *Horsch v. Terminix International Co.*, 19 Kan.App.2d 134, 865 P.2d 1044 (1994). Consider this formulation: "a material representation is one that would likely affect the conduct of a reasonable person with reference to the transaction." Is that meaning the same as the Restatement's formulation? *Campbell v. Southland Corporation*, 127 Or.App. 93, 871 P.2d 487 (1994).

48. **Examples for evaluation.** Suppose defendant is a seller of used cars. He tells a potential buyer that he has three children, all in college. This is an outright lie, used to gain confidence (or perhaps sympathy?). Such lies facilitate friendly talk, fellow-feeling, and ultimately sales. Is the statement material?

Suppose that the same salesperson knows that the next prospect is a member of the KamaSuture Sect of Surgeons and prefers to buy only from co-religionists. The seller assures the buyer that the seller, too, is a member of the sect. Is this material?

49. **Opinion, puffing, and law statements.** The plaintiff is seldom justified in relying on statements of pure opinion, implying no assertions of fact, statements that puff or praise the defendant's wares in general terms, and abstract statements of law in the absence of special circumstances.

McGowan v. Chrysler Corporation, 631 So.2d 842 (Ala. 1993). The plaintiff bought a Chrysler car, allegedly relying upon advertisements and dealer's "representations" that "the 1987 Fifth Avenue was a 'top-of-the-line' car and a 'smooth-riding' car." Whether a given representation is an expression of opinion or a statement of fact depends upon all the circumstances of the particular case, such as the form and subject matter of the representation and the knowledge, intelligence and relation of the respective parties. The mere form of the representation as one of opinion or fact is not in itself conclusive, and in cases of doubt the question should be left to the jury. Nevertheless, in this case, the statements were only puffery, not representations of fact.

Briggs v. Carol Cars, Inc., 407 Mass. 391, 553 N.E.2d 930 (1990). The plaintiff purchased a used car from the defendant on the defendant's representation that "the vehicle in question was in good condition." Shortly after she took it home, she discovered that it burned oil: in six weeks, she had to put in nine quarts. The car had a number of other difficulties, such as stalling. The defendant argued that the "good condition" statement was only a matter of opinion and not actionable. The trial judge, as trier, awarded damages to the plaintiff. *Held*, affirmed. The trial judge was warranted in her finding that the statement was one of fact. "Fraud or deceit 'may be perpetrated by an implied as well as by an express representation.' A statement that, in form, is one of opinion, in some circumstances may reasonably be interpreted by the recipient to imply that the maker of the statement knows facts that justify the opinion. Restatement (Second) of Torts § 539 (1977). Such circumstances were present in this case in which an uninformed person purchased a used vehicle from a dealer in such items. The defendant's representation that the vehicle was in good condition reasonably implied that it was safe and operable and that the vehicle's oil requirements would be far less than they turned out to be. Therefore, we reject the defendant's argument that its representation concerning the good condition of the Plymouth was not a statement of fact."

50. **Implied facts.** The Restatement recognizes that liability may be imposed for "opinion" statements where the facts are not disclosed and the statement implies that the speaker knows facts that justify the opinion. Restatement § 539.

SHAFMASTER v. SHAFMASTER

138 N.H. 460, 642 A.2d 1361 (1994)

BROCK, Chief Justice. . . .

[The parties were husband and wife who decided on divorce after 17 years of marriage.] The parties intended to proceed in a non-litigious manner, without formal discovery, in an atmosphere of cooperation.

To that end, during September 1986, the defendant's accountant provided the plaintiff's financial advisor with requested financial information including a financial statement dated April 30, 1986. By early December 1986, the plaintiff hired her own attorney. The parties, each represented by counsel, negotiated a property settlement agreement based on the financial information that had been provided to the plaintiff's financial advisor. Unknown to the plaintiff, her attorney or her financial advisor, the defendant had a new financial statement dated December 31, 1986, which he signed in March of 1987, that showed a significant increase in the value of his assets. In mid-May 1987, the plaintiff's attorney wrote to the defendant's attorney requesting that a new paragraph be added to the stipulation [which ended with this sentence]:

> Each party acknowledges that he or she has been forthright with the other regarding the current status and value of their assets and financial affairs.

The defendant's attorney refused to add the last sentence of the additional proposed language. He wrote: "Article 14 is new, per your suggestion. I have not included your suggested last sentence. We have provided you and [plaintiff's financial advisor] with all of the financial data you have requested, and I feel it is your responsibility to determine what the values are for property settlement purposes." The stipulation was signed in final form on June 23, 1987, without the suggested final sentence in paragraph fourteen.

The parties' divorce decree approved and incorporated the permanent stipulation that provided for distribution of their considerable property. ... The master's recommendation of the divorce decree incorporating the stipulation was approved by the Superior Court (Gray, J.) on June 29, 1987.

In January 1989, the plaintiff petitioned the court to modify the parties' divorce decree alleging that the stipulated property settlement was obtained by fraud through the defendant's intentional misrepresentation of material financial information. [The master denied relief.] The plaintiff appeals the denial of her petition to modify the parties' divorce decree.

... Property distributions or stipulations decreed by a court are not retained under the continuing jurisdiction of the court and will not be modified unless the complaining party shows that the distribution is invalid due to fraud, undue influence, deceit, misrepresentation, or mutual mistake. ... One who makes a representation that is true when made is under a duty to correct the statement if it becomes erroneous or is discovered to have been false before the transaction is consummated. In contract negotiations, equity imposes a duty to speak when one knows or ought to know that his silence is misleading and will induce another to act upon it to his damage.

As noted by the marital master, the primary issue in this case involves the valuation of known assets rather than concealment of assets. The defendant contends that values included in his financial statements were opinions rather than facts, and, as such, cannot be the basis for fraud. The law is to the contrary. Opinions of value, if made to mislead, are fraudulent representations.

We agree with the marital master that once financial information was requested and provided, the defendant had an ongoing obligation to provide current and accurate financial information. ...

In equity, we will not allow the defendant to perpetrate a fraud based on an eleventh hour change of negotiating posture from cooperation to combat. Because the defendant failed to provide the plaintiff with updated financial statements in violation of his duty to do so, he allowed her to rely on information which he knew was dated and false when she signed the permanent stipulation for property distribution. Therefore, we conclude that the defendant fraudulently induced the plaintiff to sign the property settlement and that the plaintiff, under these circumstances, did not have a duty to conduct discovery or further investigate the defendant's representations. ...

---

51. **Reliance on valuation statements.** Statements of value by an adversarial bargainer are obviously suspect. *Mitchell v. Mitchell*, 888 S.W.2d 393 (Mo. App. 1994), insisted that, in a divorce negotiation, the husband's representations about the value of his assets, would be action-

able only if he had "special knowledge" about value, otherwise his statements would be only opinion.

Yet in *Westby v. Gorsuch,* 112 Wash.App. 558, 50 P.3d 284 (2002), the plaintiff had inherited an item from the Titanic. Needing immediate funds, he took it to a local antique dealer who first told him the item would not even bring as much as $500. The dealer nevertheless then agreed to pay the plaintiff $1,000 for the item and an album of post cards, some of which had Titanic associations, although the plaintiff said the dealer told him they were worth nothing. The dealer later auctioned the ticket for a total of $110,000. Would a reasonable seller think (a) the dealer's low-value statement was merely dealer's talk, the buyer's version of puffing? (b) the dealer was a philanthropist in disguise, paying more than twice the value of the article? The court upheld a judgment for the plaintiff. Maybe the plaintiff thought he was consulting the buyer as an expert first, and then the roles changed so his consultant became his buyer?

GOLDMAN V. BARNETT, 793 F.Supp. 28 (D. Mass. 1992). Barnett was an art dealer. He owned a painting by Milton Avery and held other Milton Averys on consignment for resale. He sold his own and one of the consigned paintings to the plaintiff, along with other art for a total of $1 million. The Averys constituted most of the value. The defendant had appraised the paintings on a letterhead stating that he was a member of the Appraisers Association of America. Although the plaintiff paid less than the values attributed to the paintings by the defendant's appraisals, he became suspicious that he had nevertheless paid too much. He sued, claiming that the appraisals were fraudulent. On summary judgment motion, *held*, (Keeton, J.): jury issues were raised on the issue of falsity. "First, there is evidence that his appraisals were, on average, roughly four times higher than the fair market value as found by at least one other expert. Second, Barnett received a commission on his sales giving him inducement to inflate the purchase price. Third, a jury could find that Barnett held himself out as an expert appraiser; thus, a jury could reasonably infer that he did know the true market values." And because "a jury could find that Barnett held himself out as an expert art appraiser, particularly of the paintings of Milton Avery," the jury could also find that his market value representation was made "by one possessing knowledge rather than mere opinion."

MILWAUKEE AUCTION GALLERIES, LIMITED v. CHALK

13 F.3d 1107 (7th Cir. 1994)

POSNER, Chief Judge.

Two art dealers brought this diversity suit for fraud and breach of contract against O. Roy Chalk, the well-known entrepreneur (and now

Russia's Washington representative). Megan Rosenfeld, "Russia's Capitalist on the Potomac," Washington Post, June 20, 1991, p. D1. The district judge granted the defendant a directed verdict on the fraud count, and the jury rendered a verdict for the defendant on the breach of contract count. The law of Wisconsin governs the substantive issues.

An octogenarian, Chalk decided the time had come to sell part of his extensive art collection, which is housed in his apartment in New York City. Distrusting New York art dealers, he made an oral contract with the two plaintiffs whereby each would be entitled to a 5 percent commission, to be paid by the buyer, if they presented to Chalk someone who was ready, willing, and able to buy a work of art that he wanted to sell, and if the sale was made. These were nonexclusive contracts, so there was no question of taking the art to the gallery of either plaintiff to be shown—and anyway Chalk refused to let the art leave his apartment. To allay the plaintiffs' concern that Chalk would meet and deal directly with prospective buyers whom the plaintiffs brought him, cutting the brokers out, Chalk promised the plaintiffs that he would "protect" their commissions.

One prospect whom the plaintiffs brought to Chalk's apartment to view his art, Mr. Morishita, expressed particular interest in Renoir's "L'Enfant a la Pomme" but thought the price of $3.5 million too high. A year later a company controlled by Morishita bought the painting from Chalk for $2 million. Chalk refused the plaintiffs' demand for a commission on the sale. The same story was repeated with another buyer of another painting—Mary Cassatt's "Sara in a Dark Bonnet." These two sales are the foundation of the lawsuit.

The claim of fraud is based on two alleged misrepresentations by Chalk. The first was the promise to protect the plaintiffs' commissions. The making of a promise normally implies at the very least that the promisor does not have a fixed intention not to honor it; so, if he does have that intention, he is guilty of misrepresentation. But courts naturally are concerned lest every breach of contract be levered into fraud by the too-facile expedient of asking the jury to infer from the fact that the defendant did not perform his promise that he never intended to perform it. So the rule has grown up that nonperformance is not enough to ground such an inference; there must be additional evidence of the defendant's intentions at the time he made the promise. There was no additional evidence here.

The second alleged misrepresentation is that when the plaintiffs inquired about their commission for the sale of the Cassatt, Chalk told them that the buyer was no one they knew, so they hadn't earned any commission. This misrepresentation, if it occurred (there is evidence that Chalk didn't know the connection between the buyer and the plaintiffs), constituted fraudulent concealment of the original (and nonactionable) fraud. Fraudulent concealment of legal liability is a form of fraud for which damages or other relief (most commonly, tolling the statute of limitations, as in City of Madison v. Hyland, Hall & Co., 73 Wis.2d 364,

243 N.W.2d 422, 431 (1976)), can be obtained in an appropriate case. The plaintiffs, who sued within the statutory period, want damages. But as with any other tort, there must be evidence of injury before damages can be awarded; there was none. Another possibility not pursued—so we needn't discuss it—is that the fraudulent concealment alleged in this case was evidence of a fraudulent disposition that might provide the missing evidence on the original claim of fraud.

So the district judge was right to direct a verdict for the defendant on the claim of fraud. . . .

BIBERSTINE v. NEW YORK BLOWER CO., 625 N.E.2d 1308 (Ind. App. 1993). "The law in this jurisdiction is well-settled that actual fraud may not be based on representations regarding future conduct, or on broken promises, unfulfilled predictions or statements of existing intent which are not executed. NYB's representations that it would allow Biberstine to keep his stock in the event his employment was terminated were not misrepresentations of past or existing fact but rather were representations regarding future conduct. Biberstine thus failed to present materials supporting an essential element of his claim for fraud. The trial court properly granted summary judgment in favor of NYB on this claim."

---

52. **Advantages of a fraud claim to the plaintiff.** Why would a plaintiff aggrieved by a broken promise like that alleged in Chalk's case ever need to claim fraud as distinct from a breach of contract? Some possibilities include these: the statute of limitations for fraud is more favorable (not likely); the parol evidence rule, or the statute of frauds bars a claim on the unwritten promise but not on actual fraud.

53. **Evidence of fraudulent intent in "promissory fraud" cases.** Nonperformance of a promise is not sufficient evidence to show that the promisor had a fraudulent intent when the promise was made. What *is* sufficient? Suppose a client tells you the following story:

> I purchased a condo for $200,000 from the CanDoCondo Company. They told me that by summer, they would have tennis courts, racquetball courts, an olympic pool, and some other stuff for the common use of the owners. But they never built any of it and I don't think they will. When I talked to them about it they said, we'll build it all if we can, but its not in the contract, so I should have no complaint. They are right; there is nothing about it in the contract.

If you hope to prove promissory fraud or fraudulent intent, what specific kinds of evidence might you seek?

§ 7. SCOPE OF DUTY

(a) Third Persons

54. **Scienter fraud and liability to third persons.** Privity is not required to impose liability for scienter fraud. A defendant guilty of scienter fraud is subject to liability to all those he intends or expects to influence, provided they reasonably rely on his statement in the type of transaction he intends or expects to influence. See RESTATEMENT (SECOND) OF TORTS § 531 (1977). Short of actual intent, reason to expect that the statement will influence a transaction or a class of persons is sufficient. However, "reason to expect" is more demanding than mere foreseeability. See *Ernst & Young, L.L.P. v. Pacific Mut. Life Ins. Co.,* 51 S.W.3d 573 (Tex. 2001).

55. **Applying the person and transaction limitation.** Suppose: (a) The defendant intentionally misrepresents to X that certain officers or managers of the World Energy Corporation are honest when he knows they are not. The plaintiff is a butler listening at the keyhole and invests in World Energy Corporation. He is then financially wiped out when it crashes. (b) Defendant advertises his home for sale with the statement that the neighborhood is not contaminated by a scandalous dump two miles west. In fact the defendant knows it is seriously contaminated. The plaintiff, relying on the ad, buys property in the neighborhood, though not the defendant's. Cf. RESTATEMENT (SECOND) OF TORTS § 531, illus. 7.

NORTH AMERICAN SPECIALTY INS. CO. v. LAPALME

258 F.3d 35 (1st Cir. 2001)

SELYA, Circuit Judge. . . .

In the 1980s, Jeffrey Canty formed Canty Roofing and Sheetmetal, Inc. (CRS). . . . For much of CRS's existence, the firm of Dias & Lapalme (D & L) rendered accounting services to it. The partner in charge was David Lapalme. For the most part, the work was mundane, involving, inter alia, the preparation of annual financial statements and tax returns.

Over the years, CRS installed and repaired roofs on a variety of public and private buildings. Contractors working on public construction projects in Massachusetts are required by statute to post payment and performance bonds on a project-by-project basis. CRS routinely bid on public works jobs and, thus, from time to time required bonds.

. . . [After inspecting CRS's financial records and Canty's personal finances] NASI entered into a bonding relationship with CRS. Once this relationship commenced, NASI told Canty that CRS would be required to provide updated financial statements, prepared by an independent certified public accountant, for each succeeding calendar year.

In late 1995, Canty agreed to sell CRS to a group composed of three businessmen, namely, Robert Cote, Paul Flynn, and David Beasley. The transfer of ownership, structured as a sale of stock, occurred on December 29, 1995. Shortly thereafter, D & L prepared an independent, review-level financial statement for CRS with respect to calendar year 1995. This statement, issued by D & L on March 25, 1996, lacked specific information about the change in ownership. To make matters worse, the notes to the financial statement contained three arguably misleading comments that implied Canty's continuing participation as CRS's sole shareholder. . . .

CRS thereafter obtained new contracts for work on public buildings. To facilitate these engagements, NASI wrote bonds (relying, it claims, on the 1995 financial statement) totaling $847,630 on June 14, 1996, and bonds totaling $874,500 on August 21, 1996. But CRS foundered under the stewardship of its new owners and eventually defaulted on these bonds. This calamity forced NASI, *qua* surety, to step into the breach. Doing so cost it nearly $2,000,000.

[In NASI's diversity suit against D & L and Lapalme, NASI claimed negligent misrepresentation under Massachusetts law, alleging it would not have issued bonds and suffered the losses on them had the defendants' financial reports been accurate. The trial court gave summary judgment for defendants.]

[The Supreme Judicial Court of Massachusetts has accepted Restatement (Second) of Torts § 552, noting its limitation on liability to third persons for negligent misrepresentation as follows:]

> That liability is [(2)] limited to loss suffered (a) by the person or one of a limited group of persons for whose benefit and guidance he intends to supply the information or knows that the recipient intends to supply it; and (b) through reliance upon it in a transaction that he intends the information to influence or knows that the recipient so intends or in a substantially similar transaction.

The SJC recognized that § 552 was not self-elucidating, and that courts had been erratic in interpreting and applying it. This lack of uniformity seemed most readily apparent in respect to the level of knowledge—actual or constructive—required on the part of the putative defendant. The SJC opted to demand actual knowledge. In so doing, it interpreted § 552 "as limiting the potential liability of an accountant to noncontractual third parties who can demonstrate actual knowledge on the part of accountants of the limited—though unnamed—group of potential third parties that will rely upon the [accountant's work product], as well as actual knowledge of the particular financial transaction that such information is designed to influence." The accountant's actual knowledge, the court added, should be ascertained at the time the audit report or financial statement is issued.

Despite this emphasis on actual knowledge, the SJC added a caveat. It cautioned that accountants could not avoid liability by burying their heads in the sand: "the Restatement standard will not excuse an accountant's 'willful ignorance.' "

... Although substantially similar transactions can serve as a basis for an accountant's liability to a third party under the Restatement rule, the dimensions of that doctrine remain in doubt.

The Restatement does not attempt to define the phrase "substantially similar transactions." Nevertheless, the commentary offers some insight into what is meant by the term. Thus, when a corporation seeking a bank loan asks an accountant to audit the books and prepare a report for the prospective lender, liability for negligence will attach even though the corporation delays for a month in obtaining the loan. The transaction, though later in time, remains substantially similar because its "essential character"—the amount and terms of the credit—has not changed. So too if the amount of the anticipated loan varies slightly. ...

Quite plainly, this definition is fact-sensitive and requires case-by-case development. We think that, under it, an accountant's liability for substantially similar transactions must be determined in two steps. First, the rule implicitly recognizes that the risk perceived by the accountant at the time of the engagement cabins the extent of the duty that he owes to known third parties. Thus, an inquiring court initially must consider, from the preparer's standpoint, what risks he reasonably perceived he was undertaking when he delivered the challenged report or financial statement.

Second, the court must undertake an objective comparison between the transaction of which the accountant had actual knowledge and the transaction that in fact occurred. This comparison cannot be hypertechnical, but, rather, must be conducted in light of "[t]he ordinary practices and attitudes of the business world." The goal of this inquiry is to determine whether the two transactions share essentially the same character. If so, the actual transaction is substantially similar to the contemplated transaction (and, therefore, liability-inducing). Elsewise, the third party has no recourse against the accountant for negligent misrepresentation. ...

First, NASI argues that the bonds which it issued in 1996 were part of a regular "bonding program" and that D & L prepared the financial statement with this program in mind. ...

To establish the defendants' actual knowledge and intent to influence, NASI relies most heavily on Cote's deposition. Cote testified in substance that once he and his partners had acquired the stock of CRS, he met with Lapalme to discuss the preparation of the 1995 financial statement. At that time, he informed Lapalme that CRS's new owners planned to use the financial statement to meet the corporation's obligations for "ongoing" bonds (which he described as "projects that were currently being worked on by [CRS] for which bonds had been issued"). ...

Taken at face value, Cote's testimony does not support a conclusion that the defendants knowingly undertook the substantial risks inherent in the issuance of *future* bonds. ...

Lapalme was keenly aware that the preparation of the 1995 financial statement was likely to be D & L's last engagement for CRS. Cote testified that he and his partners had begun looking for a new accountant by the time that D & L completed its work on the 1995 financial statement. This was to be expected: D & L had been retained to handle the CRS account by the former owner, Canty, and the purchase-and-sale agreement obligated the new owners to retain D & L only until the firm had completed the tax returns and other financials necessary to close out calendar year 1995. It strains credulity to believe that an experienced C.P.A. would undertake liability for indeterminate amounts of bonds not yet written when he had no reasonable anticipation of working for the principal in the future.

NASI next contends that the defaulted bonds represented transactions which were substantially similar to those that the defendants intended to influence. . . .

To be sure, determinations of this type involve matters of degree. If, for example, D & L had agreed to release the 1995 financial statement in anticipation of allowing NASI to review it before issuing a $500,000 bond for a specific future project, and NASI thereafter issued a bond for that project in an amount that varied by, say, $50,000, D & L would be liable to NASI for any loss occasioned by a negligent misrepresentation. . . .

In this context, there is no scientific formula for ascertaining substantial similarity. Even if the change involves a new transaction, rather than merely a modification of the earlier (known) transaction, the accounting firm might still be held liable if the identity of the third party is unchanged, the type of transaction pretty much the same, and the firm's exposure relatively constant. Imagine, for example, that D & L agreed to provide the financial statement in anticipation that NASI would review it in deciding whether to write a $500,000 bond referable to a specific roofing contract that CRS hoped to secure. Imagine, too, that the project fell through, but CRS instead obtained a different, roughly comparable roofing contract, likewise requiring a $500,000 bond, and NASI, relying on the financial statement, provided the bond. In that hypothetical situation, D & L likely would be liable to the surety for misinformation.

There is an obvious difference between these examples and the case at hand. The examples presume that the accountants knew the general nature of the risk they were taking and the approximate dollar amount of their potential liability. In this case, however, D & L accepted potential liability only for ongoing work—known projects in various stages of completion—but NASI seeks to hold the firm liable for unknown future projects not yet begun (or even bid) when the financial statement was delivered. The increased degree of risk is patent. By like token, D & L accepted potential liability only for bonds previously issued—bonds with fixed, easily ascertainable dollar limits—but NASI seeks to hold D & L liable for bonds which, at the relevant time, were not yet issued (and which, therefore, had no monetary limit). . . .

Affirmed.

---

56. **The Ultramares case.** The leading case is *Ultramares Corporation v. Touche,* 255 N.Y. 170, 174 N.E. 441, 74 A.L.R. 1139 (1931), where Cardozo expressed concern lest "a thoughtless slip" "expose accountants to a liability in an indeterminate amount for an indeterminate time to an indeterminate class." The *Ultramares* case allowed a little leeway, but not much, saying that when the suit is for negligence, liability "is bounded by the contract, and is to be enforced between the parties by whom the contract has been made." The problem of third persons who rely on negligent misrepresentations is not limited to accountants, but it is true that many cases do involve lenders or investors who rely on an audit report of a company as a basis for lending money or investing in that company.

57. **The Restatement rule and its support.** Of the contemporary positions on liability to third persons, the Restatement § 552 attempts what is ostensibly a middle position. It would impose liability for negligent misrepresentations to, but only to, persons or a limited class of persons—those he intends to reach and those he "knows" will get the information from his client. As with scienter fraud, the Restatement also limits the liability to the type of transaction he intends to influence or knows will be influenced. Most cases appear to support the Restatement, although exact terms and applications differ. See *Boykin v. Arthur Andersen & Co.*, 639 So.2d 504 (Ala. 1994); *Bily v. Arthur Young & Co.,* 3 Cal.4th 370, 11 Cal.Rptr.2d 51, 834 P.2d 745 (1992); *Bethlehem Steel Corporation v. Ernst & Whinney*, 822 S.W.2d 592 (Tenn. 1991).

58. **The more restrictive rule of "near privity" with a "link."** New York developed a more restrictive rule. In *Security Pacific Business Credit, Inc. v. Peat Marwick Main & Co.*, 79 N.Y.2d 695, 597 N.E.2d 1080, 586 N.Y.S.2d 87 (1992), the defendants' audit of a retailer, Top Brass, was negligent in failing to recognize that 30% the Top Brass' accounts receivable were uncollectible. The plaintiff loaned funds to the Top Brass in reliance on the accountant's 1984 audit report. The loans were secured by accounts receivable. Top Brass filed for bankruptcy and the plaintiff lender sued the accountants. The accountants had prepared the audit knowing it would be used to satisfy Securities Exchange Commission annual reporting requirements. The accountants knew that Top Brass was negotiating for a loan from the plaintiff, and that report would also be relevant to that loan. The plaintiff lender had called the accountants during or virtually at the end of the auditing process and had received assurances that the firm was comfortable with giving an unqualified audit opinion, that the audit had uncovered nothing untoward. Nevertheless, the court held the claim was not actionable under New York's rules announced in *Credit Alliance Corp. v. Arthur Andersen & Co.,* 65 N.Y.2d 536, 483 N.E.2d 110, 493 N.Y.S.2d 435 (1985): "(1) the accountants must have been aware that the financial reports were to be

used for a particular purpose or purposes; (2) in the furtherance of which a known party or parties was intended to rely; and (3) there must have been some conduct on the part of the accountants linking them to that party or parties, which evinces the accountants' understanding of that party or parties' reliance." The phone call was an insufficient link. If a phone call were enough, every lender would make one and thus acquire "deep pocket surety coverage." New York's linking rule got support in *Walpert, Smullian & Blumenthal, P.A. v. Katz,* 361 Md. 645, 762 A.2d 582 (2000), where, however, the court concluded that an adequate link was shown on the facts.

59. **The more liberal foreseeability rule.** A tiny bit of authority rejects the limits of the Restatement rule and allows recovery by third persons for negligent misrepresentation if they would foreseeably rely, whether or not they were known or intended users of the financial information. See *Citizens State Bank v. Timm, Schmidt & Co.,* 113 Wis.2d 376, 335 N.W.2d 361 (1983); *Touche Ross v. Commercial Union Ins.*, 514 So.2d 315 (Miss. 1987). New Jersey also so held in *H. Rosenblum, Inc. v. Adler*, 93 N.J. 324, 461 A.2d 138 (1983), but legislation changed the rule in that state.

SIDELIGHT: AUDIT REPORTS AND THE SARBANES–OXLEY ACT

Audit reports on publicly held companies make the financial system work. The reports are provided to the federal Securities Exchange Commission (SEC), where they are public records. They are also used in giving information to prospective investors, stockholders who may wish to sell their shares, and prospective lenders. The market will not work well at all without audit reports that investors and others believe to be reliable. Misrepresentations in audits as well as other securities frauds are thus a public as well as a private concern.

In the 1990s, Congress reversed its historical emphasis on protecting stockholders, potential investors, and others from securities-related fraud by corporations, their insiders, and the securities market players. As we saw in an earlier sidelight, the 1990s saw Congressional efforts to protect corporate defendants and managers from fraud suits, especially class actions, which were regarded as opportunistic strike suits organized by lawyers and countenanced by courts.

In 2002, after the devastating losses inflicted by the corruption at Enron and many other companies, Congress came to perceive, more or less, that somewhat honest audits were the foundation of securities regulation. It thus became concerned that auditors, far from being independent, had an incentive—future business—to represent financial affairs of the company in the way the company wished.

In the Sarbanes-Oxley Act of 2002, PL 107–204, Congress addressed a number of corporate fraud potentials in publicly held companies, including auditing. Among the auditing provisions, it provided a new regulatory agency for the auditing industry, required that companies' internal audit committees be composed of independent directors, and required chief officers of corporations to sign off on the audit reports. The act does not expressly create a private cause of action except for employees who are wrongfully discharged for reporting misconduct. However, the act's regulatory and criminal provisions may be relevant in existing causes of action, and it is possible that courts will recognize some implied causes of action. See Lewis D. Lowenfels, Alan R. Bromberg, *Implied Private Actions under Sarbanes-Oxley,* 34 SETON HALL L. REV. 775 (2004).

Whether or not a new private right of action can be brought, the Sarbanes-Oxley Act highlights a public recognition that incentives for auditors' may undermine or eliminate their independence and suggests that their "negligence" may in fact be more culpable than that.

BARRIE v. V.P. EXTERMINATORS, INC., 625 So.2d 1007 (La. 1993). The plaintiffs purchased a dwelling from the Secor Bank in reliance upon a termite inspection secured by the bank and a certificate by the inspector given to the bank and passed to the plaintiffs. Within days after purchase, the plaintiffs discovered heavy damage that allegedly rendered the house uninhabitable. They sued the inspector, Palumbo, and his company, V.P., claiming negligence. The trial court held for Palumbo and V.P. on the ground that they were not in privity with the purchasers. *Held*, reversed. V.P. and Palumbo owed the purchasers the duty of reasonable care and competence "in obtaining or ascertaining facts for and/or in communicating the facts or opinion in the wood destroying insect report. The duty was owed to the Barries even though they were a third party to V.P., without privity of contract or direct or indirect contact, because they were known to V.P. as the intended users of the report.

"V.P. was manifestly aware of the use to which Secor would put the wood destroying insect report. Like the situation in Justice Cardozo's *Glanzer*, the Barries' use of the termite inspection report was "not merely one possibility among many, but the end and aim of the [Secor-V.P.] transaction." Moreover, V.P. intended to supply it for that purpose. The concerns evoked in *Ultramares*, the fear of liability with indeterminate limits of amount, time and class, were not present. Palumbo's knowledge of the intended use of the report, enlarged his duty to perform his service carefully, not only for the vendor who ordered the report, but for the vendee who was to use it."

---

60. **The single liability pattern.** Some cases that purport to apply Restatement § 552 are actually cases in the *Barrie* pattern. See, e.g., *Burbach v. Radon Analytical Labs., Inc.,* 652 N.W.2d 135 (Iowa 2002) (home inspector reporting to A is liable to buyer from A). What is distinctive about cases in the *Barrie* pattern? Should a court applying

New York's restrictive rule impose liability in cases like *Barrie*? Look back at the facts in *Glanzer v. Shepard*, 233 N.Y. 236, 135 N.E. 275 (1922), summarized in ¶ 15. On the question of liability to third persons, is it simply a case in the *Barrie* pattern?

61. **Contract versus tort: architects and engineers.** Suppose a landowner retains an architect or engineer to provide plans or specifications for a project. The landowner's contractors or subcontractors rely on the plans, which in effect make negligent representations of fact, perhaps about the nature of the soil, perhaps about the type of construction that will work. The contractor relying upon the plans or specs either underbids or is forced to do additional work. Has the contractor a claim against the architect or engineer? Is this the same as the accountant-audit problem? Some courts, supposedly a majority, have said that the contractor has a claim. See *Century Ready-Mix Co. v. Campbell County School Dist.*, 816 P.2d 795 (Wyo. 1991). Others have opposed liability. E.g., *Berschauer/Phillips Construction Co. v. Seattle School District No. 1*, 124 Wash.2d 816, 881 P.2d 986 (1994). The Washington Court said: "A bright line distinction between the remedies offered in contract and tort with respect to economic damages also encourages parties to negotiate toward the risk distribution that is desired or customary. We preserve the incentive to adequately self-protect during the bargaining process."

(b) Harms Within or Outside the Risk

OREGON STEEL MILLS, INC. v. COOPERS & LYBRAND, LLP

336 Or. 329, 83 P.3d 322 (2004)

BALMER, J. . . .

Plaintiff Oregon Steel Mills, Inc., a company whose stock is traded on the New York Stock Exchange, retained defendant Coopers & Lybrand, LLP, for many years to provide accounting and auditing services. In 1994, plaintiff entered into a transaction that involved the sale of stock in one of plaintiff's subsidiaries. Defendant advised plaintiff that the transaction should be reported as a $12.3 million gain on plaintiff's financial statements and reports. Pursuant to that advice, plaintiff reported the transaction as a gain and, when defendant audited plaintiff's 1994 financial statements in early 1995, defendant gave its opinion that plaintiff's consolidated financial statements fairly represented plaintiff's financial position in accordance with generally accepted accounting principles. Plaintiff alleges in its complaint, and for purposes of its summary judgment motion defendant does not dispute, that defendant's accounting advice regarding the 1994 transaction was incorrect and that defendant gave that advice negligently.

During late 1995 and early 1996, plaintiff was planning to make a public offering of its stock and debt. Defendant knew of plaintiff's plans and had known, since at least 1994, that plaintiff would be selling stock and debt at some time in the future. Plaintiff anticipated that it would file the necessary documents with the Securities and Exchange Commission (SEC) on February 27, 1996, and that, barring unforeseen problems in the SEC approval process, the securities would be priced and sold on or about May 2, 1996. Defendant provided accounting advice to plaintiff in connection with the planned offering, and the documents that plaintiff filed with the SEC included the 1994 financial statements that defendant had audited.

Shortly before the initial SEC filing, defendant advised plaintiff that the 1994 transaction might have been reported incorrectly and that defendant would not approve the audit of plaintiff's 1995 financial statements or allow use of the 1994 audit unless the SEC approved the accounting treatment of the 1994 transaction. Subsequently, the SEC concluded that the accounting treatment for the 1994 transaction was incorrect and required plaintiff to restate its 1994 financial statements. Because of the time required to restate the 1994 financial statements and change other documents related to the planned offering, plaintiff was unable to make its initial filing with the SEC until April 8, 1996, and the public offering did not occur until June 13, 1996. On that date, plaintiff sold $80 million of newly issued stock and $235 million of debt. Although the price of plaintiff's stock was $13.50 on February 22, 1996, when defendant discovered the accounting error, and, coincidentally, also was $13.50 when plaintiff issued the stock on June 13, 1996, the stock price had risen and fallen between those dates. On May 2, 1996, the date that plaintiff alleges that it would have issued the stock but for defendant's negligence, plaintiff's stock sold for $16 per share. . . .

[The plaintiff sued for damages based on the difference between $13.50 per share it received and the $16 per share it would have received but for the defendant's delay. The trial court granted summary judgment for the defendant on this issue, holding that the defendant could not be liable for such damages, since the defendant's negligence did not cause the market to drop, even though it caused the delay. The Court of Appeals held otherwise, reversed the trial court.]

On review, defendant argues, as it did in the trial court, that a plaintiff in a professional malpractice case may not recover economic damages that are caused by market forces unrelated to the defendant's wrongful conduct. . . . In defendant's view, the extent of the economic damages for which a defendant may be held liable depends on the relationship between a plaintiff and a defendant. Defendant argues that, because plaintiff did not allege that defendant had any duty to protect plaintiff from changes in the market price of plaintiff's stock, defendant can be liable to plaintiff for harm resulting from adverse changes in that price only if its wrongful conduct was the cause of those changes.

Even when a special relationship is the basis for the duty of care owed by one person to another, this court has held that, if the special relationship (or status or standard of conduct) does not prescribe a particular scope of duty, then "[c]ommon law principles of reasonable care and foreseeability of harm are relevant." ...

Our discussion above of recent Oregon tort cases sets the stage for consideration of that issue. The Court of Appeals concluded that the issue of whether plaintiff's damage was "foreseeably" caused by defendant's negligent acts should be tried to a jury. The problem with that conclusion is that no one could foresee, at the time of defendant's accounting errors in 1994 and early 1995, the risk that plaintiff would suffer a loss because its securities would be sold at market-determined prices on June 13, 1996, rather than on May 2, 1996. Plaintiff argues that it is foreseeable that stock prices will fluctuate, and that is certainly true. It also is foreseeable, as the trial court stated, that negligent conduct by an accounting firm may harm a client by impairing its ability to raise capital. With appropriate proof, the client of a negligent accounting firm may recover damages for lost profits or lost business opportunities that result from the accounting firm's negligent acts. Here, however, plaintiff seeks damages based solely on a decline in the price of plaintiff's stock during the delay that defendant caused in getting the offering to market, yet plaintiff admits that the price decline affected all steel stocks and was unrelated to defendant's misconduct.

... In this case, defendant's conduct caused the delay in the offering that led to an "unintended adverse result." However, the intervening action of market forces on the price of plaintiff's stock was the "harm-producing force," and defendant's actions did not "cause" the decline in the stock price so as to support liability for that decline. As a matter of law, the risk of a decline in plaintiff's stock price in June 1996 was not a reasonably foreseeable consequence of defendant's negligent acts in 1994 and early 1995. ...

Plaintiff argues that, even if losses due to market forces are not recoverable from a defendant whose negligent behavior did not cause those losses, the losses in this case were foreseeable because defendant knew that plaintiff intended to enter the market and sell its securities at a specific and favorable time. The Court of Appeals relied on that argument, stating that the offering date was timed to take advantage of higher-than-expected first-quarter earnings and favorable market conditions. However, the record does not support plaintiff's assertion or the Court of Appeals' statements. First, plaintiff's second amended complaint does not allege that the securities offering was scheduled to occur at a specific, advantageous time. The only negligent acts alleged in the complaint are defendant's improper tax advice in 1994 and its audit and approval of the financial statements for the year ended December 31, 1994. Yet, according to the complaint, plaintiff planned the securities offering "during the later part of 1995 and early 1996." Although defendant knew in 1994 that plaintiff contemplated a public offering at some point, the timing of that offering, at least according to the record here, was known only in the most general sense at the time of defendant's wrongful conduct.

Second, ... [f]or plaintiff to have been harmed because the offering was delayed too long after the release of the favorable earnings report, plaintiff would have to present evidence that defendant knew or should have known that plaintiff's stock would have risen briefly after the release of the earnings report and then *fallen* back to its post-release level. Such a market prediction would be surprising—as well as quite speculative—but, in any event, plaintiff made no such contention in any affidavit, deposition, or document submitted as part of the summary judgment record. Nor does the summary judgment record contain any other suggestion by plaintiff that it expected that market conditions would be favorable at the time the offering was originally planned, why those conditions were favorable, or why conditions would be any less favorable six weeks later. On the contrary, the uncontroverted evidence in the record shows (1) that plaintiff wished to issue its securities as expeditiously as possible because it needed cash to finance a capital improvement program and to remain in compliance with bank covenants, and (2) that the increase and then decrease in steel company stock prices, including plaintiff's, between April and June 1996 was due to market forces unrelated to plaintiff's financial condition or to defendant's conduct. ...

For the reasons discussed above, we conclude that, although defendant breached its duty to plaintiff by failing to provide competent accounting services, defendant had no duty to protect plaintiff against market fluctuations in plaintiff's stock price. The decline in plaintiff's stock price in June 1996 was, as a matter of law, not reasonably foreseeable, and defendant cannot be liable for damages based on that decline. The trial court correctly granted defendant's motion for summary judgment on that ground. ...

The decision of the Court of Appeals is reversed. The judgment of the circuit court is affirmed.

---

62. **Losses from extraneous forces.** Losses resulting from forces unrelated to the defendant's negligent misrepresentation are ordinarily not recoverable.

63. **Damages available under the *Oregon Steel Mills* rule.** In *Oregon Steels Mills*, what was the foreseeable risk the defendant negligently created? The answer determines for which harms the defendant is liable. If you were lawyering the case for the plaintiff, what damages would you try to claim and what evidence would you seek? To answer that question, first consider what the plaintiff might recover in an easier case:

P purchases a factory from D, paying $1,000,000 in justifiable reliance on D's documented misrepresentation that the factory building has been inspected and is in sound physical condition. In fact the factory needs serious repairs and is worth $100,000 less than paid. After P takes possession, the factory is bombed by a domestic terrorist and the building completely collapses and the factory is worth nothing.

64. **Scienter fraud and variables.** Would the limitation imposed in *Oregon Steel Mills* apply if the defendant is guilty of scienter fraud? Would it matter whether the plaintiff would not have contracted at all but for the misrepresentation or whether the plaintiff would have invested, but would have paid or invested less?

§ 8. DEFENSES

(a) Disclaimers, The Economic Loss Rule, and Parol Evidence

GIBB v. CITICORP MORTGAGE, INC.

246 Neb. 355, 518 N.W.2d 910 (1994)

CAPORALE, Justice.

[Plaintiff purchased a house from Citicorp Mortgage, who had previously foreclosed on the house when the previous mortgagee had abandoned it because of extensive termite infestation. When the plaintiff found the infestation, he sued for fraud. The trial court held for the defendant.]

Prior to the purchase, Citicorp's selling agent showed Gibb a single area where termite damage had occurred and assured Gibb that this was the only termite-damaged area and that all necessary repairs and treatments had been made to eliminate the termite problem. . . .

The purchase agreement recited that the transaction was "based upon [Gibb's] personal inspection or investigation of the Property and not upon any representation or warranties of condition by [Citicorp] or [its] agent." The agreement further provided that the property was "sold strictly in 'AS IS' condition. [Citicorp] does not make any warranties regarding the condition of the property at the time of sale and thereafter."

Nonetheless, Gibb claims to have relied on the misrepresentations made to him and asserts he has suffered damage as a consequence . . .

Gibb has pled all the essential elements for recovery based on fraudulent misrepresentation [and also fraudulent concealment].

Notwithstanding that Gibb has pled all of the elements of those two bases of recovery, Citicorp asserts that where an agreement for the sale of real estate contains a disclaimer and an "as is" clause such as those present here, the seller should not be held liable for the fraudulent misrepresentations or concealments of its agent. Citicorp further urges that Gibb had as much access to the relevant information as did Citicorp.

In so arguing, Citicorp acknowledges that under our law, a principal may be liable for the fraudulent actions of its agent, but urges that we adopt the position of New York's highest court in Danann Realty Corp. v. Harris, 5 N.Y.2d 317, 157 N.E.2d 597, 184 N.Y.S.2d 599 (1959).

Therein, the New York Court of Appeals held that a purchaser had no cause of action against a seller for false representation when the contract for the purchase of a lease contained disclaimer, "as is," and merger clauses as follows: "The Purchaser has examined the premises agreed to be sold and is familiar with the physical condition thereof. The Seller has not made and does not make any representations as to the physical condition, rents, leases, expenses, operation or any other matter or thing affecting or related to the aforesaid premises, except as herein specifically set forth, and the Purchaser hereby expressly acknowledges that no such representations have been made, and the Purchaser further acknowledges that it has inspected the premises and agrees to take the premises 'as is' .... It is understood and agreed that all understandings and agreements heretofore had between the parties hereto are merged in this contract, which alone fully and completely expresses their agreement, and that the same is entered into after full investigation, neither party relying upon any statement or representation, not embodied in this contract. ..."

... The Danann Realty Corp. majority concluded that the specific disclaimer clause, in conjunction with the merger clause, declared that the parties did not rely on representations not embodied in the contract and thus prevented the purchaser from adducing parol evidence to establish otherwise, thereby destroying the purchaser's allegations of reliance.

However, on several occasions we have addressed whether a disclaimer clause within a contract will bar a purchaser's fraud-based claim. In Schuster v. North American Hotel Co., 106 Neb. 672, 184 N.W. 136 (1921), reh'g denied 106 Neb. 679, 684, 186 N.W. 87, 89, we wrote: "It is quite generally held that a provision in a contract, to the effect that the agent cannot bind the company by any representations, statements or agreements, will not relieve the principal from responsibility for the fraudulent representations, as to the subject-matter of the contract, made by the agent, since such representations are within the scope of the agent's actual or ostensible authority ...."

In Menking, the disclaimer clause was similar to the provision in the agreement now before us. There, the purchaser stated and agreed that "he has made personal inspection of the property covered by the within contract, and is buying it solely on his own investigations, and not on any representations made by any one else as to any material matter affecting said property, or his purchase thereof."

Considering whether such a provision barred the purchaser from maintaining any action for fraud or deceit, we reiterated: "A provision in such a contract, to the effect that the agent cannot bind the company by any representations, statements or agreements, will not relieve the principal from responsibility for the fraudulent representations, made by its agents, concerning the subject-matter of the contract ... for a sales agent has ostensible authority to make representations as to the subject-matter of the sale, and his fraud, committed within the limits of such authority, will fix responsibility upon his principal." . . .

We have also concluded that an "as is" clause does not necessarily bar a purchaser's fraud-based claim, writing in Wolford v. Freeman, 150 Neb. 537, 547, 35 N.W.2d 98, 103 (1948), that "[a] provision that the buyer takes the article in the condition in which it is, or in other words, 'as is,' does not prevent fraudulent representations relied on by the buyer from constituting fraud. . . ."

Thus, a clause that an article is taken in the condition in which it is, or in other words, "as is," is relevant in determining whether a claimant relied on a false representation concerning the condition of the article, but is not controlling.

. . . Thus, just as the disclaimer does not necessarily prevent Gibb from stating causes of action for fraudulent misrepresentation or fraudulent concealment, neither does the "as is" clause, nor do the two clauses together prevent him from doing so. Under these circumstances, the question as to whether Gibb acted reasonably is one of fact. . . .

---

65. **Parol evidence rule no bar to fraud claim.** In line with the result in *Gibb,* many decisions state that the parol evidence rule will not bar an action if the contract was induced by fraud. Fraud, it is said, vitiates everything. E.g., *Wood v. Phillips,* 849 So.2d 951 (Ala. 2002); *Ferrell v. Cox*, 617 A.2d 1003 (Me. 1992).

66. **Parole evidence rule and other traditional rules of law.** But in other cases, rules of law reflected in the statute of frauds, merger by deed doctrine, and the parol evidence rule may bar the fraud claim in certain instances. The parol evidence rule—which is also reflected in the merger clause in *Danann*—bars admission of oral representations to contradict a contract in writing that is intended to state the parties' complete agreement. *Pinnacle Peak Developers v. TRW Investment Corp.,* 129 Ariz. 385, 631 P.2d 540 (App. 1980), is worth considering. The court there thought that two factors determined whether the fraud claim would be barred by the parol evidence rule. The claim would be barred if (1) relatively sophisticated parties entered into a formal contract and (2) the contradiction between the purportedly fraudulent statement and the writing was clear and direct. At the other end of the spectrum, evidence of fraud might be admitted if the plaintiff was not a sophisticated bargainer in an entrepreneurial contract and/or the contradiction was not clear.

67. **Examples of the conflict test.** If *Pinnacle Peak* is right, how should these cases come out on admission of evidence of fraud?

Case A. Seller orally promises to deliver a new, latest model car of a certain make, intending to deliver last year's model instead. He provides a purchase contract that says the buyer is to buy a car model of last year.

Bank of America Nat. Trust & Sav. Ass'n v. Pendergrass, 4 Cal.2d 258, 48 P.2d 659 (1935).

Case B. A vendor falsely represents that the property is not subject to zoning restrictions against business. The contract provides that the title is subject to all restrictions on record, but does not mention the zoning restrictions particularly. *Fox v. Southern App., Inc.*, 264 N.C. 267, 141 S.E.2d 522 (1965).

68. **Disclaimers, economic loss rule, and negligent misrepresentations.** In *negligent* misrepresentation cases, shouldn't defendants be permitted to use any form of disclaimer clause as a defense against a negligent misrepresentation claim? The court so held in *Richey v. Patrick,* 904 P.2d 798 (Wyo. 1995). Some cases have done the same by invoking the economic loss rule as to negligent misrepresentations where the parties have an integrated contract. *Duquesne Light Co. v. Westinghouse Electric Corp.,* 66 F.3d 604 (3d Cir. 1995); *Apollo Group, Inc. v. Avnet, Inc.,* 58 F.3d 477 (9th Cir. 1995) (forecasting Arizona law); *Van Lare v. Vogt, Inc.,* 274 Wis.2d 631, 683 N.W.2d 46 (2004) (negligence and "strict liability" misrepresentation claims barred by economic loss rule; plaintiff might have been able to sue for intentional misrepresentation, but did not do so). In *All-Tech Telecom, Inc. v. Amway Corp.,* 174 F.3d 862 (7th Cir. 1999), Judge Posner said, speaking of negligent misrepresentations: "Where there are well-developed contractual remedies, such as the remedies that the Uniform Commercial Code (in force in all U.S. states) provides for breach of warranty of the quality, fitness, or specifications of goods, there is no need to provide tort remedies for misrepresentation. The tort remedies would duplicate the contract remedies, adding unnecessary complexity to the law. Worse, the provision of these duplicative tort remedies would undermine contract law." What is to be done in the case of intentional misrepresentation, scienter fraud?

Huron Tool and Eng'g Co. v. Precision Consulting Servs., Inc., 209 Mich.App. 365, 532 N.W.2d 541 (1995). The plaintiff contracted to purchase software and services from the defendant and paid the full price. Alleging defects, the plaintiff asserted both breach of warranty and fraud claims. The trial court dismissed both claims. *Held*, dismissal of the fraud claim affirmed. "The economic loss doctrine provides that [w]here a purchaser's expectations in a sale are frustrated because the product he bought is not working properly, his remedy is said to be in contract alone, for he has suffered only economic losses. ... Although the issue has been addressed in only a handful of jurisdictions, the emerging trend is clearly toward creating an exception to the economic loss doctrine for a select group of intentional torts. ... Fraud in the inducement presents a special situation where parties to a contract appear to negotiate freely—which normally would constitute grounds for the economic loss doctrine—but where in fact the ability of one party to negotiate fair terms and make an informed decision is undermined by the other party's fraudulent behavior. In contrast, where the only misrepresentation by the dishonest party concerns the quality or character of the goods sold, the other party is still free to negotiate warranty and other terms to account for possible defects in the goods. . . . The distinction between fraud in the inducement and other kinds of fraud is the same as the distinction drawn by a New Jersey federal district court between fraud extraneous to the contract and fraud interwoven with the breach of contract. With respect to the latter kind of fraud, the misrepresentations relate to the breaching party's performance of the contract and do not give rise to an independent cause of action in tort." In this case, "[t]he fraudulent representations alleged by plaintiff concern the quality and characteristics of the software system sold by defendants. These representations are indistinguishable from the terms of the contract and warranty that plaintiff alleges were breached." Consequently the plaintiff cannot maintain a fraud action.

69. **Disclaimers, economic loss rule, and intentional misrepresentations.** Some courts have held that disclaimers written into the contract between sophisticated parties will bar the fraud claim. See *CERAbio LLC v. Wright Med. Techn., Inc.,* 410 F.3d 981 (7th Cir.2005) (a clause disclaiming any reliance on information furnished by the defendant). What if the fraud induced the plaintiff to sign the contract with the disclaimer clause in it?

Sometimes, apart from disclaimers, courts invoke the economic loss rule to bar scienter fraud claims. The occasions for barring those claims are less than clear, but *Huron Tool* has been cited repeatedly. If the economic loss rule seeks to honor the contract, leaving contract parties to bargain for what they want, then it would work in fraud cases much like the parol evidence rule, barring the fraud claim if the alleged fraud contradicted a contract provision. Should courts ever take the economic loss doctrine further, using it, even in scienter fraud cases, to bar the fraud claim merely because the fraud was interwoven with the contract provisions? Or because, where the fraud concerns only the quality or character of the goods covered by the contract, the plaintiff *should have* insisted on contractual protection and *should be* barred from tort recovery? This is worth some meditation. You can read more on the topic in the Professional and Academic Enhancements to this chapter.

70. **Reference.** On exculpatory clauses and the like, see generally DOBBS ON TORTS § 482 (2000).

(b) Immunity

71. **Rule of immunity.** The United States government (and state governments as well) are immune from suit except to the extent the relevant government has waived immunity. The Federal Tort Claims Act waives the federal immunity for some tort claims, but it retains sovereign immunity for claims based upon misrepresentation by the government or its agent. Suppose a federal bean-weigher negligently adjusts the scales so that the seller's beans appear to weigh 30,000 pounds when in

fact they weigh 33,000 pounds. Acting on the error, the plaintiff sells the beans for 10% less than their value. Is the government immune? See *Block v. Neal,* 460 U.S. 289, 103 S.Ct. 1089, 75 L.Ed.2d 67 (1983).

(c) First Amendment Effects

KEIMER v. BUENA VISTA BOOKS, INC.

75 Cal.App.4th 1220, 89 Cal.Rptr.2d 781 (1999)

WALKER, J. . . .

In 1983 a group of retired women from Beardstown, Illinois, formed a financial investment club which came to national attention in 1991 because of its claimed 10-year-average annual investment return of 23.4 percent, a return higher than the Standard and Poors Index, and 3 times higher than that obtained by mutual funds and professional money managers during the same period. News of the women who became known as "The Beardstown Ladies" and their financial investment savvy spread to television, then to a videotape produced by respondent Central Picture Entertainment entitled "Cookin' Up Profits on Wall Street—A Guide to Common Sense Investing." Eventually respondent Seth Godin Productions acquired the rights to The Beardstown Ladies' story and developed a ghost-written book for them, which it sold to Hyperion Press, the Disney-owned publisher. Disney titled the book, "The Beardstown Ladies' Common-Sense Investment Guide—How We Beat the Stock Market—and How You Can, Too" which was first published in hardcover, and later in paperback. Four other books, entitled "The Beardstown Ladies' Stitch-in-Time Guide to Growing Your Nest Egg"; "The Beardstown Ladies' Guide to Smart Spending for Big Savings"; "The Beardstown Ladies' Little Book of Investment Wisdom"; "The Beardstown Ladies' Pocketbook Guide to Picking Stocks"; and a video entitled "The Beardstown Ladies—Cookin' Up Profits on Wall Street—A Guide to Common Sense Investing" followed. Displayed prominently on the front and back covers and the packaging of these materials there often appeared statements such as "23.4% ANNUAL RETURN"; "59.5% returns in 1991"; "find [the Beardstown Ladies'] secret recipe for success"; and "learn how to outperform mutual funds and professional money managers 3 to 1."

[Keimer sued defendants, the publisher and related entities, collectively called Disney, on behalf of the public, claiming statutory false advertising and unfair trade practices.] Keimer's complaint alleged that these statements, extolling The Beardstown Ladies' annual rate of return and investment success record as compared with investment industry professionals, were used as the primary basis for advertising and marketing the books and videotape to the general public. The complaint further alleged that these statements were false and misleading, because the verifiable fact was that the investment club's actual average rate of return from 1984 to 1994 was 9.1 percent as opposed to the advertised 23.4 percent, and did not outperform mutual funds and investment professionals by a ratio of 3 to 1. [As reflected in *Lacoff,* summarized below, the Standard and Poor's 500 average return was 14.9%, and the average general stock fund return was 12.6% during the same period.] ... Keimer claimed that Disney had engaged in false advertising and unfair business practices because it knew or should have known that the advertising claims were false, misleading and/or likely to deceive the public.

The complaint's allegations were supplemented by the books and videotape themselves, of which Disney asked the trial court to take judicial notice, a request which received no opposition from Keimer. The judicially noticed materials substantiated the complaint's allegations regarding the text of statements made on the covers of the books and videotape. They also supported Disney's claim on demurrer that the advertising statements made on those covers were contained in the text of the books themselves. Finally, they bolstered Keimer's allegation that Disney "knew, or by the exercise of reasonable care should have known, that the advertisements were untrue or misleading," because the Library of Congress page of the first best seller's paperback reprint contained the following disclaimer: "NOTE: Investment clubs commonly compute their annual 'return' by calculating the increase in their total club balance over a period of time. Since this increase includes the dues that the members pay regularly, this 'return' may be different from the return that might be calculated for a mutual fund or a bank. ..." The judicially noticed materials also reveal that this disclaimer was not repeated in any of the subsequent publications, and that the inflated investment return claims continued to be used to advertise the club's books. For these alleged wrongs, the complaint sought an injunction barring Disney from continuing to use the false statements in advertising and requiring it to publish retractions or corrections in future publications. The complaint also sought disgorgement of Disney's profits from the sale of the books and videotape. ...

Keimer's complaint alleged that Disney violated the Unfair Trade Practices Act by disseminating advertisements for The Beardstown Ladies' books and videotape which it knew were false and misleading, and which it should have known in the exercise of reasonable care were false and misleading. ... [Disney argued] that the advertising statements were entitled to First Amendment protection because they repeated statements made in the books and videotape themselves. In making this claim, Disney characterized the statements in question as noncommercial speech, entitled to full free speech protection. ... [The trial judge sustained Disney's demurrers.]

The commercial speech doctrine was first enunciated by the United States Supreme Court in *Va. Pharmacy Bd. v. Va. Consumer Council* (1976) 425 U.S. 748, 96 S.Ct. 1817, 48 L.Ed.2d 346 (*Virginia State*). There, the court acknowledged that commercial speech, characterized as "speech that does 'no more than propose a commercial transaction' " was entitled to a degree of First Amendment protection, but that the protection was limited: commercial speech could be regulated and restricted in a manner that could be justified by legitimate state interests. In explaining the rationale for the limitation, the court pointed out some "commonsense differences" between commercial speech and other varieties, which justified a different degree of protection: "The truth of commercial speech, for example, may be more easily verifiable by its disseminator ... in that ordinarily the advertiser seeks to disseminate information about a specific product or service that he himself provides and presumably knows more about than anyone else," and because advertising is indispensable in the commercial world it may be more durable than other types of speech, as "there is little likelihood of its being chilled by proper regulation and foregone entirely." These differences, the court reasoned, justified less tolerance for inaccurate statements. They also rendered appropriate those restrictions designed to prevent commercial speech from being deceptive, such as by requiring the message to include any necessary warnings and disclaimers. ... Finally, the Supreme Court in *Virginia State* stated, in no uncertain terms, that provably false commercial speech was entitled to *no First Amendment protection at all.*

As noted, *Virginia State* defined commercial speech as speech which does no more than propose a commercial transaction. This type of speech has been labeled "core" commercial speech. Some speech, however, cannot be characterized as core commercial speech, because it serves some purpose beyond the pure proposition of a commercial transaction. (*Bolger v. Youngs Drug Products Corp.* (1983) 463 U.S. 60, 66, 103 S.Ct. 2875, 77 L.Ed.2d 469 (*Bolger*).) In *Bolger,* the Supreme Court considered the constitutionality of a federal statute prohibiting the unsolicited mailing of advertisements for contraceptive products. The court was faced with evaluating a variety of written materials sent by a contraceptive manufacturer and distributor, most of which it determined were core commercial speech, proposing nothing more than a commercial transaction because they consisted primarily of price and quantity information. Other mailing materials were not so easily categorized. For example, two of the mailings were informational pamphlets which discussed topics such as human sexuality and venereal disease, but also made mention of the contraceptive products.

In determining whether the pamphlets were commercial or noncommercial speech, the *Bolger* court identified three characteristics of the mailings which, taken together, convinced it that the speech in question was commercial, in spite of the fact that the pamphlets also contained discussions of important public issues. First, the pamphlets were conceded to be advertisements; second, the materials made reference to a specific product; and finally, the disseminator of the information had an economic motivation for mailing the pamphlets. ...

[T]he complaint alleges that the advertising campaign for the books and videotape was based primarily on The Beardstown Ladies' investment returns, and were made material features of Disney's marketing and advertising of the publications. This language can be interpreted as a claim that the entire purpose of the statements was to urge the public to buy the books, that is, to propose a commercial transaction. These allegations, which we must accept as true on review of a ruling on demurrer. ... Of course, we do not resolve this issue, but merely conclude that on demurrer any argument that a commercial transaction was not proposed is premature and will have to await further court proceedings.

Even assuming the complaint's allegations and the judicially noticed materials were not sufficient to support the inference that the statements were core commercial speech, we reach the same conclusion by considering the three *Bolger* characteristics applicable when the nature of the speech is not obvious. First, Disney has conceded that the book covers are advertisements, but claims, correctly, that this is not the end of the inquiry. We must also determine whether the speech refers to a specific product, which in the case of a book or videotape cover it obviously does. The covers are touting the content of the material inside, which the consumer can only discover by purchasing the product. And finally, we consider whether Disney had an economic motivation in making the statements. We must conclude that it did, for what other reason would it have for publishing the books? It is true, of course, that the subject matter of the books—achieving economic security by investing—is of interest to the general public. However, speech can be considered commercial even though it contains information which enables the public to "... cope with the exigencies of their period." The Supreme Court has "made clear that advertising which 'links a product to a current public debate' is not thereby entitled to the constitutional protection afforded non-commercial speech." We hold that the statements made on the book and videotape covers are commercial speech, entitled only to qualified free speech protection.

By holding that the statements at issue constitute commercial speech we do not strip them of all free speech protections. We do, however, limit those protections by allowing rational and carefully crafted restrictions. In *Central Hudson Gas & Elec. v. Public Serv. Comm'n* (1980) 447 U.S. 557, 100 S.Ct. 2343, 65 L.Ed.2d 341 (*Central Hudson*), the Supreme Court articulated a four-pronged analysis for evaluating the validity of commercial speech restrictions. As we shall see, under the allegations of appellant's complaint, the statements on the book and videotape covers lose any hope of constitutional protection under *Central Hudson*'s very first prong. That prong asks, as a threshold, whether the commercial speech concerns lawful activity and is *not misleading.* As explained in *Bolger,* "[t]he State may deal effectively with false, deceptive, or misleading sales techniques." Appellant's complaint alleges that the investment return claims made on the book and videotape covers, which we have held to be commercial speech, were false. Accepting these allegations as true, we must conclude that the complained of statements are entitled to no First Amendment free speech protections. ...

Disney [asserts that] if a book's content is noncommercial and entitled to First Amendment protection, then material taken from that content and used in advertising is also entitled to full First Amendment protection. We do not dwell at length on the argument, because a review of Disney's authorities reveals that each is materially distinguishable from the matter before us in one of two ways. They either involved advertising statements which were true, or were opinion or "rhetorical hyperbole" and thus were not verifiably false or misleading, as were the investment return figures here; or they involved the infringement on rights which are less zealously protected than the right of consumers to be free from false advertising. . . .

In *Lane v. Random House, Inc.* (D.C.1995) 985 F.Supp. 141, Lane, a well-known Kennedy conspiracy theorist, sued Random House for defamation and other related claims, because advertisements for a book disputing the conspiracy theory claimed that Lane was "guilty of misleading the American public." Summary judgment was entered for Random House, in part because the court held the speech in question was not commercial. The basis for the finding, which Disney has glossed over, was the court's legitimate concern in protecting "advertising which summarizes *an argument or opinion* contained in the book" as contrasted with statements that are objectively verifiable as true or false. The statement Lane complained of, being "rhetorical hyperbole [which] cannot be proven true or false" was not actionable. . . .

Finally, respondents contend that they had no duty to investigate the accuracy of the investment return claims made in The Beardstown Ladies' books, which eventually made their way to the book covers. While this may be the case, the argument has no relevance here. Appellant has alleged that respondents knew or should have known that the *advertising statements* were false or misleading. He has not alleged that they should have investigated the truth of the statements contained in the books. The distinction is critical, because the Unfair Trade Practices Act imposes liability upon an advertiser for untrue or misleading statements which the advertiser, in the exercise of reasonable care, should have known were false. Disney cannot shield itself from the statute's mandates by linking its advertising to the books' contents.

[Reversed.]

LACOFF V. BUENA VISTA PUB. INC., 183 Misc.2d 600, 705 N.Y.S.2d 183 (Sup. Ct. 2000). [The facts were essentially similar to those in Keimer.] "The Book here is noncommercial speech—it was clearly not designed to sell another product. The main purpose of the work is to tell the story of the Beardstown Ladies, to educate as to investment clubs and the Beardstown Ladies' investment strategy, and to entertain.

"[T]he challenged statement which is the focus of plaintiffs' claims, the 23.4% annual return, explicitly comes from within the contents of the Book. It cannot be transformed into purely commercial speech simply because of its change in location. As the Second Circuit has stated, 'it is important to distinguish between advertising statements made to summarize an argument or opinion within a book and those made about a book as a product.' [Citing Groden v. Random House, Inc., 61 F.3d 1045 (2d Cir. 1995), a case similar to the *Lane* case discussed in *Keimer,* supra.]

"Further, advertising that promotes noncommercial speech, such as a book, is accorded the same constitutional protection as the speech it advertises. It is actionable only if it fails to accurately reflect the contents of the protected speech being promoted.

"Accordingly, the claims against defendants for false and deceptive advertising under GBL §§ 349 and 350 are dismissed.

"With respect to the common-law causes of action, they are also dismissed. Plaintiffs' allegations fail to state a claim, because defendants have no duty to investigate the accuracy of the contents of the book they published. Moreover, with respect to the fraud cause of action, plaintiffs provide no factual basis whatsoever for their conclusory allegations that defendants knew and intended to mislead book buyers as to the Beardstown Ladies' annual rate of return. . . ."

§ 9. REMEDIES FOR MISREPRESENTATION

KLAIBER v. FREEMASON ASSOCS. INC.,

266 Va. 478, 587 S.E.2d 555 (2003)

OPINION BY Justice LAWRENCE L. KOONTZ, JR .....

[Defendants developed a condominium. They sold units in the condominium to the plaintiffs Klaiber and Sienicki. The plaintiffs claimed that the roof was defective and sued for fraudulent misrepresentation as well as breach of warranty.] Klaiber purchased unit four in February 1999 for $200,000. Sienicki purchased unit one in January 1999 for $135,000. K.B.B. Corp., (K.B.B.), d/b/a Re/Max Central Realty, acted as the seller's real estate agent in these transactions.

By an order dated April 18, 2001, the trial court severed the claims of the individual plaintiffs and the Association, and directed that each case thereafter proceed independently, except for purposes of conducting discovery. At that time, Klaiber had sold his condominium unit for $216,000, and Sienicki had sold his unit for $170,000. In both transactions, agreements were executed purporting to continue the voting rights of Klaiber and Sienicki in the Association with respect to the pending litigation so that each would bear the costs of any assessment made by the Association for repairs to the condominium building but would also receive the proceeds of any settlement reached in the litigation. . . .

During discovery, it was established that the Association had paid $37,120 to replace the roof of the condominium and had incurred ongoing attorney's fees in the pending litigation. The Association had imposed special assessments on the individual unit owners to recover those costs. It was further established that Klaiber and Sienicki had paid $14,884 each to satisfy those assessments. In addition, Klaiber had paid $3,852.13 to repair water damage to his unit resulting from the defective roof, and Sienicki had paid $155.90 to remove the gas logs in the fireplace in his unit. Both parties also stated that they claimed "damages in the amount of any future special assessments for roof replacement, attorney's fees and repair and refurbishment of the fireplaces and chimneys."

On June 3, 2002, Freemason filed a joint motion for summary judgment asserting, among other things, that neither Klaiber nor Sienicki could prove actual damages with respect to any of their claims because they had sold their units at a "profit" and would have no further liability with respect to the repair of the alleged defects in the roof, chimneys, fireplaces, and flues in question. [The plaintiffs] contended that they had alleged an adequate measure of their damages because each had paid the special assessments related to the "cost of the replacement of the roof, attorney's fees, and is subject to their proportionate share of the cost of correcting the problem with the chimneys, flues and fireplaces." . . .

In *Community Bank,* we observed that "the rule as to what constitutes damage [for fraud], in any case, may broadly be stated to be that there is no damage where the position of the complaining party is no worse than it would be had the alleged fraud not been committed." Where the alleged fraud occurs in a commercial transaction involving the transfer of real property, we have more succinctly defined the measure of damages as "the difference between the actual value of the property at the time the contract was made and the value that the property would have possessed had the [fraudulent] representation been true." *Prospect Development Co. v. Bershader,* 258 Va. 75, 91, 515 S.E.2d 291, 300 (1999). Similar to the situation in *Prospect Development,* Klaiber and Sienicki did not allege facts to support a conclusion that the actual value of their condominium units at the time they purchased them was less than the value those units would have had absent the fraudulent acts of Freemason and K.B.B. Moreover, to the extent that Klaiber and Sienicki alleged damages in the form of costs of repair or replacement of defective elements of the condominium, we expressly declined to adopt this measure of damages in fraud cases. . . .

[T]he measure of damages for breach of contract or breach of warranty is not necessarily limited to the same measure of damages applicable to fraud torts or statutory false advertising. Under certain circumstances, a party seeking to restore the benefit of a bargain or to enforce a warranty is permitted to show that the cost of remedying the breach is the appropriate measure of damages. "The cost measure is calculated on the basis of the cost to complete the contract according to its terms or the cost to repair what has been done so that the contract terms are met. The cost measure is appropriate unless the cost to repair would be grossly disproportionate to the results to be obtained, or would involve unreasonable economic waste."

[The court held the plaintiffs could proceed with claims for breach of warranty/breach of contract for certain repair costs to fireplaces and flues, but not for repair of the roof, because the condominium association had recovered damages for that.]

Damages

72. **Damages measures.** Courts have used several different damages measures in misrepresentation cases.

(a) *Loss of bargain.* Damages based upon the loss of the bargain: the plaintiff is awarded the difference between value of the thing received in the bargain from the value it would have had if the representation had been true.

(b) *"Out of pocket."* Damages based upon actual loss sustained by the plaintiff because the thing received in the transaction is worth less than the price paid: the plaintiff is awarded the difference between the price paid and value received.

(c) *Consequential damages.* Consequential damages not based upon the value of the thing transferred but upon the plaintiff's losses or failure to obtain gains in other transactions in consequence of the misrepresentation. Consequential damages are recoverable only if foreseeable and if proved with reasonable certainty.

73. **Cost of making the representation good.** If the defendants' misrepresentations led the plaintiffs to buy property with defects, why not permit the plaintiffs to recover for cost they suffered in repairing the defects?

74. **Scienter, negligent, or innocent misrepresentation.** Many courts allow the plaintiff to recover the loss of bargain measure of damages, or to choose the most favorable measure of damages. Some, however, restrict the plaintiff to the so-called out of pocket measure. In addition, the out of pocket measure may be the only appropriate measure of damages for economic loss resulting from negligent or innocent misrepresentation. If the plaintiff would be entitled to rescind for an innocent-but-basic misrepresentation, see ¶ 22, supra, the plaintiff is entitled to recover damages that put the parties in substantially the same financial condition as rescission, ordinarily out of pocket damages.

75. **Evidence of lost bargain; the governing date.** The *Klaiber* court holds that the plaintiffs did not allege facts sufficient to permit proof showing the difference between the value plaintiffs received and the value they would have received if the representations had been true. The normal date used for the valuations required by this rule is the date of performance, that is, the date of purchase. What specific information would the plaintiffs be required to plead and prove? Would the fact that the plaintiffs sold the property for more than they paid for it necessary show they had no damages?

76. **Emotional harm damages.** Damages for emotional harm resulting from the misrepresentation are not recoverable in purely pecuniary transaction cases; such damages may be recovered if the misrepresentation amounts to some other kind of tort or if the misrepresentation is an assurance intended to secure emotional tranquility rather than pecuniary values.

77. **Punitive damages.** Punitive damages may be awarded in intentional misrepresentation cases, but some decisions hold that punitive damages are to be awarded only for aggravated forms of fraud. When the recovery is made under a statute rather than under common law scienter fraud, punitive damages may be excluded by the statute. Other statutes provide for double or treble damages.

78. **Losses from extraneous causes.** Recall that the measure of relief may depend upon the scope of the risk for which the defendant is liable. See *Oregon Steel Mills* and the paragraphs following, § 7 (b), supra.

Rescission and Reformation

79. **Reformation.** If the defendant's scienter, negligent, or innocent misrepresentation induces the plaintiff to subscribe to a writing that does not reflect the true agreement, the court may reform the writing to reflect the true agreement and then enforce it as reformed.

80. **Restitution.** (a) If the defendant's scienter or negligent misrepresentation induces the plaintiff to enter into a transaction, the plaintiff may timely restore to the defendant any values the plaintiff has received, rescind the transaction, and recover any values the plaintiff has transferred to the defendant in the transaction.

(b) If the defendant's innocent misrepresentation induces the plaintiff to enter into a transaction and that misrepresentation concerns a fact basic to the bargain and not merely material, the plaintiff may timely rescind, restoring values received and recovering values transferred. See 2 DOBBS ON REMEDIES § 9.3 (1) (2d ed. 1993).

81. **Restitution by way of constructive trust.** If the defendant's misrepresentation induces the plaintiff to transfer specific property, the court may order the defendant to make restitution of that particular property. See DOBBS ON REMEDIES § 9.3 (4); RESTATEMENT (THIRD) OF RESTITUTION AND UNJUST ENRICHMENT § 13 (Tentative Draft 2005). Typically this is expressed by saying the defendant is held as a constructive trustee and then required to convey the property. Although constructive trusts can furnish an important remedy in bargaining-transaction misrepresentation cases, they are not limited to such cases, but can be granted to prevent any kind of unjust enrichment.

82. **Restitution of the defendant's gains from the transaction.** Suppose the defendant, by misrepresentation, induces the plaintiff to sell shares of stock to the defendant. The defendant retains the shares and they double in value. At that point, the plaintiff discovers the

misrepresentation upon which he justifiably relied. The court can hold that the defendant is a constructive trustee and that he therefore must transfer the shares back to the plaintiff. Notice that such a transfer will give the plaintiff the increased value of the shares. *Estate of Jones v. Kvamme,* 449 N.W.2d 428 (Minn. 1989). The conceptual principle is that the plaintiff, in the eyes of equity, remains the "owner" of the shares throughout.

83. **Defendant's gains from sale or use of the property obtained by misrepresentation.** The same legal conception leads to the rule that if the defendant has sold the property, he is liable to make "restitution" of the gains he received in the sale. If he has used the property in a business, he may be liable for the use value as well as for the return of the property itself. See generally, DOBBS ON REMEDIES § 4.3 (2) (2d ed. 1993).

84. **Liability of defendant's donees of property obtained by misrepresentation.** Finally, the plaintiff who parts with property in justifiable reliance on the defendant's material misrepresentation is entitled to recover the property not only from the defendant, but from those to whom the defendant has donated the property. Again, the conception that the plaintiff has remained the owner (in the eyes of equity courts) explains the result. The donee is not entitled to keep property that belongs to another. Contrast, though, the rule that applies to a purchaser who does not know of the plaintiff's interests and pays value to the defendant for the property. In that case, the purchase cuts off the plaintiff's "equity" in the property. The plaintiff would still have her claims against the fraudulent defendant.

Professional and Academic Enhancements
Chapter 14

The Economic Loss Rule as a Bar To Intentional Misrepresentation Claims

DIGICORP, INC. v. AMERITECH CORP.

262 Wis.2d 32, 662 N.W.2d 652 (2003)

N. PATRICK CROOKS, J. . . .

[Digicorp was an authorized Ameritech distributor. Wishing to sell Ameritech's "Value-Link" calling plan through Bacher Communications, which was not an Ameritech authorized distributor, Digicorp entered into a new agreement with Ameritech that superseded its old one. Under this new contract, Digicorp was responsible for both Digicorp and Bacher employees. The new agreement contained a new provision that Ameritech could terminate the contract without any notice, if Digicorp submitted any sales agreements subsequently found to contain forged customer signatures. Ray Taylor, acting for Ameritech in arranging the new contract, did not inform Digicorp that one of Bacher's salesmen, Dann Krinsky (Krinsky) had engaged in fraudulent acts of forging customers' signatures when Krinsky had worked for Northeast Communications (NCS), another authorized Ameritech distributor.]

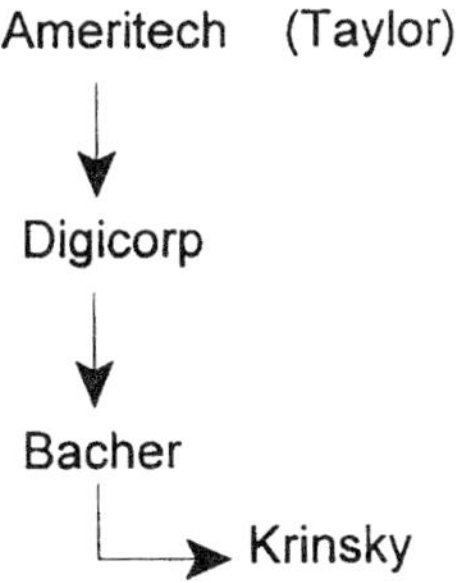

Unaware of Krinsky's past fraudulent actions, Digicorp entered into an agreement, superseding its earlier one with Ameritech, and incorporating Bacher (and its employees) as part of the distribution plan for Ameritech products.

Krinsky, through his employment at Bacher, continued to sell Ameritech Value-Link plans as one of Digicorp's 1099 employees. A few weeks later, an Ameritech employee discovered that the customer signatures on two Ameritech contracts submitted by Krinsky were forgeries. Digicorp was notified of the investigation; Krinsky then quit Bacher.

Bacher thereafter retrieved the Ameritech contracts from Krinsky's files and discovered that, during the two and a half months Krinsky had been employed by Bacher, only two or three of the over 250 Value-Link contracts he sold had genuine signatures. All of the rest were forged. ... Ameritech exercised its right under its agreement with Digicorp and terminated Digicorp's status as an Ameritech authorized distributor. Following that, Bacher was unable to sell Ameritech products.

[Digicorp sued Ameritech, asserting a number of theories, including intentional misrepresentation. Ameritech counterclaimed with its own misrepresentation claims. Bacher was brought in and it also claimed against Ameritech. The trial court held that the economic loss doctrine did not bar Digicorp's claim for fraudulent inducement. The jury awarded Digicorp $13,000 for Ameritech's breach of contract, and over $250,000 for intentional misrepresentation. Ameritech and Bacher recover some items of damages, too. The court of appeals affirmed Digicorp's recovery.]

This court is presented with the following issues:

(1) Does Wisconsin law recognize the so-called "fraud exception" to the economic loss doctrine and, if so, what are its elements?

(2) May a subcontractor of the party to whom the alleged misrepresentations were made avoid the operation of the economic loss doctrine because it was not in contractual privity with the party that made the alleged misrepresentation?

(3) Assuming that the economic loss doctrine does not bar a given claim for fraud in the inducement of a contract, may the allegedly defrauded party recover the benefit of the bargain premised upon the continuing vitality of the contract?

With respect to the first issue, we answer in the affirmative. Wisconsin recognizes a narrow fraud in the inducement exception, such as the one adopted in *Huron Tool and Engineering Co. v. Precision Consulting Services, Inc.,* 209 Mich.App. 365, 532 N.W.2d 541 (1995). This exception is not as broad as the one set forth by the court of appeals in *Douglas-Hanson Co. v. BF Goodrich Co.,* 229 Wis.2d 132, 598 N.W.2d 262 (1999). We hold that, consistent with the on *Huron Tool* decision, the economic loss doctrine acts as a bar where the fraud is interwoven with the contract, and not extraneous to it.

With respect to the second issue, this court answers in the negative. ... The economic loss doctrine precludes recovery in tort for solely economic losses, regardless of whether privity of contract exists between the parties.

We also answer the third issue in the negative, based on consistent interpretations of Wisconsin case law prohibiting recovery for the benefit of the bargain under the circumstances set forth. Where the fraud in the inducement exception applies, recovery for the benefit of the bargain is not permitted.

Accordingly, we reverse the court of appeals' decision and remand these matters to the circuit court for a new trial on contract remedies. . . .

[T]he economic loss doctrine requires transacting parties in Wisconsin to pursue only their contractual remedies when asserting an economic loss claim, in order to preserve the distinction between contract and tort law. As we noted in *Wausau Tile, Inc. v. County Concrete Corp.,* 226 Wis.2d 235, 265, 593 N.W.2d 445 (1999), "[w]e refuse to pass on to society the economic loss of a purchaser such as Wausau Tile who may have failed to bargain for adequate contract remedies."

. . . It is well settled that the economic loss doctrine was created to maintain the fundamental distinction between tort law and contract law; protect commercial parties' freedom to allocate economic risk by contract; and encourage the party best situated to assess the risk of economic loss, the commercial purchaser, to assume, allocate, or insure against that risk.

However, there are valid policy reasons why a party engaging in fraud should not be allowed to hide behind the protections of the economic loss doctrine. Wisconsin has a long-standing principle that parties need a background of truth and fair dealing in commercial relationships.

Furthermore, "[a] party to a business transaction is under a duty to disclose facts basic to the transaction if he knows the other is about to enter into it under a mistake as to them, and the other party could reasonably expect a disclosure of those facts". . . .

According to *Douglas-Hanson,* Wisconsin law does not allow the party perpetrating the fraud to hide behind contractual remedies. *Douglas-Hanson* at 148–50, 598 N.W.2d 262. In *Douglas-Hanson,* the court of appeals adopted a broad exception permitting tort claims to be asserted whenever the contract was induced by fraud. The court held that the economic loss doctrine did not preclude the plaintiff's claim for intentional misrepresentation, when the misrepresentation fraudulently induced the plaintiff to enter into the contract. In that case, the court of appeals reasoned that when an intentional misrepresentation fraudulently induces a party to enter into a contract, the parties appear to negotiate freely; but, in fact, one party's ability to negotiate fair terms and make an informed decision is undermined by the other party's fraudulent conduct. . . .

On appeal, this court was evenly split, in reviewing the *Douglas-Hanson* decision, on whether there should be a fraud in the inducement exception to the economic loss doctrine. Consequently, the precise issue of whether a fraud in the inducement exception to the economic loss doctrine is recognized in Wisconsin was left open to further debate by our split decision in *Douglas-Hanson.* . . .

Decisions from the United States District Court for the Eastern District of Wisconsin have recognized an exception to the economic loss doctrine for fraudulent inducement claims, but only when the claim is extraneous, rather than "interwoven" with the subject matter of the contract. ... In defining extraneous versus interwoven, the *Huron Tool* court said that extraneous fraud concerns those matters whose risk and responsibility were not expressly or impliedly dealt with in the contract.[9]

Turning to the facts of this case, as noted above, Ameritech argues that Wisconsin should recognize the narrow fraud in the inducement exception of *Huron Tool,* rather than the broad exception from the court of appeals' decision in *Douglas-Hanson,* which permits tort claims to be asserted whenever the contract in question was induced by fraud.

Digicorp agrees with Ameritech on this point, maintaining that public policy supports a narrow fraud in the inducement exception to the economic loss doctrine, because it promotes honesty, good faith and fair dealing during contract negotiations. Relying on the policies set forth in *Douglas-Hanson* and *Budgetel,* Digicorp reiterates that there can be no effective bargaining if contract negotiations begin with the assumption that the other party is lying.

As noted previously, we hold that there is indeed a fraud in the inducement exception to the economic loss doctrine. However, that exception is not as broad as the rule set forth by the court of appeals' decision in *Douglas-Hanson.* Instead, we adopt the narrow approach set forth in *Huron Tool,* and overrule the *Douglas-Hanson* decision to the extent that it is contrary to that narrow exception. The fraud in the inducement exception we adopt is wholly consistent with the policies underlying the economic loss doctrine. ...

Having determined the proper analytical framework for evaluating claims of fraud in the inducement, we now turn to the facts of this case. Our task is to determine whether the fraud involved matters for which risks and responsibilities were extraneous to, or interwoven into, the contract. ...

The subject of the alleged misrepresentation in this case does not involve the actual Value-Link service, but instead, deals with the responsibility and risk of the 1099 employee, Krinsky.

Here, we find that based on the evidence in the record, the fraud involved matters for which risks and responsibilities were interwoven into the contract. It is clear from the record that the parties expressly and impliedly assigned and allocated the responsibilities and risks for the 1099 employees.

9. We take strong issue with the broad, sweeping assertion in the dissent that "the *Huron* limitation fatally undermines the viability of the tort of fraud in the inducement." The fraud exception to the economic loss doctrine that we adopt is not dead on arrival. We expect that, through the years, there indeed will be circumstances where there is extraneous fraud, concerning matters whose risk and responsibility were not expressly or impliedly dealt with in the contract.

First, The Digicorp Fox Valley Division Sales Program Agreement Section Five states:

> Conduct of employees—DIGICORP reserves the right to approve all individuals engaged by Contractor in the sale and marketing of Ameritech services covered by this agreement. DIGICORP'S reputation in the industry is mutually agreed to be a valuable asset. *If DIGICORP becomes aware of any representations not in conformity with this agreement or sales activities deemed harmful to its reputation or business interests, we will immediately advise Contractor.* Contractor agrees to take corrective action, up to and including termination of the employee, to expeditiously address the improper activities or representations. Continuation or recurrence of unacceptable activities will be deemed a material breach of this agreement.

Pet'r App. to Opening Br. of Pet. Ameritech at 043 (emphasis added). Section Five of the Sales Program Agreement illustrates that Digicorp, during pre-contract negotiations, anticipated and allocated the risks and responsibilities associated with entering into an agreement with Ameritech.

Second, the letter from Taylor to the President of Digicorp, Clark, lists the duties and responsibilities of Ameritech and Digicorp 1099 employees. In particular, the letter unequivocally sets forth the criteria that must be met for an Ameritech Authorized Distributor to use sales people employed by another company to sell Ameritech services. In addition to the list of criteria, Taylor included the following statement in the letter:

> I want to make it clear that Ameritech holds its' [sic] Authorized Distributors responsible for the actions of 1099 sales representatives.
>
> Any activity by a 1099 sales person, as with any other sales representative, that is contrary to the standards established by Ameritech, will place in jeopardy your status as an Ameritech Authorized Distributor.

The detailed discussion included in this letter demonstrates that both Ameritech and Digicorp understood the terms of their agreement, and had an opportunity to allocate the risks involved during contract negotiations.

Finally, the June 1996 Non-Exclusive Authorized Distributor Agreement between Ameritech and Digicorp, clearly sets forth in Section 5.01 what happens if forged signatures are discovered. Section 5.1(c) states in relevant part:

> Notwithstanding 5.1(a) and (b) above, it is agreed that Ameritech may terminate this Agreement without notice in the event of ... submission of any sales agreement by the AD, any of its representatives, or its agents which is *subsequently found to contain forged*

customer signatures or of which the customer denies any knowledge of placing an order with AD. . . .

The entire relationship among Ameritech and Digicorp and Bacher was governed by contract. . . . The duties, responsibilities and risks of both Ameritech and Digicorp were set forth in great detail. The parties clearly allocated, by use of the contract terms, the risks and responsibilities of entering into the agreement.

It is clear from this information that the parties expressly and impliedly assigned responsibility and risk for the 1099 employees—the subject of the alleged misrepresentation.

Contrary to Digicorp's argument, the June 1996 contract between Digicorp and Ameritech was not a new contract, but a modification of a prior one. It was a routine renewal of a pre-existing contract. Even assuming, arguendo, that the misrepresentation made by Taylor with regard to knowledge of Krinsky's past fraudulent behavior, was a material inducement to Digicorp to enter into its replacement agreement with Ameritech, it was part and parcel of an overall allocation of risks and responsibilities for 1099 employees.

This information shows that the alleged misrepresentations by Taylor were interwoven with the subject matter of the contract. . . . The misrepresentations concerned matters related to the performance of the contract itself, and as such, cannot be found to be extraneous to the contractual dispute. Accordingly, Digicorp is limited to contract remedies. The fraud in the inducement exception to the economic loss doctrine is inapplicable under these circumstances.

Ameritech argues that Bacher should not be able to escape application of the economic loss doctrine just because there was no privity between them.

We answered the question in *Daanen & Janssen,* 216 Wis.2d 395, 573 N.W.2d 842, and unequivocally held there that even in the absence of privity, the economic loss doctrine bars one party in the distributive chain from recovering economic losses in tort from another party in that chain. For the reasons discussed herein, the economic loss doctrine applies to Bacher as well, and the fraud in the inducement exception is not applicable to its claims.

With regard to Bacher, it is important to note that it hired Krinsky before any representation was made by Ameritech. . . .

Accordingly, we reverse the court of appeals' decision and remand to the circuit court for a new trial limited to contract remedies. . . .

SHIRLEY S. ABRAHAMSON, Chief Justice and JON P. WILCOX, J., did not participate.

DIANE S. SYKES, J. (*concurring in part, dissenting in part*).

I would not adopt a fraud exception to the economic loss doctrine. The economic loss doctrine precludes commercial contracting parties from recovering tort damages for purely economic losses associated with the contract relationship. That is, the doctrine restricts commercial contracting parties to contract remedies when they allege an economic loss stemming from the contract relationship. . . .

The creation of a fraud exception to the economic loss doctrine undermines these important purposes and distinctions. A contracting party who alleges that he was fraudulently induced to enter into the contract already has adequate contract remedies: he can affirm the contract and seek damages for breach, or he can pursue the equitable remedy of rescission and seek restitutionary damages. A contract fraudulently induced is void or voidable; a party fraudulently induced to enter into a contract "has the election of either rescission or affirming the contract and seeking damages." This election of remedies requirement does not confer upon the aggrieved party the option of pursuing either contract or tort remedies, but, rather, involves a choice between two different contract remedies: damages for breach or rescission/restitution. . . .

The lead opinion concludes that there is a fraud in the inducement tort but disallows benefit-of-the-bargain tort damages. The lead opinion apparently restricts recovery in this new tort to that which would be allowed in an equitable action in contract for rescission and restitution, although it does not directly say so.

I certainly do not disagree with this outcome, because I would leave the parties to their contract remedies in the first place. However, the lead opinion's hybrid cause of action blurs rather than preserves the distinction between tort and contract remedies.

The lead opinion's narrow fraud exception does less damage to the second and third purposes underlying the economic loss doctrine, because it bars a tort claim for fraud in the inducement concerning matters that are "interwoven with" or "expressly or impliedly dealt with in the contract." I agree that the facts of this case do not support a claim under the lead opinion's narrow exception to the economic loss doctrine. As a general matter, however, we should refrain from attempting to articulate new legal rules where the factual predicates to do so are not present in the case. . . .

The facts of this case do not warrant the creation of a fraud-in-the-inducement exception to the economic loss doctrine, even one that is narrowly drawn. Digicorp had a pre-existing, ongoing, terminable-at-will distributorship agreement with Ameritech, and there is no evidence that the June 1, 1996, renewal of that agreement was induced by Ameritech's failure to disclose what it knew about the past forgeries of an employee that Digicorp's subdistributor, Bacher, had already hired. That is, there is no causal link between the fraudulent nondisclosure and the June 1, 1996, contract, the termination of which provided the premise for the award of lost profits and punitive damages in this case. There is no factual basis for the recognition of a fraud exception to the economic loss doctrine in this case, but the lead opinion purports to recognize one anyway.

Contracting parties can protect themselves against economic losses associated with pre-contract misrepresentations by appropriate contract language, and, in the event that one party's fraud frustrates the other party's ability to do so, contract law renders the contract voidable at the option of the aggrieved party and allows recovery of restitution. I would not adopt a fraud-in-the-inducement exception to the economic loss doctrine. In other respects, I concur in the majority opinion.

ANN WALSH BRADLEY, J. (*dissenting*).

Typically, when you narrow the viability of a cause of action, you chip away at the edges while being careful to preserve its core essence. However, by endorsing the *Huron* limitation, the lead opinion eviscerates the core of the tort of fraud in the inducement while purportedly leaving the edges of this cause of action intact. Because the *Huron* limitation essentially eliminates the viability of the tort of fraud in the inducement and undermines the purpose of the economic loss doctrine, I respectfully dissent.

While I agree with the lead opinion that there is a fraud in the inducement exception to the economic loss rule, I disagree with the lead opinion's endorsement of the limitation on that exception set forth in *Huron Tool.* Like the court of appeals, I would uphold the rule set forth in *Douglas-Hanson Co.* that "the economic loss doctrine does not preclude a plaintiff's claim for intentional misrepresentation when the misrepresentation fraudulently induces a plaintiff to enter into a contract." ...

Black's Law Dictionary defines "fraud in the inducement" as "fraud occurring when a misrepresentation leads another to enter into a transaction with a false impression of the risks, duties, or obligations involved." *Black's Law Dictionary,* 671 (7th ed.1999). As this definition reflects, the core of a fraud in the inducement action addresses misrepresentations regarding the risks, duties or obligations to be set forth in, and therefore "interwoven" with, a contract. It is hard to see how any of this core can survive under the lead opinion's formulation of the rule which bars a fraud in the inducement action where the fraud "is interwoven with the contract in that it involved matters for which risks and responsibilities were addressed."

The use of the *Huron* limitation creates an analytical disconnect in cases that involve a tort claim of fraud in the inducement. The disconnect is created because the type of case that the tort of fraud in the inducement is designed to address is the same type of case that the *Huron* limitation prevents from being brought. The court in *Budgetel* highlighted this problem:

> The tort, after all, is inducing someone to enter into a contract, so to say it does not apply where the tort involves the contract or its subject matter analytically makes no sense. ...

Daanen & Janssen held that privity is not required for the economic loss doctrine to bar a remote commercial purchaser from recovering economic losses from a manufacturer under theories of strict liability and negligence. The lead opinion prefers a significant expansion of this rule to cover situations such as this case in which the plaintiff is not a remote commercial purchaser, the defendant is not a manufacturer, and the tort claim is not strict liability or negligence. . . .

Since Bacher had no contract with Ameritech, presumably the lead opinion's application of *Daanen & Janssen* leaves Bacher without a tort remedy or a contract remedy. It acknowledges that Bacher raised the concern that if the economic loss doctrine prevents its intentional tort claim, it will be left without a remedy for Ameritech's fraud. However, the opinion does not explain why Bacher being left without a remedy is the correct result. Perhaps it did not address this question because it cannot fairly answer it. . . .

[Justice Bablitch joined this dissent]

1. **The fraud claim.** Notice that the claim is for intentional misrepresentation, but that the misrepresentation takes the form of concealment or nondisclosure—Ameritech knew of Krinsky's fraudulent behavior in the past, yet without disclosing the fact, inserted a clause that would eliminate Digicorp and Bacher if Krinsky lived up to this potential for criminality.

2. **The lineup of the justices.** Two justices of the Wisconsin Court did not participate. That left five justice to determine *Digicorp.* Only two of the five recognized the *Huron Tool* "exception." The justices lined up this way: two, the dissenters, wanted to *always* permit a scienter fraud action; two who wanted to permit it *sometimes* under the narrow *Huron Tool* view, and one, Justice Sykes, who wanted *never* to permit the action. That pretty well sorts out the major options on the table.

3. **The "exception" terminology and the types of economic loss rule.** Supporters of the economic loss rule to bar scienter fraud claims gained rhetorical advantage when courts adopted the "exception" terminology, which suggests that the economic loss rule by its own terms would apply to protect the defendant from responsibility for his own intentional fraud. Yet, historically the *Seely* type of economic loss rule (Chapter 12, § 1) did not deal with fraud of any kind, barring only negligence and strict liability suits, not intentional tort claims. And the *Robins* types rule (Chapter 12, § 3) only addressed negligence claims by a plaintiff who had no property interest in the damaged goods. To allow the fraud claim does not look like an "exception" to rules that never covered fraud in the first place.

4. **The broad and narrow "exceptions."** As the Justices in *Digicorp* recognize, the broad exception to the economic loss rule always allows the plaintiff to recover for intentional fraud that induces the contract. The "broad exception" view is equivalent to the view that the

economic loss rule does not apply to intentional fraud cases. The "narrow" exception is frequently associated with *Huron Tool*, supra, this chapter. It would permit recovery for scienter misrepresentations that induce a contract, but only if that fraud was somehow extraneous from the contract and not interwoven with it. If the misrepresentation is material (as it must be if it is actionable), then how could it ever be extraneous? Can you tell from Justice Crooks' opinion what he thinks operates to interweave the fraud and the contract?

5. **Disclaimers and economic loss rule.** As between the contracting parties, is the economic loss rule merely new language adopted to give effect to all forms of contractual disclaimers? Does some of the Crooks opinion seem to rely on implicit disclaimers?

6. **Bargaining for protection against fraud.** If the economic loss rule protects the defendant even when there is no disclaimer, how can the plaintiff bargain for protection? Would corporate counsel ever permit the defendant to contractually agree that it would be liable if it defrauded the plaintiff?

7. **Justice Sykes' views.** If you adopt Justice Sykes' views, would you be eliminating the misrepresentation or fraudulent inducement action altogether? Securities law requires corporations selling shares or bonds to provide accurate information about their financial condition. If an investor is harmed by corporate fraud, he has a cause of action. Do you think the logic of Justice Sykes' view would suggest abolition of the securities law? What if a large investor like a pension fund purchased shares directly from the corporation, which turned out to be an Enron, leaving large numbers of retirees without a pension?

8. **Negotiation costs.** If fraud actions—in securities cases and otherwise—are largely or entirely eliminated, would costs of negotiation rise? Costs of investigation? Imagine the investigation required to buy shares in a corporation if there were no reliable figures anywhere.

9. **Missing the effect of fraud?** Do any of the opinions miss the point that if the plaintiff was induced to enter the contract by fraud, the plaintiff is not really a consenting party? Or, on the contrary, do you think that the plaintiff can be fully protected by contract remedies?

10. **Barring those not in privity.** Why is it that someone like Bacher who is not a party to the contract should be barred? First, notice that Bacher is not barred by the principle in *Robins,* which holds that negligent tortfeasors are not liable to strangers for damaging the property of another person. Second, consider whether any rule or principle of fraud liability would make Ameritech liable to Bacher in the first place, irrespective of any economic loss rule.

Remedies for Misrepresentation

SMALL v. FRITZ COMPANIES, INC.

30 Cal.4th 167, 132 Cal.Rptr.2d 490, 65 P.3d 1255 (2003)

KENNARD, J. . . .

Stockholder Harvey Greenfield filed this action in 1996 against Fritz Companies, Inc., a corporation, and against three officers: Lynn Fritz, the company president, chairman of the board, and owner of 39 percent of the common stock; John Johung, the chief financial officer and a director; and Stephen Mattessich, the corporate controller and a director. The action was filed as a class action on behalf of all shareholders in Fritz "who owned and held Fritz common stock as of April 2, 1996 through at least July 24, 1996, in reliance on defendants' material misrepresentations and omissions ... and who were damaged thereby." The complaint alleged causes of action for common law fraud and negligent misrepresentation, and for violations of Civil Code sections 1709 and 1710, which codify the common law actions for fraud and deceit.

Before us is the validity of plaintiff's second amended complaint. It alleged that Fritz provides services for importers and exporters. Between April 1995 and May 1996, Fritz acquired Intertrans Corporation and then numerous other companies in the import and export businesses. Fritz encountered difficulties with these acquisitions, and in particular with the Intertrans accounting system, which it adopted for much of its business. Nevertheless, on April 2, 1996, Fritz issued a press release that reported third quarter revenues of $274.3 million, net income of $10.3 million, and earnings per share of $29. The same figures appeared in its third quarter report to shareholders, issued on April 15, 1996, for the quarter ending February 29, 1996. According to plaintiff, that report was incorrect for a variety of reasons: the inadequate integration of the Intertrans and Fritz accounting systems led to recording revenue that did not exist; Fritz failed to provide adequate reserves for uncollectible accounts receivable; and Fritz misstated the costs of its acquisitions.

The complaint alleged that on July 24, 1996, Fritz restated its previously reported revenues and earnings for the third quarter. Estimated third quarter earnings were reduced from $10.3 million to $3.1 million. Further, Fritz announced that it would incur a loss of $3.4 million in the fourth quarter. . . .

With respect to damages, the complaint alleged: "In response to defendant's disclosures on July 24, 1996, Fritz's stock plunged more than 55% in one day, dropping $15.25 to close at $12.25 per share. ... Had defendants disclosed correct third quarter revenue, net income and earnings per share on April 2, 1996, as required by GAAP [generally accepted accounting practices], Fritz's stock price would likely have declined on April 2, 1996, and plaintiff and the Class would have disposed of their shares at a price above the $12.25 per share closing price of that day."

[The trial court sustained a demurrer, but the Court of Appeals reversed. The Supreme Court of California granted petition for review. The court held that forbearance in reliance on a misrepresentation is indeed sufficient reliance. The fact that some suits like this one might be non-meritorious strike suits, intended to coerce a settlement, does not justify dismissing all such suits by holders of securities who, in reliance on misrepresentations, failed to sell. The judicial goal instead was to separate the wheat from the chaff. The federal Private Securities Litigation Reform Act of 1995 and the Uniform Standards Act of 1998, were almost entirely concerned with preventing nonmeritorious suits. But in more recent years, the reality of corporate fraud on an important scale has become apparent. "Eliminating barriers that deny redress to actual victims of fraud now assumes an importance equal to that of deterring nonmeritorious suits." However, plaintiffs must allege reliance with specificity in holder suits, even if they are based on negligent rather than fraudulent misrepresentation. The plaintiff's conclusory statements that he relied are insufficient and the case is remanded to permit him to state reliance. The plaintiff must allege actions, as distinguished from unspoken and unrecorded thoughts and decisions, that would indicate that the plaintiff actually relied on the misrepresentations. Although the plaintiff did not adequately plead reliance, the requirement we set forth here has not been stated in previous cases. Consequently the plaintiff is permitted to amend the complaint.]

BAXTER, J., concurring. . . .

[T]he most fundamental flaw is the complaint's utter failure to state whether, or how, the described shareholders have suffered a *realized loss* as a result of the alleged fraud. The complaint does not allege that any such investor *sold* shares at a price depressed by revelation of the scandal. Nor does it articulate any other way in which this group of Fritz shareholders sustained *actual out-of-pocket* damage as a direct result of the July 24, 1996, disclosures. The complaint simply suggests that because these persons *were holding* Fritz shares on July 24, they are entitled to recover any difference between the price to which the shares actually fell on that date, and the price at which the shares could have been promptly sold if the true third quarter results had been announced in timely fashion.

These allegations are insufficient to support monetary recovery for the alleged fraud and deceit. . . .

Of course, persons who held Fritz shares on July 24 suffered at least momentary *paper* losses when the price of those shares dropped. These investors' balance sheets of assets and liabilities, computed as of July 24, would show lower values for their Fritz shares than on July 23. However, such shareholders did not necessarily suffer *permanent realized* losses, and the law may compensate only the latter. Only those who sold the shares on the bad news, or otherwise incurred measurable, irretrievable out-of-pocket losses as a result, should be deemed to have suffered actual damage subject to recovery. Otherwise, damages are entirely speculative, and the opportunity for windfall recoveries is manifest.

If a company's stock was held for a substantial period after the fraud and its disclosure, intervening events may have obliterated the effect of the fraud on the value of the shareholders' investments. An efficient public securities market responds rapidly and accurately both to changing general economic conditions, and to the shifting prospects of each business whose shares are traded therein. Transitory events that affected the price of the company's shares on certain days during a particular year may have little to do with the value of the shares months or years later. A company's fortunes may rebound from fraud, perhaps under new and honest management, such that an investment retained for the long term may ultimately be worth more than if the fraud had never occurred. Certainly an attempt to trace the effect of a fraud that occurred in 1996 on the current value of the company's shares is an exercise in futile speculation. . . .

Even if my reasoning means that, in some cases, investors would have to sell their shares in order to recover, I foresee no dire market consequences.

BROWN, J., Concurring and Dissenting. . . .

First, plaintiff suffered *no* injury due to the content of the alleged misrepresentations. All of the alleged misrepresentations concerned *public* information that defendants had to disclose. In an efficient market, the market price of a stock reflects *all* publicly available information. Therefore, the price of Fritz stock after the April 2 misrepresentations was unlawfully inflated. If Fritz had timely reported its true third quarter results on April 2, then the market price of Fritz stock would have reflected this information and would have dropped accordingly. Even assuming plaintiff would have sold his stock immediately after a timely announcement of Fritz's true third quarter results, he would have suffered *a drop in share price commensurate to the inflation in share price caused by the content of the misrepresentations*. Because the market accurately and efficiently assimilates *all* public information this drop in share price would have been equal to any drop in share price attributable to the representations made on July 24. As such, plaintiff could not have profited from a timely announcement of Fritz's third quarter results absent "insider trading in violation of the securities laws." Thus, as a matter of law, plaintiff suffered no damages due to the misrepresentations themselves.

Second, plaintiff suffered no cognizable injury from the timing of the announcement of Fritz's true third quarter results. Plaintiff contends the drop in Fritz's stock price was more dramatic on July 24 because Fritz simultaneously announced its restated third quarter and disappointing fourth quarter results. Plaintiff, however, ignores his own allegations. According to plaintiff, defendants concealed the costs of Fritz's acquisitions on April 2 and did not reveal these costs until July

24. Specifically, plaintiff alleged that defendants deliberately concealed that Fritz would have to take an $11 million charge in the third quarter and *an additional $11.5 million charge in the fourth quarter.* Thus, even if Fritz had timely announced these charges on April 2, the announcement would have not only resulted in lower reported third quarter earnings, but also *presaged Fritz's fourth quarter loss.* ... [A]ny psychological effect allegedly caused by the timing of the announcement would have occurred even if defendants had timely reported the information allegedly concealed by Fritz's management for three months. Any damages attributable to the combined effect of the negative third and fourth quarter earnings announcement on July 24 are therefore illusory.

In any event, plaintiff forgets that stock prices in an efficient market react quickly and in an *unbiased* fashion to publicly available information. Stock prices in an efficient market are by definition fair ... [and] it is impossible for investors to be cheated by paying more for securities than their true worth. The true worth of Fritz's stock on July 24 necessarily reflected the fact that the restated third quarter results should have been reported on April 2. Thus, the price of Fritz stock on July 24 was, by definition, the same price the stock would have had on that date if defendants had reported Fritz's true third quarter results on April 2.

Third, any drop in stock price due to an alleged loss in investor confidence in Fritz management caused by the delayed announcement is either illusory or too speculative to constitute cognizable damages. ...

KENNARD, J., Concurring. ...*

The majority opinion, which I authored, upholds the right of stockholders to sue for fraudulent or negligent misrepresentation when they reasonably rely on the misrepresentation to refrain from selling their stock. It does not discuss whether the plaintiff here has adequately pled damage, because defendants did not raise that question. I write separately to explain my disagreement with the separate opinions of Justices Baxter and Brown. ...

Justice Baxter begins his discussion with the correct proposition that a plaintiff must show *actual* damages. But he asserts two more propositions that are unsound and unsupported by any authority. First, he asserts that defrauded stockholders incur no damages unless the value of their stock was *permanently* diminished. Second, he maintains that if, after an initial decline when the fraud is revealed, the price of the stock at any later time rises *for reasons unrelated to the fraud,* this rise reduces or eliminates the plaintiff's loss. The possibility of such a rise, he maintains, would make damages too speculative. These premises lead Justice Baxter to conclude that in most instances stockholders must sell their stock in order to sue, because there is no other way they can fix the amount of damages suffered and prove they will not benefit from an

* In the printed reporters, this opinion appeared immediately after the majority opinion. Editors changed placement for ease in following the arguments.

increase in the value of the stock, at some unknown future date, arising from unknowable future circumstances.

But Justice Baxter's premises are wrong. Temporary injury is legally compensable. Examples abound. One who sustains personal injuries may sue even if the injuries will eventually heal. A temporary taking of property is compensable, even if the property is later returned. To state a cause of action, a plaintiff whose property is damaged need not plead that its value will be forever impaired. In *Mears v. Crocker First Nat. Bank* (1948) 84 Cal. App. 2d 637, 191 P.2d 501, the appellate court upheld a cause of action for conversion when a company wrongfully refused for six weeks to transfer title to stock on its books.

... The economy is filled with what could derisorily be termed "paper assets"—the appreciated value of real estate, the goodwill of a business, uncollected accounts receivable, the balance of a checking account, etc. Business and individual investors make decisions based on the value of such assets. A decline in the value of stock, like a decline in the balance of a bank account or in the worth of a physical asset, is a decline in the net worth of the stockholder, whether or not the stock is sold. For individual stockholders, it affects such matters as whether the stockholders will take a vacation, whether they can get a mortgage, and what other investments they make or do not make. It can have drastic effects on retirement plans. Businesses and institutions also hold stock. A decline in the value of the stock it holds can lead a college to raise tuition or an insurer to raise premiums. It affects a company's ability to borrow money or issue new stock. In sum, ours is a paper economy, and declines in stock prices have real and serious effects *whether or not the stockholders sell the stock.*

I disagree also with Justice Baxter's second premise—that the damages defrauded stockholders should receive would become unduly speculative if they continued to hold the stock because of the possibility that the price of the stock might increase later, at any time into the indefinite future, because of matters unrelated to the fraud. The accepted rule is to the contrary. In a securities fraud case, the loss is calculated by using the "market price after the fraud is discovered when the price ceases to be fictitious [i.e., based on false data] and represents the consensus of buying and selling opinion of the value of the securities." (Rest.2d Torts, § 549, com. c, p. 110.) Later prices changes, in either direction, do not affect the calculation of the loss.

This rule does not necessarily mean that damages must be computed on the basis of the market price of the stock on the day the possible fraud is revealed; the market may take longer to digest and react to the news. In 1995 Congress, in the Public Securities Litigation Reform Act of 1995 (PSLRA), addressed proof of damages in cases in which a plaintiff who was fraudulently induced to purchase securities sued the corporation and its officers after the fraud was revealed and the price fell. (15 U.S.C. § 78u–4(e).) The PSLRA calculates damages based on the mean trading price of the security within a 90-day period after the date when the misstated or omitted fact is disclosed to the market. (Kaufman, Securities Litigation: Damages (2002) § 3.13, pp. 3–95 to 3–102.) (The mean trading price is the average of the closing prices of the security throughout the 90-day period.) If, however, the plaintiffs sell the security before the expiration of the 90-day period, damages are based on the mean trading price in the postdisclosure period ending on the date of the sale. (*Ibid.*) There are differences between the buyer's actions regulated by the PSLRA and the holder's actions at issue here, but they share a common need: to fix a postdisclosure date and price to use in calculating damages. In this respect the two actions are analogous, and the federal legislation regulating buyer's action suggests a workable rule for computing damages in holder's actions: It recognizes that the market may overreact to news of fraud, and that a later price may be a better indicator of the true postdisclosure value of the stock, but it does not diminish a plaintiff's damages because of the possibility that long-term economic factors may eventually cause the stock price to rise to its predisclosure level. . . .

I disagree also with Justice Brown's concurring and dissenting opinion. Justice Brown notes that plaintiff pled that Fritz's shares were traded in an "efficient market," and she declines to accept or reject the efficient capital market hypothesis[5] but despite her disclaimer she relies on that economic theory for her analysis. The efficient capital markets hypothesis, however, does not support her analysis.

I agree with Justice Brown that plaintiff here is not entitled to damages on the theory that he would have sold Fritz stock at artificially high prices maintained through Fritz's concealment of adverse information. "Plaintiffs cannot claim the right to profit from what they allege was an unlawfully inflated stock value". . . .

Justice Brown, however, relies on the efficient capital market hypothesis to argue that as a matter of law plaintiff sustained no damage. She asserts: "The true worth of Fritz's stock on July 24 necessarily reflected the fact that the restated third quarter results should have been reported on April 2. Thus, the price of Fritz's stock on July 24 was, by definition, the same price the stock would have had on that date if defendants had reported Fritz's true third quarter results on April 2." This argument is logically unsound. Under the semi-strong version of the efficient capital market hypothesis, the price of Fritz's stock on July 24 necessarily reflected the fact that the third quarter results should have been reported on April 2. But that does not mean the price on July

5. There are three versions of the efficient capital market hypothesis. The weak version holds that market prices eventually reflect all publicly available information. The semi-strong version says that prices do so rapidly. The strong version holds that prices reflect all material information, even that not available to the public. The weak version obviously does not aid Justice Brown's position. For reasons stated in text neither does the semi-strong version. The strong version, which would imply that the market knew Fritz's financial reports were false long before Fritz disclosed this fact, would assist Justice Brown, but "[n]o one these days accepts the strongest version of the efficient capital market hypothesis, under which non-public information automatically affects prices. That version is empirically false. . . ."

24 was the same price the stock would have had on that date if Fritz had reported those results on April 2. Here is why: On July 24 the market had additional information—that the April 2 report was false and that the true facts had been concealed for over three and one-half months. Justice Brown asserts that in an efficient market, "the market price of a stock reflects *all* publicly available information." The efficient capital market hypothesis does *not* presume that investors consider only hard economic data and ignore other information casting doubt on the integrity or competence of management. There is no logical reason under the efficient capital market hypothesis to assume that investors would disregard information showing false earnings reports and concealment of true data and would value the stock as if no such things had occurred. . . .

In sum, disclosures during the past three years have revealed extensive fraud involving numerous corporations, often involving false financial reports and the concealment of true financial data—fraud so massive that it contributed to an overall decline in the stock market and perhaps to a decline in the economy generally. The victims include not only those who bought or sold stock in reliance upon the false statements, but also those who held stock in reliance. The majority opinion allows such holders to sue for damages. That remedy should not be so hedged and qualified that only a fraction of those actually injured would be able to gain redress.

General Rules Permitting and Restricting Recovery for Unrealized Harm

Dan B. Dobbs

The Law of Torts § 483A (Supp. 2005)

Economic entitlement or market-measured damages. Damages rules in misrepresentation cases can be called economic entitlement rules. They aim to give the plaintiff damages in a sum that will give her the value she was entitled to have under the representation or breach of warranty. Specifically, they attempt to place the plaintiff in the economic position she would have enjoyed if the representation had been correct or (under the out of pocket rule) in the position she would have enjoyed if the items she received had been worth what she paid.

These rules require the plaintiff to prove a loss, but they do not require the plaintiff to *realize* a loss. That is, they do not require the plaintiff to re-sell the purchased goods at a loss, to pay for repair or upgrading of the goods, or to suffer any kind of physical injury as a result of the item's poor qualities. There is nothing unusual in the law of damages about using this kind of entitlement or bookkeeping measure of damages. In fact, the damages measure is like the buyer's measure of damages for breach of warranty which is codified in the UCC.

Example. For example, suppose the seller fraudulently represents that a house has a new roof in excellent condition when in fact the roof is rotting and ready to leak at the first rain. With a roof like that represented, the house would be worth $300,000, but with the bad roof it is worth only $290,000. The misrepresentation puts the plaintiff purchaser at risk for rain damage in the future, but that future risk also creates a present loss in value. The plaintiff's claim in such a case is a market-based loss for her economic entitlement. Under the loss of bargain measure of damages, the plaintiff is entitled to recover $10,000, even though she has not actually sold at a loss, incurred expenses of repair, or suffered damage from leaks.

Consequential damages—when harm must be realized or likely to be realized. The rule is different when the plaintiff seeks to recover consequential damages. Consequential damages are not based on the market value of the very thing to which the plaintiff is entitled but upon collateral costs incurred or profit losses suffered. For example, the defendant who misrepresents the condition of the roof to the home buyer is liable to make the plaintiff's economic entitlement good by paying damages based on the difference between the value of the house with the roof as represented and the value the plaintiff received. In contrast, though, if the plaintiff claims that the rains came and the roof leaked, causing rain damage to the plaintiff's antique furniture, the claim is for consequential damages and the plaintiff will be required to prove that the damages were in fact realized or will more likely than not be realized in the future. Consequential damages claims are also limited by a series of other rules, requiring rather clear proof as to causation and damage and also requiring the plaintiff to minimize damages.

The upshot is that in the ordinary misrepresentation claim (and the claim of economic damages for breach of warranty as well), the buyer-plaintiff can claim economic damages if the property is worth less than the value she was entitled to; but if she claims consequential damages, she must prove that the loss has been realized or will probably be realized in the future by way of physical harm, repair costs, or sale-at-a-loss.

Cases Requiring Physical Injury or Harm

Fact pattern. One group of cases seems facially at odds with the rules permitting recovery of unrealized economic harm based on the difference in value between what the buyer paid and what she got. In these cases, the plaintiff purchases a mass-produced product such as a motor vehicle. She later sues the manufacturer asserting that some feature of the vehicle is defective because it is unreasonably dangerous, for example, that the vehicle is prone to rollover, or the door latch is prone to pop open. In most of these, the plaintiff asserts both breach of warranty and misrepresentation. The harm claimed is economic harm, not physical harm. What economic harm? Because of its defect, the product does not have the economic value the plaintiff is entitled to. On this basis, the normal rules of misrepresentation and the normal rules of warranty would both permit recovery. In fact, the Uniform Commercial Code statutorily prescribes damages measured by "the difference ... between the value of the goods accepted and the value they would have had if they had been as warranted. ..." The benefit of the bargain rule in misrepresentation cases is essentially similar.

The cases. Many of the courts that have addressed this situation in the case of vehicles or their accessories, and some that have addressed it in the case of medical devices, have said that until physical injury occurs, the plaintiff has no claim. Courts requiring physical injury as a prerequisite to the economic loss claim usually assert in various language that the plaintiff has no harm or damage until a physical injury manifests itself, although some of the cases denying the claim may not support such departures from the usual economic measure of damages.

Aspinall v. Philip Morris Companies, Inc., 442 Mass. 381, 813 N.E.2d 476 (2004). Cigarette smokers sued Philip Morris under a consumer protection statute, claiming that the defendant deceptively advertised "light cigarettes" with "lowered tar and nicotine," knowing that most consumers would not get the benefit of these qualities. The trial court certified the claim as a class action. A judge on the court of appeals decertified the class. On appeal, *held*, over dissents, the trial court's certification of the class is affirmed. If the plaintiff sought damages for personal injury, the "unique and different experiences of each individual member of the class would require litigation of substantially separate issues and would defeat the commonality of interests in the certified class." But here, "plaintiffs need not prove individual physical harm in order to recover for the defendants' deception." What the plaintiffs allege is that because of the "defendants' deceptive advertising, all consumers of Marlboro Lights in Massachusetts paid more for the cigarettes than they would have otherwise paid. The plaintiffs expect to offer proof at trial that the amount that all purchasers of Marlboro Lights paid for the cigarettes exceeded their true market value (what purchasers would have paid had they known the truth). If they succeed in their proof, the plaintiffs argue that the correct model for measuring actual damages is the difference between the price paid by the consumers and the true market value of the 'misrepresent[ed]' cigarettes they actually received. (Thus, the exact amount of actual damages may be determined by multiplying the number of cigarettes sold, in the years defined by the certification order, by the difference between the price paid and actual fair market value.) This is a variation on the traditional 'benefit of the bargain' rule that awards a defrauded party the monetary difference between the actual value of the product at the time of purchase and what its value would have been if the representations had been true."

Chapter 15

STATUTORY PROTECTION AGAINST MISREPRESENTATION AND DECEPTIVE PRACTICES

A variety of state and federal statutes prohibit certain types of fraud and misrepresentation. These statutory causes of action are often pleaded alongside common law claims. In the states, a broad range of unfair and deceptive practices are subject to private challenge through state consumer fraud or deceptive practices acts. At the federal level, certain patterns of unlawful practice can be challenged under the civil RICO statute. Specific federal acts preclude other forms of fraud.

This chapter focuses on key state and federal statutes that provide consumers, and sometimes businesses, with a private right of action. The focus is on tort claims. Although not directly addressed in this chapter, misrepresentation also may be subject to administrative regulation, as it is under the Federal Trade Commission Act, 15 U.S.C. § 45(a)(1), which declares unlawful "unfair methods of competition in or affecting commerce, and unfair or deceptive practices in or affecting commerce." Or misrepresentation may be subject to criminal prosecution, as it is under RICO (§ 2 below). In addition, contract claims, such as Uniform Commercial Code breach of warranty claims, can be (and frequently are) asserted alongside consumer fraud actions.

§ 1. CONSUMER PROTECTION AND UNFAIR TRADE PRACTICES

The most widely applicable statutes protecting consumers from fraud are state consumer protection acts. These statutes, which protect consumers from many types of deception, have been enacted in every state of the union as well as the District of Columbia. State consumer protection acts have varied titles, and are sometimes referred to as consumer fraud acts, uniform deceptive practices acts ("UDAPs"), unfair competition acts, or "little FTC acts."

As with any statutory cause of action, understanding the scope and elements of a particular consumer fraud act necessarily begins with a careful reading of the statutory language itself. But while consumer fraud acts vary considerably among the states, many of the acts stem from model acts proposed by the Federal Trade Commission and the National Conference of Commissioners on Uniform State Laws. For this reason, the state statutes share a number of common elements.

(a) Common Elements

(1) Unfair and Deceptive Practices

FLORIDA DECEPTIVE AND UNFAIR TRADE PRACTICE ACT
WEST'S FLORIDA STATUTES ANNOTATED

§ 501.204 Unlawful Acts and Practices

(1) Unfair methods of competition, unconscionable acts or practices, and unfair or deceptive acts or practices in the conduct of any trade or commerce are hereby declared unlawful.

(2) It is the intent of the Legislature that, in construing subsection (1), due consideration and great weight shall be given to the interpretations of the Federal Trade Commission and the federal courts relating to s. 5(a)(1) of the Federal Trade Commission Act, 15 U.S.C. s. 45(a)(1) as of July 1, 2001.

TEXAS DECEPTIVE TRADE PRACTICES ACT
VERNON'S TEXAS STATUTES AND CODES ANN.

§ 17.46 Deceptive Trade Practices Unlawful.

(a) False, misleading, or deceptive acts or practices in the conduct of any trade or commerce are hereby declared unlawful. . . .

(b) Except as provided in [a later section involving damages actions brought by consumers], the term "false, misleading, or deceptive acts or practices" includes, but is not limited to, the following acts:

(1) passing off goods or services as those of another;

(2) causing confusion or misunderstanding as to the source, sponsorship, approval, or certification of goods or services. . . .

(5) representing that goods or services have sponsorship, approval, characteristics, ingredients, uses, benefits, or quantities which they do not have or that a person has a sponsorship, approval, status, affiliation, or connection which he does not;

(8) disparaging the goods, services, or business of another by false or misleading representation of facts;

(9) advertising goods or services with intent not to sell them as advertised. . . .

(11) making false or misleading statements of fact concerning the reasons for, existence of, or amount of price reductions. . . .

(13) knowingly making false or misleading statements of fact concerning the need for parts, replacement, or repair service;

(14) misrepresenting the authority of a salesman, representative or agent to negotiate the final terms of a consumer transaction. . . .

(16) disconnecting, turning back, or resetting the odometer of any motor vehicle so as to reduce the number of miles indicated on the odometer gauge;

(20) representing that a guarantee or warranty confers or involves rights or remedies which it does not have or involve. . . .

(24) failing to disclose information concerning goods or services which was known at the time of the transaction if such failure to disclose such information was intended to induce the consumer into a transaction into which the consumer would not have entered had the information been disclosed;

(27) taking advantage of a disaster declared by the governor under Chapter 418, Government Code, by:

(A) selling or leasing fuel, food, medicine, or another necessity at an exorbitant or excessive price; or

(B) demanding an exorbitant or excessive price in connection with the sale or lease of fuel, food, medicine, or another necessity. . . .

(c)(1) It is the intent of the legislature that in construing Subsection (a) of this section in suits brought under Section 17.47 of this subchapter the courts to the extent possible will be guided by Subsection (b) of this section and the interpretations given by the Federal Trade Commission and federal courts to Section 5(a)(1) of the Federal Trade Commission Act [15 U.S.C.A. § 45(a)(1)].

(2) In construing this subchapter the court shall not be prohibited from considering relevant and pertinent decisions of courts in other jurisdictions.

---

1. **General restrictions—the problem of vagueness.** What constitutes an unfair or deceptive practice is "notoriously undefined." In states with acts that bar unfair and deceptive practices in general terms, as in Florida, do defendants have fair notice that their conduct is prohibited? In one Florida case, the defendant sponsored a "puzzle contest." Entrants were not initially required to pay a fee to enter. Once entrants solved an elementary puzzle correctly (as 97% of the entrants did), they were notified that they were tied for first prize and given a chance to compete for cash prizes up to $1000 by paying a fee and solving another elementary "tiebreaker" puzzle. This process continued for several rounds. A public agency sued under Florida's Deceptive and Unfair Trade Practice Act. Although the case did not note what relief

was sought, the court noted that possible sanctions "consist of injunctive relief, declaratory reliefs, damages and cease and desist orders." The defendant argued that no relief should be granted because Florida's "little FTC act" was so vague, uncertain and indefinite that one could not know from the statute what is permitted and what is prohibited. Should this argument prevail? See *Department of Legal Affairs v. Rogers,* 329 So.2d 257 (Fla. 1976).

2. **Federal Trade Commission interpretations.** As in Florida and Texas, many states place great weight on Federal Trade Commission interpretations of unfair and deceptive practices. The Federal Trade Commission Act prohibits such practices but does not create a private right of action. See *Holloway v. Bristol-Myers Corp.*, 485 F.2d 986, 988 (D.C. Cir. 1973). Federal Trade Commission interpretations of deceptive and unfair practices may be found in cases brought by the agency in administrative proceedings or federal court. In addition, the Federal Trade Commission has issued trade regulation rules which can be found in the code of federal regulations. See, e.g., FTC Retail Food Store Advertising and Marketing Practices, 16 C.F.R. § 424.1 (2003) (requiring food stores advertising products at a stated price to have the advertised products in stock and available to customers during the effective period of the advertisement or else to disclose that supplies are limited). One particularly significant trade regulation rule is the FTC's rule on franchising. Titled "Disclosure Requirements and Prohibitions Concerning Franchising and Business Opportunity Ventures," 16 C.F.R. § 436, the rule requires prospective franchisees to be given a disclosure document, copies of franchise documents and related agreements. The federal trade commission has also published a number of industry guides addressing fair and unfair trade practices. Should every violation of FTC precedents, regulations or guides, which govern public enforcement, also set the standards for private enforcement under state consumer fraud statutes? Should the fact that the FTC has *not* barred a practice provide evidence that it is not unfair or deceptive?

3. **Specific prohibitions—loopholes.** Acts that create detailed "laundry lists" of prohibited conduct are subject to different kinds of challenges. The maxim of statutory interpretation—"expresio unius est exclusio alterius"—counsels that expressing one or more items in a statute indicates an intent to exclude other items which are not expressed. When states' statutes have specifically enumerated prohibited acts, should courts bar recovery for acts that were not mentioned in the statute? In one Texas case, sellers of a mobile home park did not disclose to the purchasers information about defects in the water system. The failure to disclose occurred the year before failure to disclose was added to Texas's laundry list of prohibited practices. Should the action for failure to disclose nevertheless be permitted? See *Cobb v. Dunlap*, 656 S.W.2d 550 (Tex. Ct. App. 1983). Is it preferable for state legislatures to provide a general standard barring unfair practices or more detailed lists of the conduct to be prohibited?

4. **Overlap with common law torts.** Many of the unfair and deceptive practices prohibited by state consumer fraud acts overlap with common-law torts and other violations of law. See *Bernardo v. Planned Parenthood Federation of America*, 115 Cal.App.4th 322, 9 Cal.Rptr.3d 197, 222 (2004) (noting that California's unfair competition law by proscribing "any unlawful business practice," "borrows violations of other laws and treats them as unlawful practices that the unfair competition law makes independently actionable"). Can you identify items barred by the Texas consumer fraud act that would seem to be actionable at common law or under other statutes we have studied? Courts often hold that consumer fraud act liability rules add to any existing causes of action. Does the addition of a statutory cause of action for conduct covered by a common law cause of action or another statute undermine or strengthen those rules?

5. **Transactions that affect the public interest.** In many jurisdictions even a single unfair or deceptive practice can serve as the basis for a consumer fraud act claim. See *PNR, Inc. v. Beacon Property Mgmt., Inc.*, 842 So.2d 773 (Fla. 2003). However, to be actionable in other jurisdictions an unfair or deceptive practice must impact "consumers at large," or be "affected with the public interest." In jurisdictions that have adopted these standards, precisely which practices affect the public interest is the subject of ample litigation. See *Sloan v. Thompson*, 115 P.3d 1009 (Wash. Ct. App. 2005) (builder's sale of home with a defective first floor had no impact on the public interest and thus was not actionable under the state consumer fraud act); *New York Univ. v. Continental Ins. Co.*, 87 N.Y.2d 308, 639 N.Y.S.2d 283, 662 N.E.2d 763 (1995) (holding that complex issue of non-standard commercial insurance coverage was not actionable under state deceptive practices act because it did not have a broad impact on consumers at large). Typically, breach of contract claims do not count as unfair or deceptive acts under state consumer fraud acts. *PNR*, 842 So.2d at 777 n.2.

6. **Interaction with other state statutes.** Some freestanding statutes—not formally a part of the consumer fraud or deceptive practices acts—in effect add to the laundry list of forbidden practices. For example, some statutes condemn misleading web information or e-mail messages. See, e.g., WASH. REV. CODE § 19.190.030. In Texas, a separate statute forbids representing products as authentic Indian arts and crafts when they are not. TEX. BUS. & COM. CODE ANN. § 17.853. Likewise, a person may not represent that a food is kosher if the person knows or was reckless in determining whether it was. TEX. BUS. & COM. CODE ANN. § 17.823. Do these additional statutes duplicate coverage under the general consumer protection statutes? One important type of statute that adds to the laundry list provisions are state unfair claims settlement practices acts. See, e.g., WASH. ADMIN. CODE 284–30–330 et seq. These acts make violation of certain minimum insurance standards a per se unfair practice under the state consumer fraud act. See, e.g., *American Manufacturers Mut. Ins. Co. v. Osborn* , 104 Wash.App. 686, 17 P.3d 1229 (2001) (noting that insureds may bring a private action against insurers

for both bad faith and breach of the duty of good faith under the Consumer Protection Act).

7. **Free speech concerns.** Not only may consumer fraud act claims overlap with other economic and dignitary torts, but the free speech concerns in these suits may overlap with the concerns that arise in other economic and dignitary torts. For instance, in *Bernardo v. Planned Parenthood Federation of America*, 115 Cal.App.4th 322, 9 Cal.Rptr.3d 197 (2004), the plaintiff, a person who opposed abortion, sought an injunction against defendant Planned Parenthood under California's Unfair Competition Law and False Advertising Law. Plaintiff argued that Planned Parenthood made misleading statements on its website—specifically, that abortion is safe or safer than childbirth, and that medical research has not established a link between abortion and breast cancer. Plaintiff alleged that these statements caused women to make decisions about abortion without full information. The California Superior Court granted a motion to strike the complaint under the state's anti-SLAPP statute, touched on in Chapter 8, supra. The appellate court affirmed the dismissal on the ground that the challenged statements were "expressions of opinion about an issue of genuine scientific debate," and were "noncommercial speech fully protected under the First Amendment." The court also upheld an award of costs and attorneys' fees to Planned Parenthood.

(2) Duty to Disclose

Many consumer fraud acts, such as the Texas statute, require disclosure of information that would be important to a consumer in deciding whether or not to enter into a transaction for goods and services. Failure to disclose such information would constitute an unlawful practice. Recall that in common law fraud cases, nondisclosure of material information often was not actionable.

STRAWN v. CANUSO

140 N.J. 43, 657 A.2d 420 (1995)

O'HERN, J.

[This] case concerns the claims of more than 150 families seeking damages because the new homes that they bought in Voorhees Township, New Jersey, were constructed near a hazardous-waste dump site, known as the Buzby Landfill. The complaint named as defendants John B. Canuso, Sr., and John B. Canuso, Jr., and their companies: Canetic Corporation and Canuso Management Corporation. Fox & Lazo Inc. (Fox & Lazo), the brokerage firm that was the selling agent for the development, was also named as a codefendant.

Plaintiffs base their claims on common-law principles of fraud and negligent misrepresentation, and the New Jersey Consumer Fraud Act, *N.J.S.A.* 56:8–1 to –66 ....

[The court describes the Buzby Landfill. Although it "was not licensed to receive liquid-industrial or chemical wastes, large amounts of hazardous materials and chemicals were dumped there. ... Toxic wastes dumped in the Buzby Landfill began to escape because it had no liner or cap." Tests done by the New Jersey Department of Environmental Protection and Energy (DEPE) determined that hazardous waste was seeping from the landfill into a downstream lake and contaminating the ground water. Although a system was installed at the landfill to vent excessive levels of methane gas, DEPE's site manager discovered gas leaks in the venting system that released contaminants, including benzene and other volatile organic compounds. EPA recommended that the site be considered for a Superfund cleanup.

Plaintiffs allege that the developers were specifically aware of the existence and hazards of the landfill, but did not disclose those facts to plaintiffs when they bought their homes. In particular, the Canuso defendants had a copy of a 1980 EPA report that warned: "The proposed housing development on land adjacent to the site has all the potential of developing into a future Love Canal if construction is permitted" (though later agency reports described any risk as "indeterminate"). DEPE representatives warned defendants of the problems of building a large development near the landfill and one of Fox & Lazo's marketing directors urged his firm and the individual Canuso defendants to disclose the existence of the Buzby Landfill to home buyers. Despite this knowledge, defendants' representatives were instructed never to disclose the existence of the landfill even when asked about such conditions.

The trial court rejected class certification and on defendants' motions for summary judgment ruled that "there is no duty that the owner of lands owe[s] to a prospective purchaser to disclose to that prospective purchaser the conditions of somebody else's property." However, the trial court added that if the sellers had made a statement concerning someone else's property, they could be liable for their affirmative misrepresentations.

Upon appeal by seven plaintiff-families who alleged nondisclosure but not affirmative misrepresentations by the defendant, the Appellate Division held that the builders and brokers of the new multi-home development had a duty to disclose to potential buyers the existence of a nearby, closed landfill. The court detailed the appellate division rulings, and then began its own analysis.]

Justice Holmes once noted that "whenever we trace a leading doctrine of substantive law far enough back, we are very likely to find some forgotten circumstance of procedure at its source." The forgotten circumstance in this case is not one of procedure, but Justice Holmes' observation is relevant to the law of real property, which is firmly grounded in history. For example, the concept of estates in land continues to influence our law of landowners' liability to the extent that liability depends on the status of the person on the property. Was the person a trespasser, a licensee, or an invitee?

Only gradually has the law of real property assimilated other principles of law. One commentator observed that "the law offers more protection to a person buying a dog leash than it does to the purchaser of a house." For years, "[c]ourts continued to cling to the notion that a seller had no duty whatsoever to disclose anything to the buyer." That attitude endured, though the purchase of a home "is almost always the most important transaction [one] will ever undertake."

The lack of protection afforded to purchasers of real property remained even though principles of commercial marketability had long since been infused into most business transactions. Professor Karl Llewellyn stated during the New York Law Revision Commission's hearings in 1954 that "good faith has been a part of mercantile obligation since American law began." In calling for securities reform in his message to Congress in 1933, President Franklin D. Roosevelt suggested that to the rule of *caveat emptor* should be added, "[L]et the seller also beware."

However, in the field of real property, the doctrine of *caveat emptor* survived into the first half of the twentieth century. Generally speaking, the principle of *caveat emptor* dictates that in the absence of express agreement, a seller is not liable to the buyer or others for the condition of the land existing at the time of transfer ....

Whatever its origins or purposes, the rule of *caveat emptor* has not retained its original vitality. With time, and in differing contexts, we have on many occasions questioned the justification for the rule. [The court then outlined exceptions to the rule of *caveat emptor* in the sale of land, including the development of the doctrine of implied warranty of habitability and the duty to disclose latent defects in the home.]

In short, *[c]aveat emptor,* the early rule, no longer prevails in New Jersey. [After examining the limits that other jurisdictions have placed on the doctrine of caveat emptor through common law and by statute, the court then turned to the question of whether its common-law precedent required not only disclosure of on-site defective conditions, but also disclosure of off-site conditions that materially affect the value of the property. The court focused on differential bargaining power between the professional seller of residential real estate and the purchaser of such housing as a factor shaping the duty to disclose.]

Practices prohibited by the Consumer Fraud Act include affirmative acts and acts of omission. Consumer fraud consisting of affirmative acts does not require a showing of intent. To hold a defendant liable for an act of omission, however, requires a finding that defendant acted "knowingly." The Consumer Fraud Act states that "the *omission of any material fact* with intent that others rely upon such ... omission, in connection with the sale ... of ... real estate" is an "unlawful practice." A "material fact" is not confined to conditions on the premises. Defendants, however, would have us limit their liability to nondisclosures violative of *Restatement (Second) of Torts* § 551. That is, the conduct must be the equivalent of "swindling" or "shocking to the ethical sense of the community." When conduct rises to that level, a purchaser may recover treble damages for any ascertainable loss, plus reasonable attorney's fees under the Consumer Fraud Act.

Short of that showing of unconscionability, a purchaser may establish a common-law claim by showing that the seller's or the broker's nondisclosure of material facts induced the purchaser to buy. [The court discussed a previous case in which "a seller of residential property was held liable for failing to disclose that tennis courts would be constructed on an adjoining property," because the plaintiff-buyer in that case relied on the seller's representations "as to the character of the surrounding neighborhood."]

[The court returned to the present case and wrote that the silence of the Canuso defendants' representatives] "created a mistaken impression on the part of the purchaser." Defendants used sales-promotion brochures, newspaper advertisements, and a fact sheet to sell the homes in the development. That material portrayed the development as located in a peaceful, bucolic setting with an abundance of fresh air and clean lake waters. Although the literature mentioned how far the property was from malls, country clubs, and train stations, neither the brochures, the newspaper advertisements nor any sales personnel mentioned that a landfill [was] located within half a mile of some of the homes ... [T]hese materials address factual matters.

[The court referred to an earlier case in which a seller of condominium units failed to disclose to buyers that use of the complex's recreational facilities was not encompassed in the individual purchase agreements of the buyers.]

> The fact that no affirmative misrepresentation of a material fact has been made does not bar relief. The suppression of truth, the withholding of the truth when it should be disclosed, is equivalent to the expression of falsehood. The question under those circumstances is whether the failure to volunteer disclosure of certain facts amounts to fraudulent concealment, or, more specifically, whether the defendant is bound in conscience and duty to recognize that the facts so concealed are significant and material and are facts in respect to which he [or she] cannot innocently be silent. Where the circumstances warrant the conclusion that [the seller] is so bound and has such a duty, equity will provide relief.

[In that case, as] in the instant case, a sales brochure misled the purchasers.

Is the nearby presence of a toxic-waste dump a condition that materially affects the value of property? Surely, Lois Gibbs would have wanted to know that the home she was buying in Niagara Falls, New York, was within one-quarter mile of the abandoned Love Canal site. See Lois M. Gibbs, LOVE CANAL: MY STORY (1982) (recounting residents' political struggle concerning leaking toxic-chemical dump near their homes). In the case of on-site conditions, courts have imposed affirmative obligations on sellers to disclose information materially affecting the value of property. There is no logical reason why a certain class of sellers and brokers should not disclose off-site matters that materially affect the value of property. ...

The duty that we recognize is not unlimited. We do not hold that sellers and brokers have a duty to investigate or disclose transient social conditions in the community that arguably affect the value of property. In the absence of a purchaser communicating specific needs, builders and brokers should not be held to decide whether the changing nature of a neighborhood, the presence of a group home, or the existence of a school in decline are facts material to the transaction. Rather, we root in the land the duty to disclose off-site conditions that are material to the transaction. That duty is consistent with the development of our law and supported by statutory policy.

We note that in some instances the Legislature has required disclosure of information to certain classes of home buyers. However, we have previously acted in this field absent a specific legislative mandate. The Legislature will often refine the contours of a judicially-imposed duty, as it did with The New Home Warranty and Builders' Registration Act.

We hold that a builder-developer of residential real estate or a broker representing it is not only liable to a purchaser for affirmative and intentional misrepresentation, but is also liable for nondisclosure of off-site physical conditions known to it and unknown and not readily observable by the buyer if the existence of those conditions is of sufficient materiality to affect the habitability, use, or enjoyment of the property and, therefore, render the property substantially less desirable or valuable to the objectively reasonable buyer. Whether a matter not disclosed by such a builder or broker is of such materiality, and unknown and unobservable by the buyer, will depend on the facts of each case.

We realize that there is considerable debate regarding the nature and extent of the hazard imposed by the Buzby Landfill. For example, defendants note that the Buzby Landfill has never been on the Superfund list or the New Jersey Priority List, both of which delineate toxic landfill sites; that much of the information on which plaintiffs rely postdates their purchase of the property; that [the selling agent] was involved in only a portion of the sales (those between 1985 and 1986); and that some of the plaintiffs have already sold their homes at a profit. Those and other facets of the case will bear on its final resolution.

Ultimately, a jury will decide whether the presence of a landfill is a factor that materially affects the value of property; whether the presence of a landfill was known by defendants and not known or readily observable by plaintiffs; and whether the presence of a landfill has indeed affected the value of plaintiffs' property. Location is the universal benchmark of the value and desirability of property. Over time the market value of the property will reflect the presence of the landfill. Professional builders and their brokers have a level of sophistication that most home buyers lack. That sophistication enables them better to assess the marketability of properties near conditions such as a landfill, a planned superhighway, or an office complex approved for construction. With that superior knowledge, such sellers have a duty to disclose to home buyers the location of off-site physical conditions that an objectively reasonable and informed buyer would deem material to the transaction, in the sense that the conditions substantially affect the value or desirability of the property.

The judgment of the Appellate Division is affirmed.

---

8. **Subsequent New Jersey legislation.** Five months after the *Strawn* case, the New Jersey Legislature enacted the New Residential Real Estate Off–Site Disclosure Act. N.J. STAT. ANN. § 46:3C–1—12 (West 2003). This act defines the "entirety of the disclosure duties of the sellers of newly-constructed residential real estate." The Act requires sellers to provide to the municipal clerk each year a list of nine specific off-site conditions—Superfund sites, certain hazardous discharge sites, wastewater treatment facilities and others. The seller satisfies its disclosure duties by furnishing notice of the availability of the list. The New Jersey Supreme Court examined this legislation in detail in *Nobrega v. Edison Glen Assoc.,* 167 N.J. 520, 772 A.2d 368 (2001). Should professional sellers of newly-constructed residential real estate have duties different from those of other sellers of residential real estate? Is an information repository more or less helpful to consumers than would be individual disclosures?

9. **Disclosures after *Strawn* and *Nobrega*.** After *Strawn* and *Nobrega,* a number of New Jersey plaintiffs have argued that defendants who are not subject to the new disclosure act violated the state consumer fraud act by failing to disclose material information. Does the seller of a special order yacht have a duty to disclose the manufacturer's bankruptcy to the buyer before the contract is signed? See *Judge v. Blackfin Yacht Corp.*, 357 N.J.Super. 418, 815 A.2d 537 (2003). Does the developer of a single new home have a duty to disclose that the neighbor is abusive and sent a torrent of profane correspondence promising to make the purchaser's life in the house miserable? See *Levine v. The Kramer Group*, 354 N.J.Super. 397, 807 A.2d 264 (2002). Other than landfills, what disclosures should sellers be required to make?

10. **Scope of duty to disclose.** Some cases, oddly saying that liability can be established for nondisclosure even if there is no duty to disclose, seem in effect to be saying that there is always a duty to disclose. See *Minnesota v. Fleet Mortgage Corp.*, 158 F.Supp.2d 962 (D. Minn. 2001). At the other end of the spectrum, some courts have severely limited the duty of disclosure. In *Wright v. Brooke Group Ltd.*, 652 N.W.2d 159 (Iowa 2002), the Iowa Supreme Court held that a manufacturer's failure to disclose material information to a consumer generally did not give rise to a fraud action unless 1) the manufacturer has made misleading statements of fact intended to influence consumers, or 2) the manufacturer had previously made true statements of fact

intended to influence consumers and subsequently acquired information rendering the prior statements untrue or misleading.

11. **Specific disclosure obligations.** While many consumer fraud acts include provisions barring concealment or omission of material facts, statutes may also require specific disclosures. For instance, a person who uses the title "doctor" when making representations in advertisements can be required to conspicuously disclose the profession in which the person is licensed. N.Y. GEN. BUS. LAW § 350–b (McKinney 2003). In a similar vein, a mail order catalog business conducted from a site used for the receipt of mail may be required to disclose its legal name and actual business address on promotional materials and order forms. 815 ILL. COMP. STAT. 505/2B.1 (West 2003).

12. **Disclosure forms: real property sales.** One important kind of specific disclosure statute passed in some states requires home sellers to fill out a formal disclosure statement answering specific questions about the home they are selling. See, e.g., CAL. CIV. CODE § 1102.1 et seq. In *Beaux v. Jacob,* 30 P.3d 90 (Alaska 2001), the state statute required sellers to answer the disclosure form question: "Is there any indication of water/seepage/dampness in basement/crawl space? If yes, explain." The seller checked "no" but added in hand writing, "Sump Pumps must be maintained and used." When the buyers suffered water damage at the basement level, they sued. The court held that the seller was negligent in failing to indicate that two separate sump pumps had to be used, not merely one, even though the seller's answer mentioned sump pumps in the plural. (The court also approved the trial court's finding that the plaintiff-buyers were not chargeable with comparative fault or failure to minimize damages.) Is it preferable to have a state statute that specifically defines sellers' required disclosures rather than a common law standard requiring disclosure of material information affecting the value of the property? Will sellers likely reveal more material information to buyers when detailed disclosure forms are required?

MD. CODE, REAL PROPERTY

§ 2–120 Disclosure of material fact or latent defect.

(a) Matters not constituting material fact or latent defect.—Under this title, it is not a material fact or a latent defect relating to property offered for sale or lease that:

(1) An owner or occupant of the property is, was, or is suspected to be:

(i) Infected with human immunodeficiency virus; or

(ii) Diagnosed with acquired immunodeficiency syndrome; or

(2) A homicide, suicide, natural death, or felony occurred on the property.

(b) Immunity.—An owner or seller of real property or the owner's or seller's agent shall be immune from civil liability or criminal penalty for failure to disclose a fact contained in subsection (a) of this section.

13. **Disclosure exceptions: statutory immunity.** Although the bulk of state statutes have broadened the duty to disclose material facts, a number of states have passed statutes substantially like Maryland's. What rationales might support the statute? (a) The legislature should make buyers think rationally about such things as AIDS and homicide in a house? (b) The seller's privacy rights should be protected as more important that the buyer's self-determination? (c) The seller should be protected from the buyer's irrational fears? Would buyers really care about whether a prior occupant had AIDS? If they did care, could they avoid the immunity provided by the statute to the seller?

(3) Scienter

MILLER V. KEYSER, 90 S.W.3d 712 (Tex. 2002). Defendant, Barry Keyser, worked as a sales agent selling homes in a new subdivision in Pearland, Texas. "The homeowners informed Keyser that they were interested in larger backyards, many wanting extra space for their children and pets. Keyser represented to the homeowners that [the lots in the development] were oversized and that they were in fact larger than the lots of a competing builder in the subdivision. Keyser told the homeowners that even with the existence of [a twenty-five foot drainage] easement, the lots could be fenced along the back of the property line. The homeowners paid a premium for these 'oversized' lots. In 1994, after the homeowners built their homes, some received a letter from the Brazoria County Drainage District telling them that all fences in the easement must be removed at the owners' expense." The homeowners sued the owner of the corporation that built the subdivision, and sales agent, Barry Keyser, for common-law fraud and misrepresentations in violation of the Deceptive Trade Practices Act [DTPA]. "The homeowners claim that Keyser misrepresented the size of the lots and where the fencing could be placed at the back of the lots. The homeowners sought to recover damages for the fence and landscaping repairs and a return of the excess charges paid for the lots." The trial court granted a directed verdict in favor of the owner of the corporation, finding that he had no direct communication with the homeowners, and he therefore made no misrepresentations about the lots. However, the trial court rendered judgment against Keyser. The appellate court reversed the trial court's judgment with respect to Keyser on the ground that Keyser had not acted fraudulently and under the DTPA, a corporate agent cannot be held personally liable for company misrepresentations. *Held*, the judgment of the court of appeals is reversed. "Keyser argues that he should not be held liable because he did not, in fact, know that his representations were false. But a DTPA claim does not require that the consumer prove the employee acted knowingly or intentionally. The DTPA requires that the consumer show that the misrepresentation was false and that the false misrepresentation was the producing cause of the consumer's damages. A consumer is not required to prove intent to make a misrepresentation to recover under the DTPA. The DTPA was enacted to 'protect consumers against false, misleading, and deceptive business practices, unconscionable actions, and breaches of warranty' and to provide consumers with a means to redress deceptive practices 'without the burden of proof and numerous defenses encountered in a common law fraud or breach of warranty suit.' Misrepresentations that may not be actionable under common law fraud may be actionable under the DTPA. Thus, Keyser may be held liable under the DTPA even if he did not know that his representations were false or even if he did not intend to deceive anyone. ... [A]n agent may be held personally liable for his own violations of the DTPA. ... The Homemaker [the corporation that built the subdivision] is an entity that may have liability for the homeowners' harm. If Keyser was truly just passing along company information, then he has a right to seek indemnity against The Homemaker."

---

14. **Strict liability.** State consumer fraud acts often seem to impose strict liability by failing to require a showing of intentional or negligent misstatement. California has said that "the plaintiff need not show that a UCL [Unfair Competition Law] defendant intended to injure anyone through its unfair or unlawful conduct. The UCL imposes strict liability when property or monetary losses are occasioned by conduct that constitutes an unfair business practice." *Cortez v. Purolator Air Filtration Prods. Co.,* 23 Cal.4th 163, 999 P.2d 706, 96 Cal.Rptr.2d 518 (2000). More specifically, innocent misrepresentations violate some consumer fraud acts. See *Martin v. Heinhold Commodities, Inc.,* 163 Ill.2d 33, 205 Ill.Dec. 443, 643 N.E.2d 734 (1994) (a cause of action can be maintained even where the defendant did not know or believe its statement was untrue). Is it fair to hold the defendant liable if he or she did not know that a representation was false, or that a disclosure should have been made?

15. **Rejecting strict liability.** Other states require the plaintiff to show that a defendant knowingly engaged in a deceptive practice. See *Omega Eng'g, Inc. v. Eastman Kodak Co.*, 908 F.Supp. 1084, 1100 (D. Conn. 1995). Still others treat acts and omissions differently. For example, in *Strawn, supra*, the court wrote that holding a defendant liable for an omission requires that the defendant acted "knowingly," however holding a defendant liable for an affirmative act, unlike an omission, "does not require a showing of intent."

16. **Scienter and damages.** Strict liability could result in substantial damages. In *Gray v. North Carolina Ins. Underwriting Ass'n,* 352 N.C. 61, 529 S.E.2d 676 (2000), the court, echoing other authority, specifically commented that good faith was no defense. The defendant insurer was found guilty of an unfair business practice, perhaps because, to protect itself against double claims, it insisted on issuing its check payable both to the insureds and to a person claiming to hold a mortgage. The plaintiffs recovered the amount of insurance payment due, $256,000, plus $117,000 in damages and attorney fees for violation of the deceptive practice statute. This latter was trebled under the

statutory authorization, so the defendant was liable for a total of $607,000. Should scienter influence the amount of damages awarded?

(4) Reliance

STUTMAN v. CHEMICAL BANK

95 N.Y.2d 24, 731 N.E.2d 608, 709 N.Y.S.2d 892 (2000)

Chief Judge KAYE. . . .

In November 1991, plaintiff Michael Stutman and his wife, plaintiff Jeanette Rodriguez, borrowed $175,000 from defendant Chemical Bank (now merged into the Chase Manhattan Bank) to finance the purchase of a cooperative apartment. The loan was secured by plaintiffs' shares in the co-op. The note covering the loan permitted plaintiffs to prepay the principal at any time without incurring "any prepayment charge." The note stated:

> I have the right to make payments of principal at any time before they are due. . . . I may make a full prepayment or partial prepayments without paying any prepayment charge.

In February 1994, plaintiffs sought to refinance their loan with a new loan from Citibank, using the same shares of stock as collateral. Chemical, however, would not release the collateral until it received the funds to satisfy the loan, and Citibank would not release the funds for the new loan until it received the collateral.

Chemical informed plaintiffs that it would charge a $275 "attorney's fee" to arrange a simultaneous transfer in which Chemical would deliver the collateral and other documents to Citibank in exchange for the funds. Plaintiffs initially objected to the fee, but then decided to pay it, under protest, in order to complete the refinancing. About a day after plaintiffs "closed" the loan with Citibank, a representative from Chemical—who plaintiffs allege was not an attorney—delivered the collateral and other unidentified documents to Citibank. Simultaneously, Citibank gave the representative a check which retired the Chemical Bank loan. . . . [Plaintiffs brought this suit, asserting various common law and statutory claims. Complicated procedures in various courts finally brought the claim up to the New York Court of Appeals for review.]

Section 349 of the General Business Law, enacted in 1970 as a broad consumer protection measure, begins:

> Deceptive acts or practices in the conduct of any business, trade or commerce or in the furnishing of any service in this state are hereby declared unlawful

General Business Law § 349[a].

A decade later, in 1980, the Legislature added section 349(h), giving private citizens a right of action for deceptive trade practices. Citizens can enjoin an unlawful business practice, recover actual damages (or $50, whichever is greater) and obtain attorney's fees. In addition, if a defendant knowingly or willfully engages in a deceptive practice, the court may, in its discretion, award treble damages up to a maximum of $1,000 (*see*, General Business Law § 349[h]).

A plaintiff under section 349 must prove three elements: first, that the challenged act or practice was consumer-oriented; second, that it was misleading in a material way; and third, that the plaintiff suffered injury as a result of the deceptive act. Whether a representation or an omission, the deceptive practice must be "likely to mislead a reasonable consumer acting reasonably under the circumstances." A deceptive practice, however, need not reach the level of common-law fraud to be actionable under section 349. In addition, a plaintiff must prove "actual" injury to recover under the statute, though not necessarily pecuniary harm.

Further, as we have repeatedly stated, reliance is not an element of a section 349 claim. The plaintiff, however, must show that the defendant's "material deceptive act" caused the injury.

In the case at hand, plaintiffs allege that defendant violated section 349 by promising, in the note, that there would be no "prepayment charge," but then assessing a $275 "attorney's fee" when plaintiffs sought to refinance their loan. Plaintiffs contend that the $275 fee was a "prepayment charge" in disguise and that the note was deceptive for not revealing that fee.

The Appellate Division dismissed plaintiffs' claim, holding that they failed to show justifiable reliance: that is, that the note's failure to disclose the $275 attorney's fee "had any effect on plaintiffs' decision to borrow from defendant in the first place." That, however, was the wrong standard, because reliance is *not* an element of a section 349 claim.

Reliance and causation are twin concepts, but they are not identical. . . . [T]here is a difference between reliance and causation, as illustrated by the facts of this case. Here, plaintiffs allege that because of defendant's deceptive act, they were forced to pay a $275 fee that they had been led to believe was not required. In other words, plaintiffs allege that defendant's material deception caused them to suffer a $275 loss. This allegation satisfies the causation requirement. Plaintiffs need not additionally allege that they would not otherwise have entered into the transaction. Nothing more is required.

Nevertheless, we uphold the Appellate Division's dismissal of plaintiffs' claim, for a different reason: plaintiffs have failed to show that defendant committed a deceptive act. The nub of plaintiffs' complaint is that the $275 "attorney's fee" was really a prepayment charge in disguise. Even taking plaintiffs' allegations as true, as we must in deciding defendant's motion to dismiss, plaintiffs have not demonstrated that the fee was a prepayment charge.

It is undisputed that the $275 fee was not a "prepayment charge" in the classic sense: defendant did not impose a penalty on plaintiffs for early repayment of the loan. Indeed, plaintiffs acknowledge in their complaint that, had they shown up at Chemical Bank with cash or a certified check for the balance of their loan, they "would not have been charged for the calculation of the pay-off amount or the review of the check or file."

Rather, the $275 fee was assessed for the special arrangement in which a Chemical representative was required to go to Citibank, attend the closing and tender the collateral in exchange for a check satisfying the balance of the loan. Plaintiffs acknowledge that defendant properly charged a fee for these special services, but argue that an "attorney's fee" was not justified because the services of an attorney were not required to deliver the collateral to Citibank in exchange for the check. Plaintiffs allege:

> defendant charged the plaintiffs an attorney fee for essentially the services of a delivery person or a title company which agrees to hold documents or a check in escrow pending the termination of the sale.

Amended complaint, ¶ 22.

Thus, at bottom, plaintiffs' argument is not that the note was deceptive in stating that there would be no prepayment charge. Clearly, no such charge was assessed. Rather, plaintiffs' argument is that the $275 fee was excessive because it was not necessary for Chemical to retain an attorney. There might, or might not, be merit to that assertion. But it is in any event unnecessary to consider it because plaintiffs have abandoned their excessiveness claim on appeal to this Court, and argue only that defendant committed a deceptive act under General Business Law § 349. Since no "prepayment charge" was assessed, plaintiffs have failed to show that the note was deceptive.

Accordingly, the order of the Appellate Division should be affirmed, with costs.

SHANNON v. BOISE CASCADE CORP., 208 Ill.2d 517, 281 Ill.Dec. 845, 805 N.E.2d 213 (2004). Homeowners purchased homes covered with a Boise Cascade composite wood siding, which was installed on the homes when they were built in the 1980s. The homeowners alleged that the siding was defective in that it was subject to rotting, buckling, warping and other failures. Plaintiffs filed a claim against Boise Cascade under Illinois' consumer fraud act alleging that the company had deceptively advertised the siding as "of inherent good quality," "durable" and so forth, when in fact it had a high rate of failure that the company did not disclose. Most of the plaintiffs themselves had not seen any of this advertising. However, they claimed that "in the absence of the promotion and marketing activities of Boise Cascade a market would not have developed for composite wood siding and thus the siding would not have been sold in the State of Illinois and therefore it would not have been installed on the residences of plaintiffs and the other members of the class." The trial court granted summary judgment for Boise Cascade against the plaintiffs who had not read the advertising materials, but not against the one who had. The appellate court reversed the grant of summary judgment on the ground that no "direct contact between the plaintiffs and the representations made" need be shown. On appeal to the Illinois Supreme Court, *held*: summary judgment had been properly granted. "The teaching of [the court's previous case law] is that deceptive advertising cannot be the proximate cause of damages under the Act unless it actually deceives the plaintiff. Plaintiffs' complaint in this case does not allege that any deceptive advertising by Boise Cascade was received by any plaintiff, or that it was received by any builder, architect, engineer, or other like person somehow connected with a plaintiff. Instead, plaintiffs claim that Boise Cascade's alleged deceptions created a market for their product that would not otherwise exist, thus resulting in its use on their homes and the plaintiffs' ultimate damages. ... The advertising in [the court's previous opinion in] *Oliveira* and in this case did not in any way deceive the plaintiffs, and thus could not have proximately caused the claimed damages, whatever their nature.

"It is certainly possible that evidence might demonstrate that the siding would not have been installed on plaintiffs' homes but for Boise Cascade's promotional literature. It does not follow, however, that the literature distributed to unnamed persons 20 or more years ago, who may or may not have been deceived, induced plaintiffs to accept the siding. Without such a nexus, the alleged deception is simply too remote from the claimed damages to satisfy the element of proximate cause.

"Although proof of actual deception of a plaintiff is required, this is not to say that the deception must always be direct between the defendant and the plaintiff to satisfy the requirement of proximate cause under the Act. For instance, if the product literature had in fact deceived a particular builder, architect, or contractor, resulting in the installation of defective siding on a home, the damage could arguably have occurred 'as a result of' the indirect deception, as required by section 10a(a) of the Act. In those circumstances, the purchaser, who may have no independent knowledge of the qualities or expected performance standards of siding, is deceived because of the deception of the builder, architect or contractor, who reasonably should have had correct knowledge. Plaintiffs did not plead any facts to support that theory at any time."

17. **Reliance in public versus private actions.** As illustrated in *Stutman,* reliance is not required under the New York statute. Why wouldn't the statute drafters and the court want to require reliance? Part of the answer may lie in the original idea that the state statute would be enforced by the attorney general, who would not seek damages or imprisonment but an injunction against deceptive practices. For example, if a retailer used bait and switch ads or advertised goods as being on sale when in fact the retailer was charging the ordinary price, the attorney general might obtain an injunction against such a practice. Given that the ads had potential for harming consumers and that the enforcement was by injunction rather than damages, reliance would be superfluous. Put differently, injunctions frequently attempt to avert

harm before it arises rather than to repair damage already done; hence the harm shown by reliance is not necessary. Some courts have held that a public official enforcing the state consumer fraud act need not prove reliance, while a private individual must do so. See *Weinberg v. Sun Company, Inc.*, 565 Pa. 612, 618, 777 A.2d 442, 446 (Pa. 2001) ("There is no authority which would permit a private party to pursue an advertiser because an advertisement might deceive members of the audience and might influence a purchasing decision when the plaintiff himself was neither deceived nor influenced."); *Parkhill v. Minnesota Mutual Life Ins. Co.*, 188 F.R.D. 332 (D. Minn.1999) (distinguishing damages cases from cases in which injunctive or other equitable relief is sought).

18. **Reliance versus causation.** The *Stutman* court treats reliance and causation as similar but not identical concepts, saying that the plaintiff who proves causation need not prove reliance. *Group Health Plan v. Philip Morris*, 621 N.W.2d 2, 12–13 (Minn. 2001), said essentially the same, but then also found that where plaintiffs allege that their damages were caused by fraudulent advertising, "it is not possible that the damages could be caused by a violation without reliance on the statements" and thus plaintiffs must prove reliance to prove causation. Are there situations in which causation without reliance can be shown?

19. **Actual cause versus proximate cause.** The Illinois consumer fraud statute in *Shannon* creates a cause of action for "any person who suffers actual damage as a result of a violation of the act." The Illinois courts interpret that provision to require a private plaintiff to show that the damages were "proximately caused" by the defendant's fraud. Is this a requirement of cause in fact? Or some kind of foreseeability?

20. **Reasonable reliance.** Courts interpreting the New York statute cited in *Stutman* have defined deceptive acts as acts likely to mislead a reasonable consumer. See *Boule v. Hutton*, 328 F.3d 84, 94 (2d Cir. 2003). And yet, a plaintiff need not show reasonable reliance, or any reliance, in order to prove a claim. Do these rules simply shift the reasonable reliance requirement to another part of the case? Why require the plaintiff to show that a reasonable person would have been misled by the statements but not that she was? Other states also forego proof of reliance. See *Searle v. Wyndham Internat. Inc.*, 102 Cal.App.4th 1327, 1333, 126 Cal.Rptr.2d 231, 236 (2002). Within states that require reliance, some require reasonable reliance. See *Taylor v. McCollom*, 119 Or.App. 1, 849 P.2d 1123, 1125 (1993) (determining that reasonable reliance was an issue of fact for the jury). Others find that actual reliance is enough. See *Holeman v. Neils*, 803 F.Supp. 237, 242 (D. Ariz. 1992). If the defendant has committed a deceptive act and the plaintiff has relied on it though unreasonably, which ought to prevail? What about some sort of comparative fault in this situation?

(b) Scope of Coverage

Many state consumer fraud acts protect consumers from unfair practices "in the conduct of any trade or commerce" or "in connection with the sale or advertisement of any merchandise." Trade or commerce and the sale of merchandise may be defined to include the sale of services as well as goods. 73 PA. STAT. ANN. § 201–2; ARIZ. REV. STAT. § 44–1521. Although state consumer fraud acts often specifically exempt some entities from suit, such as TV, radio, and print media, questions arise about whether additional defendants are exempted as well.

(1) Professional Services

CRIPE v. LEITER

184 Ill.2d 185, 703 N.E.2d 100, 234 Ill.Dec. 488 (1998)

BILANDIC, Justice. . . .

The question presented in this appeal is whether a client may state a cause of action against an attorney under the Consumer Fraud and Deceptive Business Practices Act (Consumer Fraud Act or Act) (815 ILCS 505/1 *et seq.*) based upon alleged overbilling by the attorney. [Plaintiff's complaint alleged that Roberta Schmitz, the sole beneficiary of two trusts worth $583,000, had discharged her family attorney, retained attorney Thomas E. Leiter, and with Leiter's assistance transferred the trusts from First National Bank to South Side Trust and Savings Bank of Peoria, where Leiter was appointed attorney for the trusts. Plaintiff Roberta Cripe, Mrs. Schmitz's daughter and present guardian, filed a petition for appointment of guardian for disabled person in probate court, alleging that Mrs. Schmitz lacked sufficient capacity to make responsible decisions about her own care and the management of her estate. Mrs. Schmitz retained Leiter to defend her and the first guardianship petition was ultimately dismissed on Mrs. Schmitz's motion. One year later, after Mrs. Schmitz began living with the plaintiff, a probate court found that Mrs. Schmitz was legally incapacitated based upon the report of a physician that her condition was consistent with a progressive illness that causes dementia such as Alzheimer's disease. A public guardian was appointed for Mrs. Schmitz and the probate court subsequently appointed the plaintiff as successor guardian.]

The plaintiff, in her capacity as Mrs. Schmitz's guardian, filed this action against Thomas Leiter and The Leiter Group in the circuit court of Peoria County on October 24, 1994. The complaint alleged that, between February 12, 1992, and June 1, 1994, South Side Bank paid $65,933.50 out of the Schmitz trusts to the defendants as fees for legal services. The complaint charged that the defendants' fees for legal services were "outrageously excessive and unreasonable and bear no relationship to the actual time spent by Attorney Leiter in allegedly representing Mrs. Schmitz as her personal attorney and as her trust attorney." As ultimately amended, the plaintiff's complaint charged the defendants with: (1) violation of the Consumer Fraud Act; (2) common law fraud; (3) breach of fiduciary duty; (4) legal malpractice; and (5) constructive fraud. Each of the counts was premised on the allegation that the defendants charged excessive and unreasonable legal fees. The complaint alleged that the defendants' overbilling caused the Schmitz trust accounts to be depleted in excess of $40,000 in order to pay the defendants' excessive legal fees.

Only counts I and VI, the Consumer Fraud Act counts, are at issue in this appeal. ... [The Circuit court dismissed the Consumer Fraud Act counts on the ground that the Act does not apply to legal services or the billing of those services. The appellate court determined that the Consumer Fraud Act, although not applicable to the actual practice of law, is nonetheless applicable to the "commercial aspects" of a law practice, which include billing for legal services. The Supreme Court then addressed this issue.]

The Consumer Fraud Act is a regulatory and remedial statute intended to protect consumers, borrowers and business persons against fraud, unfair methods of competition, and other unfair and deceptive business practices. The Act is to be liberally construed to effectuate its purpose. Section 2 of the Act declares unlawful the following conduct:

> Unfair ... or deceptive acts or practices, including but not limited to the use or employment of any deception, fraud, false pretense, false promise, misrepresentation or the concealment, suppression or omission of any material fact, with intent that others rely upon the concealment, suppression or omission of such material fact ... in the conduct of any trade or commerce. ...

Section 10a(a) of the Act provides that "[a]ny person who suffers damage as a result of a violation of this Act committed by any other person may bring an action against such person." The elements of a claim under the Act are: (1) a deceptive act or practice by the defendant; (2) the defendant's intent that the plaintiff rely on the deception; and (3) that the deception occurred in the course of conduct involving trade or commerce. The plaintiff need not establish any intent to deceive on the part of the defendant because even an innocent misrepresentation may be actionable under the Act. The Act allows for the imposition of punitive damages and for the award of attorney fees to the prevailing party.

This court has not previously addressed the applicability of the Act to the legal profession. Our appellate court has considered this question in several cases. [The court describes prior Illinois appellate court decisions that address the application of the state deceptive practices act to attorneys, and the court then notes the varied conclusions that other state courts have reached on this issue].

Our Consumer Fraud Act, like those discussed in the preceding cases from other jurisdictions, contains no language expressly excluding or including the legal profession within its ambit. Despite the absence of such language, there appears to be little dispute among the decisions addressing this issue that consumer protection statutes do not apply to claims arising out of the "actual practice of law." The plaintiff in this case concedes that the Act does not apply to such claims. We are called upon here to decide whether an attorney's billing for legal services is included within that exemption. ... We find no indication that the legislature intended the Consumer Fraud Act to apply to regulate attorneys' billing practices.

Historically, the regulation of attorney conduct in this state has been the prerogative of this court. In the exercise of this power, this court administers a comprehensive regulatory scheme governing attorney conduct. The Illinois Rules of Professional Conduct adopted by this court set forth numerous requirements to which attorneys in this state must adhere. Violation of these rules is grounds for discipline. This court has appointed an Attorney Registration and Disciplinary Commission (ARDC) to supervise the "registration of, and disciplinary proceedings affecting, members of the Illinois bar." This court has also created a procedural scheme under which the ARDC operates, providing detailed regulations involving inquiry, hearing and review boards. The purpose of this regulatory scheme is to protect the public and maintain the integrity of the legal profession.

This court's regulatory scheme extends to the area of attorneys' fees. ... An attorney who charges or collects an excessive fee in violation of this court's rules may be subjected to discipline. This court has also ordered an attorney to make restitution to a client who was charged excessive legal fees. The Rules of Professional Conduct further provide for discipline of an attorney who engages in conduct involving fraud, dishonesty, deceit or misrepresentation. In addition, this court has created a client protection program operating under the auspices of the ARDC to reimburse losses caused by the dishonest conduct of attorneys in the course of the attorney-client relationship.

Accordingly, the attorney-client relationship in this state, unlike the ordinary merchant-consumer relationship, is already subject to extensive regulation by this court. The legislature did not, in the language of the Consumer Fraud Act, specify that it intended the Act's provisions to apply to the conduct of attorneys in relation to their clients. Given this court's role in that arena, we find that, had the legislature intended the Act to apply in this manner, it would have stated that intention with specificity. Absent a clear indication by the legislature, we will not conclude that the legislature intended to regulate attorney-client relationships through the Consumer Fraud Act. [The court noted that the legislature amended other provisions of the Act after Illinois appellate courts had ruled that the Act was inapplicable to claims arising out of the attorney-client relationship and thus presumed that the legislature endorsed that interpretation].

[A]n attorney's billing for legal services cannot be separated from the attorney-client relationship. Unlike ordinary merchant-consumer relationships, the relationship between attorney and client is fiduciary in nature. Although an attorney's fees in a particular case will generally be governed by the contractual arrangement between the attorney and the client, the attorney's fiduciary position prohibits the attorney from charging an excessive fee. Fraudulent or excessive billing of a client violates the attorney's fiduciary duty to the client. Thus, an attorney's billing of a client is not simply a "business" aspect of the practice of law, but is tied to the attorney's fiduciary obligation to the client. Because of that fiduciary relationship, the attorney's fees are subject to scrutiny and regulation not applicable to the fees for most commercial services. The Consumer Fraud Act therefore was not intended to apply to an attorney's billing of a client for legal services.

Accordingly, we conclude that the legislature did not intend the Consumer Fraud Act to apply to regulate the conduct of attorneys in representing clients. We hold that, where allegations of misconduct arise from a defendant's conduct in his or her capacity as an attorney representing a client, the Consumer Fraud Act does not apply. An attorney's billing of a client for legal services is a part of the attorney's representation of the client and is therefore exempt from the Act. The circuit court properly dismissed the plaintiff's Consumer Fraud Act counts against the defendants in this case. [Accordingly, the court affirmed the circuit court's dismissal of counts I and VI].

Justice HARRISON, dissenting:

The majority engages in a protracted discussion of the legislative intent behind the Consumer Fraud Act (815 ILCS 505/1 *et seq.*). It is axiomatic, however, that the best indication of the legislature's intent is the language it employed in drafting the law. Where the language of a statute is clear and unambiguous, the court should not resort to other tools of statutory interpretation. The court's only legitimate function is to enforce the law as written. [The dissent then details the language in the Illinois statute].

Had the General Assembly intended to exclude attorneys from the scope of the Act, it could easily have done so, just as it excluded real estate salesmen and brokers, newspaper and periodical publishers, and individuals associated with television and radio stations. Attorneys, however, are nowhere mentioned. . . .

Holding attorneys to the same standards of honesty and fair dealing that apply to other business people will inevitably affect the practice of law. In my view, the results can only be positive. Unlike my colleagues, I am not concerned about encroachment on this court's authority. While it is true that responsibility for regulating the legal profession and disciplining attorneys is vested in our court, the General Assembly has made specific provision in the Consumer Fraud Act to avoid separation of power problems. Section 10b(1) of the Act exempts from coverage "[a]ctions or transactions specifically authorized by laws administered by any regulatory body or officer acting under statutory authority of this State or the United States." Accordingly, if an attorney's conduct were permissible under the rules we have enacted and the standards we have set, it would not be actionable under the Consumer Fraud Act.

The conduct alleged in this case, if proven, would not be permissible under the rules of our court. Although the attorneys involved might ultimately be subject to discipline, that is no reason to deny plaintiff her right to bring a statutory damage action against them. If what the attorneys did constituted a crime, we would surely not say that they are exempt from prosecution merely because they are subject to disbarment by us. The same principle applies here.

For the foregoing reasons, counts I and IV of plaintiff's complaint should not have been dismissed, and the judgment of the appellate court should be affirmed. I therefore dissent.

---

20. **Attorney liability.** Whether attorneys should be subject to state consumer fraud acts has been the subject of much controversy in state courts and among commentators. Courts and commentators have also addressed whether other kinds of regulated professionals such as accountants and physicians should be subject to litigation under state consumer fraud actions. Are there special reasons to exempt professionals from consumer fraud act obligations? Should professionals, who may have heightened obligations to their clients, at least be required to live up to ordinary consumer fraud act protections that apply to others?

21. **Insurer liability.** Answering another significant coverage issue, a number of states hold that claims against insurers may not be brought under state consumer fraud acts. See, e.g., *Wilder v. Aetna Life & Cas. Ins. Co.,* 140 Vt. 16, 433 A.2d 309, 310 (1981) (insurance does not fall under definition of goods or services in the state consumer fraud act); *O.K. Lumber Co. v. Providence Wash. Ins. Co.*, 759 P.2d 523, 528 (Alaska 1988) (state consumer fraud act expressly exempts activities covered by the state insurance code). However, other statutes do allow claims against insurers. See Texas Deceptive Trade Practices Act § 17.50 (a)(4). Even when consumer protection codes do not apply, many state statutes specifically require fair conduct by insurers.

(2) Businesses as Plaintiffs

Consumer fraud acts often protect consumers from fraud in the inducement of a contract as well as unfair practices such as harassment or invasion of privacy in debt collection. At times a business is in the role of a consumer and in that role may have standing under broadly worded statutes. See *Downers Grove Volkswagen v. Wigglesworth*, 190 Ill.App.3d 524, 137 Ill.Dec. 409, 546 N.E.2d 33 (1989) (permitting suits in which a business acting as a consumer sues another business under the state consumer fraud act if there is a consumer nexus). Under some statutes, issues about businesses as consumers may be paired with issues about whether the transaction concerned covered "goods and services" rather than intangible interests. See *Texas Cookie Co. v. Hendricks & Peralta, Inc.*, 747 S.W.2d 873, 877 (Tex. Ct. App. 1988) (permitting franchisee to maintain action against franchisor under state consumer fraud act). Texas, however, excludes standing under the statute for corporations with assets of $25 million or more. In some states, businesses can sue under consumer fraud acts on an equal footing with individuals. See

N.C. GEN. STAT. § 75–16 (2005) (stating that if any person or "the business of any person, firm or corporation" is injured by another person, a private right of action applies).

Apart from the possibility that a business is also a consumer, however, the statutes may focus on business rights as competitors. They are thus often a part of the law of unfair competition, prohibiting passing off, misuse of trademarks, and false advertising. To a large extent these may overlap federal statutes, particularly the Lanham Act, covered in Chapter 12, § 4, supra. The federal statutes are more commonly invoked. See *Alderman v. Iditarod Properties, Inc.,* 32 P.3d 373 (Alaska 2001) (relying on federal trademark precedent to interpret state unfair competition statute). Still other statutes aim at a specific industry or specific practices. For example, various state acts regulate unfair settlement practices by insurers. See ¶ 23, supra.

(c) Procedures and Remedies

22. **Special procedural rules.** Some states require pre-suit demand letters or special notices. Some statutes impose detailed requirements, see TEX. BUS. & COM. CODE § 17.505(a), while others are only designed to provide notice, see *Cassano v. Gogos,* 20 Mass.App.Ct. 348, 480 N.E.2d 649, 651 (1985). In some jurisdictions failure to file a demand letter is considered a jurisdictional defect. *Id.* The plaintiff's recovery may be limited if the plaintiff does not accept a reasonable settlement offer in response. See ALA. CODE § 8–19–10(e) (limiting plaintiff's recovery to actual damages without attorneys fees or costs if the defendant's offer was sufficient to cover actual damages).

23. **Jury trial rights.** Defendants in some jurisdictions can require plaintiffs to submit consumer fraud act claims to arbitration, rather than judicial processes. *Pick v. Discover Financial Services, Inc.,* 2001 WL 1180278 (D. Del. 2001) (credit card issuer can unilaterally require plaintiff to arbitrate state consumer fraud act disputes). A plaintiff in a consumer fraud action may be entitled to a jury trial because the statute is construed to require such a trial in a private action for damages. *Zorba Contractors, Inc. v. Housing Auth. of City of Newark,* 362 N.J.Super. 124, 827 A.2d 313 (2003). When the statute does not so provide, courts look to their state constitutions to determine whether a jury trial is constitutionally guaranteed. Illinois has stated a broad rule that no new statutory rights are to be tried to a jury, even if the plaintiff is seeking damages, the quintessential common law remedy. Thus the statutory consumer fraud rights carry with them no jury trial right. *Martin v. Heinold Commodities, Inc.,* 163 Ill.2d 33, 643 N.E.2d 734, 205 Ill.Dec. 443 (1994). Some other courts appear to focus on the nature of the relief sought, withholding a jury trial only if the plaintiff seeks equitable relief. See *Nunley v. State,* 628 So.2d 619 (Ala. 1993) ("Nunley had no right to a trial by jury in the State's action for an injunction against him. An injunction is an equitable remedy, as to which there is no jury trial right"). Conversely, if the proceeding is a criminal enforcement by the state, a jury trial would be required. Cf.

People v. Toomey, 157 Cal.App.3d 1, 203 Cal.Rptr. 642 (1984) (if state seeks civil, not criminal penalty, no jury is required). In *Meyers v. Cornwell Quality Tools, Inc.,* 41 Conn.App. 19, 674 A.2d 444 (1996), the court thought that the Unfair Trade Practices Act "creates an essentially equitable cause of action," so that there was no constitutional jury trial right, but that a jury trial was *permissible* even though not required.

24. **Remedies: statutory minimum, treble and punitive damages.** State consumer fraud acts provide favorable damage claims to the plaintiff. Certain states provide minimum statutory damages for violation of consumer fraud statutes. See IDAHO CODE § 48–608(1) (plaintiff may "recover actual damages or one thousand dollars ($1000), whichever is the greater"). In addition, treble damages and punitive damages may be available. See *Johnson v. Ford Motor Co.,* 35 Cal.4th 1191, 29 Cal.Rptr.3d 401, 113 P.3d 82 (2005) (noting state's interest in awarding punitive damages in consumer fraud act case, but also noting restrictions on punitive damage awards imposed by *State Farm Mut. Auto Ins. Co. v. Campbell,* 538 U.S. 408, 123 S.Ct. 1513, 155 L.Ed.2d 585 (2003), and remanding for reconsideration court's reduction of punitive damage award from $10 million to $53,000 in consumer fraud act claim in which car manufacturer concealed car's history of transmission repairs and replacements when reselling the car). Some statutes permit additional civil penalties to be assessed when the defendant attempts to victimize members of a vulnerable group such as the elderly or especially impaired, with penalties going to a state fund. See FLA. STAT. ANN. § 501.2077 (2004) (up to $15,000).

25. **Remedies: attorney fees.** Perhaps the greatest difference in damages between common law and statutory actions concerns attorney fees. The common law fraud action comes under the general common law rule that requires each party to pay her own attorney fees. In contrast, consumer or deceptive practice statutes may authorize an award of attorney fees to the plaintiff. Given the availability of attorney fees, consumer fraud actions may be the only alternative when the individual suffers only small damages.

ETHRIDGE V. HWANG, 105 Wash.App. 447, 20 P.3d 958 (2001). Mary Ethridge owned a mobile home in a mobile home park owned by Anna Hwang. Ethridge attempted to sell her home to a buyer, Mr. Qualls, but Hwang refused to permit the sale. Ethridge also alleged that she found another buyer, Ms. Cubine, but Hwang again unreasonably and wrongfully refused to approve the sale. According to Ethridge, Hwang's refusal to permit the sales was unreasonable, and further Hwang had a widespread pattern and practice of refusing to permit the assignment of tenants' rental agreements, denying applications for tenancy in the mobile home park, and refusing to approve sales of mobile homes in the park on idiosyncratic, frivolous, unreasonable, and unlawful grounds. Ethridge alleged that as a result of Hwang's unfair and deceptive conduct, Ethridge was forced to live and work in an area in which she no longer wished to live, thereby causing her emotional distress, and causing her injury to business or property. In Ethridge's claim against Hwang, *held*: Hwang violated the consumer protection act, the state common law of tortious interference and the Mobile Home Landlord Tenant Act and in light of her successful CPA claim, Ethridge was entitled to damages and attorney fees. "Hwang argues that the trial court erred in awarding Ethridge fees for her non-CPA claims. However, the court is not required to artificially segregate time in a case, such as this one, where the claims all relate to the same fact pattern, but allege different bases for recovery. Ultimately, the fee award must be reasonable in relation to the results obtained. Here, Ethridge prevailed on all three theories alleged in the complaint: MHLTA, CPA, and tortious interference. Each claim involved the same core facts—Hwang's unreasonable rejection of prospective buyers at the park. Proof of the tortious interference claim involved the same preparation as the other claims—establishing that Hwang acted unreasonably. Because nearly every fact in this case related in some way to all three claims, segregation of the fee request was not necessary and the trial court did not abuse its discretion in awarding fees as it did. ... Both parties have requested attorney fees on appeal. Because Hwang failed to improve her position on this appeal following her request for a trial de novo over what she obtained at arbitration, Ethridge is entitled to attorney fees on appeal. We affirm.

---

26. **Attorney fees when plaintiff prevails on both consumer fraud and other claims.** One issue that arises with respect to attorney fees is to what extent those fees should be available when a plaintiff pursues both a common law and a statutory claim. Should the plaintiff be entitled to full damages, as in *Ethridge*, even though some of the claims her attorney researched and pursued carried no right to attorney fees? On the other hand, is it fair for the plaintiff to recover less when she prevails on two claims (one common law and one statutory) than she would if she prevailed on just one statutory claim? Should the plaintiff who prevails on both get only one half the attorney fees?

27. **Calculation of fee awards.** Often a court will award attorney fees based on a lodestar calculation. Under this approach the court multiplies a reasonable hourly rate times the number of hours reasonably expended on the matter. At times, courts permit adjustments for other factors such as difficulty of the questions involved, the benefit to the client, and the contingency of collecting a fee. See DOBBS ON REMEDIES §§ 3.10(7)–3.10(10). What if the value of the legal fees exceeds the value of the amount of money in controversy? In *Scott Fetzer Co. v. Weeks*, 122 Wash.2d 141, 859 P.2d 1210 (1993), a prevailing defendant requested attorney fees of $180,914 for its successful defense of a claim for the return of merchandise valued at $19,000. Should the court permit

recovery for the hours actually expended by the attorneys or limit that recovery on the ground that fees of this magnitude are unreasonable on a case with such a small amount of money in controversy? See Dobbs, supra, § 3.10(8) (discussing the problem in civil rights fee awards).

28. **Rescission or revocation of acceptance.** When a buyer accepts goods, but finds that the goods delivered are nonconforming and substantially impaired in value, the buyer may revoke acceptance of the goods. For example, an automobile lessee who finds that the car's odometer has been turned back can return the car and obtain a refund. See *Cuesta v. Classic Wheels, Inc.*, 358 N.J.Super. 512, 818 A.2d 448 (2003) (where the lessor would not take back the goods and so ultimately had to pay treble damages and attorney fees in addition to rescission).

29. **Remedies requiring judicial supervision.** Courts are reluctant to mandate remedies that require the court to supervise business operations. In *Gregory v. Albertson's, Inc.*, 104 Cal.App.4th 845, 128 Cal.Rptr.2d 389 (2002), a citizen filed suit against Albertson's for securing a 70–year leasehold interest in a shopping center, not to open a store there but instead to prevent a competitor from opening a store. The court held that the citizen had not stated a claim for unfair competition and registered its concern that affording plaintiff a remedy would "impose a difficult burden on the court." "A judicially supervised marketing of the property would, at best, put the court in the untenable position of making or approving commercial decisions without clear guidelines and, at worst, would involve a level of dominion over the property raising constitutional issues." However, what if the shopping mall owner relet the property to a new grocery store? Would the court restrain the breach of contract, or find that the contract was a violation of public policy?

§ 2. FEDERAL STATUTES RELATED TO CONSUMER PROTECTION

(a) Civil RICO

The civil Racketeer Influenced and Corrupt Organizations ("RICO") statute, like its criminal counterpart, was intended to combat organized crime. Initially courts were wary of its sweeping language and were reluctant to permit broad use of the statute by businesses and other organizations. However, the Supreme Court has held that RICO cannot be limited to suits against mobsters and organized criminals, but instead applies to respected and legitimate enterprises as well. See *Sedima, S.P.R.L. v. Imrex Co., Inc.*, 473 U.S. 479, 499, 105 S.Ct. 3275, 87 L.Ed.2d 346 (1985).

Because the RICO statute is designed to combat racketeering activity, it is easy to overlook its applicability to a number of contexts that are not traditionally understood to involve organized crime. However, civil RICO actions can pertain to a wide range of fraudulent activities, including many that hurt consumers or competitors.

(1) Federal Statutes

RACKETEER INFLUENCED AND CORRUPT ORGANIZATIONS (RICO)
18 U.S.C.A. §§ 1961—1964

§ 1961. Definitions

As used in this chapter—

(1) "racketeering activity" means (A) any act or threat involving murder, kidnaping, gambling, arson, robbery, bribery, extortion, dealing in obscene matter, or dealing in a controlled substance or listed chemical (as defined in section 102 of the Controlled Substances Act), which is chargeable under State law and punishable by imprisonment for more than one year; (B) any act which is indictable under any of the following provisions of title 18, United States Code: [the statute here lists 60 sections of title 18, including "section 1341 (relating to mail fraud), section 1343 (relating to wire fraud)"; subsections (C) through (F) list acts chargeable under sections in other titles of the U.S. Code.]

§ 1962. Prohibited activities

(a) It shall be unlawful for any person who has received any income derived, directly or indirectly, from a pattern of racketeering activity or through collection of an unlawful debt in which such person has participated as a principal within the meaning of section 2, title 18, United States Code, to use or invest, directly or indirectly, any part of such income, or the proceeds of such income, in acquisition of any interest in, or the establishment or operation of, any enterprise which is engaged in, or the activities of which affect, interstate or foreign commerce. [The statute exempts some purchases of securities on the open market. Subsection (b) ties off some loopholes in this prohibition.]

. . .

---

30. **Construing § 1962(a).** Notice that § 1962(a) does not prohibit racketeering activity. Instead it prohibits a person who has participated in racketeering activity from investing or using the proceeds to acquire or engage in an enterprise. "Person" is defined in § 1961 to include an entity. Congress was thinking here of racketeer-associated individuals or businesses moving in on a legitimate business, or, alternatively, starting an enterprise with money from the racketeering.

(c) It shall be unlawful for any person employed by or associated with any enterprise engaged in, or the activities of which affect, interstate or foreign commerce, to conduct or participate, directly or indirectly, in the conduct of such enterprise's affairs through a pattern of racketeering activity or collection of unlawful debt.

31. **Construing § 1962(c).** This section prohibits racketeering activity. The specific statutory requirements of § 1962(c) have been listed in a number of ways. At a minimum, proof of a private violation

under this section has been said to require: (1) the existence of an enterprise and the association of a person with the enterprise, (2) a pattern of racketeering activity that violates the RICO statute, and (3) an injury to business or property which occurs "by reason of" the violation. See *United HealthCare Corp. v. American Trade Ins. Co.,* 88 F.3d 563 (8th Cir. 1996). The predicate acts used to establish a pattern of racketeering activity, such as mail fraud or Hobbs Act violations, contain their own legal requirements as well.

32. **Association with an enterprise.** Can you sue an enterprise under § 1962(c)? Yes, at least theoretically, because an enterprise can be a person. But the "person" who is associated with or employed by an enterprise and participating in the conduct of the enterprise must be separate from the enterprise itself. For purposes of the RICO statute, an enterprise can be a private entity, a public entity, or even a government agency. Nicholas Berg and Christopher Kelly, *Racketeer Influenced and Corrupt Organizations,* 41 Am. Crim. L. Rev. 1027, 1038–39 (2004).

§ 1964. Civil remedies

(a) The district courts of the United States shall have jurisdiction to prevent and restrain violations of section 1962 of this chapter by issuing appropriate orders, including, but not limited to: ordering any person to divest himself of any interest, direct or indirect, in any enterprise; imposing reasonable restrictions on the future activities or investments of any person, including, but not limited to, prohibiting any person from engaging in the same type of endeavor as the enterprise engaged in, the activities of which affect interstate or foreign commerce; or ordering dissolution or reorganization of any enterprise, making due provision for the rights of innocent persons ....

(c) Any person injured in his business or property by reason of a violation of section 1962 of this chapter may sue therefore in any appropriate United States district court and shall recover threefold the damages he sustains and the cost of the suit, including a reasonable attorney's fee, except that no person may rely upon any conduct that would have been actionable as fraud in the purchase or sale of securities to establish a violation of section 1962. [The statute excepts from this last sentence, an action against any person who is criminally convicted in connection with the fraud, in which case a special date for accrual of the statute of limitations applies].

(d) A final judgment or decree rendered in favor of the United States in any criminal proceeding brought by the United States under this chapter shall estop the defendant from denying the essential allegations of the criminal offense in any subsequent civil proceeding brought by the United States.

(2) Pattern of Racketeering Activity

CORLEY v. ROSEWOOD CARE CENTER, INC. OF PEORIA

142 F.3d 1041 (7th Cir. 1998)

Ilana Diamond ROVNER, Circuit Judge. . . .

[In 1989 Corley and his mother arranged for her care in Rosewood Care Center, Inc. of Peoria ("Rosewood").] [T]he contract was conditioned on Rosewood's guarantee that Mrs. Corley would be provided a private suite for the duration of her stay. Under the contract, the initial base rate for that private suite was $70 per day. Corley maintains that defendants induced him to execute the contract by making a series of promises relating to the quality of care his mother would receive at Rosewood. In addition to the guarantee of a private suite, defendants told Corley that his mother would be provided a choice of two entrees at every meal and that she would be permitted to remain in the Peoria facility as a Medicaid patient even if she were to exhaust her personal resources. Defendants also told Corley that in the event of a price increase, the differential between the rate for a private suite and the rate for a semi-private room would remain constant. Corley contends that Rosewood never had any intention of honoring these promises.

According to Corley, defendants began to implement the "switch" component of their scheme shortly after he executed the contract and settled his mother into the Peoria facility. After only two months, Corley received a letter from Rosewood's administrator indicating that the demand for Rosewood's services had exceeded expectations and that as a result, Rosewood would be required to limit the number of residents residing in private suites. The letter urged Corley to consider transferring his mother to a semi-private room and warned that if he did not, the price of her private suite would increase by $14 per day. Corley refused to give up his mother's private suite, however, and on March 1, 1990, Rosewood raised the per-day rate for that suite to $84. Rosewood subsequently raised the rate to $88 per day as of March 30, 1990, and then to $122 per day as of October 29, 1990. In the meantime, Rosewood also began to offer residents only one entree choice at meals, despite its earlier promise that it would provide Mrs. Corley two entree choices. If Mrs. Corley refused the available entree on any given day, she was served leftovers from the previous day. Finally, in the fall of 1990, Rosewood notified residents that its Peoria facility would not be honoring the promise of continuing care if residents should exhaust their personal resources. Residents would instead be required to relocate to Rosewood's East Peoria facility in order to obtain that guarantee of continuing care. With respect to Corley and his mother, the complaint alleges that defendants utilized the United States mails in furtherance of their scheme to defraud when they mailed the executed contract to Corley sometime after October 25, 1989, when Rosewood's administrator sent his December 1989 letter urging Corley to transfer his mother to a semi-private room, when they mailed notices of rate increases to Corley on March 30, 1990 and October 24, 1990, and when they mailed him bills on a monthly basis from March 1, 1990 through March 1, 1992. On March 31, 1992, Corley removed his mother from Rosewood's Peoria nursing home.

The predicate acts of racketeering alleged in the complaint are not limited to Corley and his mother, however, for the complaint alleges that similar acts of mail fraud were directed against other Rosewood residents and their relatives.

Corley alleges that the foregoing acts violated ... 18 U.S.C. § 1962(c). ... The complaint further alleges that Vander Maten and Hoefling conducted the affairs of the enterprise through the predicate acts of mail fraud detailed above for the purpose of maximizing their income and net worth. ... According to the complaint, the predicate acts of mail fraud are sufficient to form a pattern of racketeering activity under the statute. Corley also alleges that by investing income derived from this racketeering activity in the operations of the enterprise, the corporate defendants violated 18 U.S.C. § 1962(a).

[The District Court granted summary judgment for the defendant.]

As is so often the case with civil RICO, the viability of Corley's claims turns on whether he has established a pattern of racketeering activity. Such a pattern is an essential element of a claim under both sections 1962(a) and 1962(c). The RICO statute itself is not particularly helpful in defining the all-important pattern requirement, as it notes only that a pattern requires at least two acts of racketeering activity within a ten-year period. 18 U.S.C. § 1961(5). And "racketeering activity" is defined to include, among other things, any act indictable under specified provisions of the United States Code, including 18 U.S.C. § 1341 (mail fraud) and 18 U.S.C. § 1343 (wire fraud). See 18 U.S.C. § 1961(1)(B); The Supreme Court has indicated that although two predicate acts of racketeering are necessary to form a pattern, two acts alone generally will not suffice. *H.J. Inc. v. Northwestern Bell Tel. Co.*, 492 U.S. 229, 237 (1989). Rather, in addition to at least two predicate acts, a RICO plaintiff must show "that the racketeering predicates are related, and that they amount to or pose a threat of continued criminal activity." In other words, a RICO plaintiff like Corley must show continuity plus relationship with respect to the alleged predicates.

The "relationship" prong is relatively uncontroversial here. The predicate acts of racketeering satisfy the relationship test if they "have the same or similar purposes, results, participants, victims, or methods of commission, or otherwise are interrelated by distinguishing characteristics and are not isolated events." Neither defendants nor the district court have suggested that the core predicate acts comprising the alleged "bait and switch" scheme are insufficiently related to satisfy the relationship prong. So we accept that the core predicate acts are related and proceed to consider continuity.

The Supreme Court dealt extensively with this more controversial aspect of the pattern requirement in *H.J. Inc.* There, the Court explained that a RICO plaintiff must show "that the predicates themselves amount to, or that they otherwise constitute a threat of, continuing racketeering activity." "Continuity," the Court observed, is both a closed- and open-ended concept, in that it refers "either to a closed period of repeated conduct, or to past conduct that by its nature projects into the future with a threat of repetition."

Continuity over a closed period may be demonstrated by proof of "a series of related predicates extending over a substantial period of time." The Court cautioned, however, that "[p]redicate acts extending over a few weeks or months and threatening no future criminal conduct do not satisfy this requirement" because "Congress was concerned in RICO with long-term criminal conduct." Prior to *H.J. Inc.*, this circuit had looked to five factors in analyzing whether predicate acts are sufficiently continuous to give rise to a pattern of racketeering activity: "the number and variety of predicate acts and the length of time over which they were committed, the number of victims, the presence of separate schemes and the occurrence of distinct injuries." *Morgan v. Bank of Waukegan*, 804 F.2d 970, 975 (7th Cir.1986). We have continued to look to the *Morgan* factors after *H.J. Inc.* when considering whether a closed period of related conduct is sufficient to establish continuity.

"Open-ended continuity," by contrast, may involve predicate acts occurring over a short period of time so long as there is a threat that the conduct will recur in the future. Such a threat is present when: (1) a specific threat of repetition exists, (2) the predicates are a regular way of conducting [an] ongoing legitimate business, or (3) the predicates can be attributed to a defendant operating as part of a long-term association that exists for criminal purposes.

The district court viewed Corley's complaint as closed-ended and found its span of 14 months insufficient to meet the continuity requirement. Corley blamed the lack of evidence relating to other residents on the district court's restriction of his ability to investigate and obtain additional discovery.

[W]e think it clear that once Corley's allegations with respect to other Rosewood residents are considered, his complaint is sufficient. In light of those allegations, defendants' "bait and switch" mail fraud scheme is much broader than merely the five predicate acts considered by the district court at the summary judgment stage below. Corley alleges, for example, that defendants made similar misrepresentations to other prospective Rosewood residents and their relatives about the availability of private suites, the availability of two entree choices at each meal, and the guarantee of continuing care with Medicaid reimbursement first at the Peoria facility and then at the Rosewood facility in East Peoria, Illinois. He also alleges that numerous others were overcharged for the services defendants provided. As with defendants' execution of the scheme with respect to Vera Corley, numerous mailings to other residents and their relatives allegedly furthered defendants' scheme. Thus, with reference to the *Morgan* factors, this broader scheme, even if closed-ended, involved innumerable predicate acts of mail fraud occurring over a significant period of time, and it was directed against a substantial number of victims, all of whom experienced distinct injuries. It is not entirely clear to us, in fact, that the scheme as alleged by Corley could not be described as "open-ended" in the sense that it reflects defendants' ongoing way of conducting a legitimate business enterprise. But in any event, the scheme clearly does not have the natural end point that has caused us to find a lack of continuity in some closed-ended cases. Rather, the nature of the conduct alleged here would seem to carry with it the threat that defendants may continue to conduct business at their various nursing homes in what may be a fraudulent way. We believe, then, that if Corley's allegations are accepted as true, he could indeed prove a set of facts consistent with those allegations that would establish a pattern of racketeering activity under the RICO statute.

Yet defendants contend that the allegations on which we have focused should not be considered because they are not sufficiently specific to satisfy Fed.R.Civ.P. 9(b), which requires that "the circumstances constituting fraud ... be stated with particularity." We have indicated that this rule applies to allegations of mail and wire fraud, including where those offenses are alleged to comprise predicate acts of a RICO pattern. To satisfy the particularity requirement, we have required a RICO plaintiff to allege the time, place, and content of an allegedly fraudulent communication, as well as the parties to that communication. In this case, Corley generally identifies the content of allegedly fraudulent communications, but in a number of instances is unable to state the specific time or place that a communication was made, nor does he identify the particular Rosewood resident or relative to whom the communication was directed. But Corley's complaint also emphasizes that such specific information is in the hands of defendants, who at the time had resisted his attempts in discovery to obtain a list of other Rosewood residents affected by the alleged scheme. We have noted on a number of occasions that the particularity requirement of Rule 9(b) must be relaxed where the plaintiff lacks access to all facts necessary to detail his claim, and that is most likely to be the case where, as here, the plaintiff alleges a fraud against one or more third parties. Corley's complaint identifies certain other Rosewood residents to whom the various misrepresentations were communicated, and with respect to the identified residents, he details the circumstances of the alleged frauds with sufficient particularity. To the extent the complaint makes allegations relating to other classes of unidentified Rosewood residents, however, we believe that Rule 9(b)'s particularity requirement must be relaxed if, at the time the complaint was filed, Corley had been denied access in discovery to information that would identify those residents. Predicate acts of racketeering relating to those residents may be pled more generally, as Corley has done here by referencing his own experiences with Rosewood in contracting for the care of his mother and alleging in some detail that other residents and their relatives also were victimized by the identical scheme. In sum, then, we agree with the district court that Corley's fourth amended complaint satisfies the particularity requirements of Rule 9(b) and sufficiently alleges a pattern of racketeering activity. It was therefore not subject to dismissal for failure to state a claim.

[The court then held that summary judgment for the defendant was error because the plaintiff should have been permitted to discover evidence relating to possible predicate acts directed at other residents.]

33. **Predicate acts.** In order to establish liability under § 1962(c), the plaintiff must show that the defendant committed offenses listed in § 1961 as "racketeering activity." These offenses are then referred to as predicate acts. Although predicate acts can include physical injury torts such as murder and kidnaping, a number of those acts involve economic injury. A predicate act that is frequently invoked in litigation between businesses is mail fraud. Mail fraud that violates 18 U.S.C. § 1341, is proven by just a few elements: (1) the defendant's participation in a scheme to defraud; (2) the defendant's intent to defraud; and (3) the defendant's use of the mails in furtherance of the fraudulent scheme. Furthermore, the evidence must establish that the false representations were material. *United States v. Henningsen* 387 F.3d 585, 589 (7th Cir. 2004).

34. **Pattern of racketeering.** Just how many and what kind of predicate acts it takes to make a pattern of racketeering activity has created some confusion. As *Corley* discusses, a pattern requires at least two predicate acts. In addition, the predicates must be related and pose a threat of continued criminal activity. Despite the open nature of the inquiry after that point, the pattern of racketeering requirement has survived a number of vagueness challenges. See, e.g, *United States v. Keltner*, 147 F.3d 662, 667 (8th Cir. 1998) (rejecting vagueness challenge and citing other circuits that had also done so). In a civil RICO claim, it is enough to prove the predicate acts which form the basis of the pattern of racketeering in the civil case itself, presumably under a preponderance of the evidence standard. Ordinarily, the defendant need not have been criminally convicted of these acts. *Sedima, S.P.R.L. v. Imrex Co., Inc.*, 473 U.S. 479, 105 S.Ct. 3275, 87 L.Ed.2d 346 (1985). However, because of statutory language added to § 1964(c) by the Private Securities Litigation Reform Act of 1995, a special rule applies in securities cases. See *Popp Telecom, Inc. v. American Sharecom, Inc.*, 361 F.3d 482, 488 (8th Cir. 2004). Moreover, as § 1964(d) makes clear, if the defendant *has* been convicted of the offenses which serve as the predicate acts, the defendant is estopped from denying them in the civil case.

35. **Situations involving a pattern of racketeering activity.** Because a false communication that violates federal mail or wire fraud requirements can satisfy the predicate act of racketeering, the RICO statute has been invoked in a wide variety of circumstances. See, e.g.,

Cadle Co. v. Flanagan, 2005 WL 1039005 (D. Conn. 2005) (genuine issue of material fact with regard to whether lawyers violated RICO by intentionally misrepresenting source of client funds and hiding client assets in order to help client avoid paying a debt); *Procter & Gamble Co. v. Amway Corp.,* 242 F.3d 539, 565 (5th Cir. 2001) (P & G stated a RICO claim sufficient to survive rule 12(b)(6) dismissal where its competitor had allegedly spread a rumor that caused consumers to stop buying P & G's products); *Westways World Travel v. AMR Corp.,* 182 F.Supp.2d 952 (C.D. Cal. 2001) (travel agencies could maintain a civil RICO claim against airlines and airline ticket clearinghouse for requiring travel agencies to pay large penalties for purported "tariff" violations for passengers who purchased airline tickets from them if agencies wanted to continue doing business with airlines); *Humana Inc. v. Forsyth* 525 U.S. 299, 119 S.Ct. 710, 142 L.Ed.2d 753 (1999) (health insurance policy beneficiaries could sue group health insurer and hospital under RICO for scheme regarding discounts on hospital services that were not disclosed or passed on to policy beneficiaries, resulting in insurer's payment of considerably less than 80% of actual hospital charges that were covered by policy). Even early on, civil RICO suits often involved businesses. A 1984 ABA Task Force found that (before the Private Securities Law Reform Act amendments) of the 270 known civil RICO cases at the trial court level, 40% involved securities fraud, 37% involved common-law fraud in a commercial or business setting, and only 9% involved "allegations of criminal activity of a type generally associated with professional criminals." Report of the Ad Hoc Civil RICO Task Force of the ABA Section of Corporation, Banking and Business Law at 55–56 (1985).

36. **State RICO acts.** Many states have passed civil RICO statutes that are similar to the federal acts. See, e.g., *Rosier v. First Financial Capital Corp.,* 181 Ariz. 218, 221, 889 P.2d 11, 14 (1994). These statutes may be broader or narrower than the federal statute that they parallel. In states that have broad acts, state civil RICO claims may make frequent appearances in business tort litigation. See A. Laxmidas Sawkar, *From the Mafia to Milking Cows: State Rico Act Expansion,* 41 ARIZ. L. REV. 1133 (1999).

37. **Stigma.** For a defendant, being accused of "racketeering" can carry a significant stigma. Thus a business which files a civil RICO suit against its competitor may damage its competitor's reputation just by filing suit. Is it an abuse of process to file a civil RICO claim for this purpose?

(3) Injury "by Reason of" the Violation

COMMERCIAL CLEANING SERVS. v. COLIN SERVICE SYS., INC.

271 F.3d 374 (2d Cir. 2001)

LEVAL, Circuit Judge.

Plaintiff-appellant Commercial Cleaning Services, L.L.C. (Commercial) appeals from the dismissal of its suit. . . . The complaint alleges that

Colin engaged in a pattern of racketeering activity by hiring undocumented aliens for profit in violation of Section 274 of the Immigration and Nationality Act (INA), 8 U.S.C. § 1324(a), a RICO predicate offense. According to the complaint, Colin's illegal hiring practices enabled it to lower its variable costs and thereby underbid competing firms, which consequently lost contracts and customers to Colin. ... The district court granted Colin's motion and dismissed the complaint without leave to amend, granting judgment in Colin's favor, on the grounds that (i) Commercial had no standing to sue because it did not allege a direct injury proximately caused by Colin's illegal hiring, and (ii) Commercial failed to provide a sufficiently detailed RICO case statement as required by the Connecticut district court's Standing Order in Civil RICO Cases (Standing Order). ...

Commercial and Colin each provide janitorial services for commercial buildings. According to the complaint, Commercial is a small company that has bid against Colin for competitively awarded janitorial service contracts in the Hartford area. Colin operates throughout the Eastern seaboard and is described in the complaint as one of the nation's largest corporations engaged in the business of cleaning commercial facilities. The complaint was filed as a national class action on behalf of Colin's competitors.

The complaint alleges that Commercial and the members of the plaintiff class are victims of Colin's pattern of racketeering activity in violation of 18 U.S.C. § 1962(c), referred to as "the illegal immigrant hiring scheme." The theory of the case, succinctly stated, is that Colin obtained a significant business advantage over other firms in the "highly competitive" and price-sensitive cleaning services industry by knowingly hiring "hundreds of illegal immigrants at low wages." Colin's illegal immigrant hiring scheme allows it to employ large numbers of workers at lower costs than its competitors must bear when operating lawfully. Colin allegedly pays undocumented workers less than the prevailing wage, and does not withhold or pay their federal and state payroll taxes, or workers' compensation insurance fees. The complaint refers to Colin's prosecution in 1996 by the United States Department of Justice for, among other things, hiring at least 150 undocumented workers, continuing to employ aliens after their work authorizations had expired, and failing to prepare, complete, and update employment documents.

The allegations assert that Colin is part of an enterprise composed of entities associated-in-fact that includes employment placement services, labor contractors, newspapers in which Colin advertises for laborers, and "various immigrant networks that assist fellow illegal immigrants in obtaining employment, housing and illegal work permits." The complaint neither describes how the undocumented workers allegedly hired by Colin entered the country, nor claims that Colin had knowledge of how those workers came to the United States. It alleges that Colin's participation in the affairs of the enterprise through the illegal immigrant hiring scheme violates 8 U.S.C. § 1324(a), which prohibits hiring certain undocumented aliens, and which is a RICO predicate offense if committed for financial gain. . . .

The complaint alleges that, through the illegal immigrant hiring scheme, Colin could offer Pratt & Whitney and other potential customers access to "a virtually limitless pool of workers on short notice" at significantly lower prices than other firms could offer by operating lawfully. As a result, Pratt & Whitney and other large contractors for cleaning services accepted Colin's lower bids over Commercial's.

The [district] court dismissed the complaint primarily on the ground that Commercial had no standing to bring suit because its injury did not bear a "direct relation" to Colin's racketeering activity as required by *Holmes v. Securities Investor Protection Corp.,* 503 U.S. 258, 268, 112 S.Ct. 1311, 117 L.Ed.2d 532 (1992). . . .

RICO grants standing to pursue a civil damages remedy to "[a]ny person injured in his business or property by reason of a violation of [18 U.S.C. § 1962]." 18 U.S.C. § 1964(c). In order to bring suit under § 1964(c), a plaintiff must plead (1) the defendant's violation of § 1962, (2) an injury to the plaintiff's business or property, and (3) causation of the injury by the defendant's violation. . . .

RICO's use of the clause "by reason of" has been held to limit standing to those plaintiffs who allege that the asserted RICO violation was the legal, or proximate, cause of their injury, as well as a logical, or "but for," cause. See *Holmes*, 503 U.S. at 268. . . . In marking that boundary, the Supreme Court has emphasized that a plaintiff cannot complain of harm so remotely caused by a defendant's actions that imposing legal liability would transgress our "ideas of what justice demands, or of what is administratively possible and convenient." *Holmes,* 503 U.S. at 268 (internal quotation marks omitted) (quoting W. Page Keeton et al., *Prosser and Keeton on the Law of Torts* § 41, at 264 (5th ed.1984)).

Colin contends that the chain of causation between its alleged hiring of undocumented workers and Pratt & Whitney's decision to award cleaning contracts to Colin instead of Commercial is too long and tenuous to meet the proximate cause test of *Holmes.* [The court then addressed the facts in *Holmes*].

The *Holmes* Court applied a proximate cause test requiring a "direct relation between the injury asserted and the injurious conduct alleged." The "direct relation" requirement generally precludes recovery by a "plaintiff who complain[s] of harm flowing merely from the misfortunes visited upon a third person by the defendant's acts."

[The *Holmes* Court] expressly warned against applying a mechanical test detached from the policy considerations associated with the proximate cause analysis at play in the case. See *id.* ("[O]ur use of the term 'direct' should merely be understood as a reference to the proximate-cause enquiry that is informed by the [policy] concerns set out in the [opinion].") . . .

The *Holmes* Court gave three policy reasons for limiting RICO's civil damages action only to those plaintiffs who could allege a direct injury. First, the less direct an injury is, the more difficult it becomes to determine what portion of the damages are attributable to the RICO violation as distinct from other, independent, factors. Second, if recovery by indirectly injured plaintiffs were not barred, courts would be forced, in order to prevent multiple recovery, to develop complicated rules apportioning damages among groups of plaintiffs depending on how far each group was removed from the defendant's underlying RICO violation. Third, there was no need to permit indirectly injured plaintiffs to sue, as directly injured victims could be counted on to vindicate the aims of the RICO statute, and their recovery would fix the injury to those harmed as the result of the injury they suffered.

[The first factor.] The difficulty of proof identified in *Holmes,* however, was quite different from the circumstances of this case. Here, the plaintiffs bid against the defendant as direct competitors. The complaint asserts that Pratt & Whitney chose Colin because Colin submitted "significantly lower" bids in a "highly competitive" price-sensitive market. According to the complaint, Colin was able to underbid its competitors because its scheme to hire illegal immigrant workers permitted it to pay well below the prevailing wage for legal workers. Although we do not deny that there may be disputes as to whether the plaintiff class lost business because of defendant's violation of § 1324(a) or for other reasons, the plaintiff class was no less directly injured than the insolvent broker-dealers in *Holmes,* whose trustees, the Court indicated, would be proper plaintiffs. . . .

Colin objects that any reduced labor costs were due to its alleged underpayment of workers and failure to pay other employment-related costs of doing business, not its participation in the illegal immigrant hiring scheme. In other words, Colin claims that Commercial complains of an injury caused by the low wages paid to Colin's workers—and not by their immigration status. Of course, paying workers less than the prevailing wage and failing to withhold payroll taxes are not RICO predicate acts. Nonetheless, the purpose of the alleged violation of 8 U.S.C. § 1324(a), the hiring of illegal alien workers, was to take advantage of their diminished bargaining position, so as to employ a cheaper labor force and compete unfairly on the basis of lower costs. By illegally hiring undocumented alien labor, Colin was able to hire cheaper labor and compete unfairly. The violation of § 1324(a) alleged by the complaint was a proximate cause of Colin's ability to underbid the plaintiffs and take business from them.

[The second factor.] . . . Colin contends that its business competitors are not the only aggrieved parties who could recover under Commercial's theory and that the difficulty of apportioning damages among potential plaintiffs will be severe. Colin's response misses the point. The point made in *Holmes* was that, if damages are paid both to first tier plaintiffs—those directly injured by defendant's alleged acts—and to second tier plaintiffs—those injured by the injury to the first tier plaintiffs—

then the payment of damages to the first tier plaintiffs would cure the harm to the second tier plaintiffs, and the payment of damages to the latter category would involve double compensation. Colin's answer is no answer to this point. If a defendant's illegal acts caused direct injury to more than one category of plaintiffs, the defendant may well be obligated to compensate different plaintiffs for different injuries. It does not follow that any plaintiff will have been twice benefitted, which was the concern in *Holmes.*

Unlike the situation in *Holmes,* Commercial and its fellow class members are not alleging an injury that was derivative of injury to others. . . .

[The third factor.] Colin argues that this factor weighs against Commercial's standing, because other parties, such as state and federal authorities charged with collecting unpaid taxes and workers' compensation fees, may sue to vindicate the statute. Moreover, the INS, which enforces § 1324(a), has already obtained Colin's agreement to pay $1 million for violations of the immigration laws.

Once again, Colin misses the point. If the existence of a public authority that could prosecute a claim against putative RICO defendants meant that the plaintiff is too remote under *Holmes,* then no private cause of action could ever be maintained, for every RICO predicate offense, as well as the RICO enterprise itself, is separately prosecutable by the government. In *Holmes,* those directly injured could be expected to sue, and their recovery would redound to the benefit of the plaintiffs suing for indirect injury. Here, in contrast, suits by governmental authorities to recover lost taxes and fees would do nothing to alleviate the plaintiffs' loss of profits. There is no class of potential plaintiffs who have been more directly injured by the alleged RICO conspiracy than the defendant's business competitors, who have a greater incentive to ensure that a RICO violation does not go undetected or unremedied, and whose recovery would indirectly cure the loss suffered by these plaintiffs. . . .

The judgment of the district court is vacated, and the case is remanded for further proceedings consistent with this opinion.

---

38. **Injury to business or property.** Notice that § 1964(c) provides a damages remedy for "any person injured in his business or property by reason of a violation of section 1962." *Commercial Cleaning* examines the "by reason of" aspect of the cause of action, which has been thought to include not only an actual cause but also a proximate cause element, and which excludes plaintiffs with "derivative" losses much as *Robins Dry Dock* did in a different setting. At least one court has held that an injury to the plaintiff's dignitary interests, as in the case of false arrest, is not actionable as an injury to business or property. See *Walker v. Gates*, 2002 WL 1065618 (C.D. Cal. 2002).

39. **Actions when injury to business or property is absent.** Section 1964(a) grants district courts the jurisdiction "to prevent and restrain violations of section 1962," even when a person has not been injured by reason of the violation. However § 1964(a) has been held to provide jurisdiction only for forward-looking remedies. In *United States v. Philip Morris USA Inc.*, 396 F.3d 1190 (D.C. Cir. 2005), the United States brought a civil RICO claim against cigarette manufacturers and research organizations based on an alleged fraudulent pattern of covering up the dangers of tobacco use, and marketing tobacco products to minors. The United States sought damages to recover health-related costs it incurred because of the pattern of fraudulent activity. However, the District of Columbia Court of Appeals held that these costs were not recoverable under § 1964(a) because the remedies under that section do not include disgorgement of ill-gotten gains, but rather provide only for remedies directed toward preventing future violations.

40. **Related causes of action.** The RICO statute may bear on other kinds of claims involved in this book. *Commercial Cleaning* brings to mind interference with business opportunity if nothing else. Consider also whether privacy and other claims might turn out to be RICO claims in some instances. Was ABC engaged in a pattern of racketeering activity when it secretly recorded activities of the plaintiffs in *Food Lion* and *Desnick,* Chapter 7?

41. **RICO and organized protests.** The U.S. Supreme Court twice examined application of the Civil RICO statute to organized protests. In *National Organization for Women v. Scheidler*, 510 U.S. 249, 114 S.Ct. 798, 127 L.Ed.2d 99 (1994), the Court ruled that the civil RICO statute could be applied to coalitions of anti-abortion protestors who interfered with and disrupted abortion clinics through lawful and unlawful means, even though that organization was not motivated by an economic purpose. In a subsequent decision in the same case, *Scheidler v. National Organization for Women,* 537 U.S. 393, 123 S.Ct. 1057, 154 L.Ed.2d 991 (2003), the Court ruled that the plaintiffs' alleged predicate acts of extortion were insufficient to maintain a claim. In a concurring opinion, Justice Ginsburg noted that under a different interpretation, RICO could have been applicable to the civil rights sit-ins and expressed reluctance "to extend RICO's domain further by endorsing the expansive definition of 'extortion' adopted by the Seventh Circuit." *Id.* at 1069. Are these concerns reminiscent of other first amendment concerns we have seen?

(b) Other Significant Federal Statutes

42. **Specific statutes.** Some statutes proscribing fraud are very narrow, simply enacting a rule for a particular situation. For instance, 15 U.S.C. §§ 1988—1989 requires correct odometer readings on cars.

43. **Regulatory systems.** More important statutes may affect whole industries, or create whole system of liability, often with public as well as private enforcement. These include federal and state statutes

regulating transactions in securities like stocks and bonds, lending practices, mass real estate sales, and unfair consumer practices.

44. **The False Claims Act and qui tam.** (a) Under the Federal False Claims Act, anyone who knowingly presents a false claim against the United States is criminally liable and also liable for a civil fine and treble damages. 18 U.S.C.A. § 287 & 31 U.S.C.A. § 729.

(b) A bounty hunter provision in the False Claims Act allows private citizens to sue on behalf of the government for False Claims Act violations. The government can then take over the lawsuit or not, but even if it does, the private plaintiff who brought suit in the government's name is paid a percentage of the recovery. These private citizen actions are called "qui tam" actions, from the first words of a Latin phrase used in common law actions to describe the plaintiff—one who sues for the king as well as for himself.

(c) Some special limitations apply to the private qui tam actions. Two of these are found in the statutory rules that if the facts have been publicly disclosed, no qui tam action can be brought; and if someone else has already brought a qui tam action on similar facts, the plaintiff cannot sue, even though the previous suit has been dismissed and the plaintiff has better knowledge of the facts. Examples of false claims suits include (1) assertions that a government contractor was misallocating costs from one government project to another to maximize costs to the government, see *United States v. Hughes Aircraft Co.,* 243 F.3d 1181 (9th Cir. 2001); and (2) assertions that healthcare entities such as doctors, clinics, or nursing homes, are falsifying claims for medicare or medicaid reimbursement, or even that a nursing home receiving such reimbursement is not providing the quality of services required, see *United States v. NHC Healthcare Corp.,* 115 F.Supp.2d 1149 (W.D.Mo. 2000).

45. **Securities statutes—10b–(5).** Federal statutes and regulations affecting transactions in securities such as stocks and bonds contain a number of different provisions aimed at preventing or redressing misrepresentations. One of the main sources of litigation occurs under a regulation known as 10b–5. 17 C.F.R. § 240.10b–5 (2002). The 1934 statute prohibits the use of "any manipulative or deceptive device or contrivance" in dealing with securities and a more detailed rule of the Securities Exchange Commission prohibits the use of "any devices, scheme or artifice to defraud" and also prohibits any "act, practice, or course of business which operates or would operate as a fraud or deceit upon any person".

These provisions were analyzed in *Ernst & Ernst v. Hochfelder*, 425 U.S. 185, 96 S.Ct. 1375, 47 L.Ed.2d 668 (1976), where the Supreme Court concluded that the statute applied to intentional but not negligent conduct. The Court left open the question whether reckless behavior might suffice for liability.

Federal securities laws do impose strict liability for a limited class of misrepresentations. These are representations found in registration and prospectus statements. 15 U.S.C. §§ 77k, 77l. Sellers may be strictly liable under some anti-fraud clauses even when they are not liable under others. See *Aaron v. Securities and Exchange Comm'n*, 446 U.S. 680, 100 S.Ct. 1945, 64 L.Ed.2d 611 (1980), holding that 15 U.S.C. § 17(a)'s provisions like those of 10b–5 require *Hochfelder* scienter, but provisions against obtaining money by means of untrue material statements or omissions and against engaging in any transactions that would *operate* as a fraud impose strict liability.

States often impose their own securities laws, often similar to federal laws. Arizona, for example, parallels the federal rules, requiring scienter under statutory language similar to that found in 10b–5, but imposing strict liability under the *Aaron* type language. See *Greenfield v. Cheek*, 122 Ariz. 57, 593 P.2d 280 (1979) (§ 44–1991–1, 10b–5 language, no strict liability, scienter required); *State v. Gunnison*, 127 Ariz. 110, 618 P.2d 604 (1980) (§ 44–1991–2 and–3, *Aaron* type language, strict liability). These state laws are important even if you don't deal with formal securities like corporate stocks, because a lot of things may count as a security, including, for example, an interest in an apple orchard where the seller has a management contract to operate it. *Rose v. Dobras*, 128 Ariz. 209, 624 P.2d 887 (1981).

46. **The Interstate Land Sales Full Disclosure Act.** Rules are imposed under the Interstate Land Sales Full Disclosure Act, 15 U.S.C. §§ 1701, 1703, 1709, aimed at protecting consumers from artful sales of land such as "vacation" spots. Again, state statutes may make similar provisions. Relief may be limited to rescission. See *Alaface v. National Investment Co.*, 181 Ariz. 586, 892 P.2d 1375 (Ct. App.1994).

47. **References.** NATIONAL CONSUMER LAW CENTER, UNFAIR AND DECEPTIVE ACTS AND PRACTICES (6th ed. 2004); Dee Pridgen, CONSUMER PROTECTION AND THE LAW (2003 edition); Michael M. Greenfield, CONSUMER LAW: A GUIDE FOR THOSE WHO REPRESENT SELLERS, LENDERS, AND CONSUMERS (1995).

Chapter 15

Class Action Litigation

As originally enacted, many state consumer fraud statutes provided only for public enforcement by state attorneys general. Consequently, when state legislatures amended these acts to permit a private right of action, these claims were well suited for class action treatment. Private attorneys general could force disgorgement of improperly obtained profits on behalf of fellow consumers, even when the amount at stake for any single consumer was too small to justify individual litigation. Unlike many private actions, the stakes in class action cases can be very high. With the availability of multi-state classes and punitive or treble damages, courts have entered *billion* dollar judgments on behalf of classes of consumers. One of the crucial issues in class action cases is whether a class will be certified. These enhancements focus on the issue of class certification in private damages actions filed under state consumer protection statutes, and at times, civil RICO provisions as well.

Procedural Rules Governing Class Certification

Rule 23 of the Federal Rules of Civil Procedure provides the basic framework for resolving whether a class action case should be certified. Rule 23(a) outlines the prerequisites to a class action suit, which are often characterized as numerosity, commonality, typicality, and adequacy of representation. In addition to meeting these four prerequisites of Rule 23(a), a class action can only be maintained if it meets one of the additional prerequisites stated in Rule 23(b). Plaintiffs can meet this requirement by showing that the prosecution of separate actions risks inconsistent or varying adjudications or would substantially impair plaintiffs' ability to protect their interests; or that the defendant has acted or refused to act on grounds generally applicable to the class. However, frequently the prerequisite at issue in consumer fraud act or civil RICO class actions is the one found in Rule 23(b)(3):

RULE 23 OF THE FEDERAL RULES OF CIVIL PROCEDURE

(b)(3) the court finds that the questions of law or fact common to the members of the class predominate over any questions affecting only individual members, and that a class action is superior to other available methods for the fair and efficient adjudication of the controversy. The matters pertinent to the findings include: (A) the interest of members of the class in individually controlling the prosecution or defense of separate actions; (B) the extent and nature of any litigation concerning the controversy already commenced by or against members of the class; (C) the desirability or undesirability of concentrating the litigation of the claims in the particular forum; (D) the difficulties likely to be encountered in the management of a class action.

1. **State and federal standards.** Federal Rule of Civil Procedure 23 governs certification of federal class action cases. Consumer fraud class actions are often certified in state courts under state procedural rules. However, state rules frequently parallel the basic concepts and terminology used in Rule 23. See, e.g., CAL. CIVIL CODE § 1781(b) (West 2005); 735 ILL. COMP. STAT. ANN. 5/2–801; N.Y. C.P.L.R § 901 (McKinney 2005).

2. **Availability of private class action suits.** Class action suits asserting violation of state consumer protection statutes can have significant impact on businesses. A number of state legislatures have chosen not to permit private consumers to file class claims. In addition, states may limit the awards that even state actors may recover on behalf of the class. See ALA. CODE § 8–19–10(f) (stating that a consumer "may not bring an action on behalf of a class" although the office of the Attorney General or district attorney may do so, and restricting even the latter's ability to obtain minimum or treble damages). See also GA.CODE ANN. § 10–1–399(a); LA. REV. STAT. ANN. § 51:1409(A); MISS. CODE ANN. § 75–24–15(4). Meanwhile, other jurisdictions expressly sanction private class action claims. See CAL. CIVIL CODE § 1781(a) ("Any consumer entitled to bring an action under [the state consumer protection act] may, if the unlawful method, act, or practice has caused damage to other consumers similarly situated, bring an action on behalf of himself and such other consumers to recover damages or obtain other relief as provided for in [the state consumer protection act]."). Similarly, New Jersey courts have instructed that "the class action rule should be construed liberally in a case involving allegations of consumer fraud." *Strawn v. Canuso,* 140 N.J. 43, 68, 657 A.2d 420, 432–33 (1995).

3. **Class Action Fairness Act of 2005.** Differences in state class action standards may extend beyond differences in statutes themselves. As a practical matter, businesses and litigators believe that certain jurisdictions provide a more fertile ground for class recovery under consumer protection statutes and other causes of action. In response to this concern, Congress recently passed the federal Class Action Fairness Act of 2005 ("CAFA"), which expands federal court diversity jurisdiction over class action lawsuits. Under CAFA, codified at 28 U.S.C. § 1332(d), class actions based on state law may be removed to federal court if the aggregate damages sought by all class members exceeds $5 million, and at least one class member resides outside the forum state. The federal court may remand the suit to state court, however, if one of the primary defendants is a resident of the state and at least one-third of the putative class members reside in the state. Before remanding, the court must consider choice of law, national interests, and whether similar actions are pending elsewhere.

In part, CAFA was designed to discourage the trial of putative nationwide class actions arising under state law in particular state courts perceived to be more likely fora for "class action abuse." Commentators have debated whether this purpose addresses reality or is based on misperceptions, and whether CAFA will simply cause defendants to defend a number of simultaneous regional class actions in the same state courts CAFA was meant to avoid.

Elements of Class Certification

(a) Predominance—Individual Versus Common Questions.

In most suits seeking certification of a class to recover damages for violation of a consumer protection statute, the central certification battle is satisfaction of the two requirements contained in federal Rule 23(b)(3)—"predominance" and "superiority." The predominance requirement—whether "questions of law or fact common to the members of the class predominate over any questions affecting only individual members"—is more stringent than, and to a large extent envelops, the "commonality" requirement of Rule 23(a)(2).

MOORE v. PAINEWEBBER, INC.

306 F.3d 1247 (2d Cir. 2002)

SOTOMAYOR, J.

Plaintiffs based their RICO and fraud claims on the oral misrepresentations made by PaineWebber's brokers, arguing that PaineWebber engaged in a common scheme to misrepresent one of its products. ...

Plaintiffs allege that changes in the federal tax code in the late 1980s prompted many investors to reduce the amount of money they put into IRAs, thus making the IRA business less lucrative for PaineWebber. Plaintiffs further allege that, in order to recapture its lost IRA investment stream and boost life insurance sales, PaineWebber decided to market a universal life insurance policy—the "Provider"—as if it were an IRA or an IRA substitute.

According to the complaint, PaineWebber used a variety of deceptive techniques in its attempt to present the Provider as a kind of IRA. PaineWebber is alleged to have advertised the Provider as a retirement savings plan offering "cash accumulation," competitive interest rates, and tax-advantaged status. The size of the investment that clients were told to make in their Provider accounts—$2000 each year—was allegedly chosen because $2000 is both the maximum and the typical amount that people contribute annually to IRAs. PaineWebber, in its marketing of the Provider, deliberately avoided insurance-associated terms like "premium" and instead used misleading words such as "contribution" or "deposit." Finally, plaintiffs allege PaineWebber's internal training materials explicitly acknowledged that the targeted customer base could be easily persuaded to invest large amounts of money in the Provider, so long as the customers did not think of the Provider as a life insurance policy. PaineWebber did tell some clients that purchasers of the Provider would get life insurance coverage, but presented this insurance as an added benefit rather than the investment itself. In reality, the Provider was a universal life insurance policy and nothing more.

[Both of the named plaintiffs were PaineWebber clients who were told that the Provider "would be a good replacement for their existing IRAs." They received statements listing their "deposits" as though they were a cash savings plan. However, the money was not held as a deposit but used to pay insurance premiums on universal life policies. The named plaintiffs assert that "had they known the true nature of the Provider, they would not have purchased it, but instead would have invested their money in actual IRAs." The district court dismissed the RICO suits on the ground that the misrepresentations were not the proximate cause of their damages. The Second Circuit reversed. On remand, the plaintiffs moved for class certification.]

In support of their motion for class certification, plaintiffs presented evidence that PaineWebber developed a centralized marketing scheme through which it marketed the Provider as an IRA alternative. Specifically, plaintiffs demonstrated that PaineWebber prepared marketing materials and information pieces presenting the Provider as an IRA alternative; PaineWebber's brokers used these materials in promoting the Provider. Moreover, PaineWebber held training sessions in which brokers were instructed to emphasize the Provider's investment features. One of these seminars, "David Macchia Presents: The Alternative Plan," encouraged brokers to market the Provider as an IRA alternative while downplaying the insurance aspects. A memo to all divisional vice-presidents stated that it was PaineWebber's "intention to mobilize our efforts around the David Macchia client seminar," and commanded the vice-presidents to memorize a script prior to an upcoming marketing meeting. Plaintiffs further point to a document entitled "New York Version—Sales Presentation," which again emphasized the investment aspects of the Provider package, and a certification submitted by a former PaineWebber divisional vice-president, which discusses the fact that the "overriding theme" of all the marketing materials prepared by PaineWebber was that, if sales brokers wished to sell the Provider, they could not focus on the insurance aspects of the product.

Plaintiffs also presented evidence that PaineWebber's brokers used at least three different telephone scripts for "cold calling" prospective investors. [One of the three did not mention life insurance at all and referred to the Provider as a "retirement program." The other two scripts referred to some relation to insurance. The scripts suggest meeting with a broker for further information. In addition, client complaint letters claimed that the purchasers were not informed that life insurance was part of the product, were informed that insurance was a part for tax purposes but that they would not be charged administrative fees, or were told that the rate of return would be high enough that after insurance charges their return would still be about 8%.]

In opposition to plaintiffs' motion, PaineWebber submitted affidavits from brokers who testified that they did not employ a standardized sales presentation, and had not participated in the training sessions plaintiffs mentioned.

[The district court denied plaintiffs motion to certify a class under Federal Rule of Civil procedure 23(b)(3) from which plaintiffs appeal. After discussing the standard of review, which is for an abuse of discretion, the court reviewed the requirements of Rule 23(a) and then began it's discussion of the predominance requirement in Rule 23(b)(3).]

The Rule 23(b)(3) predominance inquiry tests whether proposed classes are sufficiently cohesive to warrant adjudication by representation. It is a more demanding criterion than the commonality inquiry under Rule 23(a). Class-wide issues predominate if resolution of some of the legal or factual questions that qualify each class member's case as a genuine controversy can be achieved through generalized proof, and if these particular issues are more substantial than the issues subject only to individualized proof.

PaineWebber argues that fraud claims founded upon oral misrepresentations may not form the basis of a class action unless the misrepresentations are materially uniform in nature. On appeal, plaintiffs argue that liability for the allegedly fraudulent misrepresentations follows from a common course of conduct and, thus, class-wide issues predominate over individualized factual and legal issues. . . .

[T]o recover for a defendant's fraudulent conduct, even if that fraud is the result of a common course of conduct, each plaintiff must prove that he or she personally received a material misrepresentation, and that his or her reliance on this misrepresentation was the proximate cause of his or her loss. Fraud actions must therefore be separated into two categories: fraud claims based on uniform misrepresentations made to all members of the class and fraud claims based on individualized misrepresentations. The former are appropriate subjects for class certification because the standardized misrepresentations may be established by generalized proof. Where there are material variations in the nature of the misrepresentations made to each member of the proposed class, however, class certification is improper because plaintiffs will need to submit proof of the statements made to each plaintiff, the nature of the varying material misrepresentations, and the reliance of each plaintiff upon those misrepresentations in order to sustain their claims. As these are questions that more than likely will be the central disputed issues in a fraud action, certification of the class will not negate the need for a series of mini-trials where there are material variations in the nature of the misrepresentations made.

The question posed in the present case is whether the oral misrepresentations made to the individual plaintiffs fall within the first or the second category. The district court followed the lead of the Third, Fourth, Fifth, Sixth, and Seventh Circuits which have held that oral misrepresentations are presumptively individualized. These circuits therefore treat class certification of fraud claims based upon oral misrepresentations as improper, absent a showing that the misrepresentations were made pursuant to a written, standardized sales script and that the sales agent participated in a common training program that emphasized uniformity in sales techniques.

[The Third Circuit considered the issue in great depth in *In re Prudential Insurance Co. of America Sale Practices Litigation*, 148 F.3d 283 (3d Cir. 1998). In that case,] the complaint alleged that Prudential engaged in a systematic fraudulent marketing scheme, which it implemented through the use of false and misleading sales presentations, policy illustrations, marketing materials, and other information approved, prepared, and disseminated by Prudential to its nationwide sales force. The sales force was not permitted to use any marketing material that had not been centrally approved. Moreover, because Prudential had given its agents extensive training, the agents' oral sales presentations were uniform. Given these findings, the district court certified the class because Prudential had engaged in a "common course of conduct" with materially uniform misrepresentations to the plaintiff class. The Third Circuit approved the certification of the class as within the district court's discretion.

In a subsequent case, the Third Circuit clarified that the *Prudential* holding rested upon the district court's finding of uniformity in the oral sales presentations. See *In re LifeUSA Holding Inc.*, 242 F.3d 136 (3rd Cir. 2001). . . . The Third Circuit distinguished *Prudential* on the grounds that *Prudential* involved "uniform, scripted, and standardized" sales presentations that were "virtually identical" in all material respects, while the claims in *LifeUSA* arose from individual misrepresentations, neither uniform nor scripted, made by some 30,000 independent agents to over 280,000 purchasers. [T]he Third Circuit held that, the predominance requirement had not been met and commonality of claims did not exist. . . .

We agree with these courts that a common course of conduct is not enough to show predominance, because a common course of conduct is not sufficient to establish liability of the defendant to any particular plaintiff. In order to establish PaineWebber's liability, each plaintiff must prove that he or she personally received a material misrepresentation, and that his or her reliance on this misrepresentation was the proximate cause of his or her loss. But a common course of conduct does not demonstrate that any specific statements made pursuant to that scheme were actionable. In contrast, evidence of materially uniform misrepresentations is sufficient to demonstrate the nature of the misrepresentation; an individual plaintiff's receipt of and reliance upon the misrepresentation may then be simpler matters to determine.

We disagree with these courts, however, insofar as they require specific forms of proof, for example, uniform written scripts for any oral communications and uniform training of sales agents. While training and the existence of scripts are relevant factors, the inquiry should remain focused on whether material variations in the misrepresentations existed. No particular form of evidentiary proof is mandated. The absence of uniform written sales scripts and training informs the determination whether material variations existed; it does not mandate a particular result. Thus, the fact that sales agents submitted affidavits that they did not participate in training programs or follow scripts, even if uncontroverted, is insufficient to demonstrate by itself that the misrepresentations themselves were not materially uniform.

Even though we believe that material uniformity in the misrepresentations may be established without the use of a standardized sales script, in the present case the district court did not abuse its discretion in denying the motion for class certification. Plaintiffs provided substantial evidence of a centralized sales scheme. For example, PaineWebber prepared marketing materials centrally and trained its brokers to emphasize the Provider's investment features. Several scripts provided evidence that PaineWebber sought to sell the Provider by downplaying the fact that the Provider was, simply, life insurance. But this evidence does not answer the relevant question—whether members of the class received materially uniform misrepresentations. Only if class members received materially uniform misrepresentations can generalized proof be used to establish any element of the fraud. The common scheme presented here does not demonstrate that the individual misrepresentations made were uniform. . . .

Even the evidence presented by plaintiffs shows that there were, in fact, material variations in the sales pitches used by their brokers. One customer complaint states that the broker misrepresented the Provider as a retirement program with insurance benefits; another states that the broker represented that the Provider was an IRA; a third specifically states that the broker never mentioned that the Provider was a life insurance product. Similarly, the telephone scripts upon which plaintiffs rely vary significantly. . . . Plaintiffs' evidence demonstrates that PaineWebber's disclosures regarding the Provider's insurance nature varied dramatically. . . .

For the reasons stated, we affirm the district court's denial of plaintiffs' class certification motion.

1. **Material Variation.** The Federal Rules of Civil Procedure Advisory Committee attempted to provide guidance about weighing predominance in a fraud case. In notes to the 1966 amendment of federal Rule 23(b)(3), the Advisory committee stated:

> [A] fraud perpetrated on numerous persons by the use of similar misrepresentations may be an appealing situation for a class action, and it may remain so despite the need, if liability is found, for separate determination of the damages suffered by individuals within the class. On the other hand, although having some common core, a fraud case may be unsuited for treatment as a class action if there was material variation in the representations made or in the kinds or degrees of reliance by the persons to whom they were addressed.

The *Moore* court cited this note and applied the "material variation" standard.

2. **Disposition of common issues and the individualized issues that remain.** When deciding whether common issues predominate, a court may also look to "what value the resolution of the class-wide issue will have in each class member's underlying cause of action." *Klay v. Humana, Inc.,* 382 F.3d 1241, 1255 (11th Cir. 2004). If after the class-wide issues have been adjudicated, "plaintiffs must still introduce a great deal of individualized proof or argue a number of individualized legal points to establish most or all of the elements of their individual claims, such claims are not suitable for class certification under Rule 23(b)(3)." *Id.* If a class had been certified in *Moore*, what individualized proof would have been required after adjudication of class-wide issues? Would resolution of the class-wide issues first have materially assisted the plaintiffs in establishing their individual cases?

3. **Discovering and proving common representations and differences.** In a class certification fight, plaintiffs attempt to highlight the defendant's conduct that is common with respect to each class member. Not surprisingly, the defendants attempt to discover and note differences between class member claims. In *Moore*, what evidence did the court note that tended to establish common representations? What evidence did the court note that showed material variations among the class members? If you represented the plaintiff or the defendant, what kind of information would you seek in discovery and how would you present that information to the court?

MILES v. AMERICA ONLINE, INC.

202 F.R.D. 297 (M.D. Fla. 2001)

MOODY, J. . . .

Plaintiff Marguerite Miles ("Miles") filed a class action Complaint against Defendant America Online, Inc. ("AOL") for violations of Florida's Deceptive and Unfair Trade Practices Act, § 501 *et seq.,* Fla. Stat. ("FDUTPA") and for fraud and fraudulent inducement by omission. . . .

Plaintiffs' claims focus on AOL's conduct in signing up customers for its internet access service through what Plaintiffs describe as a "uniform, standardized advertising and promotional campaign" that induced consumers to subscribe to and use AOL's internet access service for a "low monthly fee varying in price but averaging $19.95 per month for the use of the service." Plaintiffs further allege that AOL deceived its subscribers by stating that their monthly fee would be "fixed" at $19.95 for "unlimited" internet access. It is Plaintiffs' contention that AOL failed to disclose, or failed to effectively disclose, that its subscribers would most likely incur long distance telephone charges in addition to their monthly AOL fee. . . .

[Plaintiffs proposed two national classes, one of which "includes all AOL consumers from February 15, 1996, to present who subscribed to

AOL through an access number and who incurred long distance charges through a "local access number." The other concerned consumers whose computer configurations were damaged. The court discussed its subject matter jurisdiction and then addressed the class certification arguments.]

The parties do not appear to contest the requirements of Rule 23(a), commonly referred to as numerosity, typicality, commonality, and adequacy of representation. Instead, the central class certification dispute is in the application of Rule 23(b)(3), commonly referred to as the predominance of common issues of fact or law.

... Plaintiffs' argument in support of class certification is founded upon the contention that their proof of AOL's deceptive advertising scheme so clearly presents common and predominant factual and legal issues, that class certification is the only reasonable and efficient way for this Court to address the hundreds of claims that exist as a result of AOL's conduct. [Furthermore, Plaintiffs point out that AOL's defense to this action is that it has adequately disclosed to its consumers in its "Terms of Service" agreement the potential of incurring long distance charges in connection with its internet service. Plaintiffs contend that this "adequate and uniform disclosure" defense is just another example of how common issues predominate this case, making it an appropriate one for class action status.]

AOL's central theme in opposition to class certification is that individualized issues of reliance and causation defeat any commonality of fact and law and clearly predominate over class-wide issues. ... AOL's response highlights the deposition testimony of Plaintiff Miles to show that she knew that she was dialing a long distance number when she accessed AOL. Thus, AOL urges that class status is inappropriate because there is undisputed evidence from one of the named Plaintiffs that establishes individual circumstances that bear directly on the issue of reliance, a necessary element of Plaintiff's fraud and deception claims. AOL contends that individual issues of other potential class members' knowledge of long distance and local access numbers and their reliance thereon preclude class certification. In summary, AOL's argument is that "individualized proof" of facts required in what AOL calls a "classic fraud case" make this lawsuit inappropriate for class action status.

[After the court concluded that plaintiffs had established numerosity, commonality, typicality and adequacy of representation under Rule 23(a), the court began its analysis of Rule 23(b)(3).]

As Rule 23's Advisory Notes warn, a fraud case may not be well-suited for class status due to "material variations in the representations made or in the kinds or degrees of reliance by the persons to whom they were addressed." However, the Advisory Notes also find it appealing to use a class device to resolve cases involving "fraud perpetrated on numerous persons by the use of similar misrepresentations." The Court is persuaded that this case is more similar to the latter circumstance and finds common issues of law and fact predominate over questions affecting individual members as to the provision of internet access service to AOL's customers. Mindful of the issue of individualized reliance that Defendant argues apply to the facts of this case, the Court has fashioned a more narrowly defined class to achieve the economics of time, effort and expense and promote uniformity of decision to similarly situated individuals without sacrificing procedural fairness.

Under Rule 23(b)(3), the predominance of common questions is not the only inquiry to determine whether class certification is appropriate. The Court must also look to determine if class representation is "superior" to other available methods for fair and efficient adjudication of the controversy. To do so, the Rule 23(b)(3) identifies a "non exhaustive" list of "matters pertinent to these findings: (A) the interest of members of the class in individually controlling the prosecution or defense of separate actions; (B) the extent and nature of any litigation concerning the controversy already commenced by or against members of the class; (C) the desirability or undesirability of concentrating the litigation of the claims in the particular forum; (D) the difficulties likely to be encountered in the management of a class action."

As to these other issues, Plaintiffs have supplemented the record with numerous letters from AOL customers complaining of excessive long distance bills. Plaintiffs explain that these letters (a "representative sample" of 4700 written complaints) are from only one of AOL's six call centers. Accordingly, there are likely to be thousands of potential class members, most of whom would probably not pursue individual lawsuits (especially if the individual had to pursue the claim in Virginia pursuant to AOL's forum selection clause). Each individual's amount is fairly minimal and the cost large for each member to proceed individually against AOL. Plaintiffs' counsel contends that they know of no other lawsuits concerning this controversy.

.... the Court is satisfied that the economic reality of this case, in terms of time, effort and expense, makes class litigation the superior method for adjudication.

The Class Definition

In order to be certified, a class must be identifiable and clearly defined so as to be "ascertainable without a prolonged and individualized analytical struggle". ...

Thus, to identify a class in this case, the Court finds that Plaintiffs are entitled to certification of a class of individuals who they claim may have been harmed by AOL's conduct, but a class that reflects Defendant's concern that individualized issues of reliance predominate in a proposed class consisting of all consumers using AOL's internet access service. Accordingly, the Court hereby certifies a class of those individuals targeted by AOL's marketing program for its internet access service, who used AOL's service and incurred long distance charges and for whom reliance may be inferred by the class members conduct. Specifically, the class shall include all AOL members, past or present, who received long distance charges incurred in connection with using AOL's internet access service (through the promotional campaign in question) and who either (1) discontinued AOL's service within seventy-five (75) days of the date of incurring the first long distance charge, or (2) changed their AOL access number within seventy-five (75) days of incurring the first long distance charge, or (3) communicated with AOL in writing within six (6) months of incurring the first long distance charge.

[The court then refused to certify a second class and directed the plaintiffs to provide written notice to class members.]

1. **Defining the class.** A court looking at class certification issues need not only accept a proposed class or reject it. As in *Miles*, the court may redefine the class to include only claimants for whom common issues predominate. Often under state statutes which require proof of reliance, or even causation, defendants will focus on the need to establish individual reliance for each class member in order to defeat class certification. Look at the way in which the *Miles* court got around the need for an individualized showing of reliance by each class plaintiff.

2. **Proving Reliance and Causation By Circumstantial Evidence.** In *Miles*, the court permitted certain objective actions, such as changing an access number or discontinuing service, to provide circumstantial evidence of reliance. In some cases, courts have gone further and ruled that merely entering into a transaction may provide sufficient evidence to establish plaintiffs' reliance or causation on a class-wide basis. For example, in *Klay v. Humana, Inc.*, 382 F.3d 1241 (11th Cir. 2004), a purported class of physicians asserted RICO claims against HMOs alleging that the HMOs engaged in a variety of predicate acts systematically designed to withhold or substantially delay reimbursements due to the physicians. The court held that the physicians could establish reliance class-wide simply because the physicians entered into provider agreements with the HMOs. "It does not strain credulity to conclude that each plaintiff, in entering into contracts with the defendants, relied upon the defendants' representations and assumed they would be paid the amounts they were due."

3. **Presuming reliance or causation.** However, courts sometimes also say that they will not presume reliance or causation for absent class members, which would impermissibly permit class plaintiffs to avoid proving an element of their claim. In *Oshana v. The Coca–Cola Company*, 225 F.R.D. 575 (N.D. Ill. 2005), the court rejected certification of a class which alleged, under the Illinois Consumer Fraud Act, that Coca–Cola employed a deceptive marketing scheme that concealed and misled consumers into believing that Diet Coke from the fountain is the same product as Diet Coke sold in a can or bottle. For each of the class plaintiffs to establish "proximate cause" he or she had to prove awareness of the allegedly deceptive acts and misstatements as well as causation—that he or she would not have purchased Diet Coke without the deception. The plaintiffs could not establish these requirements simply by proof of the plaintiffs' purchase.

4. **Circumstantial evidence or prohibited presumption?** It is a fine line between letting individual entry into a transaction count as circumstantial evidence of reliance or causation, which courts sometimes permit, and presuming reliance or causation for absent class members, which courts say they would not permit. Perhaps the issue is what inferences can fairly be drawn from the plaintiffs' conduct. Can an inference of reliance or causation be proved by the consumer's entry into the transaction in the following circumstances? Consumers were sold automobile "waxes" but the products applied contained no wax and are allegedly inferior to protectants that contain actual wax. *Garner v. Healy,* 184 F.R.D. 598 (N.D. Ill. 1999). Casino patrons challenged as deceptive the design of computerized, video poker games whose appearance suggests that the probability of obtaining a particular result is the same as if the game were played with an actual deck of cards, when in fact the probabilities differ because of the nature of the computer programming. *Poulos v. Caesars World, Inc.*, 379 F.3d 654 (9th Cir. 2004).

5. **Damages.** The presence of individualized issues in calculating the amount of damages in itself will generally not prevent a finding that common issues of fact predominate. "Particularly where damages can be computed according to some formula, statistical analysis, or other easy or essentially mechanical methods, the fact that damages must be calculated on an individual basis is no impediment to class certification." *Klay v. Humana, Inc.*, 382 F.3d 1241, 1259–60 (11th Cir. 2004).

6. **Statutory Damages.** Under a number of state statutes, statutory minimum damages are available, allowing plaintiffs to recover the greater of actual damages or from twenty-five dollars, see MASS. GEN. LAWS ch. 93A § 9(3), to two thousand dollars per violation, see UTAH CODE § 13–5–14. The availability of such remedies for violations resulting in smaller monetary damages may ease class plaintiffs' burden to obtain class certification when the class can establish liability but no effective means to calculate damages class wide. See *Smilow v. Southwestern Bell Mobile Sys.,* 323 F.3d 32, 42–43 (1st Cir. 2003). But see, N.Y. C.P.L.R. § 901(b) (McKinney 2005) (not allowing class action recovery of statutory minimum damages unless specifically authorized by statute).

7. **Nationwide Classes.** If the court decides that it can exercise jurisdiction over a nationwide class action, but the substantive laws of a number of states would apply to the class claims, class plaintiffs must show through an " 'extensive analysis' of state law variances, 'that class certification does not present insuperable obstacles' " to a finding that common issues predominate. *Walsh v. Ford Motor Company,* 807 F.2d 1000, 1017 (D.C. Cir. 1986). If variations in state law are substantial, the need to account for these variations at trial would "swamp any common issues and defeat predominance." *Castano v. American Tobacco Co.,* 84 F.3d 734, 741 (5th Cir. 1996); *Fisher v. Bristol–Myers Squibb Co.*, 181 F.R.D. 365, 371–72 (N.D. Ill. 1998).

Given the impediments to nationwide class actions based on state law causes of action, federal statutes such as RICO may become more attractive vehicles for plaintiffs seeking to maintain a nationwide class. Nonetheless, differences in state law may also prevent the certification of nationwide RICO claims alleging racketeering activity defined under 18 U.S.C. § 1961(1)(A), criminal violations under state law. For example, in *Schwartz v. The Upper Deck Company*, 183 F.R.D. 672 (S.D. Cal. 1999), the court refused to certify a class alleging that the inserting of special "chase cards" (containing for example an autograph or a piece of a jersey) into a small percentage of packages of sports cards constituted an illegal lottery or gambling, because of the need to evaluate the defendant's alleged conduct under the gambling laws of 50 states.

(b) Superiority

The second prong of federal Rule 23(b)(3) requires the court to make a final determination that a "class action is superior to other available methods for the fair and efficient adjudication of the controversy." The focus is not on the convenience or burden of a class action suit *per se*, since any class action will be a burden, but on "the relative advantages of a class action suit over whatever other forms of litigation might be realistically available to the plaintiffs." *Klay v. Humana, Inc.*, 382 F.3d 1241, 1269 (11th Cir. 2004).

CARNEGIE v. HOUSEHOLD INTERNATIONAL, INC.,

376 F.3d 656 (7th Cir. 2004).

POSNER, J. . . .

The litigation arose out of refund anticipation loans made jointly by the defendants, who for simplicity we'll refer to as "the bank" and "the tax preparer." When the tax preparer files a refund claim with the Internal Revenue Service on behalf of one of its customers, the customer can expect to receive the refund within a few weeks unless the IRS decides to investigate the return. Even a few weeks is too long for the most necessitous taxpayers, and so the bank will lend the customer the amount of the refund for the period between the filing of the claim and the receipt of the refund. The annual interest rate on such a "refund anticipation loan" (RAL) will often exceed 100 percent. Although the bank is the lender, the tax preparer arranges the loan. It is contended that the customer is told neither that the bank pays the tax preparer a fee for having generated the loan nor that the tax preparer receives an ownership interest in the loan.

Beginning in 1990 a number of class-action suits were brought against the defendants on behalf of a total of 17 million refund-anticipation borrowers, charging violations of various state and federal laws, including RICO. The basic claim is that the defendants lead the borrowers to believe that the tax preparer is their fiduciary, much as if they had hired a lawyer or an accountant to prepare their income tax returns, as affluent people do, whereas, unbeknownst to them, the tax preparer is engaged in self-dealing. This conduct is alleged to constitute a scheme to defraud in violation of the federal mail-and wire-fraud statutes. Violations of those statutes are "predicate offenses" that can form the basis of a RICO charge.

In 1999 the named plaintiff in one of the suits entered into a settlement agreement with the bank and the tax preparer. This was to be a "global" settlement: the members of all the classes would divide up a $25 million fund put up by the defendants in exchange for the release of all claims arising out of the RALs. The district judge approved the settlement and enjoined (with one exception) the other RAL class actions, but we reversed, on the ground that the district judge had failed to scrutinize the fairness of the settlement adequately. We were concerned that the settlement might have been the product of collusion between the defendants, eager to minimize their liability, and the class lawyers, eager to maximize their fees.

The district judge to whom the case was reassigned on remand concluded that the settlement had indeed been unfair and disapproved it. There was no appeal. The proceedings continued in the district court, with both the named plaintiff and the class counsel replaced. Although no class had formally been certified in the earlier proceedings, rather than require the new plaintiff to move for certification the judge asked the defendants for their objections to certification, and they responded. She agreed with some of the objections, rejected others, and, in effect, certified the same class that had been contemplated by the rejected settlement, which is to say all RAL borrowers (with a few exceptions) whose claims weren't barred by the statute of limitations. But she limited the certification to prosecution of just the RICO claim, plus one breach of contract claim involving the law of only one state.

The defendants object mainly to the procedure the judge employed and to the brevity with which she pronounced the class manageable despite its vast size. In the previous round of this protracted litigation the defendants had urged the district court to accept the giant class as appropriate for a global settlement, had prevailed in their urging, and so are now precluded by the doctrine of judicial estoppel, from challenging its adequacy, at least as a settlement class (the significance of this qualification will appear in due course). . . . The reason lies in the purpose of the doctrine. . . . [which is] to reduce fraud in the legal process by forcing a modicum of consistency on a repeating litigant.

. . . [T]he defendants benefited from the temporary approval of the settlement, which they used to enjoin other RAL litigation against them; and having reaped a benefit from their pertinacious defense of the class treatment of the case for purposes of settlement they cannot now be permitted to seek a further benefit from reversing their position.

. . . The defendants are correct, however, that a class might be suitable for settlement but not for litigation. The class might be unmanageable if the case were actually tried yet manageable as a settlement class because the settlement might eliminate all the thorny issues that the court would have to resolve if the parties fought out the case. *Amchem Products, Inc. v. Windsor,* 521 U.S. 591, 620, 117 S.Ct. 2231, 138 L.Ed.2d 689 (1997). But although the district judge might have said more about manageability, the defendants have said nothing against it except that there are millions of class members. That is no argument at all. The more claimants there are, the more likely a class action is to yield substantial economies in litigation. It would hardly be an improvement to have in lieu of this single class action 17 million suits each seeking damages of $15 to $30. The rejected settlement capped damages at these amounts for single and multiple RALs respectively, and while the amounts may be too low they are indicative of the modest stakes of the individual class members. The *realistic* alternative to a class action is not 17 million individual suits, but zero individual suits, as only a lunatic or a fanatic sues for $30. But a class action has to be unwieldy indeed before it can be pronounced an inferior alternative—no matter how massive the fraud or other wrongdoing that will go unpunished if class treatment is denied—to no litigation at all.

... We are mindful that no district judge has as yet explicitly addressed whether the other criteria for class certification, besides adequacy of representation of the class, have been met in this case. Those criteria are whether "(1) the class is so numerous that joinder of all members is impracticable; (2) there are questions of law or fact common to the class; (3) the claims or defenses of the representative parties are typical of the claims or defenses of the class." Fed.R.Civ.P. 23(a). There is no need for a remand on these questions, however. Criteria (1) and (2) have been met; and the satisfaction of (3) is implicit in Judge Bucklo's rejection of the defendants' contention that to handle their dispute with the class members in the class action format would be unmanageable. There has been substantial compliance with the requirements of the rule, and no more is required, especially in a case in which the defendants were enthusiastic proponents of class treatment until their opportunistic change of heart.

AFFIRMED.

1. **Factors for determining superiority of a class action.** Although the superiority test permits the court to weigh a variety of factors, two factors generally determine whether a class action suit is considered to be superior to other methods of adjudication—predominance of common issues and the size of individual claims. Predominance, is of course, the first criterion in the Rule 23(b)(3) test, but it is also "intertwined" with the efficiency factor in the second part of the standard. Typically, the more that common issues predominate over individual issues, the more efficient a class action will be and the more manageable trial of the suit will be. See *Jackson v. Motel 6 Multipurpose, Inc.,* 130 F.3d 999, 1006 n.12 (11th Cir. 1997). Under the second factor, to preserve a remedy for individuals with smaller claims, courts are more likely to overlook other factors arguing against class certification. As Judge Posner noted in *Carnegie*, the realistic alternative to a class action when class member claims are small would be no action at all, "as only a

lunatic or fanatic sues for $30." Yet even after class certification and litigation of the liability issue in *Carnegie*, the court notes that further proceedings could be needed to determine the relief to which individual class members would be entitled. If only a lunatic or fanatic would have pursued such small-scale litigation before class certification, would you expect many more claimants to take part in a damages phase after liability had been determined? If not, why certify a class?

2. **Rethinking *Moore*.** In a later part of *Carnegie*, the court took issue with a case that refused to certify a RICO class action on the ground that issues about whether defendant had engaged in a pattern of racketeering would be swamped in the litigation by individual issues about whether each plaintiff had been injured by reason that violation. The *Carnegie* court wrote, "whether RICO was violated can be separated from the question whether particular intended victims were injured, and thus can ... be resolved in a single proceeding with the issue of injury parceled out to satellite proceedings, as is frequently done in class action tort litigation." *Id.* At 663. Looking back at the *Moore* case, should the court have certified a class action there with respect to the misrepresentations themselves if not with respect to issues about the damages caused to individual claimants?

3. **Size of Individual Claims.** One difference between *Moore* and *Carnegie* is that the amount of money at issue for each claim holder in *Moore* was much greater. As the stakes and sophistication of the potential class members increase, it may be more appropriate to deny class status. As noted in Rule 23(b)(3) the court should consider "the interest of members of the class in individually controlling the prosecution or defense of separate actions." Presumably, plaintiffs with a greater amount of money at issue will have a greater interest in controlling the litigation themselves. See, e.g., *Liberty Mutual Insurance Co. v. Tribco Construction Co.,* 185 F.R.D. 533 (E.D. Ill. 1999) (noting that each of the 220 purported corporate class plaintiffs paid annual insurance premiums of $690,000 and that several similarly situated firms had separately brought suit). However, in practice, could granting class action status for very small claims but not for mid-size claims result in plaintiffs receiving recoveries for deceptive practices that cause them small injuries (through class action litigation), but not for claims that are somewhat larger (and would require the filing of an individual action)?

4. **Settlement Classes.** In many cases, as in *Carnegie*, the named plaintiff and the defendant reach a settlement agreement prior to the plaintiff's moving for class certification. So-called "settlement classes" eliminate the manageability requirement of Rule 23(b)(3), but still require the court to protect the interests of absent class members who will be bound by any class settlement entered:

> Confronted with a request for settlement-only class certification, a district court need not inquire whether the case, if tried, would present intractable management problems for the proposal is that there be no trial. But other specifications of the Rule—those de-

> signed to protect absentees by blocking unwarranted or overbroad class definitions—demand undiluted, even heightened, attention in the settlement context. Such attention is of vital importance, for a court asked to certify a settlement class will lack the opportunity, present when a case is litigated, to adjust the class, informed by the proceedings as they unfold.
>
> Settlement, though a relevant factor, does not inevitably signal that class-action certification should be granted more readily than it would be were the case to be litigated. Proposed settlement classes sometimes warrant more, not less, caution on the question of certification.

Amchem Products, Inc. v. Windsor, 521 U.S. 591, 620–21 (1997). The opinion in *Carnegie*, which cites *Amchem,* seems to be animated in part by condemnation for the defendants' tactics—being "enthusiastic proponents of class treatment" when a vast class meant a broad-ranging and relatively cheap release, but having an "opportunistic change of heart" when class certification might yield more significant relief for the class.

5. **Strawn v. Canuso.** In *Strawn*, presented in § 1 of this chapter, the trial court had originally denied class certification and granted summary judgment against the named plaintiffs based on its ruling that the defendant developers and brokers had no duty to disclose. Once the New Jersey Supreme Court held that there was a duty to disclose and remanded, should the district court on remand certify a class?

Chapter 16

THE SPECIAL CASE OF LAWYER MALPRACTICE

NOTE: THE SCOPE OF LAWYER MALPRACTICE AND THE ECONOMIC LOSS RULE

In Chapter 12, ¶ 10, supra, we saw that the economic loss rule does not foreclose malpractice claims against lawyers, where courts have emphasized the special relationship of lawyer and client. See *Collins v. Reynard,* 154 Ill.2d 48, 180 Ill.Dec. 672, 607 N.E.2d 1185 (1992); *Clark v. Rowe,* 428 Mass. 339, 701 N.E.2d 624 (1998). Perhaps the central point is that, when you retain someone for the express purpose of being on your side, he cannot rightly contract to be your adversary instead. That may not be the end of the story, because surely lawyers can limit the scope of their representation by contract, even if they cannot avoid their duties of care and fiducial responsibility within that relationship. But we turn to malpractice claims in tort, leaving to some other book the lawyer's contractual opportunities for limiting liability.

Lawyer malpractice claims assert negligence or other breach of duty by a lawyer to a client as part of, or at least in the course of, a representation. In this respect, a "client" can sometimes include a third-party beneficiary. However, claims by clients that do not involve matters included in the representation are not malpractice claims. The lawyer who runs his client down in a crosswalk is guilty of negligence, but not the kind of negligence we call malpractice. Strangers may have good claims against lawyers for, say, interference with contract, but if the stranger is not entitled to the lawyer's representation or fiduciary duty, the claim is not for malpractice but something else altogether.

The lawyer is a fiduciary to the client. Some claims against lawyers are ordinary professional negligence claims, such as those based on the lawyer's failure to file a complaint within the statute of limitations. Other claims, though, are grounded in the special duties of a fiduciary, whether these are considered to be "malpractice" or something else.

§ 1. THE BASES OF LIABILITY

WINNICZEK v. NAGELBERG

394 F.3d 505 (7th Cir. 2005)

POSNER, Circuit Judge.

The district court dismissed for failure to state a claim a diversity suit that charges breach of contract, legal malpractice, and breach of fiduciary duty, all in violation of Illinois law. The plaintiffs are Hilary Winniczek and his wife, Danuta; the defendant is a lawyer, Sheldon Nagelberg. The complaint, our only source of facts, alleges the following. Winniczek was charged with a variety of federal criminal offenses arising from his participation in a scheme to help people obtain commercial drivers' licenses fraudulently. He hired a lawyer named Petro to represent him. Nagelberg got wind of the matter and advised the Winniczeks that Petro was inexperienced in federal criminal matters and they should fire Petro and hire him; and they did so. Nagelberg then told them that Winniczek had a good defense to the criminal charges but that it would cost the Winniczeks $150,000 in fees, plus $20,000 in expenses, to present the defense. They paid him the $170,000 over the course of the year preceding the scheduled date of the criminal trial. As soon as Nagelberg was fully paid, he told the Winniczeks that he wouldn't take the case to trial because Winniczek had made statements to the authorities when he was represented by Petro that scotched any defense he might have had, and as a result Winniczek had no choice but to plead guilty. Nagelberg then departed the scene and another lawyer represented Winniczek at the plea hearing. Winniczek pleaded guilty and was sentenced to 22 months in prison.

Winniczek does not claim to be innocent of the crimes for which he was convicted, and this dooms his claim for legal malpractice. (His wife, not having been represented by Nagelberg, obviously has no malpractice claim.) Under Illinois law, as that of other states, a criminal defendant cannot bring a suit for malpractice against his attorney merely upon proof that the attorney failed to meet minimum standards of professional competence and that had he done so the defendant would have been acquitted on some technicality; the defendant (that is, the malpractice plaintiff) must also prove that he was actually innocent of the crime, which Winniczek cannot prove. This "actual innocence" rule presumably has an exception for the case in which, although the defendant is guilty, he received an unlawful penalty; ... but the exception would not be applicable to Winniczek either.

The "actual innocence" rule differs from the rule applicable to malpractice arising out of civil matters. There the only requirement is, as in all tort cases, that the plaintiff prove he was injured by the defendant's negligence. If the malpractice involved the handling of a lawsuit, all he has to prove is that he would have won had it not been for the lawyer's negligence. It would be irrelevant that the negligence had consisted in failing to make a purely technical argument.

The reason for the difference is not that criminals are disfavored litigants, though there are hints of such a rationale in some cases. It is that the scope for collateral attacks on judgments is broader in criminal than in civil matters. A criminal defendant can establish ineffective assistance of counsel, the counterpart to malpractice, and thus get his conviction vacated, by proving that had it not been for his lawyer's failure to come up to minimum professional standards, he would have been acquitted. He can do this even if, as in a case in which his only defense was that illegally seized evidence had been used against him, the ground for acquittal would have been unrelated to innocence. Since a criminal defendant thus has a good remedy for his lawyer's malpractice—namely to get his conviction voided—he has less need for a damages remedy than the loser of a civil lawsuit, who would have no chance of getting the judgment in the suit set aside just because his lawyer had booted a good claim or defense.

This analysis shows that the logic of the "actual innocence" rule does not extend to a case in which the complaint is not that the plaintiff lost his case because of his lawyer's negligence, but that he was overcharged. The fact that one of the plaintiffs, namely Mrs. Winniczek, wasn't even charged with a crime merely underscores the district court's error. She is seeking restitution of money obtained from her by false pretenses or breach of an implied contract. But so is Winniczek, in count one of the complaint, which is for breach of contract or, what need not be distinguished in this case ... breach of the fiduciary obligation that Nagelberg, as Winniczek's lawyer, owed him. ...

To see why count one is not about malpractice, imagine that Nagelberg had promised to represent Winniczek for a fee of $50,000, plus $25,000 in prepaid expenses of which any amount not expended was to be returned to Winniczek. Suppose further that Nagelberg had done a superb though ultimately unsuccessful job in representing Winniczek but had incurred expenses of only $5,000 and refused to refund the balance of the $25,000 in prepaid expenses. There would be no malpractice, in the sense of incompetent representation—and there would be nothing in the thinking behind the actual-innocence rule to suggest that Winniczek should not be allowed to enforce his contract just because he had been convicted. So we are not surprised that the courts that have confronted this type of case—no Illinois court has—have held that the actual-innocence rule is not a bar. [Citing *Bird, Marella, Boxer & Wolpert v. Superior Court,* 106 Cal. App. 4th 419, 130 Cal. Rptr. 2d 782 (2003), and other cases.]

It is true that the narrative portion of count one accuses Nagelberg not only of overcharging and of charging for services not rendered but also of being careless, for example in failing to read the statements by Winniczek to the authorities that showed he had no defense. But the fact that a breach of contract is negligent rather than willful does not change the character of the breach. Sometimes a contract is broken willfully, sometimes unavoidably (circumstances beyond the promisor's control, but not rising to the level at which he would have a defense of impossibility or *force majeure,* might have prevented him from fulfilling his promise), and sometimes carelessly (the promisor should have realized he couldn't fulfill his promise—that he had bitten off more than he could chew). Since liability for breach of contract is, in general, strict liability, the cause, character, and mental element of the breach usually are immaterial. . . .

[T]here is no basis in Illinois law for supposing that filing a complaint with the ARDC is a condition precedent to bringing a suit against one's attorney for breach of contract just because the breach may also have involved a violation of the attorney's ethical duties.

Nor is there a basis for supposing that only the court in which, as it were, the breach of the lawyer's contract with his client occurred has exclusive jurisdiction over the contract suit. That is not the rule in ordinary civil malpractice, and there is no reason to make it the rule in a case—which is not even a malpractice case—arising from a criminal proceeding. . . .

The dismissal of count two is affirmed, but the dismissal of count one is reversed and the case remanded for further proceedings consistent with this opinion.

1. **Actual innocence or guilt-in-fact as affirmative defense.** A number of courts follow the rule in *Winniczek* that the plaintiff complaining of a criminal conviction must prove innocence in fact. In *Shaw v. State,* 861 P.2d 566 (Alaska 1993), the court agreed that the plaintiff's innocence or guilt-in-fact was relevant, but did not require the plaintiff to prove it. Instead, the court cast guilt-in-fact as an affirmative defense with the burden upon the defendant.

2. **Exoneration.** Most courts require that the plaintiff must prove exoneration through post-conviction proceedings of some kind independent of the innocence-in-fact rule. See *Gibson v. Trant,* 58 S.W.3d 103 (Tenn. 2001) (relying on the practical impossibility of proving that malpractice caused harm and on collateral estoppel/issue preclusion); *Peeler v. Hughes & Luce,* 909 S.W.2d 494 (Tex. 1995). The Texas Court thought that absent such proof, the conclusion was inescapable that the plaintiff's own crime was the sole proximate cause of her conviction. In *Canaan v. Bartee,* 276 Kan. 116, 72 P.3d 911 (2003), the court listed arguments for requiring exoneration: "[P]rinciples against shifting responsibility for the consequences of the criminal's action; the paradoxical difficulties of awarding damages to a guilty person; theoretical and practical difficulties of proving causation; the potential undermining of the postconviction process if a legal malpractice action overrules the judgments entered in the postconviction proceedings; preserving judicial economy by avoiding relitigation of settled matters; creation of a bright line rule determining when the statute of limitations runs on the

malpractice action; availability of alternative postconviction remedies; and the chilling effect on thorough defense lawyering."

3. **Where the lawyer has a conflict of interest.** *Krahn v. Kinney,* 43 Ohio St. 3d 103, 538 N.E.2d 1058 (1989), rejected any rule requiring the plaintiff to show that her conviction was reversed or that she had ineffective assistance of counsel. The plaintiff there was a bar manager who allowed Shaffer to place a game machine in the bar. The plaintiff gave customers credits for their successes on the machine, which led to a charge of first degree misdemeanor gambling. Her attorney allegedly represented both her and Shaffer without revealing that fact. Shaffer wanted to get the confiscated machine back. Here's the alleged malpractice: the prosecutor offered to drop charges against the plaintiff if she'd testify against Shaffer. The attorney did not advise the plaintiff of this opportunity. In the end, she pleaded guilty to a first degree misdemeanor. These allegations, if true, would represent a terrible conflict of interest. Should Krahn be regarded as a "minority view" or as a case distinguishable from cases like *Winniczek v. Nagelberg*?

4. **Exoneration rule and the statute of limitations.** In *Coscia v. McKenna & Cuneo,* 25 Cal. 4th 1194, 108 Cal. Rptr. 2d 471, 25 P.3d 670 (2001), the court held that the plaintiff claiming criminal-law malpractice leading to a conviction by plea or trial must show that (a) he is innocent and (b) has been exonerated on appeal or in post-conviction proceedings. To avoid unfair application of the statute of limitations, the plaintiff can file the malpractice suit before he is exonerated and move to stay it while he establishes his innocence. Saying the majority was otherwise, *Morrison v. Goff,* 91 P.3d 1050 (Colo. 2004), adopted a similar view. What if the trial judge, in his discretion, denies the stay?

5. **Scope of the rules?** Why should the plaintiff be barred if she is guilty in fact of a lesser included crime but not the crime of which she was negligently convicted?

6. **A demanding proof standard for the plaintiff?** In *Bailey v. Tucker,* 533 Pa. 237, 621 A.2d 108 (1993), the court accepted the innocence in fact and the exoneration rules and added that the criminal-law malpractice plaintiff must also prove not only that the lawyer was chargeable with professional negligence but was also reckless or wanton in his disregard of the client's interests. The court expressed concern that without these limitations, criminal defense attorneys would practice defensive lawyering, substituting client wishes for independent judgment.

WARTNICK v. MOSS & BARNETT

490 N.W.2d 108 (Minn. 1992)

GARDEBRING, Justice.

This case arises out of a malpractice action filed by Norman Wartnick against his attorney Phillip Gainsley and Gainsley's law firm Moss & Barnett. After Norman Wartnick's former employee and recent competitor Robert Nachtsheim, Sr. (the decedent) was murdered in May 1973, Wartnick retained Gainsley as counsel during the police investigation. Gainsley also advised and assisted Wartnick in recovering the proceeds of a life insurance policy Wartnick's company, Midwest Florist Supply Company (Midwest), had held on the decedent. Gainsley continued to represent Wartnick after Betty Nachtsheim (Nachtsheim), the decedent's widow, sued Wartnick and Midwest for unjust enrichment. Nachtsheim's suit was later consolidated with a wrongful death suit against Wartnick alone.

Gainsley represented Wartnick at the trial of the consolidated actions, in which the jury awarded Nachtsheim $350,000 in damages and $2,000,000 in punitive damages on the wrongful death action. The unjust enrichment action was dismissed. Gainsley also represented Wartnick in his appeal to the court of appeals in which the jury's verdict was affirmed.

[Wartnick's malpractice action against Gainsley was dismissed on summary judgment. The Court of Appeals affirmed the dismissal. Wartnick appeals.]

The underlying facts of this matter are as follows: Norman Wartnick was a shareholder and officer of Midwest, where the decedent [Robert Nachtsheim, Sr.] was a salesperson between 1959 and 1972. In 1970, Wartnick purchased from Prudential Life Insurance Company (Prudential) a $100,000 "key man" life insurance policy on the decedent's life, with Midwest as the named beneficiary. The decedent left Midwest's employ in August 1972, and started a competing business. On May 11, 1973, Wartnick paid the annual life insurance premium on the policy to keep it in effect, despite the fact that the decedent was no longer an employee of Midwest. On May 24, 1973, the decedent was shot in the head at close range, shortly after he arrived for work. No one was ever charged with the murder.

After the decedent's death, Wartnick retained Gainsley to represent him and Midwest in connection with the claim for the life insurance proceeds. Gainsley also represented Wartnick in the on-going police investigation of the murder, advising him not to take a lie detector test, and recommending that Wartnick hire a criminal lawyer to assist Gainsley. Prudential also investigated the murder and, after receiving notice that the Hennepin County Attorney's office would not be indicting Wartnick, paid the life insurance policy proceeds to Midwest.

[Betty] Nachtsheim [the deceased's widow] hired an attorney to represent her in a suit to obtain the insurance proceeds from Wartnick and Midwest. She also wanted to sue Wartnick for wrongful death, because she believed that her husband had been killed for the insurance proceeds. Her attorney was reluctant to bring a suit for wrongful death with so little evidence, and inadvertently let the wrongful death statute of limitations expire before bringing suit. The attorney did, however, file a claim for unjust enrichment against Wartnick and Midwest in 1976.

During the discovery period of this civil suit, Wartnick was deposed. Gainsley and Wartnick have different accounts of the preparation and decision making that took place prior to the deposition. Gainsley asserts that he researched the ramifications of having Wartnick plead the fifth amendment in response to any questions about the murder of the decedent. Gainsley also reports discussing the issue with other lawyers at his firm, and discussing it with Wartnick in "numerous phone conversations," and at a meeting several days before the deposition. Gainsley asserts that Wartnick made an informed decision to take Gainsley's advice and plead the fifth.

Wartnick does not remember meeting with Gainsley prior to the deposition, or receiving any information about the possible negative consequences of pleading the fifth. The only meeting or conversation he remembers regarding the decision to plead the fifth was a meeting in the men's room immediately prior to the deposition. There, according to Wartnick, Gainsley advised him to respond to any questions about the decedent's murder by asserting his fifth amendment privilege against self-incrimination. He gave Wartnick a card to read at the appropriate times. Wartnick followed Gainsley's advice.

[The court noted in a footnote that the "United States Supreme Court has held that the fifth amendment allows an adverse inference to be drawn by the jury in a civil case where a party invokes the fifth amendment privilege against self incrimination. See Baxter v. Palmigiano, 425 U.S. 308, 318, 96 S.Ct. 1551, 1558, 47 L.Ed.2d 810 (1976). In Minnesota, the rule is also that a jury may draw such an adverse inference in a civil case. See Ralph Hegman Co. v. Transamerica Ins. Co., 293 Minn. 323, 198 N.W.2d 555, 557 (1972). . . . In the instant case, after the statute of limitations was amended, it appears that the finder of fact's ability to make an adverse inference on the basis of Wartnick's answers in the deposition may have helped the case go to the jury."]

Furnished with Wartnick's unresponsive answers in the deposition Nachtsheim's attorney proceeded to lobby the legislature to amend the wrongful death statute to remove any limitations period for actions to recover damages for "a death caused by an intentional act constituting murder." The attorney drafted and promoted this change as a victim's rights bill. After two unsuccessful attempts, and continued lobbying by the attorney, the bill passed. The amendment applied to "any death or cause of action arising prior to its enactment which resulted from an intentional act constituting murder."

No longer barred by the statute of limitations, Nachtsheim promptly brought a wrongful death action against Wartnick. The unjust enrichment and wrongful death actions were consolidated by stipulation. Prudential, a party in the unjust enrichment suit, settled with Nachtsheim prior to trial. While preparing for the case, Gainsley offered Wartnick for another deposition if opposing counsel would agree not to use the first one. Nachtsheim's attorney refused. Gainsley relied principally on the police file and a deposition of Nachtsheim to gather information about the decedent's murder and construct a defense.

In his opening arguments at trial, Gainsley revealed that although Wartnick had been asked to take a polygraph examination regarding the murder, and was willing, Gainsley had advised against it. Because of his lack of an independent investigation and his reliance on the police reports, during the trial Gainsley had some difficulty getting information into the record. Wartnick's responses in the deposition were read to the jury, and Wartnick testified at the trial. After being instructed that it could draw an adverse inference from Wartnick's fifth amendment assertions in the deposition, the jury found Wartnick had murdered or caused the murder of the decedent. However, the unjust enrichment claim was dismissed because the jury found for Midwest.

In his action against Gainsley, Wartnick asserts five counts of malpractice. These counts, as summarized in Wartnick's brief, are: 1) Instructing Wartnick to assert the Fifth Amendment privilege at his deposition without understanding the legal ramifications of that instruction; 2) Failing to permit Wartnick to make his own informed decision whether to assert the Fifth Amendment privilege; 3) Injecting inadmissible and highly prejudicial evidence into the trial by advising the jury in opening statement that Wartnick had refused to take a polygraph test when requested to do so by the police lieutenant investigating the Nachtsheim murder; 4) Failing to conduct a minimum adequate investigation into the Nachtsheim murder, including failing to interview and depose key witnesses and suspects in the murder; 5) Failing to mitigate the damage caused by his Fifth Amendment instruction by not offering Wartnick unconditionally for a second deposition. . . .

In support of his motion for summary judgment, Gainsley provided deposition testimony of two experts. One of them testified regarding all five malpractice counts, concluding that Gainsley's actions in representing Wartnick were not negligent. The other testified regarding Gainsley's introduction of the polygraph issue in the opening statement, stating that raising the issue himself was in accord with good trial practice. Wartnick provided deposition testimony of five experts, all of whom testified regarding the fifth amendment and polygraph issues, and all of whom believe that Gainsley's actions were negligent. Four of Wartnick's five experts testified on the failure to investigate and failure to mitigate counts, believing that Gainsley's conduct was negligent. . . .

To prove that Gainsley acted negligently, Wartnick must demonstrate a standard of care and show that Gainsley did not meet it. "An attorney is only bound to exercise that degree of care and skill that is reasonable under the circumstances, considering the nature of the undertaking." An attorney's error in judgment will not create liability if it is "within the bounds of an honest exercise of professional judgment." However, this court has qualified the "honest error in judgment" language, stressing that a professional must use reasonable care to obtain the information needed to exercise his or her professional judgment, and failure to use such reasonable care would be negligence, even if done in good faith.

The first two malpractice counts concern Gainsley's advice to Wartnick prior to the deposition taken on February 16, 1979, during discovery in the unjust enrichment action. The record suggests the existence of questions of material fact as to Gainsley's understanding of the ramifications of his fifth amendment advice, the nature of Wartnick's informed decision on the fifth amendment privilege, and the applicable standard of care for attorneys in advising clients faced with the threats of both civil liability and possible criminal prosecution.

However, even if Gainsley was negligent in the delivery of legal services, Wartnick's malpractice claims may still be barred if Gainsley's advice was not the proximate cause of Wartnick's damages. This court has defined proximate cause as follows: For negligence to be the proximate cause of an injury, it must appear that if the act is one which the party ought, in the exercise of ordinary care, to have anticipated was likely to result in injury to others, then he is liable for any injury proximately resulting from it, even though he could not have anticipated the particular injury which did happen. While the general rule is that a negligent actor is responsible for all injuries which proximately result from a negligent action, there is an exception: the doctrine of superseding cause. The doctrine of superseding cause recognizes that although an actor's negligent actions may have put the plaintiff in the position to be injured, and therefore contributed to the injury, the actual injury may have been caused by an intervening event. That intervention prevents the original negligent actor from being liable for the final injury.

The trial court and the court of appeals concluded, and Gainsley now argues, that the action by the legislature in creating a cause of action which did not even exist at the time of deposition was a superseding cause which vitiates any liability associated with the allegedly negligent advice on the fifth amendment issue. In essence, Gainsley argues, in the words of the trial court, that "the legislative enactment intervened not to insulate the original negligent person, but rather to create a basis for liability that did not otherwise exist."

For an intervening cause to be considered a superseding cause, the intervening cause must satisfy four elements: (1) Its harmful effects must have occurred after the original negligence; (2) it must not have been brought about by the original negligence; (3) it must actively work to bring about a result which would not otherwise have followed from the original negligence; and (4) it must not have been reasonably foreseeable by the original wrongdoer. Unless all four elements are satisfied, an intervening cause cannot be considered superseding.

We conclude that the first element is satisfied because Gainsley's advice was taken and given in 1979 and the statute's amendment and its harmful effects came after the advice was given. We also find that the second element is satisfied, because the statute's amendment was not "brought about" by the advice. Wartnick argues that the advice did indeed bring about the statute's amendment, since Nachtsheim's attorney, armed with Wartnick's responses in the deposition, drafted the statute's amendment and actively lobbied for its passage in the legislature. However, analysis of this element suggests that in this case the connection between the act and the intervening cause is not sufficient to meet the test.

This court earlier held that an intervening cause which is "a normal response to the stimulus of a situation created by [the original] negligence ... will not be considered a superseding cause such that it relieves the original negligent actor." More recently, we held that where an intervening event was "a normal, foreseeable consequence" of the original act, the subsequent act was not a superseding intervening cause as a matter of law. ...

The issue thus becomes whether a change in the wrongful death statute is a "normal response" to Gainsley's advice and Wartnick's answers at the deposition. We conclude that it is not. First, Wartnick hardly maintained a unique position by pleading the fifth amendment to questions regarding his role in a serious felony. It is extraordinary that a change in the law would result from pleading the fifth amendment in a deposition. Second, the legislative action to amend the statute was only indirectly related to Gainsley's advice. While the deposition testimony may have provided incentive for Nachtsheim's attorney to seek a change in the wrongful death statute, the legislative process is exceedingly complex; it is subject to a variety of pressures and forces that are totally outside the power of a lobbyist alone to impact. Consequently, we hold that the change in the statute of limitations cannot be said to be a normal consequence of the advice and subsequent testimony.

The third element will be satisfied if the intervening cause actively works to bring about a result different from that which would have followed from the original negligence. Wartnick argues that the statute's amendment worked to bring about the very same result which Gainsley's alleged negligence brought about: a costly adverse verdict in a civil action. Whether this element is satisfied will depend on the definition of "result." The Restatement calls for an examination of whether: (a) the ... intervention brings about harm different in kind from that which would otherwise have resulted from the actor's negligence. RESTATEMENT (SECOND) OF TORTS, § 442(a) (1965). The issue could be stated as follows: Whether the extension of the statute of limitations for the wrongful death statute brought about a result "different in kind" from that which would have come about from Gainsley's advice alone. By framing the ultimate outcome in terms of pecuniary damage resulting from civil liability, Wartnick has chosen to construe the "result" very broadly. We believe the resulting harm is more narrow, one of liability for a particular cause of action, that of wrongful death. This harm is very different in kind from what would have happened had the law not been changed; a wrongful death action was not even possible before the intervening change in the law. Accordingly, the fact that Wartnick's subsequent liability in the wrongful death action could not "have otherwise resulted" from Gainsley's advice without the intervening change in the statute of limitations persuades us that the third element is satisfied.

The fourth element necessary to establish the presence of a superseding cause is the foreseeability of the intervening act. We have said in earlier cases that "the foreseeability of intervening causes is to be determined as of the time of defendant's acts or omissions." While Wartnick argues that Rieger controls and mandates a conclusion that the legislative enactment was foreseeable, we hold that Gainsley could not foresee a change in the statute of limitations. At the time of Gainsley's allegedly negligent advice, the statute of limitations had run on the wrongful death action and there was no indication that the legislature would act to, in essence, create a cause of action to be applied retroactively. ... Thus, we find the fourth element of the test for superseding cause is met.

The determination of proximate cause is normally a question of fact for the jury. However, if reasonable minds cannot disagree, proximate cause becomes a question of law. We believe reasonable minds cannot disagree that the amendment of the statute to create a whole new cause of action was a superseding cause of Wartnick's damages, and therefore Gainsley's fifth amendment advice, if originally negligent, was not the proximate cause of Wartnick's damages.

We affirm the decision of the trial court and the court of appeals dismissing the first two counts of malpractice regarding the fifth amendment advice.

As to the remaining three counts of malpractice, both Wartnick and Gainsley have provided expert testimony regarding Gainsley's representation of Wartnick at the trial itself. Wartnick asserts that Gainsley's introduction of the polygraph issue in the opening statement, failure to investigate the murder adequately, and failure to mitigate the damage done by original deposition answers did not meet the standard of care of the community. In granting summary judgment on these issues, despite the conflicting expert testimony on the applicable standard of care, the trial court essentially held as a matter of law that Gainsley had not breached the standard of care. The trial court found that the errors, if any, were errors in judgment.

In a professional malpractice action, the plaintiff must present evidence of the applicable standard of care, and that the standard of care was breached. Generally expert testimony is required to establish these issues, unless the conduct can be evaluated by a jury in the absence of expert testimony. This court has never explicitly held that these determinations are for the finder of fact. However, when conflicting expert testimony is given, these questions normally go to the jury. If there are no factual disputes as to the standard of care and whether it was breached, if, for example the plaintiff does not provide necessary expert testimony on the issue, summary judgment is properly granted. There may be errors made by attorneys which do not constitute malpractice as a matter of law but are errors in judgment. However, a failure to meet the minimum standard of care required is not a "mere error in judgment."

Because judges in reviewing courts are lawyers, there is a normal tendency to act as a finder of fact when addressed with these issues of trial preparation and strategy, in a way a judge might not do if the experts were from a field outside law. However, it is the job of the reviewing court when reviewing the grant of a summary judgment motion to determine whether there are any questions of material fact and whether the trial court has erred in the application of the law. The record in this case is filled with conflicting testimony, by legal experts, on the applicable standard of care and whether Gainsley breached it. These conflicts are questions of fact, and are most appropriately answered by the jury.

The conflicting expert testimony on the questions of Wartnick's introduction of the polygraph issue in the opening statement, failure to investigate, and failure to mitigate the damage done by the original deposition answers provides questions of material fact as to what the applicable standard of care is within the community on these issues, and whether it was breached. We reverse the grant of summary judgment on these issues and remand to the district court for trial.

Affirmed in part, reversed in part and remanded.

7. **Standard of care.** Sometimes courts state the standard of care for attorneys rather casually—"an attorney is negligent if he fails to exercise reasonable diligence and skill on behalf of his client." *Callahan v. Clark,* 321 Ark. 376, 901 S.W.2d 842 (1995). Commonly, however, courts state the professional standard of care. So the malpractice plaintiff must establish that the lawyer's representation departed from the standard of care a reasonably prudent attorney, perhaps one in the same jurisdiction, would exercise in similar circumstances. *Wood v. Parker,* 901 S.W.2d 374 (Tenn. App. 1995); ("a plaintiff must establish that the lawyer's conduct fell below that degree of care, skill, and diligence which is commonly possessed and exercised by attorneys practicing in the same jurisdiction"); *Simko v. Blake,* 448 Mich. 648, 532 N.W.2d 842 (1995) (standard is that of an attorney "of ordinary learning, judgment or skill . . . under the same or similar circumstances. . . ."); *Peterson v. Scorsine,* 898 P.2d 382 (Wyo. 1995) (plaintiff must establish lawyer's "representation departed from the standard of care a reasonably prudent attorney would exercise under similar circumstances" in same jurisdiction).

8. **Expert testimony.** Does the professional standard imply, as it does in medical malpractice cases, that expert testimony will ordinarily be required to establish the standard of care and its breach? Since judges know or presumably know a good deal about standards of care for lawyers, and in fact are sometimes called to testify about the lawyer's performance in litigation, it would might be thought that (a) no expert is required to establish the standard, or at least that (b) the judge could grant summary judgment where appropriate on the basis of her own knowledge of the standard. But where negligence is not obvious or

definitionally proved, courts have required expert testimony in the first place and have acted on it in granting or denying summary judgment. Besides the stringent example in *Wartnick,* see, e.g., *Jim Mitchell and Jed Davis, P.A. v. Jackson*, 627 A.2d 1014 (1993).

9. **Codes of professional conduct or ethics.** The codes of professional responsibility, violation of which may lead to disciplinary action against the attorney, do not create civil cause of action. An expert witness does not establish the standard of care by testifying that the lawyer violated the code of professional responsibility. *Lazy Seven Coal Sales, Inc. v. Stone & Hinds, P.C.,* 813 S.W.2d 400 (Tenn. 1991).

10. **Statute of limitations.** Where the lawyer has opportunity to sue within the statute of limitations period but fails to do so, courts may find negligence as a matter of law without resort to expert testimony.

11. **Tactical choices.** Courts often repeat the idea that mere error of judgment is not of itself negligent, although that statement reveals little: if the attorney is negligent, it is not a mere error of judgment; if it is a mere error of judgment, the attorney is not negligent. However, courts have shown themselves reluctant to find negligence on the basis of tactical decisions in trying a case. For example, a decision not to call a witness or not to cross-examine a witness is often regarded as a tactical decision that cannot be readily judged and hence counts as, at worst, "mere error." See *Simko v. Blake,* 448 Mich. 648, 532 N.W.2d 842 (1995). Would it be clear that expert testimony would be required if you were to have any hope of holding a lawyer liable for a tactical choice?

12. **Research and investigation.** It is also difficult to know how much investigation to pursue and how much research to do. In lines that will always be dear to the heart of the malpractice defendant, the Michigan Court in *Simko*, supra, observed: "There is no motion that can be filed, no amount of research in preparation, no level of skill, nor degree of perfection that could anticipate every error or completely shield a client from the occasional aberrant ruling of a fallible judge or an intransigent jury. To impose a duty on attorneys to do more than that which is legally adequate to fully vindicate a client's rights would require our legal system, already overburdened, to digest unnecessarily inordinate quantities of additional motions and evidence that, in most cases, will prove to be superfluous. And, because no amount of work can guarantee a favorable result, attorneys would never know when the work they do is sufficiently more than adequate to be enough to protect not only their clients from error, but themselves from liability."

§ 2. CAUSATION

PHILLIPS v. CLANCY

152 Ariz. 415, 733 P.2d 300 (App. 1986)

MEYERSON, Judge. . . .

On May 23, 1980, plaintiff-appellant Wesley E. Phillips, then 42 years old, filed an application for disability insurance benefits with the

Social Security Administration claiming that he was unable to work due to stomach ailments. ... Plaintiff's application for Social Security disability benefits was denied after the information he submitted was reviewed by an examiner and a physician. ...

After his request for reconsideration was denied, Phillips retained defendant-appellee Kenneth Clancy to present his claim at a hearing before an administrative law judge. Clancy, however, failed to file a timely request. When Clancy realized the time to file the request had run, he advised Phillips merely to file another application for benefits and to retain another attorney.

Despite repeated efforts, Phillips never succeeded in obtaining a hearing on his claim or an award of disability benefits. ...

In August, 1982, plaintiff and his wife filed suit for legal malpractice. Clancy filed a motion for summary judgment and submitted the affidavit of Judge Patterson. Judge Patterson stated that he had been an administrative law judge with the Social Security Administration for ten years. He stated that he had reviewed the entire file containing all documents, medical records and Phillips' deposition testimony. He then stated, based on his review of the case, that even if the request for hearing had been timely filed and he had heard the case, he would not have reversed the district examiner's decision because it was his opinion that Phillips did not qualify for disability benefits.

In response to the motion for summary judgment, Phillips submitted the affidavit of Dale D. Tretschok, an attorney experienced in representing applicants for Social Security disability benefits. Tretschok stated that based on his review of the case, and his experience in handling similar matters, there was an excellent chance for success before an administrative law judge. ...

As in any negligence action, a plaintiff in a legal malpractice action must show the following basic elements: duty, breach of duty, causation, and damages. One claiming legal malpractice must therefore establish (1) the existence of an attorney-client relationship which imposes a duty on the attorney to exercise that degree of skill, care, and knowledge commonly exercised by members of the profession, (2) breach of that duty, (3) that such negligence was a proximate cause of resulting injury, and (4) the fact and extent of the injury.

The trial court granted summary judgment in favor of Clancy based upon its determination that Judge Patterson's affidavit established that even if Clancy had timely requested a hearing, Phillips would have been unsuccessful in his claim for disability benefits. We conclude that this ruling was in error.

In legal malpractice cases, the impact of the lawyer's negligence in the underlying action is judged against an objective standard rather than a subjective one, such as was applied by the trial court. In a legal malpractice action, the plaintiff must prove that but for the attorney's negligence, he would have been successful in the prosecution or defense of the original suit. This is commonly called a "case within the case." Under a subjective standard, such as was applied by the trial court, the arbiter from the first suit would be asked to testify concerning the effect, if any, of the attorney's actions on the outcome of the underlying case. Under an objective standard, the trier in the malpractice suit views the first suit from the standpoint of what a reasonable judge or jury would have decided, but for the attorney's negligence. We hold that the objective standard is most appropriate. . . .

In applying the foregoing authorities to the case before us, we conclude that the objective standard is most appropriate. First, we are concerned with the appearance of impropriety created when a judge, in effect, sides with one of the litigants in an ongoing proceeding. See Code of Judicial Conduct, Canon 2(B). In testifying as a witness for either party in a malpractice action, it may appear that the judge is shedding his cloak of impartiality and "throwing the weight of his position and authority behind one of two opposing litigants." The prospect that a jury would attach undue weight to a judge's testimony is, indeed, readily apparent.

Second, it is infeasible to allow judicial testimony of this kind. The interference and disruption of the work of the judiciary would be overwhelming. . . .

Accordingly, the trial court here erred in giving any consideration to the affidavit of Judge Patterson.

An issue raised in the briefs and which will arise on remand, is whether a judge or jury should decide the merits of the underlying action—Phillips' eligibility for Social Security disability benefits. Phillips contends this task is for the jury; Clancy argues that it is for the judge. Two factors determine the appropriate arbiter: (1) whether appellate level or trial level malpractice is involved, and (2) whether issues of law or issues of fact must be resolved.

Appellate level malpractice commonly occurs when the original trial has ended and the attorney fails to timely file an appeal. The plaintiff must prove that an appellate court would have (1) granted review, and (2) rendered a favorable judgment. Courts have consistently found that these determinations are questions of law for the trial judge, rather that questions of fact for the jury. We agree. Resolving legal issues on appeal is reserved for the exclusive province of judges. . . .

In trial level malpractice, the attorney's negligence either precluded a trial on the merits, or prevented the client's case from being presented according to professional standards. If the underlying suit would have been tried to a jury, or a judge sitting as a trier of fact, we conclude that the jury in the malpractice case should decide the disputed factual issues pertaining to the original suit. But see Legal Malpractice § 672.

. . . Although the proceeding before the Social Security Administration involved an administrative appeal from an examiner's ruling to an administrative law judge, see 20 C.F.R. § 404.918 (1980), it is clear that the alleged malpractice falls on the trial level side of the continuum. At the proceeding before the administrative law judge, the judge would have been sitting as both judge and jury. See 20 C.F.R. § 404.939 (1980). A hearing would have been held where evidence was submitted and factual determinations made concerning the scope and nature of Phillips' disability. Therefore, on remand, in the "case within the case," the jury should be instructed on the applicable Social Security law and regulations and be asked if, based on the facts presented, but for the alleged negligence, Phillips would have been entitled to disability benefits. In short, legal issues are to be decided by the judge; factual issues are to be decided by the jury.

For the foregoing reasons, the summary judgment is reversed and this matter is remanded to the trial court for further proceedings consistent with this opinion.

13. **Litigation malpractice: substituted liability.** Litigation malpractice is commonly asserted. Among the litigation malpractice cases, a failure to file a pleading or motion in a timely way is the most commonly asserted fault. This kind of case produces the "case within the case" problem seen in *Phillips*. The lawyer is substituted for the defendant and takes on the defendant's liability. This is an application of the but-for test of causation and but-for proof will be required in transactional malpractice as well as litigation malpractice. *Viner v. Sweet,* 30 Cal. 4th 1232, 70 P.3d 1046, 135 Cal. Rptr. 2d 629 (2003).

14. **Testimony of judges.** Courts disfavor the testimony of judges. In *Glenn v. Aiken,* 409 Mass. 699, 569 N.E.2d 783, 4 A.L.R.5th 1060 (1991), the plaintiff claimed malpractice because the attorney failed to make a certain objection. The attorney responded with the affidavit of the very judge who tried the criminal case. The judge swore that he would have overruled the objection even if it had been made. The Massachusetts Court disregarded the affidavit. "Probing the mental processes of a trial judge, that are not apparent on the record of the trial proceeding, is not permissible."

15. **Judge or jury.** If the issue in the underlying action was decided by a judge, should that mean that a judge will decide the issue in the malpractice case-within-the-case? Certainly if the issue is one of law. Suppose, though, the issue is one of fact but in the underlying action judges are triers of fact. That happened in *Phillips* because the underlying action was administrative and no jury ever decided administrative proceedings. Was *Phillips* right, though, in leaving the decision to the jury in the case-within-the-case? In *Harline v. Barker,* 912 P.2d 433 (Utah 1996), the underlying case was in bankruptcy and issues of fact are decided by the bankruptcy judge. The Utah Court disagreed with Phillips on this point, saying

> While the fact versus law distinction followed by these courts has some superficial analytic appeal, we reject its application in this context. Harline seeks to have a jury determine what only a bankruptcy judge could have determined in the first instance. We see no

reason why a malpractice plaintiff should be able to bootstrap his way into having a lay jury decide the merits of the underlying "suit within a suit" when, by statute or other rule of law, only an expert judge could have made the underlying decision. It is illogical, in effect, to make a change in the law's allocation of responsibility between judge and jury in the underlying action when that action is revisited in legal malpractice actions and thereby distort the "suit within a suit" analytic model.

16. **Comparing criminal-case malpractice.** Is the case-within-the-case approach the only one reasonably available? Think back about criminal-case malpractice claims. Recall that most courts require the malpractice-suit plaintiff to prove that he was in fact innocent. Is that a case-within-the-case approach?

17. **Substituted liability standard and collectibility.** Consider how substituted liability works in the following cases if the lawyer's negligence prevents the client-plaintiff from proceeding with suit:

(A) The jury estimates that the plaintiff would have received a judgment against the original defendant for $100,000 but would not have been able to collect anything.

(B) The jury estimates that the plaintiff would not have won if he went to trial but that he could have settled the case for $50,000.

18. **Substituted liability and the lawyer's fee.** What is the lawyer's net liability if the plaintiff would have recovered a collectible judgment of $100,000 and would have paid the lawyer $50,000 in contingent fees? If you think the plaintiff should recover only $50,000 from the lawyer, you will find support in *Moores v. Greenberg,* 834 F.2d 1105 (1st Cir. 1987). But some other cases have said the plaintiff should recover the entire $100,000. E.g., *Strauss v. Fost,* 213 N.J. Super. 239, 517 A.2d 143 (1986); *Kane, Kane & Kritzer, Inc. v. Altagen,* 107 Cal. App. 3d 36, 165 Cal. Rptr. 534, 538 (1980). Notice: the lawyer did not earn any fee and the plaintiff may have incurred attorney fees in bringing the malpractice suit. Does either of these reasons suggest that $100,000 is the correct measure of damages? *Distefano v. Greenstone,* 357 N.J.Super. 352, 815 A.2d 496 (2003), goes a step further, allowing the plaintiff to recover the full $100,000 plus the contingent fee of her present attorney in suing on the malpractice claim.

19. **Second layer damages.** Should the client be permitted to recover a second layer of damages, say for emotional distress or damages to her credit resulting when the suit did not go forward?

20. **Punitive damages based on the attorney's serious misconduct.** A punitive issue might arise because the lawyer was malicious in his malpractice and he deserved to suffer a punitive judgment. For instance, in *Metcalfe v. Waters,* 970 S.W.2d 448 (Tenn. 1998), the lawyer for a personal injury plaintiff suffered a nonsuit when he wasn't ready for trial, and on re-filing the complaint failed to pay the filing fee or get summons issued. In the end the whole thing was finally dismissed. He

then lied to his clients, telling them it was pending. Finally, he told them it was dismissed and not worth appealing, but didn't reveal his own culpability. The jury awarded $100,000 in punitive damages. The court held that fraudulent, malicious, or even merely reckless misconduct would suffice to justify punitive damages and that the attorney here was at least reckless. Concealing his wrongs was one reason for punitive damages; it did not matter that his fraud in doing so occurred after rather than contemporaneously with his malpractice.

21. **Punitive damages based upon the adverse party's misconduct.** Should the lawyer who negligently represents a plaintiff in the underlying law suit be liable for the punitive damages that would have been levied against the original defendant? Such damages are not compensation and they would not have gone to the plaintiff in the original action as a matter of right. Paid by the lawyer, they will not perform their punitive function against the original defendant. *Elliott v. Videan,* 164 Ariz. 113, 791 P.2d 639 (Ariz. App. 1989), allowed recovery against the lawyer whose only fault was negligence, not the evil mind required for punitive damages. *Ferguson v. Lieff, Cabraser, Heimann & Bernstein, LLP,* 30 Cal.4th 1037, 69 P.3d 965, 135 Cal.Rptr.2d 46 (2003), goes the other way on several grounds. One was that to allow recovery "of lost punitive damages would defeat the very purpose behind such damages." Another was the danger of driving attorneys, or their insurers, out of business. Still another was that the complexity of allowing such a recovery would be too great: "[T]he standard of proof for lost punitive damages will be, in essence, a standard within a standard. To recover lost punitive damages, a plaintiff must prove by a preponderance of the evidence that but for attorney negligence the jury would have found clear and convincing evidence of oppression, fraud or malice. In light of this complex standard, '[t]he mental gymnastics required to reach an intelligent verdict would be difficult to comprehend much less execute.' "

22. **Informed consent.** You are familiar with the kind of medical malpractice that results in an informed consent claim. Is there any legal malpractice that would be analogous? One judge said, "As part and parcel of this duty, a lawyer must keep his client seasonably apprised of relevant developments, including opportunities for settlement." *Moores v. Greenberg,* 834 F.2d 1105 (1st Cir. 1987). What damages could there be if an attorney fails to inform a client of a settlement offer? In *Moores,* supra, the client was allowed to recover the amount of the settlement offer not transmitted by the lawyer, minus the contingent fee. The client may assert an informed consent (or no consent) type claim without referring to consent at all, only to the attorney's unauthorized action, such as entering a plea without consulting the client. *Hauschulz v. Michael Law Firm,* 306 Mont. 102, 30 P.3d 357 (2001).

JONES MOTOR CO., INC. v. HOLTKAMP, LIESE, BECKEMEIER & CHILDRESS, P.C.

197 F.3d 1190 (7th Cir. 1999)

POSNER, Chief Judge.

The plaintiffs in this legal malpractice suit appeal from its dismissal on the defendants' motion for summary judgment, raising a novel issue concerning the law of legal malpractice. The issue, which arises when as in this case the plaintiff is complaining that his lawyer booted a procedural entitlement, such as the right to a jury trial, is whether the plaintiff must show that his lawyer's negligence not only caused him to lose but brought about an unjust result—the wrong party won. The plaintiffs are the Jones Motor Company, a trucker, and its insurer. The defendants are lawyers who represented Jones in a personal injury lawsuit brought against it by Elston Cannon. Federal jurisdiction is based on diversity of citizenship; and the applicable law, the parties agree, is Illinois's common law of malpractice.

The underlying suit had been filed in a state court in St. Clair County and assigned to a judge who we are told, and accept for purposes of deciding this appeal, has the reputation of favoring plaintiffs in personal injury suits. Jones's lawyers negligently failed to make a timely effective request for a jury because they failed to accompany the request with payment of the fee for a jury trial. As a result the case was tried to the judge, who entered a judgment of $2.8 million for the plaintiff; the suit was then settled for $2.5 million. In the present case, the malpractice case, Jones tendered the opinion of an experienced lawyer in St. Clair County that had the case been tried to a jury, the verdict would have been in the neighborhood of $500,000. Jones and its insurer, which paid a part of the $2.5 million settlement, are suing for the $2 million difference. . . .

We come to the most important issue, which is whether, and if so when, the loss of a procedural advantage can give rise to a malpractice suit even if the advantage was not essential to the protection of the client's substantive rights. Through the defendants' negligence Jones and its insurer lost their right to a jury trial and were forced to submit to a bench trial—which means they got a trial before an authorized tribunal. They allege no error in the conduct of the trial by the judge whom they did not want to try the case, and they did not appeal from the judgment that he rendered, large as it was. The plaintiffs thus got a fair trial and there is no basis for supposing that the judgment was excessive, albeit it may have been higher than it would have been had Jones's lawyers not thrown away their client's right to a jury trial. Some Illinois cases say or imply that you cannot get a judgment for malpractice against a lawyer unless you can show that you had a meritorious claim (or defense, when the client had been a defendant rather than a plaintiff), and Jones's lawyers argue correctly that their client had no entitlement not to be mulcted by a judgment of $2.8 million.

But we think the real thrust of these cases is that a malpractice plaintiff cannot prevail merely by showing that his claim which his lawyer booted, though baseless, had some nuisance value. Imagine a situation in which a class action is brought and is thrown out as a result of a negligent mistake by the lawyer for the class, who is then sued for tens or hundreds of millions of dollars in another class action, in which it is argued that although the suit was frivolous it is well known that frivolous class actions can sometimes extort sizeable settlements from the defendants. ... To impose malpractice liability for booting a nuisance suit would—like deeming a plaintiff who obtains a nuisance settlement a prevailing party for purposes of entitlement to an award of attorneys' fees, which courts also refuse to do—simply encourage nuisance suits, of which we have enough already.

But to say that the plaintiff's loss of a nuisance suit is not a ground for the plaintiff's suing his lawyer is not the same thing as saying that the plaintiff must prove that had it not been for his lawyer's negligence he would have won the suit for sure. Take the classic case of legal malpractice in litigation—failure to file suit before the statute of limitations expires. If the suit thus aborted had only nuisance value, then, as we have just said, the lawyer's negligence would not support a malpractice suit. But if as with most suits the probability of a successful outcome was less than 100 percent, the plaintiff in the malpractice suit could not "prove" that he would have won. The outcome of the suit (had there been no malpractice) might have turned on which of two witnesses the jury would have believed, and if there were a reasonable probability that the defendant would have won the swearing contest then it could not be said that a loss of the case by the plaintiff could only have reflected injustice. Such possibilities do not defeat malpractice liability.

There is a difference, however, between saying that a claim can be meritorious without its being certain to prevail at trial and saying that one of the parties would have done better than the other, had it not been for the negligence of his lawyer, regardless of the relative merits of the parties' positions. And that is (at most) this case. Although the judge who tried the case against Jones may have a reputation of being more liberal in personal-injury suits than the average jury in his county, it is impossible to infer from this that the $2.8 million judgment that he rendered against Jones was too high; the average jury verdict in such a case might be too low. Of course if this judge were prejudiced against motor carriers, or litigants named Jones, or defendants in personal injury cases, there would be a basis for inferring that the negligence of Jones's lawyer had cost Jones a shot to which he was entitled at a lower damages award, albeit an entitlement not certain to be enforced even by a jury; but of this there is no evidence.

Yet this analysis is not satisfactory either. We must ask why Illinois allows a defendant in a civil suit to elect to be tried by a jury even though the plaintiff would prefer a bench trial. The answer must be that each party is deemed entitled to seek the "protection" of the jury against being tried by a judge. "Developments in the Law: The Civil Jury," 110

Harv. L.Rev. 1408, 1429–32 (1997). That entitlement, a real legal entitlement and not just a tactical opportunity to obtain a more favorable tribunal, was worth something to Jones, and it was kicked away by the defendants' negligence. The only reason for treating it differently from other entitlements, such as the entitlement to introduce evidence or to enforce a substantive right, is practical; it is the difficulty of valuing its loss. The difficulty becomes impossibility in a case (which is not this case, however) in which, at the time the right to a jury trial is forfeited, the identity of the judge who will try the case in lieu of the jury is not known. There is variance among judges as well as among juries, and it is very hard to say that the average jury is likely to be more favorable to a defendant than the average judge. Hence the foreseeable loss in such a case would be extremely hard to estimate. . . .

Partly because the precise issue has never arisen before, so far as the parties' research or our own discloses, either in Illinois or in any other jurisdiction, we hesitate to rule out the possibility of convincing an Illinois court to allow a malpractice suit to go forward on the basis of an argument that the plaintiff lost a procedural entitlement even though it was not an entitlement necessary to avert an unjust outcome. But given the uncertainty of harm we think the plaintiff in such a case must do more than the plaintiffs have done here to show that they can prove damages to a reasonable certainty. Some degree of speculation is permissible in computing damages, because reasonable doubts as to remedy ought to be resolved against the wrongdoer; but there are limits. Although there is plenty of evidence that [the defendant in[?]]any personal-injury case assigned to the judge who presided at Cannon v. Jones Motor Group, Inc. would want a jury rather than this judge to determine damages, there is no credible evidence of what a jury might have awarded. The principal evidence is the opinion of the lawyer who thought Cannon's case worth to a jury in the range of $500,000, but this was offered as a bare conclusion without data of actual verdicts in St. Clair County in comparable cases from which some reasonable confidence interval, some range in which any jury verdict would be quite likely to lie, might have been computed. No reasonable trier of fact could have been allowed to award damages to Jones and its insurer on the basis of such unsubstantiated expert testimony.

The plaintiffs argue that the way to compute damages in this case is simply to try the malpractice claim to a jury. That is a bad suggestion quite apart from the fact that a jury in a federal district court is not drawn from the same pool as the jury in a state court. The suggestion overlooks the fact that given the variance among juries, it would be necessary to try the malpractice claim a number of times in order to get a sense of the average performance of a jury in this case, and it is the difference between the judge's judgment and the judgment that Jones could have expected from a jury, which would be an average jury performance, that is the measure of what Jones lost as a result of its lawyers' negligence. So the suit was rightly dismissed after all.

Affirmed.

23. **Alternative proof of causation?** Is Judge Posner rejecting the case-within-the-case proof of causation? At least for cases involving booted procedural entitlements? Is he (also?) rejecting expert testimony? What does that leave available as a means of proving damages?

§ 3. LIABILITY TO THIRD PERSONS

Safeway Managing General Agency, Inc. v. Clark & Gamble, 985 S.W.2d 166 (Tex. App. 1998). The plaintiff issued a liability insurance policy protecting Manning up to the limits of $20,000. Garcia obtained a default judgment against Manning for almost $500,000. At that point the plaintiff retained the defendant attorneys to represent Manning and conclude a settlement with Garcia. The attorneys reached a settlement for almost $24,000. They represented to the insurer-plaintiff that this settlement released all claims. In reliance on that, the insurer released the funds. Thereafter, it discovered that the settlement only released Garcia's claims for excess-of-policy liability. The insurer was therefore required to pay an additional $20,000 to Garcia for its basic policy coverage. It then sued the attorneys for breach of fiduciary duty and for negligent misrepresentation. *Held*, (1) the insurer is not the client when it retains attorneys to represent the insured and the attorneys owe no fiduciary duty to the insurer; but (2) the attorneys are liable to the insurer for negligent misrepresentation.

24. **Lawyer-client relationship.** The lawyer-client relationship is consensual, and it is that relationship that creates the lawyer's professional duty of care. Ordinarily, the client must manifest an intent for the lawyer to provide legal services and the lawyers must manifest a consent or fail to correct the putative client's reasonable impression that the lawyer is undertaking to provide services. It is also possible that a lawyer-client relationship can be created when a court appoints a lawyer. See Restatement of the Law Governing Lawyers § 14 (1998).

25. **Liability insurer retaining lawyer to defend insured.** Liability insurers undertake in their policies to provide a defense for the covered insured who is sued. The insurer has the right to and does select the lawyer. Once the lawyer is selected for the insured, the lawyer-client relationship exists between the lawyer and the insured.

26. **Both insurer and insured as clients?** Can the insurer also be a client of the same lawyer with respect to the same situation? According to *Paradigm Ins. Co. v. Langerman Law Offices*, 200 Ariz. 146, 24 P.3d 593 (2001), when an insurer assigns a lawyer to defend its insured, the insured is a client, but it is possible that the insurer is also a client until a conflict of interest is imminent, or that a duty of care is owed to the insurer even if it is not a client, so that the lawyer may be obliged to defend the insured but also to investigate the possibility that other carriers furnish primary liability coverage.

27. **Confidentiality.** By the insurance contract, the insured permits the insurer to control the defense and settlement within the limits

of the policy. Case evaluations and other communications between the lawyer and insurer should be considered privileged whether the insurer is the client or not. See RESTATEMENT OF THE LAW GOVERNING LAWYERS § 134, cmt. f. (1998).

PIZEL v. ZUSPANN

247 Kan. 54, 795 P.2d 42, 10 A.L.R.5th 1098 (1990)

[A lawyer, Zuspann, attempted to create an inter vivos trust for his client, Charles. Charles wanted it to be secret and the deeds to land that would count as the corpus were not recorded. Before Charles died Zuspann left the firm and the representation was taken over by Whalen. Then Charles died. The trust failed and the beneficiaries lost out. The beneficiaries brought this suit against both Zuspann and Whalen. The trial court granted summary judgment for Zuspann, on the ground that Whalen could have corrected his error. The jury brought in a verdict against Whalen for a sum deemed to be his share.]

[Zuspann's liability.] Zuspann had a continuing duty to assure that Charles' intent to pass the land to his nephews was realized. Zuspann's alleged failure to adequately advise Charles of the steps needed to effectuate the trust constituted a special obligation that was continuous in nature and that resulted in injury to Pizel and his intended third-party beneficiaries. . . . The mere fact that Whalen subsequently represented Charles does not relieve Zuspann of liability for his acts of negligence prior to the termination of his attorney-client relationship with Charles. The fault of each attorney, if any, is for the jury to determine and compare. . . .

[Liability to third persons.] But here, the jury found that Whalen did not breach his contract with Charles and that the appellants were not third-party beneficiaries. We must therefore decide whether to allow nonclients to recover under a legal duty owed directly to the nonclient. California has adopted such a theory, utilizing a multi-criteria balancing test. Although it is viewed as a separate theory, its criteria are closely related to the analysis and policy reasons used to justify permitting a third-party beneficiary to recover in a contract action.

The California Supreme Court first addressed the multi-criteria balancing test in Biakanja v. Irving, 49 Cal.2d 647, 320 P.2d 16 (1958), which challenged the validity of a will. A notary public, who was not an attorney, prepared a will for a testator. The will was later found invalid due to the notary's negligence. The court concluded that the notary had a duty to the sole beneficiary to exercise due care. . . . [T]he court listed the following criteria: ". . . the extent to which the transaction was intended to affect the plaintiff, the foreseeability of harm to him, the degree of certainty that the plaintiff suffered injury, the closeness of the connection between the defendant's conduct and the injury suffered, the moral blame attached to the defendant's conduct, and the policy of preventing future harm."

Next, the California Supreme Court held, in Lucas v. Hamm, 56 Cal.2d 583, 15 Cal.Rptr. 821, 364 P.2d 685 (1961), that liability should be extended to beneficiaries who were injured by a will negligently drafted by an attorney. Listing an additional factor to be balanced in such cases, the court reasoned such extension did not place an undue burden on the profession because, otherwise, the innocent beneficiary would have to bear the loss.

In Heyer v. Flaig, 70 Cal.2d 223, 74 Cal.Rptr. 225, 449 P.2d 161 (1969), daughters of the deceased filed an action against an attorney for negligently failing to fulfill testamentary directions of his client, the deceased. In discussing whether a third party could recover against an attorney on a theory of tort liability for a breach of duty owed directly to the third party, the court stated: "When an attorney undertakes to fulfill the testamentary instructions of his client, he realistically and in fact assumes a relationship not only with the client but also with the client's intended beneficiaries. ... In Bucquet v. Livingston, 57 Cal.App.3d 914, 922, 129 Cal.Rptr. 514 (1976), the court found no rational basis for distinguishing inter vivos trusts and applied the principles set forth in Heyer v. Flaig to intended beneficiaries of such trusts.

Relying upon the analysis from the California courts, the Arizona Court of Appeals concluded that an attorney can be held liable to a third person not in privity if a duty arises based upon the balancing of the various factors listed in the California cases. Fickett v. Superior Court of Pima County, 27 Ariz. App. 793, 795–96, 558 P.2d 988 (1976).

Not all courts have adopted the balancing test developed by the California courts. The Supreme Court of New York [a trial court] refused to recognize a duty owed by attorneys who prepared decedents' wills and assisted the executor in Kramer v. Belfi, 106 App.Div.2d 615, 482 N.Y.S.2d 898 (1984). The beneficiaries alleged the attorneys negligently failed to advise the executor to renounce the trust created in the will of the deceased wife, which caused severe tax consequences to the deceased husband's estate. The court found defendant attorneys were entitled to dismissal of all causes of action brought by all plaintiffs except for the plaintiff who sued in his capacity as executor of the decedents' estates. The court stated: "Defendants were retained by the executor only and are not liable to the beneficiaries of the decedents' estates in the absence of fraud, collusion, or malice, none of which is alleged here."

We find the California cases persuasive. We conclude that an attorney may be liable to parties not in privity based upon the balancing test developed by the California courts. Applying that test to the present case, appellants' claim would state a cause of action against Whalen under a theory of negligence ... (1) The extent to which the transaction was intended to affect the plaintiffs: Appellants here were the intended beneficiaries of the inter vivos trust. ... (2) The foreseeability of harm to the plaintiffs: Appellants were the intended beneficiaries of the trust. If the inter vivos trust failed, their inheritance from Charles would be limited to the provisions of the will, which did not mention the trust. (3)

The degree of certainty that the plaintiffs suffered injury: Because the inter vivos trust was found to be invalid, the property that was intended for the trust passed through the residuary clause of Charles' will. (4) The closeness of the connection between the attorney's conduct and the injury: Although Whalen did not draft the original trust, he did draft an amendment to it that included Herb as a trustee. He also took over as the attorney for Charles for several years while the trust was supposedly in operation. (5) The policy of preventing future harm: If the intended beneficiaries of the inter vivos trust here are not allowed to pursue a negligence claim against the attorneys who drafted the trust and its amendments, then the beneficiaries will have no avenue of recovery. (6) The burden on the profession of the recognition of liability under the circumstances: The trial court here correctly instructed the jury that a lawyer is negligent if he does not use the degree of care and skill which a reasonably competent attorney would use in similar circumstances. The legal profession will not be unduly burdened by requiring a lawyer to act in a reasonably competent manner in the representation of his or her clients. . . .

The judgment of the district court is reversed as to the plaintiffs' appeal and affirmed as to the defendants' cross-appeal. The case is remanded for a new trial.

28. **Entering appearance for non-clients.** A citizen sues a city and its police officers, A and B, claiming a civil rights violation. Officer B was never served, but the city attorney, in the course of defending for the city, entered an appearance on behalf of A and B. The suit against the city was later dismissed. He did not continue in the defense of A and B and a default judgment was entered against Officer B, though he had never known of the suit. Officer B then sued the city attorney for malpractice. The attorney argued that as he had never represented Officer B, he could not be liable for malpractice. Although the argument was supported by a decision from the same jurisdiction, the court held it had no application here because a court rule specified that when an attorney entered an appearance, he was the attorney of record for that case unless released by the court. *Warren v. Williams,* 313 Ill. App. 3d 450, 246 Ill. Dec. 487, 730 N.E.2d 512 (2000). Should courts ever have made a rule that encourages attorneys to defend such a patently meritorious claim?

LEYBA V. WHITLEY, 120 N.M. 768, 907 P.2d 172 (1995). Corrine retained defendant Whitley to recover for the wrongful death of her unmarried son, Philip. Philip, though unmarried, was the father of a child born posthumously. Under the New Mexico wrongful death statute, the wrongful death action was to be brought by the personal representative of the estate. The lawyers had Corrine appointed personal representative. They ultimately settled the claim for almost $550,000. The net proceeds were paid to Corrine in the sum of $324,816. Corrine did not turn the money over to the child as statutory beneficiary but dissipated most of it. On behalf of the child-beneficiary, this suit charges the lawyers with negligence (1) in failing to pay for a guardian or conservator for the child and (2) in failing to inform Corrine that she held the money as a fiduciary and subject to a duty to pay on behalf of the child. *Held*: an attorney owes a duty to the statutory beneficiary to use reasonable care to protect his interests.

29. **Balancing vs. third-party beneficiary test.** The multi-factored "balancing test" of the California cases can be contrasted with the "third party beneficiary theory" of lawyer liability to third persons. However, the two approaches are largely consistent if you add to the balancing test that a proven intent to benefit a third person weighs heavily (or totally) in favor of the duty. *Donahue v. Shughart, Thomson & Kilroy, P.C.*, 900 S.W.2d 624 (Mo. 1995).

GREYCAS, INC. v. PROUD

826 F.2d 1560 (7th Cir. 1987)

POSNER, Circuit Judge.

Theodore S. Proud, Jr., a member of the Illinois bar who practices law in a suburb of Chicago, appeals from a judgment against him for $833,760, entered after a bench trial. The tale of malpractice and misrepresentation that led to the judgment begins with Proud's brother-in-law, Wayne Crawford, like Proud a lawyer but one who devoted most of his attention to a large farm that he owned in downstate Illinois. The farm fell on hard times and by 1981 Crawford was in dire financial straits. He had pledged most of his farm machinery to lenders, yet now desperately needed more money. He approached Greycas, Inc., the plaintiff in this case, a large financial company headquartered in Arizona, seeking a large loan that he offered to secure with the farm machinery. He did not tell Greycas about his financial difficulties or that he had pledged the machinery to other lenders, but he did make clear that he needed the loan in a hurry. Greycas obtained several appraisals of Crawford's farm machinery but did not investigate Crawford's financial position or discover that he had pledged the collateral to other lenders, who had perfected their liens in the collateral. Greycas agreed to lend Crawford $1,367,966.50, which was less than the appraised value of the machinery.

The loan was subject, however, to an important condition, which is at the heart of this case: Crawford was required to submit a letter to Greycas, from counsel whom he would retain, assuring Greycas that there were no prior liens on the machinery that was to secure the loan. Crawford asked Proud to prepare the letter, and he did so, and mailed it to Greycas, and within 20 days of the first contact between Crawford and Greycas the loan closed and the money was disbursed. A year later Crawford defaulted on the loan; shortly afterward he committed suicide.

Greycas then learned that most of the farm machinery that Crawford had pledged to it had previously been pledged to other lenders.

The machinery was sold at auction. The Illinois state court that determined the creditors' priorities in the proceeds of the sale held that Greycas did not have a first priority on most of the machinery that secured its loan; as a result Greycas has been able to recover only a small part of the loan. The judgment it obtained in the present suit is the district judge's estimate of the value that it would have realized on its collateral had there been no prior liens, as Proud represented in his letter.

That letter is the centerpiece of the litigation. Typed on the stationery of Proud's firm and addressed to Greycas, it identifies Proud as Crawford's lawyer and states that, "in such capacity, I have been asked to render my opinion in connection with" the proposed loan to Crawford. It also states that "this opinion is being delivered in accordance with the requirements of the Loan Agreement" and that

> I have conducted a U.C.C., tax, and judgment search with respect to the Company (i.e., Crawford's farm) as of March 19, 1981, and except as hereinafter noted all units listed on the attached Exhibit A ("Equipment") are free and clear of all liens or encumbrances other than Lender's perfected security interest therein which was recorded March 19, 1981 at the Office of the Recorder of Deeds of Fayette County, Illinois.

. . . Proud never conducted a search for prior liens on the machinery listed in Exhibit A. His brother-in-law gave him the list and told him there were no liens other than the one that Crawford had just filed for Greycas. Proud made no effort to verify Crawford's statement. The theory of the complaint is that Proud was negligent in representing that there were no prior liens, merely on his brother-in-law's say-so. No doubt Proud was negligent in failing to conduct a search, but we are not clear why the misrepresentation is alleged to be negligent rather than deliberate and hence fraudulent, in which event Greycas's alleged contributory negligence would not be an issue (as it is, we shall see), since there is no defense of contributory or comparative negligence to a deliberate tort, such as fraud. Proud did not merely say, "There are no liens"; he said, "I have conducted a U.C.C., tax, and judgment search"; and not only is this statement, too, a false one, but its falsehood cannot have been inadvertent, for Proud knew he had not conducted such a search. The concealment of his relationship with Crawford might also support a charge of fraud. But Greycas decided, for whatever reason, to argue negligent misrepresentation rather than fraud. . . .

He also does not, and could not, deny or justify the misrepresentation; but he argues that it is not actionable under the tort law of Illinois, because he had no duty of care to Greycas. (This is a diversity case and the parties agree that Illinois tort law governs the substantive issues.) He argues that Greycas had an adversarial relationship with Proud's client, Crawford, and that a lawyer has no duty of straight dealing to an adversary, at least none enforceable by a tort suit. In so arguing, Proud is characterizing Greycas's suit as one for professional malpractice rather than negligent misrepresentation, yet elsewhere in his briefs he insists that the suit was solely for negligent misrepresentation—while Greycas insists that its suit charges both torts. Legal malpractice based on a false representation, and negligent misrepresentation by a lawyer, are such similar legal concepts, however, that we have great difficulty both in holding them apart in our minds and in understanding why the parties are quarreling over the exact characterization; no one suggests, for example, that the statute of limitations might have run on one but not the other tort. So we shall discuss both.

Proud is undoubtedly correct in arguing that a lawyer has no general duty of care toward his adversary's client; it would be a considerable and, as it seems to us, an undesirable novelty to hold that every bit of sharp dealing by a lawyer gives rise to prima facie tort liability to the opposing party in the lawsuit or negotiation. The tort of malpractice normally refers to a lawyer's careless or otherwise wrongful conduct toward his own client. Proud argues that Crawford rather than Greycas was his client, and although this is not so clear as Proud supposes—another characterization of the transaction is that Crawford undertook to obtain a lawyer for Greycas in the loan transaction—we shall assume for purposes of discussion that Greycas was not Proud's client.

Therefore if malpractice just meant carelessness or other misconduct toward one's own client, Proud would not be liable for malpractice to Greycas. But in Pelham v. Griesheimer, 92 Ill.2d 13, 64 Ill.Dec. 544, 440 N.E.2d 96 (1982), the Supreme Court of Illinois discarded the old common law requirement of privity of contract for professional malpractice; so now it is possible for someone who is not the lawyer's (or other professional's) client to sue him for malpractice. The court in Pelham was worried, though, about the possibility of a lawyer's being held liable "to an unlimited and unknown number of potential plaintiffs," so it added that "for a nonclient to succeed in a negligence action against an attorney, he must prove that the primary purpose and intent of the attorney-client relationship itself was to benefit or influence the third party." That, however, describes this case exactly. Crawford hired Proud not only for the primary purpose, but for the sole purpose, of influencing Greycas to make Crawford a loan. . . .

All this assumes that Pelham governs this case, but arguably it does not, for Greycas, as we noted, may have decided to bring this as a suit for negligent misrepresentation rather than professional malpractice. We know of no obstacle to such an election; nothing is more common in American jurisprudence than overlapping torts.

The claim of negligent misrepresentation might seem utterly straightforward. It might seem that by addressing a letter to Greycas intended (as Proud's counsel admitted at argument) to induce reliance on the statements in it, Proud made himself prima facie liable for any material misrepresentations, careless or deliberate, in the letter, whether or not Proud was Crawford's lawyer or for that matter anyone's lawyer. Knowing that Greycas was relying on him to determine whether the collateral for the loan was encumbered and to advise Greycas of the results of his determination, Proud negligently misrepresented the situation, to Greycas's detriment. But merely labeling a suit as one for negligent misrepresentation rather than professional malpractice will not make the problem of indefinite and perhaps excessive liability, which induced the court in Pelham to place limitations on the duty of care, go away. So one is not surprised to find that courts have placed similar limitations on suits for negligent misrepresentation—so similar that we are led to question whether ... these really are different torts, at least when both grow out of negligent misrepresentations by lawyers. ...

The absence of a contract between the lender and the accountant defeated the suit in Ultramares—yet why should privity of contract have been required for liability just because the negligence lay in disseminating information rather than in designing or manufacturing a product? The privity limitation in products cases had been rejected, in another famous Cardozo opinion, years earlier. See MacPherson v. Buick Motor Co., 217 N.Y. 382, 111 N.E. 1050 (1916). Professor Bishop suggests that courts were worried that imposing heavy liabilities on producers of information might cause socially valuable information to be underproduced. See Negligent Misrepresentation Through Economists' Eyes, 96 L.Q.Rev. 360 (1980). Many producers of information have difficulty appropriating its benefits to society. The property-rights system in information is incomplete; someone who comes up with a new idea that the law of intellectual property does not protect cannot prevent others from using the idea without reimbursing his costs of invention or discovery. So the law must be careful not to weigh these producers down too heavily with tort liabilities. For example, information produced by securities analysts, the news media, academicians, and so forth is socially valuable, but as its producers can't capture the full value of the information in their fees and other remuneration the information may be underproduced. Maybe it is right, therefore—or at least efficient—that none of these producers should have to bear the full costs. [But Illinois cases impose liability.]

Proud, in the practice of his profession, supplied information (or rather misinformation) to Greycas that was intended to guide Greycas in commercial dealings with Crawford. Proud therefore had a duty to use due care to see that the information was correct. He used no care.

Proud must lose on the issue of liability even if the narrower, ad hoc approach of Rozny is used instead of the approach of section 552 of the Restatement. Information about the existence of previous liens on particular items of property is of limited social as distinct from private value, by which we mean simply that the information is not likely to be disseminated widely. There is consequently no reason to give it special encouragement by overlooking carelessness in its collection and expression. Where as in this case the defendant makes the negligent misrepresentation directly to the plaintiff in the course of the defendant's business or profession, the courts have little difficulty in finding a duty of care. Prosser and Keeton on the Law of Torts, supra, § 107, at p. 747. . . .

A final point. The record of this case reveals serious misconduct by an Illinois attorney. We are therefore sending a copy of this opinion to the Attorney Registration and Disciplinary Commission of the Supreme Court of Illinois for such disciplinary action as may be deemed appropriate in the circumstances. Affirmed.

[A concurring opinion is omitted.]

FIRE INSURANCE EXCHANGE v. BELL

643 N.E.2d 310 (Ind. 1994)

DICKSON, Justice. . . .

[Allegations included these.] On May 28, 1985, sixteen-month-old Jason Bell was severely burned in a fire at the Indianapolis home of Joseph Moore (Moore), Jason's grandfather. Gasoline had leaked onto the floor of Moore's utility room and was ignited by a water heater. The fire department cited Moore for the careless storage of gasoline. The carrier for Moore's homeowner's policy was Farmer's, whose claims manager was Dennis Shank (Shank) and whose attorney was Scaletta. Jason's mother, Ruby Bell (Bell), retained attorney Robert Collins to represent Jason regarding his claims for injuries sustained in the fire. . . . Collins claimed that Scaletta and Shank told him on separate occasions that Moore had a $100,000 policy limit [when in fact the limit was $300,000, as Scaletta knew.] Scaletta confirmed his misrepresentation to Collins in a letter he wrote to Shank on February 14, 1986. When Jason's condition stabilized, Shank and Scaletta each represented to Collins that Farmers would pay the $100,000 policy limit. As a result of these conversations, Collins advised Bell to settle. The agreement was approved by the probate court, and after settling with Farmers, [Bell learned that the policy limit was actually $300,000. Bell filed suit against the defendants, including the lawyers, alleging misrepresentation.]

[Scaletta's firm, Ice Miller,] and Scaletta each contend that they were entitled to summary judgment because of the absence of the right to rely, a component of the reliance element required to prove fraud. They contend that Bell's attorney had, as a matter of law, no right to rely on the alleged misrepresentations because he was a trained professional involved in adversarial settlement negotiation and had access to the relevant facts. With respect to the claims of Farmers, we agree with the analysis of the Court of Appeals, including. . . . its conclusion that whether Collins had the right to rely upon the alleged misrepresentations by Farmers is a question of fact for the jury to decide. As to the appellate contentions of Farmers, we summarily affirm the opinion of the Court of Appeals.

With respect to the alleged misrepresentations of Scaletta and Ice Miller, however, we grant transfer to recognize a separate and more demanding standard. This Court has a particular constitutional responsibility with respect to the supervision of the practice of law. The reliability and trustworthiness of attorney representations constitute an important component of the efficient administration of justice. A lawyer's representations have long been accorded a particular expectation of honesty and trustworthiness.

Commitment to these values begins with the oath taken by every Indiana lawyer; it is formally embodied in rules of professional conduct, the violation of which may result in the imposition of severe sanctions; and it is repeatedly emphasized and reinforced by professional associations and organizations. The Indiana Oath of Attorneys includes the promise that a lawyer will employ "such means only as are consistent with truth." Indiana Professional Responsibility Rule 8.4 declares that it is professional misconduct for a lawyer to "engage in conduct involving dishonesty, fraud, deceit or misrepresentation." Numerous other sources of guidelines and standards for lawyer conduct emphasize this basic principle. The Preamble of the Standards for Professional Conduct within the Seventh Federal Judicial Circuit begins with the following statement: A lawyer's conduct should be characterized at all times by personal courtesy and professional integrity in the fullest sense of those terms. In fulfilling our duty to represent a client vigorously as lawyers, we will be mindful of our obligations to the administration of justice, which is a truth-seeking process designed to resolve human and societal problems in a rational, peaceful, and efficient manner. Similarly, the Tenets of Professional Courtesy adopted by the Indianapolis Bar Association declare, "A lawyer should never knowingly deceive another lawyer or the court."

Ice Miller and Scaletta contend that the plaintiff's attorney "had no right to rely on the representations he claims because he had the means to ascertain relevant facts, was in an adverse position, was educated, sophisticated and not involved in any dominant-subordinate relationship." They further argue "that the relationship was adverse, the negotiations were protracted and that both sides were at all times represented by counsel," and emphasize that policy limits information was available to Bell's attorney from a variety of sources, including the rules of discovery.

We decline to require attorneys to burden unnecessarily the courts and litigation process with discovery to verify the truthfulness of material representations made by opposing counsel. The reliability of lawyers' representations is an integral component of the fair and efficient administration of justice. The law should promote lawyers' care in making statements that are accurate and trustworthy and should foster the reliance upon such statements by others.

We therefore reject the assertion of Ice Miller and Scaletta that Bell's attorney was, as a matter of law, not entitled to rely upon their representations. However, rather than finding this to be an issue of fact for determination at trial, as did our Court of Appeals, we hold that Bell's attorney's right to rely upon any material misrepresentations that may have been made by opposing counsel is established as a matter of law. The resolution of the questions of what representations were actually made and the extent of reliance thereon are, along with any other remaining elements of plaintiff's case, issues of fact which must be determined at trial. . . .

Gilbert v. Board of Medical Examiners of the State of Arizona, 155 Ariz. 169, 745 P.2d 617 (App. 1987). Gilbert's license to practice as a physician was revoked by the Board of Medical Examiners. He did not seek review but brought a tort action against various persons involved. He claimed civil rights violations under § 1983, interference with contract and relations, and infliction of emotional distress. The civil rights count was dismissed by stipulation. The trial judge ultimately granted a motion for summary judgment and also awarded attorney fees. The fees were awarded against both the plaintiff, the former doctor, and his attorney. Held: affirmed. (1) The failure to exhaust administrative remedies precluded the tort suit. (2) Fees against attorney. Rule 11 holds the lawyer liable and justifies a sanction when the "position asserted by a lawyer, after reasonable inquiry, will not support a reasonable belief that there is a sound basis in law or in fact for the position asserted." Experts were listed by the attorney but when deposed by defendants, they testified that the attorney had not contacted them and they knew nothing of the law suit. "The filing of a list of 450 witnesses and the failure of counsel to contact witnesses is substantial evidence to support appellees' contention that Attorney Rappeport by filing an amended list of more than 450 witnesses which he intended to have testify at trial caused unnecessary delay and needless increase in the cost of the litigation. Sanctions . . . are appropriate. . . . An attorney is obligated to review and examine his position as the facts of the case are developed. . . . During a substantial period of time available for discovery, Attorney Rappeport did not discover any facts to support claims of malice and bad faith against the Iveys. Additionally, Attorney Rappeport failed to undertake any discovery directed at the Iveys regarding facts and the circumstances of the lawsuit. He apparently acted instead upon mere assumptions and suspicions of Dr. Gilbert. An attorney may have to rely on his client for facts. However, whether those facts are sufficient to form an appropriate basis for filing or continuing a lawsuit is within the attorney's judgment and expertise. It requires inquiry into both the facts and the law." Fees are also allowable under the civil rights statute because, though dropped by stipulation, there was initially a civil rights claim by the plaintiff; this subjects him to a fee award if the claim is frivolous.

Wyatt v. Wehmueller, 163 Ariz. 12, 785 P.2d 581 (App. 1989), rev'd in part, Wyatt v. Wehmueller, 167 Ariz. 281, 806 P.2d 870 (1991) (see paragraph (3) below). Plaintiffs purchased real estate from defendant, giving a promissory note and a deed of trust to secure payment. Defendants allegedly did not convey the full acreage contracted and plaintiffs sued for damages. About the same time, plaintiffs defaulted on the note. Defendants, at a proper time, scheduled a trustee's sale for the property. Plaintiffs attempted to stop this by a preliminary injunction which failed. The plaintiffs' attorney then recorded a notice of lis pendens. After a hearing, the court quashed the lis pendens notice. The court then ruled that "the lis pendens filed by plaintiffs' attorney was groundless in that it had been filed in an action where the only relief sought was monetary damages and that the filing contained a material misstatement of plaintiffs' actual claims with respect to the trustee sale. The trial court granted defendants' judgment against plaintiffs in the amount of $5,000 under A.R.S. § 33–420 and judgment against their attorney Richard N. Brandes for $2,762 in attorney's fees pursuant to A.R.S. § 12–349." In the Court of Appeal, Held, affirmed.

(1) Lis pendens is justified under the statute only when the action will affect title. "Under the complaint ... success for plaintiffs would not have resulted in cancellation of their liability under the promissory note. Plaintiffs' complaint sought only damages for breach of contract. It included no alternative request for rescission of the contract or cancellation of plaintiffs' liability on the promissory note secured by the deed of trust. Plaintiffs' conclusion that plaintiffs' action would involve an adjudication of rights incident to title to the real property in question is therefore simply wrong."

(2) Damages of $5,000 were awarded under Ariz. Rev. Stats. § 33–420A, which provides for $5,000 damages or treble actual damages, whichever is greater, and also for attorney fees when a document asserting an interest, lien or encumbrance is filed without grounds or filed containing a material misstatement. The court also awarded attorney fees under § 12–349, which authorizes fees when an action is brought without substantial justification or for delay or harassment.

(3) Although the client did not know of or authorize filing the lis pendens, this was part of the ongoing litigation and well within the authority of the attorney; so the client is liable for that action. On review in the Supreme Court of Arizona, Held, reversed on this point. The client is not liable under the statute, which is punitive and requires personal scienter; although the attorney had authority to bind the client at common law, the client is not liable under the statute.

30. **Slander of title, abuse of process liability?** Would the attorney have been liable for slander of title or abuse of process or the like?

31. **Where only the client is liable.** Suppose the attorney is not liable in a case like *Wyatt* but that the client is. Won't the attorney be liable indirectly because he or she has caused the client to be liable? Or would that be determined by a different standard?

32. **Restitution to adversaries.** Another basis of liability to an adversary arises when grounds for restitution appear. Suppose the plaintiff recovers a judgment. The defendant appeals but cannot post a supersedeas bond to postpone payment during an appeal. Consequently,

the defendant pays the judgment. When the appeal is heard, the defendant prevails and obtains a final judgment. In such a case, the defendant can recover payments made to the plaintiff under the erroneous judgment. If the plaintiff has paid part of the sum to her attorney as a fee, does the general rule that no duty is owed to an adversary bar recovery from the attorney? In *Berger v. Dixon & Snow,* 868 P.2d 1149 (Colo. App. 1993), the court in a somewhat similar situation held that the no-duty-to-adversaries rule had no application to a claim for restitution, which is "based on the general principle that one should not be permitted to keep that which 'in equity and good conscience' should be restored to another, and it encompasses, among others, the theories of recovery asserted here by trustee: unjust enrichment, quasi-contract, money had and received, and constructive trust. 1 D. DOBBS, LAW OF REMEDIES §§ 4.1–4.3 (2d ed. 1993). . . ."

33. **Reference.** On lawyer malpractice generally, see R. MALLEN & J. SMITH, LEGAL MALPRACTICE § 16.18 (3d ed. 1989); DOBBS ON TORTS §§ 484–492 (2000).

§ 4. DEFENSES

(a) Comparative Fault

34. **Client negligence reducing the award.** In *Pizel v. Zuspann,* 247 Kan. 54, 795 P.2d 42, 10 A.L.R.5th 1098 (1990), considered above in connection with liability of lawyers to third persons, the jury applied comparative negligence fault rules. It assigned 60% to the beneficiaries and Charles Pizel, 35% to defendant Whalen, and 5% to defendant Zuspann. The plaintiffs' total damages came to $204,550. The plaintiffs recovered only $71,592.50 from Whalen as his comparative fault share. On appeal, the court first observed that precedent supported a refusal to reduce a punitive award, but that different considerations arose for compensatory damages. The court said:

"Other jurisdictions that have considered the matter have allowed the negligence of the client to be considered in comparing fault. . . . 'Legal malpractice is a form of negligence. In other negligence contexts, findings of comparative fault can be based on the plaintiff's failure to take reasonable measures which might have prevented or reduced the injury caused by the defendant's negligence. We discern no convincing reason why that should not be true in this context.' " Here, "the trial court here correctly instructed the jury to compare the fault of the parties. The evidence would support the finding by the jury that the trustees here should have taken steps based upon their knowledge of real estate and the existence of the trust to manage the property that was contained within the trust." However, the court thought that the negligence of Charles should not be imputed to all the others.

35. **Comparative fault statutes limiting application in lawyer cases.** Some comparative fault statutes address cases of personal injury and wrongful death. Would these implicitly exclude comparative

fault in lawyer malpractice cases? Would lawyers ever have a duty to protect a client from her own fault, so that the client's comparative fault would not be held against her?

36. **Finding client fault.** Given that lawyers undertake to represent clients' interests, should courts be cautious about finding a client at fault for not protecting himself rather than for relying upon the lawyer? There are certain cases in ordinary negligence law in which the plaintiff is not charged with contributory fault because the defendant has undertaken to protect the plaintiff. For example, if a mental hospital undertakes the care of a depressed patient, the hospital may be liable for the patient's suicide. Suicide is one of the things professional care is supposed to prevent. In the lawyer malpractice area, perhaps clients should be chargeable with contributory fault for failure to follow the attorney's instructions or advice, but perhaps not for relying upon the attorney to act professionally.

Consider *Greycas, Inc. v. Proud,* 826 F.2d 1560 (7th Cir. 1987) (an excerpt from which is printed above). Recall that the lawyer actually lied to the lender, advising the lender that the lawyer had conducted a UCC search and in effect that the lender would have a good lien on farm machinery. When it turned out that the lawyer had conducted no search and the lender got no effective lien with the result that it lost most of its loan, the lender sued. The lying lawyer sought to defend on the ground of contributory fault of the lender. Here is what Judge Posner said:

> Due care is the care that is optimal given that the other party is exercising due care. It is not the higher level of care that would be optimal if potential tort victims were required to assume that the rest of the world was negligent. A pedestrian is not required to exercise a level of care (e.g., wearing a helmet or a shin guard) that would be optimal if there were no sanctions against reckless driving. Otherwise drivers would be encouraged to drive recklessly, and knowing this pedestrians would be encouraged to wear helmets and shin guards. The result would be a shift from a superior method of accident avoidance (not driving recklessly) to an inferior one (pedestrian armor).
>
> So we must ask whether Greycas would have been careless not to conduct its own UCC search had Proud done what he had said he did—conduct his own UCC search. The answer is no. The law normally does not require duplicative precautions unless one is likely to fail or the consequences of failure (slight though the likelihood may be) would be catastrophic. One UCC search is enough to disclose prior liens, and Greycas acted reasonably in relying on Proud to conduct it. Although Greycas had much warning that Crawford was in financial trouble and that the loan might not be repaid, that was a reason for charging a hefty interest rate and insisting that the loan be secured; it was not a reason for duplicating Proud's work. It is not hard to conduct a UCC lien search; it just requires checking the records in the recorder's office for the county

where the debtor lives. So the only reason to backstop Proud was if Greycas should have assumed he was careless or dishonest; and we have just said that the duty of care does not require such an assumption. Had Proud disclosed that he was Crawford's brother-in-law this might have been a warning signal that Greycas could ignore only at its peril. To go forward in the face of a known danger is to assume the risk. But Proud did not disclose his relationship to Crawford.

Suppose the lawyer prepares a document for the client to sign, mistakenly telling the client that it specified the agreed amounts of money in a settlement with another person. The client signs the document without reading it, only to find later that the document had understated the amounts of money due the client. Does the usual rule that one is bound by a document he signs whether he has read it or not bar the client? See *Arnav Industries, Inc. v. Brown, Raysman, Millstein, Felder & Steiner, L.L.P.*, 96 N.Y.2d 300, 751 N.E.2d 936, 727 N.Y.S.2d 688 (2001).

(b) Pari Delicto

37. **Following the lawyer's advice to commit a legal wrong.** In *General Car & Truck Leasing System, Inc. v. Lane and Waterman*, 557 N.W.2d 274 (Iowa 1996), a client wanted to register a service mark for its business, which included leasing cars and other vehicles. The lawyer retained for the purpose of applying for registration with the Patent and Trademark Office prepared an affidavit asserting that the mark was in use for rentals of a number of vehicles and for boats and aircraft as well. In fact, the client had never leased boats or aircraft and knew that the statement was false. Several years later, a similar procedure was repeated to maintain the registration. Again, the client knew that false statements were made, but signed the affidavit anyway, after being specifically advised by the attorney that his concern was misplaced. A year later, a competitor with a similar name petitioned the PTO to cancel the mark because it had been obtained by fraud. The PTO ultimately did so and a court affirmed the cancellation.

The client then sued the attorneys who advised use of the false affidavit. The attorneys defended in part on the ground that the client was in pari delicto, in equal fault. The court explained: "The doctrine of in pari delicto is the legal counterpart to the equitable doctrine of unclean hands. The doctrines are not, however, the same. The doctrine of unclean hands considers whether the party seeking relief has engaged in inequitable conduct that has harmed the party against whom he seeks relief. 1 DAN B. DOBBS, DOBBS LAW OF REMEDIES § 2.4(2), at 97–99 (2d ed.1993). In pari delicto, in contrast, focuses on the relative culpability of the parties. See 3 DOBBS § 13.6, at 573. The culpability element of the in pari delicto doctrine requires that the plaintiff has been guilty of illegal or fraudulent conduct. ... The purpose of the in pari delicto doctrine is to deter future misconduct by denying relief to one whose losses were substantially caused by his own fraud or illegal conduct." The court concluded that the pari delicto doctrine could apply in any case of scienter fraud, regardless of "intent to deceive," and that this was such a case. The final question was whether the client was in equal fault. After all, it had relied on advice of the defendants, who represented the client as counsel. But the court thought that the wrongfulness of lying in the affidavit was clear and that it was enough to put the client in pari delicto. That defeated the client's claim.

What do you think? Should lawyers who advise lying be liable to the client who is caught at it? Should lawyers be liable at least when they fail to warn the client of the risks and consequences?

(c) Statute of Limitations

38. **Accrual times.** Courts may adopt one of at least four different times as the time of accrual of a lawyer malpractice action, starting the statutory clock running at that time. These are:

The occurrence rule—the right of action accrues at the time of the negligent act or omission. See 2 Ronald Mallen and Jeffrey Smith, Legal Malpractice 18.10 (1989).

The damage rule—the right of action accrues at the time damage first occurs so that the plaintiff can bring suit. E.g., *Tingley v. Harrison*, 125 Idaho 86, 867 P.2d 960 (1994). This is the rule most consistent with negligence cases generally.

The discovery rule—the right of action accrues when the plaintiff discovered or should have discovered the relevant information. As always with discovery rules, there is room for difference about what it is that must be discovered. In *Beesley v. Van Doren*, 873 P.2d 1280 (Alaska 1994), for instance, the Alaska Court held that discovery was sufficiently complete to start the statute when the plaintiff discovered either the negligence or the injury that resulted from it. Perhaps a more subtle version would be justified: postpone the statute's start until the plaintiff discovers facts that would put her on notice that investigation is appropriate. In many instances, mere loss of the case will do this, but not in all. The difficulty with this more subtle rule is that there is no obvious termination; discovery might be postponed indefinitely.

Continuous representation rule—the action accrues only when the lawyer-client relationship terminates with respect to the particular representation. E.g., *O'Neill v. Tichy,* 19 Cal.App.4th 114, 25 Cal.Rptr.2d 162 (1993). Termination of the relationship is sometimes a useful trigger only because termination is a good index of the client's discovery of the negligence or claim, because it is possible that, as long as the relationship has not been terminated, the lawyer can rectify the negligence or at least minimize damages.

39. **Accrual vs. tolling.** The effects of a statute of limitations is controlled in part by deciding when the claim accrues so that the statutory clock starts running. However, to say that the claim does not accrue until, say, the lawyer-client relation has terminated, implies that

the plaintiff could not sue earlier. That might be a good idea in some cases, but maybe not in all cases. If it is not a good idea for all cases, courts can say that the claim actually accrues at some earlier point—when harm is done, for example—but that the statute can be tolled at the plaintiff's option until the representation is completed.

40. **Limitations and repose.** Although traditional statutes of limitations were described as statutes of repose, the "repose" term has now come to be used to describe a special kind of no-matter-what bar to the claim. For example, the straight statute of limitations might be tolled because of the plaintiff's incapacity, or it might not begin to run until the plaintiff discovered or should have discovered negligence or injury. A statute of repose in effect caps the amount of leeway the plaintiff can gain from tolling or discovery. It might provide, for example, that even the plaintiff who was incompetent or a minor is barred at some point after the lawyer's negligence. Many such statutes apply to personal injury, but it is possible to enact them for malpractice as well.

41. **Malpractice statutes.** Some statutes address "malpractice" without distinguishing among the forms of professional malpractice. Under such statutes, an initial question is whether the statute applies to lawyers at all. A few other states have passed statutes of varying complexity, addressed specifically to lawyer malpractice. The California statute, Cal. Code Civ. Proc. § 340.6., represents a carefully considered scheme and resolves many of the issues. First, actual fraud cases aside, the statute provides a discovery and repose system. The plaintiff has one year to sue after she discovers or should have discovered "the facts constituting the wrongful act or omission," but not longer than four years from the date of the wrongful act. Second, the statute provides for tolling, without respect to the four year limit. The statute is tolled until actual injury occurs, and during continued representation or wilful concealment by the attorney. It is also tolled for legal or physical disabilities. A separate provision covers documents like wills that will have an effective date depending upon a future event. For these, the statute begins to run upon the happening of the event.

TOWER v. GLOVER, 467 U.S. 914, 104 S.Ct. 2820, 81 L.Ed.2d 758 (1984). The plaintiff was convicted of robbery. He was represented by Tower as a public defender. The plaintiff sued Tower under § 1983, claiming that Tower conspired with state officials to obtain the plaintiff's conviction. In the Supreme Court, *held*, (1) the plaintiff adequately alleges that the public defender acted under color of law and (2) state public defenders are not absolutely immune from liability in such cases. The legislation was not made against a background of any similar immunity, the closest analogy in the 19th century being a private attorney, who was not and is not immune from liability for intentional misconduct like that alleged here.

42. **Civil rights action against the negligent public defender.** What if the public defender or appointed defense counsel is merely negligent? In that case, the defender may not be in violation of § 1983. First, the public defender may not be acting under color of state law in that case, but more like private counsel. Second, the public defender who is merely negligent may not be violating any substantive federal rights of the client.

43. **Public defender liability under state law.** What about suing the public defender under state malpractice law? In *Bradshaw v. Joseph,* 164 Vt. 154, 666 A.2d 1175 (1995), the malpractice plaintiff had been charged with sexual assault. The defendant here was appointed as public defender and eventually the plaintiff was acquitted. The plaintiff's complaint was that the lawyer failed to notify the plaintiff that his bail had been reduced, with the effect that he remained incarcerated until acquittal. Under Vermont's scheme of immunities, state employees are not liable for negligence, but the state may be. The public defender's office was created by statute. The plaintiff argued that as matter of policy, immunity is undesirable because of the "inconsistency between the role of the criminal defender, who is responsible only to his client, and the state employee, who presumably reports to and is under the control of a supervising official of the state—which is the entity prosecuting the defendant." The court was unmoved. "The apparent paradox of having the government support and pay for a constitutionally adequate system of legal representation for those charged by the government with criminal offenses was inherent in the public defender system from the outset. It is a variant of numerous interbranch conflicts that inhere in our system of separation of powers, including the clear paradox of having the judicial branch decide constitutional challenges to legislative enactments whereas the Legislature appropriates the funds that sustain the judicial branch." In the end, the court concluded that the public defender was a state employee and hence immune under the statute.

44. **Federal public defenders.** Where does that leave federal public defenders? In *Ferri v. Ackerman,* 444 U.S. 193, 100 S.Ct. 402, 62 L.Ed.2d 355 (1979), the defendant had been appointed to defend the plaintiff against a federal criminal charge. The plaintiff sued for malpractice under state law. The Supreme Court held that a federal-court-appointed defender was not entitled to absolute immunity as far as federal law was concerned. The Court did not consider whether states might provide an absolute immunity as a matter of state tort law.

Index

About This Index

This index refers to key words, legal rules or ideas, legal issues, key parties, and, important factual settings. It is *not* a concordance or a computer generated word list. Hence not every instance of a word is listed in this index. Equally, the referenced page may discuss or exemplify the legal idea indexed without using the indexing word. References are to pages on which materials on the referenced rule or issue *begin*. Discussion of the issue may continue on one or more pages following the referenced page. For example, liability of an agent for misrepresentation under state consumer protection statutes is indexed to page ___, where the case mentioning that point begins, even though the case does not state the rule on an agent's personal liability until page ___. In the same way, a note discussing a topic may begin on the page preceding the specific mention of that topic; the index refers to the page on which the note begins. Additional notes or other materials may follow without separate indexing. However, in a few instances involving large topics, inclusive reference are provided.

About This Index

About This Index

About This Index

About This Index

About This Index

About This Index

About This Index

About This Index

†